JIM MURRAY'S
WHISKY
BIBLE
2017

This 2017 edition is dedicated
with affection to the memory
of
Michael Steele
and
Harold Currie

This edition first published 2016 by Dram Good Books Ltd

10 9 8 7 6 5 4 3 2 1

The "Jim Murray's" logo and the "Whisky Bible" logo are trade marks of Jim Murray.

For information regarding using tasting notes from Jim Murray's Whisky Bible contact:
Dram Good Books Ltd, Unit 2, Barnstones Business Park, Litchborough, UK, NN12 8JJ
Tel: 44 (0)117 317 9777. Or contact us via www.whiskybible.com

A CIP catalogue record for this book is available from the British Library

ISBN: 978-0-9932986-1-5

Printed in Belgium by Graphius Group Eekhoutdriesstraat 67, B-9041 Gent.

Written by: Jim Murray
Edited by: David Rankin and Peter Mayne
Design: Rob-indesign, Jim Murray, Vincent Flint-Hil
Maps: James Murray, Rob-indesign
Production: Rob-indesign, Vincent Flint-Hill, Billy Jeffrey
Chief Researcher: Vincent Flint-Hill
Sample Research: Vincent Flint-Hill, Ally Telfer, Julia Nourney, Mick Secor
Other Research: Emma Thomson
Sales: Billy Jeffrey
European Dictionary: Julie Nourney, Tom Wyss, Mariette Duhr-Merges, Stefan Baumgart,
Erik Molenaar, Jürgen Vromans, Henric Molin and Kalle Valkonen.

Author's Note
I have used the spelling "whiskey" or "whisky" depending on how the individual distillers
prefer. All Scotch is "whisky". So is Canadian. All Irish, these days, is "whiskey", though
that was not always the case. In Kentucky, bourbon and rye are spelt "whiskey", with the
exception of the produce of the early Times/Old Forester Distillery and Maker's Mark which
they bottle as "whisky". In Tennessee, it is a 50-50 split: Dickel is "whisky", while Daniel's is
"whiskey".

JIM MURRAY'S
WHISKY
BIBLE
2017

DRAM GOOD BOOKS

Contents

Introduction

Have you ever noticed the similarities between people and whisky?

I don't mean in the way that a person is like the dog they own which, apparently, is not an unusual phenomenon. No, I mean the way a whisky has a personality. One which changes over time as age and events sculpt its character.

Doubtless you have met many people over the years who on first, brief introduction appear charming and thoroughly good company. But only on spending time with them do you realise that perhaps they are not what they seem, and they have a mean or niggardly streak to them; or that the slightly outgoing trait which first appeared attractive ends up as an annoyance. Or, conversely, you don't like them at all on first meeting but, when you have taken time to discover what they are about, you then find them possessing hidden depths and even a certain charisma which keeps bringing you back for even more of their company.

It is like that with people. It is like that with whisky.

So, for Jim Murray's Whisky Bible 2017, I am pleased to introduce you to no less than 1,241 new characters, the number of new whiskies I have tasted for this very latest edition. Some you will like on first meeting and continue to like; some you will dislike and no amount of getting to know you time will change your first impression. But there will be many here which, as they did to me, surprise and even delight.

Surprise and delight is exactly what happened when I named a Canadian, Crown Royal Northern Harvest Rye, World Whisky of the Year for 2016. And horrification. Probably in equal measure. Of course the brainless, know-nothing rent-a-quotes came out from under their stones claiming the award was ridiculous as Canadian is known to be inferior to Scotch or that I had taken back handers, or was seeking publicity or whatever the reason was. The one thing they could not accept, or even get their tiny minds around, was the possibility that the greatest Canadian could be more than a match for anything. Also that I had met someone – sorry, I mean a whisky – I had fallen completely in love with. It was love at first flight: the initial time I raised the sample glass to my nose I knew I had met something of exquisite beauty. And while I waited for my first impression to change as I got to know this whisky better, quite the opposite happened. My attraction to the whisky grew deeper and deeper. Until I had to declare it was, improbable as it seemed, the best whisky I had tasted that year amongst more than a 1,000 newbies. Even when I tasted the three whiskies that were battling it out for this year's grand award and I compared it to that very same sample of breath-taking Canadian that had blown me away a year ago...it was the Canadian which narrowly won.

Except it lost. Because unknown to me at the time the whisky I gave the award to was a single batch of many for that brand. As it turned out, this particular batch was for sale only in the US. The couple of later bottlings I got my hands on were exceptionally good – but not quite good enough for the Bible's World Whisky awards. You see, your girlfriend may have many sisters...but it is only her you love...

As usual, the World Whisky Award caused mayhem. To the extent that not only did the Northern Harvest Rye sell out in days, but new batches lasted little more than moments before likewise vanishing. There was, in one Canadian store, even a fight over the last bottle - needing police to be called in to restore order. It means the Bible has inadvertently, as it did – and still has - in Japan, slightly skewed stocks of whisky of a particular type. Rye doesn't grow on trees. It does so in fields on stems, of course. But that takes a year and there has never been quite enough of the high quality stuff to go around the distilling industry. So with further years required for maturation demand has outstripped supply and people have become annoyed. That is both a shame. And a wonderful thing.

Because the entire purpose since the Whisky Bible was conceived – indeed, the very first day of my becoming the world's first full time whisky writer 25 years ago - is to get people to discover whiskies they may not have found or tried before. And that is by telling you straight as I see it. No marketing hype. No advertising. No snobbery. Just good old fashioned plain honesty coupled with a little bit of knowledge that goes back a long way. And then an introduction to someone – sorry, something! – you might care to get to know. And if a whisky is already well known and marketed and the best I can find, then that will win an award, also. No bias. No discrimination, positive or otherwise. For sometimes it is worth spending time with old friends because you might just remember what it was you may have taken for granted but now discover you are missing.

Jim Murray
Willow Cottage,
Somewhere in rural Northamptonshire.
August 2016

How to Read The Bible

The whole point of this book is for the whisky lover – be he or she an experienced connoisseur or, better fun still, simply starting out on the long and joyous path of discovery – to have ready access to easy-to-understand information about as many whiskies as possible. And I mean a lot. Thousands.

This book does not quite include every whisky on the market... just by far and away the vast majority. And those that have been missed this time round – either through accident, logistics or design – will appear in later editions once we can source a sample.

WHISKY SCORING

The marking for this book is tailored to the consumer and scores run out just a little higher than I use for my own personal references. But such is the way it has been devised that it has not affected my order of preference.

Each whisky is given a rating out of 100. Twenty-five marks are given to each of four factors: nose (n), taste (t), finish (f), balance and overall complexity (b). That means that 50% of the marks are given for flavour alone and 25% for the nose, often an overlooked part of the whisky equation. The area of balance and complexity covers all three previous factors and a usually hidden one besides:

Nose: this is simply the aroma. Often requires more than one inspection as hidden aromas can sometimes reveal themselves after time in the glass, increased contact with air and changes in temperature. The nose very often tells much about a whisky, but – as we shall see – equally can be quite misleading.

Taste: this is the immediate arrival on the palate and involves the flavour profile up to, and including, the time it reaches maximum intensity and complexity.

Finish: often the least understood part of a tasting. This is the tail and flourish of the whisky's signature, often revealing the effects of ageing. The better whiskies tend to finish well and linger without too much oak excess. It is on the finish, also, that certain notes which are detrimental to the whisky may be observed. For instance, a sulphur-tarnished cask may be fully revealed for what it is by a dry, bitter residue on the palate which is hard to shake off. It is often worth waiting a few minutes to get the full picture of the finish before having a second taste of a whisky.

Balance: This is the part it takes a little experience to appreciate but it can be mastered by anyone. For a whisky to work well on the nose and palate, it should not be too one-sided in its character. If you are looking for an older whisky, it should have evidence of oak, but not so much that all other flavours and aromas are drowned out. Likewise, a whisky matured or finished in a sherry butt must offer a lot more than just wine alone and the greatest Islay malts, for instance, revel in depth and complexity beyond the smoky effects of peat.

Each whisky has been analysed by me without adding water or ice. I have taken each whisky as it was poured from the bottle and used no more than warming in an identical glass to extract and discover the character of the whisky. To have added water would have been pointless: it would have been an inconsistent factor as people, when pouring water, add different amounts at varying temperatures. The only constant with the whisky you and I taste will be when it has been poured directly from the bottle.

Even if you and I taste the same whiskies at the same temperature and from identical glasses – and even share the same values in whisky – our scores may still be different. Because a factor that is built into my evaluation is drawn from expectation and experience. When I sample a whisky from a certain distillery at such-and-such an age or from this type of barrel or that, I would expect it to offer me certain qualities. It has taken me 30 years to acquire this knowledge (which I try to add to day by day!) and an enthusiast cannot be expected to learn it overnight. But, hopefully, Jim Murray's Whisky Bible will help...!

SCORE CHART
Within the parentheses () is the overall score out of 100.
0–50.5 Nothing short of absolutely diabolical.
51–64.5 Nasty and well worth avoiding.
65–69.5 Very unimpressive indeed.
70–74.5 Usually drinkable but don't expect the earth to move.
75–79.5 Average and usually pleasant though sometimes flawed.
80–84.5 Good whisky worth trying.
85–89.5 Very good to excellent whiskies definitely worth buying.
90–93.5 Brilliant.
94–97.5 Superstar whiskies that give us all a reason to live.
98–100 Better than anything I've ever tasted!

KEY TO ABBREVIATIONS & SYMBOLS
% Percentage strength of whisky measured as alcohol by volume. **b** Overall balance and complexity. **bott** Date of bottling. **db** Distillery bottling. In other words, an expression brought out by the owners of the distillery. **dist** Date of distillation or spirit first put into cask. **f** Finish. **n** Nose. **nc** Non-coloured. **ncf** Non-chill-filtered. **sc** Single cask. **t** Taste. ⋇ New entry for 2017. ⊙ Retasted – no change. ⊙⊙ Retasted and re-evaluated. **v** Variant WB17-001 Code for Whisky Club bottling.

Finding Your Whisky
Worldwide Malts: Whiskies are listed alphabetically throughout the book. In the case of single malts, the distilleries run A–Z style with distillery bottlings appearing at the top of the list in order of age, starting with youngest first. After age comes vintage. After all the "official" distillery bottlings are listed, next come other bottlings, again in alphabetical order. Single malts without a distillery named (or perhaps named after a dead one) are given their own section, as are vatted malts.

Worldwide Blends: These are simply listed alphabetically, irrespective of which company produce them. So "Black Bottle" appears ahead of "White Horse" and Japanese blends begin with "Ajiwai Kakubin" and end with "Za". In the case of brands being named after companies or individuals the first letter of the brand will dictate where it is listed. So William Grant, for instance, will be found under "W" for William rather "G" for Grant.

Bourbon/Rye: One of the most confusing types of whiskey to list because often the name of the brand bears no relation to the name of the distillery that made it. Also, brands may be sold from one company to another, or shortfalls in stock may see companies buying bourbons from another. For that reason all the brands have been listed alphabetically with the name of the bottling distiller being added at the end.

Irish Whiskey: There are four types of Irish whiskey: (i) pure pot still; (ii) single malt, (iii) single grain and (iv) blended. Some whiskies may have "pure pot still" on the label, but are actually single malts. So check both sections.

Bottle Information
As no labels are included in this book I have tried to include all the relevant information you will find on the label to make identification of the brand straightforward. Where known I have included date of distillation and bottling. Also the cask number for further recognition. At the end of the tasting notes I have included the strength and, if known, number of bottles (sometimes abbreviated to btls) released and in which markets.

PRICE OF WHISKY
You will notice that Jim Murray's Whisky Bible very rarely refers to the cost of a whisky. This is because the book is a guide to quality and character rather than the price tag attached. Also, the same whiskies are sold in different countries at varying prices due to market forces and variations of tax, so there is a relevance factor to be considered. Equally, much depends on the size of an individual's pocket. What may appear a cheap whisky to one could be an expensive outlay to another. With this in mind prices are rarely given in the Whisky Bible.

How to Taste Whisky

It is of little use buying a great whisky, spending a comparative fortune in doing so, if you don't get the most out of it.

So when giving whisky tastings, no matter how knowledgable the audience may be I take them through a brief training schedule in how to nose and taste as I do for each sample included in the Whisky Bible.

I am aware that many aspects are contrary to what is being taught by distilleries' whisky ambassadors. And for that we should be truly thankful. However, at the end of the day we all find our own way of doing things. If your old tried and trusted technique suits you best, that's fine by me. But I do ask you try out the instructions below at least once to see if you find your whisky is talking to you with a far broader vocabulary and clearer voice than it once did. I strongly suspect you will be pleasantly surprised – amazed, even - by the results.

Amusingly, someone tried to teach me my own tasting technique some years back in an hotel bar. He was not aware who I was and I didn't let on. It transpired that a friend of his had been to one of my tastings a few years earlier and had passed on my words of "wisdom". I'd be lying if I said I didn't smile when he informed me it was called "The Murray Method." It was the first time I had heard the phrase... though certainly not the last!

"THE MURRAY METHOD"

1. Drink a black, unsweetened, coffee or chew on 90% minimum cocoa chocolate to cleanse the palate, especially of sugars.

2. Find a room free from distracting noises as well as the aromas of cooking, polish, flowers and other things which will affect your understanding and appreciation of the whisky.

3. Make sure you have not recently washed your hands using heavily scented soap or are wearing a strong aftershave or perfume.

4. Use a tulip shaped glass with a stem. This helps contain the alcohols at the bottom yet allows the more delicate whisky aromas you are searching for to escape.

5. Never add ice. This tightens the molecules and prevents flavours and aromas from being released. It also makes your whisky taste bitter. There is no better way to get the least from your whisky than by freezing it.

6. Likewise, ignore any advice given to put the bottle in the fridge before drinking.

7. Don't add water! Whatever anyone tells you. It releases aromas but can mean the whisky falls below 40%...so it is no longer whisky. Also, its ability to release flavours and aromas diminish quite quickly. Never add ridiculous "whisky rocks" or other supposed tasting aids.

8. Warm the undiluted whisky in the glass to body temperature before nosing or tasting. Hence the stem, so you can cradle in your hand the curve of the thin base. This excites the molecules and unravels the whisky in your glass, maximising its sweetness and complexity.

9. Keep an un-perfumed hand over the glass to keep the aromas in while you warm. Only a minute or two after condensation appears at the top of your glass should you extend your arms, lift your covering hand and slowly bring the glass to your nose, so the alcoholic vapours have been released before the glass reaches your face.

10. Never stick your nose in the glass. Or breathe in deeply. Allow glass to gently touch your top lip, leaving a small space below the nose. Move from nostril to nostril, breathing normally. This allows the aromas to break up in the air, helping you find the more complex notes.

11. Take no notice of your first mouthful. This is a marker for your palate.

12. On second, bigger mouthful, close your eyes to concentrate on the flavour and chew the whisky - moving it continuously around the palate. Keep your mouth slightly open to let air in and alcohol out. It helps if your head is tilted back very slightly.

13. Occasionally spit – if you have the willpower! This helps your senses to remain sharp for the longest period of time.

14. Look for the balance of the whisky. That is, which flavours counter others so none is too dominant. Also, watch carefully how the flavours and aromas change in the glass over time.

15. Assess the "shape" and mouth feel of the whisky, its weight and how long its finish. And don't forget to concentrate on the first flavours as intensely as you do the last. Look out for the way the sugars, spices and other characteristics form.

16. Never make your final assessment until you have tasted it a third or fourth time.

17. Be honest with your assessment: don't like a whisky because someone (yes, even me!), or the label, has tried to convince you how good it is.

18. When you cannot discriminate between one whisky and another, stop immediately.

Immortal Drams:
The Whisky Bible
Winners 2004-2016

	World Whisky of the Year	Second Finest Whisky of the Year	Third Finest Whisky of the Year
2004	George T Stagg	N/A	N/A
2005	George T Stagg	N/A	N/A
2006	George T Stagg	Glen Moray 1986 Cask 4696 distillery bottling	N/A
2007	Old Parr Superior 18 Years Old	Buffalo Trace Experimental Collection Twice Barreled	N/A
2008	Ardbeg 10 Years Old	The Ileach Single Islay Malt Cask Strength	N/A
2009	Ardbeg Uigeadail	Nikka Whisky Single Coffey Malt 12 Years	N/A
2010	Sazerac Rye 18 Years Old (bottled Fall 2008)	Ardbeg Supernova	Amrut Fusion
2011	Ballantine's 17 Years Old	Thomas H Handy Sazerac Rye (129 proof)	Wiliam Larue Weller (134.8 proof)
2012	Old Pulteney Aged 21 Years	George T Stagg	Parker's Heritage Collection Wheated Mash Bill Bourbon Aged 10 Years
2013	Thomas H Handy Sazerac Rye (128.6 proof)	William Larue Weller (133.5 proof)	Ballantine's 17 Years Old
2014	Glenmorangie Ealanta 1993	William Larue Weller (123.4 proof)	Thomas Handy Sazerac Rye (132.4 proof)
2015	Yamazaki Single Malt Sherry 2013	William Larue Weller (68.1 abv)	Sazerac Rye 18 Years Old (bottled Fall 2013)
2016	Crown Royal Northern Harvest Rye	Pikesville 110 Proof Straight Rye	Midleton Dair Ghaelach

Who has won it this year?
Find out on page 14

Bible Thumping
Rejoice With Me
For I Have Found

Stand back and observe, as I sometimes do, the buyer.

Before him, or her, is a wall of glass glittering gold or green, shepherding the shop's lights and sending fragmented, diaphanous rays of promise and mystery into eager, enquiring eyes of the man or woman on a mission. This brickwork of bottles is cemented by lines of prices which act as a sobering counter to the giddying alcohol on show.

And, gingerly, a 25-year-old malt is teased from the shelf and held carefully and nearer the light for closer inspection. What does this potential buyer see beyond the sheen and clarity of the gold or amber? Usually a bottle expensively and expansively fashioned, sleek, sensual to hold and hinting at the suggestive curvature of the malt inside. And upon it a label which a design artist has used his greatest skills to capture the essence of the distillery and your attention, though not always in that order. Invariably, there will be words – crafted by a copy writer in all probability possessing a lot less knowledge of whisky than the person consuming his work. And because so many whiskies claim very much the same thing and engage the same mesmeric form of romanticism it is hard for the buyer to decide which whisky in the end they would prefer to be seduced by.

If that isn't enough, they will also inspect the expensive coffin in which the whisky is laid when paid for, or the tube or tin which is every bit as much an art form as the the label on the stylised bottle. In the end, do they go for the one whose name they have heard the best reports about or seen advertised, a distillery they have tried and enjoyed at younger ages, the one whose writer is most winning or will it be decided by price? I do, truly, feel sorry these days for anyone who has to make a decision on what to buy if it is based only on the details set before them on the whisky shelf.

By contrast, when holding a 25-year-old malt, what do I see? Not the packaging artwork or general blurb which adorns it. That is all background noise, irrelevant, like the audience's expectant babble quietened and silenced as the conductor strikes the baton upon his podium. I hurl myself back in time and remember the distillery as it was 25 years ago. The manager if I knew him (and I most probably did), the stillman, the warehouseman, the blender who worked with the whisky and what he wanted from it.

Most blurb paints a picture of a cask filled two and half decades ago by skilled craftsmen, in the time-honoured tradition, and laid down with intent and purpose so now, a quarter of a century on, you will be able to marvel at the contents of this carefully planned time capsule.

My memory, which even after a quarter of a century can still play back the vivid sights, smells and sounds as if they happened only this morning, will most probably be of a distillery which, more likely than not, was laying down casks for blends; whiskies unlikely to spend more than five years in the warehouse, let alone 25 years. And distillery managers fretting about the quality of their casks having just emerged from a whisky loch which had seen empty barrels piled high for more years than was healthy but grateful, at least, that theirs was not a distillery that had not been closed down in the cull of the 1980s designed to prevent overproduction ever again. Well, with there now being a whisky shortage and prices forever rising at least that plan worked...

I will remember the romance of an industry that was still barely written about and very little traversed or observed. One where there was just a handful of visitor centres throughout Scotland, no websites and magazines. Where the distillery manager would take you round in person when he could create a spare 20 minutes, or maybe just before he disappeared into his house on site to set about the supper prepared for him by his wife. Or just after, maybe, after the washing up had been done.

Recollections of 25 years ago takes in urgent, occasionally irritated, sometimes heated discussions between the warehouseman and the manager, quite often about the quality of the sherry butts which had been offloaded from a truck that day. Each one they discovered with dismay had an unpleasant sulphur note. The manager had contacted head office. He was under orders to fill the butts anyway. The warehouseman would shake his head and return back to a warehouse or filling hall head bowed against the winds, both meteorological and, now I see looking back, those of change, too, chuntering unhappily. And the manager would explain to me that those butts would end up in a blend and no-one would be the wiser.

11

Except now I had a 25-year-old malt in my hand from that very distillery. It was sherry cask, maybe even one I had seen delivered that day. And it had not ended up as a blend as planned and expected. Because about 25 years ago something dramatic happened. The Single Malt Revolution began. Sales of blends declined, the number of brands reduced and the generation of blend drinkers do what all older generations do...they died.

I think of this now because it was 25 years ago in the first months of 1992 that I made the step, that huge stride into the unknown, that no-one had ever taken before. I became a full-time whisky writer. So from a personal viewpoint 2017 marks a very special landmark year for me. Hence the cover of the Bible. How I was then, when the myriad nuances of the world's many whisky styles – including, it is hard to believe, single malt Scotch - was still to be discovered; when many of these casks now fetching extraordinary, scary prices, were being filled for blends which no-one bought. And now.

It is as though I have travelled between worlds from one dimension of space and time to another.

Because if you could come back with me to the whisky world I once knew and inhabited, I doubt if you would believe your eyes. Or ears or even taste buds. It is as though I was then standing atop a mountain, behind me a chasm left by the last great quake to hit the industry, one that reverberated around the globe often to catastrophic effect; and before me more undulating, sunnier, friendly plains with gentle hills rather than vast mountain ranges to climb, the fault lines smaller and much more stable.

Indeed, what fun if you could hold my hand and jump back with me even further in time to 1975, when I visited my first distillery: Talisker on the Isle of Skye. No internet to 'Google Earth It' first and plan your route. Not even a bridge as there is today so you can drive there quickly and in comfort. Instead, a rusty old ferry, a rotting prop it seemed from Whisky Galore, that chugged you across to an island bathed in purple but with gloomy, forbidding outlines beyond. And it was there I entered my first warehouse and drank from the thief at full strength, the curtain of my future life opening that very moment. Oh, and the smells. Not just from the warehouse, but a different aroma for every quarter of the distillery; a signature pungency to every section of the mashing, distilling and warehousing process. Return there today and health and safety regulation means that the most thrilling of those unique odours have been piped away: like most others, it is now a relatively sterile environment by comparison to that living, breathing one I first encountered a lifetime ago.

My good fortune was that my journalistic career meant I was often seconded to Scotland, living and working there for weeks, even months, at a time, allowing me over the next decade to visit every single distillery, even quietly work in some, meet blenders and begin to learn the varied arts and crafts of the industry. I felt then, and feel it even more keenly today, that it was my great honour and privilege to come face-to-face with the inwardly tough, hugely skilled, largely unrecognised, almost invisible workforce, then being away from prying eyes and cameras, who manned each distillery – women then were usually found only in the offices – to encounter first-hand their pride, their joy, their dedication. And their fears. Because Fridays always used to be half days at the distilleries, so the manager and other staff could disappear to the local golf course for a round, a blether and finally a dram with their rival colleagues. Except during the 1980s fewer had to be in work the following Monday. For blends spent longer time sitting on the shelves, single malt was yet to be discovered by even the British let alone the world... and distilleries closed down. Rather than just find Scotland's whisky talent on the greens on a Friday afternoon, you might now come across them on a Tuesday or Wednesday also...

And this wasn't a problem found exclusively in Scotland. Even 25 years ago. When then it was like meeting a lover-to-be that was still shy and demure, largely unaware of its own charm and beauty, thinking itself plain and uninteresting. It was like that in Scotland. But I discovered it was even more so in Kentucky when I courted bourbon and rye for the very first time on its own back porch. After a lifetime of seeing suitors disengage and turn their backs on her, she was in no mind or mood to be told it was the drinker's loss: that one day soon the world would discover the flame-tinted beauty that had been there all the time.

A quarter of a century ago some of the distillers of Kentucky told me, with something as close to certainty as they would ever allow themselves, rye would be gone within a generation. The rot had set in after prohibition and speeded on by the Second World War when people became used to drinking lighter and lighter spirits and cocktails. I remember being laughed at, not unkindly but just in bemused disbelief, when I predicted that rye as well as the bigger bourbons would take off around the world as people, now discovering the smoky depths of Islay, would be looking for full bodied, rich-bloodied whiskeys irrespective of wherever they were made. One distillery even offered to sell me all their rye stocks over four years old if that was what I genuinely believed. Had I taken the offer I would today be a very wealthy man, but I declined (foolishly, perhaps) on the grounds of maintaining my independence.

The Irish likewise did not believe it when I told them that pure Pot Still would one day become greatly desired and prized for the very same reason as rye. Not at first, but I did, in about 1995, at last manage to persuade the directorate of Irish Distillers, though not before a raised-voice, finger-jabbing argument, to significantly up the amount of Pot Still whisky in their standard Jameson blend...and they have never looked back since.

Back in 1992 that, and so much more, was still to come. The whisky landscape was then a very quiet one, save for the distant rumble of economic uncertainty, with one glance forward into the future, but two behind hoping that the past was not catching up with them. That bottle of 25-year-old malt the buyer today has in their hand - translucent, sparkling, beckoning - was distilled in another age entirely and one that would not have foretold the suave shop it was being viewed in, the price being asked for it, the desire for climbing new whisky tasting heights from the prospective purchaser. It was made by good people mostly no longer still working, some, alas, no longer with us at all. Sometimes for people then still to be born.

For those of you not there at the time it is a barren landscape hard to imagine. And I am sometimes asked which world I prefer. The innocent one of then; the glitzy, brash, slightly cynical one of today.

It is almost impossible to answer with a certainty. Certainly uncovering an undiscovered world, exploring unknown distilling territory as I have done through my career was fun then because you really were plotting and marking the contours of previously blank maps. It is hard to believe that when I visited the distilleries of Canada in the early 1990s I became the first person living to have visited them all coast to coast. Today there are whisky tours and people spending extended holidays on whisky sojourns, the internet – and the Whisky Bible, of course – always there to guide them. So yes, the intimacy and the charming naivety of the distillers, mainly free from controlling PR and marketing departments, of that bygone age is so much more romantic than the scene today.

But now the whisky loving world has a diversity of whiskies to choose from, encapsulating every corner of the planet, and a choice which was beyond even our wildest dreams two score and five years ago.

Two whisky universes and time dimensions. Both enthralling and captivating in their own ways. Hopefully captured and brought together in this little book of mine. So when you hold a bottle of whisky 25, 30, 35 years old, ignore the brilliant design and hype. Look, instead, into the liquid past and try to picture, if you can, the true romance of a vanished whisky world....

Join our Tasting Club

How would you like to compare your own tasting notes from the very same bottle I have used for each whisky? Set your nose and taste buds against mine.

That is the concept we are now going to make happen. Since the very first edition was launched way back in 2003 readers have asked if we could sell samples of the whiskies I have tasted. I have also had numerous approaches by business types over the years asking me to sell whisky off the back of the Bible...and been offered vast sums to do so.

In order to underline this book's impartiality, the very bedrock of its existence, I declined those offers. I did not want to be incorrectly perceived favouring a whisky; people thinking I was feathering my own nest by making a profit from increased sales of whiskies I had given high scores or even awards to...which would be entirely opposite to absolutely everything I believe in and stand for. So, just like advertising, I turned my back on that potential source of revenue. But for simple health reasons I have had to drastically rethink how to make the Bible happen. Because during the writing of the 2014 edition I developed two blood clots which could easily have had fatal consequences. They came about because samples were, as usual, sent to me by some distillers and bottlers so late in the day I had to spend almost six weeks tied to a desk. Tasting twelve to fourteen hours a day, seven days a week in order to somehow hit the publishing deadline. Deep vein thrombosis was, not surprisingly, the result.

So we will, whenever possible, be buying the whiskies as they are launched and I will be tasting them throughout the year to even the burden, rather than just in the summer months prior to publication. The whiskies we bought in over the last two editions have been split into seven sealed 10cl bottles: one for me to work from, the others to be made available to Whisky Club members on a first-come, first-served basis. We are still in the development phase of making this happen and investigating the final mechanics of how. Because of the enormous pressure on time to hit the deadline for this edition we have yet to fully determine just how the samples will be made available. But they will be and we ask you keep a close eye on **Whiskybible.com** to monitor developments and instructions how to join the Whisky Bible Club. The money we raise from this means we then have the funds to buy more whiskies as they become available. Not just the whiskies the distillers and bottlers want us to have. But the ones my researchers find out there. You will know my score for the samples available for the 2015 and 2016 Bibles. For the 2017 edition onwards you will not. You will have to use your judgement to guess which will be the high flyers because scores will still not be given until the Whisky Bible is launched each October. And the chance to build your own whisky library.

I will look forward to welcoming you to the Jim Murray Whisky Bible Tasting Club very soon.

Jim Murray's Whisky Bible Awards 2017

It is hard to know which is the more difficult.

Nosing and tasting some 1,250 different whiskies of every conceivable hue and variety in just a matter of a few months? Or working your way through the absolute top scorers, in the painstaking way a forensic scientist might inspect complex evidence, to decide which is the champion whisky of its type in just a couple of weeks? Probably the latter.

For this edition, it was a question as to whether any were going to catch the Booker's Rye. It was one of those rare whiskeys which on first tasting you knew, instantly, was most probably going to carry off the title of Jim Murray Whisky Bible's World Whisky of the Year. There are any number of whiskies which delight, enthral, simply blow you away; but those with that specific X Factor, as opposed to ex factor, are thin on the ground. So when I tasted this, it edged ahead of the rest – and though the chase was keen, it could not be caught.

Indeed, this year has seen a far greater polarisation of quality than I have before seen. But the great news was that amongst the 1,250 new whiskies to market this year an impressive number had scored in the mid 90s. Still a small number, but almost certainly better than any year before: one got the overall feeling that massive work had gone into the fine-tuning or very careful selection of an above average number of brands.

The Whisky Bible has in recent years raised hackles because it has taken a swipe at the Scotch whisky industry: the fact that last year none of its whiskies got into my world's top five drew headlines globally. Well, no such problem this year. The only whisky that was a realistic threat to the Booker's Rye was the Glen Grant 18-year-old, a single malt unveiled for the first time in 2016. What was so remarkable, was that you had the feeling that there could be more to come from this malt, that it was coasting and performing well within itself. It is a 43% volume dram: unleashed at 46%, non-chill-filtered, and Scotland might well be champion again.

Indeed, it was Speyside which dominated amongst the Scots, with Glen Grant, complete with its Ardbegian purifiers, picking up a staggering four gongs, and the largely unknown but truly brilliant Glentauchers two more. A sublime 25-year-old Macallan from That Boutique-y Whisky Company caught one's breath as well as eye. The only disappointing aspect was that in the latter two cases the awards went to independent bottlers rather than the owner of the distilleries, which begs an obvious question.

But there is still no getting away from the fact that for the second successive year – and indeed third time in five – a rye whisk(e)y has lorded over the others. I remember speaking by phone to old Booker Noe not that long before he died and him telling me, in a Kentuckian drawl thick enough to paint a warehouse door with, about some rye he had been "messing" with, if I recall his phrase correctly, that was of a higher rye percentage in the mash bill than the standard Jim Beam Rye. This was probably it.

A very big, unforgettable whiskey from a very big, unforgettable man. What a legacy...!

2017 World Whisky of the Year

Booker's Rye 13 Years, 1 Month, 12 Days

Second Finest Whisky in the World
Glen Grant Aged 18 Years Rare Edition

Third Finest Whisky in the World
William Larue Weller (134.6 Proof)

SCOTCH

Scotch Whisky of the Year
Glen Grant Aged 18 Years Rare Edition
Single Malt of the Year (Multiple Casks)
Glen Grant Aged 18 Years Rare Edition
Single Malt of the Year (Single Cask)
That Boutique-y Whisky Macallan 25 batch 5
Scotch Blend of the Year
The Last Drop 1971 Blended Scotch Whisky
Scotch Grain of the Year
Whiskyjace Invergordon 24 Year Old
Scotch Vatted Malt of the Year
Compass Box Flaming Heart 15th Anniversary

Single Malt Scotch

No Age Statement (Multiple Casks)
The Glenlivet Cipher
No Age Statement (Runner Up)
Port Askaig 100 proof
10 Years & Under (Multiple Casks)
Glen Grant Aged 10 Years
10 Years & Under (Single Cask)
Kilchoman 2 Isles Guze Cask Finish
11-15 Years (Multiple Casks)
Lagavulin 12 Year Old
11-15 Years (Single Cask)
The Single Cask Glentauchers 14 Year Old
16-21 Years (Multiple Casks)
Glen Grant Aged 18 Years Rare Edition
16-21 Years (Single Cask)
Scyfion Mortlach 1996
22-27 Years (Multiple Casks)
Dalwhinnie 25 Years Old
22-27 Years (Single Cask)
The Boutique-y Macallan 25 Batch 5
28-34 Years (Multiple Casks)
Port Ellen 32 Year Old
28-34 Years (Single Cask)
Cadenhead's Caol Ila 31 Year Old
35-40 Years (Multiple Casks)
Brora 37 Year Old
35-40 Years (Single Cask)
Cadenhead's Glentauchers 38 Year Old
41 Years & Over (Multiple Casks)
Gordon & MacPhail Glen Grant 1952
41 Years & Over (Single Cask)
Gordon & MacPhail Glen Grant 65 Year Old

BLENDED SCOTCH

No Age Statement (Standard)
Ballantine's Finest
No Age Statement (Premium)
Ballantine's Limited
5-12 Years
Johnnie Walker 12 Year Old
13-18 Years
Chivas 18 Ultimate Cask Collection
19 - 25 Years
Royal Salute 21 Years Old
26 - 50 Years
The Last Drop 1971 Blended Scotch Whisky

IRISH WHISKEY

Irish Whiskey of the Year
Redbreast Aged 21 Years

Irish Pot Still Whiskey of the Year
Redbreast Aged 21 Years
Irish Single Malt of the Year
Bushmills 21 Year Old
Irish Blend of the Year
Jameson
Irish Single Cask of the Year
Teeling Whiskey Single Cask 2004

AMERICAN WHISKEY

Bourbon of the Year
William Larue Weller 134.6 Proof
Rye of the Year
Booker's Rye 13 Years 1 Mo 12 Days
US Micro Whisky of the Year
Garrison Brothers Cowboy Bourbon 2009
US Micro Whisky of the Year (Runner Up)
Koval Four Grain

BOURBON

No Age Statement (Multiple Barrels)
William Larue Weller 134.6 Proof
No Age Statement (Single Barrel)
1792 Single Barrrel Kentucky Straight Bourbon
9 Years & Under
Garrison Brothers Cowboy Bourbon 2009
10 Years & Over (Multiple Barrels)
Blade & Bow 22 Year Old

RYE

No Age Statement
Thomas Handy
Up to 10 Years
Pikesville 110 Proof
11 Years & Over
Booker's Rye 13 Years 1 Mo 12 Days

WHEAT

Wheat Whiskey of the Year
Bernheim Original

CANADIAN WHISKY

Canadian Whisky of the Year
Crown Royal Northern Harvest Rye

JAPANESE WHISKY

Japanese Whisky of the Year
Yamazaki Sherry Cask
Single Malt of the Year (Multiple Barrels)
Yamazaki Sherry Cask

EUROPEAN WHISKY

European Whisky of the Year (Multiple)
English Whisky Co. Chapter 14 (England)
European Whisky of the Year (Single)
Langatun 6YO Pinot Noir Cask
(Switzerland)

WORLD WHISKIES

Asian Whisky of the Year
Kavalan Solist Moscatel (Taiwan)
Southern Hemisphere Whisky of the Year
Heartwood Any Port in a Storm (Australia)

*Overall age category and/or section
winners are presented in **bold**.*

The Whisky Bible Liquid Gold Awards (97.5-94)

Jim Murray's Whisky Bible is delighted to again make a point of celebrating the very finest whiskies you can find in the world. So we salute the distillers who have maintained or even furthered the finest traditions of whisky making and taken their craft to the very highest levels. And the bottlers who have brought some of them to us.

After all, there are over 4,600 different brands and expressions listed in this guide and from every corner of the planet. Those which score 94 and upwards represents only a very small fraction of them. These whiskies are, in my view, the élite: the finest you can currently find on the whisky shelves of the world. Rare and precious, they are Liquid Gold.

So it is our pleasure to announce that all those scoring 94 and upwards automatically qualify for the Jim Murray's Whisky Bible Liquid Gold Award. Congratulations!

97.5

Scottish Single Malt
Ardbeg Uigeadail
Glenmorangie Ealanta 1993 Vintage
Gordon & MacPhail Linkwood
Old Pulteney Aged 21 Years

Scottish Blends
Ballantine's 17 Years Old

Bourbon
George T Stagg
William Larue Weller
William Larue Weller bott Spring 2001

American Straight Rye
Booker's Rye 13 Years, 1 Month, 12 Days
Pikesville Straight Rye Whiskey aged at least 6 years
Thomas H. Handy Sazerac Straight Rye Whiskey

Canadian Blended Malt
Crown Royal Northern Harvest Rye

Japanese Single Malt
Yamazaki Single Malt Whisky Sherry Cask

97

Scottish Single Malt
Ardbeg 10 Years Old
Ardbeg Day Bottling
Ardbeg Supernova
Ardbeg Supernova 2015
Cadenhead's Small Batch Caol Ila 31 Year Old
Glen Grant Aged 18 Years Rare Edition
Glenfiddich 50 Years Old
That Boutique-y Whisky Company Macallan 25 Year Old
Port Ellen 32 Year Old

Scottish Blends
Johnnie Walker Blue Label The Casks Edition
The Last Drop 50 Year Old
The Last Drop 1971 Blended Scotch Whisky
Old Parr Superior 18 Years Old

Irish Pure Pot Still
Redbreast Aged 12 Years Cask Strength

Irish Blend
Midleton Dair Ghaelach

Bourbon
Four Roses 2013 Limited Edition Single Barrel #3-4P Aged 13 Years
Parker's Heritage Collection Wheated Mash Bill Bourbon Aged 10 Years
William Larue Weller

American Straight Rye
Colonel E.H. Taylor Straight Rye
Sazerac Rye 18 Year Old
Sazerac 18 Years Old

Japanese Single Malt
Nikka Whisky Single Coffey Malt 12 Years
The Yamazaki Single Malt Whisky Mizunara

Czech Rebublic Single Malt
Gold Cock Single Malt Whisky 1992 Limited Release Whisky Festival.cz

French Single Malt
Kornog Taouarc'h Chwec'hved 14

German Single Malt
Spinnaker Single Cask Malt Whisky Fassstärke

Indian Single Malt
Amrut Fusion

Taiwanese Single Malt
Kavalan Solist Fino Sherry Cask
Kavalan Single Malt Amontillado Sherry

96.5

Scottish Single Malt
Ardbeg 21 Years Old
Ardbeg Corryvreckan
Ardbeg Supernova
Balblair 1965
Balblair 1983 Vintage 1st Release
The Balvenie Single Barrel Aged 12 Years
Bowmore Black 50 Year Old
Octomore Edition 7.1 Aged 5 years
Port Charlotte PC6
Caol Ila 30 Year Old
Old Malt Cask Caol Ila Aged 29 Years
Acla Selection Clynelish 21 Years Old
Kingsbury Silver Craigellachie 18 Year Old 1995
Dalwhinnie 25 Year Old
The GlenDronach 18 Years Old
Glenfarclas The Family Casks 1957
Glenfarclas The Family Casks 1966
Glenfarclas The Family Casks 1967
Glenfarclas The Family Casks 1985
Glen Grant 50 Year Old
Gordon & MacPhail Distillery Label Glen Grant 50 Year Old
Gordon & MacPhail Rare Vintage Glen Grant 1952
The Glenlivet Cipher
The Glenlivet Single Cask Inveravon 21 Yrs
Glenmorangie Sonnalta PX

Svenska Eldvatten Glen Moray 1991
The Single Cask Glentauchers 14 Year Old
Highland Park 50 Years Old
AnCnoc Cutter 20.5 ppm
AnCnoc Rutter 11 ppm
That Boutique-y Whisky Company
Lagavulin 10 Year Old
  Lagavulin 12 Years Old
Special Release 2011
  Laphroaig Aged 25 Years
Cask Strength 2011
  Signatory Cask Strength Collection
Laphroaig Aged 15 Years
  Berry's Own Selection Linkwood 1987
Aged 26 Years
  The Cooper's Choice Lochside 1967
Aged 44 Years
  Hidden Spirits Longmorn LNG.315 11
Years Old
  Scyfion Mortlach 1996
  Tomatin 36 Year Old
  Master Of Malt Speyside 50 Years Old 3rd
Edition
  Port Askaig 100 Proof
  Saar Whisky Gruwehewwel
Scottish Grain
  Clan Denny Cambus Vintage Aged 25
Years Old
  The Sovereign Dumbarton Aged
50 Years Old
Scottish Vatted Malt
  Compass Box Flaming Heart Fifteenth
Anniversary
  The Last Vatted Malt
Scottish Blends
  Ballantine's Limited Release no. L40055
  The Last Drop 1965
  Teacher's Aged 25 Years
Irish Pure Pot Still
  Midleton Single Pot Still Single Cask 1991
  Powers John's Lane Release
Aged 12 Years
Irish Single Malt
  Teeling Whiskey Single Cask 2004
Bourbon
  Blanton's Gold Original Single Barrel
  Blanton's Uncut/Unfiltered
  Elmer T. Lee Bourbon 1919 - 2013
  Four Roses 125th Anniversary Small Batch
Bourbon
  George T. Stagg Limited Edition
  George T Stagg
  Virgin Bourbon 7 Years Old
American Straight Rye
  Sazerac Rye 18 Year Old
American Microdistilleries
  Garrison Brothers Cowboy Bourbon
Aged Four Years
  The Notch Aged 12 Years
Canadian Blended
  Masterson's 10 Year Old Straight Rye
Japanese Single Malt
  Chichibu 'The Peated' 2013
  The Hakushu Single Malt Whisky
Sherry Cask
  Scotch Malt Whisky Society Cask 119.14
Aged 11 Years
  Yamazaki Single Malt Sherry Cask 2016

Swiss Single Malt
  Langatun Single Malt Whisky 6 Year Old
  Langatun 10 Years
Welsh Single Malt
  Penderyn Portwood
Indian Single Malt
  Amrut Greedy Angels 10 Years Old
  Paul John Edited
New Zealand Single Malt
  The New Zealand Whisky Collection
Willowbank 1988 25 Years Old

96
Scottish Single Malt
  Aberfeldy Single Cask Unravel
  Aberlour A'Bunadh Batch No. 54
  Ardbeg 1977
  Ardbeg Kildalton 1980
  Ardbeg Provenance 1974
  Octomore 5 Years Old
  Port Charlotte PC10
  Gordon & MacPhail Cask Strength
Bruichladdich 1994
  The Whisky Barrel Port Charlotte 2003
  Burns Malt 12 Years Old
  Eiling Lim Bunnahabhain
34 Years Old 1980
  The Golden Cask Caol Ila 13 Years Old
  The Dalmore Candela Aged 50 Years
  Gordon & MacPhail Rare Vintage Glen
Albyn 1976
  Gordon & MacPhail Connoisseurs Choice
Glencadam 1993
  Maltbarn Glen Elgin 1995
  Glenfarclas 1966 Fino Cask
  The Last Drop Glen Garioch 47 Year Old
  Glenglassaugh 45 Years Old 1968
  Glen Grant Aged 10 Years
  Gordon & MacPhail Glen Grant 1948
  Gordon & MacPhail Connoisseurs
Choice Glenlossie
  Glen Scotia 1989 23 Years Old
  The Glenturret Fly's 16 Masters Edition
  Highland Park Sigurd
  Highland Park Loki Aged 15 Years
  Highland Park Aged 25 Years
  Highland Park 1973
  Kilchoman Port Cask Matured
  Master of Malt Single Cask Kilchoman
5 Years Old
  Laphroaig PX Cask
  Laphroaig Quarter Cask
  Gordon & MacPhail Rare Vintage
Glen Grant 1948
  Single Cask Collection Longmorn
Aged 23 Years
  Rosebank 25 Years Old
  Ledaig Dùsgadh 42 Aged 42 Years
  Elements of Islay BR5
  Ben Bracken Islay Single Malt 22 Years Old
  Old Malt Cask Probably Speyside's Finest
28 Years Old
  Whisky-Fässle Speyside Malt 20 Year Old
  Whisky-Fässle Speyside Region 1975
Scottish Grain
  The Clan Denny Cambus Aged 25 Years
  The Last Drop Dumbarton 54 Year Old

Cadenhead's Small Batch Port Dundas
Aged 25 Years
Whiskyjace Invergordon 24 Years Old 1991
Scottish Blends
Ballantine's Finest
Oishii Wisukii Aged 36 Years
Irish Pure Pot Still
Redbreast Aged 12 Years Cask Strength
Redbreast Aged 21 Years
Irish Single Malt
Scotch Malt Whisky Society Cask 118.3
Aged 22 Years
Irish Single Blends
Powers Gold label
Bourbon
1792 Full Proof Kentucky Straight Bourbon
Ancient Ancient Age 10 Years Old
Buffalo Trace Single Oak Project
Barrel #101
Old Weller Antique 107
Pappy Van Winkle's Family Reserve 15 YO
American Straight Rye
Bulleit 95 Rye
John David Albert's Taos Lightning
Very Rare 21 YO Barrel 28
Rittenhouse Rye Single Barrel Aged 25 Years
Barrel 19
American Microdistilleries
Balcones Crooked Texas Bourbon Barrel
McCarthy's Oregon Single Malt
Aged 3 Years
Cowboy Bourbon Texas Straight Bourbon
Whiskey Aged Three Years
Koval Single Barrel Four Grain Whiskey
Canadian Blended
Crown Royal Special Reserve
Japanese Single Malt
Scotch Malt Whisky Society Cask 124.5
The Yamazaki Single Malt Aged 18 Years
SMWS Cask 116.17 Aged 25 Years (Yoichi)
Belgian Single Malt
Gouldys 12 Years Old Distillers Range
English Single Malt
Hicks & Healey Cornish Whiskey 2004
The English Whisky Co. Chapter 6 English
Single Malt Not Peated
The English Whisky Co. Chapter 14
German Single Malt
Eifel Whisky Einzelfass Single Rye 2015
Swedish Single Malt
Mackmyra Moment "Malström"
Swiss Single Malt
Langatun Old Bear Châteauneuf-du-Pape
Welsh Single Malt
Penderyn Bourbon Matured Single Cask
Penderyn Single Cask PT9 LMDW Vintage
Australian Single Malt
The Good Convict Port Cask
Heartwood Any Port in a Storm
Timboon Single Malt Whisky
Indian Single Malt
Amrut Greedy Angels 10 Years Old
Amrut Greedy Angels
Paul John Single Malt Single Cask No 164
Paul John Single Malt Cask No 780
Paul John Single Malt Cask No 1846

95.5
Scottish Single Malt
Aberlour A'bunadh Batch No. 50
Cadenhead's Authentic Collection Ardbeg
Aged 20 Years
Kingsbury Gold Ardmore 6 Year Old 2008
Gordon & MacPhail Rare Old Banff 1966
The BenRiach Aged 12 Years Matured In
Sherry Wood
Benromach 30 Years Old
Scotch Malt Whisky Society Cask 50.75
Aged 25 Years
Cadenhead's Authentic Collection
Bowmore 15 Year Old
Gleann Mór Bowmore 30 Year Old
Port Charlotte The Peat Project
Caol Ila 14 Years Old Unpeated Style
Whisky-Fässle Clynelish 16 Year Old
The Dalmore Visitor Centre Exclusive
Glenfarclas The Family Casks 1955
Glenfarclas The Family Casks 1956
Glenfarclas The Family Casks 1963
Glenfarclas 105
Glenfarclas 1994
Glenglassaugh 1978 35 Years Old
Glen Grant Distillery Edition Cask Strength
Aged 20 Years
Gordon & MacPhail Rare Vintage Glen
Grant 1956
Eiling Lim Glen Keith 21 Years Old
Glengoyne 25 Year Old
The Glenlivet Archive 21 Years of Age
The Glenlivet Nàdurra First Fill Selection
The Glenlivet Archive 21 Years of Age
The Glenlivet Nadurra Aged 16 Years
Glenmorangie 25 Years Old
Cadenhead's Authentic Collection
Glen Ord 11 Year Old
Cadenhead's Authentic Collection
Glentauchers 38 Year Old
Old Particular Highland Glenturret 28
Years Old
Hazelburn Rundlets & Kilderkins 10 Years
Hazelburn Rundlets & Kilderkins 11 Years
Highland Park Aged 18 Years
Highland Park Vintage 1978
The Peated Arran "Machrie Moor" 4th Ed.
Kilchoman 2007 Vintage
Kilchoman 100% Islay The 5th Edition
Kilchoman Single Cask Release
AnCnoc 1999
Lagavulin 12 Year Old
The First Editions Laphroaig Aged 19
Years 1996
Scotch Malt Whisky Society Cask 7.129
Aged 30 Years
The Macallan Fine Oak 12 Years Old
The Macallan Oscuro
The Warehouse Collection Macduff Aged
18 Years
Cadenhead Single Cask Mannochmore
37 Year Old
Gordon & MacPhail Connoisseurs Choice
Mannochmore 1994
Rosebank 21 Year Old
Cadenhead's Tamdhu-Glenlivet Port Cask
Aged 22 Years
Le Gus't Selection V Ledaig 2008

Old Particular Highland Leidag Aged 21 Yrs
Cù Bòcan Highland Single Malt 1989
Vintage
Tomatin 1988
Tomintoul Aged 33 Years
Glen Fahrn Airline Nr 05 Tomintoul 1968
Aged 43 Years
Old Malt Cask Tormore 26 Years Old
Celtique Connexion Origine Islay Affine
Sauternes cask
Wemyss 30 Years Islay "Heathery Smoke"

Scottish Grain
A.D. Rattray Girvan
The Pearls of Scotland North of Scotland
1971
The Pearls of Scotland Invergordon 1997
The Sovereign Port Dundas 27 Years Old
The Sovereign Port Dundas Aged 36 Years
The Pearls of Scotland Strathclyde 1988

Scottish Vatted Malt
Compass Box Flaming Heart
Compass Box The Lost Blend
Compass Box The Spice Tree

Scottish Blends
Ballantine's Aged 30 Years
Ballantine's Limited Release no. J13295
The Chivas 18 Ultimate Cask Collection
First Fill American Oak
Glenalba Aged 34 Years Sherry Cask Finish
Johnnie Walker Black Label 12 Years Old
John Walker & Sons Private Collection
2015 Edition
Royal Salute "62 Gun Salute"
William Grant's 25 Years Old

Irish Single Malt
Eiling Lim Irish Single Malt
22 Years Old 1991
The Tyrconnell Single Cask 11 Year Old
Bushmills Aged 21 Years
Whisky-Fässle Irish Single Malt 1989

Bourbon
Blade and Bow 22 Year Old
Buffalo Trace Single Oak Project Barrel #27
Buffalo Trace Single Oak Project Barrel #30
Buffalo Trace Single Oak Project Barrel #63
Buffalo Trace Single Oak Project Barrel #183
Buffalo Trace Experimental Collection 12
Year Old Bourbon From Floor #9
Charter 101
Elijah Craig Barrel Proof Bourbon 12 Years
Knob Creek Aged 9 Years
Smooth Ambler Old Scout Straight
Bourbon 10 Years Old
Willett Pot Still Reserve

American Straight Rye
George Dickel Rye
Michter's No. 1 Straight Rye
Sazerac Kentucky Straight Rye 18 Years Old
Thomas H. Handy Sazerac
Thomas H. Handy Sazerac Straight Rye

American Straight Wheat
Parker's Heritage Collection Original Batch
Kentucky Straight Wheat Whiskey Aged
13 Years

American Microdistilleries
291 M Colorado Whiskey Rye Malt
Bad Guy Bourbon
Hillrock Single Malt Whiskey

Reservoir Distillery Rye Whiskey
Rock Town Arkansas Rye Whiskey
Stranahan's Snowflake Cab Franc
The Notch Aged 8 Years
The Notch Aged 10 Years
Westland American Single Malt Whiskey
Single Cask 115

Other American Whiskey
Buffalo Trace Experimental Collection
French Oak Barrel Head Aged

Canadian Blended
Alberta Premium
Forty Creek Port Wood Reserve
Gibson's Finest Rare Aged 18 Years

Japanese Single Malt
SMWS Cask 120.7 Aged 14 Years
Ichiro's Malt Aged 20 Years

Japanese Single Grain
Kawasaki Single Grain

Austrian Single Malt
Peter Affenzeller Single Malt Whisky 7
Years Old

Czech Republic Single Malt
Gold Cock Single Malt Whisky Aged 24
Years 1992

English Single Malt
The English Whisky Co. Chapter 6 English
Single Malt Not Peated
The English Whisky Co. Chapter 15 Heavily
Peated
Stephen Notman Whisky Live Taipei 2013

French Single Malt
Kornog Saint Ivy 2015

German Single Malt
Valerie Amarone Single Malt Whisky 4
Years Old

Swiss Single Malt
Langatun Old Deer Cask Strength
Langatun Old Mustang Bourbon 4 Year
Old recipe
The Swiss Malt

Swedish Single Malt
Gute Single Malt Whisky
Mackmyra Moment "Rimfrost"

Australian Single Malt
Heartwood 2 of /3 Tasmanian Malt Whisky
Heartwood The Beagle 3 Tasmania Vatted
Malt Whisky
Heartwood Devil in the Detail
Sullivan's Cove American Oak Single Cask

Indian Single Malt
Paul John Indian Single Malt Bold
Paul John Single Cask No 1833
Paul John Single Malt Cask No 692
Paul John Single Malt Cask No 784
Paul John Single Malt Cask No 1444

Indian Blends
Rendezvous

Taiwanese Single malt
Kavalan Single Malt Manzanilla Sherry
Cask

95 (New Entries Only)
Scottish Single Malt
Gordon & MacPhail Connoisseurs Choice
Aberfeldy 1999
Aberlour A'Bunadh Batch No. 53
Simon Brown Aberlour 1991

Cadenhead's Authentic Collection Ardbeg 21 Year Old
Acla Selection Bladnoch 25 Years Old
Old Malt Cask Blair Athol Aged 20 Years
Reifferscheid Private Cask Port Charlotte 9 Year Old
Clynelish Select Reserve
Scotch Malt Whisky Society Cask 37.70 Aged 15 Years
Cadenhead's Rum Cask Dalmore 24 Year Old
Dalwhinnie Winter's Gold
Glen Grant Aged 12 Years
Spirits Shop Selection & Sansibar Whisky Glenlossie 1992
Glenmorangie Tarlogan
Kininvie 23 Years Old
Old Particular Islay Laphroaig 14 Years Old
Old Particular Islay Laphroaig 15 Years Old
Old Malt Cask Linkwood Aged 18 Years
Tomatin 2002 Whisky L Beijing - Shanghai 2015
Spirits Shop Selection & Sansibar Whisky Speyside Malt 1977

Scottish Vatted Malt
Five Lions Westport 18 Years Old

Scottish Grain
Whiskybroker Caledonian 28 Year Old
Old Particular Cambus 27 Years Old
The Sovereign Carsebridge 50 Years Old

Unspecified Grain
Svenska Eldvatten Grain 1964

Bourbon
Baker's Aged 7 Years Kentucky Straight Bourbon Whiskey
Buffalo Trace Experimental Collection Old Fashioned Sour Mash Entry Proof 125
Knob Creek Single Barrel Reserve Aged 9 Years

American Microdistilleries
77 Whiskey Local Rye & Corn 483 Days Old
A.D. Law Origins Four Grain Straight Bourbon Bottled in Bond
Rock Town Arkansas Bourbon Whiskey Flavour Grain
Wyoming Barrel Strength Bourbon Whiskey

Japanese Single Malt
Ichiro's Malt Chichibu Peated 2015

Austrian Single Malt
Broger Burn Out Single Malt Whisky

Czech Republic Single Malt
Gold Cock Single Malt Whisky 1992 Slivovitz Finish

Denmark Single Malt
Stauning Peated 6th Edition
Stauning Young Rye 2013

French Single Malt
Kornog Roc'h Hir

German Single Malt
Valerie Amarone Cask Single Malt
Derrina Roggenmalz Schwarzwälder Single Malt Whisky

Italian Single Malt
PUNI Alba 3 Year Old

Swedish Single Malt
BOX The Archipelago 2016

Swiss Single Malt
Johnett Single Cask Swiss Single Malt Whisky Rum Trinidad Finish

Welsh Single Malt
Penderyn Madeira Finish
Penderyn Myth
Penderyn Portwood Single Cask PT165

Australian Single Malt
Bakery Hill Classic Malt

Indian Single Malt
Paul John Mars Orbiter
That Boutique-y Whisky Company Paul John Batch 1

94.5 (New Entries Only)

Scottish Single Malt
Hunter Laing's Old & Rare Aberlour Aged 25 Years
Old Particular Speyside Aberlour 21 Years Old
The First Editions Bowmore Aged 15 Years 2000
Five Lions Braes of Glenlivet Aged 20 Years
Brora 37 Year Old
Whic Port Charlotte 12 Years Old
Whic Port Charlotte 12 Years Old
Hepburn's Choice Caol Ila 5 Years Old
Old Particular Islay Caol Ila 19 Years Old
Cadenhead's Small Batch Dalmore 25 Year Old
That Boutique-y Whisky Company Glenburgie
Sansibar Whisky Glen Garioch Aged 23 Years 1991
Gordon & MacPhail Rare Vintage Glenlivet 1974
Eiling Lim Glenlossie 23 Years Old 1992
Glen Scotia Single Cask Distillery Edition No. 002
That Boutique-y Whisky Company Lagavulin
MacAlabur Laphroaig 16 Year Old
Scotch Malt Whisky Society Cask 29.181 Aged 20 Years
Highlander Inn Longmorn Aged 23 Years
Old Particular Speyside Miltonduff 15 Years Old
Simon Brown The Speyside Distillery
Whiskybroker Speyside 15 Year Old
Tobermory 42 Year Old
Tomintoul Five Decades
Old Ballantruan Aged 10 Years
The Classic Cask 40 Year Old

Scottish Vatted Malt
Chapter 7 Peatside 2009
Compass Box Enlightenment

Irish Pure Pot Still
Teeling Whiskey Single Cask
Teeling Whiskey Vintage Reserve Silver Bottling 23 Years Old

Bourbon
1792 Single Barrel Kentucky Straight Bourbon
Eagle Rare 17 Years Old
Jack Daniel's Single Barrel Proof Tennessee Whiskey
Governor's Reserve Taos Lightning Straight Rye Whiskey

American Micro Distilleries
Garrison Brothers Texas Straight Bourbon
Single Barrel Aged Two Years
  Iron Smoke Apple Wood Smoked Whiskey
A.D. Law Four Grain Straight Bourbon
Aged No Less Than 3 Years
  Ghost Owl Pacific Northwest Rye Whisky
Canadian Single Malt
  Crown Royal Hand Selected Barrel
J.P. Wiser's Last Barrels Aged 14 Years
Austrian Single Malt
  STGB Tiroler Single Malt Whisky Aged
3 Years
  Dark Single Malt J.H. Cask Strength
Denmark Single Malt
  Braunstein Danish Single Malt Cask
Edition no. 6
  Stauning KAOS
English Single Malt
  English Whisky Co. Chapter 14
German Single Malt
  Blaue Maus Single Cask Malt Whisky
Fassstärke
  Otto's Uisge Beatha Single Cask Malt
Whisky
Litchenstein Single Malt
  Telser Liechtenstein Single Malt Whisky IX
Swiss Single Malt
  Buechibärger Whisky Single Malt
Fassstärke 2006
Welsh Single Malt
  Penderyn Celt
Australian Single Malt
  Bakery Hill Classic Malt
  Mackey Tasmanian Single Malt Aged 6
Years
Taiwanese Single Malt
  Kavalan Solist Moscatel

94 (New Entries Only)

Scottish Single Malt
  Acla Selection Ardmore 14 Years Old
  Old Malt Cask Auchentoshan Aged
21 Years
  Provenance Aultmore Aged 7 Years
  Hunter Laing's Distiller's Art Braeval
Aged 13 Years
  Old Malt Cask Braeval Aged 14 Years
  Cragganmore 25 Year Old
  The Dalmore 30 Year Old
  Dalwhinnie The Distillers Edition Double
Matured
  The Singleton of Glendullan 38 Year Old
  Old Malt Cask Glen Elgin Aged 25 Years
  Glenfarclas The Family Casks
2000 Release W15
  Gordon & MacPhail Rare Vintage
Glen Grant 1965
  Glenmorangie Grand Vintage Malt 1990
  Glen Moray Elgin Heritage Aged 18 Years
  Scotch Malt Whisky Society Cask 35.137
Aged 25 Years
  That Boutique-y Whisky Company
Highland Park
  Romantic Rhine Collection Isle of Arran
19 Year Old
  Scotch Malt Whisky Society Cask 121.82
Aged 15 Years
  Laphroaig Lore

Old Particular Islay Laphroaig 15 Years Old
  Best Dram Linkwood 14 Years Old
  The Deveron 18 Year Old
  Old Malt Cask Macduff Aged 18 Years
  Cadenhead's Wine Cask Miltonduff
21 Year Old
  C&S Dram Collection Speyside Aged
22 Years
  Romantic Rhine Collection Speyside 23
Year Old
  Cadenhead's Authentic Collection
Strathisla 25 Year Old
  Hepburn's Choice Tobermory Smoky &
Peaty 8 Years Old
  The Warehouse Collection Tomatin Aged
20 Years
  Tomintoul Aged 15 Years Portwood Finish
  William Cadenhead Islay 7 Year Old
Irish Pure Pot Still
  Chapter 7 Irish Single Malt 1999
16 Years Old
Bourbon
  Elijah Craig Single Barrel Aged 18 Years
  That Boutique-y Whisky Company
Heaven Hil
  Turley Mill Straight Rye Western Whiskey
  Whiskey Del Bac Dorado Mesquite
Smoked Single Malt
  Kings County Distillery Peated Bourbon
Whiskey
  Nelson's Green Brier Tennessee White
Whiskey
  Rock Town Arkansas Single Barrel Reserve
Bourbon Whiskey Aged 15 Months
Canadian Single Malt
  Crown Royal Northern Harvest Rye
  Gooderham & Worts Four Grain
  J.P. Wiser's Double Still Rye
Austrian Single Malt
  Broger Medium Smoked Single Malt
Whisky
  Original Rye Whisky J.H. Selection
Denmark Single Malt
  Braunstein Danish Single Malt Cask
Edition no. 2
  Braunstein Danish Single Malt Cask
Edition no. D28
  Stauning Danish Single Malt Virgin
Oak 2010
English Single Malt
  Cotswolds Distillery Single Malt Spirit
20 Months Old
  Master of Malt Single Cask English Whisky
Co. 5 Year Old Heavily Peated
German Single Malt
  Saillt Mór Pfälzer Eiche Single Malt Whisky
  Spreewälder Sloupisti Single Malt Whisky
Swedish Single Malt
  Spirit of Hven Organic Single Malt 7
Stars No. 4 Megrez
Welsh Single Malt
  Penderyn Madeira Finish
  Penderyn Peated
Australian Single Malt
  Belgrove Distillery Rye Whisky 100% Rye
  Heartwood Spiritual Journey
Indian Single Malt
  Paul John Brilliance

Scottish Malts

For those of you deciding to take the plunge and head off into the labyrinthine world of Scotch malt whisky, a piece of advice. And that is, be careful who you take your advice from. Because, too often, I hear that you should leave the Islays until you have tackled the featherlight Speysiders and the bolder, weightier Highlanders. This is just complete, patronising nonsense. The only time that rings true is if you are tasting a number of whiskies in one day. Then leave the smoky ones till last, so the lighter chaps get a fair hearing.

I know many people who didn't like whisky until they got a Talisker from Skye inside them, or a Lagavulin to swamp their tastebuds with oily iodine. The fact is, you can take your map of malt whisky, start at any point and head in whichever direction you feel. There are no hard and fast rules. Certainly with nearly 3,000 tasting notes for Scottish malts here you should have some help in picking where this journey of a lifetime begins.

It is also worth remembering not always to be seduced by age. It is true that many of the highest scores are given to big-aged whiskies. The truth is that the majority of malts, once they have lived beyond 25 years or so, suffer from oak influence rather than benefit. Part of the fun of discovering whiskies is to see how malts from different distilleries perform to age and type of cask. Happy discovering.

LEWIS

Abhainn Dearg

SKYE

Talisker

Ardnamu

Tobermory

MULL

Oban

Isle of Ju

ISLAY

Isle of Ar

Springbank
Glen Scotia
Glengyle

Islay

Bunnahabhain

Caol Ila

Kilchoman

Bruichladdich

Bowmore

Port Ellen   Ardbeg
Laphroaig   Lagavulin

ORKNEY
ISLANDS
Highland Park
Scapa

Wolfburn

Pultney

Clynelish
Brora

Balblair
Glenmorangie
Dalmore
Invergordon
Teaninich
Glenglassaugh   Banff
Speyside see page 24
Glenglassaugh   Macduff
Glen Ord
Royal Brackla   Knockdhu
Inverness   Glenugie
Glen Albyn   Glendronach
Glen Mhor   Tomatin   Ardmore
Millburn   Glen Garioch
The Speyside Distillery
Royal Lochnagar   Aberdeen

Dalwhinnie
Glenury Royal
Fettercairn
Glencadam
Blair Athol   North Port   Glenesk
Fort William   Lochside
Ben Nevis   Edradour   Arbikie
Glenlochy   Aberfeldy
Strathearn   Dundee
Glenturret   Perth
Daftmill
Tullibardine   Eden Mill   Kingsbarns
Deanston   Cameronbridge
Glengoyne
Rosebank   Glenkinchie
Loch Lomond   St. Magdelene
Dumbarton   Starlaw   Edinburgh
Interleven   Glasgow   North British
Littlemill   Strathclyde
Auchentoshan   Port Dundas
Kinclaith

Girvan
Ailsa Bay
Ladyburn

Annandale

Bladnoch

Key

● **Major Town or City**
▲ **Single Malt Distillery**
▲ **(*Italics*) Grain Distillery**
✝ **Dead Distillery**

Speyside

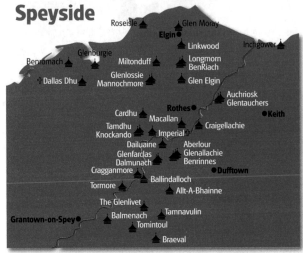

Roseisle   Glen Moray

Elgin ●

Linkwood   Inchgower

Glenburgie

Benromach

Glenlossie
Mannochmore

Dallas Dhu

Miltonduff

Longmorn
BenRiach

Glen Elgin

Auchriosk
Glentauchers

Cardhu
Macallan

Rothes ●

● Keith

Tamdhu
Knockando

Imperial

Craigellachie

Dailuaine

Aberlour

Glenfarclas
Dalmunach

Glenallachie
Benrinnes

Cragganmore

● Dufftown

Tormore

Ballindalloch

Allt-A-Bhainne

The Glenlivet

Balmenach

Tamnavulin

Grantown-on-Spey ●

Tomintoul

Braeval

Distilleries by Town	Mortlach	Glenrothes
Dufftown	Dufftown	Glenspey
Glenfiddich	Pittyvaich	**Keith**
Convalmore	**Rothes**	Aultmore
Balvenie	Speyburn	Strathmill
Kininvie	Glen Grant	Glen Keith
Glendullan	Caperdonich	Strathisla

SINGLE MALTS
ABERFELDY

Highlands (Perthshire), 1898. John Dewar & Sons. Working.

Aberfeldy 12 Year Old db **(81) n21 t21 f19 b20.** A puzzling malt. Aberfeldy makes and matures some of the greatest whisky on this planet, make no mistake. So why this conservative, ultra safe toffee-sultana-fudge offering when their warehouses are crammed with casks which could blow the world away? Pleasant. But so relentlessly dull and disappointing. And 40% abv...? Really...? 40% WB16/031

⬧ **Aberfeldy 16 Year Old** db **(89.5) n22.5** ight, leathery and with a citrus freshness; **t23.5** succulent, with a ripe melon sweetness meeting an earthier, almost semi-phenolic, substrata; a beautiful match; **f21.5** should recede in layers. Yet, despite some lingering sugars, fades with a surprising flatness; **b22** finishes far too fast and tamely. But the thrust of the malt is wonderful. 40%

Aberfeldy 21 Year Old db **(88) n22** not exactly faultless, but there is at least an attractive degree of landscaping to this fruity aroma; **t22.5** exactly the silky toffee-laden delivery one might expect from the nose. But some charming spices burst through, and even some voluptuous and juicy malts; **f21.5** coffee cake with an irritating injection of light sulphur; **b22** the kind of malt I wish I could be let loose on...this really could be world class. But... 40% WB16/032

Aberfeldy Aged 25 Years db **(85) n24 t21 f19 b21.** Just doesn't live up to the nose. When Tommy Dewar wrote, "We have a great regard for old age when it is bottled," as quoted on the label, I'm not sure he had as many as 25 years in mind. 40%.

Aberfeldy Bits of Strange 16 Year Old db **(94.5) n24 t23.5 f23 b24** One of those lovely casks which combines oaky and sugary bits in just the right proportions. A cracker of a cask – and sublime by present day sherry standards. The perfect way to start or end a day... 55.1%. sc..

Aberfeldy Single Cask Unravel db **(96) n24 t24 f24 b24** This completes the best set of single cask malts I have tasted from any Scottish distillery for the last four or five years. Restores one's faith, it does... Oh, and this is supposed to be savoured while listening to some music. Don't bother; it conjures a major symphony of its own...56.5%. sc. John Dewar & Sons.

Gordon & Macphail Cask Strength Aberfeldy refill sherry hogsheads, cask no. 2488, 2489 & 2491, dist 07 Apr 1995, bott 29 Jan 2014 (93) n22 t23.5 f24 b23.5 a fabulous meal of a malt. What a wonderful distillery this is. *55.8%. WB15/113*

◇ **Gordon & MacPhail Connoisseurs Choice Aberfeldy 1999** (95) n23.5 such a seductive degree of light smoke: almost like Arbroath Smokies on a plate in the next room; freshly planed wood and a tart, salty seasoning and roasted cashews: not exactly what you might expect from a malt distilled in the middle of Scotland...but so very Aberfeldy...! t24 no less seductive mouth feel: soft yet with just enough firmness for the barley to stand up and be counted; slowly, a gorgeous heather-honey sweetness emerges, alongside a milky mocha and vague mintiness; f23.5 that milky mocha lasts the pace, perhaps with a little molasses now just to see it to the end; b24 this is a great distillery: I am always a little disappointed when bottlings of it aren't up to this standard. Gordon and MacPhail set the benchmark. One of the most old-fashioned styles of malt still found in the Highlands and almost perfectly weighted. *46%*

Provenance Aberlour Over 7 Years refill barrel, cask no. 10766, dist Summer 08, bott Summer 15 (89) n22 t23 f22 b22 Tasted on the hottest July day on record in Britain, this refreshing youngster could not have come along at a better time. *46%. nc ncf sc.*

Wemyss Malts 1999 Single Highland Aberfeldy "Snuffed Candle" hogshead, bott 2014 (88) n23 t23.5 a freshly blasted shotgun offers the earthier tones to this where elsewhere glazed fruit abounds; t23 voluptuous mouth-feel. There is an immediate impact of spice, half-hearted at first but grows – and glows – quickly. After an initial malty spurt, the fruit holds ground; f20 curiously bitter and rigid; b21.5 some disappointing oak at the death puts the dampeners on an otherwise full blood malt. *46%. sc. 379 bottles.*

ABERLOUR

Speyside, 1826. Chivas Brothers. Working.

Aberlour 10 Years Old db (87.5) n22.5 t22 f21 b22. Remains a lusty fellow though here nothing like as sherry-cask faultless as before, nor displaying its usual honeyed twinkle. *43%*

Aberlour 10 Years Old Sherry Cask Finish db (85) n21 t21 f21 b22. Bipolar and bittersweet with the firmness of the grain in vivid contrast to the gentle grape. *43%*

Aberlour 12 Years Old Double Cask Matured db (88.5) n22 t22.5 f22 b22. Voluptuous and mouth-watering in some areas, firmer and less expansive in others. Pretty tasty in all of them. *43%*

Aberlour 12 Years Old Non Chill-Filtered db (87) n22.5 t22 f21 b21.5. There are many excellent facets to this malt, not least the balance between barley and grape and the politeness of the gristy sugars. But a sulphured butt has crept into this one, taking the edge off the excellence and bringing down the score like a cold front drags down the thermometer. *48%. ncf.*

Aberlour 12 Years Old Sherry Cask Matured db (88) n23 t22 f21 b22. Could do with some delicate extra sweetness to take it to the next level. Sophisticated nonetheless. *40%*

Aberlour 15 Years Cuvee Marie d'Ecosse db (91) n22 t24 f22 b23. This always was a deceptive lightweight, and it's got lighter still. It is sold primarily in France, and one can assume only that this is God's way of making amends for that pretentious, over-rated, caramel-ridden rubbish called Cognac they've had to endure. *43%*

Aberlour 15 Year Old Double Cask Matured db (84) n23 t22 f19 b20. Brilliant nose full of vibrant apples and spiced sultana, but then, after a complex, chewy, malt-enriched kick-off, falls surprisingly flat on its face. *40%*

Aberlour 15 Year Old Sherry Finish db (91) n24 exceptionally clever use of oak to add a drier element to the sharper boiled cooking apple. And a whiff of the fermenting vessel, too; t22 the sharp fruit of the nose is magnified here ten times; f23 wave upon wave of malt concentrate; b22 quite unique: freaky, even. Really a whisky to be discovered and ridden. Once you acclimatize, you'll adore it. *43%*

Aberlour 18 Years Old db (91) n22 thick milkshake with various fruits and vanilla; t22 immediate fresh juice which curdles beautifully as the vanilla is added; f24 wonderful fruit-chocolate fudge development: long, and guided by a gentle oiliness; b23 another high performance distillery age-stated bottling. *43%*

Aberlour 100 Proof db (91) n23 t23 f22 b23. Stunning, sensational whisky, the most extraordinary Speysider of them all...which it was when I wrote those official notes for the bottling back in '97, I think. Other malts have superseded it now, but on re-tasting I stand by those original notes, though I disassociate myself entirely with the rubbish: "In order to savour Aberlour 100 at its best add 1/3 to 1/2 pure water. *57.1%*

Aberlour A'Bunadh Batch No. 45 Spanish oloroso sherry butts db (95) n24 t24 f23 b24 Faultless sherry of the old school. *60.2%. sc nc ncf. WB15/332*

Aberlour A'Bunadh Batch No. 47 db (88.5) n22 t24 f20.5 b22 A valued friend of mine, Byron Rodgers, one of Britain's greatest living essayists, asked me over a pint the other night what I thought of the A'Bunadh batch 47 they were selling at our nearest Waitrose. You see, I had recently brought him, wide eyed and innocent, into a world of cask strength whisky; and being a man of infinite curiosity he was determined to learn more very much in the manner of an astronaut having landed on an alien and wondrous landscape. I couldn't tell him, as I had not yet tasted it. Well, I have now. And tomorrow I will advise him to go forth and invest in a bottle, though with a warning. Because as learning curves go, by and large this is a pretty delicious one. Yet perhaps better still for the explorer, it contains a fault from which much can be learned. Like what happens when you pit one bad butt against many good ones. 60.7%.

Aberlour A'Bunadh Batch No. 48 Spanish oloroso sherry butts db (92) n24 grape must and nippy mixed spice; t22 for once, the barley is heard early. But not for long, as lots of natural caramels mix with the grape to make for a thick mouth feel. Elsewhere the spices kick in with a degree of venom; f23 still nips and tingles, though Demerara sugar tries to heal the wounds; b23 delicious. But surprisingly aggressive for an a'bunadh. 59.7%. sc nc ncf. WB15/333

Aberlour A'Bunadh Batch No. 50 db (95.5) n23.5 t24.5 f24 b23.5 It seems a long time ago now. But I can remember sitting with the good people of Aberlour when they showed me what they had planned for batch 1 of a new brand called a'bunadh. I was thrilled that they were going for it with a no-holds barred malt...but nervous they were using sherry butts. That was some time ago...and now they have reached 50 not out. Miraculously, they have managed, usually, to avoid the worst excesses of present day sherry butts. And they have done so again here to bring their half century up in style. Ladies and gentlemen of Aberlour: I raise a glass to you in celebration. 59.6% WB16/027

◇ **Aberlour A'Bunadh Batch No. 53** db (95) n23 dry oloroso at play: clean, sulphur-free, though with an intriguing playdough edge to the fruit and nut; t24 the spices are off like a rocket, so waspish that for a moment they make you jolt! But slowly things calm into a more structured and sensible procession of rich grape notes, mainly of the burnt raisin variety; a little dark muscovado backs up the fruit; f24 lush, oily and, unusual for an a'bunadh, a vague wave of malt can be clearly heard, though not for too long. The dates and molasses on the finish are scrummy! Oh, and a final salivating rush of green apple and barley at the end for a late juicy surprise...; b24 a truly beautiful whisky. But, oh! Had only Batch 54 been this sulphur free we would have entered a new experience of whisky perfection. 59.7%

◇ **Aberlour A'Bunadh Batch No. 54** db (96) n23.5 quite a tight nose, on account of the almost opaque intensity of the grape and a mild dose of the 'S' word.; t25 not sure I can remember an A'Bunadh quite this totally switched on and in control from the moment it first passes your lips. The delivery is, quite simply, perfection. As oloroso goes, this is the highest ranking intensity and this is borne out by the truly unbelievable and mesmeric layering which follows for the next two or three minutes. Indeed, it is hard to know just where the middle ends and the finish starts, so mind-blowingly well-orchestrated is the structure. What is most amazing is that the first ten or twelve flavour waves are ones of salivating lightness, as both the fruit and grain makes the juices flow like you have rarely felt them do so before. Then we move towards the mid-ground where the earlier menacing spices – which themselves whip up a further frenzy of salivation – now weave and bob about with the ever-growing tannin and earthier fruit. And when we say fruit, we are talking thick plum pudding, slightly overcooked fruitcake where someone forgot to stop adding the raisins, all sweetened by molasses and maple syrup. And maybe some liquorice added for extra depth before the molasses arrives. Layer, upon, layer, upon layer...seemingly unable to end; meanwhile the spices nip and buzz; f23 not easy to pick up where the start actually begins, maybe perhaps just after where those fabulous cocoa notes (definitely a Venezuelan style at play here) begin to gain more than a foothold. But at least a dozen more ever-lightening layers of the above. Until a very slight sulphur note pricks the tongue and roof of the mouth...; b24.5 had the nose and finish been quite up there with the delivery, we would have had a record score. Just a slight sulphur trace, but probably enough to dash the World Whisky of the Year (indeed, this is the closest to a Yamazaki 17 I have yet unearthed) this might have otherwise so fully deserved. For just the delivery alone – and for the ensuing two minutes with its perfect weight, oils, distribution of flavours and pace of evolvement – no whisky will be better this year, or probably next. It had even crossed my mind to give it 25.5...! A privilege to experience... 60.7%

Cadenhead's Small Batch Aberlour-Glenlivet Aged 23 Years bourbon hogsheads, dist 1989, bott 2013 (93.5) n23 thin-ish and warming...the spirit safe was taking a bit of a pounding. But the cut was true, leaving the malt to show a late, warming clarity. The cask is in perfect sync, offering just a light banana and custard accompaniment; t24.5 astonishingly clean and salivating. The grist appears to have been set in icing sugar; the warm buzz does not appear to be oak-induced spice...; some gorgeous heather-honey adds perfect weight; **f23** more of the same...forever, it seems; and still warms...; **b23** one of the cleanest, sweetest 23 year olds you'll ever encounter. But I suspect the distiller manager of the time, Puss Mitchell, had the stills at full revs when this was made. A hottie! *54.9%. 522 bottles. WB15/069*

Darkness! Aberlour Aged 20 Years Oloroso Cask Finish (95) n23.5 t24 f23.5 b24 "Subtlety, poise and elegance have no place here" claims the back label. Now, I wonder where they get that phrase from...? But, as it happens, this is exactly what the whisky has, helped enormously by the fact that sulphur is wonderfully conspicuous by its absence... *53.4%. 96 bottles. WB15/199*

⬥ **Distilleries Collection Aberlour Aged 19 Years 1994** bott 2014 **(89.5) n22.5** a buzzing maltiness also shows a distinct move towards the first hints of eucalyptus; **t22** the age is evident on delivery, with the tannins off to a flyer. Slowly, though, the honey begins to take effect, very much of a heather-honey style; **f22.5** a little salty and sharp, the honey now better defined and allowing only so much spice; **b22.5** a steady, confident bottling with massive accent on the honey. *56.8%. Bottled for Scotch Malt Sales Ltd.*

⬥ **Hunter Laing's Old & Rare Aberlour Aged 25 Years** refill hogshead, cask no. 15133, dist Oct 90, bott Mar 16 **(94.5) n24** just love the orange peel mixing in with the ulmo honey; the slightly salty oak and barley gel to form a fascinating sub strata; **t23.5** deep barley: rich and thick. But the orange blossom honey is always within touching distance; a lovely salivating thread is always apparent; **f23.5** a salt and pepper fade as the tannins ramp up the sharper notes; **b23.5** a seriously classy dram from the first magnificent sniff onwards. *50.3%. nc ncf sc. 150 bottles.*

The Maltman Aberlour Aged 19 Years bourbon cask **(94.5) n23 t23.5 f24 b24** Absolutely brilliant to see Aberlour naked and not hiding behind sherry: there is rare beauty to behold... *46%*

⬥ **Old Particular Speyside Aberlour 20 Years Old** refill hogshead, cask no. 10779, dist Feb 95, bott Feb 15 **(86.5) n21.5 t22 f21.5 b21.5.** A steady old dram concentrating on the high propane barley which, early on, is juicy, thick and intense. The oak element is a touch tangy. *51.5%. nc ncf sc. 300 bottles.*

⬥ **Old Particular Speyside Aberlour 21 Years Old** refill hogshead, dist Feb 95, bott Feb 16 **(94.5) n23.5** a perky nose, one with a surprising degree of smoke. Not huge phenols, but enough to raise a greying eyebrow, as peat is something hardly ever associated with the Speysider. There is a charming gristiness to this, and weight also thanks to the phenols...; **t23.5** clean, intense and chewy. Not the Aberlour one might expect, bristling with lively malt and apples. But instead ponderous and weighed down with dark sugars and the outline of something distinctly phenolic; **f23.4** a lovely liquorice and smoked molasses mix; the oak conjures up a delightfully well weighted last few layers; **b24** well, an Aberlour with a dab of smoke. Some smoked malt accidentally got into the mix? Or matured in an old Laphroaig or Ardbeg cask? Who knows? Really doesn't matter as the result is truly wonderful. *51.5%. nc ncf sc. 278 bottles.*

⬥ **Simon Brown Aberlour 1991** bourbon casks, dist Sept 91, bott Jun 05 **(95) n24** freshly diced, early autumnal apples: clean yet gorgeously layered, with the malt and oak showing exceptional poise and refinement; dashes of cedar wood and even the tiniest pinch of allspice season things rather enigmatically; some captivating cocoa notes also thread through the narrative; **t23.5** taste when insufficiently warmed and the dryness of the cedar translates emphatically. Warm a little and the oils and sugars raise their game and the overall intensity and balance of the malt itself; **f23.5** long, thanks to those oils, with a vague spice buzz to the languid dried molasses; **b24** a stunner of a bottling which rewards time spent with it handsomely. *46%. nc ncf.*

That Boutique-y Whisky Company Aberlour batch 3 **(90.5) n23.5** superb Speyside-style nose; clean malt showing both confidence and a shrill austerity; **t23** superb delivery: a bunch of sugars – mainly from the maple syrup family – cling to the malty coattails; **f21.5** bitters slightly, but that malt carries on undeterred; **b22.5** some 30 years ago Aberlour had very little body and would not have impressed in this form. Certainly not the case today: though a light whisky, enough oils cling to the frame to make for something substantial. *49.2%.*

⬥ **That Boutique-y Whisky Company Aberlour 23 Year Old** batch 4 **(92) n22** well mannered oak shows you its soft vanilla side. The malt, clean and uncompromised, promises much...; **t23.5** wow! And it doesn't let you down as it arrives in almost thick syrup form with the barley grist being made up into a slightly oily paste when mixed with light muscovado. The spices show plenty of oak is at play; **f23** long with an almost German-style malty-hoppy bitterness towards the end; **b23.5** not a malt interested much in complexity. But the malt and muscovado show it puts on is pretty dazzling! *51%. 432 bottles.*

⬥ **Xtra Old Particular Speyside Aberlour 25 Years Old** sherry butt, dist Nov 90, bott Nov 15 **(90) n24** classic dry oloroso in all its nutty splendour; **t24** a beautiful combination of mouth-watering barley and eye-wateringly dry oloroso; sublime spices weave into the middle ground to excellent effect; **f20** more nuttiness and dries further as a little sulphur says hello; **b22** a near Puss Mitchell Special. The then distillery manager at Aberlour set great store by the quality of his sherry-matured stock. And was deeply offended – to the point of near anger – if he was delivered one of the new breed of sulphur-treated butts which had just begun creeping into the system and which he so roundly detested. As an affront to all he was trying to achieve, he would reject them on sight and send them back to whence they came. Or, mischievously, tell the driver to take them to nearby Macallan, where they were welcome to them... This one does have a trace of sulphur that can be detected on the finish, but is initially so well hidden it would have evaded even the sensitive and censorial nose of old Puss. *51.7%. nc ncf sc. 289 bottles.*

ABHAINN DEARG
Highlands (Outer Hebrides), 2008. Marko Tayburn. Working.
Abhainn Dearg New Make db (92.5) **n23 t23 f23.5 b23**. Exceptionally well made with no feints and no waste, either. Oddly salty – possibly the saltiest new make I have encountered, and can think of no reason why it should be – with excellent weight as some extra copper from the new still takes hold. Given a good cask, no reason this impressive new born son of the Outer Hebrides won't go on to become something significant. *67%*

AILSA BAY
Lowland, 2007. William Grant & Sons. Working.
⬩ **Ailsa Bay** db (92.5) **n23.5** tangy, tart, exceptionally dry nose with a little salt added to the classically coastal reek: fulsome and very attractive; **t23.5** brilliant mix of grist and soot, as the phenols get in early and hard. Predominantly dry, exactly as the nose suggests, but just enough molasses to keep the balance honest; **f22.5** thins quite dramatically as the distillery style begins to make its mark. Smoke sticks around as the vanillas and spices build. Curiously oil-less for a peaty scotch malt; **b23** I remember years back being told they wanted to make an occasional peaty malt at this new distillery different in style to Islay's. They have been only marginally successful: only the finish gives the game away. But they have certainly matched the island when it comes to the average high quality. A resounding success of a first effort, though I'd like to see the finish offer a little more than it currently does. Early days, though. *48.9%.*

ALLT-Á-BHAINNE
Speyside, 1975. Chivas Brothers. Working.
⬩ **Big Market Sonderabfüllung Nr. 14 Allt-a-Bhainne 1995** bott 2015 (88) **n22** boiled over-ripe gooseberries; no shortage of dry tannin; **t22** a chunky chap, fat on barley; **f22** vanilla grabs hold and dries – a little salty as the oak takes control; **b22** puts me in mind of an unsugared gooseberry tart. *54.8%. 50th Anniversary bottling.*
Chapter 7 Allt-A-Bhainne 1995 18 Year Old bourbon hogshead, cask no. 166300 (91.5) **n22.5 t24 f21.5 b23.5** Have been disappointed with the quality of the offering of this distillery in recent times, knowing that it is capable of something much better. This is a much better representation of the distillery in form, though the finish is thin. *59.2%. sc. 264 bottles.*
⬩ **The First Editions Allt-A-Bhainne Aged 22 Years 1993** refill hogshead, cask no. 12123, bott 2015 (89.5) **n22.5** a charming Kentucky edge to this, with softening ulmo honey; **t22.5** puckering delivery, sharp and barley fisted; **f22** a light vanilla and butterscotch fade; **b22.5** a good all-rounder flexing its malt and oak muscles in equal measure. *51.4%. nc ncf sc. 177 bottles.*
⬩ **Hepburn's Choice Allt-a-Bhainne 7 Years Old** refill hogshead, dist 2008, bott 2016 (80) **n19 t21 f20 b20**. A boiled sugar candy sweetness to this. But wrapped in an unkind cask. *46%. nc ncf sc. 300 bottles.*
Master of Malt Single Cask Allt-a-Bhainne 18 Year Old sherry hogshead, dist 25 Sept 92, bott 24 Mar 15 (86) **n21.5 t22 f21 b21.5**. Warming, spicy and thinly malty, the cask intervention may be what you expect of a 22-year-old. *55.2%. sc. 166 bottles.*
Old Malt Cask Allt-A-Bhainne Aged 18 Years refill hogshead, cask no. 10825, dist Jun 96, bott Aug 14 (85.5) **n21.5 t22 f20.5 b21.5** A slightly lazy cask has subtracted slightly from what might otherwise been a stunner. Really well constructed at the still: the malt and oils are in harmony with no apparent power struggle. The sugars are also clean and striking, at times heading into acacia honey territory but for its age, undercooked with not quite enough oak added to the recipe. *50%. nc ncf sc. 337 bottles. OMC2407*
⬩ **Old Particular Speyside Allt-A-Bhainne 22 Years Old** refill hogshead, dist Mar 93, bott Dec 15 (87) **n21 t23 f22 b21.** Clean, well made and refreshing, the oak has kept a distance, giving this a much younger, rather immature feel. But if you like concentrated, juicy barley this might just be your bag. *51.5%. nc ncf sc. 295 bottles.*

Provenance Allt A Bhaine Over 12 Years sherry butt, cask no. 9513, bott Winter 13 (**91.5**) n22.5 t23.5 f22 b23.5. From the boiled gooseberry school of deliciousness. And about as clean a Speysider as you'll find this year. 46%. nc ncf sc.

Signatory Vintage Single Malt Allt-A-Bhainne 1995 Aged 18 Years, hogsheads, cask no. 147071+147072, dist 22 Sep 95, bott 07 Feb 14 (**87.5**) n22 t22 f21.5 b22. A kind of Chivas blending blueprint malt. Cut glass and clean barley: simple with no frills. 43%. nc. WB15/015

ARDBEG
Islay, 1815. Glenmorangie Plc. Working.

Ardbeg 10 Years Old db (**97**) n24 more complex, citrus-led and sophisticated than recent bottlings, though the peat is no less but now simply displayed in an even greater elegance; a beautiful sea salt strain to this; t24 gentle oils carry on them a lemon-lime edge, sweetened by barley and a weak solution of golden syrup; the peat is omnipotent, turning up in every crevice and wave, yet never one once overstepping its boundary; f24 stunningly clean, the oak offers not a bitter trace but rather a vanilla and butterscotch edge to the barley. Again the smoke wafts around in a manner unique in the world of whisky when it comes to sheer élan and adroitness; b25 like when you usually come across something that goes down so beautifully and with such a nimble touch and disarming allure, just close your eyes and enjoy... 46%

Ardbeg 10 bottling mark L10 152 db (**95**) n24.5 t23.5 f23.5 b23.5 A bigger than normal version, but still wonderfully delicate. Fabulous and faultless. 46%. Canadian market bottling in English and French dual language label.

Ardbeg 17 Years Old earlier bottlings db (**92**) n23 t22 f23 b24. OK, I admit I had a big hand in this, creating it with the help of Glenmorangie Plc's John Smith. It was designed to take the weight off the better vintages of Ardbeg whilst ensuring a constant supply around the world. Certainly one of the more subtle expressions you are likely to find, though criticised by some for not being peaty enough. As the whisky's creator, all I can say is they are missing the point. 40%

Ardbeg 17 Years Old later bottlings db (**90**) n22 t23 f22 b23. The peat has all but vanished and cannot really be compared to the original 17-year-old: it's a bit like tasting a Macallan without the sherry: fascinating to see the naked body underneath, and certainly more of a turn on. Peat or no peat, great whisky by any standards. 40%

◇ **Ardbeg 21 Years Old** db (**96.5**) n24 it is as though there are three levels of smokiness working in tandem: the layering is ridiculously well-structured. The deepest notes are earthy, rich with even a hint of unpicked tomato; the middle layer is flightier and spiced, seemingly in league with the gristier notes. And a third layer of phenols are sooty and wispy, like thin clouds scudding across on a windy day...amazing....; t24 the delivery by contrast is only two-toned. The malt, sans smoke, is gristy, lemon tinged and juices up with intense barley as the sugars strike home. But it is kept in check by the phenols which hit first with a combined weight, but then scatters about the palate until it reforms later on in liquorice and chocolate vogue; f24 much more ethereal now, though we have moved more towards crystalline sugars only too willing to melt and discreet spices which occasionally nip. To say the finish is long is a little bit of an understatement...; b24.5 tap into Ardbeg with great care, like someone has done here, and there is no describing what beauty can be unleashed. For much of the time, the smoke performs in brilliant fashion somewhere between the ethereal and profound. 46%

Ardbeg 1977 db (**96**) n25 t24 f23 b24. When working through the Ardbeg stocks, I earmarked '77 a special vintage, the sweetest of them all. So it has proved. Only the '74 absorbed that extra oak that gave greater all-round complexity. Either way, the quality of the distillate is beyond measure: simply one of the greatest experiences – whisky or otherwise – of your life. 46%

Ardbeg 1978 db (**91**) n23 t24 f22 b22. An Ardbeg on the edge of losing it because of encroaching oak, hence the decision made by John Smith and I to bottle this vintage early alongside the 17-year-old. Nearly ten years on, still looks a pretty decent bottling, though slightly under strength! 43%

Ardbeg Alligator 1st Release db (**94**) n24 t22.5 f24 b23.5 An alligator happy to play with you for a bit before sinking its teeth in. The spices, though big, are of the usual Ardbegian understatement. 51.2%. ncf. Exclusive for Ardbeg Committee members.

Ardbeg Alligator 2nd Release db (**93**) n24 t23 f23 b23 Something of a different species to the Committee bottling having been matured a little longer, apparently. Well long enough for this to evolve into something just a little less subtle. The nose, though, remains something of striking beauty – even if barely recognisable from the first bottling. 51.2%. ncf.

Ardbeg Almost There 3rd release dist 1998, bott 2007 db (**93**) n23 t24 f23 b23. Further proof that a whisky doesn't have to reach double figures in age to enter the realms of brilliance... 54.1%

Ardbeg Ardbog The Ultimate db ex-Manzanilla sherry cask **(78.5) n20 t22 f17.5 b19**. The best advice one can be given about bogs is to avoid them. *52.1%. Glenmorangie PLC.*

Ardbeg Aurivedes American oak casks with specially toasted cask lids. db **(91.5) n22 t22.5 f24 b23** I have spoken to nobody at Ardbeg about this one but from the slight bourbon character of the nose and the heavy vanilla, this version appears to be about the casks, possibly the char of the barrels. Fascinating, enjoyable...but whatever this is, the usual complexity of the peat feels compromised in the same way a wine cask might. Except here I detect no telling fruit. A real curiosity, whatever it is... *49.9%. Moet Hennessy.*

Ardbeg Blasda db **(90.5) n23.5 t22.5 f22 b22.5** A beautiful, if slightly underpowered malt, which shows Ardbeg's naked self to glowing effect. Overshadowed by some degree in its class by the SMWS bottling, but still something to genuinely make the heart flutter. *40%*

Ardbeg Corryvreckan db **(96.5) n23 t24.5 f24 b25** As famous writers – including the occasional genius film director (stand up wherever you are my heroes Powell and Pressburger) – appear to be attracted to Corryvreckan, the third most violent whirlpool found in the world and just off Islay, to boot, - I selected this as my 1,500th whisky tasted for the historic Jim Murray Whisky Bible 2009. I'm so glad I did because many have told me they thought Blasda ahead of this. To me, it's not even a contest. Currently I have only a sample. Soon I shall have a bottle. I doubt if even the feared whirlpool is this deep and perplexing. *57.1%. 5000 bottles.*

⬦ **Ardbeg Dark Cove** db **(86) n22.5 t22.5 f19.5 b21.5.** For whatever reason, this is a much duller version than the Committee Edition. And strength alone can't explain it, or solely the loss of the essential oils from reduction. There is a slight nagging to this one so perhaps any weakness to the sherry butts has been accentuated by the reduction of oil, if it has been bottled from the same vatting – which I doubt. Otherwise, the tasting notes are along the lines of below, except with just a little less accent on the sugars. *46.5%*

⬦ **Ardbeg Dark Cove Committee Edition** db **(90.5) n23.5** oh, sherry! And some! Gives the wrong signal about the depth of the peat involvement, as the grape is sticky enough to hide some of the phenols, though not the more sooty types. Liquorice and dates at play. Sticky, indeed...; **t23** an immediate blast of dark molassed sugars point towards Melton Hunt Cake at first, but the smoke arrives in droves to drive you off that particular scent. Spices begin to compensate; chewy until your jaw hurts...; **f21.5** just leans towards a slight burnt bitterness and a cloying of the fruit; **b22.5** big sherry and bigger peat always struggle somewhere along the line. This one does pretty well until we reach the finale when it unravels slightly. But sulphur-free. And challenging. *55%*

Ardbeg Day Bottling db **(97) n24.5 t24.5 f23.5 b24.5** I left this to be one of the last whiskies I tasted this year. I had an inkling that they might come up with something a little special, especially with the comparative disappointment of the fundamentally flawed Galileo. On first sweep I thought it was pretty ordinary, but I know this distillery a little too well. So I left the glass for some 20 minutes to breathe and compose itself and returned. To find a potential world whisky of the year... *56.8%. Available at distillery and Ardbeg embassies.*

Ardbeg Guaranteed 30 Years Old db **(91) n24 t23 f21 b23**. An unusual beast, one of the last ever bottled by Allied. The charm and complexity early on is enormous, but the fade rate is surprising. That said, still a dram of considerable magnificence. *40%*

Ardbeg Kildalton db **(94) n23.5 t23 f23.5 b24** Youthful and lightly smoked, unlike the days when I blended the first-ever Kildalton which was middle aged and, for all intents and purposes, peat free. The most subtle of Ardbegs which whispers its beauty, though quite audibly... *46%*

Ardbeg Kildalton 1980 bott 2004 db **(96) n23 t24 f24 b25**. Proof positive that Ardbeg doesn't need peat to bring complexity, balance and Scotch whisky to their highest peaks... *57.6%*

Ardbeg Lord of the Isles bott Autumn 2006 db **(85) n20 t22 f22 b21.** A version of Ardbeg I have never really come to terms with. This bottling is of very low peating levels and shows a degree of Kildalton-style fruitiness. No probs there. But some of the casks are leaching a soft soapy character noticeable on the nose. Enjoyable enough, but a bit frustrating. *46%*

Ardbeg Mor db **(95) n24 t24 f23 b24** Quite simply... more the merrier... *57.5%*

Ardbeg Perpetuum db **(94.5) n23.5 t23.5 f23.5 b24** what a beautifully structured malt. There is no escaping the youth of some of the phrases. But you can't help enjoying what it says. *47.4%. ncf.*

Ardbeg Provenance 1974 bott 1999 db **(96) n24 t25 f23 b24.** This is an exercise in subtlety and charisma, the beauty and the beast drawn into one. Until I came across the 25-year-old OMC verson during a thunderstorm in Denmark, this was arguably the finest whisky I had ever tasted: I opened this and drank from it to see in the year 2000. When I went through the Ardbeg warehouse stocks in 1997 I earmarked the '74 and '77 vintages as something special. This bottling has done me proud. *55.6%*

Ardbeg Renaissance db **(92) n22.5 t22.5 f23.5 b23.5.** How fitting that the 1,200th (and almost last) new-to-market whisky I sampled for the 2009 Bible was Renaissance... because that's what I need after tasting that lot...!! This is an Ardbeg that comes on strong, is not afraid to wield a few hefty blows and yet, paradoxically, the heavier it gets the more delicate, sophisticated and better-balanced it becomes. Enigmatically Ardbegian. 55.9%

Ardbeg Rollercoaster db (90.5) n23 t23 f23 b21.5 To be honest, it was the end of another long day – and book – when I tasted this and I momentarily forgot the story behind the malt. My reaction to one of my researchers who happened to be in the tasting room was: "Bloody hell! They are sending me kids. If this was any younger I'd just be getting a bag of grist!" This malt may be a fabulous concept. And Rollercoaster is a pretty apt description, as this a dram which appears to have the whisky equivalent of Asperger's. So don't expect the kind of balance that sweeps you into a world that only Ardbeg knows. This, frankly, is not for the Ardbeg purist or snob. But for those determined to bisect the malt in all its forms and guises, it is the stuff of the most rampant hard-ons. 57.3%

Ardbeg Supernova db (96.5) n24.5 t24 f23.5 b24.5 A spot on bottling which upholds the brand's unique style and never compromises: shows Ardbeg at its biggest and meanest, yet still somehow charms with wondrous intensity and ease. 55%

Ardbeg Supernova db (97) n24.5 t24 f24 b24.5 Apparently this was called "Supernova" in tribute of how I once described a very highly peated Ardbeg. This major beast, carrying a phenol level in excess of 100ppm, isn't quite a Supernova...much more of a Black Hole. Because once you get dragged into this one, there really is no escaping... 58.9%

Ardbeg Supernova 2010 db (93.5) n24 t23.5 f23 b23 There are Supernovas and there are Supernovas. Some have been going on a bit and have formed a shape and indescribable beauty with the aid of time; others are just starting off and though full of unquantifiable energy and wonder have a distance to travel. By comparison to last year's blockbusting Whisky Bible award winner, this is very much in the latter category. 60.1%

Ardbeg Supernova 2015 db (97) n24 gosh! Few whiskies pulse so impressively, or for quite so long, with a slight mocha subplot to the ever-interchanging peat one moment smoky, the next gritty, then acidic... Not peat on steroids, as someone once described it to me...this is far too natural and beautiful..! t24.5 a consuming delivery: frisky, smoky, sugary, ashy, playful, stern... and naturally, as Ardbeg will, amid all the enormity, comes the counterpoint of delicate citrus...; f24 long, with the grist still leaving behind its smoky essence, like a comet might leave its lingering tail... b24.5 in many ways an essay in balance. This is a huge beast of a malt with seemingly insurmountable peat...until it encourages, then allows you to climb upon its back. Magnificent. 54.3%

Ardbeg Uigeadail db (97.5) n25 t24.5 f23.5 b24.5. Massive yet tiny. Loud yet whispering. Seemingly ordinary from the bottle, yet unforgettable. It is snowing outside my hotel room in Calgary, yet the sun, in my soul at least, is shining. I came across this bottling while lecturing the Liquor Board of British Columbia in Vancouver on May 6th 2008, so one assumes it is a Canadian market bottling. It was one of those great moments in my whisky life on a par with tasting for the first time the Old Malt Cask 1975 at a tasting in Denmark. There is no masking genius.The only Scotch to come close to this one is another from Ardbeg, Corryvreckan. That has more oomph and lays the beauty and complexity on thick...it could easily have been top dog. But this particular Uigeadail (for I have tasted another bottling this year, without pen or computer to hand and therefore unofficially, which was a couple of points down) offers something far more restrained and cerebral. Believe me: this bottling will be going for thousands at auction in the very near future, I wager. 54.2%

Ardbeg Uigeadail db (89) n25 t22 f20 b22. A curious Ardbeg with a nose to die for. Some tinkering - please guys, as the re-taste is not better - regarding the finish may lift this to being a true classic 54.1%

Cadenhead's Authentic Collection Ardbeg Aged 20 Years bourbon barrel, dist 93, bott Jun 14 (95.5) n24.5 t24 f23 b24 As this was the 666th new Scottish malt tasted for the Bible 2015, I chose an Ardbeg from one of the most consistently excellent bottlers: I just knew it would be devilishly good.... 55.9%. 186 bottles. WB15/274

⬦ **Cadenhead's Authentic Collection Ardbeg 21 Year Old** bourbon hogshead, dist 1993 (95) n24 frail diced apple and pear offer a subtleness which fits wonderfully with the sharp, salty but delicate – even by Ardbeg's standards – peat. No other distillery on the planet...; t24 eye-wateringly sharp! Belies its years with the most profound of fresh, gristy, barley sugar and sherbet lemon effervescence. But the smoke continues in elegant form, bordering on breath-taking sophistication; f23 some old Allied barrel bitterness creeps in at the death, but even that can't undo the sublime melting of the smoky grist; b24 simply Ardbeg. 53.2%. sc.

⬦ **Gleann Mór Ardbeg 2004** (85.5) n21.5 t22 f21 b21. First of all, there is not a sulphur note to be had: the cask is cleaner than the cleanest whistle. But I must place my hand on heart here and say I am just not the greatest fan of big, ostentatious fruit mixing with big peat. Just too soupy and unsubtle for my book, though I am sure there are those out there who will willingly swap their mother-in-law for a bottle of this. OTT doesn't even begin to sum this one up... 60.9%. sc.

Master of Malt Single Cask Ardbeg 23 Year Old refill bourbon hogshead, dist Feb 91, bott Jan 15 **(94.5) n23** buttery phenols make for a heavy experience; allotment bonfires on a seashore prevail...; **t24** surprisingly, it's the sugar – most pretty sharp and tart and of a processed white variety – which make the early running before the gristy phenols make up ground...; **f23.5** soft oils descend to maximise the length of the smoke's stay. Butterscotch intertwangles with the fading peat; **b24** long, and of a variety of hues and humours. Ridiculously complex....and it doesn't even try! 50.6%. sc. 216 bottles.

⬦ **That Boutique-y Whisky Company Ardbeg 12 Year Old** batch 7 **(92.5) n23** it's that unique Ardbeg intensity: in other words, the peat first strikes you as big and bold, but on closer, more studied sniffing reveals itself to be layered, bewildering and borderline light; **t23** deep molasses and fruitier muscovado sugars pipe up early on. The smoke rumbles in meaningful layers but never once gets the better of the sugar; **f23** some oaky intent slaps down some extra weight; **b23.5** essential, effortless Ardbeg. 52%. 203 bottles.

ARDMORE

Speyside, 1899. Beam Inc. Working.

⬦ **Ardmore 12 Year Old Port Wood Finish** db **(90) n21.5** really tight with neither the fruit or the cask giving ground, leaving an austere imprint; (having said that, leave the empty glass overnight and you have something not far off perfection)...; **t23.5** fabulous mouth feel with the smoke slowly displaying before being choked off by the intensity of the fruit. The middle ground is no less intense, though here we have vanilla battling through; **f22** long, yet still clinging to that biting austerity, despite the smoke and spices trying to make special things happen; **b23** not sure how many years it took me to get the owners of this great distillery to get the malt out there in to the public domain (it certainly runs to well into double figures), but I will never forget the day when the executive at the time met up with me and told me they had listened to my arguments and were going for it. Since then the personnel have changed, more the pity. Because I genuinely understand this distillery better than most and just wish they'd come to me before unleashing a bottling such as this. Yes, this is in part a beautiful whisky. But forget all this hand-crafted stuff on the label: this is a blending whisky criminally overlooked for a century. Here we have a lovely fruit-rich malt, but one which has compromised on the very essence of the complexity which sets this distillery apart. Lovely whisky I am delighted to say...but, dammit, by playing to its unique nuances it could have been so much better...I mean absolutely sensational...! 46%. ncf.

Ardmore 25 Years Old db **(89.5) n21 t23.5 f22.5 b22.5** A 25-y-o box of chocolates: coffee creams, fudge, orange cream...they are all in there. The nose maybe ordinary: what follows is anything but. 51.4%. ncf.

Ardmore 30 Years Old Cask Strength db **(94) n23.5 t23.5 f23 b24** I remember when the present owners of Ardmore launched their first ever distillery bottling. Over a lunch with the hierarchy there I told them, with a passion, to ease off with the caramel so the world can see just how complex this whisky can be. This brilliant, technically faultless, bottling is far more eloquent and persuasive than I was that or any other day... 53.7%. nc ncf. 1428 bottles.

Ardmore 1996 db **(87) n22 t22 f21 b22.** Very curious Ardmore, showing little of its usual dexterity. Perhaps slightly more heavily peated than the norm, but there is also much more intense heavy caramel extracted from the wood. Soft, very pleasant and easy drinking it is almost obsequious. 43%.

Ardmore 100th Anniversary 12 Years Old dist 1986, bott 1999 db **(94) n24 t23.5 f22.5 b24.** Brilliant. Absolutely stunning, with the peat almost playing games on the palate. Had they not put caramel in this bottling, it most likely would have been an award winner. So, by this time next year, I fully expect to see every last bottle accounted for... 40%

Ardmore Fully Peated Quarter Casks db **(89) n21 t23 f23 b22.** This is an astonishingly brave attempt by the new owners of Ardmore who, joy of all joys, are committed to putting this distillery in the public domain. Anyone with a 2004 copy of the Whisky Bible will see that my prayers have at last been answered. However, this bottling is for Duty Free and, due to the enormous learning curve associated with this technique, a work in progress. They have used the Quarter Cask process which has been such a spectacular success at its sister distillery Laphroaig. Here I think they have had the odd slight teething problem. Firstly, Ardmore has rarely been filled in ex-bourbon and that oak type is having an effect on the balance and smoke weight; also they have unwisely added caramel, which has flattened things further. I don't expect the caramel to be in later bottlings and, likewise, I think the bourbon edge might be purposely blunted a little. But for a first attempt this is seriously big whisky that shows enormous promise. When they get this right, it could – and should – be a superstar. Now I await the more traditional vintage bottlings... 46%. ncf.

Ardmore Legacy db (71.5) n17 t19 f17.5 b18. Must win an award as the most disappointing whisky of the year. Not least because this is one of the world's great distilleries. The nose is dirty and off-key. After a too brief fight back on delivery, it soon descends on the palate to the same mess found on the nose. As this distillery's first and oldest advocate, frankly, for me, a massive shock and disappointment. 40%

Ardmore Traditional Cask db (88.5) n21.5 t22 f23 b22. Not quite what I expected. "Jim. Any ideas on improving the flavour profile?" asked the nice man from Ardmore distillery when they were originally launching the thing. "Yes. Cut out the caramel." "Ah, right..." So what do I find when the next bottling comes along? More caramel. It's good to have influence... Actually, I can't quite tell if this is a result of natural caramelization from the quarter casking or just an extra dollop of the stuff in the bottling hall. The result is pretty similar: some of the finer complexity is lost. My guess, due to an extra fraction of sweetness and spice, is that it is the former. All that said, the overall experience remains quite beautiful. And this remains one of my top ten distilleries in the world. 46%. ncf.

◇ **Acla Selection Ardmore 14 Years Old** hogshead, dist 2000, bott 2014 (94) n23.5 a slightly fizzy smokiness; like peated sherbet; t23.5 very exact weight on delivery: vague oils and peated dark sugars arrive early and to mesmerising effect. Classic stuff....and the spices enter the fray at just the right time and with just enough puff...; f23 the light coating of smoked spices continue to the very end, though the vanilla takes a greater interest late on; b24 nutshells the distillery quite beautifully. And the best blends always have a little bite: here you can see exactly why this malt is a blender's dream. 51.6%. nc ncf.

◇ **C & S Dram Collection Ardmore Aged 4 Years** hogshead, cask no. 804208, dist 28 Jun 11, bott 18 Jan 16 (85.5) n22 t21.5 f21 b21. Wow, this is young! Has something of the pre-pubescent Bowmore about it, as there appears to be an upped peating level. This sugar-laden fledgling whisky still hasn't found its legs as the smoke and oak clash. But you have to be a right miserable git not to enjoy the fun on offer! 60.8%. sc.

Chieftain's Ardmore Aged 21 Years barrel, dist Jun 92, bott Jun 14 (89.5) n22.5 t23.5 f21 b22.5 Some of the smoke has been replaced by pure silk... 46%. nc ncf.

Crom Ardmore 13 Years Old Warlords & Warriors Edition Peated sherry hogshead, dist Apr 01, bott Aug 14 (92.5) n23 t23.5 f23 b23 A slightly more angular and fruity Ardmore bottling than most. Delicious, though! 56.4% sc

◇ **The Golden Cask Ardmore 14 Years Old** cask no. CM 217, dist 2000, bott 2015 (91) n23 not sure if you can get an Ardmore nose more nutshelled than this. The smoke is confident, yet refuses to dictate – allowing a nutty maltiness to merge gracefully with the vanilla; t22.5 thumping gristy malt, at first younger in aspect than the actual age states. At first. your fillings are tested, then calms down as the concentrated and lighted peated malt infuses with the part-time acacia honey; f22.5 a fade of spiced, honeyed, lightly smoked cocoa; b23 a fierce, yet brutally and sometimes deliciously honest, account of the distillery in its more fiery mode. No frills, but plenty of thrills. 57.3%. sc. 178 bottles.

Gordon & MacPhail Distillery Label Ardmore 1996 (92) n23.5 relaxed peat works well with the minty vanilla; even a little dried date has crept in from the sugars; expect some oak further down the line as the big tannin is here to stay; t23.5 the smoke works wonderfully with the sugars to help form a cocoa-covered fudge, with a bit of molasses thrown in to add some weighty drama; f22 some serious oak bite shows that age has caught up with this a little; b23 even when the oak is beginning to get the upper hand, this distillery has the charisma to charm you into pouring another glass before you know you've done it... 43%

◇ **Gordon & MacPhail Distillery Label Ardmore 1998** (92.5) n22.5 the smoke in its most apologetic form, but still offering reassuring weight; t23 chewy mix of malt and delicate tannins, bound together by Demerara sugar and light smoke; f23 mint mocha; b24 from one of its lesser peating days. But the overall weight and structure is superb! 43%

◇ **Kingsbury Gold Ardmore 6 Year Old 2008** hogshead, cask no. 800006 (95.5) n24 for the age you can ask for absolutely nothing more: a minty smokiness with a just about equal split between the sugars and the drier, though light, oaks; t23.5 slightly above average peating for the distillery: the smoke appears at ground level amid the barley and sugars, and in the roof of the mouth as the oils stick; f24 about the longest finish for a 6-year-old you'll find for this and many a year. Those smoked mocha notes, indulged with a mix of maple syrup and molasses, really do the trick...; b24 young, adorable and fabulous example of why this is one of the great blending malts in the world at this age. Truly faultless. 59.5%. sc. 187 bottles.

Teacher's Highland Single Malt quarter cask finish db (89) n22.5 t23 f21.5 b22. This is Ardmore at its very peatiest. And had not the colouring levels been heavily tweaked to meet the flawed perceptions of what some markets believe makes a good whisky, this malt would have been better still. As it is: superb. With the potential of achieving greatness if only they have the confidence and courage... 40%. India/Far East Travel Retail exclusive.

⬩ **The Whisky Agency Acla Selection Ardlair Aged 5 Years** sherry cask, dist 2009, bott 2015 **(72) n17 t19 f17 b19.** Memo to the guys at Ardlair. You have one of the great distilleries of the world here: great selection, so well done – especially at an age it rarely appears in the market place. But always (and I mean, like, 100% of the time) go for ex-bourbon. Don't fuck about with sulphur-screwed sherry. Whatever the guys flogging you the cask say. Capiche? 47.6%. nc ncf. 391 bottles.

AUCHENTOSHAN
Lowlands, 1800. Morrison Bowmore. Working.

Auchentoshan 10 Years Old db **(81) n22 t21 f19 b19.** Much better, maltier, cleaner nose than before. But after the initial barley surge on the palate it shows a much thinner character. 40%

Auchentoshan 12 Years Old db **(91.5) n22.5** sexy fruit element – citrus and apples in particular – perfectly lightens the rich, oily barley; **t23.5** oily and buttery; intense barley carrying delicate marzipan and vanilla; **f22.5** simplistic, but the oils keep matters lush and the delicate sugars do the rest; **b23** a delicious malt very much happier with itself than it has been for a while. 40% ⊙

Auchentoshan 14 Years Old Cooper's Reserve db **(83.5) n20 t21.5 f21 b21.** Malty, a little nutty and juicy in part. 46%. ncf.

⬩ **Auchentoshan 18 Years Old** db **(78) n21 t21.5 f17 b19.** Although matured for 18 years in ex-bourbon casks, as according to the label, this is a surprisingly tight and closed malt in far too many respects. Some heart-warming sugars early on, but the finish is bitter and severely limited in scope. 43%

Auchentoshan 21 Years Old db **(93) n23.5** a sprig of mint buried in barely warmed peat, all with an undercoat of the most delicate honeys; **t23** velvety and waif-like, the barley-honey theme is played out is hushed tones and unspoiled elegance; **f23** the smoke deftly returns as the vanillas and citrus slowly rise but the gentle honey-barley plays to the end, despite the shy introduction of cocoa; **b23.5** one of the finest Lowland distillery bottlings of our time. A near faultless masterpiece of astonishing complexity to be cherished and discussed with deserved reverence. So delicate, you fear that sniffing too hard will break the poor thing...! 43%. ⊙

Auchentoshan 1975 db **(88) n22.5 t22.5 f21 b22** Goes heavy on the natural caramels. Does not even remotely show its enormous age for this distillery. I detest the word "smooth". But for those who prefer that kind of malt...well, your dreams have come true...; 45.6%

Auchentoshan 1977 Sherry Cask Matured oloroso sherry cask db **(89) n23 t22 f22 b22.** Rich, creamy and spicy. Almost a digestive biscuit mealiness with a sharp marmalade spread. 49%. sc. Morrison Bowmore. 240 bottles.

Auchentoshan 1979 db **(94) n23.5 t24 f23 b23.5** It's amazing what a near faultless sherry butt can do. 50.1%

Auchentoshan 1988 25 Year Old Wine Cask Finish db **(94.5) n23 t24 f23.5 b24** The thing about a triple distilled malt is that a confident influence can have a very loud say. And the clean wine here certainly calls the shots, though some pretty high quality oak ensures the speech is balanced. A delightful malt which makes a very respectful nod to the combined skills of distiller, wood manager and blender. 47%

Auchentoshan 1998 Sherry Cask Matured fino sherry cask db **(81.5) n21 t22 f18.5 b20.** A genuine shame. Before these casks were treated in Jerez, I imagine they were spectacular. Even with the obvious faults apparent, the nuttiness is profound and milks every last atom of the oils at work to maximum effect. The sugars, also, are delicate and gorgeously weighted. There is still much which is excellent to concentrate on here. 54.6%. ncf. 6000 bottles.

Auchentoshan American Oak db **(85.5) n21.5 t22 f20.5 b21.5.** Very curious: reminds me very much of Penderyn Welsh whisky before it hits the Madeira casks. Quite creamy with some toasted honeycomb making a brief cameo appearance. 40% ⊙

⬩ **Auchentoshan Blood Oak** French red wine & American bourbon casks db **(76.5) n20.5 t19 f18 b19.** That's funny: always thought blood tasted a little sweet. This is unremittingly bitter. 48%. ncf.

Auchentoshan Classic db **(80) n19 t20 f21 b20.** Classic what exactly...? Some really decent barley, but goes little further. 40%

⬩ **Auchentoshan Noble Oak Aged 24 Years** Oloroso sherry casks & American bourbon hogsheads db **(87.5) n22 t23 f21 b21.5.** Normally a skinny soul on account of its triple distillation, unusual to find a 'Toshan with so much muscle. The fruit from the sherry is piled on high, yet it is a massive toffee effect which takes the firmest grip, presumably tannins from the oak. So the finish is a little flat. But the good news is that this is one fruit cake that is happily sulphur-free. *50.3%. ncf. 2015 Limited Release.*

Auchentoshan Select db (85) n20 t21.5 f22 b21.5. Has changed shape of late, if not quality. Much more emphasis on the enjoyable juicy barley sharpness these days. *40%*

Auchentoshan Silveroak 1990 Limited Release db (94.5) n23.5 t23 f24 b24. Okay... tasting pretty blind on this: have only the sample bottle, showing the name of the brand and the strength, but no accompanying production notes. Appears to have good age, probably above 17, and the sherry butts used here (and I don't think it is exclusively wine oak at work) are of rare high quality for these days. Appears to have the imprint of outstanding blender Rachael Barry. *50.9%. Exclusive for Global Travel Retail.*

Auchentoshan Solera db (88) n23 t22 f22 b21. Enormous grape input and enjoyable for all its single mindedness. Will benefit when a better balance with the malt is struck. *48%. ncf.*

Auchentoshan Three Wood db (76) n20 t18 f20 b18. Takes you directly into the rough. Refuses to harmonise, except maybe for some late molassed sugar. *43%* ⊙

Auchentoshan Virgin Oak db (92) n23.5 like a busy bourbon with the accent on the buzzing small grains: all the regulation manuka honey and liquorice there in respectful amounts; t23 big, sugary delivery, but a cushion of hickory and vanilla keeps the sweetness under control; a little molasses adds extra weight to the middle; f22.5 pretty dry, with a bit of a coppery sheen, as though some work had recently been done to a still; b23 not quite how I've seen 'Toshan perform before: but would love to see it again! *46%*

◇ **Cadenhead's Authentic Collection Auchentoshan Aged 24 Years** bourbon barrel, dist 90, bott Jun 14 (88) n22 t24.5 f20 b21.5. The high point is the delivery: fabulously juicy and defying the years. But here we have the unusual case of an Auchentoshan being let down by the cask, rather than the other way round as the slight milkiness on the nose develops into a minor fault on the finale as the cask tires beyond endurance. *52.3%. 150 bottles. WB15/273*

◇ **Eiling Lim Auchentoshan 23 Years Old 1992** bott 2015 (93) n23.5 wonder if this was matured in an ex-Bowmore cask: definitely the very faintest hint of smoke. That, mixing comfortably with the busy bourbon thrust, provides the heaviest tone, and one of no little complexity; t23 unusually oily for a 'Toshan, with the malt providing a chewy thickness while the lemon sherbet fizz sticks truer to the distillery style. Some light manuka honey takes us back towards a bourbon path; f23 light cocoa mingles with the vanilla as the sugars wear thin; the spices continue unabated; b23.5 a quite beautiful and well percussioned rendition of a usually light song. *45.7%. nc ncf sc. 132 bottles. 9th Release.*

◇ **Hepburn's Choice Auchentoshan 12 Years Old** refill hogshead, dist 2003, bott 2015 (83) n21 t21 f20 b21. Zesty, malty, salivating. But never far from the feel of a new make, despite its age. *46%. nc ncf sc. 152 bottles.*

◇ **Hunter Laing's Distiller's Art Auchentoshan Aged 12 Years** refill hogshead, dist 2003, bott 2015 (85) n21.5 t21.5 f21 b21. A degree of oaky chunkiness and some extra spice fizz help eek out the most of an otherwise light, borderline austere, offering. *48%. nc ncf sc. 257 bottles.*

Kingsbury Gold Auchentoshan 16 Year Old 1997 hogshead, cask no. 10370 (94) n23 t24 f23.5 b23.5 Amazed: sampled blind, would not have recognised it as a 'Toshan in a 1,000 tastings...*53.5%. 308 bottles.*

Old Malt Cask Auchentoshan 17 Years Old refill hogshead, dist Oct 97, bott Feb 15 (90.5) n23 soft malt, yet beautifully textured and full. A slight herbal note to the delicate vanilla; t23 much fuller now. The sub-current of vanilla appears to give an impression of primness. But the malt, as on the nose, has a deceptively rich texture; f22 reverts to a more gristy feel; excellent late spice; b22.5 so elegant. *50%. nc ncf sc. 313 bottles.*

◇ **Old Malt Cask Auchentoshan Aged 18 Years** refill hogshead, cask no. 11294, dist Sept 97, bott Apr 16 (89) n22.5 gorgeously grassy: light, refreshing barley with a hint of butter and lemon zest; t22.5 clean, salivating with a little maple syrup to accompany the fresh malt; f22 still juicy and barley rich, but with a dose of vanilla and spice; b22 proving that clean simplicity can be quietly beautiful... *50%. nc ncf sc. 150 bottles.*

◇ **Old Malt Cask Auchentoshan Aged 18 Years** refill hogshead, cask no. 12128, dist Oct 97, bott Nov 15 (87.5) n21.5 t22 f22 b22. A very enjoyable, though only gently challenging dram which makes the most of its triple distillation to allow the oak to offer an almost bourbon sweetness. Perhaps lacks complexity, though the spices more than make amends. What it does, it does especially well indeed. *46.9%. nc ncf sc. 258 bottles.*

◇ **Old Malt Cask Auchentoshan Aged 21 Years** refill hogshead, cask no. 11782, dist Oct 93, bott Aug 15 (94) n23.5 wow...!! You don't often see the distillery offer such a wide array of aromas: mainly mango-based, but so many strands of bourbon-style dark sugar as well as a coppery sheen to this. Rich, but so subtle...; t23.5 the sugars on the nose melt on the palate early on. No shortage of barley at play – almost an Irish pot still hardness to this. Juicy, crisp and with a firm, metallic edge and lilting citrus. The bourbon notes are very easily accessible;

f23 the copper reverberates around the palate; the spices caress rather than bite; the oak has a Kentucky burr..; **b24** a classic must find 'Toshan. As rich as it gets with what appears to be a coppery depth to this integrating sublimely with the liquorice-bourbon lustre of the oak. Must have put in a new still, or done some coppery repair work just prior to this being distilled 50%. nc ncf sc. 156 bottles.

Old Particular Auchentoshan 14 Years Old refill hogshead, cask no. 10716, dist Sept 00, bott Feb 15 **(91) n23 t23 f22.5 b22.5** A more compact and richer-bodied example from this distillery than most. 48.4%. nc ncf sc. 324 bottles.

The Pearls of Scotland Auchentoshan 1998 cask no. 2197, dist Sept 98, bott May 15 **(93) n23.5** you'll be taken aback by the enormity of the malt; spices and malted milk biscuits pitch in; **t24** no less intense on delivery – actually even more so with the barley coming through at its most distinguished and clean. Almost one dimensional, but what a dimension...! **f23** the concentrated grist and the surprise manuka honey make for a thumping send off; **b23** rare to find the distillery this chunky and weighty. 55.3%. sc.

Whisky Fair Auchentoshan 23 Years Old bourbon barrel, dist 1992, bott 2015 **(88.5) n23** beautifully demure and complex: confident, dry oak which offsets the clementine and honeyed barley; **t22.5** early juicy barley is soon extinguished by marauding oak. Good spice; **f21** heavy tannin; **b22** with such a light body, oak encircles the malt threateningly. But just enough sugar to do the job. 46.3%. 69 bottles.

Whisky-Fässle Auchentoshan 21 Year Old sherry hogshead, dist 1992, bott 2014 **(88) n23 t23 f20 b22** Good, clean grape until it falls at the very last hurdle. 52.1%. nc ncf.

Whisky-Fässle Auchentoshan 23 Year Old hogshead, dist 1990, bott 2014 **(92) n22 t23 f23.5 b23.5** Neat, tidy, beautifully clean and nutty. A must experience charmer. 47.7%. nc ncf.

Whisky Tales Auchentoshan Aged 19 Years sherry cask, dist 1995, bott 2015 **(90) n22 t23 f22.5 b22.5** 'Toshan showing a little muscle and grace. Delicious. 48%. nc ncf sc. 110 bottles.

AUCHROISK

Speyside, 1974. Diageo. Working.

Auchroisk Aged 10 Years db **(84) n20 t22 f21 b21.** Tangy orange on the nose, the malt amplified by a curious saltiness on the palate. 43%. Flora and Fauna.

Auchroisk 30 Years Old Special Release 2012 American and European Oak refill casks, dist 1982, bott 2012 db **(91.5) n22 t23 f23 b23.5** A hugely – and surprisingly - impressive singleton of tannins. 54.7%. nc ncf. Diageo.

◇ **Distilleries Collection Auchroisk Aged 17 Years 1997** bott 2015 **(84.5) n21 t20.5 f22 b21.** At times a thin but firebrand dram, branding the barley on to your taste buds. But as it settles, the malt offers a more sensible, sober and enjoyable presence. 55%. Bottled for Scotch Malt Sales Ltd.

Drams By Dramtime Auchroisk 14 Year Old 1999 sherry hogshead, dist 3 Dec 99, bott 21 Oct 14 **(93) n23** lush grape: clean, intense with an enticing salty nip; **t23.5** a knife and fork might be useful to cut through the seasoned sultana. A surprising, vague phenol note followed by some zippy spices; a half-hearted juiciness adds a degree of levity; **f23** long, with spices showing more of an oak bent by the minute...; **b23.5** amazing the beauty that can be had from a clean, top-notch wine cask. 46%. nc ncf sc. 63 bottles.

◇ **The Golden Cask Auchroisk 17 Years Old** cask no. CM 209, dist 1997, bott 2014 **(78.5) n19 t19.5 f21 b19.** Salivating, almost concentrated malt. But the oak's contribution is very limited, leaving a Speyside malt much closer to seven years in style (if that!) than 17... 53%. sc. 280 bottles.

◇ **Hepburn's Choice Auchroisk 12 Years Old** refill hogshead, dist 2003, bott 2016 **(85) n21.5 t21 f21.5 b21.5.** Untaxing, simplistic malt. Excellent oak has sparked off a bit of a bourbony trait, though displayed on a thin malty body. Quite pleasant, though. 46%. nc ncf sc. 375 bottles.

◇ **Old Malt Cask Auchroisk Aged 15 Years** refill hogshead, cask no. 11944, dist Oct 00, bott Oct 15 **(82) n20 t21.5 f20 b20.5.** Pleasant, intensely malty, sweet in part and very clean. But rather bereft of character. 50%. nc ncf sc. 645 bottles.

Old Malt Cask Auchroisk 21 Years Old refill hogshead, cask no. 11238, dist Jan 94, bott Feb 15 **(90) n22 t23 f22.5 b22.5** A beautiful – and unusual - example of this distillery going into well weighted malty overdrive. Simple, but wonderfully effective. 50%. nc ncf sc. 264 bottles.

AULTMORE

Speyside, 1896. John Dewar & Sons. Working.

Aultmore 12 Year Old db **(85.5) n22 t22 f20 b21.5.** Not quite firing on all cylinders due to the uncomfortably tangy oak. But relish the creamy malt for the barley is the theme of choice and for its sheer intensity alone, it doesn't disappoint; a little ulmo honey and marzipan doff their cap to the kinder vanillas. *46% WB16/028*

⬩ **Aultmore 18 Year Old** db **(88.5) n22.5** soft, though with a vague spice nip. Otherwise, a mix of ulmo honey, treacle and cream toffee combine; **t22.5** the barley makes the first play on delivery, a grassy volley which slowly vanishes into a mist of caramel; **f22** that caramel persists – again of Toffo variety - but at least the spices can be heard; **b21.5** charming, but could do with having the toffee blended out... *46%*

Aultmore 25 Year Old db **(92.5) n23 t23.5; f23 b23** Now here's a curiosity: this is the first brand I have ever encountered which on the label lists the seasons the distillery was silent (1917-19, 1943-45, 1970-71) like a football club would once list on the front page of their official programme the years they won the FA Cup! Strange, but rather charming. And as for the whisky: succulent stuff!! *46% WB16/029*

Cadenhead's Small Batch Aultmore-Glenlivet Aged 17 Years bourbon hogsheads, dist 97, bott 14 **(88) n22 t22.5 f21 b22.5** Most whiskies would succumb to the tightness of the bitter oak. But this is so well endowed with explosive barley and lightly sugared citrus, it gets away with it. Some great moments. *54.9%. 450 bottles. WB15/261*

⬩ **Endangered Drams Aultmore 7 Year Old** bourbon hogshead, cask no. 100149, dist 03 Apr 08, bott 02 Sept 15 **(86) n21 t22.5 f21 b21.5.** Rather puts the tart in tartan. A light smokiness offers a minor degree of weight, but it is the vaguely salty, juicy barley which dominates. Sadly, a jaded old cask subtracts from the balance slightly. *62.3%. sc*

Gordon & MacPhail Connoisseurs Choice Aultmore dist 2000, bott 2013 **(91) n22 t24 f22 b23** The kind of malt I can drink all day and every day. Just so wonderfully refreshing and alive. *46%. nc ncf. WB15/145*

⬩ **Provenance Aultmore Aged 7 Years** sherry cask, bott Mar 16 **(94) n23** a touch of apricot on the marzipan leads a very enticing nose; **t24** not sure if it is the barley, the green apple or the developing greengage which is making me salivate so much. Adore the slow build in intensity and even slower build up of spices; **f23** slightly fat now and the barley again regains control. But those spices...just so confident and intense; **b24** clean and beautifully subtle: now, that's the kind of sherry influence I want to see...! *46%. nc ncf sc.*

⬩ **That Boutique-y Whisky Company Aultmore** batch 6 **(84) n21 t22 f21 b20.** Not a particularly bad barrel. But this is smothered in fruit in the same way a child would be swamped in his parent's clothes: the malt, indeed the whisky, makes no impact whatsoever. Juicy, with a pleasant degree of herbal notes. But just too much of a good thing, I'm afraid. *52.5%. 98 bottles.*

Whic.de Aultmore 8 Year Old sherry butt, cask no. 900016, dist 12 Mar 07, bott 12 Mar 15 **(88.5) n22 t23.5 f21 b22** A lovely, fresh malt let down slightly in the latter stages. *53.9%. sc. 60 bottles.*

Whiskybroker Aultmore 8 Years sherry butt, cask no. 900016, dist 12 Mar 07 **(92) n23 t24 f22 b23.** From the same sherry butt as Whic.de at identical strength. Yet this one can claim a more concentrated fruit factor on the nose and a massively more confident – borderline aggressive – taste on delivery with the grape coming out with rare richness and bravado. And acting more like an 8-year-old. Also, there is cocoa on the finish which doesn't appear on its twin bottling. A sulphur bite does hit a little later, though. Two identical whiskies from the same cask...yet one very different from the other. Go figure... *53.9%. sc.*

⬩ **The Whisky Barrel Aultmore 1990 Burns Malt 25 Years Old** cask no. 2341 **(76) n19 t20 f18 b19.** One of those heart-breakers. What a whisky this would have been except for that nagging sulphur. *57.8%. sc.*

⬩ **Xtra Old Particular Speyside Aultmore 25 Years Old** sherry butt, cask no. 11066, dist Feb 90, bott Feb 16 **(83) n19 t22 f20 b22.** Is this a perfect cask? No. Has it been ruined by the sulphur? No. Is there still plenty to find for the sherry lover? Yes. Because the sherry is also beautifully supported by the malt which weighs in to give extra depth. *44.2%. nc ncf sc. 302 bottles.*

BALBLAIR
Highlands (Northern), 1872. Inver House Distillers. Working.

Balblair 10 Years Old db **(86) n21 t22 f22 b21.** Such an improved dram away from the clutches of caramel. *40%*

Balblair Aged 16 Years db **(84) n22 t22 f20 b20.** Definitely gone up a notch in the last year. The lime on the nose has been replaced by dim Seville oranges; the once boring finish reveals elements of fruit and spice. It's the barley- rich middle that shines, though, and some more work will belt this up into the high 90s where this great distillery belongs. *40%*

Balblair 1965 db **(96.5) n23 t24.5 f24.5 b24.5** Many malts of this age have the spirit hanging on in there for grim life. This is an exception: the malt is in joint control and never for a moment allows the oak to dominate. It is almost too beautiful for words. *52.3%*

Balblair 1969 db (94.5) n22.5 t23.5 f24 b24.5. A charmer. Don't even think about touching this until it has stood in the glass for ten minutes. And if you are not prepared to give each glass a minimum half hour of your time (and absolutely no water), then don't bother getting it for, to be honest, you don't deserve it... 41.4%

Balblair 1975 db (94.5) n24.5 t23.5 f23 b23.5. Essential Balblair. 46%

Balblair 1978 db (94) n24 t24 f23 b23. Just one of those drams that exudes greatness and charm in equal measures. Some malts fall apart when hitting thirty: this one is totally intact and in command. A glorious malt underlining the greatness of this mostly under-appreciated distillery. 46%

Balblair 1983 Vintage 1st Release dist 1983 bott 2013. db (96.5) n24.5 t24 f23.5 b24.5 Very few malts are this comfortable, or vibrant, by the time they reach their third decade in the cask. A Highland gathering of sensational casks resulting in a celebration of what great Scotch whisky is really all about. Magnificent. 46%. nc ncf. Inverhouse Distilleries.

Balblair 1983 Vintage 1st Release dist 1983, bott 2014 db (95) n23.5 hmmm: that oak has much to say for itself. Orange blossom honey at its softest and drier hickory/cocoa and spice when it growls; t23 not surprisingly, a tad aggressive on delivery. The drier spices bite hard but there is a superb oiliness (weirdly, very similar to corn oil in bourbon) which soothes and dresses the oak burn, all framed by excellent sugars; f24.5 now at its very best, as the spiced oak has calmed allowing a clearer view of the still intact barley notes and the wide range of cocoa (including Nutella) and honey notes, manuka at the fore...; b24 the last Balblair 83 I tasted fair won my heart and undying devotion with its beauty and complexity. This may also be a beautiful and shapely morsel, but the over exuberance of the oak means this is more of a spicy, pleasure-indulging, hedonistic one night-stand than lasting, tender love. Mind you... 46%. nc ncf.

Balblair 1989 db (91) n23 t23 f22.5 b22.5. Don't expect gymnastics on the palate or the pyrotechnics of the Cadenhead 18: in many ways a simple malt, but one beautifully told. Almost Cardhu-esque in the barley department. 43%

Balblair 1989 db (88) n21.5 t22 f22.5 b22. A clean, pleasing malt, though hardly one that will induce anyone to plan a night raid on any shop stocking it... 46%

Balblair 1990 db (92.5) n24 t23.5 f22 b23. Tangy in the great Balblair tradition. Except here this is warts and all with the complexity and greatness of the distillery left in no doubt. 46%

Balblair 1990 Vintage 2nd Release dist 1990 bott 2013. db (83.5) n22 t21 f20 b20.5. Full bodied yet tight and tangy. 46%. nc ncf. Inverhouse Distilleries.

◇ **Balblair 1990 Vintage 2nd Release** dist 1990, bott 2014 db (93) n23.5 dense thanks to a near inpenetrable forest of oak with a big fruity canopy; t23 juicy, slightly fizzy even. Again, thick enough to stand a spoon in and we are in major old fruitcake country, with no shortage of black cherry and a little liquorice for good measure; the tannin really is in the red zone, yet somehow doesn't self-destruct; f23.5 fabulous finish: just so long, wonderfully toasty and still a little effervescence to maximise the effect. An inevitability to the late spice and cocoa; b23 this is major malt. It does not try to take a polite course but hurls the tannins in all directions with abandon. Luckily, the overall lushness absorbs the greatest impacts. 46%. nc ncf.

Balblair 1997 2nd Release db (94) n23.5 gooseberry tart with a curious salt and sugar seasoning; a shaving of ginger and a little physalis adds no end of complexity; t23.5 sharp, tangy, pulsing barley both salivating and showing verve and a complex drier side: quintessential Balblair...; f23 the vanillas walk hand-in-hand with the barley towards a cocoa-rich, late-spiced finale; b24 a very relaxed well-made and matured malt, comfortable in its own skin, bursting with complexity and showing an exemplary barley-oak ratio. A minor classic. 46%. nc ncf.

Balblair 1999 Vintage 1st Release dist 1999 bott 2014. db (92.5) n23 t23.5 f23 b23 The same colour as the cockerel which wakes me each morning...and crows as loudly. Gorgeous. 46%. nc ncf. Inverhouse Distilleries.

Balblair 1999 Vintage 2nd Release dist 1999, bott 2014 db (83.5) n22 t22.5 f19 b20. You know one of those old vintage sports cars which looks amazing, sounds just the thing but when you get inside and put your foot down nothing happens...? Well this is a bit like that. The dried dates have flattened all the higher notes so everything is a bit nondescript and shapeless. There are, of course, some attractive toffee-fruit moments. But a certain furriness on the finish negates the good. 46%. nc ncf.

◇ **Balblair 1999 Vintage 2nd Release** dist 1999, bott 2015 db (91.5) n23.5 has the pull of a tractor beam – drags you towards its mesmerising vanilla and milky nougat interplay, all sharpened by some of the most brittle citrus imaginable; t22.5 not quite so three-dimensional as the nose, accentuating the natural caramels; the barley gives a full salivating display; f23 a little praline goes a long way, especially with the oils now getting to work; takes time for the spices to rise, but they do; b22.5 always subtle and sensual. 46%. nc ncf.

Balblair 2000 db (**87.5**) n21.5 t22.5 f21.5 b22. No toffee yet still a clever degree of chewy weight for all the apparent lightness. *43%*

Balblair 2001 db (**90.5**) n23.5 t23.5 f21.5 b22.5 A typically high quality whisky from this outrageously underestimated distillery. *46%*

Balblair 2002 1st release bott 2012 db (**90.5**) n22 t23 f22.5 b23. A malt which reminds you how cold it is during Scottish winters...there is a lot of fresh-faced youth to this. But just so beautiful thanks to its understated complexity and honesty. *46%. nc ncf.*

Balblair 2003 Vintage 1st Release dist 2003 bott 2013. db (**88.5**) n20 strangely tart, at times off key. Not Balblair's nose showing by any means its greatest profile...; t23.5 ...yet the delivery is an absolute treat, churning out a succession of confident barley themes in classic Balblair style, from eyewateringly salivating and rich to crisp and precise. The sugars are crunchy and follow a gristy route; f22 a rather lovely succession of vanilla and butterscotch notes, always with a barley theme; b23 the nose maybe a bit odd, even unattractively flawed. But this a tale with a happy ending. *46%. nc ncf. Inverhouse distilleries.*

Balblair 2003 Vintage 1st Release dist 2003, bott 2015 db (**89**) n21 a fidgety, ill-at-ease aroma where the oak tentatively dominates but without establishing a character; t23 mainly citrus flavours at work, though the barley is clean and bright. Excellent, delicate oak sub-text, leading into light mocha; f22.5 a bit of spice buzz and praline; b22.5 just like their 2013 bottling, gets off to an uncertain start on the nose but makes its mark on delivery. *46%. nc ncf.*

Balblair 2004 Vintage 1st Release bourbon Matured, dist 2004, bott 2014. db (**88**) n22 t22.5 f21.5 b22 Maybe could have done with a higher percentage of 2nd fill casks to soften the experience and magnify the complexity. *46%. nc ncf. Inverhouse Distilleries.*

Balblair 2004 Vintage 1st Release Sherry Matured dist 2004 bott 2014. db (**68**) n16 t19 f16 b17. The sadness, of course, is that there are some pretty decent sherry butts amongst duds. *46%. nc ncf. Inverhouse Distillers.*

◇ **Balblair 2005 Vintage 1st Release** dist 2005, bott 2015 db (**86.5**) n20 t23 f21.5 b22. The nose is tight and has problems expanding, while the finish is short and quickly out of puff. But the delivery and follow through are superb with the malt really on maximum volume, and not without a little saline sharpness. Some good citrus, too. *46%. nc ncf.*

Gordon & MacPhail Cask Strength Balblair 1993 (**87**) n21.5 t23.5 f21 b21. No damaging sulphur: hurrah! But the grape is very loose fitting, swamping the whisky like granny's oversized knitted jumper engulfs a toddler. Little shape, though the spiced juiciness is delightful. *53.4%*

◇ **Gordon & MacPhail MacPhail's Collection Balblair 10 Year Old** (**87**) n21.5 t22 f22 b21.5. Enjoyable and very true to the distillery at this age and from cross-sectional bourbon cask: tart with a malty abrasiveness. A distillery where the complexity levels take off further down the line. *43%*

◇ **Gordon & MacPhail MacPhail's Collection Balblair 21 Year Old** (**90.5**) n23 lovely green banana adds a fruity edge to the malty grassiness; t23 salivating, of course, then varying layers of salted vanilla and chalky grist; the sugars keep their heads down, though always present; f22 shortish and with a marked Digestive biscuit quality; b22.5 oh, if only they had kept this at a bigger strength: the reduction breaks up the oils somewhat so we don't get the full story told. Even so, still a delight. *43%*

BALMENACH
Speyside, 1824. Inver House Distillers. Working.

Balmenach Aged 25 Years Golden Jubilee db (**89**) n21 t23 f22 b23. What a glorious old charmer this is! An essay in balance despite the bludgeoning nature of the beast early on. Takes a little time to get to know and appreciate: persevere with this belter because it is classic stuff for its age. *58%. Around 800 decanters.*

◇ **Old Malt Cask Balmenach Aged 14 Years** refill hogshead, cask no. 12129, dist Nov 01, bott Nov 15 (**86.5**) n20.5 t23 f21.5 b21.5. A very curious cask, this. A tad feinty on the nose, with the ultra oily, thickset finish confirming the problem. But a massive delivery of concentrated malt and even a little ulmo honey ensuring some quite wonderful moments in mid stream. A chewing whisky with excellent late caramel and cocoa, too. *50%. nc ncf sc. 348 bottles.*

THE BALVENIE
Speyside, 1892. William Grant & Sons. Working.

The Balvenie Aged 10 Years Founders Reserve db (**90**) n23 astonishing complexity: the fruit is relaxed, crushed sultanas and malty suet. A sliver of smoke and no more: everything is hinted and nudged at rather than stated. Superb; t24 here we go again: threads of malt binding together barely detectable nuances. Thin liquorice here, grape there, smoke and vanilla somewhere else; **f20** Light muscovado-toffee flattens out the earlier complexity. The bitter-sweet balance remains brilliant to the end; **b23** just one of those all-time-great standard 10-year-olds from a great distillery – pity they've decided to kill it off. 40%

The Balvenie Double Wood Aged 12 Years db (80.5) **n22 t20.5 f19 b19**. OK. So here's the score: Balvenie is one of my favourite distilleries in the world, I confess. I admit it. The original Balvenie 10 is a whisky I would go to war for. It is what Scotch malt whisky is all about. It invented complexity; or at least properly introduced me to it. But I knew that it was going to die, sacrificed on the altar of ageism. So I have tried to get to love Double Wood. And I have tasted and/or drunk it every month for the last couple of years to get to know it and, hopefully fall in love. But still I find it rather boring company. We may have kissed and canoodled. But still there is no spark. No romance whatsoever. 40%

The Balvenie 14 Years Old Cuban Selection db (86) **n20 t22 f22.5 b21.5**. Unusual malt. No great fan of the nose but the roughness of the delivery grows on you; there is a jarring, tongue-drying quality which actually works quite well and the development of the inherent sweetness is almost in slow motion. Some sophistication here, but also the odd note which, on the nose especially, is a little out of tune. 43%

The Balvenie 14 Years Old Golden Cask db (91) **n23.5 t23 f22 b22.5** A confident, elegant malt which doesn't stint one iota on complexity. Worth raiding the Duty Free shops for this little gem alone. 47.5%

The Balvenie 16 Year Old Triple Cask db (84.5) **n22 t22.5 f19 b21**. Well, after their single cask and then double wood, who saw this coming...? There is nothing about this whisky you can possibly dislike: no diminishing off notes (OK, well maybe at the very death) and a decent injection of sugar, especially early on. The trouble is, when you mix together sherry butts (even mainly good ones, like here) and first fill bourbon casks, the intense toffee produced tends to make for a monosyllabic, toffeed, dullish experience. And so it proves here. 40% WB16/030

The Balvenie Double Wood Aged 17 Years db (84) **n22 t21 f20 b21**. Balvenie does like 17 years as an age to show off its malt at its most complex, & understandably so as it is an important stage in its development before its usual premature over maturity: the last years or two when it remains full of zest and vigour. Here, though, the oak from the bourbon cask has offered a little too much of its milkier, older side while the sherry is a fraction overzealous and a shade too tangy. Enjoyable, but like a top of the range Mercedes engine which refuses to run evenly. 43%

The Balvenie Double Wood Aged 17 Years bott 2012 db (91) **n22.5 t23.5 f22 b23** A far friskier date than the 12-year-old. Here, maturity equals a degree of sophistication. Still not as outrageously sexy as a straightforward high grade bourbon cask offering from the distillery. But easily enough to get you hot under the collar. Lip smacking, high quality entertainment. 43%

The Balvenie Roasted Malt Aged 14 Years db (90) **n21 t23 f22 b24**. Balvenie very much as you've never seen it before. An absolute, mouth-filling cracker! 47.1%

The Balvenie Rum Wood Aged 14 Years db (88) **n22 t23 f21 b22**. Tasted blind I would never have recognized the distillery: I'm not sure if that's a good thing. 47.1%

Balvenie 17 Years Old Rum Cask db (88.5) **n22 t22.5 f22 b22**. For all the best attentions of the rum cask at times this feels all its 17 years, and perhaps a few Summers more. Impossible not to love, however. 43%

Balvenie New Wood Aged 17 Years db (85) **n23 t22 f19 b21**. A naturally good age for Balvenie; the nose is lucid and exciting, the early delivery is thick with rich malt. This, though, has sucked out lots of caramel from the wood to leave an annoyingly flat finish. 40%

The Balvenie 17 Year Old Sherry Oak db (88) **n23 t22.5 f21 b21.5**. Clean as a nut. High-class sherry it may be but the price to pay is a flattening out of the astonishing complexity one normally finds from this distillery. Bitter-sweet in every respect. 43%

The Balvenie Aged 21 Years Port Wood db (94.5) **n24** chocolate marzipan with a soft sugar-plum centre; deft, clean and delicate; **t24** hard to imagine a delivery more perfectly weighted: a rich tapestry of fruit and nut plus malt melts on the palate with a welter of drier, pithy, grape skin balancing the vanillas and barley oils; **f23** delicately dry with the vanilla and buttered fruitcake ensuring balance; **b23.5** what a magnificently improved malt. Last time out I struggled to detect the fruit. Here, there's no escaping. 40%

The Balvenie Aged 50 Years cask no. 4567 db (74.5) **n18.5 t20 f17.5 b18.5**. The milky, soapy nose gives the game away from the first minute: the spirit has gone through the cask and is now extracting some unwanted oaky residue. This re-emerges on the finale. There is, betwixt these hefty oaky footprints, a few moments of charm and cocoa-enriched enjoyment. But it is fleeting. 45.4%

The Balvenie Aged 50 Years cask no. 4570 db (84) **n21 t22 f20 b21**. It's like an elegant aircraft trying to take off and barely making it because of all the timber on board. The best bits have a bourbon tendency, with a special nod towards liquorice and hickory. But the truth is: it's simply too old and lumbering for greatness. *45.9%*

The Balvenie Single Barrel Aged 12 Years 1st fill ex bourbon, cask no. 12755 db **(96.5)** **n24.5 t24.5 f23.5 b24** About as close to perfection as a single cask may get. David Stewart, the finest blender of the last decade, may have half retired. But a cask like this shows he has lost none of his magic touch. Sublime. *47.8%. sc ncf. WB15/283*

The Balvenie Single Barrel Aged 15 Years sherry cask, cask no. 609 db **(95)** **n24 t24 f23.5 b23.5** A faultless cask – not a shadow of sulphur anywhere. But a case of where the grape has overwhelmed the barley, meaning balance has been compromised: and on the palate it feels as though you have been mugged by an oloroso butt. That said, this is still a stunning experience - a silky delight to be savoured. *47.8%. sc ncf. No more than 650 bottles. WB15/334*

The Balvenie Thirty Aged 30 Years db **(92)** **n24 t23 f22 b23** Rarely have I come across a bottling of a whisky of these advanced years which is so true to previous ones. Amazing. *47.3%*

The Balvenie 1993 Port Wood db **(89)** **n21 t23 f22 b23.** Oozes class without getting too flash about it: the secret is in the balance. *40%*

The Balvenie TUN 1401 batch 6 db **(90)** **n22.5 t23 f22 b22.5.** I'm amazed my stemmed nosing glass hasn't cracked under the weight of this Speyside monster of a dram. With the mix of fruit and big oak, probably distilled in lead stills... *49.8%. nc ncf.*

The Balvenie TUN 1401 batch 7 db **(87)** **n22.5 t23 f20 b21.5.** More juiciness to the fruit and sugar allows more clarity than the previous batch. *49.2%. William Grant & Sons.*

The Balvenie Tun 1401 Batch 9 db **(88)** **n22 t22 f22.5 b21.5** The kind of rough-house oak which grabs you when you are looking for a quiet night in and gives you a good duffing up. *49.3%*

The Balvenie Tun 1509 Batch 1 db **(89)** **n23 t22.5 f21.5 b22** Balvenie is a distillery which struggles with age. And this is hanging on for life by its bloodied claws... *47.1%*

The Balvenie TUN 1509 batch 2 db **(94)** **n23.5 t24 f23 b23.5** A far happier and all round better balanced bottling than Batch 1. A big whisky, though you won't at first realise it... *50.3%*

BANFF
Speyside, 1863–1983. Diageo. Demolished.

Gordon & MacPhail Rare Old Banff 1966 (95.5) n24 t24 f23.5 b24 A rare whisky on at least two major counts: one because casks of this are harder to come by than Millwall wins under Ian Holloway. And, secondly, because few casks get to this kind of age with its honey and sugars still intact. What a loss this distillery was. But what a gain it is for anyone who finds this bottle: it is a true classic. *45.2%*

BEN NEVIS
Highlands (Western), 1825. Nikka. Working.

Ben Nevis 10 Years Old db **(88)** **n21 t22 f23 b22.** A massive malt that has steadied itself in recent bottlings, but keep those knives and forks to hand! *46%*

Ben Nevis Synergy 13 Years Old db **(88)** **n22 t22 f21.5 b22.5** One of the sweetest Ben Nevis's for a long time, but as chewy as ever! A bit of a lady's dram to be honest. *46%*

⬩ **Acla Selection Ben Nevis 16 Years Old** dist 1997, bott 2013 **(77.5) n19.5 t20.5 f18 18.5** Didn't even have to taste this to write these notes: the nose told the sorry tale. Of course, I did taste it. And it confirmed the work of a substandard cask, resulting in a sharp, thin malt. The spirit never stood a chance from day one. *52.9%. nc ncf.*

⬩ **Acla Selection Ben Nevis 43 Years Old** bourbon hogshead, dist 1970, bott 2014 **(77) n21.5 t20 f17.5 b18.** Weirdly, most things I come across these days from 1970 appear to have gone off the rails rather badly – Vintage Port, apart. Doubtless once beautiful, this now has unappetising rancid notes, the early honey giving way to bitterness, confusion and structural decay: a very unpleasant, classless, finish after the lovely, sweet start. Doubtless someone will find this quite wonderful, on account of its age. But more fool them... *44.7%. nc ncf.*

⬩ **Best Dram Ben Nevis 18 Years Old** **(86.5) n21 t22.5 f21.5 b21.5.** The huge oak takes absolutely no prisoners here. There is an imbalance of tannin over barley from the word go and the malt seems at least double its 18 years. Still, the chunky sugars do their best to take the sting from the oak, though it proves an unequal battle. *51.2%*

⬩ **Big Market Sonderabfüllung Nr. 16 Ben Nevis 1997** bott 2015 **(90.5) n21.5** A nervous nose: there are elements here which can go either way. Very much of the crushed pip school as the very active barley find a non-specific fruitiness to hassle. Not a single jot of balance, but so much delicious intrigue...; **t23.5** barley on steroids. The malt comes at you intense and sharp...and then comes at you again...and again! Clean and effervescent; **f23** long, with a little lemon curd tart trailing into vanilla; **b23** tart....in every sense. A great, enlivening whisky to come home from work to. 56.5%. 50th Anniversary bottling.

⬦ **Chapter 7 Ben Nevis 1996 18 Years Old** (90.5) **n22.5** oak has made some attractive inroads: shows age but doesn't make a big thing about it; **t22.5** a typically thick and intense barley theme for the distillery with a cocoa undercoat; **f22.5** remains simple as the barley hangs on to the slightly minty chocolate; **b23** an usually singular and understated whisky in that it barely departs from the track it first starts out upon. Highly attractive. 51.8%. sc. 273 bottles.

⬦ **Eiling Lim Ben Nevis 43 Years Old 1970** bott 2014 (81) **n22 t19 f20 b20**. The nose is as puzzling as it is intriguing. A real mish-mash of suet and stewed fruit, and porridge, too..!! A kind of spotted dog pudding breakfast. Less joy on delivery, though. An unhappy cask makes for a tangy, bitter unstructured free for all. 44.8%. nc ncf sc. 60 bottles. 2nd Release.

⬦ **The First Editions Ben Nevis Aged 18 Years 1996** refill hogshead, cask no. 11790, bott 2015 (90.5) **n23** rare to find a Nevis quite so provocative: so much malt, yet the fruity theme is more along the lines of boiled sweets than from the fruit bowl or barrel; **t23** sensationally salivating: the barley really does coat the palate with several handsome layers of malt. Light traces of maple syrup adds depth before the salty oak arrives; **f22** a shade tangy as the vanilla tannin begins to take command **b22.5** though delightful as a single malt in its own right, just love to think what I could do with this in a blend...!! 46.5%. nc ncf sc. 339 bottles.

⬦ **Grindlay's Selection Ben Nevis 1997** (91) **n22.5** impressive nose: balanced cleverly between the butterscotch, lime and grist; **t23** fabulous sugars act as pathfinders with the oak respectfully in its train; **f22.5** a surprising late puff of citrus offers an unscheduled lightness to the finish; **b23** the sugars sparkle quite beautifully. 52.6%. nc ncf. 228 bottles.

⬦ **Hunter Laing's Distiller's Art Ben Nevis Aged 19 Years** refill hogshead, dist May 96, bott 2016 (90) **n22** a little diced up pear breaks up the crisp barley beautifully; **t23** just adore the sugar-salt edge to the malt, maximising the flavour from the go; the oak has a mildly bitter undertone, but this settles into a spiced mocha middle; **f22.5** traces of light citrus to the clean vanilla fade; **b22.5** exemplary, high class Nevis. 48%. nc ncf sc. 111 bottles.

⬦ **Kingsbury Gold Ben Nevis 17 Year Old 1998** sherry butt, cask no. 11336 (73) **n18 t23 f15 b17**. Loads of chocolate spiced fruit cake, if such a thing exists. Well, it does in liquid form, make no mistake! But if you are into sulphur, here's your lad! If you are one of those genetically unable to pick up sulphur, this might well be your whisky of the year! 57.9%. sc. 460 bottles.

⬦ **Maltbarn Ben Nevis 1996** ex-bourbon cask, bott 2015 (81.5) **n20 t21 f20 b20.5**. The odd malty sharpness entertains. But just a little too rough and ready for its own good. 50.9%. sc. 121 bottles.

⬦ **Old Malt Cask Ben Nevis 14 Years Old** (81) **n21 t20 f20 b20**. Thick and glutinous. Little layering to the intense barley or tangy, tired oak. A tad hot, too. 48.4%. sc.

Old Malt Cask Ben Nevis 16 Years Old sherry butt, cask no. 10982, dist Jun 98, bott Oct 14 (72.5) **n18 t19 f17.5 b18**. Ticks lots of boxes...but few of them are the right ones. Stodgy though occasionally juicy, there is a definite grubbiness to this which may appeal to some, though not the purists. 50%. nc ncf sc. 714 bottles.

⬦ **Old Malt Cask Ben Nevis Aged 19 Years** sherry butt, cask no. 12148, dist Jun 96, bott Nov 15 (93.5) **n23.5** a little tight, though not from sulphur. Instead the grape seems to have a mix of fresh juiciness and a more austere dry style which is determined to keep the oak in its place; **t23.5** big delivery which improves with each arriving wave. Begins a little uncertainly, but the fruit intensifies as it progresses. Yet it is the spice which really commands; **f23** the simplicity of the dram is confirmed as the fruit begins to diminish. Surprising lack of weight, but the layering of the drying vanilla is profound; **b23.5** good grief! A sulphur-free sherry butt from 1996! Not the most common of happenings. The grape pings around the palate like a whisky possessed. But still cannot get the better of the spice. Delightful and intriguing. 50%. nc ncf sc. 572 bottles.

⬦ **That Boutique-y Whisky Company Ben Nevis** batch 2 (91.5) **n22** busy sugars, plus Brazilian biscuit and vanilla; **t23.5** you could drown in your own saliva – this is so ridiculously juicy. Profoundly light, gristy sugars; **f23** a beautiful malt fade...but those spices...my word!! **b23** if anyone remembers Batch 1 – more of the same but much more spice! 48.7%. 52 bottles.

⬦ **That Boutique-y Whisky Company Ben Nevis 19 Year Old** batch 4 (84.5) **n21.5 t21.5 f19.5 b21**. A distinctly bitter-sweet experience. 49.5%. 166 bottles.

⬦ **Whic Ben Nevis 18 Years Old** bourbon hogshead, dist Jun 96, bott Apr 15 (88) **n21.5** some chewing gum sticking to the nose; **t22.5** good, crisp barley. A very lazy hint of citrus and ulmo honey, but really it is the lightly spiced vanilla which makes the running; **f22** dries with almost indecent haste. But the malt battles on gamely; **b22** very simplistic bending malt, but pleasant. *53.7%. 126 bottles.*

◈ **Whiskybroker Ben Nevis 18 Year Old** hogshead, cask no. 596, dist 22 May 97, bott 24 Sept 15 (**87**) **n21.5 t22.5 f21.5 b22.** Very malty. But the sugars star too briefly. Just a tad too warm, thin and austere. *53.4%. sc.*

◈ **Whisky-Fässle Ben Nevis 1996** sherry butt, bott 2015 (**91.5**) **n23** Danish pastry, warm with the raisins still radiating a slightly burnt fruitiness amid the lighter sugars and doughy, buttery tones; **t23** house-style heftiness, though a few glazed cherries emphasise the fruit with aplomb. Spicy, too; **f22.5** a little chunkiness to the distillate as the oils collect. Remains formidably of fruitcake substance; **b23** a beautiful sherry butt has done a good job here. *52.7%*

◈ **Whiskyjace Ben Nevis 16 Years Old** 1998 bourbon hogshead, bott 2015 (**88**) **n22** malt concentrate riddled with toasty oak; **t22.5** tangy, salivating barley. Not exactly stylish, but very effective...and thick! **f21.5** just a little bit too much tang from a tired cask. But the spices amid the still juicy barley save the day...; **b22** for a simplistically malty dram, this is pretty big stuff...! *52.6%*

BENRIACH

Speyside, 1898. The BenRiach Distillery Co. Working.

The BenRiach db (**86**) **n21 t22 f21.5 b21.5.** The kind of soft malt you could wean nippers on, as opposed to Curiositas, which would be kippers. Unusually for a BenRiach there is a distinct toffee-fudge air to this one late on, but not enough to spoil that butterscotch-malt charm. No colouring added, so a case of the oak being a bit naughty. *40%*

BenRiach 10 Year Old db (**87.5**) **n20 t23 f22.5 b22.** A much fatter spirit than from any time when I worked those stills. The dry nose never quite decides where it is going. But there's no doubting the creamy yet juicy credentials on the palate. Malty, with graceful fruit sugars chipping in delightfully. *43%*

The BenRiach Aged 12 Years db (**82.5**) **n21 t20 f21 b20.5.** More enjoyable than the 43% I last tasted. But still an entirely inoffensive malt determined to offer minimal complexity. *40%*

The BenRiach Aged 12 Years db (**78.5**) **n21.5 t20 f18 b19.** White peppers on the nose, then goes uncharacteristically quiet and shapeless. *43%*

The BenRiach Aged 12 Years Dark Rum Wood Finish db (**85.5**) **n21 t22 f21 b21.5.** More than a decade ago, long before it ever became fashionable, I carried out an extensive programme of whisky maturation in old dark rum casks. So, if someone asked me now what would happen if you rounded off a decently peated whisky in a rum cask, I'd say – depending on time given for the finish and type of rum – the smoke would be contained and there would be a ramrod straight, steel-hard sweetness ensuring the most clipped whisky you can possibly imagine. And this here is exactly what we have... *46%*

The BenRiach Aged 12 Years Matured In Sherry Wood db (**95.5**) **n23.5 t24 f24 b24** Since I last tasted this the number of instances of sampling a sherry wood whisky and not finding my taste buds caked in sulphur has nosedived dramatically. Therefore, to start my tasting day at 7am with something as honest as this propels one with myriad reasons to continue the day. A celebration of a malt whisky in more ways than you could believe. *46%. nc ncf.*

The BenRiach Aged 15 Years Dark Rum Finish db (**86**) **n20 t22 f22 b22.** Drier, spicier than before. Old Jamaica chocolate candy. *46%. nc ncf.*

The BenRiach Aged 15 Years Madeira Wood Finish db (**89.5**) **n22.5 t21.5 f23 b22.5.** Very much drier than most Madeira finishes you will find around. Once the scramble on delivery is over, this bottling simply exudes excellence. A collector's must have. *46%*

The BenRiach Aged 15 Years Pedro Ximénez Sherry Wood Finish db (**94.5**) **n25 t23.5 f22.5 b23.5.** Some of the strangest Scotch malts I have tasted in the last decade have been fashioned in PX casks. And few have been particularly enjoyable creations. This one, though, bucks the trend thanks principally to the most subtle of spice imprints. All the hallmarks of some kind of award-winner. *46%*

The BenRiach Aged 15 Years Tawny Port Wood Finish db (**89.5**) **n21.5 t23 f22.5 b22.5.** Now that really is the perfect late night dram. *46%*

The BenRiach Aged 16 Years db (**85.5**) **n21.5 t21.5 f20 b21.** Although maltily enjoyable, if over dependent on caramel flavours, you get the feeling that a full works 46% version would offer something more gripping and true to this great distillery. *40%*

The BenRiach Aged 16 Years db (**83.5**) **n21.5 t21 f20 b21.** Pleasant malt but now without the dab of peat which gave it weight; also a marked reduction of the complexity that once gave this such a commanding presence. *43%. nc ncf.*

The BenRiach Aged 16 Years Sauternes Wood Finish db (85) n19.5 t23 f21.5 b21. One of the problems with cask finishing is that there is nothing like an exact science of knowing when the matured whisky and introduced wood gel to their fullest potential. BenRiach enjoy a reputation of getting it right more often than most other distillers and bottlers. But here it hasn't come off to quite the same effect as previous, quite sensational, versions I have tasted of the 16-y-o Sauternes finish. No denying the sheer joy of the carpet bombing of the taste buds on delivery, though, so rich is the combination of fresh grape and delicate smoke. 46%

The BenRiach Aged 17 Years "Septendecim" Peated Malt db (93.5) n24 t24.5 f23 b24 proof, not that it is now needed, that Islay is not alone in producing phenomenal phenols... 46%. nc ncf.

The BenRiach Aged 18 Years Gaja Barolo Wood Finish db (89) n22 t23 f21.5 b22.5. The delivery gives one of the most salivating experiences of the year. 46%

The BenRiach Aged 18 Years Moscatel Wood Finish db (92.5) n23.5 t23.5 f22 b23.5 One of those rare whiskies which renews and upholds any belief I have for cask finishing. Superb. 46%

The BenRiach Aged 20 Years db (85.5) n21.5 t23 f19 b22. A much more attractive version than the American Release 46%. The barley offers a disarming intensity and sweetness which makes the most of the light oils. Only a bittering finish shuts the gate on excellence. 43%. nc ncf.

The BenRiach Aged 20 Years db (78) n19 t20 f19 b20. This is big, but not necessarily for the right reasons or in the right places. A big cut of oiliness combines with some surging sugars for a most un-BenRiachy ride. 46%. US Market.

The BenRiach Aged 21 Years "Authenticus" Peated Malt db (85.5) n22 t21.5 f21 b21. A heavy malt, though the smoke only adds a small degree to its weight. The barley is thick and chewy but the oak has a very big say. 46%

The BenRiach 25 Years Old db (87.5) n21.5 t23 f21 b22. The tranquillity and excellent balance of the middle is the highlight by far. 50%

The BenRiach 30 Years Old db (94.5) n24 the fruit, though very ripe and rich, remains uncluttered and clean and is helped along the way by a superb injection of sweetened cloves and Parma Violets; the oak is present and correct offering an egg custard sub-plot; t24 how ridiculously deft is that? There is total equilibrium in the barley and fruit as it massages the palate in one of the softest deliveries of a 30-y-o around; the middle ground is creamy and leans towards the vanilla; even so, there are some amazingly juicy moments to savour; f23 very lightly oiled and mixing light grist and rich vanilla; b23.5 it's spent 30 years in the cask: give one glass of this at least half an hour of your time: seal the room, no sounds, no distractions. It's worth it...for as hard as I try, I can barely find a single fault with this. 50%

BenRiach 35 Year Old db (90) n23 juicy dates and plums are tipped into a weighty fruitcake; t24 sit right back in your armchair (no..? Then go and find one...!!) having dimmed the lights and silenced the room and just let your taste buds run amok: those plums and toasted raisins really do get you salivating, with the spices also whipping up a mid-life storm; f21.5 angular oak dries and bitters at a rate of knots; b22 sexy fruit, but has late oaky bite. 42.5%

◇ **The BenRiach 1995 19 Year Old** Port hogshead, cask no. 3616, dist 1993, bott Sept 14 db (79) n19 t22.5 f18.5 b19. Any port in a storm, eh? Sadly, this was partially sunk before it could even reach safe haven. Can't fault the delivery, though. 53.7%. nc ncf sc. Bottled for The Tasting Room, Norway.

◇ **BenRiach Cask Strength** batch 1 db (93) n22.5 very green and grassy malt; t24 masterful: how many layers of maltiness can you count? I have made five – before it moves into a delightful and very milky Malteser middle; f23 those of you into vaguely fruity fudge will adore this...; b23.5 if you don't fall in love with this one, you should just stick to vodka... 57.2%

The BenRiach Curiositas Aged 10 Years Single Peated Malt db (90.5) n23 t23 f22 b22.5 "Hmmmm. Why have my research team marked this down as a 'new' whisky" I wondered to myself. Then immediately on nosing and tasting I discovered the reason without having to ask: the pulse was weaker, the smoke more apologetic...it had been watered down from the original 46% to 40%. This is excellent malt. But can we have our truly great whisky back, please? As lovely as it is, this is a bit of an imposter. As Emperor Hadrian might once have said: "ifus itus aintus brokus..." 40%

The BenRiach "Heart of Speyside" db (85.5) n21.5 t22 f21 b21. A decent, non-fussy malt where the emphasis is on biscuity barley. At times juicy and sharp. Just a tease of very distant smoke here and there adds weight. 40%

The BenRiach "Horizons" db (87) n22 t22.5 f21 b21.5. Few mountains or even hills on this horizon. But the view is still an agreeable one. 50%. nc ncf.

⟡ **BenRiach Peated Quarter Casks** db **(93)** n23.5 there's a lot of peat in them barrels. The citrus is vital...; **t24** a plethora of sugars and caramel leached from the casks make for a safe landing when the smoke and malt – with a slightly new make feel - arrive in intensive form; **f22.5** the caramel continues, now with spice; **b23** though seemingly youthful in some phases, works a treat! 46%

The BenRiach "Solstice" db **(94)** n23.5 t24 f23 b23.5. On midsummer's day 2011, the summer solstice, I took a rare day off from writing this book. With the maximum light available in my part of the world for the day I set off at daybreak to see how many miles I could walk along remote country paths stopping, naturally, only at a few remote pubs on the way. It was a fraction under 28 miles. Had this spellbinding whisky been waiting for me just a little further down the road, I am sure, despite my troubled left knee and blistered right foot, I would have made it 30... 50%. nc ncf.

The BenRiach "Solstice" 17 Years Old 2nd Edition port finish, heavily peated db **(94)** n23.5 t23 f23.5 b24 Well, it's the 21st June 2012, the summer solstice. And, naturally, pouring down with rain outside. So what better time to taste this whisky? With all that heart-warming, comforting peat as thick as a woolly jumper, this is the perfect dram for a bitterly cold winter's day the world over. Or midsummer's day in England... 50%. nc ncf.

The BenRiach Vintage 1999 Bottling Aged 13 Years finished in virgin American oak casks, dist 12 Aug 99 db **(91)** n24.5 t22.5 f22 b22 Doesn't quite live up to the billing on the nose... but then not much would. 46%. ncf nc. WB15/330

Birnie Moss Intensely Peated db **(90)** n22 youthful, full of fresh barley and lively, clean smoke; **t23.5** juicy, fabulously smoked, wet-behind the ears gristy sugars; **f22** some vanillas try to enter a degree of complexity; **b22.5** before Birnie Moss started shaving... or even possibly toddling. Young and stunning. 48%. nc ncf.

⟡ **The First Editions Ben Riach Aged 26 Years 1989** refill puncheon, cask no. 12002, bott 2015 **(90)** n22 shouts wine cask before you even know what it is! To be more precise, a style more normally associated with Cognac, and sometimes Port. The sugars are crisp and form an outer shell around the barley; **t23.5** enormous. And as it progresses, quite beautiful. The barley which had been itching to escape on the nose is fully unleashed here. But the muscovado sugars remain crunchy and bring out the delicate fruits as far as they can take them; quite eye-watering in its fresh intensity; **f21.5** the oak tires a little towards the end, making for a sharp finale; **b22.5** so brittle and clipped. you feel like it could chip your teeth. But doesn't stint on the big flavours. 56.1%. nc ncf sc. 258 bottles.

Old Masters BenRiach 22 Year Old cask no. 110693, dist 1991, bott 2014 **(88.5)** n22.5 t22 f22 b22 a steady as she goes oldie, surprisingly consistent throughout. 54.2%. sc. James MacArthur & Co Ltd

The Single Malts of Scotland Benriach 24 Year Old bourbon cask, cask no. 100142, dist 1990, bott Jul 14 **(91)** n23 t22.5 f22.5 b23 pleasant, malty, confident Speysider for its age, happy to underline the passage of time and the way it has, mostly, cocked a snook at it.... 50.2%. 315 bottles. WB16/011

⟡ **That Boutique-y Whisky Company BenRiach** batch 3 **(88)** n22 malt; t22 malt; f22 malt; **b22** this is not far off the most basic and simplistic of styles I encountered at this distillery when I first worked there so many years ago... 48.9%. 103 bottles.

BENRINNES
Speyside, 1826. Diageo. Working.

Benrinnes Aged 15 Years db **(70)** n16 t19 f17 b18. What a shame that in the year the independent bottlers at last get it right for Benrinnes, the actual owners of the distillery make such a pig's ear of it. Sulphured and sicklysweet, this bottling has little to do with the very good whisky made there day in day out by its talented team. Depressing. 43%. Flora and Fauna.

⟡ **Benrinnes 21 Year Old** ex-sherry European oak casks, dist 1992 db **(83.5)** n21 t22 f19 **b21.5**. Salty and tangy. Some superb cocoa moments mixing with the muscovado sugars as it peaks. But just a little too furry and bitter at the finish. 56.9%. 2,892 bottles. Diageo Special Releases 2014.

Cadenhead's Authentic Collection Benrinnes Cask Strength Aged 25 Years bourbon hogshead, bott Jul 13 **(84)** n20.5 t21 f21.5 b21. You'll do well to find a thinner 25-year-old all year. Warming, at times aggressive with crisp barley sugar. 53%. 270 bottles. WB15/095

⟡ **Chapter 7 Benrinnes 1997 18 Years Old** bourbon hogshead, cask no. 898 **(89)** n22 custard cream biscuits dunked in milk; **t23.5** now that is one beautiful delivery: concentrated malt slowly unravels to reveal stunning oak-infused spices; **f21** a bit tangy towards the finish, though not before an excellent paprika and sandalwood burst; **b22.5** the high intensity of the barley has just enough clout to fend off the strong-arm oak. A big Benrinnes. 61.5%. sc.

⟡ **The First Editions Benrinnes Aged 18 Years 1997** refill hogshead, cask no. 12124, bott 2015 **(85.5)** n21 t22.5 f21 b21. Plenty of old oak tang to get you puckering. Very good texture and even a degree of saltiness creeps in. Enough barley to keep the balance honest. 52.8%. nc ncf sc. 285 bottles.

◇ **Hepburn's Choice Benrinnes 6 Years Old** European oak quarter cask, dist 2009, bott 2015 **(92.5) n22.5** the North American signature expected is there, in that the European tannins have taken hold to ensure a spiced red liquorice lead...; **t23.5** this is beautifully structured on delivery: the tannin builds a platform, but not remotely at the cost of the gentle sugars. The barley remains intact and at times unusually intense for this distillery. Though not before the surprising oils and ginger biscuit have ganged happily together; **f23** long, with the earlier muscovado sugars now virtually spent. Dries but remains intact and confident; **b23.5** now there's a fascinating proposition: take Speyside's lightest malt and place it in a quarter cask. Well, the outcome is obvious. The oak will dominate throughout. The questions are: how and will the barley make any telling mark at all? The answer given here might surprise you, for this is a very fine malt from many angles. Satisfying and, as expected, big for its age. 46%. nc ncf sc. 86 bottles.

◇ **Hepburn's Choice Benrinnes 6 Years Old** European oak quarter cask, dist 2009, bott 2015 **(73.5) n17.5 t19 f18 b19.** An honest whisky: the less than pleasant, discordant nose tells you that you are in for an unhappy time of it on the palate. And it certainly doesn't lie... 46%. nc ncf sc. 84 bottles.

◇ **Hepburn's Choice Benrinnes 6 Years Old** European oak quarter cask, dist 2009, bott 2015 **(87) n20 t22.5 f22 b22.5.** There's some gristle on the meaty nose, and a little hoarseness to the finish. But between the odd unhappy moment, there is plenty to get on with and enjoy, especially on the chunky, malty delivery which moves into barley-sugary country within no time. 46%. nc ncf sc. 82 bottles.

◇ **Hepburn's Choice Benrinnes 11 Years Old** sherry butt, dist 2002, bott 2014 **(84) n20.5 t22 f20 b21.5.** A crisp, juicy edge to this one. Fruit doesn't for a moment enter the fray, though spice certainly does. 46%. nc ncf sc. 761 bottles.

◇ **Old Malt Cask Benrinnes Aged 15 Years** sherry butt, cask no. 10891, dist Jul 99, bott Oct 14 **(85.5) n21 t22.5 f20.5 b21.5.** Steams in from the word go with no shortage of malty muscle. A better Benrinnes. The barley impacts beautifully on both nose and delivery and its positive all the way. 50%. nc ncf sc. 567 bottles.

◇ **Old Masters Benrinnes 15 Year Old** cask no. 306771, bott 2016 **(92.5) n22.5** weighty... hang on... did I just type "weighty" on a Benrinnes tasting note? I had better nose it again.... Yep, weighty. What the f....? And with some earthy smoke.... Nope, just pinched myself and hit my head three times against the table...it hurt. I am not dreaming. I have a slightly smoky, weighty Benrinnes...; Next, I'll be seeing my beloved Millwall playing the ball on the deck... no, that's just being ridiculous..; **t23** seriously intense...hang on did I just write "intense" with a Benrinnes...better taste this again. Yep. Intense...and oily... OILY???? What the f....? Plus delicate smoke, spices and honey...on a Benrinnes?; **f23** long, chewy, smoky...hang on let me read that again. And check the bottle. And taste it again. I am living in some weird parallel universe...; **b24** this is Benrinnes? My flabber is fully gasted... 57.5%

◇ **Provenance Benrinnes Aged 8 Years** bott Mar 16 **(79) n19 t21 f19.5 b19.5.** The barley-rich sugars try to keep this malt buoyant for as long as possible. But an unfriendly cask takes its toll. Unusually oily and fat for this triple-distilled malt. 46%. nc ncf sc.

Riegger's Selection Cask Strength Benrinnes 16 Year Old 2nd fill sherry butt, bott 12 Mar 15 **(91) n23.5 t23 f22 b22.5** Benrinnes singing in its very finest voice. And, for once, in tune... 53.6%

◇ **Scotch Malt Whisky Society Cask 36.99 Aged 9 Years** 1st fill barrel, dist 08 Nov 06, bott 22 Feb 16 **(84.5) n21 t21.5 f20.5 b21.5.** Typically torch-like, the intense yet strangely thin malts are blasted seeringly onto the palate. As a blender, I would not be too happy to see this wasted as a single malt. Rather, it should be used to impact on a low-ish malt content blend, and one using the softer grains. 57.8%. nc ncf sc. 234 bottles.

Stronachie 18 Years Old (83.5) n21.5 t21 f20 b21. This is so much like the older brother of the Stronachie 12: shows the same hot temper on the palate and even sharper teeth. Also, the same slim-line body. Have to say, though, something strangely irresistible about the intensity of the crisp malt. 46%

◇ **Whiskybroker Benrinnes 17 Year Old** bourbon barrel, cask no. 893, dist 15 Oct 97, bott 28 Aug 15 **(86) n22 t21 f21.5 b21.5.** A tad fierce on the palate – and we ain't talking spice. But rather enjoy the vanilla ice cream theme, especially on the nose. 57%. sc.

◇ **Whiskybroker Benrinnes 18 Year Old** refill bourbon barrel, cask no. 906, dist 15 Aug 97, bott 01 Feb 16 **(87) n22 t21.5 f22 b21.5.** Carries many similar traits to their 17-year-old version, especially with the thin burn. But here the vanilla-rich oak and barley travel more hand in hand. *50%. sc.*

⬦ **The Whisky Chamber Benrinnes 18 Years Old** ex-bourbon hogshead, cask no. 890/1997, dist 12 Oct 95, bott 08 Mar 16 **(84.5) n20.5 t21.5 f21 b21.5**. A warming malt, with the barley forming some attractive layering – often sandwiched between molten light refined sugars. Decent caramelised biscuit. But just a tad too hot for comfort. *56.6%. nc sc.*

BENROMACH
Speyside, 1898. Gordon & MacPhail. Working.
Benromach 10 Years Old matured in hand selected oak casks db **(87.5) n22 t22 f21.5 b22.** For a relatively small still using peat, the experience is an unexpected and delicately light one. *43%*

Benromach 15 Year Old db **(78) n20 t22 f17 b19**. Some charming early moments, especially when the grape escapes its marker and reveals itself in its full juicy and sweet splendour. But it is too short lived as the sulphur, inevitably takes over. *43%*

Benromach 21 Years Old db **(91.5) n22 t23.5 f23 b23** An entirely different, indeed lost, style of malt from the old, now gone, big stills. The result is an airier whisky which has embraced such good age with a touch of panache and grace. *43%*

Benromach 22 Years Old Finished in Port Pipes db **(86) n22 t23 f20 b21**. Slightly Jekyll and Hyde. *45%. 3500 bottles.*

Benromach 25 Years Old db **(92) n24** seriously sexy with spices interplaying with tactile malt: the bitter-sweet balance is just so. There is even the faintest flicker of peat-smoke to underscore the pedigree; **t22** an early, surprising, delivery of caramel amongst the juicy barley; **f23** lots of gentle spices warm the enriched barley and ice-creamy vanilla; **b23** a classic old-age Speysider, showing all the quality you'd hope for. *43%*

Benromach 30 Years Old db **(95.5) n23.5** spiced sultana, walnuts and polished bookcases; **t24** no malt has the right to be anything near so silky. The sugars are a cunning mix of molasses and muscovado; the honey is thinned manuka. Still the barley gets through, though the vanilla is right behind; **f24** drier, but never fully dries and has enough spotted dog in reserve to make for a moist, lightly spiced finish. And finally a thin strata of sweet, Venezualan cocoa; **b24** you will struggle to find a 30-year-old with less wrinkles than this.. Magnificent: one of the outstanding malts of the year. *43%*

Benromach 100° Proof db **(94) n23** proof positive that toasty oak, a dash of fruit and several puffs of peat can go a long, long way...; **t23.5** beautiful mouth-feel, as thick as anything I have seen from the new Benromach before. The fabulous spice really does make a name for itself, but all those notes recognised on the nose are present and correct here; **f23.5** more of the same, but a layer of Jaffa Cake towards the finish, though it is short-lived as it dries...; **b24** for any confused US readers, the strength is based on the old British proof strength, not American! What is not confusing is the undisputed complexity and overall excellence of this malt. *57%*

Benromach 2002 Cask Strength db **(88.5) n22 t22.5 f22 b22**. Most peaty malts frighten those who aren't turned on by smoky whisky. This might be an exception: they just don't come any friendlier. *60.3%*

Benromach 2002 Sassicaia Wood Finish db **(86) n21 t22 f21 b22**. Again this entirely idiosyncratic wood-type comes crashing head to head with the smoke to form a whisky style like nothing else. Dense, breathless and crushed, there is little room for much else to get a word in, other than some oak-extracted sugars. A must experience dram. *45%*

Benromach 2005 Sassicaia Finish db **(92.5) n22.5 t24 f23 b23**. A sassy dram in every way... *45%*

Benromach Cask Strength 1981 db **(91) n21.5 t23 f23.5 b23**. Really unusual with that seaweedy aroma awash with salt: stunningly delicious stuff. *54.2%*

Benromach Cask Strength 2001 db **(89) n21.5 t23 f22 b22.5**. Just fun whisky which has been very well made and matured with total sympathy to the style. Go get. *59.9%*

Benromach Cask Strength 2003 db **(92) n22.5 t23.5 f23 b23.5** Hats off to the most subtle and sophisticated Benromach I have tasted in a while. *59.4%*.

⬦ **Benromach Heritage 35 Year Old** db **(87) n22 t21.5 f22 b21.5**. A busy exchange of complex tannin notes, some backed by the most faded spice and caramel. All charming and attractive, but the feeling of decay is never far away. *43%*

⬦ **Benromach Heritage 1974** db **(93) n23.5** a brilliant interplay between sandalwood and old oak floorboards; **t23** the tannins show early and with spiced intent. Muscovado sugars cover some fruity ground, the caramels making a softer landing for the crisper elements; **f23** a massive break out of malt, though the oak still shows who's boss...; **b23.5** made in the year I left school to become a writer, this appears to have survived the years in better nick than I... *49.1%*

Benromach Madeira Wood db (92) n22 t24 f23 b23. If you want a boring, safe, timid malt, stay well away from this one. Fabulous: you are getting the feeling that the real Benromach is now beginning to stand up. 45%

Benromach Marsala Wood db (86.5) n21.5 t22 f22 b21. Solid, well made, enjoyable malt, which in some ways is too solid: the imperviousness of both the peat and grape appears not to allow much else get through. Not a dram to say no to, however, and the spices in particular are a delight. 45%

Benromach Organic db (91) n23 t23 f22 b23. Young and matured in possibly first fill bourbon or, more likely, European (even Scottish) oak; you cannot do other than sit up and take notice of this guns-blazing big 'un. An absolute treat! 43%. nc ncf.

Benromach Organic Special Edition db (85.5) n22 t21 f21.5 b21. The smoky bacon crisp aroma underscores the obvious youth. Also, one of the driest malts of the year. Overall, pretty. But pretty pre-pubescent, too... 43%

Benromach Organic 2008 bott 2014 db (93) n23 huge toasty oak: a degree of bourbon-style liquorice and ulmo honey, pepped up further by barley on heat...; t23.5 good grief: just didn't expect that! The sugars from the oak have linked with the sweeter bits of the barley and rocketed off, with spices forming when the energy begins to dip; f23 long, with the barley sugar refusing to allow any oaky bitterness to climb onboard at all; b23.5 for a whisky at a meagre 43%, the most astonishing explosion of intense barley and oak. More orgasmic than organic... 43%

Benromach Peat Smoke Batch 3 db (90.5) n22 excellent nose: pretty decent levels of peat reek evident but dried, rather than cured...; t23 the dry peat builds in intensity, though not after the clean and powering barley makes the first speech; f22.5 dry, chalky and compact; damn it – this is very good, indeed! b23 an excellent malt that has been beautifully made. Had it been bottled at 46 we would have seen it offer an extra degree of richness. 40%

Benromach Peat Smoke 2005 67ppm db (88.5) n22 t22.5 f21.5 b22.5 This may be 67 parts per million phenols when it started. But size, so I have been told, is not important. Stamina and finesse both are. And while this may enjoy a degree of the latter, it has little of the former. 46%.

Benromach Peat Smoke 2006 db (90.5) n22.5 a soothing softness to the peat reveals attractive degrees of mint and vanilla; t23.5 the gristy sugars are up front and carry with them a surprisingly dense smokiness, which soon dissipates; beautifully even middle, with that weak mint humbug touch drifting in; f22 long, a little tart as a few tannins nip; b22.5 a more measured malt than the previous vintage. 46%

Benromach Traditional db (86) n22 t21 f21.5 b21.5. Deliciously clean and smoky. But very raw and simplistic, too. 40%

Benromach Vintage 1968 db (94.5) n23 t23 f24.5 b24. A 40 year plus whisky of astonishing quality...? A piece of cake... 45.4%

Benromach Vintage 1969 db (92) n22 t22 t24 f23 b23. The odd branch of the old oak too many. But still has many magical mahogany moments. 42.6%

Benromach Vintage 1976 db (89.5) n23 exotic fruit is expected...and doesn't disappoint; yawns a little from tiredness here and there; t23.5 silky, mouth-watering though attractively tart. Any blender looking to ensure the malty but exotic frame to an old blend would be searching in his arsenal for a series of Speysiders just like this; f21 mainly vanilla and cocoa milkshake; bitters out slightly as the oak bites; b22 hardly complex and shows all the old age attributes to be expected. That said...a very comfortable and satisfying ride. 46%

⬥ **Benromach Wood Finish 2007 Sassicaia** db (86.5) n22 t22 f21 b21.5. Now back to the new distillery. Problem with this wood finish is that even when free from any taint, as this is, it is a harsh taskmaster and keeps a firm grip of any malty development – even on a dram so young. A brave cask choice. 45%

Benromach Wood Finish Hermitage dist 2001 db (84) n19 t23 f21 b21. A sweet, tight dram with all the shape crushed out of it. It does have its moment of greatness, though: about three or four seconds after arrival when it zooms into the stratosphere on a massively fruity, sensuously spiced rocket. Then it just fades away... 45%

Benromach Wood Finish Pedro Ximénez dist 2002 db (85.5) n21 t22.5 f21 b21. Combining PX with peated whisky is still probably the hardest ask in the maturation lexicon. Lagavulin are still to get it right. And they have not quite managed it here, either. It's a bumpy old ride, though some of the early chewing moments are fun. Not a bad attempt, at all. Just the learning curve is still on the rise... 45%

Gordon & MacPhail Benromach Vintage 1976 db (89) n22.5 t22 f22 b22.5. For all the massive oak which shapes every inch of this dram, the degree of ulmo honey at work is extraordinary. 46%. ncf.

Gordon & MacPhail Benromach Port Wood finish 2000 db (86.5) n22 t21 f22 b21.5. A pleasant experience with a distinctive chocolate liqueur feel to it. Just a little too heavily laden with grape (though thankfully clean and entirely sulphur-free) for greatness as the malt is all but obliterated, though the spices rack up the complexity levels. 45%. ncf

BLADNOCH
Lowlands, 1817. David Prior. Working.

Bladnoch Aged 6 Years Bourbon Matured db (91) n21.5 t22.5 f24 b23 The fun starts with the late middle, where those extra oils congregate and the taste buds are sent rocking. Great to see a Lowlander bottled at an age nearer its natural best and even the smaller cut, in a roundabout way, ensures a mind-blowing dram. 57.3%

Bladnoch Aged 6 Years Lightly Peated db (93) n23 t23 f23.5 b23.5 The peat has nothing to do with the overall score here: this is a much better-made whisky with not a single off-note and the cut is spot on. And although it claims to be lightly peated, that is not exactly true: such is the gentle nature of the distillate, the smoke comes through imperiously and on several levels. "Spirit of the Lowlands" drones the label. Since when has outstanding peated malt been associated with that part of the whisky world...?? 58.5%

Bladnoch Aged 6 Years Sherry Matured db (73.5) n18 t19 f18.5 b18. A sticky, lop-sided malt where something, or a group of somethings, conjures up a very unattractive overture. Feints on the palate but no excellent bourbon cask to the rescue here. 56.9%

Bladnoch Aged 10 Years db (94) n23 t24 f23 b24 This is probably the ultimate Bladnoch, certainly the best I have tasted in over 25 years. This Flora and Fauna bottling by then owners United Distillers should be regarded as the must-get-at-all-costs Bladnoch. If the new owner can create something even to hang on to this one's coat-tails then he has excelled himself. For those few of us lucky enough to experience this, this dram is nothing short of a piece of Lowland legend and folklore. 43%.

Bladnoch Aged 15 Years db (91) n22.5 remnants of zest and barley sit comfortably with the gentle oaks; t22.5 excellent delivery and soon gets into classic Bladnoch citric stride; f23 wonderfully clean barley belies the age and lowers the curtain so delicately you hardly notice; b23 quite outstanding Lowland whisky which, I must admit, is far better than I would have thought possible at this age. 55%

Bladnoch Aged 16 Years "Spirit of the Lowlands" db (88) n22 t22 f22 b22. Really lovely whisky and unusual to see a Lowlander quite this comfortable at such advanced age. 46%. ncf.

Bladnoch 18 Years Old db (88.5) n21 t23.5 f22 b22. The juiciness and clarity to the barley, and especially the big gooseberry kick, early on makes this a dram well worth finding. 55%

◈ Acla Selection Bladnoch 25 Years Old barrel, dist 1990, bott 2015 (95) n24 few Lowlanders will be so sensually structured this year: the layering is faultless with so many strands of clean, rich malt harmonising with a saline-crusted oak and spiced heather-honey; t24 now the sugars lead, always pepped up with spice. Molten icing sugars relax into barley sugar; the oak reminds you of its age without domineering; never less than salivating; f23 drier, with a more tannic signature; still the barley integrates and accelerates; b24 the distillery in top gear. 52.2%. nc ncf.

◈ Fadandel.dk Bladnoch 9 Years Old cask no. 536, dist 17 Mar 07, bott 9 Jun 16 (88.5) n22 malt x2; t23.5 malt x 6; f22 malt x3; b21 quite shiny on the palate with a degree of gloss attached to the massive barley. Indeed, the delivery is like grist on steroids, but after that initial shockwave of ultra-intense, super-concentrated malt, it has little more involving complexity to say. Possibly one of the maltiest malts you'll ever find. 61.3%. nc ncf sc. 258 bottles.

Scotch Malt Whisky Society Cask 50.58 Aged 24 Years refill barrel, dist 26 Jan 90 (89) n22 t21.5 f23.5 b22 A kinder cask allows the malt to progress at full throttle. 55%. sc. 90 bottles.

◈ Scotch Malt Whisky Society Cask 50.71 Aged 25 Years refill barrel, dist 26 Jan 90, bott 21 Sept 15 (86.5) n21.5 t23.5 f20 b21.5. Ostensibly, a gloriously honeyed dram full of dark, brooding corners and spices willing to kill without asking questions. But deeper down there are questions about the cask which are not satisfactorily answered. Even so, the better moments are sheer, unadulterated bliss. 58.2%. nc ncf sc. 165 bottles.

◈ Scotch Malt Whisky Society Cask 50.75 Aged 25 Years refill barrel, dist 26 Jan 90, bott 30 Nov 15 (95.5) n23.5 the gentle waters lapping beside the distillery hardly accounts for the salty incursion into the acacia honey and maple syrup; t24 sublime mouth feel: light oils spread the honey notes evenly around the palate, but not so thick as to prevent the saltier, earthier, eye-wateringly spiced tones to register. The barley builds into an impressive crescendo...; **f24** dries quickly as the vanilla builds but the butterscotch and manuka honey survive all...; oh, and those spices...wow!!! **b24** a much sturdier cask than 50.71 pays handsome dividends. A little honeyed nugget.. 54.1%. nc ncf sc. 108 bottles.

BLAIR ATHOL
Highlands (Perthshire), 1798. Diageo. Working.
Blair Athol Aged 12 Years db **(77)** n18 t19 f21 b19. Thick, fruity, syrupy and a little sulphury and heavy. The finish has some attractive complexity among the chunkyness. 43%. Flora and Fauna.

Berry's Own Selection Blair Athol 1989 Aged 23 Years cask no. 6333, bott 2013 **(87.5)** n21.5 t22 f21.5 b22. Bold, full bodied and fat. Slightly puckering and a little greasy. 46%. ncf. WB15/243

⬦ **Best Dram Blair Athol 26 Years Old** wine treated butt **(66.5)** n17 t18.5 f15 b16. I think they meant "sulphur ruined butt". 578%

⬦ **C & S Dram Collection Blair Athol Aged 5 Years** sherry butt, cask no. 301878, dist 05 Mar 10, bott 18 Jan 16 **(76)** n18 t20 f19 b19. Chugging away pleasantly, I was, with a bunch of ex-bourbon malts. Then picked this up by mistake: my nose alerted me to the error. Harsh, off-key and irritatingly unyielding. 58.5%. sc.

⬦ **Cadenhead's Sherry Cask Blair Athol 26 Year Old** dist 1989 **(91.5)** n24.5 now, I could nose that all day: beautifully rich fruitcake – almost of a Christmas pudding variety – with the oak really upping the substance and spice; the big cherry and sultana personality has much to say; **t23** a gorgeous delivery, with crystalline sugars giving the fruit a lighter touch than the nose suggests. Where is the oak and malt, though...? **f22** thins and tires a little as it dries; **b22** a rather lovely, predominantly clean wine cask at work here. However, not quite enough body in the malt to do it full justice 48.9%. sc.

⬦ **Gordon & MacPhail Connoisseurs Choice Blair Athol 2006 (88.5)** n22.5 the timber is already showing; the malt is buttery; **t22.5** pleasingly lush with attractive spices; remains buttery with an almost apologetic ulmo honey thread; **f21.5** just becomes a little bit bitter as that oak re-emerges; **b22** attractive, though quite a few splinters for its age. 46%

Hepburn's Choice Blair Athol Aged 12 Years refill hogshead, dist 2002, bott 2015 **(87.5)** n21.5 t21.5 f22.5 b22. Thumping liquid barley. The nose and early delivery both on the meagre side. But the maltiness, catching the sugars and drier oak notes just right, more than makes amends. 46%. nc ncf sc. 165 bottles.

⬦ **Hidden Spirits Blair Athol BLA.214 11 Years Old** cask no. 10614, dist 2002, bott 2014 **(91)** n22 youthful for its age, but the light marzipan sits comfortably with the clean malt; **t23.5** such a beautiful delivery: the barley is fresh, juicy, clean and intense. But the mix of light citrus and clever, delicate sugars – especially the thinned maple syrup – really does the job; **f22.5** the oaky rings offer a light tannin-rich distraction from the malt; **b23** for those looking for a juicy malt. This is deceptively delicious. 48%. sc.

⬦ **Kingsbury Silver Blair Athol 18 Year Old 1995** sherry butt, cask no. 10459 **(68)** n16 t19 f16 b17. Malty and sugary. But can't escape the confines of the sulphur. This is a lovely company who work hard to bottle great whisky. But 20 years ago I warned them to avoid sherry butts unless they were 100% certain of their quality. With the greatest respect and fondness, I warn them again...! 46%. sc. 762 bottles.

⬦ **Old Malt Cask Blair Athol Aged 20 Years** sherry butt, cask no. 12149, dist Jun 95, bott Nov 15 **(95)** n23.5 clean, edifying and intriguing fruit notes: almost a mix of fruit and chocolate cake blended together; **t24** much more tannin on delivery than you might expect from a sherry butt. But no complaints here. Because the cocoa-rich tannic works well with the juicier toasted raisin notes; **f23.5** busy, lightly spiced and a lovely oak-induced red liquorice and sherry-slanted plum pudding mix: very unusual...; **b24** as close to a chocolate liqueur as you are likely to find in a bottle! 50%. nc ncf sc. 597 bottles.

⬦ **Old Masters Blair Athol 28 Year Old** cask no. 4865, bott 2016 **(88.5)** n22.5 serious pear drops; serious age, too...; **t22.5** freshly salivating; helped by a light oil which maximises the malt; pretty thin middle with good vanilla injection; **f21.5** thin malt and butterscotch; **b22** this one falls into the category of pretty unimpressive spirit when first distilled but over the best part of three decades has mellowed into something charming and almost elegant. 56.5%

⬦ **Provenance Blair Athol Aged 12 Years** bott Mar 16 **(81.5)** n20.5 t21 f20 b20. Even after a dozen years there is far more a new make quality than old matured malt about this. Not at all unpleasant, especially when the pithy dryness gets to work. But for the age... 46%. nc ncf sc.

⬦ **Old Single Cask Blair Athol Aged 22 Years** cask no. 7284, dist 13 Aug 91, bott 23 Sept 13 **(88)** n21 oak sap...; **t23.5** hard hats required here: this is a car crash of a malt! Massive tannins career into rock hard sugars with explosive force. Only the ulmo honey offers any soothing comfort. Plus the chocolate fudge middle. Bloody marvellous, I have to say...!! **f21.5** oak sap...with residual honey...; **b22** OTT in so many ways. But you have to give the honeyed sugars attached to snarling tannins some credit for bravery here...! *54.8%. nc ncf sc.*

BOWMORE
Islay, 1779. Morrison Bowmore. Working.

Bowmore Aged 12 Years db **(91) n22.5** light peats, the air of a room with a man sucking cough sweets; sweet pipe smoke; **t23.5** soft, beautiful delivery of multi-layered peats; lots of effervescent spices and molassed sugars; spices abound; **f22.5** much drier with sharper berries and barley; the peat still rumbles onwards, but has no problems with the light, sawdusty oaks; **b23.5** this new bottling still proudly carries the Fisherman's Friend cough sweet character, but the coastal, saline properties here are a notch or three up: far more representative of Islay and the old distillery style. Easily by far the truest Bowmore I have tasted in a long while with myriad complexity. Even going back more than a quarter of a century, the malt at this age rarely showed such relaxed elegance. Most enjoyable. *40%* ⊙

Bowmore "Enigma" Aged 12 Years db **(82) n19 t22 f20 b21.** Sweet, molassed and with that tell-tale Fisherman's Friend tang representing the light smoke. This Enigma hasn't quite cracked it, though. *40%. Duty Free.*

Bowmore "Darkest" Aged 15 Years db **(83) n20 t23 f19 b21.** In recent years a dram you tasted with glass in one hand and a revolver in the other. No more. But for the sulphur present, this would have been a much higher score. *43%* ⊙

Bowmore Gold Reef oak casks db **(79) n19.5 t21 f19 b19.5.** Simple, standard (and rather boring and safe) fare for the masses gagged by toffee. *43% WB15/280*

Bowmore "Mariner" Aged 15 Years db **(79) n19 t21 f19 b20.** There are two ways of looking at this. As a Bowmore. Which is how I have marked it. Or a something to throw down your neck for pure fun. Which is probably worth another seven or eight points. Either way, there is something not entirely right here. *43%. Duty Free.*

Bowmore Aged 17 Years db **(77) n18 t22 f18 b19.** For all the attractiveness of the sweet fruit on delivery, the combination of butt and cough sweet makes for pretty hard going. *43%*

Bowmore Aged 18 Years db **(79) n20 t21 f19 b19.** Pleasant, drinkable Fisherman's Friend style – like every Bowmore it appears around this age. But why so toffee-dull? *43%* ⊙

Bowmore Aged 23 Years Port Matured db **(86) n22 t22 f21 b21.** Have you ever sucked Fisherman's Friends and fruit pastels at the same time, and thrown in the odd Palma Violet for good measure...? *50.8%*

Bowmore Aged 25 Years db **(86) n21 t22 f21 b22.** Not the big, chunky guy of yore: the age would surprise you if tasted blind. *43%*

◈ **Bowmore Aged 25 Years Small Batch Release** db **(85.5) n21 t22 f21 b21.5.** Distilled at the very heart of Bowmore's peculiar and uniquely distinctive Fisherman's Friend cough sweet era. You will never find a more vivid example. *43%*

Bowmore Aged 30 Years db **(94) n23** intense burnt raisin amid the intense burnt peat; a deft rummy sweetness strikes an improbable chord with the sweetened lime; the oak is backward coming forward but binds beautifully with both peat and fruit; **t24** near flawless delivery showing a glimpse of Bowmore in a form similar to how I remember it some 25 years ago. The peat, though intense does have a hint of the Fisherman's Friend about it, but not so upfront as today. For all the peat, this is clean whisky, moulded by a craftsman into how a truly great Islay should be; **f23** dries sublimely as the oak contains the peat and adds a touch of coffee to it in unsugared form. Gentle oils cling tightly to the roof of the mouth; **b24** a Bowmore that no Islay scholar should be without. Shows the distillery at its most intense yet delicate; an essay in balance and how great oak, peat and fruit can combine for those special moments in life. Unquestionably one of the best Bowmores bottled this century. *43%*

◈ **Bowmore Black 50 Year Old** db **(96.5) n25** the blackest of black cherries embedded in the most delicately smoked cake...; probably the nose of the year. Almost too subtle to describe as justice simply cannot be done...; **t24** if that most gifted of blenders, Rachel Barrie, worked on this, then I think she would have gone to bed a very happy woman over a great number of days. This delivery is sheer sex in a bottle; an orgy on a palate. The peat and spices are now no more than a caress of the most tender parts of your being; the tannins offer the whip, the malt lubricates the taste buds beyond belief; **f23** long, with a spicy sting and further dark tannins which inflict pain and pleasure in equal measure; **b24.5** a little known fact: a long time ago, before the days of the internet and a world of whisky experts which outnumbers the stars that puncture the sky on the very darkest of nights, I actually tasted the first Black Bowmore in their very basic blending lab and gave it the required seal of approval before they allowed it to hit the shelves. It wasn't a 50-year-old beast like this one, though. And it proves that though something may have reached half a century, it knows how to give pleasure on at least a par with anything younger ... *41%*

Bowmore 1985 db (89) n21.5 t24 f22 b21.5. I may have tasted a sweeter Islay. Just not sure when. This whisky is so wrong..it's fantastically right...! 52.6%

Bowmore 100 Degrees Proof db (90.5) n22 low key smoke. Anyone who has been to Arbroath looking for where the Smokies are cured and homed in on the spot by nose alone will recognise this aroma...; t23 delicate in all departments, including the peat. The barley is sweet but it is the tenderness of the oils which stars; f22.5 long with a tapering muscovado finale; b23 proof positive! A real charmer. 57.1%. ncf

Bowmore Black Rock oak casks db (87.5) n22.5 t22 f21 b22. A friendly, full bodied dram whose bark is worse than its bite. Smoked toasted fudge is the main theme. But that would not work too well without the aid of a vague backdrop cinnamon and marmalade. If you are looking for a gentle giant, they don't come more wimpish than this. 40% WB15/336

Bowmore Devil's Cask db (87.5) n22 t23 f21 b21.5. Not really my style of whisky, for all its obvious fun...and this little devil doesn't really even to try and balance itself out. 56.9%

Bowmore Devil's Cask II db (80.5) n19.5 t22 f19 b20. Another huge experience, like Devil's Cask I. And, also like that bottling, brimstone can be detected. Still not my cup of tea. 56.3%

 Bowmore Devil's Casks III db (92.5) n23 as many rum notes here as whisky ones, except the smoke is rather distinctive. And mildly evil...; As in as evil as a farm byre, as there is something a little agricultural about this, too; t23 a real symphony of sugars hammer home hard and fast...like the Devil's Gallop. The pace of the changes to this whisky on the palate remain frenetic; f23.5 normally, this is where sulphur will ensure a hellish finale. Okay, a bit of a wobble, as it is not entirely free. But there is something deliciously satanic about the smoky verses...... b23.5 a whisky created by Charles Williams, surely. So, at last....I'm in league with the devil...! Hawwww-hhaaaa-haaaaaa!!!! 56.7%

Bowmore Laimrig Aged 15 Years db (90.5) n22.5 thumping oloroso smashed head first into Bowmore in its Fisherman's Friend mode. The result is unique...and not for the faint-hearted...; t23.5 a genuinely attractive delivery which concentrates on the silky mouth-feel at first before getting on with the business of the molasses, dates and outrageous spice. And of course, the smoke...; f22 some wonderful chocolate on show, comfortable with the now busy rather than raging spices and those dark, vaguely dirty, sugars; b22.5 first things first: absolutely spot on sherry butts at work here with not a hint of an off note. But often it is hard to get smoke and sherry to gel. The exercise here is not without success, but you feel it is straining at every sinew to hit the high spots. 53.7%. 18,000 bottles.

Bowmore Laimrig III db (92) n23.5 so delicate is the ultra clean grape, I am assuming this is a sherry cask finish. Not usually a fan of smoke and grape, but when it is this delicate, what isn't there to like?; t23.5 the softness found on the nose is continued on the palate. The sweetness is cleverly controlled and when the Fisherman's Friend personality arrives, it is quietly muffled, if not smothered to death, by a combination of silky grape, teasing spice and melting muscovado sugars; f22.5 the oak now raises its profile, the deep vanillas and hint of honeycomb underlining a reasonable age; b23 I must ask my research team: where the hell are Laimrigs I and II....? 53.7%

Bowmore Legend db (88) n22 t22.5 f22 b22.5. Not sure what has happened here, but it has gone through the gears dramatically to offer a substantial dram with both big peat and excellent balancing molasses. Major stuff. 40%

 Bowmore Mizunara Cask Finish db (90.5) n22.5 a very different Bowmore nose: unique, in fact. Curious mix of rose petal and bubblegum, lightly coated with soft phenol; gun smoke with a metallic edge; t22 a tight delivery. Hard, crisp, unyielding and biting on the palate. Much more spice and oomph than the sleepy nose warns of; f23.5 dry, sooty cocoa with an assertive spice burn; b22.5 a Bowmore like no other: not always happy in its own skin, but when it relaxes towards the finish, it positively pulses its Islay credentials. 53.9%. 2,000 bottles.

Bowmore Small Batch "Bourbon Cask Matured" db (86) n22 t22 f21 b21. A big improvement on the underwhelming previous Small Batch from this distillery, then called "Reserve", though there appears to be a naievity to the proceeding which both charm and frustrate. The smoke, hanging on the grist, is very low key. 40%.

Bowmore Small Batch Reserve db (80.5) n20 t21 f19 b20.5. With a name like "Small Batch Reserve" I was expecting a marriage between intense Kentucky and Islay. Alas, this falls well short of the mark. 40%

Bowmore Tempest Aged 10 Years Small Batch Release V db (90.5) n23 t23 f21.5 b23 if you like your Islays on the subtle side but with a bold undercurrent, here you go..! 55.9%. ncf. WB15/279

Bowmore White Sands Aged 17 Years db (88) n20 not quite the most exciting Bowmore nose but a winner if you like hesitant peat and irrepressible caramel; t22 chewy dates to start, then a slow working through the peat. Again, the caramel seems to have fingers everywhere, smothering the spices in particular; **f23** ridiculously soft mouth-feel. Now the spices have spread and try to nip but have no teeth. The sugars appear to be an amalgam of muscovado, molasses, maple syrup and caramel...but all watered down; **b23** a muzzled malt which shouldn't work – but somehow does. *43%*

⟡ **Acla Selection Bowmore 11 Years Old** bourbon barrel, dist 2002, bott 2014 **(89.5) n22** the distillery showing its vaguely acrid peat and anthracite style; **t23.5** magnificent delivery: a volley of honey – ulmo mostly but heather-honey, too – pins the smoke right up against the palate. The battle is delicious and beautifully weighted; **f21.5** not the greatest oak statement, with a bitterness creeping in, but the spices remain excellent; **b22.5** a slightly better cask would have furthered the enormous strides made by the honey and spice. *52.4%. nc ncf.*

⟡ **Cadenhead's Authentic Collection Bowmore 15 Year Old** bourbon hogshead, dist 2001, bott Apr 16 **(95.5) n23.5** heavy duty acrid anthracite, with the peat forming a sweeter, heavier bottom layer..very clever; **t24** the intensity to the delivery can hardly be bettered: the smoke takes a back pew while we worship at the alter of melt-in-the-mouth barley sugar and acacia honey; inevitable spices decorate the proceedings; **f24** long, a little sticky as the honey and light oils linger. The smoke has a decided hickory slant to it...; dries slowly and elegantly; **b24** you have to take your hat off to Cadenhead: they really do bottle some stunners. This is no exception. *54.8%. sc. 264 bottles.*

⟡ **The First Editions Bowmore Aged 15 Years 2000** refill hogshead, cask no. 11783, bott 2015 **(94.5) n23.5** lively oak tries to interweave through the delicate smoke notes: older than its years. The light saltiness sits comfortably among the acacia honey and vague, oaky paprika; **t24** everything I look for from a Bowmore at least three years older! Classic distillery style with the peat landing lightly amid a fabulous intermingling of malt and Lubek's finest; a little liquorice seeps in and goes a long way...; **f23** the marzipan effect wears off to leave a much drier oak and smoke residue; **b24** the real deal. Bowmore groaning under the distillery's unique character: like a vatting in a cask...!! Takes me back to the early '80s, that! *58.7%. nc ncf sc. 101 bottles.*

Gleann Mór Bowmore 12 Year Old dist May 03, bott Jun 15 **(93) n22.5 t23.5 f23.5 b23.5** The most succulent and lively Bowmore I have encountered for a very long while! *53.3%. sc.*

Gleann Mór Bowmore 30 Year Old dist Mar 85, bott May 15 **(95.5) n23.5 t24.5 f23.5 b24** After what first appears as an underwhelming, if pleasant, nose, what happens next is spectacular...! *52.3%. sc.*

⟡ **The Golden Cask Bowmore 13 Years Old** cask no. CM 201, dist 2000, bott 2014 **(86) n20.5 t23 f21 b21.5**. A surging malt which really thumps out the peat in no uncertain terms, the highlight of the show being the first three or four waves after delivery. But the nose and finish reveal a slight niggardliness to the oak which refuses to play ball. *55.5%. sc. 300 bottles.*

⟡ **The Golden Cask Bowmore 15 Years Old** cask no. CM 219, dist 2000, bott 2015 **(92) n23** some serious saline: as if bottled straight from a rock pool...The smoke at first seems flash, but settles to become subtle and sexy; **t23** a big bite to this one – and not just from the strength. There is a crispness to this which appears to come from the juicy barley, so a salivating smokiness ensues; a wonderful honey note absorbs any drier excesses; ridiculously chewy; **f22.5** some cocoa and remarkably botanical in its fallout, too... **b23.5** complex, satisfying whisky which forever shape-shifts on the palate. *58.5%. sc. 185 bottles.*

⟡ **Old Particular Islay Bowmore 15 Years Old** sherry butt, dist May 00, bott Jun 15 **(68) n17 t19 f15 b17**. My first sulphur-hammered bottling of the 2017 edition. Also, my first sherry butt... *48.4%. nc ncf sc. 468 bottles.*

⟡ **Scotch Malt Whisky Society Cask 3.249 Aged 14 Years** refill hogshead, dist 08 May 01, bott 17 Aug 15 **(89) n22** sharp, angular yet tidy. The smoke has a degree of attitude...; **t22.5** nips, bites and growls. But the layering is magnificent with a lovely red liquorice edge to the smoke, dark muscovado and booming spices; **f22** remains a hot dram, though as much for the spice as the distillate; **b22.5** if it wore hats, it'd have a punk-style baseball cap... *56.4%. nc ncf sc. 252 bottles.*

⟡ **Scotch Malt Whisky Society Cask 3.250 Aged 20 Years** refill hogshead, dist 06 Apr 95, bott 21 Sept 15 **(83) n21 t21 f20.5 b20.5**. Neither a great cask, nor quite the best distillate at work. Tangy, aggressive and ill-at-ease. Some good demerara sugars at work, though. *54.3%. nc ncf sc. 254 bottles.*

Single Malts of Scotland Bowmore 15 Year Old dist 1999 **(85.5) n20.5 t23 f20.5 b21.5**. An entirely enjoyable Bowmore which keeps things simple. A bit of the old Fisherman's Friend nose warns you this won't be a classic, but the light peat unites with the intense dark sugars and late butter very attractively. *55.2% WB16/012*

⬦ **Svenska Eldvatten Bowmore 2002** ex-bourbon hogshead, dist Mar 02 **(92) n22** the light hint of Fisherman's Friend cough sweet leaves you in no doubt of the distillery; attractive light molasses, too; **t23.5** outstanding weight to delivery: near perfect degree of oils. Superb spices mix in with the slight Hovis wholemeal gristiness; again, light liquorice and molasses; **f23** attractive fade, though bitters out slightly; **b23.5** a gorgeous little bottling. *57.1%. sc.*

BRAEVAL
Speyside, 1974. Chivas Brothers. Working.

⬦ **Chapter 7 Braes of Glenlivet 1994 20 Years Old** bourbon barrel, cask no. 165681 **(88.5) n23** a pastoral setting of dank straw and cut grass. Beautifully refreshing; **t22** quite fat, intense, juicy barley with a gentle nod to the lightest of oaky spices; **f21.5** retains the barley footprint but vanilla dominates alongside some chocolate fudge; **b22** revels gloriously in a distinct Chivas, barley-centric style. *50.4%. sc. 172 bottles.*

⬦ **Five Lions Braes of Glenlivet Aged 20 Years** 1st fill American bourbon barrel, dist Dec 94, bott Nov 15 **(94.5) n23** no kidding about the bourbon barrel...! Red liquorice and spiced up tannin lead with a superb maple syrup and treacle sub plot; **t24** the sugars deliver immediately, increasingly upping the toastiness. The barley is still sound and at first offers a shrill, mouth-watering intensity. The vanilla and butterscotch are quickly on the scene but have to make way for the marauding spices; **f23.5** busy spices with a little Fisherman's Friend as the hickory bites deep; the unwavering Demerara is highly impressive; **b24** more eye-watering than a Virginia McKenna film....and about as clean and wholesome, too. A top grade cask, for sure. *55.3%. nc ncf.*

⬦ **Hunter Laing's Distiller's Art Braeval Aged 13 Years** sherry butt, dist May 02, bott 2016 **(94) n23.5** clean, edifying and intriguing fruit notes: almost a mix of fruit and chocolate cake blended together; **t23.5** much more tannin on delivery than you might expect from a sherry butt. But no complaints here. Because the cocoa-rich tannin works well with the juicier toasted raisin notes; **f23** busy, lightly spiced and a lovely oak-induced red liquorice and sherry-slanted plum pudding mix: very unusual...; **b24** as close to a chocolate liqueur as you are likely to find in a bottle! *48%. nc ncf sc. 438 bottles.*

⬦ **Maltbarn Braes of Glenlivet 1994** ex-bourbon cask, bott 2016 **(87) n20 t23 f21.5 b21.5.** A very mild butyric note does not quite scupper an otherwise delicious dram. The chocolate input is borderline insane. And the expected oils do ensure a well dispersed degree of muscovado sugar. If I wasn't such a miserable git demanding faultless whisky, I'd mark this much more highly. *51.7%. sc. 197 bottles.*

⬦ **Old Malt Cask Braeval Aged 14 Years** sherry butt, cask no. 11999, dist May 01, bott Oct 15 **(94) n23.5** thick toffee apple relaxes to let in the barley and dry Lubec marzipan; **t24** one of the great deliveries of the year so far: the sugars, sherry and barley appear to meld into a rich, stunningly structured coating which offers varying degrees of sweetness and fruit, never seemingly sitting still; **f22.5** a very late furriness still cannot spoil a lovely experience; **b24** oh, it gives the soul so much joy to spend half an hour in the company of a mainly unspoiled sherry butt... *50%. nc ncf sc. 612 bottles.*

⬦ **Old Malt Cask Braeval Aged 18 Years** sherry butt, cask no. 12292, dist Dec 97, bott Feb 16 **(79) n19 t21 f19 b20.** No doubting its sherry cask credentials! Lightly tainted by you-know-what. But still plenty of blood orange to be getting on with. *50%. nc ncf sc. 369 bottles.*

⬦ **Old Particular Speyside Braeval 14 Years Old** sherry butt, dist May 01, bott Dec 15 **(90.5) n23** superb pippy grape to this: clean as a whistle and almost as shrill once the barley gets involved; **t22.5** it is as if someone has squeezed all the juice out of some unmalted barley and mixed it with dry oloroso: juicy and at first seemingly dry, but some muscovado sugars creeps cleverly into the mix; **f22.5** long, mainly dry but subtle caramelised biscuit helps retain the balance; **b22.5** plays the delicate sugars to near perfection. *51.5%. nc ncf sc. 383 bottles.*

⬦ **Signatory Vintage Single Malt Braeval 1998 Aged 14 Years** bourbon barrels, cask no. 168894+168895, dist 12 Nov 98, bott 22 Mar 13 **(94.5) n23.5 t24 f23 b24** Quintessential Speyside malt. Not overly complex. Just does what it does very beautifully helped by some exceptional oak. If you see it, grab it and be seduced... *43%. nc. 668 bottles. WB15/014*

⬦ **Single Cask Collection Braeval 1997 17 Year Old** hogshead **(93) n23** clean, juicy barley with just the right degree of firmness. Subtle hazelnut oil thickens the expectation; **t24** intense, beautifully clean, barley concentrate. Molten muscovado sugars adds extra sparkle before a meringue light sweetness melts on the palate; **f22.5** dries gently while the barley somehow intensifies and pulses; **b23.5** when this distillery shines, it positively glistens... *54.7%*

BRORA
Highlands (Northern), 1819–1983. Diageo. Closed.

◈ **Brora 37 Year Old** refill American oak hogsheads, dist 1977 db **(94.5) n23** the toasty tannins mark every single one of the passing 37 years. But a buttery smokiness, further enriched by the beguiling complexities of a mature herb garden, keeps the braying oak at bay...; **t24** much more intact: the smoke and tannin collide with wonderful results, the phenols appearing to be riding on the back of soothing molasses and the oak aligning with a dark chocolate thread; **f23.5** the earlier oils thin slightly allowing the vanilla a much louder voice; the chocolate persists...but so do the more sawdusty elements of the tannins; **b24** as it was I who first discovered the hidden and unloved hoards of Brora casks over 25 years ago, I feel a proprietorial claim to this distillery – especially as the 1977 stocks were among the first I managed to get bottled as a 12-year-old. A quarter of a century on, one has to say that the journey continues against the odds, perhaps with a creaking malt on the wane but one still defiantly refusing to concede that its days of outstanding beauty are over.... Make no mistake: it is still a stunner, after all these years... *50.4%. 2,976 bottles. Diageo Special Releases 2015.*

BRUICHLADDICH
Islay, 1881. Rémy Cointreau. Working.

Bruichladdich 10 Years Old db **(90) n22** beautifully clean and zesty, the malt is almost juvenile; **t23** sweet, fruity then malty charge along the tastebuds that geets the mouth salivating; **f23** the usual soft vanilla and custard but a bigger barley kick in the latter stages; **b22** more oomph than previous bottlings, yet still retaining its fragile personality. Truly great stuff for a standard bottling. *46%*

Bruichladdich 12 Years Old 2nd Edition db **(88) n23 t22 f22 b21.** A similar type of wine involvement to "Waves", but this is oilier in the old-fashioned 'Laddie style and lacks a little of the sparkle. The fruit on the finish is outstanding, though, and I don't think you or I would turn down a third glass... *46%*

Bruichladdich 15 Years Old 2nd Edition db **(86) n22 t23 f20 b21.** Delicious, as usual, but something, possibly fruity, appears to be holding back the show. *46%*

Bruichladdich 16 Years Old bourbon cask db **(89) n22.5 t22.5 f22 b22.** Plucked from the cask in the nick of time. In this state rather charming, but another Summer or two might have seen the oak take a more sinister turn. *46%*

Bruichladdich XVII Aged 17 Years bourbon/renegade rum db **(92) n23 t23.5 f22 b23.5.** Always good to see the casks of drier, more complexly structured rums being put to such intelligent use. My sample doesn't tell me which rum casks were used, but I was getting vivid flashbacks here of Ruby-Topaz Hummingbirds flitting from flower to flower in the gardens of the now closed Eigflucht distillery in Guyana in the long gone days when I used to scramble around the warehouses there. That distinctive dryness though is pure Enmore, though some Barbadian rum can offer a similar effect. Something very different and a top quality experience. *46%. nc ncf.*

Bruichladdich 18 Years Old bourbon/cognac cask db **(84.5) n23.5 t21 f20 b20.** Big oak-spice buzz but thin. Sublime grapey nose, for sure, but pays a certain price, ultimately, for associating with such an inferior spirit... *46%*

Bruichladdich 18 Years Old 2nd Edition bourbon/jurancon db **(86) n22 t21.5 f21 b21.5.** Plenty of fruit, including medium ripe greengages and slightly under-ripe grape. Juicy and sweet in the right places. *46%*

Bruichladdich Flirtation Aged 20 Years 2nd Edition db **(86) n21 t22 f22 b21.** Hi sugar! A Laddie for those with a sweet tooth. *46%*

Bruichladdich 21 Years Old oloroso cask db **(76.5) n18.5 t21 f18 b19.** Oops! *46%*

Bruichladdich Black Art 1990 Aged 23 Years 4th Edition cask no. 13/161 db **(79) n20 t21 f18 b20.** The same wobbly weaknesses found in the 3rd edition are back here in force once again. Big, juicy fruit notes will form a degree of compensation for some. *49.2%. nc ncf sc.*

Bruichladdich 2004 Islay Barley Valinch fresh sherry butt db **(89.5) n22.5 t24 f21 b22.** Yet another quite fabulous bottling form Bruichladdich, this one really cranking up the flavours to maximum effect. Having said all that, call me mad if you will...but seeing as this is Islay barley, would it not have been a good idea to shove it into a bourbon barrel, so we could see exactly what it tastes like? Hopefully that is on its way... *57.5%*

Bruichladdich Infinity Third Edition refill sherry tempranillo db **(94.5) n24 t24 f23 b23.5.** I dare anybody who says they don't like smoky whisky not to be blown away by this. Go on...I dare you... *50%*

Bruichladdich Islay Barley Aged 5 Years db **(86) n21 t22.5 f21.5 b21.** The nose suggests a trainee has been let loose at the stills. But it makes amends with an almost debauched degree of barley on delivery which lasts the entirety of the experience. Heavens! This is different. But I have to say: it's bloody fun, too! 50%. nc ncf.

Bruichladdich Laddie Classic Edition 1 db (89.5) n23 t23 f21 b22.5. You probably have to be a certain vintage yourself to fully appreciate this one. Hard to believe, but I can remember the days when the most popular malt among those actually living on Islay was the Laddie 10. That was a staunchly unpeated dram offering a breezy complexity. Not sure of the age on this Retroladdich, but the similarities almost bring a lump to the throat... 46%

Bruichladdich Scottish Barley The Classic Laddie db (78.5) n20 t21.5 f18 b19. Not often a Laddie fluffs its lines. But despite some obviously complex and promising moves, the unusual infiltration of some sub-standard casks has undone the good of the local barley. If you manage to tune out of the off-notes, some sublime moments can still be had. 50%. nc ncf sc.

Bruichladdich Sherry Classic Fusion: Fernando de Castilla bourbon/Jerez de la Frontera db (91) n23 t23 f22 b23. What a fantastically stylish piece of work! I had an overwhelming urge to sing Noel Coward songs while tasting this: for the Dry Martini drinkers out there who have never thought of moving on to Scotch... 46%

Bruichladdich X4 db (82) n18 t22 f21 b21. Frankly, like no new make I have ever come across in Scotland before. Thankfully, the taste is sweet, malty and compact: far, far better than the grim, cabbage water nose. Doesn't really have the X-Factor yet, though. 50%

The Laddie Ten American oak db (94.5) n24 t23.5 f23 b24 This, I assume, is the 2012 full strength version of an Islay classic which was the preferred choice of the people of Islay throughout the 70s, 80s and early 90s. And I have to say that this is already a classic in its own right.... 46%. nc ncf.

The Laddie Sixteen American oak db (88) n22 huge natural caramels dipped in brine; t22.5 very even and gentle with a degree of citrus perking it up; f21.5 reverts to caramels before the tannins strike hard; b22 oak 'n' salt all the way... 46%

The Laddie Twenty Two db (90.5) n24 a breakfast plate of three pieces of toast: one with salted butter, another with ulmo honey and the last one with marmalade; light spices, too. Busy yet understated; t23 silky salted butters again on delivery immediately backed by intense barley sugar; f21.5 the oak cranks up significantly; b22 fabulous coastal malt, though the oak is a presence always felt. 46%

Octomore 5 Years Old db (96) n23.5 t24.5 f24 b24. Forget about the age. Don't be frightened by the phenol levels. Great whisky is not about numbers. It is about excellent distillation and careful maturation. Here you have a memorable combination of both... 63.5%

Octomore 3rd Edition Aged 5 Years db (95) n24.5 t24 f23 b23.5. I usually taste this late on in the Bible writing cycle: it is so important to be rewarded at the end of a long journey. This hasn't let me down and here's the rub: how something which looms so large be made from so many traits so small...? 59%

Octomore 4th Edition Aged 5 Years (167 ppm) db (92) n21.5 t23.5 f23.5 b23.5 Choctomore, surely? 62.5%

Octomore Edition 5.1 db (91.5) n23 t22.5 f23 b23. A slightly less complex version, probably because of the obvious lack of years. Great fun, though. 59.9%

Octomore Edition 6.1 Aged 5 Years bourbon cask db (91.5) n24 t23 f22 b22.5 a slightly different Octomore, a little more tart than usual and wears its youth with pride. 57%

Octomore Edition 6.1 Aged 5 Years Scottish Barley (167 ppm) db (94) n23.5 t24 f24 b22.5 Talk about can't see the wood for the trees: here you can't see the peat for the moss. It appears that when you get to a certain degree of phenol saturation, the smokiness suggests less rather than more. On the nose that is. Then you taste it...and you are then in for the peatiest experience of your life... 57% WB15/314

Octomore Edition 6.2 Aged 5 Years Cognac cask db (90) n22.5 the peat is already crushed, the fruit strangles any possible movement; t23.5 hard to imagine the smoke playing second fiddle, but it does: the sugars are so intense and the barley so salivating, for a few moments you even forget it is there; f22 even tighter oak and crisp enough to break all your teeth; b22 one of the sweetest bottlings from this distillery of all time. Some warming late spice, too; 58.2%.

Octomore Edition 7.1 Aged 5 years (208 ppm) db (96.5) n24 at first the wall of peat is so thick, it is opaque and barely noticeable. But as your nose acclimatises, it recognises the ever-gathering intensity of the phenols, its shape, its depth...its enormity! And then, finally, its scariness...!! t24.5 certainly no doubts when it comes to delivery and immediate follow through. In some ways, the secondary fruit presence becomes the dominant theme. Hang on...it isn't fruit. No, it is concentrated sugars, as you might get from a mouthful of noble rot. This is pushed to the fore by the tidal wave of phenols. Then that peaty wave breaks and the "fruit" is lost under the crashing smoke; leaving splinters of mocha, fragments of liquorice, flotsam of citrus...; f24 amid the swirl and haze of smoke, spices begin their serious work...; b24 a gargantuan malt which will make short work of the feint hearted... This, also, was the whisky which Islay whisky maker par excellence Jim McEwen decided to bow out on. Farewell, Jim, my dear old friend of some 35 years. You have been to Scotch whisky what Jock Stein was to Scottish football; what Octomore is to Islay malt.... *59.5%*

Octomore 10 db **(95) n24 t24 f23 b24** When I am tasting an Octomore, it means I am in the home straight inside the stadium after running (or should I say nosing and tasting) a marathon. After this, there is barely another 20 more Scotch malts to go and I am closing in on completing my 1,200 new whiskies for the year. So how does this fair? It is Octomore. It is what I expect and demand. It gives me the sustenance and willpower to get to that crossing line. For to tell you guys about a whisky like this is always worth it...whatever the pain and price. Because honesty and doing the right thing is beyond value. Just ask David Archer... *50%. nc ncf.*

Port Charlotte Heavily Peated db **(94.5) n23** smoke comes scudding into the nose, vigorously, giving the joint effect of death by peat and acrid burnt toast; **t24** a youthful livewire delivery a pretty surprising degree of maple syrup and treacle latching onto the phenols: the effect and balance is wonderful; pay attention and you'll spot some juicy fruit notes popping up here and there, too; **f23.5** the lack of major oak means the finish is fractionally lighter than it might be, but the smoke is now even and pretty soft despite the late spice; **b24** rearrange the following two words: "giant" and "gentle". *50%*

Port Charlotte PC6 db **(96.5) n24.5 t24 f24 B24** Not many whiskies have a truly unmistakable nose... and... but this is, this... is... this... mmmmmmm..., arrrrrhh. Ohhhhhhhh... *61.6%*

Port Charlotte PC7 dist 2001 db **(93.5) n24 t24 f22 b22.5** Not quite as orgasmic as last year, sadly. But should still be pretty stimulating... *60.5%*

Port Charlotte PC8 bourbon, dist 2001, bott 2009 db **(88) n22 t23 f21 b22.** Enjoyable, but muted by PC standards... *60.5%. 30,000 bottles.*

Port Charlotte PC10 db **(96) n24 t24.5 f23.5 b24** Just so right....!!! *59.8%*

Port Charlotte The Peat Project db **(95.5) n24.5** the smoke drifts through in varying degrees of intensity and types of mood. Whenever it darkens, a burst of citrus appears to brighten its countenance; **t24** soft sugars form a guard of honour as the smoke tip-toes into the arena. The peat does not seem so prominent here as it does on the nose, a light vanilla infusion also detracting from the smoke; **f23** dries slowly, allowing in a delicate cocoa oil intensity to the smoke; **b24** this is not peat for peat's sake. This appears to be crafted and layered, offering a pleasing timbre and unusual gracefulness. *46% WB15/339*

⬙ **Dramfool Lochindaal Aged 5 Years** refill bloodtub, cask no. 4411, dist Dec 10, bott Feb 16 **(93.5) n24** well, there's peat. And under that...peat. Just when you begin to get used to that some peat arrives...; **t23.5** phenols. Smoke. Peat. And some light muscovado sugars; **f23** peaty vanilla; pretty dry...; **b23** can you have too much of a good thing? Well, this is staggering whisky, for sure. And Peat Heads the world over can now happily write their wills and curl up and die once they have tasted this. But, for all the fun, the balance has been compromised by the sheer outrageousness of the phenols. But would I have another glass full....? I'd chop yer bloody fingers off for it...! *61.4%. nc ncf sc. 42 bottles.*

⬙ **Dramfool Lochindaal 9 Years Old** sherry cask, dist 1 Jun 10, bott 20 May 16 **(92) n24** someone has seriously smoked the fruitcake...; **t23** such a charming bunch of grape notes: sharp, mouth-watering, eye-watering yet always in a massive phenolic halo; always has a particularly young feel to it; **f22** a surprising degree of vanilla mounts the fruity dais; **b23** question. What do you get if you cross a massively peated malt with a big, clean, unlsuphured sherry cask? Answer. This. *58.2%. nc ncf sc. 187 bottles.*

⬙ **Gordon & MacPhail Cask Strength Bruichladdich 1994 (96) n24** there was me thinking: "oh, black pepper"...and I sneezed! But I'm also thinking: "Jesus H Christ...!! This is amazing". Because we have that rarest of combinations of near faultless distilling with totally faultless maturation. So the malt is pristine and precise, the smoke discreet, the sugars harmonious...and the peppers...not to be sneezed at..! **t24** those peppers don't hang around to make it to the vanguard of the delivery. The malt arrives in so many intonations; the sugars are sparkling in their Demerara clarity; **f24** just maybe the hint of a late smoky thread with a little extra clarity now. But those vanillas...the malt...wow! **b24** hear that purring noise? That's me tasting this exquisite original style Bruichladdich which just gives an almost imperceptible nod towards the newer persona. *56.2%*

⬙ **Hidden Spirits Bruichladdich BRC.315 12 Years Old** cask no. 0311A, dist 2003, bott 2015 **(92) n23** heavily smoked moist fruitcake....with more than a touch of the sherry trifles about it; **t24** brilliant! Seldom does fruit and peat mingle and balance almost immediately, but it does here. Juicy grape meets the maple syrup head on; the light smoke is relaxed; **f22** the sync fails slightly towards the end as a little bitterness arrives; **b23** a rather lovely cask at play here. *48%. sc.*

Master of Malt Single Cask Bruichlddich 12 Year Old first-fill bourbon cask, dist Jul 02, bott Nov 14 **(67) n17 t18 f16 b16.** A bourbon cask by name. A poor sherry butt by nature. *573%. sc. 114 bottles.*

Master of Malt Single Cask Bruichlddich 12 Year Old first-fill sherry hogshead, dist Jun 02, bott Nov 14 **(82) n21.5 t21.5 f19 b20.** Thumping fruitiness and a silk delivery. But a bitter furriness is not far below the tannin and sugar surface. *62.3%. sc. 86 bottles.*

◇ **Old Malt Cask Bruichladdich Aged 12 Years** bourbon barrel, cask no. 12144, dist Nov 03, bott Nov 15 **(92) n23** charming, almost textbook marriage between medium smoke and confident, complex, toasty tannins lightly sprinkled with spice: so much promise...; **t23** superb delivery: this is beautifully made spirit, clean and bursting with salivating barley despite the smoky shackles. Spices abound in tandem with a phenolic marzipan sweetness, and even slightly gritty texture; dries early but a sub-strata of sweeter grist slows the process; **f23** now impressively dry, with a sooty thread. The tannins are of the bourbon kind, but now without the accompanying sugars; **b23** a busy malt which never gives your taste buds a moment's peace... *50%. nc ncf sc. 284 bottles.*

◇ **Old Particular Islay Bruichladdich 13 Years Old** refill hogshead, dist Aug 02, bott Nov 15 **(77) n19 t20 f19 b19.** Not sure if they mean 19 months rather than 19 years. A spent cask means little colour or oaky value is added, so the new make gristiness rules without the modest smoke ever finding a rhythm or balance. *48.4%. nc ncf sc. 199 bottles.*

Old Particular Islay Bruichladdich 21 Years Old refill hogshead, cask no. 10706, dist Nov 93, bott Feb 15 **(91.5) n23 t23 f22.5 b23** One of the old school 'Laddies, devoid of smoke but beautifully endowed with charm. *51.5%. nc ncf sc. 306 bottles.*

◇ **Old Particular Islay Port Charlotte 10 Years Old** refill hogshead, dist Oct 05, bott Feb 16 **(89) n21.5** curious smoked Cognac signature; **t22.5** mouth-watering for the first few waves, then settles into something a little more soft and vanilla-lined. Slowly the peat comes out to play and gathers momentum fast, as does the light spice; **f22.5** long, retaining that spice buzz − and cocoa! **b22.5** the one thing you can say about PC is that it is wildly variable. And here is one which, unexpectedly, comes up on the cocoa side of things. *48.4%. nc ncf sc. 415 bottles.*

◇ **Reifferscheid Private Cask Port Charlotte 9 Year Old** sherry bloodtub, cask no. 887 **(95) n23.5** a real nip to the nose as the spices try to take the limelight away from the intense − clean! − sherry and the even more intense youthful peat. Not sure noses were built for this kind of warfare...; not really my style. But have to admit: there are a few dazzling, truly awe-inspiring moments on this; **t24** again, I have to admit to being confounded. The grape, with a slight slew towards young dates, is phenomenal, the peat phenolic...; **f23.5** you better have an evening free, as this finish, still full of juicy grape, muscovado and smoke, takes its time...; **b24** rarely does this kind of whisky work. Aided by a faultless sherry cask, this does. And how! *54.9%. sc. 48 bottles.*

◇ **That Boutique-y Whisky Company Port Charlotte** batch 1 **(87.5) n21.5 t22.5 f22 b21.5.** There is obviously more than one Port Charlotte on Islay...A bewildering dram refusing to give up its peat in time-honoured PC style − lets the smoke out like traffic lights allowing cars onto a motorway at peak time. Certainly youthful and refreshing. But the peat just refuses to play nicely. Enjoyable, but really hard to join up the dots. *52.4%. 183 bottles.*

◇ **That Boutique-y Whisky Company Port Charlotte 13 Year Old** batch 2 **(93.5) n23.5** beautifully made: a little fatter than usual, the sugars more from a maple syrup direction. The peat, of course, is doing some serious business; **t23.5** sweet delivery with a sublime Digestive biscuit element which goes heavy on the salt; the smoke is held within the thick body of the malt; **f23** bitters very slightly and extra weight is applied to the smoky oil; **b23.5** by no means the most phenolic PC you'll find, though the oils make it travel a long distance. *54.7%. 84 bottles.*

◇ **Whic Bruichladdich 9 Years Old** bourbon cask, cask no 317, dist 10 May 06, bott 14 Aug 15 **(86.5) n21.5 t22 f21 b22.** Old school unpeated Laddie at times shows just what a malty and complex baby this can be. But there are a few too many rough edges to this, both from cask and distillate, to make the heart swoon. Austere. *55.2%. sc. 48 bottles.*

◇ **Whic Bruichladdich 11 Years Old** sherry hogshead, cask no 1333, dist 26 Nov 03, bott 27 Aug 15 **(93) n22.5** not the greatest fan of sherry and peat. But when the grape is this clean...; **t23** succulent and beautifully soft. The peat jerks out at some strange Escher-esque angles at first but slowly settles; **f24** now a much happier chappie, with the sugars and cocoa thickening things further; **b23.5** a fruity soup of a dram. *46%. sc. 36 bottles.*

◇ **Whic Port Charlotte 12 Years Old** bourbon hogshead, cask no 660, dist 07 Jul 03, bott 01 Sept 15 **(94.5) n23.5** errr...peat!!! And lots of it...!! **t24** the ashy, monosyllabic phenols on the nose open up here into something far more rotund and interesting. A light zestiness is caught in the undercarriage as this one takes off; excellent malt thread straight through the middle; **f23.5** some brave sugars hang on to the end as the smoke continues its voluptuous bombardment; a really decent vanilla sideshow; **b23.5** new school Laddie...!! *56%. sc. 180 bottles.*

❖ **The Whisky Barrel Port Charlotte 2003 Burns Malt 12 Years Old** cask no. 671 **(96) n24** the peat may be huge to the point of gargantuan. Yet not once does it overstep the mark or become pompous. The vanilla, cocoas and light muscovado sugars are there to offer a softening charm; **t24** the sugars are the red carpet laid for the eventual procession of the massive, yet measured smoke. The tannins are so respectful, they almost bow. But, best of all, are the light oils that stick to every corner of the palate; **f24** beautifully elegant spices caress the palate; the layering of tannin and peat has a sandwich of lightly roasted molasses. Not a single off note, or hint of weakness or failure....anywhere...; **b24** the essential Port Charlotte. *56.2%. sc.*

BUNNAHABHAIN
Islay, 1881. Burn Stewart Distillers. Working.

Bunnahabhain 12 Years Old (Older Bottling) db **(80) n19 t21 f20 b20.** Pleasant in its own clumsily sweet, smoky way. But unrecognisable to the masterful, salty Bunna 12 of old. *43.3%. nc ncf.*

Bunnahabhain Aged 12 Years db **(85.5) n20 t23 f21 b21.5.** Lovers of Cadbury's Fruit and Nut will adore this. There is, incongruously, a big bourbony kick alongside some smoke, too. A lusty fellow who is perhaps a bit too much of a bruiser for his own good. Some outstanding moments, though. But, as before, still a long way removed from the magnificent Bunna 12 of old... *46.3%. nc ncf.*

Bunnahabhain Aged 16 Years Manzanilla Sherry Wood Finish db **(87) n20.5 t23 f21.5 b22.** The kind of undisciplined but fun malt which just makes it up as it goes along... *53.2%*

Bunnahabhain Aged 18 Years (Older Bottling) db **(94) n24.5 t24 f22.5 b23** A triumph for the sherry cask and a reminder of just how good this distillery can be. It's been a long time since I've enjoyed a distillery bottling to this extent. *43%*

Bunnahabhain Aged 18 Years db **(93.5) n24** a sumptuous amalgam of lightly salted roasted hazelnut shimmering within its own oil. Oloroso bulging with toasted, slightly singed currants, a sliver of kumquat and topped by thick vanilla. Irresistible... **t24.5** almost impossible to fault: the oloroso grandly, almost pompously, leads the way exuding thick, Christmas pudding depth; a light muscovado sugar top dressing counters the deeper, lightly salted vanillas which begin to emerge; **f22** a very slight sulphury note sullies the tone somewhat, but there is still enough rich vanilla and spotted dick for some enjoyable afters; **b23** only an odd cask has dropped this from being a potential award winner to something that is merely magnificent... *46.3%. nc ncf.*

Bunnahabhain XXV Aged 25 Years (Older Bottling) db **(91.5) n23 t23 f22.5 b23.** An intense and fun-packed malt for those who like a fine sherry and a sea breeze. *43%*

Bunnahabhain XXV Aged 25 Years db **(94) n23** you almost need a blow torch to cut through the oloroso, so thick is it. A little tight thanks to a minor distortion to a butt, but I am being picky. Salty and seaweedy, the ocean hangs in the air...; **t24** glorious weight and sheen to the delivery. The early balance is nearly perfect as the thick fruit is thinned by the proud barley. The early, contemplative sweetness, buttressed by a wonderful mixture of sultana and Demerara, gives way to the drier oaks and the tingly, chalky signs of a mildly treated butt; **f23** despite the winding down of the sugars the residual fruit manages to overcome the small obstacles placed before it; **b24** no major blemishes here at all. Carefully selected sherry butts of the highest quality (well, except maybe one) and a malt with enough personality to still gets its character across after 25 years. Who could ask for more...? *46.3%. nc ncf.*

Bunnahabhain Ceòbanach db **(87.5) n21.5 t22.5 f21.5 b22.** An immensely chewable and sweet malt showing little in years but much in character. A charming liquorice and acacia honey lead then a developing, dry smokiness. Great fun. *46.3%*

Bunnahabhain Darach Ùr Batch no. 4 db **(95) n24 t24.5 f23 b23.5** Because of my deep love for this distillery, with my association with it spanning some 30 years, I have been its harshest critic in recent times. This, though, is a stunner.. *46.3%. nc ncf.*

Bunnahabhain Toiteach db **(78) n19 t21 f19 b19.** Cloying, sweet, oily, disjointedly smoky. Had you put me in a time capsule at the distillery 30 years ago, whizzed me forward to the present day and given me this, it would have needed some serious convincing for me to believe this to be a Bunna. *46%*

Bunnahabhain Toiteach Un-Chillfiltered db **(75.5) n18 t21 f17.5 b19.** A big gristy, peaty confrontation on the palate doesn't hide the technical fault lines of the actual whisky. *46%. ncf.*

❖ **Acla Selection Bunnahabhain 23 Years Old** refill sherry butt, dist 1990, bott 2013 **(84) n20 t23 f20 b21.** Back in the summer of 1990, in the days when it was owned by Highland Distillers, I was staying at Bunna when a batch of sherry butts turned up. The warehouseman, a friend of mine, was not impressed: "If I had it my way, every bugger would be sent back" he complained. Then adding with weary resignation, "but what's the point? I'd just get another consignment every bit as bad as these..." Well, the good news is that this is not from the awful sherry butts I saw delivered all those years back. But it is no oil painting, either. This is a clumsy dram where the frailties of the sherry diminish from the absolute brilliance of the honeyed, almost Highland Park style, body of the malt. Tarnished gold if ever there was.... *47.2%. nc ncf sc.*

⬩⬩⬩⬩ **Eiling Lim Bunnahabhain 34 Years Old 1980** bott 2014 **(96) n24** profound sea salt and a more austere ozone lead. A vague citrus note ensures a different kind of freshness; **t24** lands as lightly as the red-breasted flycatcher I saw jump up and down from the distillery's telephone pole all those years ago...; a sharpness indicates a degree of tiredness, but as soon as this shows, a squadron of spices and varied honey tones make an elegant entrance...; **f23.5** begins as a light layering of tannin which skips towards a medium roast Java before more spices intervene...then re-settles as a mocha with a splash of cream; late on, the vanilla makes a peaceful exit; **b24** when this dram was made, the people at the distillery told me that their whisky peaked at about 18 years and anything older than that really needed to be carted off for blending. Oh, if only those lovey folk of those days could taste this now: how can something survive so long yet be so delicate? We would have such a ceilidh to celebrate. *46.2%. nc ncf sc. 50 bottles. 7th Release.*

⬩⬩⬩ **The First Editions Bunnahabhain Aged 25 Years 1989** refill hogshead, cask no. 11783, bott 2015 **(93.5) n23.5** fresh, intensely malty with the vaguest wisp of coastal peat reek; **t24** superbly busy delivery: myriad honey tones and more prosaic barley notes bunch up early for a mouth-watering entrance. A light smoky coffee begins to take up the mid ground; **f23** much saltier here as the oak begins to offer a sharp prod; **b23** an angular, moody dram which never sits still for a moment. Pretty delicious, though! *49.4%. nc ncf sc. 136 bottles.*

⬩⬩⬩ **Gordon & MacPhail MacPhail's Collection Bunnahabhain 2006 (88.5) n22** a malty accent with the most vague salty accompaniment; **t22** soft, relaxed and malt intense. Lacks those more profound notes of yore, especially the delicate fruit; **f22.5** an attractive interaction with the oak, as the vanilla begins to make an impact; **b22** having stayed in the distillery's long defunct workmen's cottages as storms lash against the distillery and my windows, offering the perception that both would give way at any moment, it is strange to encounter a Bunna so placid in temperament... *43%*

⬩⬩⬩ **Gordon & MacPhail MacPhail's Collection Peated Bunnahabhain 8 Year Old (87) n22 t22 f21 b22.** An exceptionally polite and understated Bunna. The peat is of the unyielding variety: hard and abrupt. Opens very slowly but closes at thrice the speed. *43%*

⬩⬩⬩ **Hepburn's Choice Bunnahabhain 8 Years Old** refill hogshead, dist 2007, bott 2015 **(71) n17 t19 f17 b18.** Very poorly made whisky. From a distillery as great as Bunna, one expects so much better. *46%. nc ncf sc. 364 bottles.*

⬩⬩⬩ **Hidden Spirits Bunnahabhain 7 Years Old** cask no. BU815, dist 2008, bott 2015 **(79) n19 t20.5 f19 b20.5.** Malty, at times intense, a little wisp of salt on the delicate phenols and light powdering of muscovado sugar. But, for all that, not a great spirit and fails to sit comfortably. *48%. sc.*

⬩⬩⬩ **Kingsbury Gold Bunnahahbain 17 Year Old 1997** hogshead, cask no. 5382 **(91.5) n22.5** a few half-hearted smoky tendrils clamp around the vanilla-led oak; **t23.5** much more biting delivery, mainly thanks to the tannin and spice. Builds to an intense heather-honey, juicy crescendo The juicy malt, then the lazy smoke drift in when bothered; **f22.5** good light sugaring to the fade; **b23** everything is laid back and/or in slow motion...and very much closer to a Highland Park in character than a usual Bunna. *52.5%. sc. 289 bottles.*

⬩⬩⬩ **The Loch Fyne Bunnahabhain 14 Year Old** sherry cask, cask no. 1606, dist Dec 01, bott Dec 15 **(86) n22 t22 f20.5 b21.5.** Curiously lacking in the riveting coastal feel which was once the byword and trademark of this distillery. Instead offers an attractive fudge and raisin malt with a little bit of a tang at the finish. *48%. sc. 960 bottles.*

⬩⬩⬩ **Old Malt Cask Bunnahabhain Aged 26 Years** refill hogshead, cask no. 12142, dist Oct 89, bott Nov 15 **(87.5) n22 t22 f21 b21.5.** Maybe just a little too eye-watering for its own good. Sharp and uncompromising, this has much more to do with the state of the cask than the distillate, which is honest and massively malt-proud. *50%. nc ncf sc. 215 bottles.*

Old Masters Bunnahabhain 14 Year Old cask no. 87, dist 1991, bott 2014 **(91) n23** sharp minty marmalade and myriad other signs of a great whisky having been left the odd summer too long, but plucked from the cask in the nick of time...; **t23.5** still soft and a slow deployment of random sugars which, crucially, see off the excesses of the oak; **f22** a little ulmo honey moves in to settle things. The tannin keeps on wailing their frustration and intent...; **b22.5** a Bunna hanging onto life like a hill walker might hang on to a cliff edge of the Paps opposite the distillery after having taken a tumble... *44.7%. sc. James MacArthur & Co Ltd.*

⫸ **Xtra Old Particular Islay Bunnahabhain 25 Years Old** refill hogshead, cask no. 10894, dist Nov 90, bott Nov 15 **(84.5) n23.5 t21 f20 b20.** Disappointing, as the nose carries you to rocky shorelines and throws in a dab of light orange blossom honey for good measure. But on the palate it is hard to escape from the cramped confines of the tangy oak. That said, a brief blast of juicy barley does try to inject something more luxurious. *44.2%. nc ncf sc. 269 bottles.*

CAOL ILA
Islay, 1846. Diageo. Working.

Caol Ila Aged 10 Years "Unpeated Style" bott Aug 09 db **(93.5) n24** a beautiful medley of pear and lime with a thin spread of peanut butter for good measure...not exactly what one might expect...!!! **t23.5** the barley is just so juicy from the kickoff: the citrus on the nose reappears, though any hopes of pear vanishes; the barley, so rarely heard in a Caol-Ila grows in confidence and intensity as the delivery develops; **f23** not as oily as you might expect, allowing extra oak to emerge; **b23** always fascinating to see a traditional peaty Islay stripped bare and in full naked form. Shapely and very high class indeed. *65.4%. Only available at the Distillery.*

Caol Ila Aged 12 Years db **(89) n23 t23 f21 b22.** A telling improvement on the old 12-y-o with much greater expression and width. *43%*

Caol Ila 12 Years Old Special Release 2011 db **(89) n21.5 t23.5 f22 b22.** A sideways look at a big distillery allowing the casks to have the loudest say over the malt: not at all common with this Islay. *64%. nc ncf.*

Caol Ila 14 Years Old Unpeated Style First fill ex-bodega European Oak Casks, dist 1997, bott 2012 db **(95.5) n22.5 t24 f23 b24.** What a night's entertainment to battle your way through this. In normal circumstances the astonishing machinations of this malt would be lost under a sea of peat. But the malt here – 14 going on 40 – never ceases to amaze. A whisky grey and hunched way beyond its years...but what a story it tells...! A malt that lives long on the palate...and in the memory... *59.3%. nc ncf.*

⫸ **Caol Ila 17 Year Old** American oak ex-bourbon casks, dist 1997 db **(90) n23** the smoke is in pretty low revs: indeed, hard to tell the peat engine has started at all. This is much more about the ulmo honey and vague seaweed.; **t23.5** the sugars can't arrive quick enough, leaving the tannins to form a series of layered and orderly queues...; **f21.5** bitters out late on; **b22** a charming malt. But not one the serious Peat Heads out there will much appreciate. *55.9%. Diageo Special Releases 2015.*

Caol Ila Aged 18 Years db **(80) n21 t20 f19 b20.** Another improvement on the last bottling, especially with the comfortable integration of citrus. But still too much oil spoils the dram, particularly at the death. *43%*

⫸ **Caol Ila 30 Year Old** refill American oak & European oak casks, dist 1983 db **(96.5) n24** wow! Like being back on Islay: the peat mixes quite brilliantly with rock pools with the tide out...you half expect to see crabs running about and starfish trying not to get stranded.; **t24.5** one of the deliveries of the year: the silky oil one expects from this distillery, landing at first with a wave of rounded, understated peat plus salt and malt galore, then thickening with rich fruitcake and ulmo honey. The coastal saltiness bolsters the flavour profile, but not to the extent of overcooking it; **f24** just more of the same, but with the slowest of fades...; **b24** indisputably, one of the most complex, well-rounded and complete Caol Ilas I have tasted since they rebuilt the distillery... *55.1%. 7,638 bottles. Diageo Special Releases 2014.*

Caol Ila 1979 db **(74) n20 t19 f17 b18.** Disappointing. I could go on about tropical fruit yada, yada, yada. Truth is, it just conks out under the weight of the oak. Too old. Simple as that. *58.6%*

Caol Ila 1997 The Manager's Choice db **(93.5) n24 t23.5 f23 b23.** When this malt is not enveloped in taste bud-clogging oil, it really can be a little special. Here's further proof. *58%*

Caol Ila Moch db **(87) n22 t22 f21 b22.** Easy drinking, but I think they mean "Mocha"... *43%*

Caol Ila Stitchell Reserve "Unpeated Style" bott 2013 db **(89) n23 t24 f20 b22** Not really a patch on the 2012 bottling, mainly due to inferior sherry butts, any smoke which does appear is like a half-imagined movement in the shadows. The delivery, though, is superb! *59.6% WB15/344*

⫸ **Cadenhead's Small Batch Caol Ila 31 Year Old** bourbon hogshead, dist 1984, bott 2016 **(97) n24** a near perfect Caol Ila nose: its entire 30-plus years is etched onto the aroma. Salted celery, sea brine, morning kippers on the pan, an old oak chest opened for the first time in decades, pepper on toast...; **t24.5** oh, my god....! The only thing the nose lacked was honey. And it is the first thing to turn up on the delivery: a blend of acacia and manuka. Dig your spoon in and soon the smoke emerges, spicy and noble ; **f24** long, the sugars refusing to fade beyond significance. The spices continue to probe; the smoke's presence is always felt, though at times you have to remind yourself it is there...; **b24.5** dream how you'd like your ultimate Caol Ila to be... Well, you've just found it...! This is one of the most complete single casks I have ever encountered. In fact, I had no idea a single cask could be this complex. *52.1%. 432 bottles.*

⟐ **Cadenhead's Small Batch Caol Ila 32 Year Old** bourbon hogshead, dist 1984, bott 2016 **(90.5) n23** big oak. But the peat is punchy enough to absorb the blows without noticeable damage; **t23** explosive spices on delivery, aided by attractive honey. But the oak follow-through is near brutal; **f22.5** dry tannins have a chalky element. The smoke just about keeps a sugary grip; **b22** you can count the rings... *52.9%. sc. 234 bottles.*

⟐ **Eiling Lim Caol Ila 9 Years Old 2006** bott 2015 **(91.5) n23** bluebells in full bloom with orange blossom honey and delicate phenols; **t23.5** fabulous structuring: the oak assists the peat to compartmentalise and offer various layering. Adorable sweet-dry inter-locking; **f22** errs to the dry side for the fade as the ash and light tannins unite; **b23** an enormous degree of depth for something seemingly so delicate.... *51.2%. nc ncf sc. 109 bottles. 11th Release.*

⟐ **The Golden Cask Caol Ila 13 Years Old** cask no. CM 207, dist 2001, bott 2014 **(96) n24** none of the usual oils to gum up the works. So here we have true smoky sophistication as the light Arbroath Smokies allows the salted butter to melt into it and a sprinkling of sugar to reveal a delightful French toast element, too...; **t24** such a difficult whisky for a taster to spit out...! There is a near perfect meeting of ulmo and manuka honeys, offset by a drier, vaguely burnt molasses, while the peat enters on a sooty level and positively growls as it dries and embraces the vanilla; the spices vibrate with a big, bourbon-rich oakiness: this is profound stuff...; **f23.5** much drier and still no oils to speak of. Long, a light dusting of grist and cocoa powder: just so remarkably satisfying... **b24.5** Caol Ila at its most subtle and sexy. Just so understatedly beautiful...One of the single casks of the year! *55%. sc. 268 bottles.*

Gordon & MacPhail Cask Strength Collection Caol Ila 2004 9 Years Old refill sherry cask, cask no. 306655, bott Aug 14 **(77.5) n20 t22.5 f17 b18.** Even through the thick smoky fog of the intense peat, you can tell something is not quite right with the sherry butt. Just for maybe two or three seconds after the initial, off key, hit on the palate, you doubt yourself as the fruity sugars surge. But slowly, and very surely, the sulphur returns to do its worst... *58.5%. nc ncf sc. The Whisky Exchange exclusive. WB16/005*

Gordon & MacPhail Cask Strength Caol Ila 2004 (82) n22.5 t21 f19 b19.5. At first the sultanas and smoke on the nose work in acceptable synchronisation, especially due to some serious juiciness on offer. But there is a background weakness, and so it proves on the palate, the finish in particular showing a nagging degree of furriness. *60.1%*

Gordon & MacPhail Connoisseurs Choice Caol Ila 2001 (91.5) n22 dry, slightly minty phenols; **t23.5** sharp grassy, salivating barley, as though a crisp Speysider has been blended into the peaty mix. The spices lead the counter attack while the smoke slowly envelopes, builds and intensifies...; **f23** lightly molassed peat, then vanilla; **b23** simple but very effective. *46%. WB15/112*

Gordon & MacPhail Connoisseurs Choice Caol Ila 2003 (90) n23 something of the Bavarian lightly smoked sausage about this, except for the background gristy sugars; **t23** excellent mouth feel: nothing like as oily as it can be, but just enough body weight to handle the sugars with purpose. Chewy, although slightly less to get your teeth into than normal for a Caol Ila; **f21.5** bitters slightly, but now the smoke grows and oils develop...; **b22.5** paradoxically, understated...yet confident. *46%*

⟐ **Hepburn's Choice Caol Ila 5 Years Old** European oak quarter cask, dist 2009, bott 2015 **(94.5) n23.5** a blanket of thick, youthful peat crashes into a wall of oak: the oily result will keep you mesmerised for a good ten minutes...; **t24** it had to be a massive delivery...and it is! The sugars are found on as many levels as the smoke. The lighter ones melt early on, leaving viscous molasses to join forces with the ever intensifying phenols. Meanwhile, the oak stands its ground...; **f23** something of a smoky, well oiled chocolate roll...; **b24** now what we have here is Caol Ila in all its oily mastery and oak at full volume. The result isn't for the faint hearted. Few five year old Scotch whiskies will take up so much of your time as this one... *46%. nc ncf sc. 98 bottles.*

⟐ **Old Malt Cask Caol Ila Aged 19 Years** refill hogshead, cask no. 12159, dist Aug 96, bott Nov 15 **(93) n22.5** the smoke is slapped on, with a little green apple to thin the effect: we are in for a ride...; **t24** beautiful delivery: this is a 35 part per million phenol kick somehow controlled like an engine at full revs and the clutch just about to bite. Wonderful counterpointing between the insane smoke and the sharper, still piercing barley; **f23** long, thanks to the subtle oils, with wave after wave of peat crashing onto a shore of vanilla and almost rum-soaked marzipan; **b23.5** revels in all its oily glory. A real smoke fest! *50%. nc ncf sc. 239 bottles.*

Old Malt Cask Caol Ila Aged 29 Years refill hogshead, cask no.10069, dist Jan 84, bott Oct 13 **(96.5) n24 t24 f24 b24.5** One of the most chocolate-rich smokies you'll ever come across.

Rare to find a whisky of this age so beautifully weighted and balanced: shows absolutely no signs of wear. Sublime. *50%. nc ncf sc. 131 bottles. WB15/136*

⬧ **Old Particular Islay Caol Ila 19 Years Old** refill hogshead, dist Dec 96, bott Dec 15 **(94.5) n23** defies the years as the sugars on the barley sparkle and a delicate buttery note mingles with the crisp and pronounced peat; even a slight floral element; **t24** translates from the nose perfectly onto the palate: a gorgeous clarity allows a sublime interplay between the controlled smoke and still bright and nubile barley; the oak does little other than spectate; **f23.5** a long finish with a dull spicy throb which fits well with the heavier phenols and growing oak; **b24** a Caol Ila of very rare poise and beauty. Unusually, don't warm too well in the hand for the best results. *51.5%. nc ncf sc. 313 bottles.*

⬧ **Old Particular Islay Caol Ila 20 Years Old** refill hogshead, cask no. 10870, dist Jan 95, bott Aug 15 **(86.5) n21.5 t22 f21.5 b21.5.** A fascinating contrast to their 19-year-old bottling this year: where the other is an exhibition of grace as it moves around the palate like a ballet dancer, this is a duller, flatter malt where the relatively dullard oak and smoke crash head-first and care little for the consequences. *51.5%. nc ncf sc. 282 bottles.*

⬧ **Provenance Caol Ila Aged 5 Years** bott Mar 16 **(85.5) n22 t21.5 f21 b21.** Very little meaningful oak or unfurled peat: pleasant, malty and refreshing – but barely out of nappies. *46%. nc ncf sc.*

⬧ **Spirits Shop Selection & Sansibar Whisky Caol Ila 1997** sherry butt, bott 2015 **(72) n18 t19 f17 b18.** Fails on so many fronts, hard to know where to start... *40.2%. 599 bottles.*

⬧ **Spirits Shop Selection & Sansibar Whisky Caol Ila 2006** bourbon cask, bott 2015 **(89.5) n22.5** the nose of a well-stocked blending lab: fresh, gristy smoke with an underlying ashy quality. Cheerfully understates the age...; **t22.5** dry delivery with that youth on the nose quickly apparent on the palate; the sugars slowly appear, like seaweed from a retreating tide; **f22** a little smoked manuka honey mixes well with the spice; **b22.5** a beautifully made Islay which makes no great attempt at complexity. *51.3%*

CAPERDONICH
Speyside, 1898. Chivas Brothers. Closed.

⬧ **Acla Selection Caperdonich 21 Years Old** bourbon hogshead, dist 1992, bott 2013 **(87) n21.5 t22 f22 b21.5.** Some older Caperdonichs have been among the most complex malts ever listed in the history of the Whisky Bible. However, this tends towards the other direction: simplistically malty. Actually, the malt itself is unerringly attractive. The hot bite which accompanies it is perhaps not quite so desired. *52.3%. nc ncf.*

Single Cask Collection Caperdonich 1994 20 Year Old sherry hogshead, dist 1994 **(87.5) n23 t22 f21 b21.5.** The nose reminds me of a muesli I used to eat a decade ago built on apple, raisin and mixed nuts...but without the milk. The delivery is quite superb thanks to the controlled oiliness of the body and the charm of the intense grist. The finish, though, works hard to cut out a threatening bitterness. It succeeds, but could have done without the battle. *53.5%*

CARDHU
Speyside, 1824. Diageo. Working.

Cardhu 12 Years Old db **(83) n22 t22 f18 b21.** What appears to be a small change in the wood profile has resulted in a big shift in personality. What was once a guaranteed malt love-in is now a drier, oakier, fruitier affair. Sadly, though, with more than a touch of something furry. *40%*

Cardhu 18 Year Old db **(88) n22.5** soft, easy going – one might even say "safe". Attractive amalgam of clean fruit, citrus especially, and vanilla-drenched barley. But perhaps not enough subtle peaks and troughs to excite; **t23** more of the same: soft, juicy malt but with a darker side as the fruit fills in the gaps; **f20.5** way too bitter for its own good; **b22** very attractive at first. But when you consider what a great distillery Cardhu is and how rare stocks of 18 year old must be, have to say that I am disappointed. The fruit masks the more intricate moments one usually experiences on a Cardhu to ensure an acceptable blandness and accounts for a poor finish. Why, though, it is bottled at a pathetic 40% abv instead of an unchillfiltered 46% – the least this magnificent distillery deserves – is a complete mystery to me. *40%*

Cardhu Amber Rock db **(87.5) n22 t23 f21 b21.5.** Amber is the right colour for this: it appears stuck between green and red, not sure whether to go or not. The delivery, in which the tangerine cream is in full flow reflects the better elements of the nose. But the finish is all about being stuck in neutral. Not helped by the useless 40% abv, you get the feeling that a great whisky is trying to get out. The odd tweak and we'll have a winner. That said, very enjoyable indeed. Just even more frustrating! *40%. Diageo.*

CLYNELISH

Highlands (Northern), 1968. Diageo. Working.

Clynelish Aged 15 Years "The Distillers Edition" double matured in oloroso-seco casks CI-Br: 169-1f, bott code L6264CM000 03847665, dist 1991, bott 2006 db **(79) n20 t20 f19 b20.** Big in places, distinctly oily in others but the overall feel is of a potentially brilliant whisky matured in unsympathetic barrels. 46%

⟨⟩ **Clynelish Select Reserve** ex-bourbon, rejuvenated & refilled American oak, and ex-bodega & refill European oak casks db **(92) n23** a few bourbon elements are weaved into the honey and marmalade; **t24** sometimes the flavours come second to a near perfect texture, though with so much honey on display, it is no that far behind; **f22** bitters out very slightly as the spices rise; **b23** does anyone do honey as well as Clynelish? The fact they can even pull it off with European oak involvement underlines the distillery's brilliance. 54.9%. 2,964 bottles. Diageo Special Releases 2014.

⟨⟩ **Clynelish Select Reserve** ex-bourbon first fill American oak barrels, rejuvenated & refilled American oak hogsheads, and ex-bodega & refill European oak butts db **(95) n23** a thick, dense aroma where the fruit slightly out-spars the acacia honey; just a hint of something slightly smoky amid the tannins; **t24.5** ridiculously beautiful: the wall of flavour is easily scalable but the way in which the ulmo honey merges with the rich and spiced peach and vanilla theme makes one actually groan with pleasure...; **f23.5** the slow fading of before, but with some extra spices taking up position; **b24** stunning. 56.1%. 2,946 bottles. Diageo Special Releases 2015.

⟨⟩ **Acla Selection Clynelish 17 Years Old** refill sherry hogshead, dist 1996, bott 2013 **(80.5) n21.5 t23 f17 b19.** Only a Clynelish can fend off a painfully tight sherry influence with such an outpouring of astonishing honey and juicy fruit. Any other distillery and this cask would have reduced the score into the 60s... Oh, had only this hoggie been clean, might well have been on course for one of the whiskies of the year... 49.7%. nc ncf.

⟨⟩ **Acla Selection Clynelish 21 Years Old** ex-bourbon hogshead, dist 1992, bott 2014 **(96.5) n24.5** ridiculous degree of weight and balance: the signature honeys are there, always delicate – especially the ulmo. I'll not be the only one to fall in love with that vanilla/kumquat mix...; just the most teasing degree of smoke on this one, too...; **t24** now near perfect weight as well as deftness. The vanillas are far more telling here with the sugars molten and of the lighter variety; the malt thickens as the story unfolds; **f23.5** late, busy spice meet the gathering citrus; **b24.5** dangerous whisky: I could drink this all day every day. Even spitting this seems like sacrilege... 49.8%. nc ncf.

⟨⟩ **Cadenhead's Sherry Cask Clynelish 20 Year Old** dist 1994 **(87) n20 t23.5 f21.5 b22.** By no means the worst sherry cask you'll find from this period and the degree of intense spice, coupled with the trademark honey, ensures it has some lovely moments. 55.4%. sc.

⟨⟩ **Gordon & MacPhail Cask Strength Clynelish 2001 (84.5) n21.5 t21 f21 b21.** A few wisps of honey, but surprisingly muffled. 54%

⟨⟩ **Kingsbury Gold Clynelish 19 Year Old 1995** hogshead, cask no. 10195 **(92) n22** quite nutty and unusually dry; **t23** a scrambled delivery finally makes sense after about the four or fifth flavour wave when the cocoa begins to settle the unruly malt and vanilla elements. A little spice kicks in, too; **f23.5** develops into full-blown mocha – but not without a light layer of acacia honey; **b23.5** a lovely, characterful malt which improves as it goes along 57.3%. sc. 250 bottles.

Whiskybroker Clynelish 17 Years hogshead, cask no. 12380, dist 29 Oct 97 **(88.5) n22.5** a salty edge to the banana sandwich nose; young grassy malt, too...; **t22.5** salivating and unusually simple. The malt is intense and sharp; **f21.5** bitters slightly, but that salivation factor barely drops; **b22** not the usual honeyfest. But makes purposeful malt statements. 54.5%. sc.

⟨⟩ **The Whisky Cask Company Clynelish 18 Years Old** sherry hogshead, dist 1997 **(86.5) n21 t23 f21 b21.5.** Somewhat on the tangy and muted side. But enjoys a few moments of honeyed high drama on delivery. 51.6%

Whisky-Fässle Clynelish 16 Year Old sherry cask, dist 1996, bott 2013 **(95.5) n24 t24.5 f23 b24** An outstandingly beautiful butt, so to speak. And so close to being sulphur free. 53.3%. nc ncf.

Whisky-Fässle Clynelish 19 Year Old hogshead, dist 1995, bott 2014 **(92.5) n23 t23.5 f23 b23** A few extra oils to go with the honey. 52.7%. nc ncf.

⟨⟩ **Whiskyjace 10th Anniversary Clynelish 18 Years Old 1996** bourbon cask, bott 2015 **(84.5) n23 t21 f20 b20.5.** Not entirely what I was expecting. The gentle strands of honey teases you into thinking we have another whisky essay of excellence from this stunning distillery. But there is a sharp, greenish catch to the nose, too. And this is realised with a serious sharpness to the delivery, despite the beauty of the early honeycomb. Excellent spirit in a very aggressively interfering old cask. 51%

CONVALMORE
Speyside, 1894–1985. William Grant & Sons. Closed.

Gordon & MacPhail Rare Old Convalmore 1975 (94) n23 t24 f23 b24 The rarest of the rare. And in tasting, the flavour map took me back 30 years, to when I used to buy bottles of this from Gordon and MacPhail as a 10-year-old...probably distilled around 1975. The unique personality and DNA is identical on the palate as it was then; except now, of course, there is far more oak to contend with. Like finding an old lover 30 years further on: a little greyer, not quite in the same lithe shape as three decades earlier...but instantly recognisable and still very beautiful... *46%*

CRAGGANMORE
Speyside, 1870. Diageo. Working.

Cragganmore Aged 12 Years db (81.5) n20 t21 f20 b20.5. I have a dozen bottles of Cragganmore in my personal cellar dating from the early 90s when the distillery was first bottled as a Classic Malt. Their astonishing dexterity and charm, their naked celebration of all things Speyside, casts a sad shadow over this drinkable but drab and instantly forgettable expression. *40%*

Cragganmore Aged 14 Years The Distillers Edition finished in port casks, dist 1993, bott 2007 db **(85) n22 t21 f21 b21.** The tightly closed fruit on the palate doesn't quite match the more expansive and complex nose. *40%*

◇ **Cragganmore 25 Year Old** American oak & refill European oak, dist 1988 db **(94) n23.5** a teasing nose, but one that is decidedly oak dominated. The spices are profound, the tannins border on the aggressive. Yet there is enough subtlety and intrigue to charm, still...; many degrees of slightly hidden dried orange peel; **t24** better still: the malt allows a beautiful softness to the delivery. Not far behind are those fabulous pithy notes and then an entire gamut of varying oak tones. The sublime spice and subtle red liquorice ensure that there is nothing vaguely one-dimensional and balance is always at the core...; **f23** when something is this subtle, and when so much oak is involved, the dry finish is almost inevitable. There is, though, an impressive sophistication at play, too...; **b24** the secret of Cragganmore is the subtle way the malt and spices intertwangle without anyone really noticing, or able to pick which of the two strands is the thickest. Here, the almost secret subtlety of the nose has been compromised for maximum effect on the palate. It was probably a chance worth taking, as the full on display of the tannins is something that lives long on the taste buds...and memory... *51.4%. 3,372 bottles. Diageo Special Releases 2014.*

◇ **Hunter Laing's Old & Rare Cragganmore Aged 30 Years** refill hogshead, dist Apr 95, bott Oct 15 **(91) n23** the malt hangs on to the oaky coat-tails...; **t24** intense with both the barley and tannins screaming at full decibels, one hoping to shout down the other; **f22.5** the tannins win, as the finish becomes dry and spicy with a distinctly botanical feel; some very late mocha soothes; **b22.5** not really a malt designed for this kind of age. But this has been matured in a high quality cask...and it shows. *50.3%. nc ncf sc. 180 bottles.*

◇ **Scotch Malt Whisky Society Cask 37.64 Aged 30 Years** refill hogshead, dist 24 Apr 85, bott 22 Jun 15 **(84) n22 t21 f21 b20.** Certainly has a story to tell. And with some deep marmalade notes and a plethora of dark sugars to hand (all this after a bourbon-esque nose), some of them are a delight. But the brooding presence of the big oak makes others harder to hear. *51.3%. nc ncf sc. 188 bottles.*

◇ **Scotch Malt Whisky Society Cask 37.67 Aged 29 Years** refill hogshead, dist 11 Jun 86, bott 17 Aug 15 **(82) n21.5 t20 f21.5 b19.** This cask should either have made its way into a blend or been bottled at least a decade ago. Far too aggressively tannin dominated, though the spices are interesting. *57.6%. nc ncf sc. 127 bottles.*

◇ **Scotch Malt Whisky Society Cask 37.69 Aged 29 Years** refill hogshead, dist 26 May 87, bott 21 Sept 15 **(93) n23** though there is some evidence of cask deterioration, there is enough in the bank to make for a superb aroma. Best of all is the orange blossom honey mingling with the liquorice...; **t23** the oils which this distillery somehow generates does a sublime job of filling in the oaky cracks. It has malt aplenty, and even more molasses, to help with the maintenance; **f23.5** more settled and subtle with an almost toasted malt effect leading to mocha; **b23.5** one that has withstood the test of time with its head held defiantly high. *58.1%. nc ncf sc. 188 bottles.*

◇ **Scotch Malt Whisky Society Cask 37.70 Aged 15 Years** refill hogshead, dist 22 Aug 00, bott 12 Oct 15 **(95) n24.5** a masterful, yet understated essay in Speyside beauty. It seems as though the malt dominates, but that is an illusion: the gap's left open for the deft oak-fed vanilla and perhaps most delicate citrus note to be found in any malt this year; **t23.5** the subtlety of the malt is extended by the surprising oils which pitch up from nowhere. The spices are but a murmur, the buttery sheen carries gentle maple syrup, while the malt and vanilla intertwine; **f23** more soothing malt, though just a degree of tiredness allows the oak to just take too firm a hand late on; **b24** if we head back four or five decades Cragganmore was often on the list of malts for "top dressing" in their blends: the highest grade malts for flavouring. But very few blends were above the 15-year-old mark and I knew one, back in the '60s and '70s, who swore by this at half the age. Here you get a pretty good idea why: the nose is pure quality *56.9%. nc ncf sc. 303 bottles.*

⬦ **Scotch Malt Whisky Society Cask 37.72 Aged 29 Years** refill hogshead, dist 11 Jun 86, bott 22 Feb 15 **(85.5) n21.5 t21 f22 b21.** Another summer, two at most, and this would have been toast. As it is, a volley of milky notes extracted from a failing cask gives it a wobbly start. But there is enough malt, cream and sugar to see it limp through, though a little unconvincingly. *57.1%. nc ncf sc. 102 bottles.*

CRAIGELLACHIE

Speyside, 1891. John Dewar & Sons. Working.

Craigellachie 13 Year Old db **(88) n21.5** an old-fashioned nose, common among Speysiders 20 years back: a seasoned maltiness busied by a mixture of ex-bourbon casks of mixed age and fortune; **t23** astonishing volley of varied sugars. The gristy ones go first, settled by a layer of ulmo honey; **f21.5** the weaknesses of the barrels begin to show. But an impressive array of peppery spices offer a keen diversion; **b22** not technically the best. But those honey and spice tones are irresistible. *46% WB16/033*

⬦ **Craigellachie 13 Year Old** db **(78.5) n20 t22 f18 b18.5.** Oily and intense, it shovels on the malt for all it is worth. That said, the sulphur notes are its undoing. *46%*

Craigellachie 17 Year Old db **(84.5) n20 t23 f20 b21.5.** A slightly dirty, earthy nose is matched with the tangy finish. But there is no doubting the deliciousness of the silky delivery which is as chewy and fruity as a bar of toffee raisin fudge. *46% WB16/034*

⬦ **Craigellachie 17 Year Old** db **(88.5) n22** chocolate Liquorice Allsort! A tad oily and boiled vegetable. But enough malt to make the difference; **t22.5** just love that delivery. Not the cleanest. But a mix of those heavy duty oils and an almost biting vanilla-barley note is attractive in an unkempt kind of way; **f22** almost like an oil slick in a sea of oak-splintered barley; **b22** technically falls flat on its face. Yet the whole is way better than the sum parts... *46%*

Craigellachie 23 Year Old db **(91.5) n23.5** easy enough to say honey on toast: accurate, too. But it is the variation of honeys which impresses, along with the salt and pepper seasoning; **t23** ulmo honey, inevitably, leads the way. But it doesn't get far before a surge of ultra intense malt washes over it – remarkable considering its age. The oak, through vanilla, isn't far behind; **f22** a little bitter, perhaps from the worm tub sulphur trace. But still spicy and biscuity; **b23.5** expected a little house smoke on this (the malt made here in the early 1990s always had delicate phenol), but didn't show. The honey is nothing like so shy. *46% WB16/035*

⬦ **Cadenhead's Authentic Collection Craigellachie 21 Year Old** sauternes cask, dist 1994 **(88.5) n22** not quite the sweet, juicy, caressing note we are used to from this kind of cask: much more tomboyish and confrontational. Crisp and very direct...; **t22** crisp again on delivery. And...yes! There are the juices: momentarily sweet and then fade as fast as they arrive. The residue is half malt and half vanilla; **f22** a little fruit returns, though the slightly fudgy sweetness is exceptionally taciturn; **b22.5** most Sauternes cask malts are a picture of subtlety; an essay in controlled degree. Here we have the exception... *53.1%*

⬦ **The First Editions Craigellachie Aged 19 Years 1995** sherry butt, cask no. 11792, bott 2015 **(87.5) n21 t23 f21 b22.** A lovely near-as-dammit sulphur-free cask which harnesses together the more juicy elements of the barley and deep toffee-rich, fudgy thread. Simplistic, but very charming. *54.6%. nc ncf sc. 543 bottles.*

⬦ **Hepburn's Choice Craigellachie 7 Years Old** European oak quarter cask, dist 2008, bott 2015 **(81.5) n21.5 t21 f19 b20.** Has something of a US single malt about this: young, with a big oak punch. Balance at a premium but some exceptionally thrusting malt at play. *46%. nc ncf sc. 89 bottles.*

⬦ **Hepburn's Choice Craigellachie 7 Years Old** European oak quarter cask, dist 2008, bott 2015 **(83.5) n20 t21.5 f21 b21.** The sugars have been purged early from the oak and nestle comfortably in the malty grist. Attractive biting spice, too. *46%. nc ncf sc. 92 bottles.*

⬦ **Hepburn's Choice Craigellachie 7 Years Old** European oak quater cask, dist 2008, bott 2015 **(75.5) n19 t20 f18 b18.5.** About as tight and dry as you can imagine. Not to mention furry at the finale. *46%. nc ncf sc. 90 bottles.*

Hepburn's Choice Craigellachie Aged 9 Years sherry butt, dist 2004, bott 2014 **(72.5) n17.5 t18 f19 b18.** Never finds balance nor synchronisation. Hefty, but at a point in its development where the distillate and oak are barely on the same page. The intriguing puff of smoke at the death is pure Craigellachie, though. *46%. nc ncf sc. 786 bottles.*

⬧ **Kingsbury Silver Craigellachie 18 Year Old 1995** sherry butt, cask no. 10389 **(96.5)** **n24.5** a quite stunning Amontillado-style sherry kick: clean, nutty and teasingly and fascinatingly found at that halfway house between sweet and dry; with the malt lurking in the background and not a single sulphur atom in site, this isn't too far from perfection; **t24** stupendous, quite stupendous. Again, that Amontillado-style theme, with the oak investing just the right amount of subtle spice to make this particularly delicious. The sugars range between malt grist and muscovado, but the pace, weight and tone are truly exceptional; some light milky mocha persists, but the spice warms it sublimely; **f23.5** long. The spices stay the course and the gorgeous clarity of the grape and grain leaves you truly astonished; the mocha sticks around, complete with Demerara sugars; **b24.5** if you think you have died and gone to heaven, here is the good news: you have been tasting this whisky. Unquestionably the best cask bottled by Kingsbury sampled since I moved on as their cask selector over 20 years ago. They have unearthed an absolute liquid gold nugget. Don't just enjoy this dram. Worship at its faultless, grapey alter. *46%. sc. 398 bottles.*

⬧ **Old Malt Cask Craigellachie Aged 12 Years** sherry butt, cask no. 11872, dist Apr 02, bott Aug 15 **(78.5) n18 t22 f19 b19.5.** The breath-taking intensity of the maltiness does much to release the malt from its straightjacket. *50%. nc ncf sc. 120 bottles.*

⬧ **Old Malt Cask Craigellachie Aged 14 Years** sherry butt, cask no. 10892, dist Feb 00, bott Oct 14 **(85) n21 t22 f20.5 b21.5.** An honest malt, essentially untroubled by its sherried origins and even offers a puff of smoke as the malt and untaxing sugars unravel. *50%. nc ncf sc. 680 bottles.*

⬧ **Old Malt Cask Craigellachie Aged 20 Years** sherry butt, cask no. 12112, dist Sept 95, bott Nov 15 **(88) n21.5** sharp, vague citrus and salty chocolate. A little unusual...; **t23** blood orange delivery and then a succession of hefty malt blows to the palate. Spices gang up in the mid ground, but all seems younger than its age; **f21** slightly untidy as the sherry butt takes effect, but the spices still work well; **b22.5** an attractively indolent dram, seemingly spoiling for a fight but always allowing its barley-fruit good nature to get the better of it. *50%. nc ncf sc. 360 bottles.*

⬧ **Old Particular Speyside Craigellachie 15 Years Old** refill butt, cask no. 10465, dist Apr 99, bott Oct 14 **(88) n21** sharp, in the distillery – and probably condenser – style. Some serious tang here; **t22.5** super-salivating delivery: non-specific fruit aligns with the mega barley kick, all further enriched by some meaningful oil; **f22** settles to allow the soothing vanilla an easy ride; **b22.5** beautifully rich, rounded and malt-lush. *48.4%. nc ncf sc. 570 bottles.*

⬧ **Old Particular Speyside Craigellachie 20 Years Old** sherry butt, dist Sept 93, bott Dec 15 **(74) n18 t20 f17 b19.** An enormous bunch of grapes. Had the silly sods in Spain not waved a lit sulphur stick in this cask, we'd have had one of the great whiskies of the Speyside year... *51.5%. nc ncf sc. 314 bottles.*

⬧ **The Whisky Chamber Craigellachie 14 Years Old** ex-bourbon hogshead, cask no. 46/2001, dist 05 Sept 01, bott 11 Jan 16 **(87) n21 t22.5 f21.5 b22.** Pleasant dram full of malty vim. The sugars are a little too stark and in your face for greatness. But when they have subsided, the barley sings an attractive ditty, eventually giving up centre stage to the late mocha. *62.8%. nc sc.*

⬧ **Whisky Live Tel Aviv Craigellachie Aged 7 Years** butt, cask no. 900771, dist 2007, bott 2015 **(80.5) n19 t21.5 f19 b21.** Technically, not the best. But despite its obvious sherry butt flaws, how can you not like the nutty intensity of the malt when it engulfs the palate? Probably the least Kosher whisky ever sold in Tel Aviv. *66%. sc. 654 bottles.*

⬧ **Whiskybroker Craigellachie 9 Year Old** refill hogshead, dist 04 Dec 06, bott 18 Feb 16 **(86.5) n21.5 t22 f21.5 b21.5.** Malty, oily, biscuity. Yet always curiously ill-at-ease with itself. *57.8%. sc.*

DAILUAINE
Speyside, 1854. Diageo. Working.

Dailuaine 1997 The Manager's Choice db **(87.5) n21.5 t23 f21 b22.** One of the most enjoyable (unpeated!!) Dailuaines I've come across in an age. There is the usual distillery biff to this, but not without a honeyed safety net. Great fun. *58.6%*

Dailuaine Aged 16 Years bott lot no. L4334 db **(79) n19 t21 f20 b19.** Syrupy, almost grotesquely heavy at times; the lighter notes of previous bottlings have been lost under an avalanche of sugary, over-ripe tomatoes. One for those who want a massive dram. *43%*

Alexander Murray & Co Dailuaine 1997 16 Years Old (84.5) n20.5 t22 f21 b21. A fudged issue. Literally. *40%*

◇◇◇ **C & S Dram Collection Dailuaine Aged 17 Years** hogshead, cask no. 12812, dist 07 Oct 97, bott 10 Aug 15 **(80) n21 t19 f20 b20.** Clean, monosyllabic malt. And hotter than Hades... 56.6%. sc. 235 bottles.

Cadenhead's Authentic Collection Dailuaine Aged 18 Years dist 1997 **(73) n18 t19 f18 b18.** Dailuaine struggles in a half decent bourbon cask. In what appears to be a sulphur-treated wine cask, it has no chance at all... 54.4%

◇◇◇ **Cadenhead's Wine Cask Dailuaine 18 Year Old** Chateau Lafitte cask, dist 1997 **(93.5) n23** austere grain but, my word, some formidable grape, resplendent with crushed pips..; do I detect either the hint of something smoky...? **t23** salivating, soaring fruit revealing a freshness defying either the cask or the malt. A puckering, explosive powder keg of fizzing spice and fruit; **f23** lasts the course like a thoroughbred, making light of the obvious aggression of the spirit to concentrate on the repairing qualities of the fruit...and, what do you know...? There's that gentle hint of smoke once again; **b23.5** if proof were required that you can turn a below average spirit into an above average malt thanks to the casks, here it proudly is. Love it – well done Cadenhead's! 54.4%. sc.

◇◇◇ **Gordon & MacPhail Connoisseurs Choice Dailuaine 2004** (80) **n19 t21 f20 b20.** A tetchy malt at the best of times, the unkempt nose suggests it just isn't going to play ball. And despite the odd phase of attractively intense barley, this never quite makes itself feel at home. 46%

◇◇◇ **Hepburn's Choice Dailuaine 7 Years Old** sherry butt, dist 2008, bott 2015 **(84) n20 t22 f21 b21.** So rough and ungainly, it is actually quite enjoyable – a bit like having a dust up when playing rugby. Still, the sherry butt is clean and malt makes itself heard. Have fun, but expect a few bruises! 46%. nc ncf sc. 389 bottles.

◇◇◇ **Old Particular Speyside Dailuaine 12 Years Old** refill butt, cask no. 11026, dist Sept 03, bott Feb 16 **(79) n19 t19 f21 b20.** Soft and nutty. 48.4%. nc ncf sc. 291 bottles.

◇◇◇ **Provenance Dailuaine Over 11 Years** refill sherry butt, dist Autumn 04, bott Autumn 15 **(74) n18.5 t19 f18.5 b18.** Bog standard single malt. Not particularly well made, harsh on delivery and finish and, beyond basic barley, proffers little else. Like a Vauxhall where seats come as extras.... 46%. nc ncf sc.

◇◇◇ **Scotch Malt Whisky Society Cask 41.70 Aged 34 Years** 2nd fill Sauternes hogshead, dist 13 Dec 80, bott 25 Jan 16 **(86) n22 t21.5 f21.5 b21.** Well done, SMWS. You have located a Dailuaine which actually puts on a show worth listening to. Distinctly nutty, as in the house style, but the sugars and spices combine rhythmically and even set up a charming coffeed finale; 48.6%. nc ncf sc. 102 bottles.

◇◇◇ **The Warehouse Dram Dailuaine Aged 8 Years** sherry finish octave, cask no. 510S23, dist 21 Feb 08, bott 04 Apr 16 **(72.5) n17.5 t18.5 f18 b18.5.** Lots of sugars at play. But not a malt I can get particularly sweet over. 46%. nc ncf. 94 bottles.

DALLAS DHU
Speyside, 1899–1983. Closed. Now a museum.
Gordon & MacPhail Rare Vintage Dallas Dhu 1979 (94.5) n23 marginally earthy but probably only there for the fruit and nuts to grow in; green banana and toasted yam lead, pecan pie follows behind; **t23.5** how can barley melt in the mouth after 32 years? It defies logic and description. What makes it work so well, is that the base and baritone sugars from the oak never for a moment attempt to drown the tenor from the grist. Often that is the key to a whisky's success and here it is demonstrated perfectly: it means the complexity levels remain high at all times and the depth of oak controlled; **f23.5** long, with the vanilla enjoying a nutty depth, moving into a more deliciously praline oiliness. The tannins are firm enough to remind us that 1979 was a long time ago now but not a single hint of oaky degradation. Clear, confident, strident notes from first to last; **b24** I can hardly recall the last time a bottling from this distillery popped along – depressing to think I am old enough to remember when they were so relatively common they were being sold on special offer! It was always a class act; it's closure an act of whisky vandalism, whether it be preserved as a museum or not. This, even after all these years, shows the extraordinary quality we are missing day in, day out. 43%

DALMORE
Highands (Northern), 1839. Whyte and Mackay. Working.
The Dalmore 12 Years Old db **(90) n22** mixed dates: both dry and juicy; **t23** fat, rich delivery with a wonderful dovetailing of juicy barley and thick, rumbling fruit; **f22.5** lots of toffee on the finish, but gets away with it thanks to the sheer depth to the barley and the busy sherry sub-plot; **b22.5** has changed character of late yet remains underpowered and with a shade too much toffee. But such is the quality of the malt in its own right it can overcome any hurdles placed before it to ensure a real mouth-filling, rumbustious dram. 40%

The Dalmore Dee Dram 12 Years Old db (63.5) n15.5 t17 f14 b16. Words fail me...40%

The Dalmore 15 Years Old db (83.5) n21 t21 f20.5 b21. Another pleasant Dalmore that coasts along the runway but simply fails to get off the ground. The odd off note here and there, but it's the blood orange which shines brightest. 40%

The Dalmore 18 Years Old db (76.5) n19 t21 f18 b18.5. Heaps of caramel and the cask choice might have been better. 43%

The Dalmore 21 Years Old db (87) n22 t23 f20 b22. Bottled elegance. 43%

◈ **The Dalmore 21 Year Old** db (88.5) n22 date and walnut cake...though light on the walnuts...; t23 fat, chewy, mouth-watering and complex...though light on the complexity; f21.5 remains chewy, bitter and sweet...though light on the sweetness; b22 fat, unsubtle, but pretty enjoyable. 42%

The Dalmore 25 db (88) n23.5 hugely attractive with a sherry-trifle signature; t22.5 a glossy delivery with the accent very much on fruit, plums in particular; an attractive degree of sharpness throughout; f20 just a little dry with a tell-tale tang towards the end; b22 the kind of neat and tidy, if imperfect, whisky which, were it in human form, would sport a carefully trimmed and possibly darkened little moustache, a pin-striped suit, matching tie and square and shiny black shoes. 42%. Whyte & Mackay Ltd.

◈ **The Dalmore 30 Year Old** db (94) n24 the grape drifts across the glass; not quite perfect but enough panache and class to carry an aura of slight wonder...; t24 so thick, so long, so dripping in fruit....; subtle spice and a slow realisation of aged, confident tannin; f22.5 undone very slightly by a very late degree of bitterness; b23.5 a malt, quite literally for the discerning whisky lover. Essays in complexity are rarely so well written in the glass as found here... 45%

The Dalmore 50 Years Old db (88) n21 t19 f25 b23. Takes a while to warm up, but when it does becomes a genuinely classy and memorable dram befitting one of the world's great and undervalued distilleries. 52%

The Dalmore 62 Years Old db (95) n23 PM or REV marked demerara potstill rum, surely? Massive coffee presence, clean and enormous, stunning, topdrawer peat just to round things off; t25 this is brilliant: pure silk wrapping fabulous moist fruitcake soaked in finest oloroso sherry and then weighed with peat which somehow has defied nature and survived in cask all these years. I really cannot fault this: I sit here stunned and in awe; f24 perfect spices with flecks of ginger and lemon rind; b24 if I am just half as beautiful, elegant and fascinating as this by the time I reach 62, I'll be a happy man. Somehow I doubt it. A once-in-a-lifetime whisky – something that comes around every 62 years, in fact. Forget Dalmore Cigar Malt – even I might be tempted to start smoking just to get a full bottle of this. 40.5%

The Dalmore 1263 King Alexander III db (86) n22 t22.5 f20 b21.5. Starts brightly with all kinds of barley sugar, fruit and decent age and oak combinations, plus some excellent spice prickle. So far, so good...and obviously thoughtfully and complexly structured. But then vanishes without trace on finish. 40%

The Dalmore 1978 db (89.5) n23.5 t22 f21.5 b22.5. A seriously lovely old dram which is much weightier on the palate than nose. 471%. 477 bottles.

The Dalmore 1979 db (84) n21 t21.5 f20 b21.5. Hard to find a more rounded malt. Strangely earthy, though. 42%. 487 bottles.

The Dalmore 1980 db (81.5) n19 t21 f20.5 b21. Wonderful barley intensity on delivery does its best to overcome the so-so nose and finale. 40%

The Dalmore 1981 Amoroso Sherry Finesse amoroso sherry wood cask db (85.5) n21 t22 f21.5 b21. A very tight, fruity, dram which gives away its secrets with all the enthusiasm of an agent under torture. Enjoyable to a degree... but bloody hard work. 42%

The Dalmore Astrum Aged 40 Years db (89) n23.5 t21 f22 b22.5. This guy is all about the nose. The oak is too big for the overall framework and the balance hangs by a thread. Yet somehow the overall effect is impressive. Another summer and you suspect the whole thing would have snapped... 42%

The Dalmore Aurora Aged 45 Years db (90.5) n25 t22 f21.5 b22. Sophisticated for sure. But so huge is the oak on the palate, it cannot hope to match the freakish brilliance of the nose. 45%

The Dalmore Candela Aged 50 Years db (96) n25 t24 f23.5 b23.5. Just one of those whiskies which you come across only a handful of times in your life. All because a malt makes it to 50 does not mean it will automatically be great. This, however, is a masterpiece, the end of which seemingly has never been written. 50% (bottled at 45%).

The Dalmore Cabernet Sauvignon db (79) n22 t19 f19 b19. Too intense and soupy for its own good. 45%

The Dalmore Castle Leod db (77) n18.5 t21 f18.5 b19. Thumpingly big and soupy. More fruit than you can wave a wasp at. But, sadly, the sting comes with the slightly obvious off note. 46%

The Dalmore Ceti db **(91.5) n24** a nose for fruitcake lovers everywhere: ripe cherries and blood orange abound and work most attractively with the slightly suety, muscovado enriched body...; **t23.5** the nose demands a silky delivery and that's exactly what you get. Rich fruit notes form the principle flavour profile but the backing salivating barley and spice is spot on; the mid ground becomes a little saltier and more coastal...; **f21.5** a vague bitterness to the rapidly thinning finale, almost a pithy element, which is slightly out of sync with the joys of before; **b22.5** a Ceti which warbles rather well... *44.7%*

The Dalmore Cigar Malt Reserve Limited Edition db **(73.5) n19 t19.5 f17 b18.** One assumes this off key sugarfest is for the cigar that explodes in your face... *44%*

The Dalmore Cromartie dist 1996 db **(78.5) n20 t22 f17.5 b19.** Always hard to forecast what these type of bottlings may be like. Sadly there is a sulphur-induced bitterness and tightness to this guy which undermines the more attractive marmalade notes. *45%*

The Dalmore Distillery Exclusive 2015 db **(85.5) n22.5 t22.5 f19.5 b21.** Dalmore, so often a thick and syrupy dram when house bottled, in thick and syrupy mode. The nose offers a sharp bite of greengage and fresh-out-of-the-oven fruitcake. But the lack of a malt perspective and, more fatally, the bitter finish, means excellence is a long way off. *48%. 450 bottles.*

⟫ **The Dalmore Dominium** db **(89.5) n22.5** thick, full-on grape; **t23** lush delivery which becomes progressively more chewy. A few spiced sultanas in there; **f22** big on the caramel; **b22** like so many Dalmores, starts brightly but as the caramels gather it just drifts into a soupy lump. Still, no taint to the fruit and though the finish is dull you can say it is never less than very attractive. *43%. Fortuna Meritas Collection*

The Dalmore Eos Aged 59 Years db **(95) n24.5 t24 f22.5 b24** For those of you who thought this was a camera, let me put you in the picture. This is one well developed whisky, but by no means over exposed, as it would have every right to be after nearly 60 years. Indeed: it is one of those drams which utterly confounds and amazes. I specially chose this as the 1001st new whisky for the 2012 Bible, and those of us old enough to be young when most of its sister casks were hauled off for blending, there was an advert in the '60s which said: "1,001 cleans a big, big carpet...for less than half a crown." Well this 1001 cleans a big, big palate. But I can't see a bottle of this majestic malt going for as little as that... *44%*

The Dalmore Gran Reserva sherry wood and American white oak casks db **(82.5) n22 t21.5 f19 b20.** An improvement on the near nonentity this once was. But still the middle and finish are basic and lacking sophistication or substance outside a broad sweet of oaky chocolate toffee. Delightful mixture of blood orange and nuts on the approach, though. *40%*

⟫ **The Dalmore Luceo** db **(87) n22 t22 f21.5 b21.5.** Pleasantly malty, exceptionally easy going and perfect for those of you with a toffeed tooth. *40%. Fortuna Meritas Collection*

The Dalmore Valour db **(85.5) n21 t22 f21 b21.5.** Not often you get the words "Valour" and "fudge" in the same sentence. *40%. Fortuna Meritas Collection* ☉

⟫ **The Dalmore Regalis** db **(86.5) n22.5 t21.5 f21 b21.5.** For a brief moment, grassy and busy. Then dulls, other than the spice. The caramel held in the bottling hall is such a great leveller. *40%. Fortuna Meritas Collection*

The Dalmore Visitor Centre Exclusive db **(95.5) n25 t24 f22.5 b24** Not exactly the easiest distillery to find but a bottle of this is worth the journey alone. I have tasted some sumptuous Dalmores over the last 30-odd years. But this one stands among the very finest. *46%*

⟫ **Cadenhead's Rum Cask Dalmore 24 Year Old** dist 1990 **(95) n23.5** not as crisp as some rum casks might be – suspect this might be from Guyana, because the slightly coffee-enriched (or do I mean Coffey...?) complexity; **t24** sublime: a superb meeting of thick vanilla, thicker malt and dark molasses...and still that Demerara-style rum intensity; **f23.5** long, toasty with a late salty blast to sharpen up and polish the late flavour profile; **b24** given an excellent cask, which this is, and kept away from overbearing caramel, ditto, Dalmore can be an outstanding malt. Just rarely see it in a suit that fits.... *54.9%. sc.*

⟫ **Cadenhead's Small Batch Dalmore 25 Year Old** sherry butt, dist 1990, bott 2016 **(94.5) n23** a sturdy mix of tannin and very healthy, unspoiled fruitcake; **t24** big 'n' juicy, the raisins fair romp across the palate. The salivating continues well into the mid-ground with vanilla slowing things down, though the spices try to kick start it again...; **f23.5** mocha with a side plate of fruitcake; **b24** mon sherry! Not a sulphur atom in sight...!! *56.3%. sc. 474 bottles.*

DALWHINNIE
Highlands (Central), 1898. Diageo. Working.

Dalwhinnie 15 Years Old db **(95) n24** sublime stuff: a curious mixture of coke smoke and peat-reek wafts teasingly over the gently honied malt. A hint of melon offers some fruit but the caressing malt stars; **t24** that rarest of combinations: at once silky and malt intense, yet at the same time peppery and tin-hat time for the tastebuds, but the silk wins out and a sheen of barley sugar coats everything, soft peat included; **f23** some cocoa and coffee notes, yet the pervading slightly honied sweetness means that there is no bitterness that cannot be controlled; **b24** as a malt it is hard to decide whether to drink or bath in: I suggest you do both. One of the most complete mainland malts of them all. Know anyone who reckons they don't like whisky? Give them a glass of this – that's them cured. Oh, if only the average masterpiece could be this good. *43%*

Dalwhinnie 25 Years Old Special Release 2012 Rejuvenated American oak hogshead, dist 1987, bott 2012 db **(92) n23.5 t23.5 f22 b23** More from the mountains of Kentucky than central Scotland. Anyone with a bourbon bent and a sweet tooth will adore this. As will bee keepers. *52.1 %. nc ncf. Diageo.*

⬩⬩⬩ **Dalwhinnie 25 Year Old** refill American oak hogsheads, dist 1989 db **(96.5) n24.5** light smoke buzzes and drifts; heather honey sweetens towards a leathery richness – indeed, a sweet saltiness suggests old riding tackle – and a beautiful crushed walnut oiliness. Together, something rather special... **t24** the mouth feel to end all mouth feels: a light oily caress, like an expert massage, with spicy pressure being applied on just the right points...; the heather honey now shifts to ulmo honey as the vanillas take effect; **f23.5** vague phenols and a spicy buzz...; **b24.5** just exemplary. If only all Scotch single malt was this magnificent... *48.8%. 5,916 bottles. Diageo Special Releases 2015.*

⬩⬩⬩ **Dalwhinnie The Distillers Edition Double Matured** special release D. SU. 312, dist 1997, bott 2013 db **(94) n24** superb! Deft use of plum jam and ulmo honey makes for a rich and very complex aroma. The tannins have a degree of toastiness, but no more than the pastry on a well cooked fruit pie...; **t23.5** soft and sensual: the ulmo honey keeps its foot on the pedal, then a light fruit and then the vaguest, most distant, dusky smokiness ensures the malt has a solid foundation; **f23** all about the vanilla and caramels; **b23.5** more like a blender's edition: I can count the number of genuinely successful double matured malts probably on both hands. There is some serious skill and understanding of this distillery at work here. Wouldn't have hurt to see it at 46%, mind... *43%*

⬩⬩⬩ **Dalwhinnie Winter's Gold** db **(95) n23.5** for such a remote and inland distillery, the coastal saltiness to this is remarkable... golden syrup and earthy heather-honey also at work here; **t24** something of the Johnnie Walker Gold about this: there is a clarity to the malt, the citrus and vanilla which reminds one of the air when looking far away into the mountains on a cool winter's morn; **f23.5** earthy to the end with the honey (ulmo, naturally!) still the dominating theme; just a late hint of bitterness; **b24** whichever blender came up with this deserves a pat of the back. *43%*

DEANSTON
Highlands (Perthshire), 1966. Burn Stewart Distillers. Working.

Deanston 6 Years Old db **(83) n20 t21 f22 b20.** Great news for those who remember how good Deanston was a decade or two ago: it's on its way back. A delightfully clean dram with its trademark honey character restored. A little beauty slightly undermined by caramel. *40%*

Deanston 12 Years Old db **(74) n18 t19 f18.5 b18.5.** It is quite bizarre how you can interchange this with Tobermory in style; or, rather, at least the faults are the same. *46%. ncf.*

Deanston Aged 12 Years db **(75) n18 t21.5 f17.5 b18.** The delivery is, for a brief moment, a malty/orangey delight. But the nose is painfully out of sync and finish is full of bitter, undesirable elements. A lot of work still required to get this up to a second grade malt, let alone a top flight one. *46.3%. ncf. Burn Stewart.*

Deanston 18 Year Old batch 2 db **(89.5) n23** celebrates a very healthy degree of ulmo honey: soft and sexy; **t22.5** big malt kick early on; soft oils bring on the vanillas; juicy and just a touch of lime to lighten things; **f22** a little spicier and deeper toned as the tannin takes charge; **b22** a soft treat for the palate... *46.3%. nc ncf.*

⬩⬩⬩ **Deanston 20 Year Old** db **(61) n15 t16 f15 b15** Riddled with sulphur. *55.4%. nc ncf.*

Deanston Virgin Oak db **(90) n22.5 t23 f22.5 b22** Quirky. Don't expect this to taste anything like Scotch... *46.3%*

Cadenhead's Small Batch Deanston Aged 19 Years butts, dist 1994, bott 2014 **(83) n20.5 t21.5 f20 b21.** A syrupy, unsubtle malt which paints on the sugar-coated barley with a spray gun. The odd fruit note, especially some diced, crunchy French apple. But counts for little when the jigsaw has been mis-printed. *56.4%. 846 bottles. WB15/067*

⬩⬩⬩ **The Golden Cask Deanston 18 Years Old** cask no. CM 208, dist 1996, bott 2014 **(83) n21 t21.5 f19.5 b21.** A stark, fiery whisky helped by the kind of molten sugars you find on very hot porridge. The lack of body allows some of the more aggressive oak to say too much. *54%. sc. 278 bottles.*

Marks & Spencer Deanston Aged 12 Years db **(84.5) n20.5 t22 f21 b21.** It's been a while since I found so much honeyed malt in a Deanston. Echoes of 20 years ago. *40%. UK.*

⟨⟩ **The Single Cask Deanston Aged 15 Years** cask no. 1958, dist 10 Dec 97, bott 01 Aug 13 **(76) n19 t21 f18 b18.** A white knuckle roller-coaster dram with more downs than ups. Lurches between over-the-top cloying sugar and an eye-watering oak tang. 45.8%. nc ncf sc.

Whiskyjace Deanston 15 Year Old bourbon hogshead, dist 1997, bott 2013 **(83) n21 t21.5 f20 b20.5.** A hot, sugary dram. Malty, simple and thin but with a hint of citrus. 54.4%

DUFFTOWN

Speyside, 1898. Diageo. Working.

Singleton of Dufftown 12 Years Old db **(71) n18 t18 f17 b18.** A roughhouse malt that's finesse-free. For those who like their tastebuds Dufft up a bit... 40%

⟨⟩ **The Singleton of Dufftown Spey Cascade** db **(80) n19 t20 f21 b20.** A dull whisky, stodgy and a little dirty on the nose. Improves the longer it stays on the palate thanks mainly to sympathetic sugars and an ingratiating oiliness. But if you are looking for quality, prepare to be disappointed. 40%

The Singleton of Dufftown "Sunray" db **(77) n20 t20 f18 b19.** One can assume only that the sun has gone in behind a big toffeed cloud. Apparently, according to the label, this is "intense". About as intense as a ham sandwich. Only not as enjoyable. 40%. WB15/121

The Singleton of Dufftown "Tailfire" db **(79) n20 t20 f19 b20.** Tailspin, more like. 40%. WB15/122

⟨⟩ **Gordon & MacPhail Connoisseurs Choice Dufftown 2006 (84) n20.5 t21.5 f21 b21.** About as fat on the palate as you'll find any Speysider, this bottling is bolstered by some highly attractive spice which manages to pierce the oily and sugary gloom. More than somewhat cloying. 46%

Scotch Malt Whisky Society Cask 91.20 Aged 37 Years refill hogshead, dist 3 Jun 76 **(72.5) n19 t18 f18.5 b18.** A harsh malt which plays lip-service to the oak which is better than the all-round experience suggests. The initial spirit was so uncompromisingly tough and steely, though, there is little direction for this whisky to take – even at such great age. 46.9%. sc. 58 bottles.

EDRADOUR

Highlands (Perthshire), 1837. Signatory Vintage. Working.

Edradour Aged 10 Years db **(79) n18 t20 f22 b19.** A dense, fat malt that tries offer something along the sherry front but succeeds mainly in producing a whisky cloyingly sweet and unfathomable. Some complexity to the finish compensates. 43%

Edradour Ballechin The Discovery Series #3 Port Cask Matured Heavily Peated, First fill port casks db **(88) n21 t23 22 b22** For Peat Freaks and masochists only... 46%. nc ncf. 6,000 bottles. WB15/033

Edradour Ballechin The Discovery Series #4 Oloroso Sherry Cask Matured Heavily Peated, First fill oloroso sherry butts db **(87) n22.5 t23.5 f20 b21** One of the fattest malts of all time. Just trips with tarry oil... 46%. nc ncf. 6,000 bottles. WB15/034

Edradour Ballechin The Discovery Series #5 Marsala Cask Matured Heavily Peated, First fill Marsala hogsheads db **(92) n23 t23.5 f22.5 b23** Challenging at first, not least because the oily spirit takes some navigating, but once you dip your shoulders under the peat, you are in...!!! Complex, well weighted and beautifully formulated. 46%. nc ncf. 6,000 bottles. WB15/035

Edradour Ballechin The Discovery Series #6 Bourbon Cask Matured Heavily Peated, First fill bourbon barrels db **(90.5) n23 t23 f22 b22.5** Edradour's tiny still give this ultra smoky malt a truly unique fingerprint. 46%. WB15/036

Edradour Ballechin The Discovery Series #7 Bordeaux Cask Matured Heavily Peated First fill Bordeaux hogsheads db **(74) n20 t21 f16 b17.** A sweet, phenolic start...but goes horribly downhill from there... 46%. nc ncf. 6,000 bottles. WB15/037

Edradour Ballechin The Discovery Series #8 Sauternes Cask Matured Heavily Peated, First fill sauternes hogsheads db **(82) n21 t22 f19 b20.** A bit like looking at the Mona Lisa through cracked glass. There is something so right with it, yet so very wrong. Massive peat enshrined in what might have been a truly stunning cask. But hardly for a moment do the two twains meet. 46%. nc ncf. 6,000 bottles. WB15/038

Edradour Barolo Cask Matured Barolo hogsheads, dist March/April 06, bott Apr 14 db **(79.5) n19 t21.5 f19 b20.** Never entirely at ease at spirit or maturation level. The wide cut doesn't suit the indisciplined grape 46%. nc ncf. batch number: One, 2450 bottles. WB15/041

Edradour Chardonnay Cask Matured chardonnay hogsheads, dist Dec 2003, bott Sep 2011 db **(72) n18 t19 f17 b18.** Crushingly dry. Grim. 46%. nc ncf. batch number: One, 1600 bottles. WB15/043

Edradour Dougie Maclean's Caledonia Selection Aged 12 Years db **(91) n23 t23 f22 b23** Gosh! Hold on to your hats. This is some ride.... 46%. nc ncf. WB15/044

Edradour Port Cask Matured port hogsheads, dist June/July 2003, bott Mar 14 db **(91.5)** n23 t23.5 f22 b23 wonderful malt, make no mistake. Hardly any small still trace, allowing for a more expansive whisky. 46%. nc ncf. batch number: One, 2400 bottles. WB15/042

Edradour Sauternes Cask Matured Sauternes hogsheads, dist Dec 03, bott Feb 13 db **(81)** n19 t24 f18 b20. For a few brief, glorious moments this malt soars to the heights obtained only by great Sauternes casks and looks imperiously down at everything else around. But to get there you have to go through a dodgy take off and an even bumpier landing... 46%. nc ncf. batch number: Three, 2150 bottles. WB15/039

Edradour Straight From The Cask Aged 10 Years sherry butt, cask no. 530, dist 06 Dec 01, bott 21 Nov 12 db **(88.5)** n22.5 t23 f21 b22 Some you know what. But otherwise sweet as a nut... 573%. sc. 984 bottles. WB15/051

Edradour Straight From The Cask Barolo Cask Finish Aged 10 Years dist 28 May 02 in hogsheads, disgorged 28 Feb 11, finished in a Barolo hogshead, bott 15 Apr 13 db **(88)** n22 t22.5 f22 b22 It packs a presence, that's for sure. 58.3%. 423 bottles. WB15/050

Edradour Straight From The Cask Burgundy Cask Finish Aged 11 Years dist 08 May 02 in hogsheads, disgorged 24 Mar 11, finished in a Burgundy hogshead, bott 09 Dec 13 db **(89.5)** n23.5 t22 f22.5 b21.5 Lurches around the palate like Ron Burgundy on a bender. Great fun, though. 58.6%. 429 bottles. WB15/048

Edradour Straight From The Cask Chardonnay Cask Finish Aged 12 Years dist 30 Jun 00 in hogsheads, disgorged 22 Nov 08, finished in a Chardonnay hogshead, bott 11 Apr 13 db **(82.5)** n20 t22 f20 b20.5. Massive grape statement and no shortage of cocoa on the furry finish. But not my type of whisky, I'm afraid, and leaves me cold. 56.3%. 451 bottles. WB15/045

Edradour Straight From The Cask Chateauneuf Du Pape Cask Finish Aged 11 Years dist 28 May 13 in hogsheads, disgorged 28 Feb 11, finished in a Chateauneuf Du Pape hogshead, bott 28 Nov 13 db **(94)** n24 t24 f22 b24 Had no idea Chateauneuf Du Papa 2002 was this good a vintage.... 576%. 440 bottles. WB15/049

Edradour Straight From The Cask Marsala Cask Finish Aged 11 Years dist 28 May 02 in hogsheads, disgorged 28 Feb 11, finished in a Marsala hogshead, bott 04 Oct 13 db **(93.5)** n23.5 t24 f22.5 b23.5 Good to see another sulphur-free wine cask. At its very height, quite stupendous. 58.6%. 603 bottles. WB15/047

Edradour Straight From The Cask Port Wood Finish Aged 13 Years dist 23 Jan 2001 in hogsheads, disgorged 10 Dec 2010, finished in a port pipe, bott 20 Feb 2014 db **(95)** n24 t24 f23 b24 One of the greatest Port Finishes for a very long time. 56.3%. 1010 bottles. WB15/046

Edradour Super Tuscan Cask Matured Super Tuscan hogsheads, dist March/April 06, bott Apr 14 db **(81)** n20.5 t23 f18 b19.5. Not sure what a non-Super cask would have been like. Imbalanced from nose to finish, at least it boasts a rousing chocolate fruit and nut middle. 46%. nc ncf. Batch number: One, 2450 bottles. WB15/040

Edradour Vintage 2006 oloroso sherry cask matured, cask no. 240, dist 1 Jun 06, bott 3 Sep 13 db **(91.5)** n24 t23 f21.5 b23 A big malt still dripping with the fresh contents of the handsome sherry butt. 59.2%. sc nc. Cask hand picked by The Whisky Exchange. WB15/282

Ballechin Aged 12 Years Burgundy wine hogsheads, dist 20 Jan 04, bott 01 Apr 16 db **(92.5)** n23 thumping peat offers the acidity of a barely cooled hearth; t23.5 again, the peat is first out of the blocks: but the grape rallies briefly with a degree of stoicism, hammering home a Demerara quality crunchiness to the grape. But it is all rather short lived....; f23 back to a slightly more tart, acidic finish even though some caramels emerge; b23 the burgundy is blasted off the planet: the Pinot Noir grape is crisp enough to usually look after itself, but here it is no match for 50ppm phenols... 52.5%. nc ncf. 905 bottles. Bottled for the Swedish Whisky Federation.

Anam na h-Alba The Soul of Scotland Edradour 2000 bourbon & oloroso sherry casks, dist May 00, bott Aug 14 **(83.5)** n21 t22 f20 b20.5. Pretty clean sherry by today's standards and viscous in body. But lacking balancing sugars: something of a dullard. 46%. 310 bottles.

FETTERCAIRN

Highland (Eastern), 1824. Whyte and Mackay. Working.

Fettercairn 12 Year Old db **(66)** n14 t19 f16 b17. If the nose doesn't get you, what follows probably will...Grim doesn't quite cover it. 40%

Fettercairn 30 Years Old db **(73)** n19 t18 f18 b18. A bitter disappointment. Literally. 46.3%

Fettercairn 40 Years Old db **(92)** n23 technically, not exactly how you want a 40-y-o to be: a bit like your old silver-haired granny knitting in her rocking chair...and sporting tattoos. But I also have to say there is no shortage of charm, too...and like some old tattooed granny, you know it is full of personality and has a tale to tell... t24 I was expecting dates and walnuts... and I have not been let down. A veritable date and walnut pie you can chew on until your jaw is numb; the sharp raisiny notes, too, plus a metallic sheen which reminds you of its provenance...; **f22** those burned raisins get just a little more burned...; **b23** yes, everyone knows my views on this distillery. But I'll have to call this spade a wonderfully big, old shovel you can't help loving...just like the memory of me tattooed ol' granny... 40%. 463 bottles.

Fettercairn 1824 db (69) **n17 t19 f16 b17**. By Fettercairn standards, not a bad offering. Relatively free from its inherent sulphury and rubbery qualities, this displays a sweet nutty character not altogther unattractive – though caramel plays a calming role here. Need my arm twisting for a second glass, though. *40%*

❖ **Acla Selection Fettercairn 24 Years Old** refill hogshead, dist 1990, bott 2014 (72.5) **n19 t17.5 f18 b18**. Nutty, though some have gone off. Cloyingly sweet in part. Always chimes a little off key. So everything normal for this distillery, then. *50.3%. nc ncf.*

Anam na h-Alba The Soul of Scotland Fettercairn 1995 bourbon cask, dist Jan 95, bott Feb 15 (86.5) **n21 t23 f21 b21.5**. Not normally a malt which impresses. But here you can only enjoy – and, to a degree, admire – the crisp juiciness of the barley sugar as well as the normal nuttiness. Have to say it: an enjoyable Fettercairn. *58.3%. 250 bottles.*

❖ **Best Dram Fettercairn 9 Years Old** (82) **n20 t21.5 f20 b20.5**. Having a label like this is about the only way to get the words "Fettercairn" and "best dram" into the same sentence. That said, this cask is above the norm in terms of average quality for this distillery and there is plenty to enjoy from the nutty, sugary, if very hot, maltiness. *55.9%*

❖ **Big Market Sonderabfüllung Nr. 11 Fettercairn 1997** bott 2014 (73.5) **n19 t17 f19 b18.5**. Sugary, nutty and hot. By Fettercairn standards, not bad. *58.5%*

❖ **C & S Dram Collection Fettercairn Aged 6 Years** hogshead, cask no. 1104, dist 31 Mar 09, bott 18 Jan 16 (87.5) **n21.5 t22.5 f21.5 b22** Guess what? A really enjoyable Fettercairn – I kid you not! No, it isn't April 1st. I know, because I just checked. But here we have this grim old distillery producing a deliciously malty number with the sugar clean and crisp and in keeping with the gristy theme. A little hot, maybe. But impressed! I mean, this really is Fettercairn, right...? *58.8%. sc.*

Gordon & MacPhail Connoisseurs Choice Fettercairn dist 1997, bott 2013 (83) **n21 t21.5 f19.5 b21**. Nutty, milky sweet (a little cloyingly at times, surprise, surprise...) and malty. A bit hot and a little oak bitterness at the death, as well as its usual house tang. That apart, perfectly drinkable. *46%. nc ncf. WB15/143*

❖ **Hepburn's Choice Fettercairn 6 Years Old** European oak quarter cask, dist 2008, bott 2015 (67.5) **n15 t18 f17 b17.5**. Nice try, lads. But typically rubbery Fettercairn like this is a whisky that needs hanging, drawing and quartering – not quarter casking... *46%. nc ncf sc. 93 bottles.*

❖ **Hepburn's Choice Fettercairn 6 Years Old** European oak quarter cask, dist 2008, bott 2015 (76.5) **n19 t19.5 f19 b19**. Chewy and rubbery but some base sugars offer a kind of synthetic cream you get in cheaper cakes. Some maltiness can be detected. *46%. nc ncf sc. 95 bottles.*

❖ **Hepburn's Choice Fettercairn 6 Years Old** European oak quarter cask, dist 2008, bott 2015 (77.5) **n20 t19.5 f19 b19**. Enjoys the odd tenable moment when the barley and oak combine comprehensively enough to see off the worst of the usual nutty-rubber tang. Still proudly maintains a stubborn grimness. *46%. nc ncf sc. 94 bottles.*

❖ **Hepburn's Choice Fettercairn 7 Years Old** red wine finished barrel, dist 2008, bott 2016 (69.5) **n18 t18 f17 b17.5**. Even if you use a top-notch cask, when the spirit starts off as poorly as this, you have no chance. After tasting a shockingly –one might even say suspiciously - good 6-y-o Fettercairn just a few moments ago, it is very much back to normal now... *46%. nc ncf sc. 383 bottles.*

❖ **Whiskybroker Fettercairn 9 Year Old** bourbon barrel, cask no. 107666, dist 20 Nov 06, bott 15 Feb 16 (85.5) **n21 t21 f22 b21.5**. Hot headed and slightly aggressive, it comes into its own when the high intensity malt and milky chocolate combine. Definitely an extra high quality ex-bourbon barrel at work here ensuring a very decent dram. *55.6%. sc.*

GLEN ALBYN
Highlands (Northern) 1846–1983. Diageo. Demolished.
Gordon & MacPhail Rare Vintage Glen Albyn 1976 (96) **n22.5** salty and nippy. And the theme thunders into an early Kentuckian drawl, with red liquorice and hickory prominent; **t24.5** I am shaking my head in disbelief. Not through disappointment, but wonder! How can something of this antiquity still fill your mouth with so much juice? The barley still offers a degree of grassiness, though this is camouflaged by the softest bourbon characters I have seen in a long time. The honeycomb is in molten form, as is the vanilla which appears to carry with it a fabulous blend of avocado pear and ulmo honey; **f24.5** a pathetic degree of oaky bitterness tries to interrupt, but it is swept aside by the residual and very complex sugars.

There remains some spicy activity and even some Kentuckian red liquorice and hickory, but that South American honey really does the business **b24.5** wow! My eyes nearly popped out of my head when I spotted this in my sample room. Glen Albyns come round as rarely as Scotsman winning Wimbledon. Well, almost. When I used to buy this (from Gordon and MacPhail in their early Connoisseur's Choice range, as it happens) when the distillery was still alive (just) I always found it an interesting if occasionally aggressive dram. This masterpiece, though, is something else entirely. And the delivery really does take us to places where only the truly great whiskies go... *43%*

GLENALLACHIE
Speyside, 1968. Chivas Brothers. Working.
Glenallachie 15 Years Old Distillery Edition db **(81) n**20 **t**21 **f**19 **b**19. Real battle between nature and nurture: an exceptional sherry butt has silk gloves and honied marzipan, while a hot-tempered bruiser lurks beneath. *58%*

⟫ **Endangered Drams Glenallachie 22 Year Old** bourbon hogshead, cask no. 5077, dist Sept 93, bott Oct 15 **(82) n**20 **t**20 **f**22 **b**20. Dear god...! It's not the dram which is endangered, but your taste buds! A fiery frolic from start to finish. One dimensional malt does its best to retain the barley on an even keel and, at the end, almost succeeds. *57.3%. sc.*

⟫ **Hepburn's Choice Glenallachie 7 Years** Old refill hogshead, dist 2008, bott 2016 **(65) n**16 **t**17 **f**16 **b**16. Just no in so many ways... *46%. nc ncf sc. 301 bottles.*

⟫ **Old Malt Cask Glenallachie Aged 24 Years** refill hogshead, cask no. 12307, dist Feb 92, bott Feb 16 **(85) n**21 **t**22 **f**20.5 **b**21.5. Pretty well built and chunky for a Glenallachie. The malt is fully buttressed by oak. Hot in part, though. *50%. nc ncf sc. 180 bottles.*

Provenance Glenallachie Over 9 Years sherry casks, cask no. 10404, dist Spring 05, bott Summer 14 **(73.5) n**18 **t**18 **f**19 **b**18.5. Malty, though astringent. Lacking any discernible charm or complexity. *46%. nc ncf sc.*

⟫ **The Warehouse Collection Glenallachie Aged 22 Years** bourbon hogshead, cask no. 5077, dist 09 Sept 93, bott 30 Oct 15 **(87.5) n**21.5 **t**23 **f**21.5 **b**21.5. Malty and juicy and even a few pears at work. Though thin in its typecast way, rather good for this distillery *57.3%. nc ncf. 244 bottles.*

GLENBURGIE
Speyside, 1810. Chivas Brothers. Working.
Glenburgie Aged 15 Years bott code L00/129 db **(84) n**22 **t**23 **f**19 **b**20. Doing so well until the spectacularly flat, bitter finish. Orangey citrus and liquorice had abounded. *46%*

⟫ **Five Lions Glenburgie Aged 20 Years** 2nd fill American bourbon hogshead, dist Jun 95, bott Nov 15 **(89) n**22 a busy, vaguely hickory-rich nip on the nose shows the oak has travelled a long way; **t**23.5 mmm! Beautifully clean, and fabulously ramped up with maple syrup and comfortably balancing the bigger tannins; **f**21.5 thins rapidly as the vanillas arrive; **b**22 solid and true throughout. *53.7%. nc ncf.*

Old Malt Cask Glenburgie 25 Years Old refill hogshead, cask no. 11218, dist Jun 98, bott Feb 15 **(86.5) n**21 **t**22.5 **f**21 **b**22. A competent, malty spirit in a less competent cask. That said, some exotic fruit manages to do the rounds. *46.9%. nc ncf sc. 223 bottles.*

⟫ **Old Particular Speyside Glenburgie 18 Years Old** refill butt, cask no. 10873, dist Jun 97, bott Aug 15 **(64) n**15 **t**17 **f**16 **b**16. Disappointing on so many levels. From the nose onwards, refuses to gel. *48.4%. nc ncf sc. 744 bottles.*

⟫ **That Boutique-y Whisky Company Glenburgie** batch 2 **(94.5) n**23.5 marries a winning freshness with a deeper, oak-stoked anchor. Salty, malty and teasing...; **t**24 sublime delivery: the mouth feel simply luxuriates in a rich malty bed, random spices popping around but the sugars emerging in a superb ulmo honey layering; **f**23 the ulmo continues, punctuated now by more urgent spice; **b**24 pretty much faultless, top grade blending malt: quite irresistible! *50.1%. 75 bottles.*

GLENCADAM
Highlands (Eastern), 1825. Angus Dundee. Working.
Glencadam Aged 10 Years db **(95) n**24 crystal clarity to the sharp, ultra fresh barley. Clean, uncluttered by excessive oak, the apparent lightness is deceptive; the intensity of the malt carries its own impressive weight and the citrus note compliments rather than thins. Enticing; **t**24 immediately zingy and eye-wateringly salivating with a fabulous layering of sweet barley. Equally delicate oak chimes in to ensure a lightly spiced balance and a degree of attitude; **f**23 longer than the early barley freshness would have you expecting, with soft oils ensuring an extended, tapering, malty edge to the gentle, clean oak; **b**24 sophisticated, sensual, salivating and seemingly serene, this malt is all about juicy barley and balance. Just

bristles with character and about as puckeringly elegant as single malt gets...and even thirst-quenching. My God: the guy who put this one together must be a genius, or something... 46%

Glencadam Aged 12 Years Portwood Finish db (89.5) n22.5 t22.5 f22 b22.5. After coming across a few disappointing Port finishes in recent weeks, just wonderful to experience one as you would hope and expect it to be. 46%

Glencadam Aged 14 Years Oloroso Sherry Cask Finish bott May 10 db (95) n24 t23.5 f24 b23.5. What a total treat. Restores one's faith in Oloroso whilst offering more than a glimpse of the most charming infusion of fruit imaginable. 46%

Glencadam Aged 15 Years db (90.5) n22.5 t23 f22 b23 The spices keep the taste buds on full alert but the richness and depth of the barley defies the years. Another exhibition of Glencadam's understated elegance. Some more genius malt creation... 46%

Glencadam Aged 17 Years Triple Cask Portwood Finish db (93.5) n23 that is one beguiling and sexy nose: so many layers of fruit and of varying intensity; the background is choc-a-bloc (almost literally) with vanilla and natural caramels in the shape of chocolate fudge; t24.5 is it the mouth feel which blows you away most? Or the way the lush, fruitcake notes take on an extra dimension – especially when the intense dark chocolate begins to form? One of the flavour profiles of the year...; f22 some dry, bitter powdery notes emphasise the wine casks, but the fruit-chocolate-alcohol mix really does underline the innate greatness and profound beauty of this whisky; b24 a 17-year-old whisky truffle. A superb late night or after dinner dram, where even the shadowy sulphur cannot spoil its genius. 46%. nc ncf. 1128 bottles.

⬦ **Glencadam Aged 19 Years Oloroso Sherry Cask Finish** db (84) n21.5 t22 f19.5 b21. Mainly, though not quite, free of sulphur so the whisky after 19 years gets a good chance to speak relatively ungagged, though somewhat muffled. 46%. nc ncf. 6,000 bottles.

Glencadam Aged 21 Years "The Exceptional" bott 2011 db (94) n23.5 t24 f23 b23.5. This distillery is emerging out of the shadows from its bad old Allied days as one of the great Scottish single malt distilleries. So good is some of their whisky, this "exceptional" bottling is almost becoming the norm. 46%. nc ncf.

⬦ **Glencadam Aged 25 Years** db (95) n25 some 1,600 of you will get the chance to discover exactly what the perfect nose looks like. Trying to describe it is like attempting to paint a picture of an orgasm. Impossible. But let's just say it carries on for a very long time, kind of peaking but not. And here, do you concentrate on the gooseberries or the lemon curd tart? The ulmo honey or the orange-blossom? The salt or the lightest white peppers...? I think I'm in love....; t24 more of the same. In fact, near identical on the delivery, except here malt - full of concentrated gristy sugar – really does seriously enter the equation; f22 this is an old Allied distillery. And for some reason many of their barrels had just a hint of bitterness to their finish. This does, but the sugars are so intact and stunningly presentable, the damage is negligible. Perhaps just enough to steer it off course from World Whisky of the Year...; b24 imagine the best-balanced team Mourinho ever produced for Chelsea. Well, it was never as good as this nose... 46%. nc ncf. 1,600 bottles.

Gordon & MacPhail Connoisseurs Choice Glencadam 1993 (96) n24 t24.5 f23.5 b24 One of the most dependable malts on the circuit: rare to come across a dud these days. This one is fabulous even by Glencadam's exceptionally high standards. World class whisky. 46%

Provenance Glencadam Over 10 Years refill hogshead, cask no. 10596, dist spring 04, bott autumn 14 (92) n23 t23 f22.5 b23.5 Glencadam is one of the little-known Highland gems and there is enough elegant nuances in the script for this to cordially entertain and quietly charm you before your evening meal. 46%. nc ncf sc.

GLENCRAIG

Speyside, 1958. Chivas Brothers. Silent.

Cadenhead's Single Malt Glencraig 31 Years Old (92) n22.5 light – hints of green apple and even a few feints getting into the act, which is odd, as you'd expect the whole to be a lot weightier. A unique nose from a one-off distillery...; t23.5 much heavier now, confirming the minor flaws detected on the nose. But still a beautifully delicate fruitiness working beautifully with the intense, biscuity malt; the sugars and light honeys bide their time before arriving – and make themselves count when they do; f23 still a few feints to be had. But so delightful are the sugary, gristy tones – and the developing lemon and butterscotch – you really don't mind. Indeed, you welcome them, as they provide the oils which ensure a finish much longer than you might ever have believed; b23 well done Cadenhead in coming up with one of the last surviving Glencraig casks on the planet. The feintiness shows why it was eventually done away with. But this is a malt with great distinction, too. 50.8%

GLENDRONACH

Highlands, 1826. The BenRiach Distillery Co. Working.

GlenDronach 8 Year Old The Hielan db **(82) n20 t22 f20 b20**. Intense malt. But doesn't quite feel as happy with the oil on show as it might. *46%*

The GlenDronach Aged 8 Years "Octarine" db **(86.5) n23.5 t23 f19 b21**. Juicy yet bitter: a bipolar malt offering two contrasting characters in one glass. *46%. nc ncf.*

The Glendronach 2003 11 Year Old pedro ximenez sherry puncheon, cask no. 3568, dist Jan 03, bott Nov 14 db **(94.5) n23** no notes to guide me, alas... looks like a PX butt at work here: the sugars, like the grape are crisp and tight, locking in both the vanilla and barley; **t24** yep, def PX!! Those sugars...only a vivid spice can punch its way though. The midground offers up chocolate and toffee...for about five minutes...then raisin fudge; **f24** total confirmation of PX...only now do we get the real picture, as the tightness loosens and the fruit begins to have some kind of a say. A little maple syrup and butterscotch tries to equal the spices; **b23.5** helped by a superb, entirely sulphur free butt, this malt is as clean as it rich as it is memorable as it is excellent. *53.3%. 625 bottles. The Whisky Shop exclusive.*

The GlenDronach 12 Years Old db **(92) n22** some pretty juicy grape in there; **t24** silky delivery with the grape teaming with the barley to produce the sharpest delivery and follow through you can imagine: exceptionally good weight with just enough oils to make full use of the delicate sweetness and the build towards spices and cocoa in the middle ground is a wonderful tease; **f22.5** dries and heads into bitter marmalade country; **b23.5** an astonishingly beautiful malt despite the fact that a rogue sherry butt has come in under the radar. But for that, this would have been a mega scorer: potentially an award-winner. Fault or no fault, seriously worth discovering this bottling of this too long undiscovered great distillery *43%*

The GlenDronach Aged 12 Years "Original" db **(86.5) n21 t22 f22 b21.5**. One of the more bizarre moments of the year: thought I'd got this one mixed up with a German malt whisky I had tasted earlier in the day. There is a light drying tobacco feel to this and the exact same corresponding delivery on the palate. That German version is distilled in a different type of still; this is made in probably the most classic stillhouse on mainland Scotland. Good, enjoyable whisky. But I see a long debate with distillery owner Billy Walker on the near horizon, though it was in Allied's hands when this was produced. *43%*

The GlenDronach Aged 12 Years db **(83) n20 t22.5 f20.5 b20**. Glendronach at 12 is a whisky which has long intrigued me...for the last three decades, in fact. Always felt Allied had problems dealing with it, though when it was right it was sumptuous. Here it is a distance from being right: odd tobacco notes creeping into the fray, though that rings a bell with this distillery as I'm sure the old "Original" showed a similar trait. A very decent malty middle but elsewhere it flounders somewhat. *43%. nc ncf.*

The GlenDronach Original Aged 12 Years Double Matured db **(88) n23 t21 f22 b22**. Vastly improved from the sulphur-tainted bottling of last year. In fact, their most enjoyable standard distillery bottling I've had for many years. But forget about the whisky: the blurb on the back is among the most interesting you are likely to find anywhere. And I quote: "Founder James Allardice called the original Glendronach, 'The Guid Glendronach'. But there's no need to imitate his marketing methods. The first converts to his malt were the 'ladies of the night' in Edinburgh's Canongate!" Fascinating. And as a professional whisky taster I am left wondering: did they swallow or spit... *40%*

GlenDronach 12 Year Old Sauternes db **(93.5) n23** the fruit, with an edgy, rounded sharpness – if that makes sense – is in tip-top condition. The malty background remains profound; **t24** the delivery of your dreams: a near perfect marriage between light grape and chunkier barley...with a wonderful vanilla-oak border to both: the result is salivating...; **f23** long, still deep with the fruit – marmalade – taking a bigger part in the play, despite the malty curtain coming down; **b23.5** despite the magnificently delicate fruit, it is the malt which wins on points. Superb! *46%*

The GlenDronach 14 Years Old Sauternes Finish db **(78.5) n18 t22 f19 b19.5**. That unique Sauternes three dimensional spiced fruit is there sure enough...and some awesome oils. But, with so much out of key bitterness around, not quite I had hoped for. *46%. nc ncf.*

The GlenDronach 14 Years Old Virgin Oak db **(87) n22.5 t22 f21 b21.5**. Charming, pretty, but perhaps lacking in passion... *46%. nc ncf.*

The GlenDronach 15 Years Old db **(77.5) n19 t18.5 f20 b20**. The really frustrating thing is, you can hear those amazingly brilliant sherry butts screaming to be heard in their purest voice. Those alone, and you could, like the 12-y-o, have a score cruising over the 95 mark. I can't wait for the next bottling. *46%*

The GlenDronach 15 Years Old db (83) n20 t22 f20 b21. Chocolate fudge and grape juice to start then tails off towards a slightly bitter, dry finish. 40%

The GlenDronach 15 Years Old Moscatel Finish db (84) n19 t22.5 f21.5 b21. Such is the intensity of the grape, its force of life, it makes a truly remarkable recovery from such a limited start. But it is hard to be yourself when shackled... 46%. nc ncf.

The GlenDronach 15 Years Old Tawny Port Finish db (84.5) n21 t22 f20.5 b21.5. Quite a tight fit for the most part. But when it does relax, especially a few beats after delivery, the clean fruit fairly drips onto the palate. 46%. nc ncf.

The GlenDronach Aged 15 Years "Revival" db (88.5) n22 t23 f21.5 b22. Unambiguously Scottish... A fantastically malty dram. 46%

The GlenDronach 18 Years Old db (96.5) n24 groaning under the weight of sublime, faultless sherry and peppers; t24 puckering enormity as the saltiness thumps home. Black forest Gateaux complete with cherries and blended with sherry trifle. The spices have to be tasted to be believed. The sugars range from Demerara to light molasses; f24 again the sugars are in perfect position to ramp up the sweetness, but the grape, vanilla and spices are the perfect foil; b24.5 the ultimate sherry cask whisky. Faultless and truly astounding! 46%. nc ncf.

The GlenDronach Aged 18 Years "Allardice" db (83.5) n19 t22 f21 b21.5. Huge fruit. But a long-running bitter edge to the toffee and raisin sits awkwardly on the palate. 46%

The GlenDronach Cask Strength batch 2 Oloroso & Pedro Ximenez sherry casks db (94) n23 t24.5 f23 b23.5. For those who like their sherried malts to take not a single prisoner. Immense, magnificent and quite unique in flavour profile. 55.2%. nc ncf.

⟨⟩ **GlenDronach 2002 11 Year Old** PX sherry puncheon, cask no. 2042, dist Jul 02, bott Nov 13 db (91) n23.5 although unquestionably grape at work, there is enough tannin around, probably in conjunction with the sugars, to offer an unexpected degree of bourbon-style notes; t23 salivating, clean, rich and a superb balance of malt and crisp sugars; f22 a little spice as those sugars crystallise further; b22.5 kept away from smoke and given a malt with sufficient identity to be an equal to the grape, PX can work well: it works well here...Oh, and 100% sulphur-free...!! 53.9%. sc. 660 bottles. Bottled for premiumcask.de.

⟨⟩ **The Glendronach 2003** Pedro Ximenez shery puncheon, cask no 4630, dist Aug 03, bott Nov 15 db (93.5) n23.5 buttery acacia honey; almost akin to corn oil at work; t23.5 the gorgeous malty sugars tenderly kiss the palate, a little custard softening the impact even further; f23 just a little "Allied" cask bitterness creeps in; b23.5 wow! What a way to start the day! Few will top this, I can assure you! 56.1%. sc. 375 bottles. Bottled for Sansibar Whisky.

GlenDronach Cask Strength Batch 3 db (90) n21.5 t23 f22.5 b23 After last year's Batch 2, I had laid a knife and fork out in my lab for this and tucked a napkin into my shirt. However, this proved just a little more bland, austere and sophisticated. 54.9%.

GlenDronach Cask Strength Batch 4 db (92.5) n23 the odd liquorice note; sweet chestnut and spice; t24 a fizzer! The malt comes at you on delivery in its thickest, most intense form; huge but controlled oak, too...more bourbon notes of liquorice and hickory. The molasses are inevitable as is the spice; the natural toffee-fudge softness is a surprise; f22 vanilla – and more toffee; b23 After the absorbing delivery, the complexity levels go down a bit. But still a belter! 54.7%

⟨⟩ **GlenDronach Cask Strength** batch 5 db (89.5) n22 gentle vanillas are straight and unerring; t23 salivating as the malt takes command on delivery; the middle is more intense malt with a Victoria sponge edge; f22 butterscotch tart with a pinch of spice; b22.5 a very safe malt which does everything to keep its shape intact. 55.3%

The GlenDronach Grandeur Aged 31 Years db (94.5) n23.5 dry, mildly peppery vanilla; crushed golden raisin counter-plot; t24 spice-dusted grapes explode on the palate on entry; the mouth-feel plays a key role as the early lushness carries the fruit only so far before it begins to break up, allowing a fabulous spicy complexity to develop; f23.5 beautiful intertwangling between those golden raisins and coffee. The spices are never far away...; b23.5 just one hell of an alpha sherry butt. 45.8%

GlenDronach Grandeur 24 Year Old Batch 5 db (93.5) n23 a busybody nose: fussing around the oak one moment, some traces of toasted malt the next....; t24 a lush delivery, as soft as you like. Thick, almost syrupy malt and then a constant pulse of spice which warms by the moment; f23 spiced butterscotch tart; and rather tart towards the finale, too...; b23.5 one to stand your spoon up in. Enormous whisky. 48.9%

⟨⟩ **GlenDronach Peated** db (93.5) n23.5 no prisoners taken here: this is one smoky dude...; t23.5 sublime clarity to the ulmo honey which underlines the malt despite the hefty smoke slowly making its presence felt; f23 good spice, confident peat still, but a little late bitterness creeps in; b23.5 I rarely mark the smoky whisky from a distillery which makes peat as an afterthought higher than its standard distillate. But here it is hard not to give massive marks. Only a failing cask at the very death docks a point or so... *46%*

⬦ **Classic Whisky & Lifestyle Glendronach 20 Year Old 1994** sherry cask **(86) n22 t22 f20.5 b21.5.** Top heavy with tannin, the sugars are in a losing battle with the proudly more bitter elements. *55%. 300 bottles.*

GLENDULLAN *(see also below)*
Speyside, 1972. Diageo. Working.

Glendullan Aged 8 Years db **(89) n20 t22 f24 b23.** This is just how I like my Speysiders: young fresh and uplifting. A truly charming malt. *40%*

Singleton of Glendullan 12 Years Old db **(87) n22 t22 f21 b22.** Much more age than is comfortable for a 12-y-o. *40%*

⬦ **The Singleton of Glendullan 38 Year Old** European oak casks, dist 1975 db **(94) n23.5** custard creams with a Garibaldi accompaniment; this nose really does take the biscuit....; **t24** lively delivery: gorgeous crushed sultana and golden syrup...; the malt, even half way through, shows some magically rich touches; **f22.5** spicy; a little tiredness has crept in to bitter effect; **b24** gather round and let me tell you a little story about the excellence of European oak casks before sulphur reared its ugly head. No, better still, take a glass of this and allow it to do it so much more eloquently... *59.8%. 3,756 bottles. Diageo Special Releases 2014.*

Singleton of Glendullan Liberty db **(73) n17 t19 f18 b19.** For showing such a really unforgiving off key bitter furriness, it should be clamped in irons... *40% WB16/036*

Singleton of Gendullan Trinity db **(92.5) n24** truly exceptional nose: Turkish Delight means things are looking rosy here while the weight is provided by a distant, indistinct smokiness which may be down to the molasses at play; **t23** not such a complex or cleverly weighted delivery, and even a little bitter oak gets in on the act. But there is no denying the intensity of those sugars again, nor their crispness. The way they melt into the barley is exceptional; **f22.5** the bitterness retains, but some fluttering spices help compensate; **b23** designed for airports, this complex little beauty deserves to fly off the shelves... *40% WB16/037*

⬦ **The Golden Cask Glendullan 18 Years Old** cask no. CM 220, dist 1999, bott 2015 **(87.5) n22 t23 f21 b21.5.** Celebrates the spiky oak which, at times, is driven like a stake through the taste buds. Early on, the barley does get the chance to show some honeyed turns during some complex moments. *59.8%. sc. 186 bottles.*

GLEN ELGIN
Speyside, 1900. Diageo. Working.

Glen Elgin Aged 12 Years db **(89) n23 t24 f20 b22.** Absolutely murders Cragganmore as Diageo's top dog bottled Speysider. The marks would be several points further north if one didn't get the feeling that some caramel was weaving a derogatory spell. Brilliant stuff nonetheless. States Pot Still on label – not to be confused with Irish Pot Still. This is 100% malt... and it shows! *43%*

⬦ **Maltbarn Glen Elgin 1995** ex-bourbon cask, bott 2015 **(96) n24.5** salty orange-blossom honey: along with the crisp barley and rich butterscotch, this is vivid, fresh and, frankly, stunning....; **t24** much heavier delivery: there is weight to the spirit itself, a slightly oily and thick cut. The orange-blossom honey translates perfectly, with a little buttery lemon curd tart for back up. My word, this is very good...; **f23** good age showing now. The weightiness has transferred from the texture to the actual intensity of the vanilla; dries towards vanilla with extraordinary finesse; **b24.5** such an old-fashioned experience. Some 30 years ago, many of the casks in Speyside boasted what is on offer here. Though seldom actually from the same barrel....This is quite brilliantly made and matured malt; if each one of Scotland's barrels were anything like this, the overall quality would be a good 30% higher than it actually is...Anyway, if you were ever to kiss your partner and swap whisky in mid-kiss, this is the dram to do it. Truly sensual and erotic stuff. *51.7%. sc. 116 bottles.*

⬦ **Old Malt Cask Glen Elgin Aged 25 Years** refill hogshead, cask no. 12155, dist Mar 90, bott Nov 15 **(94) n23** typical Glen Elgin depth and elegance: the malt is grassy but with a light hint of sharp orange blossom honey; vaguely milky; **t23.5** eye-watering, salivating. The barley is in overdrive and in concentrated form. **f23.5** a little weakness from an old cask shows its milky faults at the death. But the sheer class of the now ulmo honey repairs much of the damage; the continuous hum of the warming spice is a wonderful bonus; **b24** for a dram with some faults, the utter magnificence of the good bits ensures a gorgeous experience. *50%. nc ncf sc. 205 bottles.*

Scotch Malt Whisky Society Cask 85.30 Aged 15 Years refill hogshead, dist 6 Oct 99 (89.5) n23 a little essay in understated complexity: busy, slightly nutty oak offers the nippy, spicy counter to the lemon-drizzled barley; t22.5 more austere than the nose, but the sugars offer a little twinkle here and there; f22 dries, almost to an eye-watering degree. But this is good oak and the finale fits impressively; b22.5 a pretty standard, unremarkable cask as far as a Glen Elgin is concerned: which means it's bloody good stuff... 56.6%. sc. 321 bottles.

GLENESK
Highlands (Eastern), 1897–1985. Diageo. Demolished.
Duncan Taylor Collection Glenesk 1983 cask no. 4930 (89.5) n22 t23 f22 b22.5. By far the best Glen Esk I've tasted in years. Perhaps not the most complex, but the liveliness and clarity are a treat. 52.1%

GLENFARCLAS
Speyside, 1836. J&G Grant. Working.
Glenfarclas 8 Years Old db (86) n21 t22 f22 b21. Less intense sherry allows the youth of this malt to stand out. Mildly quirky as a Glenfarclas and enormous entertainment. 40%

Glenfarclas 10 Years Old db (80) n19 t20 f22 b19. Always an enjoyable malt, but for some reason this version never seems to fire on all cylinders. There is a vague honey sheen which works well with the barley, but struggles for balance and the nose is a bit sweaty. Still has distinctly impressive elements but an odd fish. 40%

Glenfarclas 12 Years Old db (94) n23.5 a wonderfully fresh mix of grape and mint; t24 light, youthful, playful, mouthwatering. Less plodding honey, more vibrant Demerara and juiced-up butterscotch; f23 long, with soft almost ice-cream style vanillas with a grapey topping; b23.5 a superb re-working of an always trustworthy malt. This dramatic change in shape works a treat and suits the malt perfectly. What a sensational success!! 43%

Glenfarclas 15 Years Old db (85.5) n21.5 t23 f20 b21. One thing is for certain: working with sherry butts these days is a bit like working with ACME dynamite....you are never sure when it is about to blow up in your face. There is only minimal sulphur here, but enough to take the edge off a normally magnificent whisky, at the death. Instead it is now merely, in part, quite lovely. The talent at Glenfarclas is unquestionably among the highest in the industry: I'll be surprised to see the same weaknesses with the next bottling. 46%

Glenfarclas 17 Years Old db (93) n23 just so light and playful: custard powder lightens and sweetens, sultana softens, barley moistens, spice threatens...; t23 the relaxed sherry influence really lets the honey deliver; delightfully roasty and well spiced towards the middle; f23 when I was a kid there was a candy – pretend tobacco, no less! – made from strands of coconut and sweetened with a Demerara syrup. My, this takes me back...; b24 an excellent age for this distillery, allowing just enough oak in to stir up the complexity. A stupendous addition to the range. 40%

Glenfarclas 18 Years Old db (84) n21 t22 f20 b21. Tight, nutty and full of crisp muscovado sugar. 43%. Travel Retail Exclusive.

Glenfarclas 21 Years Old db (83) n20 t23 f19 b21. A chorus of sweet, honied malt and mildly spiced, teasing fruit on the fabulous mouth arrival and middle compensates for the few blips. 43%

Glenfarclas 25 Years Old db (84) n20 t22 f20 b22. A curious old bat: by no means free from imperfect sherry but compensating with some staggering age – seemingly way beyond the 25-year statement. Enjoys the deportment of a doddering old classics master from a family of good means and breeding. 43%

Glenfarclas 30 Years Old db (85) n20 t22 f21 b22. Flawed yet juicy. 43%

Glenfarclas 40 Years Old db (94) n23 old Demerara rum laced with well aged oloroso. Spicy, deep though checked by vanilla; t23 toasty fruitcake with just the right degree of burnt raisin; again the spices are central to the plot though now a Jamaican Blue Mountain/Mysore medium roast mix makes an impressive entrance; f24 long, with the oak not just ticking every box, but doing so with a flourish. The Melton Hunt cake finale is divine... b24 couldn't help but laugh: this sample was sent by the guys at Glenfarclas after they spotted that I had last year called their disappointing 40-year-old a "freak". I think we have both proved a point... 46%

Glenfarclas 50 Years Old db (92) n24 Unique. Almost a marriage between 20-y-o bourbon and intense, old-fashioned sherry. Earthy, weighty stuff that repays time in the glass and oxidization because only then does the subtlety become apparent and a soft peat-reek reveal itself; t23 an unexpected sweet – even mouthwatering - arrival, again with a touch of peat to add counter ballast to the intense richness of the sherry. The oak is intense from the middle onwards, but of such high quality that it merely accompanies rather then dominates; **f22** warming black peppers ping around the palate; some lovely cocoa oils coat the mouth for a bitter-sweet, warming and very long finish; **b23** Most whiskies cannot survive such great age. This one really does bloom in the glass and the earthy, peaty aspect makes it all the more memorable. It has taken 50 years to reach this state. Give a glass of this at least an hour's inquisition, as I have. Your patience will be rewarded many times over. 44.4%

◇ **Glenfarclas 50 Years Old** III ex-Oloroso sherry casks db **(88.5) n23.5** just about every single note of tiring whisky can be found here, with the exception of eucalyptus... though another summer might have seen that one sprout up, too. Still offers brilliant and delicious complexity and such attractive and unusual combinations, such as Banbury cake and chocolate mousse, for instance...; **t21** here the degree of oak takes a tougher line and despite the big caramel incursion, is much less forgiving; **f22** settles slightly as the vanilla takes up a softer approach aided by the delicate Demarar sugars; **b22** you can actually hear it wheezing as it has run out of puff. But it is easy to recognise the mark of an old champion... 41.1%. ncf. *937 bottles.*

Glenfarclas 105 db **(95.5) n23.5** the youthful grape comes in clean, juicy bunches; the herbs and spices on a rack on the kitchen wall; **t24** any lovers of the old Jennings books will here do a Mr Wilkins explosive snort as the magnificent barley-grape mix is propelled with the force of dynamite into the taste buds; survivors of this experience still able to speak may mention something about cocoa notes forming; **f24** long, luxurious, with a pulsing vanilla-grape mix and a build up of spices; light oils intensify and elongate; **b24** I doubt if any restorative on the planet works quite as well as this one does. Or if any sherry cask whisky is so clean and full of the joys of Jerez. A classic malt which has upped a gear or two and has become exactly what it is: a whisky of pure brilliance... 60%

◇ **Glenfarclas £511.19s.0d Family Reserve** db **(88) n22.5** some salt has been sprinkled on the malt: slightly coastal; **t22.5** so salivating, though struggles to get away from its ultra-intense barley delivery; **f21** bitters out slightly; **b22** not the best, but this still ain't no two bob whisky, mister, and make no mistake... 43%

◇ **Glenfarclas 1966 Fino Cask** cask nos. 4194, 4195 & 4197 db **(96) n24** Glenfarclas's 1966 Cup Fino gets off to a cracking start with just as much liquorice as there is fruit: back in 1966 the main, everyday British candy were Fruit Salads and Black Jacks...so, so fitting...; **t24** runs entirely according to plan, with a grassy maltiness sliding effortlessly alongside the caramels and slinky grape; **f23.5** long, and after going into extra time, hits the bar. Finally, I think it's all over....; **b24.5** as it was exactly 50 years ago today – July 30th 1966 – that England won the World Cup, I thought it entirely fitting that I should taste this 50 year old bottling. No matter how well they fared, or even badly, none of the new whiskies I tasted this year could be any worse than the gutless, leaderless, shameful, embarrassing apology of a display England put up in the European Championships this summer. On my travels a very long time ago I once saw Alf Ramsey, manager of England on that day in 1966, on a railway platform. I had to get off – and wait an hour for another train to complete the journey - just so I could shake the great man by the hand and thank him for what he achieved. Likewise, in the course of my whisky life, I was fortunate enough to share a changing room in a TV studio with the great Kenneth Wolstenholme (who, like me, spent some of his life in Belmont, Surrey). And where, with great grace, and with only I as an audience, he gave the greatest soliloquy in English football history: "There are some people running on to the pitch: they think it's all over. (Beat) It is now...." 50.5%

Glenfarclas 2000 Vintage bott 2014 db **(76) n18.5 t22.5 f17 b18.** Surprisingly youthful in part. Wonderful early coffee and spice before the dull, bitter furriness kicks in... 43%.

Glenfarclas The Family Casks 1955 sherry butt, cask 2216 db **(95.5) n23.5 t24 f23 b24** a malt in its 60th year really has no right to survive. Remember, when the cask was filled, it wasn't designed to reach this kind of antiquity. T'was expected that this fellow would end up in a blend or possibly – though much more unlikely – as a single malt more than 50 years earlier...! So I will forgive the tiredness as the oak gains hold. It is natural and to be expected. Instead, I will savour those fruity depths on both nose and delivery and the beguiling development of the faint honey notes which guarantee and maintain the complexity to be found. This, after all these ridiculous years, is imperfect perfection... 45.4%. sc.

Glenfarclas The Family Casks 1956 sherry hogshead, cask 1767 db **(95.5) n24 t24 f23 b24** Age and logic defying Speyside whisky. Proves that great distillate in outstanding wood can comfortably withstand the test of time... 43.8%. sc.

Glenfarclas The Family Casks 1957 sherry hogshead, cask 2110 db **(96.5) n24 t24 f24 b24.5** I chose this as my 1,000th new dram for the Jim Murray's Whisky Bible 2016 as I was born in 1957 and there are very few casks of my vintage still untapped worldwide....and because Glenfarclas have some astonishingly super-quality malts in their warehouse. Well I struck lucky with this, as it ticks every single box that a great malt might, and there is not a single cross to be found. And to a very special person who should have enjoyed this celebration of a malt with me tonight, all I can say is: Mazel Tov .... *50.3%. sc.*

Glenfarclas The Family Casks 1958 sherry hogshead, cask 2061 db **(88) n22.5 t21.5 f22 b22** A substantially old whisky; in its really aged and imperfect way, it's all rather beautiful... *41.7%. sc.*

Glenfarclas The Family Casks 1959 sherry hogshead, cask 3226 db **(80) n22 t21.5 f17 b19.5**. Quite possibly the darkest uncoloured whisky I have ever encountered...and if I didn't know any better, from the evidence of the mammoth bitterness of the finish and the deep black colour, I'd say some iron had got into this somewhere along the line (a nail dropping into the cask, for instance, sometime in the last 56 years, that kind of thing) ...Maybe the best mixer for a Rusty Nail, ever! Despite this, the early fruit is monumental. *55.2%. sc.*

Glenfarclas The Family Casks 1961 sherry hogshead, cask 3056 db **(93) n23.5t24 f22.5 b23** Like all whiskies of this age, needs about 15 minutes to breathe and reveal its true self: drink direct after pouring and you will be missing the fun. Who buys this kind of malt? Well, I know some very rich Spurs supporters who would pour themselves a double of this any day... *46.7%. sc.*

Glenfarclas The Family Casks 1962 sherry hogshead, cask 3246 db **(94) n23.5 t24 f22.5 b24** The resin cuts into the whisky like a diamond drill. Remember always to give these whiskies a good ten minutes to breathe in the glass before tasting, otherwise the results can be a little tight and you get only a quarter of the picture. Most remarkable here is the closer aspect to an old bourbon whisky than an ancient sherry butt. *43.4%. sc.*

Glenfarclas The Family Casks 1963 sherry hogshead, cask 3541 db **(95.5) n24 t24 f23.5 b24** A malt which defies the years. This must have been matured in oak which today is almost impossible to find. Ensure when you've finished your glass you leave it beside your bed overnight. Should you wake in the early hours, remember to give it a sniff.... *474%. sc.*

Glenfarclas The Family Casks 1964 sherry butt, cask 4725 db **(84) n22 t22 f19 b21**. Grape and date abounds. But much too tight for its own good. Especially late on. *46.4%. sc.*

Glenfarclas The Family Casks 1965 sherry butt, cask 4512 db **(91) n23.5 t23.5 f22 b22** Three years ago or so, this might have been a whisky to die for. But for the ulmo honey it would be a spent force: there is no doubting it is a malt in descent. That said, some magnificent moments to fully savour... *51.8%. sc.*

Glenfarclas The Family Casks 1966 sherry butt, cask 4198 db **(96.5) n23.5 t25 f24 b24** When England beat West Germany 4-2 in 1966 to win the World Cup, the Scots were so delighted that they put much of their finest whisky in to their very best casks so, nearly 50 years on, we can all still celebrate that special day. It was a very fine gesture. Thank you. *50.6%. sc.*

Glenfarclas The Family Casks 1967 sherry butt, cask 6359 db **(96.5) n23.5 t24.5 f24 b24.5** Heavy duty on both fruit and oak front. And neither compromising balance or quality. Quite magnificent: almost the ultimate aged heavy sherry dram. *52%. sc.*

Glenfarclas The Family Casks 1969 refill sherry butt, cask 2458 db **(87.5) n20.5 t21 f24 b22**. Ultimately, a beautiful whisky which appears to have fallen between two stalls. Has hit that point where the oaks are having to be slightly over aggressive to see off the quiet dominance of the high class grape. The result is a rough passage as the palate is assaulted by marauding, OTT oak. And then a sublime follow through as harmony is achieved with the aid of subtler spice and mocha, which seems to be in complete accord with the molasses and dates. A challenging but rewarding experience. *56.2%. sc.*

Glenfarclas The Family Casks 1970 sherry hogshead, cask 2026 db **(78) n19 t22 f18 b19**. By no means the first thing I've encountered with a 1970 vintage that promised so much but, after flattering to deceive, was ultimately a heart-breaking let down. Looks great from a distance and is wonderful when first encountered on the palate. But on close inspection proves old, haggard and bitter with not a single trace of lingering sweetness. No amount of patience sees any improvement as time progresses, alas. *53%. sc.*

Glenfarclas The Family Casks 1974 refill sherry hogshead, cask 4077 db **(87) n22.5 t21 f22 b21.5**. When it comes to oaky brinkmanship, this can show others how it should be done. The odd moment of chewing pencils, but just enough sugar lasts the course for sufficient balance. Watch out at the death for some late chocolate cupcake. *43.9%. sc.*

Glenfarclas The Family Casks 1978 4th fill sherry hogshead, cask 746 db **(89.5) n22 t22.5 f22.5 b22.5** So oaky and old, the whisky has growth rings... *46.2%. sc.*

Glenfarclas The Family Casks 1980 refill sherry hogshead, cask 1411 db **(94.5) n23.5 t24 f23.5 b23.5** Some whiskies can show their age, yet be more sexy than ever before. You get the feeling this cask has peaked. *48%. sc.*

Glenfarclas The Family Casks 1983 refill sherry hogshead, cask 49 db **(73) n18 t20 f17 b18.** One assumes this was "refreshed" in a newer cask somewhere along the line. Anyway, sulphur has slipped in from somewhere. *53%. sc.*

Glenfarclas The Family Casks 1985 refill sherry hogshead, cask 2593 db **(96.5) n24 t24 f24 b24.5** One of the most supremely balanced Glenfarclases of all time. As beautifully mesmerising as it is memorable. If only all whisky was like this.... *49%. sc.*

Glenfarclas The Family Casks 1987 refill sherry butt, cask 1477 db **(69) n17 t19 f15 b18.** Big juicy grape. Bigger sulphur. *51.1%. sc.*

Glenfarclas The Family Casks 1988 refill sherry hogshead, cask 1993 db **(93.5) n24 t24 f22 b23.5** G is for juicy.... F is for fruity... *56.4%. sc.*

Glenfarclas The Family Casks 1992 4th fill sherry butt, cask 5850 db **(93) n23 t24 f22.5 b23.5** A dry giant of a dram. *50.9%. sc.*

Glenfarclas 1994 db **(95.5) n23.5 t24.5f23.5 b24** Very close in character and quality with to distillery's latest official 1994 release. Which means it's not far off God's gift to present day sherried malt whisky... *43%. 1200 bottles. The Whisky Shop exclusive.*

Glenfarclas The Family Casks 1994 4th fill sherry butt, cask 4319 db **(95) n24t24 f23.5 b24** Such understated elegance! *56%. sc.*

Glenfarclas The Family Casks 1995 sherry hogshead, cask 2283 db **(82.5) n21 t22 f19 b20.5.** The fruit appears to be thrown like paints on a canvas by a troubled artist. Not so troubled, though, as the tight, furry finish. *47.8%. sc.*

Glenfarclas The Family Casks 1996 sherry butt, cask 1493 db **(94) n23.5 t24 f23 b23.5** Almost exemplary sherry butt whiskying. *55.6%. sc.*

◇ **Glenfarclas The Family Casks 2000 Release W15** refill sherry butt, cask no. 4075 db **(94) n23.5** so busy: even some celery adds a spicy element to the three dimensional sugar and some playful fig and apricot; there is also a lovely aroma of barley...; **t24** and it is that barley which arrives first and in silos full...the fruit is apparent but very sluggish. My god, this is one satisfying mouthful...; **f23** spiced up barley; **b23.5** one of those malts which releases its manifold secrets at an absurdly slow pace. *58.5%. sc.*

◇ **Glenfarclas The Family Casks 2003** cask no. 1450, bott 2013 db **(87) n21.5 t22.5 f22 b21.** Not sulphured. So, Le Yay! But still just slightly oversaturated with rather course, unrefined grape to get the balance quite where we want it to be. *56.8%. Selected for Le Gus't.*

Cadenhead's Authentic Collection Glenfarclas Aged 25 Years bourbon cask, dist 1990 **(92) n21.5** such busy bourbon noises: the oak pulls all the strings and like a marionette tends to dance around a little ungainly; **t23** much better now: the oak-bestowed spices strike early to form a superb counter point to the mocha and Demerara sugars; **f24** long and mega complex: more mocha, a little Lubeck marzipan and a few late strands of hickory...almost showing as many bourbon traits as Scotch; **b23.5** just as how this light spirit allows sherry to have its merry way with it, so great American oak can shape this into something special, too... *52.6%*

◇ **Scotch Malt Whisky Society Cask 1.189 Aged 21 Years** refill hogshead, dist 24 Mar 93, bott 22 Jun 15 **(87) n22 t23 f21 b21.5.** No shortage of natural caramels. Excellent, full-blooded delivery that has plenty of spice in the mix. But a flattish, bitter finale. *54.3%. nc ncf sc. 245 bottles.*

◇ **Scotch Malt Whisky Society Cask 1.193 Aged 21 Years** refill hogshead, dist 23 Sept 93, bott 27 Jul 15 **(89.5) n22** the caramels drip from the oak; **t23** lively, salivating, rich malt. Simple in its butterscotch and spice follow through, but very effective; **f22** massive spices now, soothed by the caramels; **b22.5** similar to 1.189 but with better consistency. *53.4%. nc ncf sc. 196 bottles.*

GLENFIDDICH
Speyside, 1887. William Grant & Sons. Working.

Glenfiddich 12 Years Old db **(85.5) n21 t22 f21 b21.5.** A malt now showing a bit of zap and spark. Even displays a flicker of attractive muscovado sugars. Simple, untaxing and safe. *40%*

Glenfiddich 12 Years Old Toasted Oak Reserve db **(92.5) n22.5 t23.5 f22.5 b24.** Another bottling to confound the critics of Glenfiddich. This is as fine an essay in balance, charm and sophistication as you are likely to find in the whole of Speyside this year. Crack open a bottle... but only when you have a good hour to spend. *40%*

Glenfiddich Caoran Reserve Aged 12 Years db **(89) n22.5 t22 f21.5 b23.** Has fizzed up a little in the last year or so with some salivating charm from the barley and a touch of cocoa from the oak. A complex little number. *40%*

Glenfiddich Rich Oak Over 14 Years Old new American & new Spanish oak finish db **(90.5) n23 t22 f23.5 b22.** From the moment you nose this, there is absolutely no doubting its virgin oak background. It pulls towards bourbon, but never gets there. Apparently European oak is used, too. The result is something curiously hinting at Japanese, but without the crushing intensity. Delicious, thoughtful whisky and one to tick off on your journey of malt whisky discovery. Though a pity we don't see it at 46% and in full voluptuous nudity: you get the feeling that this would have been something really exceptional to conjure with. 40%.

Glenfiddich 15 Years Old db **(94.5) n23** such a deft intermingling of the softer fruits and bourbon notes...with barley in there to remind you of the distillery; **t23** intense and big yet all the time appearing delicate and light; the most apologetic spices help spotlight the barley sweetness and delicate fruits; **f24.5** just so long and complex; something of the old fashioned fruit salad candy about this but with a small degree of toffee just rounding off the edges; **b24** if an award were to be given for the most consistently beautiful dram in Scotland, this would win more often than not. This under-rated distillery has won more friends with this masterpiece than probably any other brand. 40%

Glenfiddich Aged 15 Years Cask Strength db **(85.5) n20 t23 f21 b21.5.** Improved upon the surprisingly bland bottlings of old, especially on the fabulously juicy delivery. Still off the pace due to an annoying toffee-ness towards the middle and at the death. 51%

Glenfiddich Distillery Edition 15 Years Old db **(93.5) n24.5 t24 f22 b23.** Had this exceptional whisky been able to maintain the pace through to the finish, this would have been a single malt of the year contender - at least. 51%. ncf

Glenfiddich Aged 15 Years Solera Reserve (see Glenfiddich 15 Years Old)

Glenfiddich 18 Years Old db **(95) n23.5** the smoke, which for long marked this aroma, appears to have vanished. But the usual suspects of blood orange and various other fruit appear to thrive in the lightly salted complexity; **t24.5** how long are you allowed to actually keep the whisky held on the palate before you damage your teeth? One to really close your eyes and study because here we have one of the most complex deliveries Speyside can conjour: the peat may have gone, but there is coal smoke around as the juicy barley embeds with big fat sultanas, plums, dates and grapes. Despite the distinct lack of oil, the mouthfeel is entirely yielding to present one of the softest and most complete essays on the palate you can imagine, especially when you take the bitter-sweet ratio and spice into balance; **f23** long, despite the miserly 40% offered, with plenty of banana-custard and a touch of pear; **b24** at the moment, the ace in the Glenfiddich pack. If this was bottled at 46%, unchilfiltered etc, I dread to think what the score might be... 40%

Glenfiddich Age Of Discovery Aged 19 Years Bourbon Cask Reserve db **(92) n23.5 t24 f22 b22.5.** For my money Glenfiddich turns from something quite workaday to a malt extraordinaire between the ages of 15 and 18. So, depending on the casks chosen, a year the other side of that golden age shouldn't make too much difference. The jury is still out on whether it was helped by being at 40%, which means the natural oils have been broken down somewhat, allowing the intensity and richness only an outside chance of fully forming. 40%

Glenfiddich Age Of Discovery Aged 19 Years Madeira Cask Finish db **(88.5) n22.5 t22.5 f21 b22.5.** Oddly enough, almost a breakfast malt: it is uncommonly soft and light yet carries a real jam and marmalade character. 40%

Glenfiddich 21 Years Old db **(86) n21 t23 f21 b21.** A much more uninhibited bottling with loads of fun as the mouth-watering barley comes rolling in. But still falls short on taking the hair-raisingly rich delivery forward and simply peters out. 40%

Glenfiddich 30 Years Old db **(93.5) n23** always expect sherry trifle with this: here is some sherry not to be trifled with... salty, too; **t23.5** the juiciest 30-y-o I can remember from this distillery for a while: both the grape and barley are contributing to the salivation factor...; the mid ground if filled with light cocoa, soft oils and a delicate hickory-demerara bourbon-style sweetness; **f23.5** here usually the malt ends all too briefly. Not this time: chunky grape carries on its chattering with the ever-increasing bourbon-honeycomb notes; a vague furry finale...; **b23.5** a 'Fiddich which has changed its spots. Much more voluptuous than of old and happy to mine a grapey seam while digging at the sweeter bourbon elements for all it is worth. Just one less than magnificent butt away from near perfection and a certain Bible Award... 40%

Glenfiddich Rare Collection 40 Years Old db **(86.5) n22.5 t23 f20 b21.** A quite different version to the last with the smoke having all but vanished, allowing the finish to show the full weight of its considerable age. The nose and delivery are superb, though. The barley sheen on arrival really deserves better support. 43.5%

Glenfiddich 50 Years Old db **(97) n25 t24 f24 b24** For the record, my actual words, after tasting my first significant mouthful, were: "fuck! This is brilliant." It was an ejaculation of genuine surprise, as any fly on the wall of my Tasting Room at 1:17am on Tuesday 4th August would testify. Because I have tasted many 50-year-old whiskies over the years, quite possibly as many as anyone currently drawing breath. For not only have I tasted those which have made it onto the whisky shelves, but, privately, or as a consultant, an untold number which didn't: the heroic but doomed oak-laden failures. This, however, is a quite different animal. We were on the cusp of going to press when this was released, so we hung back. William Grant blender David Stewart, whom I rank above all other blenders on this planet, has known me long and well enough to realise that the surrounding hype, with this being the most expensive whisky ever bottled at £10,000 a go or a sobering £360 a pour, would bounce off me like a pebble from a boulder. "Honestly, David," he told my chief researcher with a timorous insistence, "please tell Jim I really think this isn't too oaky." He offered almost an apology for bringing into the world this 50-year-old babe. Well, as usual David Stewart, doyen of the blending lab and Ayr United season ticket holders, was absolutely spot on. And, as is his want, he was rather understating his case. For the record, David, next time someone asks you how good this whisky is, just for once do away with the Ayeshire niceness installed by generations of very nice members of the Stewart family and tell them: "Actually, it's bloody brilliant if I say so myself! And I don't give a rat's bollocks what Murray thinks." 46.1%

Glenfiddich Cask Collection Select Cask db (78.5) n19 t22.5 f18 b19. Bourbon and wine casks may be married together...but they are on course for a messy divorce. The honeymoon on delivery is pretty rich and exotic. But it is all too short-lived as things soon turn pretty bitter. 40% WB16/041

Glenfiddich Cask Collection Reserve Cask db (83) n20 t22 f20 b21. Soft, chewy, occasionally sparkling but the overdose of toffee and a disappointing degree of late furriness means its speech is distinctly limited in its topic. 40% WB16/040

Glenfiddich Malt Master's Edition double matured in oak and sherry butts db (84) n21 t22 f20 b21. I would have preferred to have seen this double matured in bourbon barrels and bourbon barrels... The sherry has done this no great favours. 43%

Glenfiddich Millennium Vintage dist 2000, bott 2012 db (83.5) n21.5 t22 f20 b20. Short and not very sweet. Good juicy delivery though, reminiscent of the much missed original old bottling. 40%

GLEN GARIOCH

Highlands (Eastern), 1798. Morrison Bowmore. Working.

Glen Garioch 8 Years Old db (85.5) n21 t22 f21 b21.5. A soft, gummy, malt – not something one would often write about a dram of this or any age from Geary! However, this may have something to do with the copious toffee which swamps the light fruits which try to emerge. 40%

Glen Garioch 10 Years Old db (80) n19 t22 f19 b20. Chunky and charming, this is a malt that once would have ripped your tonsils out. Much more sedate and even a touch of honey to the rich body. Toffeed at the finish. 40%

Glen Garioch 12 Years Old db (88.5) n22 t23 f21.5 b22. A significant improvement on the complexity front. The return of the smoke after a while away was a surprise and treat. 43%

Glen Garioch 12 Years Old db (88) n22.5 t22.5 f21.5 b22. Sticks, broadly, to the winning course of the original 43% version, though here there is a fraction more toffee at the expense of the smoke. 48%. ncf.

Glen Garioch 15 Years Old db (86.5) n20.5 t22 f22 b22. In the a bottling I sampled last year the peat definitely vanished. Now it's back again, though in tiny, if entertaining, amounts. 43%

Glen Garioch 21 Years Old db (91) n21 a few wood shavings interrupt the toasty barley; t23 really good bitter-sweet balance with honeycomb and butterscotch leading the line; pretty juicy, busy stuff; f24 dries as it should with some vague spices adding to the vanilla and hickory; b23 an entirely re-worked, now smokeless, malt that has little in common with its predecessors. Quite lovely, though. 43%

Glen Garioch 1797 Founders Reserve db (87.5) n21 t22 f22.5 b22. Impressively fruity and chewy: some serious flavour profiles in there. 48%

Glen Garioch 1958 db (90) n24 t21 f23 b22. The distillery in its old smoky clothes: and quite splendid it looks! 43%. 328 bottles.

Glen Garioch 1995 db (86) n21 t22 f21.5 b21.5. Typically noisy on the palate, even though the malty core is quite thin. Some big natural caramels, though. 55.3%. ncf.

Glen Garioch 1997 db (89) n22 unusually salty, dry and subtle; t22.5 just a few semi-gristy sugars make a minor noise while the barley appears in intense bursts but happy to duck behind the oak; some early barley wine oils early on; f22 a charming fade of caramelised barley; b22.5 had you tasted this malt as a 15-year-old back in 1997, you would have tasted something far removed from this, with a peaty bite ripping into the palate. To say this malt has evolved is an understatement. 56.5%. Whisky Shop Exclusive. 204 bottles.

Glen Garioch 1997 db **(89.5) n22 t23 f22 b22.5**. I have to say: I have long been a bit of a voice in the wilderness among whisky professionals as to regards this distillery. This not so subtly muscled malt does my case no harm whatsoever. 56.7%. ncf.

Glen Garioch 1998 db **(89.5) n21** ok, not exactly the perfect nose but, the slight taint apart, the depth of the dates is pretty startling; **t23.5** a thick, three-course malt which needs a knife and fork to get through. An astonishing mix of date and grape yet still with a malty background to ensure a honeyed sweetness keeps out any unwelcome guests; **f22.5** yes, some spoiling sulphur, certainly. But, again, we have the date-malt combo sticking to the ulmo-manuka honey blend and lasting a ridiculous amount of time...; **b23** with dates this good, a chocolate-loving, non-Islamic Tuareg will adore this one...one of the best flawed whiskies I have tasted in a while... 48% WB16/039

Glen Garioch 1999 db **(64) n16 t17 f15 b16**. Massively sulphured. 56.3%. ncf.

Glen Garioch The Renaissance Aged 15 Years db **(79) n19 t23 f18 b19**. Oh...so close to absolute brilliance, this one. Certainly one of the top ten most complex whiskies this year and you need your taste buds turned up to maximum alertness to be able to tackle the depth and myriad intricacies of this malt. However, I suspect the casks plucked from the warehouse for bottling didn't match those in the blending lab: the nose and finish reveal a furry, bitter off note which does the damage. 51.9% WB16/038

Glen Garioch Sherry Cask Matured Oloroso sherry casks, batch no. 30, dist 1999, bott 2013 db **(79) n19 t23 f18 b19**. The usual sherry problems arise. Which is enough to make you weep, because for a few glorious seconds on delivery (about the third to the fifth taste beats in) the impact and beauty of the oloroso matches anything experienced in Scotland this year. But the s-word wins, as it so often does, in the end. 56.3%. ncf. WB15/157

Glen Garioch Virgin Oak db **(93) n22** a salty, unsmoked bacon feel to this with quietly controlled tannins and hickory; **t23.5** a series of complex sugar notes are first to arrive. Then come in second, third and fourth, the complexity levels rising by the second; grated coconut and Brazilian biscuit works well with the maple syrup; **f24** now the complexity peaks with modest spices cranking up the vanilla and countering the light layer of ulmo and manuka honey blend; **b23.5** Glen Garioch as probably never seen before and at its most beautifully complex. 48%

⬥ **Acla Selection Glen Garioch 21 Years Old** bourbon hogshead, dist 1992, bott 2013 **(86.5) n22.5 t20.5 f22 b21.5**. Retains a firewater house style which was not so prevalent in 1992 than it had been in previous years. The light muscovado and spiced smoke does give it a certain attractiveness, though it always speaks harshly. 52.8%. nc ncf.

⬥ **Acla Selection Glen Garioch 23 Years Old** bourbon hogshead, dist 1990, bott 2013 **(85) n21.5 t21 f21.5 b21**. The attractive smoky butterscotch does little to disguise the overly aggressive nature of this malt. 49.7%. nc ncf.

⬥ **Gleann Mór Glen Garioch 1986** db **(92.5) n23** thick and clotted: plenty of vanilla and bigger tannin making a noise; some lovely apple, too; **t24** again, gentle fruits like apples and pears make for a juicy delivery with gristy malt in its train; the malt is precise and intense; **f22.5** bitters to a degree as the butterscotch tart sets its sight; **b23** easily one of the most complex Geerys I have tasted for a long while. 49.2%. sc.

The Last Drop Glen Garioch 47 Year Old hogshead, cask no. 662 dist 23 Mar 67 **(96) n24 t23.5 f24 b24.5** When this distillery produced the whisky in the bottle before me it was making probably the smokiest malt on mainland Scotland. Which is just as well for this grizzled old greybeard. Because things preserve rather well in peat – and this Glen Garioch is no exception. Just a standard low- or non-peated malt would have vanished behind the layers of tannins which have formed a crust around some of the lighter components of the dram. But here the smoke softens the oaky blows until they become only caresses. It is a quite extraordinary - and in many ways lucky – experience. 45.4%.

⬥ **Maltbarn Glen Garioch 1993** ex-bourbon cask, bott 2015 **(85.5) n21 t22.5 f21 b21**. So many good aspects to this: not least the crisp barley sugar. But just a little of a stray lactic note from the cask takes the edge off its sparkle. 52.5%. sc. 142 bottles.

Master of Malt Single Cask Glen Garioch 20 Year Old **(87.5) n21 t23 f21.5 b22**. Magnificent delivery of concentrated barley. A minor niggle prevents development. But for those into intense malt...you'll be pouring a second glass! 58.8%. sc.

⬥ **Old Particular Highland Glen Garioch 20 Years Old** refill hogshead, dist Sept 95, bott Feb 16 **(76) n19 t20 f18 b19**. A huge injection of sugars isn't quite enough to overcome the off-key cask. 51.5%. nc ncf sc. 234 bottles.

⬥ **Sansibar Whisky Glen Garioch Aged 23 Years 1991** bott 2014 **(94.5) n23** toasty and dry but also something of the early morning baker's when the treacle tarts are in the oven...; **t24** massive. No, beyond massive! The sugars are climbing all over each other to reach the highest point. The spices positively throb with a tannin charge as the mid-ground liquorice and mocha digs deep; **f23.5** long, helped by just the faintest malty oil. But those toasty sugars now move towards a more cocoa-rich signature; **b24** presumably the cask was re-toasted because the sugars of the oak are phenomenal. Superb. *51.7%. sc. 288 bottles.*

⬦ **The Single Cask Glen Garioch Aged 19 Years** cask no. 145, dist 19 Sept 95, bott 03 Oct 14 **(87) n21.5 t21.5 f22.5 b21.5.** Blenders used to look upon this malt with a degree of trepidation: it had the reputation as one of the most fiery malts in Scotland. It has been calmed down in recent decades. But here we get a little insight into how I first found the whisky three decades ago – though then it was smoky. Now it concentrates on an intense maltiness. At times juicy and some attractive vanilla, too. *62.7%. nc ncf sc.*

⬦ **World of Orchids Glen Garioch 1991 22 Year Old** bourbon cask, cask no. 7936 **(84) n22 t23 f18.5 b20.5.** Huge, fat juicy grape, spice....and even the odd phenol or two. But a little furriness on the finish. *53.2%. sc. 204 bottles.*

GLENGLASSAUGH
Speyside, 1875. The BenRiach Distillery Co. Working.

Glenglassaugh 21 Year Old db **(94) n23.5** elegant and adroit, the lightness of touch between the citrus and barley is nigh on mesmeric: conflicting messages of age in that it appears younger and yet you feel something has to be this kind of vintage to hit this degree of aloofness. Delicate and charming...; **t24.5** again we have all kinds of messages on delivery: the spices fizz around announcing oaky intentions and then the barley sooths and sweetens even with a degree of youthful juiciness. The tastebuds are never more than caressed, the sugar-sweetened citrus ensuring neither the barley or oak form any kind of advantage; impeccably weighted, a near perfect treat for the palate; **f22.5** white chocolate and vanilla lead the way as the oak begins to offer a degree of comparative austerity; **b23.5** a malt which simply sings on the palate and a fabulous benchmark for the new owners to try to achieve in 2030...!! *46%*

Glenglassaugh 26 Years Old db **(78.5) n19 t21.5 f18.5 b19.5.** Industrial amounts of cream toffee here. Also some odd and off key fruit notes winging in from somewhere. Not quite the gem I had hoped for. *46%*

Glenglassaugh 1986 28 Years Old Batch 1 hogshead, cask no. 2101, dist 19 Feb 86, db **(93) n23.5 t24 f22.5 b23** A spotless cask which has more grey hairs than you might expect for its age. Superb, though. *43.7%. sc.*

Glenglassaugh Master Distillers' Selection Aged 28 Years dist 1983 db **(93) n23 t24 f22.5 b23.5** knowing Norway as I do, glad to see these lovely people are getting their money's worth! *49.8%. nc ncf sc. Norway exclusive. 400 bottles.*

Glenglassaugh 30 Year Old db **(89) n23 t23 f21 b22.** Sheer poetry. Or not... *43.1%*

Glenglassaugh 30 Year Old db **(87) n22.5 t23 f20 b21.5.** A gentle perambulation around soft fruitcake. Moist and nutty it still has a major job on its hands overcoming the enormity of the oak. The buzzing spices underline the oak involvement. Meek, charming though a touch furry on the finish. *44.8%.*

Glenglassaugh Rare Casks Aged Over 30 Years db **(86) n22 t21 f21.5 b21.5.** Nearly four decades in an oak cask has resulted in a huge eruption of caramels. Soft oils and citrus abounds but it is the oak which dominates. *43%. nc ncf sc. Actual age 36 years. 280 bottles.*

Glenglassaugh 1963 51 Years Old cask no. 3301 db **(88) n23.5 t22.5 f20 b22** A shame this wasn't bottled a few years back: there are some magnificent phases here. The nose and delivery possess their own morbid beauty and the battle of the fruity sugars against the passage of time is of heroic status. The final moments, though, are a little painful. *41.7%*

Glenglassaugh 1978 35 Years Old Batch 1 sherry hogshead, cask no. 1803, dist 06 Oct 78 db **(95.5) n23.5 t24 f24 b24** Truly exceptional. *41.6%. sc.*

Glenglassaugh 1978 35 Years Old Batch 1 port hogshead, cask no. 1810, dist 06 Oct 78 db **(93) n23 t23.5 f23 b23.5** One of those quiet, unassuming chaps who takes about half an hour to fully fathom. Worth the effort, though. *42.9%. sc.*

Glenglassaugh 1975 35 Years Old Batch 1 Oloroso sherry hogshead, cask no. 7301, dist 03 Sep 75 db **(94.5) n23.5 t23.5 f23.5 b24** A classy, understated little malt, one that does all it can to pass under the radar,. Sorry – but you've been outed! Also, at its best after being allowed to breathe in glass for a good half hour. *40.7%. sc.*

Glenglassaugh 1975 38 Years Old Batch 1 Moscatel hogshead, cask no. 7801, dist 18 Jun 75, db **(89) n21.5 t21.5 f22.5 b22.5** A more voluptuous, expansive version of cask 7301. But in being so, has somewhere lost its finesse and complexity down the line. Oh, not the similarity of the cask numbers: probably from being tucked away in an inaccessible part of an old warehouse... *42.4%. sc.*

Glenglassaugh 40 Year Old db **(87.5) n21.5 t23.5 f21 b21.5.** Not entirely sure what it is with this one. I wasn't too happy about my 40th birthday, I remember, and this appears to have had the same mind-set. Hasn't quite extracted some of the better qualities of the oak, so never entirely gets its game together. A few flashy clothes (mainly in the form of a brief outbreak of stunning exotic fruit) and bling. But, underneath, for all its occasionally exotic patter a bit of a dullard, really. And then, maybe late of an evening, when less analytical, I see this in a slightly different light and home in on its good points, jettisoning the bad – then it is worth half a dozen points more. Entirely a mood and/or moment thing. *42.5%.*

Glenglassaugh 1973 40 Years Old Batch 1 Manzanilla sherry puncheon, cask no. 6801, dist 05 Dec 73 db **(74) n22 t20 f15 b17.** A particularly lingering and unwanted drying note has gone traipsing over what looks like fabulous sherry. Some lovely fleeting moments, but will be tarnished for some. I was caught off guard on this one due to the overt richness of the nose. *52.1%. sc.*

Glenglassaugh 1972 41 Years Old Batch 1 refill sherry butt, cask no. 2114, dist 25 Oct 72 db **(87.5) n23 t23 f20 b21.5.** The nose has the malt's age tattooed in oak across it. But there is big grape with no intention of yielding on delivery and for a while is an essay on style. Sad, then, that it should bitter out on the finish with no less single mindedness. *50.6%. sc.*

Glenglassaugh Aged 43 Years db **(91) n23.5** a nose of rare clarity for its age. Or it is once it has been in the glass for a good 15 minutes. Then the wrinkles vanish and we are left with a vibrant, juicy nose offering a sweetness that runs the full gamut from fruit to biscuit... Not surprisingly there is a death by chocolate feel to this one, too. And even a little smoke; not entire free of the odd gremlin, but not too much damage done; **t24** you really don't spit this kind of whisky, however professional you are. Not sure if the silkworm has been bred yet that can produce something as silky as this guy. A few random spices here, a splash of walnut oil there; **f21** a slight Achilles heel: some weaknesses show as a mild bitterness leaks in. But I am not quibbling; **b22.5** another ridiculously magnificent malt from a distillery which should never have been closed in the first place... *48.7%. nc ncf.*

Glenglassaugh 45 Years Old 1968 Batch 1 sherry hogshead, cask no. 1601, dist 07 May 68 db **(96) n23.5 t23.5 f24.5 b24.5** It may be hanging on for grim death at times against the oak, but what emerges is something you'll remember forever. *44.3%. sc.*

Glenglassaugh 1973 Family Silver db **(95) n23 t24 f24 b24.** From first to last this whisky caresses and teases. It is old but shows no over-ageing. It offers what appears a malt veneer but is complexity itself. Brilliant. And now, sadly, almost impossible to find. Except, possibly, at the Mansefield Hotel, Elgin. *40%*

Glenglassaugh The Chosen Few 1978 db **(94) n24 t23 f23.5 b23.5** Hate to say it, and almost impossible to believe: but Mhairi McDonald has not seen off the years quite as well as Ronnie Routledge. Even so, still some looker! *46.5%.*

Glenglassaugh Evolution Ex-Tennessee Cask db **(87) n22 t22.5 f21 b21.5** A Bambi of a dram, youthfully stumbling around seeking balance with limited success. Interesting: the 10cl sample bottle here tells me only it is ex-Tennessee cask. I'd be willing to bet a wad of this is Dickel over Daniel any day. The giveaway is the fact that the punchier tannins are not in evidence – suggesting older maturation in the US. Nor is the residual oiliness which usually makes its mark. Having said all that, I'm sure someone will now tell me this is a JD cask! *57.2%.*

Glenglassaugh Evolution db **(85) n21 t22 f21 b21.** Cumbersome, oily and sweet, this youngster is still evolving. *50%.*

Glenglassaugh Madeira db **(93) n23.5** spices rarely come sexier: busy, pulsing and of varying tone and heat; mainly appear to be oak led, though the sultana concentrate makes its mark, also; **t23.5** thick grape dulls the expected spice kick; the sugars, at first beaming, are also quickly subdued, though of a lightly molassed style; supremely chewy, though, with just so sugar impact; **f22.5** a gorgeous creamy mocha with a tea spoon of molasses; a slightly muffled, furry finale; **b23.5** a deliciously rich but surprising malt in that the spices fanfared on the nose never quite arrive. Love it, warts and all. *44.8% nc ncf sc. 437 bottles.*

Glenglassaugh The Manager's Legacy No.1 Jim Cryle 1974 db **(90.5) n21.5 t23.5 f22.5 b23** Talk about blowing away the cobwebs! The nose trumpets all the hallmarks of a tired old malt in decline. What follows on the palate could not be more opposite. Don't you just love a surprise! *52.9%. nc ncf sc.*

Glenglassaugh Muscat Finish db **(94) n23 t23.5 f24 b23.5** You'd expect any Muscat finish to be over the top...and it is. Great to see a whisky named after a former Millwall hardman... wasn't it...? *44.1% nc ncf sc. 308 bottles.*

◇ **Glenglassaugh Octaves Classic** db **(91.5) n23** beautiful: like molten jammy dodger biscuits; **t23.5** pristine malt backed up by Demerara sugar and a light touch of ulmo honey; **f22** quietens as the vanillas begin to take control; **b23** very high quality malt with a clean, intense persona which makes the most of any sweetness going. *44%*

◇ **Glenglassaugh Octaves Peated** db **(93) n23.5** the phenols offer only the most subtle of anchors; **t23.5** fabulously crisp: Demerara sugars meet with much loftier, more fruity dark muscovado; again, the peat rumbles – though nothing like it might...; **f22.5** the oak at last gets a word in with a volley of caramels; **b23.5** because of the apparent extra degree of oil, this really is a treat. Quite splendid and scarily seductive malt. *44%*

Glenglassaugh Red Port db (85) n22 t22 f20 b21. Loads of homemade redcurrant jam on toast here. Excellent texture, good age but an off key finish. *50.2%. nc ncf sc.*

Glenglassaugh Revival new, refill and Oloroso sherry casks db (75) n19 t20 f17 b19. Rule number one: if you are going to spend a lot of money to rebuild a distillery and make great whisky, then ensure you put the spirit into excellent oak. Which is why it is best avoiding present day sherry butts at all costs as the chances of running into sulphur is high. There is some stonkingly good malt included in this bottling, and the fabulous chocolate raisin is there to see. But I look forward to seeing a bottling from 100% ex-bourbon. *46%. nc ncf.*

Glenglassaugh The Spirit Drink db (85) n20 t22 f21.5 b21.5. A pretty wide margin taken on the cut here, it seems, so there is plenty to chew over. Richly flavoured and a tad oily, as is to be expected, which helps the barley to assert itself in midstream. The usual new make chocolaty element at work here, too, late on. Just great to see this distillery back in harness after all these years. And a great idea to get the new spirit out to the public, something I have been encouraging distilleries to do since my beard was still blue. Look forward to seeing another version where a narrower cut has been made. *50%. 8,160 bottles*

Glenglassaugh The Spirit Drink Fledgling XB db (91) n22 t23.5 f22.5 b23. The barley arrives unblemished and makes a proud, juicy stand. A surprising degree of early natural caramel. Prefer this over the peat, to be honest, and augers well for the distillery's future. *50%*

Glenglassaugh The Spirit Drink Peated db (89.5) n22 t23 f22 b22.5. Enjoyable and doesn't appear close to its 50%abv. But it's not about the bite, for there is a welcome citrus freshness to this, helped along the way by a peatiness which is big but by no means out to be the only important voice. *50%*

Glenglassaugh The Spirit Drink That Blushes to Speak Its Name db (85) n22 t21.5 f21 **b21.** Not whisky, of course. New make matured for a few months in wine barrels. The result is a Rose-looking spirit. Actually takes me back to my early childhood – no, not the tasting of new make spirit. But the redcurrant aroma which does its best to calm the new make ruggedness. Tasty and fascinating, though the wine tries to minimalise the usual sweetness you find in malt spirit. *50%*

Glenglassaugh Torfa db (90) n23.5 not stinting on the phenols: the peat appears to have been shovelled into the furnace like a fireman feeding coals to the Flying Scotsman; **t22.5** crisp, sugary delivery with some meaningful smoke layering. Some Parma Violet candy nuzzles alongside the treacle-cocnut; **f22** good phenolic grist fade; **b22** appears happy and well suited in its new smoky incarnation. *50%.*

GLENGOYNE
Highlands (Southwest), 1833. Ian Macleod Distillers. Working.

Glengoyne 10 Years Old db (90) n22 beautifully clean despite coal-gas bite. The barley is almost in concentrate form with a marmalade sweetness adding richness; **t23** crisp, firm arrival with massive barley surge, seriously chewy and textbook bitter-sweet balance; but now some oils have tucked in to intensify and lengthen; **f22** incredibly long and refined for such a light malt. The oak, which made soft noises in the middle now intensifies, but harmonises with the intense barley; an added touch of coffee signals some extra oak in recent bottlings; **b23** proof that to create balance you do not have to have peat at work. The secret is the intensity of barley intertwangling with oak. Not a single negative note from first to last and now a touch of oil and coffee has upped the intensity further. *40%*

Glengoyne 12 Years Old db (91.5) n22.5 salty, sweet, lightly fruity; **t23** one of the softest deliveries on the market: the fruit, gristy sugars and malt combine to melt in the mouth: there is not a single hint of firmness; **f23** a graduation of spices and vanilla. Delicate and delightful...; **b23** the nose has a curiously intimate feel but the tasting experience is a wonderful surprise. *43%*

Glengoyne 12 Years Old Cask Strength db (79) n18 t22 f19 b20. Not quite the happiest Glengoyne I've ever come across with the better notes compromised. *57.2%. nc ncf.*

Glengoyne Aged 14 Years Limited Edition oloroso cask db (77) n19 t20 f19 b19. A vague sulphur taint. But rather underpowered anyway. *40%. nc. Marks & Spencer UK.*

Glengoyne 15 Years Old db (73.5) n18 t19 f18 b18.5. Some sub-standard, left-out-in-the-rain oak crept in from somewhere. Ouch. *40%. Travel Retail exclusive.*

Glengoyne 15 Years sherry casks db (81) n19 t20 f21 b21. Brain-numbingly dull and heavily toffeed in style. Just don't get what is trying to be created here. Some late spices remind me I'm awake, but still the perfect dram to have before bed – simply to send you to sleep. Or maybe I just need to see a Doctor... *43%. nc. Ian Macleod Distillers.*

Glengoyne 17 Years Old db **(86) n21 t23 f21 b21.** Some of the guys at Glengoyne think I'm nuts. They couldn't get their head around the 79 I gave it last time. And they will be shaking my neck not my hand when they see the score here...Vastly improved but there is an off sherry tang which points to a naughty butt or two somewhere. Elsewhere mouth-watering and at times fabulously intense. *43%*

Glengoyne 18 Years first-fill sherry casks db **(82) n22 t22 f18 b20.** Bunches of lush grape on nose and delivery, where there is no shortage of caramel. But things go downhill once the dreaded "s" word kicks in. *43%. nc. Ian Macleod Distillers.*

Glengoyne 21 Years Old db **(90) n21** closed and tight for the most part as Glengoyne sometimes has a tendency to be nose-wise, with the emphasis very much on coal gas; **t22** slow to start with a few barley heads popping up to be seen; then spices arrive with the oak for a slightly bourbony feel. Gentle butterscotch and honey add a mouth-watering edge to the drier oaks; **f24** a stupendous honey thread is cross-stitched through the developing oak to deliver near perfect poise and balance at finish; **b23** a vastly improved dram where the caramel has vanished and the tastebuds are constantly assailed and questioned. A malt which builds in pace and passion to delivery a final, wonderful coup-de-grace. Moments of being quite cerebral stuff. *43%*

Glengoyne 21 Years Old Sherry Edition db **(93) n22 t24 f23 b24.** The nose at first is not overly promising, but it settles at it warms and what follows on the palate is at times glorious. Few whiskies will match this for its bitter-sweet depth which is pure textbook. Glengoyne as few will have seen it before. *43%*

Glengoyne 25 Year Old db **(95.5) n24** an old-fashioned, sopping-with-oloroso nose, resplendent in orange peel and molasses; **t24.5** voluptuous and curvy in all the right places, hard not to be turned on by a delivery like this. Being pedantic, the sherry is slightly OTT and two decades ago I would have marked this down as being a little too gushing in grape. But such is the rarity of finding un-ruined sherry butts at work, one is easily tempted to turn a blind eye and just enjoy this soaking-moist fruitcake moment; **f22.5** slightly bitter as the ancient tannins begin to dig in; **b23.5** a beautiful sherry-matured malt from the pre-cock up sulphur days. Not a single off note of note and a reminder of what a sherry cask malt meant to those of us who were involved in whisky a quarter of a century ago... *48% WB16/042*

Glengoyne 40 Years Old db **(83) n23 t21 f19 b20.** Thick fruit intermittently pads around the nose and palate but the oak is pretty colossal. Apparent attempts to reinvigorate it appear to have backfired. *45.9%*

Glengoyne Burnfoot db **(84) n21 t21 f21.5 b21.** A clodhopping bruiser of a malt. Good honey, though. *40%. Duty Free Market.*

Glengoyne Cask Strength batch no. 002 db **(85.5) n20 t23.5 f20.5 b21.5.** Perhaps only the single slightly off-key cask has found its way into this. But it plays out far better on the palate than it does the nose, though you get the feeling that there is a grinding in the gears as it tries to run through its set-pieces. Love the lilting richness of the delivery, though, with its honey concentrate and bubbling, jammy fruit. A spicy chap, too. So close to a classic. *58.9%. nc. WB15/119*

Glengoyne Cask Strength batch 003 db **(81) n19 t20 f20 b20.** Dull, disjointed, a tad furry and bitter. Though at cask strength, refuses to fire on all cylinders. *58.2%*

Glengoyne 'Glen Guin' 16 Year Old Shiraz Finish db **(79) n18.5 t20 f19.5 b20.** Some oily depth here. *48%*

Glengoyne Port Cask Finish 1996 db **(74) n17 t20 f18.5 b18.5.** Decent fruit on delivery, but elsewhere proof that in whisky there is no such thing as any port cask in a storm... *46%*

Glengoyne Teapot Dram db **(86.5) n23 t22 f20.5 b21.** The nose, for its obvious fault, still has a truly classic oloroso-style depth. However, the light sulphur stain is not so easily covered up once tasted. A slightly cracked teapot, I'm afraid. *58.8%. nc ncf. Distillery exclusive.*

Glengoyne Vintage 1996 db **(70) n16 t18 f18 b18.** Creamy, but off key. *43%. nc ncf. USA.*

Glengoyne Vintage 1997 db **(68) n16 t18 f17 b17.** The "S" word strikes. And with a vengeance. *43%. nc ncf. German release.*

⬦ **Cadenhead's Wine Cask Glengoyne 19 Year Old** Chateau Lafitte barrel, dist 1996 **(81.5) n21.5 t21 f19 b20.** Exceptionally tight. The fruit is massive and the spices quite brilliant. But never quite comes together. *55%*

⬦ **Hepburn's Choice Glengoyne 7 Years Old** refill hogshead, dist 2007, bott 2014 **(83) n21 t21 f20 b21.** If you are looking for a jolly, juicy bottling, full of youthful fizz and fulsome malt, here you go. If complexity and the meaning of life is what you are after, then move along: there is nothing to see here. *46%. nc ncf sc. 478 bottles.*

⸜⸝ **Hunter Laing's Distiller's Art Glengoyne Aged 19 Years** refill hogshead, dist Nov 96, bott 2016 **(86) n21 t22.5 f21 b21.5.** The green nose is matched by the modest, thin finish. But there is much more to grapple with and enjoy on delivery which is oily, juicy and barley dominant. *48%. nc ncf sc. 82 bottles.*

Ian Macleod Glengoyne 25 Years Old db **(94.5) n23 t24 f23.5 b24** By far and away the best Glengoyne sherry butts I have come across for a very long time. One worth tracking down. *48%.*

Old Particular Highland Glengoyne 17 Years Old refill hogshead, cask no. 10697, dist Sept 97, bott Feb 15 **(86.5) n21 t22 f21.5 b22.** An unusual firmness to the barley for this distillery with a degree of hickory as the only clue to its age. *48.4%. nc ncf sc. 348 bottles.*

⸜⸝ **Old Particular Highland Glengoyne 28 Years Old** refill hogshead, dist Dec 96, bott Aug 15 **(89.5) n22** clean grassy barley with a slight must moment or two; **t22.5** crisp and stark, the spice and malt combination offers maximum salivation; **f22.5** thins quickly as the oak gets a foothold; a little cocoa but the malt continues unabated; **b22.5** apart from that crushed pip moment, hardly moves away from its malty, spicy path. Austere yet strangely enchanting. *48.4%. nc ncf sc. 306 bottles.*

Scotch Malt Whisky Society Cask 123.10 Aged 9 Years 1st fill barrel, dist 5 May 05 **(86.5) n22 t22 f21 b21.5.** The outline of this malt will take those of us long enough in the tooth back about quarter of century when Glengoyne made a fuss about being an unpeated malt – and that all their oak was ex-bourbon. An annoying bitterness creeps in though just to stifle the barley as it was getting into full flow. *57.6%. sc. 238 bottles.*

GLEN GRANT
Speyside, 1840. Campari. Working.

Glen Grant db **(87) n21.5 t23 f21 b21.5.** This is a collector's malt for the back label alone: truly one of the most bizarre I have ever seen. "James Grant, 'The Major'" it cheerfully chirrups, "was only 25 when he set about achieving his vision of a single malt with a clear colour. The unique flavour and appearance was due to the purifiers and the tall slender stills he designed and the decision to retain its natural colour..." Then underneath is written: "Farven Justeter Med Karamel/Mit Farbstoff"" Doh! Or, as they say in German: "Doh!" Need any more be said about the nonsense, the pure insanity, of adding colouring to whisky. *40%*

Glen Grant 5 Years Old db **(89) n22.5 t22 f21.5 b23.** Elegant malt which has noticeably grown in stature and complexity of late. *40%*

Glen Grant Aged 10 Years db **(96) n23.5** OK: let's take turns in counting the rungs on the barley ladder here....the usual crisp aroma, but softened by deft, if unspecific fruitiness (maybe the distant aroma of a very old orange and by no means unpleasant!), myriad vanilla and butterscotch notes can do without the toffee one; **t24** magnificent! A malty delivery which simultaneously melts in the mouth, yet offers granite-like barley that crashes into your teeth; the star, perhaps are the sugars which vary from caster, through golden syrup and pans out somewhere in the muscovado range – curiously honey-free, though; **f23.5** a tad tangy, though the caramel returns to turn out the lights after the butterscotch and marzipan say goodnight..; **b24** unquestionably the best official 10-y-o distillery bottling I have tasted from this distillery. Absolutely nails it! Oh, and had they bottled this at 46% abv and without the trimmings...my word! Might well have been a contender for Scotch of the Year. It won't be long before word finally gets around about just how bloody good this distillery is. *40%*

⸜⸝ **Glen Grant Aged 10 Years** db **(96) n24.5 t24 f23.5 b24** This is the new bottling purely for the UK market without, alas for a traditionalist like me, the famous, magnificent white label. The bottle design may not be a patch on the beautifully elegant one that had served the distillery with distinction for so long, but the malt effortlessly stands up to all scrutiny. The only difference between this and the original bottling available world-wide is a slight reduction in the work of the sugars, the muscovado ones in particular, and an upping in the green, grassy, sharper barley. Overall, this is a little drier yet slightly tarter, more reserved and stylish. My one and only regret is that it is not yet upped to 46% so the people of Britain could see a whisky, as I have so many times in the private and privileged enclave of my blending lab, as close to perfection as it comes... *40%*.

⸜⸝ **Glen Grant Aged 12 Years** db **(95) n23.5** a subtle nose: a little cream toffee, but a wonderful sleight of hand for a citrus slant as well as a totally unexpected hint of weak lavender; **t24** sharp malt, as though barley sugar candy has been melted down – with a bunch of grist stirred in for good measure; slightly more oils than expected; **f23.5** remains refreshing and determined to show the fresh barley is all its stunning dimensions; some very late mocha gives a nod to the oak; far more spices than the norm for a Gen Grant adding, with those oils, some welcome extra length; **b24** beautifully distilled, thoughtfully matured and deeply satisfying malt. *43%.*

⟨⟩ **Glen Grant Aged 12 Years Non Chill-Filtered** db **(91.5) n23** some lovely oils give the startling barley much extra; **t23** a much weightier cove than your average Glen Grant with the oils maximising the fruity qualities of the muscovado sugars which brood and enrich in equal measure; **f22.5** the tannins have much more to say than normal, perhaps also reflected by the above average spice. And there is also that persistent fruity note which even hints at the faintest degree of furriness. This is a rumbler: a very long finish indeed which just refuses to go quietly...or soon...; **b23** in so many ways speaks volumes about what non-filtration can do to one of the world's truly great distilleries... 48%. *Exclusive to travel retail.*

Glen Grant Aged 16 Years bott Mar 10 db **(91.5) n23 t23.5 f21.5 b22** Again the finish doesn't do justice to the earlier jousting on the nose and palate. The label talks about orchard fruits, and they are absolutely spot on. Apples are order of the day, but not sure about the ripe bit: they appear slightly green to me...and that suits the nature of the crisp malt. A gorgeous whisky I fully expect to see improve over coming batches: it's one that has potential to hit superstar status. 43%

⟨⟩ **Glen Grant Aged 18 Years Rare Edition** db **(97) n24.5** the hardest decision to make here: full marks or not. Actually, no: an even harder decision is trying to work out the leading forces behind this extraordinary nose. This is so in tune and well balanced it is impossible to nail exactly what leads and which follows. Instead, one is left mesmerised by the incredible brittleness of the barley, which seems to snap if you sniff slightly too hard; the sugars at once delicate and fruity yet with the crafted sharpness of a newly forged sword. And those tannins, somehow caught up in the overall firmness, the friability of it all. Has to be the essential Speyside nose...; **t24.5** oh, wow! When does barley arrive this beautifully manicured, not a malty molecule out of place? The sugars are as clipped as a 1940's English actor's annunciation, and probably more precise. From somewhere light oils ooze to the surface to ensure some velvet caresses the sword. The oak builds up some steam, but the tannins never once outpoint the sugars and by the mid-ground, when a little cocoa can be detected, honours are even...; so complex it was on about the fifth go I realised just what a vital role those big early spices play; **f23.5** the firmness here is so complete, that I have only tasted whisky like this in commercially bottled form in pure Irish Pot still and rye, though here without the same intensity of spice you find in either. That said, the spices teasingly impact all the same....; **b24.5** the most crystalline, technically sublime Speysider I have tasted in a very long time... I didn't expect to find a better distillery bottled Glen Grant than their superlative 10-year-old. I was wrong... 43%.

Glen Grant Distillery Edition Cask Strength Aged 20 Years cask no. 17165, dist 12 Feb 92, bott 14 Aug 12 db **(95.5) n23.5 t24 f23.5 b24.5** I can only assume that this was matured in a cask which once held a high phenol Islay. The underlying peat is as intriguing as it is delicious! Glen Grant as you may never have seen it before...and will definitely want to see again. 55.7%.

Glen Grant 40 Year Old db **(83.5) n22.5 t21 f20 b20.** Probably about ten summers too may. The nose threatens an oakfest, though there are enough peripheral sugars for balance and hope. Sadly, on the palate the cavalry never quite gets there. 40%.

Glen Grant Cellar Reserve 1992 bottled 2008 db **(94.5) n23 t24 f24 b23.5.** One of the great world distilleries being revealed to the us in its very finest colours. They tend to be natural, with no colourings added, therefore allowing the extraordinary kaleidoscope of subtle sweetnesses to be deployed and enjoyed to their fullest. I defy you not to be blown away by this one, especially when you realise there is not a single big base note to be heard... 46%. nc ncf.

Glen Grant 50 Year Old db **(96.5) n24** heavyweight malt: toasted hazelnut and fruit combine with ridiculous ease; the spryness of the spice is amazing; a few old black cherries bob around on the breeze; **t24** silky delivery with early oak signs, but these are little more than polite enquiries. Delicate molasses and black cherry combine to match the drier elements of the oak; half way through, a surprising blast of juicy malt pierces the darkness; **f24** like on delivery, the weight of the piece is extraordinary: near perfect, in fact. Just a slight hint of smoke for the first time and this sits well with the chocolate and cherry pie served up with cream on the finish. Naturally, a little treacle is mixed in for effect; **b24.5** I really don't know how G&M keep coming up with these golden oldies. The quality of the oak must have been pretty exceptional. Sexier than any 50-year-old has the right to be. For those celebrating their 50th birthday or wedding...well you'd only regret it if you missed out. 40%

Glen Grant 170th Anniversary db **(89) n23.5 t23.5 f20 b22.** The odd mildly sulphured cask has slipped through the net here to reduce what was shaping to be something magnificent. Still enjoyable, though. 46%

Glen Grant Five Decades bott 2013 db **(92) n24** the kind of aroma which leaves you transfixed: the trademark crisp, juicy barley is there in force, but the darker, deeper tones rumble with a spiced orange lead: sublimely complex; **t23.5** the delivery is full of the usual malty zest for life. There is a unique clarity to the barley of Glen Grant and here, on delivery and for a few a few moments after, this goes into overdrive. The mid ground is more muddled with tannin and burnt raisin making their presence felt; **f21.5** tangy marmalade; **b23** a nose and delivery of astonishing complexity. Hardly surprising the fade cannot keep up the pace. *46%*

Glen Grant The Major's Reserve bott Mar 10 db **(85.5) n21.5 t23 f20 b21.** Forget about the so-so nose and finish. This is one of those drams that demands you melt into your chair on delivery, such is the fresh beauty of the malt and stunning honeycomb threads which tie themselves around every taste bud. Pity about the ultra dry, caramel-rich finish, but apparently nearly all the sherry butts have now been used up at the distillery. Thank gawd for that. *40%*

⬥ **The Classic Cask Glen Grant 21 Year Old** European oak hogshead, cask no. 139, dist 1993, bott 2015 **(91) n23.5** there's a playful nose from my childhood: grassy with a hint of toffee apple and jam doughnuts – Epsom on Derby day; **t23.5** sassy and salivating on delivery in the great Glen Grant tradition: the malt really does sparkle and even offers a slightly salty edge. Though a slight weight and tang through the middle is confirmed when I notice this is from an old European oak; **f22** the sugars vanish to be replaced by a duller tang; **b22** not quite classic, but the nose and delivery are superb. *46% (92 proof). sc. 328 bottles.*

⬥ **Endangered Drams Glen Grant 20 Year Old** dist 1992, bott 2013 **(86.5) n22 t23 f20 b21.5.** Something of the newly baled straw about this. An outstanding pick up on delivery with a rich oiliness to the grist. But bitters slightly too alarmingly later. *55%. sc.*

⬥ **The Golden Cask Glen Grant 12 Years Old** cask no. CM 218, dist 2002, bott 2015 **(91) n24** anyone not entirely seduced by the interplay between the bourbon-style spiced tannin and molten acacia honey shouldn't be drinking whisky...; **t23.5** how many waves of honey?! Then juicy barley, then spice, then tannin crash into the taste buds. The nose in liquid form, but with far more energy; **f23** remnants of golden syrup laced with vanilla; dries in the manner of an older malt; **b23.5** from the sweet, sexy nose to the pulsing delivery, this malt exudes natural, naked beauty... *58.9%. sc. 213 bottles.*

Gordon & MacPhail Distillery Label Glen Grant 40 Year Old (83.5) n22.5 t21 f20 b20. Probably about ten summers too many. The nose threatens an oakfest, though there are enough peripheral sugars for balance and hope. Sadly, on the palate the cavalry never quite gets there. *40%*

Gordon & MacPhail Distillery Label Glen Grant 50 Year Old (96.5) n24 t24 f24 b24.5 I really don't know how G&M keep coming up with these golden oldies. The quality of the oak must have been pretty exceptional. Sexier than any 50-year-old has the right to be. For those celebrating their 50th birthday or wedding...well you'd only regret it if you missed out. *40%*

⬥ **Gordon & MacPhail Distillery Label Glen Grant 2005 (82) n20 t22 f20 b20.** Considering that Glen Grant and Gordon and MacPhail are almost inseparable, unusual to find they haven't quite got the balance right on this bottling. Too tangy by half. *43%*

⬥ **Gordon & MacPhail Glen Grant 65 Years Old** 1950 cask no. 2747 **(90) n22.5** when first poured: pure oak. Give it half an hour to oxidise and suddenly green apples have sprouted from somewhere..; **t22** a surprising sharpness on delivery battles the tannins, which half an hour ago had complete control of the situation; **f23** a fabulous chocolate and late smoke finale really makes the most of the growing dark sugars; **b22.5** by 'eck! This is an oldie: it's got grey whiskers, this has! Forests of intimidating oak greet you on the nose, warning you of the tannin attack to come on the palate. Timber....!!! It arrives with no holds barred but, thankfully, a legion of sugars and spices step up to the plate to try and calm matters. Ulmo honey begins the task, but proves inadequate. Treacle and spices are brought in as emergency and do a job. But it is containment, rather than balancing. So it gets a score of 85 (21-21-22-21). Then time in the glass works its magic and hey presto! Sugars and grasses galore to entertain and balance things out. Oh and a small matter of peat, as well... *63.5%. sc.*

⬥ **Gordon & MacPhail Rare Vintage Glen Grant 50 Year Old (89.5) n23** yes, the oak is way OTT. But the way it infiltrates that Melton Hunt cake...well you have to admire it...; **t22** a volley of splinters and toothpicks lead the way; the mouth feel though is luxuriant; **f22** lovely spice keeps the pulse racing...; **b22.5** shows a frightening degree of age. Yet, against the odds, hangs together as a delicious unit. *43%*

Gordon & MacPhail Glen Grant 1948 66 Year Old cask no. 1369 **(96) n24 t24 23.5 b24.5** When this was being made, my parents were getting married (they had me late!), Millwall were in the process of being relegated from the second tier under the auspices of manager Jack Cock and the Ealing classic, Whisky Galore, was being filmed on Barra. So what better whisky to choose as my 1,111 new dram for the 2015 Bible? Hearty congratulations to Gordon and MacPhail – and the extraordinary Glen Grant distillery, and those hardy, war-bitten souls who made this malt two generations ago – on somehow defying the odds and logic and, 66 years on, giving us a whisky experience which leaves you cooing with delight. My last little taste shall be to those lost men of Glen Grant distillery, 1948. I salute your memories, sirs, fittingly with your very own magnificent craftwork. *46.6%. sc.*

◇ **Gordon & MacPhail Rare Vintage Glen Grant 1948 (96) n24.5** yes, the oak is full on. But we are talking the old oak floorboards of my junior school in Belmont, Surrey, in my first days there in 1961 when much of the time was scrabbling around the ancient, wooden floor with plasticene and the vintage, long-skirted teacher Miss Scent (it had to be a sign!) casting kind eyes over me and forever encouraging with soothing Edwardian tones. A few forgiving vanillins soften the impact in a way the 1950 vintage above is unable to; please allow to oxidise for a good ten to fifteen minutes for all elements to soften, settle and integrate to astonishing effect, for even a degree of grapefruit enters the fray; very slowly the lightest possible smoke from the gentle peat and rum-like esters begins to rise...; **t23.5** brilliant! Deft sugars, seemingly a mix of muscovado and – surely not! But yes, grist!! - mix contentedly with the red liquorice and intense, dried out butterscotch tart. Even now, nearly 70 years on, oils and spice mix sublimely; still the vaguest peat rumbles reminding you of the Speyside style of yore; **f24** obviously, the tannins will return with a degree of vengeance. But the vanilla and light brown sugars combine to defuse the situation. As do the chocolate and mint which combined with understated deliciousness. So, instead, the fade is measured, if a little laboured, like an elegant old lady or gent hobbling heroically in their Sunday finest with the aid of a creaky, oaky walking frame towards the sunset... **b24** so, I bring down the curtain on another Jim Murray's Whisky Bible: this is the last of the 1,241 new whiskies I have analysed for the 2017 edition. When it began, where I wrote this was a part of Europe. Now it is destined to no longer be. But in the course of the maturing life of this malt the world has changed and changed again; in so many ways beyond recognition. The people who made this still had ration books following World War Two and are, most likely, no longer with us now. In the year this was distilled, filled into barrel and rolled into warehouse my parents were married. In the week I tasted this I placed my 95-year-old mother in an old people's home for the very first time. A poignant whisky, indeed. And I admit, without shame, that I write this with a tear in the eye. This is, indeed, the perfect whisky to reflect what this spirit represents so vividly and like no any other: the passing of time... 40%

◇ **Gordon & MacPhail Rare Vintage Glen Grant 1952 (96.5) n24** yes, the splinters arrive first. But they are docile and submissive the moment a light citrus and vanilla duet begins. And virtually vanish altogether when the Malteser chocolate turns up...; **t24** soft and inviting: like wide, tender and yielding lips. The taste buds are kissed and caressed over and over again by a gorgeous mix of ulmo honey and Horlicks, with the oak induced tannins ensuring a stiffening of the sensations at just the right time...; **f24** this is spicy stuff, though at first you don't quite notice because of the malty seduction of your palate. But the constant teasing, kissing and caressing leads, due to the spice, to an unexpectedly violent finish...which carries on and on and on before it softens and drifts away...; **b24.5** the 1952 vintage Glen Grant has always been one of the finest post war bottlings they have consistently bottled. I had expected the quality to dip. It hasn't. I can honestly tell you that there is very little that is better than tasting a 1952 vintage: it gets my vote every time... 40%

◇ **Gordon & MacPhail Rare Vintage Glen Grant 1953 (87.5) n20.5 t21.5 f23.5 b22.** For a while, the oak is in total control and allowing little but forests of tannin to make their play. But slowly the oaky sharpness throttles back and allows increasing amounts of vanilla-rich sugars to come through. Best of all, and the saviour of this malt, is the French-style praline which holds the mid ground before Manuka honey takes on the role of absorbing the oak. Some journey, this. 40%

◇ **Gordon & MacPhail Rare Vintage Glen Grant 1954 (89) n23** ye gods, this has aged! There are wrinkles on every aspect of this nose. But, somehow, the darkest of muscovado sugars do just enough to keep the massive tannins at bay; **t21.5** eye-wateringly tight with oak. But again those sugars work with colossal will to keep the balance. It is creaking and cracking but the integrity still holds...; **f22.5** much more relaxed vanilla as the tannins begin to yield; a little spiced treacle makes for a delightful fade; **b22** hangs on for dear life. But just about stays in the camp of excellence having nearly outstayed its welcome. 40%

◇ **Gordon & MacPhail Rare Vintage Glen Grant 1956 (95.5) n23** that's the trouble with reducing down to 40% at this age...every last splinter is there to be seen. Thankfully, some light kumquat is around to cover the barest bits...; **t23.5** silky soft delivery with the malt still intact after all this time: remarkable. Oak far less intrusive than on the nose, thanks mainly to the stiff upper lip grist; **f24.5** now we see some serious complexity as the malts, sugar and tannins play gently together. Remarkably intact and wonderful finesse so late on; one would feel short-changed if some chocolate didn't turn up somewhere along the storyline. It does, and in full milky form.; **b24.5** just as it appears to have done in the cask, it just improves as it goes along on the palate... 40%

⟩⟩ **Gordon & MacPhail Rare Vintage Glen Grant 1965 (94) n23** waxy apple and no shortage of crispy, chipper malt: still a freshness to this despite the loitering oak; the muscovado sugars offer a further fruity sideshow; a few teasing smoke molecules, perhaps...? **t23.5** salivating delivery, though the tannins take a harder, more aggressive, line than on the nose; **f24** the oak grips with some inevitable spice. The malt still has a part to play, offering a late and surprising gristy sweetness; there is even an intriguing late hint, again, of something on the phenolic side...; **b23.5** the casks in use here have sorely tested the resolve of this obviously high quality distillate. It nearly buckles under, but not quite... 40%

⟩⟩ **Le Gus't Selection III Glen Grant 1992** hogshead, cask no. 55415, bott 2014 **(93) n23.5** a real sharp rock pool intensity to this, though the malt remains seriously intense; **t24** good grief! That delivery! Makes the hairs on the back of your neck stand up: this really is sharp and as intensely malty as you'll find this year; **f22** just a little bitterness creeps in, though enough gristy malt still around to cope; **b23.5** as though the distillery has been moved to sit beside the sea....52.6%. sc.

GLENGYLE
Campbeltown, 2004. J&A Mitchell & Co. Working.

⟩⟩ **Kilkerran 12 Year Old** db **(90.5) n22.5** very polite phenols offer a surprisingly fresh mintiness to the countenance. Wafer light body, and a wafer light caramel has been extracted from the genteel oak; **t23** despite the dozen years in cask, this still retains a degree of youth about it. But the malts are confident and take advantage of the overall lack of body to spread out and blossom; **f22.5** light, with a chocolate chip mint finale; **b22.5** a malt far more comfortable at this age than some of the previous, younger, bottlings from a few years back. Has a fragile feel to it and the air of a malt which must be treated gently and with respect. 46%

Kilkerran Work In Progress 6 Bourbon Wood db **(92.5) n23.5 t23 f22.5 b23.5** An intriguing dram offering a style of peated malt like nowhere else in Scotland. Where WIP 5 had something of the Port Ellen about it, this has no such pretentions. Austere and disciplined, the precision of the sugar and fruit is a thing at which to marvel. 46%. WB15/100

Kilkerran Work In Progress 6 Sherry Wood db **(88.5) n21.5 t23 f22 b22** less lugubrious than WIP5, and though things here are painted with a wallpaper brush, there is some fun to be had for sure. 46%. WB15/099

GLEN KEITH
Speyside, 1957. Chivas Brothers. Working (re-opened 14th June 2013).

Glen Keith 10 Years Old db **(80) n22 t21 f18 b19**. A malty if thin dram that finishes with a whimper after an impressively refreshing, grassy start. 43%

⟩⟩ **Eiling Lim Glen Keith 21 Years Old** 1992 bott 2014 **(95.5) n24** a seductive and truly irresistible blend of gristy barley, delicate, understated smoke and citrus. Wow...! **t24** perhaps the best example of a nose being converted to an exact match on the palate you'll find this year. Except here there is extra clarity and juiciness; **f23.5** the smoke gathers, as do the spices. Elegantly, of course...; **b24** Gen Keith was used for a time by Chivas as a distillery to make their peated malt. There is peat on this, albeit in delicate amounts. But this bottling certainly underlines that on its day, it really was capable of making high grade spirit, something which at the time was in dispute. A distillery gem. 48.2%. nc ncf sc. 48 bottles. 5th Release.

⟩⟩ **Maltmountains Glen Keith 20 Years Old** hogshead, dist 1995, bott 2015 **(84.5) n21.5 t21 f21 b21.** Crisp, fragile and malty. A clean dram with few pretentions above being standard blending fodder. 48.8%

Master of Malt Single Cask Glen Keith 19 Year Old dist 8 Nov 95, bott 30 Mar 15 **(82) n21 t21 f20 b20**. More tangy second hand and second class cask spoiling the show. The barley tries to sparkle, but the battle is unequal. 56.6%. sc. 192 bottles.

⟩⟩ **The Single Cask Glen Keith 20 Year Old** cask no. 171225, dist 08 Nov 95, bott 22 Feb 16 **(88) n22** butterscotch tart with the emphasis on the pastry. A green maltiness pervades throughout; **t22** zingy, tangy, sharp barley: a light distillate meeting a tiring cask; spices briefly perform; **f22** slightly bitter oils, some leaning towards cocoa, but still the barley has the last word; **b22** a single minded single malt. And the fixation is barley... 45.8%. nc ncf sc.

⟩⟩ **Spirits Shop Selection & Sansibar Whisky Glen Keith 1995** bourbon cask, bott 2015 **(87) n22 t21.5 f22 b21.5.** A simplistic though fully enjoyable Speysider. The excellent vanilla and spice on the finish lifts it above the average. 51.4%. 210 bottles.

⟩⟩ **Whisky-Fässle Glen Keith 1996** barrel, bott 2015 **(84.5) n21.5 t21.5 f20.5 b21.** Thin, with a heated debate between the gristy, sweet malt and taciturn oak. The emphasis is on the heated. 52.3%

GLENKINCHIE
Lowlands, 1837. Diageo. Working.

Glenkinchie 12 Years Old db (85) n19 t22.5 f21.5 b22. The last 'Kinchie 12 I encountered was bloody woeful. This is anything but. Still not firing on all cylinders and can definitely do better. But there is a fabulous vibrancy to this which nearly all the bottlings I have tasted in the last few years have sadly lacked. Impressive. 43%

Glenkinchie Aged 15 Years The Distillers Edition Amontillado finished, dist 1992, bott 2007 db (94) n23.5 t24 f23 b23.5. Now this is absolutely top class wine cask finishing. One of my last whiskies of the night, and one to take home with me. Sophisticated, intelligent and classy. 46%

Glenkinchie 20 Years Old db (85.5) n21 t22 f21.5 b21. When I sampled this, I thought: "hang on, haven't I tasted this one before?" When I checked with my tasting notes for one or two independents who bottled around this age a year or two ago, I found they were nigh identical to what I was going to say here. Well, you can't say its not a consistent dram. The battle of the citrus-barley against the welling oak is a rich and entertaining one. 58.4%

Glenkinchie 1992 The Manager's Choice db (78) n19 t22 f18 b19. Has a lot going for it on delivery with a barley explosion which rocks you back in your chair and has you salivating like a rabies victim. But the rest of it is just too off key. 58.1%. Diageo.

⬦ **Cadenhead's Small Batch Glenkinchie 28 Year Old** bourbon hogshead, dist 1987, bott Apr 16 (93.5) n23.5 despite the magnificent marriage between the thick barley and the sugar-rich oak, there still appears to be a fruitier third dimension; even a vague hint of smoke from somewhere; t24 sultry and deep, there is a Marlene Dietrich feel to this: everything is laid back yet very much focussed on what it wants. The ulmo honey has a massive degree of wood to deal with, but the oils allow it to slip in easily; f22.5 less penetrating now, just a malty afterglow as the wood withdraws and softens...; b23.5 really defies belief that a 'Kinchie can eat up this number of years. Yet it does so with aplomb: goes down a treat! 53.3%. sc. 240 bottles.

THE GLENLIVET
Speyside, 1824. Chivas Brothers. Working.

The Glenlivet Aged 12 Years db (79.5) n22 t21 f18 b18.5. Wonderful nose and very early development but then flattens out towards the kind of caramel finish you just wouldn't traditionally associate with this malt, and further weakened by a bitter, furry finale. 40%

The Glenlivet Aged 12 Years Old First Fill Matured db (91) n22.5 t22.5 f23 b23. A quite wonderful whisky, far truer to The Glenlivet than the standard 12 and one which every malt whisky lover should try once in their journey through the amber stuff. Forget the tasting notes on the bottle, which bear little relation to what is inside. A gem of a dram. 40%

The Glenlivet Excellence 12 Year Old db (87) n22 t21.5 f22 b21.5. Low key but very clean. The emphasis is on delicate. 40%. Visitor Centre and Asian exclusive.

The Glenlivet 15 Years of Age db (80) n19 t21 f20 b20. Undeniable charm to the countless waves of malt and oak. But don't expect much in the way of complexity or charisma. 40%

The Glenlivet Aged 18 Years bott Feb 10 db (91) n22 attractive mixture of honeycombed bourbon and fruitcake; t23.5 oh...just didn't expect that...!! Fabulous, honey-sweet and slightly sharp edge to the barley: excellent weight and mouthfeel with the honeycomb on the nose making slow but decisive incursions; f23 a very slight technical flaw drops it half a point, but there is no taking away from the improbable length of the dissolving honey and barley...some gentle chewing is required, especially with the late juices and vanilla arriving; b23 a hugely improved bottling seriously worth discovering in this form. Appears to have thrown off its old shackles and offers up an intensity that leaves you giving a little groan of pleasure. 43%

The Glenlivet Alpha db (92) n23.5 t24 f21.5 b23. You get the feeling some people have worked very hard at creating a multi-toned, complex creature celebrating the distillery's position at the centre of Speyside. They have succeeded. Just a cask selection or two away from a potential major Bible award. Maybe for the next bottling.... 50%

The Glenlivet Archive 21 Years of Age batch 1012L db (95.5) n24 t24 f23 b24.5 Possibly the most delicate whisky of this and many years: a kind o' Ballantine's 17, but in single malt form... 43%.

⬦ **The Glenlivet Archive 21 Years of Age** batch no. 0513M db (95.5) n24 just wonderful: orange blossom honey with a little baked tomato and ulmo honey to soften things down; t24 soft and salivating: the toasty malt takes off at breakneck speed. A unison of Manuka and ulmo honeys along with Demerara and, to a lesser extent, molasses are right on its heels; f23.5 soft toffee and a succession of toasty notes make for a gentle but stirring finish; b24 less archive and more achieve. For getting so many honey tones to work together without it getting overly sweet or syrupy really is a major achievement. 43%

❧ **The Glenlivet Cipher** db **(96.5) n24.5** by no means your standard Glenlivet aroma: also one of the most delicate and teasing ever. A wonderful mix of Cape gooseberry and pear with the most distant hint of smoky bacon and vanilla; **t24** a no less sophisticated delivery: delicate ulmo honey at the core but a breakout of sophisticated tannins including playful spice and the first threads of liquorice – though all understated. The lightest muscovado sugar taps out a vague fruity tone; **f23.5** if it has any weakness at all, it is the vague bitterness which breaks out as the ulmo honey reduces in effect; **b24.5** it has taken over half an hour to distil these tasting notes into something that will fit the book: we have more new entries than normal and I'm running out of room. Few whiskies I taste this year, however, will compare to this. 48%

The Glenlivet Conglass 14 db **(92.5) n22** a curious fresh paper/vanilla nose and, while you try to work out if the sweetness or dryness is dominant, the spices enter from a side entrance; **t23** no doubt about who dominates now: the sugars take off vividly in a maple syrup/ulmo honey direction while the gristy barley also has a major presence; **f23.5** ahhh... now it settles for the complexity to totally enchant: the vanillas have stood firm while the sugars have slowly weakened...now a lovely mocha thread weaves in, with just a sprinkle of vanilla; **b24** a joyous barley and high quality oak interplay: probably what this distillery does best of all. 59.8% WB16/043

The Glenlivet Founder's Reserve db **(78.5) n20 t21.5 f18 b19**. Really can't believe what a shy and passionless whisky this is (not to mention flawed). The strength gives the game away slightly as to where the malt is positioned. But I had hoped for a little more than malty tokenism. 40%

The Glenlivet French Oak Reserve 15 Years of Age Limousin oak casks db **(91) n22.5 t23 f22.5 b23**. I have to say that after tasting nearly 800 cask strength whiskies, to come across something at the ancient 40% is a shock to the system. My taste buds say merci... And, what is more, a bottle of this shall remain in my dining room for guests. Having, a lifetime ago, lived with a wonderful French girl for three years I suspect I know how her country folk will regard that... Oh, and forgive a personal message to a literary friend: Bobby-Ann...keep a bottle of this beside the Ancient Age... 40%

The Glenlivet The Gaurdians' Chapter db **(81.5) n20 t21 f20 b20.5**. Read the chapter – but can make neither head nor tail of it. A brief moment of honeyed enjoyment. But nothing else really adds up. Just doesn't gel. 48.7%. WB15/120

The Glenlivet Master Distiller's Reserve db **(86.5) n22.5 t22 f20.5 b21.5**. I chose this as my 800th whisky to taste for the 2012 Bible against the Founder's Reserve on the strength of the nose over the first 30 seconds. Oh, well. Shows you the pricelessness of time when evaluating a whisky... 40%

❧ **The Glenlivet The Master Distiller's Reserve Small Batch** batch no. 9378/003 db **(82) n19 t22 f20 b21**. Succulent mouth feel. But just a little dull and off key in one or two vital areas. 40%

❧ **The Glenlivet The Master Distiller's Reserve Solera Vatted** bott date: 2015/11/30 db **(91) n23** a deft intertwangling of grassy malt and orange blossom honey; **t23.5** the delivery on the palate is like a butterfly landing on a lavender bush; sensual malt chimes well with the chalky vanilla and understated fruit; **f21.5** blood orange bitterness; **b23** although Solera vatted, no trace here of the dreaded 'S' word...or even grape dominance. 40%

The Glenlivet Nadurra Aged 16 Years batch no. 0712U, bott 07/12 db **(95.5) n24 t24 f23.5 b24**. So rare to find a big corporate dram like this showing every sign of grey-bearded cherry picking. A wise whisky, where care has been taken to wring every last drop of complexity from this great malt. 55.5%.

The Glenlivet Nadurra Aged 16 Years batch no. 0313W, bott 03/13 db **(88.5) n21.5 t23 f22 b22** An enjoyable enough whisky which would be more than acceptable to most distilleries. But palls by comparison with other Nadurras. 54.8%.

The Glenlivet Nadurra Aged 16 Years batch no. 0114A, bott 01/14 db **(94.5) n23 t24.5 f23 b24** Confident, rich, full-bodied and clean: exactly how a Nadurra should be. And as though this is a distilled, concentrated definition of Speyside whisky. Fabulous. 55.3% WB15/312

The Glenlivet Nàdurra First Fill Selection batch no. FF0714, first fill American white oak casks, bott 07/14 db **(95.5) n23.5** mmmm! A naughtily spicy cove: a real nose tingle. No question the oak leads the way with a dry flourish; the sweeter barley is left in its wake...; **t24.5** a sumptuously rich delivery. And though the oils are healthy, never is there a threat to the complexity. The spices on the nose arrive just after the malt has made a sweet opening. But then we hit a massive crescendo as the dry tannins thud home almost with a degree of aggression: all this in the first half dozen beats. Red liquorice and treacle pudding fills the mid ground; walnut oil subtly adds a further oaky presence; **f23.5** a long interweaving between the oak and barley, although it is the malt which fades faster...; **b24** now that is what I call a whisky... *63.1%. ncf.*

⬦ **The Glenlivet Nàdurra Peated** Cask Finish batch no. PW0715, bott Jul 15 db **(90) n22.5** the smoke is perhaps little more than an afterthought, but also a comforting light blanket covering, gently, green banana and cucumber: unusual...; **t22.5** distinctly two-toned: immediately the grassy juiciness, with all sugars on full alert, then a heavier wave of peat than anticipated; **f23** much more complexity as creamy mocha enters the fray but a late degree of bitterness, also; **b22.5** the fact that this is simply the effect of peat cask finishing, the ultra-delicate nature of Glenlivet's malt, is clearly underlined. *61.5%. ncf.*

The Glenlivet Nàdurra Oloroso Matured batch no. OL0314, bott 03/14 db **(73) n19 t21 f16 b17.** Present generation first fill sherry butts at work here...so I'll let you guess. Meanwhile, those immune to sulphur will find this this rich and many a fruity dream come true. *48%.*

The Glenlivet Nàdurra Oloroso Matured batch no. OL0614, first fill oloroso sherry casks, bott 06/14 db **(71) n17 t20 f17 b17.** Easy to see how good this might have been. But in the end, sulphur wins – or, rather, loses – the day. *60.7%. ncf.*

The Glenlivet Single Cask Inveravon Aged 21 Years cask no. 10667, bott 25 Oct 11 db **(96.5) n24 t24 f24 b24.5** This was a single cask for the Taiwanese market I think. Time to get a flight to Taipei...this is Glenlivet at its absolute best. *54.6%*

⬦ **The Glenlivet XXV Twenty Five Years of Age** batch no. 0115B, finished in first fill Oloroso sherry casks db **(88) n24.5** I don't think I'll be alone in being completely won over by this astonishing marriage of marmalade and orange blossom honey. You could almost buy this for the lady of your life as a scent...; **t22** much more straightforward collection of vanillas, though fruity signposts are found all along the road; **f20** a little spice now, with a drier feel to both the fruit and vanilla; **b21.5** what a shame this is not at 46% or even 50% to allow the oils to keep slightly tighter control. The nose, though: wow! *43%*

The Glenlivet XXV Twenty Five Years of Age Batch No. 0913A, finished in first fill OLOROSO sherry casks db **(93.5) n24** nutty, sassy, elegant but showing just a little smirk and attitude. Dried dates and cock-a-snook spice. Yet all set within walls of quiet reflection; **t24** mouth-filling, soft with fruit and malt in equal measures; the oils and spices border perfection; **f22** some cocoa and butter cream. But, alas, late on a little sulphur niggle, too; **b23.5** probably one dodgy sherry butt away from immortality: some of the passages here are lifetime memorable. *43%.*

Cadenhead's Glenlivet (Minmore) Wine Cask Aged 24 Years Claret cask, dist 1988, bott Feb 2013 **(93) n22.5 t23.5 f23.5 b23.5** How good is that? A cask from France without a trace of sulphur! A genuine – and rather delicious – collectors' item. *53.9%. 258 bottles. WB15/075*

⬦ **Edinburgh Whisky The Library Collection Glenlivet** first fill sherry cask, dist 15 Mar 07, bott 2015 **(68) n16 t19 f16 b17.** You'll find this one in the Library under Sulphur... *46%. sc.*

⬦ **Gordon & MacPhail Rare Vintage Glenlivet 1974** (94.5) **n23** creaking like an ancient oak floorboard, still the citrus is alive and sharp, breathing life into the vanillas; **t24** ridiculously juicy for its age: the malt still retains traces of a gristy character, tempered by major tannins which still offers a sugared, muscovado quality; the ulmo honey is the soothing balm which ensures everything hangs together; **f23.5** long with tingling spices; the tannins refuse to cross the threshold but make themselves known; **b24** these are the types of whisky I hope above hope at seeing a few times each year. A malt well punctuated with oak to confirm great age, but the balance not even threatened, let alone lost. *43%*

GLENLOCHY
Highlands (Western), 1898–1983. Diageo. Closed.

Gordon & MacPhail Rare Old Glenlochy 1979 (95) n23.5 t24 f23.5 b24 it has been many years since a bottle from this long lost distillery turned up and that was such a classic, I can remember every nuance of it even now. This shows far greater age, but the way with which the malt takes it in its stride will become the stuff of legend. I held back on tasting this until today, August 2nd 2013, because my lad David this afternoon moved into the first home he has bought, with new wife Rachael and little Abi. It is near Fort William, the remote west coast Highland town in which this whisky was made, and where David will be teaching next year. His first job after moving in, though, will be to continue editing this book, for he worked on the Whisky Bible for a number of editions as researcher and editor over the years. So I can think of no better way of wishing David a happy life in his new home than by toasting him with what turned out to be a stunningly beautiful malt from one of the rarest of all the lost distilleries which, by strange coincidence, was first put up for sale exactly 100 years ago. So, to David, Rachael & little Abigail... your new home! And this time I swallowed.. *46%. ncf.*

GLENLOSSIE

Speyside, 1876. Diageo. Working.

Eiling Lim Glenlossie 23 Years Old 1992 bott 2015 **(94.5) n23.5** a coastal, salty, seaweedy edge to this one, but the barley positively glows...; **t23.5** exemplary juiciness on delivery as the concentrated barley further intensifies; a good smattering of warming spice as the oak raises its flag; **f23.5** long, vanilla gilded with a sublime praline and chocolate nut fade; **b24** beautiful integrity to the barley, this positively radiates charm having spent 23 profitable years in a very good cask. *51.1%. nc ncf sc. 100 bottles. 10th Release.*

Gordon & MacPhail Connoisseurs Choice Glenlossie dist 1995, bott 2013 **(96) n24 t24 f24 b24** getting harder and harder to find a dud Lossie these days: glad people are getting a chance to be in on one of the best kept secrets in Scotland... This one is truly glorious: absolutely exceptional even by the distillery' very high standards. *46%. nc ncf. WB15/149*

Gordon & MacPhail Connoisseurs Choice Glenlossie 2004 (87) **n21.5 t23.5 f21.5 b21.** Such a pleasant malt. Boasts a little saltiness on both the nose and delivery and the first five or six waves after delivery are fizzing as a Lossie should. Especially with malt. But then goes all caramel rich and a little dull. Like buying a Ferrari, revving up the engine getting to 0-60 in four seconds...and then running out of gas and cruising to a standstill. *46%*

Old Malt Cask Glenlossie Aged 17 Years refill hogshead, cask no. 11564, dist Nov 97, bott Jun 15 **(87.5) n22 t22 f21.5 b22.** A glossy Lossie with all the emphasis on the juicy, gleaming barley. Unashamedly simplistic but with late vanilla involvement. *50%. nc ncf sc. 328 bottles.*

Old Particular Speyside Glenlossie 17 Years Old refill hogshead, cask no. 10861, dist Jan 04, bott Aug 15 **(91.5) n24** a Lossie of your dreams: refreshing, clean, perky and alive with busy spices, fresh cucumber, light red liquorice and sandalwood; **t23** bright delivery with sharp, salivating edges to the barley. An unsalted potato crisp dryness towards the middle; **f22** a gentle vanilla fade, with a little liquorice for padding; **b22.5** gorgeous stuff, but worth getting for the nose alone. *48.4%. nc ncf sc. 294 bottles.*

Scotch Malt Whisky Society Cask 46.33 Aged 22 Years refill hogshead, dist 16 Sept 92, bott 17 Aug 15 **(87) n22.5 t23 f20 b21.5.** No shortage of attractive heather-honey and spice on both nose and delivery. But, sadly, a tiring cask makes for a bitter and unforgiving finale. *52.7%. nc ncf sc. 224 bottles.*

Spirits Shop Selection & Sansibar Whisky Glenlossie 1992 bourbon cask, bott 2015 **(95) n24.5** tannin with a dab of ulmo honey and a beautiful waft of crushed Maltesers...; **t24** stupendous texture: just enough oils to coat the palate, but not too much to obscure the view. The malt really does sparkle here, aided by some honeyed spice which warms as the liquorice-led tannins accumulate; **f23.5** long, still spicy but those sweeter notes persist to ensure full balance; **b24** so effortlessly beautiful: a genuine star whisky *51.7%. 317 bottles.*

GLEN MHOR

Highlands (Northern), 1892–1983. Diageo. Demolished.

Glen Mhor 1976 Rare Malt db **(92.5) n23 t24 f22 b23.5.** You just dream of truly great whisky sitting in your glass from time to time. But you don't expect it, especially from such an old cask. This was the best example from this distillery I've tasted in 30 years...until the Glenkeir version was unleashed! If you ever want to see a scotch that has stretched the use of oak as far it will go without detriment, here it is. What a pity the distillery has gone because the Mhor the merrier... *52.2%*

GLENMORANGIE

Highlands (Northern), 1843. Glenmorangie Plc. Working.

Glenmorangie 10 Years Old db **(94) n24** perhaps the most enigmatic aroma of them all: delicate yet assertive, sweet yet dry, young yet oaky: a malty tone poem; **t22** flaky oakiness throughout but there is an impossibly complex toastiness to the barley which seems to suggest the lightest hint of smoke; **f24** amazingly long for such a light dram, drying from the initial sweetness but with flaked almonds amid the oakier, rich cocoa notes; **b24** you might find the occasional "orange variant", where the extra degree of oak, usually from a few too many first-fill casks, has flattened out the more extreme peaks and toughs of complexity (scores about 89). But these are pretty rare – almost a collector's item – and overall this remains one of the great single malts: a whisky of uncompromising aesthetic beauty from the first enigmatic whiff to the last teasing and tantalising gulp. Complexity at its most complex. *40%*

Glenmorangie 15 Years Old db **(90.5) n23** chunky and fruity: something distinctly sugar candy about this one; the barley's no slouch, either; and, just to raise the eyebrows, just the faintest waft of something smoky...; **t23** silky, a tad sultry, and serious interplay between oak and barley; a real, satisfying juiciness to this one; **f22** dries towards the oaky side of things, but just a faint squeeze of liquorice adds extra weight; **b22.5** exudes quality. 43%

Glenmorangie 15 Years Old Sauternes Wood Finish db (68) n16 t18 f17 b17. I had hoped – and expected – an improvement on the sulphured version I came across last time. Oh, whisky! Why are you such a cruel mistress...? 46%

Glenmorangie 18 Years Old db (91) n22 pleasant if unconvincing spotted dick; t23 sharp, eye-watering mix of fruit and mainly honeyed barley; nutty and, with the confident vanillas, forming a breakfast cereal completeness; f23 Cocoa Krispies; b23 having thrown off some previous gremlins, now a perfect start to the day whisky... 43%

Glenmorangie 25 Years Old db (95.5) n24 it's strap yourself in time: this is a massive nose with more layers, twists and turns than you can shake a thief at. Soft, mildly lush Lubec marzipan is sandwiched between fruit bonbons and myriad barley tones. Worth taking half an hour over this one, and no kidding... t24 the clarity on the nose is matched here. Every single wave of flavour is there in crystal form, starting, naturally, with the barley but this is soon paired with various unidentified fruits. The result is salivation. Towards the middle the oak shows form and does so in various cocoa-tinged ways; every nuance is delicately carved, almost fragile, but the overall picture is one of strength; f23.5 medium length with the cocoa heading towards medium roast Java b24 every bit as statesmanlike and elegant as a whisky of this age from such a blinding distillery should be. Ticks every single box for a 25-year-old and is Morangie's most improved malt by the distance of Tain to Wellingborough. There is a hint of genius with each unfolding wave of flavours with this one: a whisky that will go in 99/100 whisky lover's top 50 malts of all time. And that includes the Peatheads. 43%

Glenmorangie 30 Years Old db (72) n17 t18 f19 b18. From the evidence in the glass the jury is out on whether it has been spruced up a little in a poor sherry cask – and spruce is the operative word: lots of pine on this wrinkly. 44.1%

Glenmorangie Vintage 1975 db (89) n23 t23 f21 b22. A charming, fruity and beautifully spiced oldie. 43%

Glenmorangie Artein Private Edition db (94) n24 t23.5 f23 b23.5. If someone has gone out of their way to create probably the softest Scotch single malt of the year, then they have succeeded. 46%. ncf.

Glenmorangie Artein Private Edition 15 Years Old db (91) n23 t23.5 f21.5 b23. A truly sensual and complex dram, gorgeously weighted underplaying the fruit and wine aspect to a disarming degree. 46%. ncf.

Glenmorangie Artisan Casks db (93) n23 t23.5 f23 b23.5. If whisky could be sexed, this would be a woman. Every time I encounter Morangie Artisan, it pops up with a new look, a different perfume. And mood. It appears not to be able to make up its mind. But does it know how to pout, seduce and win your heart...? Oh yes. 46%

Glenmorangie Astar db (88) n21 t23 f22.5 b22. Decidedly strange malt: for quite a while it is as if someone has extracted the barley and left everything else behind. A star is born? Not yet, perhaps. But perhaps a new breed of single malt. 57.1%

⬩ **Glenmorangie Bacalta** db (87) n22 t22.5 f21 b21.5. Unusually for a Glenmorangie the narrative is muffled and indistinct. Has some lovely moments, but a bit sharp and lacking in places. 46%

Glenmorangie Burgundy Wood Finish db (72) n17.5 t19.5 f18 b18. Sulphured whisky de table. 43%

Glenmorangie Burr Oak Reserve db (92) n24 t24 f22 b22. Fades on the finish as a slightly spent force, but nose and arrival are simply breathtaking. Wouldn't be out of place in Kentucky. 56.3%

Glenmorangie Cellar 13 Ten Years Old db (88.5) n22 t22.5 f22 b22 Oh, if only I could lose weight as efficiently as this appears to have done... oh, I have! My love and thanks to Nancy, Nigel and Ann Marie. 43%

Glenmorangie Companta Clos de Tart & Rasteau casks, dist 27 Jan 99, bott 14 Nov 13 db **(74)** n17 t20 f18 b19. "I don't think you'll be a fan of this one, Jim" said the Glenmorangie blender to me, letting me know the sample was on its way. How right he was. Have to say there is some breath-taking fruit to be had before the sulphur does its worst. 46%. ncf.

Glenmorangie Dornoch db (94) n23.5 light and sea breezy: grist on a coastal wing. The gristiness extends to the sugars which stick to a simple but effective path. The secret to its charm, though, is the clarity and layering... t23 even on delivery the malt arrives on all levels and in different hues, ranging from sweet and fresh to a duller, oak-dried digestive biscuit – but quite tightly bound; f23.5 a beautiful unravelling: those tighter notes relax offering a procession of further biscuity, malty themes – not without a light sprinkling of salt – and then in a denser malt extract feel; **b24** a rare Glenmorangie which this time does not put the emphasis on fruit or oak influence. But this appears to concentrate on the malt itself, taking it through a routine which reveals as many angles and facets as it can possibly conjure. Even if the casks are from a central warehouse, at times a seascape has been created by a light salty influence – so befitting the whisky's name. A real treat. *43%*

Glenmorangie Ealanta 1993 Vintage db **(97.5) n24 t24 f24.5 b25** When is a bourbon not a bourbon? When it is a Scotch single malt...And here we have potentially the World Whisky of the Year. Free from the embarrassing nonsense which passes for today's sherry butt, and undamaged by less than careful after use care of second-hand bourbon casks, we see what happens when the more telling aspects of oak, the business end which gives bourbon that extra edge, blends with the some of the very finest malt made in Scotland. Something approaching one of the best whiskies of my lifetime is the result... *46%*

Glenmorangie Elegance db **(92) n22** quite herbal and soothing; **t24** the thinnest layer of icing sugar coats the silk-soft malt; every bit as gentle as the nose suggests; **f22** medium to short with some attractive rolling vanilla; **b24** a surprise package that is not entirely dissimilar to the Golden Rum, only a tad sweeter. *43%*

Glemorangie Finealta db **(84.5) n21 t22 f20.5 b21.** Plump and thick, one of the creamiest malts around. For what it lacks in fine detail it makes up for in effect, especially the perky oaky spices. *46%*

⬩ **Glenmorangie Grand Vintage Malt 1990** db **(94) n24** a rare nose in Scotland these days to find a few outline elements of cocoa among the complex floral and citrus – mainly, though not exclusively, kumquat - tones; **t24** my word! The sublime crispness of the barley nigh takes the breath away: after the gentle roundness of the nose, this was not expected. There is a healthy sharpness which brings both the grain and deft spices together to forge a magnificent maltscape on the palate; **f22.5** the spices remain. But the oils have broken down slightly, so the finish saunters into simplistic malt and vanilla notes slightly too easily; **b23.5** grand by name, grand by nature...almost. For a malt this outstandingly good, it really should have been at 46% minimum... *43%*

Glenmorangie Lasanta sherry casks db **(68.5) n16 t19 f16 b17.5.** The sherry problem has increased dramatically rather than being solved. *46%*

Glenmorangie Lasanta Aged 12 Years sherry cask finish db **(93) n23.5** a dry exhibition of fruit – or perhaps an exhibition of dry fruit. Either way, quietly rich and showing the range of old fruit cake depths I had hoped to find on the original Lasanta; really love the stewed plums and spotted dick; **t24** wonderfully soft delivery, backed handsomely by a two-toned sherry fruitiness, with dry and cream being just about on equal terms. The sugars appear both fruit and cask borne, though it is the deeper Eccles cake and treacle notes which carry furthest; **f22** a fluffy dryness and numbing to the tip of the tongue reveals that not every sherry butt used here was faultless, but there is enough of a chocolate and walnut butter cream sideshow to distract; **b23.5** a delightful surprise: every bottling of Lasanta I'd ever tasted had been sulphur ruined. But this new 12-y-o incarnation has got off to a flying start. Although a little bit of a niggle on the finish, I can live with that in the present climate. Here's to a faultless second bottling... *43%*

Glenmorangie Legends The Duthac db **(91.5) n23.5** a big yet tight nose: the sugars are rigid, the tannins unusually confident; **t23.5** a nutty delivery, confirming wine casks. But again, those nuts are encased in crisp sugars, then a softer cocoa follow through and gorgeous light nutty liquorice; **f21.5** a slight 's-word' furriness takes some of the gloss off the excellence, **b23** not spoken to their blender, Bill Lumsden, about this one. But he's been busy on this, though not so busy as to get rid of the unwelcome you-know-what from the wine casks. Educated guess: some kind of finish involving virgin oak, or at least first fill bourbon, and sherry, probably PX on account of the intensity of the crisp sugar. *43%. ncf.*

Glenmorangie Madeira Wood Finish db **(78) n19.5 t20.5 f19 b19.** One of the real problems with wine finishes is getting the point of balance right when the fruit, barley and oak are in harmony. Here it is on a par with me singing in the shower, though frankly my aroma would be a notch or two up. *43%*

Glenmorangie Margaux Cask Finish db **(88) n22 t22 f22 b22.** Even taking every whisky with an open mind, I admit this was better than my subconscious might have considered. Certainly better than the near undrinkable Ch. Margaux '57 I used to bring out for my birthday each year some 20-odd years ago... *46%*

Glenmorangie Milsean db **(94) n23** the odd kumquat does battle with a big vanilla oak kick...; **t23.5** opens up far more on delivery than it does on the nose: juicy barley goes on full salivating duty. Light spices pulse while a tangy marmalade (thick cut) ramps up the sharpness; **f23.5** the marmalade bitterness continues, but slowly morphs into a cocoa theme. Superb weight and pace to the development, helped by the malt being on standby at all times...; **b24** a quite beautiful malt which goes out of its way to put the orangey in 'Morangie... *46%*

Glenmorangie Nectar D'or Sauternes Finish db **(94)** n23 t24 f23 b24 Great to see French casks that actually complement a whisky – so rare! This has replaced the Madeira finish. But there are some similar sweet-fruit characteristics. An exercise in outrageously good sweet-dry balancing. *46%*

Glenmorangie Quinta Ruban Port Finish db **(92)** n24 t23 f22 b23 This replacement of the original Port finish shows a genuine understanding of the importance of grape-oak balance. Both are portrayed with clarity and confidence. This is a form of cask finishing that has progressed from experimentation to certainty. *46%*

Glenmorangie Sherry Wood Finish db **(84)** n23 t21 f20 b20. Stupendous clean sherry nose, then disappoints with a somewhat bland display on the palate. *43%*

Glenmorangie Signet db **(80.5)** n20 t21.5 f19 b20. A great whisky holed below the waterline by oak of unsatisfactory quality. Tragic. *46%. Travel Retail Exclusive.* ⊙

Glenmorangie Sonnalta PX db **(96.5)** n24 t24 f24.5 b24 Remains a giant among the tall stills. A mesmeric whisky... *46%*

Glenmorangie Taghta db **(92)** n23 t23 f23 b23 A curious Glenmorangie which, unusually, appears not to be trying to make a statement or force a point. This is an old Sunday afternoon film of a dram: an old-fashioned black and whitie, (home grown and not an Ealing, or Bogie or Edward G Robinson) where, whether we have seen it before or not, we know pretty much what is going to happen, in a reassuring kind of a way... *46%*

◇ **Glenmorangie Tarlogan** db **(95)** n24 a keen sharpness on the nose; as though fresh mown grass and newly cut straw have been bundled together: speaks vividly of the late summer fields around Tain; t24 and, of course, salivating on delivery: grassy again, with all the accompanying young sugars, aided by light shafts of Demerara; f22.5 the oak intercedes with a major caramel injection, plus a little citrus and vanilla for good measure; b23.5 interesting. I have just tasted three new Dalmore. Identical colour and some very similar toffeed characteristics. I allowed a whisky-loving visitor to taste them, without telling him what they were. He could barely tell them apart. Here, I have three new Glenmorangies. All of a different hue. I may not like them all; we will see. But at least I know there will be remarkable differences between them. This fabulous malt radiates the countryside in a way few drams have done before. As refreshing as an early morning dip in a Scottish pond... *43%*

Glenmorangie Traditional db **(90.5)** n22 orange blossom, barley sugar and chalk dust; t23 delicate delivery revelling in gentle complexity: really playful young-ish malt makes for a clean start and middle; f22.5 soft mocha notes play out a quiet finish; b23 an improved dram with much more to say, but does so quietly. *57.1%*

Glenmorangie Tayne db **(87.5)** n21 t22.5 f22 b22. Tangy back story. But also a curious early combination between butterscotch and Werther's Original candy. The malt – topped with a splash of double cream - in the centre ground, though, is the star showing. *43%. Travel Retail Exclusive.* ⊙

Glenmorangie Tùsail Private Edition db **(92)** n24.5 if you sniff this too hard, you might break the whisky into a thousand pieces... just so gentle, wafer-thin shards of barley, butterscotch, boiled pear, vanilla, marzipan...and all watched over by brittle spices; t23 the delivery mirrors the nose: the first six or seven waves are simply sketches of most of the things you find in the aroma, yet with no weight or substance at all...the mid-ground becomes little more simple and vanilla-driven, though with a delicate ulmo honey thread; f21.5 lightweight vanilla and barley; only the spices make a noise; bitters very slightly at death; b23 doesn't quite live up to the nose. But that would have been a big ask! From the Understated School of Glenmorangie. *46%. ncf.*

GLEN MORAY
Speyside, 1897. La Martiniquaise. Working.

Glen Moray Classic 8 Years Old db **(86)** n20 t22 f21 b23. A vast improvement on previous bottlings with the sluggish fatness replaced by a thinner, barley-rich, slightly sweeter and more precise mouthfeel. *40%*

Glen Moray 10 Years Old Chardonnay Matured db **(73.5)** n18.5 t19 f18 b18. Tighter than a wine cork. *40%*

Glen Moray 12 Years Old db **(90)** n22.5 gentle malt of varying pitch and intensity; t22 a duller start than it should be with the vanilla diving in almost before the barley but the juicy, grassy notes arrive in good time; f23 long, back on track with intense malt and the custardy oak is almost apologetic but enlivened with a dash of lime: mmmmm... pure Glen Moray! b22.5 I have always regarded this as the measuring stick by which all other malty and clean Speysiders should be tried and tested. It is still a fabulous whisky, full of malty intricacies. Something has fallen off the edge, perhaps, but minutely so. Still think a trick or two is being missed by bottling this at 40%: the natural timbre of this malt demands 46% and no less.... *40%*

Glen Moray 16 Years Old db **(74)** n19 t19 f18 b19. A serious dip in form. Drab. *40%*

Glen Moray 20 Years Old db **(80) n22 t22 f18 b18.** With so much natural cream toffee, it is hard to believe that this has so many years on it. After a quick, refreshing start it pans out, if anything, a little dull. 40%

◇ **Glen Moray Aged 25 Years** Port Cask Finish dist 1988 db **(88) n23** a puffy, chalky, dry nose where the fruit has to work hard to make an impact. But once its foot is established it balances out rather well; **t22.5** a slightly juicy delivery, too, with the grape well up for it. But this is all too brief as a dry bitterness creeps in; **f20.5** a strangely niggardly finish, with that bitterness still evident and the dryness in control...; **b22** thought I'd celebrate Andy Murray's second Wimbledon victory, which he completed just a few minutes ago, by having another go at a Glen Moray 25-year-old (Moray is pronounced Murray). I remember last time being slightly disappointed with this expression. Well this later bottling is a little better, but nowhere near the brilliance Murray displayed in gaining revenge for Canada last year getting World Whisky of the Year. Curiously, if this is a 25-year-old and was distilled in 1988, then presumably it was bottled in 2013...the first time Murray won Wimbledon! 43%

Glen Moray 25 Year Old Port Cask Finish batch 2 db **(95) n23.5** for all the fruit flying about, there is a massive bourbon-style oak richness to this. Very unusual light/heavy duel personality which really takes your breath away...; **t23.5** ...and no less complex on delivery, again with the fruit trying to run away with it, but the spices having none of it. The malt seems lightweight, the oak and fruit offers greater intensity; **f24** unusual, as the length of the finish – which is impressive – does not overly depend on oils. Instead, the oak now moves into a spicier phase, which lengthens the enjoyment considerably – and unexpectedly. And the biggest surprise of all...? The very late juiciness which belies the quarter of a century in wood; **b24** some quite first rate port pipes are involved here. Absolutely clean as a whistle and without any form of off-note. A distillery I have a very soft spot for showing very unusual depth – and age. Brilliant. 43%. 3295 bottles.

Glen Moray Aged 25 Years Portwood Finish Rare Vintage Limited Edition bott code. 3153, dist 1986 db **(87.5) n22.5 t22 f21 b22.** Just get the feeling that the Port pipe has not quite added what was desired. 43%

Glen Moray 30 Years Old db **(92.5) n23.5** it's probably the deftness of the old-fashioned Speyside smoke in tandem with the structured fruits that makes this so special; **t23.5** for a light Speysider, the degree of barley to oak is remarkable: soft, oil-gilde d barley is met by a wonderful, if brief, spice prickle; **f22.5** deft layering of vanilla and cocoa; a sprinkle of muscovado sugar repels any darker oak notes; **b23** for all its years, this is a comfortable malt, untroubled by time. There is no mistaking quality. 43%

Glen Moray 1959 Rare Vintage db **(91) n25 t23 f21 b22.** They must have been keeping their eyes on this one for a long time: a stunning malt that just about defies nature. The nose reaches absolute perfection. 50.9%

Glen Moray 1984 db **(83) n20 t22 f20 b21.** Mouthwatering and incredibly refreshing malt for its age. 40%

Glen Moray 1989 db **(86) n23 t22 f20 b21.** Doesn't quite live up to the fruit smoothie nose but I'm being a little picky here. 40%

Glen Moray Classic db **(86.5) n22 t21.5 f21.5 b21.5.** The nose is the star with a wonderful, clean barley-fruit tandem, but what follows cannot quite match its sure-footed wit. 40%

◇ **Glen Moray Elgin Classic Chardonnay Cask Finish** db **(73) n19 t19 f17 b18.** Juicy. But sulphur-dulled. 40%

◇ **Glen Moray Elgin Classic Sherry Cask Finish** db **(85) n21 t22 f20.5 b21.5.** Must be a cream sherry, because this is one exceptionally creamy malt. A bit of a late sulphur tang wipes off a few marks, but the delicious grapey positives outweigh the negatives. 40%

◇ **Glen Moray Elgin Heritage Aged 15 Years** db **(74) n19 t20 f17 b18.** Dulled by some poor, sulphur-laden sherry butts. Glen Moray is one of the maltiest drams on God's earth and at its most evocative in ex-bourbon. Who needs sherry? 40%

◇ **Glen Moray Elgin Heritage Aged 18 Years** db **(94) n23.5** a gorgeous blend of acacia and heather honey gives the brimming malt a sparkle; light muscovado sugars don't do any damage, either...; **t24** translates word perfect from nose to delivery: lashings of malt, but polished all the way by the honey; **f23** drier, as delicate vanilla notes mix comfortably with the late mocha; **b23.5** absolutely true to the Glen Moray style. Superb. 47%

Glen Moray Peated Classic db **(87.5) n21.5 t22.5 f21.5 b22.** Really never thought I'd see this distillery, once the quintessential Speyside unpeated dram, gone all smoky... A little bit of a work in progress. And a minor word to the wise to their blenders: by reducing to 40% you've broken up the oils a shade – but tellingly - too much, which can be crucial in peaty whiskies. Up to 46% next bottling and I think you'll find things fall into place – and not apart... Some minor erotic moments, though, especially on the fourth or fifth beats, when the sugars and smoked vanilla do work well together. Too fleeting, though. 40%

Glen Moray Classic Port Cask Finish db **(89.5) n21** a bit of a mess: the lack of integration between the harsh fruit, confused thin vanillas and seemingly young barley has been exposed through the weak strength of the spirit. Untidy and sharp...; **t21.5** not a great delivery, either. Still no telling narrative...then, suddenly, it clicks! Maybe an injection of sugars has made the difference because the fruit is now identifiable as fruit while the spice offer extra dimensions; **f23.5** my word: that chocolate fruit and nut....ridiculously yummy. The late Demerara sugars do no harm, either; **b23.5** a malt which has to somehow work its way to the exit...and finally does so with supreme confidence and a touch of class along the way... 40%

⤜ **Acla Selection Glen Moray 27 Years Old** hogshead, dist 1988, bott 2015 **(82.5) n21.5 t21.5 f19.5 b20.** Not a malt that can always travel through the years without showing wear and tear. Here the oak takes its toll, biting deep into the game, grassier elements of the barley. But the tannin dominates in the end. 46.5%. nc ncf.

Adelphi Glen Moray 22 Year Old (86.5) n21.5 t23 f20.5 b21.5. A thick, glutinous malt bounding with fruity, nutty tones. But there is an annoying, nagging bitterness, too. The highlight is the delivery, a thing of viscous, fruit-sugary intensity. What follows, though, is just a little too bitty for its own good. Other than the late cocoa, that is... 56.6% WB16/010

⤜ **Best Dram Glen Moray 17 Years Old (86.5) n22 t21 f22 b21.5**. Just a little tang to the cask detracts from a very well made malt of the intensely barley-rich Glen Moray school. 55.4%

⤜ **Big Market Sonderabfüllung Nr. 15 Glen Moray 1998** bott 2015 **(91.5) n22** pretty youthful and green in part, the malt doused in light peat reek; **t23.5** beautifully fresh and salivating. The malt has a sharp, sweet, grassy, gristy edge while some distinct phenols provide the ballast and further weight to the hickory; **f22.5** long, drying with aplomb so the oak does, finally, have a good say in matters; **b23.5** lively and chirpy, this is a clean, upbeat malt offering a surprise smoky note so there's no shortage of depth, too. A lovely way to celebrate 50 years...! 573%. 50th Anniversary bottling.

Blackadder Raw Cask Glen Moray 1995 18 Years Old single oak hogshead, cask no. 2510, dist 21 Mar 95, bott Apr 13 **(92) n22 t24 f23 b23** Not a distillery naturally given to passing this many summers. But this is rather lovely, at times wonderful, despite the obvious oak encroachment. 54.9%. nc ncf sc. 211 bottles. WB15/162

Cadenhead's Glen Moray Wine Cask Aged 21 Years Claret cask, dist 1992, bott Feb 14 **(95) n23.5 t24 f23.5 b24** Highly unusual example of Glen Moray, the least oak-damaged I have ever encountered at this age. Brilliant. Literally. 55.4%. 216 bottles. WB15/077

⤜ **Cadenhead's Wine Cask Glen Moray 23 Year Old** Sauternes cask, dist 1992, bott Apr 16 **(89.5) n22** strangely uncomfortable as the fruit and barley fail to see eye to eye; **t24** no such problem here: the intense barley is a match for the lemon-curd tart fruitiness, while the spices try not to intrude too much. And kind of fail...; **f22** quite a big jump from the intense sweetness to the tighter oak input: the fruit and tannin begin to scrap it out; **b21.5** a clean but curious malt which seems to have more dust-ups in ten minutes than the average volume of Kill Bill... 52%. sc. 252 bottles.

⤜ **Chapter 7 Glen Moray 1990 25 Years Old (93.5) n23.5** despite the obvious vanilla and tannin layering – all stylishly done – it is the fresh barley and delicate citrus which catches the eye, giving the whisky a younger profile; **t23.5** no mistaking the light layering of smoke which gives this a very old-fashioned Speyside feel. The barley remains crisp and juicy and in touch with the more sugary elements while the oak makes a polite, unfussy entrance; **f23** a slow, gentle fade with the vanilla slowly taking command; **b23.5** resplendent in the juiciest barley imaginable. Vague smoke drifts in and out teasingly. Unusually for a Gen Moray, shows no signs of wear and tear for its age. 57%

⤜ **Old Particular Speyside Glen Moray 20 Years Old** refill hogshead, cask no. 10871, dist Mar 95, bott Aug 15 **(86.5) n21.5 t22.5 f20.5 b22.** Feverishly malty in that trademark Glen Moray style. Juicy and salty, too. Tangy finish. 51.5%. nc ncf sc. 264 bottles.

⤜ **Scotch Malt Whisky Society Cask 35.137 Aged 25 Years** 1st fill barrel, dist 25 Aug 89, bott 22 Jun 15 **(94) n23.5** a Speyside aroma chiselled out of sugar: a blend of light and dark muscovado sugars at play here, with a vaguely grassy barley sugar candy background; **t24** oh...my...word...!!! The sweeter the tooth you have, the more you will adore this: the spirit appears to have dived into the barrel and extracted every last sugar atom it can find. Naturally, spices come, too. And with interest. Eventually the barley turns up – and intensifies quickly...; **f23** at last, some countering drier notes, first cocoa and then mocha led. Still those dark sugars linger, though now distinctly taking on a maple syrup persona; **b23.5** unlikely you will find a crisper and more sweet Speyside malt all year. Astonishing! 52.8%. nc ncf sc. 87 bottles.

⤜ **Svenska Eldvatten Glen Moray 1991** ex-bourbon barrel, dist Feb 91 **(96.5) n24** not quite sure what knocks me out most: the spice, the acacia honey, the clear, stunning malt or the fabulous balance of the pristine, delicate tannins...; **t24** ridiculously beautiful: buttery malt melts in the mouth to salivating effect; while the spices and tannins add texture and a playfulness; **f24** so rare to find a malt so evenly paced and weighted. The finish is just a slow fade of all the joys that had previously played out on the palate; **b24.5** if you want to see why Glen Moray should always be bottled from ex-bourbon cask, then look no further than this. A classic example of a classic but tragically misunderstood and abused distillery. *57.5%. sc.*

◈ **Whiskyjace 10th Anniversary Glen Moray 17 Years Old 1998** bourbon cask, bott 2015 **(89)** n22 a very comfortable if simplistic balance between vanilla and malt; **t23** initially light on delivery. But the way the malt goes through phases of intensity before settling into the spicy tannin is so lovely; **f22** dries, per script....; **b22** "Glen Moray" goes through this like "Blackpool" is found in a stick of rock candy. A very decent cask which maximises the malty potential. *57.6%*

GLEN ORD
Highlands (Northern), 1838. Diageo. Working.

Glen Ord Aged 12 Years db **(81)** n20 t23 f18 b20. Just when you thought it safe to go back...for a while Diageo ditched the sherry-style Ord. It has returned. Better than some years ago, when it was an unhappy shadow of its once-great self, but without the sparkle of the vaguely-smoked bottling of a year or two back. Nothing wrong with the rich arrival, but the finish is a mess. I'll open the next bottling with trepidation... *43%*

Glen Ord 25 Years Old dist 1978 db **(95)** n24 t24 f23 b24. Stupendous vatting here: cask selection at its very highest to display Ord in all its far too rarely seen magnificence. *58.3%*

Glen Ord 28 Years Old db **(90)** n22 t23 f22 b23. This is mega whisky showing slight traces of sap, especially on the nose, but otherwise a concentrate of many of the qualities I remember from this distillery before it was bottled in a much ruined form. Blisteringly beautiful. *58.3%*

Glen Ord 30 Years Old db **(87)** n22 t21 f23 b21. Creaking with oak, but such is the polish to the barley some serious class is on show. *58.8%*

Singleton of Glen Ord 12 Years Old db **(89)** n22.5 t22.5 f22 b22 A fabulous improvement on the last bottling I encountered. Still possesses blood oranges to die for, but greatly enhanced by some sublime spices and a magnificent juiciness. *40%*

Singleton of Glen Ord 32 Year Old db **(91)** n23.5 t23 f22 b22.5. Delicious. But if ever a malt has screamed out to be at 46%, this is it. *40%*

◈ **Cadenhead's Authentic Collection Glen Ord 11 Year Old** butt, dist 2004 **(95.5)** n23.5 fruit and nut. Dry oloroso dominates, but give enough time for the malt to slowly seep through: beguiling! **t23.5** an immediate spice explosion: just a few bangs at first before the big one. The fruit and malt are in constant battle for supremacy: hard call to tell the victor; **f24.5** residual spice begins to really warm things up. One of the longest finishes for a Highland malt you'll find this year, and its move from walnut and date cake to chocolate Swiss roll is borderline genius; **b24** exceptionally high quality malt from a very high quality – unspoiled! – butt...! *60.6%*

◈ **Old Particular Highlands Glen Ord 25 Years Old** refill butt, cask no. 10872, dist Jan 90, bott Aug 15 **(89.5)** n22.5 something of a Cognac hardness to the nose as the fruit fails to soften the brittle barley; **t23** fabulous delivery: massive malt, mostly of the juicy variety, showing a solidity more in keeping with a Glen Grant in its firmness and structure; **f22** some light shades of fruit to accompany the modest mocha; **b22** no negative sherry influence here. Disciplined and at times fascinatingly rigid. By no means usual for this distillery. *51.5%. nc ncf sc. 318 bottles.*

GLENROTHES
Speyside, 1878. Edrington. Working.

Glenrothes 2001 dist 25 May 01, bott 13 db **(72)** n16 t21 f17 b18. The sulphur in Spain makes this whisky very plain. *43% WB15/297*

The Glenrothes Alba Reserve db **(87.5)** n22 t22 f21.5 b22. You know that smartly groomed, polite but rather dull chap you invariable get at dinner parties? *40%*

The Glenrothes Elders' Reserve db **(75.5)** n19 t20.5 f17.5 b18.5. Now when I was a young man, young man, Scotch single malt whisky tasted a lot better than this, you know. Well, could hardly have tasted worse, could it?! That nice young Mr Lloyd George wouldn't have put up with this rubbish, oh no. He would have sent in the troops and nationalised the industry, that's what he would have done. Hung anyone guilty of using sherry butts stinking of sulphur. Or shot 'em. Only fair. These young blenders... Blenders?!? Don't know they are born... In my day.... *43% WB16/046*

The Glenrothes Manse Reserve db **(74)** n18.5 t20 f17 b18.5. More like Mansfield Reserves... *43% WB16/045*

The Glenrothes Minister's Reserve db **(91)** n22.5 trace sulphur, but by Genrothes standards this is pretty amazing: the grape really does come through with a spring in its juicy step; **t23.5** absolutely top dollar sherry at work: a gorgeous sultana-laden sweetness but backed by the most luscious mouth feel, aided by a little liquorice from the oak; **f22** a little manuka honey fights off successfully the late bitterness from the obligatory dodgy butt; **b23** I think the Minister had a little word with someone upstairs... 43% WB16/047

The Glenrothes Sherry Cask Reserve db **(68)** n16 t19 f16 b17. Inevitable, I suppose... The tragedy is that before some bloke stuffed lighted sulphur candles into these sherry butts, thereby ruining them and the whisky which would later mature in them, they were obviously the dog's...; and had they been left unmolested we would have been nosing and tasting something of intense brilliance. Exasperating doesn't even begin to cover it. 40% WB16/044

◇ **The First Editions Glenrothes Aged 19 Years 1996** refill hogshead, cask no. 12125, bott 2015 **(84.5)** n20.5 t23 f20 b21. For those turned on by the aroma of sweaty armpits, this could be a very exciting whisky for you. After an eye-watering, salty and sexily honeyed delivery, it does tail off towards a tired tanginess towards the end. Still, lacking in character it most certainly isn't...! 56.2%. nc ncf sc. 242 bottles.

Gordon & MacPhail The Macphails Collection Glenrothes 1971 (94) n22 a tiring malt, as the tannins have a firm grip. But the toasted raisins are of the best fruit cake tradition; **t23.5** not often you get eucalyptus on the delivery. But the grape is so rich, it is handled with tact and respect. The tannins continue to drive forward, but now muffled by the delicious grape; **f24.5** hits the high spots, as salt and spice combine to big up the high quality fruitcake style moistened with the very best molasses; **b24** threatens to run to old age fast. But instead we get a master class in age management by the fruit. Sublime. 43%

◇ **Hepburn's Choice Glenrothes 11 Years Old** sherry butt, dist 2004, bott 2015 **(82)** n21 t22 f20 b19. For once, no ruinous sulphur (well, not much – a little does arrive late on the finish). Brilliant! Sadly, the weight of the grape makes for a lop-sided dram. I know many will probably sell their grannies off to slavery to raise the money for such a sherried catch. But this, for me, totally lacks balance. Sorry. 46%. nc ncf sc. 341 bottles.

◇ **Old Malt Cask Glenrothes Aged 18 Years** red wine finished barrel, cask no. 12122, dist Sept 97, bott Nov 15 **(89)** n22.5 bold fruit pastille. A not quite properly cooked apple tart; **t21.5** a sharp and stark fruitiness has to wait a series of beats before it is able to comfortably embrace the full-on barley; **f23.5** an attractive chocolate fruit and nut finale; **b21.5** a good example of a cask bottled when the fruit and malt hadn't quite gelled. But there is enough quality abounding for it to work out okay in the end. 47.8%. nc ncf sc. 256 bottles.

◇ **That Boutique-y Whisky Company Glenrothes 10 Year Old** batch 2 **(68)** n16 t18 f17 b17. Clunking caramels and even clunkier you-know-what...45.8%. 294 bottles.

GLEN SCOTIA

Campbeltown, 1832. Loch Lomond Distillers. Working

Glen Scotia 2005 9 Year Old Heavily Peated cask no. 136, bourbon cask db **(92.5)** n23 t23.5 f23 b23. Peaty malts which nose like a farmyard can go either way...and usually to extremes. This settles into a beautifully compact, fabulously distilled dram where the barley gets an equal airing to the massive smoke. The sugars are on song from first to last and help bring out the best of the late cocoa. Brilliant stuff helped by the lack of aggressive oak. 57.7%. nc ncf. Taiwan exclusive.

Glen Scotia Aged 10 Years bourbon cask, bott Dec 12 db **(90.5)** n22.5 t23.5 f22 b22.5. Fabulous to see Scotia back in this excellent nick again. 46%. nc ncf.

Glen Scotia 12 Years Old db **(73.5)** n18 t19 f18 b18.5. Ooops! I once said you could write a book about this called "Murder by Caramel." Now it would be a short story called "Murder by Flavours Unknown." What is happening here? Well, a dozen years ago Glen Scotia was not quite the place to be for consistent whisky, unlike now. Here, the caramel is the only constant as the constituent parts disintegrate. 40%

Glen Scotia Aged 12 Years bourbon cask, bott Dec 12 db **(89)** n22 t22 f23 b22. Simplistic but delicious. 46%. nc ncf.

Glen Scotia 1999 14 Year Old Heavily Peated cask 528, bourbon cask db **(89)** n22.5 t22 f22.5 b22. Elegant peat and showing excellent sugars a third of the way in. At times a little thin and on the fierce side with fast still spirit burn rather than spice. But genuinely pleasing overall. 55.9% nc ncf. Taiwan exclusive.

Glen Scotia 14 Year Old Peated bourbon cask db **(87)** n21.5 t22 f21.5 b22. A very straight bat played by this one: a malty up and downer with few frills others than a slow though ineffective build up of smoke. 50%. nc ncf.

✧ **Glen Scotia Aged 15 Years** American oak barrels db **(91.5) n22.5** a serious buzz of lively, working tannin to this. All dark sugars and spice, it suggests a malt which means business; **t23** mouth-filling deep, roasty, slightly fat, vaguely salty, massively chewy. A kind of molasses feel with the sweetness reduced; **f23** long, with a lovely, buttery oiliness giving a sheen to the late liquorice; the spices really do come into their own; **b23** great to see this rather special little distillery produce something quite so confident and complex. *46%. ncf.*

Glen Scotia Aged 16 Years bourbon cask, bott Dec 12 db **(87) n22 t22 f21 b22.** Signs of a less than brilliant distillate which has been ironed out to some good effect in the cask. *46%. nc ncf.*

Glen Scotia Aged 18 Years bourbon cask, bott Dec 12 db **(77) n20 t21 f17 b19.** Malty but hot as Hades: a reminder of a less than glorious period in the distillery's history. *46%. nc ncf.*

Glen Scotia Aged 21 Years bourbon cask, bott Dec 12 db **(86.5) n21.5 t22.5 f21 b21.5.** Appears nothing like its age: the very vaguely smoked malt is entirely on top and offers little deviation. A playful spice reminds you oak is involved somewhere. *46%. nc ncf.*

Glen Scotia 1989 23 Years Old cask 310, bourbon cask db **(96) n24 t24 f24 b24.** Obviously a cherry-picked cask, as this is stunning. A riot of delicate honey notes trying to outdo each other. Majestic ulmo honey leads the way with heather honey not far behind. Light spice flickers like a butterfly on a lavender bush. Off note free and about as good a Glen Scotia I have ever seen. Like the other new Glen Scotias, arrived too late for full tasting notes. *55.6% nc ncf.*

✧ **Glen Scotia Double Cask** finished in American oak & Pedro Ximenez sherry casks db **(85.5) n22 t22 f20.5 b21.** When blending, I do not like to get too involved with PX casks, unless I know for certain I can shape the effect to further or enrich the storyline on the palate. The reason is that PX means the complexity of a malt can easily come to a sticky end. That has happened here with both the malt and grape cancelling each other out. Soft and easy drinking with an excellent early delivery spike of intensity. But a dull middle and finish. And dull has never been a word I have associated with this distillery. Ever. *46%. ncf.*

Glen Scotia Legends of Scotia 1st Release "Picture House" 10 Year Old Heavily Peated bourbon cask db **(85.5) n21 t21 f22 b21.5.** Not exactly a B Movie. But doesn't have you on the edge of your seat, either. Some smoke meanders along the thin plot line with little to say while weight takes on only a walk on part. Occasionally complex, but you'll be asleep before the lights come on... *50%. nc ncf. 6,000 bottles.*

Glen Scotia Legends of Scotia 2nd Release "Murfield" Heavily Peated bourbon cask db **(94.5) n23 t24 f23.5 b24.** The nose has about as much smoky power as me teeing off from the 5th: virtually none. But it apologetically creaks into action on the palate and actually plays a delicate and sophisticated game with the peat no more than shadowing the muscovado and liquorice. Again, a little ulmo honey shows to add understated sweetness and body. With such genius at play less Muirfeld, more Tynecastle, I'd say... *50%. nc ncf. 6,000 bottles.*

Glen Scotia Single Cask Distillery Edition 001 cask no. 196, dist Dec 02, bott May 15 db **(94) n23** the oak kicks up some busy spice. The malt swirls around a bit, but is upstaged by the oak in every quarter, to the extent that a few bourbon notes are detectable; the vaguest degree of smoke can be detected, also...; **t24** a much more co-operative delivery, with the barley pretty apparent. But, again, those superb liquorice-manuka honey bourbon notes are soon apparent; **f23.5** relaxes now and stretches. So even a slight sawdusty note creeps into the sugars which have no problem lasting the pace; meanwhile, those spices just keep on gently stinging; **b23.5** a delicious malt which makes the most of what is available. Love it! *56.1%. sc.*

✧ **Glen Scotia Single Cask Distillery Edition No. 002** cask no. 332/543-1, dist Jun 03, bott Aug 15 db **(94.5) n23** sweet and crisp: a succulent fruitiness offers a fascinating alternative thread; **t24** just adore that delivery: everything loud, yet curiously understated, perhaps with no single character allowed to dominate. The warming, firm spirit is softened by muscovado fruitiness. There is a hardness one normally associates with rum- and sometimes cognac-matured malts with the sugars crystalline, yet allowing the softer fruit to flourish. Thick, with a lovely salty liquorice late middle; **f23.5** long, with an array of spice as the oak really arrives. Those dark sugars really do linger...; **b24** so busy and alive with internecine battling for control. No overall winners, other than the lucky person tasting this. *56.4%. ncf sc.*

✧ **Glen Scotia Single Cask Distillery Edition No. 003** cask no. 536, dist Dec 06, bott Apr 16 db **(85) n20 t21.5 f22 b21.5.** Malty, juicy and all that. And good light molasses, too. But someone was in a big hurry to get home for Christmas by the look of this thin offering: appears as though the stills were run like the clappers...or do I mean sleigh bells.... *56.9%. ncf sc.*

Glen Scotia Victoriana db **(89.5) n23** adore the malt and oak stripes with vague citrus weaving in and out at random. Very soft...; **t23** initially, thick manuka honey at play, then a spice wave. Malty and keeps the oak at arm's length. That's until the toffee invades the midground; **f21.5** now the toffee dominates as the sugars from the heavy char take on a chewy, slightly one-dimensional theme; **b22** an unusual malt for a cask strength. Beyond the nose there is limited layering, instead concentrating on the malt-toffee intertwangling. *51.5%*

⬧ **Cadenhead's Sherry Cask Glen Scotia 15 Year Old** dist 2000, bott Apr 16 **(95.5) n24** easy to think this is all about spice. And easy to think it is all about fresh lime mixed with greengage and pear. Or vanilla. Is it equally all of those...?; **t24** succulent. Sensual. Creamy. Clean. Sultana-laden. At times like a fruit salad with a double cream topping; **f23.5** where the hell does this late heather-honey come from...? **b24** a clean, rich sherry butt. A malt spirit brimming with character. What's not to like...? Again, Cadenhead come up with something just a little special... *50.5%. sc. 252 bottles.*

⬧ **Maltbarn Glen Scotia 1992** ex-bourbon cask, bott 2016 **(88.5) n22** some blundering barley crashes into the hapless vanilla. Both out of control, yet somehow compliment the other; **t22.5** the delivery is one hell of a battle. The malt is bigger, the oak is bigger still. Fudge dominates, but the malt really does fight hard; plenty of uncompromising bite just as the molasses appear; **f22** a more reasonable fade of mocha and red liquorice; **b22** what it lacks in finesse, it makes up for in personality. *53.3%. sc. 144 bottles.*

GLEN SPEY
Speyside, 1885. Diageo. Working.
Glen Spey Aged 12 Years db **(90) n23** the kind of firm, busy malt you expect from this distillery plus some lovely spice; **t22** mouthwatering and fresh, a layer of honey makes for an easy three or four minutes; **f22** drier vanilla, but the pulsing oak is controlled and stylish; **b23** very similar to the first Glen Spey I can remember in this range, the one before the over-toffeed effort of two years ago. Great to see it back to its more natural, stunningly beautiful self. *43%*

Glen Spey Special Release 2010 21 Years Old sherry American oak cask, dist 1988 db **(94.5) n23 t24 f23.5 b24.** Glen Speys of this age tended to find their way into blends where they would beef up the sweeter malt content. Sometimes they were used to impart clean sherry or at least fruit, but otherwise give nothing of themselves. This bottling tends to take both strands and then ties them up in a complex and compelling fashion. Wonderful. *50.4%. nc ncf. Diageo.*

GLENTAUCHERS
Speyside, 1898. Chivas Brothers. Working.
⬧ **Cadenhead's Authentic Collection Glentauchers 38 Year Old** bourbon hogshead, dist 1976, bott April 15 **(95.5) n23.5** though the oak is now ruling the roost, it does so in benign fashion. Still, the malt is evident and it is comfortable in its complex and deceptively weighty surroundings. There is an attractively, spicy, earthy vegetable side to this, softened by a little manuka honey; **t23.5** the silky delivery is a sublime mix of acacia honey and vanilla with still enough juiciness to the barley to maximise those honey tones; **f24.5** bravo...!! You feel like applauding the age-defying way that the barley remains intact and intense enough to ensure the finale never dries to unflattering oak dominance. But a moistness to the mocha brings out those lingering molasses and manuka notes, sticking to the palate with the lightest of oils for maximum effect. Wonderful...; **b24** usually you'll find this whisky left another couple of years to find its way into a delicate, complex 40 year-old. Here, though, is a rare chance to see what one of the mainstays of great blending adds to the party. Elegance, sophistication and complexity....that's what! *50.8%. sc. 210 bottles.*

⬧ **Distilleries Collection Glentauchers Aged 18 Years 1996** bott 2014 **(88.5) n22.5** peppery, with a degree of crushed pip; **t23** salivating delivery, then warms ostentatiously. The malt claws its way back in slowly...; **f21** still juicy, but decidedly on the tangy side; **b22** 'Tauchers is always at its best when the spirit rather than the cask has the slightly louder voice. Here, the barrel pipes up above the malt, though still to highly attractive effect. *52.1%. Bottled for Scotch Malt Sales Ltd.*

Endangered Drams Glentauchers 16 Year Old dist 1996, bott 2013 **(94) n23.5 t23.5 f23 b24.** Unusually sharp and fruity for a 'Tauchers, but that doesn't detract from its usual supremely-weighted complexity. About as busy as a Speysider ever gets, and that fruit offers extra weight here, too. Excellent, chocolate-bitter orange late middle. *55.2%*

⬧ **Five Lions Glentauchers Aged 13 Years** 2nd fill American bourbon barrel, dist Jul 02, bott Nov 15 **(92) n22** dry with an emphatic chalky feel to the oak; **t23.5** the barley gains revenge by nailing the delivery: clean, salivating with just-so degrees of barley which ramps up the intensity by the passing minute; spices unfurl to very impressive effect **f23** long, with crisp, uncluttered barley. Barley sugar dovetails with butterscotch and acacia honey; **b23.5** what a beautifully honest dram! *55.6%. nc ncf.*

⋙ **Grindlay's Selection Glentauchers 1996 (89) n22.5** just a little cedar wood enriching the ultra clear malt; **t22.5** unusually, the oak chips in first, but the lightly oiled barley soon overtakes; a lovely salivating moment halfway through; **f22** untaxing vanilla; **b22** a very clean and solid Speysider with sugars at a premium. *54.5%. nc ncf. 210 bottles.*

⋙ **Hepburn's Choice Glentauchers 6 Years Old** refill hogshead, dist 2009, bott 2016 **(86) n21.5 t22 f21 b21.5.** Was shaping up quite well, this youngster. Fulsome malt, as to be expected, ably assisted by a short buttery-vanilla charge and a slightly surprising degree of spice. *46%. nc ncf sc. 397 bottles.*

⋙ **Old Particular Speyside Glentauchers 18 Years Old** refill barrel, cask no. 10779, dist Dec 96, bott May 15 **(92.5) n23.5** a nose to savour: malt on several levels, the majority of them on a fragile, sugared theme. The oak offers a light dusting of tannins hinting at bourbon, but no more. It is the perfect counter balance to the crystallised barley sugars...; **t23.5** fabulously crisp delivery – the clean barley ricocheting around the palate; the salivation levels run high for the first minute before the oak rumbles in with a nudge to fudge; **f22.5** long, remains clean despite the continuation of toasted fudge and vanilla; **b23** another beautiful 'Tauchers, just revelling in the essence of Speyside. *48.4%. nc ncf sc. 186 bottles.*

⋙ **Provenance Glentauchers Aged 9 Years** bott Mar 16 **(90) n21.5** a real nose tweak here, from a malt which normally pats your proboscis. Sharp, strangely coastal; **t22.5** much softer now, except the sharpness is puckering and eye-watering. Again, a salty element suggests an unusual sea air hue for this malt; **f23** the malt is now driven into overdrive; yet still a vaguely salty, limey sea-spray effect is evident; **b23** unusually coastal for a 'Tauchers, but it still churns out delicious malt almost with its eyes closed. *46%. nc ncf sc.*

⋙ **The Single Cask Glentauchers 14 Year Old** cask no. 15827, dist 26 Jan 02, bott 22 Feb 16 **(96.5) n24** so subtle... wispy strands of dry oak bind the vaguely salty-, diced coconut-tinged barley together using the lightest knot. The sugars are so fragile, they feel they might snap at any moment...; **t24.5** does any malt arrive on the palate with a more perfect weight? Light enough to cleanse and allow all the barley to show its rich hand, hefty enough to coat the palate for the long haul; the mid-ground offers mocha and macaroons, all doused in light muscovado sugars; meanwhile the spices rise like a moon from over the horizon...; **f24** long, with the spices playfully prodding the incumbent acacia honey and Demerara sugars...; **b24** absolute bloody nectar. I remember – it must be well over 20 years ago now; maybe 25, sitting in the brewer's office at Glentauchers discussing my appreciation bordering on love of this malt. I even nearly bought the old distillery manager's house to turn into my Scottish HQ. He was a quiet, charming man, the brewer, surprised that anyone outside of the distillery had noticed just how good their whisky was: indeed, I was the first who had ever come to pay their respects...and learn. For it was hardly ever seen as a single malt. This cask, as quiet yet true to the distillery as the old brewer, will give you some insight as to why I have banged the gong so hard and for so long for this distillery which here presents nearly as perfect a single malt as it is a blending whisky. *45.8%. nc ncf sc.*

That Boutique-y Whisky Glentauchers batch 1 **(91.5) n22 t23.5 f23 b23** Shouts "top grade Speyside blending fodder" at every opportunity. *50.7%. WB15/224*

⋙ **That Boutique-y Whisky Company Glentauchers 17 Year Old** batch 2 **(91) n22.5** quiet even for a 'Tauchers; letting the oak do the whispering...; **t23** immediate oomph on impact. Such salivating barley...wow! **f22.5** fades elegantly with the vanilla coming back into to the fray, though the barley still controls the pitch; **b23** this distillery is brilliant without even trying... *48.8%. 508 bottles.*

GLENTURRET
Highlands (Perthshire), 1775. Edrington. Working.

Glenturret Aged 8 Years db **(88) n21 t22 f23 b22.** Technically no prizewinner. But the dexterity of the honey is charming, as this distillery has a tendency sometimes to be. *40%*

The Glenturret Aged 10 Years db **(76) n19 t18 f20 b19.** Lots of trademark honey but some less than impressive contributions from both cask and the stillman. *40%*

The Glenturret Aged 15 Years db **(87) n21 t22 f22 b22.** A beautifully clean, small-still style dram that would have benefitted from being bottled at a fuller strength. A discontinued bottling now: if you see it, it is worth the small investment. *40%*

⋙ **The Glenturret Fly's 16 Masters Edition** db **(96) n24.5** mag-nif-i-cent...!! Unmistakably Glenturret with its genteel intertwangling of ulmo honey, Malteser-type barley, barely visible spice, that unmistakable coppery backbone of sharpness, which mingle well with that squeeze of lime, and seriously high class vanilla from the oak: one of the noses of the year! **t24** slightly lightweight at first, then builds and builds in intensity. Also, the oils gather thickening with the ulmo honey and a few more bitter strands of oak; **f23.5** delightful mocha and Walnut Whip fondant. The spice buzz is so teasing it is ridiculous. The copper also reminds you it is still around; **b24.5** when I first found Glenturret some 30 years so ago, their whisky was exceptionally rare – on account of their size and having been closed for a very long time – but the few bottlings they produced had a very distinctive, indeed unique, feel. Then it changed as they used more Highland Distillers sherry butts which were, frankly, the kiss of death. Here, though, we appear to have reverted back to exactly how it tasted half a lifetime ago. Rich, kissed with copper and stirred with honey. It is, as is fitting to old Fly, the dog's bollocks... 44%. 1,740 bottles.

⬦ **The Glenturret Peated Edition** db (**86**) n20.5 t22 f21.5 b22. Pleasant enough, for sure, even if the nose is a bit rough. But in the grand scheme of things, just another peated malt and one of no special distinction. Surely they should concentrate on being Glenturret: there is only one of those.... 43%

⬦ **The Glenturret Sherry Edition** db (**78**) n19 t21 f19 b19. Not sure if this sherry lark is the best direction for this great distillery to take. 43%

⬦ **The Glenturret Triple Wood Edition** db (**84**) n20 t22.5 f20 b21.5. Not the happiest of whiskies, but recovers from its obvious wounds by concentrating on the juicy grain, rather than the grape. 43%

⬦ **Old Particular Highland Glenturret 27 Years Old** refill hogshead, dist Dec 88, bott Mar 16 (**90.5**) n23.5 quintessential Glenturret: entirely encapsulates the unique, sharp, green-barley tinge to the light acacia honey nose. No other distillery on the planet bares this hallmark; **t22.5** coppery and tangy; good dispersal of gristy sugars despite the age; **f22** the most copper-rich finish in the business...; **b22.5** scores extra points for being an exemplary showing of what sets Glenturret apart. A must have for those looking to create a library of malts which perfectly represent their distillery style. 45.4%. nc ncf sc. 264 bottles.

⬦ **Old Particular Highland Glenturret 28 Years Old** cask no. 11028, dist Nov 87 (**95.5**) **n24** adore the acacia and ulmo honey play off: the distillery's coppery trademark acts as referee; the intense malt is more than just a spectator; **t23.5** silky, sensual, salivating, spicy...; **f24** long, with a keen return of copper and that soothing ulmo honey understated sweetness; **b24** as near as damn it faultless so far as a single cask of Glenturret goes. 51.5%

GLENUGIE
Highlands (Eastern). 1834–1983. Whitbread. Closed.

Deoch an Doras Glenugie 30 Years Old dist 1980, bott 2011 db (**87**) n22 t23.5 f19.5 b22. Now there's something I didn't expect to see again: a distillery bottling of Glenugie. Well, technically, anyway, as Glenugie was part of the Chivas group when it died in the 1980s. As far as I can remember they only brought it out once, either as a seven- or five-year-old. I think that went to Italy, so when I walked around the old site just after it closed, it was a Gordon and MacPhail bottling I drank from and it tasted nothing like this! Just a shame there is a very slight flaw in the sherry butt, but just great to see it in bottle again. 52.13%. nc ncf.

GLENURY ROYAL
Highlands (Eastern), 1868–1985. Diageo. Demolished.

Glenury Royal 36 Years Old db (**89**) n21 t23 f22 b23. An undulating dram, hitting highs and lows. The finish, in particular, is impressive: just when it looks on its last legs, it revives delightfully. The whole package, though far from perfect, is pretty astounding. 50.2%

Glenury Royal 40 Year Old Limited Edition dist 1970, bott 2011 db (**84**) n20.5 t20 f22 **b21.5**. Glenury is these days so rare I kept this back as a treat to savour as I neared the end of the book. The finale throws up a number of interesting citrus equations. But the oak, for the most part, is too rampant here and makes for a puckering experience. 59.4%. 1,500 bottles.

HAZELBURN (see Springbank)

HIGHLAND PARK
Highlands (Island–Orkney), 1795. Edrington. Working.

Highland Park 8 Years Old db (**87**) n22 t22 f22 b21. A journey back in time for some of us: this is the orginal distillery bottling of the 70s and 80s, bottles of which are still doing the rounds in obscure Japanese bars and specialist outlets such as the Whisky Exchange. 40%

Highland Park 10 Year Old Ambassador's Choice db (**74**) n17.5 t20 f17.5 b19. Some of the casks are so badly sulphured, I'm surprised there hasn't been a diplomatic incident... 46%

Highland Park Aged 12 Years db (**78**) n19 t21 f19 b19. Let's just hope that the choice of casks for this bottling was a freak. To be honest, this was one of my favourite whiskies of all time, one of my desert island drams, and I could weep. 40% WB16/048

Highland Park Saint Magnus Aged 12 Years 2nd edition db (**76.5**) n18.5 t21 f19 b19. Tight and bitter 2nd edition. 55%

Highland Park Aged 15 Years db **(85) n21 t22 f21 b21.** Had to re-taste this several times, surprised as I was by just how relatively flat this was. A hill of honey forms the early delivery, but then... *40%*

Highland Park Earl Magnus Aged 15 Years 1st edition db **(76.5) n20 t21 f17.5 b18.** Tight and bitter. *52.6%. 5976 bottles.*

Highland Park Loki Aged 15 Years db **(96) n24 t24 f23.5 b24.5** the weirdness of the heather apart, a bit of a trip back in time. A higher smoke ratio than the bottlings of more recent years which new converts to the distillery will be unfamiliar with, but reverting to the levels regularly found in the 1970s and 80s, probably right through to about 1993/94. Which is a very good thing because the secret of the peat at HP was that, as puffed out as it could be in the old days, it never interfered with the overall complexity, other than adding to it. Which is exactly the case here. Beyond excellent! *48.7%. Edrington.*

Highland Park 16 Years Old db **(88) n23 t23 f20 b22.** I tasted this the day it first came out at one of the Heathrow whisky shops. I thought it a bit flat and uninspiring. This sample, maybe from another bottling, is more impressive and showing true Highland Park colours, the finish apart. *40%. Exclusively available in Duty Free/Travel Retail.*

Highland Park Thor Aged 16 Years db **(87.5) n22.5 t23.5 f19 b22.5.** Now, from what I remember of my Norse gods, Thor was the God of Thunder. Which is a bit spooky seeing as hailstones are crashing down outside as I write this and lightning is striking overhead. Certainly a whisky built on power. Even taking into account the glitch in one or two of the casks, a dram to be savoured on delivery. *52.1%. 23,000 bottles.*

Highland Park Ice Edition Aged 17 Years db **(87) n22 t23 f21 b21.** Although the smoke drifts around until it finds some spices, this is frustrating: you expect it kick on but it stubbornly refuses to. Far more caramel and vanilla up front than is the norm, then bitters out. *53.9%*

Highland Park Aged 18 Years db **(95.5) n23.5 t24 f24 b24** If familiarity breeds contempt, then it has yet to happen between myself and HP 18. This is a must-have dram. I show it to ladies the world over to win their hearts, minds and tastebuds when it comes to whisky. And the more time I spend with it, the more I become aware and appreciative of its extraordinary consistency. The very latest bottlings have been astonishing, possibly because colouring has now been dropped, and wisely so. Why in any way reduce what is one of the world's great whisky experiences? Such has been the staggering consistency of this dram I have thought of late of promoting the distillery into the world's top three: only Ardbeg and Buffalo Trace have been bottling whisk(e)y of such quality over a wide range of ages in such metronomic fashion. Anyway, enough: a glass of something honeyed and dazzling calls... *43%*

Highland Park Aged 21 Years db **(82.5) n20.5 t22 f19 b21.** Good news and bad news. The good news is that they appear to have done away with the insane notion of reducing this to 40% abv. The bad news: a sulphured sherry butt has found its way into this bottling. *47.5%*

Highland Park Aged 25 Years db **(96) n24 t24 f24 b24** I am a relieved man: the finest HP 25 for a number of years which displays the distillery's unmistakable fingerprints with a pride bordering on arrogance. One of the most improved bottlings of the year: an emperor of a dram. *48.1%*

Highland Park Aged 30 Years db **(90) n22 t22.5 f23 b22.5** A very dramatic shift from the last bottling I tasted; this has taken a fruitier route. Sheer quality, though. *48.1%*

Highland Park 40 Years Old db **(90.5) n20.5** tired and over-oaked but the usual HP traits are there in just enough force to save it from failing with an extra puff of something smoky diving in to be on the safe side; **t22.5** even after 40 years, pure silk. Like a 40-year-old woman who has kept her figure and looks, and now only satin stands in the way between you and so much beauty and experience...and believe me: she's spicy...; **f24** amazing layering of peat caresses you at every level; the oak has receded and now barley and traces of golden syrup balance things; **b23.5** I have to admit to picking splinters from my nose with this one. Some of the casks used here have obviously choked on oak, and I feared the worst. But such is the brilliance of the resilience by being on the money with the honey, you can say only that it has pulled off an amazing feat with the peat. Sheer poetry... *48.3%*

Highland Park 50 Years Old dist Jan 60 db **(96.5) n24.5** mint, cloves and a thin coat of creosote usurp the usual deft heather and smoke to loudly announce this whisky's enormous age. Don't bother looking for honey, either. Well, not at first... However, there is a growling sweetness from the start: deep and giving up its part molten Demerara-part treacle character with miserly contempt, as though outraged by being awoken from a 50-year slumber. Of course, as the whisky oxidises there is a shift in pattern. And after about ten minutes a wine effect – and we are talking something much more akin to a First Growth Bordeaux than sherry - begins to make a statement. Then the sugars transmogrify from treacle to molasses to manuka honey; **t24** certain sugars present on the delivery, though at first hard to quite make out which. Some surprising oil ensures suppleness to the oak; there is also a wonderful marriage, or perhaps it is a threesome, between old nutty fruitcake, tangy orange-enriched high quality north European marzipan, and ancient bourbon...; **f24** silky with some wonderful caramels and toasted fudge forming a really chewy finale. As well as ensuring any possible old-age holes are plugged; **b24** old whiskies tend to react to unchartered territory as far as time in the oak is concerned in quite different ways. This grey beard has certainly given us a new slant. Nothing unique about the nose. But when one is usually confronted with those characteristics on the nose, what follows on the palate moves towards a reasonably predictable path. Not here. Truly unique – as it should be after all this time. *44.8%. sc. 275 bottles.*

Highland Park 1973 bott 2010 db **(96) n24 t25 f23 b24** Now that, folks, is Highland Park and make no mistake! *50.6%*

Highland Park Vintage 1978 db **(95.5) n24 t24 f23.5 b24** If you are buying this in Duty Free, a tip: get it for yourself...it's too good for a gift!! This purrs quality from first to last. And is quite unmistakably Highland Park. A noble malt. *478%. Available in Global Travel Retail.*

Highland Park 1997 "The Sword" db **(79.5) n19 t23 f18 b19.5.** Shows its cutting edge for only a brief while on delivery – when it is quite spectacular. Otherwise, painfully blunted. *43%. Available in Taiwan.*

Highland Park Dark Origins db **(80) n19 t23 f18 b20.** Part of that Dark Origin must be cocoa, as there is an abundance of delicious high grade chocolate here. But the other part is not so much dark as yellow, as sulphur is around on the nose and finish in particular - and does plenty of damage. Genuinely disappointing to see one of the world's greatest distilleries refusing to play to its strengths and putting so much of its weight on its Achilles heel. *46.8%. ncf.*

Highland Park Earl Haakon db **(92) n22.5 t24 f22.5 b23.** A fabulous malt offering some of the best individual moments of the year. But appears to run out of steam about two thirds in. *54.9%. 3,300 bottles.*

Highland Park Einar db **(90.5) n23** soft, warmingly smoky, toffee apple; **t23** fresh, salivating delivery but bordered by tannin and imbued with spice; vague heather honey; **f22** dry with the tannins and spices buzzing to the end; **b22.5** a curious style of HP which shows most of its usual traits but possesses an extra sharpness. *40% WB15/328*

Highland Park Freya 1st fill ex-bourbon casks db **(88.5) n22 t23 f21.5 b22.** The majestic honey on delivery makes up for some of the untidier moments. *52.10%.*

Highland Park Harald db **(74.5) n19 t20 f17 b18.5.** Warrior Harald has been wounded by sulphur. Fatally. *40% WB15/337*

Highland Park Hjärta db **(79.5) n18.5 t22 f19 b20.** In part, really does celebrate the honeycomb character of Highland Park to the full. But obviously a major blemish or two in there as well. *58.1%. 3924 bottles.*

⟡ **Highland Park King Christian** db **(83.5) n22 t22.5 f18.5 b20.5.** A hefty malt with a massive fruit influence. But struggles for balance and to keep full control of the, ultimately, off-key grapey input. Despite the sub-standard finale, there is much to enjoy with the early malt-fruit battles on delivery that offer a weighty and buttery introduction to the diffused molasses and vanilla. But with the spice arrives the Achilles heel... *46.8%*

Highland Park Leif Eriksson bourbon and American oak db **(86) n22 t22 f21 b21.** The usual distillery traits have gone AWOL while all kinds of caramel notes have usurped them. That said, this has to be one of the softest drams you'll find. *40%. Edrington.*

⟡ **Highland Park Ragnavald** db **(87.5) n21.5 t22 f22 b22.** Thickset and muscular, this malt offers a slightly different type of earthiness to the usual HP. Even the malt has its moment in the sun. But the overall portrait hangs from the wall at a slight tilt... *45.05%*

Highland Park Sigurd db **(96) n23.5** clever, delicate layering of exotic fruit lurking behind gentle smoke, all heightened by a shake of salt; **t24.5** truly beautiful delivery which nutshells HP at its most intense: the smoke is rounded and only marginally intense, the heather-honey forms the centre point and is equally as circular in its shape and motion around the palate. Yet all along, there is that exotic fruit, omnipresent, but so easy to miss. And, if that is not enough, the mouth feel is simply perfection...; **f23.5** just when you need spice, you really get it...; **b24.5** breath-taking, star-studded and ridiculously complex reminder that this distillery is capable of serving up some of the best whisky the world can enjoy. *43%*

Highland Park Svein db **(87) n22 t22 f21.5 b21.5.** A soft, friendly dram with good spice pick up. But rather too dependent on a tannin-toffee theme. *40% WB15/318*

⟡ **Cadenhead's Wine Cask Highland Park 27 Year Old** claret cask, dist 1988 **(89) n23.5** an astonishing, just about unique, mix of liquorice and fruit...; **t22** salivating, juicy, abrupt fruit; **f21.5** remains on the juicy side, but bitters out; **b22** very attractive, never quite lives up to the nose. *53.3%. sc.*

⟨⟩ **Edinburgh Whisky The Library Collection Highland Park 2000** first fill bourbon, dist 24 Aug 00, bott 2015 **(92) n23.5** there you go: immaculate heather-honey bang on cue...; and does it have that wisp of smoke..? Yep! **t22** a surprising degree of tannin is included in the delivery, which is momentarily bitter and uncoordinated before the honey works its magic. Gets even better as the smoke begins to make its mark...; **f23.5** happier now with the usual character traits sorted and chatting amongst themselves. The spice is a late arrival at the party...; **b23** after the uncharacteristic scramble on delivery this becomes a classic HP for its age, as is the nose. Rather lovely. 46%. sc.

⟨⟩ **The First Editions Highland Park Aged 18 Years 1997** refill hogshead, cask no. 12099, bott 2015 **(91.5) n22** needs to sit in the glass a good 20 minutes before it breaks away from some oaky shackles to allow the light smoke to finally be seen; **t23** a beautiful beeswax delivery. The spices are busy and help keep the oak at a distance until the tannins arrive and add further weight. Meanwhile, the smoke is bigging itself up...; **f23.5** after the slow start, this is now firing on all cylinders and revels in its full HP character; **b23** just a little on the tight side at first. Needs persuasion to give up its secrets, but with some cajoling, it finally does... and then doesn't stop yapping... 56.7%. nc ncf sc. 231 bottles.

⟨⟩ **Gordon & MacPhail Cask Strength Highland Park 2007 (91.5) n23** a shade more vanilla than might be expected. The smoke is shy, though present. The usual honey has made way for light, gristy sugars...; **t23** gorgeous delivery. Maybe the body is a little thinner than the norm but enough muscle to carry the standard heather-honey and drifting phenol; **f22.5** gently spiced and that thinner body now wraps itself around the mounting tannin...; **b23** beautifully structured. 59.2%.

⟨⟩ **Scotch Malt Whisky Society Cask 4.212 Aged 19 Years** refill hogshead, dist 30 Nov 95, bott 27 Jul 15 **(84) n21 t21.5 f20.5 b21.** A frustrating dram. Marked down slightly because an HP of this age should be offering so much more, especially when it comes to balance. The fault lies with the cask, which is too obtrusive and injects a tang that subtracts from both the honey and smoke. Harsh words for a harsh whisky. 55.4%. nc ncf sc. 258 bottles.

⟨⟩ **That Boutique-y Whisky Company Highland Park** batch 3 **(94) n23** what do you know? Deft peat, heather-honey...it has to be...; **t23** a surprising degree of vanilla and caramel on delivery. But satisfying and malty, too...; **f24** here we go; deft peat, heather-honey...and spice. It has to be...; **b24** a volley of ancient oaths...!! You need a grip like a Viking hell-bent on rape and pillage to get into this bloody bottle.... 45.5%. 27 bottles.

IMPERIAL
Speyside, 1897. Chivas Brothers. Silent.

Imperial Aged 15 Years "Special Distillery Bottling" db **(69) n17 t18 f17 b17.** At least one very poor cask, hot spirit and overly sweet. Apart from that it's wonderful. 46%

Gordon & MacPhail Imperial 1995 (87.5) n21.5 t23 f21 b22. Impressively sweet, with more grist than you might believe possible for a malt this old. Good spice involvement, too. Light, limited but delicious. 43%

⟨⟩ **Signatory Vintage Un-Chillfiltered Collection Imperial 20 Years Old** hogshead, cask no. 50228, dist 18 Sept 95, bott 27 Oct 10 **(89) n22** bright barley showing its juicy Speyside credentials; **t23.5** the first four waves here are on a par with any other high octane barley-dominated Speysider this year. Absolutely massive barley which waters the eye and lifts the spirits, especially when those malty maple syrup notes hit the ground running; **f21.5** thins and fades in a style recognised by blenders who used to work with this malt. But the barley, with a cocoa accompaniment, still hangs in there; **b22** an impressive and enjoyable rendition of a malt which often fails to sparkle. The glitter on delivery is sublime. 56.3%. nc ncf. Bottled for Alca da Fans.

INCHGOWER
Speyside, 1872. Diageo. Working.

Inchgower 1993 The Manager's Choice db **(84.5) n21 t21.5 f21 b21.** Like your malts subtle, delicate, clean and sophisticated? Don't bother with this one if you do. This has all the feel of a malt that's been spray painted onto the taste buds: thick, chewy and resilient. Can't help but like that mix of hazelnut and Demerara, though. You can stand a spoon in it. 61.9%

⟨⟩ **Best Dram Inchgower 35 Years Old (92) n22.5** date and walnut cake dipped in axle grease; **t23.5** good grief! It's as though the whisky is not so much caressing my taste buds as giving me a punch up the bracket. Dirty and oily, the malt, molasses and some vague fruitiness combine with the spices to make for something rather amazing; **f23** chocolate fruit and nut, dropped into an oily car engine...; **b23** this is so wrong, it's right. They were making big pungent malt like this when I first went to the distillery, at a time when this cask still hadn't matured as far as being called whisky. And though there are no shortage of rough edges, the uncompromising enormity, almost brutality, is something to inspire awe. Outrageously delicious. 47.6%

⟐ **Gordon & MacPhail Connoisseurs Choice Inchgower 2005 (74)** n18.5 t20 f17 b18.5. I have long been looking forward to the day when I get a sexy, clean, delicate Inchgower to wow me. Sadly, today certainly isn't that day... 46%

⟐ **Hepburn's Choice Inchgower 7 Years Old** European oak quarter cask, dist 2008, bott 2015 **(92)** n22.5 nutty and intense, the oak doesn't get all its own way as the still youthful malt flexes its muscle; t23.5 fabulous delivery: a powering oiliness to the barley thrashes about the taste buds, depositing oak wherever it lands; f23 a fudgy, slightly dirty mocha with liquorice. A lot better than it sounds..believe me! b23 a distillate with attitude meets some hard lining oak. The result is big, absolutely delicious...and works! 46%. nc ncf sc. 92 bottles.

⟐ **Hepburn's Choice Inchgower 7 Years Old** European oak quarter cask, dist 2008, bott 2015 **(92.5)** n23 chocolate and barley...oh, and some oak...!! t23.5 chunky, chocolatey, oily, chocolatey, oily, chunky...and did I mention the chocolate...? But it is the sub plot of Demerara sugars which works wonders here...; f23 where did that surprise chocolate come from...? b23 superb...and just brimming with chocolate, would you believe? 46%. nc ncf sc. 92 bottles.

⟐ **Hepburn's Choice Inchgower 7 Years Old** European oak quarter cask, dist 2008, bott 2015 **(84.5)** n21.5 t21.5 f20.5 b21. Similar in so many ways to the other two Hepburn's Inchgowers of this ilk to be almost a carbon copy, but there is just a little too much oil and vague feints apparent here for it to be in their league. There is little margin for error in a whisky like this. 46%. nc ncf sc. 92 bottles.

⟐ **Hepburn's Choice Inchgower 8 Years Old** wine finished hogshead, dist 2008, bott 2016 **(81)** n21 t20 f20.5 b19.5. The threads of malt and grape rarely meet. 46%. nc ncf sc. 395 botts.

Hepburn's Choice Inchgower 14 Years Old sherry butt, dist 2000, bott 2014 **(75)** n18 t19 f19 b19. For all – no, probably because – of its obvious faults, this makes for an interesting malt. Not often Jack Daniel's is compared to a scotch single malt, but it would be fair to do so here. JD possesses a slightly dirty character due to its inefficient second distillation. There is a recognisably similar dirtiness to this, also: big oils and clammy on the palate, the impurities from the distillate spread abundantly about. Some JD lovers might well enjoy this. 46%. nc ncf sc. 377 bottles.

⟐ **Maltbarn Inchgower 1990** ex-bourbon cask, bott 2015 **(86.5)** n21.5 t22.5 f21 b21.5. Barely a malt for the squeamish, both the bite and the eye-watering oiliness could easily overcome the faint hearted. But there is also something deliciously uncouth and natural to this which appeals, not least the dominating chocolate fudge. 51.4%. sc. 135 bottles.

⟐ **Old Masters Inchgower 28 Year Old** cask no. 11506, bott 2016 **(87)** n21 t22.5 f21.5 b22. A serious rarity to find a near 30-year-old malt at this kind of strength. It is just as well, for the oils in this maintain the whisky's integrity – especially on the finish. The nose remains dirty in the house style of the time but the delivery and follow-through give much to chew over in a particularly Jack Daniel's kind of way. Indeed, JD lovers might quite enjoy this, though don't expect the same sugar content. 60.2%

Old Particular Inchgower 16 Years Old refill butt, cask no. 10414, dist Aug 00, bott Oct 14 **(85)** n21 t21 f22 b21 Biting, sharp and one of the few single malts which can probably cut its way through diamonds. Yet the crunchy barley juice and molassed sugar combo overcomes the obvious weaknesses in the clarity of the narrative. A bit messy – but strangely delicious. 48.4%. nc ncf sc. 774 bottles.

⟐ **Old Particular Speyside Inchgower 20 Years Old** refill butt, cask no. 10880, dist May 95, bott Aug 15 **(87.5)** n21.5 t22 f22 b22. Even after so long a time in such excellent oak, the excesses of the still house cannot be fully corrected or the oils fully managed. But there is no little charm in the essence of must which permeates through this, the nose and delivery being particularly pippy. Lovely whisky, for all its pits and warts. 51.5%. nc ncf sc. 690 bottles.

⟐ **Old Particular Speyside Inchgower 25 Years Old** refill hogshead, cask no. 10879, dist Oct 89, bott Aug 15 **(93.5)** n24 just gorgeous. A vague hint of something smoky forms the perfect backdrop, as well as the unusual but quite beautiful lavender-citrus mix...; t23.5 a procession of sugary notes, beginning with light gristy barley and going so far as molasses, ensures a massively salivating experience. The barley is thick and concentrated, and amid it can be found the timber; f22.5 dries, as it should, with a slight salty piquancy ensuing maximum effect; b23.5 so rare to find a whisky from this distillery so yielding and complex. Big, but hides it well... 51.5%. nc ncf sc. 294 bottles.

INVERLEVEN
Lowland, 1938–1991. Demolished.
Deoch an Doras Inverleven 36 Years Old dist 1973 **(94.5)** n24 t23.5 f23 b24 As light on the palate as a morning mist. This distillery just wasn't designed to make a malt of this antiquity, yet this is to the manor born. 48.85%. nc ncf. Chivas Brothers. 500 bottles.

ISLE OF ARRAN
Highlands (Island–Arran), 1995. Isle of Arran Distillers. Working.

Isle of Arran Machrie Moor 5ᵗʰ Edition bott 2014 db (**91.5**) n22.5 t24 f22 b23 A few tired old bourbon barrels have taken the score down slightly on last year. But the spirit itself is nothing short of brilliant. *46% WB16/049*

The Arran Malt 10 Year Old db (**87**) n22.5 t22.5 f20 b22. It has been a while since I last officially tasted this. If they are wiling to accept some friendly advice, I think the blenders should tone down on raising any fruit profile and concentrate on the malt, which is amongst the best in the business. *46%. nc ncf.*

The Arran Malt 12 Years Old db (**85**) n21.5 t22 f20.5 b21 Hmmmm. Surprise one, this. There must be more than one bottling already of this. The first I tasted was perhaps slightly on the oaky side but otherwise intact and salt-honeyed where need be. This one has a bit of a tang: very drinkable, but definitely a less than brilliant cask around. *46%*

The Arran Malt 12 Years Old Cask Strength Batch 1 bott Sep 11 db (**78**) n21 t22 f17 b18. There is no questioning that Arran is now one of Scotland's Premier League quality malts. But the strength of their whisky is in their bourbon casks, not so much their sherry. And to create a batch like this was tempting fate. The sulphur present is by no means huge, but it takes only a single off butt to spoil the party. *54.1%. nc ncf. 12,000 bottles. WB15/114*

The Arran Malt Aged 12 Years Cask Strength batch no. 2, bott 09/12 db (**80**) n21 t22 f18 b19. A better dram than their 2011 bottling with a little extra depth, nuttiness and sweetness and small degree less sulphur. But there is still enough on the finish in particular to make the difference between the great whisky it should be, and this essay in off-key ordinariness it actually is. *53.6%. nc ncf. 13,200 bottles.*

The Arran Malt Aged 14 Years db (**89.5**) n22 t23.5 f21.5 b22.5. A superb whisky, but the evidence that there has been a subtle shift in emphasis, with the oak now taking too keen an interest, is easily attained. *46%. ncf.*

The Arran Malt Aged 17 Years db (**91.5**) n23.5 t23.5 f21.5 b23 "Matured in the finest ex-Sherry casks" trills the back label. And, by and large, they are right. Maybe a single less than finest imparts the light furriness to the finish. But by present day sherry butt standards, a pretty outstanding effort. *46%. nc ncf. 9000 bottles. WB15/152*

The Arran Malt Devil's Punch Bowl Chapter No. 2 Angels & Devils db (**87.5**) n22 t24 f20 b21.5. When Chapter I was launched, the whisky was what it said on the tin...for it offered little more than brimstone. I gave the devil a poke in the eye for going to the trouble of undermining one of the world's greatest distilleries with contemptuous sulphur. And it appears someone has taken heed. For this is an almost unimaginable improvement over the previous bottling. Is this entirely without blemish? The finish suggests it must. But, clearly, much greater diligence has been taken in cask selection. To the extent that those lucky ones who do not possess the genetic make up to detect sulphur will have a hell of a time. Even those of us who do cannot be but astonished by the beauty of the intense, mollassed fruit. With even more judicious care in the cherry picking of casks next time round, this could be a monster whisky that will give any devil a run for his money. *52.3%. 6,660 bottles. WB15/153*

The Arran Malt Fino Sherry Cask Finish db (**82.5**) n21 t20 f21 b20.5. Pretty tight with the bitterness not being properly compensated for. *50%*

The Arran Malt Millenium Casks db (**94**) n23.5 t24 f23 b23.5 At times hits some dizzying heights. Superbly complex the late fault line. *53.5%. nc ncf. 7,800 bottles. WB15/154*

The Arran Malt Millenium Casks db (**94**) n23.5 t24 f23 b23.5 At times hits some dizzying heights. Superbly complex the late fault line. *53.5%. nc ncf. 7,800 bottles. WB15/154*

The Arran Malt "The Sleeping Warrior" bott 2011 db (**84.5**) n19 t22.5 f21.5 b21.5. Zzzzzzzz. *54.9%. nc ncf. 6000 bottles.*

The Peated Arran "Machrie Moor" Fourth Edition 14 ppm, bott 2013 db (**95.5**) n23 t23.5 f24.5 b24.5 A masterful, gentle but wonderfully complex whisky. A complete gem. *46%. nc ncf. 12,000 bottles. WB15/343*

◇◇ **Acla Selection Arran 17 Years Old** refill sherry cask, dist 1997, bott 2014 (**89**) n22.5 a lovely salty edge to this light spotted dick pudding; busy, sharp and engaging; t23 imagine a police line-up of different sugars and you have to name those responsible for the sweet delivery: would be hard to find an innocent party; the fruit is barely noticeable as the spices dominate and maple syrup finds a treacle edge; f21.5 a shade tangy as the oak weakens; b22 a very old sherry butt, thankfully free from a sulphury curse. More of an intriguing than classy dram. *51.6%. nc ncf.*

◇◇ **Acla Selection Arran 17 Years Old** rum wood, dist 1997, bott 2014 **(88.5) n21.5** toffee apple; **t22** rock hard delivery. Salivating and malty but the spices are unforgiving; **f22.5** plenty of caramel and even more spice; **b22.5** rum casks have a tendency to give a malt a crisp, if tough, outer shell. This is no exception. *50.7%. nc ncf.*

◇◇ **A.D. Rattray Arran 2011** cask no. 5 **(80) n22 t21 f18 b19.** An eye-watering tang grips this malt. The intensity of the malt almost defies both description and belief. But another tangy note makes for a slightly uncomfortable journey... *58.5%. sc.*

◇◇ **BDRAM Isle of Arran 1996 17 Year Old** hogshead, cask no. 1293, dist Sept 96, bott Jun 14 **(92.5) n23** solid malt, polite oak and the thinnest thread of smoke; **t23** salivating, chewy, grassy, light heather honey – and the smoke persists; **f23** milky chocolate and spice – that smoke's hanging around and going nowhere; **b23.5** Arran at its least extrovert and most malty and complex. That smoke thread is intriguing: perhaps an ex-Islay cask. Stunning without even breaking sweat. *54.7%. Bottled by Morrison & Mackay Ltd.*

◇◇ **C & S Dram Collection Isle of Arran Aged 17 Years** sherry puncheon, cask no. 670, dist 28 Apr 97, bott 23 Mar 15 **(76) n19.5 t19 f18.5 b19.** A tight dram which never relaxes and veers towards an uncomfortable bitterness, despite the odd bout of juiciness. *58.7%. sc. 603 bottles.*

◇◇ **Cadenhead's Sherry Cask Arran 19 Year Old** Fino sherry cask, dist 1996, bott 2016 **(86) n23 t23 f19 b21.** Mouthwatering and clean for the most part, a nagging bitterness arrives late on. The early moments are monumental, though... *54%. sc.*

Cadenhead's Small Batch Arran Aged 16 Years 1 Hogshead and 1 butt, dist 1997, bott 2013 **(92) n23 t23.5 f22.5 b23** A busy tapestry of salt and honey. *46%. 792 bottles. WB15/089*

Càrn Mòr Strictly Limited Edition Arran Aged 16 Years hogsheads, dist 1997, bott 2014 **(92.5) n23 t24 f22.5 b23** a very simple joy... *46%. nc ncf. 568 bottles from 2 casks. WB15/053*

◇◇ **Chapter 7 Isle of Arran 1996 18 Years Old** cask no. 879 **(86) n21.5 t22 f21 b21.5.** An outwardly attractive dram, though hampered by an imbalance between the oak and the malt. A slight tanginess on the finish and sharpness throughout suggests a cask that was not prepared for another 18 years, so best to concentrate on the very fine depth to the malt instead. *57.2%. sc. 262 bottles.*

◇◇ **Gordon & MacPhail Connoisseurs Choice Arran 2006 (84) n21 t22 f20 b21.** Dry, a little tight in places and fails to relax into its normal, complex stride. *46%*

◇◇ **Kingsbury Gold Isle of Arran 18 Year Old 1996** hogshead, cask no. 11451 **(93.5) n24** a buttery note to this – salted, of course – mingles sublimely with the light marmalade and honey and toast...; **t23.5** salivating...positively brimming with sugars, especially orange blossom honey; the tingling spice hits just the right balance; **f22.5** the vanillas come in quite strongly; **b23.5** though Arran, to me, is still at its most interesting when around the dozen years mark with a mix of new and second fill ex-bourbon barrels, this at 18 really does fly the distillery's flag with great distinction. *52.9%. sc. 281 bottles.*

◇◇ **Le Gus't Selection IV Isle of Arran 1996** puncheon, cask no. 1634, bott 2015 **(68) n17 t18 f16 b17.** Yes, there are attractive sugars to be had. But you pay a high price with the unforgiving, cask-induced dryness. Grim. *51.1%. sc.*

Master of Malt Single Cask Arran 17 Years Old refill, dist 5 Aug 1995, bott 4 Feb 2014 **(94) n23.5 t23.5 f23 b24** Lovely, composed malt and, though the passing years are beginning to stretch its finer points, this is still a work of whisky art. *53.6%. 100 bottles. WB15/231*

Old Malt Cask Arran 18 Years Old refill hogshead, cask no. 10852, dist Dec 95, bott Aug 14 **(89) n22 t23 f22 b22** The unmistakable tang of a malt slightly beyond its best as the oak has a louder say than it once did. Charming, nonetheless. And always interesting to see my little baby now sporting a few grey hairs... *50%. nc ncf sc. 299 bottles.*

◇◇ **Old Malt Cask Arran Aged 19 Years** refill hogshead, cask no. 11885, dist Sept 96, bott Sept 15 **(91) n22** nutty, malty and salty; **t23** especially salty on delivery, with a crisp barley side-show. As the malt intensifies, the honey takes a more earthy character and the spices begin to play up; **f23** more relaxed, with a lovely spiced barley sugar fade; **b23** a "new" distillery entering new territory age-wise. Nothing like as integrated at when around the 12-13 mark. But has enough good habits under its belt to comfortably cruise through this test. *50%. nc ncf sc. 288 bottles.*

◇◇ **Old Particular Highland Arran 18 Years Old** refill hogshead, cask no. 10864, dist Feb 97, bott Jul 15 **(88.5) n22** the oak is in the box seat and showing the first signs of fatigue despite the malty patchwork; **t22** attractive spice and molassed sugar kick. The vanilla heads towards a distinct tannin dominance but a little spice helps divert the taste buds towards the sweeter elements; **f22.5** a sawdusty fade and ever growing spice. Vague remnants of sugars battle gamely, but that oak bites deep...; **b22** Arran peaks a good half dozen years earlier than this bottling age. So this has done well to last the course – just - and provide attractive and chewable depth. *48.4%. nc ncf sc. 252 bottles.*

◈ **Romantic Rhine Collection Isle of Arran 19 Year Old** sherry puncheon, cask no. 1306, dist 17 Sept 96, bott 12 Oct 15 **(94) n23.5** intriguing and complex: a vague fruitcake tone to this, as though mixed in with date and walnut cake; also with some diced almond; **t23.5** brilliant! Such an entertaining interplay between the sweeter elements and the tarter fruit notes coupled with a surge of tannin offering only limited sugars. The spices are testing and gloriously lively...; **f23** a little fade as the drier tannins govern. But some late date and walnut (again!) make amends; **b24** bravo! A sherry butt from this period not caked in sulphur! I remember testing many when the first couple of year's casks had been filled and the majority of sherry butts were sulphur stained. This is as clean as it is delicious: a substantial, unspoiled malt. *52.5%. sc. 120 bottles.*

◈ **Scotch Malt Whisky Society Cask 121.82 Aged 15 Years** refill hogshead, dist 2 Dec 99, bott 22 Jun 15 **(94) n23.5** delicate orange blossom honey peeking out between the saltier, spicier crevices; **t24** big, intense, for a moment deliciously chaotic as a leading character is sought. This turns out to be a salty cove, ramping up the sharpness of the barley for all it is worth; **f23** long, yet with a vanilla touch to the persistent spices; the vague Jaffa cake sweetness towards the end is both vivid and intriguing; **b23.5** an excellent representation of the distillery: appears to have its character to a tee. *57.6%. nc ncf sc. 269 bottles.*

◈ **Whiskybroker Isle of Arran 19 Year Old** hogshead, cask no. 1381, dist 23 Sept 96, bott 30 Nov 15 **(88) n22.5** the tannins are winding themselves up slightly, but the salty ulmo honey compensates; **t22** again the tannin is first out of the blocks and once more the sugars have to rush in – some of them quite gristy – to save the day; **f21.5** now the spices keep the oak from domination; **b22** fascinating stuff, but showing distinct oak fatigue. *51.5%. sc.*

◈ **Whisky Tales Arran 18 Years Old (89) n22.5** like a malty, saline drip to the nose... **t22.5** like the nose, hits home hard with a salty riff. The malts are full on but just a little aggressive and warm; **f22** sharp and tangy; **b22** entirely enjoyable. But at no moment is this an easy ride. *49.8%*

ISLE OF JURA
Highlands (Island–Jura), 1810. Whyte and Mackay. Working.

Isle Of Jura Aged 10 Years db **(79.5) n19 t22 f19 b19.5.** Perhaps a little livelier than before, but still miles short of where you might hope it to be. *40%*

Jura Elixir Aged 12 Years Fruity & Spicy db **(77) n18 t21 f18 b20.** Fruity, spicy and a little sulphury, I'm afraid. Those who can't spot sulphur will love the caramel-fruitcake enormity. *40%*

Isle of Jura Mountain of Gold 15 Years Old Pinot Noir cask finish db **(67.5) n15 t18 f17 b17.5.** Not for the first time a Jura seriously hamstrung by sulphur - for all its honeyed sweetness and promise: there are some amazingly brilliant casks in there tragically wasted. And my tastebuds partially crocked because of it. Depressing. *46%. 1366 bottles.*

Isle of Jura Mountain of Sound 15 Years Old Cabernet Sauvignon finish db **(81) n20 t21.5 f19.5 b20.** Pretty quiet. *43%*

Isle of Jura The Sacred Mountain 15 Years Old Barolo finish db **(89.5) n21.5 t24 f21.5 b22.5** Hoo-bloody-rah! One of the three from this series has actually managed to raise my pulse. Not, it must be said, without the odd fault here and there. But there really is a stunning interaction between grape and barley that sets the nerves twitching: at its height this is about as entertaining a malt as I've come across for some time and should be on everyone's list for a jolly jaunt for the taste buds. Just when I was beginning to lose faith in this distillery... *43%*

Isle Of Jura Aged 16 Years db **(90.5) n21.5** salty, coastal, seaweedy, but with an injection of honey; **t23.5** carries on from the nose perfectly and then ups the stakes. The delivery is malt dependent and rich, the salty tang a true delight; **f23** all kinds of vanillas and honeys carried on a salty wind; **b23** a massive improvement, this time celebrating its salty, earthy heritage to good effect. The odd strange, less than harmonious note. But by far and away the most improved Jura for a long, long while. *40%*

Isle of Jura 21 Years Old Cask Strength db **(92) n22 t24 f23 b23.** Every mouthful exudes class and quality. A must-have for Scottish Island collector... or those who know how to appreciate a damn fine malt *58.1%*

Isle of Jura 30 Years Old db **(89) n22.5 t22.5 f22 b22.** A relaxed dram with the caramel dousing the higher notes just as they started to get very interesting. If there is a way of bringing down these presumably natural caramels – it is a 30 years old, so who in their right mind would add colouring? – this would score very highly, indeed. *40%*

Isle of Jura 40 Years Old finished in oloroso wood db **(90)** n23 a different species of Jura from anything you are likely to have seen before: swamped in sherry, there is a vague, rather odd smokiness to this. Not to mention salty, sea-side rockpools. As a pairing (sherry and smoke), the odd couple... which works and doesn't work at the same time. Strange... **t22** syrupy sweet delivery with thick waves of fruit and then an apologetic 'ahem' from the smoke, which drifts in nervously. Again, everything is awkward... **f22** remains soft and velvety, though now strands of bitter, salty oak and molasses drift in and out; **b23** throw the Jura textbooks away. This is something very different. Completely out of sync in so many ways, but... 40%

Jura Elements "Air" db **(76)** n19.5 t19 f18.5 b19. Initially, I thought this was earth: there is something strangely dirty and flat about both nose and delivery. Plenty of fruits here and there but just doesn't get the pulse racing at all. 45%

Jura Elements "Earth" db **(89)** n23.5 t22 f21.5 b22. I haven't spoken to blender Richard Paterson about these whiskies yet. No doubt I'll be greeted with a knee on the nuts for declaring two as duds. My guess is that this is the youngest of the quartet by a distance and that is probably why it is the best. The peat profile is very different and challenging. I'd still love to see this in its natural plumage as the caramel really does put the brakes on the complexity and development. Otherwise we could have had an elementary classic. 45%

Jura Elements "Fire" db **(86.5)** n22.5 t21.5 f21 b21.5. Pleasant fare, the highlight coming with the vaguely Canadian-style nose thanks to a classic toffee-oak mix well known east of the Rockies. Some botanicals also there to be sniffed at while a few busy oaky notes pep up the barley-juiced delivery, too. Sadly, just a shade too toffee dependent. 45%

Jura Elements "Water" db **(73.5)** n18.5 t19 f18 b18. Oranges by the box-full trying to get out but the mouth is sent into puckering spasm by the same sulphur which spoils the nose. 50%

Jura Prophecy profoundly peated db **(90.5)** n23.5 something almost akin to birchwood in there with the peat and salt; there is a wonderful natural floral note as well as coastal elements to this one; **t23** impressively two-toned: on one side is the sharper, active barley and peat offering an almost puckering youthfulness and zest; on the other, a sweeter, lightly oiled buzz...a treat; **f22** thins as the vanillas enter; **b22** youthful, well made and I prophesize this will be one of Jura's top scorers of 2011... 46%

Jura Superstition db **(73.5)** n17 t19 f18 b18.5. I thought this could only improve. I was wrong. One to superstitiously avoid. 43% ☉

◈ **Jura Tastival 2016 triple sherry finish** db **(67)** n17 t18 f15 b17. Sulphur. In triplicate. 51%. ncf.

Jura Turas-Mara db **(82.5)** n20.5 t22 f19 b21. Some irresistible Jaffa Cake moments. But the oils are rather too severe and tangy. 42%. Travel Retail Exclusive.

◈ **Acla Selection Isle of Jura 24 Years Old** ex-bourbon hogshead, dist 1988, bott 2013 **(88)** n21.5 noses far more summers than it might: genuinely sharp tannin which bites deep... **t22.5** ultimate borderline OTT oak. At first you recoil from the volley of splinters. Then, slowly, some ulmo honey – complete with a sprinkling of salted cocoa – begins to seep in, making for an enjoyable middle; **f22** the cocoa lingers – thankfully...; **b22** a superb recovery from a malt I initially thought had died from old age. No shortage of wrinkles. 475%. nc ncf.

Douglas Laing's Single Minded Jura Aged 8 Years sherry butt, dist Apr 06, bott Sept 14 **(80)** n18.5 t21.5 f20 b20. Young malt, clean and juicy, despite the indifferent nose, but with very limited development. A pleasant wafer biscuit sweetness, though. 41.5%

◈ **The First Editions Jura Aged 24 Years 1991** refill hogshead, cask no. 11791, bott 2015 **(88.5)** n22 a little freshly picked tea leaf wraps itself around the pleasantly spiced marzipan; **t23** silky delivery and no apology for the sugar-sprinkled, concentrated malt which follows; lovers of Maltesers will enjoy the middle passage; **f21.5** the malt backs off and allows the vanillas from the decent oak an uncomplicated if slightly bittering path home; **b22** not always a distillery which hits the heights, but this is a sweet and charming bottling. 50.5%. nc ncf sc. 181 bottles.

◈ **Kingsbury Silver Isle of Jura 21 Year Old** 1992 hogshead, cask no. 10580 **(88)** n21 very green and underdeveloped, especially for its age; **t23** enormous delivery: the barley comes in varying shapes and forms ranging from ethereal to downright thuggish. Love the juicy aspect to this; **f22** simple vanilla; **b22** happy to project a bipolar personality. Enjoyable throughout. 46%. sc. 216 bottles.

◈ **Old Malt Cask Jura Aged 24 Years** refill hogshead, cask no. 12288, dist Feb 92, bott Feb 16 **(91.5)** n22.5 busy and tingly: not from the alcohol but from the playful spotted dog suet pudding which radiates light sugars; **t23** as soft a delivery as you could wish for: the first half dozen flavour waves all belong to the big malty theme which pervades throughout. Slowly, some salty vanilla makes a mark; **f23** dries elegantly, but the barley is not far out of sight; **b23** as enjoyable and relaxed a Jura as I can remember for a long while. *50%. nc ncf sc. 281 bottles.*

⟨⟩ **Scotch Malt Whisky Society Cask 31.30 Aged 26 Years** refill hogshead, dist 27 Sept 88, bott 31 Oct 15 **(88) n21.5** some light smoke has entered the fray here, helping to breathe life into an otherwise lacklustre nose **t22.5** a little creamy at times; at others thin. Usual so-so distillate, but there is something genuinely attractive about the balance of understated smoke and busy, nippy spices; **f21.5** minty cool; **b22.5** a curious malt showing its strengths and weaknesses equally. But the good bits are very good... *48.4%. nc ncf sc. 204 bottles.*

⟨⟩ **Xtra Old Particular Highland Jura 25 Years Old** refill hogshead, cask no. 11067, dist Feb 91, bott Feb 16 **(86.5) n21.5 t22 f21.5 b21.5.** Begins with a grudging thinness. Fattens for a short while as the barley beats its chest. But doesn't take long before it returns to its meagre tale. *50.2%. nc ncf sc. 269 bottles*

KILCHOMAN
Islay, 2005. Kilchoman Distillery Co. Working.

⟨⟩ **Kilchoman 2 Isles Single Cask Guze Cask Finish** cask no. 688/2010, dist 04 Nov 10, bott 7 Oct 15 db **(95.5) n23.5** sublime peat reek from the open fire; if there is any fruit around it is covered by soot; **t24.5** lush delivery with sparkling Demerara sugars comfortably withstanding the smoky onslaught; a soft caramel cushion also forms, along with the spices; **f24** delightfully ashy with a little late muscovado and spice; **b24.5** my first ever Guze finish, as far as I can remember. And with it keeping such a low profile, colour apart, hopefully not my last. *60.3%. nc ncf sc. 262 bottles. Bottled for Dominic & Prince.*

Kilchoman 2007 Vintage dist 2007, bott 2013 db **(95.5) n24.5 t24 f23 b24** Credit where credit is due. This malt has moved on in quality expedientially from one vintage to the next since its first unsteady, Bambiesque, feinty bottlings. Not hint of feints now. But excellence is writ large... *46%. WB15/116*

Kilchoman 100% Islay The 5th Edition db **(95.5) n23.5** young phenols let the gristy barley fall all over the nose without much ballast keeping them in line. Despite the obvious wet-behind-the-ears character, some vanilla still gets through and allows the Zambian forest honey to share the stage; **t24** big peat, yet this is the softest of softies on delivery, ulmo honey now taking control. The smoke offers a dual role of integrating with the sugars and offering an embracing, friendly, oily backdrop; **f24** the character style of central American coffee makes a later entry than normal, but intertwines with the smoke to magnificent effect...; **b24** 100% stunning. *50%. nc ncf.*

⟨⟩ **Kilchoman Guze Cask Finish** cask no. 678/2010, dist 4 Oct 10 db **(94) n23.5 t24 f23.5 b24** Different bottling and strength as the same whisky above. Curiously, the peat on this one is markedly more jagged and confident, although the overall balance and effect is only slightly altered, but enough to chip off the richer aspects of this malt. *59%. nc ncf sc. Bottled for The Wine Boutique Franks, Malta*

Kilchoman Loch Gorm sherry cask, dist 07, bott 13 db **(92.5) n23.5 t23.5 f22.5 b23** It is never a good idea to be Gorm-less...especially when a whisky is quite this scarily enormous. On this and other evidence, it could be that Kilchomen is not just challenging Caol Ila as the oiliest malt on Islay, but may well have surpassed it. *46%. nc ncf.*

⟨⟩ **Kilchoman Loch Gorm** sherry cask, dist 2010, bott 2015 db **(83) n20 t22 f20 b21.** Just not my kind of thing, this type of big peat and grape mix. I'm afraid I stand accused, rightly, of being Gormless... *50%. nc ncf.*

Kilchoman Machir Bay bott 2012 db **(93) n23 t23.5 f23 b23.5** It is over 30 years since I first tried to play football on the sands of Machir Bay. I did it because with the winds never ceasing, it was, like a latter day Canute, an attempt at the impossible. A bit like trying to get to the bottom of this malt, in fact. In some respects it works, in others I feel a degree of sherry may just have knocked out some of the more complex characters in an attempt to soften. It is, however, much more successful than my failed attempts at playing "Keepie Uppie" against the perennial winds of Machir Bay... *46%. nc ncf.*

Kilchoman Machir Bay oloroso sherry butt finish, bott 13 db **(90.5) n23 t22.5 f22 b23** I think this was more honeyed last time, but the sultanas ring a bell. Another very different but high quality offering from Kilchomen. *46%. nc ncf.*

Kilchoman Machir Bay bott 2014 db **(92) n23 t24 f22 b23** Some 25 years ago, Machir Bay would be where my children and I tried to play blow football: it was us against the impossible, relentless winds which howled off the sea with a will and singularity of mind that could not be tamed. There was only ever one winner. So, interesting to see that they have created a malt to reflect those very rare days when you can explore the length of it untroubled by nature. As lovely as this whisky is, I think I would have enjoyed it more had it reflected the Bay in all its fury... *46%. ncf nc. WB15/27*

Kilchoman Machir Bay bott 2015 db **(94.5) n23 t24 f23.5 b24** A thudding, thumping dram hitting you like a Dave Mackay tackle. Big peat, perfectly representing a big malt. *50%. nc ncf.*

Kilchoman Port Cask Matured dist 2010, bott 2014 db **(96) n23.5 t24 f24 b24.5** A rare occasion when smoke and fruit find outstanding harmony. And for its age...just ridiculously good. *55%. ncf nc.*

Kilchoman Port Cask Matured Aged 5 Years cask 285, dist 2009, bott 2014 db **(92.5) n23 t24 f22.5 b23** Delicious but a rare Kilchoman where the fruit rules the roost.. *58.3%. Abbey Whisky exclusive.*

⬧⬧⬧ **Kilchoman Sanaig** bourbon & sherry casks, bott 2016 db **(89.5) n23** full on smoke, slightly rounded down by the fruit; **t22** a distinctly muzzled delivery: the peat clears its throat to make a statement when soft grape intervenes, so little is said until the middle ground is reached and an oily smokiness is announced; **f22** slightly thin, despite the oils, and a little light grape accompanying the gentle smoke; **b22.5** never quite seen a Kilchoman tow the line this way before... *46%. nc ncf.*

Kilchoman Sherry Cask Release bott 2011 db **(83) n21.5 t21.5 f19 b21.** The thumping peat and at times almost syrupy sherry is just too much of a good thing. *46%. nc ncf.*

Kilchoman Single Cask Release bourbon, cask no.473/2008, dist 25 Sep 08, bott 16 Sep 13 db **(95.5) n23.5** a hint of Fisherman's Friend adds a menacing sharpness to the otherwise serenely sweet peat; **t24** quite outstanding mouth feel on delivery: the palate is a blur of smoke and dark sugars, though midway in, ash and coal dust bites; **f24** as long as demanded for a malt this big; the peat now layering in both intensity and sweetness. The spices buzz cleverly and almost below the taste buds' radar; **b24** most of the whiskies I have tasted from this distillery this year have been truly exceptional. Here is another one. *61%. ncf nc. Bottled in celebration of the 5th year of The Whisky Show. The Whisky Exchange. WB15/278*

Kilchoman Vintage 2006 bott 2012 db **(93.5) n24 t23.5 f22.5 b23.** A sweetly peated triumph. *46%. nc ncf.*

Master of Malt Single Cask Kilchoman 5 Years Old (96) n24 t24.5 f23.5 b24 The smoke keeps a lower than usual profile. No bad thing: the intricacy of the oak in particular takes some believing. A wonder malt. *59.6%. sc.*

KINCLAITH
Lowlands, 1957–1975. Closed. Dismantled.

Mo Òr Collection Kinclaith 1969 41 Years Old first fill bourbon hogshead, cask no. 301453A, dist 28 May 69, bott 29 Oct 10 **(85.5) n22 t22 f20.5 b21.** Hangs on gamely to the last vestiges of life, though the oak, without being overtly aggressive, is squeezing all the breath out of out of it. *46%. nc ncf sc. Release No. 2. The Whisky Talker. 164 bottles.*

KNOCKANDO
Speyside, 1898. Diageo. Working.

Knockando Aged 18 Years sherry casks, dist 1987 db **(77) n19 t21 f18 b19.** Bland and docile. Someone wake me up. *43%*

Knockando 1990 db **(83) n21 t22 f20 b20.** The most fruity Knockando I've come across with some attractive salty notes. Dry, but a little extra malty sweetness these days. *40%*

KNOCKDHU
Speyside, 1894. Inver House Distillers. Working.

AnCnoc 12 Year Old db **(94.5) n24** so complex it is frightening: delicate barley; delicate spices; delicate butterscotch-vanilla, delicate citrus... and all the while the lightest discernible sugars melt into the malt; **t23** it had to be salivating... and is! Yet there is enough oaky-vanilla roughage to ensure the citrus and barley don't get their own way; **f23.5** a slow but telling arrival of spices fit hand in glove with the complex cocoa-barley tones; **b24.5** a more complete or confident Speyside-style malt you are unlikely to find. Shimmers with everything that is great about Scotch whisky... always a reliable dram, but this is stupendous. *40%*

AnCnoc 13 Year Old Highland Selection db **(85) n21 t23 f20 b21.** A big Knockdhu, but something is dulling the complexity. *46%*

AnCnoc 16 Years Old db **(91.5) n22** sharp, pithy, salty, busy...; **t23.5** those salts crash headlong into the taste buds and then give way to massive spice and barley; soft sugars and vanilla follow at a distance; **f23** salted mocha and spice; **b23** unquestionably the spiciest AnCnoc of all time. Has this distillery been moved to the coast..? *46%*

AnCnoc 18 Years Old db **(88.5) n22.5** a curious mix of prickly spice and buttered raisin shortcake; **t23** the palate is swamped by malt and vanilla; malt sharp and two-toned, as though the third fill bourbon casks more than equal first. But the middle is a little dull, with fruit fudge the order of the day; **f21** disappointing sign of charisma: monotone fruit, perhaps, but badly lacking in lengthening sugars; **b22** cleaner sherry at work here. But again, the contours of the malt have been flattened out badly. *46%. nc ncf.*

AnCnoc 22 Year Old db **(87)** n22 t21.5 f22 b21.5. Often a malt which blossoms before being a teenager, as does the fruits of Knockdhu; struggles to cope comfortably with the inevitable oakiness of old age. Here is such a case. *46%. Inverhouse Distillers.*

AnCnoc 24 Years Old db **(94)** n23 deep...and gets deeper. Dates and spiced toasted raisin dominate, leading to a heavy, dense fruitcake feel...; **t24.5** so no surprises: thick Melton Hunt cake, with extra lashing of molasses are quickly to the fore...and linger. The spices begin early but multiply even when the manuka honey begins to kick in; ulmo honey, then Lubeck marzipan and sultana enrich the middle ground; **f22.5** dulls slightly as the sugars wear thin, but now some dough with the plums, dates and spices aplenty; there is, if you are wondering, a slight furry tang – but pretty low key; **b24** big, broad-shouldered malt which carries a lot of weight but hardly veers away from the massively fruity path. For sherry loving whisky drinkers everywhere... *46%. nc ncf.*

AnCnoc 26 Years Old Highland Selection db **(89)** n23 t22 f23 b21. There is a little flat moment between the middle and finish for which I have chipped off a point or two. That apart, superb. *48.2%*

AnCnoc 30 Years Old db **(85)** n21 t23 f19 b22. Seat-of-the-pants whisky that is just on the turn. Still has a twinkle in the eye, though. *49%*

AnCnoc 35 Years Old db **(86)** n21 t21 f22.5 b21.5. Tries to take the exotic fruit route to antiquity but headed off at the pass by a massive dollop of natural caramels. The slow burn on the spice is an unexpected extra treat, though. *43%*

AnCnoc 35 Years Old bourbon and sherry casks db **(88)** n22.5 t22 f21.5 b22. The usual big barley sheen has dulled with time here. Some attractive cocoa notes do compensate. *44.3%. nc ncf.*

AnCnoc 1975 bott 2014 db **(90)** n23.5 creaking, crumbling oak at every turn. Fortunately there's enough sugar at play – a blend of maple syrup and molasses – to see off any negative points. When some form of equality is established, the rich fruitcake comes out to play...; **t23** all kinds of timber notes up front but the fruit gushes in quickly to form a lush cushion. Two year old Melton Hunt Cake with fully burned raisin; **f21.5** just a little bit of awkward bitterness – and an odd furriness – joins the fruit; **b22.5** if it showed any more signs of age, it'd need its own Zimmer frame. But the deep, fruity sugars are a superb restorative. *44.2%. nc ncf.*

An Cnoc 1993 db **(89)** n22 t22 f24 b22. Quite an odd one this. I have tasted it a couple of times with different samples and there is a variance. This one takes an oakier path and then invites the barley to do its stuff. Delicious, but underscores the deft touch of the standard 12-year-old. *46%*

AnCnoc 1994 db **(88.5)** n22.5 t22.5 f21.5 b22. Coasts through effortlessly, showing the odd flash of brilliance here and there. Just get the feeling that it never quite gets out of third gear... *46%. ncf.*

AnCnoc 1995 db **(84.5)** n21 t22 f20.5 b21. Very plump for a Knockdhu with caramel notes on a par with the citrus and burgeoning bourbon. Some barley juice escapes on delivery but the finish is peculiarly dry for the distillery. *46%*

AnCnoc 1999 db **(95.5)** n24 t24 f23.5 b24 I noticed as I was putting the bottle away that on their back label their description includes "Colour: soft, very aromatic with a hint of honey and lemon in the foreground" and "Nose: amber with a slight yellow hue." Which would make this malt pretty unique. But this is worth getting for far more than just the collectors' item typo: this is brilliant whisky – one of their best vintage malts for a very long time. In fact, one of their best ever bottlings...period. *46%. nc ncf. WB15/160*

AnCnoc 2000 bott Sept 14 db **(87)** n21.5 t23 f21.5 b21.5. Knockdhu whisky is at its best in a judicious mix of ex-bourbon barrels, as it is they which can fully exploit – and allow unrestricted access to show - the abnormal complexity of the malt. It appears sherry butts have been introduced here. And though there is no OTT sulphur, a flattening process – similar to that experienced when caramel is inserted – has occurred. Some lovely chocolate fruit and nut notes, and all round enjoyable stuff. But the higher complexity has been trimmed. *46%. nc ncf.*

AnCnoc 2001 bott Dec 15 db **(92)** n23.5 not sure I can get enough of those citrus notes.. wow! **t23.5** tell me, 'cos I can't decide: is it the malt or that citrus that is making me drown in my own saliva...? **f22** at last the tannins get a word in, though still pretty muted as plenty of toffee makes for a chewy finish; **b23** cruises effortlessly along like a 2001 Jag... *46%. nc ncf.*

AnCnoc Barrow 13.5 ppm phenols db **(88)** n22 t21 f23 b22 A quite peculiar Knockdhu. The usual subtle richness of texture is curiously absent. As are friendly sugars. The strange angles of the phenols fascinate, however. *46%. nc ncf. Exclusive to travel retail.*

⁘ **AnCnoc Blas** db **(67)** n16 t18 f16 b17. Blast! Great chocolate. Shame about the sulphur.... *54%. nc ncf.*

AnCnoc Black Hill Reserve db **(81)** n20 t22 f19 b20. The furriness threatened on the nose and realised at the finish does this great distillery no favours at all. *46%. nc ncf. Exclusive to travel retail.*

AnCnoc Cutter 20.5 ppm phenols db **(96.5)** n24 t24 f24 b24.5 Brilliant! An adjective I am far more used to associating with anCnoc than some of the others I have had to use this year. The most Ardbeg-esque mainland malt I have ever encountered. *46%. nc ncf.*

AnCnoc Flaughter 14.8 ppm phenols db **(88.5)** n23 t22 f21.5 b22 interesting to compare the relative heavy handedness of this against the Rutter. A lovely whisky this may be, but has nothing like the poise or balance. *46%. ncf nc. WB15/345*

AnCnoc Peter Arkle Limited Edition db **(87.5)** n22.5 t22.5 f20.5 b22. A floral nose, with lavender and honeysuckle in abundance. Also offers dried orange peel. But the malt doesn't move on from there as one might hope, becoming just a little too sugary and caramel stodgy for the malt to do itself justice. All that said, a great dram to chew on for a few minutes! *46%. ncf nc. WB15/321*

⁘ **AnCnoc Rascan** 11.1ppm phenols db **(89)** n22 so light is the overall contribution from the oak, the peating level appears higher than that given; very young...; t23 ridiculously fresh: if there is oak in there, I can barely see it. Instead, the gristy smoke has fun with the lighter sugars and noisy spices; f22 only the peat keeps the finish going, though the castor sugar help; b22 not sure I've ever come across such a dainty wallflower of a peated malt. *46%. nc ncf.*

AnCnoc Rutter 11 ppm phenols db **(96.5)** n24.5 t24.5 f23.5 b24 I remember vividly, at this great distillery's Centenary party exactly 20 years ago this summer, mentioning to the then distillery manager that I thought that the style of the malt produced at Knockdhu was perfectly geared to make a lightly malted peat along the lines of its neighbour, Ardmore. Only for a few weeks of the year I ventured. I'm pretty certain this malt was not a result of that observation, but it is heartening to see that my instincts were right: it's a sensation! *46%. ncf nc. WB15/320*

⁘ **Endangered Drams Knockdhu 7 Year Old** bourbon hogshead, cask no. 7, dist 07 Apr 08, bott 02 Sept 15 **(88)** n22 a big slice of new make still attached but the malt is sharp, focussed and faultless; t22 juicy and beautifully constructed gristy malt; just a vague hint of grapefruit; f22 remains malty and intact; b22 magnificent quality malt with negligble oak interference. *59.2%. sc.*

⁘ **Whiskyjace 10th Anniversary Knockdhu 7 Years Old 2008** bourbon cask, bott 2015 **(89)** n22 an intriguing mix of pre-pubescent new make and the first outlines of a strident, intense Speysider. The oak is caught somewhere in no-man's-land... ; t23 wow!! You could almost drown in your own juices: probably the most juicy delivery of the year with the gristy barley making for spectacular salivation. This is something that could be savoured all day; f22 a little vanilla, unripened greengage and a gentle wisp of smoke; b22 despite it being too young for its own good, the glass almost explodes with character....!! Just impossible not to love. *55.2%*

LADYBURN

Lowlands, 1966–2000. William Grant & Sons. Closed.

Mo Òr Collection Rare Ayrshire 1974 36 Years Old first fill bourbon barrel, cask no. 2608, dist 10 May 74, bott 1 Nov 11 **(89.5)** n22 t23.5 f22 b22.5. I had a feeling it'd be this distillery when I saw the title on the label... it couldn't be much else! Fascinating to think that I was in final countdown for my 'O' levels when this was made. It appears to have dealt with the passing years better than I have. Even so, I had not been prepared for this. For years during the very early 1990s Grant's blender David Stewart sent me samples of this stuff and it was, to put it mildly, not great. Some were the oakiest malt I ever tasted in my life. And, to compound matters further, the distillery's own bottling was truly awful. But this cask has re-written history. *46%. nc ncf sc. Release No. 4. The Whisky Talker. 261 bottles.*

LAGAVULIN

Islay, 1816. Diageo. Working.

Lagavulin 12 Years Old 8th release, bott 2008 db **(94.5)** n24 t24.5 f22.5 b23.5. Sensational malt: simply by doing all the simple things rather brilliantly. *56.4%*

Lagavulin 12 Years Old 10th release, bott 2010 db **(94.5)** n23.5 t24 f23.5 b23.5. Keeps on track with previous Releases. Though this is the first where the lowering of the ppms from 50 to 35 really do seem noticeable. Quite beautiful, nonetheless. *56.5%*

⁘ **Lagavulin 12 Year Old** refill American oak casks db **(95.5)** n23.5 beautifully salty. A squeeze of lime heralds in the phenols which grow to manageable levels; t24 more explosive depth than a depth charger. The phenols are happy to tag along with a light molasses sweetness and vaguely liquorice drier tone; intriguingly, there is even a touch of underlying youth to this; **f24** at its most comfortable when it is steered a vaguely vanilla-enriched route into the sunset; **b24** at the age I cut my Lagavulin teeth on, long before the 16-year-old was even the twinkle in a blender's eye. Not as peaty as then, to be honest. But for subtlety, this doesn't compare unfavourably... *48.8%. Diageo Special Releases 2015.*

Lagavulin 12 Years Old Special Release 2011 db **(96.5) n24.5 t24 f23.5 b24.5.** So the peat may not pound as it did when the Whisky Bible began life in 2003: the phenols are noticeably lighter here. But it is not all about size: balance and complexity still reign supreme. *57.5%. nc ncf.*

Lagavulin 12 Years Old Special Release 2012 Refill American oak casks, bott 2012 db **(95) n23 t24 f24 b24.** Truly wonderful. A very clever, sympathetic and professional choice of casks from this superstar distillery. *56.1%. nc ncf. Diageo.*

Lagavulin 16 Years Old db **(95) n24** morning cinders of peat from the fire of the night before: dry, ashy, improbably delicate. Just a hint of Demerara sweetness caught on the edge; **t24** that dryness is perfectly encapsulated on the delivery with the light sugars eclipsed by those countless waves of ash. A tame spiciness generates a degree of hostility on the palate, but the mid-ground sticks to a smoky, coffee-vanilla theme; **f23** light spicy waves in a gentle sea of smoke; **b24** although i have enjoyed this whisky countless times socially, it is the first time for a while I have dragged it into the Tasting Room for professional analysis for the Bible. If anyone has noticed a slight change in Lagavulin, they would be right. The peat remains profound but much more delicate than before, while the oils appear to have receded. A different shape and weight dispersal for sure. But the sky-high quality remains just the same. *43%*

Lagavulin 21 Years Old Special Release 2012 dist 1991, bott 2012 db **(92.5) n23.5 t23.5 f23 b22.5.** The impact of the fruit is truly delicious in its sweet juiciness, but the smoke means complexity is slightly subdued. Fantastic whisky, though...and rather sweet. *52%. nc ncf. Diageo.*

Lagavulin Special Release 2010 12 Years Old db **(94) n24.5 t24 f22 b23.5.** Bloody hell! This is some whisky...! *56.5%. nc ncf.*

Gleann Mór Lagavulin 10 Year Old dist Mar 05, bott Apr 15 **(94) n24 t23.5 f23 b23.5** Even without being troubled by pesky things such as...oooh, oak, for instance, this bottling shows just how profoundly good the basic Lagavulin spirit is. *53.2%. sc.*

⬧ **That Boutique-y Whisky Company Lagavulin** batch 1 **(94.5) n23.5** a raw nose: young, fresh, but with most of the new-makey feel knocked out of it. The peat appears to be within itself, yet threatens so much more...; **t24** oh, what a sensational delivery: the texture is silk with some spicy pins sticking out of it; the sugars are forthright, with a glorious mix of manuka honey and molasses, thickened with a paste of heavily smoked grist...; **f23.5** long, with a slow infusion of vanilla into the smoke. The spices remain playful but significant; **b23.5** a very unusual chance to grab a Lagavulin with kindergarten characteristics: rare to find this malt with so little oak etched into it. A real last-thing-at-night malt, or after a meal of steak barely troubled by heat.... Beautifully made and a genuine treat of a dram. *54.5%. 101 bottles.*

⬧ **That Boutique-y Whisky Company Lagavulin 10 Year Old** batch 2 **(96.5) n24.5** a near perfect Islay nose: as confident in the glass as Theresa May was today at the Dispatch Box... though the peating level is back down to 35ppm, this is as close to how it was when at 50ppm more than a decade ago... **t24** such gorgeous weight: all the power, impudence and mind-blowing accuracy of an Andy Murray back hand passing shot...; **f24** what a finish: dainty, articulate, precise: like Archie Gemmill's goal for Scotland against Brazil...; **b24** a great whisky from a great distillery plucked at just the right age (indeed, being surprisingly youthful) and in all its naked beauty. Sublime. A bit like a Jim Murray Whisky Bible.... *53.7%. 239 bottles.*

LAPHROAIG
Islay, 1815. Beam Inc. Working.

Laphroaig 10 Years Old db **(90) n24** impossible not to nose this and think of Islay: no other aroma so perfectly encapsulates the island – clean despite the rampaging peat-reek and soft oak, raggy coast-scapes and screeching gulls – all in a glass; **t23** one of the crispiest peaty malts of them all, the barley standing out alone, brittle and unbowed, before the peat comes rushing in like the tide: iodine and soft salty tones; **f20.5** the nagging bitterness of many ex-Allied bourbon casks filled during this period is annoyingly apparent here... **b22.5** has reverted back slightly towards a heavier style in more recent bottling, though I would like to see that old oomph at the very death. Even so, this is, indisputably, a classic whisky. The favourite of Prince Charles apparently: he will make a wise king... *40%* ☺

Laphroaig 10 Years Old Original Cask Strength db **(92) n22** a duller nose than usual: caramel reducing the normal iodine kick; **t24** recovers supremely for the early delivery with some stunning black peppers exploding all over the palate leaving behind a trail of peat smoke; the controlled sweetness to the barley is sublime; **f23** again there is a caramel edge to the finish, but this does not entirely prevent a fizzing finale; **b23** caramel apart, this is much truer to form than one or two or more recent bottlings, aided by the fresh, gristy sweetness and explosive spices. Wonderful! *55.7%*

Laphroaig Aged 15 Years db **(79)** n20 t20 f19 b20. A hugely disappointing, lacklustre dram that is oily and woefully short on complexity. Not what one comes to expect either from this distillery or age. *43%*

Laphroaig 18 Years Old db **(94)** n24 multi-layered smokiness: there are soft, flightier, sweeter notes and a duller, earthier peat ingrained with salt and leather; **t23.5** perhaps it's the big leg-up from the rampant hickory, but the peat here offers a vague Fisherman's Friend cough sweet quality far more usually associated with Bowmore, except here it comes in a milder, Demerara-sweetened form with a few strands of liquorice helping that hickory to a gentler level; **f23** soft oils help keep some late, slightly juicy barley notes on track while the peat dances off with some spices to niggle the roof of the mouth and a few odd areas of the tongue; **b23.5** this is Laphroaig's replacement to the woefully inadequate and gutless 15-year-old. And talk about taking a giant step in the right direction. Absolutely brimming with character and panache, from the first molecules escaping the bottle as you pour to the very final ember dying on the middle of your tongue. *48%*

Laphroaig Aged 25 Years db **(94)** n23 the clean - almost prim and proper - fruit appears to have somehow given a lift to the iodine character and accentuated it to maximum effect. The result is something much younger than the label demands and not immediately recognisable as Islay, either. But no less dangerously enticing... **t24** the grapes ensure the peat is met by a salivating palate; particularly impressive is the way the sweet peat slowly finds its footing and spreads beautifully; **f23.5** no shortage of cocoa: a kind of peaty fruit and nut chocolate bar... **b23.5** like the 27-y-o, an Islay which doesn't suffer for sherry involvement. Very different from a standard, bourbon barrel-aged Laphroaig with much of the usually complexity reined in, though its development is first class. This one's all about effect - and it works a treat! *40%*

Laphroaig Aged 25 Years Cask Strength 2011 Edition oloroso and American oak casks db **(96.5)** n24 t24.5 f24 b24. Quite possibly the finest bottling of Laphroaig I have ever encountered. And over the last 35 years there have been a great many bottles... *48.6%*

Laphroaig Aged 30 Years db **(94)** n24 t23 f23 b24. The best Laphroaig of all time? Nope, because the 40-y-o is perhaps better still... just. However, Laphroaig of this subtlety and charm gives even the very finest Ardbeg a run for its money. A sheer treat that should be bottled at greater strength. *43%*

Laphroaig Aged 40 Years db **(94)** n23 t24 f23 b24. Mind-blowing. A malt that defies all logic and theory to be in this kind of shape at such age. The Jane Fonda of Islay whisky. *43%*

Laphroaig Au Cuan Mòr db **(95)** n24 the even peat appears to have a rich, fruity tint to it. But it is the influence of the bourbon barrel which stars, seemingly forging a seamless alliance with the more provocative notes to harmonise them and bring them into a charmingly Kentuckian fold; **t24** it will be hard to locate a more serene delivery on the palate for any peated malt this year. The fruit is entirely sulphur-free and polite enough to, rather than row with the smoke, combine with it to give a featherbed mouth-feel. The oak is profound and should clatter into the taste buds. But the smoke and fruit provide the buffers; **f23** drier, with a gentle smoked fruit-chocolate finale; **b24** you don't need to squint at the back label to be told that first fill bourbon barrels are at work here: this is where Kentucky, Jerez and Islay merges with breath-taking ease and harmony. *48%. Travel retail exclusive.*

Laphroaig Cairdeas bourbon barrels and Amontillado seasoned traditional hogsheads, bott 2014 db **(92.5)** n22.5 ashy...with a few dabs of TCP; **t23** something seemingly youthful bites and bites hard: the light muscovado sugars melt; a little lavender creeps up from nowhere; **f23.5** now pretty dry with the lavender and peat on equal terms; **b23.5** as dry as Laphroaig gets. Rather beautifully made and so delicate you feel it might simply crumble in your mouth. *51.4%.*

Laphroaig Càirdeas Origin quarter casks, bott 2012 db **(89)** n24 t22.5 f20.5 b22. Started like a train and hit the buffers for the finish. Still, early on it is quite superb. *51.2%. ncf.*

◇ **Laphroaig Lore** db **(94)** n23.5 dense, almost opaque, smoke. Plenty of saline moments and a slow delivery of spice...; **t24** big, wallowing in its bog of peat. The sugars are a mixture of Fisherman's Friend and molasses, dried by hickory...; **f23** the oils spread the sugars further while slowing the vanilla development. Excellent vanilla-peat mix at the end and extended by chocolate marzipan; **b23.5** seeing how much I adore this distillery – and treasure my near 40 years of tasting its exceptional malt and visiting its astonishing home – I left to become my 750th new whisky for the 2016 Whisky Bible. "Our richest expression ever" the label promised. It isn't. Big, fat and chunky? Tick. Bounding with phenols? Yep. Enjoyable? Aye! Richest expression ever. Nah. Not quite. Still, a friendly beast worth cuddling up with. And, whatever they say on the label, this is a stunner! *48%. ncf.*

Laphroaig PX Cask bourbon, quarter and Pedro Ximenez casks db **(96) n23.5 t24.5 f24 b24.** I get the feeling that this is a breathtaking success despite the inclusion of Pedro Ximenez casks. This ultra sweet wine is often paired with smoky malt, often with disastrous consequences. Here it has worked, but only because the PX has been controlled itself by absolutely outstanding oak. And the ability of the smoke to take on several roles and personas simultaneously. A quite beautiful whisky and unquestionably one of the great malts of the year...in spite of itself. *48%. Travel Retail exclusive.*

Laphroaig Quarter Cask db **(96) n23** burning embers of peat in a crofter's fireplace; sweet intense malt and lovely, refreshing citrus as well; **t24** mouthwatering, mouth-filling and mouth-astounding: the perfect weight of the smoke has no problems filling every crevice of the palate; builds towards a sensationally sweet maltiness at the middle; **f24** really long, and dries appropriately with smoke and spice. Classic Laphroaig; **b25** a great distillery back to its awesome, if a little sweet, self. Layer upon layer of sexed-up peatiness. The previous bottling just needed a little extra complexity on the nose for this to hit mega malt status. Now it has been achieved... *48%*

Laphroaig Select db **(89) n22** not just full of smoke, but vitality, too. Certain aspects of the sweetness are slightly more aligned to bourbon with a red liquorice flourish to the gristy smoke; **t22** soft – almost too soft – as the smoked toffee becomes decidedly fudgy; **f23** more of the same, only a hint of cocoa and Demerara plus some late oil and spice; **b22** missed a trick by not being unchillfiltered at 46%. An apre-taste squint at the back label revealed some virgin oak casks had been used here, which explains much! *40%. WB15/117*

Laphroaig Triple Wood ex-bourbon, quarter and European oak casks db **(86) n21 t21.5 f21.5 b21.** A pleasing and formidable dram. But one where the peat takes perhaps just too much of a back seat. Or, rather, is somewhat neutralised to the point of directional loss. The sugars, driven home by the heavy weight of oak, help give the whisky a gloss almost unrecognisable for this distillery. Even so, an attractive whisky in many ways. *48%. ncf.*

⟡ **The First Editions Laphroaig Aged 19 Years 1996** refill hogshead, cask no. 11784, bott 2015 **(95.5) n24** the distillery's fingerprints are all over this: unmistakably Laphroaig. The salty sootiness to the peat reek even after all these years shows. There is something of the cowshed about this one – pungent and natural. Some Palma Violets have also crept in as the oak has its say. This is the fanfare of a malt with a very hairy – and muddied – chest...; **t23.5** silky delivery, allowing the liquid brown sugars and salty smoke to dive in in tandem. The mid-ground offers a little coconut and mocha. But the peat rumbles like thunder around the palate; **f24** long, with liquorice and molasses ushering in the mounting vanillas. The mocha stays attached to the peat...and takes forever to fade...; **b24** the salty sootiness after even all these years suggests a whisky that started somewhere above the 35ppm phenols two decades ago. Uncompromising and confident enough to not worry about showing its age. Take your time to discover the levels of complexity here: you'll be pretty amazed. Love it! *56.5%. nc ncf sc. 188 bottles.*

⟡ **Hidden Spirits Laphroaig LPH.015 14 Years Old** cask no. 111712, dist 2000, bott 2015 **(92.5) n23** a clipped nose: brusque peat, a little acidic and sharp. But enough molasses to stare down the arrogant dryness; **t23** no less crisp and sharp on delivery. A rather beautiful theme of smoked mocha, with that molasses now coming more fully into the picture; some light oils and spice fill the middle ground; **f23** the spices tingle as a little zesty vanilla comes into play; **b23.5** a quite lovely bottling, showing the distillery in a rather starched and rigid pose. Yet the excellent oak at play ensures for the drinker that time spent equals complexity discovered. *48%. sc.*

Hunter Laing's Old & Rare Laphroaig Aged 24 Years refill hogshead, dist Mar 90, bott Jul 14 **(84) n21 t22 f20 b21.** The nose clambers through the smoke, warning of a less than perfect bourbon barrel. And this is confirmed on delivery and, especially, the finish. The burn and prickle is not space. *51.9%. ncf sc. 285 bottles.*

⟡ **MacAlabur Laphroaig 16 Year Old** bourbon barrel, cask no. 700288, dist 30 Jul 98, bott 25 Oct 14 **(94.5) n23.5** a nose to confound those who claim Laphroaig is all about the phenols. Intricate traces of lime and pink grapefruit thread through the ethereal peat, stitching it neatly with the salty sea-spray dampened oak; the gristy malt has an almost old-fashioned style more closely associated at this age with its late neighbour, Port Ellen; **t23.5** the sugars are first on the scene, tidy and measured, allowing the peat to grow without causing too much angst to the palate. The citrus, equally calming in its effect, is also a force for the good; **f23.5** an almost genteel fade. The smoke clouds up on the palate, but never so thick as to hide the growing nutty vanilla; **b24** refuses to depend on the peat, which it shows with restraint. Elegant and uses the light citrus present to great effect. Charming. *57.3%. sc. 230 bottles.*

⬩ **Old Malt Cask Laphroaig Aged 15 Years** refill butt, cask no. 11642, dist Apr 00, bott Jun 15 **(90) n22.5** dry, earthy and salty; **t23** a brooding presence immediately on the palate. Sugars at a premium and the soot takes hold; **f22** throbbing, dry, waves of peat and latterly oak; **b25.5** a moody and deep rendition which never veers off its hefty script. *50%. nc ncf sc. 479 bottles.*

⬩ **Old Malt Cask Laphroaig Aged 15 Years** cask no. 11708, dist Apr 00, bott Jul 15 **(84.5) n21 t21 f21.5 b21.** The oak has given this one a youthful edge for its age. Excellent shape to the smoke, but,overall, feels somehow thin and incomplete. *50%. nc ncf sc. 156 bottles.*

⬩ **Old Malt Cask Laphroaig Aged 15 Years** refill butt, cask no. 12537, dist Feb 01, bott Apr 16 **(88) n23.5** a major mix of peat reek and anthracite: like a smoky custard pie in the face...; **t23** much more soft-bodied and rotund on delivery than the nose suggests. The dark sugars have a field day...; **f19.5** dries vigorously, leaving a sooty residue. Just a shade too bitter; **b22** the brash, slightly bitter finale cannot take away from the earlier beauty. *50%. nc ncf sc. 357 bottles.*

⬩ **Old Particular Islay Laphroaig 14 Years Old** refill butt, cask no. 10880, dist Feb 01, bott Aug 15 **(95) n24** complex once the air gets to work on it. Sweet, vaguely flat, salty smokiness; a curious "small grain" busyness usually associated with better bourbons; **t23.5** soft and sweet delivery with a bite as the smoke arrives; yet again there is that stirring "small grain" complexity at the back of the palate: intriguing; **f23.5** continues to fizz as the vanilla tries – but fails – to match the smoke in depth; **b24** fabulously complex and busy. And always with plenty of feel-good qualities. A classic of its rather unusual type. *48.4%. nc ncf sc. 390 bottles.*

⬩ **Old Particular Islay Laphroaig 15 Years Old** refill hogshead, cask no. 10791, dist Jun 00, bott Jun 15 **(94) n23.5** textbook: the smoke runs deep and is enriched further with lavender; **t24** glorious melt-in-the mouth delivery. Just a little extra oil for Laphroaig, though well within its comfort zone. The peat shows early before the gristy sweetness begins to form. When the oak arrives, it is warmly (literally) greeted as an equal; **f23** a beautiful degree of cocoa mingles beautifully with the smoke; **b23.5** how can a whisky so big be so subtle? Fabulous pacing to this and an elegance to match its confidence. Beautiful! *48.4%. nc ncf sc. 234 bottles.*

⬩ **Old Particular Islay Laphroaig 15 Years Old** refill hogshead, cask no. 10791, dist Jun 00, bott Dec 15 **(95) n24** one of those 15 minute jobs: the peat spins a spicy tale, occasionally with some citrusy characters, too..; **t23.5** limited oil, ensuring a sooty dryness to the smoke and a crystalline feel to the Demerara sugars; **f23.5** warms as the spices take hold. A light Allied cask bitterness towards the end, but sugars enough to balance the score; **b24** very sexy malt. Just purrs at you, sometimes showing its claws...Brilliant! *48.4%. nc ncf sc. 234 bottles.*

Provenance Laphroaig Over 8 Years one refill hogshead, cask no. 10407, dist autumn 05, bott summer 14 **(94.5) n23.5 t24 f23 b24** I'd love a few casks of this in a blend I design: it'd make such an impact! But pretty much on the money as a singleton, too. Superb. *46%. nc ncf sc.*

⬩ **Scotch Malt Whisky Society Cask 29.181 Aged 20 Years** refill barrel, dist 04 Apr 95, bott 21 Mar 16 **(94.5) n23** evidence of a very decent cask at work and good times ahead: the smoke appears just a little preoccupied by the appearance of light butterscotch and a little salt. Delicate, even considering the vintage...; **t24**...and no less delicate on delivery for the first few waves. That is before a surge of Demerara sugars carry with it the smoke in a now much more intense role. And roll...; the mid ground savours the salt and spices; **f23.5** long, with moderate oils assisting. The smoke is now deft and offers a gristy hue; **b24** just love it when a big whisky like this just cruises through the gears, showing its power only as a reminder of its capabilities... *57.6%. nc ncf sc. 204 bottles.*

⬩ **Svenska Eldvatten Laphroaig 2005** ex-bourbon barrel, dist Mar 05, bott Apr 15 **(93.5) n23.5** the ultimate peat reek fire cleaning exercise, dry and sooty...but salty and sexy, too...; **t23** sootier than a chimney unswept for ten years; **f23.5** some late muscovado sugars kick in some unexpected fruit notes, while the sugars soften; **b23.5** never sets a foot wrong from nose to finale. Excellent! *56.9%. sc.*

Whisky Fair Laphroaig 16 Year Old sherry hogshead, dist 1998, bott 2015 **(87) n24 t22 f19 b22.** A rare case of fruit and phenols working merrily in tandem, with the smoke in particular having a certain swagger. But it appears that it is the oak, rather than treated sherry, which makes the finish bitter and hard going. Some beautiful moments to treasure early on, though. *46%. 246 bottles.*

⬩ **Whiskyjace Laphroaig 16 Years Old 1998** bourbon barrel & refill sherry cask, bott 2014 **(77) n19 t21 f19 b18.** A malt which lurches around the palate like Frankenstein's monster after guzzling back a crate of local slivovitz! The sherry and the peat never find a single point of common ground from start to finish. Not even sulphur at play: seems pretty clean to me. Just a malt, engulfed in discordant wine and peat notes, that refuses to work, other than the neutral early sugars. The lovely people at Whiskyjace; I have a simple question: why? Why.....??? *51.2%*

⬩ **Whisky Tales Laphroaig 18 Years Old (82.5) n20.5 t22.5 f18.5 b21.** Some way from a standard Laphroaig. The nose tells the story of a tired cask and gives away the ending: that it will interfere further down the line. And the finish is, indeed, untidy. Some major sugars on show, though, especially on the silky delivery. A buttery smokiness is not without merit. *52.9%*

LINKWOOD

Speyside, 1820. Diageo. Working.

Linkwood 12 Years Old db **(94.5) n23.5** gorgeous malt absolutely bursting at the seems with barley-rich vitality; citrus and anthracite abound; **t24** a quite stunning delivery with some of the clearest, cleanest, most crystalline malt on the market. The sugars are angular and decidedly Demerara; **f23** a long play out of sharp barley which refuses to be embattled by the oaky vanillas; light spices compliment the persistent sugars; **b24** possibly the most improved distillery bottling in recent times. Having gone through a period of dreadful casks, it appears to have come through to the other side very much on top and close to how some of us remember it a quarter of a century ago. Sublime malt: one of the most glittering gems in the Diageo crown. *43%*

Linkwood 26 Year Old port finish dist 1981, bott 2008 db **(85) n20 t24 f20.5 b20.5.** Can't say that either nose or finish do it for me. But the delivery is brilliant: the enormity and luxurious sweetness of the grape leaves you simply purring and rolling your eyes in delight. *56.9%*

Linkwood 26 Year Old rum finish, dist 1981, bott 2008 db **(89.5) n23.5 t23.5 f21 b21.5.** A real touch of the rum toffee raisin candy to this one. *56.5%*

Linkwood 26 Year Old sweet red wine, dist 1981, bott 2008 db **(89) n22.5 t23 f21 b22.** Juicy, spicy: doesn't stint on complexity. *56.5%*

Linkwood 1974 Rare Malt db **(79) n20 t21 f19 b19.** Wobbles about the palate in search of a story and balance. Finds neither but some of the early moments, though warming, offer very decent malt. The best bit follows a couple of seconds after – and lasts as long. *55%*

⬩ **Best Dram Linkwood 14 Years Old (94) n23.5** drop dead gorgeous: light mallows with crushed Maltesers, plus some apple and vague citrus; **t23.5** a quite stunning brightness to the barley sugar which proudly juts from every vantage point. Still a soft landing despite the obvious brittleness and, though the spices are fierce, they sit comfortably with the Demerara sugars on display; **f23** long, and though the sugars are mainly spent, the toasty tannin offers a gentle bourbon flourish; **b24** as I wrote these notes, a male blackcap jinked around in the bushes outside my window, and under the table in my garden. Yet its early Spring-warbled song was scarcely more lovely or in tune than this whisky... *55.9%*

⬩ **Fadandel.dk Linkwood 21 Years Old** cask no. 7127, dist 5 Jun 95, bott 6 Jun 16 **(93) n23** delicate moist marzipan with a hint of crushed green acorn: a malt that's been squirreled away for the last two decades, obviously; **t23.5** a superb balancing act between the still intact, clean, juicy barley – complete with sweetened barley water - and much more upright and slightly uptight oak; **f23** long strands of oak. But the freshness of the barley refuses to diminish; **b23.5** a quite studied, controlled and elegant dram. *47.5%. nc ncf sc. 237 bottles.*

⬩ **The First Editions Linkwood Aged 18 Years 1997** refill hogshead, cask no. 11789, bott 2015 **(83.5) n21 t21.5 f20 b21.** Typically Linkwoodian, in that you are never quite sure what mood it will arrive in. Well, this one's chewing bubblegum –as the nose confirms – and is in a fiery frame of mind. The oak is relentlessly dry at the end. *59.5%. nc ncf sc. 148 bottles.*

⬩ **Hidden Spirits Linkwood LKW.716 18 Years Old** cask no. LK9716, dist 1997, bott 2016 **(94.4) n23.5** acacia honey and beeswax; add a twist of citrus, a sprig of mint and a little barley sugar...and hey presto! **t24** much more body on delivery than can be found on the nose: the malt is thick and at times concentrated. The acacia honey (again!) and spice is dried slightly by the vanilla; **f23** some of the oils retain just enough barley sugar to balance out the powdery vanillas...; **b24** here's a great example of why this makes such superb blending malt: imagine the malty surge this would offer! As it is, as a single malt, not half bad, either... *48%. sc.*

⬩ **Hunter Laing's Distiller's Art Linkwood Aged 18 Years** refill hogshead, dist 1997, bott 2016 **(82) n21 t21 f20 b20.** A very similar cove to the First Editions Linkwood. An almost identical puckering to the huge dry oak finish, but with less oil to maximise the sugars. *48%. nc ncf sc. 148 bottles.*

Kingsbury Silver Linkwood 24 Year Old cask no. 568, dist 1989 **(85) n20.5 t23.5 f20.5 b21.** What seems like a thumping heavyweight oloroso butt has its weaknesses on both nose and finish. But there is no denying the delivery which is of the Harvey's Bristol Cream variety and is stashed with some grapey treasures. A flawed diamond, indeed... 46%.

⬧ **Maltbarn Linkwood 1998** ex-bourbon cask, bott 2015 **(89.5) n22.5** classic school butterscotch tart; **t23** a happy mix of light oak and lighter barley. The sugars have nowhere to hide, so briefly dazzle; **f22** the thin finish dries towards spiced cocoa; **b22.5** slightly anorexic. But still very pretty. 49.3%. sc. 205 bottles.

Montgomerie's Single Cask Collection Linkwood cask no. 6713, dist 05 Dec 89, bott Mar 13 **(89.5) n22.5 t23 f22 b22** in many ways a modest whisky. But what it does right can be breath-taking. 46%. nc ncf. WB15/130

Old Malt Cask Linkwood Aged 15 Years refill hogshead, cask no. 10828, dist Oct 98, bott Aug 14 **(87.5) n20 t23 f22 b22.5**. The higgledy-piggledy nose is more than compensated by a thoroughly entertaining malty richness on delivery, fully backed by complex spices and light molasses. Good oils, too. Hugely satisfying on the palate. 50%. nc ncf sc. 351 bottles.

⬧ **Old Malt Cask Linkwood Aged 18 Years** refill hogshead, cask no. 11565, dist Jun 97, bott Jul 15 **(87) n21.5 t22 f21.5 b22**. The accent is firmly on the oak from the first sniff to the last gurgle. At times, there is enough barley to offer a counter point, and a dusting of cocoa to emphasise the oaky dominance. 50%. nc ncf sc. 257 bottles.

⬧ **Old Malt Cask Linkwood Aged 18 Years** refill hogshead, cask no. 12106, dist Jun 97, bott Nov 15 **(95) n24** a spellbinding nose: the kind of aroma that needs concentration and an odour-free environment. Only then might you catch the scarily subtle interplay between the crushed muscovado sugars, the comice pear, the gristy barley and the genteel vanillas of the oak. What a treat...; **t24** deft malt caresses and kisses the tongue and palate, offering a fragile gristy sweetness to balance the busier spices. A beautiful interplay between youthful and older tones which deserves a good 20 minutes to fully appreciate; **f23** elements of Canadian grain here as the flaky vanilla melds with the last subtle sugar tones. Dry, spiced but always in happy unison with light but lingering barley; **b24** a sophisticated dram for those who prefer their Martinis very dry and their whiskies stunning. All too easy to overlook the greatness of this bottling: truly glorious. 50%. nc ncf sc. 335 bottles.

⬧ **Scotch Malt Whisky Society Cask 39.112 Aged 25 Years** refill hogshead, dist 16 Oct 89, bott 21 Sept 15 **(89.5) n23.5** a substantial oak presence **t22.5** those tannins present on the nose build a veritable fortress on delivery; softened only by the mix of honey and malt concentrate; **f22** distinctly splintery, despite the softening oils; some mocha, but drowned out by the spice; **b22** enjoys the odd spectacular moment, especially on the nose. But plucked from the warehouse about three summers too late... 49%. nc ncf sc. 248 bottles.

⬧ **Scotch Malt Whisky Society Cask 39.117 Aged 24 Years** refill hogshead, dist 29 Oct 90, bott 30 Nov 15 **(85.5) n23 t21 f21.5 b20**. The texture of this malt is exceptionally soft. Which sits in contrast to the attack of malt and oak, making for the odd uncomfortable moment. A few years beyond its optimum age. 46.5%. nc ncf sc. 204 bottles.

⬧ **The Single Cask Linkwood Aged 18 Years** cask no. 7122, dist 05 Jun 95, bott 19 Jun 13 **(93) n23** lemon sherbet meets toasted cedar; **t23.5** busy delivery. Fizzy and fulsome despite the overall lack of weight. Playful citrus enlivens the simple malt-vanilla centre stage; **f23** hello! We're back to that sherbet dab again. Even with a bit of liquorice with the late oil...! **b23.5** beautifully made. Wonderfully matured. Absolute fun! 51.2%. nc ncf sc.

⬧ **That Boutique-y Whisky Company Linkwood** batch 1 **(91)** toasted hazelnut; **t23.5** beautifully intense: the delivery, thanks to the clarity of the spirit, leaves nothing to the imagination: toasty barley stokes up the spices before a more subtle praline semi-sweetness appears; **f22.5** predominantly spiced vanilla; **b23** the nutty sugars are the star turn. A satisfying and complex malt. 51.2%. 92 bottles.

⬧ **That Boutique-y Whisky Company Linkwood** batch 2 **(85) n21 t23 f21 b20**. Reminds me of something between central European oak and horse chestnut wood at play here. The chocolate mousse intensity is lovely on one hand. But the overall bigness of the wood really does annihilate any chance of overall balance to match the intriguing flavour profile. In the meantime, any traces of malt have vanished... Still, can't say I don't absolutely love that molassed sugar kick early on. Different. 54.7%. 135 bottles.

⬧ **The Whisky Chamber Linkwood 10 Years Old** ex-bourbon barrel, cask no. 99/2005, dist 20 Jul 05, bott 05 Jan 16 **(88.5) n22** not dissimilar to a yeast-induced fruitiness to this one, but the big malt takes centre stage; **t22.5** big salivating malt with a mix of gristy sweetness falling in with a more austere sawdusty tannin; **f22** concentrates on the malt, with a lightly spiced side-dish; **b22** a warming, vaguely aggressive dram which rarely steers away from the malty path. 59.3%. nc sc.

LITTLEMILL

Lowland, 1772. Loch Lomond Distillers. Demolished.

Littlemill 21 Year Old 2nd Release bourbon cask db (**87**) n22 t21.5 f21.5 b22. So thin you expect it to fragment into a zillion pieces on the palate. But the improvement on this as a new make almost defies belief. The sugars are crisp enough to shatter on your teeth, the malt is stone hard and fractured and, on the finish, does show some definite charm before showing its less attractive teeth....and its roots... Overall, though, more than enjoyable. *47%. nc ncf.*

Littlemill 25 Year Old db (**92.5**) n22 perhaps a little reminder of the once flame-thrower nose, but this is more like a popgun amid the slightly (and characteristically) glue-like maltiness; **t24** the malt excels here in a way those of us intimately familiar with this distillery 25 years ago could scarcely imagine. Even moves into mocha and then praline mode as the intensity of the barley flies off the scale; **f23** long, with a pleasing spice pulsing alongside the flatter vanillas; **b23.5** another example of a malt which was practically undrinkable in its fiery, punkish youth but that is now a reformed, gentle character in older age. *52%*

Littlemill 1964 db (**82**) n21 t20 f21 b20. A soft-natured, bourbony chap that shows little of the manic tendencies that made this one of Scotland's most-feared malts. Talk about mellowing with age... *40%*

Littlemill 1990 Vintage Aged 22 Years bott 2013 db (**91**) n23 despite a light flame licking at the nose there is enough honey and sugar on the barley to persuade you to dive in head first; **t23** peppered barley attacks the taste buds with gusto, leaving behind a trail of tannins and honey; **f22.5** butterscotch and watered-down napalm in equal measures; **b22.5** a very tasty bit of rough. *50.6%. nc ncf. Glen Contrine Bonded Warehouse Ltd.*

Chieftain's Littlemill Aged 22 Years hogshead, dist Feb 92, bott Jun 14 (**82**) n19.5 t21.5 f20 b21. Some attractive sugar-barley moments. But never manages to quite grow out of its aggressive youth. *50.7%. nc ncf.*

◇ **Eiling Lim Littlemill 23 Years Old 1990** bott 2013 (**84**) n21.5 t22.5 f19 b21. Like an exhausted, age-weathered volcano, this has been polished by time and reduced in ferocity. Nutty throughout and still displaying a tell-tale sheen on the sugary but feisty palate, this now has more bourbon notes at play than malt ones. *498%. nc ncf sc. 68 bottles. 1st Release.*

◇ **Eiling Lim Littlemill 24 Years Old 1990** bott 2014 (**82**) n21 t20 f21 b20. The anger of its youth has been reduced to the point of this now rocking back and forth in its oaky chair, absent-mindedly singing songs of vanilla and spicy battles of yore... *46.8%. nc ncf sc. 113 bottles. 8th Release.*

LOCH LOMOND

Highlands (Southwestern), 1966. Loch Lomond Distillers. Working.

◇ **Loch Lomond Aged 12 Years** db (**93.5**) n22.5 a triangular battle between spices, malt and an almost coppery-metallic fruitiness; **t23.5** so succulent! Not sure if the distiller at the time was playing about with some high propane yeast which just explodes with fruit, but there is a richness to this malt which really does deserve applause; **f23.5** good grief! I've been through some Loch Lomond casks over the years but not sure where they dug these up from. Never before seen spice quite like it, or such a sublime balance with the fruity malt. And when I say fruit, please don't think grape..; **b24** great to see they now have the stocks to allow this malt to really flex its muscles... *46%. ncf.*

Loch Lomond 14 Year Old Peated bourbon cask db (**83**) n21 t21.5 f20.5 b20. Lomond can do a lot, lot better than this. Huge malts but entirely out of sync and never comfortable with the oils present. This isn't the Loch Lomond I know and love. *46% nc ncf.*

Loch Lomond 18 Years Old db (**78.5**) n19 t21 f19 b19.5. A demanding, oily malt which is a long way from technical excellence but is no slouch on the chocolate nougat front. *43%*

◇ **Loch Lomond Aged 18 Years** db (**89.5**) n22 subtle, Ardmore-style peat tones sinking into lightly fruited morass; **t23** silky and slick, dark muscovado sugars merge with the more intense malts; **f22.5** a slow re-kindling of almost apologetic smoky embers; the sugars – and probably esters - keep the fruitiness alive; **b22.5** there is always something slightly irresistible when you come across a single malt where the peat beats a gentle rhythm rather than its own chest... *46%. ncf.*

Loch Lomond 21 Years Old db (**89.5**) n22.5 t23 f22 b22. A little while since I last tasted this, and pretty close to exactly how I remember it. Seems to revel in its own enormity! *43%*

Loch Lomond Organic 12 Year Old bourbon cask db (**83.5**) n19 t20 f23 b21.5. A malty beast. But in some respects has more in common with a German still than a traditional pot. Definite traces of feint. *48%. nc ncf.*

Loch Lomond Original bourbon casks db **(81.5)** n20 t21 f20 b20.5. Hmmm. Surprisingly feinty, though the really wide cut does ensure a huge number of flavours. A distinctly German style to this. 40%

Glengarry 12 Year Old db **(92.5)** n22.5 the citrus edge cannot hide the big barley presence. Weighty, without being oily and cumbersome; **t23.5** good grief: it is like sucking on a tablet of concentrated malt! The oak also makes its mark, but acts no more than a prop and inserter of warming, though controlled, spice. And faint molasses; **f23** more of the same with those spices peddling to the end; **b23.5** probably the most intense malt on the market today. Astonishing. And stunning. 46%. ncf.

Inchmurrin 12 Years Old db **(86.5)** n21.5 t22 f21.5 b21.5. A significantly improved dram which is a bit of a malt soup. Love the Demerara injection. 40%

Inchmurrin Aged 15 Years bourbon cask, bott Dec 12 db **(86)** n22 t21.5 f21 b21.5. Slightly tangy with an edge to the cask which interferes with the usual malty procession. 46%. nc ncf.

Inchmurrin Aged 18 Years bourbon cask, bott Dec 12 db **(92.5)** n22.5 t23.5 f23.5 b23. Loch Lomond distillery in its brightest colours. 46%. nc ncf. Glen Catrine Bonded Warehouse Ltd.

Inchmurrin Aged 21 Years bourbon cask, bott Dec 12 db **(90)** n22 t23 f22.5 b22.5. This has spent 21 years in a very exceptional cask. Not exactly breathtaking complexity, but what it does is completed with aplomb. 46%. nc ncf. Glen Catrine Bonded Warehouse Ltd.

Inchmurrin Loch Lomond Island Collection 12 Year Old db **(87)** n21.5 t22 f21.5 b22. A thick malty offering with a weighty grist and maple syrup infusion. Big and clumsy. 46%. ncf.

⬙ **Inchmurrin Island Collection Aged 18 Years** db **(87)** n21 t22.5 f21.5 b22. Wow! That is quite a tangle of flavours and messages. Not quite sure where the "summer grass" on the label comes from. But date and walnut cake...now that would have made sense. Big and rather beautiful in an ugly kind of way... 46%. ncf. Loch Lomond Whiskies

⬙ **Inchmurrin Island Collection Madeira Wood Finish** db **(77)** n17 t23 f18 b19. Alas, it wasn't only sherry butts which were sulphur damaged. Mind you, the explosion of golden sultana on delivery is worth the discomfort. 46%. ncf. Loch Lomond Whiskies

⬙ **Old Malt Cask Inchmurrin Aged 31 Years** refill barrel, cask no. 12255, dist Jun 84, bott Apr 16 **(91.5)** n22.5 a joyous bourbon edge, with red liquorice and vanilla-clad tannin. What fun! **t23** silky, with a sugary lustre which emphasises the busy (vaguely smoky) gristiness beautifully; **f22.5** a tad chalky, but still the grist melts...though now the spices are in full flow, as is the lemon sherbet finale; **b23.5** brilliant to see this malt in such fine fettle! A rare treat from this uniquely-styled malt. And carries its years effortlessly. 47.1%. nc ncf sc. 288 bottles.

LOCHSIDE
Highlands (Eastern), 1957–1992. Chivas Brothers. Demolished.

The Cooper's Choice Lochside 1967 Aged 44 Years cask no. 807 **(96.5)** n24.5 t24.5 f23.5 b24 It is amazing that I had to travel 6,000 miles to find this in British Columbia. But, this is the kind of whisky you would travel four times that kind of distance to experience. Easily one of the top ten single casks I have tasted in the last five years. 41.5%. 354 bottles.

LONGMORN
Speyside, 1895. Chivas Brothers. Working.

Longmorn 15 Years Old db **(93)** n23 curiously salty and coastal for a Speysider, really beautifully structured oak but the malt offers both African violets and barley sugar; **t24** your mouth aches from the enormity of the complexity, while your tongue wipes grooves into the roof of your mouth. Just about flawless bitter-sweet balance, the intensity of the malt is enormous, yet – even after 15 years – it maintains a cut-grass Speyside character; **f22** long, acceptably sappy and salty with chewy malt and oak. Just refuses to end; **b24** these latest bottlings are the best yet: previous ones had shown just a little too much oak but this has hit a perfect compromise. An all-time Speyside great. 45%

Longmorn 16 Years Old db **(84.5)** n20.5 t22 f21 b21. This was one of the disappointments of the 2008 edition, thanks to the lacklustre nose and finish. This time we see a cautious nudge in the right direction: the colour has been dropped fractionally and the nose celebrates with a sharper barley kick with a peppery accompaniment. The non-existent (caramel apart) finale of yore now offers a distinct wave of butterscotch and thinned honey...and still some spice. Only the delivery has dropped a tad...but a price worth paying for the overall improvement. Still a way to go before the real Longmorn 16 shines in our glasses for all to see and fall deeply in love with. Come on lads in the Chivas lab: we know you can do it... 48%

⬙ **Longmorn The Distiller's Choice** bott 2015/12/09 db **(84.5)** n21.5 t22 f20.5 b20.5. The steam train depicted on the label would have needed some fuel to get it to its destination. Not enough coal, and it would certainly break down somewhere en route. Likewise, this is underpowered at 40%, with the oils badly broken down, thus allowing the finish to become a little too chalky and one or two less well-balanced notes to have too great a say. Pleasant in its early toffeed maltiness, but a little too tangy for its own good... and just runs out of puff... *40%*

◇ **Acla Selection Longmorn 21 Years Old** bourbon hogshead, dist 1992, bott 2014 **(89) n22.5** vaguely tart, with a non-specific citrus element giving the barley a vivid third dimension; **t22.5** mouth-watering and gristy even after all these years. Some decent soft caramel, too..; **f22** flat, other than some toffee apple as it fattens out; **b22** quite a creamy version. Ultra simplistic for its age, having taken on a fair chunk of natural caramel from the oak. *52.1%. nc ncf.*

◇ **Gordon & MacPhail Distillery Label Longmorn 2002 (77)** n19 t20 f19 b19. I have been marvelling at Longmorn, originally through G&M's astonishing old 12-year-old, longer than a great many readers of this book have been on this planet: certainly before they discovered whisky. And I have never known these great bottlers to get their cask selection for Longmorn this wrong. Despite the attractive marmalade and honey thread, this is disappointing, off-key and incoherent. A one-off, I am sure. *43%*

◇ **Hidden Spirits Longmorn LNG.315 11 Years Old** cask no. 11198, dist 2003, bott 2015 **(96.5) n24** few 12-year-olds will boast a nose quite this stunning: buttery cashew, a tweak of spice, a smattering of vanilla, the fading echoes of grist, a twist of red liquorice. Delicate, elegant, beautiful...; **t24** one of the deliveries of the year: any softer and it would barely register on delivery. Lightly malty oils, sharpened by juicy citrus and freshly cut grass; the malt rekindles and intensifies...we are now talking Maltesers...; **f24** long, elegant and a slow melting of those Maltesers, milk chocolate and all...and then those spices...wow, wow, wow...! **b24.5** the name "Hidden Spirit" is hardly lost on this pure work of art. How many years – decades even – have I been saying that Longmorn should be bottled no more than 12 years and without added colouring? And here we have it. A single cask, maybe. But the previously hidden beauty of this distillery unmasked and naked for all to see. This has to be in line for a potential Single Cask of the Year... *48%. sc.*

◇ **Highlander Inn Longmorn Aged 23 Years** cask no. 48514, dist 10 Jan 92, bott 22 Sept 15 **(94.5) n23.5** big age on this, but contained: the tannins have ensured gravitas, but a mix of treacle and liquorice have ensured the sweetness is never crushed; **t24** such a big delivery, seemingly with slightly OTT oak. But, again, the sugars – now with a bigger malt infusion – arrive in good time to shepherd the more splintery tannins to safe ground. The liquorice and maple syrup mix delights; **f23** spices tingle and fizz and again we seem to be bordering Kentucky...; **b24** a profound malt which projects its impressive personality with gusto. At times closer to bourbon than barley... *48%. sc. 228 bottles.*

◇ **Kingsbury Gold Longmorn 18 Years Old 1996** hogshead, cask no. 11443 **(92) n23** about as citrusy as Longmorn gets: lemon peel binds beautifully with the vanilla; the big, biscuity malt hovers on an entirely different plane; **t23** the zestiness on the nose ties in brilliantly with the salivating delivery. Slowly, the maltiness builds and becomes pretty estery and rich; a lovely mix of ulmo honey, light muscovado and a hint of coconut fills the mid ground; **f22.5** long, with the citrus returning, accompanied by spice; **b23.5** hugely satisfying whisky with never a dull moment. *53.9%. sc. 241 bottles.*

◇ **Old Particular Speyside Longmorn 18 Years Old** new wood hogshead, cask no. 11070, dist Oct 98, bott Feb 16 **(84) n22 t21 f20 b21.** Two distinct strands to this malt. The positive one being the high quality, intense, sweet barley. Less desired is the classic Allied bitter bourbon cask syndrome. *48.4%. nc ncf sc. 328 bottles.*

The Queen of the Moorlands Rare Cask Ipstones Edition Longmorn 1992 Aged 21 Years (93) n22.5 t23.5 f23 b24 Rarely has a malt with, strictly speaking, a slight technical flaw, been quite so entertaining. But, there again, you rarely find honey quite this switched on. Some serious Highland Park tendencies at play here. *56.2%. sc.*

◇ **Scotch Malt Whisky Society Cask 7.127 Aged 30 Years** refill hogshead, dist 24 Sept 95, bott 25 Jan 16 **(92.5) n23** some thundering oak makes for a dark and foreboding nose. But there is enough crystallised molasses and spice to suggest somewhat overcooked Manor House cake; **t23** the delivery is an instant declaration of war between the sugars and seemingly pissed off spices. It could turn ugly, but instead, a compromise is drawn, the soft malty oils being the broker...; **f23** both sides have their say towards the end, though the oak, through a build up of hefty tannins, forms the biggest splinter group...literally; **b23.5** a malt at its very age limit, but wears the wrinkles with panache. *53.1%. nc ncf sc. 24 bottles.*

◇ **Scotch Malt Whisky Society Cask 7.129 Aged 30 Years** refill hogshead, dist 24 Sept 95, bott 22 Feb 16 **(95.5) n24** bread and butter pudding, (old) banana sandwich, porridge with molten brown sugar on top, coconut in syrup, apple strudel. All this...and more...; **t23.5** the high strength takes full advantage of the sweet integrity of the malt: fabulous clarity and oomph! A parade of demerara sugar and grist; **f24** dries elegantly as the oak takes firmer command; a late creamy texture helps lengthen the delight further; **b24** Longmorn at its very finest. *57.4%. nc ncf sc. 72 bottles.*

⋘ **Single Cask Collection Longmorn Aged 23 Years** bourbon hogshead (96) **n24.5** the kind of nose you want to bury your snout into all day: though from a bourbon cask, we have light honey as the back drop to the most subtle peach and pear imaginable. Perhaps set off slightly by the vaguest sprinkle of salt; **t24** a butterfly landing of honey-tipped barley and then butterfly kisses of golden syrup with the odd, more passionate nip by spice; **f23.5** long, delicate – of course – and now concentrates on the oak with a butterscotch (from the butterflies!) and mocha interplay; **b24** almost impossible to find fault: perfectly distilled and matured in a cask shaped in heaven. A thing of profound beauty. *52.1%. sc.*

The Single Malts of Scotland Longmorn Aged 21 Years hogshead, cask no. 110979, dist 11 Sep 92, bott 25 Mar 14 (95) **n23.5 t24 f23.5 b24** Absolutely beautiful, evocative malt. A rare treat of a dram. *49.7%. 293 bottles. WB15/293*

The Single Malts of Scotland Longmorn 22 Years Old cask no. 12289, dist 90, bott 14 Sep 13 (89.5) **n22.5 t23 f22 b22** A very decent Longmorn which does the simple things attractively. *48.1%. 199 bottles. WB15/305*

⋘ **That Boutique-y Whisky Company Longmorn** batch 1 (86) **n21 t23.5 f20.5 b21.** A lovely dram where the intensity of the malt hurtles through the roof. But from the very first nose, you sense not all is dunky-hory owing to the restrictions of the old bourbon cask. And this is accentuated towards the finale. *52%. 157 bottles.*

THE MACALLAN
Speyside, 1824. Edrington. Working.

The Macallan 7 Years Old db (89) **n23 t23 f21 b22.** An outstanding dram that underlines just how good young malts can be. Fun, fabulous and in recent bottlings has upped the clarity of the sherry intensity to profound new heights. *40%*

The Macallan Fine Oak 8 Years Old db (82.5) **n20.5 t22 f20 b20.** A slight flaw has entered the mix here. Even so, the barley fights to create a distinctive sharpness. However, a rogue sherry butt has put paid to any hopes the honey and spice normally found in this brand. *40%*

The Macallan 10 Years Old db (91) **n23** oloroso appears to be the big noise here, but clever, almost meaty, incursions of spice offer an extra dimension; fruity, yet bitter-sweet: dense yet teasingly light in places; **t23** chewy fruit and the old Macallan silk is back: creamy cherries and mildly under-ripe plum ensures a sweet-sour style; **f21.5** traces of vanilla and barley remind us of the oak and barley, but the fruit reverberates for some while, as does some annoying caramel; **b23.5** for a great many of us, it is with the Mac 10 our great Speyside odyssey began. It has to be said that in recent years it has been something of a shadow of its former great self. However, this is the best version I have come across for a while. Not perhaps in the same league as those bottlings in the 1970s which made us re-evaluate the possibilities of single malt. But fine enough to show just how great this whisky can be when the butts have not been tainted and, towards the end, the balance between barley and grape is a relatively equal one. *40%*

The Macallan 10 Years Old Cask Strength db (85) **n20 t22 f22 b21.** Enjoyable and a would give chewing gum a run for its money. But over-egged the sherry here and not a patch on the previous bottling. *58.8%. Duty Free.*

The Macallan Fine Oak 10 Years Old db (90) **n23** finely tuned and balanced: everything on a nudge-nudge basis with neither fruit nor barley willing to come out and lead: really take your time over this to maximise the entertainment; **t22.5** brimming with tiny, delicate oak notes which just brush gently, almost erotically, against the clean barley; **f21.5** drier, chewier and no less laid-back; **b22** much more on the ball than the last bottling of this I came across. Malts really come as understated or clever than this. *40%*

The Macallan Sherry Oak 12 Years Old db (93) **n24** thick, almost concentrated grape with a stunning degree of light spices. Topped with boiled greengage; **t23.5** clean sherry is heralded not just by vanilla-thickened grape but a deft muscovado sweetening and a light seasoning of spice; **f22.5** cocoa, vanilla and fudge. Remains clean and beautifully layered; **b23** I have to say that some Macallan 12 I have tasted on the road has let me down in the last year or so. This is virtually faultless. Virtually a time machine back to another era... *40%*

The Macallan 12 Years Old Sherry Oak Elegancia db (86) **n23 t22 f20 b21.** Promises, but delivers only to an extent. *40%*

The Macallan Fine Oak 12 Years Old db (95.5) n24 faultless, intense sherry light enough to allow the fabulous apple and cinnamon to blend in with the greengage and grape; t24 a near perfect entry: firm, rummy sugars are thinned by a barley-grape double act; juicy yet enough vanilla to ensure structure and layering; f23.5 delicate spice keeps the finish going and refuses to let the muscovado-grape take control; b24 a whisky whose quality has hit the stratosphere since I last tasted it. I encountered a disappointing one early in the year. This has restored my faith to the point of being a disciple... 40%

Macallan Gran Reserva Aged 12 Years db (92) n23 massive cream sherry background with well matured fruit cake to the fore: big, clean, luxurious in a wonderfully old-fashioned way. Oh, and a sprinkling of crushed sultana just in case the grapey message didn't get across... t24 a startlingly unusual combination on delivery: dry yet juicy! The ultra fruity lushness is dappled with soft spices; oak arriving early-ish does little to alter the path of the sweetening fruit; just a hint of hickory reveals the oak's handiwork towards the middle; f22 dry, as oloroso does, with a vaguely sweeter edge sparked by notes of dried date; the delicate but busy spices battle through to the toffeed end; b23 well, you don't get many of these to the pound. A real throwback. The oloroso threatens to overwhelm but there is enough intrigue to make for a quite lovely dram which, as all good whiskies should, never quite tells the story the same way twice. Not entirely without blemish, but I'm being picky. A Macallan soaked in oloroso which traditionalists will swoon over. 45.6%

The Macallan Fine Oak 15 Years Old db (79.5) n19 t21.5 f19 b20. As the stock of the Fine oak 12 rises, so its 15-y-o brother, once one of my Favourite drams, falls. Plenty to enjoy, but a few sulphur stains remove the gloss. 43%

The Macallan Fine Oak 17 Years Old db (82) n19.5 t22 f19.5 b21. Where once it couldn't quite make up its mind on just where to sit, it has now gone across to the sherry benches. Sadly, there are a few dissenters. 43%

The Macallan Sherry Oak 18 Years Old db (87) n24 t22 f20 b21. Underpowered. The body doesn't even come close to matching the nose which builds up the expectancy to enormous levels and, by comparison to the Independents, this at 43% appears weak and unrepresentative. Why this isn't at 46% at the very least and unambiguously uncoloured, I have no idea. 43%

The Macallan 18 Years Old dist 1991 db (87) n22 t22.5 f21 b21.5 Honestly: I could weep. Some of the sherry notes aren't just textbook...they go back to the Macallan manuals of the early 1970s. But the achievable greatness is thwarted by the odd butt of you know what... 43%

The Macallan Fine Oak 18 Years Old db (94.5) n23.5 classic cream sherry aroma: thick, sweet but enlivened by a distinct barley sharpness; t24 juicy, chewy, clean and intense delivery. Strands of honey and syrup help pave the way for vanillas and spices to get a grip; the complexity levels are startling and the weight just about spot on; f23 a degree of blood orange bitterness amid the cocoa and raisin; the spices remain lazy, the texture creamy; b24 is this the new Fine Oak 15 in terms of complexity? That original bottling thrived on the balance between casks types. This is much more accentuated on a cream sherry persona. But this sample is sulphur-free and quite fabulous. 43%

The Macallan Fine Oak 21 Years Old db (84) n21 t22 f20 b21. An improvement on the characterless dullard I last encountered. But the peaks aren't quite high enough to counter the sulphur notes and make this a great malt. 43%

The Macallan 25 Years Old db (84.5) n22 t21 f20.5 b21. Dry with an even drier oloroso residue; blood orange adds to the fruity mix. Something, though, is not entirely right about this and one fears from the bitter tang at the death that a rogue butt has gained entry to what should be the most hallowed of dumping troughs. 43%

The Macallan Fine Oak 25 Years Old db (90) n22 coal dusty: the plate of old steam engines; a speckle of raisin and fruitcake; t23.5 despite the early signs of juicy grape, it takes only a nanosecond or two for a much drier oak-spiced spine to take shape; the weight is never less than ounce perfect, however; f22 puckering, aged oak leaves little doubt that this is a malt of advanced years, but a few liquorice notes ensure a degree of balance; b22.5 the first time I tasted this brand a few years back I was knocked off my perch by the peat reek which wafted about with cheerful abandon. Here the smoke is tighter, more shy and of a distinctly more anthracitic quality. Even so, the sweet juiciness of the grape juxtaposes gamely with the obvious age to create a malt of obvious class. 43%

The Macallan Fine Oak 25 Years Old db (89) n23 t23 f21 b22. Very similar to the Fine Oak 18. However, the signature smoke has vanished, as I suppose over time it must. Not entirely clean sherry, but much remains to enjoy. 43%

The Macallan Fine Oak 30 Years Old db (81.5) n22 t22 f18 b19.5. For all its many riches on delivery, especially those moments of great bourbon-honey glory, it has been comprehensively bowled middle stump by the sherry. Gutted. 43%

The Macallan 40 Years Old dist 10 May 61, bott 09 Sep 05 db **(90)** n23 t23 f22 b22. Very well-rounded dram that sees off advancing years with a touch of grace and humour. So often you think the oak will take control, but each time an element intervenes to win back the balance. It is as if the dram is teasing you. Wonderful entertainment. 43%

The Macallan 50 Years Old dist 29 Mar 52, bott 21 Sep 05 db **(90)** n25 t23 f19 b23. Loses it at the end, which is entirely excusable. But until then, a fabulous experience full of passion and complexity. I nosed and tasted this for over an hour. It was one very rewarding, almost touching, experience. 46%

The Macallan Millennium 50 Years Old (1949) db **(90)** n23 t22 f22 b23. Magnificent finesse and charm despite some big oak makes this another Macallan to die for. 40%

The Macallan Lalique III 57 Years Old db **(95)** n24.5 t23 f23.5 b24. I chose this as my 1,000th new whisky tasted for the 2012 Bible not just because of my long-standing deep love affair with this distillery, but also because I honestly felt it had perhaps the best chance to offer not just a glimpse at the past but also the possibility of a whisky experience that sets the hairs on the back of my neck on end. I really wasn't disappointed. It is almost scary to think that this was from a vintage that would have supplied the whiskies I tasted when getting to first discover their 21-year-old. Then, I remember, I thought the malt almost too comfortable for its age. I expected a bit more of a struggle in the glass. No less than 36 years on, the same thing crosses the mind: how does this whisky find it so easy to fit into such enormous shoes? No experience with this whisky under an hour pays sufficient tribute to what it is all about. Checking my watch, I am writing this just two minutes under two hours after first nosing this malt. The score started at 88.5. With time, warmth, oxidation and understanding that score has risen to 95. It has spent 57 years in the cask; it deserves two hours to be heard. It takes that time, at least, to not just hear what it has to say to interpret it, but to put it into context. And for certain notes, once locked away and forgotten, to be slowly released. The last Lalique was good. But simply not this good. 48.5%

The Macallan 1824 db **(88)** n24 t23.5 f19 b21.5. Absolutely magnificent whisky, in part. But there are times my job is depressing...and this is one of them.. 48%

The Macallan 1824 Estate Reserve db **(90.5)** n22 excellent clean grape with an intriguing dusting of mint; t23 almost a Jamaican pot still rum sheen and sweetness; beautiful weight and even some barley present; f22.5 satisfying, gorgeously clean with very good vanilla-grape balance; b23 don't know about Reserve: definitely good enough for the First Team. 45.7%

The Macallan 1824 Select Oak db **(82)** n19 t22 f20 b21. Soft, silky, sometimes sugary... and tangy. Not convinced every oak selected was quite the right one. 40%

The Macallan 1851 Inspiration db **(77)** n19.5 t19.5 f19 b19. Flat and uninspirational in 2008. 41%

The Macallan 1937 bott 1969 db **(92)** n23 an outline of barley can eventually be made in the oaky mist; more defined as a honeyed sweetness cuts in. Fingers of smoke tease. When nosing in the glass hours later the fresh, smoky gristiness is to die for ... and takes you back to the mill room 67 years ago; t22 pleasantly sweet start as the barley piles in – even a touch of melon in there; this time the oak takes second place and acts as a perfect counter; f24 excellent weight with soft peat softening the oak; b23 subtle if not overly complex whisky where there are few characters but each play its part exceptionally well. One to get out with a DVD of Will Hay's sublime Oh Mr Porter which was being made in Britain at the same time as this whisky and as Laurel and Hardy were singing about a Lonesome Pine on the other side of the pond; or any Pathe film of Millwall's FA Cup semi-final with Sunderland. 43%

The Macallan Gran Reserva 1981 db **(90)** n23 t22 f22 b23. Macallan in a nutshell. Brilliant. But could do with being at 46% for full effect. 40%

The Macallan Gran Reserva 1982 db **(82)** n21 t22 f20 b19. Big, clean, sweet sherry influence from first to last but doesn't open up and sing like the '81 vintage. 40%

Macallan Cask Strength db **(94)** n22 t24 f24 b24. One of those big sherry babies; it's like surfacing a massive wave of barley-sweetened sherry. Go for the ride. 58.6%. USA.

The Macallan Estate Reserve db **(84)** n22 t22 f20 b20. Doh! So much juice lurking about, but so much bitterness, too. ...grrrrr!!!! 45.7%

The Macallan Fine Oak Master's Edition db **(91)** n23 one of the most delicate of all Macallan's house noses, depending on a floral scented theme with a sweetish malty tinge to the dark bracken and bluebells; t23 so salivating and sensual! The tastebuds are caressed with sugar-coated oaky notes that have a devilish buzz about them; f22 more malt and now vanilla with a bitter cocoa death... b23 adorable. 42.8%

The Macallan Fine Oak Whisky Maker's Selection db **(92)** n22 t23 f23 b24. This is a dram of exquisite sophistication. Coy, mildly cocoaed dryness, set against just enough barley and fruit sweetness here and there to see off any hints of austerity. Some great work has gone on in the lab to make this happen: fabulous stuff! 42.8%. Duty Free.

The Macallan Gold sherry oak cask db (89.5) n22 t23.5 f21.5 b22.5. No Macallan I have tasted since my first in 1975 has been sculpted to show the distillery in such delicate form. *40%*

The Macallan Oscuro db (95.5) n24.5 t24 f23 b24. Oh, if all sherried whiskies could be that kind - and taste bud-blowingly fabulous! *46.5%*

The Macallan Ruby sherry oak cask db (92.5) n23 t24 f22 b23.5. Those longer in the tooth who remember the Macallan 10 of 30 years ago will nod approvingly at this chap. Perhaps one butt away from a gong! *43%.*

The Macallan Sienna sherry cask db (94.5) n23 t24 t23.5 b24. The pre-bottling sample presented to me was much more vibrant than this early on, but lacked the overall easy charm and readily flowing general complexity of the finished article. A huge and pleasing improvement. *43%*

The Macallan The Queen's Diamond Jubilee sherry cask matured db (94) n23.5 t23 f24.5 b23. A wonderful, high quality sulphur-free zone where Macallan unashamedly nails its sherried credentials to the union flag. *52%. 2012 bottles. UK exclusive.*

⬦ **The Macallan Rare Cask Black** db (83.5) n21.5 t22 f19 b21. Pretty rich and some intense, molasses, black cherry and liquorice notes to die for. But some pretty off-key ones, too. Overall, average fare. *48%*

The Macallan Royal Marriage db (89) n23.5 t22.5 f21 b22. Some amazing moments to remember. *46.8%*

The Macallan Select Oak db (83) n23 t21 f19 b20. Exceptionally dry and tight; and a little furry despite the early fruitiness. *40%*

The Macallan Whisky Makers Edition db (76) n19 t20 f18 b19. Distorted and embittered by the horrific "S" element... *42.8%*

The Macallan Woodlands Limited Edition Estate Bottling db (86) n21 t23 f21 b21. Toffee towards the finish brings a premature halt to a wonderfully mollased early delivery. *40%*

Heiko Thieme's 1974 Macallan 65th Birthday Bottling cask no. 16807 dist 25 Nov 74 bott Jul 08 (94) n23 t23 f24 b24 This is not whisky because it is 38%abv. It is Scottish spirit. However, this is more of a whisky than a great many samples I have tasted this year. Ageism is outlawed. So is sexism. But alcoholism isn't....!! Try and become a friend of Herr Thieme and grab hold of something a little special. *38% 238 bottles.*

⬦ **Hunter Laing's Old & Rare Macallan Aged 25 Years** refill hogshead, dist May 90, bott Jan 16 (93) n23.5 elegant citrus amplifies the gristy qualities of the faultless malt; t24 tangy, salty, citrusy and salivating: a bit lighter than a Macallan 25 of yore, but still on the money; f22.5 a docile finale, like an old timer nodding off...; b23 I can remember the day when a Macallan 25-year-old represented the highest peak of Scotland's single malt whisky range. Things have moved on over the years, though this still celebrates a Speysider showing good grace outside its usual comfort zone... *50.3%. nc ncf sc. 212 bottles.*

⬦ **That Boutique-y Whisky Company Macallan 25 Year Old batch** 5 (97) n24.5 have I just entered a time machine? Am I nosing the first Macallan 25 I tasted over 30 years ago...? There is liquorice to that deep oloroso, and spice of course...and so much more...; t24 silky, saturated with untarnished oloroso and with a magical degree of balance to the sugars – mostly molasses and Manuka honey – and the vaguely salty vanilla and barley; f24 drifting away on molassed Melton Hunt Cake at its very finest and the slightest of spices...; b24.5 see my notes for the Hunter Laing 25. Now, this I must say, is not a million miles away from how I remember ye olde Macallan from three decades back... So good I could weep... *48.8%. 126 bottles.*

MACDUFF
Speyside, 1963. John Dewar & Sons. Working.

Glen Deveron Aged 10 Years dist 1995 db (86) n19 t23 f23 b21. The enormity of the third and fourth waves on delivery give some idea of the greatness this distillery could achieve perhaps with a little more care with cask selection, upping the strength to 46% and banning caramel. We'd have a malt scoring in the low to mid 90s every time. At the moment we must remain frustrated. *40%*

⬦ **The Deveron 12 Year Old** db (87.5) n22 t22 f21.5 b22. Buttery and pleasant. But feels like driving a Ferrari with a Fiat Uno engine. Woefully underpowered and slightly too flat in too many places where it should be soaring. The trademark honey notes cannot be entirely defied, however. *40%*

⬦ **The Deveron 18 Year Old** db (94) n24.5 oh well, this is a 20 minuter. Evolves as it warms and oxidises. Almost a sherbet lemon kick at times, with freshly diced apple and halved Chinese gooseberry. The malt is present, but happy for delicate exotic fruits to quietly dominate the show; t23.5 silky, with much more malt at the helm. A vague bitter tannin note, too; **f22.5** spiced honey alongside that vaguely bitter tannin; **b23.5** each bottle should be stamped" Class: handle with care"... 40%

⬧ **Endangered Drams Macduff 8 Year Old** sherry butt, cask no. 900204, dist 05 Mar 07, bott 01 Sept 15 (**88.5**) **n22.5** heavy-handed as the ripe figs and fat sultanas are slapped on, any old way; **t23** thick, clambering fruit gives way to a charming series of sugar and honey tones, acacia and heather-honey leading the procession; **f21** as the sugars break down, a vague bitterness emerges. A bit of a bumpy landing; **b22** oooh, so close to being a really excellent dram. 65.4%. sc.

⬧ **The Golden Cask Macduff 23 Years Old** cask no. CM 222, dist 1992, bott 2015 (**93**) **n23** elegant and understated: the butterscotch intertwangles nimbly with the heather honey; **t23.5** no less poise on delivery: the sugars make a quick, orderly entrance, the slightly lighter ones giving way to a soft oak-vanilla and Manuka mix; stunning mouth feel: limited oils but soft all the same; **f23.5** long, still the vanilla showing exemplary weight as we revert to the original heather-honey; **b23** so many threads of honey which is this distillery's trademark. 64.6%. sc. 223 bottles.

⬧ **The Golden Cask Macduff 33 Years Old** cask no. CM 210, dist 1980, bott 2014 (**87.5**) **n22 t22.5 f21 b22.** A compact malt for its age, undone slightly by a bitter thread which begins on the nose and peaks on the finish. But being a Macduff, still plenty of honey tones to entertain, admire and celebrate, especially just after the initial delivery. Watch out for the Fisherman's Friend nose which underlines the age. 47.5%. sc. 125 bottles.

⬧ **Old Malt Cask Macduff Aged 18 Years** refill hogshead, cask no. 11785, dist Apr 97, bott Aug 15 (**94**) **n23** barley-sprinkled Sugar Puffs breakfast cereal; **t24** nothing so innocent as a kiddy's breakfast cereal on the palate: this is serious whisky! More Cocoa Crispies as the chocolate gets in early and fully integrates with the treacle and chocolate fudge; a light, orangey Jaffa Cake sweetness circles the more intense oak; **f23** high class oils ensure a long fade. French praline escorts the barley to the exit door...; **b24** Macduff has it within its capabilities of being a truly great distillery. Here we get a good look at the intense, delicious complexity it has to offer. A marvellous malt. 50%. nc ncf sc. 296 bottles.

⬧ **That Boutique-y Whisky Company Macduff** batch 2 (**70**) **n18 t19 f16 b17.** Just...duff... 49.6%. 101 bottles.

⬧ **The Warehouse Collection Macduff Aged 18 Years** bourbon hogshead, cask no. 5252, dist 09 Sept 97, bott 20 Jan 16 (**95.5**) **n24** complex orange blossom honey with a pinch of salt: worth 15 minutes of anyone's time; **t24** a beautifully confident delivery: the malt sits compact enough to resonate but with enough give to allow the soft honey and ever-growing spices to flourish; the mid-ground casts the spotlight on some outstanding oak; **f23.5** very long, with varying intensity of malt and mocha. Biscuity yet still traces of orange blossom. The spices never let up, nor dominate; **b24** a sound, complete whisky where the malt offers a firm texture. A classic of its type. 55.9%. nc ncf sc. 211 bottles.

⬧ **The Whisky Barrel Macduff 1990 Burns Malt 25 Years Old** cask no. 1271 (**91**) **n22.5** attractive grape intermingled with subtle spice and dried, pithy orange peel: more fruit cakey than some fruit cakes...; **t23.5** punchy, salivating, bold, thick and rich. Doesn't stint on the mocha, either. Not for the faint hearted as this radiates its flavours with the fervour of a zealot; **f22** a furry tang to the praline finish, but the spices do their best to make amends; **b23** as whisky barrels go, this is a big 'un! And the fruit fair hangs off the oaky branches. 55.4%. sc.

⬧ **Xtra Old Particular Highland Macduff 25 Years Old** sherry butt, dist Feb 90, bott Nov 15 (**74.5**) **n19 t19.5 f17 b19.** A discordant whisky which never quite finds the right key, as hard as it tries. 54.1%. nc ncf sc. 287 bottles.

MANNOCHMORE

Speyside, 1971. Diageo. Working.

Mannochmore Aged 12 Years db (**84**) **n22 t21 f20 b21.** As usual the mouth arrival fails to live up to the great nose. Quite a greasy dram with sweet malt and bitter oak. 43%.

Mannochmore 1998 The Manager's Choice db (**71.5**) **n18 t18 f17.5 b18.** A very bad cask day... 59.1%

Cadenhead's Mannochmore Port Cask Aged 32 Years dist 1982, bott Jan 15 (**89**) **n22.5** clean and fruity: over-ripe greengage and spice; **t22.5** those spices arrive early and usher in wave upon wave of yet more fruit; **f22** drier, but neither the malt or oak make much of a mark, other than a late hint of cocoa. The pithy fruit continues charmingly; **b22** hardly gets out of second gear for a malt of such age. But a deliciously comfortable, if predictable, ride nonetheless. 54.7%. 186 bottles.

⬧ **Cadenhead Single Cask Mannochmore 37 Year Old** bourbon hogshead, dist 1977 (**95.5**) **n23** perfect for those who like a little honey in their oak...; the slight OTT mint and eucalyptus also carries the very lightest traces of smoke; **t24** where did this come from...? A breath-taking blend of heather and ulmo-honey, mixed with a light smattering of treacle and liquorice. The enormity of the more aggressive oak is entirely controlled and taken in its stride by the sugars extracted from it mixing wonderfully with the barley. The light muscovado middle really does the trick, as the spices now arrive and find no shortage of softening balance; **f24** mocha with stirred in muscovado. Long, with the harsher tannins now absent altogether; **b24.5** the nose tells of a decade too many summers and out of control tannin. The experience on the palate could not be more different: if you don't have a free half hour to explore this whisky, don't even think about starting on it. Truly fantastic stuff! *49.4%. sc. 210 bottles.*

Gordon & MacPhail Connoisseurs Choice Mannochmore 1994 (95.5) n24 t24 f23.5 b24 Full of vitality, charm and class. Quite irresistible. *46%.*

MILLBURN

Highlands (Northern), 1807–1985. Diageo. Demolished.

Millburn 1969 Rare Malt db **(77) n19 t21 f18 b19.** Some lovely bourbon-honey touches but sadly over the hill and declining fast. Nothing like as interesting or entertaining as the massage parlour that was firebombed a few yards from my office twenty minutes ago. Or as smoky. *51.3%*

MILTONDUFF

Speyside, 1824. Chivas Brothers. Working.

Miltonduff Aged 15 Years bott code L00/123 db **(86) n23 t22 f20 b21.** Some casks beyond their years have crept in and unsettled this one. But some real big salty moments to savour, too. *46%*

Cadenhead's Single Malt Miltonduff-Glenlivet Aged 20 Years dist 1994, bott Jun 2014 **(82) n21 t22 f19 b20.** An "Allied Distillers" trait cask with more residual bitterness than is good for it. An untidy dram that hits the ground limping... *50.4%. 246 bottles. London exclusive. WB15/272*

Cadenhead's Small Batch Miltonduff-Glenlivet Aged 24 Years bourbon hogheads, dist 90, bott 14 **(95) n23.5 t24 f23.5 b24** Probably a first fill bourbon at play as there is more 'ye-harr' to this than 'och-eye'. Bit of a Kentucky belle. *55.3%. 474 bottles. WB15/256*

⟐ **Cadenhead's Wine Cask Miltonduff 21 Year Old** Chateau Lafitte cask, dist 1994, bott Apr 16 **(94) n23** busy, spiced grape; vaguely green and fresh; **t23.5** salivating, spicy, and ridiculously fruity. And when I say ridiculously, I mean deliciously...; **f24** a touch of Fry's Turkish Delight, only with dark chocolate; still salivating...and even malty very late on: amazing! **b23.5** almost arrogantly satisfying. *51.5%. sc. 228 bottles.*

Gordon & MacPhail Rare Vintage Miltonduff 1984 (85) n21.5 t21.5 f21 b21. Overcooked on the oak, alas. Even the spikey nose is a bourbon, sniffed blind. Has a few moments of brilliance when the barley shines and the spices bite. But would have done a way better job in a blend than as a singleton. *43%.*

⟐ **Maltduff Miltonduff 1989** ex-bourbon cask, bott 2015 **(76.5) n18.5 t21.5 f18.5 b18.** An almost classic bitter "Allied cask" element to this which sends warning signals to the nose of the bumpy ride ahead. Some cocoa notes try to intervene, as does the Demerara sugars which briefly make for a lovely (if off-key!) delivery. Disappointing. Well, it's Friday 13th, what should I have expected...?. *51.2%. sc. 156 bottles.*

⟐ **Old Particular Speyside Miltonduff 15 Years Old** refill hogshead, dist Jun 00, bott Aug 15 **(94.5) n23** an attractive crushed pip element complements the clean but intense barley; **t24** superb delivery. Spine-tingling depth and spice to the barley, which meanders hand-in-hand with top grade oak; the light marzipan and ulmo honey mix is extraordinary; **f23.5** the brilliant spices fizz to the very end. As clean a finish as can be hoped for; **b24** a great distillery going effortlessly through its paces. The span and scope of the barley is truly awesome. Hardly surprising that this malt is key to some of Scotland's very top blends. *48.4%. nc ncf sc. 294 bottles.*

⟐ **The Single Cask Miltonduff 21 Year Old** cask no. 2594, dist 07 Feb 02, bott 22 Feb 16 **(90.5) n23** good grief....! This is 21...??? Massive oak, but given time to breathe, myriad orange and citrus notes tumble forth; pretty salty, too; **t23** seems so much older than 21 years on delivery, too: the oak is outrageously forward and every note has some kind of link to the cask, especially the hickory and the continuing citrus; throughout, there is a curious oiliness that constantly breaks down; **f22.5** better balanced as the malt fights back and just a hint of heather honey gets a word in. Lovely late spice; **b22.5** simply must be a first fill cask forgotten or inaccessible at the top of a warehouse: it has the feel of a beautiful woman who had spent too many years bathing naked on sun-drenched beaches. *45.8%. nc ncf sc.*

    That Boutique-y Whisky Miltonduff batch 1 **(86)** n21 t22 f21.5 b21.5. Funny how, as generously malty as this dram is, if I get a speck of botanical where it shouldn't, my nose and taste buds focus on that to the cost of all else. A bit like the tongue on a chipped tooth. *51.4%. 122 bottles. WB15/226*

    ◈ **The Warehouse Collection Miltonduff Aged 20 Years** bourbon barrel, cask no. 12392, dist 08 Feb 95, bott 30 Oct 15 **(81.5)** n20 t21.5 f20 b20. A particular sharpness to the nose – and again after the raging delivery subsides - would have the men and women in white lab coats marking a little cross next to this one: green, malty and stark. *59.1%. nc ncf. 157 bottles.*

    The Whisky Cask Miltonduff Aged 21 Years first fill sherry butt, dist 1992, bott 2013 **(76.5)** n19 t22.5 f17 b18. A shame: no shortage of honey and fruit from this great distillery. But the S word rears its ugly head just enough to spoil the party. Those immune will find this an outstanding dram. *56.7%. nc ncf.*

    ◈ **The Whisky Chamber Miltonduff 9 Years Old** ex-sherry hogshead, cask no. 900873, dist 28 Jun 06, bott 26 Jan 16 **(88)** n22 dry, with a marked, hard new makey edge, even after these years: odd! Plenty of fruit, of course; t22.5 again, the malt appears a little ill at ease while the sherry is far more assured and offers a dense, moist fruitcake intensity without batting an eyelid; muscovado sugars fill the midground; f21.5 dries a little harshly; b22 big and spicy. And clean! But not really as balanced as it might have been given a few more years, as the youth is always apparent and argumentative. *59.6%. nc sc.*

MORTLACH
Speyside, 1824. Diageo. Working.

Mortlach Aged 16 Years db **(87)** n20 t23 f22 b22. Once it gets past the bold if very mildly sulphured nose, the rest of the journey is superb. Earlier Mortlachs in this range had a slightly unclean feel to them and the nose here doesn't inspire confidence. But from arrival on the palate onwards, it's sure-footed, fruity and even refreshing... and always delicious. *43%*

    Mortlach 18 Year Old db **(75)** n19 t19 f18 b19. When I first tasted Mortlach, probably over 30 years ago now, it really wasn't even close to this. Something went very wrong in the late '80s, I can tell you...*43.4%.*

    Mortlach 25 Year Old db **(91.5)** n23 just love the lemon grass alongside the liquorice and hickory; t23.5 thick and palate-encompassing. The sugars are pretty toasty with a light mocha element in play; f22.5 crisp finale with a return of the citrus, sitting confidently with the late spice; b22.5 much more like it. The sugars may be pretty full on, but there is enough depth and complexity for a narrative to be told. Very much a better Mortlach on so many levels. *43.4%. Diageo.*

    Mortlach 32 Years Old dist 1971 db **(88)** n22 t22 f22 b22. Big and with attitude... *50.1%*

    Mortlach Rare Old db **(79)** n20 t21 f19 b19. Not rare enough... *43.4%. Diageo.*

    Mortlach Special Strength db **(79.5)** n20 t21.5 f19 b19. Does whisky come any more cloyingly sweet than Mortlach...? Not in my experience... *49%. Diageo.*

    ◈ **Cadenhead's Authentic Collection Mortlach 26 Year Old** butt, dist 1988 **(76.5)** n19 t20 f18 b18.5. The better grape notes have a charm. But, sadly, very much a Mortlach of its time. *56.1%. sc.*

    ◈ **Crom Mortlach 16 Years Old Warlords & Warriors Edition Thorgrim's Shield** hogshead, dist Oct 97, bott Apr 14 **(85.5)** n22.5 t21.5 f20.5 b21. Typically sweet and macho and comes complete with you usual tangy weaknesses. *52.3%. sc.*

    ◈ **Gordon & MacPhail Exclusive Single Malt Mortlach 1994** 1st fill sherry butt, cask no. 8180, dist 31 Aug 94, bott Feb 15 **(92)** n22.5 hefty fruit: very much of the fruitcake groaning under toasted raisins variety...; t23 pitch perfect succulence. There is heavyweight fruit involvement here, yet with layers of butterscotch and barley to be found. And spice, of course...; f23.5 if anyone loves dark Belgian chocolate and black cherry, you may have found your perfect malt...; b23 so good to encounter a pretty unsullied sherry butt: well done G&M. *46%. nc ncf sc. 623 bottles. Bottled for the Swedish Whisky Federation.*

    ◈ **Gordon & MacPhail Rare Vintage Mortlach 1954 (93)** n22 not a nose to use as an example of great old whisky, but enough charm and grape to allow its many eccentricities; t23 ahhh...now that's better! The oak has calmed down sufficiently to integrate with the huge plummy fruit. Few fruitcakes can take this amount of fruit...; f24 the demerara sugars linger to see off anything the tannins might get up to; in the end, they merge joyously with a bitter-sweet cheerio...; b24 has defied the years to put up a very idiosyncratic performance... Wonderful! *43%*

    Gordon & MacPhail Rare Vintage Mortlach 1981 (90) n23.5 f21.5 b22 Really don't even begin to understand why this is at 43%abv rather than at least 46 and preferably at cask strength. Reducing to this strength after so many years has broken down the vital oils holding the aged elements together and subtracted from what might have been a great experience. 43%.

Gordon & MacPhail Rare Vintage Mortlach 1984 (89) n23 t22 f22 b22 Ridiculously sweet and soupy in typical Mortlach fashion. But, against the odd, this one works rather well! 43%.

Hepburn's Choice Mortlach Aged 7 Years refill hogshead, dist 2007, bott 2014 **(85.5)** n21 t22 f21 b21.5. For a malt that has been matured in older-than-normal second fill cask or, more likely, a standard third fill, enjoys some surprising buttery nuances to bring entertainment to the semi-new make. Every bit as salivating as you'd expect it to be and so light even a discreet puff of peatiness can be located. A typical Mortlach of mixed messages. 46%. nc ncf sc. 384 bottles.

◈ **Hepburn's Choice Mortlach 7 Years Old** refill barrel, dist 2007, bott 2015 **(92)** n23 clean, fresh, citrus-sharpened barley; t23 salivating as the malt strikes home with minimum fuss and complication; f23 a vague mocha note salutes the early oak involvement; b23 lovers of the original Glenfiddich brand (from just up the road) before it became a dour 12-year-old will fully appreciate this lively offering – as well as be jolted back a fair few years – and, indeed, ponder a much-missed dram. Just so beautiful.... 46%. nc ncf sc. 248 bottles.

◈ **Hepburn's Choice Mortlach 7 Years Old** refill hogshead, dist 2008, bott 2015 **(88)** n22.5 there be some oil in them barleys...; t22 and indeed there is: the malt is weighed down and slightly flattened by the surprising chewiness; f21.5 a slight tanginess to the chocolate wafer biscuit; b22 a pleasant if doughy dram missing some of the joie de vivre of Hepburn's 2007 distillation. 46%. nc ncf sc. 427 bottles.

Hepburn's Choice Mortlach Aged 10 Years refill hogshead, dist 2004, bott 2015 **(83.5)** n21 t21 f21 b20.5. Settles for a display of thick, creamy sugars. Cloying, but with the good grace to offer up late spice and barley, though the old unkempt house style is evident throughout. 46%. nc ncf sc. 153 bottles.

The Maltman Mortlach Aged 14 Years bourbon cask, cask no. 10998, dist Oct 98, bott Apr 13 **(84.5)** n22 t23 f19.5 b20. Ticks all the boxes for those looking for a big malty Speysider. But suffers from a lack of complexity and guile, unspiced heat and a thin finale. 46%. sc ncf nc. 376 bottles. WB15/228

◈ **Old Malt Cask Mortlach Aged 11 Years** refill hogshead, cask no. 12150, dist Nov 04, bott Nov 15 **(87.5)** n21.5 t21.5 f22.5 b22. Some remnants of the old Mortlach syrupy style here. Heavy duty malt, not without some charm as the muscovado sugar and manuka honey combine, and even offer some attractive liquorice, too. But, at times, it is an undignified grapple, though never less than tasty and always chewy. Oh, those who like the brown Liquorice Allsorts are in for a minor treat here... 50%. nc ncf sc. 435 bottles.

◈ **Old Particular Speyside Mortlach 11 Years Old** refill hogshead, dist Jan 04, bott Dec 15 **(88.5)** n22 a little ulmo honey on pancakes; t23 solid barley aided by some high quality grist; f21.5 just a barely detectable puff of smoke before the oak bites slightly; b22 there is no doubting that after many lean years due to its truly terrible cask portfolio, Mortlach is on the mend. A very presentable, if marginally youthful, dram. 48.4%. nc ncf sc. 381 bottles.

◈ **Provenance Mortlach Over 8 Years** refill hogshead, dist Autumn 08, bott Spring 15 **(86.5)** n21 t22 f21.5 b22. Thick, chewy and typically barley intense. But just a little too new makey in part. 46%. nc ncf sc.

◈ **Scotch Malt Whisky Society Cask 76.122 Aged 27 Years** refill hogshead, dist 22 Sept 87, bott 23 Mar 15 **(85.5)** n22 t22.5 f20 b21. The finish suggests this was an early treated cask, when the distillery owners put a sherry-like concoction into the barrel to give it a Spanish butt effect. Sadly, most had a sulphur edge. Here the sulphur is quite light, so it may have escaped the worst of the treatment. Enough juicy sweet grape to still impress. 53.6%. nc ncf sc. 211 bottles.

◈ **Scyfion Mortlach 1996** Odesskoe Chernoe cask finish, bott 2015 **(96.5)** n23.5 very different: one of the most subtle fruit noses this year. Fruit pastilles, though easy on the sugar and heavier on the lime and even pomegranate....; t24.5 wow, wow, wow...!!! What a delivery! I will be hard pressed to find one this year which actually betters the mouth feel. This is silk: so soft it makes not a single dent as it lands. The barley has not been cowered by the fruit and exudes a rich oiliness. But there is no escaping the salivating fruit, either, as myriad chocolate liqueurs burst open and spill their contents onto a grateful palate; f24 long, bolstered by gorgeous, beautifully behaved spices, molasses, liquorice and a quite astonishing flourish of cocoa; b24.5 the first time in over 15,000 whiskies tasted for the Bible I have encountered a Odesskoe Chernoe finish. I sincerely hope it shall not be the last: an absolutely inspired choice. Make no mistake: this is a masterpiece. 46%. nc ncf sc. 330 bottles.

⬦ **That Boutique-y Whisky Company Mortlach** batch 1 **(84)** n20.5 t21.5 f21 b21. A tetchy, impatient whisky, harrying the taste buds with its sharp, vaguely off key maltiness. Got to admire its eye-watering qualities, for all its limitations. *49.6%. 89 bottles.*

⬦ **That Boutique-y Whisky Company Mortlach 27 Year Old** batch 2 **(85.5)** n22 t21.5 f21 b21. Chunky, argumentative and a little dirty despite the aggressive sugars. So true to the distillery character, I named what it was before I even checked to see what the sample was. Pure Mortlach for this era... *52.6%. 162 bottles.*

MOSSTOWIE
Speyside, 1964–1981. Chivas Brothers. Closed.
Rare Old Mosstowie 1979 (84.5) n21.5 t21 f21 b21. Edging inextricably well beyond its sell by date. But there is a lovely walnut cream cake (topped off with brown sugar and spices) to this which warms the cockles. Bless... *43%. Gordon & MacPhail.*

NORTH PORT
Highlands (Eastern), 1820–1983. Diageo. Demolished.
Brechin 1977 db **(78)** n19 t21 f18 b20. Fire and brimstone was never an unknown quantity with the whisky from this doomed distillery. Some soothing oils are poured on this troubled – and sometimes attractively honeyed – water of life. *54.2%*

OBAN
Highlands (Western), 1794. Diageo. Working.
Oban 14 Years Old db **(79)** n19 t22 f18 b20. Absolutely all over the place. The cask selection sits very uncomfortably with the malt. I look forward to the resumption of normality to this great but ill-served distillery. *43%*

Oban Aged 15 Years The Distiller's Edition db finished in Montilla Fino casks, dist 1992, bott 2007 **(90)** n22.5 t23 f22.5 b22. This isn't all about complexity and layering. It's about style and effect. And it pulls it off brilliantly. *43%*

Oban Aged 15 Years The Distiller's Edition db finished in Montilla Fino casks, dist 1993, bott 2008 **(91.5)** n22 nutty, tight, a little musty; t24 much more assured: the dryness of the grape sports beautifully against the obviously more outgoing and sweeter barley: excellent balance between the two; f22.5 perhaps the Fino wins, as it dries and embraces the oak quite happily; b23 delicate and sophisticated whisky. *43%*

⬦ **Oban The Distillers Edition** special release OD 162.FX, dist 1998, bott 2013 db **(87.5)** n22.5 t22.5 f21 b21.5. Some attractive kumquat and blood orange makes for a fruity and rich malt, though just a little furry towards the finish. Decent Demerara early on, too. *43%*

Oban Little Bay db **(87.5)** n21 t23 f21.5 b22. A pleasant, refreshing simple dram. Clean and juicy in part and some wonderful oak-laden spice to stir things up a little. Just a little too much chewy toffee near the end, though. *43%*

PITTYVAICH
Speyside, 1975–1993. Diageo. Demolished.
Pittyvaich Aged 12 Years db **(64)** n16 t18 f15 b15. It was hard to imagine this whisky getting worse. But somehow it has delivered it. From fire-water to cloying undrinkability. What amazes me is not that this is such bad whisky: we have long known that Pittyvaich can be as grim as it gets. It's the fact they bother bottling it and inflicting it on the public. Vat this with malt from Fettercairn and neighbouring Dufftown and you'll have the perfect dram for masochists. Or those who have entirely lost the will to live. Jesus... *43%. Flora and Fauna.*

⬦ **Pittyvaich 25 Year Old** refill American oak hogsheads & first fill ex-bourbon barrels, dist 1989 db **(80)** n21 t20 f19 b20. No matter what collar you put on it, once a Rottweiler, always a Rottweiler... *49.9%. 5,922 bottles. Diageo Special Releases 2015.*

PORT ELLEN
Islay, 1825–1983. Diageo. Closed.
Port Ellen 1979 db **(93)** n22 mousy and retiring; a degree of oak fade and fruit on the delicate smoke t23 non-committal delivery but bursts into stride with a series of sublime, peat-liquorice waves and a few rounds of spices; f24 a surprising gathering of oils rounds up the last traces of sweet barley and ensures an improbably long – and refined – finish; b24 takes so long to get out of the traps, you wonder if anything is going to happen. But when it does, my word...it's glorious! *57.5%*

⬦ **Port Ellen 32 Year Old** refill European oak butts, dist 1983 db **(97)** n24.5 astonishing. I have scant information here, but the fruit is so fresh it is as though it is a finish. Entirely sulphur free and fruit that is as enticing as it is untarnished. The smoke is denser than a standard Port Ellen. No gristiness here: these are phenols which mean business...; **t24.5** salivating on two fronts: the muscovado, fruity sugars...and then the...grist!!! Yes, the Port Ellen trademark is there for all to see...and my god, it is so beautiful in its nakedness...; **f24** the phenols spread luxuriously about the palate on an unexpected film of oil as a lover spreads invitingly across a king size bed. The chocolate fruit tones are stupendous, the weight and pace of the phenols better still...; **b24** that was as different as it was unexpected: with all that fresh fruit, Port Ellen as you may never have seen it before (if you have ever seen it at all...!) Usually I shy away from smoke and grape. Here, though, it works like an old, priceless charm. When I was in the grounds of the old distillery this Spring, a Blackcap sang for a mate with exquisite beauty. It did not, though, match the heart-rendering song of this tragically lost distillery. 50.4%. 2,964 bottles. Diageo Special Releases 2015.

Port Ellen 32 Years Old Special Release 2011 db (88.5) n22.5 t22.5 f22 b22. Really feeling its age, though there are many superb passages of play. 53.9%. nc ncf.

Port Ellen 32 Years Old Special Release 2012 Refill American and European oak casks, dist 1979, bott 2012 db (88.5) n23 t23.5 f20 b22. Some mesmerising moments. Not sure what the finish is all about, though. 52.5 %. nc ncf. Diageo.

PULTENEY
Highlands (Northern), 1826. Inver House Distillers. Working.

Old Pulteney Aged 12 Years db (90.5) n22 pungent, busy and full of zesty zap. Enough salt to get your blood pressure up; **t23** beautifully clean barley, again showing little shortage of saltiness, but thriving in its zesty environment; **f22.5** the vanillas and cocoa carry out an excellent drying operation. The sea-breeze saltiness continues to hang on the taste buds...; **b23** a cleaner, zestier more joyous composition than the old 43%, though that has less to do with strength than overall construction. A dramatic whisky which, with further care, could get even closer to the truth of this distillery. 40%

Old Pulteney Aged 12 Years db (85) n22 t23 f19 b21. There are few malts whose finish dies as spectacularly as this. The nose and delivery are spot on with a real buzz and panache. The delivery in particular just bowls you over with its sharp barley integrity: real pulse-racing stuff! Then... toffee...!!! Grrrr!!! If it is caramel causing this, then it can be easily remedied. And in the process we'd have a malt absolutely basking in the low 90s...! 43%

Old Pulteney Aged 15 Years db (91) n21 pretty harsh and thin at first but some defter barley notes can be detected; **t24** an attention-grabbing, eye-wateringly sharp delivery with the barley in roasty mood and biting immediately with a salty incision; the barley-sugar effect is mesmerising and the clarity astonishing for its age; **f23** long, with those barley sugars working overtime; a slight salty edge there but the oak behaves impeccably; **b23** only on about the fourth or fifth mouthful do you start getting the picture here: enormously complex with a genuine coastal edge to this. The complexity is awesome. 54.9%

Old Pulteney Aged 17 Years db (95) n22 tight but does all that is possible to reveal its salty, fruity complexity with pears and lemons to the fore; **t25** one of the softest, most beautifully crafted deliveries in the whisky world. Absolutely faultless as it picks the most fabulous course among the honeyed vanilla and barley which is so delicate words simply cannot do justice; **f24** near perfect balance between the vanillas and delicate honeys; **b24** the nose confirms that some of the casks at work here are not A1. Even so, the whisky performs to the kind of levels some distillers could only dream of. 46%

Old Pulteney Aged 21 Years db (97.5) n25 if you had the formula to perfectly transform salt, citrus, the most delicate smoke imaginable, sharp barley, more gristy barley, light vanilla, toasty vanilla, roasted hazelnut, thinned manuka honey, lavender honey, arbutus blossom and cherry blossom, light hickory, liquorice, and the softest demerara sugar into the aroma of a whisky, you still wouldn't quite be able to recreate this perfection...; **t24** the sugars arrive: first gristy and malt-laden, then Demerara. This is followed by a salty, nerve-tingling journey of barley at varying intensity and then a slow but magnificently complete delivery of spice...; **f24** those spices continue to buzz, the vanillas dovetail with the malt and the fruit displaying a puckering, lively intensity. Ridiculously long fade for a malt so seemingly light, the salts and spices kiss the taste buds goodnight...; **b24.5** by far and away one of the great whiskies of 2012, absolutely exploding from the glass with vitality, charisma and class. One of Scotland's great undiscovered distilleries about to become discovered, I think... and rightly so! 46%

Old Pulteney 30 Years Old db (92) n23.5 fabulous mix of Jaffa cake and bourbon, seasoned by a pinch of salt; **t23.5** an early, unexpected, wave of light smoke and silkier oak gives immediate depth. But stunning, ultra-juicy citrus and barley ensures this doesn't get all big and brooding; **f22** thinner and oakier with a playful oak-spice tingle; plenty of vanilla controls the drier aspects; **b23** I had to laugh when I tasted this: indeed, it had me scrambling for a copy of the 2009 Bible to check for sure what I had written. And there it was: after bemoaning the over oaking I conjectured, "As Pulteney has the fascinating tendency to radically shift style over not too long a period, I can't wait for the next instalment." And barely a year on, here it is. Pretty far removed from last year's offering and an absolute peach of a dram that laughs in the face of its 30 years... 45%

Old Pulteney 35 Year Old db **(89) n23** the dry ginger doesn't do anything to make this feel younger than its 35 years; a meeting place of various forms of tannin, some sweeter than others. But it is those delicate muscovado sugars alongside the manuka honey, alongside the ginger, which are key; **t21.5** much harder to keep it together on the palate:th attractive mouth feel is undermined by the drier oa elements, some of which are very dry; **f22.5** some lovely mint chocolate does offer great charm; **b22** a malt on the perimeter of its comfort zone. But there are enough gold nuggets included to make this work. Just. 46%. Inverhouse Distilleries.

Old Pulteney Aged 40 Years db **(95) n23.5** gosh! That's pretty aged stuff with the exotic fruit hanging on by a fingernail. Some major bourbon notes now evident – and lip-smacking; **t23.5** massive delivery, again with tannins coming from every angle. But a mix of liquorice, dates, burnt raisin and honey cope well while spices tingle; **f24** settles for a long essay of happy old bourbon-style led whisky; **b24** this malt still flies as close to the sun as possible. But some extra fruit, honey and spice now grasps the tannins by the throat to ensure a whisky of enormous magnitude and complexity 51.3%

Old Pulteney 1990 Vintage American oak ex bourbon & Spanish oak ex sherry butts. db **(85) n21 t23 f21 b20.** As you know, anything which mentions sherry butts gets me nervous – and for good reason. Even with a World Great distillery like Pulteney. Oddly enough, this bottling is, as near a dammit, free of sulphur. Yee-hah! The bad news, though, is that it is also untroubled by complexity as well. It reminded me of some heavily sherried peaty jobs...and then I learned that phat ex Islay casks were involved. That may or may not be it. But have to say, beyond the first big, salivating, lightly spiced moments on delivery you wait for the story to unfurl...and it all turns out to be dull rumours. 46%. Inverhouse Distilleries.

Old Pulteney Clipper American ex bourbon and ex sherry casks db **(93) n23 t24 f22.5 b23.5** Looks like honey, tastes like honey. Most un-Pulteney like. The most delicate and disarming bottling from this distillery I can remember. 46%. ncf nc. 2013-14 commemorative bottle. WB15/276

Old Pulteney Duncansby Head Lighthouse bourbon and sherry casks db **(90.5) n23 t23 f22 b22.5** Beginning to wonder if Pulteney is into making whisky or cakes. And malt straight from the oven. 46% WB15/329

Old Pulteney Dunnet Head Lighthouse bourbon & sherry casks db **(90.5) n22** moody and broody, this is heavy going with only a hint of dusty heather honey lighting the way; **t23.5** much more expansive on delivery, showing true Pulteney depth and layering, especially when those light honey notes transfer from the nose; the sugar-spice interplay is excellent; **f22** salted caramel-vanilla and slightly tangy; dulls quickly despite the spice's best efforts; **b23** loads to chew over with this heavyweight. 46%. nc ncf. Exclusive to travel retail.

Old Pulteney Isabella Fourtuna WK499 2nd Release db **(89) n23** coconut cake, anyone? Or moist Battenburg? **t23** a brilliant delivery of Madeira cake with an extra dollop of malty icing sugar; **f21.5** bread pudding – but someone forgot to add the sugar; **b22** this sailing lark...a piece of cake! 46%. Travel retail exclusive. WB15/324

◈ **Old Pulteney Navigator** bourbon & sherry casks db **(80) n19 t23 f18 b20.** Sherry butts have clearly been added to this. Not sure why, as the sulphur only detracts from the early honey riches. The compass is working when the honey and cocoa notes briefly harmonise in beautiful tandem. But otherwise, badly off course. 46%. nc ncf.

Old Pulteney Noss Head Lighthouse bourbon casks db **(84) n22.5 t22 f19 b20.5.** If Noss Head was as light as this dram, it'd be gone half way through its first half decent storm. An apparent slight overuse of third and less sturdy second fill casks means the finale bitters out considerably. A shame, as the nose and delivery is about as fine a display of citrus maltiness as you'll find. 46%. Travel retail exclusive. WB15/327

Old Pulteney Pentland Skerries Lighthouse db **(85) n21 t22 f20.5 b21.5.** A chewy dram with an emphasis on the fruit. Sound, evens enjoys the odd chocolate-toffee moment. But a little sulphur, apparent on the nose, creeps in to take the gloss off. 46%. WB15/323

Old Pulteney WK209 db **(71) n68.5 t18 f16.5 b17.** Could well be liked by the Germans. 46%

Old Pulteney WK217 db **(88.5) n21 t22 f23 b22.5.** The WK series is named after the old fishing vessels which used to be based in the town's harbour. I suspect old WK217 rarely had a day at sea in waters as calm as this softy of a malt. 46%

◈ **Cadenhead's Authentic Collection Pulteney 25 Year Old** bourbon hogshead, dist 1990, bott 2016 **(89.5) n23** one of the saltiest Pulteney noses I've come across in the last decade: even takes on the crystalline light muscovado sugars for supremacy; **t23.5** which means the delivery is going to be robust and full-flavoured – tart even – which it is. The middle is big on the malt; **f21** some annoying Allied-type cask projects a late bitterness, though the salt does help; **b22** forget the finish. The nose and delivery have your senses on full alert! *50.5%. sc.*

◈ **Gordon & MacPhail MacPhail's Collection Pulteney 1982** (92.5) **n23.5** one of the most oak-rich noses I've come across for a while that is not suffering because of splinters. Orange blossom honey meets light muscovado sugars for an earthy encounter; **t23** superb texture: though the oils have vanished, there is body enough offered by the oak. Glorious, bitter-sweet ratio with a teasing dryness which never becomes unfriendly; **f23** long, with an increasingly milky mocha tone...with half a spoonful of molasses, of course; **b23** one of the few distilleries which takes the passing of time in its stride. Big tannin presence for sure – no problem! *43%*

◈ **Gordon & MacPhail MacPhail's Collection Pulteney 2005** (91.5) **n22.5** attractively balanced vanilla and ulmo honey, the dryness of the former arresting the sweetness of the latter; the vaguest hint of something smoky; **t23** melt-in-the-mouth sugars again tempered by a chalkier vanilla kick. The barley pops up for a grassy volley which fair waters the eye; **f23** lingering despite the oils being broken slightly, with the accent remaining on the barley; very late spice kicks in impressively, as does the laid-back, vaguely salty mocha; **b23** classy! *43%*

Gordon & MacPhail Rare Vintage Old Pulteney 1982 (87.5) **n21 t22.5 f22 b22.** So oak-soaked there is even a degree of creosote on the nose. The oak involvement makes for a tart experience to the very death, but I adore the battle put up by the barley and banana to keep this alive and kicking. *43%.*

ROSEBANK

Lowlands, 1840–1993. Diageo. Closed. (But if there is a God will surely one day re-open)
Rosebank Aged 12 Years db (95) **n24 t24 f23 b24.** Infinately better than the last bottling, this is quite legendary stuff, even better than the old 8-y-o version, though probably a point or two down regarding complexity. The kind of whisky that brings a tear to the eye... for many a reason... *43%. Flora and Fauna.*

◈ **Rosebank 21 Year Old** refill American oak casks, dist 1992 db (95.5) **n23.5** a textbook of complexity: nutty biscuits – Maryland Cookie is about the closest – meets spiced, diced runner beans as a sweet earthiness nestles into the malt and delicate honey; **t24** a surprising coastal kick of sugars and salt mixing in with the vanilla and butterscotch clad malt; **f24** long, with the light oils being used to the full to draw out the ulmo honey...and a further dusting of salt...; **b24** Rosebank is at its very best at eight-years-old. Well, that won't happen again, so great to see it has proven successful at 21... *55.3%. 4,530 bottles. Diageo Special Releases 2014.*

Rosebank 21 Years Old Special Release db (94) **n24** fabulous interplay between apple and berry fruits, though it's the pear juice which acts as the sweetening agent; a nose to spend a good 20 minutes over; **t23.5** at once fizzing and busy while soft and caressing; natural caramels combine with coconut oil to offer the weightier sheen; **f23** dries but never bitters; healthy vanilla all the way **b23.5** can any Lowland be compared to a fully blossomed Rosebank? This is whisky to both savour and worship for this is nectar in a Rose... *53.8%. nc ncf.*

Rosebank 22 Years Old Rare Malts 2004 db (85) **n22 t23 f19 b21.** One or two Rosebank moments of joyous complexity but, hand on heart, this is simply too old. *61.1%*

Rosebank 25 Years Old db (96) **n24.5 t23.5 f24 b24.** I had to sit back, take a deep breath and get my head around this. It was like Highland Park but with a huge injection of sweetened chocolate on the finale and weight – and even smoke – from a Rosebank I had never quite seen before. And believe me, as this distillery's greatest champion, I've tasted a few hundred, possibly thousands, of casks of this stuff over the last 25 years. Is this the greatest of all time? I am beginning to wonder. Is it the most extraordinary since the single malt revolution took off? Certainly. Do I endorse it? My god, yes! *61.4%*

Gordon & MacPhail Rare Old Rosebank 1989 (85.5) **n21 t22 f21 b21.5.** The once dazzling greatness of this malt has been sacrificed on the alter of time. Enjoyable whisky, but significantly limited by the degree of involvement from the vanilla and natural caramels which dominate completely. Eye-watering at times, but the juicy moments are a plus. *46%.*

Romantic Rhine Collection Rosebank refill barrel, cask no. 6492, dist Feb 90, bott Feb 11 (90.5) **n22 t23 f22.5 b23.** An unusual, busy saltiness for a Rosebank. But the weight and pace of the slow infusion of acacia honey makes for a beautiful malt, treading carefully through the oaky ruins. *50%. 120 bottles.*

Scotch Malt Whisky Society Cask 25.66 Aged 23 Years refill hogshead, dist 14 Nov 90 (94) **n23** beautifully weighted. Old school butterscotch tart; the barley bounds along playfully with a jaunty sharpness; **t24** explosive barley again, this time backed by a crisper sugar tone than that found on the nose; **f23** thinks about bittering out but decides against it as the oak offers a more fudge-laden alternative; remains lively salivating almost to the very end – when the last minute spices take over; **b24** a truly great whisky when young, it is holding out impressively. There is life in this dead distillery still. *578%. sc. 157 bottles.*

Scotch Malt Whisky Society Cask 25.69 Aged 23 Years refill barrel, dist 1 Jul 91 **(90)** **n22** pretty dull and conservative, though the delicate bourbon note is attractive; **t23** a busy delivery reminding me of the malt whisky made at Midleton in Ireland some decades ago. Juicy only for the first few waves, it settles into a much more even maltiness after; **f22.5** a good quality oak cask has added just the right degree of tannin to strengthen rather than rule the barley note; **b22.5** much less inclined to go the sugar or honey route you might expect but sets a course flatly amid the barley. *52.5%. sc. 35 bottles.*

ROYAL BRACKLA
Speyside, 1812. John Dewar & Sons. Working.

Royal Brackla Aged 10 Years db **(73)** n18 t20 f17 b18. A distinct lowering of the colours since I last tasted this. What on earth is going on? *40%*

◇ **Royal Brackla 12 Year Old** db **(82.5)** n21.5 t21 f20 b20. Just one of those bottlings which is pleasant enough if you are just looking for something to drink without too much thought, but there is a frustrating lack of harmony and purpose in this for those of us looking to be entertained. *40%*

◇ **Royal Brackla 21 Year Old** db **(91)** n23.5 wonderful dried lychee kick sets the tone for the sweetness of the malt; **t23** silky malt, with a shade of coastal salt ensuring the full flavours are wrung out; **f22** creamy chocolate ice cream before the spices arrive; **b22.5** now that's much more like it! *40%*

◇ **Cadenhead's Wine Cask Royal Brackla 23 Year Old** claret wine barrel, dist 1992 **(93)** **n23.5** sensual grape: sweeter than any claret I've met, with the malt harnessed to superb effect; **t23** outstanding oils smear the juicy fruit into all corners; lovely cocoa and spice middle; **f23.5** almost like a taste of jam on a vanilla biscuit; a vague phenolic depth towards the end; **b23** wow! This has come from a truly exceptional cask. Stunningly clean. *52.9%. sc.*

ROYAL LOCHNAGAR
Highlands (Eastern), 1826. Diageo. Working.

Royal Lochnagar Aged 12 Years db **(84)** n21 t22 f20 b21. More care has been taken with this than some other bottlings from this wonderful distillery. But I still can't understand why it never quite manages to get out of third gear...or is the caramel on the finish the giveaway...? *40%*

Cadenhead's Royal Lochnagar Rum Cask Aged 17 Years dist 1996, bott Oct 13 **(89.5)** **n23** t23.5 f21 b22. Little Royal Lochnager like you have never quite seen her before... *57.4%. 606 bottles. WB15/076*

Old Malt Cask Royal Lochnagar Aged 16 Years cask no. 10588, dist Aug 97, bott Jun 14 **(94)** n24 t23.5 f23 b23.5 It is some 30 years since I spotted a ring ouzel half way up a hill very near the Lochnagar distillery, the only time I have ever seen one. Unlike that elusive bird, there is nothing black and white about this. Absolutely champions its small stills by offering here a malt of regal depth and virtuosity. *50%. nc ncf sc.*

ST. MAGDALENE
Lowlands, 1798–1983. Diageo. Demolished.

Linlithgow 30 Years Old dist 1973 db **(70)** n18 t18 f16 b18. A brave but ultimately futile effort from a malt that is way past its sell-by date. *59.6%*

SCAPA
Highlands (Island–Orkney), 1885. Chivas Brothers. Working.

Scapa 12 Years Old db **(88)** n23 t22 f21 b22. Always a joy. *40%*

Scapa 14 Years Old db **(88)** n22 t22.5 f21.5 b22. Enormous variation from bottling to bottling. In Canada I have tasted one that I gave 94 to: but don't have notes or sample here. This one is a bit of dis-service due to the over-the-top caramel added which appears to douse the usual honeyed balance. Usually, this is one of the truly great malts of the Chivas empire and a classic islander. *40%*

Scapa 16 Years Old db **(81)** n21 t20.5 f19.5 b20. For it to be so tamed and toothless is a crime against a truly great whisky which, handled correctly, would be easily among the finest the world has to offer. *40%*

Scapa 'the' Orcadian 16 Years Old db **(87.5)** n22 t22 f21.5 b22. A thin wisp of honey is key to the weight and balance of this malt. *40%. For the Swiss market.*

⟡ **Scapa Skiren** db (89.5) n22.5 tangy, salted orange and deep vanilla; t22.5 major malt which steps on the salivation pedal almost immediately; the tannins are layered, offering some ice cream, including cone; f22 the sugars tail off leaving this a little lightweight; b22.5 chaps who created this: lovely, you really have to power this one up a bit... 40%

Gordon and MacPhail Distillery Label Scapa 2001 (94.5) n23 the fresh, slightly fruity aromas of a high class bakery on first opening its doors; the barley is so, so young...but equally unblemished; t24 the delivery is near-perfect: a light oil helps spread the juiciest of salty barley notes, young and chock-a-bloc with gristy sugars; a very light, cooling mintiness to the vanilla; f23.5 more of the same, the oils ensuring a long fade and high quality oak offering weight and keeping things on track; b24 showing Scapa exactly as it should be. One of the easiest drinking malts currently in the market place, and quite probably the most moreish. Genius. And dangerous... 43%

SPEYBURN
Speyside, 1897. Inver House Distillers. Working.

Speyburn 10 Year Old db (82) n20 t21 f20.5 b20.5. A tight, sharp dram with slightly more emphasis on the citric. A bit of toffee on the finale. 40%

Speyside 12 Years Old db (85) n22 t22 f20.5 b21.5 Copious honey and malt on delivery. Simplistic, effective but a tad bitter on finish. 40%

Speyburn Aged 25 Years db (92) n22 t24 f23 b23. Either they have re-bottled very quickly or I got the diagnosis dreadfully wrong first time round. Previously I wasn't overly impressed; now I'm taken aback by its beauty. Some change. 46%

Speyburn Bradan Orach db (76.5) n19 t20 f19.5 b18. Fresh, young, but struggles to find a balance. 40%

Gordon and MacPhail Connoisseurs Choice Speyburn 1989 (82.5) n21 t21.5 f20 b20. A kind of Speyside version of malt gruel. 46%. ncf.

Gordon & MacPhail Connoisseurs Choice Speyburn 1991 (94) n23.5 unusually dense for Speyburn: excellent oak has rubbed off just enough to give some depth to the barley while crisp barley sugar adds lustre; t23.5 gorgeously clean and salivating. The barley is beautifully defined and untainted by the years. The oak is gentle and slightly powdery. But it's the gracefulness of the light sugars – pepped by outline spice – which sets this whisky off; f23 just a little (acceptably) tired oak buzz towards the end, but clean barley sugar persists; the slow intensifying of the spice is masterful; b24 not a distillery you'd expect to negotiate two decades with such panache. About as enjoyable as anything I've seen from this distillery for a very long while. 46%

⟡ **Hepburn's Choice Speyburn 10 Years Old** sherry butt, dist 2004, bott 2015 (82) n20.5 t21 f20.5 b20. As stark and austere a Speysider as you'll find. Clean but thin and I'd say it never quite gets out of second gear – but not entirely sure it has one...! 46%. nc ncf sc. 444 bottles.

⟡ **Hidden Spirits Speyburn 8 Years Old** cask no. SP715, dist 2007, bott 2015 (84.5) n21 t22 f20.5 b21. Entirely competent though non-complex malt with a lemon sherbet kick. Light bodied even though a decent cask is at play. 48%. sc.

Provenance Speyburn Over 8 Years sherry butt, cask no. 10437, dist Autumn 05, bott Summer 14 (86) n20.5 t22 f21.5 b22. A little while since I've seen a Speyburn with this degree of oomph and body at any age. A much broader church for denser malt notes than it once was, while still light enough to easily take onboard the oak to ensure some genuine layering and depth to the finish, and even some intermittent honey. Impressed! 46%. nc ncf sc.

THE SPEYSIDE DISTILLERY
Speyside, 1990. Speyside Distillers. Working.

The Speyside 10 Years Old db (81) n19 t21 f20 b21. Plenty of sharp oranges around; the malt is towering and the bite is deep. A weighty Speysider with no shortage of mouth prickle. 40%

The Speyside Aged 12 Years db (81) n19 t22 f19.5 b20.5. Unusual to find feints to this degree after twelve years. Some short-lived honey...but it's hard work! 40%

Spey 12 Years Old limited edition, finished in new oak casks db (85.5) n21.5 t23 f19.5 b21.5. One of the hardest whiskies I have had to define this year: it is a curious mixture of niggling faults and charming positives which come together to create a truly unique scotch. The crescendo is reached early after the delivery with an amalgamation of acacia honey, barley sugar and butter notes interlocking with something bordering classicism. However, the nose and finish, despite the chalky oak, reveals that something was lacking in the original distillate or, to be more precise, was rather more than it should have been. Still, some hard work has obviously gone into maximising the strengths of a distillery that had hitherto failed to raise the pulse and impresses for that alone. 40%. nc. 8,000 bottles.

The Speyside Aged 15 Years db (75) n19 t20 f18 b18. A case of quantity of flavours over quality. 40%

Spey 18 Years Old ltd edition, fresh sherry casks db (82.5) n19 t23.5 f19 b21. What a shame this malt has been brushed with sulphur. Apparent on nose and finish, it still can't diminish from the joy of the juicy grape on delivery and the excellent weight as the liquorice and treacle add their gentle treasures and pleasures. So close to a true classic. 46%. nc.

Spey Chairman's Choice db (77) n19 t21 f18 b19. Their Chairman's Choice, maybe. But not mine... 40%

Spey Royal Choice db (87) n21 t23 f21 b22. "I'll have the slightly feinty one, Fortescue." "Of course, Your Highness. Would that be the slightly feinty one which has a surprising softness on the palate, a bit like a moist date and walnut cake? But with a touch too much oil on the finish?" "That's the blighter! No ice, Fortescue!" "Perish the thought, Sir." Or water, Forters. One must drink according to the Murray Method, don't you know!" "Very wise, Sir." 46%

Spey Tenné finished in Tawny Port casks db (90) n22.5 the usual Spey character, but made short work of by a crisp, boiled sweet fruitiness; t23 softer than marshmallow, which is odd as it has a kind of mallow quality about it: creamy, sugary and melt-in-the-mouth; the cherry-grape fruits are omnipresent; f22 long, rings out every last drop of sweetness before entering a lightly oiled, bitter phase; b22.5 upon pouring, the handsome pink blush tells you one of three things: i) someone has swiped the whisky and filled the bottle with Matheus Rose instead; ii) I have just located where I put the pink paraffin or iii) this whisky has been matured in brand spanking new port casks. Far from a technical paragon of virtue so far as distilling is concerned. But those Tawny Port casks have brought something rather magical to the table. And glass. 46%. nc. 18,000 bottles.

⬩ **Beinn Dubh** db (82) n20 t21 f21 b20. Mountains. Dogs. Who can tell the difference...? I suppose to a degree I can, as this has for more rummy undertones and is slightly less inclined to layering than the old Danish version. 43%

⬩ **C&S Dram Collection Speyside Aged 22 Years** sherry puncheon, cask no. 942, dist 11 Nov 91, bott 17 Mar 14 (94) n23.5 absolutely spot on, intense, succulent, lightly spiced sherry. Zero sulphur present...; t24 excuse me while I pick myself up from the floor. No, no use – I've swooned again... What a brilliant mouthful I have just encountered: malt and sultana infested sherry, with a just so peck of spice: magnificent; f23 butterscotch and vanilla, but the tingle of spice is just so satisfying; b23.5 the aroma of clean, untainted sherry is so rare it took me a few moments to recognise here. Superb malt... 62%. sc. 514 bottles.

⬩ **The Golden Cask Speyside 23 Years Old** cask no. CM 223, dist 1992, bott 2015 (85.5) n22 t21.5 f21 b21. Certainly some treacle at play here, as well as some decent malt. But there is an aggressive edge, too, which cannot be accounted for simply by its strength alone. 61.7%. sc. 434 bottles.

Old Malt Cask Speyside 21 Years Old sherry butt, cask no. 11404, dist Oct 93, bott Mar 15 (88) n22.5 a thick nose, mixing intense barley and a vague fruit-sweetness; t22.5 attractively silky with soft, safe layers of sugary vanilla before a few spices pep up the proceedings; f21 the spices fade as a more bourbony theme is pursued; just becomes a little more chewy and "dirty" towards the finish; b22 a pretty big whisky which, though a long way from faultless, has plenty of entertainment value. 50%. nc ncf sc. 164 bottles..

⬩ **Old Malt Cask Speyside Aged 21 Years** sherry butt, cask no. 12162, dist Dec 93, bott Nov 15 (71.5) n17.5 t19 f17 b18. Even the lashings of honey the barley has conjured up cannot entirely dampen the excesses of the sulphur. 50%. nc ncf sc. 390 bottles.

⬩ **Romantic Rhine Collection Speyside 23 Year Old** sherry puncheon, cask no. 943, dist 11 Nov 91, bott 09 Oct 15 (94) n23.5 all about the grape, which comes thick and impressively well lashed with molasses; t24 brilliant! Explodingly ripe plums, black cherries and raisins mixed in with some meaningful spice; gorgeous ulmo honey fills in any gaps; f23 at last, some tannin gets a word in, though the spices continue to growl; b23.5 wow! Absolutely nothing wrong with this sherry cask. Monumental stuff! 60.8%. sc. 68 bottles.

⬩ **Simon Brown The Speyside Distillery** bourbon casks until May 12, Nicaragun Rum cask until Jun 14, dist Feb 99, bott Jun 14 (94.5) n24 a level of sophistication and complexity I had never thought possible from this place. As though the softer tannin-sugar notes from the bourbon casks have been trapped in the crisper ones from the rum...; t23.5 sweet, soft, cherubic sweetness on delivery: surprisingly malty oils at play and a little ulmo honey spreading far and wide; f23 dries towards a slightly molassed finale; b24 as someone who has properly monitored this whisky more closely than any other independent whisky expert, I can put my hand on my heart and say I have never tasted better from this distillery. Indeed, I had no idea it could be this good. Well done to all concerned! 43%. nc ncf.

◇ **Whiskybroker Speyside 15 Year Old** hogshead, cask no. 2380, dist 26 Oct 00, bott 09 Sept 15 **(94.5) n24** gorgeous Frosties with a squeeze of lime; **t23.5** stupendously clean barley, but liberally doused with a mix of castor sugar and golden syrup; **f23** the gentle oils lock in the sugars as long as possible. Spices arrive as the oak begins to take charge; **b24** an entirely atypical malt from this distillery. The malt is loud, proud and rather wonderfully made. Nothing like I have ever seen from the Speyside distillery... 50.3%. sc.

◇ **Whiskyjace 10th Anniversary The Speyside Distillery 21 Years Old 1995** bourbon cask, bott 2016 **(90.5) n23** an outstanding barrel at work here: plenty of bourbon-style tannin and muscovado in harness; **t22.5** exceptionally friendly delivery: again, the sugars are lining up to make their speech, but the intense barley is doing its best to drown them out; **f22** back to a more north American stance, with a big tannin surge once more; **b23** the malt from this distillery at this time was varied. This is way up in the upper echelons.... 54.1%

SPRINGBANK

Campbeltown, 1828. J&A Mitchell & Co. Working.

Springbank Aged 9 Years dist Feb 04, bott Oct 13 db **(94) n24 t24.5 f22 b23.5** Can you have too much of a good thing? When you combine an undercooked malt like Springbank at half the age it is usually comfortable at being with the intense impact of these very fresh Barolo casks, then the onrush of flavours is almost too much. Certainly harmony takes a bit of a ding. Still, if you are looking for something different and quite memorable... and after a while confusion makes way for awe...! 54.7%. 11,000 bottles. WB15/074

Springbank Aged 10 Years db **(89.5) n22 t23 f22 b22.5.** Although the inherent youthfulness of the 10-y-o has not changed, the depth of body around it has. Keeps the taste buds on full alert. 46%

Springbank Aged 10 Years (100 Proof) db **(86) n21.5 t22 f21 b21.5.** Trying to map a Springbank demands all the skills required of a young 18th century British naval officer attempting to record the exact form and shape of a newly discovered land just after his sextant had fallen into the sea. There is no exact point on which you can fix...and so it is here. A shifting dram that never quite tastes the same twice, but one constant, sadly, is the bitterness towards the finale. Elsewhere, it's one hell of a journey...! 57%

Springbank Aged 12 Years Cask Strength db **(89) n21.5** tangy fruit; **t24** superb delivery: rather thick; almost overwhelming, but enough mocha escapes to lighten the load; the sugar and treacle mix takes some believing; **f22** Cadbury's dairy fruit...with an injection of spice and tannin; just a little too bitter for greatness; **b22** does well to untangle itself at critical times to make for an OTT but wonderfully intense superheavyweight whisky. 50.3%. WB15/074

Springbank Aged 12 Years Cask Strength db **(87) n21.5 t23.5 f21 b21.** Springbank is such an enormous whisky that for decades the 12 has usually struggled to cope with successfully making sense of all it has to offer. This is borderline going under its own weight, with so much fruit, oil and toffee-tannin to disperse on the palate. Best just to sit back and role with the delivery which offers more different types of sugar than you probably knew existed. Have a white flag at the ready, though.... 52.3%. WB15/072

Springbank Aged 15 Years db **(88.5) n22.5 t22 f22 b22.** Last time I had one of these, sulphur spoiled the party. Not this time. But the combination of oil and caramel does detract from the complexity a little. 46%

Springbank Aged 16 Years 10 years in refill bourbon, 6 years in fresh Madeira, cask no. 07/178-3, dist Jun 97, bott Oct 13 db **(93) n23 t23 f23.5 b23.5** A superb malt which, early on, does little quietly, but is at its best when in sedate contemplation. 56%. sc ncf nc. WB15/266

Springbank Aged 18 Years db **(90.5) n23** busy in the wonderful Springbank way; delicate greengage and date; nippy; **t23** yummy, mouthwatering barley and green banana. Fresh with excellent light acacia honey; **f21.5** fabulous oak layering, including chocolate. A little off-key furriness from a sherry butt late on; **b23** just one so-so butt away from bliss... 46%

Springbank Aged 21 Years db **(90) n22 t23 f22.5 b22.5** A few years ago I was at Springbank when they were bottling a very dark, old-fashioned style 21-year-old. I asked if I could take a 10cl sample with me for inclusion in the Bible; they said they would send it on, though I tasted a glass there and then just for enjoyment's sake. They never did send it, which was a shame. For had they, they most probably would have carried off World Whisky of the Year. This, though very good, is not quite in the same class. But just to mark how special this brand has always been to me, I have made this the 500th new single malt scotch and 700th new whisky in all of the 2015 Whisky Bible. 46%. WB15/096

Hazelburn Aged 8 Years bourbon cask, bott 2011 db **(94.5) n23** green apple represents the more dashing aspect of the very young barley; **t24** fabulously solid barley; intense and complete. The youth shimmers on the palate, the malt mixing contentedly with pleasing early butterscotch; elsewhere there is a real richness seemingly imparted from the stills themselves; **f23.5** confirmation of an excellent cask in use here as the lightly spiced vanilla enjoys the odd strand of honey; more light metals breaking into the lengthy barley; **b24** a very curious coppery sheen adds extra lustre and does no harm to a very well made spirit filled into top grade oak. For an eight year old malt, something extra special. *46%*

Hazelburn Aged 12 Years fresh sherrywood, bott 2012 db (85.5) **n22 t21 f21.5 b21.** At times nutty. At others, oily. And is that the vaguest hint of phenol I spot bouncing around at one stage...? But overall a malt which does not, at this juncture in its life, seem entirely at ease with either itself or the cask. Some lovely moments of lucidity but for the most part it's an interrupted work in progress. Still, this is the 666th new whisky I have tasted for the 2013 Bible, so it was likely to have a little bit of devil in it... *46%*

Hazelburn Rundlets & Kilderkins Aged 10 Years dist Nov 03, bott Jan 14 db (95.5) **n24 t24 f23.5 b24** Rundlets. Kilderkins. There's a blast from the past: a name I had seen now and then from my vast library of 19th and early 20th century literature on whisky and distilling, and only a handful of times in warehouses in nearly 40 years of distillery hopping. But here we have a malt matured in these tiny casks. And though the barrels may be small, the whisky they are responsible for really is quite huge. The kind of multi-faceted whisky I could so easily drink all day every day, if you know what I mean... *50.1%. 12,000 bottles. WB15/101*

Hazelburn Rundlets & Kilderkins Aged 11 Years dist Nov 01, bott Jan 13 db (95.5) **n23.5 t24.5 f23.5 b24** A fascinating comparison with the Hazelburn sister bottling. Doubtless the Peat Freaks will have this down as a clear winner. But, to me, the smoke in giving so much also subtracts some of the more intricate moments found on the non-peated version, even allowing for a ten second purple patch which is as good as whisky can get. A battle which goes the full 15 rounds, but the Hazelburn, just a little lighter on its feet and with a devastating jab, wins narrowly on points. But, if you have the opportunity, grab both bottlings and compare. It will be one of the best whisky moments you'll have this year. *51.7%. nc ncf. 9,000 bottles. WB15/118*

Longrow Aged 10 Years db (78) **n19 t20 f19 b20.** This has completely bemused me: bereft not only of the usual to-die-for smoke, its warts are exposed badly, as this is way too young. Sweet and malty, perhaps, and technically better than the marks I'm giving it – but this is Longrow, dammit! I am astonished. *46%*

Longrow Aged 10 Years 100 Proof db (86) **n20 t23 f22 b21.** Still bizarrely smokeless – well, maybe a flicker of smoke as you may find the involuntary twitching of a leg of a dying fly – but the mouthfeel is much better here and although a bit too oily and dense for complexity to get going, a genuinely decent ride heading towards Hazelburn-esque barley intensity. Love it, because this oozes class. But where's the ruddy peat...?! *57%*

Longrow Red 11 Year Old Port cask db (85.5) **n21.5 t21 f22 b21.** I know some people will take a bottle of this to bed with them...to cuddle rather than drink. But, for me, this is just too astringent with a coal gas fierceness to both nose and delivery which doesn't quite sit with the fruit. Passages to enjoy, especially at the end when some kind of compromise is reached. But otherwise just too in your face. *51.8%. 9000 bottles.*

Longrow Red Aged 11 Years Australian Shiraz Cask Peated six years in refill bourbon hogsheads & five years in fresh Shiraz casks db (91) **n23** an airless blockbuster: all done by smoke and shiraz; **t23** thick, almost impenetrable delivery: blackcurrant jam in a smoke chamber; **f22.5** tangy, still dense though fair dinkum honey seeps out at the end; **b22.5** strewth! No surprise that a combination of peat and shiraz has biffed out the complexity. But enough goodies to go round. Just. *53.7%. ncf 9000 bottles. WB15/252*

Longrow 14 Years Old refill bourbon and sherry casks db (89) **n24 t23.5 f19 b22.5.** Again, a sherry butt proves the Achilles heel. But until then, a charmer. *46%*

Longrow Aged 18 Years (94.5) **n25 t23 f23 b23.5** If you gently peat a blend of ulmo, manuka and heather honey you might end up with something as breathtakingly stunning as this. But you probably won't... *46%. WB15/103*

Longrow CV bott 2012 db (91) **n24 t24.5 f19.5 b23.** For a few moments this is heading onto the shortlist of potential Whisky Bible award winners, but a familiar furry rumble – a bit like the distant thunder currently heard from my tasting room – means vital points are lost. Even so, the nose and delivery are something very special, indeed. *46%*

Longrow Limited Edition 18 Years Old db (82) **n21 t22 f19 b20.** Spicy. Smoky. But a long way from its usual brilliant self. A cask, presumably a sherry one, has done it no favours at all. *46%. WB15/104*

⤷ **Classic Whisky & Lifestyle Springbank 15 Year Old 2000** rum cask (80.5) **n21 t21.5 f19 b19.** In the early '90s, Springbank became the first distillery to commercially bottle rum cask whisky. I know, because it was I who found the puncheons sitting forgotten in their warehouse. And hence their famous "Green" whisky was born. This, though, is not a patch on those casks of a quarter of a century ago. The sugars are slapdash, the oak input is undisciplined and the overall effect is bewildering. Only the wonderful spices make sense. *4.71%. 247 bottles.*

Dà Mhìle Organic Springbank Director's Cut 23 Years Old cask no. 233 **(91) n22.5** salty and typically deep. The interwoven acacia honey and oil, nutty fudge forms a weighty tapestry alongside the waxed oak floors; a few citrus notes try to offer a lighter side; **t23** a huge delivery: there appears to be no gaps in flavour or mouth feel, with those big oils from the wide cut thickening a chewy malt further; the oak plays it quietly at first, but soon gets into a weighty stride; the malty nuttiness is topped with molasses; **f22.5** those unmistakable feints tingle. But the malt is now in its element and jousting contentedly with the vanilla-rich oak; **b23** the first Da Mhile where the oak is in the driving seat. The complexity levels remain magnificently high and the road it takes is a panoramic one. 50%

⬨ **ePower Springbank 15 Year Old** sherry cask, dist 1999, bott 2015 **(88) n22.5** something of the boiled sweet shop about this (the sweets being boiled, not the shop). A brooding, Neanderthal, sweaty armpit and fruitcake heavy enough to use as a club...; **t23** delivery concentrates on the fruit. Again, it is thick stuff; though the sugars are surprisingly crisp and even encourage the latent malt; **f20.5** a little sulphur seeps through the cracks; **b22** heavy duty malt offering a very unusual, frankly fascinating, sherry aspect. *43%. Selected by Best Dram.*

⬨ **Hunter Laing's Old & Rare Springbank Aged 22 Years** refill hogshead, dist Dec 93, bott Jan 16 **(93) n23** seemingly matured in an underwater cave: as much kelp as malt...; **t23** the saline nose is not lost on delivery: eye-wateringly bright barley, so sharp it takes a little while for the massive spices to even register...; **f23.5** settles into a far more evenly balanced and elegant malt and the deft vanilla and spiced ulmo honey play a wonderful late duet; **b23.5** not a malt for those looking for a bland brand. *53.9%. nc ncf sc. 212 bottles.*

The Maltman Springbank Aged 17 Years sherry cask **(88.5) n23 t23.5 f20 b22.5.** A profound malt to get sherry lovers smacking their lips. 50.1%

⬨ **Old Particular Campbeltown Springbank 18 Years Old** refill hogshead, cask no. 10737, dist Oct 96, bott Feb 15 **(88) n22.5** a pleasing mix of marshmallow and malt; **t22** juicy malt which bends towards an unwieldy oiliness; the tannins seem strangely detached; **f22** a strange balance between the oaky splinters and muscular malt, though they keep their distance from the other; **b21.5** a clunky, oily malt which still hasn't quite woken up yet. *48.4%. nc ncf sc. 360 bottles.*

⬨ **Sansibar Whisky Springbank Aged 22 Years 1993** bott 2015 **(79) n19 t22 f19 b19.** Neither fish nor fowl. Springbanks aren't meant to be smoky (that's Longrow's prerogative) but this one is. Half-heartedly. Throw in a cask kicking out way too great a lactose imprint, having, presumably, been around the block once too often. And you have an unusually unsatisfactory Springbank. *51.8%. sc. 150 bottles.*

STRATHISLA
Speyside, 1786. Chivas Brothers. Working.

Strathisla 12 Years Old db **(85.5) n21.5 t22 f21 b21.** A slight reduction in strength from the old bottling and a significant ramping up of toffee notes means this is a malt which will do little to exert your taste buds. Only a profusion of spice is able to cut through the monotonous style. Always sad to see such a lovely distillery so comprehensively gagged. *40%.*

Strathisla Distillery Edition 15 Years Old db **(94) n23** flawlessly clean and enriched by that silky intensity of fruity malt unique to this distillery; **t23** the malt is lush, sweet and every bit as intense as the nose; a touch of toffeespice does it no harm; **f24** just so long and lingering, again with the malt being of extraordinary enormity: these is simply wave upon wave of pure delight; **b24** what a belter! The distillery is beautiful enough to visit: to take away a bottle of this as well would just be too good to be true! *53.7%*

⬨ **Cadenhead's Authentic Collection Strathisla 25 Year Old** bourbon hogshead, dist 1989, bott July 15 **(94) n24** you know that gorgeous orange blossom honey you get when great malts meets a superb bourbon cask...? Well, here it is, in groves...; **t23.5** pure silk: the malt is rich, biscuity and intense while the spices form with determination; **f23** deftly falls into mint chocolate mode, the decent oils helping to enrich further; **b23.5** everything that can be asked of a 25-year-old Speysider, and from this distillery in particular. *42.7%. sc. 150 bottles.*

⬨ **Gordon & MacPhail Rare Vintage Strathisla 1965 (84.5) n21.5 t22 f19.5 b21.5.** There is a type of old Speysider which appears to have drowned in a vat of ancient Oloroso. This is one such example. The degree of oak is borderline scary, but all the splinters vanish in this gloopy – if, at times, curiously delicious – mix of tinned tomato and sherry: the tomato being tinned, not the sherry. Anyway, the tiredness of the oak is underlined by the most ungracious of bitter of finishes. 43%

Gordon & MacPhail Rare Vintage Strathisla 1967 (92) n22.5 no shortage of age jabbing at you. But grape first soothes and then guides you to a softer date-like fruitiness; **t23** a svelte fruitiness is momentarily bludgeoned by determined oak, including hickory, giving a double-layered attack. Finally a compromise merges the two styles, with an oily mocha as peacemaker. As those fruitcake notes gather, so do spices and even bigger cocoa; **f23.5** true harmony at last: the spices are now in full flow while late manuka honey sees off any last oaky uprising; **b23** holds up beautifully for its antiquity. Perhaps more equally confrontational than truly balanced, but class tells in the end for the experience is charming. 43%

Gordon & MacPhail Strathisla 1999 bott 2013 **(83.5) n22 t21 f20 b20.5.** Odd that a bottling which for many years you could showcase as a "that's the way to do it" malt has been off the boil for a while now. There is a charming honey-pollen element to the nose, but beyond that balance is at a premium as the cask types clash. 43%. WB15/109

STRATHMILL
Speyside, 1891. Diageo. Working.

◇◇ **Strathmill 25 Year Old** refill American oak casks, dist 1988 db **(89) n23** charming and elegant, the barley seems to celebrate its old age by coming out in its cleanest yet most delicate and uncomplicated attire; **t22** the delivery reveals a little tiredness, a slight tannin-stained tang to the vanilla; **f22** retains its ultra-malty stance; **b22** a blending malt which reveals the kind of big malty deal it offers older brands. 52.4%. 2,700 bottles. Diageo Special Releases 2014.

Cadenhead's Authentic Collection Cask Strength Strathmill Aged 18 Years bourbon hogshead, dist 1995, bott Feb 14 **(87.5) n22 t23 f21 b21.5.** Crusty barley offers good gristiness and ultra juiciness. Lovely malt, as you'd expect from Strathmill, with excellent spice kick, too. But the oak tires slightly, injecting a late bitterness. Just revere the delivery, though! 54.4%. WB15/080

◇◇ **Cadenhead's Wine Cask Strathmill 19 Year Old** Chateau Lafitte barrel, dist 1995 **(72) n18 t19 f17 b18.** Sulphur afoot with the Laffite 55.1%

TALISKER
Highlands (Island–Skye), 1832. Diageo. Working.

Talisker Aged 10 Years db **(93) n23** Cumberland sausage and kipper side by side; **t23** early wisps of smoke that develop into something a little spicier; lively barley that feels a little oak-dried but sweetens out wonderfully; **f24** still not at full throttle with the signature ka-boom spice, but never less than enlivening. Some wonderful chocolate adds to the smoke; **b23** the deadening caramel that had crept into recent bottlings of the 10-y-o has retreated, and although that extraordinary, that wholly unique finale has still to be re-found in its unblemished, explosive entirety, this is much, much closer to the mark and a quite stupendous malt to be enjoyed at any time. But at night especially. 45.8%

Talisker 12 Years Old Friends of the Classic Malts db **(86) n22 t21.5 f21 b21.5.** Decent, sweet, lightly smoked...but the explosion which made this distillery unique - the old kerpow! - appears kaput. 45.8%

Talisker Aged 14 Years The Distillers Edition Jerez Amoroso cask, dist 1993, bott 2007 db **(90.5) n23 t23 f22 b22.5.** Certainly on the nose, one of the more old-fashioned peppery Taliskers I've come across for a while. Still I mourn the loss of the nuclear effect it once had, but the sheer quality of this compensates. 45.8%

Talisker Aged 20 Years db **(95) n24 t24 f23 b24.** I have been tasting Talisker for 28 years. This is the best bottling ever. Miss this and your life will be incomplete. 62%

Talisker 25 Years Old db **(88) n22.5 t22 f21.5 b22.** Pretty taken aback by this one: it has taken a fancy to being a bit of a Bowmore, complete with a bountiful supply of Fisherman's Friends. 45.8%

Talisker 25 Years Old db **(88.5) n23 t22 f21.5 b22.** Another Talisker almost choked with natural caramels. Chewy and undoubtedly charming. 54.8%

Talisker 25 Years Old db **(92) n23.5 t24 f22.5 b22.5.** Fabulous stuff, even though the finish in particular is strangely well behaved. 58.1%

Talisker 30 Years Old db **(93.5) n23** complex and slightly bitty, lemon-lightened phenols, sitting comfortably atop a pile of buttery egg custard tart. A lot sexier than it sounds...! **t24** the citrus leads the way here, too. It helps intensify the juiciness of the barley, though a countering liquorice and crunchy Demerara sugar sweetness amplifies the age. The smoke is restrained though not beyond offering a spice throb; **f23** just a few shuddering oaky passes, but the smoke, sugar, spice and even a little salted butter ensure the fade is long and satisfying; **b23.5** much fresher and more infinitely entertaining than the 25 year old...!!! *45.8%*

Talisker 30 Years Old db **(84.5) n21 t21.5 f21 b21.** Toffee-rich and pretty one dimensional. Did I ever expect to say that about a Talisker at 30...? *53.1%*

Talisker 1977 Special Release 2012 American and European oak refill casks, bott 2012 db **(86.5) n22 t21 f22.5 b21** Distilled just two years after I first visited the distillery, I remember being told that they bottled their whisky at 8-years-old as they felt it was the optimum age of the maturing malt. The manager pointed to some very old casks in a warehouse there but said they were for blending, as it tastes better that way rather than as a singleton. Interesting to hear those works echo around my head now. Certainly this is a malt of character, but over the time the majority of the peat has vanished and huge oak has taken its place. The highlight is somewhere near the end, when the sugars have at last come to terms with the tannins and a gorgeous, vaguely smoky mocha theme strikes up. *54.6%. nc ncf.*

Talisker 57 Degrees North db **(95) n24** salty, smoky, coastal, breezy. The distillery's location in a nose... **t24.5** peat encased in a muscovado sugar, in the same way a fly might be enveloped in amber, melts to allow the slow blossoming of a quite beautiful and peaty thing...; **f23** some welcome whip and bite; the smoke and vanillas hang in there and even the odd hint of mocha puffs around a bit; **b23.5** a glowing tribute, I hope, for a glowing whisky... *57%*

Talisker Dark Storm charred oak db **(92) n22** some pretty chunky peat and spice is blown around the glass, certainly big enough to take the muscovado sugars and red liquorice head on...; **t23.5** the sugars on the nose appear to multiply on delivery, as does the bourbon-style tannin-led liquorice and hickory. The smoke takes a bit of time to get back into the game, as if hiding behind the sofa until safe to come out again but mildly reasserts itself; **f23** even the sugars buckle under the oaky strain. But all is fresh and balanced enough to come good, even with some very late spices; **b23.5** much more like it! Unlike the Storm, which appeared to labour under some indifferent American oak, this is just brimming with vitality and purpose. *45.8%.*

Talisker Port Ruighe db **(88) n22 t22 f22 b22.** Sails into port without changing course *45.8%.*

Talisker Skye (85) n21 t22 f21 b21. The sweetest, most docile Talisker I can ever remember with the spices working hard in the background but weirdly shackled. More Toffee Sky than Vanilla... *45.8% WB16/051*

Talisker Storm db **(85.5) n20 t23 f21 b21.5** The nose didn't exactly go down a storm in my tasting room. There are some deft seashore touches, but the odd poor cask –evident on the finish, also - has undone the good. But it does recover on the palate early on with an even, undemanding and attractively sweet display showing malt to a higher degree than I have seen any Talksker before. *45.8%.*

⟡ **Hepburn's Choice Talisker 5 Years Old** refill hogshead, dist 2009, bott 2015 **(88) n21.5** just a hint of cabbage water amid the docile spice; **t22.5** outrageously, it is the sugars to show first: never usually the case for this distillery. The smoke arrives with the oils as an afterthought and some Swiss Roll-style creamy vanillas make an impact, too; **f22** a little bit of the cabbage water returns, but the spices at last turn up, long after their cue; **b22** must be about 30 years since I first came face-to-face with a Talisker of this age in a blending lab. Much more peppery then, with less oil and the smoke, I remember, standing out with an almost three-dimensional clarity against all else. It has changed in the three passing decades. Not for the better, alas, with a much more Caol Ila-esque quality. Judged as a whisky alone, though, still decent, if not outstanding. *46%. nc ncf sc. 216 bottles.*

TAMDHU

Speyside, 1897. Ian Macleod Distillers. Working (re-opened 3rd March 2013).

Tamdhu db **(84.5) n20 t22.5 f21 b21.** So-so nose, but there is no disputing the fabulous, stylistic honey on delivery. The silkiest Speyside delivery of them all. *40%*

Tamdhu Aged 10 Years oak sherry cask db **(69.5) n17 t18.5 f17 b17.** A much better malt when they stick exclusively to ex-bourbon casks, as used to be the case. *40%*

Tamdhu Aged 18 Years bott code L0602G L12 20/08 db **(74.5) n19 t19 f18 b18.5.** Bitterly disappointing. Literally. *43%.*

Tamdhu 25 Years Old db **(88) n22 t22 f21 b23.** Radiates quality. *43%*

Tamdhu Batch Strength db **(80) n19.5 t21.5 f19 b20.** A chunky bruiser of a dram. What it misses in sophistication, it makes up for with a brooding sugary, spicy oomph... *58.8%*

Cadenhead's Tamdhu-Glenlivet Port Cask Aged 22 Years dist 1991, bott Feb 2014 **(95.5) n24 t24.5 f23 b24** Can't remember the last time I tasted a Tamdhu this stunningly dressed up and with so many places to go. A belter! *57%. 258 bottles. WB15/081*

Cadenhead's Small Batch Tamdhu-Glenlivet Aged 22 Years bourbon hogsheads, dist 91, bott 14 **(87.5) n21.5 t22.5 f22 b21.5.** Hangs its very large hat on punchy sugars, but complexity is lost to the big toffee-coffee element. Pleasant, chewy and one for those who have a sweet tooth while liking a bit of bite to their dram. *56%. 522 bottles. WB15/264*

Glen Fahrn Airline Nr 08 Tamdhu 1984 Aged 28 Years cask no. 2832 **(89) n22 t23 f22 b22.** Charming and fruit-edged from age as the oak offers its most exotic notes. Silky and sensuous, the obvious limitations of the distillate is overcome by the magnificence of the cask. *56.2%. sc. 132 bottles.*

Hepburn's Choice Tamdhu 2005 Aged 8 Years refill hogshead, dist 05, bott 14 **(80) n20 t21 f19 b20.** As young whiskies mature, they tend to peak and trough. This is not peaking. The sweaty armpit nose is interesting... *46%. nc ncf sc. 381 bottles.*

⬦ **Hepburn's Choice Tamdhu 9 Years Old** refill hogshead, dist 2006, bott 2016 **(92.5) n22.5** some youthful malty fizz; **t23.5** melt-in-the-mouth grist. Rather beautifully weighted sugars to encase the clear barley; **f22.5** beautifully polite oak ensures a lovely milky mocha flourish; **b24** beautifully made malt matured in a superb cask and plucked when still in full bloom. A gem of a Tamdhu. *46%. nc ncf sc. 405 bottles.*

The Macphail's Collection from Tamdhu 1971 (91.5) n22 Nice coconut biscuits dunked in weakish milky tea, but gripping on for dear life against the oaky scars; some citrus does offer some alleviation; **t23** now that is classy! Somehow the oils have survived the last 40-odd years to smear citrus-tinged maple syrup all over the palate. Astonishing...; **f23** not a single hint of bitterness or over indulgent oak. Just more vanilla and citrus...and ths delicate sugars, of course; **b23.5** must admit: been a little let down by some of the older whiskies this year. But this unassuming guy has stepped u to the plate and done Speyside proud. *43%.*

Old Malt Cask Tamdhu 16 Years Old refill hogshead, cask no. 10923, dist Mar 98, bott Oct 14 **(77) n19 t20 f19 b19.** Just the thing for those who like a bit of malty rough... *50%. nc ncf sc. 279 bottles.*

⬦ **Old Particular Speyside Tamdhu 14 Years Old** refill hogshead, dist Oct 01, bott Dec 15 **(87) n22 t22 f21.5 b21.5.** Clean, juicy, exceptionally malty. But, for its age, pretty undercooked. *48.4%. nc ncf sc. 328 bottles.*

Old Particular Speyside Tamdhu 16 Years Old refill hogshead, cask no. 10360, dist Jun 98, bott Jun 14 **(87.5) n21.5 t22 f22 b22.** Set up as a blending malt, there is no second guessing the game plan to make this a big malt player. Well made, decently matured, if a little young for its years. No shortage of vanilla, though. *48.4%. nc ncf sc. 324 bottles.*

Old Particular Speyside Tamdhu 16 Years Old refill hogshead, cask no. 10452, dist Jun 98, bott Aug 14 **(88.5) n22** clean barley with a teasing honey edge; **t23** about as lively a malt you'll find from this distillery: the grassy malt has real grit and bite; attractively salivating; **f21.5** the delicate oak quietens the barley; **b22** what a playful, elegant little dram. *48.4%. nc ncf sc. 291 bottles.*

⬦ **Old Malt Cask Tamdhu Aged 27 Years** refill hogshead, cask no. 12004, dist Jun 88, bott Oct 15 **(87.5) n22 t21.5 f22 b22.** Eye-wateringly tart, but given an unexpected boost by a gentle fillip of peat. Rather too thin for greatness, but the phenols extract the most out of the juicy barley. *45.9%. nc ncf sc. 164 bottles.*

⬦ **Old Particular Speyside Tamdhu 17 Years Old** refill hogshead, cask no. 10768, dist Mar 98, bott May 15 **(85.5) n21.5 t21.5 f21 b21.5.** Sizzles on the palate somewhat. Neither the barley or the limited tannin can forge enough personality to overcome the bite. *48.4%. nc ncf sc. 234 bottles.*

Provenance Tamdhu Over 8 Years refill hogshead, cask no. 10570, dist autumn 06, bott autumn 14 **(87) n22 t22 f21.5 b21.5.** A slight whisky it may be, but the maltiness is attractive and pretty well held together by the uncluttered oak. Lovely lemon-honey backdrop. *46%. nc ncf sc.*

⬦ **Simon Brown Tamdhu** bourbon casks, dist Sept 89, bott Jun 05 **(90) n23** attractive from the moment you pull the cork: superb citrus and candy store vanilla entwined. Clean yet no shrinking violet – for all its floral notes....; **t22.5** kicks up a surprising degree of age on delivery: the oaky handshake is firm; gristy sugars slowly enter the fray, and even some very late light muscovado, too; **f22** returns to a malty, Speyside-style theme; **b22.5** not renowned for true excellence, the distillery does come up with the odd elegant little charmer like this now and again. *46%. nc ncf.*

TAMNAVULIN

Speyside. 1966. Whyte and Mackay. Working.

Tamnavulin 1966 Aged 35 Years cream sherry butt db **(91) n24 t22 f23 b22.** For those who love great old sherry, this is an absolute. Perhaps too much sherry to ever make it a true great, but there is no denying such quality. *52.6%*

TEANINICH

Highlands (Northern), 1817. Diageo. Working.

Gordon & MacPhail Connoisseurs Choice Teaninich 2006 (86.5) n22 t22 f21 b21.5. Sugary and unsophisticated, has all the bells and whistles required for a very decent blending malt, though one from a decent cask. Lots of spice and busyness, though thins out a little too quickly. 46%.

◇ **Gordon & MacPhail Connoisseurs Choice Teaninich 2008** (82) n19 t21.5 f21.5 b21. Disappointing malt, the nose showing that it would take an astonishing spirit to overcome the faults evident. It does recover to a degree, employing an attractive chewiness seemingly fashioned by big malt and bigger caramels. Even salivating at times. 46%

TOBERMORY

Highlands (Island–Mull), 1795. Burn Stewart Distillers. Working.

Tobermory Aged 10 Years db (67.5) n16 t17 f17.5 b17. A less than brilliantly made malt totally bereft of character or charm. I have no idea what has happened here. I must investigate. Frankly, I'm gutted. 40%

Tobermory 10 Years Old db (73.5) n17.5 t19 f18 b19. The last time I tasted an official Tobermory 10 for the Bible, I was aghast with what I found. So I prodded this sample I had before me of the new 46.3% version with all the confidence Wile E Coyote might have with a failed stick of Acme dynamite. No explosions in the glass or on my palate to report. And though this is still a long way short, and I'm talking light years here, of the technical excellence of the old days, the uncomplicated sweet maltiness has a very basic charm. The nose and finish, though, are still very hard going. 46.3%

Tobermory Aged 10 Years db (85) n20 t22.5 f21 b21.5. Bracing, nutty and malty the oils perhaps overdo it a little but there are enough sugars on hand to steer this one home for an enjoyable experience overall. 46.3%. nc ncf.

Tobermory Aged 15 Years db (93) n23.5 dripping with fresh, clean, ultra high quality oloroso there remains enough tangy malt to underscore the island location; t23.5 a fabulous marriage of juicy grape and thick, uncompromising malt. It is an arm wrestle for supremacy between the two...but it is the delicate spices which win; f23 salty chocolate raisin; b23 a tang to the oils on both nose and finish suggests an over widened middle. But such is the quality of the sherry butts and the intensity of the salt-stained malt, all is forgiven. 46.3%. nc ncf.

Tobermory Aged 15 Years Limited Edition db (72.5) n17 t18 f19 b18.5. Another poorly made whisky: the nose and delivery tells you all you need to know. 46.3%

◇ **Tobermory 42 Year Old** db (94.5) n23.5 I wonder if this was originally a Ledaig as I swear I can pick up more phenols than should be reasonably expected on a malt this old; thick soup - can pick up more phenols than should be reasonably expected on a malt this old; thick soup-like fruitiness helped by the muscovado sugars; t23.5 I know this sounds perverse, but there really is a hint of boiled tomato on the delivery: not unknown in old malt whisky... but by no means common. Again, in the thick - one is tempted at this age to say primeval - soup, there are the fading rays of phenol amongst the muscovado; f23.5 a little chocolate dribbled on a light fruit cake before the smoked spices take quiet control; b24 a real journey back in time. Wonderful. 47.7%

Ledaig Aged 10 Years db (85.5) n20 t22.5 f21.5 b21.5. Almost a Bowmore in disguise, such are its distinctive cough sweet qualities. Massive peat: easily one of the highest phenol Ledaigs of all time. But, as usual, a slight hiccup on the technical front. Hard work not to enjoy it, though. 46.3%. nc ncf.

Ledaig Aged 10 Years db (63) n14 t17 f15 b17. What the hell is going on? Butyric and peat in a ghoulish harmony on nose and palate that is not for the squeamish. 43%

Ledaig Aged 12 Years db (90) n23 serious farmyard aromas – and as someone who spent three years living on one, believe me...borderline butyric, but somehow gets away with it, or at least turns it to an advantage; t23.5 the staggering peat on the nose is no less remarkable here: chunky, clunking, entirely lacking poise and posture. And it obviously doesn't give a damn...; f21.5 strange gin-type juniper amid the smoke; b22 it has ever been known that there is the finest of lines between genius and madness. A side-by-side comparison of the Ledaig 10 and 12 will probably be one of whisky's best examples of this of all time... 43%

◇ **Ledaig 18 Year Old** batch 2 db (71) n16 t20 f17 b18. There are many ways to describe this whisky. Well made, alas, is not one of them. The nose sets off many alarms, especially on the feinty front. And though some exceptional oak repairs some of the damage, it cannot quite do enough. Sugary, too – and occasionally cloyingly so. 46.3%. nc ncf.

Ledaig Dùsgadh 42 Aged 42 Years db (96) n25 perfection: the peat – once fierce and unfettered – is now restrained and purring in aged contentment. The moist fruitcake must have a Dundee connection as nuts abound. Spices are muted, the molassed sugars thick and inert. We have found an idyllic whisky spot...; t24.5 you expect the gentlest of deliveries – and you are not disappointed. The oak has stirred like a deaf old uncle shouting above the rest, unaware of the disruption caused, but is mollified and shushed by a thin comforting blanket of peat, supported by some juicy sugars; f22.5 bitters slightly towards the finish, but compensated by busy spices which rise as all else fades; b24 it has to be about 30 years ago I tasted my first-ever Ledaig – as a 12 year old peated malt. This must be from the same stocks, only this has been housed in exceptional casks. Who would have thought, three decades on, that it would turn into some of the best malt bottled in a very long time. A smoky experience unlikely to be forgotten. 46.3%

⬩ **Ledaig 1996** db (88) n21 some annoying barrels in there have seen better days and the tang distracts from what would have been a playful smokiness; t23.5 grip your seat, fling your head back, close your eyes and chew...we are in business. Absolutely sublime mouth feel: dense yet passable, lush yet never boggy. The dark sugars and barley intertwangle quite deliciously with the underplayed smoke...; f21 long, smoky bacon and still that lovely oil trace. Thins out towards a pasty austerity just when it starts getting really interesting.... damn it...!! b22.5 a malt you feel is at times reaching for the stars. But has to settle for an, ultimately, barren planet. 46.3%

⬩ **Acla Selection Ledaig 8 Years Old** ex-bourbon hogshead, dist 2005, bott 2014 db (89) n22 a tad thin and austere, but the light smoke offers a chirpy sweetness while the odd citrus note drifts in and out; t22.5 much livelier with the salivating barley underlining its youthful credentials from the first moment; grows in complexity quite fast with an intriguing smoked Digestive biscuit middle and a pleasant laying down of oils; f22 a light mintiness to the smoke is not unwelcome; b22.5 a deft whisky which errs on the understated. 51.4%. nc ncf.

Alexander Murray & Co Tobermory 1994 19 Years Old (78) n19 t19 f20 b20. Poorly made malt. Not even a few slabs of fudge can save it. 40%

⬩ **Big Market Sonderabfüllung Nr. 13 Tobermory 1995** bott 2014 (93) n23 wow! Malt concentrate. How clean and intense is that...? t23.5 the nose doesn't lie! It's barley gone berserk. Stunningly rich malt with the oak seemingly concentrating things further: hardly complex...but what a beautiful effect, especially with those bourbon-style sugars thickening; f23 lush, lip-smacking and liquid liquorice...all topped off with that insane malt...; b23.5 you may find a maltier island whisky than this. But not many. Just love it 54.3%

⬩ **C & S Dram Collection Ledaig Aged 17 Years** hogshead, cask no. 640378, dist 01 Oct 97, bott 23 Mar 15 (81.5) n19 t21.5 f21 b20. A clumsy, massively oiled, sugar-laden dram which has matured in a very decent cask. Which is just as well, as the nose confirms that this was not particularly well made. If it's just the smoke you are after, then it might just do the job. 50.9%. sc. 295 bottles.

Cadenhead's Sherry Cask Tobermory Aged 19 Years sherrywood, dist 95, bott July 14 (67) n15 t20 f16 b16. Riddled with sulphur. 54.2%. 498 bottles. WB15/268

Cadenhead's Small Batch Ledaig Aged 21 Years bourbon cask, dist 1992 (78.5) n19 t21 f19 b19.5. Intensely malty, threateningly sugary, barely smoky and, alas, distilled to a pretty mediocre standard. 53.6%

Càrn Mòr Strictly Limited Edition Ledaig Aged 7 Years hogshead, dist 2005, bott 2013 (89) n22.5 t22.5 f22 b22 Oh, for the promise of youth... So lovely to for once see this malt uncluttered by oak. 46%. nc ncf. 785 bottles. WB15/155

The Coopers Choice Ledaig 2005 Aged 8 Years hogshead, cask no. 0062, bott 2014 (91.5) n23 t23 f22.5 b23 I really do adore young Ledaigs which allow the grist to do its thing. Oily enough to woo Caol Ila fans. 46%. 400 bottles. WB15/301

⬩ **Dramboree 2014 Ledaig 8 Years Old** sherry butt, cask no. 900173 (87) n22 t21 f22 b22 Says this is from the Ledaig distillery. I think they mean Tobermory. Don't mind the strength, but there is some heat coming from elsewhere other than the alcohol. No sulphur on the sherry – hurrah! But the big peat and grape are in a bit of a grapple which blasts balance and complexity out of the window. Still, great fun and the perfect dram to sort out any plaque. 58.8%. WB15/410

⬩ **Endangered Drams Tobermory 9 Year Old** cask no. 900095, dist Sept 05, bott Dec 14 (86.5) n21.5 t22 f21.5 b21.5. A curious creature. This is a Ledaig version of the distillery's output. Incredibly weighty though, apart from a massive explosion of peat on delivery, never feels comfortable. Particularly rough and jarring in part, which is some achievement considering the lubricating oils on show. 46%. sc.

First Edition The Freedom of 811 Ledaig 2004 10 Years Old bott 2014 **(94.5)** n23.5 the dry, ashy phenols suck you into the glass; **t24** magnificent delivery: the smoke is full on but there is more than enough sugar to cope. What's more, the sweetness ranges from grist to ulmo honey, with the vanillas also being gorgeously spruce and confident; **f23.5** the major sugars now spent, the ashy finish is beautifully structured and paced; **b23.5** one of the best younger Ledaigs I have had for many a year. A dram from the old Ledaig school... 46%. 192 bottles. WhiskyAuction.com.

⬥ **The First Editions Tobermory Aged 21 Years 1994** refill hogshead, cask no. 11833, bott 2015 **(85.5)** n21 t22.5 f21 b21. Big malt, and a twiddle of salt. But steadfastly refuses to go anywhere or further the narrative. 'Tis all about the interaction between pretty simple barley and clean but flaky oak. 58.6%. nc ncf sc. 125 bottles.

Glen Fahrn Airline Nr 07 Tobermory 1995 Aged 17 Years cask no. 446 **(85.5)** n21 t22 f21 b21.5. A typically indifferent Tobermory of so-so distillation quality. But a decent cask has helped highlight the richness of the malt itself, while helping to paper over some cracks. 56.8%. sc. 236 bottles.

⬥ **The Golden Cask Ledaig 9 Years Old** cask no. CM 212, dist 2005, bott 2015 **(91.5)** n22.5 a youthful peatiness conjures up images of Scottish coastal chimneys and a fresh sea wind...; **t23** doesn't seem any older on the palate. But just enough oil to stick to the roof of the mouth and radiate mainly phenols, but some beautifully balancing muscovado sugars, also...; **f22.5** dries, as according to the script. A little bite as the oak nibbles and the youth has a late strop; **b23.5** a thin body, perhaps. But some smoky meat on it, too. 61.3%. sc. 312 bottles.

Gordon & MacPhail Connoisseurs Choice Ledaig 1999 (69) n15 t19 f17 b18. Though well peated, the phenols aren't enough to disguise the rough, occasionally syrupy distillate at the core. Rare to find this degree of feints in Scotch whisky. 46%

⬥ **Gordon & MacPhail Connoisseurs Choice Ledaig 2000 (88.5)** n22 unprepossessing peat; a little on the rough side; **t22.5** surprising oils arrive early and keep on mounting. The smoke remains subdued; praline towards the middle; **f22** more lightly smoked oil; **b22** Ledaig at its very oiliest, though by no means smokiest. 46%

Gordon & MacPhail Exclusive Single Malt Ledaig sherry hogshead, cask no. 469, dist 23 Oct 97, bott Oct 13 **(86.5)** n21 t23.5 f21 b21. Has you gripping your seat...not in excitement but trying to hold on tight. Hardly brilliant distillate here and the peat is thrust at you like clods of turf and anthracite eggs hitting you slap on the nose: it is all rather austere, brutal and distinctly farmyardy. Peaks on delivery when a bevvy of sugars, mainly molasses and maple syrup combined, overcome the covert bitterness and soften the peaty blows. The finish is mildly less brutal, and even offers black cherries to counter the bittering oak. For peat freaks, you'll find this a hard-faced, icy-hearted lover. But you'll probably return to her for more...58.6%. nc ncf sc. 263 bottles, bottled exclusively for The Vintage House. WB15/065

⬥ **Le Gus's Selection V Ledaig 2008** first fill bourbon, cask no. 700751, bott 2016 **(95.5)** n23.5 still youthful, but the sheer enormity of the peat has the hairs of your neck standing on end...; **t24.5** good God! It is like taking in a mouthful of peat reek direct from the chimney. Thankfully, a gristy sweetness is at work to offer comfort and support...; the layering of the dark sugars is akin to an art form. But let us just say that the intervention of the acacia honey and the dogged spice saves the day, for even peats as enormous as these are kept in subtle control; **f23.5** does its best to dry. But those sugars will not be bettered and allow the reek a dignified exit...; **b24** my outstanding Chief Researcher, Vinny, had, with a very rare aberration, marked this down as a Tobermory: a mistake which, before the truth dawned, had me reaching for my smelling salts! This is as big and phenolic Ledaig I have encountered in 30 years. Something went wrong when they were sorting out the phenols levels here. And what was wrong, was so very right... 60.3%. sc.

⬥ **Hepburn's Choice Tobermory Smoky & Peaty 8 Years Old** refill hogshead, dist 2008, bott 2016 **(94)** n23.5 green, clean smoke of not inconsiderable phenol intensity; **t24** sublimely juicy thanks to a salivating freshness to the grassy, smoky barley. Light oils assist the charming liquorice and molasses to ensure good balance; **f23** not long enough in the cask for the oak to really make its mark. But the spicy glow to the phenols more than makes amends; **b23.5** though marked as "Tobermory" the smokiness reveals this as a full-blown Ledaig. Fresh, quite beautifully made and very satisfying malt. 46%. nc ncf sc. 401 bottles.

The Maltman Tobermory Aged 16 Years sherry cask, cask no. 5010, dist Jun 96, bott Apr 13 **(71.5)** n16.5 t19 f18 b18. More distilling faults in this than you can wave a whisky thief at. Feinty though sweet. 43%. sc ncf nc. 233 bottles. WB15/217

⬥ **Maltmountains Tobermory 20 Years Old** hogshead, dist 1995, bott 2015 **(86)** n21.5 t22 f21.5 b21. An intriguing, collectors' malt. Although a Tobermory, it was probably bottled after a Ledaig run – or it is a cask which once held peated malt – because the phenols play a vital role here. Like so much Tobermory, the actual distillation quality is not of Premiership quality: the oily nuttiness underlines the score there. But the phenols do help to up the mocha content to acceptable degrees. 48.4%. 48 bottles.

Master of Malt Single Cask Tobermory 18 Years Old refill, dist 22 Nov 95, bott 4 Feb 14 **(88.5) n21 t22.5 f22 b22** A better than expected malt given the nose. For its obvious technical faults it is impossible not to enjoy the overall richness of the picture. 53.9%. 100 bottles. WB15/230

Old Malt Cask Tobermory Aged 19 Years refill hogshead, cask no. 9910, dist Apr 94, bott Aug 13 **(81.5) n20 t21.5 f20 b20.** Smoky, but stringent and eye-watering, too. Those stills were running at a lick when this was made... 50%. nc ncf sc. 170 bottles.

Old Malt Cask Tobermory 18 Years Old cask no. 11235, dist Oct 96, bott Feb 15 **(87.5) n21.5 t22.5 f21.5 b22.** A wizard malty jape. Forget any pretentions to whisky greatness: this is just a dram which has hardly grown up for its age but instead is set upon all kinds of barley-rich fun and spicy adventures. If you can't enjoy this, then you need to chill out a bit. 50%. nc ncf sc. 314 bottles.

Old Malt Cask Tobermory Aged 20 Years refill hogshead, cask no. 10827, dist Apr 94, bott Aug 14 **(90) n22** a hefty cut once, the excesses have died over two decades in the barrel. Remains malty; **t22.5** chewy, with the remnants of the light feints to the fore. But the intensity of the barley, seasoned with salt makes for a salivating joy, too; **f23** fabulous layering, not least due to a metallic seam. Serious butterscotch and pastry at the death; **b22.5** work had recently been carried out on one of the stills or condenser: there is a lot of copper floating around the palate. Suitably sharp and rich. 50%. nc ncf sc. 309 bottles.

⟶ **Old Malt Cask Tobermory Aged 21 Years** sherry butt, cask no. 11891, dist Jul 94, bott Sept 15 **(73) n18 t19 f18 b18.** Don't blame the sherry butt. That is fine – indeed, it has been wasted! It is all down to the bloody awful distillate made at the distillery. Almost worth rubber-necking for... 50%. nc ncf sc. 645 bottles.

⟶ **Old Particular Highland Ledaig 10 Years Old (86) n22 t21 f22 b21.** Lazilly smoked and nutty, overall a bit of a disappointment as the stills appear to have been run ragged here. The malt barely sticks to the palate, while the smoke arrives in a gristy sweetness. 65.4%. Bottled for Big Market Berlin. 50th Anniversary bottling.

⟶ **Old Particular Highland Ledaig 10 Years Old** refill hogshead, dist Sept 05, bott Dec 15 **(83) n20 t22 f20 b21.** The pleasing peatiness does its best to mask a less than brilliant piece of distilling. Fails, though not without a fight. 48.4%. nc ncf sc. 349 bottles.

Old Particular Highland Leidag Aged 21 Years refill hogshead, cask no. 10263, dist Mar 1993, bott Mar 2014 **(95.5) n24 t24 f23.5 b24** One of the best fruit plucked from Tobermory for many a year. Sublime. 50.9%.

⟶ **Old Particular Highland Tobermory 20 Years Old** refill hogshead, cask no. 10813, dist Jul 95, bott Jul 15 **(91) n22** polite malt doffs its cap to the entering oak; **t23** impressive delivery. Delicate sugars create a buffer to absorb the impact of the malt and oak, as one hits straight after the other. The malt remains a soothing constant; **f23** lovely vanilla dovetails with the barley while the spices play quietly; **b23** effortlessly beautiful. Charming and elegant throughout. 51.5%. nc ncf sc. 288 bottles.

Old Particular Ledaig 14 Years Old refill hogshead, cask no. 10789, dist May 01, bott Jun 15 **(83.5) n21.5 t22 f19 b21.** Shame. Trace elements of milky oakiness reveal on the nose a weakness in the cask despite the very high – and slightly Fisherman's Friend style – phenols. The growing tang on the finish confirms it. 48.4%. nc ncf sc. 330 bottles.

⟶ **Provenance Ledaig Aged 7 Years** bott Mar 16 **(88) n22.5** gristy smoke; **t22.5** seriously youthful with the citrus every bit as hands-on as the phenols; **f21** dry: not yet found a happy voice; **b22** a game little blighter for its age. What it lacks in complexity it makes up for with simple, smoky charm... 46%. nc ncf sc.

Romantic Rhine Collection Ledaig 7 Years Old Heavily Peated bourbon hogshead, dist 29 Sept 97 **(91) n24 t23.5 f21 b22.5.** Unlikely you will find a better non-Islay peated nose this year: a mesmerising balance between coal and peat reek, the sweet-dry ration constantly making micro-adjustments to keep in unison, like a bird's head staying perfectly still on a swaying branch. The delivery, with its complex citrus sweetness, is almost as good, but the finish bitters out. 48%. 72 bottles.

⟶ **Scotch Malt Whisky Society Cask 42.18 Aged 9 Years** refill barrel, dist 05 Oct 06, bott 25 Jan 16 **(85) n21 t21.5 f21 b21.5.** Just from the cream soda nose – with a little smoked vanilla ice cream mixed in – you know you are in for an oily experience. While that comes true, the slight aggression to the middle, depicting a slightly hurried distillation, does come as a surprise. The light, unobtrusive smoke tries, along with the full-on sugars, to soothe. 59.3%. nc ncf sc. 234 bottles.

⟶ **Simon Brown Tobermory** American oak casks, dist Apr 94, bott Mar 06 **(71.5) n18 t19.5 f16.5 b17.5.** There are times you have to hold your hands up and say: sorry, this isn't very well made whisky. And this is one of them. Malty, for sure. But far too many crosses in the boxes. *46%. nc ncf.*

The Single Malts of Scotland Tobermory Aged 19 Years hogshead, cask no. 5174, dist 14 Dec 1994, bott 25 Mar 2014 **(74) n18 t19 f18 b19.** Furry, sweet but off key. *55.8%. WB15/311*

Spirit of Caledonia Ledaig 8 Years Old (88.5) n22.5 busy nose bursting with big phenols: the oak seems a little dodgy; **t23** sweet and oily but a real bite and juiciness to the grist; **f21** oily still, but an annoying tang; **b22** a generally sound Ledaig: this one has many components – especially the oiliness - similar to Caol Ila. *58.8%. Mr Whisky.*

Spirit & Cask Ledaig hogshead, dist 2005, bott 2015 **(91) n23** thumping, unrefined peat still to be taken down a peg or two by the oak; **t23.5** oils and sugars ganging together from the off. They need to, as the peat tries to own all it can see...; **f22** a light, buttery vanilla and deft spices emerge as the smoke runs out of steam; **b22.5** raw and young, but enough sugars to ensure a gentle landing. *48%. 324 bottles.*

Svenska Eldvatten Tobermory 1994 ex px sherry butt, dist Mar 94, bott Sept 14 **(85.5) n21 t22 f21 b21.5.** Sadly, not quite the highest ranking distillate you'll find, so the intense malt theme doesn't get the all round backing it deserves. Certainly mouthwatering and bursting with barley. *54.8%. sc.*

Svenska Eldvatten Ledaig 1997 ex bourbon hogshead, dist Oct 97, bott Sept 14 **(87) n22 t22 f21.5 b21.5.** Love the mildly minty nose to this one, which impressively uplifts the smoke. But there is no getting away from the rough edge and overall coarseness to the malt itself, becoming rather thin towards the end. *50.3%. sc.*

That Boutique-y Whisky Ledaig batch 1 **(91.5) n24 t23.5 f21.5 b22.5** Technically, not the most gifted malt. But blunders along beautifully, helped by its disarming peat profile. *57.1%. 217 bottles. WB15/209*

That Boutique-y Whisky Company Ledaig batch 2 **(84) n19 t22.5 f21 b21.5.** Pretty major peat at work. But this is rough stuff: not so much spicy as not particularly well made. The stills have been run fast on this one, hence the lack of rounded edges. The sugars ensure there is plenty to enjoy, as does the smoke and oils. The kind of malt to have after coming home on a freezing cold day when the barbed rain has been battering your face without mercy. This will be either kill or cure. *50.2%. 99 bottles.*

That Boutique-y Whisky Tobermory batch 2 **(76) n18 t19 f20 b19.** Follows pretty much in the same footsteps as Batch 1, except the finish enjoys an extra smudge of decent barley. *53.9%. 73 bottles. WB15/196*

That Boutique-y Whisky Tobermory batch 3 **(76.5) n18.5 t20 f19 b19.** Malty, hot but another one that sinks without trace like the wrecks off Tobermory... *48.1%. WB15/233*

Trader Joe's Isle of Mull Single Malt 1996 17 Years Old (83.5) n21.5 t21 f20.5 b20.5. Possibly not the greatest distillate to start off with. But does island whisky come any duller than this? *40%. Alexander Murray & Co.*

Villa Konthor Ledaig 9 Years Old ex bourbon cask, dist 2005, bott 2015 **(91.5) n23** firm phenols offer little in the way of flare or fancy footwork. Peat at its most acidic and effective; **t23.5** the sugars missing on the nose are found here in abundance. As is the lush malty softness. The smoke works on an alternative level and in a different key; **f22** lingering sugars met by growing vanilla; **b23** a very competent Ledaig, especially for the period. *46%*

◇ **Whic Tobermory 20 Years Old** bourbon hogshead, cask no 1241, dist 18 Jul 95, bott 17 Aug 15 **(90.5) n22** sweet and nutty: good oak but controlled and intriguing; **t23** the promise on the nose is fulfilled on delivery: huge malty marker, massively enhanced by the friendly oils; the spiced ulmo and manuka honey blend is gorgeously understated; **f22.5** late and lovely chocolate fudge; the butterscotch-spice follow on is a bonus, as is the salt which underlines the island character; **b23** teeming with personality. The honey and sugars do a sound job between them. *54.8%. sc. 132 bottles.*

The Whisky Barrel Tobermory 1994 Burns Malt 20 Years Old cask no. 188063 **(89.5) n21** technically a bit off, partially through the oak plus a wider cut than is usually wise. Very suety; **t23** that generous cut ramps up the malt intensity to delightful levels. The oil cling limpet-like to the palate, ensuring the spices have a slight searing quality; **f22.5** the hefty oils turn a little bitter, but a coppery sheen compensates; **b23** achieves fleeting moments of brilliance. Coppery in places but the oily spice positively sings. *51.1%*

◇ **The Whisky Cask Company Ledaig 17 Years Old** bourbon hogshead, dist 1999 **(93.5) n23** buttered kippers – right, where's my shopping list...? **t23.5** so lovely: smoked acacia honey with just the right degree of salt – and with the butter, we are back to kippers again; **f23.5** long, with dark muscovado – but the sublime peat maintains its starring role; **b23.5** a bit of a collector's item: a moderately oily and beautifully made malt from the turn of the century Tobermory. *51.5%*

Whisky-Fässle Ledaig 7 Year Old hogshead, dist 2005, bott 2013 **(93) n23.5 t24 f22 b23.5.** Someone went nuts on the peating level with this one: phenols are practically crawling

Scottish Malts

out of the glass! For all its youthful, smoky muscle, this is a thing of beauty and wonder. Superb! *55.2%. nc ncf.*

Whisky-Fässle Ledaig 8 Year Old hogshead, dist 2005, bott 2014 **(88) n22** a little bit of oak tang is brushed aside by the chunky phenols; **t23** sharp, young, lively barley - but oily peat remains the master; **f21** that tang is confirmed; **b22** decent. A better cask and this would have been a cracker. *53.3%. nc ncf.*

Wilson & Morgan Barrel Selection Ledaig 2005 oloroso sherry finish, cask no. 800069/70/71/72/75/76, dist 2005, bott 2015 **(77.5) n19 t21.5 f18 b19**. The irony that so much excellent grape is visible is not lost on us. Sadly, the whisky is as the sulphur takes hold. *48.5%*

Wilson & Morgan Barrel Selection Tobermory 18 Year Old sherry finish, dist 1997, bott 2015 **(84.5) n23 t21.5 f19 b21**. Most entertainment is provided on the nose, where the peat enjoys a piercing acidic quality. Beyond that, the smoke and fruit never quite hit it off as they might, while a tang on the finish does few favours either. *54.3%*

Whiskyjace Tobermory 18 Year Old bourbon hogshead, dist 1994, bott 2012 **(80) n18 t22 f19 b21**. The nose tells you exactly what you are in for and it doesn't let you down. Or, rather, it does... Poor oak makes for a sharp aroma; the delivery is more intense still. There are some magic moments to the mountainous malt, but it is the problem with both spirit and barrel which grabs most. *60.6%*

TOMATIN
Speyside, 1897. Takara, Shuzo and Okura & Co. Working.

⬩ **Tomatin 10 Year Old MacAlabur 10th Anniversary** first fill ex-bourbon cask, cask no. 1874, dist 7 May 03, bott 28 Apr 14 db **(92.5) n23** buttered malt just heard amid the din of the toasty tannins; **t24** an early bourbon score to the production: liquorice and light maple syrup combine, but the sugars dry up as the spices arrive; **f22.5** seriously toasty, with a rich cocoa edge to the profound spice; **b23** that must have been one underused bourbon cask in Kentucky, because the tannins never release their grip. *58.4%. sc. 228 bottles. Bottled for the MacAlabur Barrel Society.*

Tomatin 12 Years Old db **(85.5) n21 t21.5 f22 b21**. Reverted back to a delicately sherried style, or at least shows signs of a touch of fruit, as opposed to the single-minded maltfest it had recently been. So, nudge or two closer to the 18-y-o as a style and shows nothing other than good grace and no shortage of barley, either. *40%*

Tomatin 12 Year Old finished in Spanish sherry casks db **(91.5) n23** an uplifting clean grape note adds lustre to the more prosaic butterscotch and vanilla; **t23.5** beautiful delivery where both malt and fruit lift off hand-in-hand; **f21.5** the malt shines longer, while a buttery note develops. The late bitterness is a shame; **b23.5** for a great many years, Tomatin operated under severe financial restrictions. This meant that some of the wood brought to the distillery during this period was hardly of top-notch quality. This has made life difficult for those charged with moulding the stocks into workable expressions. I take my hat off to the creator of this: some great work is evident, despite the finish. *43%*

Tomatin 14 Year Old Port Finish db **(92.5) n23** under-ripe greengage shows some nip and spice; **t24** salivating, as a Tomatin delivery so ften is. But here we get all juiced up by succulent fruit, helped along by glazed muscvado; **f22.5** the fruit tails off allowing the vanilla and spice an easy ride; **b23** allows the top notch port a clear road. *46%. ncf.*

Tomatin Aged 15 Years ex bourbon cask, bott 2010 db **(86) n21 t22 f21.5 b21.5**. One of the most malty drams on the market today. Perhaps suffers a little from the 43% strength as some of the lesser oak notes get a slightly disruptive foothold. But the intense, juicy barley trademark remains clear and delicious. *43% Tomatin Distillery*

Tomatin 15 Years Old bourbon barrels and Spanish Tempranillo wine casks db **(88.5) n22 t23 f21 b22.5**. Not free from the odd problem with the Spanish wine casks but gets away with it as the overall complexity and enjoyment levels are high. *52%*

⬩ **Tomatin 15 Year Old Cadenhead's Anniversary** bourbon barrel, Pedro Ximenez first fill cask finish, cask 34876 dist 30 Nov 01, bott 11 Apr 16 db **(93) n23.5** more PX than PX: the sweetest, stickiest fruit nose you'll find this year; **t23.5** if you ain't got a sweet tooth, then scram...the fruit is soaked in runny molasses and spice; **f23** yet more molasses...and PX; **b23** I actually began nosing this in the dark, before I was aware of the distillery. But I certainly knew the cask type: the PX drips all over this malt like a murderer's fingers drip blood over a knife. Guys, you are meant to dump the PX before putting the whisky in, right...? Oh, no sulphur by the way...yippee...!! *56.1%. ncf sc. Bottled for Cadenhead's Switzerland.*

Tomatin Aged 18 Years db **(85) n22 t21 f21 b21**. I have always held a torch for this distillery and it is good to see some of the official older stuff being released. This one has some serious zing to it, leaving your tastebuds to pucker up - especially as the oak hits. *40%*

Tomatin 18 Years Old db **(88) n**22.5 **t**22 **f**21.5 **b**22. What a well-mannered malt. As though it grew up in a loving, caring family and behaves itself impeccably from first nose to last whimpering finale; *43%*

Tomatin Aged 18 Years sherry finish, bott 2010 db **(92.5) n**22.5 busy, thick milkshake maltiness with a touch of fruitcake; **t**23.5 cream sherry: creamy + sweet barley + fruity = cream sherry...; **f**23 very long with a touch of controlled spicy fizz to the proceedings. But that indomitable barley signature sings to the end; **b**23.5 finished in quite superior sherry butts. A malt brimming with character and quality. What a treat! *46%. ncf. Tomatin Distillery.*

Tomatin 25 Years Old db **(89) n**22 **t**23 **f**21.5 **b**22.5. Not a nasty bone in its body: understated but significant. *43%*

Tomatin 30 Years Old db **(91) n**22 if there was a hint of the exotics in the 25-y-o, it's here, five years on, by the barrel load. Evidence of grape, but the malt won't be outdone, either; **t**23 silky and sultry, there is every suggestion that the oak is thinking of going too far. Yet such is the purity and intensity of the malt, damage has been repaired and/or prevented and even at this age one can only salivate as the soft oils kick in; **f**23.5 probably my favourite part of the experience because the sheer deliciousness of the chocolaty finale is awesome; **b**22.5 malts of this age rarely maintain such a level of viscosity. Soft oils can often be damaging to a whisky, because they often refuse to allow character to flourish. Yet here we have a whisky that has come to terms with its age with great grace. And no little class. *49.3%*

Tomatin 30 Year Old European & American oak casks db **(85.5) n**21 **t**21 **f**22.5 **b**21. Unusually for an ancient malt, the whisky becomes more comfortable as it wears its aged shoes. The delivery is just a bit too enthusiastic on the oaky front, but the natural caramels soften the journey rather delightfully. *46%. ncf.*

Tomatin 36 Year Old American & European oak db **(96.5) n**24 the elegant, slightly erotic and truly exotic fruit means one thing only...; **t**24.5 which happens to be confirmed by the even more exotic fruit delivery: great age! The mid ground is both firm with the oak also evident with the butterscotch theme, and soft - the malt still extant having laid down a yielding carpet. A little mocha and praline seep into the mix; but the fruits just keep on giving; **f**23.5 not a hint of bitterness, no stewed pencils of exhausted oak. Just a slow re-run of all that has gone before, though now only in shadowy form...except for the busy but behaved spices...; **b**24.5 the difference between old oak and the newer stuff is brilliantly displayed here. Make no mistake: this is a masterpiece of a malt. *46%*

Tomatin 40 Years Old db **(89.5) n**21.5 **t**22 **f**23 **b**23. Not quite sure how it's done it, but somehow it has made it through all those oaky scares to make for one very impressive 40-y-o!! Often it shows the character of a bourbon on a Zimmer. *42.9%*

Tomatin 1981 Single Cask db **(93.5) n**24 classic nutty old sherry; dried dates and burnt raisin...the label really doesn't need to mention the type of cask...; **t**23.5 further indelible hallmarks of an eye-watering dry oloroso, the oak offering a degree of bitter orange but only after the clipped, spiced delivery; **f**22.5 brooding molasses offering stingy amounts of sweetness to counter that late bitterness; **b**23.5 a hand-picked beautifully rip cherry from Tomatin, one that essentially has to be tasted at body temperature for very best results. Even then, still one of the driest sherry butts you'll find this year. *43.2%*

◇ **Tomatin 2002 Whisky L Beijing - Shanghai 2015** American oak hogshead, cask no. 33196, dist 25 Jan 02, bott 10 Jun 15 db **(95) n**23.5 probably a few more toasty, orangey bourbon notes than there are malt ones: seriously spicy, with a bourbon-esque small grain busy-ness to it all. Decidedly herbal and minty, too...; **t**24 even more than the nose promises: a silky delivery in which the malt, hidden in the aroma, is an immense surprise package. The tannins are neatly packaged with no shortage of natural caramels and fudge. Naturally, the spices are up front also, which counters the buttery ulmo honey pleasantly; **f**23.5 much more stark tannin, brooding now. The spices linger, as do the dark sugars; **b**24 spectacularly serious whisky! Takes the oak element to the max without tipping over the edge, thanks to an absolutely top quality bourbon cask. About as enormous as this distillery gets. *57.8%. sc. 288 bottles.*

Tomatin Highland 1988 Vintage db **(86.5) n**22 **t**22 **f**21 **b**21.5. Few whiskies in the world shows off its malty muscle like Tomatin and here, briefly, it goes into overdrive. For the most part, a happy meeting of slightly salty malt and oak. *46%. ncf.*

Tomatin 1988 Batch 2, bourbon & port casks db **(95.5) n**23.5 a firmness to the grape plus a degree of ye olde fruitcake; **t**24.5 lush, with seemingly malt at first but soon overtaken by a huge swirl of clean fruit – mainly grape, ripe greengage and fat, sweet gooseberries burst at the skin; the undercurrent is thin acacia honey; **f**23.5 drier cocoa but with molasses and fudge; **b**24 another stunner from Tomatin. Complex, beautifully clean and delicious! *46%*

Tomatin Cask Strength Batch 1, bourbon & sherry casks db **(77) n**19 **t**20 **f**19 **b**19. I could weep: these sherry butts are dripping with juice. But then, sulphur-tainted, lead to the whisky's downfall... *57.5%*

Tomatin Contrast Bourbon Casks from 1973, 1977, 1988, 2002, 2006 db **(94.5) n24** sublime layering: the oak is captured in many phases and poses, so the characteristics stretch from the more youthful citrus notes, through dank, sea-salt caves right along to the first hints of exotic fruit. Spices nip and kiss playfully, butterscotch and heather honey vie to fill in any gaps...; **t24** my word! That is just such a satisfying delivery: a little oil, but not enough to disguise the busy honey, manuka and heather at the fore. Instead, it cushions the arrival of those inevitable spices and surprisingly solid malt notes; **f22.5** a slight bittering towards the end; the sugars are so nimble and beautifully poised, they compensate almost immediately wherever needed; **b24** this is exceptionally fine malt whisky boasting an advanced degree of structure and complexity. If you don't have half an hour to spare to do it justice, don't even open the bottle. *46%. Packaged with sherry edition.*

Tomatin Contrast Sherry Casks from 1973, 1977, 1988, 2002, 2006 db **(87) n21 t22 f22 b22.** Certainly a contrast with the bourbon, not least on the complexity front. No damaging off notes, even if the nose is a little tight. But though the grape makes itself heard, it never spreads its wings and flies in this curiously muted offering. *46%. Packaged with bourbon edition.*

◈ **Tomatin Warehouse 6 Collection 1971** db **(87) n22 t22 f21.5 b21.5.** Just one of those terribly frustrating malts where you just have to say: sorry, chaps, but you allowed this one to wallow in the warehouse a summer or two too long. Some superb vanilla and butterscotch, but the tannins have just a little bit too much of a scowl to their faces...That said, still plenty to savour and a fair bit of spice to show there's still life in the old dog... *45.8%*

Tomatin Whisky Meets Sherry Oloroso finished in oloroso sherry casks db **(78) n22 t20 f17 b19.** So powerful is the grape that the nose promises all you desire. Sadly, the bitterness on delivery and beyond makes for a punishing experience. *57.9%. Packaged with PX edition.*

Tomatin Whisky Meets Sherry Pedro Ximenez finished in PX sherry casks db **(84) n20.5 t22.5 f20 b21.** No shortage of spice. And enough sugar to cause any number of cavities. But the casks, alas, have been very mildly tainted with you-know-what. That said, those (lucky ones?) who cannot detect sulphur will probably have their minds blown by this one, especially once the grape goes into overdrive... *53.4%. Packaged with oloroso edition.*

Cù Bòcan 1988 db **(89.5) n23** quite a dry smokiness; no shortage of herbal notes, too....; **t22.5** soft oils encourage the vanillas as much as the light smoke; **f21.5** reverts to its naturally dry stance; a few spices liven things up while some late mocha does offer a sweeter edge; **b22.5** continually smoulders... *51.5%. nc ncf. 2,200 bottles.*

Cù Bòcan The Bourbon Edition fully matured in bourbon casks db **(84) n21.5 t22 f20 b20.5.** The malt battles hard to overcome the poor cask bitterness. But fails. *46%*

Cù Bòcan Highland Single Malt virgin oak, bourbon & sherry casks db **(85.5) n21 t21 f22 b21.5.** An old fashioned dram: the type Pitt the Younger, or Pitt the Embryo might remember... and appreciate. Appears to be nearer new make than fully matured Scotch: the big player is the oak which, almost, bourbon-like, shovels cart loads of caramel and muscovado into the mix. Green...and engrossing. *46%*

Cù Bòcan Highland Single Malt 1989 Vintage db **(95.5) n23** what the....??? A peaty Tomatin! And classy, too...; **t24** sure, the peat is first to show...and glistens as it does so. But where the hell has all that juicy fruit come from. Fruit and peat...not usually happy marriage. But here it is bliss...; **f24.5** now dries slightly to allow the smoke to have a slightly sharp tang, as though the phenls have risen to surprisingly high levels. Still the fruit is on song, like the citrus jelly which accompanies some of the better marzipans....; **b24** the last Cu Bocan I got my nose around, I likened to Pitt the Younger. Well, the only pit here would be a peat one... This is not only absolutely superb whisky, but a bit of a shock, too...Indeed, I am stunned! *53.2%. ncf.*

Cù Bòcan The Sherry Edition fully matured in sherry casks db **(83) n20 t22 f20 b21.** For several magic seconds, the delivery and first four or five flavour waves after offer delicious malt polished by high grade grape. But it is all far too short-lived as off-key notes abound on the nose and finish. *46%*

Cù Bòcan The Virgin Oak Edition fully matured in virgin oak casks db **(94.5) n23.5** subtly rich and strangely coastal: varying levels of honey intensity intertwangled with a light and uplifting saltiness. Darker sugars point the honey towards manuka, though the ulmo undercurrent ensures a beguiling softness; **t23.5** no surprises with the honey coming first: its sweetness is kept in check by equal amounts of vanilla and oaky chalkiness. A little red liquorice takes the side road towards hickory; ulmo and butterscotch counter the gnawing spices; **f23.5** dries, becomes a tad oilier as the malt makes its mark. But it is those buzzing spices amid the dying rays of honey which push the correct buttons; **b24** don't expect a quiet little whisky to nuzzle into. This chap has attitude, and no little complexity. Magnificent use of differing honey styles: overall a delightful box of tricks. *46%*

Anam na h-Alba The Soul of Scotland Tomatin 2006 1st fill sherry cask, dist Jan 06, bott Feb 14 **(73.5) n18 t20 f17 b18.5.** A dram which crashes around the taste buds like a blind F1 driver at Monaco. Unappealingly sweet, weird phenol-type never finds harmony with the fruit and inevitable sulphur. Just weird. 54.2%. 96 bottles.

◇ **BDRAM Tomatin 1994 19 Year Old** hogshead, cask no. 12351, dist 2 Nov 94, bott 6 Nov 13 **(89.5) n21.5** a dribble of acacia honey on the butterscotch tart; **t23** beautifully soft opening: the malt fairly kisses and caresses its way around the palate, gaining in intensity with each passing second: classic Tomatin; **f22.5** the oak dries with efficiency, but the residue remains malty; subtle, late spice; **b22.5** a slightly over-aged malt still very true to the character of the distillery: delicious! 55.5%. Bottled by Morrison & Mackay Ltd.

Cadenhead's Authentic Collection Tomatin Aged 25 Years bourbon cask, dist 1989 **(84.5) n21.5 t22 f20 b21**. When you need a dose of malt concentrate in your life, you don't have to look any further than a Tomatin. In this instance, a slightly off key cask has just undermined the star quality with a tangy input. 51.9%

Cadenhead's Small Batch Tomatin Aged 19 Years bourbon hogshead, dist 1994, bott 2014 **(89) n22 t22.5 f22.5 b22** malt at the max. The complexity is down to the kind oak rather than any magic within the spirit. A simple, very decent quality Tomatin nutshelled, really. 46%. WB15/090

◇ **The Golden Cask Tomatin 20 Years Old** cask no. CM 221, dist 1994, bott 2015 **(86.5) n21 t23 f21.5 b21.** No shortage of merit to this big, oak-infested dram. But the tannins play too fierce a role and, once the brown sugars have been washed away, what remains is just a little too splintery for its own good. 53.9%. sc. 257 bottles.

◇ **Gordon & MacPhail Cask Strength Tomatin 2004 (92.5) n23.5** a good ten-minute nosing required as it moved through the gears: love it when the salt merges with the lime and Jaffa cake – with malt never less than ever; **t23** what a delivery! A wall of salivating malt takes you through its paces, moving from barley sugar to biscuit; again the salt is evident, maximising the intensity; **f23** if that is still a biscuit mode, someone's tossed in a chocolate one; **b23** a model malt. Fabulously structured and shows all its barley-rich clarity. 61.2%

Gordon & MacPhail Connoisseurs Choice Tomatin 1997 (89.5) n22.5 unmistakable signs of elegant aging as the exotic fruits take control; **t22.5** soft and luscious at first, then grips you and warms beautifully. A superb mix of drier oak notes and those joyous fruity tones; good background barley still; **f22** drier and spicier as the oak grips tighter; **b22.5** slips onto your palate and cuddles up to your taste buds like a lover slips into bed and cuddles up with you on a cold night... 46%

◇ **Gordon & MacPhail Connoisseurs Choice Tomatin 2002 (89) n22.5** malt; **t22** malt; **f22** malt; **b22.5** so simplistically, yet deliciously, malty! Laid back and entertains without even trying. 46%

Old Malt Cask Tomatin Aged 20 Years refill hogshead, cask no. 11143, dist Oct 94, bott Dec 14 **(92) n21.5** perhaps heavy on the dry tannin; **t23** early Demerara sugars give way to the inevitable; delightfully oily, though, and very weighty; **f23** spiced mint-chocolate ice cream. In an oaky wafer... **b23.5** Heavy on the oak. But surprisingly refreshing – as well as complex – at times. A lot of whisky... 50%. nc ncf sc. 233 bottles.

Old Particular Speyside Tomatin 20 Years Old refill hogshead cask no. 9984, dist Jan 93, bott Aug 13 **(84.5) n21 t22 f20.5 b21.** Concentrates on the house big malt theme. But a few spices tag along to enliven procedings. 51.5%. nc ncf sc. 211 Bottles. OLP0037.

Single Cask Collection Tomatin 2006 9 Year Old bourbon barrel **(91) n22** the vague strains of peanut butter on toast drifting in from a distant kitchen. Green, drying grass but not the usual malty intensity...; **t23.5**...until the delivery! Ye gods!! Malt rarely comes maltier than this, while butterscotch rumbles around contentedly...; so salivating...and shows little sign of letting up; **f22.5** duller, but the malt still eclipses the growing oak; **b23.5** for me, this is a much underrated distillery, not least because it can produce, as it has done here, the almost definitive malty whisky... The kind of malt a blender might kill for. 55.7%

◇ **The Warehouse Collection Tomatin Aged 20 Years** bourbon barrel, cask no. 2798, dist 02 Nov 94, bott 30 Oct 15 **(94) n23** tomatoes! I swear...sharp, tangy, wonderful tomatoes...!! Plus a little celery and salt: being on a diet, I am now ravenous...! **t24** okay: find yourself a seat. No man or woman can take on board this degree of concentrated malt and be left standing. Enormous. The salad has been left behind: this is all about barley at its most outrageously intense and beautiful; **f23.5** long, buttery malt seemingly amplified by that soft saltiness...; **b23.5** this cask puts me in mind of a blender who a good dozen years ago now had major problems with a new brand he was working on. His budget would not allow his malt content to go so much above about 30%, and try as hard as he might, he just could not impart the lingering malty layering as he wanted. At his wits' end, he rang me for help and told me the malts he had put together. "So you are not using Tomatin, then?" I observed. He confirmed he wasn't. "Can you get any?" I asked. He thought he could. A week later he rang me. Bingo! He had cracked it, thanks to the Tomatin. Taste this and you'll see exactly why... *58.7%. nc ncf. 103 bottles.*

◇ **Whiskybroker Tomatin 21 Year Old** refill hogshead, cask no. 2323011258, dist 14 Oct 94, bott 12 Feb 16 **(82.5) n19 t22.5 f20.5 b20.5.** A creamy, malty whisky. But a few too many summers have seen the cask give up a few of its more milky elements. The late delivery does offer a pleasant chocolate lime moment or two, though. *53.4%. sc.*

World of Orchids Tomatin 2004 8 Year Old bourbon cask, cask no. 456 **(73) n18 t20 f17 b18.** Though this is from a bourbon cask, the result is of the profoundly negative sherry variety. Presumably, at some time in the cask's history it was treated with an ersatz sherry mix to turn it into a sherry-type cask, a practise used in the industry but not widely mentioned. Sadly, most of these had a sulphur tinge. *58.6%. sc. 119 bottles.*

TOMINTOUL
Speyside, 1965. Angus Dundee. Working.

Tomintoul Aged 10 Years db **(83.5) n21 t20 f21.5 b21.** Has bucked up recently to offer a juicy, salivating barley thrust. Yet still a little on the thin side, despite some late oak. *40%*

Tomintoul Aged 12 Years Oloroso Sherry Cask Finish db **(73.5) n18.5 t19 f18 b18.** Tomintoul, with good reason, styles itself as "The Gentle Dram" and you'll hear no argument from me about that one. However, the sherry influence here offers a rough ride. *40%*

Tomintoul Aged 12 Years Portwood Finish db **(87.5) n22 t22 f21.5 b22.** As Portwood finishes go, a real lightweight allowing the barley plenty of room to flex its juicier muscles. *46%. nc ncf.*

Tomintoul Aged 14 Years db **(91) n23.5 t23 f21.5.** This guy has shortened its breath somewhat: with the distinct thinness to the barley and oak arriving a little flustered and half-hearted rather than with a confident stride; b23 remains a beautiful whisky full of vitality and displaying the malt in its most naked and vulnerable state. But I get the feeling that perhaps a few too many third fills, or under-performing seconds, has resulted in the intensity and hair-raising harmony of the truly great previous bottlings just being slightly undercooked. That said, still a worthy and delicious dram! *46%. nc ncf.*

◇ **Tomintoul Aged 15 Years Portwood Finish** db **(94) n23** both the malt and grape drip from the glass – in about equal measure; **t23.5** salivating yet weighty. The spices check in early, the only luggage being some excellent vanilla notes, as the oak reminds us of the decent age. The fruit pootles along without a care in the world; **f23.5** superb, understated finish: plenty of evidence still of a plummy fruit...and still the barley carries through; **b24** so rare to find a wine finish which maximises the fruit to the full without allowing it to dominate. Charming. And so clean. Probably a brilliant whisky to help repair my damaged palate after tasting yet another s******ed sherry butt. I'll keep this one handy...*46%. nc ncf. 5,820 bottles.*

Tomintoul Aged 16 Years db **(94.5) n24.5** a fruity concoction of apples and pears topped with vanilla ice cream; even the vaguest hint of something smoky...one of the noses of the year; **t23.5** every bit as gentle as the label promises, as the light oils coat the palate with a fabulously intense and delicately sweetened barley skin. The skeleton is playful oak; **f23** a wonderful, multi-layered interplay between malt and oak-vanillas. Long, curiously spice-free, increasingly dry but hugely sophisticated; **b23.5** confirms Tomintoul's ability to dice with greatness. *40%*

Tomintoul Aged 21 Years db **(94) n24** has all the hallmarks of a malt which contains casks a lot older than the stated age: the fruit is of the exotic variety and the manner in which those fruit and defter floral notes effortlessly intertwine confirms not just the magnificence of quality but also familiarity between oak and malt **t24** silky and soft with the balance of the light sugars to barley almost perfect; the vanillas grow, as they should, but the freshness to the barley never diminishes **f22.5** a beautiful butterscotch and custard confection **b23.5** just how good this whisky would have been at cask strength or even at 46 absolutely terrifies me. *40%.*

Tomintoul Aged 25 Years db **(95) n25** the day has just begun and the sun is barely up. But I will be hard pushed to find a more quaint and gorgeously balanced nose between now and sunset. The aroma would not be out of place in the garden outside my window, a sensual breeze of orange blossom and floral scents. Ulmo honey thinly spread on toast is about as heavy as it gets; **t24** no less subtle is the array of sweet notes on delivery, melting, meringue-like, into every crevice; the malt at times stacks up to make a short Speyside-themed speech; **f23** bitters slightly, though no great detriment, as the oak quietly takes command. The malt and vague fruitiness drifts inexorably to the finale; **b23.5** a quiet masterpiece from one of Scotland's criminally underappreciated great distilleries. *43%*

Tomintoul Aged 27 Years db **(87) n22 t22.5 21.5 b21.** The last time I saw a colour like this was on antique expert David Dickinson's face. Still, lots of charm and character to go round... and on the whisky, too. *40%*

Tomintoul Aged 33 Years db **(95.5) n24.5 t24.5 f23 b24.** The point about whiskies of this age is that sometimes you have to deal with what you are given. Some 33 years ago a blender didn't decide to put these to one side for a single malt; this was made to be blended away and have arrived at this point with a pleasing randomness: the casks used here escaped the call of the warehouse foreman. Which means this breathtakingly beautiful 33 Year Old Tomintoul bares virtually no resemblance to the last one I tasted. Which is what makes this job of mine, at times, so bloody fascinating. *43%.*

⬧ **Tomintoul Aged 40 Years** db **(86) n22 t21 f21.5 b21.5.** Groans every single one of its 40 years. Some lovely malty moments still, as well as butterscotch. But the oak has just jogged on past the sign that said 'Greatness' and carried straight on into the woods... *43.1%. nc ncf. 500 bottles.*

Tomintoul 1976 Vintage bott 2013 db **(94.5) n25** stupendously classic Speyside style old timer's exotic fruit: you have to have reached a massive age to find something as juicily soft and alluring as this! **t22** all's well with the sweet, fruity-malty delivery...before the oak hits you so hard, your eyes water. But the malts fight back – aided by their fruitiest notes to soften the impact; **f23.5** to complete the recovery, we are thrown back into fruity mode – this time jelly babies without the dusting of sugar plus more exotic papaya, even with that attractive bitterness it possesses....; **b24** when you get that amount of exotic fruit on the nose, you know there is going to be a massive oaky kickback somewhere. However, this copes brilliantly and even has something fruitier up its sleeve further down the line. This can be taken as one of your five fruits a day... *40%*

⬧ **Tomintoul Five Decades** bott Jul 15 db **(94.5) n23.5** love it: slightly green tomato, the lightest of muscovado sugars and lashings of malt...; **t24** all kinds of caramel and vanillas to the fore. Then a series of brief citrus notes followed by weightier, prettily spiced, molasses; **f23** long, with spices nibbling at the taste buds like one might nibble at the chocolate smeared on one's naked lover..; **b24** writing this Bible, and the inordinate amount of time it takes, day and night, night and day, week in, month out, means that I have to turn down most invites to attend the opening of distilleries and the celebration of anniversaries. Just can't fit it in. So glad the 50th anniversary of Tomintoul came to me in the shape of this luxurious dram. Another whisky which leaves you scratching your head to wonder why Whyte and Mackay sold this brilliant distillery: as though the manager wanted to get rid of the star player to harmonise the dressing room. Anyway, happy 50th birthday, Tomintoul distillery: you are in loving hands now and able to fulfil your enormous potential. *50%. nc ncf. 5,230 bottles.*

Tomintoul With A Peaty Tang db **(94) n23 t24 f23 b24.** A bit more than a tang, believe me! Faultlessly clean distillate that revels in its unaccustomed peaty role. The age is confusing and appears mixed, with both young and older traits being evident. *40%*

Old Ballantruan db **(89.5) n23.5** ye gods!! This is packing some peat!! Young it may be... but...well...ye gods!! **t23** sugars are falling over themselves to engage before the tidal wave of peat arrives. They just about manage it...; **f21** becomes fractionally too bitter as the vanilla and lime retreats, despite the phenols; **b22** profound young malt which could easily be taken for an Islay. *50%. ncf.*

⬧ **Old Ballantruan Aged 10 Years** bott code 1706.15 db **(94.5) n23.5** oily now, in a Caol Ila style: the phenols cling to the nose. Clean, with vanilla unhindered despite the smoke; **t23.5** not sure I have ever come across a smoked whisky which is so oily yet so juicy: very odd! Just like the nose, the vanilla and peat are the two main characters, but a light smattering of maple syrup does no harm; **f23.5** long. Spices at last arrive and oils recede as it dries; **b24** can't say this is a spectacular peated malt. But everything is brilliantly in proportion and so sublimely balanced. *50%. ncf.*

Darkness! Tomintoul Aged 18 Years Oloroso Cask Finish **(91.5) n23 t23 f22.5 b23** Luscious sherry with not a sulphur of atom in sight...! *52.7%. 95 bottles. WB15/204*

Glen Fahrn Airline Nr 05 Tomintoul 1968 Aged 43 Years cask no. 4227 **(95.5) n24 t24.5 f23 b24.** Exotic fruit par excellence! Everything one might hope from such an aged Speysider. The tannins are a shade over eager at the death. But until then, the movement through the phases of vanilla, blood orange and kumquats, oily barley and cocoa tick every box of expectation. Sublime. *48.1%. sc. 180 bottles.*

Master of Malt Single Cask Tomintoul 19 Year Old dist 1 May 95, bott 1 Apr 15 **(87) n21.5 t22.5 f21.5 b21.5.** Boasts a similar type of fruitiness to their Batch 2. Quite a short, thin finish follows a refreshing, though European-style body and spirit. Youthful for its near two decades. *54.6%. sc. 186 bottles.*

That Boutique-y Whisky Company Tomintoul batch 2 **(88) n22** gorgeous (and curious) mix of grape must and grist; **t23** fresh, salivating and something of the east European slivovitz; **f21.5** continues on the sugary-fruity theme; **b21.5** malts rarely come much cleaner. An odd distinctive fruitiness more akin to brandy. *54.1%. 71 bottles.*

TORMORE
Speyside, 1960. Chivas Brothers. Working.

Tormore 12 Years Old db (75) n19 t19 f19 b18. For those who like whisky in their caramel. 40%

Tormore Aged 14 Years batch no. A1308, bott 2013 db (83.5) n21 t21.5 f20.5 b20.5. Toffeed, flat and inoffensive. Good dram to have last thing at night: chances are you'll be asleep before you finish the glass... 43% WB15/326

Tormore Aged 15 Years "Special Distillery Bottling" db (71) n17 t18 f19 b17. Even a supposed pick of choice casks can't save this from its fiery fate. 46%

Tormore Aged 16 Years batch no. B1309, bott 09 2013 db (95) n23.5 a husky nose: deep with an oaky roughage, underlined by spice. But on another plane there is a softer, oilier, dark-sugared, vaguely kumquat-ish hue, too...; t24 this is Tormore....? Wow! Succulent dates are topped with complex but effective spices. But as the ulmo honey moves in the complexity levels rise accordingly. Stunning butterscotch tart and red liquorice towards the still lightly oiled middle and cocoa can soon be expected...; f23.5...which arrives bang on cue and on time like a Japanese bullet train! Not so much predictable, but following the path of great whisky. The cocoa shimmers on different levels of intensity, with an occasional citrus moment. The spices grumble gorgeously; b24 Tormore as I have never seen it before. The label talks about the "long and dry" finish. It does the bottling such a disservice: this is magnificently complex with cocoa notes a thing of sheer beauty. A landmark bottling for Tormore. 48%

Best Dram Tormore 19 Years Old hogshead (91) n23 nuts and dates...what the...thought this was from a hoggie...?? t23.5 an implausible delivery – really not out of the usual Tormore canon. Those dates and nuts on the nose are now joined by juicy figs and greengages. Some mocha drifts through, and a little dollop of ulmo honey arrives and vanishes; f21.5 not entirely flawless with its nagging, buzzing off note. But still a lot of liquorice and raisin going on besides...; b23 a genuinely pleasant surprise. This is just bursting out of the glass with class and character... 49.9%

Chapter 7 Tormore 1995 19 Year Old bourbon hogshead, cask no. 20159 (94.5) n23.5 a real attitude between the oak and malt: fascinating and intriguing..; the oak (a little nimbler thanks to some kumquat and pear juiciness) appears to be landing some knock out blows...; t24 Tormore...? Really...? I mean...really...??? A massive delivery where the obvious fault line between the barley and tannin turns into a magnitude 8 quake, spices ripping into the taste buds without mercy. Huge...but the barley and oak are in two different camps. Meanwhile dark, satanic sugars run amok, even the odd hint of manuka honey in there....before the barley battles back; f23 you can't really follow that. And the finish doesn't even try: it just lets nature take its course. A light descending of vanilla and butterscotch from the mountainous heights of the massive sugars. Then, at last, the barley again makes its mark...before, finally, spiced cocoa: just so mmmmmm!!! b24 for a Tormore, this is right up there. No: despite its usual rough and ready antics, this is beyond all possible expectation. But just dig that delivery! Groovy, baby! 55.7%. sc. 209 bottles.

Gordon & MacPhail Connoisseurs Choice Tormore 1996, bott 2011 (86) n22 t21 f22 b21. Can't say this is an example of how scotch should be distilled, but pans out well thanks to decent oak. 46%. nc ncf. WB15/151

⬥ **Gordon & MacPhail Connoisseurs Choice Tormore 1998** (87) n21.5 t22.5 f21.5 b21.5. A sober and, at times, suave malt. Silky soft, it is comfortable in its malty skin but rarely ventures away from the barley theme. Limited in scope, but delicious in what it does. 46%

Gordon & MacPhail Cask Strength Tormore 1999 (90.5) n22 custard cream tart meets lemon merengue pie; t23.5 hugely intense eye-watering barley, crunchy sugar with a lovely gooseberry edge; f22 bitters out a tad, but the barley sugar remains on top; b23 lays it on thick with the barley. Attractive. 58%

⬥ **Gordon & MacPhail Cask Strength Tormore 2004** (85.5) n21 t22 f21 b21.5. An above standard Tormore which really blasts out its malty credentials at full volume. The sugars threaten to overdo things slightly and the heat is not all to do with the alcohol. But all this more than make up for the wallpaper paste, nutty aroma. 61.2%

Cadenhead's Small Batch Tormore Aged 30 Years dist 1984 (82) n20 t21.5 f20 b20.5. The Speyside style chiselled in stone; the aggressively smouldering delivery on the palate... the total refusal to harmonise beyond the gripping spices..Yes, no mistaking this as a Tormore,,,! 53.8%

Old Malt Cask Tormore 26 Years Old sherry butt, cask no. 10665, dist Nov 88, bott Apr 15 (95.5) n23 oddly thin for a sherry butt, but no off notes. Nutty and enticing; t24 superb delivery: probably not oloroso as that nuttiness continues (impressively, mind), though now accompanied by gentle greengage and grape. Oils build and we slowly move into moist fruitcake territory; light on the sugars, though the odd toasted cherry turns up; **f24** long, with an impressive continuation but now backed confidently by spice; **b24.5** beautifully elegant and sophisticated: an absolute class act. And it is not often in 30 years I have said that about Tormore... *50%. nc ncf sc. 183 bottles.*

⋗ **Old Malt Cask Tormore Aged 27 Years** refill butt, cask no. 12239, dist Nov 88, bott Apr 16 **(84.5) n20.5 t22.5 f20.5 b21.** From the marking, you can see it has a flaw. Yet the nuttiness, richness of the unsullied grape impresses. *50%. nc. 779 bottles. WB15/012*

Signatory Vintage Single Malt Tormore 1995 Aged 18 Years hogsheads, cask no. 3885+3886, dist 27 Apr 95, bott 07 Feb 14 **(85.5) n21.5 t22 f21 b21.** Clean, sweet, unchallenging malt. Perfectly acceptable. Easily drinkable. Safe. Just give me a nudge if it starts to do something. *43%. nc.*

⋗ **Single Cask Collection Tormore Aged 20 Years** bourbon hogshead **(77.5) n19.5 t21 f19 b18.** Thinly structured malt. Sweet, momentarily citrusy. But never forms a sensible combination of flavours. *53.1%. sc.*

The Single Malts of Scotland Tormore 25 Years Old bourbon barrel, cask no. 603, dist 03 Feb 8, bott 14 Feb 13 **(94.5) n23 t23.5 f24 b24** From the colour and strength, you'd be thinking this had been matured in Kentucky. And as for the flavour profile...OK, what have you done with the real Tormore...that guys nothing like as handsome as you! Never seen anything like it from this distillery in 30 years! A fabulous freak of a dram. *64.2%. 194 bottles. WB15/306*

That Boutique-y Whisky Company Tormore batch 2 **(83.5) n20.5 t22 f20 b21.** After it makes its malty statement, it has little else to say. Steely hard but the spices help. *51.4%. 103 bottles.*

⋗ **Whisky Live Tel Aviv Tormore 19 Years Old** hogshead, cask no. 20315, dist 1995, bott 2015 **(85.5) n19 t22.5 f22 b22.** The nose may not be up to much. But there is no denying the attractiveness of the malty, milk-chocolate theme. Like a distilled night-time cup of cocoa. *49.1%. sc. 289 bottles.*

TULLIBARDINE
Highlands (Perthshire), 1949. Tullibardine Ltd. Working.

Tullibardine 1992 Rum Finish bott 2009 db **(89.5) n22 t23 f22.5 b22.** Cracking stuff! *46%*

Tullibardine 1993 bott 2009 db **(91.5) n22 t23.5 f23 b23.** Intrinsically sweet barley. But spellbindingly charming all the way. *40%*

Tullibardine 1993 Moscatel Finish bott 2007 db **(92.5) n23.5 t23.5 f23 b22.5.** This really is how wine casks should integrate. A minor stunner. *46%*

Tullibardine 1993 Oloroso Sherry Finish bott 2008 db **(89) n23 t23 f21 b22.** Almost a trip down Memory Lane: once a pretty standard sherry butt, but now a treat. *46%*

Tullibardine 1993 Pedro Ximénez Sherry Finish bott 2009 db **(87) n21 t23 f20.5 b22.5.** Sticky and enjoyable. *46%*

Tullibardine 1993 Port Finish bott 2008 db **(83.5) n21.5 t21 f20 b21.** A bumbling, weighty kind of dram with indistinct shape and purpose, even to the extent of displaying a more bourbony gait than a fruity one. Enjoyable, decently spiced but limited in scope. *46%*

Tullibardine 1993 Sauternes Finish bott 2008 db **(84.5) n22 t22 f20 b20.5.** Sleepy and soft with the expected major grape input. Yet rather flattens out too early and to too great a degree. Pleasant, but a little disappointing, too. *46%*

Tullibardine Aged 20 Years db **(92.5) n22.5** busy and can't decide which weight to adopt; ethereal hazelnut and citrus rise above the languid tannins; **t24** no doubting the richness of body and the exceptional weight: first it is scorched yet juicy barley by the cartload, then thudding oak with just enough ulmo honey to oil the wheels. And then rampaging spice; **f22.5** settles for more prosaic butterscotch but the spices continue to bristle; **b23.5** while there are whiskies like this in the world, there is a point to this book... *43%*

Tullibardine Aged 25 Years db **(86.5) n22 t22 f21 b21.5.** There can be too much of a good thing. And although the intricacies of the honey makes you sigh inwardly with pleasure, the overall rigidity and fundamentalism of the oak goes a little too far. *43%*

Tullibardine 225 sauternes cask finish db **(85) n20 t22.5 f21 b21.5.** Hits the heights early on in the delivery when the honey and Lubeck marzipan are at full throttle. *43%*

Tullibardine 228 Burgundy cask finish db **(82) n21 t22 f18 b21.** No shortage of bitter chocolate. Flawed but a wow for those looking for mega dry malt. *43%*

Tullibardine 500 sherry cask finish db **(79.5) n19 t21 f19 b20.5.** The usual problems from Jerez, but the grape ensures maximum chewability. *43%*

Tullibardine Aged Oak bott 2009 db **(86) n21.5 t21 f22 b21.5.** Aged oak maybe. But early on this is all about the malt which is faultless. Major oaky buzz later. *40%*

Tullibardine Aged Oak Edition bott 2010 db **(88) n21 t22 f22.5 b22.5.** Beautifully made malt which is full of life. *40%. nc.*

Tullibardine Banyuls Finish bott 2011 db (68) n16 t18 f17 b17. I saw the sulphur coming on this. A steaming mug of intense black coffee and a cool glass of taste bud restorative coconut water wait in the wings. 46%. nc ncf.

Tullibardine Banyuls Finish bott 2012 db (71) n17 t19 f17 b18. A minor tragedy: take away the sulphur and you have what would have been a serious juicefest. Not for the first time with a banyuls cask, I could cry! 46%. nc ncf.

Tullibardine John Black db (84.5) n20 t21.5 f22 b21. Young, clean and bursting with all kinds of delicious maltiness. An almost perfect first dram of the day. 40%. nc.

Tullibardine Pure Pot new make db (90.5) n24 t23 f21.5 b22. Pure delight! Not whisky, of course, but a great example of how new make malt should be. 69%

Tullibardine Sauternes Finish bott 2012 db (90.5) n22 t23 f22.5 b23. The spices attached to the richness of the body makes for a very satisfying and quite intriguing malt. 46%. nc ncf

Tullibardine Sovereign bourbon barrel db (89.5) n22.5 a kind of 'what's what' of bourbon aromas: an entire regiment of delicate oaky tones from the standard butterscotch through to polished oak floors. But all tinged with a green-ish barley note. Always light and a little chalky; t23 the nose is transferred almost in identical form to the delivery: more light sugars at play here and a little nutty, too; f21.5 a slight tang to the fading milky Sugar Puffs; b22.5 beautifully salivating despite the intricate oak notes. 43%

Tullibardine Vintage Edition Aged 20 Years dist 1988, bott 2008 db (86) n22 t22 f21 b21. The malt sparkles on the nose and delivery. Fades as caramels kick in. 46%

Anam na h-Alba The Soul of Scotland Tullibardine 1989 bourbon cask, dist Apr 89, bott May 15 (84) n21 t22.5 f19 b20.5. The earthy, dank moss nose suggests not all is right with the barrel, as the sharp, tangy, ill-at-ease finale certifies. The massively intense barley on delivery is exceptional, though. 53.3%. 36 bottles.

◈ **Old Malt Cask Tullibardine Aged 21 Years** sherry butt, cask no. 12143, dist May 94, bott Nov 15 (85.5) n21 t22 f21 b21.5. Absolutely no sulphur on the cask; indeed, hard to see where the sherry makes its mark at all. Instead, we have a very basic, malt-charged offering which is never less than pleasant, though limited, in scope. 50%. nc ncf sc. 302 bottles.

Provenance Tullibardine Over 7 Years refill barrel, cask no. 10767, dist Summer 08, bott Summer 15 (84) n21 t21.5 f20.5 b21. Decidedly green, sugary and youthful. Struggles to find body beyond the malt and would have benefited from being at cask strength. 46%. nc ncf sc.

◈ **Scotch Malt Whisky Society Cask 28.30 Aged 25 Years** 2nd fill Sauternes hogshead, dist 25 Jun 90, bott 31 Oct 15 (89) n22 any fruit that may be present appears lost in a forest of light tannins. Salty, spicy and quietly threatening; t22.5 beautiful weight to the light oils, there is a strange sub-current of almost youthful malt. Busy, bustling and veering towards vanilla; f22 the salty sharpness continues, though now a light mocha tone filters through... spices pulse out the finale...; b22.5 impressively understated. 53.3%. nc ncf sc. 228 bottles.

◈ **Spirit & Cask Tullibardine** barrel, dist 2007, bott 2015 (85) n21 t22 f21.5 b21.5. Young, malty and refreshing. 46%. 294 bottles.

◈ **That Boutique-y Whisky Company Tullibardine** batch 1 (89) n21 a slightly churlish cask tries to undo the great work of the intense, lightly salted, vaguely green malt; t23 you'll have to go a long way to find a texture as soft as this. Just a vaguest hint of smoke clinging to the uninterrupted malt; f22.5 good length. Some tannin nibbles lightly. And a little spice plays out a simple theme charmingly; b22.5 lovely, untaxing whisky with enough going on to keep the taste buds on full alert. 50.1%. 159 bottles.

WOLFBURN

◈ **Wolfburn Single Malt Scotch Whisky** db (91.5) n23 the tannins have just taken enough shine off the new make to ensure this has all the right whisky vibes. Still very youthful, with the grist retaining citrus-imbued fizz, but an elegant smokiness drifts around ensuring weight and substance; t23 mmm! Superb delivery! Yes, this may be a youngster, but the weight of the barley-enriched oil is wonderful, especially seeing as there is not a single note of feintiness to be had. With this oil, the smoke, so apparent on the nose, plays a lesser part, though it still hangs around to give a lightly peated accent to the gentle cocoa; f22.5 the finish always undoes the young-uns, though here just enough oak is involved to ensure the lingering malt doesn't fade alone; b23 this is a very young malt showing an intriguing wispy smokiness, its evenness more in line with having been matured in ex-Islay casks than using low phenol barley. Still, it might have been, and, if so, perhaps reveals a style that would not have been entirely unknown to the people of Thurso when they last drank this during Victorian times. It is probably 30 years ago I was shown to a spot in the town where I was told the original distillery had been. Now it is back, and eclipses Pulteney as the producers of the most northerly mainland Scottish whisky. For all its youth, its excellence of quality glimmers from the glass: a malt as beautifully flighted as a cricket ball delivered by the most crafted of spinners. And offers a delightful turn on the palate, too. The building of a new distillery, no matter how romantic its location or story, does not guarantee good whisky. So I am delighted for those involved in a project as exhausting as this that a very good whisky is exactly what they have on their hands. *46%. nc ncf.*

UNSPECIFIED SINGLE MALTS (CAMPBELTOWN)

Cadenhead's Campbeltown Malt (92) n22 t24 f23 b23. On their home turf you'd expect them to get it right... and, my word, so they do!! *59.5%*

Cadenhead's Classic Campbeltown (92) n23 t24 f22 b23. What a dram! Must be what they gave Lazarus... *50%*

UNSPECIFIED SINGLE MALTS (HIGHLAND)

Alexander Murray & Co Bon Accord Highland Single Malt (82.5) n21 t21.5 f20 b20. Fudge whisky. Pleasant, but way too simple. *40%*

Alexander Murray & Co Highland Single Malt 1964 49 Years Old (88) n22 t23 f21.5 **b21.5**. For a malt bottled on the cusp of its 50th anniversary of being distilled, beyond the delivery it is hard to find a narrative here. Often malts of this age are simply too oaky and lopsided to be of any significance on the greatness front. This certainly has its fair share of tannin, and even a hint of bourbon on the nose. But it is the reticence of the malt to give much of a clue to what's been happening all these years which is perplexing: I cannot remember a bottled whisky of this age which is so comprehensively gagged on the mid-ground and finish. The delivery has a bit more going for it, and at times you can almost chew the golden syrup-dripping sawdust. And the spices at the death are superb. No doubting it has some genuinely lovely moments, and if you are looking for a very old malt which simply exudes soft, aged, occasionally charming benevolence, then this could be for you. But, overall, it is all so frustratingly fuddled and fudged. *40%*

Alexander Murray & Co Highland Single Malt 1995 19 Years Old (85) n21 t22 f21 b21. Agreeably spiced toffee. *40%*

Trader Joe's Highland Single Malt 1996 17 Years Old (86.5) n21.5 t22 f21.5 b21.5. Some serious juiciness and spice on the delivery. The spices last the course. *40%.*

UNSPECIFIED SINGLE MALTS (ISLAND)

Master Of Malt Island Single Malt (91.5) n22.5 t23 f22.5 b23.5. Don't know about Lord of the Isles. More like Lord of the Flies...Fruit flies, that is...! They would be hard pressed to find even an over-ripe mango any juicier than this gorgeous malt... *40%*

UNSPECIFIED SINGLE MALTS (ISLAY)

Ben Bracken Islay Single Malt 22 Years Old dist 1993 **(96)** n24.5 a rare, absolutely spot on marriage between grand old oak, but beautifully manicured and controlled peat reek; with the vaguest citrus peeping from just around the corner, this is just glorious...; **t24** a beautifully soft delivery, smoky, velvet fingers caressing the taste buds. The oak is tinged with a bourbony signature; **f23.5** soft spices play out, at first with a delicate sweetness, then dries powerfully as the oak and soot take hold. Would not like to have seen this go another summer: this has somehow kept its integrity; **b24** a real old timer showing its oaky scars with pride. A serious late night dram. And with an unspoiled palate, for this will be one of your smoky treats of the year... *40%*

Blackadder Peat Reek Raw Cask Islay single oak hogshead, bott Jul 13 **(88.5)** n23 t23 f21 b21.5 a more sympathetic hoggy and this would have scored very highly. *60.6%. nc ncf sc. 216 bottles. WB15/060*

Blackadder Smoking Islay cask. BA2013/450, bott Jun 13 **(88)** n22 t23 f21 b22 Attractive, but not quite up to the usual very high standards for this bottling. *55%. nc ncf sc. 386 bottles. WB15/161*

Blackadder Smoking Islay Raw Cask cask no. BA2013/449 **(92.5)** n24 t23.5 f22 b23 Almost a curious re-run of Blackadder's Peat Reek, with the fun threatening to end as the bitterness of the cask bites, adder-like. But just many good points compensate. Really lovely. *59.9%. nc ncf sc. 318 bottles. WB15/061*

Cask Islay (91.5) n22.5 ashy and dry. Oh, and smoky; **t23** soft oils dissolve to be replaced by lively spice, citrus and polite Demerara sugar. Oh, and some smoke...; **f22.5** good length thanks to the remaining oil with a light smattering of vanilla. The sugars also linger...as does the smoke; **b23** does what it says on the tin. *46%. A.D. Rattray*

Celtique Connexion Origine Islay Affine Sauternes cask dist 1999, bott 2013 **(95.5)** n23 t24 f24 b24.5 that rarest of beasts: a heavily peated malt happy to mature in a wine cask. Not surprised it required a spotless Sauternes cask to do the job. Mind-blowingly gorgeous. *46%*

Douglas Laing's Single Minded Islay Aged 6 Years (84.5) n21 t22.5 f20 b21 Oily, sweet and moderately smoky. Don't look for complexity. Or a particularly great finish, either. *48.4%. nc ncf.*

Elements of Islay AR4 (93.5) n23.5 t23.5 f23 b23.5. Massive oak infusion: the slow burn of smoke leaves no doubt to distillery. Clever oily-dry interplay plus hickory and cocoa-orange. 58.1% WB15/341

Elements of Islay Ar5 (76) n19 t20 f18 b19. One element too many in this fruity and off-key version. 57.8% WB16/017

Elements of Islay Bn5 (82.5) n19.5 t22 f20 b21. Peat a'plenty, but perhaps a few too many tangy moments than is desirable. 54.9% WB16/014

Elements of Islay BN6 (80) n20 t22 f19 b19. Simply too sweet and cloying for its own good. Zero complexity as the molasses, golden syrup and manuka honey go ballistic. Off key finale. 56.9% WB15/346

Elements of Islay BR5 (96) n24 t24.5 f23.5 b24. An unpeated masterpiece of the Laddie old school. Possibly the most complete and harmonious alloy of honeys bottled this year. Genius. 53.8% WB15/296

Elements of Islay BW3 (90.5) n22.5 t23.5 f22 b22.5. A playful Bowmore showing a copper sharpness amid the more languid smoke. Fabulous delivery: acacia and ulmo honey starring. 51.6% WB15/289

Elements of Islay Bw4 (87) n22 t22.5 f20.5 b22. Low peated and highly sugared; the spices are more than welcome. 51.6% WB16/016

Elements of Islay CI7 (91) n22 t23.5 f22.5 b23. At times thick enough to be like dementedly peated clotted cream...with vanilla and Demerara sugar stirred in. 58.5% WB16/015

Elements of Islay CL6 (94) n23 t24 f23 b24. Less oil means more balance for this stunning Caol Ila. The major citrus element cuts through the peat; light sugar and malt salivates. 61.2% WB15/290

Elements of Islay LG4 (87.5) n22 t23 f21 b21.5. Typical huge Lagavulin but untypical sharpness on delivery & sweet finish. The phenols are of a smoked mackerel variety. 55.7% WB15/287

Elements of Islay LP4 (89) n22.5 t22.5 f22 b22. Profound peat at its earthiest. A tangy delivery but then soothing, as muscovado sugars & vanillas arrive. A gentle giant. 54.8% WB15/286

Elements of Islay LP5 (92) n23.5 t22.5 f22 b22. Elements is right for this Laphroaig: what we are getting here is the malt at its gristiest with the sugars releasing the smoke beautifully. 52.4% WB15/288

⟜ **Eilan Gillan Islay Single Malt** bourbon refill casks, dist 2010, bott 2015 (91.5) n23 vibrant peat, not overly troubled by oak. Clean, textbook malt with just the first traces of something attractively coastal. Just a few strands of citrus lightens the load; t23 there are times I adore that blend-style bite, even with a single malt. And this is perfect. The youth of the spirit gouges into the palate, but then offers an oily, smoky kiss to apologise; f22.5 dry, despite the first strains of vanilla coming though. The peat throbs, dries and intensifies to the last sooty moment; b23 it's Leap Year's Day and a charming way to officially kick off tasting for the 2017 Bible! No doubting the youth and I especially chose a youngster hoping it would have enough bite and attitude to slap my taste buds back into action. It has not disappointed me in any way. A little belter! Ignore the descriptor on the label, though. It is nothing like...Oh well, one down, another 999 (at least!) to go... 43%. nc ncf.

⟜ **ePower Islay Malt** bourbon cask, dist 2009, bott 2015 (93) n23.5 beautifully bright: a crisp Demerara glaze to the fulsome peat; t23.5 sugars arrive early and concentrate fast. The smoke sneaks in through the back door before taking command; lots of juicy barley at play; f22.5 spicy, plus a little acacia honey on the vanilla; b23.5 some stunning moments for a malt so young. 52.3%

⟜ **ePower Islay Malt** Port cask, dist 2009, bott 2015 (88.5) n22 hard-nosed boiled fruit candy – smoked, of course; t22.5 much softer, sugar-prominent, arrival, though the fruit and peat soon begin to bicker; f22 some reedy vanilla undermines the smoky integrity; b22 some really lovely moments, but the youthful discord has nowhere to hide. 52.7%

Finlaggan Old Reserve Cask Strength (94) n23 t23.5 f23.5 b24. I can imagine even people who proclaim not to like peaty whisky slowly falling in love with this...it is so enormous, that it would be a case of kill or cure. 58%. The Vintage Malt Whisky Co Ltd.

Mystery Lochside (95) n24.5 t24 f22.5 b24. The kind of malt that deserves all the time you can afford it. It will repay you handsomely, especially on the nose and delivery and will never come at you at the same speed or angle. Subtle and sublime.

⟜ **Port Askaig 100 Proof** (96.5) n24 can't ask for much more: the clarity matches the purity of the pale yellow colour, and that tint helps explain the nose. Deft vanillas can be heard here, alongside gristy malt; confident, yet never arrogant or boastful peat. Astonishing...; t24 the sugars melt in the moth on impact. Just a light oiliness coats the mouth sufficiently for the citrus phenols to ensure there are two distinct weights on display. Yet, somehow, they seem equally poised...; f24 what perfect oak must have been deployed here. No off notes or buzz. Just the insistent and steadying hand of vanilla/butterscotch to add a gentle counter to the spice and smoke; b24.5 just exemplary, high quality Islay: a must experience malt. If you find a more beautifully paced, weighted and elegant Islay this year, I'd really like to hear about it.... 57.1%

Port Askaig Harbour Aged 19 Years (94) n23.5 t23.5 f23 b24. One of those gorgeous offerings which basks in its simplicity, but takes what it does to the max. *50.4%.*

Smokey Joe Islay Malt (94.5) n23 high level phenols are broadcast on an oily, salty, coastal wind...; **t24** the delivery, snug in its peaty overcoat, is good...the following waves of smoke are truly exceptional. A just-so degree of dark sugar and liquorice embrace the phenols...; **f23.5** a vague bitterness, but caught in its tracks by the gradual ascent of delicious cocoa notes; **b24** a high quality Islay ticking all the required boxes. *46%*

⬥ **Spirits Shop Selection & Sansibar Whisky Islay Malt 2007** bourbon cask, bott 2015 **(92.5) n24** adorable balance on the sweet-dry front; the salt lifts the many understated segments; the grapefruit adds a beguiling lightness of touch; **t23** just like on the nose, the smoke borders on the belligerent but thinks better of it. Some youthful notes counter the punchy peat; **f22.5** light vanilla with gentle phenolic layering; **b23** very satisfying. *51.6%. 323 bottles.*

Wemyss Aged 30 Years Islay "Heathery Smoke" hogshead, bott Aug 11 **(95.5) n24 t24 f23.5 b24.** One of those magical malts which never noses or tastes the same twice and always offers a different perspective and new facets each time it is sampled. A true gem. *46%. sc. 272 bottles. USA exclusive.*

⬥ **The Whisky Agency Acla Selection South of Islay Aged 7 Years** bourbon hogshead, dist 2007, bott 2015 **(86) n21.5 t22 f21.5 b21.** A smoky, new-makey rough diamond that is still to be cut. Some enjoyable individual traits, especially from the marauding smoke, but at that juncture in its life where the harmonisation is yet to kick in. But for sheer fun... ten out of ten!! *53.6%. nc ncf. 120 bottles.*

Whisky Fair Islay Malt 8 Year Old bourbon hogshead, dist 2007, bott 2015 **(88.5) n22.5** simple, straightforward, clean, powdery, spicy phenols; **t22** very youthful, juicy delivery. Simple and straightforward with attractive butterscotch in the midground; **f22**....errr... straightforward...? **b22** clean, gristy and irresistibly charming. *54.4%. 144 bottles.*

⬥ **Whisky-Fässle Southshore Islay Malt 2007** hogshead, bott 2015 **(91) n23** classic dry peat embers. So salty and coastal...; **t23** dense delivery: excellent spice buzz and Manuka honey mix; **f22** a degree of Fleetwood's finest cough sweet...; **b23** no great age, but certainly some excellent interplay. Superb use of honey tones to offset yet compliment the peat. *55.7%*

⬥ **Whisky-Fässle Southshore Islay Malt 2009** hogshead, bott 2015 **(87) n22 t22.5 f21 b21.5.** A curiously flat sample from a distillery where I would expect better balance, even at this age. Certainly has some excellent early moments but, just a tad too young for the composition to have hit a point of equilibrium. *52.3%*

⬥ **William Cadenhead Islay 7 Year Old** claret wine barrel, dist 1992 **(94) n23.5** a curious mix of boiling blackcurrant and peat...! Rather lovely, and very unusual (unique, in fact) it must be said...; **t24** the wine has ensured one of the softest landings imaginable: this is rich stuff with the peat pungent and intense. But it lands in a velvet glove of moist fruitcake; **f23** fabulously long: the youth and natural strength means the oils are still intact and radiate clever sugars, mostly dark muscovado, before a delicate smoked cocoa note oversees the fade; **b23.5** a rather lovely offering from Chateau Phenol. For a 7-year-old malt, truly brilliant! *59.1%. sc.*

Wilson & Morgan House Malt Single Islay Malt cask no. 6158, 6266, dist May 06, bott Jan 15 **(86.5) n23 t22.5 20 b21.** The nose is a success with its Arbroath Smokies on newly-baked bread. Oily and pugnacious. But the strangely metallic and off-key finish leaves you scratching your head... *43%*

UNSPECIFIED SINGLE MALTS (LOWLAND)

Tweeddale Single Lowland Malt Scotch Whisky 14 Years db **(89) n21.5** sharp citrus and basic vanilla; **t23.5** lively, clean and salivating, the grist positively pulses; **f22** back to simple vanilla basics...but attractively done; **b22** busy, bustling, elegant and old-fashioned...like a small borders town. *62%. nc ncf sc. Stonedean Ltd.*

UNSPECIFIED SINGLE MALTS (SPEYSIDE)

⬥ **Acla Special Edition No.1 Somewhere in Speyside 38 Years Old** refill sherry wood, dist 1977, bott 2015 **(82.5) n20 t21.5 f20 b21.** Some lovely cocoa moments. But elsewhere, too bitter and out of sorts. *46.8%. nc ncf.*

Alexander Murray & Co Speyside Single Malt 1972 41 Years Old (90) n22.5 t23 f22 b22.5. The fascinating nose is worth a good ten minutes of anyone's time: earthy, pungent, with some fruit and nut amid the oak. But you can't escape the tannin on the palate, as this reached its prime maybe a decade earlier. Even so, as oaky mountains go, this is scalable and there are some half decent views when you get to the top. *40%*

◇ **Ben Bracken Speyside Single Malt Aged 8 Years** American white oak bourbon barrels **(85.5) n21.5 t22.5 f20 b21.5.** Juicy and pleasant, with an attractive honey and molasses middle. But the caramel wipes out any meaningful complexity. *40%*

◇ **Ben Bracken Speyside Single Malt 28 Years Old** dist 1987 **(84.5) n22 t21 f21.5 b20.** The early promise on delivery – where the malt powers through with spice on its coattails – isn't backed up quite as one may wish. Goes through a number of tangy turns, where even after 28 years the tannin appears to be uneasy with the malt, or perhaps the other way round, before it settles down for a light vanilla finish, tinged with the lightest coating of ulmo honey. *40%*

◇ **Eilan Gillan Speyside Single Malt 2009** sherry casks, bott 2015 **(73) n18.5 t19 f17.5 b18.** Some sugar and spice wades in to try and save the day. But never gets going and a very average distillate is attacked by light sulphur. *43%. nc ncf.*

◇ **ePower Speyside Malt 19 Years Old** refill sherry hogshead, dist 1996, bott 2015 **(91.5) n23** an extra measure of salt to the light fruitcake; **t24** unusually silky textured. Some plum pudding soon moves along for a saltier butterscotch tart; **f21.5** just a fraction too bitter; **b23** a sherry cask from the 90s which is just about sulphur-free: ePower to the person responsible for this bottling...! *49.6%*

Glen Fahrn Airline Nr 13 Red Baron of Speyside 1971 Aged 40 Years bourbon cask **(87.5) n22 t21 f22.5 b22.** I'd say this is the product of big stills. Because a lightweight body to the malt has allowed the oak to run riot. Thankfully, enough muscovado and maple syrup has been extracted for tannins to be controlled. More Kentucky than Speyside, but with none of the depth, richness and complexity of a good bourbon. *51.7%. sc. 139 bottles.*

Kirkland Speyside 20 Year Old (88) n22 an enticing, marginally complex nose: tannins and creamy chocolate mix comfortably while gentle spices massage; **t23** attractive delivery with a supine mouth feel. The spice is gentle but upfront while a soft toffee and raisin theme develops; **f21** a little tangy and fades a shade too fast; **b22** pleasant and workmanlike. *40%. Bottled for Costco. Alexander Murray & Co.*

Malt Mountain Speyside Region 20 Year Old dist 1994, bott 2015 **(89) n22** fat, sugar-laden gooseberries being gently boiled; **t24** sumptuous mouth feel; divine arrival of over-ripe greengage, gooseberry, vanilla and spices almost at the very same moment; **f20** back to a drier, lightly salted gooseberry tart...but some cask taint, as well; **b23** not flawless, but the depth and freshness of the fruit is astonishing...and stunning! *52.4%*

Master of Malt Speyside 30 Years Old 6th edition (95) n24.5 t24 f22.5 b24 Hmmmm. My 13th whisky of the day...and this comes from bottle number 13 of 238. The omens may be bad but in fact it has proved to be the best of the session so far. From the understated school of Speysiders where subtlety is key. *43.7%. 238 bottles. WB15/229*

Master Of Malt Speyside 40 Years Old 2nd Edition (95) n23.5 t24 f23.5 b24. Magnificent. has no problem mastering the years. *43%.*

Master Of Malt Speyside 50 Years Old 3rd Edition (96.5) n24 t23.5 f24.5 b24.5. Like many an old 'un, it seems to forget where it's going for a while. But when it reaches its destination, it just charms you to death. *43%.*

Old Malt Cask Probably Speyside's Finest 28 Years Old sherry butt, cask no. 11272, dist Nov 86, bott Feb 15 **(96) n24** a seemingly quiet nose, but on concentrated listening, far more is going on than first meets the nostril: the fruit is little more than a whisper, but the honey notes star, with a blend of manuka and rape constantly fidgeting about; **t24.5** so subtle: a charming re-run of the nose with almost the same points arriving with similar timing. Only the spice is more outgoing, while the mouth feel is gently oiled and exceptionally soft; **f23.5** drier, of course, as 28 years worth of oak is intent on making some impression. But still we are in the land of caresses and hints...; **b24** a clean bill of health for this quietly intriguing and drop-dead gorgeous sherry bottling. *48%. nc ncf sc. 285 bottles.*

Riegger's Selection Cask Strength Eagle of Spey 1993 sherry cask finish, bott 24 Dec **13 (87.5) n22.5 t23 f20 b22.** A joyful, fruity –and beautifully juicy – ride until we get to the very bitter finish. *52.9%*

Spirit & Cask El Máximo No. 7 sherry butt, dist 2008, bott 2015 **(86.5) n21.5 t22 f21.5 b21.5.** A clean sherry butt. No sulphur, so bravo! But because of the age, the fruit, malt and oak haven't yet found a happy medium. Not unpleasant - indeed, at times very pleasant - just plucked from the cask at the wrong time. *65%. 675 bottles.*

◇ **Spirits Shop Selection & Sansibar Whisky Speyside Malt 1975** sherry butt, bott 2015 **(93.5) n24** as though lightly salted butter has been stirred into ulmo honey and then geed up with a further dash of orange blossom honey; **t24** one of the deliveries of the year – certainly the best for this Bible – and I am on sample number 251. The malt is concentrated and thick but those delicate honey tones buzz contentedly as a perfect foil; a few panting notes of exhaustion towards the late middle; **f22** just bitters out slightly as the oak tires...; **b23.5** if you want to see what a sherry butt tasted like the first time I went to a Scottish distillery – way back in 1975 – give this a sniff and swirl around the chops. Absolutely clean and faultless... Make no mistake: this is absolutely top quality, Premier League whisky. *51.3%. 425 bottles.*

◇◇ **Spirits Shop Selection & Sansibar Whisky Speyside Malt 1977** sherry butt, bott 2015 **(95) n24** wears its oaky age lines with pride: dry oloroso sherry, but still something of a fruit pudding to this; **t24** impressive: the oak is upfront, but the dried dates are matched only by the big salt surge. You can count the flavour rungs, like you might circles on a tree. Profound and high quality stuff! **f23.5** very long, beautifully spiced and radiates class....as well as wrinkly tannins..; **b24** an OAP malt that is past its best, for sure. But still has enough depth and pride and utter beauty to seduce and then entirely enrapture. Superb! *46.1%*

◇◇ **Spirits Shop Selection & Sansibar Whisky Speyside Malt 1980** sherry butt, bott 2015 **(85) n21 t22.5 f20 b21.5.** Exceptionally salty for a Speysider, with an eye-watering tang to the fruit also. Not a malt which stands on ceremony or on the fence. Bitter finale, but only after some attractive vanilla. *473%. 387 bottles.*

Trader Joe's Speyside Single Malt 2001 12 Years Old (85) n21.5 t22.5 f20 b21. For a moment on both nose and delivery it appears this little bird can sing, especially when the muscovado sugars kick off early and appear to ignite the grist. But the caramel middle and fade are a disappointment. *40%. Alexander Murray & Co.*

Whisky-Fässle Speyside Malt 6 Year Old sherry butt, dist 2008, bott 2014 (85) n21 t22 f21 b21. A sweet and syrupy cove. The spices appear to be the harbinger of something a little less desired. Superficially enjoyable but never finds a rhythm or happy medium. *46.9%. nc ncf.*

Whisky-Fässle Speyside Malt 20 Year Old sherry butt, dist 1994, bott 2015 **(96) n23** doughy. Jam doughnut...? **t24** oh, oh, oh....!!! That's how a sherry cask should be: a few tantalising glimpses of malt, but the rest is clean, beautifully spiced and rounded fruit..; **f24.5** the freshness of the juicy dessert wine continues, until finally met by weightier, liquorice-edged oak. Such full on complexity..; **b24.5** old school sherry cask – as clean as a whistle. And one which not only hits all the high notes but possesses the ability to stay on the mark. Just fantastic stuff! *53.2%. nc ncf.*

◇◇ **Whisky-Fässle Speyside Region 1975** Fino butt, bott 2016 **(96) n24** delicate, complex, sophisticated: a mix of putty and sultana; age seeps from this like grey hair on the temple of Cary Grant...; **t24** so ridiculously juicy after all these years: the ulmo honey, maple syrup and sultana have ganged up alongside some intense vanilla..; **f24** a long fade where the age is only hinted at rather than mentioned and the myriad layers of vanilla clasp to the last remnants of the sultana; **b24** from a butt pre-dating the sulphur disaster. Truly the stuff of legend – and a pointer to whisky lovers of what real sherry-matured whisky should be. *474%*

◇◇ **Whisky-Fässle Speyside Region 1977** sherry butt, bott 2015 **(89.5) n22** nutty and rich; **t23** some unsubtle but enjoyable molasses and dates; **f22** a little bitter, but retains the nutty thread; **b22.5** effectively delicious, though a little slapdash. *46.2%*

UNSPECIFIED SINGLE MALTS (GENERAL)

◇◇ **Abbey Whisky Anon The Rare Casks Batch One Aged 13 Years** oloroso sherry cask finish, dist 2001, bott 2015 **(89.5) n23.5** sublimely rich Oloroso, with the grape absolutely singing from the glass; **t24** puckeringly dry sherry arrives with a creamy gait and ulmo honey as an accompaniment; **f20** dries, but those grapes are still evident; a little bitterness creeps in late on; **b22** a little sulphur hangs around at the finish, but better than most. No need for this brand to be Anon whatsoever. *51.5% sc. 90 bottles.*

Blackadder The Legendary Cask Strength (93) n23 t24 f23 b23 if the legendary Blackadder, complete with trusted sword, reappeared through the "swirling mists of time" and came back as a whisky, then I think he'd prefer to be something a little more butch than this essay of gentility bordering on femininity. *58.1%. WB15/055*

Blackadder The Legendary 20 Years Old cask no. LT132013-02 (87.5) **n22 t22 f21.5 b22.** Appears to have spent a significant part of the passing 20 years trapping all the soft caramel notes it can find. This overcomes the more stark oakiness, but at the cost of complexity. Hardly challenging but very pleasant, though. *46%. nc ncf sc. WB15/057*

◇◇ **The Classic Cask 40 Year Old** batch no. SW.107, dist 1972, bott 2012 **(94.5) n24** adorable: rich dates, figs, molasses...I think you get the picture; **t24** liquorice and manuka honey sets the bar high...; almost a rum feel to the esters; **f23** a slight thread of tiring oak ensures a degree of gentle bitterness accompanies the toasty sugars and spices; **b23.5** defies the years with a compelling and erudite display. *43% (86 proof)*

◇◇ **The Corriemhor Cigar Reserve** sherry & bourbon casks **(84.5) n21 t22 f20.5 b21.5.** You must forgive me if I judge this as a whisky alone. I have never smoked a cigar in my life; not even taken as much as an unlit cigarette to my lips. Not once. Ever. Some doctors and medical specialists in the field reckon it is why my nose and taste buds are so synchronised and alert. So if this is brilliant with a cigar, Cuban or otherwise, I will take your word for it. As a single malt in its own right, it is nutty, lush and pleasant. But rather lacking in complexity, scope or excitement. Dull, in fact. 46%

◇ **Hepburn's Choice Nice & Peaty 9 Years Old** refill hogshead, dist 2006, bott 2016 **(88) n22** youthful grist with lightly tangy phenols; **t22.5** sweet, soft, a little on the cough tablet side of things; **f22** though the spices rise, as does the cocoa, always seems a little underpowered; **b21.5** very easy to find when searching on my computer for this entry: I have never used the word "nice" for any whisky since the first Bible tasting note was written way back in 2003...Anyway, this is a modest little dram which is, indeed, nice and peaty....Doh! 46%. nc ncf sc. 404 bottles.

◇ **Peat's Beast (88.5) n22** bit of a pussy, this beast. No snarl to the phenols: a gentle, teasing of peat with an attractive underlayering of caramelised biscuit, vanilla and a sprig of mint; **t22.5** quite a thin body on delivery with the sugars ganging up early before the peat finds a way through; **f22** the light oils prolong the brown sugars as the vanilla dries; **b22** "to tame the beast we recommend a dash of water." I don't. Recommend, instead, you use the Murray Method to warm up to body temp; otherwise you fracture the delicate oils and the sugars which hold this together vanish way too soon. 46%. ncf.

◇ **Raasay While We Wait** finished in Tuscan red wine casks **(77) n18 t21.5 f18.5 b19.** I have always maintained that it is a dangerous tactic to link the name of a planned distillery with a malt which doesn't actually come from it. When in professional advisor mode, I always warn against it. I sincerely hope the distillery is built on Raasay one day by R&B, but to say that certain whiskies from other distilleries will taste like what theirs, not yet even constructed, one day might is fraught with dangers: the truth is, you never know exactly what you'll get –with as much meticulous planning as you like - until you get it. However their whisky one day turns out, they must ensure they don't ruin it by putting it into wine casks as poor as these. 46%. nc ncf. R&B Distillers.

Saar Whisky Bliesgau 2007 bott 2015 **(83.5) n22 t22.5 f19 b20.** A beautiful start with sugars abounding. But the finish is a little too tangy. 53.2%. ncf sc.

Saar Whisky Gruhewwwel 2007 bott 2015 **(96.5) n24.5** textbook phenolic nose: dry and ashy yet clever muscovado sugars ensuring softness and balance; **t24** again the sugars get up close and personal early on. And they need to for the peat is as outlandishly big as it is majestic **f23.5** long, elegant, the sugars and oils lasting long enough to ensure a peaty complexity carries on for a very good while; **b24.5** just outstandlingly good, fault-free peaty whisky. One of the great independent bottlings of the year. 51.9%. ncf sc.

◇ **Saar Whisky Gruhewwwel 2nd Edition** bourbon cask, dist 2007, bott 2015 **(91) n23** very decently peated – up around the 35ppm, I'd guess – making the most of the friendly cask which offers charming vanillas; **t23** beautifully weighted delivery. The oils are up early with the smoke and spices. Demerara sugars compliment the view; **f22.5** dries gently as we head back towards the vanilla and butterscotch – all topped with oily phenols, of course...; **b22.5** an oily Islay if ever there was one... 55.2%. nc ncf sc.

◇ **Saar Whisky Hüttengold** bourbon cask, dist 2007, bott 2015 **(85.5) n22.5 t22 f20 b21.** A little tart, but high quality distillate saves the day. The nose is the star of the show, with its sooty dryness. 52.3%. nc ncf sc.

Saar Whisky Mandelbachtal 2007 bott 2015 **(93.5) n23.5** just so honeyed: heather honey, ulmo honey, rape honey all there in varying amounts and to differing depths. But excellent slightly salted butterscotch tart to keep the sugars in check; **t23.5** and there they are again: a surge of lightly oiled honeys – mainly heather honey, as on the nose – beautifully shaped by the Brazilian biscuit-style flour of the oak; **f23** drier, saltier, lingering beeswax; **b23.5** distilled by bees. 52.7%. ncf sc.

Saar Whisky Schwenker 2005 bott 2015 **(89) n22.5** beautiful dry, salty peat. A charmer; **t23** early gristy peat, then a slow blossoming of ever intensifying phenols; sugars are sprinkled liberally; **f21.5** just a little biter at death; **b22** a competent, easy going malt for peat lovers. 53.7%. ncf sc

◇ **Saar Whisky Schwenker 2nd Edition** bourbon cask, dist 2008, bott 2015 **(89) n23** so salty and evocative of rock pools, one expects a starfish to be swimming around the glass. A real coastal feel to the peat reek; **t22.5** a brief blast of phenols makes way for a growing degree of toasted mallow. But the salt, like the oils, won't give way...; tannin begins to rise...; **f21** a little off key as the oak throws in the odd discordant note; **b22.5** if "schwenker" means salty, then they've called it! 53.5%. nc ncf sc.

Spirit & Cask Maximum Peat 2008 No. 14 butt, bott 2015 **(95) n23.5** dry, acidic peat...errr, to the max...!! **t24** huge marriage of phenols, muscovado sugar and ulmo honey....sublime!

f23.5 dry, tingling smoke with a light vanilla coating; that said, enough lingering sugars to ensure balance throughout; **b24** this may be from a butt, but let me reassure you: this kicks ass...!! No sulphur nonsense present here. 61.6%. 624 bottles..

Scottish Vatted Malts
(also Pure Malts/Blended Malt Scotch)

100 Pipers Aged 8 Years Blended Malt (74) n19 t20 f17 b18. A better nose, perhaps, and some spice on arrival. But when you consider the Speysiders at their disposal, all those mouth-wateringly grassy possibilities, it is such a shame to find something as bland as this. 40%

◇ **Abrachan Triple Oak Matured (77)** n19 t21 f18 b19. Some superb sugars on delivery, but a fuzzy, furry bitterness sadly gives the game away. 42%

◇ **Acla Selection Burnside 23 Years Old** bourbon hogshead, dist 1992, bott 2015 **(93)** **n23.5** outstanding finesse to the malt and weight, and the lemon drizzle is a treat; **t23** salivating, clean and with a sublime and almost perfectly weighted balance between the malt and the vanilla. The late spices are a bit of a bonus; **f23** vanilla and spice – and still clean as a whistle; **b23.5** what a magnificent piece of oak this was given the chance to grow up in. As I taste this in my remote garden, a song thrush is celebrating the setting of the sun in spectacular triple-whistled fashion: between the whisky and the bird, nature's harmony cannot be better represented. 50.4%. nc ncf.

Angels' Nectar (81) n21 t21 f19 b20. This angel has a bitter tooth... 40%

◇ **Angel's Nectar Blended Malt Rich Peat Edition (90.5)** n22.5 peat and coal dust; **t23** soft smoke on delivery followed through with ulmo honey and a twist of lemon. The sugars are profound; **f22.5** slight vanilla, but the peat is more assured now; **b22.5** excellently-made malt: sticks unerringly to the script. 46%

Ballantine's Pure Malt Aged 12 Years bott code. LKAC1538 **(88.5)** n22.5 t23 f21 b22. No sign of the peat being reintroduced to major effect, although the orange is a welcome addition. Remains a charmer. 40%. Chivas.

Bell's Signature Blend Limited Edition (83.5) n19 t22 f21 b21.5. The front label makes large that this vatted malt has Blair Athol and Inchgower at the heart of it as they are "two fine malts selected for their exceptionally rich character". Kind of like saying you have invited the Kray twins to your knees up as they might liven it up a bit. Well those two distilleries were both part of the original Bell's empire, so fair dos. But to call them both fine malts is perhaps stretching the imagination somewhat. A robust vatting to say the least. And, to be honest, once you get past the nose, good back-slapping fun. 40%. 90,000 bottles.

◇ **Ben Bracken Blended Malt Aged 12 Years (85.5)** n22.5 t21 f21 b21. Quite a tight malt with a predominantly toffee theme. 40%

Berrys' Best Islay Vatted Malt Aged 8 Years (82) n20 t21 f20 b21. Smoky, raw, sweet, clean and massive fun! 43%. Berry Bros & Rudd.

Berry's Own Selection Blue Hanger 5th Release bott 2010 **(81)** n20 t21 f20 b20. Not a lot – but enough – sulphur has crept in to take the edge of this one. 45.6%. nc ncf.

Berry's Own Selection Islay Reserve 2nd Edition (86.5) n22 t22 f21 b21.5. Maybe an Islay reserve but has enough smoky weight and hickory/chocolate charisma to be pushing for the first team squad. 46%. nc ncf. Berry Bros & Rudd.

Berry's Own Selection Speyside Reserve 2nd Edition (79.5) n21 t21.5 f18 b19. Some excellent early sharpness and honey depth but falters. 46%. nc ncf. Berry Bros & Rudd.

Big Peat Batch 31 (90.5) n23 love it: superb mix of allotment bonfire and peat reek. Some young spirit offering great energy; **t22** gristy sweet delivery pounded by spicy attitude; a blast of hickory and cocoa; **f22.5** the smoke rumbles along, but there is no letting up in intensity of peat or spice; **b23** good to see it has maintained its cheery high standard. Youthful, boisterous and challenging throughout. 46%. nc ncf. Douglas Laing & Co.

◇ **Big Peat Bärlin Edition (91.5)** n23 clean, big, youthful peat, where oak is having a day off; **t22.5** a sugared onslaught; the oily peat slips in almost apologetically; **f23** the citrus and smoke mingle to delightful effect...and for a long time; **b23** I imagine the Peat Heads of Berlin are, rightly, very happy fellows... 50%. ncf. Bottled for Big Market Berlin, 50th Anniversary bottling.

The Big Smoke 40 (83) n22 t21 f20 b20. Pure grist. 40%

The Big Smoke 60 (92) n23 t23.5 f22.5 b23. Much more delicate and in touch with its more feminine self than was once the case. A real beauty. 60%. Duncan Taylor & Co.

Black Face 8 Years Old (78.5) n18.5 t22 f19 b19. A huge malt explosion in the kisser on delivery, but otherwise not that pretty to behold. 46%. The Vintage Malt Whisky Co Ltd.

Burns Nectar (89.5) n22 t22 f23 b22.5. A delight of a dram and with all that honey around, "Nectar" is about right. 40%

Carme 10 Years Old (79) n21.5 t20 f18.5 b19. On paper Ardmore and Clynelish should work well together. But vatting is not done on paper and here you have two malts cancelling each other out and some less than great wood sticking its oar in. *43%*

Cask Islay Vatting No. 1 (89) n23 t22 f22 b22. Those looking for a soft, smoky, inoffensive little Islay to keep them company had better look elsewhere... *46%. ncf. A.D. Rattray Ltd.*

Castle Rock Aged 12 Years Blended Malt (87) n22.5 t23 f19.5 b22. Stupendously refreshing: the finish apart, I just love this style of malt. *40%*

Cearban (79.5) n18 t21.5 f20 b19. The label shows a shark. It should be a whale: this is massive. Sweet with the malts not quite on the same wavelength. *40%. Robert Graham Ltd.*

⬩ **Chapter 7 Peatside 2009** Barrique cask, Port finish, cask no. 5511 **(94.5) n23.5** a rare example of grape and peat reek being entirely on the same wavelength; **t23.5** silky delivery. A touch of the Fisherman's Friend, but this is harnessed and used to great effect by the softening, voluptuous fruit. Salivating and satisfying; **f24** just keep on chewing until your jaw aches. Exceptional harmony and even a superb spiced fruit flourish at the last; **b23.5** there is a touch of genius to this... *46%. sc.*

Clan Campbell 8 Years Old Pure Malt (82) n20 t22 f20 b20. Enjoyable, extremely safe whisky that tries to offend nobody. The star quality is all on the complex delivery, then it's toffee. *40%. Chivas Brothers.*

Clan Denny (Bowmore, Bunnahabhain, Caol Ila and Laphroaig) **(94) n24 t23 f23 b24**. A very different take on Islay with heavy peats somehow having a floating quality. Unique. *40%*

Clan Denny Islay (86.5) n21.5 t23 f21 b21. A curiously bipolar malt with the sweetness and bitterness at times going to extremes. Some niggardly oak has taken the edge of what might have been a sublime malt as the peat and spices at times positively glistens with honey. *46.5%. nc ncf sc. Douglas Laing & Co.*

Clan Denny Speyside (87) n22 t22 f21 b22. A Tamdhu-esque oiliness pervades here and slightly detracts from the complexity. That said, the early freshness is rather lovely. *46%*

Compass Box Canto Cask 10 bott Jul 07 **(86.5) n20.5 t21 f23.5 b21.5**. One the Canto collection which slipped through my net a few years back, but is still around, I understand. Typical of the race, this one has perhaps an extra dollop of honey which helps keep the over vigorous oaks under some degree of control. Sublime finish. *54.2%. nc ncf. 200-250 bottles.*

Compass Box Eleuthera Marriage married for nine months in an American oak Hogshead **(86) n22 t22 f20 b22**. I'm not sure if it's the name that gets me on edge here, but as big and robust as it is I still can't help feeling that the oak has bitten too deep. Any chance of a Compass Box Divorce...? *49.2%. Compass Box for La Maison du Whisky.*

⬩ **Compass Box Enlightenment** bott Apr 16 **(94.5) n24.5** so delicate: a Clynelish-like orange blossom honey element, the malt seemingly burnished and clean and dipped in a puree of Cape gooseberry and lime; **t24** well, after a nose like that it really did have to taste as good as this, really. Ulmo honey sets the bar for controlled, vanilla-clad sweetness, then a posse of pastel tones follow along, some no strangers to the sweet shop: butterscotch, buttery Werthers' Originals, barley sugar...; **f22.5** just more of the same, with a very late oaky bitterness creeping in towards the finale; **b23.5** after the run of disappointing vatted malts I have tasted today, trust Compass Box to come to the rescue. This is not a whisky to have when in a hurry: the nose alone is worth a good 15 minutes... *46%. nc ncf. 5,922 bottles.*

Compass Box Flaming Heart second batch, bottling no. FH16MMVII **(95.5) n23.5 t24.5 f23 b24.5**. The Canto range was, I admit, a huge over-oaked disappointment. This, though, fully underlines Compass Box's ability to come up with something approaching genius. This is a whisky that will be remembered by anyone who drinks it for the rest of their lives as just about the perfect study of full-bodied balance and sophistication. And that is not cheap hyperbole. *48.9%. nc ncf. 4,302 bottles.*

Compass Box Flaming Heart 4th Edition bott Aug 12 **(95) n23.5 t24.5 f23 b24**. Vatted malt at its very best. A genuine celebration of great Scotch malt whisky. *48.9%. 9,147 bottles.*

Compass Box Flaming Heart 10th Anniversary bott Sep 10 **(92) n24 t23 f22 b23**. This one, as Flaming Heart so often is, is about counterweight and mouth feel. Everything appears just where it should be... *48.9%. nc ncf. 4186 bottles.*

⬩ **Compass Box Flaming Heart Fifteenth Anniversary** bott Jul 15 **(96.5) n24** my very old friend at Compass Box appears to have mellowed with age. Once, this would have been a test to see how many splinters my nose could withstand. Now it is simply teased, then kissed. And there is nothing flaming at all; rather, a sigh of malty memories and the most gentle nod towards a smoky peace in life...; **t24.5** I should have known better. He lulled me into a false sense of security. The delivery is a peach (actually, there does appear to be something peach-like in there, or is it melon..?) The dexterity of the smoke, now in total harmony with the mocha is something that warms not just the palate but the heart. It is not aflame, just glowing pleasantly...; **f23.5** the vanillas make their excuses and stay, the smoke fades with aplomb while the muscovado inspired fruit hangs around to give balance; **b24.5** Really, John? Fifteen years? I mean: 15 years....??? Fucking hell! Oh, by the way, mate. It's a bloody masterpiece... *48.9%. nc ncf. 12,060 bottles.*

Compass Box The Lost Blend (95.5) **n23** there are gristy, vanilla notes....but these cower as the peat begins to grasp hold of the situation and ushers in the spice; **t23.5** sensuously soft, sweet and oily: a little gristiness returns but the spices are proinent; a thin layer of ulmo honey breaks free of the smoke; **f24.5** an elegant finish allowing all parties an even say. Vanilla and caramel naturally complete the tale, though not before high class marzipan makes its welcome mark. The smoke lingers contentedly and without threat; **b24.5** I may be wrong, but I have a feeling that when the nose and flavour profile was being constructed, a little extra smoke than first planned was added. Seems that way by the manner in which the phenols just pipe up a little louder than it first seems... *46%*

Compass Box Lady Luck bott Sep 09 (91) **n22 t24 f23 b22.** Just a shade too sweet for mega greatness like The Spice Tree, but quite an endearing box of tricks. *46%.*

Compass Box Oak Cross bott May 10 (92.5) **n23 t24 f22.5 b23.** The oak often threatens to be just too big a cross to bear. But such is the degree of complexity, and cleverness of weight, the overall brilliance is never dimmed. Overall, a bit of a tart of a whisky... *43%. nc ncf.*

Compass Box The Peat Monster bott May 10 (82) **n21.5 t21.5 f19 b20.** It is as though Victor Frankenstein's creation has met Bambi. Monsters don't come much stranger or more sanitised than this... *46%. nc ncf.*

Compass Box The Peat Monster first fill and refill American Oak Casks, bott 18 Aug 12 (94) **n23.5 t23.5 f23 b24.** Wonderful to see peat working on so many levels. The sugars are perhaps more judicially used this time around. *46%. nc ncf.*

Compass Box The Peat Monster Cask Strength (89) **n23.5** fascinating arm wrestle between the drier, ashy notes and a more expansive peatiness, rich in dark sugars; some delicate citrus furthers the complexity; **t23** superb weight: just the right amount of oils help maximise the heather honey; the smoke is happy to hint rather than holler; **f20.5** just a little bit of oak bitterness but countered by the persistent sweetness; the smoke now blends with the spices; **b22** plenty of peat between your teeth but deserving of some better oak. *57.3%*

Compass Box The Peat Monster Reserve (92) **n23 t23.5 f22.5 b23.** At times a bit of a Sweet Monster...beautiful stuff! *48.9%*

Compass Box The Peat Monster Tenth Anniversary Release bott Sept 13 (95) **n24 t24 f23 b24** here we appear to see a mix, or compromise, between the sweeter bottling of two years ago and last year's searing dryness. And, unlike most compromises, this one works... *48.9%. 5,700 bottles.*

Compass Box The Spice Tree first-fill and refill American oak. Secondary maturation: heavily toasted new French oak (95.5) **n24.5 t24.5 f23 b23.5.** Having initially been chopped down by the SWA, who were indignant that extra staves had been inserted into the casks, The Spice Tree is not only back but in full bloom. Indeed, the blossom on this, created by the use of fresh oak barrel heads, is more intoxicating than its predecessor – mainly because there is a more even and less dramatic personality to this. Not just a great malt, but a serious contender for Jim Murray Whisky Bible 2011 World Whisky of the Year. *46%*

Compass Box The Spice Tree Inaugural Batch (93) **n23 t23 f23 b24.** The map for flavour distribution had to be drawn for the first time here: an entirely different whisky in shape and flavour emphasis. And it is a map that takes a long time to draw... *46%. 4150 bottles.*

Co-operative Group (CWS) Blended Malt Aged 8 Years (86.5) **n22 t22 f21 b21.5.** Much, much better! Still a little on the sticky and sweet side, but there is some real body and pace to the changes on the palate. Quite rich, complex and charming. *40%*

Crom Westport 16 Years Old Warlords & Warriors Edition Thulsa's Choice bourbon hogshead, dist Oct 97, bott Feb 14 (92) **n23** bananas in custard – a kind of trifle but without the sherry...; **t24** wow! Ulmo and acacia honeys blended with a smidge of spice. A few vanilla notes reprise the custard effect; **f22.5** a little drier and tighter as the oak gets a little more agressive; **b23.5** a genuine treat! Someone has done a great job finding complimentary casks... *53.7%. sc.*

Cutty Sark Blended Malt (92.5) **n22 t24 f23 b23.5.** Sheer quality: as if two styles have been placed in the bottle and told to fight it out between them. What a treat! *40%.*

Deerstalker Blended Malt Highland Edition (94) **n23.5** top quality nose: the malt shows no great age but there is fresh, grassy barley by the bushel and a vague suggestion of some phenols to ensure weight; **t23.5** cut-glass clarity to the barley on delivery and as squeaky clean as the nose states. And just like the nose, some phenols come lurking up from the depths to guarantee length...; **f23** ...which is accomplished; **b24** a quite beautiful whisky by any standards. *43%*

Douglas Laing's Double Barrel Ardbeg & Aultmore (85) n21.5 t22.5 f20 b21. Fruity, juicy and fulsome, the smoke has an adroit presence. But, ultimately, a little too tangy for its own good. 46%.

Douglas Laing's Double Barrel Ardbeg & Craigellachie (95) n24 moody and brooding, the smoke, despite the gentle veins of molasses, positively scowls from the glass; **t24** my word! What a delivery! Intense and massive, it somehow lands on the palate with all the force of a feather. Soon, though, the peat again gathers momentum, deepened in its intensity by a chocolate-liquorice injection; **f23** delicate spice buzz on the smoke; bitters out a little; **b24** I doubt if any whisky I taste today will display the same simmering beauty as this. 46%. ncf.

Douglas Laing's Double Barrel Ben Nevis & Caol Ila (87.5) n22.5 t22 f21 b22. One of the lightest coloured malt whiskies I have ever seen bottled so, unsurprisingly, oak appears to play no part in either nose or flavour profile other than a very late tang at the finish. The Ben Nevis has thinned both the oils and smoky intensity if the Islay, which shows a delicate charm on both nose and delivery in particular. 46%.

Douglas Laing's Double Barrel Bowmore & Inchgower (69) n16.5 t18 f17 b17.5. Too dry and austere with very little smoke to bind the two styles. Not happy bedfellows at all. 46%. ncf.

Douglas Laing's Double Barrel Caol Ila & Braeval 4th Release (92.5) n23 t23.5 f22.5 b23.5. After a few failures with this combination, a hit. A real egg and bacon of a vatted malt with the two personalities this time complimenting each other beautifully. 46%

Douglas Laing's Double Barrel Caol Ila & Tamdhu (86.5) n22 t22.5 f21 b21. Positivly shimmers on the palate while the smoke blasts its way through any encumberences. But there is something a little too youthful about the malt and too inhibited about the oak to make the most of the occasion. 46%.

Douglas Laing's Double Barrel Glenallachie & Bowmore 1st Release (89) n22 t22.5 f22 b22.5. The delicate smoke of the Bowmore has tamed the wilder elements of the Glenallachie. A good mix. 46%

Douglas Laing's Double Barrel Highland Park & Bowmore (95) n23 t24.5 f24 b23.5. The vital spark of fury to this one keeps the palate ignited. A standing ovation for such a magnificent performance on the palate. 46%. Douglas Laing & Co Ltd.

Douglas Laing's Double Barrel Islay & Highland (91.5) n23 delicate smoke hangs above the weightier malt; **t23** a volley of gristy sugars is sprinkled with a dusting of peat; **f22.5** dries and spices up slightly; **b23** a charmingly understated and mellifluous dram. 46%.

Douglas Laing's Double Barrel Mortlach & Laphroaig 4th Release (85.5) n21.5 t21.5 f21 b21.5. All kinds of sugars heading off every which way. Juicy and punchy, interests and entertains without harmonising. 46%

Douglas Laing's Double Barrel Speyside & Lowland (84) n21 t21.5 f20.5 b21. Pleasant, sweet, exceptionally new makey throughout but, while simple and unchallenging, always refreshing. 46%. ncf.

Douglas Laing's Double Barrel Talisker & Craigellachie 2nd Release (94.5) n23 t24 f23.5 b24. These two malts go together like bacon & eggs. And very smoky bacon at that... 46%

Douglas Laing's Rock Oyster (84.5) n21 t21.5 f21 b21. So hugely salty – and weirdly phenolic into the bargain – not quite sure what it's done for my blood pressure... 46.8%

Duncan Taylor Regional Malt Collection Islay 10 Years Old (81) n21 t22 f19 b19. Soft citrus cleanses the palate, while gentle peats muddies it up again. 40%

Duthies Campbeltown Region Blended Malt Scotch Whisky (76) n18 t21 f18 b19. Off key and furry: one suspects the hand of a naughty sherry butt...Those not troubled by such things will lap up the rich delivery in particular. 46%. WB15/360

Duthies Highland Region Blended Malt Scotch Whisky (85) n22.5 t22 f20 b21. Nose stars with its sweet; untoasted marshmallow. Delivery has attractive nip to the barley; accent on the malt; exceptionally creamy but then bitters out. Competent and pleasant other than an unforgiving bourbon cask. 46% WB15/361

Duthies Islay Region Blended Malt Scotch Whisky (94) n23.5 t23.5 f23 b24 has no great pretentions to enormity of complexity. But just displays a decent degree of peat in a thoroughly enjoyable and classical Islay manner. 46% WB15/359

Duthies Lowland Region Blended Malt Scotch Whisky (89.5) n22 lovely citrus freshens up the barley; **t22** the barley jags into the palate from various, unsatisfied angles until settling on a light massaging style full of lightly sugared, soothing oils; **f23** happier now, reverts to citrus and simple, caressing vanilla; **b22.5** a classic gentle pre-prandial top up. 46% WB15/356

◈ **Eiling Lim Older Than Old Blended Malt Whisky (87.5) n21.5 t22 f22 b22.** Charming malt. Entirely non-taxing with a light Arbroath Smoky element as the main thread and genteel vanilla notes filling most of the gaps. 46.5%

◈ **Elements of Islay Peat (91.5) n23** is it possible to have too much peat? Not for some I know and for serious peat heads the uncompromising enormity and acidic bite of this will get them very excited, indeed...; **t24** even I had to take a few moments to get my baring and senses back together after this delivery. As though copious barrels of concentrated peat juice has been added to maple syrup. Eye-watering....; **f22** fades surprisingly quickly as vanilla begins to build and a slight bitterness creeps in; **b22.5** this is rather more than elementary Islay, trust me.... *46%*

⬦ **ePower Westport 14 Years Old** bourbon hogshead, dist 1999, bott 2014 (93) n23 a complex malt bordering on a bourbon personality: the light liquorice, borderline hickory and molasses harmonise beautifully with the crisp barley; **t23.5** brilliantly agile delivery: even a light smattering of Love Heart candy on this with an effervescent fizz to the barley; **f23** long, clean and determined barley; faultless vanilla; **b23.5** a cask which just knew how to make the most of the malt it contained. *52.1%*

The Famous Grouse 10 Years Old Malt (77) n19 t20 f19 b19. The nose and finish headed south in the last Winter and landed in the sulphur marshes of Jerez. *40%. Edrington Group.*

The Famous Grouse 15 Years Old Malt (86) n21 t22 f21.5 b21.5. Salty and smoky with a real sharp twang. *43%. Edrington Group.*

The Famous Grouse 15 Years Old Malt (86) n19 t24 f22 b21. There had been a hint of the "s" word on the nose, but it got away with it. Now it has crossed that fine – and fatal – line where the petulance of the sulphur has thrown all else slightly out of kilter. All, that is, apart from the delivery which is a pure symphony of fruit and spice deserving a far better introduction and final movement. Some moving, beautiful moments. Flawed genius or what...? *40%*

The Famous Grouse 18 Years Old Malt (82) n19 t21.5 f21 b20.5. Some highly attractive honey outweighs the odd uncomfortable moment. *43%. Edrington Group.*

The Famous Grouse Malt 21 Years Old (91) n22 t24 f22 b23. A very dangerous dram: the sort where the third or fourth would slip down without noticing. Wonderful scotch! *43%.*

The Famous Grouse 30 Years Old Malt (94) n23.5 t24 f23 b23.5. Whisky of this sky-high quality is exactly what vatted malt should be all about. Outrageously good. *43%*

⬦ **Five Lions Burnside 22 Years Old** 2nd fill Oloroso sherry hogshead, dist May 93, bott Nov 15 (93) n23 classical cream sherry nose; **t23.5** gorgeous bite to the crisp Demerara sugars before a gentle sultana and sponge cake softness arrives; **f23** dries with the grape; **b23.5** an unimpeachable sherry butt - amazing! *55.5%. nc ncf.*

⬦ **Five Lions Westport 18 Years Old** 1st fill sherry butt, dist Oct 97, bott Nov 15 (95) n23.5 quite dazzling display of spiced dates and nuts; **t24** a top-ranking sherry butt working in great harmony with top ranking Glenmorangie. Oh, sorry it isn't is it... Anyway, Melton Hunt Cake to the fore; **f23.5** long, rich deep fruit continues, the spices rumbling still and tannins just getting a little weighty; **b24** brilliant! *59.7%. nc ncf.*

Glenn (89.5) n22 no shortage of nip and nibble on the grassy nose: **t23** clean, salivating and fresh. Gets even more malty as it progresses on the palate, the oak making a low-key, vaguely honeyed entrance about half way in; **f22** the oak takes a tangy twist; **b22.5** a forceful malt. Seems as though at least two strands of the thread are trying to outdo each other. Enjoyable, but erratic towards the end. *50%. Svenska Eldvatten.*

Glenalmond 2001 Vintage (82.5) n22 t21.5 f19 b20. Glenkumquat, more like: the most citrusy malt I have tasted in a very long time. *40%. The Vintage Malt Whisky Co Ltd.*

Glenalmond "Everyday" (89.5) n21.5 t23.5 f22 b22.5. They are not joking; this really is an everyday whisky. Glorious malt which is so dangerously easy to drink. *40%*

Glen Brynth Aged 12 Years Blended Malt (87) n22.5 t23 f19.5 b22. Deja vu...! Thought I was going mad: identical to the Castle Rock I tasted this morning, right down to the (very) bitter end ..!!! *40%. Quality Spirits International.*

Glenbrynth Blended Malt 12 Years (87.5) n22.5 t22.5 f21 b21.5. Heavyweight malt which gets off to a rip-roaring start on the delivery but falls away somewhat from the mid ground onwards. *43%. OTI Africa.*

Glenbrynth Ruby 40 Year Old Limited Edition (94) n23.5 t24 f23 b23.5. Has all the hallmarks of a completely OTT, far too old sherry butt being brought back to life with the aid of a livelier barrel. A magnificent experience, full of fun and evidence of some top quality vatting at work, too. *43%. OTI Africa.*

Glendower 8 Years Old (84) n21.5 t21 f20.5 b21 Nutty and spicy. *43%*

The Glenfohry Aged 8 Years Special Reserve (73) n19 t19 f17 b18. Some of the malt used here appears to have come from a still where the safe has not so much been broken into, but just broken! Oily and feinty, to say the least. Normally I would glower at anyone who even thought of putting a coke into their malt. Here, I think it might be for the best.. *40%*

Glen Talloch Blended Malt Aged 8 Years (85.5) n21 t23 f20.5 b21. An invigorating and engulfing vatting, full of intrinsic barley tones on delivery. But the caramel is too strident for further complexity. *40%*

Glen Turner Heritage Double Wood Bourbon & Madeira casks, bott code. L311657A **(85.5)** n21.5 t22 f21 b21. A very curious amalgamation of flavours. The oak appears to be in shock with the way the fruit is coming on to it and offers a bitter backlash. No faulting the crisp delivery with busy sugar and spice for a few moments brightening the palate. *40%.*

Glen Turner Pure Malt Aged 8 Years L525956A **(84)** n20 t22 f22 b20. A lush and lively vatting annoyingly over dependent on thick toffee but simply brimming with fabulously mouth-watering barley and over-ripe blood oranges. To those who bottle this, I say: let me into your lab. I can help you bring out something sublime!! *40%*

⬥ **Gleann Mór Vatted Whisky Over 40 Years Old (92.5)** n23.5 deep tannins escape from every pore: marmalade on slightly overdone toast; **t23.5** magnificent landing! Cruises in with a velvety concoction of intense malt and vanilla, sweetened gently by a little ulmo honey and mildly overbaked caramelised biscuit; **f22.5** a few serious tannins make themselves heard, as do the politer spices; **b23** an oldie and a goodie...Mor, please...!!! *47%*

Glen Orchy (80.5) n19.5 t21.5 f19.5 b20. Not exactly the most subtle of vatted malts though when the juicy barley briefly pours through on delivery, enjoyable. *40%. Lidl.*

Glen Orchy 5 Year Old Blended Malt Scotch Whisky (88.5) n22 t22.5 f22 b22. Excellent malt plus very decent casks equals light-bodied fun. *40%. Lidl.*

Glen Orrin (68) n16.5 t17.5 f17 b17. In its favour, it doesn't appear to be troubled by caramel. Which means the nose and palate are exposed to the full force of this quite dreadful whisky. *40%.*

Glen Orrin Six Year Old (88) n22 t23 f21 b22. A vatting that has improved in the short time it has been around, now displaying some lovely orangey notes on the nose and a genuinely lushness to the body and spice on the finish. You can almost forgive the caramel, this being such a well balanced, full-bodied ride. A quality show for the price. *40%*

Hedges and Butler Special Pure Malt (83) n20 t21 f22 b21. Just so laid back: nosed and tasted blind I'd swear this was a blend (you know, a real blend with grains and stuff) because of the biting lightness and youth. Just love the citrus theme and, err...graininess...!! *40%*

Highland Harvest Organic Blended Malt 7 Casks batch 002 **(86.5)** n21.5 t22.5 f21 b21.5 Not even remotely complex. But pleasant enough. *40% WB15/371*

Highland Journey Blended Malt (94.5) n23.5 a lovely mix of very lightly minted butterscotch with small dabs of acacia and ulmo honey. Delightfully indolent; **t23.5** when I taste this much honey I am always reminded of Perthshire. That mix of acacia and ulmo on the nose was not a ruse; some curious young notes appear to lighten the intensity a little; **f23.5** the journey ends, as it began and continued, without a single jolt. Very late, understated spices offer an unexpected viewpoint at the end of the line; **b24** I have been on some memorable Highland journeys in my life, but few have been quite as comfortable as this one. *46.2%. Hunter Laing & Co.*

Imperial Tribute (83) n19.5 t21.5 f21 b21. I am sure – and sincerely hope – the next bottling will be cleaned up and the true Imperial Tribute can be nosed and tasted. Because this is what should be a very fine malt... but just isn't. *46%. Spencer Collings.*

Islay Trilogy 1969 (Bruichladdich 1966, Bunnahabhain 1968, Bowmore 1969) Bourbon/ Sherry **(91)** n23 t23 f22 b23. Decided to mark the 700th tasting for the 2007 edition with this highly unusual vatting. And no bad choice. The smoke is as elusive as the Paps of Jura on a dark November morning, but the silky fruits and salty tang tells a story as good as anything you'll hear by a peat fire. Take your time...the whiskies have. *40.3%. Murray McDavid.*

J & B Exception Aged 12 Years (80) n20 t23 f18 b19. Very pleasant in so many ways. A charming sweetness develops quickly, with excellent soft honeycomb. But the nose and finish are just so...so...dull...!! For the last 30 years J&B has meant, to me, (and probably within that old company) exceptionally clean, fresh Speysiders offering a crisp, mouth-watering treat. I feel this is off target. *40%. Diageo/Justerini & Brooks.*

J & B Nox (89) n23 t23 f21 b22. A teasing, pleasing little number that is unmistakably from the J&B stable. *40%. Diageo.*

John Black 8 Years Old Honey (88) n21 t22.5 f22.5 b22. A charming vatting. *40%*

John Black 10 Years Old Peaty (91) n23 salty and peaty; **t23** soft and peaty; **f22** delicate and peaty; **b23** classy and er...peaty. *40%. Tullibardine Distillery.*

Johnnie Walker Green Label 15 Years Old (95) n24 t23.5 f23.5 b24. God, I love this stuff...this is exactly how a vatted malt should be and one of the best samples I've come across since its launch. *43%. Diageo.*

Jon, Mark and Robbo's The Rich Spicy One (89) n22 t23 f22 b22. So much better without the dodgy casks: a real late night dram of distinction though the spices perhaps a little on the subtle side... *40%. Edrington.*

Jon, Mark and Robbo's The Smoky Peaty One (92) n23 t22 f23 b24. Genuinely high-class whisky where the peat is full-on yet allows impressive complexity and malt development. A malt for those who appreciate the better, more elegant things in life. *40%. Edrington.*

The Last Vatted Malt bott Nov 11 (96.5) n24 t25 f23.5 b24. Being an American, Compass Box founder and blender, John Glaser, knows a thing or two about pouring two fingers of whisky. So I join John in raising two fingers to the SWA and toast them in the spirit they deserve to thank them for their single-minded and successful quest to outlaw this ancient whisky term. *53.7%. nc ncf. 1,323 bottles.*

The Loch Fyne The Living Cask 1745 (94.5) n23.5 an intriguing two-toned nose which, if you concentrate on one side, offers firm smokiness giving further edge to the unyielding malts; and from the other angle is a complete softie...! t23.5 the delivery takes the path of the second option with an immediate eiderdown softness on delivery but doesn't duck out of juicy and, at times, forceful barleysugar then Fisherman Friend notes...all very sweet shop; f23.5 remains silky; now with a few spices joining the rolling smoke; b24 one of the best whiskies ever created at quarter to six in the evening....and one quite impossibe not to love. *46.3%*

The Loch Fyne The Living Cask Batch One (92) n22 the harsh smoke generates little more than a wispy buzz; the banana, ulmo honey, gristy malt and growing spice is the perfect foil; t23.5 a volley of intense sugars, further enlivened by prickly spice makes for a memorable kick off. The smoke continues to drift and offer anchor; unusually, the texture actually becomes silkier as the flavours develop; f23 a series of liquorice, fudge and crisp sugar notes, all on top of a blend of genteel and tangy phenols, makes for an easy exit; b23.5 absolutely charming. *46.3%*

⬦ **The Loch Fyne The Living Cask Batch Two** (78) n18 t21 f19 b20. A charming coincidence today: the first time I visited the Loch Fyne whisky shop, about 30 years ago, I spotted my first ever Spotted Flycatcher at Inveraray Castle. Just a few minutes before tasting this, a spotted flycatcher visited my garden for the first time this summer – and it is now late July. It must have known... Thirty years ago, though, the sherry-influenced bottlings available were so much better than today... *43.6%*

⬦ **The Loch Fyne The Living Cask Batch Four** (88) n21 an intriguing mix of Lincoln biscuits and oily vanilla...; t22.5 a real malt fest for the delivery: light castor sugar sprinkled on the tame vanilla; f22 the oily texture on delivery lasts the course, but reduces enough for the spice to make a meaningful entrance; b22.5 oh well, batch 3 gave us the slip but we caught up with Batch 4 which is a vast improvement on 2. A genuinely oily cove; and astonishingly malty, too... *43.6%*

⬦ **The Lost Distillery Company Stratheden** batch no. 2/II (86) n22 t21.5 f21 b21.5. A dry malt boasting sporadic muscovado fruity sweetness and the vaguest of underlying phenols. Pleasant, though by no means perfect. I wish the company well, but have to say that putting today's casks together to recreate a malt last distilled in 1926 (and which no-one living has probably ever tasted) is fanciful, to put it mildly. In those days bourbon casks weren't available so not in use, sherry ones were then of a significantly higher standard and the peat, almost certainly, would have been a little more punchy than here. *46%. nc ncf.*

Mackinlay's Rare Old Highland Malt (89) n22 t22 f22 b23. Possibly the most delicate malt whisky I can remember coming from the labs of Whyte and Mackay. Thought it still, on the palate, must rank as heavy medium. This is designed as an approximation of the whisky found at Shackleton's camp in the Antarctic. And as a life-long Mackinlay drinker myself, it is great to find a whisky baring its name that, on the nose only, briefly reminds me of the defter touches which won my heart over 30 years ago. That was with a blend: this is a vatted malt. And a delicious one. In case you wondered: I did resist the temptation to use ice. *47.3%*

Master of Malt Reference Series I (82) n19.5 t23 f19 b20.5. Not quite the happiest of bunnies at times, as it occasionally struggles to find a balance in the face of big, not entirely desired, oils. That said, nothing to stop you embracing the enormity of the date & sugar-drizzled barley soon after delivery & during the period it has escaped a certain feintiness. *47.5% WB15/349*

Master of Malt Reference Series I.1 (87.5) n21 t23 f21.5 b22. No enormous age – or at least oak involvement - as confirmed by the nose. But some wonderful moments as the juicy, clean barley hits the palate running. *47.5%*

Master of Malt Reference Series I.2 (93) n23 the delicate smokiness is accentuated by the crispness of the barley sub strata; t23 the barley is first to hit, juicy and clean; delicate sugars dissolve merrily; f23.5 the phenols slowly reassert themselves, but never at the cost of the delicate barley tones; b23.5 a charming marriage between Fisherman's Friend phenols and balletic barley. *47.4%*

Master of Malt Reference Series I.3 (91) n22 dry, oak-steered with a nod towards mocha; t22.5 a deft, peaceful delivery with no drama but loads of development; f23.5

lightly sweetened cocoa powder makes for a fabulous ending: reminiscent of Merlin lollies of yesteryear; **b23** it's all about the chocolate... 47.1%

Master of Malt Reference Series II (84.5) **n20 t22 f21.5 b21.** The oils have been toned down for this one, though the sugars have reached shrieking point. Malty, but perhaps a tad too cloying for its own good. 47.5% WB15/350

Master of Malt Reference Series II.1 (88) **n21** nothing wrong with it: just dull and uninspiring; **t23** a rich seam of malt appears to be of an oily disposition; **f22** again, technically sound. Plenty of rich malt and all that plus a hint of spice; **b22** an oily cove... 47.5%

Master of Malt Reference Series II.2 (87) **n22 t22.5 f21 b21.5.** Soft lemon drizzle on chunky malt plus an enjoyable volley of sugary grist early on. 47.4%

Master of Malt Reference Series II.3 (89) **n21.5** floral – a dank bluebell wood; **t22.5** mouth-filling malt. Playful oils and a steady ramping up of the malt intensity; **f22.5** something of a malt cereal about the finale; a little butterscotch tart thickens the effect; **b22.5** reminiscent of a Kentucky maltshake. 47.2%

Master of Malt Reference Series III (88) **n22 t23 f21 b22** Still one for the sweet toothed, but you don't need a diagram at the back to tell you some decent age has been added to this vatting. The odd blemish, but great fun. 47.5% WB15/351

Master of Malt Reference Series III.1 (89.5) **n22.5** a squeeze of blood orange and grapefruit set the malt off beautifully; **t23** thrusts malt at the taste buds like a politician rams his party line down your earhole; **f21.5** a little vanilla and spice, though the malt lingers; a tad bitter late on; **b22.5** if you like your malt malty, vote for this. 47.7%

Master of Malt Reference Series III.2 (92.5) **n22.5** earthy, yet enticingly malty. And thick...; **t23** superb Malteser style delivery: massive malt with an attractive milk chocolate element; **f24** good grief!! That malt just doesn't know when to call it a day. A little ulmo honey has joined in to intensify the sweetness slightly; even some late spice adds to the ultra late complexity; **b23** similar to III.1, except without the bitter bits. 47.5%

Master of Malt Reference Series III.3 (78) **n19.5 t21.5 f18 b19.** Fruity, fat, sweet. A tad furry. And somewhat one-dimensional. 47.5%

Matisse 12 Year Old Blended Malt (93) **n23.5 t23 f22.5 b23.** Succulent, clean-as-a-whistle mixture of malts with zero bitterness and not even a whisper of an off note: easily the best form I have ever seen this brand in. Superb. 40%. *Matisse Spirits Co Ltd.*

Matisse Aged 12 Years (79) **n17 t21 f20 b21.** Not sure if some finishing or re-casking has been going on here to liven it up. Has some genuine buzz on the palate, but intriguing weirdness, too. Don't bother nosing this one. 40%. *The Matisse Spirits Co Ltd.*

Milroy's of Soho Finest Blended Malt (76) **n18 t19 f20 b19.** Full flavoured, nutty, malty but hardly textbook. 40%. *Milroy's of Soho.*

Moidart Aged 10 Years (89.5) **n23** wonderfully clean and blends malty promise with youth; **t23** superb! The delivery is rich in oils which makes the light, gristy-citrus notes just a little heavier; salivating and satisfying; **f21.5** some of the more well-used casks radiating a degree of tiredness which slightly detracts from the delicate malts; **b22** just love the fresh, crystal clarity of this whisky. 46% WB15/358

Mo'land (82) **n21 t22 f19 b20.** Extra malty but lumbering and on the bitter side. 40%.

Monkey Shoulder batch 27 (79.5) **n21 t21.5 f18 b19.** Been a while since I lasted tasted this one. Though its claims to be Batch 27, I assume all bottlings are Batch 27 seeing as they are from 27 casks. This one, whichever it is, has a distinctive fault found especially at the finale, which is disappointing. Even before hitting that point a big toffeed personality makes for a pleasant if limited experience. 40%. *William Grant & Sons.*

⟐ **New Town Blends The Advocate's Batch** (87.5) **n21.5 t22.5 f21.5 b22.** Attractive, pleasant and, though a vatting, simplistic. A youthful catch on the nose suggests development might be limited, but it makes amends by the sheer charm of the light, clean, earnest malt. A lovely dram before lunch, I suggest. 43%. *Edinburgh Whisky Ltd.*

"No Age Declared" The Unique Pure Malt Very Limited Edition 16-49 Years (85) **n22.5 t19.5 f22 b21.** Very drinkable. But this is odd stuff: as the ages are as they are, and as it tastes as it does, I can surmise only that the casks were added together as a matter of necessity rather than any great blending thought or planning. Certainly the malt never finds a rhythm but maybe it's the eclectic style on the finish that finally wins through. 45%. *Samaroli.*

Old St Andrews Fireside (88.5) **n22 t22.5 f21.5 b22.5.** Beautifully driven... 40%.

Old St Andrews Nightcap (89) **n21.5 t24 f21 b22.5.** Some delightful weight and mass but perhaps a bit too much toffee takes its toll. 40%. *Old St Andrews Ltd.*

Old St Andrews Twilight (94.5) **n23 t24 t23.5 f23 b24.** Less Twilight as Sunrise as this is full of invigorating freshness which fills the heart with hope and joy: Lip-smacking Scotch malt whisky as it should be. Anyone who thinks the vatted malt served up for golf lovers in these novelty bottles is a load of old balls are a fair way off target... 40%. *Old St Andrews Ltd.*

The Pearls of Scotland Burnside 1992 20 Year Old cask no. 7350, dist Dec 92, bott Nov 13 **(85) n22 t22 f20 b21.** You can tell this is 99% Balvenie: it just has real problems handling the oak at this age. Nothing too much wrong with the nose for those into over-ripe banana. And the delivery boasts excellent mouth feel and early sugars until the merciless tannin bites deep. *55.8%.*

Poit Dhubh 8 Bliadhna (90) n22.5 t23.5 f21.5 b22.5. Though the smoke which marked this vatting has vanished, it has more than compensated with a complex beefing up of the core barley tones. Cracking whisky. *43%. ncf. Pràban na Linne.*

Poit Dhubh 12 Bliadhna (77) n20 t20 f18 b19. Toffee-apples. Without the apples. *43%. ncf. Pràban na Linne.*

Poit Dhubh 21 Bliadhna (86) n22 t22.5 f21 b20.5. Over generous toffee has robbed us of what would have been a very classy malt. *43%. ncf. Pràban na Linne.*

The Pot Still Scotch Vatted Malt Over 8 Years Old (90) n22 t24 f22 b22. Such sophistication: the Charlotte Rampling of Scotch. *43.5%. ncf. Celtic Whisky Compagnie, France.*

Prime Blue Pure Malt (83) n21 t21 f21 b20. Steady, with a real chewy toffee middle. Friendly stuff. *40%*

Prime Blue 12 Years Old Pure Malt (78) n20 t20 f19 b19. A touch of fruit but tart. *40%*

Prime Blue 17 Years Old Pure Malt (88) n23 t21 f22 b22. Lovely, lively vatting: something to get your teeth into! *40%*

Prime Blue 21 Years Old Pure Malt (77) n21 t20 f18 b18. After the teasing, bourbony nose the remainder disappoints with a caramel-rich flatness. The reprise of a style of whisky I thought had vanished about four of five years ago *40%*

◈ **Queens & Kings Mary, Queen of Scots (91.5) n22.5** attractive mix of green apple and light smoke; **t23** inspired delivery: the sugars arrive in droves, mainly Demerara, though the later smoke and spice tangle is a delight; **f23** a beautiful vanilla and butterscotch fade; the delicate smoke ensures a gentle base note; the spices ensure a degree of late liveliness...; **b23** a very comfortable assembling of malt. Impressed. *55.6%. Mr. Whisky.*

Queens & Kings Robert The Bruce (88) n21 the light smoke seems to be neutered by toffee; **t23.5** the brilliant delivery lifts the malt out of the doldrums. Smoked manuka honey to the fore; much, much better! **f21.5** some dull cocoa and spice, but oak bitterness, too; **b22** a bit of a wobbly vatting, where the part of the peat and its effects have not been thoroughly thought through. *54%. Mr Whisky.*

Rattray's Selection Blended Malt 19 Years Old Batch 1 Benrinnes sherry hogsheads **(89.5) n22 t23.5 f21.5 b22.5.** Absolutely love it! Offers just the right degree of mouth-watering complexity. not a malt for those looking for the sit-on-the-fence wishy-washy type. *55.8%. Auchentoshan, Bowmore, Balblair & BenRiach. A.D. Rattray Ltd.*

Sainsbury's Malt Whisky Finished in Sherry Casks (70) n18 t19 f16 b17. Never the greatest of the Sainsbury range, it's somehow managed to get worse. Actually, not too difficult when it comes to finishing in sherry, and the odd sulphur butt or three has done its worst here. *40%. UK.*

◈ **Sansibar Whisky Very Old Vatted (74.5) n19 t19 f18 b18.5.** Pretty smoky for a Speyside. But bitter and off key. *45.6%*

Scottish Collie (86.5) n22 t23 f20.5 b21. A really young pup of a vatting. Full of life and fun but muzzled by toffee at the death. *40%. Quality Spirits International.*

Scottish Collie 5 Years Old (90.5) n22.5 t23 f22 b23. Fabulous mixing here showing just what malt whisky can do at this brilliant and under-rated age. Lively and complex with the malts wonderfully herded and penned. Without colouring and at 50% abv I bet this would have been given a right wolf-whistle. Perfect for one man and his grog. *40%.*

Scottish Collie 8 Years Old (85.5) n22 t21.5 f21 b21. A good boy. But just wants to sleep rather than play. *40%. Quality Spirits International.*

Scottish Collie 12 Years Old (82) n20 t22 f20 b20. For a malt that's aged 84 in Collie years, it understandably smells a bit funny and refuses to do many tricks. If you want some fun you'll need a younger version. *40%. Quality Spirits International.*

Scottish Leader Imperial Blended Malt (77) n20 t20 f18 b19. Now don't be confused here: this isn't Imperial malt from Speyside. And although it says Blended, it is 100% malt. What is clear, though, is that this is pretty average stuff. *40%. Burn Stewart.*

Scottish Leader Aged 14 Years (80) n21 t21 f19 b19. A cleaner, less peaty version than the no-age statement vatting, but still fails to entirely ignite the tastebuds *40%. Burn Stewart.*

Scott's Selection Burnside 1994 (93) n23.5 t24 f22.5 b23.5. I may well be wrong. But I think this is the first time I have seen a Burnside, which is a cask of Balvenie spoiled as a single malt by having a spoonful of same age Glenfiddich added to it, in a commercial bottling rather than as a sample in my blending lab! Believe me: it was well worth waiting for...! *56.7%.*

Sheep Dip (84) n19 t22 f22 b21. Young and sprightly like a new-born lamb, this enjoys a fresh, mouthwatering grassy style wth a touch of spice. Maligned by some, but to me a clever, accomplished vatting of alluring complexity. 40%

Sheep Dip 'Old Hebridean' 1990 dist in or before 1990 **(94) n23 t24 f23.5 b23.5.** You honey!! Now, that's what I call a whisky...!! 40%. The Spencerfield Spirit Co.

⟡ **Simon Brown The Captain's Pure Scotch Malt Islay** bourbon casks, dist 2010, bott 2015 **(91) n22.5** a dense aroma, like oily smoke; **t23** silky oils hold in the golden syrup and spices with ease; **f22.5** a touch of grist is a late reminder of the youth; a lovely powdery peat fade; **b23** a young malt delighted to display its sugary side. Exceptionally easy going. 43%. nc ncf.

⟡ **Simon Brown The Captain's Pure Scotch Malt Speyside Highlands** sherry casks, dist 2009, bott 2015 **(80) n18.5 t21.5 f20 b20.** As present day sherry butts go, not too bad. It bounces back from a poor nose with some impressive honey on delivery – and this manages to keep going long into when the less attractive notes of the sherry return. 43%. nc ncf.

The Six Isles Pomerol Finish Limited Edition French oak Pomerol wine cask no. 90631-90638, dist 03, bott 10 **(85.5) n19 t23 f21.5 b22.** What makes the standard Six Isles work as a vatted malt is its freshness and complexity. With these attributes, plus the distinctive distilleries used, we consistently have one the world's great and truly entertaining whiskies. With this version we have just a decent malt. The wine finish has levelled the mountains and valleys and restricted the finish dramatically, while the nose doesn't work at all. Perfectly drinkable and the delivery is extremely enjoyable. But as a Six Isles, delighted it's a Limited Edition. 46%.

S'Mokey (88) n22.5 t22 f21.5 b22. Delicate, sweet and more lightly smoked than the nose advertises. 40%.

Smokey Joe Islay Malt (87) n21.5 t22 f21.5 b22. A soft, soporific version of a smoky Islay. No thumping of waves here: the tide is out. 46%. ncf. Angus Dundee Distillers.

Speyside Mysteria 24 Years Old Blended Malt bourbon cask, dist 90, bott 14 **(90) n22.5** hangs on against the advancing years with gritty determination...and a dollop of gooseberry jam; **t23.5** fruity delivery: black cherry preserve and strawberry jam and cream Swiss roll, aided by delicate ulmo honey; **f21.5** just a little too much oak, perhaps; **b22.5** a malt which has lived a long and rich life...and has plenty of wrinkles to show for it. 54.2%. ncf.

Spirit of Caledonia Flaitheanas 18 Years Old (94) n23.5 oak shavings and tannin-based spices quietly and attractively dominate: so elegant..; **t24** superb arrival of both spice and ulmo honey, then a slow malty infusion; **f23** long, with butterscotch in the driving seat; **b23.5** now that is a proper vatted malt...!!! 57.8%. Mr Whisky.

⟡ **Svenska Eldvatten Blended Malt 1994** ex-sherry butt, dist Aug 94 **(71) n18 t18 f17 b18.** There is nothing I need to say... 54.5%. sc.

Sweet Wee Scallywag Sherry butts & bourbon hogsheads **(72) n17 t20 f17 b18.** And a sulphured Scallywag at that...! 46%. ncf. Douglas Laing & co.

Tambowie (84.5) n21.5 t21.5 f20.5 b21. A decent improvement on the nondescript bottling of yore. I have re-included this to both celebrate its newly acquired lightly fruited attractiveness...and to celebrate the 125th anniversary of the long departed Tambowie Distillery whose whisky, I am sure, tasted nothing like this. 40%. The Vintage Malt Whisky Co Ltd.

That Boutique-y Whisky Company Blended Malt #2 batch 1 **(72) n17.5 t19 f17.5 b18.** Unmolested , the grape would have been spectacular, especially with the big cocoa finish. But the cask has done its damage. 48.3%. 370 bottles.

⟡ **That Boutique-y Whisky Company Blended Malt No. 2** batch 2 **(84.5) n21.5 t21 f21.5 b20.5.** The sugars are a bit too flash and uncouth. Elsewhere, just a tad too tart and struggles to find a balance. 43.1%. 415 bottles.

⟡ **That Boutique-y Whisky Company Islay Blended Malt No. 2 27 Year Old** batch 1 **(84.5) n20 t21.5 f21.5 b21.5.** That unique and vivid Fisherman's Friend character, alongside Love Hearts candy, suggests Bowmore is at the heart of this one. 47.3%. 88 bottles.

Treasurer 1874 Reserve Cask (90.5) n23 t23 f22.5 b22. Some judicious adding has been carried out here in the Robert Graham shop. Amazing for a living cask that I detect no major sulphur faultlines. Excellent! 51%. Live casks available in all Robert Graham shops.

Triple Wood Blended Malt Scotch Whisky (77) n17.5 t22 f18.5 b19. At least one wood too many. Tangy...for all the wrong reasons. 42%. Lidl.

Vintner's Choice Speyside 10 Years Old (84) n21.5 t22 f20 b20.5. Pleasant. But with the quality of the Speysiders Grants have to play with, the dullness is a bit hard to fathom. 40%.

Waitrose Pure Highland Malt (86.5) n22 t22 f20.5 b22. Blood orange by the cartload: amazingly tangy and fresh; bitters out at the finish. This is one highly improved malt and great to see a supermarket bottling showing some serious attitude...as well as taste!! Fun, refreshing and enjoyable. 40%

⬦ **The Warehouse Dram Braon Peat** batch 4, bott 11 Dec 15 **(81.5)** n21.5 t22 f18 b20. An unusual nose: for some reason reminds me of washing on the line – soapy, perhaps? Strange! Actually, also the smell outside the kitchen of my old school mate Phil Rush's house when his mum had been doing the washing, back in the early '70s. A pattern is forming here... 57%

Wemyss Velvet Fig (64) n15 t19 f15 b15. Either vatted by someone who smokes 20 a day minimum or on purpose for the German and Chinese market which appears to enjoy this sort of thing. I eat a lot of figs which, on song, are sweet and spicy. This isn't. Although another "S" element plays a very big, debilitating, part... 46%. ncf.

Wemyss Vintage Malt The Peat Chimney Hand Crafted Blended Malt Whisky (80) n19 t22 f20 b19. The balance is askew here, especially on the bone-dry wallpapery finish. Does have some excellent spicy/coffee moments, though. 43%. Wemyss Vintage Malts Ltd.

Wemyss Vintage Malt The Smooth Gentleman Hand Crafted Blended Malt Whisky (83) n19 t22 f21 b21. Not sure about the nose: curiously fishy (very gently smoked). But the malts tuck into the tastebuds with aplomb showing some sticky barley sugar along the way. 43%

Wemyss Vintage Malt The Spice King Hand Crafted Blended Malt Whisky (84) n22 t22 f20 b20. Funnily enough, I've not a great fan of the word "smooth" when it comes to whisky. But the introduction of oily Caol Ila-style peat here makes it a more of a smooth gentleman than the "Smooth Gentleman." Excellent spices very late on. 43%. Wemyss Vintage Malts.

⬦ **The Whisky Agency Acla Selection Burnside Aged 23 Years** bourbon barrel, dist 1992, bott 2015 **(87.5)** n22.5 t22 f21 b22. Burnside peaks at around the ten year mark. Here you can see how the oak does impact in a lopsided way against the fine barley. The spices, though, are a treat! 51.9%. nc ncf. 253 bottles.

⬦ **The Whisky Cask Company Burnside 19 Years Old** bourbon hogshead, dist 1996 **(88)** n22.5 rich and biscuity; t23 creamy textured, with a massive malt surge of superbly salivating quality; excellent sugars, too; f20.5 irritatingly bitter oak; b22 wow! This is so much like a Balvenie! 55%

Whisky-Fässle Burnside 24 Year Old barrel, dist 1989, bott 2014 **(71)** n18 t21 f15 b17. Exceptionally sweet, but this is a cask on the turn: the good tannins have been extracted and we are now entering into less than briliant lactose-type notes. You will find it takes quite a while to clean your palate after this. 51.1%

⬦ **Whisky-Fässle Fine Blended Malt 1980** sherry butt, bott 2015 **(87.5)** n21 t22 f22.5 b22. No problems with the sherry – a decent butt. But a rather processional display of sugars alongside the odd deep tannin note. Delicious, for sure. But seriously uncomplicated and a little over-aged. 46.7%

Whyte & Mackay Blended Malt Scotch Whisky (78) n19 t22 f18 b19. You know when the engine to your car is sort of misfiring and feels a bit sluggish and rough...? 40%. Waitrose.

Wild Scotsman Scotch Malt Whisky (Black Label) batch no. CBV001 **(91)** n23.5 t23.5 f21 b23. The type of dram you drink from a dirty glass. Formidable and entertaining. 47%

Wild Scotsman Aged 15 Years Vatted Malt (95) n23 t24 f24 b24. If anyone wants an object lesson as to why you don't screw your whisky with caramel, here it is. Jeff Topping can feel a justifiable sense of pride in his new whisky: for its age, it is an unreconstituted masterpiece... 46% (92 proof). nc ncf. USA.

William Grant & Sons Rare Cask Reserves 25 Years Old Blended Malt Scotch Whisky (82) n21 t22 f19 b20. Mouth-filling, chewy and mildly fruity, doesn't quite grow into the decent start offered and finishes untidily. 47%. Exclusive to The Whisky Shop.

Wilson & Morgan Barrel Selection Speybridge sherry wood, dist 2001, bott 2015 **(94)** n23.5 the malt has a distinctly vanilla-rich slant, but it is the gentle, clean grape which dominates; t24 the golden syrup and spices need no invitation to head the cast and ensure a sweet and caressing delivery. The fruit tones turn up only when the sugars have receded; f23 a slow spice burn plus a gentle tang. Butterscotch tart represents the oak; b23.5 almost spot on sherry butts at work here. No sulphur involvement to speak of, so you can simply concentrate on the embracing beauty of the sugars. And so rare to encounter a sherried malt with no bitterness on the finish whatsoever. 45.9%

Wilson & Morgan Barrel Selection Westport sherry wood, dist 1997, bott 2014 **(93.5)** n23.5 dripping with sweet grape and green toffee-apple; t24 close on perfection for a present day sherry butt delivery. The taste buds are caressed by grape of initially rare clarity, clean enough to allow the molten Demerara sugars full range to mingle with the grist; f22.5 tightens up ever so slightly, but the spices buzz away beautifully; b23.5 oh...!!! The charm of virtually clean sherry butts!! Almost no sulphur here....just magnificent whisky! 48%

Mystery Malts

Chieftain's Limited Edition Aged 40 Years hogshead **(78)** n22 t22 f16 b18. Oak-ravaged and predictably bitter on the death (those of you who enjoy Continental bitters might go for this..!). But the lead up does offer a short, though sublime and intense honey kick. The finish, though... 48.5%. Ian Macleod.

Scottish Grain

It's a bit weird, really. Many whisky lovers stay clear of blended Scotch, preferring instead single malts. The reason, I am often told, is that the grain included in a blend makes it rough and ready. Yet I wish I had a twenty pound note for each time I have been told in recent years how much someone enjoys a single grain. The ones that the connoisseurs die for are the older versions, usually special independent bottlings displaying great age and more often than not brandishing a lavish Canadian or bourbon style.

Like single malts, grain distilleries produce whisky bearing their own style and signature. And, also, some display characteristics and a richness that can surprise and delight. Most of the grains available in (usually specialist) whisky outlets are pretty elderly. Being made from maize and wheat helps give them either that Canadian or, depending on the freshness of the cask, an unmistakable bourbony style. So older grains display far greater body than is commonly anticipated.

During the last year the grain whisky lover has been spoiled for choice. Especially those with deep pockets seeking the rarest of the grains, those which were seldom available to blenders even when those now lost distilleries were in full production. Top of the tree comes Garnheath, one of the lighter grains in its youth though now offering a unique charm whenever it surfaces. Two new casks yielded just 300 bottles between them - each of them nectar.

The Last Drop, as is their speciality, somehow unearthed a 44-year-old Lochside; there were some fine Carsebridges to be had from both Hunter and Douglas Laing, each company bringing out 50-year-olds; and four new bottlings of Caledonian passed through my tasting room, the Whiskybroker's 28-year-old racking up no less than 95 points to top them all, including one from the distillery's former owners, Diageo.

But it was that more prosaic, and still breathing, distillery of Invergordon which eclipsed them all, the independent bottlers Whiskyjace honouring us with a stunning 24-year-old.

Jim Murray's Whisky Bible Scotch Grain of the Year Winners	
2004-07	N/A
2008	Duncan Taylor Port Dundas 1973
2009	The Clan Denny Dumbarton Aged 43 Years
2010	Duncan Taylor North British 1978
2011	The Clan Denny Dumbarton Aged 40 Years
2012	The Clan Denny Cambus 47 Years Old
2013	SMWS G5.3 Aged 18 Years (Invergordon)
2014	The Clan Denny Dumbarton 48 Years Old
2015	The Sovereign Single Cask Port Dudas 1978
2016	The Clan Deny Cambus 25 Years Old
2017	Whiskyjace Invergordon 24 Year Old

Single Grain Scotch
CALEDONIAN

⬧ **The Cally 40 Year Old** refill American oak hogsheads, dist 1974 db **(88.5) n23.5** the vanilla merges with the ulmo honey, in total control; **t23** sharper than a butcher's knife: eye-watering explosion of what seems like unmalted barley and sugar-laden corn; **f20** bitters out as the oak begins to disintegrate; **b22** this poor old sod is tiring before your nose and taste buds. But it hangs on grimly to give the best show it can. Quite touching, really...we are witnessing first hand the slow death of a once great distillery. *53.3%. 5,060 bottles. Diageo Special Releases 2015.*

⬧ **The Sovereign Caledonian 41 Years Old** refill hogshead, cask no. 11836, dist Mar 74, bott Sept 15 **(88) n22.5** there's trouble ahead on this one, as the oak is already kicking up. But the Brazilian-style biscuit sugars do a great job of resuscitation; **t23** a cornucopia... of corn...; **f20.5** tired oak (as perfectly forecast on the nose) intervenes, though light sugars and vanilla come to the rescue; **b22** a long way from a perfect old grain. But enough character and flavour to see it through. *50.2%. nc ncf sc. 200 bottles.*

⬧ **Spirit of Caledonia Invergordon 34 Years Old** **(84.5) n21 t22 f20.5 b21.** Soft and yielding, as an Invergordon should be. And spicy in part, too. But a little tobacco on the nose and overbearing bitterness on the finish. *56%. Mr. Whisky.*

⬧ **Whiskybroker Caledonian 28 Year Old** refill hogshead, cask no. 23882, dist 20 Apr 87, bott 29 Jan 16 **(95) n23.5** high grade grain: both the red liquorice of the oak and the lighter sugars are very relaxed; **t24** busy and buzzing, the sugars and spices don't hold back; initially light but oils up slowly, becoming a tad buttery; **f23.5** a very classy vanilla fade; **b24** very unusually, I can't tell for sure if wheat or corn is at play here. The spice prickle suggests the former, as does the limitations to the oils. But the depth to the sugar and vanilla, especially towards the end is of a corn style. Probably wheat, but whichever – a stunner. *54.6%. sc.*

CAMBUS

The Clan Denny Cambus Aged 25 Years refill hogshead, cask no 10595, dist 1988 **(96) n24** the tapestry of delicate sugars are woven faultlessly into the corn-rich buttery neo bourbon silk. A kind of mix between high class Canadian and mid-aged top-drawer bourbon; **t24** one can only purr as the sugars and honeys flit around the palate. A welcome tautness to the proceedings, ensuring a crispness to the ulmo honey-butterscotch blend; **f24** long, unusual depth to the oils of the grain, confirming corn domination. The liquorice-cocoa fade presses all the right buttons; **b24** just about the perfect grain from the perfect distillery. *58.1%. sc.*

⬧ **Old Particular Cambus 27 Years Old** refill hogshead, cask no. 10940, dist Sept 88, bott Sept 15 **(91) n23** so delicate. Doughy with strands of butterscotch tart. Disciplined sugars and acacia honey are well balanced; **t23** trademark richness to the weight and texture. Soft oils blended with thinned golden syrup, all sticking to the roof of the mouth before light spices enter; **f22** a little dry as the tannins slowly take control; **b23** even as this whisky nears its third decade, it acts slightly differently than most grain but keeping its style and character rather than giving way to the march of the oak. Quite lovely. *51.5%. nc ncf sc. 270 bottles.*

⬧ **Old Particular Cambus 27 Years Old** cask no. 11047, dist Sept 88, bott Jan 16 **(95) n24** complex, subtle, delicate yet never for a moment a wilting flower. Quite beautiful degrees of biscuit and vanilla, curiously and confusingly surrounded by a slightly salty coastal sea air...and spice; **t24** brilliant...! So ridiculously soft...the delivery imparts at once the most yielding of oils enriched with vanilla and sugar, with a little ground honey-roast almond for depth; **f23** clean and stays along the vanilla pathway; **b24** spectacular! Will outperform on both nose and palate the majority of single malts you are likely to taste this year. *48.9%. nc ncf sc. 36 bottles.*

The Pearls of Scotland Cambus 1988 cask no. 59232, dist Sept 88, bott May 15 **(89) n22.5 t23.5 f21 b22.** A déjà vu moment here: "I've tasted this one before." Looked through my notes for the Sov Cambus 26-y-o...and found they were distilled in the same month. Peas in a pod. The notes for that are spot on for here, except this has a bit of extra oily toffee... *47.8%. sc.*

Scotch Malt Whisky Society Cask G8.5 Aged 25 Years refill hogshead, dist 12 Jun 89 **(93.5) n22** exceptionally quiet by Cambus standards: clean, vaguely peppery and with an even vaguer celery note; **t24** erupts into life to cofound the nose: spices starburst about the palate to offer the perfect counter to the ulmo honey and Lubeck marzipan theme; a touch of rummy esters at work in the midground; **f23.5** the near perfect cask influence allows for the sweetness to lessen in a beautifully timed fade. The last notes of Brazilian coconut and German caramelised biscuit could not be better; **b24** the politeness of the nose gives little indication of the outstanding experience on the palate which awaits. *59.6%. sc. 240 bottles.*

The Sovereign Cambus Aged 50 Years refill bourbon barrel, cask no 11031, dist Aug 64, bott Nov 14 **(89.5) n22.5** no shortage of oak, or polished oak floors. Someone in the last

50 years has trod some dried dates into them...; **t23.5** a surprising degree of oil holds out against the tannin, capturing the sugars and refusing to let them go; **f21.5** a few bitter notes, as might be expected, but the buttery ones carry the dark sugars furthest; some last minute spices and a furry buzz...; **b22** not quite a picture of whisky wisdom and at times fails to find the adequate balance. But, the very last moments apart, and for a whisky which was hardly expected to reach more than three years, a remarkable old survivor. 49.2% nc ncf sc.

The Sovereign Cambus Aged 26 Years refill hogshead, cask no 11116, dist Sept 88, bott Nov 14 (**89.5**) **n23** pretty floral for a Cambus; corn thick but a bit of bite, too; **t23.5** usual silky start, plus the standard opening of delicate sugars to be associated with Cambus; **f21** dries and bitters out just a little too quickly; **b22** a fabulous spirit looked for better support from the cask than it received. Some pretty mercurial and magical moments, though. 46.9% nc ncf sc.

◇ **The Sovereign Cambus 27 Years Old** refill hogshead, cask no. 12279, dist Sept 88, bott Feb 16 (**93**) **n23** seemingly light, yet a heaviness abounds! Beautifully buttery while the golden syrup holds back; **t24** a glorious delivery! Acacia honey, though thinly spread on the chewy dough; **f22.5** dries and spices just as one might hope; **b23.5** an outstanding piece of oak has ensured that we can all bow to the full majesty of the honey. 46.7%. nc ncf sc. 287 bottles.

The Sovereign Cambus Aged 40 Years refill hogshead, cask no. 11266, dist Feb 75, bott Feb 15 (**95**) **n23** a wonderful and possibly unique mix of corn whisky and Shredded Wheat cereal; the sugars are of the dark variety, the tannin more Canadian than Kentucky in style; **t24** corn oil coats the palate with a friendly, ulmo-honeyed swoosh; then the sugars and spices come out to play. Elements of fruit pastilles juice things up further while the oak is content in a buttery role; **f23.5** not a trace of bitterness or tiredness of any sort. Just a gentle wind down of the more intense flavours of before, with maybe only a further nod to the oak in its buttered toast finale; **b24.5** just about defies belief that a whisky can reach this number of years and still retain sugar-honey at its core. Remarkable and majestic whisky from a once remarkable and majestic distillery. 57.7%. nc ncf sc. 114 bottles.

The Sovereign Cambus Aged 30 Years refill hogshead, cask no. 11591, dist Feb 85, bott May 15 (**93**) **n23** remember that coconut "tobacco" candy moistened with treacle when we were very, very young...?; **t23.5** taste buds are met with a wall of lightly oiled, but beautifully seasoned tannin, but covered in golden syrup; the oaky spices punch through beautifully; **f23** a slow dissolving of the sugars and tannins; **b23.5** satisfying whisky on just about every level bar the certain knowledge there is little more of this nectar still to come. 53.4%. nc ncf sc.

◇ **That Boutique-y Whisky Company Cambus** batch 1 (**94**) **n23** sharp and robust, we are heading into Canadian territory here; **t23.5** superb oils: presumably corn oil dominating. The distillery's little nod to honey moves towards a fuller, molassed middle; **f23.5** oh, those darling little spices...! **b24** a brilliant bottling very much of the top quality Canadian school. Leaves you in no doubt of the magnitude of our loss with this ex-distillery. 45.1%. 41 bottles.

CAMERONBRIDGE

Cadenhead's Small Batch Cameronbridge Aged 24 Years bourbon hogsheads, dist 1989, bott 2013 (**92**) **n21.5 t23.5 f23 b23.5** A pleasing grain with idea above its supposedly lowly station. Kicks the crap out ofa great many single malts it is supposed to kow-tow to. 46%. 618 bottles. WB15/167

◇ **Old Particular Cameronbridge 25 Years Old** refill butt, cask no. 10806, dist Jun 90, bott Jun 15 (**91.5**) **n22.5** a tangy nose with an almost gin-like botanical feel, though heavy on the orange peel; **t23.5** prisoners don't stand a chance as a tidal wave of oil and liquorice-tinged dark sugar spill onto the taste buds with murderous intent. Salivating throughout and even overcomes a slight wobble from the oak; **f22.5** a mild tang but well covered by the mocha which skimps on the sugar; **b23** a blistering grain which, at this strength, shows you an old grain warts and all. As fabulous as it is fascinating. 60.6%. nc ncf sc. 282 bottles.

Signatory Single Grain Collection Cameronbridge 1995 dist 31 Jan 95, bott 18 Mar 14 (**87**) **n22 t22 f21.5 b21.5**. Although with nearly 20 years on the clock, living nearly two decades in presumably a third fill cask has done little for colour or complexity: it has the demeanour of a grain very much younger. The good news is that this is still high quality oak, so although a simple dram the mix of sugars and light vanilla is a pleasing one. 43%. WB15/170

CARSEBRIDGE

◇ **The Sovereign Carsebridge 42 Years Old** refill hogshead, cask no. 11848, dist Jan 73, bott Sept 15 (**88.5**) **n22.5** the natural caramels escape from the glass and fog up the room..; **t22** corn oil and caramel; **f21.5** bitters out slightly but spices compensate; **b22.5** had no idea it was possible to cram so much natural caramel from a cask into one bottle...! 48.9%. nc ncf sc. 221 bottles.

⟡ **The Sovereign Carsebridge 50 Years Old** refill hogshead, cask no. 11847, dist Oct 65, bott Oct 15 **(95) n24** quite fabulous: Manuka and ulmo honey blending harmoniously: the light degree of salt is a touch of genius...; the oak breezes in and out with the most deft of vanillas; **t24** the natural caramels are out in force but spices immediately give them an extra dimension. The sugars are conservative, but do enough to balance the drying vanilla; **f23** medium length, with the corn oil lasting longest; **b24** cannot ask for much more with a grain of this age. How can oak and sugars be in near perfect sync after half a century —amazing! 41.5%. nc ncf sc. 267 bottles.

⟡ **Xtra Old Particular Carsebridge 50 Years Old** refill hogshead, dist Oct 65, bott Nov 15 **(91.5) n23** a slightly more aggressive oak stance compared to the Sovereign bottling. Though by aggressive I mean a kiss involving a bit of a suck as opposed to the peck offered by its sister cask...; **t22.5** the custard cream vanillas make for a pretty gentle journey; **f23** brilliantly comes alive later on as the spices build and extend; **b23** as delicious as it is fascinating. 40.1%. nc ncf sc. 101 bottles.

DUMBARTON

The Last Drop Dumbarton 54 Year Old 2nd fill bourbon barrel, dist 19 Jan 61 **(96) n24.5** no splinters apparent on this golden oldie. Instead, we see a little coconut water adding lustre to the corn bread. Reminds me of Waterloo, one of the lost original distilleries of Canada, as there is a subtle layering which ensures the weight is neither too hefty nor restrictive. A once common nose world-wide, now just about unique...; **t24.5** an unmistakable Canadian-style corn and oak marriage in which the ulmo honey melts with the golden syrup but still can't outperform the clean corn oils. The spices are at exactly the right volume; **f23** a little bitterness from the old cask creeps in. But the spices counter immediately, and even up their game as we near the end; **b24** Dumbarton here displays, with an ease almost bordering arrogance, why it is the doyen of grain whiskies. It is no coincidence that the greatest ancient blended whiskies I have tasted include liberal amounts of Dumbarton. As you can see here, it has the ability to be firm enough for backbone to form, yet soft enough to ensure a yielding countenance, too. A grain, glorying in its 55th year... 43.5%. sc. 34 bottles.

The Sovereign Dumbarton Aged 50 Years refill hogshead, cask no 11227, dist Dec 64, bott Feb 15 **(91) n22.5** a light interplay between corn and polite oak. Clean, quiet and undemonstrative; **t23** soft, silky corn is massaged by ulmo honey...; **f22.5** the sugars meander through some bittering oak; **b23** despite the late tanginess, the overall elegance of this grain after half a century takes some believing. 43.8% nc ncf sc. 93 bottles.

The Sovereign Dumbarton Aged 50 Years refill hogshead, cask no 11592, dist Dec 64, bott May 15 **(96.5) n24** a comfortable marriage of fruit and oak, neither dominating the other. Dates, prunes and nose-tickling spices. The dark sugars are lurking in the recesses; **t24.5** now that is staggering: the weight of the mouth feel could hardly be better – after 50 years it is astonishing. No aggression, and though the tannins are apparent early, there is not a single splinter. Just silk made from corn and fruit tones woven throughout...; **f24** mocha – a bit heavier on the coffee – sweetened with a dollop of manuka honey. The spices pick up the pace during the very long fade; **b24** an astonishing bottling. No wonder why Ballantine's ancient blends are that little bit special. For this a fabulous example as to why this was the king of all Scotland's grain distilleries until its brainless dismantling, one of the most grievous injuries inflicted on blended Scotch in living memory. 49.1% nc ncf sc. 162 bottles.

GARNHEATH

⟡ **Xtra Old Particular Garnheath 41 Years Old** refill barrel, dist Feb 74, bott Dec 15 **(94) n24** a surprising hint of ginger amid the more modest vanilla notes; **t24** wow! More than a hint of ginger here! Really a very warmed-up dram with spices holding the tiller and contrasting sublimely against the muscovado sugar and big butterscotch; **f22.5** bitters slightly as the oak – having obviously pumped out so much – tires; **b23.5** the rarest of the rare grains and - as though aware of its unique place in the lexicon of vanishing scotch - doesn't disappoint for a moment. 48.9%. nc ncf sc. 141 bottles.

⟡ **Xtra Old Particular Garnheath 42 Years Old** refill barrel, dist Feb 74, bott Feb 16 **(93) n23** the Love Heart candy gives a fizzing lift to the Werther's Originals...; **t23** salivating sugars, yet the intense oak- enriched natural caramels are always nearby; **f23.5** a superb cask means no bitterness, though little happens to divert your attention away from that sublime caramel and vanilla: like a Custard Cream dunked in slightly spiced milk; **b23.5** sticks firmly to a caramel and vanilla script. 48.2%. nc ncf sc. 162 bottles.

GIRVAN

⟡ **The Girvan Patent Still Over 25 Years Old** db **(84.5) n21.5 t21.5 f20.5 b21.** A pretty accurate representation of the character these stills were sometimes quietly known for at this time, complete with some trademark sulphury notes – presumably from the still, not cask, as I do pick up some balancing American white oak character. 42%. nc.

The Girvan Patent Still No. 4 Apps db **(87) n21.5 t22 f21.5 b22.** A first look at probably the lightest of all Scotland grain whiskies. A little cream soda sweetens a soft, rather sweet, but spineless affair. The vanillas get a good, unmolested outing too. 42% WB15/369

A.D. Rattray Girvan cask no. 2 dist 1964 **(95.5) n23.5** toasty with natural fudge notes now gathered from the cask. Non specific fruit give a cake-like quality. But there is no sign of degeneration...; **t24** sumptuous and luxurious, the spices and vanillas dominate hand-in-hand. A light brushing of ulmo honey guarantees the complex sweetness, though again there is a light jammy fruitiness leaking in from somewhere; **f23.5** dries into toasted fudge. The corn oils offer the most ridiculously gentle fade after half a century you could imagine; **b24.5** even after half a century, not a hint of an off note. 47.1%

Cadenhead's Small Batch Girvan Aged 33 Years bourbon barrels, dist 1979 bott 2013 **(85) n22 t23 f19 b21.** Some parts of this are light and citrusy enough to be a gin or flavoured rum. The fact this is 33 years old at times defies belief. But where it does work is on delivery when the citrus notes are under control thanks to the butterscotch tart. Then the sugars go on a rampage. 46% 222 bottles. WB15/165

Old Masters Girvan 26 Year Old cask no. 57869, dist 1988, bott 2015 **(88.5) n22** oily, spicy and busy; **t23** beautifully rich delivery where the honey is given full scope to dominate; sweetened vanilla abounds, too; the silky texture impresses no less; **f21.5** a little sharp, as though copper deprived; **b22** a curious Girvan, showing a distinctive Strathclyde style tartness at times at the end, but excellent compensating honey for the remainder. 59.8%. sc.

⬦ **Old Particular Girvan 21 Years Old** refill barrel, dist May 94, bott Nov 15 **(85) n21 t22.5 f20 b21.5.** Fat, monosyllabic and, after the initial juicy delivery, makes little attempt to move into complex lands. The finish has a number of oaky constraints. 51.5%. nc ncf sc. 215 bottles.

⬦ **Old Particular Girvan 25 Years Old** refill barrel, cask no. 10805, dist Dec 89, bott Jun 15 **(91) n22** not unlike a light Canadian with the tannins tucked into healthy vanilla; **t23.5** superbly salivating. A lively opening, much lighter in body than some Girvans, with oils at a premium. Not sure if some barley was included in the mash bill as there is a distinctive grassiness; **f22.5** very pleasing spice throb; **b23** clean and deeply satisfying. With so many warming spices at work, this would add possibly more to a blend than a blender might be happy with. 51.5%. nc ncf sc. 232 bottles.

⬦ **Old Particular Girvan 25 Years Old** refill barrel, cask no. 10939, dist Mar 90, bott Sept 15 **(87.5) n21.5 t22.5 f21.5 b22.** Not quite such an accommodating barrel as cask 10805. But the juiciness and spices are there, though the tannins are a bit more argumentative. 51.3%. nc ncf sc. 162 bottles.

⬦ **Old Particular Girvan 27 Years Old** refill barrel, dist Jun 88, bott Nov 15 **(94.5) n23** a little green apple – not expected on a 27-y-o grain! Penetrating vanilla and sugar mix: very clean; **t23.5** good grief! If I find a more salivating grain over 20 years old this year I'll be pretty amazed. Benefits from a major oil bypass which allows the sugar and spice clear access to the palate. The vanillas are no less sparkling; **f24** superb oak ensures no tang and a slow fade of spice, vanilla and butterscotch; **b24** any time of the day restorative... Truly beautiful. 62.6%. nc ncf sc. 192 bottles.

Scotch Malt Whisky Society Cask G7.5 Aged 28 Years hogshead, dist 84 **(91) n23.5 t23.5 f22 b22.** Keep bottling gems like this and they'll have to form the Grain Whisky Society. 58.9%

The Sovereign Girvan Aged 26 Years refill hogshead, cask no 11119, dist Oct 88, bott Nov 14 **(90.5) n22** touch of the rum about this...with a vague hint of smoke on the horizon; **t23** delivery is sublime, showing magnificent texture and unexpected weight. The sugars are of the acacia honey variety. Serious depth; **f22.5** takes an attractively spicy turn and with the light praline development sees off the slight oak bitterness; **b23** a spicy cove which may well have matured for the last quarter of a century in a former Islay cask as there are some feeble smoke notes attached. 56.3% nc ncf sc. 283 bottles.

⬦ **The Sovereign Girvan 36 Years Old** refill hogshead, cask no. 12276, dist May 79, bott Feb 16 **(91.5) n23** full on with the age but softened with Manuka honey amid the Canadian-style vanilla; **t23** fabulous delivery: the vanilla pitches its tent first but the earthy, though understated, sugars and warming spice ensure plenty of chewy company; **f22.5** very good oak at play, ensuring a delicious, unsullied edge to the vanilla-tannin fade; **b23** robust and rich. 51%. nc ncf sc. 322 bottles.

⬦ **That Boutique-y Whisky Company Girvan 52 Year Old** batch 1 **(92.5) n24** yessiree...! This is the dang tooting' finest scotch bourbon style you'll find this side of the Rockies... The corn radiates vanilla while the oak beats out a spicy drum; **t23.5** a kind of gin-style juniper makes a surprising pitch for early dominance before ulmo honey filters through; **f22.5** back to pretty sedate vanilla; **b22.5** over 50 years old and still this strength! What's all that about??? There again, if a Scotch is going to be for all intents a bourbon, what do you expect...? *51.1%. 114 bottles.*

INVERGORDON

Best Dram Invergordon 23 Years Old hogshead **(87) n22 t23 f20.5 b21.5**. Not quite the best hoggie to have carried grain, as the finish clearly testifies. But there's no faulting the silky delivery, or the myriad sugar notes – the golden syrup in particular. *50.7%*

◇ **Maltbarn Invergordon 1988** ex-bourbon cask, bott 2015 **(87.5) n21.5 t22.5 f21.5 b22.** Pure blending fodder: a fat floozy which would go with anything. The slight tang to the cask does little damage, but lacks complexity. Knows how to give a brief but fun time. *51.3%. sc. 132 bottles.*

Master of Malt Single Cask Invergordon 23 Year Old refill sherry hogshead, dist Apr 91, bott Jul 14 **(77.5) n22 t21.5 f16 b18**. Very similar to their Invergordon Batch 3, perhaps with a kinder nose – which makes the bitter finish even more disappointing. Not sure of the point of sherry and grain: the Invergordon doesn't have enough about it to make a mark on the grape while the bitterness carries on unchecked... *52.8%. sc. 82 bottles.*

Old Masters Invergordon 23 Year Old cask no. 77733, dist 1991, bott 2014 **(89) n22.5** intense vanilla-corn mix – expect to see the Rockies when I look out of my tasting room window...; **t23** gorgeous texture: spices arrive early to ensure immediate complexity with the honeyed corn oils; **f21** a little on the oak-bitter side; **b22.5** presumably distilled from maize, as this has "Canadian" stamped all over it... *59.1%. sc. James MacArthur & Co Ltd*

◇ **Old Particular Invergordon 21 Years Old** refill barrel, dist Oct 94, bott Nov 15 **(73) n18 t19 f18 b18**. A bad day or two at the fermenters hasn't been corrected after over 20 years... *50.7%. nc ncf sc. 206 bottles.*

◇ **Old Particular Invergordon 28 Years Old** refill butt, dist Aug 87, bott Nov 15 **(87.5) n20.5 t23.5 f22 b22**. A sugary procession. Though oily, the tannins do get through alongside some considerable spices. Juicy and delightfully nippy at times, though deprived of greatness by a dullard nose and a slightly nagging tanginess. *56.5%. nc ncf sc. 490 bottles.*

The Pearls of Scotland Invergordon 1972 dist Dec 72, bott Apr 15 **(90.5) n23.5** a big Canadian signature here, with light liquorice and muscovado sugars lining with the big corn; **t22.5** pure silk: a featherbed delivery full of corn and acacia honey; **f22** a complete take over by the corn; **b22.5** amazing that something so old can be so simple and untaxing! *46.6%*

The Pearls of Scotland Invergordon 1997 cask no. 105, dist Apr 97, bott May 15 **(95.5) n24** much firmer nose than usual Invergordon. And spicier. The sugars are crisp and clean, of a Demerara style; **t24** wow!! A stunning delivery – an ulmo honey and maple syrup mix, bought down to earth by highly spiced vanilla. The silky texture is textbook...; **f23.5** long, with those sugars and spices never knowing when to stop...; **b24** yet another true pearl of a grain unleashed by Pearls of Scotland. Congrats – you guys have absolutely excelled! *59.1%. sc.*

◇ **The Single Cask Invergordon Aged 27 Years** cask no. 8118, dist 1 Feb 88, bott 1 Feb 16 **(94) n23** a burst of smoke suggests an ex-Islay cask installing some depth and backbone not expected when I first opened the bottle; **t24.5** wow!! Works so beautifully well: the smoke charges as the phenolic spices explode on delivery. Lovely weight, helped by unusually well controlled oils for this distillery. The sugars are of the molassed variety – and that peat just keeps on building...; **f22.5** now the oils assemble – and with some interest. Corn oil, presumably, sticks to the roof of the mouth. But the smoke makes it hard to judge exactly; **b24** with the smoke in situ, it is as if a smoky blend is at play here. Highly unusual for a single grain. But one I think most people will ask for a second glass of. Superb! *45.8%. nc ncf sc.*

◇ **The Sovereign Invergordon 27 Years Old** refill hogshead, cask no. 11853, dist Feb 88, bott Sept 15 **(83) n21 t22 f20 b20**. A few vegetable notes are briefly outshone by the sugars. But never quite finds a happy balance. *51.1%. nc ncf sc. 299 bottles.*

The Sovereign Invergordon Aged 30 Years refill butt, cask no. 11237, dist Oct 84, bott Feb 15 **(93.5) n24.5 t24 f22 b23** refilled into a sherry butt which dates before the days of the big sulphur cock-up...and it shows in the beauty of its soul... *59.6%. nc ncf sc. 687 bottles.*

The Sovereign Invergordon Aged 50 Years refill bourbon barrel, cask no 11047, dist Nov 64, bott Nov 14 **(90.5) n23.5 t22 f22.5 b23** hangs on in there...and finally reaches its biblical time in the cask gracefully... *42.5%. nc ncf sc. 252 bottles.*

◇ **Spirits Shop Selection & Sansibar Whisky Invergordon 1973** bourbon cask, bott 2015 **(94.5) n23.5** oooh, get that honey. Both acacia and ulmo in harmony as we enter serious Canadian territory: the oak is quietly profound; **t23.5** the spices kick into place almost immediately. They find a comfortable spot between the soothing sugars and the more robust oak; the tannin means we flit between Canada and Kentucky, as the liquorice and heather honey take effect; **f23.5** long, with a light mocha touch but the gentle tannins always steer the direction; the light sugars last alongside the teasing spice; **b24** a cracking grain with more buzz than a bee on performance-enhancing drugs.. *52.2%. 240 bottles.*

⋄ **Svenska Eldvatten Invergordon 1972** ex-bourbon barrel, dist Dec 72, bott Mar 16 **(91.5) n23.5** love the kumquat edge to this Demerara sugar laden grain; **t23** Demerara...and some! Light spices integrate effortlessly; **f23** the distillery's oily, silky nature is revealed late on as the vanillas find an easy and accommodating vehicle on which to travel **b22** an oily cove absolutely bursting at the seams with sugars. *48.9%. sc.*

⋄ **That Boutique-y Whisky Company Invergordon 43 Year Old** batch 5 **(88.5) n23** such an oily display of vanilla...; **t22** just when you think the vanilla can't get more intense...; the mix of castor and gristy sugars take no time to melt; **f21** a little bitterness as the darker side of the tannins come through; **b22.5** the oils are perhaps a little too consuming here *47.7%. 528 bottles.*

That Boutique-y Whisky Invergordan batch 2 **(88.5) n22** lightly spiced toffee; **t23** a Demerara-treacle mix melts as the spices evolve; **f21.5** vanilla and toffee; **b22** unassuming, easy going and just-so spiced. *58.3%. 160 bottles. WB15/347*

That Boutique-y Whisky Company Invergordon batch 3 **(79) n21.5 t22 f17 b18.5.** On the nose, blind, one would take this for a rum whisky made on a continuous still with insufficient sulphur-killing copper in the system – and the poor, bitter finish would bear this out. Absolutely nothing wrong with the big fruity delivery, though. *49.8%. 60 bottles.*

Wemyss Malts 1988 Single Grain Invergordon "Caribbean Crème" barrel, bott 2014 **(88) n22** the distillery's trademark softness wafts from the glass like feathers caught in the breeze. Delicately sweet, a little oily...not unlike the fondant in a chocolate Swiss Roll....; **t23.5** remarkably tart launch, almost a citrus kick before the oak and corn begin to lay claim to the taste buds; **f20.5** bitterish and a little dull; **b22** somewhat moody. But when in good form, chewy and balanced. *46%. sc. 171 bottles.*

The Whisky Barrel Invergordon 2006 Burns Malt 7 Years Old oloroso cask, cask no. 901446 **(91) n23** fresh and fruity, but tight and even vaguely smoked; **t23** that weird smoke turns up early, only to give way to burnt raisin and Melton Hunt cake; **f23** some cocoa and diced hazelnut; at times quite sharp; **b23** Cadbury's Fruit and Nut, the beauty of which will be lost on American candy executives. Admittedly, Invergordon as I have never seen it before in some 40 years tasting...though at times feeling as though it is operating in a strait jacket..!! Off the wall, but a joy! *61.5%*

The Whisky Barrel Invergordon 2006 Burns Malt 7 Years Old px cask, cask no. 901446 **(84) n21 t22 f20 b21.** Crisp, uniform and with a rumbling dark sugar singularity. A little tainted on the finish, though. *60.2%*

⋄ **Whiskybroker Invergordon 43 Year Old** bourbon barrel, cask no. 1300000003, dist 13 Dec 72, bott 14 Dec 15 **(91.5) n23** just exceptional: though the spirit has leeched into some of the cask's weaker lactic notes, the integrity of the corn is something else; **t23.5** a volley of soft sugars, beginning with acacia honey, then moving through red liquorice, a little juicy green apple and then a more ponderous fudgy quality; **f22** just a little tang on the fade – in keeping with the lactic nose - as the cask begins to buckle under its age...; **b23** Canadian whisky lovers will fight over a grain like this one.. *49.9%. sc.*

⋄ **Whiskyjace Invergordon 24 Years Old 1991** bourbon hogshead, bott 2015 **(96) n24** a sublime mixing of soft vanilla, dry peach and thin ulmo honey; **t24** oh, oh, oh...!! Such a beautifully demure delivery. Often has a tendency to go in a little too soft, but here gets the firmness spot on, helped by a really top quality cask. The vanilla, fudge and Manuka honey middle will make you purr...; **f23.5** no bitterness or off notes. Just an elegant fade with the cocoa notes amplified slightly towards the end; **b24.5** a truly exceptional example of this distillery at this age at its absolute richest. Great Scotch, grain or not. A lot of money has been spent securing this distillery over the last two decades: too much, really. Taste a whisky like this, and maybe you can find a reason.. *55.8%*

Wilson & Morgan Barrel Selection Invergordon 30 Year Old sherry wood, dist 1984, bott 2015 **(68) n17 t21 f14 b16.** I'd be amazed if this spent its life in only the one sherry butt since 1984 – a dreadful flavour profile such as this didn't exist in those halcyon days. Sulphur apart, the delivery has an unusual gin quality to it, though for a brief moment on arrival it sparkles quite wonderfully. *57%*

LOCH LOMOND

Loch Lomond Single Grain db **(93) n23** crisp sugars are willing to absorb the vanilla; **t23.5** indeed, the sugars on the nose are indicative of a sweet grain, for the delivery centres around the maple syrup lead. The oak is something like most anchors at work: barely visible to invisible; **f23** the oaks do have a say, though you have to wait a while on the long finale. A little spice arrives, too; **b23.5** elegant grain; keeps the sweetness controlled. *46%*

Master of Malt Single Cask Loch Lomond 16 Year Old (89) n22 t23 f21.5 b22.5. On this evidence, Loch Lomond is filled with malt and malt alone.... *62.7%. sc.*

Master of Malt Single Cask Loch Lomond 18 Year Old sherry hogshead, dist Dec 94, bott Apr 15 **(92.5)** n23 big, chunky: the impressive oak may spread its trunk but there are sugars and spices to meet its demands; **t24** easily the most dense grain of the year. There appear to be malt notes abounding, the sugars shine and sparkle with even a layer of ulmo honey for good measure; **f22** thinner and much more vanilla dependent; **b23.5** a five course meal with all the trimmings and silver service. For a grain, malty and massive. *60.5%. sc. 96 botts.*

That Boutique-y Whisky Loch Lomond batch 1 **(89.5)** n22 t23.5 f22 b22 A sometimes unloved and often misunderstood distillery, shown here to excellent fruity effect with the yeast ensuring the citrus is working at full blast. *52.4%. 191 bottles. WB15/348*

◈ **That Boutique-y Whisky Company Loch Lomond** batch 2 **(89)** n22 house style bubble-gum...; **t23** more bubble-gum, except on about the fifth major flavour wave comes an incredible kick of malt, of all things... **f22** back to slightly spiced bubble-gum safety; **b22** one of the softest grains ever produced in Scotland and here it shows all its accommodating sugars to the full... *478%. 91 bottles.*

Rhosdhu 2008 Cask No. 2484 bourbon barrel, dist 17/03/08, bott 27/07/11 **(84)** n21.5 t21.5 f20.5 b21. The barley battles with some aggressive oak, even at this tender age. The spice count is pretty high. *45%. nc ncf sc.*

LOCHSIDE

◈ **The Last Drop Lochside 1972 44 Years Old** 2nd fill American oak hogshead, cask no. 346 **(94)** n24 so lively, it almost arrogantly defies the years: a little green tea and watered down eucalyptus confirms the age, a squeeze of lemon the age-defying devil within it. Charming sugars as deft as they are dexterous ensures the tannins always stay at a low level; **t24** there go those sugars once more, though with a curious bitterness interwoven throughout them. The oak has worked hard for a prominent position but the corn offers an almost cake-like resistance, especially when the vanilla arrives; **f22.5** some tiring oak cannot be entirely contained and some late bitterness seeps through. The sugars battle manfully, though: this must have been an astonishing grain a decade back; **b23.5** a friend of mine, just a day or two before I tasted this, by coincidence sent a message saying how lovely it would be if an old Scottish Grain got World Whisky of the Year. Indeed, it would – and it may one day happen. But not this year, despite the excellence of this ancient whisky. Oh, 1972, eh! As a 14-year-old I was running 4 minutes 46 seconds in the 1500 metres for Kettering Harriers and qualifying for the England trials. Montrose, under player-manager Alex Stuart, began the year with a first-footing 3-1 win at neighbours Brechin and went on to have probably their best calendar year in the club's history on the road with a 6-1 win at Hampden over Queens Park; another win at Brechin, this time 4-1; at Stranraer they were 6-3 victors, 3-1 at Cowdenbeath and 5-1 at East Stirling. Not too much happened at their Links Park home, but just up the road at the Lochside Distillery some of Scotland's finest grain was being produced by happy distillery workers drunk on their club's comparative success. What heady days...now re-lived and not just grainy memories... *44.6%. sc.*

NORTH BRITISH

Berry's Own Selection North British 2000 cask no. 4312, bott 2011 **(87.7)** n22 t22.5 f21. Bitters thanks to some indifferent oak; **b22** neutral whisky....? I don't think so. *46%. nc ncf sc.*

Cadenhead's Small Batch North British Aged 24 Years bourbon barrel, dist 1989, bott 2014 **(94)** n23.5 t24 f23 b23.5 made on another continent, and we might have had Canadian Whisky of the Year.. *46%. 240 bottles. WB15/168*

Darkness! North British Aged 18 Years Oloroso Cask Finish **(89.5)** n22 t22.5 f23.5 b21.5 A rule of thumb is that putting grain into fresh sherry tells you far more about the cask than the distillate. And it hangs true here. Very good cask, by the way... *50.4%. 94 bottles. WB15/352*

Deerstalker Limited Release North British 1994 aged 20 years 3 months (91) n22.5 beautiful rhubarb and custard...while going easy on the sugars; **t23** must be rhubarb tart – as few grains arrive on the palate quite as tart as this. Eye-wateringly lively with what appears to be a corn oil sheen offering the softer tones; **f22.5** at last the sugars arrive, with a reintroduction of the custard. So soft, with the taste buds being massaged in oils to the very end; **b23** a grain which has more life and complexity than a great many malts. Superb! *48%.*

◈ **Friends Over A Couple of Casks Port Sgioba 4 25 Years Old** bourbon barrel, cask no. 3227, dist 22 Jan 91, bott 26 Jan 16 **(92)** n23 rich, almost a sultana sweetness with excellent accompanying spices; **t23.5** sultry delivery with a measured intensity to the sugars. Salivating, still fresh, but with the spices keen to be rid of their shackles; a gossamer-thin layering of ulmo honey does just the right job; **f22.5** thinner, much more vanilla and a vague banana and custard depth, plus the lingering honey. Some tiring oak tang, but the spices remain fit; **b23** as a 15-year-old, would tick every box for a blender. Sweet, lush, impeccably constructed and offering just the right amount of honey. 54.8%. nc ncf sc. 229 bottles.

◇ **Old Particular North British 21 Years Old** refill hogshead, cask no. 10797 **(91)** n22 corn oil? **t23** salivating sugars dissolve on the palate. A few strands of vanilla and banana inject a delicious sweetness; **f23** drier, and again the vanilla is at work. The oils are spent, allowing a more flaky mouth feel; **b23** superbly made and makes the most of an untroubled cask to show just how rich the corn can be. A very shapely frame for a blend. 50.9%. nc ncf sc. 294 bottles.

◇ **Old Particular North British 24 Years Old** refill hogshead, dist Oct 91, bott Nov 15 **(94)** **n23** smoke. Smoke....??? Yep peat is there for sure. Happens...but not very often! **t24** light bodied delivery soon fattens but then the bewildered brain is pushed into peat-encrusted corners. Some serious sugars running around in there too; watch out also for the stunning French praline; **f23.5** a long, smoky spiciness; **b23.5** A smoky grain! Wonder which distillery on Islay this cask is from! A hundred barrels of this in a blend would give the unsuspecting poor old blender a heart attack! Understatedly delicious. 49.4%. nc ncf sc. 256 bottles.

◇ **Old Particular North British 27 Years Old** refill barrel, cask no. 10938, dist Jul 88, bott Sept 15 **(93.5)** n23.5 presses so many of the right buttons: a real sharpness to this which belies its age. Would be at the heart of the most delicate of ancient blends; **t24** here we go! The nose hints at possibilities of a juicy grain and this is realised by an almost eye-watering introduction, the outside of the tongue being particularly affected. Lazy oak may punish later... **f22.5** and after a little spice and vanilla, that's exactly what happens as the tanginess of the old bourbon wood begins to grip; **b23.5** if anyone tells you grain is neutral, then shove a glass of this in their hand! 50.2%. nc ncf sc. 168 bottles.

Master of Malt Single Cask North British 20 Year Old refill bourbon barrel, dist Dec 94, bott Apr 15 **(84.5)** n21.5 t22 f20 b21. Quirky stuff, with a degree of gin-like botanicals floating around. Pleasant, but never quite reaches satisfying... 51.7%. sc. 115 bottles.

Signatory Single Grain Collection North British 1997 dist 14 May 97, bott 28 Nov 13 **(92.5)** n22.5 t23 f23 b24 The vague, distant smokiness adds further intrigue to a fine grain whisky. 43%. WB15/169

The Sovereign North British Aged 52 Years refill hogshead, cask no 10883, dist May 62, bott Sept 14 **(92)** n23.5 the corn almost bulges on the nose as it gathers full intensity to overcome the French toast oakiness; **t23** mouth-watering and fresh, totally making a lie of its age. The corn oils drip with toasty sugars, the sweetness forever gathering in intensity; **f22.5** long, the spices upping the ante; **b23** yet another grain whisky at 50 which not only defies the years, but asks searching questions of the wood deployed today in which whisky is matured. For an oldie, in many ways still a relative youngster... 40.8% nc ncf sc. 155 bottles.

The Sovereign North British Aged 25 Years refill bourbon barrel, cask no. 11226, dist Sept 89, bott Feb 15 **(86.5)** n22 t22.5 f20.5 b21.5. A steady-as-she-goes, moderate grain with all the emphasis on the natural caramels and deeper molassed sugars. 59.7% nc ncf sc.

Director's Cut North British Aged 52 Years first fill hogshead, cask no. 10356, dist 1962 **(85)** n23 t22.5 f19.5 b20. As you can see from the strength, this oldie was bottled just in the nick of time. Hard to imagine that when this was made, just the other side of the distillery walls, Hearts were sitting top of the Scottish League, their Tynecastle ground packed every other week, and that year won the League Cup. Now as I taste this, they are acclimatising to life in a lower league being watched by only a fraction of that once solid support. Curiously, in 1962 they got off to a bright start and then faded badly at the end. Odd that 52 years on a cask of whisky filled just a few yards away did exactly the same thing... 41.1%. sc. 195 bottles.

The Sovereign Single Cask North British 1962 cask no. 9930, dist 1962, bott Aug 13 **(94.5)** n24 t23 f24 b23.5. Bottlings such as these really do re-draw the map of truly great whisky... And as for this: one of the most gentle rides you will ever enjoy around a whisky bottle, entirely sans bumps; indeed, a 50-year-old without a single wrinkle...57.2%. sc.

That Boutique-y Whisky Company North British batch 1 **(73.5)** n18 t19 f18 b18.5. Didn't know they were making gin at North British. What the bloody hell is this...? 51.1%.

◇ **That Boutique-y Whisky Company North British** batch 2 **(87)** n22 t22.5 f21 b21.5. Hard to imagine a grain being more sweet and lush than this one on delivery, helped on the complexity front by a squeeze of citrus. As is so often the case with sweet whiskies, severe bitterness follows later. An enormous degree of Canadian character to this, especially on the nose, 49.3%.

The Sovereign Single Cask North British 1962 cask no. 9930, dist 1962, bott Aug 13 **(94.5)** n24 t23 f24 b23.5. Bottlings such as these really do re-draw the map of truly great whisky... And as for this: one of the most gentle rides you will ever enjoy around a whisky bottle, entirely sans bumps; indeed, a 50-year-old without a single wrinkle...57.2%. sc.

That Boutique-y Whisky Company North British batch 1 (**73.5**) **n18 t19 f18 b18.5**. Didn't know they were making gin at North British. What the bloody hell is this...? *51.1%.*

That Boutique-y Whisky Company North British batch 2 (**87**) **n22 t22.5 f21 b21.5**. Hard to imagine a grain being more sweet and lush than this one on delivery, helped on the complexity front by a squeeze of citrus. As is so often the case with sweet whiskies, severe bitterness follows later. An enormous degree of Canadian character to this, especially on the nose, *49.3%.*

NORTH OF SCOTLAND

The Pearls of Scotland North of Scotland 1971 dist Dec 71, bott Apr 15 (**95.5**) **n25** oh, that nose...sublime! About as soft as it gets and if you find a kinder infusion of tannins amid light sugars this year, then please let me know. A fruitiness has developed, but we are talking pastel tones of genteel understatement. Lime, greengage, pink grapefruit, peach...all are there. And so too are the spices which quietly announce the great age of this grain. As polite and enticing as a whisky nose ever gets...and shows virtually every malt of this age a thing or two. Perfection; **t23.5** the grapefruit arrives upfront and offers more bite and aggression in the first three seconds than you get in 20 minutes of nosing. Still no sign of the oak wanting to spoil the party. The vanillas merge with butterscotch; **f23** again, a grapefruit tartness begins to descend, the spicy buzz is distant; **b24** what a beautifully elegant old lady...and one with virtually no wrinkles... *43.6%*

PORT DUNDAS

Port Dundas 20 Years Old Special Release 2011 db (**90**) **n21.5 t22 f23.5 b23**. Can a whisky be a little too silky. This one tries, especially on the non-committal nose and over friendly delivery. But once the spices rise, things get very interesting... *57.4%. nc ncf sc.*

Cadenhead's Small Batch Port Dundas Aged 25 Years bourbon hogshead, dist 88, bott 14 (**96**) **n24.5 t24 f23.5 b24** As grain whisky goes, and Port Dundas in particular, just about perfect. Certainly represents one of the best three nose and delivery combinations of the year. *46%. 246 bottles. WB15/363*

◇ **Old Particular Port Dundas 11 Years Old** cask no. 11224, dist Jul 04, bott Apr 16 (**90.5**) **n22.5**, sharp, spicy and ridiculously oily for a continuous still spirit. Absorbed a lovely degree of nuttiness, too; **t23** early sugars are crisp, in contrast to the oozing oils. Limited oak input really allows the spices to buzz; **f22.5** stays on the sugary trail; **b22.5** a beautifully sticky grain, the style of which we will never see again. Top notch either as a straight grain or in a blend. *48.4%. nc ncf sc. 840 bottles.*

◇ **Old Particular Port Dundas 25 Years Old** refill hogshead, cask no. 10941, dist Feb 90, bott Sept 15 (**87**) **n22 t22 f21.5 b21.5**. Displays that attractive creamy fruitiness that makes for the filling of a Jammy Dodger. Pity, then, the tangy barrel is just a tad dodgy... *51.5%. nc ncf sc. 258 bottles.*

◇ **The Sovereign Port Dundas 27 Years Old** refill hogshead, cask no. 12135, dist Oct 88, bott Oct 15 (**95.5**) **n23.5** some lovely oak at play; the sugars almost point in the direction of rum; **t23.5** textbook delivery. Very rich combination of oil and molasses which allows the slow filtering of spice-clad vanilla. The midground offers some impressive Java coffee; **f24** long, with an intriguing re-introduction of late sugars and spices into that coffee, though now more Demerara than molassed; **b24.5** compact and deliciously intense. Just so right in so many aspects. *56.7%. nc ncf sc. 221 bottles.*

◇ **Old Particular Port Dundas 27 Years Old** refill hogshead, cask no. 10941, dist Oct 88, bott Nov 15 (**92.5**) **n23.5** a little green tea and attractive nuttiness; **t23** light on its feet when it arrives with the spices first to make the running. Fudgy sugars follow; **f23** back to the nuttiness detected on the nose as some praline sets in; **b23** makes as little fuss as possible, but still gives the palate a busy workout. Elegant stuff. *54.8%. nc ncf sc. 218 bottles.*

The Sovereign Port Dundas Aged 25 Years refill hogshead, cask no 10876, dist Oct 88, bott Sept 14 (**93**) **n23.5** anyone over a certain age will remember the smell of the dedicated pipe tobacco/sweetshop...this takes me right back...; **t24** massive delivery: spices explode on impact while maple syrup dribbles over the taste buds; **f22** tires and bitters out quite rapidly; **b23.5** what a treat! *58.5% nc ncf sc. 246 bottles.*

The Sovereign Port Dundas Aged 25 Years refill hogshead, cask no 11593, dist Feb 90, bott May 15 (**84**) **n22 t21.5 f20 b20.5**. A promising outburst of attractive early sugars is done in by the encroaching bitterness. *51.9% nc ncf sc. 236 bottles.*

The Sovereign Port Dundas Aged 36 Years refill hogshead, cask no 11052, dist Jan 78, bott Nov 14 (**95.5**) **n24** a magnificent soup-like amalgamation of Bakewell pudding, buttered muffins and corn oil; **t24** thick corn oil has plenty of molten muscovado sugar and ulmo honey stirred in; **f23.5** long sizzling spice embraces the vanilla; **b24** a classy, though intense, act which makes the perfect late night dram. *59.7% nc ncf sc. 177 bottles.*

⬦ **The Sovereign Port Dundas 40 Years Old** refill hogshead, cask no. 11844, dist Nov 74, bott Sept 15 **(86) n22 t23 f19 b21.5.** Some bitterness from the cask just shows how delicate this grain is. Impacts upon, but doesn't spoil, the fabulous liquorice and molassed triumph of the early tones. *4.76%. nc ncf sc. 102 bottles.*

⬦ **The Sovereign Port Dundas 50 Years Old** refill hogshead, cask no. 11838, dist Jun 65, bott Sept 15 **(85.5) n21.5 t22 f21 b21.** The grain has stayed the course over the last half century without a blemish. Sadly, it is the cask that has cracked under the weight of years and allowed a slight bitterness to infiltrate the tender complexities. *41.2%. nc ncf sc. 96 bottles.*

STRATHCLYDE

Cadenhead's Small Batch Strathclyde Aged 24 Years bourbon barrels, dist 1989, bott 2013 **(79.5) n20.5 t22 f18 b19.** Quaffable enough – providing you don't concentrate too hard on what's going on on your palate. Two dozen years ago there wasn't enough copper in the distilling system by half. And even all these years on, it shows! A bit of an Allied bitter cask doesn't help, either. *46%. 504 bottles. WB15/166*

Chivas Brothers Cask Strength Edition Strathclyde Aged 12 Years batch no. ST 12 001, dist 01, bott 13 **(88.5) n22 t23 f21.5 b22.** The back label informs us: "You may notice a slight natural haze for when you add water or ice. This is perfectly natural." I am sorry but there is nothing natural about adding ice... *62.1%. ncf nc. WB15/370*

The Clan Denny Strathclyde Aged 9 Years sherry butt, cask no. 10710, dist 2005 **(86) n21 t21 f22 b21.5.** Relax. No nasty notes despite the cask: all is good. But the grain itself doesn't make quite enough impact against the sherry influence for the balance to be quite right. Loads of sugar and spice at work - all rather like a fruit pastille with attitude. *55.7%. sc.*

Clan Denny Strathclyde Aged 38 Years refill barrel, cask no. HH9486 **(88) n23.5 t22 f20.5 b22.** Appears to be wheated grain as opposed to corn. Very early if so. *55.5%. sc.*

⬦ **Old Particular Strathclyde 10 Years Old** sherry butt, cask no. 11062, dist Nov 05, bott Feb 16 **(72) n18 t20 f15 b19.** Despite traces of the 'S' word found on both nose and finish (well, a lot on the finish, as it happens), some attractive silkiness at least. *50.9%. nc ncf sc. 221 bottles.*

⬦ **Old Particular Strathclyde 25 Years Old** refill barrel, cask no. 11987, dist Aug 90, bott Feb 16 **(93) n23** a gorgeous lemon sherbet fizz; **t23.5** fizzy, salivating delivery – almost malty in its grassiness! Icing sugars melt in the mouth; **f23** stupendously clean vanilla: almost like a trifle before you get to the sherry bit; **b23.5** punchy, beautifully lively and relentlessly juicy. *50.5%. nc ncf sc. 119 bottles.*

⬦ **Old Particular Strathclyde 27 Years Old** refill barrel, cask no. 10804, dist Sept 87, bott Jun 15 **(86) n22 t23 f20 b21.** A punchy, tart grain which pays little heed to its ungainly finish. But happily packs all its charms into the refreshing, juicy and explosive start. *51.5%. nc ncf sc. 198 bottles.*

⬦ **Old Particular Strathclyde 27 Years Old** refill barrel, cask no. 10934, dist Jun 88, bott Sept 15 **(91) n22** grassy and lively – almost gassy; **t23.5** intense grassy freshness; a little pear and then moves towards a deep mocha; **f22.5** long, with the residual oils allowing the mocha to fade into praline; **b23** superficially a similar card to cask 10804 above. But just a little fatter, spicier and, essentially, cleaner. *57.9%. nc ncf sc. 198 bottles.*

The Pearls of Scotland Strathclyde 1988 cask no. 62111, dist Jun 88, bott May 15 **(95.5) n23.5** hugely impressive –and confusing: think it is corn, but there are enough belligerent spices to suggest this could be from early wheat mash. Not often I get confused on this, but an infusion of particularly dark weighty sugars has muddied the waters; **t24** those big spices attacking at full pelt while the profound sugars try to soften the blows. Light oil... but is it corn? Probably not...; **f23.5** medium length as the oak now gathers traction. No off notes, no tiredness: very pleasant and impressive...; **b24.5** the full on nature of this little beast means it has coped with the encroaching years without breaking sweat... *55.5%. sc.*

The Sovereign Strathclyde Aged 25 Years refill hogshead, cask no 10875, dist Feb 89, bott Sept 14 **(83) n21 t22.5 f19 b20.5.** A roaring blast of sugars early on does its best to compensate for the clear deficiencies in the body and balance. A combo of lack of copper and a typical Allied cask means the finish is lacking somewhat. *59.7%. nc ncf sc. 186 bottles.*

⬦ **The Sovereign Strathclyde 25 Years Old** refill barrel, cask no. 12281, dist Aug 90, bott Feb 16 **(88) n21.5** tight, well-used oak nips at the blossoming sugars; **t23** a lightly spiced maple syrup bursts forth; **f21.5** a little tiredness to the cask results in a late tang; **b22** many of the characteristics found in the OP of the same vintage (see above) but a far less accommodating cask. *51.2%. nc ncf sc. 176 bottles.*

Xtra Old Particular Strathclyde 40 Years Old refill hogshead, cask no. 10598, dist Oct 74, bott Dec 14 **(87) n22.5 t23 f20 b21.** In many ways more rum in character than whisky! The

Strathclyde is lost under a syrupy, sticky mass which makes the bitter finish all the more accentuated. 55.4%. nc ncf sc. 150 bottles.

UNSPECIFIED SINGLE GRAIN

◇ **Borders** finished in Oloroso sherry casks **(66) n15 t18 f15 b18.** Finished being the operative word. Has no-one been listening regarding the total mess sherry butts are in. I wonder why I bother sometimes. Jeez... 51.7%. nc ncf. R&B Distillers.

Haig Club toasted oak casks **(89) n21.5 t23 f22.5 b22** When I first saw this, I wasn't quite sure whether to laugh or cry. Because 25 years ago bottles of single grain whisky were the unique domain of the flat cap brigade, the miners and other working class in the Kirkcaldy area of Scotland. Their grain, Cameron Brig, would be drunk with a splash, mixed with Coke or ginger, even occasionally with Irn Bru, or straight and unmolested as a chaser to the ubiquitous kegged heavy, McEwan's lager or a bottle of Sweetheart stout. When I suggested to the hierarchy at United Distillers, the forerunners of Diageo, that in their finer grains they had a product which could conquer the world, the looks I got ranged from sympathy for my lack of understanding in matters whisky to downright concern about my mental wellbeing. I had suggested the exquisite Cambus, now lost to us like so many other grain distilleries in those passing years, should be brought out as a high class singleton. It was pointed out to me that single grain was, always had been and always will be, the preferred choice of the less sophisticated; those not wishing to pay too much for their dram. Fast forward a quarter of a century and here sits a gorgeously expensive bottle in a deep cobalt blue normally associated with Ballantine's and a very classy, heavyweight stopper. In it is a grain which, if the advertising is to be believed, is the preferred choice not of the back street bar room idlers carefully counting their pennies but of its major ambassador David Beckham: it is the drop to be savoured by the moneyed, jet-set sophisticates. My, oh my. Let's not call this hype. Let's just say it has taken some genius exec in a suit half a lifetime – and probably most of his or hers - to come around to my way of thinking and convince those in the offices on the floor above to go for it. Wonder if I qualify for 10 percent of profit for suggesting it all those years back...or, preferably, five percent of their advertising budget. Meanwhile, I look forward to watching David pouring this into some of his Clynelish and Talisker. After all, no-one can Blend it like Beckham... 40%. WB15/408

Lady of the Glen Twenty Four Year Old (89.5) n21.5 t23 f22.5 b22.5. Squelchy-sift Invergordon at its sugary best. 56%. Hannah Whisky Merchants.

◇ **Svenska Eldvatten Grain 1964** ex-bourbon barrel, dist Dec 72, bott Mar 16 **(95) n23.5** have to be in North America, surely: the maize is absolutely leaping from this glass: wonderful...; **t24** silky sugars - a kind of popcorn buttery style – melds with the deft vanilla from the oak; the spices still have much to say; **f23.5** spicy, with more accent now on the oak; **b24** I remember a couple of years back someone publicly poured scorn on me for saying blends now are vastly different to yesteryear because of the grain. Well, look at the way corn has shaped this baby: far closer to Canadian or even bourbon (or US Corn Whiskey to be more precise) than today's Scotch because of the extraordinary effect of the maize... 52.1%. sc.

Tweeddale Single Lowland Grain Scotch Whisky Aged 16 Years (88) n23 t22 f21 b22. A quiet speech of understatement. 46%. nc ncf sc. Stonedean.

Vatted Grain

Compass Box Hedonism first fill American oak cask, bott 20 Feb 13 **(84) n22 t22 f19 b20.** Just too fat, too sweet and too bitter at the finale to work to great effect. Some decent oak on both nose and delivery, though. 43%. nc ncf. Compass Box Whisky Company.

Compass Box Hedonism Maximus (93.5) n25 t22.5 f23 b23. Bourbon Maximus... 46%

Compass Box Hedonism Quindecimus (88.5) n22.5 a drizzle of lemon on custard; **t22** simple sugars and a little oil; **f22** even late on, a hint of juiciness; **b22** sweet and refreshingly ordinary grain. Well made and unspectacularly delicious. 46%

The Last Vatted Grain bott Nov 11 **(88.5) n23 t22 f21.5 b22.** Not just sad that the term "vatted" is now pointlessly outlawed on the bottle. But also that half of the four grain distilleries used in this vatting are equally consigned to history. 46%. nc ncf. Compass Box.

William Grant & Sons Rare Cask Reserves 25 Years Old Blended Grain Scotch Whisky (92.5) n23 t23.5 f23 b23. A really interesting one, this. In the old days, blenders always spent as much time vatting the grains together as they did the malts, for if they did not work well as a unit it was unlikely harmony would be found in their blend. A long time ago I was taught to, whenever possible, use a soft grain to counter a firmer one, and vica versa. Today, there are far fewer blends to choose from, though 25 years ago the choice was wider. So interesting to see that this grain is soft-dominated with very little backbone at all. Delicious. But screams for some backbone. 47%. Exclusive to The Whisky Shop.

Scottish Blends

If any whisky is suffering an identity crisis just now, it must be the good old Scottish blend.

Once the staple, the absolute mainstay, of the Scotch whisky industry it has seen its market share increasingly buried under the inexorable, incoming tide that is single malt. But worse, the present-day blender has his hands tied in a way no previous generation of blenders have had before.

Now stocks must be monitored with a third eye, one that can judge the demand on their single malt casks and at increasingly varied ages. Worse, the blender cannot now, as was once the case, create blends with subtly shifting textures - the result of carefully using different types of grain. So many grain distilleries have closed in the last quarter of a century that now most blends seem remarkably similar to others. And there is, of course, the problem of sherry butts which has been fully documented over the years in the Whisky Bible.

So perhaps it is hardly surprising that for the third year running Jim Murray's Whisky Bible Scotch Blend of the Year has gone to a whisky containing ancient malts and, for the third year, to the The Last Drop company. In 2015 it was their 1965 edition, last year they conquered all with their 50-year-old. This year it is their relatively younger 1971 bottling. Yet what they all have in common are grains from now lost distilleries - and made from much more lush and full-flavoured corn, as opposed to wheat. Back in the day, the blenders would spend nearly as much time perfecting their blend balance, playing softer, more yielding distillate against the crisper, firmer spirit, with the same precision they gave the malts. After all, the grain would usually make up between 60% and 75% of the blend, so needed to be on the money. It is not just age, then, which makes the difference when you encounter these astonishing old blends. It is the skill of the blender in crafting a desired style and maximum complexity. Couple that with extra oak, the results now can be as good as anything you are ever likely to encounter.

Perhaps it is no coincidence that just as we go to press the news has been announced that The Last Drop has been bought by a distilling company which is no stranger to ancient barrels: Sazerac. With at least one of their Antique Collection of ryes and bourbons annually being named among the Whisky Bible's top three, it appears to be a blend made in heaven.

Jim Murray's Whisky Bible Scottish Blend of the Year Winners	
2004	William Grant's 21 Year Old
2005	William Grant's 21 Year Old
2006	William Lawson Aged 18 Years
2007	Old Parr Superior 18 Years Old
2008	Old Parr Superior 18 Years Old
2009	The Last Drop
2010	Ballantine's 17 Years Old
2011	Ballantine's 17 Years Old
2012	Ballantine's 17 Years Old
2013	Ballantine's 17 Years Old
2014	Ballantine's 17 Years Old
2015	The Last Drop 1965
2016	The Last Drop 50 Years Old
2017	The Last Drop 1971

Scottish Blends

100 Pipers (74) n18.5 t18 f19 b18.5. An improved blend, even with a touch of spice to the finish. I get the feeling the grains are a bit less aggressive than they for so long were. I'd let you know for sure, if only I could get through the caramel. *40%. Chivas.*

Aberdour Piper (88.5) n22 t23 f21.5 b22. Always great to find a blend that appears to have upped the stakes in the quality department. Clean, refreshing with juicy young Speysiders at times simply showing off. *40%. Hayman Distillers.*

Alexander Murray & Co Monumental Blend 30 Years Old (89.5) n23.5 Now there's a nose! The oak is quietly prominent with gorgeous layering of kiwifruit jam and moist Lubeck marzipan...wow!! Lurking somewhere appears to be a hint a four-fifths-hidden smoke...; t23 the softest delivery imaginable: a combination of soft oils and molten sugars. Again, the tannins are pretty upfront, but the clever semi fruitiness – something akin to glace cherries on a sponge; f21 a little messy by comparison: tangy and toffeed; b22 forget the average finish, the nose and delivery are a treat. *40%*

Antiquary 12 Years Old (92) n23.5 t23.5 f22 b23 A staggering about turn for a blend which, for a very long time, has flown the Speyside flag. *40%. Tomatin Distillery.*

Antiquary 21 Years Old (93) n23.5 t23.5 f23 b23 A huge blend, scoring a magnificent 93 points. But I have tasted better, and another sample, direct from the blending lab, came with even greater complexity and less apparent caramel. A top-notch blend of rare distinction. *43%*

Antiquary 30 Years Old (86) n22 t23 f20 b21. Decidedly odd fare but the eccentric nose and early delivery are sublime, with silky complexity tumbling over the palate. *46%*

The Antiquary Blended Scotch Whisky (81) n20 t21 f20 b20. A slightly richer version than its predecessor, Antiquary Finest, this still could do with some extra complexity from the malts to help distract from the monotony of the firm grain. Clean and enjoyable, though. *40%*

Antiquary Finest (79.5) n20 t21 f19 b19.5. Pleasantly sweet and plump with the accent on the quick early malt delivery. *40%. Tomatin Distillery.*

Arden House Scotch Whisky (86) n19.5 t22 f22.5 b22. Another great bit of fun from the Co-op. Very closely related to their Finest Blend, though this has, for some reason or other, a trace of a slightly fatter, mildly more earthy style. If only they would ditch the caramel and let those sweet malts and grains breathe! *40%. Co-Operative Group.*

Asda Blended Scotch Whisky (76.5) n19 t21 f17.5 b19. A scattergun approach with sweet, syrupy notes hitting the palate early and hard. Beware the rather bitter finish, though. *40%*

Asda Extra Special 12 Years Old (78) n19 t21 f19 b19. Pleasantish but dragged down by the dreaded S word. *40%. Glenmorangie for Asda.*

The Bailie Nicol Jarvie (B.N.J) (95) n24 t24 f23 b24. I know my criticism of BNJ, historically one of my favourite blends, over the last year or two has been taken to heart by Glenmorangie. Delighted to report that they have responded: the blend has been fixed and is back to its blisteringly brilliant, ultra-mouth-watering self. Someone's sharpened their ideas up. *40%*

Ballaglass Blended Scotch Whisky (85) n21 t22 f21 b21. Perfectly enjoyable, chewy – but clean – blend full of toffee and fudge. Very good weight and impressive, oily body. *40%.*

Ballantine's Aged 12 Years (84.5) n22.5 t22 f19 b21. Attractive but odd fellow, this, with a touch of juniper to the nose and furry bitter marmalade on the finish. But some excellent barley-cocoa moments, too. *43%. Chivas.*

Ballantine's 12 Years Old (87) n21 t22 f21 b23. The kind of old-fashioned, mildly moody blend Colonel Farquharson-Smythe (retired) might have recognised when relaxing at the 19th hole back in the early '50s. Too good for a squirt of soda, mind. *40%. Chivas Bros.*

Ballantine's 17 Years Old (97.5) n24.5 deft grain and honey plus teasing salty peat; ultra high quality with bourbon and pear drops offering the thrust; a near unbelievable integration with gooseberry juice offering a touch of sharpness muted by watered golden syrup; t24 immediately mouthwatering with maltier tones clambering over the graceful cocoa-enriched grain; the degrees of sweetness are varied but near perfection; just hints of smoke here and there; f24 lashings of vanilla and cocoa on the fade; drier with a faint spicey, vaguely smoky buzz; has become longer with more recent bottlings with the most subtle oiliness imaginable; b25 now only slightly less weighty than of old. After a change of style it has comfortably reverted back to its sophisticated, mildly erotic old self. One of the most beautiful, complex and stunningly structured whiskies ever created. Truly the epitome of great Scotch. *43%.*

Ballantine's Aged 17 Years Limited Edition Miltonduff Signature Distillery (91.5) n22.5 t24 f21.5 b23.5. The usual alto libretto of the Ballantine's 17 has been replaced here by a much weightier composition, even though the usual subtle smoke is missing. Using sherry butts is to enter a minefield in this day and age, I'm afraid, there is no clear path through. The ones here are of mixed quality, but the overall effect is pleasing. *43%*

Ballantine's Aged 21 Years (93) n24 t24 f22 b23 One of the reasons I think I have loved the Ballantine's range over the years is because it is a blenders' blend. In other words, you get the feeling that they have made as much, and probably more, as possible from the stocks available and made complexity and balance the keystones to the whisky. That is still the case, except you find now that somehow, although part of a larger concern, it appears that the spectrum of flavours is less wide, though what has been achieved with those available remains absolutely top drawer. This is truly great whisky, but it has changed in style as blends, especially of this age, cannot help but doing. *43%*

◇ **Ballantine's Aged 21 Years (94)** n23.5 not sure any blend has a more clever use of smoke: used not just as a gentle anchor but as a slight sweetener, too. Excellent mix of grain, showing both crisp and soft sides but also the biscuity malt mixing with the light Cape gooseberry and those fleeting Demerara tones...just lovely! **t24** silk delivery, again with a malty theme. Just melts on the palate into a gorgeous vanilla mush and there are several beats before the smoke makes an apologetic and distant entrance; Of course, as with all the very best blends, there is a degree of bite and firmness, too...; **f23.5** now the oils, previously undetected, swing into action to allow the last complex rays to fade at length; **b24** even though the strength has been reduced, presumably to eek out rare stocks, the beauty of this blend hasn't. *40%*

Ballantine's Aged 30 Years (94) n23.5 t24 f23.5 b23.5. Quite a different animal to that which I tasted last year...and the year before. Having come across it in three different markets, I each time noted a richer, more balanced product: less a bunch of old casks being brought together but more a sculpted piece from preferred materials. That said, I still get the feeling that this is a work in progress: a Kenny Jackett-style building of a team bit by bit, so that each compartment is improved when it is possible, but not to the detriment of another and, vitally, balance is maintained. *43%*

◇ **Ballantine's Aged 30 Years (95.5)** n24.5 some of the notes here could be marked as borderline too old, were they not part of the most astonishing balancing act. Instead the heady tannin brings a linear feel to the much lighter vanillas, some of them boasting a citrusy outer shell. Vague lavender notes mixes with the mint and shadowy phenols as though blended by Gertrude Jekyll...; **t24** if Jekyll sculpted the nose, then Lutyens designed the taste profile: two toned, with a thick, chocolatey paste of a delivery on one hand and a far more ethereal and juicy barley, corn and vanilla notes on the other, lightened further by, once again, the most delicate citrus. In classic blend style bite meets kiss; **f23** long, languid and lush. The oils appear to have come together to mean business, but only so they can soften any hint of a greater intensity to the attack; the finish hints at the vaguest furriness alongside the crumbling oak; **b24** a fascinating malt, slightly underpowered perhaps, which I have had to put to one side and keep coming back to see what it will say and do next... *40%.*

Ballantine's Finest (96) n24 a playful balance and counter-balance between grains, lighter malts and a gentle smokiness. The upped peat of recent years has given an extra weight and charm that had been missing; **t24** sublime delivery: the mouthfeel couldn't be better had your prayers been answered; velvety and brittle grains combine to get the most out of the juicy malts: a lot of chewing to get through here; **f23.5** soft, gentle, yet retains its weight and shape with a re-emergence of smoke and a gristy sweetness to counter the gentle vanillas and cocoa from the oak **b24.5** as a standard blend this is coming through as a major work of art. Each time I taste this the weight has gone up a notch or two more and the sweetness has increased to balance out with the drier grain elements. Take a mouthful of this and experience the work of a blender very much at the top of his game. *40%. Chivas Bros.*

◇ **Ballantine's Hard Fired (86.5)** n22 t22 f21 b21.5. Despite the smoky and toasty elements to this, you're left waiting for it to take off....or even go somewhere. Perhaps just a little too soft, friendly and grain indulgent. Decent, enjoyable blend, of course, but a little out of the Ballantine's usual circle of high class friends. *40%*

Ballantine's Limited brown bottle, bott code D03518 **(94.5)** n23.5 t24 f23 b24. When it comes to Ballantine's I am beginning to run out of superlatives. The last time I tasted Limited, I remember being disappointed by the un-Ballantine's-like bitter finish. Well, from nose to finale, there is a barely perceptible trace of a rogue cask costing half a point from each stage: indeed, it may have cost it World Whisky of the Year. But so magnificent are all those keeping it company there has been no such falling at the last hurdle here. This bottle, rather than finding its way back into my warehouse library, will be living at my home for offering an ethereal quality unmatched by any other whisky in the world. *43%. Chivas.*

Ballantine's Limited 75cl royal blue bottle **(89)** n22 t24 f21 b22. Hadn't tasted this for a little while but maintains its early style and quite glorious delivery. *43%*

Ballantine's Limited Release no. J13295 (95.5) n24.5 t25 f22 b24 I absolutely take my hat off to the blender. When it comes to the weight, complexity, subtlety, suaveness, balance, pace of flavour development, charm and just all-round yessss!!!!ness, I am not sure how the delivery can be bettered. A slight mix of exhausted bourbon cask (allowing some bitterness) and a degree of perhaps sherry-induced furriness means the finish can't quite reach those heights of seemingly effortless perfection and rob this of the World Whisky of the Year for this Bible it most likely would have picked up. But for the combination of nose and delivery I will take those losses. Yet again a Ballantine's which just makes me purr and celebrate the greatness some whiskies can reach. *43%.*

Ballantine's Limited Release no. L40055 (96.5) n24 sherry can be as dry as it might be sweet, and here the grape is in its most austere form of dryness. Excellent use of Speyside malts in particular generates both the sugars and the fuller structure and oils; the vaguest degree of phenol also makes for a both ethereal yet weighty experience; **t25** a silky landing, though hard to tell if that is through the malt or delicate, yielding fruit: that really is a sign of exceptional blending! Astonishingly, one starts salivating on very first contact with the palate and the spices, never more than a buzzing murmur, begin their important work nanoseconds later. The mid-ground is a busy mesh of malt, vanilla and delicate fruit notes before the cocoa begins to make an impact; you try to count the flavour waves, but on the third or fourth time of trying, give up: there are simply too many; **f23** there is a vague furriness which shows that not every cask was perhaps reaching perfection, though it must have been only the odd one or two. Despite this the peek-a-boo played between the still slightly juicy malt and the aloof grape keeps the senses entertained and the mind enthralled; **b24.5** a vaguely weightier incarnation than the last bottling I came across, and here the oils have a much more emboldening role. Indeed, this is a more embracing and confiding version, increasing even more the slightly austere part of its character, and, in doing so, just slightly upping the degree of sophistication. Even though this is only by fractions, it is enough to make it not only a world class whisky, but one of the great whiskies of 2015. And without that late, lightly furry finish, that audible whisper of a taint, almost certainly World Whisky of the Year. *40%*

◈ **Ballantine's Limited Release No. L88960 (94.5) n24 t24 f23 b23.5.** This goes over much of the same ground as L40055, so in the interests of conserving space I'll keep this brief. Whenever you taste a Ballantine's Limited, you get the feeling of an old genius at work: that brilliant blend of bite and genteel sophistication. The main difference I feel here is a slight change in the grain structure, so when the vague weakness from the odd less-than-perfect sherry butt arrives, there isn't quite the sweet body to see it off. Still magnificent, though. And a cocoa shading is sublime. *40%*

Ballantine's Master's (82) n21 t22 f19 b20. Excellent lively grain and chewy malt, but the always suspect, grain-drizzled finish has become even more nondescript in recent bottlings. *40%*

Ballantine's Rare Limited (89.5) n23.5 t22.5 f21.5 b22 A heavier, more mouth watering blend than the "Bluebottle" version. *43%. ncf. Chivas.*

Barley Barony (83) n21.5 t21 f20 b20.5. Faintly furry finish follows from firm, fruity front. *40%.*

Bell's Original (91) n23 t22.5 f22.5 b23 Your whisky sleuth came across the new version for the first time in the bar of a London theatre back in December 2009 during the interval of "The 39 Steps". To say I was impressed and pleasantly surprised is putting it mildly. And with the whisky, too, which is a massive improvement on the relatively stagnant 8-year-old especially with the subtle extra smoky weight. If the blender asks me: "Did I get it right, Sir?" then the answer has to be a resounding "yes". *40%*

Bells 8 Years Old (85) n21.5 t22.5 f20 b21. Some mixed messages here: on one hand it is telling me that it has been faithful to some of the old Bells distilleries – hence a slight dirty note, especially on the finish. On the other, there are some sublime specks of complexity and weight. Quite literally the rough and the smooth. *40%. Diageo.*

Benmore (74) n19 t19 f18 b18. Underwhelming to the point of being nondescript. *40%*

Big "T" 5 Years Old (75) n19 t20 f18 b18. Still doesn't have the finesse of old and clatters about the tastebuds charmlessly. *40%. Tomatin Distillery.*

Black & White (91) n22 t23 f22.5 b23.5 This one hasn't gone to the dogs: quite the opposite. I always go a bit misty-eyed when I taste something this traditional: the crisp grains work to maximum effect in reflecting the malts. A classic of its type. *40%. Diageo.*

Black Bottle (74.5) n18 t20.5 f17 b18. Barely a shadow of its once masterful, great self. *40%.*

Black Bottle 10 Years Old (89) n22 t23 f22 b23 A stupendous blend of weight and poise, but possessing little of the all-round steaming, rampaging sexuality of the younger version... but like the younger version showing a degree less peat: here perhaps even two. Not, I hope, the start of a new trend under the new owners. *40%*

Black Dog 12 Years Old (92) n21 t23 f24 b24. Offering genuine sophistication and élan. This minor classic will probably require two or three glass-fulls before you take the bait... *42.8%*

Black Dog Century (89) n21 t23 f23 b22. I adore this style of no-nonsense, full bodied bruising blend which amid the muscle offers exemplary dexterity and finesse. What entertainment in every glass!! 42.8%. McDowell & Co Ltd. Blended in Scotland/Bottled in India.

Black Grouse (94) n23 t24 f23 b24. A superb return to a peaty blend for Edrington for the first time since they sold Black Bottle. Not entirely different from that brand, either, from the Highland Distillers days with the smokiness being superbly couched by sweet malts. 40%

The Black Grouse Alpha Edition (72.5) n17 t19.5 f17 b18. Dreadfully sulphured. 40%

Black Knight (85.5) n21 t22 f21 b21.5. More of a White Knight as it peacefully goes about its business. Not many taste buds slain, but just love the juicy charge. 43%. Quality Spirits Int.

Black Ram Aged 12 Years (85) n21 t23 f21 b20. An upfront blend that gives its all in the chewy delivery. Some major oak in there but it's all ultra soft toffee and molasses towards the finish. 40%. Vinprom Peshtera, Bulgaria.

Blend No. 888 (86.5) n20 t21.5 f23 b22. A good old-fashioned, rip-roaring, nippy blend with a fudge-honey style many of a certain age will fondly remember from the 60s and 70s. Love it! 40%. The House of MacDuff.

Boxes Blend (90) n22.5 t23.5 f21 b23. A box which gets plenty of ticks. 40.9%. ncf.

Broadford (78.5) n19 t19.5 f20 b20. Boringly inoffensive. Toffee anyone? 40%. Burn Stewart.

Buchanan's De Luxe 12 Years Old (82) n18 t21 f22 b21. The nose shows more than just a single fault and the character simply refuses to get out of second gear. Certainly pleasant, and some of the chocolate notes towards the end are gorgeous. But just not the normal brilliant show-stopper! 40%. Diageo.

Buchanan's Red Seal (90) n22 t23 f22 b23 Exceptional, no-frills blend whose apparent simplicity paradoxically celebrates its complexity. 40%. Diageo.

Budgen's Scotch Whisky Finely Blended (85) n21 t22 f21 b21. A sweet, chunky blend offering no shortage of dates, walnuts, spice and toffee. A decent one to mull over. 40%

Cadenhead's Putachieside Aged 12 Years (91) n23 no shortage of citrus and vanilla: fresh, and the flaky, puff-pastry topping is fitting; t23 the sugars and oils make an early assault. A little bitterness from the oak creeps in; f22 malty-lemon sawdust; b23 not tasted for a while and delighted to re-discover this understated little gem. Also, has to be one of the best labels of any scotch going... 40% WB15/357

Cadenhead's Creations Light Creamy Vanilla Aged 17 Years batch no. 1, bott 2014 **(91)** n22 t23 f23 b23 Just adore clean, refreshing blends like this: says so much while appearing to do so little. For the record: Ardmore, Auchroisk, Caperdonich, and Clynelish are the malts involved, while Invergordon represents the grain. 46%. ncf nc. WB15/362

Callander 12 Years Old (86) n21 t22 f21.5 b21.5. No shortage of malt sparkle and even a touch of tangy salt. Very attractive and enjoyable without ripping up trees. 46.3%. Burn Stewart.

Campbeltown Loch (94) n23 t24 f23.5 b23.5 Over 30 years ago, this blend was one of my preferred drams at home. Not seen it for a while, so disappeared from The Bible. Found again and though it has changed a little in structure, its overall excellence takes me back to when I was a young man. 40% WB15/355

Campbeltown Loch Aged 15 Years (88) n22.5 t22.5 f21 b22 Well weighted with the age in no hurry to arrive. 40%. Springbank Distillers.

Cambletown Loch 21 Years Old db **(83)** n21 t23 f19 b20 Neither the nose or finish are much to write home about, the latter being a little tangy and bitter. But the delivery is rich and comforting: like a Digestive biscuit dunked in coffee. A seemingly decent malt content and a bit of toffee before the furry finale. 46%. WB15/102

Castle Rock (81) n20 t20.5 f20 b20.5. Clean and juicy entertainment. 40%

Catto's Aged 25 Years (85.5) n22 t22.5 f19.5 b21.5. A hugely enjoyable yet immensely frustrating dram. The higher fruit and spice notes are a delight, but it all appears to be played out in a padded cell of cream caramel. One assumes the natural oak caramels have gone into overdrive. Had they not, we would have had a supreme blend scoring well into the 90s. Elsewhere the increased furriness on the finale has not improved matters. 40%

Catto's Deluxe 12 Years Old (79.5) n20 t21.5 f18 b20. Refreshing and spicy in part, but still a note in there which doesn't quite work. 40%. Inverhouse Distillers.

Catto's Rare Old Scottish (92) n23.5 t23.5 f22 b23 Currently one of my regular blends to drink at home. Astonishingly old-fashioned with a perfect accent on clean Speyside and crisp grain. In the last year or so it has taken on a sublime sparkle on the nose and palate. An absolutely masterful whisky which both refreshes and relaxes. 40%. James Catto & Co.

Chequers Deluxe (78.5) n19.5 t20 f19 b20. Charm, elegance, sophistication...not a single sign of any of them. Still if you want a bit of rough and tumble, just the job. 40%. Diageo.

⟨⟩ **The Chivas 18 Ultimate Cask Collection First Fill American Oak (95.5)** n24 another blend that has taken about 20 minutes to get the picture, such is the complexity. Some delightful saltiness to this heightens the sharpness of the grassier, Speyside malts – which is unusual. The sugars are low key, of the lighter more muted muscovado type, while the deft vanilla reminds you of the age rather than tells you it...; **t23.5** majestic delivery: at once salivating and sharp...yet dense! Again, an unusual combination, making full use of the grain; **f24** just brilliant...brilliant!!! Lasts forever with ridiculously clever use of both grain and oilier malts. The vanillas stay entirely in balance with the spices and lingering, slightly citric, malt; **b24** immeasurably superior to any Chivas 18 I have tasted before. A true whisky lover's whisky... 48%. ncf.

Chivas Regal Aged 12 Years (83.5) **n**20.5 **t**22.5 **f**20 **b**20.5. Chewy fruit toffee. Silky grain mouth-feel with a toasty, oaky presence. 40%. Chivas.

Chivas Regal Aged 18 Years (73.5) **n**17.5 **t**20 **f**17.5 **b**18.5. The nose is dulled by a whiff of sulphur and confirmation that all is not well comes with the disagreeably dry, bitter finish. Early on in the delivery some apples and spices show promise but it is an unequal battle against the caramel and off notes. 40%

Chivas Regal 25 Years Old (95) **n**23 **t**23.5 **f**24 **b**24.5. Unadulterated class where the grain-malt balance is exemplary and the deft intertwangling of well-mannered oak and elegant barley leaves you demanding another glass. Brilliant! 40%

Chivas Regal Extra (86) **n**20 **t**24 **f**20.5 **b**21.5. Chivas, but seemingly from the Whyte and MacKay school of thick, impenetrable blends. The nose may have the odd undesirable element and the finish reflects those same trace failings. But if chewy date and walnuts in a sea of creamy toffee is your thing, then this malt is for you. This, though, does show genuine complexity, so I have to admit to adoring the lush delivery and early middle section: the mouth-feel is truly magnificent. Good spice, too. Flawed genius comes to mind. 40%

Clan Campbell (86.5) **n**21.5 **t**22.5 **f**21 **b**21.5. I'll wager that if I could taste this whisky before the colouring is added it would be scoring into the 90s. Not a single off note; a sublime early array of Speysidey freshness but dulls at the end. 40%. Chivas.

Clan Gold 3 Year Old (95) **n**23.5 **t**24 **f**23.5 **b**24. A blend-drinkers blend which will also slay the hearts of Speyside single malt lovers. For me, this is love at first sip... 40%

Clan Gold Blended 15 Years Old (91) **n**21.5 **t**23 **f**23.5 **b**23 An unusual blend for the 21st century, which steadfastly refuses to blast you away with over the top flavour and/or aroma profiles and instead depends on subtlety and poise despite the obvious richness of flavour. The grains make an impact but only by creating the frame in which the more complex notes can be admired. 40%

Clan Gold Blended 18 Years Old (94.5) **n**23 **t**24 **f**23.5 **b**24. Almost the ultimate preprandial whisky with its at once robust yet delicate working over of the taste buds by the carefully muzzled juiciness of the malt. This is the real deal: a truly classy act which at first appears to wallow in a sea of simplicity but then bursts out into something very much more complex and alluring. About as clean and charming an 18-year-old blend as you are likely to find. 40%

Clan MacGregor (92) **n**22 **t**24 **f**23 **b**23 Just gets better and better. Now a true classic and getting up there with Grant's. 43%

Clan Murray Rare Old (84) **n**18 **t**23 **f**21 **b**22. The wonderful malt delivery on the palate is totally incongruous with the weak, nondescript nose. Glorious, mouth-watering complexity on the arrival, though. Maybe it needs a Murray to bring to perfection... 40%. Benriach Distillery.

Clansman (80.5) **n**20.5 **t**21 **f**19 **b**20. Sweet, grainy and soft. 40%. Loch Lomond.

Clansman (78.5) **n**20 **t**21.5 **f**18 **b**19. Plenty of weight, oil and honey-ginger. Some bitterness, too. 43%. Loch Lomond Distillers.

The Claymore (85) **n**19 **t**22 **f**22 **b**22. These days you are run through by spices. The blend is pure Paterson in style with guts etc, which is not something you always like to associate with a Claymore; some delightful muscovado sugar at the death. Get the nose sorted and a very decent and complex whisky is there to be had. 40%. Whyte & Mackay Distillers Ltd.

Compass Box Asyla 1st fill American oak ex-bourbon, bott May 10 (93) **n**24 **t**24 **f**22.5 **b**23.5 If you can hear a purring noise, it is me tasting this... 40%. nc ncf.

Compass Box Asyla Marriage nine months in an American oak barrel (88) **n**22 **t**23 **f**21 **b**22 A lovely blend, but can't help feeling that this was one marriage that lasted too long. 43.6%. Compass Box Whisky for La Maison du Whisky in commemoration of their 50th Anniversary.

Compass Box Delilah's Limited Release American oak, bott Jul 13 (89.5) **n**23 **t**22 **f**22 **b**22.5. A clean and satisfying blend which ramps up the sugars when need be. I'll be surprised if you get to the point where you couldn't take any more... 40%. 6400 bottles.

Compass Box Delilah's Limited Release Small Batch American oak (92.5) **n**23 **t**23.5 **f**23 **b**23 blends rarely come more honeyed, or even sweeter, than this with every last sugary element seemingly extracted from the oak. My only sorrow for this whisky, given its American theme, was that it wasn't bottled as a 101 (ie 50.5% abv) instead of the rather underpowered

80 proof – because you have the feeling this would have become pretty three dimensional and leapt from the glass. And then down your throat with serious effect. *40%. nc ncf. WB15/171*

Compass Box The Entertainer Limited Edition bott Aug 12 **(88.5) n21.5 t22.5 f22 b22.** A pleasant blend, though the tanginess is perhaps a little too sharp. *46%. Compass Box Whisky Company. 1000 bottles. Commissioned by Selfridges.*

Compass Box Great King St. Artist's Blend (93) n24 t23 f22.5 b23.5. The nose of this uncoloured and non-chill filtered whisky is not dissimilar to some better known blends before they have colouring added to do its worst. A beautiful young thing this blend: nubile, naked and dangerously come hither. Compass Box's founder John Glaser has done some memorable work in recent years, though one has always had the feeling that he has still been learning his trade, sometimes forcing the issue a little too enthusiastically. Here, there is absolutely no doubting that he has come of age as a blender. *43%. nc ncf.*

Compass Box Great King Street Experimental Batch #00-V4 bott Sep 13 **(93) n22.5 t24 f23 b23.5.** A blend combining astonishing vibrancy with oaky Russian roulette. Not a dram to do things by halves... *43%. 3,439 bottles.*

Compass Box Great King Street Experimental Batch #TR-06 bott Sep 13 **(92) n22** the most dense of all the GKS I have yet tasted. All, including batch 00-V4 have shewn signs of younger malts offering a bright outlet. This, though, is a distant rumble, like highway traffic a mile off, of tannin, toast and smoke; **t23.5** unlike on the nose, the first to display is a sweet, buttery maltiness, mixed with the gentle elements of the grain. And there is sweet smoke, too which holds the middle until the tannins return; **f23** long, oily, with a smoked Demerara theme. The oak, though, rumbles and grumbles on; **b23.5** I think this one's been rumbled... *43%.*

Compass Box Great King Street Glasgow Blend (88.5) n22 playful phenols delight, but a strange wrong un of a note detracts and distracts; **t23.5** some clever interplay on delivery: the smoke appears to have its own way early on, but the grain clears a path of clarity, along which brighter, more honeyed notes occasionally travel; **f21** soft oils ensure a gentle landing, but those odd discordant notes detected on the nose bob up again, especially at the death; **b22** just the odd note seems out of place here and there: delicious but not the usual Compass Box precision. *43%*

◈ **Compass Box The Circus** bott Mar 16 **(93) n23** roll up, roll up and nose a fascinating juxtapositioning of the Fisherman's Friend-style smokiness with a sharp citric malt/grain mix...; **t23.5** eye-wateringly tart start: a strange mix of undercooked and overcooked jam tarts, with a smoked liquorice middle; **f23** remains, thick, dark and brooding: no high wires here – these are all base notes; **b23.5** Scotland's very own Clown Royal... *49%. nc ncf. 2,490 bottles.*

◈ **Compass Box This Is Not A Luxury Whisky** bott Aug 15 **(81) n20 t21.5 f19.5 b20.** Correct. *53.1%. nc ncf. 4,992 bottles.*

Consulate (89) n22 t22 f22.5 b22.5. One assumes this beautifully balanced dram was designed to accompany Passport in the drinks cabinet. I suggest if buying them, use Visa. *40%*

Co-operative Finest Blend (92.5) n23.5 t23 f22.5 b23.5 A fabulous and fascinating blend which has divested itself of its peaty backbone and instead packed the core with honey. Not the same heavyweight blend of old, but still one which is to be taken seriously – and straight – by those looking for a classic whisky of the old school. *40%*

Co-operative Premium Scotch 5 Years Old (91.5) n22 t24 f22.5 b23 From the nose I thought this blend had nosedived emphatically from when I last tasted it. However the delivery remains the stuff of legend. And though it has shifted emphasis and style to marked degree, there is no disputing its overall clout and entertainment value remains very high. *40%*

Craigellachie Hotel Quaich Bar Range (81) n20 t21 f20 b20. A delightful malt delivery early on, but doesn't push on with complexity as perhaps it might. *40%*

Crawford's (83.5) n19 t21 f22 b21.5. A lovely spice display helps overcome the caramel. *40%.*

Cutty Black (83) n20 t23 f19 b21. Both nose and finish are dwarfed and flung into the realms of ordinariness by the magnificently substantial delivery. Whilst there is a taint to the nose, its richness augers well for what is to follow; and you won't be disappointed. At times it behaves like a Highland Park with a toffeed spine, such is the richness and depth of the honey and dates and complexity of the grain-vanilla background. But those warning notes on the nose are there for good reason and the finish tells you why. Would not be surprised to see this score in the 90s on a different bottling day. *40%. Edrington.*

Cutty Sark (78) n19 t21 f19 b19. Crisp and juicy. But a nipping furriness, too. *40%*

Cutty Sark Aged 12 Years (92) n22 t24 f23 b23 At last! Cutty 12 at full sail...and blended whisky rarely looks any more beautiful! *40%. Edrington.*

Cutty Sark Aged 15 Years (82) n19 t22 f20 b21. Attempts to take the honey route. But seriously dulled by toffee and the odd sulphured cask. *40%. Edrington.*

Cutty Sark Aged 18 Years (88) n22 t22 f22 b22 Lost the subtle fruitiness which worked so well. Easy-going and attractive. *43%*

Cutty Sark Aged 25 Years (91) n21 t23.5 f22.5 b23 Magnificent, though not quite flawless, this whisky is as elegant and effortlessly powerful as the ship after which the brand was named... 45.7%. Berry Bros & Rudd.

Cutty Sark Storm (81.5) n18 t23.5 f19.5 b20.5. When the wind is set fair, which is mainly on delivery and for the first six or seven flavour waves which follow, we really do have an astonishingly beautiful blend, seemingly high in malt content and really putting the accent on ulmo honey and marzipan: a breath-taking combination. This is assisted by a gorgeous weight to the silky body and a light raspberry jam moment to the late arriving Ecuadorian cocoa. All magnificent. However, the blend, as Cutty sadly tends to, sails into sulphurous seas. 40%. Edrington.

Demijohn's Finest Blended Scotch Whisky (88) n21 t22 f23 b22 A fun, characterful blend that appears to have above the norm malt. Enjoy. 40%. Adelphi.

Dew of Ben Nevis Blue Label (82) n19 t22 f20 b21. The odd off-key note is handsomely outnumbered by deliciously complex mocha and demerara tones. Ditch the caramel and you'd have a sizzler! 40%. Ben Nevis Distillery. Replacement for Dew of Ben Nevis Millennium Blend.

Dew of Ben Nevis Special Reserve (85) n19 t21 f23 b22. A much juicier blend than of old, still sporting some bruising and rough patches. But that kind of makes this all the more attractive, with the caramel mixing with some fuller malts to provide a date and nuts effect which makes for a grand finale. 40%. Ben Nevis Distillery.

Dew of Ben Nevis Supreme Selection (77) n18 t20 f20 b19. Some lovely raspberry jam swiss roll moments here. But the grain could be friendlier, especially on the nose. 40%

Dewar's Special Reserve 12 Years Old (84) n20 t23 f19 b22. Some s... you know what... has crept onboard here and duffed up the nose and finish. A shame because elements of the delivery and background balance shows some serious blending went on here. 40%

Dewar's 18 Years Old (93) n23 t24 f22.5 b23.5 Here is a classic case of where great blends are not all about the malt. The grain plays in many ways the most significant role here, as it is the perfect backdrop to see the complexity of the malt at its clearest. Simply magnificent blending with the use of flawless whisky. 43%. John Dewar & Sons.

Dewar's 18 Year Old Founders Reserve (86.5) n22.5 t22 f20.5 b21.5. A big, blustering dram which doesn't stint on the fruit. A lovely, thin seam of golden syrup runs through the piece, but the dull, aching finale is somewhat out of character. 40%. John Dewar & Sons.

Dewar's Signature (93) n24 t23.5 f22 b23.5. A slight departure in style, with the fruit becoming just a little sharper and juicier. Top range blending and if the odd butt could be weeded out, this'd be an award winner for sure. 43%. John Dewar & Sons.

Dewar's White Label (78.5) n19 t21.5 f19 b19. When on song, one of my preferred daily blends. But not when like this, with its accentuated bitter-sweet polarisation. 40%

Dhoon Glen (85.5) n21 t22 f21 b21.5 Full of big flavours, broad grainy strokes and copious amounts of dark sugar including toffee. 40%. Lombard Brands Ltd.

Dimple 12 Years Old (86.5) n22 t22 f21.5 b21. Lots of sultana; the spice adds aggression. 40%.

Dimple 15 Years Old (87.5) n20 t21 f24 b22.5. Only on the late middle and finish does this particular flower unfurl and to magnificently complex effect. The texture of the grains in particular delight while the strands of barley entwine. A type of treat for the more technically minded of the serious blend drinkers among you. 40%. Diageo.

Drummer (81) n20 t21 f20 b20. Big toffee. Rolos...? 40%. Inver House Distillers.

Drummer Aged 5 Years (83) n19 t22.5 f20.5 b21. The nose may beat a retreat but it certainly gets on a roll when those fabulous sharp notes hit the palate. However, it deserves some stick as the boring fudge finishes in a cymbal of too much toffee. 40%. Inver House.

The Famous Grouse (89) n22 t23 f21.5 b22.5 It almost seems that Grouse is, by degrees, moving from its traditional position of a light blend to something much closer to Grant's as a middle-weighted dram. Again the colouring has been raised a fraction and now the body and depth have been adjusted to follow suit. Have to say that this is one very complex whisky these days: I had spotted slight changes when drinking it socially, but this was the first time I had a chance to sit down and professionally analyse what was happening in the glass. A fascinating and tasty bird, indeed. 40%. Edrington Group.

The Famous Grouse Aged 16 Years Special 2013 Edition (84) n22 t22 f19 b21. A completely different type of Grouse which on one hand offers a pretty comprehensive guide of the sugar shelves, yet somehow manages, for all its apparent esters, to bitter out violently at the finish. Intriguing, to put it mildly. 40%. Edrington Group.

The Famous Grouse Gold Reserve (90) n23.5 t23 f21.5 b22 Great to know the value of the Gold Reserve is going up...as should the strength of this blend. The old-fashioned 40% just ain't enough carats. 40%. Edrington Group.

The Famous Grouse Married Strength (82.5) n19 t22 f20 b21.5. The nose is nutty and toffeed. But despite the delightful, silky sweetness and gentle Speyside-style maltiness which forms the main markers for this soft blend, the nose, like the finish, also shows a little bitter furriness has, sadly, entered into the mix. Not a patch on the standard Grouse of a decade ago. *45.9% WB16/019*

The Famous Grouse Mellow Gold sherry & bourbon casks **(85) n20 t23.5 f20 b21.5**. While the nose and finish tell us a little too much about the state of the sherry butts used, there is no harm tuning into the delivery and follow though which are, unquestionably, beautiful. The texture is silk normally found on the most expensive lingerie, and as sexy as who you might find inside it; while the honey is a fabulous mix of ulmo and orange blossom. *40%*

◈ **The Famous Grouse Smoky Black (87) n22 t22 f21 b22**. Black Grouse by any other name. Flawed in the usual tangy, furry Grouse fashion. But have to say there is a certain roughness and randomness about the sugars that I find very appealing. A smoky style that Bowmore lovers might enjoy. A genuinely beautiful, smoky, ugly, black duckling. Sorry, I mean Grouse. *40%*

The Famous Jubilee (83.5) n21.5 t22.5 f18.5 b21. A heavyweight, stodgy, toffee-laden kind of blend a long way from the Grouse tradition. With its ham-fisted date and walnut middle I would have sworn this was the work of another blender entirely. There are redeeming rich honey tones that are a joy. But the dull, pulsing sulphur on the finish has almost an air of inevitability. I promise you this: go back 60 years, and there would have been no blend created with this signature...not only did the style not exist, but it would have been impossible to accomplish. *40%. Edrington.*

The Formidable Jock of Bennachie (82) n19 t22 f21 b20. "Scotland's best kept secret" claims the label. Hardly. But the silky delivery on the palate is worth investigating. Impressive roastiness to the malt and oak, but the caramel needs thinning. *40%. Bennachie Scotch Whisky.*

Fort Glen The Blender's Reserve Aged 12 Years (88.5) n21.5 t23 f21.5 b22.5 An entirely enjoyable blend which is clean and boasting decent complexity and weight. *40%*

Fort Glen The Distiller's Reserve (78) n18 t22 f19 b19. Juicy, salivating delivery as it storms the ramparts. Draws down the portcullis elsewhere. *40%. The Fort Glen Whisky Company.*

Fraser MacDonald (85) n21 t21.5 f21 b21.5. Some fudge towards the middle and end but the journey there is an enjoyable one. *40%. Loch Lomond Distillers.*

Gairloch (79) n19 t20 f20 b20. For those who like their butterscotch at 40% abv. *40%*

◈ **Gleann Mór Blended Whisky 18 Year Old (87) n21.5 t23 f20.5 b22**. A few passages in this are outstanding, especially when the delicate honey appears to collide with the softest smoke. A slight bitterness does jar somewhat, though the softness of the grain is quite seriously seductive *43.9%*

◈ **Glenalba Aged 22 Years Sherry Cask Finish** batch no. JS/322, lot no. 0745C, dist 1993 **(90) n22** hard to get past the clean grape. No bite. No layering, as such. Just very pleasant fruit..., perhaps with chocolate shavings; **t23.5** silky delivery: about as soft and caressing as whisky comes. The grains must be at work here, for the grape has a rounded, airy feel that is not at all common. Hard to distinguish the malt and the course it is trying to take; **f23.5** a rather superb mix of chocolate and sherry...rather like an expensive Belgium liqueur...; **b21** a pristine sherry effect. No off notes whatsoever. If there is a downside, it is the fact that the sherry evens out the complexity of the blend. I mean, surely...that has to be the purpose of a blend: complexity and balance, right....? That said, for the experience alone...all rather lovely and deserving of further exploration...! *40%*

◈ **Glenalba Aged 25 Years Sherry Cask Finish** batch no. SE/425, lot no. 0274J, dist 1990 **(89) n22** salty, seaweedy but the sherry is almost glutinous...; **t23.5** wow! What's not to love about this? Intense grape, like the 22-year-old slowly giving way to high percentage cocoa – and that liqueur effect is in full swing; **f22.5** the drying experience gets even drier; **b21.5** a lovely whisky, though again the unreconstructed sherry effect does few favours to the overall layering and balance. Maybe the vaguest hint of something with the 'S' word, though very low key... *40%*

◈ **Glenalba Aged 34 Years Sherry Cask Finish** batch no. JM/012, lot no. 0862B, dist 1981 **(95.5) n24** now that is one hell of a sherry-infested nose: exceptionally clean, high quality butts only deployed here. And this one allows the layering and structure demanded of a high-class blend: it is not all about the grape. A few telling tannin notes filter through, but it is the malt, clearly recognisable under a slightly salty skin, which really ramps up the complexity; **t24** magnificent! Gosh, where does one begin?! A beautiful liquid Jaffa Cake effect, with the fruit converting into tangy citrus, under a crisp cocoa shell; something akin to smoke makes a meandering appearance. But the spices are so busy yet beautifully balanced against the softness of the grape; **f23.5** long and perfectly assisted by the light oils which coat the palate with the high class sherry. The spices buzz with contentment, while a late interplay of tannin and malt underlines lingering complexity; **b24** a beautifully dry, sophisticated blend. Benefits from the use of what is about as good a sherry butt as I have encountered: not even the hint of a hint of an off-note. Where the 22 and 25 year editions are rather overcome by the magnitude of the grape, this one has enough in reserve to take the sherry in its stride and use it to excellent effect. Truly superb Scotch. *40%*

Glen Brynth (70.5) **n18 t19 f16 b17.5.** Bitter and awkward. *43%*

Glenbrynth 8 Year Old (88) **n21.5 t22 f22.5 b22.** An impressive blend which improves second by second on the palate. *40%. OTI Africa.*

Glenbrynth Pearl 30 Year Old Limited Edition (90.5) **n22.5 t23.5 f21.5 b23** Attractive, beautifully weighted, no off notes...though perhaps quietened by toffee. Still a treat of a blend. *43%. OTI Africa.*

Glen Gray (84.5) **n20 t22.5 f21 b21.** A knife and fork blend you can stand your spoon in. Plain going for most of the way, but the area between delivery and middle enjoys several waves of rich chocolate honeycomb...and some of the cocoa resurfaces at the finale. *43%*

Glen Lyon (85) **n19 t22.5 f22 b21.5.** Works a lot better than the nose suggests: seriously chewy with a rabid spice attack and lots of juices. For those who have just retired as dynamite testers. Unpretentious fun. *43%. Diageo.*

Glen Orrin Aged 5 Years (77) **n19 t21 f18 b19.** Glen Orrible more like. A step up from the no age statement version, thanks mainly to a very delicate underlying smokiness. But the core malt is still of that ilk that will drive people to bourbon. *40%. Aldi.*

Glen Orin 30 Years old Blend (95) **n24 t24 f23 b24** a clean, charming blend from the old school and of a style too rarely seen today, alas. The accent, as it should be, is on the grain, and its very brittleness accentuates just how delicate this whisky is. A perfect pre-prandial dram to be taken straight and at body temperature, without water or ice, so its astonishing complexity can be fully explored. Or very late at night when you might find time for all its mysteries to unravel. Top notch Scotch where subtlety is the watchword. Delicacy and understatement is the key; yet with enough life and juiciness to entertain even the most fatigued taste buds. Truly outstanding. *40%. Aldi.*

Glen Talloch Choice Rare & Old (85.5) **n20.5 t22.5 f21 b21.5.** A very pleasing sharpness to the delivery reveals the barley in all its Speyside-style finery, The grain itself is soothing, especially when the caramel notes kick in. *40%. ncf.*

Glen Talloch Gold Aged 12 Years (85) **n21 t22 f21 b21.** Impressive grain at work insuring a deft, velvety caress to the palate. Mainly caramel speaking, despite the age, though there is an attractive spice buzz towards the thin-ish finish. *40%*

⟐ **Glory Leading Aged 32 Years** (88.5) **n22.5** just get a load of those beautifully spiced apples and pears...; **t22.5** an alloy of some of the softest grains in the market means the malt has a problem establishing a foothold. The early imbalance stabilises as the spices begin their assault, the malt following in timidly behind; **f21.5** much better balance now: outstanding spice radiation plus some beguiling soft malt. A strange tobacco note at the death; **b22** at times a little heavy handed and out of sync. But the overall experience is one of stunningly spiced enjoyment. *43%*

Glory Leading Blended Scotch Whisky 30 Years Old American oak casks (93) **n22.5 t23 f23.5 b24** a big, clever, satisfying blend which just gets better and better... though not too sure about the Crystal Palace style eagle on the label. Even so, love it! *43%*

Golden Piper (86.5) **n22 t21 f22 b21.5.** A firm, clean blend with a steady flush through of diverse sugars. The grain does all the steering and therefore complexity is limited. But the overall freshness is a delight. *43%. Whisky Shack.*

Grand Sail (87) **n21 t22 f22 b22.** Sweet, attractive with enough bite to really matter. *40%*

Grand Sail Aged 10 Years (79) **n20 t22 f18 b19.** Pleasant and at times fascinating but with a tang that perhaps the next vatting will benefit from losing. *40%. China market.*

Grand Sail Rare Reserve Aged 18 Years (94) **n23 t24 f23 b24.** A truly beautiful whisky which cuts effortlessly and elegantly through the taste buds. *40% Angus Dundee. China market.*

Glenross Blended (83) **n20 t22 f20 b21.** Decent, easy-drinking whisky with a much sharper delivery than the nose suggests. *40%. Speyside Distillers.*

Glen Simon (77) **n20 t19 f19 b19.** Simple. Lots of caramel. *40%. Quality Spirits International.*

The Gordon Highlanders (86) **n21 t22 f21 b22.** Lush and juicy, there is a distinctive Speysidey feel to this one with the grains doing their best to accentuate the developing spice. Plenty of feel good factor here. *40%. William Grant & Sons.*

Grand Macnish (79) **n19 t21 f19 b20.** Welcome back to an old friend...but the years have caught up with it. Still on the feral side, but has exchanged its robust good looks for an unwashed and unkempt appearance on the palate. Will do a great job to bring some life back to you, though. *43%. MacDuff International Ltd.*

Grand Macnish 12 Years Old (86) n21 t22 f21.5 b21.5. A grander Grand Macnich than of old with the wonderful feather pillow delivery maintained and a greater harmonisation of the malt, especially those which contain a honey-copper sheen. *40%. MacDuff.*

Grant's Aged 12 Years bott 30/09/10 **(89.5)** n23 t23 f21.5 b22 Can't argue too much with the tasting notes on the label (although I contend that "full, rich and rounded" has more to do with its body than taste, but that is by the by). Beautiful whisky, as can be reasonably expected from a Grant's blend. If only the sharpness could last the distance. *40%.*

Grant's Cask Edition No.1 Ale Cask Finish Edinburgh ale casks **(88.5)** n22 t23 f21.5 b22. Aways loved this concept: a whisky and chaser in one bottle. This was has plenty of cheer in the complex opening, but gets maudlin towards the end. *40%. William Grant & Sons.*

Great MacCauley (81) n20 t20.5 f20 b20.5. Reminds me of another whisky I tasted earlier: Castle Rock, I think. Identical profile with toffee & spice adding to the juicy & youthful fun. *40%.*

Green Plaid 12 Years Old (89) n22 t23 f22 b22 Beautifully constructed; juicy. *40%.*

Guneagal Aged 12 Years (85.5) n21 t22.5 f20.5 b21.5. The salty, sweaty armpit nose gives way to an even saltier delivery, helped along by sweet glycerine and a boiled candy fruity sweetness. The finish is a little roughhouse by comparison. *40%. William Grant & Sons.*

Haddington House (85.5) n21 t21.5 f22 b21. Mouth-watering and delicate. *40%*

Haig Gold Label (88) n21 t23 f22 b22 What had before been pretty standard stuff has upped the complexity by an impressive distance. *40%. Diageo.*

Hankey Bannister (84.5) n20.5 t22 f21 b21. Lots of early life and even a malt kick early on. Toffee later. *40%. Inverhouse Distillers.*

Hankey Bannister 12 Years Old (86.5) n22 t21.5 f21 b22. A much improved blend with a nose and early delivery which makes full play of the blending company's Speyside malts. Plenty of toffee on the finish. *40%. Inverhouse Distillers.*

Hankey Bannister Regency 12 Year Old (84.5) n22.5 t22 f19 b21 Plenty of honey and some fine, silky structuring. Just a tad too bitter and furry on the finish, though. *40%.*

Hankey Bannister 21 Years Old (95) n23.5 a fruity ensemble, clean, vibrant and loath to show its age **t24** as juicy as the nose suggests, except for the odd rumble of distant smoke; a firm, barley-sugar hardness as the grains keep control; **f23.5** the arrival of the oak adds further weight and for the first time begins to behave like a 21-y-o; long, now with decent spice and with some crusty dryness at the very death; **b24** with top dressing like this and some obviously complex secondary malts, too, how can it fail? *43%.*

Hankey Bannister 25 Years Old (91) n22.5 t24 f21.5 b23 Follows on in style and quality to 21-year-old. Gorgeous. *40%*

Hankey Bannister 40 Years Old (89) n22 t23 f22 b22. This blend has been put together to mark the 250th anniversary of the forging of the business relations between Messrs. Hankey and Bannister. And although the oak creaks like a ship of its day, there is enough verve and viscosity to ensure a rather delicious toast to the gentlemen. Love it! *44%. Inverhouse.*

Hankey Bannister 40 Year Old (94) n23.5 t23.5 f23 b24. Pure quality. The attention to detail is sublime. *44.3%. Inverhouse Distillers.*

Hankey Bannister Heritage (84.5) n21 t22 f20.5 b21. So softly spoken sometimes you struggle to hear it. Makes a juicy, malty chuntering mid-way through, though. *46%.*

Hankey Bannister Heritage Blend (92) n23 despite the evidence of sherry the spiced chocolate fudge keeps you spellbound; **t24** at moments like this, one's taste buds are purely in love. They are being caressed, serenaded and kisses by the most glorious of old grains, encrusted with a Speyside-syle maltiness which makes you purr with pleasure; **f22** the weakness on the nose returns, though sparingly. Outstanding late Malteser candy style confirms a very decent malt depth; **b23** just so soft and sensual... *46%. Inverhouse Distillers.*

Harveys Lewes Blend Eight Year Old (89.5) n23 t23.5 f20.5 b22.5 When a blend is this good you can forgive them the missing apostrophe... A superb whisky, despite its unfortunate hiccup, from a gem of a British brewery. *40%.*

⟐ **Harveys Lewes Blend Eight Year Old** batch 4 **(93)** n23.5 it is amazing what a clever introduction of smoke, sharpened with a hint of liquorice, can do to a blend if not overdone. Earthy, weighty...yet that is only the base to a sophisticated higher symphony vanilla and demerara led mix of grains and malts; memorable; **t23** lush delivery. Superb grain arrival, coating the palate with friendly vanillas, while the smoke bounces about always with a sweet edge; always borderline salivating; **f23** long, with the phenols now tingling in spice form. Drier oak is gentle but has a say, but the juiciness persists; **b23.5** first tasted this in the front parlour of legendary Harvey's brewer Miles Jenner's home just after Christmas. It tasted quite different from their previous bottlings – and quite superb. Nosed and tasted now several months on in the cold analytical light of a tasting room...helped along with that deft addition of subtle peat, it still does. Superb! *40%*

⁂ **Hazelwood 18 Year Old (88)** n23.5 top-notch dispersal of subtle notes: walnut cream cake with a pinch of vanilla. The malt is low key but distinctly Speyside-style in its clarity, despite the odd wisp of something a little heavier; **t22.5** creamy-textured. Soft ulmo honey gives way to the thickening vanilla and toffee; **f20.5** bitters slightly at the turned-up ending; **b22** until the final furry moments, a genuine little, understated, charmer. 40%. *William Grant & Sons.*

⁂ **Hazelwood 21 Year Old (74)** n19 t20 f17 b18. Some decent acacia honey tries to battle against the bitter imbalance. 40%. *William Grant & Sons.*

⁂ **Hazelwood 25 Year Old (89.5)** n22 full on fruit underscored by the muscular tannins: simple, but satisfying; **t23** wonderful delivery: a momentous mix of muscovado and maple syrup but with the toasty tannins offering an even more roasty depth; **f22** a slight, non-spiced buzz to the finish. But that roastiness − akin to burnt fudge − gives much to chew over; **b22.5** distinctly chunky. 40%. *William Grant & Sons.*

Hedges & Butler Royal (92) n22.5 t23.5 f23 b23 Massively improved to become a juicy and charming blend of the very highest order. 40%.

High Commissioner (88.5) n22.5 t22.5 f20.5 b22.5 Now I admit I had a hand in cleaning this brand up a couple of years back, giving it a good polish and much needed balance complexity. But I don't remember leaving it in quite this good a shape. Just a bitter semi-off note on the finish, otherwise this guy would have been in the 90s. What a great fun, three-course dram this is... 40%. *Loch Lomond Distillers.*

Highland Baron (85.5) n21 t22 f21 b21.5. A very clean, sweet and competent young blend showing admirable weight and depth. 40%. *Loch Lomond Distillers.*

Highland Bird (77) n19 t19 f19 b20. I've has a few of these over the years, I admit. But I can't remember one quite as rough and ready as this... 40%. *Quality Spirits International.*

Highland Black 8 Years Old Special Reserve (85.5) n22 t22.5 f20 b21. A lovely blend which has significantly improved since my last encounter with it. A touch too much grain on the finish for greatness, perhaps. But the nose and delivery both prosper from a honey-roast almond sweetness. 40%. *Aldi.*

Highland Dream 12 Years Old bott Jan 05 **(94.5)** n23.5 t24 f23 b24. Now that is what I call a blend! How comes it has taken me two years to find it? A wet dream, if ever there was one... 43%. *J & G Grant. 9000 bottles.*

Highland Dream 18 Years Old bott May 07 **(88.5)** n22.5 t22.5 f21.5 b22. Perhaps doesn't get the marks on balance that a whisky of this quality might expect. This is due to the slight over egging of the sherry which, while offering a beautiful delivery, masks the complexities one might expect. Lovely whisky, and make no mistake. But, technically, doesn't match the 12-year-old for balance and brilliance. 43%. *J & G Grant. 3000 bottles.*

Highland Earl (77) n19 t20 f19 b19. Might have marked it higher had it called itself a grain: the malt is silent. 40%. *Aldi.*

Highland Gathering Blended Scotch Whisky (78) n19 t20 f19 b20. Attractive, juicy stuff, though caramel wins in the end. 40%. *Lombards Brands.*

Highland Glendon (87.5) n21.5 t22.5 f21.5 b22 An honest, simple but effectively attractive blend. 43%. *Quality Spirits International.*

Highland Harvest Organic Scotch Whisky (76) n18 t21 f19 b18. A very interesting blend. Great try, but a little bit of a lost opportunity here as I don't think the balance is quite right. But at least I now know what organic caramel tastes like... 40%

Highland Mist (88.5) n20.5 t23 f22.5 b22.5 Fabulously fun whisky bursting from the bottle with character and mischief. Had to admit, broke all my own rules and just had to have a glass of this after doing the notes... 40%. *Loch Lomond Distillers.*

Highland Piper (79) n20 t20 f19 b20. Good quaffing blend − if sweet - of sticky toffee and dates. Some gin on the nose − and finish. 40%

Highland Pride (86) n21 t22 f21.5 b21.5. A beefy, weighty thick dram with plenty to chew on. The developing sweetness is a joy. 40%. *Whyte & Mackay Distillers Ltd.*

Highland Queen db **(88.5)** n22 classic grain, clean, soft and a little toffeed; **t22.5** no less classically silky and soft: again a bit toffee heavy, but not so much that you can't revel in this brief burst of Speyside-style malt bursting through for a quick, juicy blast; **f22** long and remains silky soft; **b22** this is a young blend, so maybe the controlled toffee inclusion can be forgiven as the whole works beautifully well. An improved whisky by some way. 40%

Highland Queen Blended Scotch Whisky (86.5) n22 t21 f21.5 b22. Lots of grains at play here. But what grains?! Clean and crisp with a superb bite which balances the softening mouth feel attractively. Old fashioned and delicious. 40%

Highland Queen Aged 8 Years Blended Scotch Whisky (90) n22.5 t23.5 f21.5 b22.5. Lots of entertainment value from a high quality whisky. The blender has done a great job in the lab. 43%

Highland Queen Aged 12 Years Blended Scotch Whisky (87) n22 t22 f21 b22. A polite, slightly more sophisticated version of the 8-year-old...but without the passion and drama! 40%

Highland Reserve (82) n20 t21 f20 b21. You'll probably find this just off the Highland Way and incorporating Highland Bird and Monarch of the Glen. Floral and muddy. 40%

Highland Reserve Aged 12 Years (87) n21 t22 f22 b22 Anyone who has tasted Monarch of the Glen 12 will appreciate this. Maybe a bit more fizz here, though, despite the big caramel. 43%. Quality Spirits International.

Highland Warrior (77.8) n19 t19 f19.5 b20. Just like his Scottish Chief, he's on the attack armed with some Dufftown, methinks... 40%. Quality Spirits International.

Highland Way (84) n19 t20.5 f22.5 b22. This lovely little number takes the High Road with some beautiful light scenery along the way. The finish takes a charming Speyside path. 40%

Inverarity Limited Edition cask no. 698, dist 1997, bott 2009 (84.5) n20.5 t22 f21 b21. A heady, heavy-duty blend where honeycomb rules on the palate and thick dates offer a more intense sweetness. But don't go looking for subtlety or guile: those whose palates have been educated at the Whyte and Mackay school of delicate sophistication will have a ball. 40%

Islay Mist 8 Years Old (84) n20 t22 f21 b21. Turned into one heavy duty dram since last tasting a couple of years back. This appears to absorb everything it touches leaving one chewy, smoky hombre. Just a little tangy at the end. 40%. MacDuff International Ltd.

Islay Mist 12 Years Old (90) n22 t23 f22 b23. Adore it: classic bad cop - good cop stuff with an apparent high malt content. 40%

Islay Mist 17 Years Old (92.5) n22.5 t23.5 f23 b23.5 Always a cracking blend, this has improved of late into a genuine must have. 40%. MacDuff International Ltd.

Islay Mist Delux (85) n21.5 t22 f21.5 b20. Remains a highly unusual blend with the youthful peat now more brilliant than before, though the sugar levels appear to have risen markedly. 40%

Isle of Skye 8 Years Old (94) n23 t24 f23.5 b23.5. Where once peat ruled and with its grain ally formed a smoky iron fist, now honey and subtlety reigns. A change of character and pace which may disappoint gung-ho peat freaks but will intrigue and delight those looking for a more sophisticated dram. 40%. Ian Macleod.

Isle of Skye 21 years Old (91) n21 t23.5 f23 b23.5 What an absolute charmer! The malt content appears pretty high, but the overall balance is wonderful. 40%. Ian Macleod.

Isle of Skye 50 Years Old (82.5) n21.5 t21 f20 b20. Drier incarnation than the 50% version. But still the age has yet to be balanced out, towards the end in particular. Early on some distinguished moments involving something vaguely smoked and a sweetened spice. 41.6%

The Jacobite (78.5) n18 t18.5 f22 b20. Neither the nose or delivery are of the cleanest style. But comes into its own towards the finish when the thick soup of a whisky thins to allow an attractive degree of complexity. Not for those with catholic tastes. 40%. Booker.

Jackson McCloud Premium Blended Scotch Whisky (81) n20 t21 f20 b20. Absolutely standard fare, full of grainy bite and caramel. 40%. Galleon Liqueurs.

Jackson McCloud Rare Batch Blended Scotch Whisky (85.5) n20 t22.5 f22 b21. Pleasant, but with little or no effort to overcome the dominating grain. As it happens, it turns out to be pretty decent silky grain with some attractive fruit notes. 40%. Galleon Liqueurs.

James Alexander (85.5) n21 t21.5 f21.5 b21.5. Some lovely spices link the grassier Speysiders to the earthier elements. 40%. Quality Spirits International.

James King (76.5) n20 t18 f20 b18.5. Young whiskies of a certain rank take their time to find their feet. The finish, though, does generate some pleasant complexity. 43%

James King Aged 5 Years (85) n21 t21.5 f21 b21.5. Very attractive, old fashioned and well weighted with a pleasing degree of fat and chewy sweetness and chocolate fudge. Refreshingly good quality distillate and oak have been used in this: I'd drink it any day. 40%

James King 8 Years Old (78.5) n18.5 t21.5 f19 b19.5. Charming spices grip at the delivery and fine malt-grain interplay through the middle, even showing a touch of vanilla. But such a delicate blend can't fully survive the caramel. 43%. Quality Spirits International.

James King 12 Years Old (81) n19 t23 f19 b20. Caramel dulls the nose and finish. But for some time a quite beautiful blend soars about the taste buds offering exemplary complexity and weight. 40%. Quality Spirits International.

James King 15 Years Old (89) n22 t23 f21.5 b22.5. Now offers extra spice and zip. 43%

James King 21 Years Old (87.5) n20.5 t23.5 f22 b22. Attractive blend, but one that could do with the strength upped to 46% and the caramel reduced if not entirely got rid of. One of those potentially excellent yet underperforming guys I'd love to be let loose on! 43%

James Martin 20 Years Old (93) n21 t23.5 f24.5 b24. I had always regarded this as something of an untamed beast. No longer: still something of a beast, but a beautiful one that is among the most complex found on today's market. 43%. Glenmorangie.

James Martin 30 Years Old (86) n21.5 t22 f21 b21.5. Enjoyable for all its exotic fruitiness. But with just too many creaking joints to take it to the same level as the sublime 20-y-o. Even so, a blend worth treating with a touch of respect and allowing time for it to tell some pretty ancient tales... 43%. Glenmorangie.

J&B Jet (79.5) n19 t20 f20.5 b20. Never quite gets off the ground due to carrying too heavy a load. Unrecognisable to its pomp in the old J&B days: this one is far too weighty and never properly finds either balance or thrust. 40%. Diageo.

J&B Reserve Aged 15 Years (78) n23 t19 f18 b18. What a crying shame. The sophisticated and demure nose is just so wonderfully seductive but what follows is an open-eyed, passionless embrace. Coarsely grain-dominant and unbalanced, this is frustrating beyond words and not worthy to be mentioned in the same breath as the old, original J&B 15 which, by vivid contrast, was a malty, salivating fruit-fest and minor classic. 40%. Diageo.

J&B Rare (88.5) n21.5 t22.5 f22 b22.5 I have been drinking a lot of J&B from a previous time of late, due to the death of their former blender Jim Milne. I think he would have been pretty taken aback by the youthful zip offered here: whether it is down to a decrease in age or the use of slightly more tired casks – or both – is hard to say. 40%. Diageo.

Jim McEwan's Blended Whisky (86.5) n20 t22 f22.5 b22. Juicy and eye-watering with clever late spices. 46%. Bruichladdich.

John Barr (85.5) n20 t22 f21.5 b22. I assume from the big juicy dates to be found that Fettercairn is at work. Outwardly a big bruiser; given time to state its case and it's a bit of a gentle giant. 40%. Whyte & Mackay Distillers Ltd.

Johnnie Walker Black Label 12 Years Old (95.5) n23.5 pretty sharp grain: hard and buffeting the nose; a buffer of yielding smoke, apple pie and delicate spice cushions the encounter; t24.5 if there is a silkier delivery on the market today, I have not seen it: this is sublime stuff with the grains singing the sweetest hymns as they go down, taking with them a near perfection of weighty smoke lightened by brilliantly balanced barley which leans towards both soft apple and crème broulee; f23.5 those reassuringly rigid grains re-emerge and with them the most juicy Speysidey malts imaginable; the lovely sheen to the finish underlines the good age of the whiskies used; b24 here it is: one of the world's most masterful whiskies back in all its complex glory. A bottle like this is like being visited by an old lover. It just warms the heart and excites. 40%. Diageo.

Johnnie Walker Blue Label (88) n21 t24 f21 b22 What a frustrating blend! Just so close to brilliance but the nose and finish are slightly out of kilter. Worth the experience of the mouth arrival alone. 43%. Diageo.

Johnnie Walker Blue Label The Casks Edition (97) n24.5 t24.5 f23.5 b24.5. This is a triumph of scotch whisky blending. With not as much as a hint of a single off note to be traced from the tip of the nose to tail, this shameless exhibition of complexity and brilliance is the star turn in the Diageo portfolio right now. Indeed, it is the type of blend that every person who genuinely adores whisky must experience for the good of their soul....if only once in their life. 55.8%.

Johnnie Walker Double Black (94.5) n23 t23.5 f24 b24. Double tops! Rolling along the taste buds like distant thunder, this is a welcome and impressive addition to the Johnnie Walker stable. Perhaps not as complete and rounded as the original Johnnie Walker Black... but, then, what is? 40%.

Johnnie Walker Explorers' Club Collection The Gold Route (89) n23.5 t24 f19.5 b22. Much of this blend is truly the stuff of golden dreams. Like its Explorer's Club stable mate, some attention has to be paid to the disappointing finish. Worth sending out an expedition, though, just for the beautiful nose and delivery... 40%. Diageo.

Johnnie Walker Explorer's Club Collection 'The Royal Route' (93) n24.5 t24 f21.5 b23 A fabulous journey, travelling first Class most of the way. But to have discovered more, could have been bottled at 46% for a much more panoramic view of the great whiskies on show. 40%. Diageo

Johnnie Walker Explorers' Club Collection The Spice Road (84.5) n22 t23.5 f18 b21. Sublime delivery of exceptionally intense juiciness: in fact, probably the juiciest blend released this year. But the bitter, fuzzy finish reveals certain casks haven't helped. 40%.

Johnnie Walker Gold Label Reserve (91.5) n23 t24 f22 b23. Moments of true star quality here, but the finish could do with a polish. 40%. Diageo.

Johnnie Walker King George V db (88) n23 t22 f21 b22 One assumes that King George V is no relation to George IV. This has genuine style and breeding, if a tad too much caramel. 43%

Johnnie Walker Platinum Label Aged 18 Years (88) n22 t23 f21 b22. This blend might sound like some kind of Airmiles card. Which wouldn't be too inappropriate, though this is more Business than First... 40%. Diageo.

Johnnie Walker Red Label (87.5) n22 t22 f21.5 b22. The ongoing move through the scales quality-wise appears to suggest we have a work still in progress here. This sample has skimped on the smoke, though not quality. Yet a few months back when I was in the BA Business Lounge at Heathrow's new Terminal Five, I nearly keeled from almost being overcome by peat in the earthiest JW Red I had tasted in decades. I found another bottle and I'm still not sure which represents the real Striding Man. 40%. *Diageo.*

Johnnie Walker Select Casks Aged 10 Years Rye Cask Finish (90) n22.5 curiously, more Canadian than ol' Kentucky! The rye definitely nibbles deepest and earliest. But there is a distinctive corny feel I didn't expect which begins to dominate. Also, look out for a sharp tangerine and ground pistachio note. Very different; **t23** a curious delivery: both hard and soft tones try to baffle the taste buds. The predominant note is one of crisp sugars, not surprisingly tinged with a deep tannin note; citrus still to be had; **f21.5** a little bitter and sketchy once the sugars wear thin; the spices, though, are sincere and busy; **b23** with the use of first fill bourbon casks and ex-rye barrels for finishing, hardly surprising this is the Johnnie Walker with the most Kentuckian feel of them all. Yet it's even more Canadian, still. 46% (92 Proof)

Johnnie Walker X.R Aged 21 Years (94) n23.5 t24 f23 b23.5. How weird: I nosed this blind before seeing what the brand was. My first thought was: "mmm, same structure of Crown Royal XR. Canadian???" No, there's smoke!" Then looked at what was before me and spotted it was its sister whisky from the Johnnie Walker stable. A coincidence? I don't think so... 40%.

⬦ **John Walker & Sons Private Collection 2014 Edition (90) n23.5** the odd clump of peat here and there mingles with a fascinating vegetable note: lovely, but not remotely what I was expecting...; **t23.5** stupendous delivery! Such clever use of malts: the grist positively dances on the tongue, resulting in full blown salivation. Indeed, for a blend, the malt input is exceptional, if a little one sided; **f21** dulls out with vanilla and even bitters up slightly and rather annoyingly after all that earlier complexity; **b22** delicious and frustrating in equal measure. 46.8%

⬦ **John Walker & Sons Private Collection 2015 Edition (95.5) n24** this is sublime: blood orange, heather honey and vague phenols offering an earthier richness; **t24** one of the softest deliveries of the year, showing some serious age as the vanillas have a real vintage air about them; the malt is yielding, the fruits a little more ripe...lastly, ulmo honey ensuring the spice has balancing company for the finale; **f23.5** ulmo honey and spice still, with a distant and vague furry feel to the fruit; **b24** possibly one less than perfect cask away from World Whisky of the Year... 46.8%

Kenmore Special Reserve Aged 5 Years bott code L07285 **(75) n18 t20 f19 b18.** Recovers to a degree from the poor nose. A must-have for those who prefer their Scotch big-flavoured and gawky. 40%

Kingsbury Gold Mhain Baraille 1980 32 Year Old diss 1980 **(92) n23 t23.5 f22.5 b23.** A distinguished blend with just a little grey around the temples... A rather brilliant first bending attempt by Kingsbury after all these years. 473%. nc ncf. Cask Strength. 424 bottles.

King Glenorsen (81) n20 t21 f20 b20. Pleasant and easy drinking enough. But the young grains dominate completely. Designed, I think, to be neutralised by ice. 40%

King Robert II (77) n19 t19 f20 b19. A bustier, more bruising batch than the last 40 per cent version. Handles the OTT caramel much better. Agreeably weighty slugging whisky. 43%.

Kings Blended 3 Years Old (83) n21 t21.5 f20 b20.5. A young, chunky blend that you can chew forever. 40%. *Speyside Distillers.*

King's Crest Scotch Whisky 25 Years Old (83) n22 t22 f19 b20. A silky middle weight. The toffee-flat finish needs some attention because the softly estered nose and delivery is a honey-rich treat and deserves better. 40%. *Speyside Distillers.*

Kirkland Blended Whisky 21 Year Old (84.5) n21 t22 f20.5 b21. Frustrating stuff: hard to see what's going on through all the caramel. 40%. *Bottled for Costco.*

Kirkland Blended Whisky 24 Year Old (87) n22 t22 f21.5 b21.5. A weighty blend with some attractive oaky moments on the nose to underscore the age and chewy fudge after the hefty, though controlled, tannin arrival. Mild mocha on the fade. 40%.

Label 5 Aged 18 Years (84.5) n20.5 t22 f21 b21. A big mouthful and mouth-feel. Has changed course since I last had this one. Almost a feel of rum to this with its estery sheen. Sweet, simple, easy dramming. 40%. *La Martiniquaise, France.*

Label 5 Classic Black (75) n18 t20 f18 b19. The off-key nose needs some serious re-working. Drop the caramel, though, and you would have a lot more character. Needs some buffing. 40%. *The First Blending for La Martiniquaise, France.*

Label 5 Classic Black bott code L3060 **(84.5) n20.5 t22 f21 b21.** A better whisky than when last tasted with more even use of the date and walnut theme. Caramel still substantial, but complexity levels are higher. 40%. *La Martiniquaise, France.*

Label 5 Classic Black bott code L3084 **(83.5) n**20 **t**21.5 **f**21 **b**21. Like L3060. Except the nose is even harsher and here the grain have a much more jarring effect. *40%*.

Label 5 Classic Black bott code L3144 **(85) n**20.5 **t**22 **f**21 **b**21.5. Stays in the same areas as two previous bottlings, but slightly better use of spices. Still needs a nose job, though... 40%.

Label 5 Gold Heritage (92) n22.5 a tad milky, but compensated by delicate honey and date sugar notes, without being particularly fruity... well, except for the crushed physalis, maybe...; **t**23.5 the grain is as soft as it can possibly come, dissolving on the palate, but not before harmonising sublimely with coconut and some meandering smoke atoms seemingly attached to a maple syrup/molasses blend. The malts also have a melt-in-the mouth quality, leaving behind a gorgeously weighted degree of fine cocoa; **f**22 a few struggling barrels leave a lactic imprint. But the spices gang together to form a delightful diversion while the Walnut Whip vanilla and walnut oil combo takes you to the exit; **b**24 a very classy blend very skilfully constructed. A stunningly lovely texture, one of the very best I have encountered for a while, and no shortage of complexity ensures this is a rather special blend. I'll even forgive the dulling by caramel and light milkiness from the tired bourbon barrel. The overall excellence outweighs the odd blemish. *40%*

Label 5 Reserve No. 55 sherry cask finish, bott code B-3695 **(89) n**22 **t**23 **f**21.5 **b**22.5. The last one of these I had a couple of years back was a sulphur-damaged disaster. This is anything but. A real bold treat. *43%. La Martiniquaise, France.*

Label 5 Reserve No. 55 sherry cask finish, bott code F-4482 **(87) n**20.5 **t**22.5 **f**22 **b**22. Lacking the suave sweetness of the B-3695 bottling, but excellent spice. *43%*.

Label 5 Reserve No. 55 Single Cask sherry cask finish, bott code no. E-1067 **(75) n**19 **t**20 **f**18 **b**18. The cordite on the nose suggests fireworks. But somehow we end up with a damp squib. *43%. La Martiniquaise, France.*

Lang's Supreme Aged 5 Years (93.5) n23.5 **t**23.5 **f**23 **b**23.5. Every time I taste this the shape and structure has altered slightly. Here there is a fraction more smoke, installing a deeper confidence all round. This is blended whisky as it should be: Supreme in its ability to create shape and harmony. *40%. Ian Macleod Distillers Ltd.*

The Last Drop 1965 American Standard Barrel **(96.5) n**24 **t**24.5 **f**23.5 **b**24.5 Almost impossible to imagine a blended whisky to be better balanced than this. If there is a cleverer use of honey or less intrusive oak in any blended whisky bottled in the last year, I have yet to taste it. An award winner if ever I tasted one. Magnificent doesn't quite cover it... *48.6%. Morrison Bowmore. The Last Drop Distillers Ltd.*

⟨⟨⟨ **The Last Drop 1971 Blended Scotch Whisky 45 Years Old (97) n**24.5 if you can find a blend where the smoke has this perfect an effect, please point me to it. Somehow the delicate phenols possess a duel role acting as both ballast and, paradoxically, the more ethereal element as well. Sandwiched between is the handy work of the stunning grain: firm yet just about soft enough to have absorbed the complex oak-led vanillas...; **t**24 silk... with a little itching powder. The delivery moulds into every crevice of the palate, but just as you settle there is a tingling of light spice. Weak ulmo honey heads the understated sugary parade, with a little Tunnock's Teacake-style marsh mallow helping to lay down the tannins as a little red liquorice and butterscotch formulate; **f**24 just so long and elegant, with a dull ache of phenol and tannin to occupy the faint spice; **b**24.5 even though I now know many of the people involved in the Last Drop, I am still not entirely sure how they keep doing it. Just how do they continue to unearth whiskies which are truly staggering; absolute marvels of their type? This one is astonishing because the grain used is just about faultless. And the peating levels can be found around about the perfect mark on the dial. Like an old Ballentine's which has sat and waited in a cask over four decades to be discovered and tell it's wonderful, spellbinding and never-ending tale. Just mesmerically beautiful. *47%*.

The Last Drop 50 Year Old Sherry Wood **(97) n**24 a curious mix of cherry drop candy and shoe polish: pungent, fruity and lively. None of the tired oak you might expect to turn up arrives, though the vanillas do have the odd few grey hairs; **t**24.5 those cherry drops are there on impact, intensely so, with a further oily spiciness making for a busy, warming and juicy experience; the midground is still controlled by the fruit – a little more burnt raisin in style now – but those spices are the forerunner of a much toastier effort from the oak; **f**24 here's the thing: you expect those gathering oak tones to turn a tad tired and worn. But they never do. Instead, the spices buzz and a little manuka and heather honey face the oak to inject just that small degree of sweetness required for a happy ending; **b**24.5 you'd expect, after half a century in the cask, that this would be a quiet dram, just enjoying its final years with its feet up and arms behind its head. Instead we have a fairly aggressive blend determined to drive the abundant fruitiness it still possesses to the very hilt. It is backed up all the way by a surprising degree of warming, busy spice. There is a hell of a lot of life in this beautiful ol' dog... *51.2%*

Lauder's (74) n18 t21 f17 b18. Well, it's consistent: you can say that for it! As usual, fabulous delivery, but as for the rest...oh dear. *40%. MacDuff International Ltd.*

Lauder's Aged 12 Years (93.5) n23 t24 f23 b23.5 This is every bit as magnificent as the standard Lauder's isn't. *43%*

The Loch Fyne (89.5) n22 t23 f21.5 b23. This is an adorable old-style blend....a bit of a throwback. But no ruinous sherry notes...just clean and delicious. Well, mainly... *40%*

Loch Lomond Blended Scotch (89) n22 t22.5 f22 b22.5 A fabulously improved blend: clean and precise and though malt is seemingly at a premium, a fine interplay. *40%*

Loch Lomond Reserve db **(86.5)** n21.5 t22 f21.5 b21.5. A spongy, sweet, chewy, pleasant blend which is more of a take as you find statement than a layering of flavours. *40%*

Lochranza (83.5) n21 t21.5 f21 b20. Pleasant, clean, but, thanks to the caramel, goes easy on the complexity. *40%. Isle of Arran.*

Lochside 1964 Rare Old Single Blend (94.5) n24 t23.5 f23 b24. A unique and entirely fitting tribute to a distillery which should never have been lost. *42.1%. nc ncf.*

Logan (78.5) n19 t19 f20 b19.5. Entirely drinkable but a bit heavy-handed with the grains and caramel. *40%. Diageo.*

Lombard's Gold Label (85) n21 t22 f21 b21. Big and chewy, not as complex as of old but those who like chunky toffee will be in for a treat. *40%. Lombard Brands Ltd.*

Lord Elcho (76) n19 t20 f18 b19. Oh, Lord...! *40%. Wemyss Malts.*

Lord Elcho Aged 15 Years (84) n21 t21 f21 b21. A straight wicket with no turn at all. A degree of coppery sharpness and caramel, but low key. *40%. Wemyss Malts.*

Lord Hynett (88.5) n21.5 t23 f22 b22 Just perfect after a shitty day. *40%.*

Lord Hynett (87) n22 t22 f21.5 b21.5. An honest, beautifully made blend with a welcome degree of attitude. *43%. Loch Lomond Distillers.*

Lord Scot (77.5) n18.5 t20 f19.5 b19.5. A touch cloying but the mocha fudge ensures a friendly enough ride. *40%. Loch Lomond Distillers.*

Lord Scot (86.5) n20 t22 f22.5 b22. A gorgeously lush honey and liquorice middle. *43%*

The Lost Distilleries batch 2 **(94)** n22.5 t24 f23.5 b24. Whoever lost it better find it again: this is how you dream every whisky should be. *53.2%.*

The Lost Distilleries Blend Batch 6 **(91)** n23.5 huge grain presence....some old grain, too, with corn oils abounding. The vague fruity sweetness, not unlike stewed and lightly sweetened rhubarb, has much more to do with the grain than the oak: no, the oak is responsible for the custard...; **t23** soft, silky, lithe...the corn oils are working at full speed, the light sugars working flat out to keep pace; **f22** spices arrive for a late wake up call. A little tiredness from the oak, but dealt with quickly; **b22.5** the Lost Malt as well: completely grain dominant – but wonderfully lush and tasty. *49.3%*

Mackessack Premium Aged 8 Years (87.5) n21.5 t23 f21.5 b21.5. Claims a high Speyside content and the early character confirms it. Shoots itself in the foot, rather, by overdoing the caramel and flattening the finish. *40%. Mackessack Giovenetti. Italian Market.*

Mac Na Mara (83) n20 t22.5 f20 b20.5. Absolutely brimming with salty, fruity character. But just a little more toffee and furriness than it needs. Enjoyable, though. *40%*

Mac Na Mara Rum Finish (93) n22 t24 f23 b24 High quality blending, and the usage of the rum appears to have retained the old Mac Na Mara style. *40%. Praban na Linne.*

MacQueens (89) n21.5 t22.5 f22.5 b22.5. I am long enough in the tooth now to remember blends like this found in quiet country hotels in the furthest-flung reaches of the Highlands beyond a generation ago. A wonderfully old-fashioned, traditional one might say, blend of a type that is getting harder and harder to find. *40%. Quality Spirits International.*

Master of Malt 8 Years Old (88) n22.5 t22.5 f21 b22. Understated and refined. *40%*

Master Of Malt 8 Year Old Blended Whisky (83.5) n21 t22 f20.5 b20. Never quite makes up its mind what it wants to do, or where it wants to go. A few intriguing vaguely Irish Pot Still-style moments on delivery, though. *40%*

Master of Malt Blended 10 Years Old 1st Edition (84.5) n21.5 t22.5 f20 b20.5. A pleasant enough, though hardly complex, blend benefitting from the lovely malty, then silky pick-up from delivery and a brief juicy barley sharpness. But unsettled elsewhere due, mainly, to using the wrong fit of grain: too firm when a little give was needed. *47.5%. ncf. WB15/353*

Master Of Malt St Isidore (84) n21 t22 f20 b21. Sweet, lightly smoked but really struggles to put together a coherent story. Something, somewhere, is not quite right. *41.4%*

Matisse 12 Years Old (90.5) n23 t23 f22 b22.5 Moved up yet another notch as this brand continues its development. Much more clean-malt oriented with a Speyside-style to the fore. Majestic and charming. *40%. Matisse Spirits Co Ltd.*

Matisse 21 Years Old (86) n23 t22 f20 b21. Begins breathtakingly on the nose, with a full array of exotic fruit showing the older bourbon casks up to max effect. Nothing wrong with the early delivery, which offers a touch of honeycomb on the grain. But the caramel effect on the finish stops everything in its tracks. Soft and alluring, all the same. *40%*

Matisse Old (85.5) n20 t23 f21 b21.5. Appears to improve each time I come across it. The nose is a bit on the grimy side and the finish disappears under a sea of caramel. But the delivery works deliciously, with a chewy weight which highlights the sweeter malts. *40%*

Matisse Royal (81) n19 t22 f20 b20. Pleasant, if a little clumsy. Extra caramel appears to have scuppered the spice. *40%. Matisse Spirits Co Ltd.*

McArthurs (89.5) n22 t22.5 f22 b23 One of the most improved blends on the market. The clever use of the peat is exceptional. *40%. Inverhouse Distillers.*

Mitchell's Glengyle Blend (86.5) n21.5 t22 f21.5 b21.5. A taste of history here, as this is the first blend ever to contain malt from the new Campbeltown distillery, Glengyle. Something of a departure in style from the usual Mitchell blends, which tended to put the accent on a crisper grain. Interestingly, here they have chosen one at least that is soft and voluptuous enough to absorb the sharper malt notes. *40%. Springbank Distillers.*

Monarch Of The Glen Connoisseurs Choice (80) n20 t21 f19 b20. Has changed shape a little. Positively wallows in its fat and sweet personality. *40%. Quality Spirits International.*

Monarch Of The Glen Connoisseurs Choice Aged 8 Years (76.5) n19 t20.5 f18 b19. Leaves no doubt that there are some malts in there... *40%. Quality Spirits International.*

Monarch Of The Glen Connoisseurs Choice Aged 12 Years (88) n21.5 t22.5 f22 b22. Charming, fruity and a blend to put your feet up with. *40%. Quality Spirits International.*

Monarch Of The Glen Connoisseurs Choice Aged 15 Years (83) n21 t22 f19 b21. Starts off on the very same footing as the 12-y-o, especially with the sumptuous delivery. But fails to build on that due to toffee and bitters at the death. *40%. Quality Spirits International.*

Montrose (74.5) n18 t20 f18 b18.5. A battling performance but bitter defeat in the end. *40%.*

Morrisons The Best 8 Years Old (87) n21 t23 f22 b21. Some of the traces of its excellence are still there, it remains highly drinkable, but that greatness has been lost in a tide of caramel. When, oh when, are people going to understand that you can't just tip this stuff into whisky to up the colour without causing a detrimental effect on the product? Is anybody listening? Does anyone care??? Someone has gone to great lengths to create a sublime blend – to see it wasted. Natural colour and this'd be an experience to die for. *40%*

Morrisons Fine Blended Whisky (77) n18.5 t21 f18.5 b19. Sweet, chewy; rough edges. *40%.*

Muirhead's (83) n19 t22 f23 b21. A beautifully compartmentalised dram that integrates superbly, if that makes sense. *40%. MacDonald & Muir.*

Muirhead's Blue Seal (83) n21 t21 f20.5 b20.5. Goes to town quite heavily on the grain. If this is the new version of the old McDonald and Muir brand, then this is a lot oilier, with a silkier mouthfeel. *40%. Highland Queen Scotch Whisky Company.*

The Naked Grouse (76.5) n19 t21 f17.5 b19. Sweet. But reveals too many sulphur tattoos. *40%.*

Northern Scot (68) n16 t18 f17 b17. Heading South bigtime. *40%. Bruce and Co. for Tesco.*

◈ **Oishii Wisukii Aged 36 Years** (96) n24.5 I am nosing this from a little fluffy cloud about a mile above where you are sitting now: I am savouring tannins that have gone as far as they dare...but no further; a smokiness which is measured in degrees of imagination; elements of bourbon - with an almost rye-like Demerara crispness – which offer a third dimension. This is fabulous...; t23.5 how silky is that?! The palate appears to be absorbed into a grain which completely envelops it, sweet and bitter notes lurching about with brilliant randomness. Though not before the malt – probably a high proportion of the blend – has made an early statement by offering a vivid, gristy juiciness; f24 if you have about half an hour, then just listen to this fade. All I have mentioned before, dying slowly with only the spices fighting against the fading of the light...; b24 normally, I'd suggest popping into the Highlander for a pint of beer. But if they happen to have any of this stuff there...break his bloody arm off: it's magnificent! *46.2%. The Highlander Inn, Craigellachie.*

Old Crofter Special Old Scotch Whisky (83) n18 t22 f21 b22. A very decent blend, much better than the nose suggests thanks to some outstanding, velvety grain and wonderfully controlled sweetness. *40%. Smith & Henderson for London & Scottish International.*

Old Masters "Freemason Whisky" (92) n24 t23 f22 b23. A high quality blend that doesn't stint on the malt. The nose, in particular, is sublime. *40%. Supplied online. Lombard Brands*

Old McDonald (83.5) n20 t22 f20.5 b21. Attractively tart and bracing where it needs to be with lovely grain bite. Lots of toffee, though. *43.%. The Last Drop Distillers. For India.*

Old Mull (84.5) n22 t21 f20.5 b21. With dates and walnuts clambering all over the nose, very much in the house style. But this one is a shade oilier than most – and certainly on how it used to be – and has dropped a degree or two of complexity. That said, enjoyable stuff with the spices performing well, as does the lingering sweetness. *40%*

Old Parr 12 Years Old (91.5) n21.5 t23.5 f23 b23.5 Perhaps on about the fourth of fifth mouthful, the penny drops that this is not just exceptionally good whisky: it is blending Parr excellence... 40%. Diageo.

Old Parr Aged 15 Years (84) n19 t22 f21 b22. Absolutely massive sherry input here. Some of it is of the highest order. The nose, reveals, however, that some isn't... 43%

Old Parr Classic 18 Years Old (84.5) n21 t21.5 f21 b21. A real jumbled, mixed bag with fruit and barley falling over each other and the grains offering little sympathy. Enough to enjoy, but with Old Parr, one expects a little more... 46%. Diageo.

Old Parr Superior 18 Years Old batch no. L5171 **(97) n25 t25 f23 b24.** Year in, year out, this blend just gets better and better. This bottling struck me as a possible Whisky of the Year, but perhaps only an outsider. Familiarity, though, bred anything but contempt and over the passing months I have tried to get to the bottom of this truly great whisky. Blended whisky has long needed a champion. This grand old man looks just the chap. This is a worthy, if unexpected (even to me), Jim Murray' Whisky Bible 2007 World Whisky of the Year. 43%.

Old Smuggler (85.5) n21 t22 f21 b21.5. A much sharper act than its Allied days with a new honeyed-maple syrup thread which is rather delightful. Could still do with toning down the caramel, though, to brighten the picture further. 40%. Campari, France.

Old St Andrews Clubhouse (82) n18 t22 f21 b21. Not quite the clean, bright young thing it was many years back. But great to see back in my nosing glass after such a long while and though the nose hits the rough, the delivery is as sweetly struck as you might hope for. 40%

Old Stag (75.5) n18.5 t20 f18.5 b18.5. Wants shooting. 40%. Loch Lomond Distillers.

The Original Lochlan Aged 8 Years (80.5) n19 t21 f20 b20.5. Doused in caramel. So much so it's like a toffee and nut bar. One to chew on until your fillings fall out, though the spices compensate on the finish to a degree. Pleasant and sweet, but don't expect great refinement. 40%. Tesco.

The Original Mackinlay (83) n19 t21 f22 b21. A hard nose to overcome and the toffee remains in force for those addicted to fudge. But now a degree of bite and ballast appears to have been added, giving more of a story to the experience. 40%. Whyte & Mackay Distillers Ltd.

Passport (83) n22 t19 f21 b21. It looks as though Chivas have decided to take the blend away from its original sophisticated, Business Class J&B/Cutty Sark, style for good now, as they have continued this decently quaffable but steerage quality blend with its big caramel kick and chewy, rather than lithe, body. 40%. Chivas.

Passport v (91) n23 23.5 f22 b22.5. Easily one of the better versions I have come across for a long time and impressively true to its original style. 40%. Bottled in Brazil.

Passport v (91) n22.5 t22 f23.5 b23.5. A lovely version closer to original style with markedly less caramel impact and grittier grain. An old-fashioned treat. 40%. Ecuador.

Parkers (78) n17 t22 f20 b19. The nose has regressed, disappearing into ever more caramel, yet the mouth-watering lushness on the palate remains and the finish now holds greater complexity and interest. 40%. Angus Dundee.

Prince Charlie Special Reserve (73) n17 t20 f18 b18. Thankfully not as cloyingly sweet as of old, but remains pretty basic. 40%. Somerfield, UK.

Prince Charlie Special Reserve 8 Years Old (81) n18 t20 f22 b21. A lumbering bruiser of a dram; keeps its trademark shapelessness but the spices and lush malt ensure an enjoyable experience. 40%. Somerfield, UK.

⬩⬩⬩ **Queen Margot (85.5) n21.5 t22 f21 b21.** A clean, silky-textured, sweet and caramel-rich blend of disarming simplicity. 40%

Queen Margot (86) n21 t22 f21.5 b21.5. A lovely blend which makes no effort to skimp on a spicy depth. Plenty of cocoa from the grain late on but no shortage of good whiskies put to work. 40%. Wallace and Young for Lidl.

Queen Margot v (83.5) n20.5 t22 f20 b21. Same brand, but a different name on the back label. And certainly a different feel to the whisky with the grains having harsher words than before. 40%. Clydesdale Scotch Whisky Co for Lidl.

⬩⬩⬩ **Queen Margot Aged 5 Years (89) n22** pretty brooding for a blend, especially as there is no smoke influence; **t22.5** deceptively big: grows on the palate and as the spices increase, so does the coffee and marmalade; **f22** the spices warm as the layering gets more complex; **b22.5** a very attractive blend with a most agreeable level of chewability. The chocolate orange which bolsters the yielding grain appears to suggest some good, clean sherry influence along the way. 40%

⬩⬩⬩ **Queen Margot Aged 8 Years (85) n21 t22 f21 b21.** Pleasant, untaxing, with a hint of oaky vanilla after the sugary crescendo. 40%

Queen Margot Aged 8 Years (89) n22 t22.5 f22 b22.5. A satisfying blend with a delicious clarity to the light malts and high class grains. Just the right touch of sweetness, too. 40%.

Queen Margot Aged 8 Years (84) n20.5 t21 f21.5 b21. Here's the variant. Darker in colour I notice and a bit of a dullard and simpleton by comparison, though not without an acceptable degree of charm. Much weightier. *40%. Clydesdale Scotch Whisky Co for Lidl.*

Real Mackenzie (80) n17 t21 f21 b21. As ever, try and ignore the dreadful nose and get cracking with the unsubtle, big bruising delivery. A thug in a glass. *40%. Diageo.*

Real Mackenzie Extra Smooth (81) n18 t22 f20 b21. Once, the only time the terms "Real Mackenzie" and "Extra Smooth" were ever uttered in the same sentence was if someone was talking about the barman. Now it is a genuine descriptor. Which is odd, because when Diageo sent me a sample of their blend last year it was a snarling beast ripping at the leash. This, by contrast, is a whimpering sop. "Killer? Where are you...???" *40%. Diageo.*

Red Seal 12 Years Old (82) n19 t22 f20 b21. Charming, mouthwatering. But toffee numbs it down towards the finish. *40%. Charles Wells UK.*

Reliance PL (76) n18 t20 f19 b19. Some of the old spiciness evident. But has flattened out noticeably. *43%. Diageo.*

Robert Burns (85) n20 t22.5 f21 b21.5. Skeletal and juicy: very little fat and gets to the mouthwatering point pretty quickly. Genuine fun. *40%. Isle of Arran.*

Robertson's of Pitlochry Rare Old Blended (83) n21 t20 f21 b21. Handsome grain bite with a late malty flourish. Classic light blend from Pitlochry's landmark whisky shop. *40%*

The Royal & Ancient (80.5) n20 t21.5 f19 b20. Has thinned out dramatically in the last year or so. Now clean, untaxing, briefly mouth-watering and radiating young grain throughout. *40%*

Royal Castle (84.5) n20 t22 f21 b21.5. From Quality Street, or Quality Spirits? Sweet and very well toffeed! *43%. Quality Spirits International.*

Royal Castle 12 Years Old (84.5) n22 t22 f20 b20.5. Busy nose and delivery with much to chew over. Entirely enjoyable, and seems better each time you taste it. Even so, the finish crumbles a bit. *40%. Quality Spirits International.*

Royal Clan Aged 18 Years (85) n21.5 t21 f21.5 b21. For those giving up gum, here's something to really chew on. Huge degree of cream toffee and toasted fudge which makes for a satin-soft blend, but also one which ensures any big moves towards complexity are nipped in the bud. Very enjoyable, all the same. *40%. Quality Spirits International.*

Royal Household (90.5) n21.5 t23 f23 b23 We are amused. *43%. Diageo.*

Royal Park (85) n21.5 t22.5 f20 b21. Pretty generic with an attractive silky sheen, Demerara sugars and decent late spice swim around in an ocean of caramel. *40%*

Royal Salute 21 Years Old (92.5) n23 t23.5 f23 b23.5 If you are looking for the velvety character of yore, forget it. This one comes with some real character and is much the better for it. The grain, in particular, excels. *40%. Chivas.*

Royal Salute 62 Gun Salute (95.5) n24.5 t24 f23 b24 How do you get a bunch of varying whiskies in style, but each obviously growing a grey beard and probably cantankerous to boot, to settle in and harmonise with the others? A kind of Old People's Home for whisky, if you like. Well, here's how...*43%. Chivas.*

Royal Salute The Diamond Tribute (91) n23.5 t23 f21.5 b23. Ironic that a diamond is probably the hardest natural creation, yet this whisky is one of man's softest... *40%. Chivas.*

⟨⟩ **Royal Salute The Eternal Reserve (89.5)** n23 chocolate fudge, with a few sultanas tossed in for good measure; t23.5 salivating to an eye-watering scale. Huge caramel charge perhaps flattens the expected follow up, but the spices bubble to the surface like a hidden spring in a distant field; f21 way too much caramel for its own good. But that spring of spice has moved on to form a stream...; b22 one of those strange whiskies where so much happens on the nose and delivery, but much less when we head to the finish *40%*

Royal Salute The Hundred Cask Selection Limited Release No. 7 (92) n22 t23.5 f23 b23.5 As blends go, its entire countenance talks about great age and elegance. And does so with a clipped accent. *40%. Chivas.*

Royal Silk Reserve (93) n22 t24 f24 b23 I named this the best newcomer in 2001 and it hasn't let me down. A session blend for any time of the day, this just proves that you don't need piles of peat to create a blend of genuine stature. A must have. *40%*

⟨⟩ **Royal Warrior (86)** n21 t22 f21.5 b21.5. An entirely pleasant grain-rich, young, old fashioned blend which masters the prevalent sugars well when they appear to be getting out of hand. Extremely clean and beautifully rounded. *40%*

Sainsbury's Basics Blended Scotch Whisky (78.5) n19 t20.5 f19.5 b19.5. "A little less refined, great for mixing," says the label. Frankly, there are a lot of malts out there far less enjoyable than this. Don't be scared to have straight: it's more than decent enough. *40%*

Sainsbury's Scotch Whisky (84.5) n20 t22 f21 b21.5. A surprisingly full bodied, chewy blend allowing a pleasing degree of sweetness to develop. No shortage of toffee at the finish – a marked improvement on recent years. *40%. UK.*

Sainsbury's Finest Old Matured Aged 8 Years (86) n21.5 t21 f22 b21.5. A sweet blend enjoying a melt-in-the-mouth delivery, a silky body and toffee-vanilla character. The spices arriving towards the end are exceptionally pleasing and welcome. *40%. UK.*

Sandy Mac (76) n18 t20 f19 b19. Basic, decent blend that's chunky and raw. *40%. Diageo.*

Scots Earl (76.5) n18 t20 f19 b19.5. It's name is Earl. And it must have upset someone in a previous life. Always thrived on its engaging disharmony. But just a tad too syrupy now. *40%.*

Scottish Chief (77) n19 t19 f19 b20. This is one big-bodied chief, and not given to taking prisoners. *40%. Quality Spirits International.*

Scottish Collie (77) n19 t19 f19 b20. Caramel still, but a Collie with a bit more bite. *40%*

Scottish Collie 12 Years Old (85) n22 t22 f20 b21. On the cusp of a really classy blend here but the bitterness on the finish loses serious Brownie points. *40%. Quality Spirits Int, UK.*

Scottish Collie 18 Years Old (92) n24 t23 f22 b23. This, honey-led beaut would be a winner even at Crufts: an absolute master class of how an old, yet light and unpeated blend should be. No discord whatsoever between the major elements and not a single hint of over-aging. Superb. *40%. Quality Spirits International, UK.*

Scottish Glory dist 2002, bott 2005 (85) n21 t21 f22 b21. An improved blend now bursting with vitality. The ability of the grain to lift the barley is very pleasing. *40%. Duncan Taylor.*

Scottish Leader Original (83.5) n17.5 t22.5 f21 b22.5. About as subtle as a poke in the eye with a spirit thief. The nose, it must be said, is not great. But I have to admit I thoroughly enjoy the almost indulgent coarseness from the moment it invades the palate. A real chewathon of a spicy blend with a wicked, in-yer-face attitude. Among all the rough-'n-tumble and slap-'n-tickle, the overall depth, weight, balance and molassed charm ain't half bad. *40%. Burn Stewart.*

Scottish Leader Aged 12 Years (91) n22.5 t23 f22 b22.5 Absolutely unrecognisable from the Leader 12 I last tasted. This has taken a plumy, fruity route with the weight of a cannonball but the texture of mallow. Big and quite beautiful. *40%. Burn Stewart.*

Scottish Leader 30 Years Old (87) n23.5 t21.5 f20.5 b21.5 A little too docile ever to be a great whisky, but the nose is something rather special. A bit of attention on the finish and this could be a real corker. *40%. Burn Stewart.*

Scottish Leader Select (91.5) n23 t23.5 f22.5 b22.5 Don't make the mistake of thinking this is just the 40% with three extra percentage points of alcohol. This appears to be an entirely different bottling with an entirely different personality. A delight. *43%. South African Market.*

Scottish Leader Select (74) n18.5 t19 f18 b18.5. I assume the leader is Major Disharmony. *40%*

Scottish Leader Supreme (72.5) n17 t19 f18 b18.5. Jings! It's like an old-fashioned Gorbals punch-up in the glass – and palate. *40%. Burn Stewart.*

Scottish Piper (80) n20 t20 f20 b20. A light, mildly- raw, sweet blend with lovely late vanilla intonation. *40%*

Scottish Prince (83.5) n21 t22 f20 b20.5. Muscular, but agreeably juicy. *40%*

Scottish Reel (78.5) n19 t19 f20 b19.5. Non fussy with an attractive bite, as all such blends should boast. *40%. London & Scottish International.*

Scottish Rill (85) n20 t20.5 f22.5 b22. Refreshing yet earthy. *40%. Quality Spirits Int.*

Sheep Dip Amoroso Oloroso 1999 Oloroso sherry casks, bott Mar 12 (92) n23.5 t24 f21 b23.5. More like Sherry Dip than Sheep Dip. Actually, chocolate dip wouldn't be too far off the mark, either. To create this, malt which had spent three years maturing in bourbon cask was then shipped to Jerez where it spent a further nine years in presumably fresh sherry. It was worth the trouble... *41.8%. Spencerfield Spirits.*

⟡ **Sia Blended Scotch Whisky** (87) n21 t22.5 f21.5 b22. Rare to find a blend that's so up front with its smoke. Doesn't scrimp on the salivation stakes or sheer chewiness, either. *43% (86 proof)*

Something Special (85) n21.5 t22 f20.5 b21. Mollycoddled by toffee, any murderous tendencies seem to have been fudged away, leaving just the odd moment of attractive complexity. You suspect there is a hit man in there somewhere trying to get out. *40%. Chivas.*

⟡ **Something Special Legacy** (92) n23 fabulously roasty, with a serious treacle and toasted mallow theme; t22.5 silky and seductive, the lighter sugars are soon matched by a molassed and tannin-spiced intensity; f23 a light liquorice outline, then those crispy, frazzled sugars once more. A teasing spice fade is the perfect match; b23.5 good, solid blender is David Boyd. And here he has married substance with subtlety. Lovely stuff. *40%*

Something Special Premium Aged 15 Years (89) n22 t23 f21 b23 Fabulous malt thread and some curious raisiny/sultana fruitiness, too. A blend-lover's blend. *40%*

Spar Finest Reserve (90.5) n21.5 t22.5 f23.5 b23 One of Britain's best value for money blends with an honest charm which revels in the clean high quality grain and earthier malts which work so well together. *40%*

Spirit of Freedom Aged 30 Years (91) n23.5 t22.5 f22 b23 A blend created to mark the 700th anniversary of Bannockburn has a battle of its own against so many aging casks. Somehow, it just about wins. 46%. 2014 bottles. WB15/364

⟡ **Stag's Head Blended Scotch Whisky** (85.5) n21.5 t21.5 f21 b21.5. A thick, hefty nose and body, lush grain and lashings of caramel. Pleasant, sweet, nutty standard stuff. 40% (80 proof)

Stewart's Old Blended (93) n22.5 t24 f23 b23.5 Really lovely whisky for those who like to close their eyes, contemplate and have a damned good chew. 40%

Storm (94) n23 t23.5 f24 b23.5. A little gem of a blend that will take you by storm. 43%.

Swords (78) n20 t21 f18 b19. Beefed up somewhat with some early smoke thrusting through and rapier grains to follow. 40%. Morrison Bowmore.

Talisman 5 Years Old (85.5) n22 t22 f20.5 b21. Unquestionably an earthier, weightier version of what was once a Speyside romp. Soft peats also add extra sweetness. 40%

Teacher's 50 - 12 Years Old batch 2-16, bott Sep 11 (85.5) n20.5 t22.5 f21.5 b21. Once, before entering the Indian bottling hall, this must have been a strutting peacock of a Scotch blend. But after being doused in a far too liberal amount of caramels it has been reduced to a house sparrow: outwardly common and dull but at least with an engaging personality. The usual Teacher's smoke shows itself only at the death, alas. And all else is a silky honeyed sweetness pleading for an extra degree of complexity. The very complexity, indeed, which was almost certainly there before being coloured to death. If they could sort out the caramel levels in the bottling hall, this would be a blend that would put on a spectacular display.... 42.8%

Teacher's Aged 25 Years batch 1 (96.5) n24 t24.5 f23.5 b24.5 Only 1300 bottles means they will be hard pushed to create this exact style again. Worth a go, chaps: considering this is India bound, it is the karma sutra of blended scotch. 46%. Beam Inc. 1300 bottles. India & Far East Travel Retail exclusive.

Teacher's Highland Cream (90) n23 t23 f22 b22 Not yet back to its best but a massive improvement on the 2005 bottlings. Harder grains to accentuate the malt will bring it closer to the classic of old. 40%

Teacher's Highland Cream v (90) n23 t22.5 f22 b22.5 A very curious, seriously high grade, variant. Although the Ardmore distillery is on the label, it is the only place it can really be seen. Certainly - the least smoky Teacher's I've come across in 35 years of drinking the stuff: the smoke is there, but adds only ballast rather than taking any form of lead. But the grain is soft and knits with the malts with ease to make for a sweeter, much more lush version than the rest of the world may recognize. 40%

⟡ **Teacher's Origin** (92) n23 I could nose this all day: the smoke is so subtle it plays hide and seek with the vanilla and malt, seemingly cocking a snook whenever it takes command... spellbinding stuff! t23 brilliantly creamy (remember: Teacher's Highland Cream...!!) with a slightly inferior, thin grain being greatly boosted by the most stunning and complex malt signatures you'll find. Against this, the smoke drifts about warmly; f23 long, again with the creamy-textured thrust working late into the piece. Excellent late spice and real depth to the slightly rice-pudding and molasses style finale..; b23 almost brings a tear to the eye to taste a Scotch blend that really is a blend. With a better grain input (Dumbarton, say), this perhaps would have been one of the contenders for World Whisky of the Year. Superb! 40%

Teacher's Origin (88.5) n22 t23.5 f21 b22 A fascinating blend among the softest on the market today. That is aided and abetted by the exceptionally high malt content, 65%, which makes this something of an inverted blend, as that, for most established brands, is the average grain content. What appears to be a high level of caramel also makes for a rounding of the edges, as well as evidence of sherry butts. The bad news is that that has resulted in a duller finish than perhaps might have been intended, which is even more pronounced given the impressive speech made on delivery. Lovely whisky, yes. But something, I feel, of a work in progress. Bringing the caramel down by the percentage points of the malt would be a very positive start... 42.8%. ncf.

Té Bheag (86) n22 t21 f21.5 b21.5. Classic style of rich caramels and bite. 40%. ncf.

Tesco Finest Reserve Aged 12 Years (74) n18.5 t19 f18 b18.5. The most astonishing thing about this, apart from the fact it is a 12 year-old, is that it won a Gold "Best in Class" in a 2010 international whisky competition: it surely could not have been from the same batch as the one before me. Frankly, you have to go a long way to find a whisky as bland as this and for a 12-y-o it is monumentally disappointing. 40%.

Tesco Special Reserve Minimum 3 Years Old (78) n18.5 t21.5 f19 b19. Decent early spice on delivery but otherwise anonymous. 40%. Tesco.

Tesco Value Scotch Whisky (83) n19 t21 f22 b21. Young and genuinely refreshing whisky. Without the caramel this really would be a little darling. 40%

Traquair (78) n19 t21 f19 b19. Young, but offering a substantial mouthful including attractive smoke. 46%. Burn Stewart.

That Boutique-y Whisky Blended Whisky #1 batch 1 **(72) n18 t19 f17 b18.** Fuzzy, furry and generally out of sorts. 50.3%. 148 bottles. WB15/354

That Boutique-y Whisky Company Blended Whisky No. 1 batch 2 **(94.5) n23.5** a butch nose with a superb mix of smoke, vanilla and even something vaguely (deliciously and mysteriously) akin to fried onions.; **t23.5** myriad crispy salivating, sugars – malt grist included - bathed in smoke; **f23.5** far more vanilla now, plus some docile ulmo honey – and spiced smoke; **b24** one hell of a substantial blend, seemingly with a Bowmore-style smokiness! Love it! 52%. 417 bottles.

That Boutique-y Whisky Company Blended Whisky No. 1 35 Year Old batch 3 **(78.5) n19 t21.5 f19 b19.** Some off-key, unkind oak involvement. Some interesting spices at work, though! 46.5%. 1,428 bottles.

The Tweeddale Blend Aged 10 Years (89.5) n22 t23.5 f21.5 b22.5 The first bottling of this blend since World War 2, it has been well worth waiting for. 46%. ncf. 50% malt. Stonedean.

The Tweeddale Blend Aged 12 Years bott code 28, Feb 13 **(95) n23.5 t24 f23 b24.5** For the tasting notes see the 2011 bottling above. Very, very similar, except more crisp grain on the nose and a slightly more clever use of citrus throughout. How heart-warming to see a blend not just keep faithfully to its style, but appears to somehow up the quality a fraction. A treat of a whisky experience. 46%. nc ncf. Stonedean. 3rd release.

The Tweeddale Blended Scotch Whisky Aged 14 Years batch 5 **(92) n22.5** zesty and grassy, this really does give your nose a tweak; **t23.5** the massive degree of salivation is no surprise after that nose: the barley goes into Speyside-style overdrive, revealing all its malty charms simply and cleanly. The citrus notes have a say throughout; **f23** here it changes from the last bottling, the complexity and spices at a premium with the yielding grains having the major say and ensuring the softest landing imaginable; **b23** I was salivating just at the prospect of this one, as I remember what a fresh article Batch 4 was. Well, this is even sharper in some places...yet curiously far more laid back and docile in others. 46%. nc ncf.

Ushers Green Stripe (85) n19 t22.5 f21.5 b22. Upped a notch or two in all-round quality. The juicy theme and clever weight is highly impressive and enjoyable. 43%. Diageo.

VAT 69 (84.5) n20 t22 f21 b21.5. Has thickened up in style: weightier, more macho, much more to say and a long way off that old lightweight. A little cleaning up wouldn't go amiss. 40%

Walton Royal Blend Deluxe Reserve (91.5) n22.5 the unusual experience of encountering a blend which hoists and then flies the peaty flag with gay abandon: smoky and exceptionally soft; **t23** and yes....there it is again: the smoke building slowly into something substantial, but only after the spongy grains have made a sugary entrance; **f23** remains soft, not very complex but friendly and adds some late cocoa and spice to the lingering smoke; **b23** it's amazing what a dose of good quality peaty whisky can do to a blend. Certainly ensures it stands out as a deliciously chewy – and smoky – experience. 43%

White Horse (90.5) n22 t23 f22.5 b23 A malt which has subtlety changed shape. Not just the smoke which gives it weight, but you get the feeling that some of Diageo's less delicate malts have been sent in to pack a punch. As long as they are kept in line, as is the case here – just – we can all enjoy a very big blend. 40%. Diageo.

White Horse Aged 12 Years (86) n21 t23 f21 b21. Enjoyable, complex if not always entirely harmonious. For instance, the apples and grapes on the nose appear on a limb from the grain and caramel and nothing like the thoroughbred of old. Lighter, more flaccid and caramel dominated. 40%. Diageo.

Whyte & Mackay 'The Thirteen' 13 Year Old (92) n22.5 t23.5 f23 b23. Try this and your luck'll be in...easily the pick of the W&M blended range. 40%. Whyte & Mackay Distillers Ltd.

Whyte & Mackay Luxury 19 Year Old (84.5) n21 t22 f20 b21.5. A pleasant house style chewathon. Nutty, biting but with a tang. 40%. Whyte & Mackay Distillers Ltd.

Whyte & Mackay Supreme 22 Year Old (87) n21 t23 f20.5 b22.5. Ignore the nose and finish and just enjoy the early ride. 43%

Whyte & Mackay Oldest 30 Year Old (87.5) n23 t23 f20 b21.5. What exasperating whisky this is. So many good things about it, but... 45%

Whyte & Mackay Original Aged Blended 40 Years Old (93) n23 t24 f22 b24. I admit, when I nosed and tasted this at room temp, not a lot happened. Pretty, but closed. But once warmed in the hand up to full body temperature, it was obvious that Richard Paterson had created a quite wonderful monster of a blend offering so many avenues to explore that the mind almost explodes. Well done RP for creating something that further proves, and in such magnitude, just how warmth can make an apparently ordinary whisky something bordering genius. *45%*

Whyte & Mackay Special (84.5) n20 t23 f20 b21.5. If you are looking for a big-flavoured dram and with something approaching a vicious left uppercut, this might be a useful bottle to have on hand. The nose, I'm afraid, has not improved over the years but there appears to be compensation with the enormity and complexity of the delivery, a veritable orgy of big, oily, juicy, murky flavours and tones if ever there was one. You cannot but like it, in the same way as you may occasionally like rough sex. But if you are looking for a delicate dram to gently kiss you and caress your fevered brow, then leave well alone. *40%*

William Grant's 12 Years Old Bourbon Cask (90.5) n23 t22.5 f22 b23. Very clever blending where balance is the key. *40%*

William Grant's 15 Years Old (85) n21 t23 f20 b21. Grain and, later, caramel dominates but the initial delivery reveals the odd moment of sheer genius and complexity on max revs. *43%*

William Grant's 25 Years Old (95.5) n23.5 t24 f24 b24 Absolutely top-rank blending that appears to maximize every last degree of complexity. Most astonishing, though, is its sprightly countenance: even Scottish footballing genius Ally MacLeod struggled to send out Ayr Utd. sides with this kind of brio. And that's saying something! A gem. *40%*

William Grant's 100 US Proof Superior Strength (92) n23 t24 f22 b23. A fruitier drop now than it was in previous years but no less supremely constructed. *50% (100 US proof)*

William Grant's Ale Cask Reserve (89) n21 t23 f22 b23. A real fun blend that is just jam-packed with jagged malty notes. The hops were around more on earlier bottlings, but watch out for them. Nothing pint-sized about this: this is a big blend and very true in flavour/shape to the original with just a delicious shading of grain to really up the complexity. *40%*

William Grant's Family Reserve (94) n25 t23 f22 b24. There are those puzzled by my obvious love affair with blended whisky - both Scotch and Japanese - at a time when malts are all the rage. But take a glass of this and carefully nurture and savour it for the best part of half an hour and you may begin to see why I believe this to be the finest art form of whisky. For my money, this brand - brilliantly kept in tip-top shape by probably the world's most naturally gifted blender - is the closest thing to the blends of old and, considering it is pretty ubiquitous, it defies the odds for quality. It is a blend with which you can start the day and end it: one to keep you going at low points in between, or to celebrate the victories. It is the daily dram that has everything. *40%*

William Grant's Rare Cask Reserves 25 Years Old Blended Scotch Whisky (88) n22.5 busy without offering a narrative. Punchy, salty notes, dried dates and a vague fruitiness; **t23** confident delivery: silky textured and mouth-filling; a little ulmo honey mingles with dull fruit and butterscotch; **f20.5** fudgy and furry; **b22** an appealing blend that appears to be designed to come at you as a concept rather than allowing the different instrumentalists to have the odd solo. Not helped by what appear to be some less than perfect casks. *47%.*

William Grant's Sherry Cask Reserve (82) n20 t22 f20 b20. Raspberry jam and cream from time to time. Attractive, but somewhat plodding dram that's content in second gear. *40%*

William Lawson's Finest (85) n18.5 t22.5 f22 b22. Not only has the label become more colourful, but so, too, has the whisky. However that has not interfered with the joyous old-fashioned grainy bite. A complex and busy blend from the old charm school. *40%*

William Lawson's Scottish Gold Aged 12 Years (89) n22 t23 f22 b22. For years Lawson's 12 was the best example of the combined wizardry of clean grain, unpeated barley and good bourbon cask that you could find anywhere in the world: a last-request dram before the firing squad. Today it is still excellent, but just another sherried blend. What's that saying about if it's not being broke...? *40%*

Windsor 12 Years Old (81) n20 t21 f20 b20. Thick, walloped-on blend that you can stand a spoon in. Hard at times to get past the caramel. *40%. Diageo.*

Windsor Aged 17 Years Super Premium (89) n23 t22 f22 b22. Still on the safe side for all its charm and quality. An extra dose of complexity would lift this onto another level. *40%*

Windsor 21 Years Old (90) n20 t23 f24 b23. Recovers fabulously from the broken nose and envelopes the palate with a silky-sweet style unique to the Windsor scotch brand. Excellent. *40%. Diageo.*

Ye Monks (86) n20 t23 f21.5 b21.5. Just hope they are praying for less caramel to maximize the complexity. Still, a decent spicy chew and outstanding bite which is great fun and worth finding when in South America. *40%. Diageo.*

Yokozuna Blended 3 Years Old (79.5) n18.5 t20.5 f20 b20.5. It appears the Mongols are gaining a passion for thick, sweet, toffeed, oily, slightly feinty whisky. For a nation breastfed on airag, this'll be a doddle... *40%. Speyside Distillers. Mongolian market.*

Irish Whiskey

Of all the whiskies in the world, it is Irish which probably causes most confusion amongst both established whisk(e)y lovers and the novices.

Ask anyone to define what is unique to Irish whiskey - apart from it being made in Ireland and the water likewise coming from that isle - and the answer, if the audiences around the world at my tastings are anything to go by, are in this order: i) it is triple distilled; ii) it is never, ever, made using peat; iii) they exclusively use sherry casks; iv) it comes from the oldest distillery in the world; v) it is made from a mixture of malted and unmalted barley.

Only one of these answers is true: the fifth. This is usually the final answer extracted from the audience when the last hand raised sticks to his guns after the previous four responses have been shot down.

And it is this type of whiskey, known as Irish Pot Still, which has again been named as Irish Whiskey of the Year. Last year it was the Midleton Dair Ghaelach, in 2014 and 2013 it was the Redbreast 12-years-old and in 2012 Power's John's Lane. This year it was, just as in 2015, the Jameson Redbreast 21-years-old. Remarkable, considering that 25 years ago Irish Distillers had decided to end the bottling of Pure Pot Still. Just shows what a little campaigning can do.

Jim Murray's Whisky Bible Irish Whiskey of the Year Winners

	Irish Whiskey	Irish Pot Still Whiskey	Irish Single Malt	Irish Blend	Irish Single Cask
2004	Jameson	N/A	N/A	N/A	N/A
2005	Jameson	N/A	N/A	N/A	N/A
2006	Bushmills Rare 21	N/A	N/A	N/A	N/A
2007	Redbreast 15 Year Old	N/A	N/A	N/A	N/A
2008	Tyrconnel 10 Madeira Fin	N/A	N/A	N/A	N/A
2009	Jameson 2007 Vintage Reserve	N/A	N/A	N/A	N/A
2010	Redbreast 12 Year Old	N/A	N/A	N/A	N/A
2011	Sainsbury's Dun Leire 8	N/A	N/A	N/A	N/A
2012	Powers John's Lane Release 12	N/A	Sainsbury's Dun Leire 8	N/A	Jameson Rarest 07 Vintage Reserve
2013	Redbreast 12 Year Old	Redbreast 12 Cask Strength	Bushmills Aged 21	Jameson	Tyrconnell S C 11 Year Old
2014	Redbreast 12 Cask Strength	Redbreast 12 Cask Strength	Bushmills Aged 21	Jameson	N/A
2015	Redbreast Aged 21	Redbreast Aged 21	Bushmills Aged 21	Jameson	N/A
2016	Midleton Dair Ghaelach	Midleton Dair Ghaelach	SMWS 118.3 (Cooley) 1991	Powers Gold Label	N/A
2017	Redbreast Aged 21	Redbreast Aged 21	Bushmills 21 Year Old	Jameson	Teeling S C 2004

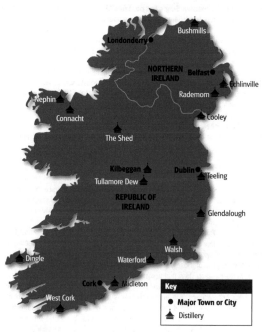

Pure Pot Still
MIDLETON (old distillery)

Midleton 25 Years Old Pot Still db **(92) n24 t24 f21 b23**. A really enormous whiskey that is in the truest classic Irish style. The un-malted barley really does make the tastebuds hum and the oak has added fabulous depth. Interesting when tasted against an American rye – the closeness of the character is there to be experienced, but also the differences. A subtle mature whiskey of unquestionable quality. Superb. *43%*

Midleton 30 Years Old Pot Still db **(85) n19 t22 f22 b22**. A typically brittle, crunchy Irish pot still where the un-malted grains have a telling say. The oak has travelled as far as it can without having an adverse effect. A chewy whiskey which revels in its bitter-sweet balance. An impressively tasty and fascinating insight into yesteryear. *45%*

Midleton 1973 Pure Pot Still db **(95) n24 t24 f23 b24**. The enormous character of true Irish pot still whiskey (a mixture of malted and unmalted barley) appears to absorb age better than most other grain spirits. This one is in its element. But drink at full strength and at body temp (it is pretty closed when cool) for the most startling – and memorable effects. I have no idea how much this costs. But if you can find one and afford it... then buy it!! *56%*

MIDLETON (new distillery)

Green Spot db **(94.5) n23.5 t24 f23.5 b23.5**. This honeyed state has remained a few years, and its sharpness has now been regained. Complex throughout. Unquestionably one of the world's greatest branded whiskies. *40%. Irish Distillers for Mitchell & Son, Dublin.*

Green Spot Château Léoville Barton finished in Bordeaux Wine Casks db **(83.5) n21.5 t22.5 f19 b20.5**. Have a kind of proprietarily, fatherly feel about Green Spot, as it was an unknown whiskey outside Ireland until revealed to the world 21 years ago in my Irish Whiskey Almanac. And fitting this is finished in Ch. Leoville Barton as I have a fair bit of that from the 70s and 80s in my cellar – and the creators of Green Spot was Dublin's oldest wine shop. However, after all that, have to say that this is a disappointment. There are warning signs on the nose and confirmation on the finish that the wine barrel did not escape the dastardly sulphur treatment. Which means it is dull where it should be bright, though the delivery does reach out for complexity and there are some excellent light cocoa moments. But the sulphur wins. *46%*

Master Distiller's Selection Single Pot db **(94) n23.5** something of the cake shop about this: sweet with random honey, apples, citrus and flour notes mixing together eloquently and enticingly; **t23.5** the first two waves are soft and welcoming. What follows is a ram-rod firm thwack of barley, which is as crunchy as it is chewy. Slowly, some fruit notes unravel, mainly of the plummy type, though the odd pear shows its hand. The spices are beginning to warm; **f23** maybe some sherry at work as there is a vague furriness now. But the spices and the crisp barley remain on course to the end; **b24** at the sweeter end of the Pot Still spectrum. The use of fruit as a background noise, rather than a lead, is a masterstroke. *46%. 500 bottles. ncf.*

Midleton Barry Crockett Legacy db **(94) n23.5 t24.5 f22.5 b23.5.** Another fabulous Pot Still, very unusual for its clever use of the varied ages of the oak to form strata of intensity. One very sophisticated whiskey. *46%. ncf.*

Midleton Dair Ghaelach db **(97) n23.5** a plethora of bourbon-style liquorice and honey – though, here, closer to heather honey. Polished oak floors, melt-on-the-nose grain...and so it goes on...and on...and on... An odd hybrid of Kentucky and Irish...but a thoroughbred, of course...; **t25** that is probably one of the great deliveries of the year. Absolutely abounds in pot still character, both being hard as nails and soft as a virgin's kiss. But the way it interacts with the ulmo honey/red liquorice/heather-honey-vanilla/embracing grain is something of a once in a lifetime experience. And, what's more, barely a hint of spice throughout...; **f24** just long, gorgeously silky and soft and a delicious furtherance of the spellbinding flavour compounds of before...; **b24.5** for heaven's sake. This is just too ridiculously beautiful...and so unmistakably Irish for all the virgin oak. Truly world class. *58.1%*

Midleton Single Pot Still Single Cask 1991 cask no. 48750, dist Nov 91, bott Oct 12 db **(96.5) n23.5** usual mix of beech honey, manuka honey and an indistinguishable fruit-like sweetness, somewhere between pear and strawberry; a fascinating blend of bourbon and rye styles; **t24** just one of those deliveries you pray for: magnificent mouth feel and weight, just about perfect in fact. Then that unique iron rod of sweet barley couched in velvet. The salivation levels are off the scale, while the hard-nosed unmalted barley offers up their standard crisp honey tones. The enormous age is supported by a crypto-bourbon attack of liquorice and hickory; **f23.5** softens, elongates and really kicks in with more bourbon/ rye-style molasses, though this only adds weight to the strawberry and chocolate mousse towards the very death; **b24.5** like the majority of Pot Still whiskeys, takes a little time to settle in the glass: always give it time to breath and come alive. When it finally does...just....wow!! *54.1%. ncf. Irish Distillers. Warehouse No. M09, exclusive to The Whisky Exchange.*

Midleton Single Pot Still Single Cask 1994 cask no. 74060, dist 15 Nov 94 db **(93) n23 t23 f23.5 b23.5.** Probably a mod pot as opposed to a heavy one. A charming bottling, though if only they had been braver and gone for full cask strength... *46%. ncf. Irish Distillers. Exclusive to the Celtic Whiskey Shop.*

Paddy Centenary Edition db **(93) n22 t23.5 f24 b23.5.** This 7-year-old Pure Pot Still whiskey really is a throwback. All Paddy's original whiskey from this era would have been from the old Midleton distillery which sits, in aspic, beside the one opened in 1975. Even with the likelihood of oats being in the mash in those days, still can't believe the original would have been quite as sweet on the palate – and soul – as this. *43%*

Powers John's Lane Release Aged 12 Years db **(96.5) n24** unmistakable. Unique. Utopian. Irish pure pot still at its most embracing and magnificent. That bizarre bipolar character of rock hard grain so at home in the company of silky, molten honey. Some light, non-specific fruit – a bit like boiled sweets in a candy shop. But a vague menthol note, too...; **t25** as Irish whiskey goes: perfection! The delivery can come only from Irish Pot still – I have encountered it nowhere else. And it is a replay of the nose: soft, dissolve-on-the-palate honey and elsewhere strands of something much firmer – hardening more and more as it moves to the middle ground; **f23.5** wonderful fade: a distant medium roast Java, the Lubec marzipan which you just knew would be coming; a little caramel; some orangey notes... **b24** this is a style of Irish Pot Still I have rarely seen outside the blending lab. I had many times thought of trying to find some of this and bottling it myself. No need now. I think I have just tasted Irish Whiskey of the Year, and certainly one of the top five world whiskies of the year. *46%*

Powers John's Lane Release Aged 12 Years bott 13 Nov 12 db **(91) n24 t23.5 f21 b22.5.** Researchers some time ago discovered the American accent is derived from an Irish one (and the Canadian from Scots). As pure Irish pot still is the foundation stone of all Irish whiskey, there is no little irony that so many aspects of this bottling is more recognisable as Kentuckian than it is from Cork. Only a slightly off beam cask undermines the finish a tad. Otherwise, superb. *46%. Irish Distillers.*

Powers Signature Release bott code. L3065 db **(91) n23.5 t22.5 f22 b23.** When I first tasted pure pot still over three decades ago, virtually all that I came across was maturing in oloroso butts. Often, the quality of the casks was better than the spirit from the dilapidated distilleries which produced it. Here again the sherry butts are of the highest quality. Maybe one is below par and this is evidenced, very vaguely, on the finish. But, overall, superb! *46%*

Powers Signature Release db **(92.5)** n23 complex: a great deal of bourbon-style tannin digs deep, assisted by the rigidity of the grain. Something sherry-related lurks in the shadows; t24 a truly beautiful delivery: marmalade on toast and a quick burst of spices. A little ulmo honey has been stirred into the pot (still!) but it is the combination of tannin and barley which sparks off a fabulously juicy phase; f22 the ulmo honey moves closer towards vanilla, but then a rapid drying process occurs as a dulling, tingling furriness from the sherry takes effect – a shame...; b23 I have lately become a little nervous of Irish matured in sherry. At the turn of this century there was plenty in the warehouse and sulphur was not a problem. Something has changed, for now it is. Here, there is not much, but just enough to it take the edge off what had been, until then, a wonderful experience. Hopefully in future bottlings this can be more carefully monitored and the oak profile adjusted. If so, greatness awaits... *46%. ncf.*

Redbreast Aged 12 Years bott 7 Jan 13, bott code: L3007 db **(89)** n22 t23.5 f21.5 b22. This one took me aback. One of the softest Irish pot stills I have encountered, in or outside a lab. Delicious, but displaying very little of the trademark steel which sets this whiskey apart. *40%. Irish Distillers.*

Redbreast Aged 12 Years Cask Strength batch B1/11 db **(96)** n24.5 just about the ultimate in Irish whiskey noses. Absolutely rock hard: you feel you could cut diamonds with an aroma like this. It is curiously fruity in that unique Irish Pot Still way, and not just from the obvious sherry involvement, yet shows clearly it's a relation to another whiskey style: American rye. A little hint of mint and lavender goes a long way and offers the only softness in this glorious bitter-sweet aroma; t24.5 my, oh my, oh my, oh my...one of those deliveries which takes your breath away and it is a few moments before you can compose yourself to think. Or, in my case, to compose myself to compose. The first thing is the sweetness which is never apparent on the nose: here we have the crunchiest Demerara sugar meeting even crunchier muscovado; then a litany of varied fruit and quasi-rye juicy bits...mmmmmm; f23 majestically long and moves in fabulously mysterious chocolatey ways - chocolate and raisin to be more precise - generating even more salivating moments right until the big chocolate sponge/sherry trifle finale. Late spices, even the faintest possible bitterness of a rogue treated sherry butt, though for once it does no serious damage, other than costing it a possible place in the world's top three. The vanillas come into action for the first time here, too...; b24 this is Irish pot still on steroids. And sporting an Irish brogue as thick as my great great grandfather John Murray's. To think, had I not included Redbreast in Jim Murray's Irish Whiskey Almanac back in 1994, after it had already been unceremoniously scrapped and discontinued, while championing the then entirely unknown Irish Pot Still cause this brand would no longer have been with us. If I get run over by a bus tomorrow, at least I have that as a tick when St Peter is totting up the plusses and minuses... And with the cask strength, he might even give me two... *57.7%. ncf. Irish Distillers.*

Redbreast Aged 12 Years Cask Strength Edition batch B1/12 bott 4 Apr 12, bott code: L2095 db **(97)** n24.5 t24 f24 b24.5. For the sake of space, it is best I refer you to the tasting notes for Batch B1/11. Except here there is less fruit and absolutely no off notes. It is, as Irish whiskey is concerned, nigh-on perfection. *58.6%. ncf. Irish Distillers.*

Redbreast Aged 12 Years Cask Strength batch no. B1/13 db **(95.5)** n24 quintessential pot still: a double bill of soft and rock hard notes, one vanishing behind the other and, occasionally, co-starring. There is a blood orange and marmalade fruitiness, plus a liquorice and molasses weightiness; t24 salivating delivery, to the point where I am nearly drooling all over the computer. A slight note from the odd cask dulls matters, but the sparkle is so profound elsewhere it doesn't matter for now. Crystalline Demerara sugars conjure up a bit of sweet smokiness, as does the rumbling liquorice and vanilla...and even Fisherman's Friend cough sweet; f23.5 the cough sweet continues while the odd degree of bitterness creeps in. But that is more than offset by the magnificently long cocoa and praline tail... b24 oh, for that bitterness. A potential World Whisky of the Year otherwise? Perhaps... *59.9%. ncf.*

Redbreast 15 Years Old db **(94)** n23 t24 f23 b24. For years I have been pleading for Irish Distillers to launch a pot still at 46%, natural colour and unchillfiltered. Well, I've got two out of three wishes. And what we have here is a truly great Irish whiskey and my pulse races in the certain knowledge it can get better still... *46%. ncf. France.*

Redbreast Aged 21 Years db **(96)** n24 so rare to find age so obvious on a nose, yet so positive in all it does. The pot still is easily recognised with its unique firmness and playful bite, surrounded by a vague fruitiness and encrusted muscovado. But the honey astonishes: so deft and calming, offering acacia in sweetness and heather in floral weight; a half mark is lost through for a light dustiness revealing, surely, added caramel; t25 perfection: at once the palate is met by a two-toned delivery - a voluptuous silkiness enwrapping steel-hard spine which a great pot still whiskey demands. The sugars melt first, then the malt and this opens the way for a delicate spice to throw a deft contrast against the cough-sweet style mentholated citrus and honey; **f23** concentrates now on the more simple aspects; the vanilla-honey balance, the fading malt, the chalkiness of the cask against the buzzing spice....though, sadly that buzzing goes on to reveal the weakest of sulphur inputs, and all the standard off-key bitterness which follows; **b24** I have tasted no shortage of 21-year-old pot still before in my career, but that was some time back when the whiskey in question was usually from the original Jameson distillery in Dublin, or Power's. I also managed to get my hands on some old stuff from the original Midleton as well as Tullamore Dew and few others. That old spirit had been made at a time when those distilleries were in the process of being closed down and the quality was nothing like it once was. This, I admit, is the first I can remember from Midleton's rebuilt distillery and it knocks the spots off the Jameson and Power's. Those did not have the balance or the insouciance so far as the honey involvement was concerned or the all-round world-class star quality which positively radiates from the glass. Hopefully this gentle giant amongst the world's truly great whiskies and near blue print for the perfect pot still Irish is here to stay. Only for the next bottling absolutely no need for the pointless caramel and the damaging sherry, both which contribute in tarnishing the dazzling sheen. There are times when less is so significantly more. *46%. ncf. WB15/417*

⤜ **Redbreast All Sherry Single Cask** db (73.5) n17 t23.5 f15 b18. I mean: seriously guys....??? A single cask pure pot still whiskey and you bottle one with sulphur fingerprints all over it? I don't have the number of what cask this is from, so I hope yours will have come from clean sherry. If you have, you are in for a treat, because the sheer brilliance and magnitude of this whiskey was able to blot out the sulphur for a good seven or eight seconds as it reached heights of near perfection. A bowl of raspberries now and a 20 minute break to help cleanse my palate and relieve my tongue which is still seriously furred up. So frustrating, as I could see a clean butt of this getting Single Cask Whisky of the Year ... *59.9%. sc.*

Redbreast Mano a Lámh db (85) n22.5 t22.5 f19 b21. Curious that on an all sherry butt bottling, the most enjoyable flavour profile is a spiced chocolate one which begins about four or five beats after the original big, soppy, lush delivery. No prizes for guessing why the score goes down towards the finish. By the way: love the robin on the label – a kind of weird cross between an immature and adult robin with the face of a white wagtail thrown in. Like the whiskey type: unique! *46%. ncf.*

Yellow Spot Aged 12 Years bourbon, sherry and Malaga casks db (88.5) n23.5 t22.5 f20 b22.5. If anything, just a shade too many wine casks used which somewhat drowns out the unique IP character. Reminds me of when Barry Walsh was working on the triple maturation theme of the Bushmills 16, probably about 15 years ago. Not until the very last days did all the components click. Just before then, it went through a phase like this (though obviously with malt, not IPS). Knowing current blender Billy Leighton as I do, I can see this whiskey improving in future batches as lessons are learned. not that there isn't already much to enjoy... *46%.*

OLD COMBER

Old Comber 30 Years Old Pure Pot Still (88) n23 t24 f20 b21. A classic example of a whiskey spending a few Summers too many in wood: increasing age doesn't equal excellence. That said, always very drinkable and early on positively sparkles with a stunning mouthfeel. Out of respect for the old I have made the markings for taste cover the first seven or eight seconds... *40%*

Single Malt
COOLEY

Connemara bott code L9042 db (88) n23 t22.5 f20.5 b22. One of the softest smoked whiskies in the world which though quite lovely gives the impression it can't make its mind up about what it wants to be. *40%*

Connemara Aged 8 Years db (85) n22.5 t21.5 f20 b21. Another Connemara lacking teeth. The peat charms, especially on the nose, but the complexity needs working on. *46%*

Connemara Aged 12 Years bott code L9024 db (85.5) n23 t21.5 f20 b21. The nose, with its beautiful orange, fruity lilt, puts the shy smoke in the shade. *40%*

Connemara Cask Strength bott code L9041 db (90) n21.5 t23 f22 b22.5. A juicy negative of the standard bottling: does its talking on the palate rather than nose. Maybe an absence of caramel notes might have something to do with that. *57.9%*

Connemara Distillers Edition db (86) n22 t22.5 f20 b21.5. When I give whisk(e)y tastings around the world, I love to include Connemara. Firstly, people don't expect peated Irish. Secondly, their smoked whisky stock is eclectic and you never quite know what is going to come out of the bottle. This is a particularly tight, sharp style. No prisoners survived... *43%*

Connemara Turf Mór Limited Edition Small Batch Collection bott code L10215 db **(94)** n23.5 t23.5 f23.5 b23.5. At Burnley FC, the wine served in their boardroom is The Claret's Claret, naturally. I will not be surprised to find this the whiskey on offer... The tasting notes to this just about perfectly match the ones above. *58.2%*

Cooley Poitín Origin Edition dist 26 July 2011, rotation 232/11 db **(92.5)** n23.5 t23 f23 b23. Full bloodied and rumbustious, this is high quality new make Irish that absolutely thumps the salivation button on palate. And, apparently, a mix of malted and unmalted barley in the traditional Irish Pot Still style....though this neither noses nor tastes anything like the new spirit from Midleton. The label waffles on about 1,000 years of Irish tradition. But the use of unmalted barley came into use only when distillers found a way of avoiding tax on the malted stuff. Were there taxes on alcohol in Ireland 1,000 years ago...? *65%*

Inish Turk Beg Maiden Voyage db **(91.5)** n22 t23.5 f22.5 b22.5 Brooding and quite delicious. *44%*

Locke's Aged 8 Years bott code L9005 db **(88)** n22.5 t22 f22 b21.5. A beautiful malt at probably this distillery's optimum age. *40%*

Locke's Aged 8 Years Crock (92) n23 t24 f22 b23. Much, much better cask selection than of old: some real honey casks here. A crock of gold...! *40%*

Locke's Aged 10 Years Premier Crew cask no. 713, dist Feb 00, bott Jul 10 db **(88)** n22 t23 f21 b22. The cask does its best to try and spoil the barley fun. Here's a tip: stick to younger malts. Cooley is brilliant and relatively undiscovered at between seven and nine years. And there is less time for cask to bite back... *46%. Cooley for The Irish Whisky Society. 292 bottles.*

Scotch Malt Whisky Society Cask 117.4 Aged 22 Years refill sherry hogshead, dist 16 Sept 91 **(94.5)** n24 huge clean fruit just bursting with juice; the background noise suggests very old oak - old enough to offer a second fruity string to the bow....this time of the exotic variety; t23.5 perhaps the most silky texture of any Cooley I have ever encountered – and I have sampled quite literally thousands of their casks. Despite the age, the salivation factor rockets through the roof, the spice cow-towed by the juiciness of it all; f23 some real complexity here as the fruit settles down and the malt actually comes out to play with its buttery, biscuit friends; b24 the oldest unpeated Cooley I have ever encountered. And fully upholds my belief that this was a malt built for age, unlike its triple-distilled counterpart north of the border. *50.3%. sc. 266 bottles.*

Scotch Malt Whisky Society Cask 117.5 Aged 22 Years refill sherry hogshead, dist 16 Sept 91 **(94)** n23.5 a pithy, fruity number, clean and clever despite its antiquity. The fruit element is clear, but takes a humbled stance, allowing the oak to show its equally understated depth; t23 much more lively and assertive on delivery – indeed, the magnitude of the flavour profile arrives as a shock. The spices are seismic, the grape – compared to the nose – tight and borderline aggressive; f24 cools and calms down into something far more genteel as the oak begins to show a certain bourbon degree of honeycomb and liquorice. But the fruit is never far away...; b23.5 good grief. A tempestuous ride – a genuine rollercoaster which somehow offers subtlety amid the fireworks. Well done SMWS for landing three of the best Irish whiskeys you'll taste for many a year. *55.5%. sc. 236 bottles.*

Scotch Malt Whisky Society Cask 118.3 Aged 22 Years 2nd fill barrel, dist 14 Oct 91 **(96)** n24 fading beauty: early peated malt designed for their Connemara brand could sometimes be of low phenolic value. This appears to be of that style, but what remains is bolstered by the first movements of an exotic fruit concerto.; t23.5 ...and it is that very same exotic fruit which shows first, though hand-in-hand with delightfully explosive spice: a little pineapple and mango marry together despite those peppery spices, though now it is the peat's turn to slowly creep into the picture; f24.5 one of the great finishes of the year: the smoke has transformed into a mint-chocolate fade with the spices gaining a second, busier wind; a little desiccated coconut and caramelised biscuit fits delightfully with those lingering fruit tones; b24 presumably a different number (118) has been given to Cooley's peated malt, though made in the same stills. Odd. Anyway, whatever it is...it's bloody magnificent. *57.9%. sc. 206 bottles.*

Tullamore Dew Single Malt 10 Years Old db **(91.5)** n23 t23 f22.5 b23. The best whiskey I have ever encountered with a Tullamore label. Furtively complex and daringly delicate. If only they could find a way to minimise the toffee... *40%. William Grant & Sons.*

The Tyrconnell Aged 10 Years Madeira Finish bott code L8136 db **(91)** n23 t23 f22 b23. Not quite the award-winning effort of a few years back, as those lilting high notes which so complimented the baser fruit tones haven't turned up here. But remains in the top echelon and still much here to delight the palate. *46%*

The Tyrconnell Single Cask 11 Year Old db **(95.5)** n23.5 t25 f23 b24. Well, if there weren't enough reasons to go to Dublin, you now have this... *46%. sc. Exclusive to the Celtic Whiskey Shop.*

Clonmel Peated Aged 8 Years (86) n22 t23 f20 b21. Take the toffee away and you would have one hell of an Irish. Claims to be "Pure Pot Still". It isn't (in Irish terms): it's malt. 40%

Craoi na Mona Irish Malt Whiskey (68) n16 t18 f17 b17. I'm afraid my Gaelic is slipping these days: I assume Craoi na Mona means "Feinty, badly made smoky malt"... (that's the end of my tasting for the day...) 40%

Glendalough Single Malt Irish Whiskey Aged 7 Years bourbon casks **(79)** n18 t22 f20 b19. Disappointing on so many levels. Malt at Cooley at 7-year-old, should, if the casks are picked assiduously, be vibrant and brimming with barley and vitality. That only happens for the odd moment or two on delivery. The nose reveals some pretty poor barrels at work while two much toffee flattens the experience. Love the spice, though. 46%. ncf.

Glendalough Single Malt Irish Whiskey Aged 13 Years bourbon casks **(90)** n22.5 fresh dates sprinkled, like a Shrove Tuesday pancake, with sugar and lemon...and a touch of lime, too; t23 superb texture: the barley bristles with oaky spice while the light oils help get the spices established; f21.5 dies slightly as the oak dries vividly and toffee kicks in; a touch milky, too; b23 a rather beautiful whiskey, spilling over with spices. A few tired casks evident, though. 46%. ncf.

Glen Dimplex (88) n23 t22 f21 b22. Overall, clean and classically Cooley. 40%

Liquid Sun Cooley 1999 bott 2012 **(87)** n22 t22 f21.5 b21.5 Awash with natural caramels and enjoyable in a horrible way...without the horrible. 53.2%. nc ncf sc. The Whisky Agency.

Magilligan Cooley Pure Pot Still Single Malt (91) n22 t22 f24 b23. A touch of honey for good measure ...or maybe not..!! 43%. Ian MacLeod Distillers.

Magilligan Irish Whiskey Peated Malt 8 Years Old (89) n21 t23 f22 b23. Such a different animal from the docile creature that formally passed as Magilligan peated. Quite lovely...and very classy. 43%. Ian Macleod Distillers.

Merry's Single Malt (83) n20 t22 f20 b21. Ultra-clean barley rich nose is found on the early palate. The finish is flat, though. 40%

Michael Collins Irish Whiskey Single Malt db **(68)** n17 t18 f17 b16. Bloody hell, I thought. Didn't anyone get my message from last year? Apparently not – and it's our fault as the tasting notes above were accidentally edited out before they went in. Sorry. But the caramel in the latest bottling has been upped to take the whisky from deep gold to bronze. Making this among the most over-coloured single malt I have tasted in years. Please guys. For the love of whiskey. Please let us taste exactly what a great malt this could be. 40% (80 proof)

Milroy's of Soho Single Malt Cooley Aged 11 Years first fill bourbon, cask no. 3442, dist 22 Oct 01, bott 5 Nov 12 **(91)** n23.5 t23 f22.5 b23. Seriously enjoyable. Just what the doctor ordered...! 46%

Sainsbury's Single Malt Irish Whiskey bott code L10083/16 **(87.5)** n22 t22 f21.5 b22. Classic Cooley showing its big, malty depth. 40%

Shannahan's (92) n23 t22 f24 b23. Cooley natural and unplugged: quite adorable. 40%

Slieve Foy Single Malt Aged 8 Years bott code L9108 **(88)** n23 t22.5 f21 b21.5. Never deviates from its delicate touch. 40%. Cooley for Marks & Spencer.

⟨⟩ **Tyrconnell 16 Year Old Single Malt (92)** n22.5 seriously odd. Like the fruit and vanilla you get from ice cream...; t24 any more salivating and you are likely to expire from dehydration. Again, there is a non-specific fruitiness to the fore, followed up by intensely fresh barley...and then spice; f22.5 the vanilla reverts back to its ice cream quality, with that strange fruit in tow and malt enough to supply a brewery...; b23 if anyone on here is old enough to remember Zoom lollies – and miss them as much as I after a gap of nearly half a century – then here's your chance to wallow down Memory Lane. So different. And so delicious! 46%

Vom Fass Cooley Irish Single Malt 8 Years Old (88) n22 t22.5 f21.5 b22. A very decent, if undemonstrative, example of the distillery at an age which well suits. 40%

The Wild Geese Single Malt (85.5) n21.5 t21 f22 b21. "A Rare Blend of Pure Aged Irish Malt Whiskies" says the front label. Yet it is a single malt. Confusing. And very unhelpful to a whisky public already being totally bamboozled by the bizarre and misguided antics of the Scotch Whisky Association. It is not a blend. It is a mixing of Cooley malt whiskey, as I understand it. The back label's "Smoother Because We Distil it Longer" is also a bit of a blarney. It's made in a pot still and whilst it is true that if you distil faster (by higher temperatures) you could well end up with "hot" whiskey, I am not aware of this being distilled at a significantly slower rate than at either Bushmills or Midleton. Or do they mean the cut of the run from the spirit still is longer, which would impart more oils – not all of them great? Just ignore the Wild Goose chase the labels send you on and enjoy the malt, with all its failings, for what it is (and this is pretty enjoyable in an agreeably rough and ready manner, though not exactly the stiff of Irish whiskey purists): which in this case for all its malt, toffee and delicate smoke, also appears to have more than a slight touch of feints - so maybe they were right all along...!!! 43%. Cooley for Avalon.

OLD KILBEGGAN

Kilbeggan Distillery Reserve Malt matured in quarter casks, batch no. 1, bott Jun 10 db **(89) n22.5 t22.5 f22.5 b22.** An endearingly soft malt to see Kilbeggan distillery back into the whiskey world. Shame it has been reduced to 40%, as this one demanded to be at least 46% - indeed, preferably naked - and allowing those delicate, elegant but marginalised characters a chance to bloom. But welcome back...and I look forward to many an evening with me tasting you as you blossom, as I am sure you will. It has been nearly 20 years since I first discovered the beauty of Kilbeggan Distillery and I have countless times since then dreamed of that moment. *40%. 1500 bottles. Available only in the distillery gift shop.* ⊙

The Spirit of Kilbeggan 1 Month (90.5) n22 t23 f23 b22.5. Wow!! They are really getting to grips with the apparatus. Full bodied and lush small still feel to this but radiating complexity, depth, barley and cocoa in equal measures. The development of the oils really does give this excellent length. Impressed! *65.5%*

The Spirit of Kilbeggan 1 Year (85) n20.5 t21 f22 b21.5. A veritable Bambi of a spirit: a typical one year old malt which, as hard as it tries, just can't locate its centre of gravity. Even so, the richness is impressive and some highly sugared chocolate mousse near the end is a treat. *62.7%*

The Spirit of Kilbeggan 2 Years (84) n20 t21 f22 b21. A tad raw and a little thin. There is some decent balance between oak and malt, but the overall feeling is that the still has not yet been quite mastered. *60.3%*

OLD BUSHMILLS

Bushmills Aged 10 Years matured in two woods db **(92.5) n23 t23 f23 b23.5.** Absolutely superb whiskey showing great balance and the usual Antrim 19th century pace with its favour development. The odd bottle of this I have come across over the last couple of years has been spoiled by the sherry involvement. But, this, as is usually the case, is absolutely spot on. *40%*

Bushmills Select Casks Aged 12 Years married with Caribbean rum cask db **(95) n23** unusual moist rum and raisin cake effect: effective and just enough spice to deliver extra complexity. Just the very slightest hint of bourbon, too; **t24** adorable malt richness; biscuity and stupendously seasoned yet always remains fresh and mouthwatering. The sweetness is very cleverly controlled; **f24** there are just so many layers to this: the oak is a growing force, but restricts itself to a vanilla topping; **b24** one of the most complex Bushmills in living memory, and probably since it was established in 1784. *40%*

Bushmills Aged 16 Years db **(71) n18 t21 f15 b17.** In my days as a consultant Irish whiskey blender, going through the Bushmills warehouses I found only one or two sulphur-treated butts. Alas, there are many more than that at play here. 40%

Bushmills Aged 21 Years db **(95.5) n24.5** this remains something of a Chinese puzzle on the nose: just how do all those different notes , sometimes soft and rounded, sometimes hard and angular, many of them fruity, manage to intertwine...yet never clash? And why can you never detach one without another clinging on to it. If Sherlock Holmes tried to solve it, this would be a three pipe conundrum...except the use of tobacco would ruin the experience. Just marvel at the greengage and physalis, the flaked vanilla and liquorice, the ulmo honey and hickory... so much else besides; **t24** as melt-in-the-mouth as a whiskey can be: amazingly juicy barley offers the cutting edge and lead while a plethora of delicate sugars dissolve on impact; the fruit is served as a perpetual mixed salad; **f23.5** this is where I am really impressed. Despite all the complexity of the nose and delivery, at the finish the Bushmills trademark flaky vanilla and delicate barley comes through...a signature unique to one distillery in the world; **b24** an Irish journey as beautiful as the dramatic landscape which borders the distillery. Magnificent. *40%*

◈ **Bushmills Sherry Cask Reserve Single Malt Whiskey** first-fill Oloroso sherry butts db **(80) n20.5 t22 f18 b19.5.** Although I am always 100% impartial, I would be lying if I didn't say I wanted this whiskey to be not just a high scorer, but a potential Bible world champion. Because in my tasting room stands a fine and very large - oil portrait of the Bushmills Distillery, and it is a place I have enjoyed special moments at - and love the people there dearly. And, also, in a few moments Northern Ireland's miracle-making football team are about to take on Wales in the last 16 of the Euros. But, sadly, the news, from here at least, is not good. Among the sherry butts selected has been one - and I am sure it is only one - that has been lightly sulphur treated. It means that the fruit, rather than taking off and going into complexity overdrive, crumples slightly as the vague bitterness and tightness spreads around the palate. There are some lovely fruit moments, so there are. But Bushmills should be so much better than this. As an Irish whiskey blender of old, I have been lucky enough to work with Bushmills sherry butts in pristine condition...and they can be among the best whiskeys you'll ever find on this planet. Sadly this is not fully representative. I just hope the boys in green rise to greater heights than this bottling and don't fall to an own goal like the one scored here.... 40%

Clontarf Single Malt (90.5) n23 t23 f22 b22.5. Beautiful in its simplicity, this has eschewed complexity for delicious minimalism; 40%. *Clontarf Irish Whiskey Co.*

Connemara Original Peated Single Malt db **(81.5)** n21 t21.5 f19 b20. It's been about a week since I last tasted a whisk(e)y at 40% abv...a shock to the system! Also a bit of a while since the first thing I got off the nose and last thing on the finish was caramel. Not the Connemara I witnessed being launched in a blaze of defiant glory those decades back. This rather meek, pleasant, safe, lightly smoked version appears to have been sanitised. Today's Connemara it may sadly be. Original Connemara it is most certainly NOT...! 40%

The Irishman Single Malt bottle no. E2496 **(83)** n20 t21 f21 b21. Highly pleasant malt but the coffee and toffee on the finish underline a caramel-style whiskey which may, potentially, offer so much more. 40%. *Hot Irishman Ltd.*

The Irishman Single Malt 12 Years Old 1st fill bourbon barrels, casks no. 70691 & 70692, bott Nov 2012 **(88)** n22 t22.5 f21.5 b22. Very pleasant but, ultimately, docile thanks to the caramels at work. Putting my Irish blender's hat on for a moment, I think the whiskey would had offered a lot more had it been carefully selected first and second fill bourbon casks at play, rather than two very similar B1s. 43%. ncf. *Hot Irishman Ltd.*

The Irishman Small Batch Single Malt batch no. 1703/2013, sherry and bourbon casks **(86.5)** n22 t22 f21 b21.5. A pleasant, sticky malt with early fudge and raisin sweetness and then an over dependence on a single caramel note. 40% *WB15/403*

Knappogue Castle Aged 12 Years bourbon cask matured **(90)** n23.5 t23 f21 b22.5. The massive toffee influence deflects from the huge character elsewhere which springs a few surprises. 40%. *Castle Brands Group.*

⬧ **The Whisky Cask Company Cù Chulainn 27 Years Old** rum cask, dist 1988 **(89)** n22.5 typically rock-hard rum effect: the sugars have to be blasted from the nose before as much as a simple vanilla can be detected; t22.5 a first-class delivery which really does make the most of that brittle malt: the barley is encrusted in sugars which slowly melt to reveal not only vivid spices but a superb butterscotch and ulmo honey mix, seemingly spread on a corn cereal; f22 lighter and slightly more bitter, which is usual for rum casks; b22.5 apparently this is from Bushmills, so the whiskey I decided to taste before Northern Ireland's game against Poland, their first in international Finals since 1986. And the first time a player from my beloved Millwall, Shane Ferguson, has taken part since Tony Cascarino represented the Republic of Ireland in 1988. 45.7%

UNSPECIFIED SINGLE MALTS

⬧ **Barr an Uisce 1803 Irish Single Malt Aged 10 Years** bourbon barrel **(92)** n22.5 red liquorice and peat so distant it could be on another planet; t23.5 just so magnificently mouth-watering. The barley really is in the finest shape...and again the smoke drifts almost invisibly though the piece; f23 long, lightly oiled with a lovely interweaving of vanilla and slightly spicy peat; b23 not sure if I have ever come across an Irish whiskey with such a pathetically weak phenolic signature. Even so, a delicious offering...! Unspecified, but Cooley for sure. 46%. ncf.

Black Corbie Boyne Single Malt 2001 refill sherry cask, cask no. 15283, dist 18 Sept 01, bott 09 Feb 15 **(93)** n23 full blown fruitcake at its most lush; t24 the palate is awash with an all consuming tidal wave of thick grape and greengage, maple syrup and treacle mix, a bit more molasses for good measure...and about as many spices as you can possibly fit in; f23 once the sugars begin to fade, a bitterness emerges – rather like the severely burnt raisins on a fruitcake; b23 balance doesn't really come into it: there is hardly any. Like Gyles Brandreth warming to a tale, this is all about effect! Just such great fun! 57.1%. sc. 221 bottles.

⬧ **Chapter 7 Irish Single Malt 2001 13 Years Old** sherry butt, cask no. 10836 **(67.5)** n17.5 t18 f15 b18. Sorry Chaps. Sweet as a nut it may be. But you have been seriously sulphured. 59.5%. sc. 293 bottles.

⬧ **Chapter 7 Irish Single Malt 1999 16 Years Old** rum cask, cask no. 5409 **(94)** n23 classic rum style: the sugars are compact and set in stone. Dark muscovado offers a degree of fruit; t23.5 sharp, brittle sugars appear to fragment on the palate. As though Maltesers have a molasses coating; f23.5 long, lightly spiced with lovely dovetailing of those dark sugars and chocolate; b24 genuinely impressive. 57.3%. sc.

Dublin in the Rare Ould Times Single Malt Irish Whiskey Aged 10 Years bourbon barrel **(81.5)** n21 t21 f19 b20.5. It was a rare old time when they made single malt whiskey like this in Dublin, for they hardly ever did. The city was the centre of Pot Still Irish and though single malt was not unknown there, it was a scarce order at the bar. When it did come along, it is hard to believe it would have been this kind of age. And, indeed, this malt would have been happier had it been a couple of years younger: the bourbon barrel at work here has allowed little malty punch to get through, while the toffee middle and finish is disappointingly dull. *40%. Bottled by Glendalough Distillery for Pete St John.*

⬧ **Eiling Lim Irish Single Malt 22 Years Old 1991** bott 2014 **(95.5) n23.5** buttered kippers (22-year-old kippers...); **t24** silky arrival. That butter is still there but the phenols have zapped up few levels to the extent that spices are seriously involved; **f24** back to the buttered kippers, amazingly! But now ulmo honey moves in to ensure a multi-faceted finale; white chocolate fills the gaps; **b24** after 22 years, this must have been one of the most highly smoked whiskeys ever produced at Cooley. A genuine landmark malt in Irish whiskey history. *48.6%. nc ncf sc. 116 bottles. 6th Release.*

Hotel Essener Hof Single Malt Irish Whisky Aged 16 Years ex rum cask **(85.5) n21.5 t22.5 f20.5 b21**. The trouble with some ex-rum casks is that they don't allow the malt to breathe or develop its own personality: whisky in a sugar-toffee straight jacket, if you like. That has happened here, though the spices are a treat. *55.7%. 211 bottles.*

Jack Ryan Single Malt Irish Whisky Aged 12 Years bourbon cask **(92.5) n23.5** mainly oak on the rise: playful diced toasted hazelnut intermingles with lemongrass and orange blossom honey; **t23** early barley offers a fresh, semi-juicy delivery; the malt is confident, elegant and clean and handles the spice with tact; **f22.5** the inevitable cocoa notes arrive in force. But the malt lingers; **b23.5** deft, very clean malt whisky where decent bourbon wood adds all kinds of beautifully paced complexity. Not even a hint of an off note. Impressive. *46%*

Limburg Dramclub Irish Malt 6 Year Old dist 2009, bott 2015 **(89) n22** lightly smoked: exceptionally clean, with little more than hints of smoke or oak; **t23** delightful delivery: probably the most salivating smoked malt you'll come across this year as the gristy sugars are left to their own devices; **f22** a tad thin, thanks to the lack of oaky input; **b22** a young, shy malt and as clean as it comes. *51.4%. 141 bottles.*

⬧ **Maltbarn Irish Malt 2001** bourbon cask, bott 2016 **(85) n21 t23 f20 b21**. A curious cask. Not happy either on nose or finish, where a degree of tightness restricts complexity. But the delivery is as beautiful as it is profound with a big Malteser signature. *48.3%. sc. 167 bottles.*

⬧ **The Quiet Man 8 Year Old Single Malt Irish Whiskey** bourbon casks **(89) n22** sharp malt and sharper citrus; underlying caramels; **t23** soft delivery with a toffee and lime intensity, moving to a meltier depth; **f21.5** caramel rich. Still the malt delivers, though...; **b22.5** had the finish not dulled quite so quickly this would have scored a lot higher. Nothing less than pleasant throughout. *40%*

⬧ **Saar Whisky No. 7 Irish Single Malt** bourbon cask, dist 2002, bott 2015 **(87.5) n21.5 t23 f21 b22.** Pleasingly malty. A few scars from the tiring cask but the overall experience is bright and one to savour. *48.7%. nc ncf sc.*

⬧ **Single Cask Collection Teeling Aged 13 Years** bourbon hogshead **(91.5) n22** effervescent, gristy sweetness; **t23** again, that grist bursts onto the scene with amazing confidence. Sharp and salivating with mid range sugars, even displaying a touch of Love Heart candy fizz; **f23.5** a more sober and integrated marriage of quality malt and impressive vanilla; **b23.5** absolutely bursting with life. Gorgeous stuff! *54.2%. sc.*

⬧ **Teeling Whiskey Single Cask 2002** bourbon cask no. 7920, filled May 02, bott Jan 16 **(93) n23** freshly sliced grapefruit, going easy on the sugars...; **t23.5** stunningly clean malt with a charming intertwangle of cap-doffing vanillas show a respectful aging process; the citrus is never far from the surface and occasionally breaks it; **f23** lightly spiced lemon easing back for the final ride with the vanilla; **b23.5** one of the most deliciously citrus-laden Irish whiskeys you'll find for a while. A superb early evening glass filler. *59.9%. ncf sc.*

⬧ **Teeling Whiskey Single Cask** sherry cask, cask no. 10811, filled Sept 01, bott Jan 16 **(94.5) n23** spices nag at the nostrils while a little Melton Hunt Cake shows its full molasses and raisin make up; **t24** what a delivery! So rare these days, this could almost make me weep... That amazing feeling that the intense fruit – complete with dazzling spice – is not going to morph into something dark and unpleasant. Instead, it delves deeper into its date and walnut script; **f23.5** a superb denouement of date and fruitcake alongside Manuka honey and treacle...; **b24** congratulations to Jack Teeling and his team for finding an unspoiled sherry butt. What a difference it makes not to be spitting out sulphur! If you find this bottling, for feck's sake just buy it. Then find out what untainted sherry matured malt should taste like. You'll soon notice the difference between this masterpiece and the failed whisky you are so often dealt with sherry cask bottlings. *59%. ncf sc.*

⟐ **Teeling Whiskey Single Cask 2004** white burgundy cask, cask no. 1404, filled Oct 04, bott Sept 15 **(96.5) n24** this isn't mucking about. The grape offers varying degrees of complexity. All of them, though, are so elegant and beautifully poised it is hard to move on to the tasting part. The sugars are first, with no wishy-washy havering between style. They are precise, while the fruit is crisp and stern. A little heather honey envelopes the saltiness; **t24.5** not sure if I have ever come across a nose so accurately transplanted onto the palate. Same again, except the chocolate raisin middle; **f23.5** vanillas begin to play an active role, perhaps reducing the complexity of the sugars. Light spices gently kiss the palate; **b24.5** one of the best single cask malts I have tasted from anywhere in the world for a long time. No sulphur, so don't worry about that. This is unadulterated, unreconstructed magnificence...! Faultless whisky. *58.8%. ncf sc.*

⟐ **Teeling Whiskey Single Malt** bott 07/2015 **(87.5) n21.5 t23.5 f21 b21.5.** Charming and, at times, intense malt impact with a lovely light fruit side-line. But a late bitterness confirms a degree of negativity from a tiring cask. The delivery, though, is pretty special. *46%. ncf.*

⟐ **Teeling Whiskey The Revival Aged 15 Years** rum barrels, bott Oct 2015 **(95) n23.5** the sugars form a tight nucleus from which vanillas and light citrus notes are slowly released. A fascinating, teasing and seductive aroma; **t24** spot on crispness that perfectly represents the rum. But the almost gristy sugars, alongside the creamy ulmo honey and soft, plummy sweeter elements combine to almost make you swoon with delight; **f23.5** a spicy farewell with the sugars from the rum, still crisp but happily integrated and friendly; **b24** an altogether better bottling than their rum-finished effort. This is happy, complex and falls into place in truly impressive fashion. Quite superb. *46%. ncf.*

⟐ **Teeling Whiskey Vintage Reserve Silver Bottling 23 Years Old** cask no. 6894 **(94.5) n23** screams old, rich molassed fruitcake, though someone's put in an extra pinch of salt; the tannins are seriously, seriously heavy and ancient...; **t24** spices arrive from almost every direction. And salt from the remainder. All this with a whoosh of intense dates and liquorice; **f23.5** long, thick and with a massive fade of treacle and dark muscovado; **b24** big, substantial with a big fruity essence, though it is the oak which always holds power. And what power....! Beautiful! *54%. sc. 187 bottles. Bottled for Shinanoya Tokyo.*

⟐ **Teeling Whiskey Vintage Reserve Silver Bottling 23 Years Old** cask no. 10680 **(88.5) n22.5** such is the depth, it takes a little while for the bourbon-esque notes to unravel into a stream of vanillins. Vaguely salty with a light muscovado fruitiness to the sweeter notes. Red liquorice abounds...; **t22** the oak thumps against the taste buds with a degree of protest having been shackled for so long; bitterness from oak creeps in; again there is a fruitiness, this time of slightly under-ripe greengages; **f22** the late bitterness is met by some busy spice; **b22** a cask caught right on the edge of its age-range. *48.2%. sc. 192 bottles.*

⟐ **The Whisky Agency Acla Selection Irish Single Malt North of Ireland Aged 24 Years** bourbon barrel, dist 1991, bott 2015 **(92.5) n23.5** a gentle peat does little more than soothe and caress; the vanillas point towards age rather than antiquity; **t23** rich barley with an elegant chocolate mint theme; the smoke is hand-in-hand with the light treacle; **f22.5** the smoky fade teases to the end; **b23.5** a beautiful cask which has held off the years with aplomb and uses its deft smokiness to the most delicate of effects. Beautiful, so it is. *51.8%. nc ncf. 218 bottles.*

Whisky-Fässle Irish Single Malt 10 Year Old hogshead, dist 2003, bott 2014 **(71) n18 t21.5 f15 b16.5.** A strangely soapy dram. The finish really is in distress. Malty on delivery. But as for the rest....bejabers! *49.5%. nc ncf.*

⟐ **Whisky-Fässle Irish Single Malt 1989** barrel, bott 2015 **(95.5) n24** such astonishingly elegant peat. Doddering, grey-haired, yet possesses the glass like a lord occupies his castle; **t24** the delivery is an extraordinary head-on meeting between the fading phenols and the oak. Somehow juices flow with a coppery sheen which suggests a fresh still...; **f23.5** long, with spices kicking in alongside the phenols; hickory represents the aging oak; **b24** I may be wrong about this. But I doubt it so much and would bet a hundred smackers, minimum. Distilled originally as a smoky whisky by Cooley, it has been matured by them or was sold to Irish Distillers (who bought a lot more than they are happy to let on). Either way, it has found its way back into private hands as one of the oldest smoky Irish whiskeys of all time. And a sacred masterpiece from the green isle...An important whiskey of great historical significance. *47.2%*

⟐ **Whisky-Fässle Irish Single Malt 1997** barrel, bott 2015 **(89) n22** a little tired oak, but the malt itself is still fizzing; **t22.5** tannins land heavily and a touch awkwardly. But again the malt has a spiced-up, souped-up effervescence; **f22** big malt, big spice and shy citrus; **b22.5** Irish malt practically dancing a jig. *46.7%*

Single Grain
COOLEY

Greenore 6 Year Old bott code L9015 db **(89) n23.5 t22.5 f21 b22.** Very enjoyable whiskey. But two points: cut the caramel and really see the baby sing. And secondly, as a "Small Batch" bottling, how about putting a batch number on the label...? *40%. Cooley.*

Greenore 8 Year Old bott code L8190 db **(86.5) n20 t22 f23 b21.5.** The vague hint of butyric on the nose is more than amply compensated by the gradual build up to something rather larger on the palate than you might have expected (and don't be surprised if the two events are linked). The corn oil is almost a meal in itself and the degree of accompanying sugar and corn flour is a treat. *40%. Cooley.*

Greenore 15 Years Old bott code L8044 db **(90) n23 t22.5 f22 b22.5.** The advent of the Kilbeggan 15 reminded us that there must be some grain of that age around, and here to prove it is a superb bottling of the stuff which, weirdly, is a lot better than the blend. Beautiful. *43%*

Greenore 18 Years Old db **(91) n22.5 t22.5 f23 b23.** This continuous still at Cooley should be marked by the State as an Irish national treasure. One of the most complex grains you'll ever find, even when heading into uncharted territory like this one. *46%. ncf. 4000 bottles.*

GLENDALOUGH

Glendalough Double Barrel Irish Whiskey first aged in American bourbon casks, then Spanish oloroso casks **(88.5) n22.5** vague fruit, mainly of pears; **t23** succulent mouth feel with a juicy surge of barley and spice; **f21** dulls out but remains silky, though dry; **b22** a very pleasant malt but rather vague and at time a little dull. *42%*

MIDLETON

◇ **Irish Whiskey Society Midleton Aged 18 Years** cask no. 21885, bonded 13 Mar 97, bott 8 Sept 15 **(91) n22** two toned. Rock hard and able to chisel into diamond on one hand. And a much more subtle fruitiness lurks on the other....; **t23.5** and there goes that insane bipolar personality, with the backbone carved from granite yet the sweeter, richer, notes still hanging onto an intense muscovado/fruitcake framework; **f22.5** a little tangy. And still dishing out the juice; enormous – truly massive - late vanilla; a few flickers of mocha; **b23** Midleton grain is the hardest, most unyielding of all the world's grain whiskies. Yet a certain implementation of fruit appears to have softened and honed this into a distinguished Irish, indeed. Wonderfully sculpted whiskey. *50.6%. sc. 114 bottles.*

TEELING

Teeling Single Grain Irish Whiskey (94) n23.5 how can something be this clean yet so complex? A beautiful marriage of custard and kumquats with a touch of astringent rhubarb tart for good measure; **t23.5** much sweeter as ulmo honey shows first before slowly giving way to a jam Swiss roll sweetness and oiliness; **f23** more of the same, but more quietly...; **b24** presumably Cooley grain – as good as anything of its ilk on this planet. And showing it has enough about it to combine to stunning effect with some high quality wine casks. I've just had that Teeling feeling....wonderful! *46%. ncf.*

Teeling Single Malt Irish Whiskey (80.5) n20 t22 f19 b19.5. Sometimes in a whiskey, complexity can be overdone – especially if different wine casks are in use. Then finding the balance, the very essence, can be a nightmare. I have but a small sample before me here and know nothing of the make-up of this malt....other than what my taste buds are telling me. It appears like a multi-cask style, but one – probably the sherry - has not been of the highest standard. A dangerous game...and always worth remembering in whiskey that less can so often be more... *46%*

UNSPECIFIED SINGLE GRAIN

◇ **Teeling Whiskey Single Grain** wine cask finish, bott Aug 2015 **(89) n22** an oily air and a vanilla edge; much firmer and less yielding when cool; **t23** silky soft with a corn-like oiliness and vanilla ice cream fade; **f22** a few spices dig in alongside the red liquorice; a vague late bitterness; **b22** exceptionally soft and satisfying. *46%. ncf.*

Blends

◇ **Barr an Uisce Wicklow Rare Blended Irish Whiskey** bourbon barrel, sherry cask finish **(87.5) n22.5 t22 f21 b22.** Busy whiskey with a creamy nose and sugar-gorged middle. However, the finish turns a tad bitter. *43%. ncf.*

Bushmills 12 Years Old Distillery Reserve db **(86) n22.5 t22.5 f20 b21.** This version has gone straight for the ultra lush feel. For those who want to take home some 40% abv fruit fudge from the distillery. *40%*

Bushmills 1608 anniversary edition **(94) n23.5 t23.5 f23 b24.** This whiskey is talking an entirely different language to any Irish blend I have come across before, or any blend come to that. Indeed, nosed blind you'd not even regard it a blend: the malt calls to you like a Siren. But perhaps it is the crystal malt they have used here which is sending out such unique signals, helping the whiskey to form a thick cloak of roasty, toasty, burnt toffeed, bitter-sweetness which takes your breath away. What a fabulous whiskey! And whether it be a malt or blend, who cares? Genius whiskey is genius whiskey. *40%*

Bushmills 1608 400th Anniversary (83) n21 t21.5 f20 b20.5. Thin-bodied, hard as nails and sports a peculiarly Canadian feel. *46%. Diageo.*

Bushmills 1608 db **(87) n22 t23 f20 b22.** A blend which, through accident, evolution or design, has moved a long way in style from when first launched. More accent on fruit though, predictably, the casks aren't quite what they once were. Ignoring the furriness on the finish, there is much to enjoy on the grape-must nose and how the fruit bounces off the rigid grain on delivery. *46%*

Bushmills Black Bush (91) n23 t23 f21.5 b23.5. This famous old blend may be under new management and even blender. But still the high quality, top-notch complexity rolls around the glass and your palate. As beautiful as ever. *40%*

Bushmills Original (80) n19 t21 f20 b20. Remains one of the hardest whiskeys on the circuit with the Midleton grain at its most unflinching. There is a sweeter, faintly maltier edge to this now while the toffee and biscuits qualities remain. *40%*

Cassidy's Distiller's Reserve bott code L8067 **(84.5) n21.5 t22 f20 b21.** Some salivating malt on flavour-exploding delivery, but all else tame and gentle. *40%. Cooley.*

Clancey's bott code L8025 **(87) n22 t21 f22 b22.** Remains an excellent blend for all the toffee. The spice balance excels. *40%. Cooley for Wm Morrison.*

Clontarf Classic Blend (81) n20 t22 f19.5 b19.5. A hard as nails blend softened only by the heavy use of caramel which, though chewy, tends to obliterate any complexity from elsewhere. Ouch! 40%. Castle Brands Group.

Delaney's (85.5) n20 t21.5 f22 b22. Young, clean, citrusy, refreshing and proud. Thoroughly enjoyable and dangerously moreish. *40%. Cooley for Co-operative UK.*

Delaney's Special Reserve (84) n21.5 t20.5 f22 b21. An attractive blend with a big late spicy blast. The toffee dominates for long periods. *40%. Cooley for Co-operative Group.*

Feckin Irish Whiskey (81) n20 t21 f20 b20. Tastes just about exactly the feckin same as the Feckin Strangford Gold... *40%. The Feckin Drinks Co.*

Golden Irish bott code L7064 **(93) n23 t23 f23.5 b23.5.** By far one of the most enjoyable Irish blends around. Simple, but what it does, it does deliciously well. *40%. Cooley.*

The Irishman Superior Irish Whiskey bott code L6299L059 **(93) n23 t23 f23 b24.** What a quite wonderful blend: not of the norm for those that have recently come onto the market and there is much more of the Irish Distillers about this than most. Forget about the smoke promised in the tasting notes on the label...it gives you everything else but. And that is one hell of a lot!! *40%. Hot Irishman Ltd.*

Jameson (95) n24.5 Swoon...bizarrely shows even more Pot Still character than the Redbreast I tasted yesterday. Flinty to the point of cracking. The sherry is there but on reduced terms, allowing the firm grain to amplify the unmalted barley: truly brilliant; **t24** mouth-watering delivery and then wave upon wave of diamond-hard barley and grain; the odd eclectic layer of something sweetish and honeyed, but this is eye-watering stuff; **f22.5** an annoying touch of caramel creeps in, costing points, but even beyond that you still cannot other than be charmed by the layering of cocoa, barley and light grape; **b24** I thought I had detected in bottlings I had found around the world a very slight reduction in the Pot Still character that defines this truly classic whiskey. So I sat down with a fresh bottle in more controlled conditions...and was blown away as usual. The sharpness of the PS is vivid and unique; the supporting grain of the required crispness. Fear not: this very special whiskey remains in stunning, truly wondrous form. *40%*

Jameson 12 Years Old Special Reserve (88) n22 t23 f21 b22. Much more sherry than of late and the pot still makes inroads, too. Just needs to lose some of the caramel effect; *40%*

Jameson 18 Years Old Limited Release bott 08/10/14 **(93.5) n24** one of the first high quality Irish whiskeys I've encountered where you are drawn in by bourbon-style tannins – virgin oak, perhaps? - rather than by the unique pot still experience. There are pot still echoes, reverberating the ulmo honey and thin lime marmalade; mega complex, fascinating and beautiful; **t23.5** so no let down on delivery. Indeed, it is even better for the first 12 to 15 seconds as the clear and thin honey melts into the hickory and liquorice; **f22.5** just bitters slightly at the end with a furry flourish; **b23.5** I've always found an Irish beauty irresistible... 40%

Jameson Black Barrel (91.5) n23 t23 f22.5 b23. Here's the problem faced by any Jameson blender: the column still grain from Midleton is the hardest on the palate made anywhere in the world. So how do you get it to mould into what you want? Usually you can't, so you have to make the whiskeys around it reflect and deflect for maximum effect. And that's what's going on here: a brittle whisky where the pot still element is magnified very cleverly indeed. Lovely stuff: New Yorkers are a lucky bunch! 40%. NY exclusive.

⟡ **Jameson Bold (92) n24** sublime use of the Midleton grain here, using its reflective qualities to heighten the spices. So now we appear to have a pinch of ginger and nutmeg at play, alongside the greengages. Something of the freshly baked light American-style fruitcake about this...; **t23.5** now the honey comes steaming in from the very first moment, a gorgeous blend of acacia and ulmo honey with a light dollop of golden syrup for good measure. As the oak asserts itself, so the spices raise their game; **f21.5** gentle spice and a light bitterness from the cask for company; **b23** delicious stuff. But not to be confused with the excellent Indian malt, Bold, from Paul John, which is a lot Bolder than this... That said, a blender's blend with the nose making one purr with delight and appreciation. 40%. The Deconstructed Series.

⟡ **Jameson The Blender's Dog (92) n23** oak plays a surprising part in this: no shortage of liquorice-led tannin. The substrata is one of light, playful grain, weighed down with an almost earthy heather-honey theme; **t23.5** luxurious delivery: a subtle fatness to the weight and a pulsing orange blossom honey sweetness; a firmer, grainier thread chisels into the palate; **b23.5** a hint of milky mocha and a late, vague tang; **b23.5** a clever blend, as this is just as much about mouth feel as it is flavour construction. You have made this dog do some entertaining tricks, Billy Leighton, my dear old friend... 43%. ncf. The Whisky Makers Series.

⟡ **Jameson Caskmates (91.5) n23.5** positively sparkles on the nose: a lovely mix of golden syrup and acacia honey alongside some earthier green leaves crushed in the fingers; **t23** the sugars offer a benevolent presence throughout and ensure the vanillas never get too far in control; **f22** a vaguely bitter edge, though the honey lasts the distance; **b23** some serious elements of Jameson Gold involved in this, especially the acacia honey thread. Delightful. 40%

⟡ **Jameson The Cooper's Croze (95) n24** quite delightful: a variety of soft fruits ranging from citrus to pear and even a suspicion of oily lychee are all drawn out in pastel shading; **t23.5** no less soft than the nose: a caressing of the taste buds with some juicy, grassy notes melding in with the slightly jammy porridge; **f23.5** an elegant fade of light muscovado sugars and butterscotch; **b24** this is one of the most softly spoken great orations on Irish whiskey in recent years. An understated masterpiece. 43%. ncf. The Whisky Makers Series.

⟡ **Jameson Crested (90) n23** a veritable fruit basket with over-ripe plums to the fore. Also some suety spotted dog, with a full complement of raisins; **t24** stunning delivery: all the grape and the dark muscovado arrive in one oily "whoosh" which coats the palate until a few timid spices begin to formulate; **f20.5** still spicy, but a little bit of a tang hangs on to its coat-tails...; **b22.5** when first introduced back in the early 1960s as Jameson's first-ever bottled whiskey, this was known as Crested 10. Now probably ditched the number so not to confuse with age. 40%

⟡ **Jameson The Distiller's Safe (95) n23.5** wow! Can't get quite enough of that delicate ulmo honey and the lemon judiciously squeezed into it. Midleton grain is probably the firmest anywhere in the world and one of the hardest to handle. But here it is used to perfectly reflect and amplify the more crystalline sweet notes quite wonderfully; **t24** an immediate spice buzz immediately peppers – literally – the tongue before heading in search of any hiding taste buds. The salivating properties of the Demerara sugars defy description. Such beautiful weight and pace; **f23.5** clean to a point which defies belief and a light buttery feel spread onto the toasted vanilla stretches the finale even longer; **b24** not sure if head distiller Brian Nation is any relation to former comedy scriptwriter Terry Nation, creator of The Daleks. Either way, this is Dalektable stuff and as beautifully timed as the funniest skits ever written. 43%. ncf. The Whisky Makers Series.

Jameson Gold Reserve (88) n22 t23 f20 b22. Enjoyable, but so very different: an absolute re-working with all the lighter, more definitively sweeter elements shaved mercilessly while the thicker oak is on a roll. Some distance from the masterpiece it once was. 40%

⟡ **Jameson Lively (84.5) n21 t21.5 f21 b21.** The belligerent grain of Midleton appears to be coming at you at full throttle and from all direction. The nose appears to be all grain, though a little toffee apple does creep in. The delivery is uncompromising: as hard as nails. 40%. The Deconstructed Series.

Jameson Signature Reserve (93) n23.5 t23.5 f22.5 b23.5. Be assured that Signature, with its clever structuring of delicate and inter-weaving flavours, says far more about the blender, Billy Leighton, than it does John Jameson. 40%. Irish Distillers.

Kellan American oak cask **(84) n21 t22 f20 b21**. Safe whisky which is clean, sweet and showing many toffeed attributes. Decent spices, too. *40% (80 Proof). Cooley.*

Kilbeggan bott code L7091 db **(86) n21 t22 f21.5 b21.5**. A much more confident blend by comparison with that faltering one of the last few years. Here, the malts make a significant drive towards increasing the overall complexity and gentle citrus style. *40%. Cooley.*

Kilbeggan 15 Years Old bott code L7048 db **(85.5) n21.5 t22 f21 b21**. My word! 15 years, eh? How time flies! And on the subject of flying, surely I have winged my way back to Canada and am tasting a native blend. No, this is Irish albeit in sweet, deliciously rounded form. However, one cannot help feeling that the dark arts have been performed, as in an injection of caramel, which, as well as giving that Canadian feel has also probably shaved off some of the more complex notes to middle and finish. Even so, a sweet, silky experience. *40%. Cooley.*

Kilbeggan 18 Year Old db **(89) n23 t21.5 f22.5 b22**. Although the impressive bottle lavishly claims "From the World's Oldest Distillery" I think one can take this as so much Blarney. It certainly had my researcher going, who lined this up for me under the Old Kilbeggan distillery, a forgivable mistake and one I think he will not be alone in making. This, so it appears on the palate, is a blend. From the quite excellent Cooley distillery, and it could be that whiskey used in this matured at Kilbeggan... which is another thing entirely. As for the whiskey: apart from some heavy handedness on the toffee, it really is quite a beautiful and delicate thing. *40%*

Kilgeary bott code L8063 **(79) n20 t20 f19 b20**. There has always, and still proudly is, something strange about this blend. Cold tea on the nose and a bitter bite to the finish, sandwiches a brief flirtation with something sweet. *40%. Cooley.*

Locke's bott code L8056 **(85.5) n21 t22 f21.5 b21**. Now, there you go!! Since I last really got round to analysing this one it has grown from a half-hearted kind of a waif to something altogether more gutsy and muscular. Sweeter, too, as the malts and grains combine harmoniously. A clean and pleasant experience with some decent malt fingerprints. *40%*

Michael Collins A Blend (77) n19 t20 f19 b19. Michael Collins was known as the "big fellow". This pleasant, impressively spiced dram, might have enjoyed the same epithet had it not surrendered to and then been strangled by caramel on the finish. *40% (80 proof). Cooley.*

Midleton Distillery Reserve (85) n22 t22 f20 b21. A whiskey which, for all its muscovado sweetness offers some memorable barley moments. *40%. Irish Distillers Midleton Distillery only. Changes character slightly with each new vatting. This one is some departure.*

Midleton Very Rare 30th Anniversary Pearl Edition db **(91) n23.5** one of the best Midleton noses over the last decade: toffee at a minimum with the emphasis on a sexy, soft and come-hither alluring bourbon notes, especially of the red liquorice variety; one presumes the harder middle note is the pot still; **t24** brilliant delivery and follow-through: the pot still is first to crash land into the taste buds, followed by a gorgeous passion fruit sharpness. The Pot Still forms its usual backbone, but then a bitterness creeps in; the passion fruit continues, joined now by soft pear and vanilla; **f21** bitter and slightly out of sync; **b22.5** the nose and delivery will go down in Irish whiskey folklore... *53.1%*

Midleton Very Rare 1984 (70) n19 t18 f17 b16. Disappointing with little backbone or balance. *40%. Irish Distillers.*

Midleton Very Rare 1985 (77) n20 t20 f18 b19. Medium-bodied and oily, this is a big improvement on the initial vintage. *40%. Irish Distillers.*

Midleton Very Rare 1986 (79) n21 t20 f18 b20. A very malty Midleton richer in character than previous vintages. *40%. Irish Distillers.*

Midleton Very Rare 1987 (77) n20 t19 f19 b19. Quite oaky at first until a late surge of excellent pot still. *40%. Irish Distillers.*

Midleton Very Rare 1988 (86) n23 t21 f21 b21. A landmark MVR as it is the first vintage to celebrate the Irish pot-still style. *40%. Irish Distillers.*

Midleton Very Rare 1989 (87) n22 t22 f22 b21. A real mouthful but has lost balance to achieve the effect. *40%. Irish Distillers.*

Midleton Very Rare 1990 (93) n23 t23 f24 b23. Astounding whiskey: one of the vintages every true Irish whiskey lover should hunt for. *40%. Irish Distillers.*

Midleton Very Rare 1991 (76) n19 t20 f19 b18. After the Lord Mayor's Show, relatively dull and uninspiring. *40%. Irish Distillers.*

Midleton Very Rare 1992 (84) n20 t20 f23 b21. Superb finish with outstanding use of feisty grain. *40%. Irish Distillers.*

Midleton Very Rare 1993 (88) n21 t22 f23 b22. big, brash and beautiful – the perfect way to celebrate the 10th-ever bottling of MVR. *40%. Irish Distillers.*

Midleton Very Rare 1994 (87) n22 t22 f21 b22. Another different style of MVR, one of amazing lushness. *40%. Irish Distillers.*

Midleton Very Rare 1995 (90) n23 t24 b21 b22. They don't come much bigger than this. Prepare a knife and fork to battle through this one. Fabulous. *40%. Irish Distillers.*

Midleton Very Rare 1996 (82) n21 t22 f19 b20. The grains lead a soft course, hardened by subtle pot still. Just missing a beat on the finish, though. 40%. *Irish Distillers.*

Midleton Very Rare 1997 (83) n22 t21 f19 b21. The piercing pot still fruitiness of the nose is met by a countering grain of rare softness on the palate. Just dies on the finish when you want it to make a little speech. Very drinkable. 40%. *Irish Distillers.*

Midleton Very Rare 1999 (89) n21 t23 f22 b23. One of the maltiest Midletons of all time: a superb blend. 40%. *Irish Distillers.*

Midleton Very Rare 2000 (85) n22 t21 f21 b21. An extraordinary departure even by Midleton's eclectic standards. The pot still is like a distant church spire in an hypnotic Fen landscape. 40%. *Irish Distillers.*

Midleton Very Rare 2001 (79) n21 t20 f18 b20. Extremely light but the finish is slightly on the bitter side. 40%. *Irish Distillers.*

Midleton Very Rare 2002 (79) n20 t22 f18 b19. The nose is rather subdued and the finish is likewise toffee-quiet and shy. There are some fabulous middle moments, some of flashing genius, when the pot still and grain combine for a spicy kick, but the finish really is lacklustre and disappointing. 40%. *Irish Distillers.*

Midleton Very Rare 2003 (84) n22 t22 f19 b21. Beautifully fruity on both nose and palate (even some orange blossom on aroma). But the delicious spicy richness that is in mid launch on the tastebuds is cut short by caramel on the middle and finish. A crying shame, but the best Midleton for a year or two. 40%. *Irish Distillers.*

Midleton Very Rare 2004 (82) n21 t21 f19 b21. Yet again caramel is the dominant feature, though some quite wonderful citrus and spice escape the toffeed blitz. 40%.

Midleton Very Rare 2005 (92) n23 t24 f22 b23. OK, you can take this one only as a rough translation. The sample I have worked from here is from the Irish Distillers blending lab, reduced to 40% in mine but without caramel added. And, as Midleton Very Rares always are at this stage, it's an absolute treat. Never has such a great blend suffered so in the hands of colouring and here the chirpiness of the pot still and élan of the honey (very Jameson Gold Label in part) show just what could be on offer given half the chance. Has wonderful natural colour and surely it is a matter of time before we see this great whiskey in its natural state. 40%

Midleton Very Rare 2006 (92) n22 t24 f23 b23. As raw as a Dublin rough-house and for once not overly swamped with caramel. An uncut diamond. 40%

Midleton Very Rare 2007 (83) n20 t22 f20 b21. Annoyingly buffeted from nose to finish by powering caramel. Some sweeter wisps do escape but the aroma suggests Canadian and insufficient Pot Still gets through to make this a Midleton of distinction. 40%. *Irish Distillers*

Midleton Very Rare 2008 (88.5) n22 t23 f21.5 b22. A dense bottling which offers considerably more than the 2007 Vintage. Attractive, very drinkable and without the caramel it might really have hit the heights. 40%. *Irish Distillers.*

Midleton Very Rare 2009 (95) n24 t24 f23 b24. I've been waiting a few years for one like this to come along. One of the most complex, cleanest and least caramel-spoiled bottlings for a good few years and one which makes the pot still character its centre piece. A genuine celebration of all things Midleton and Barry Crockett's excellence as a distiller in particular. 40%. *Irish Distillers.*

Midleton Very Rare 2010 (84) n21 t22 f20 b21. A case of after the Lord Mayor's Show. Chewy and some decent sugars. But hard to make out detail through the fog of caramel. 40%

Midleton Very Rare 2011 (81.5) n22.5 t20 f19 b20 Another disappointing version where the colour of its personality has been compromised for the sake of the colour in the bottle. A dullard of a whiskey, especially after the promising nose. 40%. *Irish Distillers.*

Midleton Very Rare Irish Whisky 2012 db (89.5) n22 t23 f22 b22.5. Much more like it! After a couple of dud vintages, here we have a bottling worthy of its great name & heritage. 40%.

Midleton Very Rare Irish Whisky 2014 db (78.5) n20.5 t22 f17 b19. Hmmm. Somehow we have missed the 2013 Midleton Very Rare...only the second of all the Midleton Rares to get away - ever. We shall try to remedy that for Jim Murray's Whisky Bible 2016. Must say how odd it looks to see Brian Nation's signature scrawled across the label and not Barry Crockett's. Also, I was a bit worried by this one when I saw the depth of orange hue to this whiskey. Sadly, my fears were pretty well founded. Toffee creaks from every corner making for a mainly flat encounter with what should be an uplifting Irish. Some lift at about the midway point when something, probably pot still, throws off the shackles of its jailer and emerges briefly with spice. But all rather too little, especially in the face of a dull, disappointingly flawed, fuzzy finale. Midleton Very Rare should be, as the name implies, a lot, lot better than this safe but flabby, personality bypassed offering. The most frutrating aspect of this is that twice I have tasted MVR in lab form just prior to bottling. And both were quite stunning whiskeys. That was until the colouring was added in the bottling hall. 40% WB15/416

Millars Special Reserve bott code L8069 **(86) n21 t22 f21.5 b21.5.** Now that's some improvement on the last bottling of this I found, with spices back with abandon and grains ensuring a fine mouthfeel. Even the chocolate fudge at the death is a treat. *40%. Cooley.*

Morrisons Irish Whiskey bott code L10028 **(78) n19 t20 f19 b20.** Sweet, pleasant and inoffensive. *40%. Wm Morrison Supermarket.*

Paddy (74) n18.5 t20 f17.5 b18. Cleaned its act up a little. Even a touch of attractive citrus on the nose and delivery. But where does that cloying sweetness come from? As bland as an Irish peat bog but, sadly, nothing like so potentially tasty. *40%. Irish Distillers.*

Powers (91) n23 t24 f22 b22. Is it any coincidence that in this bottling the influence of the caramel has been significantly reduced and the whiskey is getting back to its old, brilliant self? I think not. Classic stuff. *40%. Irish Distillers.*

Powers Gold Label (87) n22 t22 f21 b22. The solid pot still, the very DNA of what made Powers, well, Powers is vanishing in front of our very noses. Yes, still some pot still around, but nothing like so pronounced in the way that made this, for decades, a truly one-off Irish and one of the world greats. Still delightful and with many charms but the rock hard pot still effect is sadly missed. What is going on here? *40%. Irish Distillers.*

Powers Gold Label (96) n23 a bold mixing between caramel and Powers' famous high potstill content. Here the potstill even appears to have an edge which cuts effortlessly through the grains and toffee...; **t24.5** oh gosh! That is just such a fabulous delivery: a biting, jolting Irishness that is entirely unique to the genre. The sugars and honeys arrive easily and are profound – maple syrup linking arm in arm with the crisp post still to ensure some serious thrust and counter-thrust moment...; **f24** there appears to be plenty of caramel on this fella, yet somehow it is disgarded and counts for virtually nought as the pot still runs rings around anything trying to prevent it making a ful impact. How do those sugars keep so lively and going for so long...? **b24.5** a slightly dfferent breed. This is not all about minute difference in strength...this is also about weight distribution and flavour pace. It is a subtly different blend... and all the better for it...Make no mistake: this is a truly classic Irish. *43.2%*

◈ **The Quiet Man Traditional Irish Whiskey** bourbon casks **(88.5) n22** a little bite from the oak, but the caramel offers an arm round the shoulder; **t22** lovely salivating qualities. Clean, juicy but again a real toffee warmth; **f22.5** the vanillas mount up as the oak finally makes a meaningful entrance; **b22** a gentle and genteel whiskey without an unfriendly voice. And with it I toast the memory of John Mulgrew. *40%*

Redbreast Blend (88) n23 t23 f20 b22. Really impressed with this one-off bottling for Dillons the Irish wine merchants. Must try and get another bottle before they all vanish. *40%.*

Sainsbury's Blended Irish Whiskey (86.5) n22 t22 f21 b21.5. A beautifully relaxed blend showing pretty clearly – literally, thanks to an admirable lack of colouring - just how good the Cooley grain whiskey is even at no great age. Clean with a deceptively busy and intense flavour profile. Far too good for the cola the back label says this should go with... *40%. UK.*

St Patrick bott code L030907 **(77) n19 t20 f19 b19.** Good grief! No prisoners here as we have either a bitter oakiness or mildly cloying sweetness, rarely working in tandem. A few gremlins for the Kremlin. *40%. Cooley for Russia.*

Strangford Gold (81) n20 t21 f20 b20. A simplistic, exceptionally easy drinking blend with high quality grain offering silk to the countering spice but caramel flattens any malt involvement. *40%. The Feckin Drinks Co.*

Teeling Small Batch Irish Whiskey (87.5) n21 t23 f21.5 b22. Pleasant enough, and again showing high class grain. But a sharper liquorice/phenol note is out of kilter here and disrupts the natural flow of things, especially on the finish. *46%. ncf.*

The Teeling Whiskey Company Poitin (85) n21 t22 f21 b21. Intense and makes the eyes water to the required levels. Much cleaner, if not as sweet, though a lot safer than the illegal stuff I've tasted over there for the last 20-odd years! *61.5%*

◈ **Teeling Whiskey Small Batch Rum Cask Finish** bott 11/2015 **(85.5) n21 t22.5 f20.5 b21.** An attractive malt, showing both its rum qualities and, sadly, a slight strain of tired oak. Curiously, the blurb on the label says that the rum gives the whiskey a "smooth" flavour. Well, as probably the first blender to pioneer work with Irish whiskey matured in rum casks, I can tell you for a certainty the one thing rum doesn't give you is "smoothness". Rather, it always imparts a clipped, staccato tone, as it does here especially towards the tart finish. And it is tart because you have to wait until rum finishing until the sugars imparted from the cask fuse with the more natural caramel tones from the oak. Not easy. And no guarantee it will happen. Still, the delivery offers much to enjoy. *46%. ncf.*

Tesco Special Reserve Irish Whiskey bott code L8061 **(89.5) n21.5 t23.5 f22 b22.5.** A cracker of a blend which allows the malts full scope to do their juicy bit. Possibly more malt than usual for a Cooley blend, but as they say: every little bit helps. *40%. Cooley.*

Tullamore Dew (85) n22 t21.5 f20.5 b21. The days of the throat being savaged by this one appear to be over. Much more pot still character from nose to finish and the rough edges remain, attractively, just that. *40%. Campbell & Cochrane Group.*

Tullamore Dew 10 Years Old (81.5) n21 t21.5 f19 b20. A bright start from this new kid on the Tullamore block. Soft fruit and harder pot still make some kind of complexity, but peters out at the death. 40%. *Campbell & Cochrane Group.*

Tullamore Dew 12 Years Old (84.5) n21.5 t21.5 f20 b21.5. Silky thanks to some excellent Midleton grain: there are mouthwatering qualities here that make the most of the soft spices and gentle fruit. An improved whiskey, if still somewhat meek and shy. 40%. *Campbell & Cochrane Group.*

Tullamore Dew Black 43 (85) n19 t22 f22.5 b21.5. "Black". Now there's an original name for a new whiskey. Don't think it'll catch on, personally: after all, who has ever heard of a whisky being called "This or That" Black...?? But the whiskey might. Once you get past the usual Tullamore granite-like nose, here even more unyielding than usual, some rather engaging and complex (and especially spicy) things happen, though the caramel does its best to neuter them. 43%. *William Grant & Sons.*

◇ **Tullamore D.E.W Cider Cask Finished** bott code. L2 65TD, bott 05/05/2015 **(85.5)** n21.5 t22 f21 b21. Experienced Whisky Bible readers will know that over the years I have tasted whisky matured either in cider casks or, more usually, in an environment where cider brandy is also maturing. That has always been with a single malt, though, and without exception the apple shines through. Here, though, the apple has to work overtime to get any change out of the hardest, least yielding grain on the planet. The result is an, at times, attractive blend, but also one which has its more unforgiving moments... 40%

Tullamore Dew Heritage (78) n20 t21 f18 b19. Tedious going with the caramel finish a real turn off. 40.0%. *Campbell & Cochrane Group.*

Uisce Beatha Real Irish Whiskey ex-Bourbon cask **(81)** n21 t20.5 f19.5 b20. The label blurb claims this is soft and subtle. That is, about as soft and subtle as if distilled from granite. Hard as nails with dominant grains; takes no prisoners at the death. 40%

Waitrose Irish Whiskey (86.5) n21.5 t22 f21.5 b21.5. Cooley's grain whiskey, about as good a grain made anywhere in the world, is in fine voice here. Pity some toffee stifles it slightly. 40%

Walker & Scott Irish Whiskey "Copper Pot Distilled" (83) n20 t22 f20 b21. A collectors' item. This charming, if slightly fudgy-finished blend was made by Cooley as the house Irish for one of Britain's finest breweries. Sadly, someone put "Copper Pot Distilled" on the label, which, as it's a blend, can hardly be the case. And even if it wasn't a blend, would still be confusing in terms of Irish whiskey, there not being any traditional Irish Pot Still, that mixture of malted and unmalted barley. So Sam's, being one of the most traditional brewers in Britain, with the next bottling changed the label by dropping all mention of pot still. Top marks, chaps! The next bottling can be seen below. 40%. *Sam Smith's.*

Walker & Scott Irish Whiskey (85) n21 t22 f21 b21.5. Oddly, sharper grain has helped give his some extra edge through the toffee. A very decent blend. 40%

The Wild Geese Classic Blend (80.5) n20 t21 f19.5 b19. Easy going, pretty neutral and conservative. If you are looking for zip, zest and charisma you've picked the wrong goose *(see below)*. 40%. *Cooley for Avalon.*

The Wild Geese Limited Edition Fourth Centennial (93) n23 t23.5 f23 b23.5. A limited edition of unlimited beauty. One of the lightest, subtle, intriguing and quite simply disarming Irish whiskeys on the market. As a bird and whiskey lover, this is one goose that I shall be looking out for. 43%. *Cooley for Avalon.*

The Wild Geese Rare Irish (89.5) n22 t23 f22 b22.5. Just love this. The Cooley grain is working sublimely and dovetails with the malt in the same effortless way wild geese fly in perfect formation. A treat. 43%. *Cooley for Avalon.*

Writers Tears (93) n23.5 t24 f22 b23.5. Now that really was different. The first mix of pure Pot Still and single malt I have knowingly come across in a commercial bottling, but only because I wasn't aware of the make up of last year's Irishman Blend. The malt, like the Pot Still, is, I understand from proprietor Bernard Walsh, from Midleton, but the two styles mixed shows a remarkably similar character to when I carried out an identical experiment with pure pot still and Bushmills the best part of a decade ago. A success and hopefully not a one off. Which is more than I can say for the label, a whiskey collectors – sorry, collector's – item in its own right. There is a wonderfully Irish irony that a whiskey dedicated to Ireland's extraordinary literary heritage should be represented by a label, even a brand name, so punctually inept; it's almost brilliant. The reason for the Writers (sic) Tears, if from the spirits of James Joyce, Samuel Beckett, George Bernard Shaw, Oscar Wilde and perhaps even Maurice Walsh, author of The Quiet Man whose even quieter grandson, Barry, became a legendary blender at Irish Distillers, will be open to debate: we will never know whether they laughed or cried. As far as the actual whiskey is concerned, though, I am sure they, to a man, would have no hesitation but to pen the most luminous and positive critiques possible. 40%. *Writers Tears Whiskey Co.*

American Whiskey

It is now eleven years since a bourbon won the coveted title of Jim Murray's Whisky Bible World Whisky of the Year. And you might think that with Kentucky going a record-equalling three years without the top award the greatest days may be in the past. Wrong.

For the consistency of the great bourbon and rye means that year on year it is found in the top three world whisky spots - sometimes occupying all positions. And it's probably for that reason on my tours around the globe I am asked by whisky shop owners and distributors if I know any good Kentucky and Tennessee brands, or contacts in their marketing departments, so they might bring a great American onboard. Because at last, after years of being in the shadows of Scotch whisky, bourbon and rye are being rightly recognised for their greatness, diversity and, increasingly often, enormity. Certainly, their consistency is the very thing which is winning over so many friends.

Not that Kentucky and Tennessee is having it all its own way at the moment. Yes, the quality continues to improve there - providing you ignore the nonsense and lemming-like move towards cask finishes which despoils the unsullied name of bourbon. But this year a distillery in Texas really does show that great bourbon can be made on both sides of the North American continent: Garrison Brothers in Hye. It is the kind of bourbon which demands to be served in a dirty glass and slid to you after you flick the bartender the required cash. It is brutal. It is beautiful. It is young. But it feels that it ages you. I have named it the second best bourbon of the year, partly out of how well it is made, partly out of the excellent way it has handled the cruel Texas heat. Partly because it is one of the few whiskies from any country this year that punched me off my chair but had me coming back for more. Indeed, the quality of the microdistiller of America is moving ahead of his European counterpart at almost warp factor. Partly, this is because of the fact that whisky in the US matures a lot faster than northern Europe. And, also, they tend to use grains which are no shrinking violets on the flavour front. Whichever way you look at it, America is a very good place to make whiskey.

Bardstown	Woodford Reserve
Heaven Hill	**Louisville**
Tom Moore	Early Times
Frankfort	Bernheim
Buffalo Trace	Stitzel Weller

Bourbon Distilleries

Bourbon confuses people. Often they don't even realise it is a whiskey, a situation not helped by leading British pub chains, such as Wetherspoon, whose bar menus list "whiskey" and "bourbon" in separate sections. And if I see the liqueur Southern Comfort listed as a bourbon one more time I may not be responsible for my actions.

Bourbon is a whiskey. It is made from grain and matured in oak, so really it can't be much else. To be legally called bourbon it must have been made with a minimum of 51% corn and matured in virgin oak casks for at least two years. Oh, and no colouring can be added other than that which comes naturally from the barrel.

Where it does differ, from, say Scotch, is that the straight whiskey from the distillery may be called by something other than that distillery name. Indeed, the distillery may change its name which has happened to two this year already and two others in the last three or four. So, to make things easy and reference as quick as possible, I shall list the Kentucky-based distilleries first and then their products in alphabetical order along with their owners and operational status.

BUFFALO TRACE Leestown, Frankfort. Sazerac. Operating.

BROWN-FORMAN Shively, Louisville. Brown-Forman. Operating.

FOUR ROSES Lawrenceburg. Kirin. Operating

HEAVEN HILL BERNHEIM DISTILLERY Louisville. Heaven Hill. Operating.

JIM BEAM Boston and Clermont. Fortune Brands. Operating.

MAKER'S MARK Loretto. Fortune Brands. Operating.

TOM MOORE Bardstown. Sazerac. Operating.

WILD TURKEY Lawrenceburg. Campari Group. Operating.

WOODFORD RESERVE Near Millville. Brown-Forman. Operating.

Jim Murray's Whisky Bible American Whiskey Award Winners				
	Overall Winner	Bourbon	Rye	Microdistilleries
2004	George T. Stagg	George T. Stagg	Sazerac Rye 18 Years Old	McCarthy's Oregan Single Malt 3
2005	George T. Stagg	George T. Stagg	Sazerac Rye 18 Years Old	McCarthy's Oregan Single Malt
2006	George T. Stagg	George T. Stagg	Sazerac Rye 18 Years Old	McCarthy's Oregan Single Malt
2007	Buffalo Trace Experimental	Buffalo Trace Experimental	Rittenhouse Rye 21 Barrel No.28	McCarthy's Oregan Single Malt
2008	George T. Stagg 70.3%	George T. Stagg 70.3%	Old Potrero Hotaling's 11 Essay MCMVI-MMVII	Old Potrero Hotaling's 11 Essay MCMVI-MMVII
2009	George T. Stagg (144.8 Proof)	George T. Stagg (144.8 Proof)	Rittenhouse Rye 23 Barrel No.8	Stranahan's Colorado 5 Batch 11
2010	Sazerac Rye 18 (Fall 2008)	George T. Stagg (144.8 Proof)	Sazerac Rye 18 (Fall 2008)	N/A
2011	Thomas H. Handy Rye (129 Proof)	William Larue Weller (134.8 Proof)	Thomas H. Handy Rye (129 Proof)	N/A
2012	George T. Stagg (143 Proof)	George T. Stagg (143 Proof)	Thomas H. Handy Rye (126.9 Proof)	N/A
2013	Thomas H. Handy Rye (128.6 Proof)	William Larue Weller (133.5 Proof)	Thomas H. Handy Rye (128.6 Proof)	Balcones Brimstone
2014	William Larue Weller (123.4 Prof)	William Larue Weller (123.4 Proof)	Thomas H. Handy Rye (132.4 Proof)	Cowboy Bourbon Whiskey 3
2015	William Larue Weller	William Larue Weller	Sazerac Rye 18 (Fall 2013)	Arkansas Single Barrel Reserve #190
2016	Pikesville Straight Rye (110 Proof)	William Larue Weller	Pikesville Straight Rye (110 Proof)	Notch 12 Year Old
2017	Booker's Rye 13 Years 1 Mo 12 Days	William Larue Weller (134.6 Proof)	Booker's Rye 13 Years 1 Mo 12 Days	Garrison Brothers Cowboy 2009

Bourbon

◇ **1792 Full Proof Kentucky Straight Bourbon** db **(96)** n24 even though the tannin is profound, somehow this distillery's small grains – the busiest in Kentucky – have withstood the test and show their extraordinary dexterity; **t23.5** it is like being beaten up by one you love dearly, then being kissed tenderly on the taste buds and being beaten up again. This is enormous, and not just regarding the abv. The sugars and darkening, brooding tannins appear to be evenly matched and heavyweights in their class. The intense mocha – with the emphasis on the coffee – makes for an amazing middle...; **f24** can't get over the black cherry on the fade. That and the liquorice, both black and red; **b24.5** if all the 1,000 plus whiskies and whiskeys I taste for the Bible were of this standard, not only would the world be one bloody fantastic place but, at 40 minutes a go – the time it has taken to unravel this beast – this book would never get finished. But then you'd have no need for it... *62.5% (125 proof)*

◇ **1792 Single Barrel Kentucky Straight Bourbon** bott no K16 015 db **(94.5)** n23.5 slightly less small grain apparent as the tannins had added some soft liquorice; **t23.5** silkier than a Chinese Emperor. The corn oils have taken on a sheen seemingly magnified by the rye deposits and the gentle molasses. The slow build of the spice is a thing of wonder; **f24** now this is how bourbon should taste: a fabulous spice buzz works alongside the fantastic tannin, represented here by a sublime liquorice and hickory mix, sweetened by a small, measured dollop of Manuka honey; **b23.5** surely it can be only a matter of time before this distillery pulls off a very major Whisky Bible award...Effortlessly brilliant. *49.3% (98.6 proof). sc.*

1792 Sweet Wheat Kentucky Straight Bourbon db **(94.5)** n23.5 rich honeycomb threatened by spice: a brilliant, almost dizzying interweaving of grain and oak; **t24** mmmm!!! That delivery! Just too good! The corn oils are present enough to ensure a soft landing, but sufficiently light to allow the small grains full scope (something peculiar to these stills, whoever operates them); the spices ramp up slowly but not insignificantly; **f23** in fifth gear here, cruising from honeyville to downtown cocoa; excellent slow dry build, arrested by the lingering manuka; **b24** Barton has long been one of the wasted distilleries of the world, its product once bottled and sold way before its intricate, busy bourbon was able to sing to its fullest potential. Under the new management of Sazerac, we are now consistently seeing the greatness from this distillery that for decades was found only in its 6-year-old. This is a wheated, honeyed stunner. *45.6% (91.2 proof)*

◇ **Abraham Bowman Pioneer Spirit High Rye Bourbon Release No 12** dist 9/28/07, bott 7/24/15 db **(92)** n22 quite a tight nose: the firm rye notes have become tied up with the Demerara; **t23.5** the rye appears to crash head first into the taste buds, rather than land softly. But soon after impact, the softer butterscotch and treacle notes are released. Impressive spices, too; **f23** a superb liquorice-rich drawl...; **b23.5** takes a little time to open up. But when it does it flowers better than a White Cornel... *50% (100 proof)*

Ancient Age Bonded (92) n23 t24 f23 b23. Unmistakably Buffalo Trace... with balls. *50%*

Ancient Ancient Age 10 Star (94.5) n23 t24 f23.5 b24. A bourbon which has slipped effortlessly through the gears over the last decade. It is now cruising and offers so many nuggets of pure joy this is now a must have for the serious bourbon devotee. Now a truly great bourbon which positively revels in its newfound complexity: a new 10 Star is born... *45%*

Ancient Ancient Age 10 Years Old (96) n23.5 t24 f24 b24.5. This whiskey is like shifting sands: same score as last time out, but the shape is quite different again. Somehow underlines the genius of the distillery that a world class whiskey can reach the same point of greatness, but by taking two different routes...However, in this case the bourbon actually finds something a little extra to move it on to a point very few whiskeys very rarely reach... *43%*

◇ **Baker's Aged 7 Years Kentucky Straight Bourbon Whiskey** batch no. B-90-001 **(95)** n24 magnificent. So, so subtle. Jim Beam have really been getting their small grains to talk in recent years, and here they simply refuse to shut up. Busy, bitty and perfectly matched by the mix of molasses and almost earthy heather honey; **t23.5** a much more sugary affair than the nose. As though every sweet note has been pulled out of the cask for presentation. The corn oils are profound, chewy and buttery. The liquorice is light until the golden syrup and molasses get to work...; **f23.5** fabulously long with a superb toasty edge...yet never a hint of bitterness or exhaustion; **b24** one of those uncompromisingly delicious bourbons which makes spitting, as I have to do with each sample tasted, a very unnatural act... *53.5% (107 proof)*

◇ **Basil Hayden's Kentucky Straight Bourbon Whiskey** bott code L5222 **(87)** n22.5 t22 f21 b21.5. Bigs up the bitter marmalade but a relatively thin bourbon with not enough depth to entirely manage the flattening and slightly unflattering vanilla. The usual rye-based backbone has gone missing. *40% (80 proof)*

Big Bottom Straight Bourbon 91 (95) n23 tight, in that small grain dominates over the corn, while making the most of its oils, and the oak is chunky, salty and chocolaty; **t24** again, a big salty tang to this, but this then serves to bring out the enormity of the grains, in which the corn has fought back pole position; the middle is full of honey, liquorice and burgeoning spices; **f24** and now the small grains are back behind the wheel for a tantalisingly complex finale; **b24** stupendous bourbon. *45.5% (91 proof) ncf.*

Big Bottom Straight Bourbon 111 (85.5) n21.5 t20.5 f22.5 b21. An aggressive bourbon and that has nothing to do with the strength. The delivery is tart and lopsided. The sharpness recedes towards the middle and, finally, the lights shine as the praline and mocha enter the fray on the spicy finish. *55.5% (111 proof) ncf.*

Blade & Bow batch SW-B1 **(84) n21.5 t21.5 f20 b21.** A simple, if at times massively sweet, offering which minimises on complexity. *45.5%*

◈ **Blade and Bow 22 Year Old (95.5) n24** older than Zeus' dad! A far bigger tannin kick than any 23-year-old you might find in the market. Massive mix of marmalade and mint with just enough seemingly toasted Manuka honey to ensure enough sugar for balance; essentially, doesn't go over the edge...; **t24** fabulous delivery: a blend of various honey tones, perhaps Manuka and ulmo being the two guiding lights. The liquorice also has a little vanilla and Demerara blended in just to lighten things slightly; **f23.5** great length and without any permanent age scars, despite the fact that huge tannins are at work: those residual honeys are doing a fine job; **b24** this may not be the oldest bourbon brand on the market, but it creeks along as though it is. Every aspect says "Old Timer". But like many an old 'un, has a good story to tell... in this case, exceptional. *46% (92 proof)*

Blade & Bow DeLuxe batch WLCFSS-2 **(88.5) n22.5** major liquorice contribution; **t22.5** manuka honey and molasses counter the big toasty notes; **f21** as the sugars fade, the toast burns...; **b22.5** a steady ship which, initially, is heavy on the honey. *46%*

Blanton's (92) n21.5 t24 f23 b23.5. If it were not for the sluggish nose this would be a Whisky Bible Liquid Gold award winner for sure. On the palate it shows just why little can touch Buffalo Trace for quality at the moment... *40%*

Blanton's Gold Original Single Barrel (96.5) n24 t24.5 f24 b24. It is improbable that a whiskey this enormous and with so many star turns can glide so effortlessly over the palate. One of the best Blanton's in years, this is true Gold standard... *46.5% (93 Proof)*

Blanton's Takara (91.5) n24.5 t23 f22 b22. Not quite how many people might envisage a bourbon: certainly not butch enough to keep the wild west gunslingers happy. No this is a bourbon which searches for your feminine side. And being so light, leaves itself open for any off-key bitter notes which might just happen along the way. *49% (98 proof)*

Blanton's Uncut/Unfiltered (96.5) n25 t24 f23.5 b24. Uncut. Unfiltered. Unbelievable. *65.9%*

◈ **Booker's Bourbon 6 Years, 11 Months, 0 Days** batch no. 2016-01 db **(92.5) n24** pretty damn classic! Almost belligerent in its small grain attack. There is a doughy softness to the background vanillin...; **t23.5** immediately on the mark with a rich, deeply honeyed launch. The bite accentuates the liquorice and hickory but the sweetness is ably represented by a proud treacle and maple syrup blend; **f22** pretty tame by comparison despite the echoing spice; a little late bitterness; **b23** an usually fast tail off barely detracts from another beguiling bourbon. *63.95% (1279 proof)*

Booker's 7 Years 2 Months 28 Days batch no. 2015-03 db **(92.5) n23** big in intensity by normal standards: modest by Booker's. Less rigid tannin than normal – more emphasis on softer liquorice and friendly rye; **t23.5** makes amends on delivery where normal service is resumed. All kinds of manuka honey and maple syrup is at play. The rye range is a little muted as fudge and hickory storm the mid-ground; **f22.5** distinctly light with toffee notes intertwangled with deft liquorice; **b23.5** one very gentle giant. *63.6% (127.2 Proof)*

Booker's 7 Years 5 Months batch no. C2014-05 db **(95) n24** the essence of Jim Beam: almost clotted rye as sweet custard powder radiates. Strangely gentle outwardly, but is wilfully withholding a massive punch; **t24** ker-powww!! And there it is! Right on delivery, the rye notes thud relentlessly against the taste buds as corn oil clings to the palate, allowing spices to sizzle contentedly. Intense molasses and hickory deal firmly with the deep oak which has just made its play while all the time there is a honeyed beat; **f23** oaky splinters and mocha fatten out the thinning, corn-rich, finale; **b24** not for the simpering or squeamish. There's an oaky ambush to deal with. And if you ain't man (or woman) enough, then best to mosey on over to the sarsaparilla counter... *63.95%*

Booker's Big Man, Small Batch 7 Years 2 Months 16 Days batch no. 2015-01 db **(89.5) n22** presumably from the buzzard's roost: the amount of tannin floating around the nose is almost scary for its age...; **t23** sugars appear early. But they are pretty burnt and the toasty notes continue to arrive in droves. Liquorice concentrate and hickory reminds you this has been distilled in Kentucky, not cooked by King Alfred; f22 the cindered sugars and intense cocoa powder are enough to make your eyes water...; b22.5 the driest Booker's I've happened across for a good while: probably ever. Matured for seven years in a warehouse located somewhere near the centre of the sun, one assumes... *64.35% (128.7 Proof)*

Bowman Brother's Virginia Straight Bourbon (90) n21 t23 f23 b23. Quietly confident and complex: a bit of a gem waiting to be discovered. *45% (90 proof)*

Buffalo Trace (92.5) n23 t23 f23.5 b23. Easily one of the lightest BTs I have tasted in a very long while. The rye has not just taken a back seat, but has fallen off the bus. *45%*

Buffalo Trace Single Oak Project Barrel #132 (r1yKA1 *see key below*) db **(95)** n24 t23.5 f23.5 b24. This sample struck me for possessing, among the first batch of bottlings, the classic Buffalo Trace personality. Afterwards they revealed that it was of a profile which perhaps most closely matches their standard 8-year-old BT. Therefore it is this one I shall use as the tasting template. *45% (90 Proof)*

Key to Buffalo Trace Single Oak Project Codes

Mash bill type: r = rye; w = wheat   **Entry strength:** A = 125; B = 105
Tree grain: 1 = course; 2 = average; 3 = tight   **Seasoning:** 1 = 6 Months; 2 = 12 Months
Tree cut: x = top half; y = bottom half   **Char:** All #4 except * = #3
Warehouse type: K = rick; L = concrete

Buffalo Trace Single Oak Project Barrel #1 (r3xKA1*) db **(90.5)** n22 t23 f23 b22.5. Soft corn oil aroma, buttery, big sugars building, silky texture, long. *45% (90 Proof)*

Buffalo Trace Single Oak Project Barrel #2 (r3yKA1*) db **(91.5)** n23 t23 f22.5 b23. Bright rye on nose and delivery. Juicy red liquorice and soft corn oil to chew on... *45%*

Buffalo Trace Single Oak Project Barrel #3 (r2xKA1) db **(90.5)** n22.5 t23 f22.5 b22.5. Nutty, dry aroma; apple fruitiness and brown sugars. *45% (90 Proof)*

Buffalo Trace Single Oak Project Barrel #4 (r2yKA1) db **(92)** n23 t23 f23 b23. Exceptionally crisp; sharp rye, honeycomb, big liquorice. *45% (90 Proof)*

Buffalo Trace Single Oak Project Barrel #5 (r2xLA1*) db **(89)** n23 t22.5 f21.5 b22. Dullish after a rye-intense and busy nose. Early muscovado followed by vanilla and spice. *45%*

Buffalo Trace Single Oak Project Barrel #6 (r3yLA1) db **(90)** n22.5 t22 f23 b22.5. Toast with salted butter and maple syrup. Prickly, mildly aggressive spice throughout. *45%*

Buffalo Trace Single Oak Project Barrel #7 (r3xLA1) db **(90.5)** n23 t22.5 f22.5 b22.5. Prominent rye on nose and delivery; tannin rich, toasty with big liquorice fade. *45%*

Buffalo Trace Single Oak Project Barrel #8 (r3yLA1) db **(92.5)** n23 t23 f23.5 b23. Crisp rye aroma. Fruity, firm, salivating. Spiced toffee and muscovado; toasty. *45% (90 Proof)*

Buffalo Trace Single Oak Project Barrel #9 (r3xKA2*) db **(90)** n22 t22.5 f23 b22.5. Marmalade on singed toast. Soft oils: slow release of natural caramels and mocha. *45%*

Buffalo Trace Single Oak Project Barrel #10 (r3yKA2*) db **(93)** n23.5 t23.5 f22.5 b23.5. Rich, delicate rye. Complex, busy body; rye oils, tannins; slow sugar build. Bitters. *45%*

Buffalo Trace Single Oak Project Barrel #11 (r3xKA2) db **(94.5)** n23 t24 f23.5 b24. Pronounced accent on rye, especially on delivery. Oak nose upfront; good muscovado fade. *45%*

Buffalo Trace Single Oak Project Barrel #12 (r3yKA2) db **(92)** n24 t23 f22.5 b22.5. The floral, supremely balanced nose isn't matched on the palate in weight or complexity. *45%*

Buffalo Trace Single Oak Project Barrel #13 (r3xLA2*) db **(89.5)** n22 t23 f22 b22.5. Soft, yielding tactile. Early juicy, rye stance, slow build of duller light vanilla. Late spice. *45%*

Buffalo Trace Single Oak Project Barrel #14 (r3yLA2*) db **(95)** n24 t24 f23 b24. Chocolate rye nose and body; silky texture; brown sugar and vanilla; rye-rich sweet finish. *45%*

Buffalo Trace Single Oak Project Barrel #15 (r3xLA2) db **(90.5)** n22.5 t23 f22 b23. Mouth feel concentrates on sugars and spices, which grow well. Fruity on nose and finish. *45%*

Buffalo Trace Single Oak Project Barrel #16 (r3yLA2) db **(91.5)** n22.5 t23.5 f22.5 b23. Explosive delivery: big spices, juicy, firm rye. Silky middle butterscotch & ulmo honey finish. *45%.*

Buffalo Trace Single Oak Project Barrel #17 (r3xKB1*)db **(88.5)** n21.5 t22.5 f22.5 b22. Liquorice nose; oily body sweetens; big vanilla, caramel; dull spice. *45%*

Buffalo Trace Single Oak Project Barrel #18 (r3yKB1*) db **(92.5)** n23 t23 f23.5 b23. Full bodied from nose to finish. Cocoa mingles with rye and rich corn oil. Deep, intense, even. *45%*

Buffalo Trace Single Oak Project Barrel #19 (r3xKB1) db **(93)** n23 t23.5 f23 b23.5. Solid, crisp rye hallmark on nose, delivery. Sugars firm and fractured. Precise whiskey. Salivating. *45%*

Buffalo Trace Single Oak Project Barrel #20 (r3yKB1) db **(95)** n23.5 t24 f23 b23.5. Buttery nose; profound rye kick on delivery; ulmo honey body; complex toasty fade. *45%*

Buffalo Trace Single Oak Project Barrel #21 (r3xLB1*) db **(92)** n23 t23 f23 b23. Estery, clipped rye nose; salivating delivery, dark sugars, moderate spice. *45%*

Buffalo Trace Single Oak Project Barrel #22 (r3yLB1*) db **(91)** n22 t23.5 f22.5 b23. Corn/rye mix nose with manuka honey; silky corn oil throughout. Sweet, soft. *45%.*

Buffalo Trace Single Oak Project Barrel #23 (r3xLB1) db **(89) n21 t22.5 f22.5 b23.** Massive spices throughout; juicy, rye-dominated middle. Soft corn oil and rounded. 45%

Buffalo Trace Single Oak Project Barrel #24 (r3xLB1) db **(90) n22 t23 f22.5 b22.5.** Big liquorice nose and delivery; toffee raisin; big corn oil; medium spice; even ulmo honey. 45%

Buffalo Trace Single Oak Project Barrel #25 (r3xKB2*) db **(90.5) n22.5 t23 f22.5 b22.5.** Much more accent on the rye and a slow revealing of rich caramels and Demerara. 45%

Buffalo Trace Single Oak Project Barrel #26 (r3yKB2*) db **(89.5) n22 t23.5 f22 b22.** A sugary volley follows a shy nose. Quietens quickly; small grains add complexity. 45%

Buffalo Trace Single Oak Project Barrel #27 (r3xKB2) db **(95.5) n23 t24 f24.5 b24.** Bold timber on nose and delivery; hickory and liquorice evident; a big spiced honey finale. 45%

Buffalo Trace Single Oak Project Barrel #28 (r3yKB2) db **(94.5) n23 t24 f24.5 b24.** Sublime balance between sugars and grains on body. Controlled spice; layered cocoa. 45%

Buffalo Trace Single Oak Project Barrel #29 (r3xLB2*) db **(91) n23 t22.5 f23 b22.5.** Crisp rye nose; more precise grain. Excellent spices. 45% (90 Proof)

Buffalo Trace Single Oak Project Barrel #30 (r3yLB2*) db **(95.5) n23.5 t24 f24 b24.** One of the most delicate yet: crisp rye and sugars, minty forthright oak. Clean yet deep. 45%

Buffalo Trace Single Oak Project Barrel #31 (r3xLB2) db **(87.5) n22 t22 f21.5 b22.** Dull, rumbling and herbal; oily caramel and sugars. Soft. 45% (90 Proof)

Buffalo Trace Single Oak Project Barrel #32 (r3yLB2) db **(90.5) n23.5 t23 f21.5 b22.5.** Soft corn oils dominate. Buttery, molten muscovado. Late hickory. Bitterish finish. 45%

Buffalo Trace Single Oak Project Barrel #33 (w3xKA1*) db **(94.5) n24 t23.5 f23 b24.** Huge, busy baking spiced cake; muscovado sugar delivery; remains sweet, silky and spicy; 45%

Buffalo Trace Single Oak Project Barrel #34 (w3yKA1*) db **(90) n21.5 t23.5 f22.5 b22.5.** Lazy nose but big succulent spiced molasses on delivery, with a mint cocoa finale. 45%

Buffalo Trace Single Oak Project Barrel #35 (w3xKA1) db **(89.5) n22 t22 f23 b22.5.** Soft mint, yeasty; soft toffee delivery, builds in spice. 45% (90 Proof)

Buffalo Trace Single Oak Project Barrel #36 (w3yKA1) db **(91.5) n23 t23 f22.5 b23.** Vague rum and toffee; bold, salivating, slow spice. 45% (90 Proof)

Buffalo Trace Single Oak Project Barrel #37 (w3xLA1*) db **(90) n21 t23 f22 b22.** Typical big spice beast. Complex, doughy middle with accent on butterscotch and citrus. 45% (90 Proof)

Buffalo Trace Single Oak Project Barrel #38 (w3yLA1*) db **(87.5) n22 t23.5 f20.5 b21.5.** Fizzy, busy nose matched by massive spice attack on delivery. Bitter, thin finish. 45% (90 Proof)

Buffalo Trace Single Oak Project Barrel #39 (w3xLA1) db **(87) n21.5 t22 f21.5 b22.** Oak dominated: a degree of bitterness runs from nose to finish. Spices build slowly. 45%

Buffalo Trace Single Oak Project Barrel #40 (w3xLA1) db **(93) n23 t23 f23.5 b23.5.** Soft, spiced cake, big citrus; silky, oily, bananas and golden syrup; late spice, balancing bitters. 45%

Buffalo Trace Single Oak Project Barrel #41 (w3xKA2*) db **(92.5) n22 t23 f23.5 b24.** Less spice than expected. Docile start, builds in intensity. Buttery, big sugars. Balanced. 45%

Buffalo Trace Single Oak Project Barrel #42 (w3yKA2*) db **(85.5) n22 t21.5 f21 b21.** Tight nose opens slowly; sultana pudding with maple syrup. Sweet, late bitterness. 45%

Buffalo Trace Single Oak Project Barrel #43 (w3xKA2) db **(89) n22 t23 f22 b22.** Dates & plum nose; succulent fruit with broad maple syrup & molasses flourish. Big late spice. 45%.

Buffalo Trace Single Oak Project Barrel #44 (w3yKA2) db **(89) n23 t23 f21 b22.** Spice rack nose; superb warm liquorice eruption on palate but dull finale. 45%

Buffalo Trace Single Oak Project Barrel #45 (w3xLA2*) db **(87) n23 t22 f21 b21.** Ginger and allspice nose; body thick corn oil and toffee. Short finish. 45%.

Buffalo Trace Single Oak Project Barrel #46 (w3yLA2*) db **(88) n21.5 t22 f22.5 b22** Doughy aroma. Big corn oils and sugars. Late spice growth. Big vanilla. Quietly complex. 45%

Buffalo Trace Single Oak Project Barrel #47 (w3xLA2) db **(88.5) n22.5 t22 f22 b22.** Floral, waxy aroma; sugars dominate on palate with vanilla-butterscotch-ulmo theme. 45%.

Buffalo Trace Single Oak Project Barrel #48 (w3yLA2) db **(90.5) n22 t23 f22.5 b23.** Sound, rounded from first to last. Greater accent on sugar intensity and vanilla inclusion. 45%.

Buffalo Trace Single Oak Project Barrel #49 (w3xKB1) db **(93) n24 t23 f23 b23.** Chocolate spice, apples, oaky aroma; treacle pudding, soft oils; banana and custard; bitters. 45%

Buffalo Trace Single Oak Project Barrel #50 (w3yKB1*) db **(88) n21.5 t23 f22.5 b22.** Flat nose. Muscovado delivery. Slow spices. Late liquorice. Even. Limited depth. 45% (90 Proof)

Buffalo Trace Single Oak Project Barrel #51 (w3xKB1) db **(89.5) n23 t23 f21.5 b22.** Firm and well spiced from start. Oils play bigger role as sugar develops. 45%.

Buffalo Trace Single Oak Project Barrel #52 (w3yKB1) db **(87.5) n21.5 t22 f22 b22.** Yeasty nose; blend of molasses and toffee on delivery then slow spice increase. 45%

Buffalo Trace Single Oak Project Barrel #53 (w3xLB1*) db **(91) n22 t23 f23 b23.** Full bodied on nose and palate. Toasty, big liquorice and molasses. Even and elegant. 45%

Buffalo Trace Single Oak Project Barrel #54 (w3yLB1*) db **(89)** n22 t23 f22.5 b22.5. Crisp sugars and coconut nose; big molassed delivery, nutty and gentle oil. Late vanilla. 45%

Buffalo Trace Single Oak Project Barrel #55 (w3xLB1) db **(89)** n22 t22 f23 b22. Mocha nose with sturdy tannin and vanilla early on delivery. Red liquorice and vanilla late on. 45%.

Buffalo Trace Single Oak Project Barrel #56 (w3yLB1) db **(91)** n24 t22.5 f22 b22.5. Chocolate vanilla and tannins; soft, slow build up of spice, oily; bitters. 45% (90 Proof)

Buffalo Trace Single Oak Project Barrel #57 (w3xKB2*) db **(94)** n23 t23.5 f23.5 b24. Immediate spice kick on nose and delivery. Caramels and marmalade. Busy, balanced. 45%

Buffalo Trace Single Oak Project Barrel #58 (w3yKB2*) db **(90.5)** n22.5 t23 f22.5 b22.5. Liquorice and Fisherman's Friend nose; molassed middle and big spice finish. 45%

Buffalo Trace Single Oak Project Barrel #59 (w3xKB2) db **(92)** n22 t23.5 f23 b23.5. Lighter Fisherman's Friend; roasted fudge; busy small grains attack. Mega complex. 45%

Buffalo Trace Single Oak Project Barrel #60 (w3yKB2) db **(87.5)** n22.5 t22.5 f21 b21.5. Aggression to spice nose; tame delivery and body. Soft corn oil and muscovado. 46%

Buffalo Trace Single Oak Project Barrel #61 (w3xLB2*) db **(94.5)** n24 t23 f23.5 b24. Classic spiced wheat; Demerara sugars and spices abound. Big. 45% (90 Proof)

Buffalo Trace Single Oak Project Barrel #62 (w3yLB2*) db **(88)** n22 t22.5 f21.5 b22. Caramel is leading theme; soft, big wheated spice. Oily. 45% (90 Proof)

Buffalo Trace Single Oak Project Barrel #63 (w3xLB2) db **(95.5)** n24 t23 f24 b24.5. Subtle dates, spice, cocoa; gentle, oily, perfect spice build. Ultra complex. 45% (90 Proof)

Buffalo Trace Single Oak Project Barrel #64 (w3yLB2) db **(91)** n22.5 t23.5 f22.5 b23. Citrus nose. Big oak and spice delivery; treacle tart and liquorice. Softens into caramel. 45%

Buffalo Trace Single Oak Project Barrel #65 (r2xKA1) db **(91)** n23.5 t22 f23 b22.5. Small grain nose; crunchy muscovado, corn oil; liquorice, vanilla; late spice. Complex. 45%

Buffalo Trace Single Oak Project Barrel #66 (r2yKA1*) db **(88.5)** n22.5 t22.5 f21.5 b22. Dry tannin dominates on nose and palate; good spice kick and treacle. Short finish. 45%

Buffalo Trace Single Oak Project Barrel #67 (r2xKA1) db **(89.5)** n22 t23 f22 b22.5. Blandish nose; tart, tight, sharp, some toffee raisin. 45% (90 Proof)

Buffalo Trace Single Oak Project Barrel #68 (r2yKA1) db **(92)** n22.5 t23 f23.5 b23. Rye depth; deeper, warmer spices, liquorice and light molasses. 45% (90 Proof)

Buffalo Trace Single Oak Project Barrel #69 (r2xLA1*) db **(94.5)** n23 t24 f23.5 b24. Crisp, sharp rye on nose and delivery. Jagged muscovado and spice. Goes down a treat... 45%

Buffalo Trace Single Oak Project Barrel #70 (r2yLA1*) db **(91.5)** n22.5 t23 f23 b23. Yielding caramel and vanilla. Rye and hot spice breaks up the sleepy theme. 45% (90 Proof)

Buffalo Trace Single Oak Project Barrel #71 (r2xLA1) db **(92)** n22.5 t23 f23.5 b23. Busy, small grain and citrus nose; rye backbone then darker sugars and tannin. 45%

Buffalo Trace Single Oak Project Barrel #72 (r2yLA1) db **(89)** n22.5 t23 f21.5 b22. Floral nose; juicy, tangy, citrus. Liquorice, sugary vanilla. Bitter marmalade finish. 45%

Buffalo Trace Single Oak Project Barrel #73 (r2xKA2*) db **(87.5)** n21.5 t22 f22 b22. Tight, unyielding nose. Initially crisp rye then thick vanilla and baked apple blanket. 45%

Buffalo Trace Single Oak Project Barrel #74 (r2yKA2*) db **(88)** n22 t22 f22 b22. Corny nose; more corn oil early on; syrup, huge rye sure on finish; bitters slightly. 45% (90 Proof)

Buffalo Trace Single Oak Project Barrel #75 (r2xKA2) db **(91.5)** n23 t22.5 f23 b23. Clean with accent firmly on grain throughout. Spiced minty mocha middle and fade. 45%.

Buffalo Trace Single Oak Project Barrel #76 (r2yKA2) db **(89)** n22.5 t22.5 f22 b22. Bristling rye on nose and delivery; fruity edge then dullish spiced fudge and mocha. 45%

Buffalo Trace Single Oak Project Barrel #77 (r2xLA2*) db **(88)** n22 t23 f21 b22. Busy, bitty nose; sugary blast on delivery; spice follow through then vanilla overload. 45%.

Buffalo Trace Single Oak Project Barrel #78 (r2yLA2*) db **(89)** n22.5 t22.5 f22.5 b22. Small grain busy nose; light spice to oils; light rye, late sugars; chewy caramels. 45% (90 Proof)

Buffalo Trace Single Oak Project Barrel #79 (r2xLA2) db **(93)** n23 t23.5 f23 b23.5. Juicy crisp sugars. Toasty with slow liquorice burn. Creamed spiced hickory fade. Complex. 45%.

Buffalo Trace Single Oak Project Barrel #80 (r2yLA2) db **(91.5)** n23 t22.5 f23 b23. Broad oily strokes on nose, delivery. Simple vanilla tannins and ulmo honey. 45%.

Buffalo Trace Single Oak Project Barrel #81 (r2yKB1*) db **(94)** n23 t23 f24 b24. Candy shop fruitiness; delicate oils and flavour development; big yet subdued brown sugars. 45%

Buffalo Trace Single Oak Project Barrel #82 (r2yKB1*) db **(91.5)** n22.5 t23.5 f22.5 b23. Liquoice, manuka honey; lurid rye bite and lychee fruitiness; mocha and Demerara. 45%

Buffalo Trace Single Oak Project Barrel #83 (r2xKB1) db **(92)** n22.5 t23 f23.5 b23. Sharp, angular grain, rye dominant. Softer salty praline fade. 45%.

Buffalo Trace Single Oak Project Barrel #84 (r2yKB1) db **(94)** n23.5 t24 f23 b23.5. Hefty nose mixing tannin, rye and hickory. Huge sugar and corn oil theme. 45%.

Buffalo Trace Single Oak Project Barrel #85 (r2xLB1*) db **(88.5) n21.5 t22.5 f22 b22.5.** Shy nose of soft vanilla; firm body with more vanilla and butterscotch; low level sugar. 45%

Buffalo Trace Single Oak Project Barrel #86 (r2yLB1*) db **(90) n22.5 t22 f23 b22.5.** Salty, sweaty nose; sharp delivery with rye, red liquorice dominant; spiced mocha finish. 45%

Buffalo Trace Single Oak Project Barrel #87 (r2xLB1) db **(93.5) n22.5 t23.5 f23.5 b24.** Citrus-led nose; slow, corn oil start then explosive grain; rye, liquorice & honey to the fore. 45%

Buffalo Trace Single Oak Project Barrel #88 (r2yLB1) db **(89) n23.5 t22 f21.5 b22.** Hickory, rye nose; liquorice delivery big caramel surge; bitters on finish. 45% (90 Proof)

Buffalo Trace Single Oak Project Barrel #89 (r2xKB2*) db **(89.5) n22 t22.5 f22 b22.5.** Rye radiates on nose and delivery. Big spice surge to the middle. Late mocha, liquorice. 45%

Buffalo Trace Single Oak Project Barrel #90 (r2yKB2*) db **(94) n23.5 t24 f23 b23.5.** Big tannin, cocoa and caramel throughout. Major peppery spice. Complex. 45% (90 Proof)

Buffalo Trace Single Oak Project Barrel #91 (r2xKB2) db **(86.5) n21.5 t22 f21.5 b21.5.** Half-cooked: dull caramel throughout. Short spice peak. Sweet, oily, lacking complexity. 45%

Buffalo Trace Single Oak Project Barrel #92 (r2yKB2) db **(91) n22 t23 f23 b23.** Silky texture. Big corn oil but intense tannin thinned by beech honey. Hickory and maple syrup. 45%

Buffalo Trace Single Oak Project Barrel #93 (r2xLB2*) db **(89) n22.5 t22 f22 b22.5.** Soft rye and sugars; juicy grain, tangy citrus, muscovado. 45% (90 Proof)

Buffalo Trace Single Oak Project Barrel #94 (r2yLB2*) db **(92.5) n22.5 t24 f23 b23.** Rich, hefty. Slightly salty, crisp rye. Light caramel, hint of Guyanese rum. Delicate spice. 45%

Buffalo Trace Single Oak Project Barrel #95 (r2xLB2) db **(94) n23 t23.5 f23.5 b24.** Citrus, banana; soft vanilla, profound rye sharpness, spices. Big. 45% (90 Proof)

Buffalo Trace Single Oak Project Barrel #96 (r2yLB2) db **(89) n22 t23.5 f21.5 b22.** Bright, grainy delivery in contrast to oily nose and finish. Heavy, dry molasses at the death. 45%

Buffalo Trace Single Oak Project Barrel #97 (w2xKA1*) db **(87) n22.5 t22 f21.5 b21.5.** Toffee apple nose; heavy corn oil, light muscovado sugar, bitters out; 45% (90 Proof)

Buffalo Trace Single Oak Project Barrel #98 (w2yKA1*) db **(93) n23 t23.5 f23 b23.5.** Peppers on at full blast on nose and delivery; big oily liquorice and treacle counter. 45%

Buffalo Trace Single Oak Project Barrel #99 (w2xKA1) db **(86.5) n22 t22 f21 b21.5.** Malty, vanilla; thin maple syrup, caramel. Dull. 45% (90 Proof)

Buffalo Trace Single Oak Project Barrel #100 (w2yKA1) db **(94) n23 t23.5 f23.5 b24.** Busy, green, fresh; big juicy, vanilla, muscovado, spices. 45% (90 Proof)

Buffalo Trace Single Oak Project Barrel #101 (w2xLA1) db **(96) n23.5 t24 f23.5 b25.** Unerring chocolate and mint aided by even muscovado, vanilla and spice. Hugely complex. 45%

Buffalo Trace Single Oak Project Barrel #102 (w2yLA1*) db **(88.5) n22 t22 f22.5 b22.** Insane tannin on nose; overcooked caramel. Massive sugar-spice mix. 45% (90 Proof)

Buffalo Trace Single Oak Project Barrel #103 (w2xLA1) db **(89) n22.5 t22 f22 b22.5.** Early spice on nose; prominent brown sugars on deliver; corn oil follow through. 45%

Buffalo Trace Single Oak Project Barrel #104 (w2xLA1) db **(91) n23 t23 f22.5 b22.5.** Apple, cinnamon; light spice; corn oil; vanilla and ulmo honey; spices, bitters out. 45%

Buffalo Trace Single Oak Project Barrel #105 (w2xKA2*) db **(89) n22.5 t22 f22.5 b22.** Spiced, lively nose; hot cross buns; oils and sugars build slowly; spices intensify at end. 45%

Buffalo Trace Single Oak Project Barrel #106 (w2yKA2*) db **(92.5) n24 t23 f23 b23.5.** Mega complex nose: busy sugars and spices; silky texture; nougat, caramel. 45%

Buffalo Trace Single Oak Project Barrel #107 (w2xKA2) db **(93.5) n23.5 t23 f23 b24.** Bold, rich nose; pepper bite; thick body: maple syrup, molasses, cocoa. Classic wheat recipe. 45%.

Buffalo Trace Single Oak Project Barrel #108 (w2yKA2) db **(94) n22.5 t24 f23.5 b24.** Soft, delicate. Ulmo honey leads the sugars; corn oil but complex liquorice and lavender. 45%

Buffalo Trace Single Oak Project Barrel #109 (w2xLA2*) db **(87.5) n21.5 t23.5 f21 b21.5.** Dull nose and finish. Delivery lush, souped-up spiced caramel-toffee fudge. 45%.

Buffalo Trace Single Oak Project Barrel #110 (w2yLA2*) db **(90) n22 t22.5 f22.5 b23.** Intense caramel; liquorice and toffee middle, citrus and salt; caramel finish. 45% (90 Proof)

Buffalo Trace Single Oak Project Barrel #111 (w2xLA2) db **(89) n22.5 t22.5 f22 b22.** Intriguing sugar operatic. Vary from castor to muscovado. Countering spices make it work. 45%.

Buffalo Trace Single Oak Project Barrel #112 (w2yLA2) db **(90) n21.5 t23 f22.5 b23.** Caramel fudge lead. Usual whited spice before heavier, liquorice development. 45%.

Buffalo Trace Single Oak Project Barrel #113 (w2xKB1*) db **(88) n22.5 t22 f22 b21.5.** Big vanilla nose; minor spice, oily, buttery vanilla. Simple. 45% (90 Proof)

Buffalo Trace Single Oak Project Barrel #114 (w2yKB1*) db **(90) n22 t23 f22 b23.** Elements of citrus. Oily corn. Controlled spice. Earthy and sweet. 45% (90 Proof)

Buffalo Trace Single Oak Project Barrel #115 (w2xKB1) db **(88.5) n22 t22.5 f22 b22.** An even mix of corn oil and persistant light sugars. Low level spice until finish. A tad dull. 45%.

Buffalo Trace Single Oak Project Barrel #116 (w2yKB1) db (90.5) n22 t22 f23.5 b23. Caramelised biscuit nose; polite, corny start; finish rich with hickory, manuka honey. 45%

Buffalo Trace Single Oak Project Barrel #117 (w2xLB1*) db (82.5) n20 t20.5 f22 b20. Weird pineapple nose; fruity delivery with spices trying to escape. Entirely different. 45%

Buffalo Trace Single Oak Project Barrel #118 (w2yLB1*) db (86) n20.5 t21.5 f22 b22. Fruity (less than 117); big toffee body, busy spice, developing ulmo honey. Soft. 45%

Buffalo Trace Single Oak Project Barrel #119 (w2xLB1) db (93.5) n22.5 t24 f23.5 b23.5. Spices from nose to fade, accompanied by chewy burnt fudge. French toast finale. Big. 45%.

Buffalo Trace Single Oak Project Barrel #120 (w2xLB1) db (89.5) n23 t22 f22.5 b22. Controlled oak throughout. Intermittent dry vanilla. Delicate sugars. 45% (90 Proof)

Buffalo Trace Single Oak Project Barrel #121 (w2xKB2*) db (89) n22.5 t23 f21.5 b22. Citrusy corn oil apparent and dominates. Sugars rampant, spices shy. Rather flat finale. 45%

Buffalo Trace Single Oak Project Barrel #122 (w2yKB2*) db (93) n22 t23.5 f23.5 b24. Serious wheat-spice with cocoa back up. Demerara sugars evenly spread. Complex. 45%

Buffalo Trace Single Oak Project Barrel #123 (w2xKB2) db (85.5) n21 t22 f21 b21.5. One of the dullest yet: limited sparkle despite light spice. Big caramel. 45% (90 Proof)

Buffalo Trace Single Oak Project Barrel #124 (w2yKB2) db (90) n22.5 t23 f22.5 b22.5. The startling, extra sugars over #123 impact hugely. Juicy; oak (liquorice) support. 45%

Buffalo Trace Single Oak Project Barrel #125 (w2xLB2*) db (93) n24 t22 f22.5 b22.5. Heavy oak, spices; firm, juicy. Softer caramel fade. 45% (90 Proof)

Buffalo Trace Single Oak Project Barrel #126 (w2yLB2*) db (90) n22 t23 f22.5 b22.5. Floral nose (primroses); elaborate delivery of spice and creamed mocha plus molasses. 45%

Buffalo Trace Single Oak Project Barrel #127 (w2xLB2) db (85.5) n21.5 t22 f21 b21. Off balance, citrus; juicy at first, bitters later. 45% (90 Proof)

Buffalo Trace Single Oak Project Barrel #128 (w2yLB2) db (89) n21.5 t22 f22.5 b22.5. Conservative nose; OTT spice on delivery. Molassed dates and walnut. 45% (90 Proof)

Buffalo Trace Single Oak Project Barrel #129 (r1xKA1*) db (88) n22.5 t22 f22 b22. Firm grainy, tannin nose; nougat, nutty, corn oil; clean but dim vanilla fade. 45% (90 Proof)

Buffalo Trace Single Oak Project Barrel #130 (r1yKA1*) db (92.5) n22 t23.5 f23 b24. Macho: cloaked in oak. Kumquats on nose, oily, punchy tannins on sharp, silky delivery. 45%

Buffalo Trace Single Oak Project Barrel #131 (r1xKA1) db (92.5) n23 t23 f23.5 b23. Relaxed vanilla, light tannin; corn oily, icing sugars, marzipan. 45% (90 Proof)

Buffalo Trace Single Oak Project Barrel #132
See above.

Buffalo Trace Single Oak Project Barrel #133 (r1xLA1*) db (89) n22.5 t23 f21 b22.5. Small grain busyness does the business: rye leads the dark sugar procession. Bitters out. 45%

Buffalo Trace Single Oak Project Barrel #134 (r1yLA1*) db (91.5) n22 t23.5 f23 b23. Velvet delivery: big spice cushioned by muscovado and butterscotch. Mixed honey finale. 45%

Buffalo Trace Single Oak Project Barrel #135 (r1xLA1) db (92.5) n23 t23 f23.5 b23. Chocolatey theme, except on firm, grainy nose. Silky oils, intense flavours, rye rigidity. 45%

Buffalo Trace Single Oak Project Barrel #136 (r1yLA1) db (92) n23.5 t22.5 f23 b23. Liquorice on nose and delivery. Spicy. Richer oils. Demerara. Spice. 45% (90 Proof)

Buffalo Trace Single Oak Project Barrel #137 (r1xKA2*) db (90.5) n22 t23.5 f22 b23. Fruity opening with a hardening rye presence and emphasis on muscovado. Late cocoa. 45%

Buffalo Trace Single Oak Project Barrel #138 (r1yKA2*) db (87) n22.5 t21.5 f21.5 b21.5. Marzipan, citrus nose; dull delivery, slow build of muscovado and vanilla. Soft. 45%

Buffalo Trace Single Oak Project Barrel #139 (r1xKA2) db (88) n22.5 t22 f21.5 b22. More or less flatlines throughout. Big corn oil with limited spice and cocoa. 45%.

Buffalo Trace Single Oak Project Barrel #140 (r1yKA2) db (93) n23 t24 f23 b23. Classic bourbon: citrus-rich nose, thumping spicy molassed liquorice-hickory delivery. 45%

Buffalo Trace Single Oak Project Barrel #141 (r1xLA2*) db (90) n23.5 t22 f22.5 b22. Busy nose & finish. Corn dominates the mid ground. Sugar, spice growth. Complex finale. 45%.

Buffalo Trace Single Oak Project Barrel #142 (r1yLA2*) db (89.5) n23.5 t22.5 f22 b22.5. Light tannin nose; oils, liquorice, spice bite. More corn oil. Sugars, spicy vanilla. 45%

Buffalo Trace Single Oak Project Barrel #143 (r1xLA2) db (88.5) n22.5 t22.5 f21.5 b22. Hickory drifts in and out of narrative. Light rye & vanilla. Very soft – overly gentle. 45%

Buffalo Trace Single Oak Project Barrel #144 (r1yLA2) db (91) n23 t23 f22.5 b22.5. Tannin led. Bristling dark sugars. Oily with comforting vanilla. 45%.

Buffalo Trace Single Oak Project Barrel #145 (r1xKB1*) db (91) n22.5 t22 f23.5 b23. Nougat, cocoa; busy small grains; oily corn; spiced chocolate. 45% (90 Proof)

Buffalo Trace Single Oak Project Barrel #146 (r1yKB1*) db (93) n23 t24 f22 b24. Rye dominates with clarity and aplomb. Crystal clean nose and delivery: Dundee cake. 45%

Buffalo Trace Single Oak Project Barrel #147 (r1xKB1) db (93) n23.5 t23 f23.5 b23. Macho rye & tannins. Toasty & dry delivery; liquorice, sugars, soft spice gain ascendency. 45%.

Buffalo Trace Single Oak Project Barrel #148 (r1yKB1) db **(94)** n22.5 t24 f23.5 b24. Quiet aroma but intense delivery. Big sugar up front, liquorice and manuka honey fade. 45%

Buffalo Trace Single Oak Project Barrel #149 (r1xLB1*) db **(92)** n22.5 t23.5 f23 b23. Massive tannin influence. Heavy nose; heavier body with toasty liquorice and cocoa. 45%

Buffalo Trace Single Oak Project Barrel #150 (r1yLB1*) db **(93)** n23 t23.5 f23 b23.5. Huge tannin softened by big dark sugars, hickory, sharp rye notes. Long, chewy finish. 45%

Buffalo Trace Single Oak Project Barrel #151 (r1xLB1) db **(91.5)** n22 t23 f23.5 b23. Diced citrus; light body with busy grains. Powerful dark sugars gain upper hand. 45%.

Buffalo Trace Single Oak Project Barrel #152 (r1yLB1) db **(81.5)** n21 t20.5 f20 b20.5. Vaguely butyric; harsh, hot fat corn, light rye; bitters out. 45% (90 Proof)

Buffalo Trace Single Oak Project Barrel #153 (r1xLB2*) db **(94)** n23.5 t23.5 f23 b24. Complex nose, delivery. Big spice with crisp, juicy rye. Praline, delicate oils. Big but elegant. 45%

Buffalo Trace Single Oak Project Barrel #154 (r1yKB2*) db **(92)** n22.5 t23 f23 b23.5. Rye dominates. Hard on palate; yet burnt raisin, lychee and muscovado soften. 45% (90 Proof)

Buffalo Trace Single Oak Project Barrel #155 (r1xKB2) db **(93)** n23 t24 f22.5 b23.5. Fierce spice. Dynamic rye shapes all directions. Hickory and manuka honey combine. 45%

Buffalo Trace Single Oak Project Barrel #156 (r1yKB2) db **(85.5)** n22 t21 f21.5 b21. Doesn't work. Spices too hot. Caramels and oils negate development. 45% (90 Proof)

Buffalo Trace Single Oak Project Barrel #157 (r1xLB2*) db **(84.5)** n21 t21.5 f20.5 b21. Vague butyric; sharp, juicy corn with slow rye build. Bitter. 45% (90 Proof)

Buffalo Trace Single Oak Project Barrel #158 (r1yLB2*) db **(88)** n22 t22 f22 b22. Another brawny, corn-oily, oaky effort. Excellent cocoa, citrus and spice development. 45%

Buffalo Trace Single Oak Project Barrel #159 (r1xLB2) db **(88)** n20.5 t22.5 f22 b22.5. Vague butyric; firm sugars then watery, confident spices, soft honey. Complex. 45% (90 Proof)

Buffalo Trace Single Oak Project Barrel #160 (r1yLB2) db **(92.5)** n23.5 t23 f22 b23. A salty style with fruity, crisp rye right behind. Steady and firm. 45% (90 Proof)

Buffalo Trace Single Oak Project Barrel #161 (w1xKA1*) db **(87)** n21 t22 f22 b22. Cream caramel candy; juicy corn, oily; more caramel, Light spice. 45% (90 Proof)

Buffalo Trace Single Oak Project Barrel #162 (w1yKA1*) db **(88.5)** n22 t22 f22.5 b22. Cream soda and minty fudge. Early treacle kick then settles for simple life. 45%

Buffalo Trace Single Oak Project Barrel #163 (w1xKA1) db **(90)** n23 t22.5 f22 b22.5. Citrus, bubble gum; spiced muscovado sugars at first, bitters. 45% (90 Proof)

Buffalo Trace Single Oak Project Barrel #164 (w1yKA1) db **(94.5)** n23.5 t23 f24 b24. Citrus and vanilla; massive spice, building. Demerara. Warm and complex. 45% (90 Proof)

Buffalo Trace Single oak Project Barrel #165 (w1xLA1*) db **(91.5)** n22.5 t23 f23 b23. Lively, spice dominated. Ulmo honey offers superb back up. 45% (90 Proof)

Buffalo Trace Single Oak Project Barrel #166 (w1yLA1*) db **(91)** n22 t23 f23 b23. Heady, leathery. Sublime spice middle; molasses and liquorice enrich the tail. 45% (90 Proof)

Buffalo Trace Single Oak Project Barrel #167 (w1yLB1) db **(94)** n23.5 t23.5 f23 b24. Demerara, rummy; intense liquorice, hickory; dark sugars and big spice. 45% (90 Proof)

Buffalo Trace Single Oak Project Barrel #168 (w1xLA1) db **(89.5)** n22 t23 f22 b22.5. Clean, spiced nose; juicy grains with toffee and raisin. Mocha and liquorice on finish. 45%

Buffalo Trace Single Oak Project Barrel #169 (w1xKA2*) db **(94)** n23.5 t23.5 f23 b24. Spice, lavender & leather on delivery; spicy nose. Honey & corn oil follow through. 45% (90 proof)

Buffalo Trace Single Oak Project Barrel #170 (w1yKA2*) db **(92.5)** n22.5 t23 f23.5 b23.5. Sweet, spiced nose; firm, spicy delivery; Demerara and ulmo honey. 45% (90 Proof)

Buffalo Trace Single Oak Project Barrel #171 (w1xKA2) db **(88.5)** n22 t23 f21.5 b22. Friendly corn oils dominate. Estery. Dry finish after sugar and spice crescendo. 45%.

Buffalo Trace Single Oak Project Barrel #172 (w1yKA2) db **(90.5)** n22.5 t23 f22.5 b22.5. Tannins prevalent on nose and spiced delivery. Good bite, esters and oils. Late mocha. 45%

Buffalo Trace Single Oak Project Barrel #173 (w1xLA2*) db **(91)** n23.5 t23 f22 b22.5. Bold nose & delivery: honeycomb, tannins. Liquorice & vanilla middle; good spice balance. 45%.

Buffalo Trace Single Oak Project Barrel #174 (w1yLA2*) db **(89)** n22 t22.5 f22.5 b22. Delicate oak; juicy corn, liquorice, light spices, buttery corn. Bitter marmalade. 45% (90 Proof)

Buffalo Trace Single Oak Project Barrel #175 (w1xLA2) db **(91.5)** n21.5 t23 f24 b23. Lazy nose, juicy delivery. Big vanilla profile. Buttery caramel; light honey & spice. Long. 45%

Buffalo Trace Single Oak Project Barrel #176 (w1yLA2) db **(89)** n21.5 t22.5 f22.5 b22.5. Light caramel aroma; sharp, juicy (rye-esque) delivery with mocha & butter toffee finale. 45%.

Buffalo Trace Single Oak Project Barrel #177 (w1xKB1*) db **(87)** n21.5 t22 f22 b21.5. Vaguely spiced corn oil; soft, nutty, marzipan sweetness, citrus. Late mocha. 45% (90 Proof)

Buffalo Trace Single Oak Project Barrel #178 (w1yKB1*) db **(88.5)** n22.5 t23 f21.5 b21.5. Complex marzipan and Demerara nose and delivery; runs out of things to say. 45%

Buffalo Trace Single Oak Project Barrel #179 (w1xKB1) db (88) n21 t22 f22.5 b22.5 Dull caramel nose. Toffee caramel continues on palate. Late fudge sweetness. Growing spice. 45%

Buffalo Trace Single Oak Project Barrel #180 (w1yKB1) db (92) n22 t23.5 f23 b23.5. Molasses/cough sweet nose; scrambled grains and citrus; thickens with corn at end. 45%

Buffalo Trace Single Oak Project Barrel #181 (w1xLB1*) db (94.5) n22.5 t24.5 f23 b23.5. Silky chocolate fudge delivery with perfect spice. Nose more austere, finish intense. 45%

Buffalo Trace Single Oak Project Barrel #182 (w1yLB1*) db (86) n21.5 t21.5 f22 b21. Nose over fruity; profound sugars but tart, thin body. Vanilla and mocha on finish. 45%

Buffalo Trace Single Oak Project Barrel #183 (w1xLB1) db (95.5) n24 t24 f23.5 b24. Intense. Brilliant fudge/honey/molasses delivery; cocoa finish; perfect spices: mini Weller! 45%

Buffalo Trace Single Oak Project Barrel #184 (w1yLA1) db (93) n23.5 t23 f23 b23.5. Tannins, walnut oil; nutty, corn oils. Light spice, firm Demerara. Late fruity spice. Complex. 45%

Buffalo Trace Single Oak Project Barrel #185 (w1xKB2*) db (92.5) n23 t23.5 f23 b23. Dry, riveting nose; liquorice dominates the palate. Cocoa, hickory enlivened by sugars. 45%

Buffalo Trace Single Oak Project Barrel #186 (w1yKB2*) db (90) n21.5 t22.5 f22 b22.5. Rampant spice from delivery onwards. Burnt fudge and toasted raisin. 45% (90 Proof)

Buffalo Trace Single Oak Project Barrel #187 (w1xKB2) db (88) n22 t22 f22 b22. Exceptionally even and caramel rich. Unbalanced tannin and lack of spice. 45% (90 Proof)

Buffalo Trace Single Oak Project Barrel #188 (w1yKB2) db (90) n21.5 t23.5 f22.5 b22.5. Lazy nose. Bright delivery; citrusy corn oil and muscovado. Late mocha and liquorice. 45%

Buffalo Trace Single Oak Project Barrel #189 (w1xLB2*) db (88.5) n24 t22 f21 b21.5. Complex citrus, delicate yet big; tart, sweet, fresh, strangely off balance. 45% (90 Proof)

Buffalo Trace Single Oak Project Barrel #190 (w1yLB2*) db (94) n23.5 t24 f23 b23.5. Ulmo/manuka honey mix on nose and delivery; silky corn oil; spiced mocha. Complex. 45%

Buffalo Trace Single Oak Project Barrel #191 (w1xLB2) db (94.5) n23 t23.5 f24 b24. Big, spicy, classic; firm wheaty spiciness, juicy, thick caramels. Complex. 45% (90 Proof)

Buffalo Trace Single Oak Project Barrel #192 (w1yLB2) db (94.5) n23 t24 f23.5 b24. Demerara rum nose; heavy, dry liquorice body; late spice; molassed butterscotch finish. 45%

Buffalo Trace Experiment #7 Heavy Char Barrel charred white oak, dist 21 Jan 97, bott Oct 12 db (77) n20 t21.5 f17 b18.5. The very nature of experiments means that, sometimes, they go wrong. Perhaps a bit harsh for this one which, to be more precise, has not gone right. The nose has an almost bizarre sherry feel to it, the fruitiness really striking home on the attractive delivery. From then on, it's downhill, leaving an unattractive tang at the death. 45%

⬧ **Buffalo Trace Experimental Collection 15 Minute Infrared Light Wave Barrels** dist 10/13/09, barrelled 10/14/09, bott 03/31/16, still proof: 140, entry proof: 125, warehouse/floor: I/5, rick/row/slot: 1/5/1-4, age at bottling: 6 Years, 5 Months, evaporation: 32% db (92) n24 a real softie: buttery vanilla and warm croissant; traditional, heartier, molassed bourbon tones arrive late, almost as an afterthought; t23 possibly the most gentle delivery this year, and not just from the US. More buttery tones, with the corn oils now escaping to add a further softening effect; f22 only late on do we get any form of tangible oak, again of a molassed style; b23 astonishing that it is now some 25 years since I first discussed infrared cask treatment with a Scottish distiller (and was sent samples of maturing spirit in such treated barrels) but it is only now that I have seen it commercially available. Good ol' Buffalo Trace for keeping the public on its toes! 45% (90 proof)

⬧ **Buffalo Trace Experimental Collection 30 Minute Infrared Light Wave Barrels** dist 10/13/09, barrelled 10/14/09, bott 03/31/16, still proof: 140, entry proof: 125, warehouse/floor: I/5, rick/row/slot: 1/5/1-8, age at bottling: 6 Years, 5 Months, evaporation: 32% db (91) n23 a little spice nip, totally absent in the sister bottling. The sugars are more of a muscovado style, fruitier and weightier from the start; t23 seemingly soft with the corn oil to the fore. But right behind is a far more macho line of tannins, making a mix of liquorice and hickory to dry the middle; f22.5 dry, spent molasses. Late spice and a little rough-house tactics for good measure; b22.5 has quite a different gait to the 15 minute version, being far more oak dependent as well as aggressive. 45% (90 proof)

⬧ **Buffalo Trace Experimental Collection Old Fashioned Sour Mash Entry Proof 105** dist 05/01/02, barrelled 05/01/02, bott 08/20/15, still proof: 135, warehouse/floor: I/7, rick/row/slot: 22/2/1, age at bottling: 13 Years, 3 Months, evaporation: 66.2% db (93) n23.5 thumping and hefty. All liquorice and ersatz coffee; t23.5 fat, with the corn oils forming the picture, crisper rye and demerara the formwork; f23.5 long, with a fabulous liquorice fade. The oils stick around...; b23.5 fascinating comparison to the 125 entry. Much more liquorice and tannin, much less acacia honey. Seems older and hairier, which I would not necessarily have expected. 45% (90 proof)

❧ **Buffalo Trace Experimental Collection Old Fashioned Sour Mash Entry Proof 125**
dist 05/01/02, barrelled 05/01/02, bott 08/20/15, still proof: 135, warehouse/floor: I/7, rick/row/
slot: 50/2/1, age at bottling: 13 Years, 3 Months, evaporation: 54.8% db **(95) n24** wow...just get
that honeycomb...: like acacia honey on melting vanilla ice cream...; **t24** brilliant delivery: spot
on oils, tightened slightly by the liquorice-laced tannin. Still that vanilla and honey double bill
mesmerises....; **f23** the tannin sticks, but softened by mocha and demerara sugar; **b24** an
experiment which should be turned into reality... *45% (90 proof)*

Buffalo Trace Experimental Collection 12 Year Old Bourbon From Floor #1 dist
11/29/01, barreled 11/30/01, bott 3/12/14, still proof: 140, entry proof: 125, warehouse/
floor: K/1, rick/row/slot:1/1/1-4, age at bottling, 12 years, 3 months,
evaporation: 27% db **(91.5) n23.5 t23 f22.5 b22.5** Delicate bourbon with limited fight. *45%.*

Buffalo Trace Experimental Collection 12 Year Old Wheated Bourbon From Floor #1
dist 04/24/02, barrelled 04/26/02, bott 11/03/14, still proof: 130, entry proof: 125, warehouse/
floor: K/1, rick/row/slot: 1/3/1-5, age at bottling: 12 Years, 6 Months, evaporation: **(88.5) n22**
relatively inert: muscovado sugar and vanilla dominates; a hint of cough sweet; **t22** sharp
tannins; the vanillas are missing their normal sugars; **f22.5** dry, liquorice enriched and, at last,
some late muscovado sugars and melt-in-the-mouth caramelised biscuit **b21.5** pleasant, but
feels as though it is lurching around; not entirely convincing. *42% db 45%*

Buffalo Trace Experimental Collection 12 Year Old Wheated Bourbon From Floor #5
dist 04/24/02, barrelled 04/26/02, bott 11/03/14, still proof: 130, entry proof: 125, warehouse/
floor: K/5, rick/row/slot: 51/1/1-5, age at bottling: 12 Years, 6 Months, evaporation: **(91) n22
t23 f22.5 b23.5** A gorgeously weighted whiskey and the pace of development on the palate
is sublime. *47% db 45%*

Buffalo Trace Experimental Collection 12 Year Old Wheated Bourbon From Floor #9
dist 04/24/02, barrelled 04/26/02, bott 11/04/14, still proof: 130, entry proof: 125, warehouse/
floor: K/9, rick/row/slot: 44/1/1-5, age at bottling: 12 Years, 6 Months, evaporation: **(89)
n23** white chocolate, liquorice cough sweet, molasses, light spices. Big, but everything in
perspective; **t21.5** duller than the nose hints at: massive degree of natural caramel; **f22.5** yet
more caramel, with soft vanilla; good spice fade; **b22** technically very good, but a little overly
simple and single paced. *51% db 45%*

Buffalo Trace Experimental Collection 12 Year Old Bourbon From Floor #5 dist
11/29/01, barreled 11/30/01, bott 3/12/14, still proof: 140, entry proof: 125, warehouse/
floor: K/5, rick/row/slot:51/1/21-24, charred white oak, age at bottling, 12 years, 3 months,
evaporation: 25% db **(91) n22** corn oil and citrus; a touch minty with a hint of eucalyptus;
t23 quite a heavy delivery: much more rich, molassed tannin than Floor #1, and a greater
depth of the natural caramels, too; **f23** pulsing spices; **b23** though heavier, lacks some of
the grace and complexity of its lower-matured stablemate. *45%.*

Buffalo Trace Experimental Collection 12 Year Old Bourbon From Floor #9 dist
11/29/01, barreled 11/30/01, bott 3/12/14, still proof: 140, entry proof: 125, warehouse/
floor: K/9, rick/row/slot:44/1/13-16, charred white oak, age at bottling, 12 years, 3 months,
evaporation: 49% db **(95.5) n24 t24 f23.5 b24** Floorless...and confirms about bourbon
maturation what we already know. And this distillery in particular... *45%.*

❧ **Bulleit Bourbon (87) n21.5 t22 f21.5 b22.** Vanilla-fashioned on both nose and flavour
development. If it was looking to be big and brash, it's missed the target. If it wanted to be
genteel and understated with a slightly undercooked feel yet always friendly, then bullseye...
45% (90 proof)

❧ **Bulleit Bourbon 10 Year Old (90) n23** just the right chunkiness to balance the mint
with the spiced honeycomb; **t22.5** the house vanilla style returns, except now a little extra
lightly fruity muscovado sugar moves in; the corn oil is much more confident and rich; **f22**
good length and some sound seasoning to the red liquorice and vanilla; **b22.5** not remotely
spectacular. But does the simple things deliciously. *45.6% (91.2 proof)*

❧ **Bulleit Bourbon Barrel Strength (91.5) n22.5** lazy muscovado and light layering
of orange blossom honey; **t22.5** the tannins and sugars are neck and neck, with neither
giving ground. Juicy, with a brief small grain effervescence; **f23.5** such a satisfying finish: how
many strands and variations of chocolate can one whiskey get through...?; **b23** the extra oils at full strength make such a
huge difference in seeing the fuller picture. *59.6% (119.2 proof)*

Cadenhead's World Whiskies Heaven Hill Aged 17 Years bott 14, **(93.5) n24.5 t23 f23
b23** Although it says "distilled at Heaven Hill Bardstown," the distillery was by then a burnt
out husk and production had shifted to various other distilleries around Kentucky who were
happy to distil to contract, or sell spare parcels of maturing distillate to help plug the huge
stock gap. Not sure exactly where this single cask was from but has a certain touch of the
Old Forester from Louisville, which often displayed the heavy liquorice and honey character
apparent here. *58%. WB15/378*

Calhoun Bros Straight Bourbon (84.5) n20.5 t22 f21 b21. Very different! A much wider cut than the norm on straight bourbon whisky results in an oily fellow which you can chew until your jaws ache. Massively toasty, vanilla gorged and intense. *43% (86 proof)*

Charter 101 (95.5) n23.5 t24.5 f23.5 b24. Now here is a whiskey which has changed tack dramatically. In many ways it's like the Charter 101 of a year back. But this bottling suggests they have turned a warehouse into a giant beehive. Because few whiskeys offer this degree of honey. You can imagine that after all these years, rarely does a whiskey genuinely surprise me: this one has. No wonder there is such a buzz in the bourbon industry right now... *50.5%*

Clarke's Old Kentucky Straight Sour Mash Whisky Bourbon (88.5) n22.5 t22 f22 b22. Honest and hugely impressive bourbon. The rich colour – and remember straight bourbon cannot be falsely coloured – tells its own tale. *40%. Aldi.*

Colonel E H Taylor Barrel Proof (91) n23.5 t23 f22 b22.5. A big boy which turns out to be a bit of a softy in the end... *67.25% (134.5 Proof). nc ncf.*

Colonel E H Taylor Cured Oak (93.5) n23 one assumes the cured oak has resulted in a maximising of early sugars being released in maturation. Because this nose has more in common with a Caribbean pot still rum than it does whiskey. Or whisky..; **t24** and, as predicted, sugars of all forms and denominations gather on delivery: one of the sweetest starts to a bourbon for this and many a year. But there is much more besides, especially a veritable creaminess to the vanilla which is bursting out in all directions; **f23** a dissenting vague bitterness lasts for a second or two before it is shackled and led away by the remaining sugars; **b23.5** not sure about the oak being cured: coming from Buffalo Trace, I doubt if there was anything wrong with it in the first place...In many ways a much quieter than normal and delicate bourbon with the tannins harnessed and led to a path quite different from the normal toasty/liquorice style. *50%. (100 Proof)*

Colonel E. H. Taylor Old Fashioned Sour Mash (94) n24 t23.5 f23 b23.5. When they say "old fashioned" they really aren't joking. This is a style which takes me back to my first bourbon tasting days of the mid 1970s. And, at the moment, it is hard to name another bourbon offering this unique, technically brilliant style. Outstanding! *50% (100 Proof)*

⬩⬩⬩ **Colonel E.H. Taylor Seasoned Wood** db **(93.5) n25** if someone asked me to sculpt a true Bourbon nose, it would most probably turn out something almost identical to this: the tannins are bold, but delicate enough to allow the varying shades of blood orange and kumquat to come through with such subtlety. The light orange blossom honey affords a translucence while the ulmo honey shapes the creamier texture to the aroma; the playful spices and toastiness point perhaps towards a wheat recipe? The secret, though, is the truly perfect weight of everything: confidence without brashness, subtle without being coy. Truly, a perfect bourbon nose..; **t24** whoever distilled this knew exactly what they were doing: beautifully clean with just enough oil to help rather than hinder. Definitely wheat as the unique spice kick from that grain melds into the much more earthy spices from the tannins. Just a twist of orange blossom honey; salivating beyond description or belief..; **f21.5** long, with the spices now having a say. Honey and cocoa intertwine, then fade; slowly a curious, off-key murkiness creeps in and hangs around..; **b23** I am sitting in my garden in near darkness tasting and writing this, the near-thousand-year-old church just 75 yards or so behind me clanging out that it is ten of the clock. Although mid-July, it is the first day warm enough in this apology of a British summer where I have been able to work outside. Oddly, it reminded me when I used to write my books and chapters on bourbon in the grounds of Buffalo Trace in the 1990s, the sun also set and a warm breeze kissing my face. No possums here for company, although the bats are already circling me, kindly protecting me from midges. And as I can't read the label of the whiskey, it makes my senses all the more alive. A whiskey, though not perfect, for when the sun sets but your day is really about to begin... *50% (100 proof)*

Colonel E H Taylor Single Barrel (93) n23.5 t23 f23 b23.5. An exceptionally bright barrel that's a bit of a tease. *50% (100 Proof)*

Colonel E.H. Taylor Small Batch (94.5) n23 pretty effortlessly classic: a friendly layering of crisp sugars and teasing spice as well as a thin hint of mint and eucalyptus; the natural vanillas are out in force, too; **t24** pretty perfect weight: the oils have just enough clout to ensure the sugars remain in check and on the Demerara side of things; the small grains do stir, also, and herald the arrival of the toastier elements; **f23.5** long, again with the sweetness in harmony with the butterscotch tart and late peppery bite; **b24** from first nose, to last, the exemplary high quality of this bourbon is not for a second in dispute. *50% (100 Proof)*

Cougar Bourbon Aged 5 Years (95) n25 t24 f23 b23. If Karl Kennedy of Neighbours really is the whisky buff he reckons he is, I want to see a bottle of this in his home next to Dahl. By the way: where is Dahl these days...? (And by the way, Karl, the guy who married you and Susan in London is a fan of mine. So you had better listen up...!) *37% (74 proof). Foster's Group, Australia.*

Daniel Stewart 8 Years Old (92.5) n22 t23 f23.5 b24. Stellar sophistication. Real complexity here, and, as 8-year-olds go, probably among the most complex of them all. A deep notch up on the previous bottling I encountered. *45%*

Eagle Rare Aged 10 Years Single Barrel (89) n21.5 t23 f22 b22.5. A surprising trip, this, with some dramatic changes en route. *45%*

Eagle Rare 17 Years Old bott Spring 2013 db **(94)** n23 t24 f23 b24 A much more profound bottling than the 2012 edition with the accent firmly on the heavy, chocolatey sugars. Shows BT to enormous advantage and is, above all, great fun. *45%. Buffalo Trace Antique Collection.*

Eagle Rare 17 Year Old bott Spring 2014 db **(95)** n23 has someone thrown in a sprig of mint into that famous chocolate fudge...? t24 sensual delivery with the corn oils licking around the taste buds in a rather sexy manner. The sugars keep apace with a mollassed depth; f23.5 late spice harmonise with that lovely sweetened corn oil. As the oak rumbles back into play the chocolate fudge returns...; b23.5 one of the most relaxed and confident Eagle Rares I've encountered for a while. More telling sugar around than usual and a little less weighty. *45%.*

⬧ **Eagle Rare 17 Years Old** bott Spring 2015 db **(94.5)** n24 the bourbon with the famous chocolate fudge nose – now at its very chocolate fudgiest...; t23.5 a corny-copia of rich oils. A little extra treacle to this one, though the Manuka honey remains a constant. A slightly rough bite despite the lubrication; f23.5 continues in that slightly rough manner with a sprig of mint now on board as, is usually the case, the chocolate fudge returns with a vengeance; b23.5 one very consistent, big and serious bourbon... *45% (90 proof)*

Elijah Craig Barrel Proof Bourbon 12 Years of Aging db **(95.5)** n23.5 t24 f24 b24 Not sure when I saw a darker bourbon at 12 years commercially available. Remember that in straight bourbon colour represents interaction between spirit and barrel. So expect big oak presence and you will not be disappointed! A bourbon for bourbon lovers with very hairy chests – male or female.. *67.1% (134.2 proof) ncf.*

Elijah Craig 18 Years Old Single Barrel barrel no. 3328, dist 8/9/91 **(94.5)** n25 t23.5 f22.5 b23.5. Masterful. Don't even bother opening the bottle unless you have an hour to spend. *45%*

⬧ **Elijah Craig Single Barrel Aged 18 Years** barrel no. 4090, barrelled 6/14/97 db **(94)** n24 astonishing nose: as though the honey is breaking down into its myriad constituent pollen parts. This is probably what a flower smells like to a bee...; t23.5 seemingly intense dark sugars, then a swathe of vanilla lightens the impact; the spices continuously tingle; f23 seriously toasty as the tannins take a firmer grip still. Slightly salty towards the end, also...; b23.5 a substantial bourbon. Busy, intense, never quite staying in one spot long enough to settle down: sounds like we are back to the bees again... *45% (90 proof). sc.*

Elijah Craig 21 Year Old Single Barrel barrelled 26/11/90, barrel no. 41 db **(95.5)** n23.5 the busy nose shows no discomfort despite the major age: a real jumble of seasonings ranging from the nonchalantly sweet toasted honeycomb through to the much more abrupt ginger and coriander mix and diced, dried orange peel. A light sprinkling of salt brings everything out to the full; t24 and, of course, it is that oak-weighted seasoning which shows first, semi explosively and almost like botanicals of a dry gin. The sugars, flanked by minute amounts of ulmo honey, take their time to evolve and thread their way into the complex tapestry; f23.5 still mainly dry with the vanillas building alongside the increasingly peppery spices; light corn oil helps spread the limited sugar and honey; b24.5 even by bourbon's high standards, this is a thing of rare beauty and of a type. One of the most subtle and sophisticated bottlings you'll ever find at this age and one for those who prefer their Martinis and gins dry. And I mean very dry.... *45%.*

Elijah Craig Aged 23 Years Single Barrel barrel no. 26, barrelled 2.26.90 db **(87)** n21 t23 f21 b22. The citrus on this old boy is working overtime to ensure a degree of freshness combats the encroaching years. But it is a somewhat unequal battle and, finally, as was inevitable, slips under the tide of ancient oak like a man pushing a boulder up an interminable hill finally falls, spent, to the ground for the great rock to run over him on its way back downhill. That said, plenty of magic moments to be getting on with here, especially on delivery when there's a greater evenness between the light muscovado sugars and the more dogged tannins. Of course, the tannins win out in the end as the nose has accurately forecast, with a bitter –ish fade. But there is no shortage of understated elegance and charm along the way. *45%*

Elmer T Lee Single Barrel (91) n22 t23.5 f(22.5) b23. A sturdy, dense bourbon with above average sweetness. So effortless, it is hard to immediately realise that greatness has entered your glass. *45%*

Elmer T. Lee Single Barrel Bourbon 1919 - 2013 db **(96.5)** n24.5 t24 f24 b24 I left this as the 1,145th and final new whisk(e)y to be tasted for the 2015 Jim Murray's Whisky Bible. Elmer, once a neighbour of mine, loved his garden and more than once I helped him safely remove squirrels without them being hurt in any way. Which makes this whiskey, seemingly gentle but with a backbone of American steel - yet on the nose flowing with floral notes, a touching and entirely apposite marker to his memory. And it delights me to say that I know, with absolute certainty, he would have been blown away by this barrel of glorious complexity. Elmer: with a glass of this rare genius I salute your memory, my friend. *46.5%*

Evan Williams 23 Years Old (94) n22 t23.5 f24.5 b24. Struts itself, refusing to allow age to slow him or dim the shine from his glowing grains. Now oak has taken its toll. This seems older than its 23 years... Or so I first thought. Then a light shone in my soul and it occurred to me: hang on...I have wines going back to the last century. For the older ones, do I not allow them to breathe? So I let the whiskey breathe. And, behold, it rose from the dead. This Methuselah of a whiskey had come alive once more...and how!! *53.5%*

Evan Williams Single Barrel 2004 Edition barrel no. 1, dist 19/03/2004, bott 16/11/2013 db **(89.5) n22** relatively simplistic: ulmo honey and vanilla enlivened by a faint dash of tangerine peel; **t24** profound early sugars, mainly of an icing and syrupy variety. The spices are dull, though weighty and plod and prod rather than stimulate; **f21.5** thins and vanillas out with surprising abruptness; **b22** demure: wouldn't say boo to a goose. *43.3%. 19th in the series.*

Four Roses 125th Anniversary Small Batch Bourbon OBSV - 18 years, OBSK - 13years, OESK- 13 years db **(96.5) n24 t24.5 f24 b24** Nosing and tasting a whiskey like this and, after a morning of sulphur-ruined horrors, I am reminded why I still do this job. A celebration of bourbon; a triumph of blending. *51.6%. ncf. 12468 bottles. WB15/385*

Four Roses 2013 Limited Edition Single Barrel #3-4P Aged 13 Years db **(97) n24.5 t24.5 f24 b24** In that great horse racing state of Kentucky, the home of the Derby, only one distillery is seriously threatening Buffalo Trace's position of supreme bourbon maker. Coming fast up on the rails is Four Roses. Here is another truly sensational bottling. In many ways this is the quintessential bourbon displaying just about every character you can as for. The fact that so much has come from just a single barrel is truly astonishing, as usually you require several mixed together to offer such a rich and classic diversity on nose and palate. Indeed, this is probably the best single barrel bourbon I have ever encountered...from anywhere. *63.4%. WB15/173*

Four Roses Limited Edition 2014 Small Batch (94) n23.5 t24 f23 b23.5 just a little youthful undercurrent means, as beautiful as this whiskey is, it doesn't quite hit the heights of the 2013 version. Still a beauty, though...; *60% approx 11,200*

Four Roses 2014 Limited Edition Single Barrel Aged 11 Years Recipe OESF db **(88.5) n22 t23.5 f21 b22** A pretty quiet cask refusing to scale the highest peaks. *60%.*

George T. Stagg (97.5) n24 t25 f24 b24.5. Astonishing how so much oak can form and yet have such limited negative impact and so few unpleasant side effects. These tasting notes took nearly four hours to compile. Yet they are still in a simplified form to fit into this book... George T Stagg is once again... staggering. *71.5% (143 Proof). ncf.*

George T. Stagg (Barrel Proof) db **(95) n24 t24 f23 b24** Quite beautiful bourbon of the top order. But not quite so breathtakingly complex and brain-shatteringly vivid as Staggs of past times. *64.1%. Buffalo Trace Antique Collection.*

George T. Stagg (96.5) n24.5 when I die it is unlikely I'll go to heaven. But if wherever I go smells like this, then I'll be happy enough. The rye in the mash pulls the strings here, ensuring a clipped sweetness and vague fruitiness to proceedings. Concentrated dates and crispy Demerera sugars combine with a mocha middle for something rather special...; oh, and the spices...mmmm....those spices....; **t24** salivating...which you would hardly expect from something of 138 proof...then opens out into a more complex, truly labyrinthine. Coffee fudge dominates alongside the rye...and for a very long time; **f24** the usual liquorice and hickory fade; **b24** the alcohol by volume of one of the sexiest whiskeys on the planet is 69...and it goes down a treat. Much harder to spit than swallow...*69.05% Buffalo Trace Antique Collection.*

George T. Stagg Limited Edition (96.5) n24 t24.5 f24 b24 As spectacular as a sunset from the hilltop village of Coldharbour in my beloved Surrey *71.4% (142.8 proof). ncf.*

⬦ **George T. Stagg** db **(96.5) n24** never found sticky toffee pudding on a Stagg before, but it appears to have turned up here. Alongside the dates, teasing spices and complex array of dark sugars which makes this whiskey so unmistakable. So dense you feel it would make the most delicious possible swamp in another world, one you wouldn't too much mind being sucked into...; **t24** and those toasty sugars really make a big stand on delivery, swiftly joined by a concentrated blend of hickory and coffee and slowly moulded into shape by the ever-hardening and increasingly more crystalline rye which, at last, makes itself heard; **f24** now the corn oils make their stand, gluing themselves to the palate for a very long finale as the liquorice really does make a loud speech. The drier hickory tones detach themselves from the coffee to show that the tannins really do mean business...; **b24.5** it is impossible not to finish a mouthful of George T without letting out a long, contented, slightly awe-felt and entirely fulfilled sigh, just as one might make after listening to the final strains of Vaughan Williams' London Symphony or Strauss' Tod und Verklärung. Most of the usual traits to be had in abundance, plus one or two slight differences as the pot was stirred for another dip into one of world's whisky's deepest caverns.... 69.1% (138.2 proof)

Hancock's Reserve Single Barrel (92) n25 t23 f21.5 b22.5. A slightly quieter example of this consistently fine brand. The nose, though, is the stuff of wet whiskey dreams... 44.45%

I.W. Harper Kentucky Straight Bourbon (87.5) n22 t22 f21.5 b22. The puckeringly dry delivery and finish forms the toast for the well spiced light sugar sandwich. 41% (82 Proof)

I.W. Harper Kentucky Straight Bourbon 15 Year Old (94.5) n23.5 a well-balanced nose: the small grains are all but dancing a jig while light ulmo honey and butterscotch put a friendly face on the oak; t23.5 the first note or two threatens an explosion – and then there are second thoughts. Instead, we have an almost genteel procession of half-hearted but brilliantly weighted sugars bathed in soft corn oil. The spice rises quickly and falls even faster..; f24 those oils ensures a ridiculously long finish. Which means the praline is given all the time it needs to strut its stuff, as does the curiously salty oak notes...; the spices hum gently, but just loud enough to be heard; b23.5 class in a glass. 43% (86 Proof)

Jefferson's Reserve batch no. 84 (91) n23 t23.5 f22 b23. Once a 15-year-old, no age statement here. But this has seen off a few Summers, sweetening with each passing one. 45.1%.

Jim Beam Black Double Age Aged 8 Years (93) n23 t24 f22.5 b23.5. Rather than the big, noisy, thrill-seeking JB Black, here it is in quiet, reflective, sophisticated mode. Quite a shift. But no less enjoyable. 43% (86 proof)

Jim Beam Bonded 100 Proof db (92.5) n22.5 a little lazy at first, but by degree begins to reveal light layers of small grain and slightly larger oak...; t23.5 soft, vaguely sugared start... then the small grains go berserk. The mouth is peppered with shotgun blasts of rye-infused small grain and then complex sugars, wide-ranging in style; so beautifully busy; f23 now a sublime toastiness kicks in, making the most now of the molasses and chicory; b23.5 takes its time to get going. But when it does, it just won't shut up.... Complex and compelling, the toastiness takes time to make itself felt but does so with panache. 50%

Jim Beam Signature Craft Aged 12 Years db (92.5) n23 gorgeous roasted coffee and liquorice. The rye pokes through gamely; t23.5 soft delivery with a wonderful toasted fudge quality. Takes time for the rye to arrive but it does as the spices mount; f23 softly spiced with plenty of creamy mocha; b23 classic Beam: big rye and massive fruit. Quite lovely. 43% WB15/386

John B. Stetson Straight Bourbon Whiskey (92) n23.5 t23.5 f22 b23. Absolutely love it! Quality: I take my hat off to you...42%

Jim Beam Signature Craft Brown Rice 11 Year Old db 45% (78) n20.5 t21 f18 b18.5. A whiskey I nosed and tasted before looking to see what it was. And immediately alarm bells rang and I was reaching to inspect the bottle in a state of panic and shock. RICE!!! Well that explains the unsatisfying simplicity to the finish where, really, only oak can be heard....apart from the wallpaper paste, that is. And the fact the whiskey never quite gets off the ground despite an attractive cocoa thread. Or was that actually real cocoa...? Sorry, but in the great name of Jim Beam, this is one that should have just stayed in the lab. (90 Proof)

Jim Beam Signature Craft Soft Red Wheat 11 Year Old db (92) n22 buttery with touches of seasoned oak and lightly spiced liquorice; t23.5 mouth-filling delivery yet with a sugary crispness. The spices go to town almost immediately, offering an almost spiced fruit loaf feel; f23 happy to take its time to disappear and rolls out the sugars for a last, gently spiced hurrah...; b23.5 a beautifully weighted bourbon making a big deal of the sugar-spice interplay. Hugely enjoyable and at times fascinating. 45% (90 Proof)

Jim Beam Signature Craft Small Batch Quarter Cask Finished 3rd Release db (92) n23.5 delicate for any type of quarter cask: emphasis on citrus and subtlety rather than thumping oak; t23.5 soft delivery with beautifully weighted molten sugar and oils forming a match for the early spicy attack; light hickory forms the backbone; f22 a touch grainy with a little rye bite on the semi-thin finale; b23 quarter casks are not normally associated with deftness and poise. This one certainly is. Elegant, if a little lightweight at the end. 43% (86 Proof)

John E. Fitzgerald Larceny (94) n23 t23.5 f23.5 b24. If this doesn't win a few converts to wheated bourbon, nothing will. A high quality, stunningly adorable whiskey, pulsing with elegance and personality. Every drinks cabinet should have this wonderful new addition to the bourbon lexicon. 46%

⟐ **John E. Fitzgerald Very Special Reserve Aged 20 Years** (93) n22.5 the tannins are at full stretch here but remain intact thanks to a slight citrus tone which rescues the treacle and eucalyptus intro...; t24 the nose may be about to go twang. But the delivery is another matter: a stunning marriage of corn oils that soothe and tannins which just begin to make you pucker slightly. Such yin and yang...! f23 butterscotch and vanilla had a plate of molasses tipped over it...; b23.5 a bourbon lover's bourbon! 45% (90 proof)

John J Bowman Virginia Straight Bourbon Single Barrel (94) n23 t24 f23 b24. One of the biggest yet most easily relaxed and beautifully balanced bourbons on the market. *50%*

Johnny Drum (Black Label) (89.5) n22 t23 f21.5 b23. How often does that happen? The same whiskey, different strength, virtually same quality (though this has a little more depth) but gets there by a slightly different route. *43%*

Johnny Drum (Green Label) (89) n22.5 t23 f21 b22.5. Much more honey these days. Worth making a bee-line for. *40%*

Johnny Drum Private Stock (90.5) n22.5 t22.5 f23 b22.5. One of those bourbons where a single glass is never quite enough. Great stuff! *50.5% (101 proof)*

◇ **Kentucky Owl Kentucky Straight Bourbon Whiskey** batch no. 2 (91) n22.5 liquorice, toasted mallow and no little tannin; t23.5 a beautifully delivery: the corn and sugars are evenly matched, though the darker, toastier notes eventually come through louder. Quite tangy and eye-watering in part with a spicy attack to the tongue; f22.5 a vague marmalade fruitiness which had been lurking around the perimeters now enter the fray, though the corn dictates; b22.5 a big, corn-led bourbon but with some extra oaky depth. *58.6% (117.2 proof). 1,380 bottles.*

Kentucky Vintage batch 08-72 (94.5) n23.5 t24.5 f23 b23.5 Staggered! I really didn't quite expect that. Previous bottlings I have enjoyed of this have had hair attached to the muscle. This is a very different Vintage, one that reaches for the feminine side of a macho whiskey. If you want to spend an hour just getting to know how sensitive your taste buds can be, hunt down this batch... *45%*

◇ **Knob Creek 2001 Limited Edition Kentucky Straight Bourbon** batch 1, bott 2016 (89.5) n22.5 unusually tame for a Knob Creek, seemingly happy to concentrate on the vanilla; t22.5 and same for the delivery: the tannins hold all the early cards, though once more it is gentle vanilla which has the controlling hand; some heather honey does help support a light leathery structure; f22 so demure for a KC with light liquorice and butterscotch; b22 lovely bourbon, but not of a style one automatically associates with a usually hefty bourbon. *50% (100 proof)*

◇ **Knob Creek Aged 9 Year**s bott code L6154 (95.5) n23.5 delicate: not short of a few banana notes amid the treacle and golden syrup; t24 so salivating! We are back with the golden syrup again, with a firmer thread – perhaps rye starred – with the liquorice alternating between the red and black variety; f23.5 more molasses at play, with light ulmo honey and butterscotch on the fade; b24.5 seems like more barrels have been included from the lower echelons of the warehouse. Lighter, sweeter and more feminine. One of the most complex Knob Creeks I have ever encountered: a true Kentucky belle! *50% (100 proof)*

Knob Creek Aged 9 Years (94.5) n23.5 almost arrogantly consistent: you know pretty well what you are going to get...and there it is. In this classic whiskey's case a whole bunch of honeycomb and vanilla, always more delicate than it first appears...; t24 salivating delivery with rye and barley absolutely hammering on the palate. The corn oil is there not for flavour but effect – it is a fabulous mixture of dates and Demerara rum having the biggest say; f23.5 wonderfully long with the oak toastiness now really beginning to bite...; b23.5 no whiskey in the world has a more macho name, and this is not for the faint-hearted. Big, hard in character and expansive, it drives home its point with gusto, celebrating its explosive finish. *50%*

◇ **Knob Creek Single Barrel Reserve Aged 9 Years** bott no L6133 (95) n23 love the impact of the small grain which is never less than equal to the weighty, honeyed tannin; so much vivid citrus at play...; t24 just so busy and beautiful! Like on the nose, the small grains impact immediately sending the taste buds into spasms of juicy glee. Ribald and juicy, the rye ensures a fruity edge while the spices man up early and with gusto; f24 long, with more of a cocoa link to add to the established liquorice; b24 a macho bourbon of a wonderfully high standard. Just a degree juicier than you normally find with a Knob Creek. *60% (120 proof)*

Maker's 46 (95) n23.5 t24.5 f23 b24 Some people have a problem with oak staves. I don't: whisky, after all, is about the interaction of a grain spirit and oak. This guy is all about the nose and, especially, the delivery. With so much controlled honey on show, it cannot be anything other than a show-stopper. Frankly, magnificent. I think I've met my Maker's... *47% (94 proof)*

Maker's Mark (Red Seal) (91) n22.5 t23.5 f22 b23. The big honey injection has done no harm whatsoever. This sample came from a litre bottle and the whiskey was darker than normal. What you seem to have is the usual steady Maker's with a helping hand of extra weight. In fact this reminds me of the old Maker's Gold wax. *45%*

Michter's No. 1 Bourbon (87) n23 t22.5 f20 b21.5. This one is mainly a nose job: all kinds of heavy liquorice and diced kumquat. But there is also a brooding tannin menace lurking in the shadows, which revel themselves more fully – and with a tad of bitterness - on delivery and finish. *45.7%*

Noah's Mill batch 10-170 **(93) n23.5 t23.5 f23 b23**. This monster of a bourbon just rumbles along on the palate like one of the four thunderstorms I have encountered in Kentucky today... *57.15%*

Noah's Mill batch 13-81 **(93.5) n23** gorgeous glazed almonds; a little citrus & cold coffee; **t23.5** oddly enough, doesn't taste like the nose: much more macho, with the full blooded hickory & Demerara; enormous weight & depth; assorted honey notes begin to form; **f22.5** gentle finale, reverting back to the style of the aroma. Excellent vanilla on sugars & weightier liquorice; **b23.5** a full bodied classic bourbon which undulates over the palate. *57.15% (114.3 proof)*

Old Fitzgerald Very Special 12 Years Old (93) n24 t23.5 f22.5 b23. There is always something that makes the heart sing when you come across a whiskey which appears so relaxed in its excellence. At the moment my heart is in the shower merrily lathering itself... *45%*

Old Grand-Dad (90.5) n22 t23 f23 b23.5. This one's all about the small grains. A busy, lively bourbon, this offers little to remind me of the original Old Grand-Dad whiskey made out at Frankfort. That said, this is a whisk(e)y-lover's whiskey: in other words the excellence of the structure and complexity outweighs any historical misgivings. Enormously improved and now very much at home with its own busy style. *43%*

Old Grand-Dad Bonded 100 Proof (94.5) n22.5 t24 f23.5 b24.5 Obviously Old Grand-dad knows a thing or two about classy whiskey: this is a magnificent version, even by its own high standards. It was always a winner and one you could bet your shirt on for showing how the small grains can impact upon complexity. But this appears to go a stage further. The base line is a touch deeper, so there is more ground to cover on the palate. It has been a whiskey-lover's whiskey for a little while and after a few barren years, has been inching itself back to its great Frankfort days. The fact that Beam's quality has risen over the last decade has played no insignificant part in that. *50% (100 proof)*

Old Rip Van Winkle 10 Years Old (93) n24 t23 f23 b23. A much sharper cookie than it once was. And possibly a Maryland Cookie, too, what with the nuts and chocolate evident. As graceful as it is entertaining. *45% (90 Proof). Buffalo Trace.*

Old Weller Antique 107 (96) n24.5 t24 f23.5 b24 This almost blew me off my chair. Always thought this was pleasant, if a little underwhelming, in the past. However, this bottling has had a few thousands volts past through it as it now comes alive on the palate with a glorious blending of freshness and debonair aging. One of the surprise packages of 2012. *53.5% (107 proof)*

Orphan Barrel 'Barterhouse' 20 Years Old (91) n22.5 t22.5 f23 b23 To think: this was still white dog when I first visited Old Stitz! *45.1%.*

Orphan Barrel Forged Oak (87) n22 t22 f21 b22. Decent bourbon, but a little stiff and mechanical in its development. The finish has a tad too much toast for its own good. Still, a good chewing bourbon. *45.25%*

Orphan Barrel Lost Prophet batch tul-tr-1 **(92) n22.5** hickory and butterscotch pair off beautifully; **t23.5** and in steams the liquorice, the old fashioned way, with molasses as its sidekick; **f23** comfortable as the spices rise; **b23** markedly more relaxed than Forged Oak and understands the value of good sugar-spice interplay. *45.05%*

Orphan Barrel 'Old Blowhard' 26 Years Old (95) n23.5 t24 f23.5 b24 I do get my hands on a few samples of very old bourbon, but this seems to have a style more recognisable in the 1980s and early to mid '90s than now. Time warp whisky in every sense. Wonderful! *45.35%. Bottled in Tullahoma, aged 26 years, "found in Stitzel Weller".*

Orphan Barrel Rhetoric 21 Year Old batch 0109-67 **(94.5) n23.5** fabulous intensity from the get go: toasty and honeyed in the classic way with the small grains taking over the show to fizz and simper; **t24** gosh....this really is something a little special: the sugars stand tall and proud, despite being swamped by lush corns oils bathed in liquorice-coated tannins: the sweetness, as with all great bourbons, appears to be in league with the spices; **f23** dries but without bitterness and in perfect pace with the growing vanilla; **b24** a bourbon drinker's bourbon. How's that for rhetoric...? *45%*

⬩ **Orphan Barrel Rhetoric 22 Year Old** batch no. L6063J3 **(87) n20.5 t23.5 f21 b22**. Certainly has a few proud war wounds to show for 22 searing hot Kentucky summers. Some outstanding tannins and roasty sugars at play on delivery, and a few grapefruit notes for good measure. But some bitterness, also, as the oak gives up a degree of its less impressive qualities. Very hard to call it right on whiskeys this age. This comes home just the right side of very good, but another summer might have done some fair damage. *45.2% (90.4 proof)*

Pappy Van Winkle's Family Reserve 15 Years Old (96) n24.5 the usual blood oranges by the cartload...the lilting mix of plum juice and white bread kneaded until it has become a sweet, sugary ball. All that plus a shy spiciness and some broad oak. But what makes it all work is the lightness of the mix...so big...yet so delicate...; **t23.5** lush but with those threatening oaks on the nose exploding on impact. For a moment just a little OTT, but then several huge waves of cocoa-lined vanilla and marmalade puts the world to rights again...; **f24** long and back to unbridled elegance. Cocoas flit around, as do those wheated softly, softly spices and layers of thinned manuka honey... stunning...; **b24** at a book signing in Canada a Bible enthusiast asked me which well-aged, wheated bourbon he should look for. I told him Pappy 15. He looked at me quizzically and said: "Well, that's what I thought, but in the Bible you have it down as rye-recipe." I told him he was wrong...until I checked there and then. And discovered he was right. Of course, Pappy has always been wheated and the lushness on the palate and spices radiating from it has always confirmed this. I'll put it down to not spitting enough. Or perhaps the speed at which I type whilst tasting. Sometimes you mean one thing – then another word comes out. Like when a member of my staff asks for a pay rise. I mean no. But somehow say yes. So apologies to any other I fooled out there. For not only is this a wheated bourbon. With its improbable degree of deftness for something so big, it has edged up a notch or two into a truly world great whiskey...whatever the recipe. *53.5% (107 proof)*

Parker's Heritage Collection "Promise of Hope" Single Barrel 10 Years db **(95)** n24 hard to imagine how so much complexity can evolve from a single barrel...a deep aroma lightened by sublime layering of sugars, mainly muscovado, aided and abetted by watered maple syrup. Gentle hints of orange and marzipan add depth and direction **t24** this has "Parker Beam" stamped all over the taste buds: a man who prefers his whisky lush, sweet and profound; a whiskey which the average north American bear would make a lethal swipe for, so full it is of yummy honey. But it needs the injection of almost perfectly infused spices to launch this to the next level and act as the perfect counter to the blend of ulmo and manuka honeys which, combining with the liquorice, make for a sublime experience of riches engulfing the palate; **f23** thins as the corn oils accelerate, but the spices persist; **b24** in an age when masters Distillers assume that noble title after about ten minutes in the job and for marketing reasons alone, it is touching to find a whiskey bottled in honour of a genuine Master Distiller, a man who has probably forgotten more about whiskey than the majority of the recent intake have so far learned. It is no less touching that part of the money raised from the sale of this whiskey will go to ALS charities, a condition under which Parker Beam now labours. *48%.*

Parker's Heritage Collection Sixth Edition Master Distillery's Blend Of Mashbills Aged Since 2001 db **(94.5)** n24 my word! The small grains have a field day: the rye really ups the crisp fruit levels while the wheat shovels on the spice; elsewhere its big, sweetened liquorice to confirm the dozen years in barrel; **t23.5** the sugars arrive as though blasted from a cannon: hard as rock and crystalline they positively burrow into the taste buds and if explosives are required the wheat provides it with some wicked spices; that all said, the mid-ground is a depository for the more elegant, teasing by-products; **f23** settles contentedly along a vanilla route. Some burnt toasty notes, as expected; the sugars more even now, almost quiet with a lovely fried yam fade...and spice, of course! **b24** shows plenty of muscle, but subtlety and sophistication in equal measures, too. *63.5% (127 proof). ncf.*

Parker's Heritage Collection Wheated Mash Bill Bourbon Aged 10 Years (97) n24 t24 **f24.5 b24.5.** Hard to find the words that can do justice. I know Parker will be immensely proud of this. And with every good reason: I am working exceptionally hard to find a fault with this either from a technical distillation viewpoint or a maturation one. Or just for its sheer whiskeyness...A potential World Whisky of the Year. *61.1% (124.2 Proof). ncf.*

Redemption High Rye Bourbon (74.5) n19 t20 **f17.5 b18.** Hugely disappointing bottling. Vaguely butyric, and its failure to reach any high point of quality is really driven home by the car-crash finish, complete with less than pleasant tang. Seriously needs to redeem itself next time round. *46%*

Ridgemont Reserve 1792 Aged 8 Years (94.5) n23.5 t24 f23.5 b23.5 Now here is a whiskey which appears to have come to terms with its own strengths and, as with all bourbons and malts, limitations. Rarely did whiskey from Barton reach this level of maturity, so harnessing its charms always involves a bit of a learning curve. Each time I taste this it appears a little better than the last...and this sample is no exception to the rule. Excellent. *46.85% (93.7 Proof)*

Rowan's Creek Batch 13-88 **(82)** n20 t21.5 f20.5 b20. A modest bourbon short on complexity and weight but big on spice and delicate sugars. *50.05% (100.1 proof)*

Russell's Reserve Single Barrel (94) n23.5 t24 f23 b23.5. Old-fashioned, thick as treacle bourbon. Delicious. *55%. ncf. Wild Turkey.*

Russell's Reserve Small Batch 10 Year Old (92.5) n24.5 t23 f22 b23. Had the quality and complexity on the palate followed on from the nose I may well have had the world's No 1 whisky for 2012 in my glass. Just slum it with something quite wonderful, instead. Still waiting for an official explanation as to why this is a miserly 90 proof, when Jimmy Russell's preferred strength is 101, by the way... 45%. *Wild Turkey.*

Smooth Ambler Old Scout Straight Bourbon Aged 7 Years bott 13 **(94.5)** n23.5 t23.5 f23.5 b24 There is an argument that if you wanted to present someone with a bottle of bourbon to show them all its main and unique characteristics, this should be the one: very useful, indeed. 'Andy Ambler – a lion among the scouts. *49.5% WB15/372*

Smooth Ambler Old Scout Straight Bourbon 10 Years Old batch 2, bott 4 May 13 **(95.5)** n24 t24 f23.5 b24 One of the most delicate and sophisticated bourbons of the year. Absolutely every aspect of this glorious whisky is disarmingly understated...how un-American! *50% WB15/374*

Spring 44 Single Barrel Bourbon batch 2, barrel no 8 **(93)** n22 t23.5 f23.5 b24. Pure entertainment. Ticks many of the boxes the Spring 44 bourbon misses. And, to be brutally honest, barrels properly blended should always outperform a single one. *50% (100 proof)*

Spring 44 Straight Bourbon batch 2 **(84.5)** n21 t22.5 f20.5 b20.5. A straight Kentucky bourbon blended from two distinctly different rye recipe styles. The result is something very different, indeed – and sadly doesn't always work. In short, chocolate orange meets Yorkshire Tea. Odd. *45% (90 proof)*

Stagg Jn (91.5) n22.5 t24 f22.5 b22.5. A whiskey of staggering brinkmanship. Who will blink first? The massive oak or the taste buds. To be honest, this is the kind of bourbon that sorts out the men from the boys, the women from the girls. Doesn't have quite enough covering sweetness of varying type and intensity to match the complexity found in the original Stagg. One that needs a very long time to get to the bottom of. *67.2% (134.4 proof)*

⬦ **That Boutique-y Whisky Company Heaven Hill** batch 1 **(94)** n23 Fisherman's Friend cough sweet meets red liquorice; t23.5 chewy, with a bevvy of molasses and light muscovado notes; presumably a rye-inclusive mash as the juiciness is pretty profound; f24 long, with all the emphasis on hickory and vanilla; b23.5 now that's what I call bourbon! Travel back 30 years and taste some Heaven Hill, and – though a different distillery - you wouldn't be too far off! This bottling does the HH name proud! *50%. 240 bottles.*

Trails End Bourbon 8 Year Old (87) n21.5 t22.5 f21.5 b21.5. A light bourbon, where the end of the trail begins early. The citrus outpoints the tannins all too easily. *45% (90 Proof). Hood River Distillers, Inc.*

Very Old Barton 6 Years Old (92) n23 t23 f23 b23. One of those seemingly gifted bourbons that, swan-like, appears to glide at the surface but on closer inspection has loads going on underneath. *43%*

Very Old Barton 90 Proof (94) n23 t24 f23.5 b23.5. One of the most dangerously drinkable whiskeys in the world... *45% (90 proof)*

Virgin Bourbon 7 Years Old (96.5) n24 t24.5 f24 b24 This takes me back nearly 40 years to when I first began my love affair with bourbon and was still a bit of a whisky virgin. This was the very style that blew me away: big, uncompromising, rugged...yet with a heart of honeyed gold. It is the type of huge, box-ticking, honest bourbon that makes you get on your hands and knees and kiss Kentucky soil. *50.5% (101 proof)*

Virgin Bourbon 15 Years Old (92.5) n23.5 t23 f23.5 b23. The kind of bourbon you want to be left in a room with. *50.5% (101 proof)*

Virginia Gentleman (90.5) n22 t23 f23 b23.5. A Gentleman in every sense: and a pretty sophisticated one at that. *40% (80 Proof)*

Weller 12 Years Old (93) n24 t23.5 f22.5 b23. Sheer quality. And an enormous leap in complexity and grace from the 7-y-o. *45%*

Western Gold 6 Year Old Bourbon Whiskey (91.5) n22 t23 f22.5 b23 Taken from barrels sitting high in the warehouse, that's for sure. You get a lot for your six years... *40%.*

⬦ **Whiskey Thief Straight Bourbon (87)** n22 t22 f21.5 b21.5. Straight as a die, unwavering bourbon which sticks to an uncomplicated, intense vanilla theme. Very pleasant. *40%*

Wild Turkey 101 (91) n22 t23.5 f22.5 b23. By far the best 101 I have tasted in a decade: you simply can't do anything but go weak at the knees with that spice attack. *55.5% (101 proof)*

Wild Turkey American Spirit Aged 15 Years (92) n24 t22.5 f22.5 b23. A delightful Wild Turkey that appears under par for a 100 proofer but offers much when you search those nooks and crannies of your palate. *50.0% (100 proof)*

Wild Turkey Rare Breed bott code L0049FH **(94)** n22.5 t24.5 f23 b24. It is hard to credit that this is the same brand I have been tasting at regular intervals for quite a long while. Certainly nothing like this style has been around for a decade and it is massively far removed from two years ago. The nose threatens a whiskey limited in direction. But the delivery is as profound as it is entertaining. Even on this bottling's singular though fabulous style, not perhaps quite overall the gargantuan whiskey of recent years. But, seeing as it's only the nose which pegs it back a point or two, still one that would leave a big hole in your whiskey experience if you don't get around to trying. *54.1%*

Willett Pot Still Reserve barrel no. 2421 **(95.5)** n24.5 t23 f24 b24. Another fabulous whiskey from Willett. You can so often trust them to deliver and here they have given us a bourbon showing serious oak injection, yet a sweetness which counters perfectly. *47%.*

◇ **William Larue Weller** db **(97)** n24 there is a clever layer of kumquat here I didn't expect: when I finish tasting, I'll thumb through my back notes and see if I have ever mentioned this before; don't think so. But the real star is the interplay between sweet and dry: the tannins are working hard to dry this out with a series of ground coffee notes, backed up by a distinct herbal note that moves towards spice. Balancing this out is a gorgeous mollassed tone, roasty and delicate. The tannins, though, are taken to the very edge...; t24.5 talk about controlled explosions... The intensity is breath-taking, but most astonishing is the way all the myriad flavours, no matter their size, are controlled and seemingly measured so, again, no one factor dominates. The tannins, for some, might be a little too vigorous. But for old hand big bourbon lovers, the supreme confidence in the way the sugars temper the proceedings is a sign of brilliance; f24 Fisherman's Friend cough sweets on steroids. Just so long with the corn oils doing their job with astonishing panache, also adding to the most subtle sweetening imaginable; b24.5 probably the driest WLW I have yet encountered. Yet the way the barely perceptible sugars react is one of the whisky wonders of the world... *67.3% (134.6 proof)*

William Larue Weller (97.5) n24 t24.5 f24 b25 For any whiskey with a proof of 123.4, the only way is up...! Last year's Whisky Bible World Whisky of the Year Runner-up is going for the full title big time, no holds barred. Again, this is absolutely supreme class. *61.7% (123.4 proof). ncf. Buffalo Trace Antique Collection.*

William Larue Weller dist Spring 2001 db **(97.5)** n24.5 t24.5 f24 b24.5 I always save this as one of the last whiskeys I taste for each Bible. In life you always need something to look forward to... *68.1%.*

William Larue Weller (97) n24 which dominates? The wheat-induced spices? The burnt golden syrup? The liquorice-molasses mix? None? All...? t24.5 just a slow drip-dripping of spices and acacia honey, then manuka. Probably the silkiest mouth feel to any wheated whiskey on the planet and unquestionably the most glorious intertwangling of honey-dripping dark sugars and even thicker but non-threatening tannins you'll encounter in this and many other years. For all this, salivating and just dripping with fresh juices; f24 the spices continue surprisingly tamely but all those notes found earlier continue but in a lower key...; b24.5 just one of those whiskeys which makes sense of life, of whiskey. A collection and collaboration of flavours and shapes on the palate which simply beguile... *70.1% (140.2 proof).*

Woodford Reserve Batch 98 (85.5) n23 t21.5 f20 b21. The promise of the nose, full of the kind of liquorice and mollasess lovers of Old Forester rightly drool over will be as disappointed as I at the bitterness which digs in hard from the mid-point onwards. *43.2%.*

Woodford Reserve Batch 115 (90) n22 soft, delicate. Perhaps missing some complexity; mainly lemon-soaked vanilla; t22 soft delivery; some citrus and coconut water amid the deeper tannin; f23 late praline with no shortage of oily depth and demerera; really lovely spices come into their own as the story unfolds; b23 for those who prefer their bourbons a little nutty and creamy. And spicy... *43.2%*

Woodford Reserve Batch 124 (87) n22.5 t22 f21 b21.5. Pleasant enough bourbon. Perhaps the tannins could do with a little muzzling, as they have too much to say when there are so few counter notes. The thickness of the oils hardly helps, either. Enjoyable squeezes of citrus and do enjoy the cocoa and lime theme. *43.2%*

Woodford Reserve Batch 126 (87.5) n21.5 t23 f21.5 b22. A very tame bourbon poodling along the Bourbon Highway at a steady 40mph. A slight over dependence on sugars make for a limitation in complexity, badly requiring some of the oak prevalent in batch 124 to make things happen. This lack of body allows a degree of over bitterness at the end. But plenty of citrus and at the late middle a welcome, if short-lived, burst of mocha. With plenty of Demerera, of course... *43.2% . WB15/172*

◇ **Woodford Reserve Batch 183 (89)** n21.5 slight, a little flaky and with a random scattering of citrus and nutty tones; t22 slightly oilier than usual, the corn planting its flag with determination; f23 mocha and caramel work charmingly together; b22.5 a bourbon which at times enters the glass as a pleasant though undercooked offering. This batch has just enough in Reserve (geddit?) to make for a satisfying rather than slightly frustrating experience. *43.2%*

Woodford Reserve Distiller's Select batch 95 **(91)** n23 t23 f22 b23. Few bourbons so beautifully pits sweet against dry to such excellent effect. *43.2%*

Woodford Reserve Double Oaked (95) n24.5 oh-my-word...!!! The best nose from Woodford Reserve yet: it appears enormous, yet has been muffled so the intensity is controlled and spreads gorgeously. Dried dates with fig rolls, red liquorice and hickory. Not a single note, though, tries to upstage another...; t23.5 soft delivery, as it just had to be, though the spices arrive earlier than might be expected. Even so, those lush fruit notes soften the more intense liquorice and molasses; f23 thins, leaving the lighter sugars and spices to play out the end game; a little bitterness creeps in at the death; b24 the old Labrot and Graham Distillery has just entered a new phase of excellence since its reopening. Well done blender on creating a bourbon not just of beauty but of great significance. *43.2% WB16/052*

Woodford Reserve Master's Collection Four Grain (95) n24 t24 f23 b24. Sod's law would have it that the moment we removed this from the 2006 Bible, having appeared in the previous two editions without it ever making the shelves, it should at last be belatedly released. But a whiskey worth waiting for, or what? The tasting notes are not a million miles from the original. But this is better bourbon, one that appears to have received a significant polish in the intervening years. Nothing short of magnificent. *46.2%*

◇ **Yellowstone Select Kentucky Straight Bourbon** (87) n22 t22 f21 b22. Now there's a name from the past! Fatter and much more chewy than the Yellowstone of yesteryear. No shortage of molasses. *46.5% (93 proof). Bottled by Limestone Branch Distillery.*

Tennessee Whiskey
BENJAMIN PRICHARD
Benjamin Prichard's Tennessee Whiskey (83) n21.5 t21 f20 b20.5. Majestic fruity rye notes trill from the glass. Curiously yeasty as well; bounding with all kinds of freshly crushed brown sugar crystals. Pleasant enough, but doesn't gel like Prichard's bourbon. *40%*

GEORGE DICKEL
◇ **George Dickel Barrel Select** (90.5) n21 a little shy, almost indifferent. Vanilla at its most basic; maybe a strand of rye making any kind of move; t23 ah, much more like it! Crisp, firm sugars helped along by even firmer rye...; ridiculously juicy from the start; f23.5 more emphasis on liquorice, hickory and Manuka honey. Beautifully controlled spice...and that rye stars crisp and true...; b23 the limited nose makes the heart sink. What happens once it hits the palate is another story entirely. Wonderful! *43%*

◇ **George Dickel Distillery Reserve Collection 17 Year Old** (91.5) n23.5 complex: nutty with a soft doughy appeal. The subtle vanilla is laced with subtler citrus while powdery muscovado sugar further keeps any growing tannin at bay; t23.5 silky, melt-in-the-mouth delivery with corn oil having an early say before juicy, vaguely brittle rye offers a degree of backbone. The tannins roll in arm in arm with the Manuka honey f21.5 a late bitterness has crept in but the sugar and spice see off most of the threat; b23 outside of a warehouse, I'm not sure I've encountered a Tennessee whiskey of this antiquity before. I remember one I tasted some while back, possibly about a year older or two older than this, was black and like tasting eucalyptus concentrate. This is the opposite, showing extraordinary restraint for its age, an almost feminine charm. *43.5%*

◇ **George Dickel Rye** (95.5) n24 sharper than a barber's blade. The fruity notes sparkle like a crystal chandelier. The rye is as crisp as you like, and no less clean: beautiful! t23.5 like molten amber, there is a sublime rock-like quality to this. The grain is hard-edged, the spices every bit as jagged as the solidified, non-specific fruit radiating form the rye; f24 long, with an excellent degree of vanilla. The finale is lengthy, with an ever gathering amount of cocoa thickening the proceedings: stunningly complex...; b24 dare I say it? On this evidence, they do rye probably a fraction better than they produce straight Tennessee. This is a belter! *45%*

George Dickel Superior No 12 Brand Whisky (90.5) n22.5 t23 f22.5 b22.5. A different story told by George from the last one I heard. But certainly no less fascinating. *45%*

JACK DANIEL
Jack Daniel's 120th Anniversary of the White Rabbit Saloon (91) n22.5 lighter ulmo honey to this, which just lowers the temperature and intensity of the liquorice. Complex stuff...; t23.5 magnificent delivery: early corn oil carries the deft molasses; both black and red liquorice slowly builds but the middle is pure vanilla; f22 a mix of dry molassed notes and a little muscovado. Excellent late balance; b23 on its best-behaved form. After the delivery, the oils are down a little, so not the usual bombastic offering from JD. Nonetheless, this is pure class and the clever use of sugars simply make you drool... *43%. Brown-Forman.*

Jack Daniel's Holiday Select 2013 Limited Edition db (91.5) n23 t23 f22.5 b23 Just never seen a JD like this...some pretty well cooked barrels in play here. Doubtless all this is by judicious barrel choice. Now the Americans are tampering with their casks, for the first time ever I began to wonder if the flavouring wasn't all natural. I am sure it is, but see what happens once you begin trying to change the rules...? 49% WB15/381

Jack Daniel's Old No.7 Brand (Black Label) (92) n23 t23 f22.5 b23.5. Actually taken aback by this guy. The heavier oils have been stripped and the points here are for complexity...that should shock a few old Hell's Angels I know. 40%

⁓ **Jack Daniel's No. 27 Gold Double Barrelled** extra matured in maple barrels (82) n21 t21.5 f19 b20.5. Pleasant enough. But it appears the peculiar tannins from the maple barrels have just done slightly too good a job of flattening out the higher, more complex notes from the grains themselves. Slightly bitters towards the finish also. Tennessee Gold with precious little sparkle at all... 40%

Jack Daniel's Master Distiller Series No 1 db (90.5) n24 wonderful dose of extra tangy kumquat over the normal JD signature; something of the fruity cough sweet about this one; t22 a massive, pleasantly oiled mix of molassed fudge and liquorice; f22 drier, toastier hickory; b22.5 no mistaking the JD pedigree. Just a few telling extra degrees of fruit. 43% WB15/387

Jack Daniel's Rested Tennessee Rye batch 2 (88.5) n22 oily and lightly honeyed. Beyond the house style liquorice, surprisingly docile...; t23 and there is no explosion on the palate, either. Just a dull thud as the fruity rye notes collide with the taste buds. There are some gentle spices sprinkled here and there, plus a little ulmo honey to accompany the liquorice; f21 and now all is quiet, except for that light spice buzz and muscovado sugar. The bitterness of the oils strike late on; b22.5 possibly the most intriguing whiskey of the year: America's most flavour-enhancing stills take on the world's most flavoursome grain. The result is surprisingly well mannered, though the oils from both the stills and grain do help obliterate any meaningful complexity. Probably the only world whiskey type I have never tasted in a warehouse at full strength (though I now intend to correct that). Instinct tells me a trick has been missed by not making this a 101...Oh, and one important thing. Normally I suggest you take your whiskey at body temperature. This is one whiskey which needs to be tasted at normal room temperature to keep the oils to a minimum and allow the rye maximum airtime. 40% WB16/022

Jack Daniel's Single Barrel Holiday Select 2014 (93) n23.5 only one distillery on this planet produces a nose this oily and heavy, so full of the joys of liquorice, hickory and molasses; t23 if you ever want to know what a nose tastes like, try this...; f23 long, supremely chewy and thick enough to stand Syke's Hydrometer in; the manuka honey on the finish is rather wonderful...; b23.5 if anybody puts a Coke in this, they want shooting. JD, warts 'n' all... Magnificent! One gripe: a single barrel, but no way of knowing which barrel...grrrrr!!! 48% WB16/020

⁓ **Jack Daniel's Single Barrel Proof Tennessee Whiskey** barrel no. 16-2572, rick no. L-19, bott 14 Apr 16 db (94.5) n23.5 a kind of roast fest: toasted fudge, slightly overcooked treacle tart, Manuka honey, spice, slightly burnt oak...some very serious char; t23.5 a thinner delivery than I anticipated – or is normal for JD - with the corn oil taking a long time to gather itself together. Meanwhile, a mind-blowing array of toasty sugar notes mingle with intense hickory and a dab of aniseed and eucalyptus; f24 all the same notes remain, but the waves between each one is longer, their intensity a little more diluted; b23.5 now that is what you call Tennessee whiskey... 66.25% (132.5 proof). sc.

⁓ **Jack Daniel's Single Barrel Tennessee Rye Whiskey** barrel no. 16-1340, rick no. L-3, bott 24 Feb 16 db (86.5) n21 t22 f21.5 b22. I remember tasting a JD Rye last year which didn't come at me the way I expected. This, too, is surprisingly flat and oily in the places you expect it to sing. Yes, the burnt honey notes are lovely and it does have some of that heavyweight JD swagger we all love. But somehow the finer points of the grain are lost amid it all and we end up with a pretty muted whiskey. 45%. sc.

Corn Whiskey

Dixie Dew (95) n22.5 t24 f24 b24.5 I have kept in my previous tasting notes for this whiskey as they serve a valuable purpose. The three matured corn whiskeys I have before me are made by the same distillers. But, this time round, they could not be more different. From Mellow Corn to Dixie we have three whiskeys with very differing hues. This, quite frankly, is the darkest corn whiskey I have ever seen and one of world class stature with characteristics I have never found before in any whiskey. Any true connoisseur of whisk(e)y will make deals with Lucifer to experience this freak whiskey. There is no age statement...but this one has gray hairs attached to the cob... 50%

Georgia Moon Corn Whiskey "Less Than 30 Days Old" (83.5) n21.5 t22 f20 b20. If anyone has seen corn whiskey made – either in Georgia or Kentucky – then the unique aroma will be instantly recognisable from the fermenters and still house. Enjoyable stuff which does exactly what it says on the jar. *50%*

J. W. Corn (92.5) n23 t23.5 f23 b23. In another life this could be bourbon. The corn holds the power, for sure. But the complexity and levels are so far advanced that this – again! – qualifies as very high grade whiskey. Wonderful that the normal high standard is being maintained for what is considered by many, quite wrongly, as an inferior spirit. *50%*

Mellow Corn (83) n19 t21 f22 b21. Dull and oily on the nose, though the palate compensates with a scintillating array of sweet and spicy notes. *50%*

Single Malt Rye
ANCHOR DISTILLERY

Old Potrero Single Malt Straight Rye Whiskey Essay 10-SRW-ARM-E (94) n24 t23 f24 b23 The whiskey from this distillery never fails to amaze. With the distillery now under new management it will be fascinating to see what lands in my tasting lab. Even at 75% quality we will still be blessed with astonishing whiskeys. *45% (90 proof)*

Straight Rye

Benjamin Prichard's Tennessee Rye Whiskey (86) n20 t21.5 f23 b21.5. Bit of a scruffy nose, but polishes up pleasantly. The rye itself is not of the sharp variety and at times is hard to identify. But the ulmo honey and lush butterscotch offer the gloss at the finish. *43%*

◆◇◆ **Booker's Rye 13 Years, 1 Month, 12 Days** batch no. 2016-LE db (97.5) n25 for a big, well matured rye, it just doesn't come better than this. In fact, it probably can't. It's as though a bar of rye and chocolate has been created for the nose to inspect. There is nibble and bite to the dominating rye, yet it is not all about the spices and grain. Such varying weight and depth, as well as an almost random detection of vanilla and citrus makes for exhaustively brain-draining, mind-blowing but quite glorious nosing....; t24 salivating...oh, so salivating! The perfect weight of grain and sugars make for a delivery of astonishing presence. Almost immediately, the cocoa, which teases on the nose, makes its presence felt here with a series of intense waves, all the time crashing against the rye and Demerara sugar rocks which act as the backbone; f24 those oils I mentioned...this is where they come into their own: gathering up the amazing depth, like starlings in Autumn. Still the cocoa beats out, but never far away is that breath-taking rye as its accomplice and commander. And it all leaks and leaches for a very long time...; b24.5 this was a rye made in the last days of when Jim Beam's Yellow Label was at its very peak. Then, it was the best rye commercially available. Today, it is simply a staggering example of a magnificent rye showing exactly what genius in terms of whiskey actually means. If this is not World Whisky of the Year for 2017, it will be only fragments of molecules away... *68.1% (136.2 proof)*

Bulleit 95 Rye (96) n25 t24.5 f22.5 B23.5 This is a style of rye, indeed whiskey, which is unique. Buffalo Trace makes an ultra high-quality rye which lasts the course longer. But nothing compares in nose and delivery to this...in fact few whiskies in the world get even close... *45%. Straight 95% rye mash whiskey.*

Colonel E.H. Taylor Straight Rye (97) n24 t24.5 f24 b24.5 reminds me of the younger ryes when Sazerac Handy first hit the shelves, with the emphasis on the clarity of the grain and the fallout of oak and spice. Really, a bottle which should never be left on a liquor store shelf. *50%*

Cougar Rye (95) n25 t24 f23 b23. The Lawrenceburg, Indiana Distillery makes the finest rye I have ever tasted - and that is saying something. Here is a magnificent example of their astonishing capabilities. Good luck hunting the Cougar. *37%. Foster's Group, Australia.*

Crater Lake Rye Whiskey Batch no. JA 08 db (83.5) n20 t22 f20.5 b21. A distinctly warming, peppery whiskey with an obvious high rye content. Would do itself better justice as a 100 proof whiskey as here the oils are broken down a little too enthusiastically, allowing unhelpful freedom to a tobacco note. Good early use of dark sugars, though. One to keep an eye on. *40%.*

Devil's Bit Seven-Year-Old Single Barrel (93.5) n22.5 t24 f23 b24. A must-find rye from one of the most impressive small distilleries in the world. *47.7%. Edgefield Distillery.*

◆◇◆ **Governor's Reserve Taos Lightning Straight Rye Whiskey** (94.5) n24 classic: the grain is clean, brittle, fruity – especially in crisp green apple - and radiates its type like an unerring beacon. Brilliant! t24 absolutely more of the same, except a surprising oiliness cushions the impact on delivery; f23 bitters out as a little spiced mocha takes its turn; b23.5 now this is rye, believe me!!! Those who love the Lawrenceburg, Indiana, type rye (and who doesn't?!?) will adore this... *45% (90 proof). sc. Bottled by KGB Spirits LLC.*

High West 12 Years Old Rye (92.5) n22 t24 f23 b23.5. A very clever rye which will hit a chord of appreciation for those who savour this whiskey style. *46%*

High West Whiskey Rendezvous Rye Batch 12431 db **(94.5) n23.5 t24 f23 b24** After a few disappointing batches, this one appears to have found that vital spark. It could be a whole new set of whiskeys, a change of one barrel, or even the same whiskey re-stirred before bottling. It doesn't matter: something has clicked. *46%. ncf. WB15/176*

Jim Beam Pre-Prohibition Style Rye db **(95) n23** crisp muscovado and rye: clean, precise and slightly dazzling; **t24.5** brilliant delivery: the old-fashioned juicy crispness on the palate of a Jim Beam rye has been restored, despite a background fudgy smokiness which dovetails with amazing finesse; a little manuka honey goes a long, long way; **f23.5** long, with the spices now grabbing hold. Fabulous mocha makes the most of the lingering sugar and fading rye; **b24** very similar to how Jim Bean Yellow Label was over 20 years ago. In other words: simply superb! *45% (90 Proof)*

⬦ **John David Albert's Taos Lightning Straight Rye Whiskey** batch no. A1 **(96) n24** some vanilla concentrated tannins have dulled the usual crispness of the rye and thrown in extra spice for good measure; **t24.5** again, the oak is upfront and gets in on the grain's act. But this liquorice and chocolate addition still cannot douse the magical juiciness of the rye, which still enjoys a solo performance before rejoining the group. The spices are pretty warming; **f23.5** a little praline with the vanilla. But the spice and rye carry on together for a good while yet; **b24** some decent age to this has really ensured enormous complexity. And astonishing beauty. *45% (90 proof). sc. Bottled by KGB Spirits LLC.*

Knob Creek Straight Rye Whiskey (92.5) n23.5 classic rye firmness: a light dose of citrus and mango tries to gently thin the intensity; **t23.5** salivating small grain action with the rye making its biggest mark at the base of the tongue. For all the light oils and juiciness, there is no escaping the crispness at the centre, or the surrounding spices; **f22.5** an attractive rye-vanilla mix, with just a late frisson on liquorice; **b23** a slightly more genteel rye than I expected, if you compare standard Knob Creek to their usual bourbon. *50% (100 proof).* ⊙

Knob Creek Straight Rye Whiskey batch L5349CLA **(92.5) n23.5** pretty oily and soft, though the rye still holds the majority of shares...; **t23.5** that is one very intense delivery: still a surprising amount of oil at work with the floral and then fruity majesty begins to power through in no uncertain terms. So chewy, the middle spreads and spreads with molasses and a little ginger for company; **f22.5** long and no less dense. If anything the oils are bigger still...; **b23** curious: just checked...see I scored a batch from last year at 92.5 also. Can't say this isn't consistent quality...! *50% (100 proof).*

Michter's 10 Years Old Single Barrel Straight Rye barrel no. 16A113 **(88) n22.5** thicker than the thickest of thick things. Dense with enough oil to get the Clampett family staking their claim. The rye has a slightly muffled richness due to the unfortunate wideness of the still's cut...; **t23** yep, big rye! The fruitiness and cocoa battle it out for early dominance, and it is the grain which in its chiselled state, naturally, wins; **f20.5** long, vaguely off key with a slightly uncouth oiliness; **b22** Michter's and rye go together like all the great names of America and success: like David Beckham and football, Christopher Nolan and Hollywood directing , Hugh Laurie and Hollywood acting, my old Fleet Street colleague Piers Morgan and chat shows, my girlfriend's old chum Simon Cowell and talent shows. This, though, isn't quite in the same league as the bottle I tasted from them last year, which was in a Saville Row suite compared to the dowdy hand-me-down here. Enjoyable, but by Michter's high standards... *46.4% (92.8 proof).*

Michter's No. 1 Straight Rye (95.5) n23.5 fabulous cut glass clarity to the rye, sparkling with almost crystalline sugars; **t24** crunchy, rock hard and palate teaming with rye particles of the most clean and uncompromising style; the oils are clever and couched amid the juicier, fruity notes; **f24** drier now, though the spices pick up as the tannins begin to get a grip; but the grain absolutely refuses to take a back seat; **b24** truly classic rye whiskey. The stuff which makes one write swoonerisms... *42.4%*

Pappy Van Winkle's Family Reserve Rye 13 Years Old (94) n24 outwardly, the aroma basks in a crisp rye flourish; scratch below the surface and there are darker, more sinister oaky forces at work; **t23.5** crisp, almost crackling rye offers both the fruity-clean and burned fruitcake options; **f23** dulls out a bit as the liquorice/toffee oak takes hold but remains alluringly spicy and sensual; **b23.5** uncompromising rye that successfully tells two stories simultaneously. A great improvement on the Winkle rye of old. *47.8%*

Pikesville Straight Rye Whiskey Aged at Least 6 Years (97.5) n24.5 textbook: the fruitiness of the rye shimmers on the nose; a light spice tingles in Demerara rum fashion. Carry on nosing and you will, if patient and able enough, find unusual depths to which few whiskies reach. The tantalising chocolate-liquorice at about three quarters depth is one of the aromas of the year; **t24.5** after that nose, the delivery just had to be majestic. And it is. The rye grain fair rattles against the teeth, the sugars – crystalline, dark and tinged with both molasses and muscovado – help bring its salivating qualities to maximum. Then those spices...those wonderful, bustling, fizzing spices...; **f24** a lovely mix between ulmo and Zambian forest honey keeps the sweetness lingering to the end. The rye, of course, continues to sparkle and spice its way to the last embers of the fade...which is a long way away...; **b24.5** the most stunning of ryes and the best from Heaven Hill for some time. *55% (110 Proof)*

Redemption Riverboat Rye (78) n19 t21 f19 b19. Dry, weirdly off key and oily – and holed below the water line. *40%*

Redemption Rye (85.5) n22 t22.5 f20 b21. The tobacco nose is a bit of a poser: how did that get there? Or the spearmint, which helps as you try to chew things over in your mind. The big rye wave on delivery is supported by mixed dark sugars. But there is something ashy about the finish. *46%*

Rittenhouse Very Rare Single Barrel 21 Years Old (91) n25 t23 f21 b22. I may be wrong, but I would wager quite a large amount that no-one living has tasted more rye from around the world than I. So trust me when I tell you this is different, a genuine one-off in style. By rights such telling oak involvement should have killed the whisky stone dead: this is like someone being struck by lightning and then walking off slightly singed and with a limp, but otherwise OK. The closest style of whisky to rye is Irish pot still, a unique type where unmalted barley is used. And the closest whiskey I have tasted to this has been 35 to 50-year-old pot still Irish. What they have in common is a massive fruit base, so big that it can absorb and adapt to the oak input over many years. This has not escaped unscathed. But it has to be said that the nose alone makes this worthy of discovery, as does the glory of the rye as it first melts into the tastebuds. The term flawed genius could have been coined for this whisky alone. Yet, for all its excellence, I can so easily imagine someone, somewhere, claiming to be an expert on whiskey, bleating about the price tag of $150 a bottle. If they do, ignore them. Because, frankly, rye has been sold far too cheaply for far too long and that very cheapness has sculpted a false perception in people's minds about the quality and standing of the spirit. Well, 21 years in Kentucky equates to about 40 years in Scotland. And you try and find a 40-year-old Scotch for £75. If anything, they are giving this stuff away. The quality of the whiskey does vary from barrel to barrel and therefore bottle to bottle. So below I have given a summary of each individual bottling (averaging (91.1). The two with the highest scores show the least oak interference...yet are quite different in style. That's great whiskey for you. *50% (100 proof). ncf.*

Barrel no. 1 (91) n25 t23 f21 b22. As above. *50%*
Barrel no. 2 (89) n24 t23 f20 b22. Dryer, oakier. *50%*
Barrel no. 3 (91) n24 t23 f22 b22. Fruity, soft. *50%*
Barrel no. 4 (90) n25 t22 f21 b22. Enormous. *50%*
Barrel no. 5 (93) n25 t23 f22 b23. Early rye surge. *50%*
Barrel no. 6 (87) n23 t22 f20 b22. Juicy, vanilla. *50%*
Barrel no. 7 (90) n23 t23 f22 b22. Even, soft, honeyed. *50%*
Barrel no. 8 (95) n25 t24 f23 b23. The works: massive rye. *50%*
Barrel no. 9 (91) n24 t23 f22 b22. Sharp rye, salivating. *50%*
Barrel no. 10 (93) n25 t24 f22 b22. Complex, sweet. *50%*
Barrel no. 11 (93) n24 t24 f22 b23. Rich, juicy, spicy. *50%*
Barrel no. 12 (91) n25 t23 f21 b22. Near identical to no.1. *50%*
Barrel no. 13 (91) n24 t24 f21 b22. Citrus and toasty. *50%*
Barrel no. 14 (94) n25 t24 f22 b23. Big rye and marzipan. *50%*
Barrel no. 15 (88) n23 t22 f21 b22. Major oak influence. *50%*
Barrel no. 16 (90) n24 t23 f21 b22. Spicy and toffeed. *50%*
Barrel no. 17 (90) n23 t23 f22 b22. Flinty, firm, late rye kick. *50%*
Barrel no. 18 (91) n24 t24 f21 b22. Big rye delivery. *50%*
Barrel no. 19 (87) n23 t22 f21 b21. Major coffee input. *50%*
Barrel no. 20 (91) n23 t24 f22 b22. Spicy sugar candy. *50%*
Barrel no. 21 (94) n24 t23 f24 b23. Subtle, fruity. *50%*
Barrel no. 22 (89) n23 t22 f22 b22. Mollased rye. *50%*
Barrel no. 23 (94) n24 t23 f24 b23. Soft fruit, massive rye. *50%*
Barrel no. 24 (88) n23 t22 f21 b22. Intense oak and caramel. *50%*
Barrel no. 25 (93) n25 t22 f23 b23. Heavy rye and spice. *50%*
Barrel no. 26 (92) n23 t23 f23 b23. Subtle, delicate rye. *50%*
Barrel no. 27 (94) n25 t23 f23 b23. Delicate rye throughout. *50%*
Barrel no. 28 (96) n25 t24 f23 b24. Salivating, roasty, major. *50%*
Barrel no. 29 (88) n23 t22 f21 b22. Hot, fruity. *50%*
Barrel no. 30 (91) n24 t23 f22 b22. Warming cough sweets. *50%*
Barrel no. 31 (90) n25 t22 f21 b22. Aggressive rye. *50%*

Rittenhouse Rye Single Barrel Aged 25 Years (93.5) n24.5 t24 f22 b23. This is principally about the nose: a thing of rare beauty even in the highest peaks of the whiskey world. The story on the palate is much more about damage limitation with the oak going a bit nuts. But remember this: in Scottish years due to the heat in Kentucky, this would be a malt well in excess of 50 years. But even with the signs of fatigue, so crisp is that rye, so beautifully defined are its intrinsic qualities that the quality is still there to be clearly seen. Just don't judge on the first, second or even third mouthful. Your taste buds need time to relax & adjust. Only then will they accommodate and allow you to fully appreciate and enjoy the creaky old ride. At this age, though, always worth remembering that the best nose doesn't always equal the best tasting experience... *50% (100proof).*

Barrel no. 1 (93.5) n24.5 t24 f22 b23. As above. *50%*
Barrel no. 2 (88) n22 t24 f20 b22. Intense. Crisp, juicy; a tad soapy, bitter. *50%*
Barrel no. 3 (89.5) n23 t23.5 f21.5 b21.5. Fabulously crisp. Fruity. Mollassed. *50%*
Barrel no. 4 (85) n21.5 t21.5 f21 b21. Subdued fruit. Massive oak. *50%*
Barrel no. 5 (90.5) n25 t22.5 f21.5 b21.5. Complex. Mega oaked but spiced, fruity. *50%*
Barrel no. 6 (91.5) n24.5 t22 f23 b22. Tangy. Honeyed and hot. Spiced marmalade. *50%*
Barrel no. 7 (83.5) n20 t22 f20.5 b21. Treacle toffee amid the burnt apple. *50%*
Barrel no. 8 (90) n23.5 t23.5 f21 b22. Flinty, teeth-cracking rye. Crème brulee. *50%*
Barrel no. 9 (91) n23.5 t23.5 f22 b22. Massive ryefest. Mocha coated. *50%*
Barrel no. 10 (86.5) n22 t23 f20 b21.5. Early zip and juice. Tires towards caramel. *50%*
Barrel no. 11 (89) n24 t22 f21 b22. Honeycomb. Hickory. Caramel. Oil. *50%*
Barrel no. 12 (84.5) n22.5 t21 f20 b21. Delicate. Vanilla and caramel. Light. *50%*
Barrel no. 13 (89.5) n22.5 t23 f22 b22. Succulent. Yet rye remains firm. *50%*
Barrel no. 14 (88) n22 t23 f21 b22. Very similar to 13 but with extra caramel. *50%*
Barrel no. 15 (86) n21 t23 f20.5 b21.5. Lazy grain. Warming but flat. Caramel. *50%*
Barrel no. 16 (92) n23 t23 f23 b23. Sculpted rye: sugared fruit; a twist of juniper. *50%*
Barrel no. 17 (86.5) n22.5 t21.5 f21 b21.5. Fizzy, fruity spice calmed by caramel. *50%*
Barrel no. 18 (91) n23.5 t23.5 f21.5 b22.5. Pristine rye. Spice. Juicy molasses. Crisp. *50%*
Barrel no. 19 (96) n24 t23.5 t24.5 b23.5. Concentrated honeycomb and chocolate. *50%*
Barrel no. 20 (89.5) n23 t22 f22.5 b22. Cream toffee. Fruit and spice. *50%*
Barrel no. 21 (85) n21 t20 f23 b21. Severe oak delivery. Recovers with mocha toffee. *50%*
Barrel no. 22 (81) n20 t20 f21 b20. Mild sap. Fruity. Oily. *50%*
Barrel no. 23 (94) n23.5 t24 f23.5 b23. Rich. Fruity. Juicy. Clean. Corn oil. Cocoa. *50%*
Barrel no. 24 (88.5) n22.5 t22 f21 b22. Huge vanilla. Slow spice. *50%*
Barrel no. 25 (88) n22.5 t21.5 f22 b22. Custard and sugared fruit. Sharpens. *50%*
Barrel no. 26 (90.5) n22 t23 f23 b22.5. Classic crisp rye. Big, manageable oak. *50%*
Barrel no. 27 (88) n23 t22 f21.5 b21.5. Huge, honeyed oak. Oily. Dries at end. *50%*
Barrel no. 28 (91) n22.5 t23.5 f22.5 b22.5. Exemplary honeycomb-rye delivery. Spices. *50%*
Barrel no. 29 (94) n23.5 t24 f23 b23.5. Juicy rye; crisp sugar-vanilla-hickory fade. *50%*
Barrel no. 30 (94.5) n23 t24 f24 b23.5. Thick rye. Cocoa. Spices. *50%*
Barrel no. 31 (79) n21 t20 f19 b19. Lethargic. Bitter. *50%*
Barrel no. 32 (88) n21.5 t22.5 f22 b22. Relaxed honeycomb. Hint of mint. *50%*
Barrel no. 33 (88.5) n22.5 t22 f22 b22. Powering oak-rye battle. *50%*
Barrel no. 34 (84) n23 t21 f20 b20. Thick oak throughout. Corn oil. *50%*
Barrel no. 35 (93.5) n22.5 t23.5 f24 b23.5. Big rye. Demerara-hickory. Complex. *50%*
Barrel no. 36 (77) n21 t19 f18 b19. Bitter oak. *50%*

Russell's Reserve Rye 6 Year Old Small Batch bott. code L0194FH) (93.5) n24 t23.5 f22.5 b23.5. Lost none of its wit and sharpness: in fact has improved a notch or two in recent times. *45%*

Sazerac Kentucky Straight Rye Whiskey 18 Years Old bott 2012 (95.5) n24 t23 f24 b24.5. Unquestionably showing a different side to its personality this time out, allowing the rye to show its fruity personality to the full. *45%*

Sazerac Rye 18 Year Old bott Fall 2013 db (97) n24.5 t24.5 f24 b24 Another stir of the pot and up comes Sazerac 18 polished and wallowing in its own enormity. Rye whiskey exactly how it should be. *45%*

Sazerac Rye 18 Year Old bott Spring 2014 db (96.5) n24.5 a little less oil than normal means getting a particularly vivid sight of the rye in all its crisp, subtly fruity pomp; a bit like how the stars are brighter when you view them away from the lights. Last year was a little less sharp, if memory serves, but again the weight of the spice and the tannin cannot be bettered; also with this little less oil we can now recognise something of the herb garden...; t24.5 dark and deep on the palate, there is a mischievous chocolate character abroad and this chimes in stunningly with the crunchy grain and promiscuous pices; f23.5 the oak lays down the law slightly, with the spices its gun-happy deputy. The rye is now hiding a little; **b24** always one of the great and most fascinating whiskeys on the planet - essentially the same stuff year after year - plays out with each roll of the bottling dice. Here someone has cut off much of the oil...with stunning results. Way better than than last year's offering and much closer to its old self. *45%. Buffalo Trace Antique Collection*

⬦ **Sazerac 18 Years Old** bott Spring 2015 db **(97) n25** cut-glass rye: crystalline rye notes don't get any more...well...crystalline than this. Spices nibble, bite and nip with a beguiling mix of playfulness and attitude, but it is the perfect foil for the more serene, herbal notes. Not sure how a nose can be so soft, yet diamond hard at one and the same moment...; **t24** there you go! As though the nose has arrived on the palate. Except here there are far more brassy sugars immediately at work, but with a squeeze of lime to slightly break up the intensity. Mocha and praline notes add an almost phenolic weightiness in the same way smoke does on a light Islay. All the time, though, the rye can traced on every outline sharp, rigid and delicious; **f24** long, making the most of the modest and so subtle oils which have, literally, stuck around. The tannins are evident but refuse to dominate and, instead, concentrate only on adding a further degree of weight and gravitas to the unruffled rye; **b24** it is as though all excess oils have been drained from this whiskey in the last year or two and we are seeing something stark, naked and even more desirable than before. Technically sublime. *45% (90 proof).*

Smooth Ambler Old Scout Straight Rye Aged 7 Years batch 17, bott 9 Nov 13 **(82) n21 t22 f19 b20.** Now this is odd. What do you get when you combine the characteristics of rye and gin? Something, probably, like this. Never been to these guys in West Virginia, though I'll try and make a point of paying a visit when next in that stunning state. No idea if they are involved with gin. But something about the botanical feel to the nose and finish in particular suggests they might. Perhaps a bottling problem for this single batch? Intrigued. *49.5% WB15/373*

Sonoma County Rye pot distilled from grain db **(83.5) n21 t21.5 f20 b21.** Sweet nougat, heavy duty, wide-cut oily. Quite German in style. *48%. 1512 Spirits. WB15/384*

⬦ **Thomas H. Handy Sazerac** db **(95.5) n23.5** a hefty nose, the natural fruitiness of the rye given enormous weight by a dull but intense orange peel note on top of a crushed leaf (hang on, rings a bell..... yep, just checked with last year's bottling "crushed green leaves" I noted: spooky!), slightly herbal tea effect; **t24.5** the oils missing in the Sazerac 18 have turned up here. So oily at first it takes a little while for the rye to really battle though and make its mark. But when it does...oh, boy! But for its enormity, the boom of the explosion, there is no carnage or collateral damage. Just a mouth-watering, juicy spume of spiced rye and wave after wave hits the taste buds with controlled power, reducing in time elegance; **f23.5** retires to a more deft, cocoa-enriched and sober fade, with oak-enriched caramels and ulmo honey softening the buzz of the spice; **b24** with each bottling, the style of the Thomas Handy moves away from the Sazerac 18 in style *63.45% (126.9 proof).*

Thomas H. Handy Sazerac Straight Rye Whiskey (97.5) n24 t24.5 f24.5 b24.5 This was World Whisky of the Year last year and anyone buying this on the strength of that will not be disappointed. Huge whiskey with not even the glimmer of a hint of an off note. Magnificent: an honour to taste and rye smiles all round... *66.2%. ncf.*

Thomas H. Handy Sazerac Straight Rye (95.5) n24 about as herbal as I've ever known this brand: crushed green leaves, including eucalyptus, make for a sharpness which isn't the usual crisp rye character you might expect; **t24** not so much enters the mouth as kisses it: for something around 130% proof you expect a thudding entry - instead, you get a controlled explosion with no casualties. All relatively free of angst or burn and concentrates on the delightful marriage between the intense grain and the calmer, sweeter ulmo honey. The oak pulses in the background, but without recourse to a full spice attack; **f23.5** curious how these big oils seem to carry with it so much natural caramel...makes for the softest finish you imagine for a whiskey so gargantuan...; **b24** perhaps because this has become something of a softie, without all those usual jagged and crisp rye notes, it doesn't quite hit the spot with quite the same delicious drama. Still a beauty, though. *64.6%*

⬦ **Turley Mill Straight Rye Western Whiskey** aged 6 years, batch no. 12 **(94) n23.**5 the spicy rye makes no secret of its presence; **t24** absolutely brilliant delivery: the rye is bursting out from every molecule: salivating, warming, rich, crisp, deep, multi-layered and every single nuance is rye related, even those the tannins have got their teeth into; **f23** some late oils develop alongside the hesitant ulmo honey; **b23.5** so, with this from KGB Spirits, here's my Cold War: don't add ice to this superb rye under any circumstances...*58% (118 proof). sc. Bottled by KGB Spirits LLC.*

Whistlepig Aged 10 Years db **(88) n21 t22 f23 b22.** Having tasted this after the Sazarac beasts, this could have disappeared without trace. But had enough sharpness and rye freshness to make for a very pleasant and worthwhile experience. *50% (100 proof)*

WhistlePig Old World 12 Year Old European casks **(87) n23 t23.5 f20 b20.5**. What a tragedy! The spirit itself is magnificent. The grain positively glistens on both nose and delivery and is on a par with Kentucky's finest. Sadly, a pretty rough finish thanks to the cask...which is always the danger when dealing with European wine barrels. *45% (90 Proof)*

Willett Family Estate Bottled Single Barrel Rye 4 Years Old Barrel no 45 (94) n23.5 t24 f23 b23.5. Truly satisfying rye which has in style more than a passing resemblance to the old Jim Beam yellow label rye of about 15 years ago. *55%*

Straight Wheat Whiskey

Bernheim Original (91.5) n22 t23 f23 b23.5. By far the driest of the Bernheims I have encountered showing greater age and perhaps substance. Unique and spellbinding. *45%*

Parker's Heritage Collection Original Batch Kentucky Straight Wheat Whiskey Aged 13 Years db **(95.5) n23.5** quite a firm, feisty nose threatening spice on all fronts. A little starchy as well as toasty. The sugars seem surrounded and unable to offer more than a softening to the citrus; **t24** a mesmeric delivery, full of soft, bready oils and liquorice....for about a second and a half. Then the spices are in like Flint; or maybe the flint is in like spices...because this has suddenly become a rock hard, brittle bourbon softened only by background oil and a manuka honey-cocoa mix; **f23.5** more manuka and mocha, though the spices have left leaving a much more serene fade, while the liquorice and hickory underline the age to the relaxed finale; **b24.5** not sure if they get Bassett's Liquorice Allsorts in the US. But, if they did, they would immediately recognise the brown ones in this...though in an insanely beautiful mutated form. So, so delicious....! *63.7%. ncf.*

American Microdistilleries
ALASKA DISTILLERY

◇ **Alaska Proof Bourbon** db **(86) n22 t22.5 f20 b21.5.** It must be Alaska and the lack of pollution or something. But how do these guys make their whiskey quite so clean....? For a rugged, wild land, it appears to concentrate on producing a bourbon which is borderline ethereal and all about sugary subtlety. The downside is that such lightness allows any weakness in the wood or distillation to be flagged up, though with nobody saluting. *40% (80 proof)*

ALLTECH Lexington, Kentucky.

Pearse Lyons Reserve (85) n22 t21 f21 b21. A fruity, grainy, pleasant whisky with the higher notes citrus dominant. Never quite finds a place to land or quite tells its story. Attractive but incomplete. *40% (80 proof)*

Town Branch Kentucky Straight Bourbon (88.5) n22.5 red liquorice, under-ripe greengages, nutmeg and polished oak floors...mmmm! **t21.5** a soft landing with lashing of vanilla and muscovado; **f23** thickens out as the treacle and liquorice re-emerge; some kumquats, too; **b22** a delicious Kentucky bourbon of considerable depth and charm. I think they have found their niche: bourbon. In Kentucky. Go for it, guys! *40% (80 proof)*

AMERICAN CRAFT WHISKEY DISTILLERY Redwood Valley, California.

Low Gap Bavarian Hard Wheat Aged 2 Years dist 31 Dec 10, bott 23 Jan 13 **(76.5) n18 t21 f18.5 b19.** There appears to be butyric on the nose and the finish bitters uncompromisingly. Despite the odd juicy, spicy high spot, not this distillery's finest moment. *43.1%*

ARIZONA DISTILLING Tempe, Arizona

Desert Durum Wheat Whiskey Batch no. 2 db **(87.5) n21.5 t23 f21.5 b21.5.** Another hairy-chested gung-ho whiskey which pins you back in your chair. And my notes for the first edition fits this one equally as well. Except here it loses out slightly by having a slightly too wide cut, meaning the feints bite on the nose and finish. But still about as macho as a whiskey gets. And as chocolatey, too. *46%.*

BAINBRIDGE ORGANIC DISTILLERS Bainbridge Island, Washington

Battle Point Organic Washington Wheat Whiskey (88.5) n21 surprisingly placid with a light spice nibble; **t23** brilliant delivery, full of quick-tempered spicy attitude. The oils are sublime and the sugars mostly of a muscovado bent; **f22** some vanilla and butterscotch show light oaky intent while the sugars remove the spices completely; **b23** soft and satisfying. The spices demanded from wheat whiskey, though short-lived, hit all the right spots. Very well made and impressive. *43%*

BALCONES DISTILLERY Waco, Texas.

Balcones Crooked Texas Bourbon Barrel American Oak, cask no. 3017, bott 21/01/14 db **(96) n24 t24.5 f23.5 b24** Like a concentrated form of bourbon, though with far more sugars evident than is normal. Profound. And ridiculously yummy. *62.8%. ncf. no age statement.*

Balcones Fifth Anniversary Single Barrel Texas Straight Malt American oak, Brimstone Resurrection finish, cask no. 2696, bott 20/12/13 db **(93) n23.5 t24 f22.5 b23** You could stand a knife and fork as well as a spoon up in this. The depth of sugar is startling. *58.3%. ncf. no age statement. 204 bottles.*

Balcones Fifth Anniversary Single Barrel Texas Straight Bourbon American oak cask no. 1613, bott 05/07/13 db **(91.5) n23.5 t23.5 f21.5 b23** Just so profound. Had the cut been just a little more niggardly, might well have had an award-winner here. But early days for this great but young distillery: they will learn. *64.2%. ncf. no age statement. 176 bottles.*

Balcones Fifth Anniversary Single Barrel Texas Straight Bourbon v.ii American oak, cask no. 1142, bott 11/18/13 db **(93.5) n23.5 t24.5 f22 b23.5** A bourbon version of a Texas steak: pleasing fat, full of succulent red juice and absolutely bloody enormous... *65.7%. ncf. 167 bottles.*

Balcones Fifth Anniversary Single Barrel Brimstone Resurrection Straight Corn Whisky American oak, cask no. 1200, bott 2013 db **(94) n23 t24 f23.5 b23.5** When you start your tasting day 5.30am, as I do, there are fewer whiskies more capable of waking you up - or sending you straight back to bed – than this. Absolutely shakes the body and mind into submission... Beautiful. *60.5%. ncf. no age statement. 167 bottles.*

BALLAST POINT San Diego, California

Devil's Share Single Malt Aged Four Years (batch 001) **(84) n20 t22.5 f20.5 b21.** Enough feints on the nose and finish to take the gloss off an attractive first bottling from Ballast Point. Beyond the nougat, plenty of honey around to enjoy. But every distiller should remember that to move from a decent to a very good whiskey, the devil is in the detail... *46%*

BENJAMIN PRICHARD'S DISTILLERY Kelso, Tennessee.

Benjamin Prichard's Lincoln County Lightning Tennessee Corn Whiskey (89) n24 t22.5 f21 b22. Another white whiskey. This one is very well made and though surprisingly lacking oils and weight has more than enough charm and riches. *45%*

BERKSHIRE MOUNTAIN DISTILLERS Great Barrington, Massachusetts.

Berkshire Bourbon Whiskey (91.5) n23 t23.5 f23 b23. A bourbon bursting with character: I am hooked! Another micro-gem. *43%*

BLUE RIDGE DISTILLING CO. Golden Valley, North Carolina.

Defiant American Single Malt Whisky 100% malted barely db **(80.5) n19 t21 f20.5 b20.** A wide cut ensures a chewy, honey and nougat feel to this. Barley, though, does not have the same flavour compounds to compensate for the oils. Undeniably tasty, if a little flawed! *41% (82 proof)*

Blue Ridge Rye Whisky db **(87) n21.5 t22.5 f21 b21.** I remember once, when giving a talk about rye whiskey maybe 20 years ago now, I was asked about what the first ryes of Pennsylvania would have tasted like. And I remember saying that they would have been heavy beasts of a liquor: the distillers would have made the cut pretty wide and the oils would have anchored the heavier rye traits. I also said that the ryes which were floated down the river to market would have been a lot sweeter than those consumed in its home market, on account of the sugars coming in off the fresh oak barrels, if that was what they used. And on nosing and tasting this, I was put in mind of that lecture I gave, for this would have been one that was sent out to market. This is heavy and feinty, though the intensity of the rye papers over the smaller to medium sized cracks. And the sugars are intense. This is big, imperfect rye with character spilling out of the glass. But great fun and more than a nod to America's distilling past. *46% (92 proof)*

BRECKENRIDGE DISTILLERY Breckenridge, Colorado.

Breckenridge Colorado Bourbon Whiskey Aged 2 Years (86) n22.5 t22 f20.5 b21. Full of character, big-hearted, chewy, slightly rugged bourbon where honey and cocoa thrives; spices make a telling impact. How apposite that probably the one and only town in Colorado named after a Kentuckian should end up making bourbon. Being close on 10,000 feet above sea level you'd think ice would come naturally with this. But it does pretty well without it, believe me... *43%*

BREUCKELEN DISTILLING Brooklyn, New York.

◈ **77 Whiskey Local Rye & Corn 483 Days Old,** American oak barrels, db **(95) n24** simply fabulous: the rye is so crisp you could cut diamonds with it; the spices have an edge, too...; just love that balancing tangerine note...; **t24** masterfully two-toned: corn softness against the jabbing rye. Juicy and quite riveting; **f23** rich ulmo honey, peppered and punctuated by rye and spices to the very end; just a little bitterness from the oak creeps in late on; **b24** an absolute gem of a whiskey just dripping with rye. 45%

◈ **77 Whiskey New York Wheat 622 Days Old** American oak barrels db **(89.5) n22** surprisingly low key...if you ignore the spiced cookie, with diced kumquat peel; **t23** there's a hell of a lot of vanilla to keep the wheat's many spices under control; eye-watering at times and a little sticky on the palate; **f22** biscuity: dries and spices up as molasses compensate; some late bitterness; **b22.5** a very busy whiskey which never quite decides which direction it wishes to take. Still, there's something to say for a mystery tour... 45%

CADÉE DISTILLERY Clinton, Washington.

◈ **Cadée Distillery Cascadia Rye Whiskey** finished in Port barrels db **(87) n21.5 t23 f21 b21.5.** Works quite well. A vaguely wide cut does ramp up the oils. But the rye has enough crystalline firmness to cut through the fruit. Think this pretty high quality rye actually deserves better than being masked by the Port which, though clean and juicy, has a flattening effect. 43.5% (87 proof)

◈ **Cadée Distillery Deceptivus Bourbon Whiskey** finished in Port barrels db **(87) n21 t22 f22.5 b22.** The sweet corn and the fruit combine to form a formidable chewiness. Attractive with some lovely ulmo honey also. The spiced chocolate fruit and vague nougat really does ensure an entertaining finale. 42.5% (85 proof)

CATOCTIN CREEK DISTILLERY Loudoun County, Virginia.

Catoctin Creek Cask Proof Roundstone Rye Organic Single Barrel Whisky batch B12E1 **(88.5) n21 t23 f22 b22.5.** A truly huge rye that, from a technical standpoint, fails its exams. But through a combination sheer delicious belligerence and chutzpah has your taste buds swooning. Great fun! 58%. Distilled from 100% rye. 134 bottles.

CEDAR RIDGE DISTILLERY Swisher, Iowa.

Twelve Five Rye recipe: rye, corn & malted barley, batch no. 131304-A db **(87.5) n23 t22.5 f20.5 b21.5.** Some seriously big rye at work here and the nose is something to enjoy if not marvel at. Once the distillers can just narrow the middle cut, this will be a rye of serious magnitude. As it is, the feints just take the edge off an otherwise impressive rye. 47.5%

CHAMBERS BAY DISTILLERY University Place, Washington.

◈ **Greenhorn Bourbon** aged for a minimum of 1 year, batch 1, bott 13 Dec 15 db **(74.5) n18.5 t21 f17 b18.** A sharp, eye-watering experience where an interesting fermentation has given the distiller little room for manoeuvre. 44% (88 proof)

CHARBAY DISTILLERY Napa Valley, California.

Charbay Hop Flavoured Whiskey release II, barrels 3-7 **(91) n22 t22 f23 b24.** Being distilled from beer which includes hops, it can – and will - be argued that this is not beer at all. However, what cannot be disputed is that this is a rich, full-on spirit that has set out to make a statement and has delivered it. Loudspeaker and all. 55%

CLEAR CREEK DISTILLERY Portland, Oregon.

McCarthy's Oregon Single Malt Aged 3 Years batch W14-01 Bott Sept 8 2014 **(96) n24** the house style smoky bacon sizzles with perhaps a little extra degree of phenol this time. There is almost an Islay – now lost young Port Ellen aspect to this...though the sea-breeze salt is replaced by a drier tannin; **t24** if you find a softer, cleaner, malt-true delivery in the US this year, lease let me know. The sugars from the grist spill over every aspect of the delivery and follow through. The smoke treads softly, but covers al the ground to be discovered. The overall texture borders perfection as it is both soft and firm, yet neither...; **f23.5** a beautifully adroit interplay between vanilla and a slightly tingly smoke; the oaks buzz at the death; **b24.5** Steve McCarthy's hands may not still be on the tiller. But they might well as be: this plots the same course he charted a great many years back in American micro distilling's very earliest days. Still the guiding star by which all other micro distilleries must follow: a kind of World Whiskey mile and sign post.... 42.5%

◈ **McCarthy's Oregon Single Malt Aged 3 Years** batch W16-01, bott 6 May 16 db **(88.5) n22** not the normal smoky bacon style peat: dry and abrupt; **t23** excellent texture and a sublime display of smoky, gristy sugars mixed in with no less smoky Demerara; **f21.5** the finish is short, miserly spiced, and strangely lacking in its usual depth; **b22** for the first time since I tasted their first bottlings – in the days when my beard was still black – this whiskey has changed. Appears to have far less copper in the system to give the normal all-round richness; this is quite apparent on the nose and finish in particular. But they appear to have upped the peat ratio to good effect. *42.5% (85 proof)*

COLORADO GOLD DISTILLERY Cedaredge, Colorado.

⬧ **Colorado Gold Rye** charred oak barrel no. 23, bott 31 Oct 15 db **(80) n20 t21 f19.5 b19.5.** Insane sugars – Manuka honey concentrate – still can't fully overcome the tobacco bitterness. A certain dirtiness when a rye should sparkle. *45% (90 proof). sc.*

⬧ **Colorado Gold Straight Bourbon** aged 3 years, new oak barrel no. 43, bott 1 Dec 15 db **(91) n22.5** coconut strands dipped in treacle. Some major golden syrup and tannin at work, too...; **t23** amazingly syrupy delivery: about as sweet as bourbon gets – yet always delicious. The only dry notes kick in as the tannin really takes hold. But those golden syrup tones dominate; **f23** long, and now better-structured as light spices kick in; **b22.5** if you have a sweet tooth, buy a case...!! *45% (90 proof). sc.*

Colorado Gold Straight Bourbon Over Two Years Old Single Barrel bott 8 Oct 11 **(86.5) n21 t23 f21 b21.5.** A bit of a whippersnapper of a bourbon. The nose and finish may lack depth. But it is a whiskey bursting with personality and the delivery is an understated treat. A light mocha thread weaves in and out of the muscovado. Fun. *40%*

COPPER FOX DISTILLERY Sperryville, Virginia.

Copper Fox "Rye Whisky" Aged 14 Months bott 11 Jul 13 **(91) n22.5 t23 f22.5 b23** When is rye whisky not a rye whisky? When it is matured in ex-bourbon barrels, rather than virgin oak for a start. Like this whisky is. So the quote marks are mine, not the label's. That said, purely from a tasting perspective: beautiful! Probably as good a rye type yet to come out of Sperryville. Just need to work on the label... *45%*

Wasmund's Single Malt Whisky 13 Months Old batch 94 **(94.5) n23 t23.5 f24 b24** distiller Rick Wasmund gets flavours into and out of his whisky like a magician conjures a dove from a hat. Here he has exceeded himself by removing the taughtness which comes with over aging or overdoing the apple and cherry wood smoke. Here he has called it right. Superb. *48% (96 Proof) ncf*

Wasmund's Single Malt Whisky 14 Months Old Batch No. 52 (91.5) n22 t23 f23 b23. Makes a huge lightly honeyed statement: superb! *48%. ncf.*

CORNELIUS PASS ROADHOUSE DISTILLERY Hillsboro, Oregon.

McMenamins C.P.R. White Owl Distillery (93) n23.5 t23 f23 b23.5. Top dollar White Dog. Huge amount of copper helps expose all the honey available, especially on the nose. Superbly distilled and surging with barley and spice. *49.3%*

CORSAIR ARTISAN DISTILLERY Nashville, Tennessee.

Corsair Rye Moon (85) n20 t22.5 f21 b21.5. A sweet, well-weighted white dog with surprisingly little bite. The odd intense, crystalline rye moment is a joy. *46% (92 proof)*

Corsair Aged Rye (73.5) n18 t18 f19 b18.5. Hot and anarchic, not as well made as the Rye Moon. But has enough playful character to keep you guessing what's coming next. *46%*

Corsair Triple Smoke (92.5) n24 t23 f22 b23.5. The odd technical flaw, to pick nits. But, overall, a lovely whiskey with a curiously polite smoke style which refuses to dominate. Teasingly delicate and subtle...and different. *40%*

DAD'S HAT RYE DISTILLERY Bristol, Pennsylvania

Dad's Hat Pennsylvania Rye db **(89.5) n22 t23.5 f21.5 b22.5** Being a hat-wearing man all my adult life, the world's first international champion for rye whiskey and a parent, this whiskey fitted me to a T. *45% WB16/023*

Dad's Hat Pennsylvania Rye Finished in Vermouth Barrels db **(86.5) n22 t22 f21 b21.5.** A strange hybrid between powerful rye whiskey and Swedish aquavit. *47% WB16/024*

DARK CORNER DISTILLERY Greenville, South Carolina

Dark Corner Moonshine Corn Whiskey (77.5) n18.5 t22 f18 b19. Full blooded sweet corn on delivery. But could do with some extra copper elsewhere. *50%*

DARK HORSE DISTILLERY Lenexa, Kansas

Dark Horse Reserve Bourbon Less Than Four Years Old Batch 2 **(93) n23 t23.5 f23 b23.5** Even though they appear to have used oak chips to bolster the overall richness of this bourbon, there is no taking away that this is the closest any whiskey produced by a microdistiller comes to the true Kentucky style. But even there, there are few which display so much vanilla. *44.5% (89 proof)*

Dark Horse Reunion Rye Less Than Four Years Old Batch 2 **(89) n22 t23 f22 b22** Another enormous, and truly memorable, offering from Dark Horse which is unambiguous in its style. Here, though, the cut was perhaps a little over generous (costing a point or two) with the very sharpest notes sacrificed. That said: just so big and delicious! *44.5% (89 proof)*

Long Shot White Whiskey bourbon mash **(88.5) n22 t22.5 f22 b22.** Seriously good, honest white dog: well made and gives the corn a free hand to shine. Love it. *40% (80 proof)*

DELAWARE PHOENIX DISTILLERY Walton, New York.
Rye Dog Batch 11-1 (78.5) n19 t21.5 f18 b19. Sweet, distinctive rye tang but a little short on copper sheen. *50% (100 proof)*

DISTILLERY 291 Colorado Springs, Colorado.
291 Colorado Bourbon Whiskey Aspen Stave Finished distilled from a bourbon mash, aged less than 2 years, barrel no. 1 db **(91) n23 t23.5 f22 b22** The usual house style of taking the cut as far as it can go and maybe a fraction more: serious brinkmanship but, again, some very serious whiskey, too. Excellent! *50%*

291 Colorado Whiskey Aspen Stave Finished rye malt mash, barrel no. 21 db **(86) n23.5 t21.5 f20 b21.** A pretty wide cut on the still means every element from the rye has been magnified. But so has much else. Which means a dry whiskey at its happiest when nosing. A huge rye curiously still dry despite the massive honeycomb. Astonishingly herbal, too. *50%*

291 Colorado Whiskey Aspen Stave Finished distilled from a rye malt mash, aged less than 2 years, barrel no. 22 db **(92) n24 t23 f22 b23** Wow! A rye whiskey for those who prefer theirs warts and all. 50.5% and 50.8% (two bottlings). *50.8%*

291 Colorado Whiskey Aspen Stave Finished distilled from a rye malt mash, aged less than 2 years, barrel no. 23 db **(91.5) n22 t23 f23 b23.5** A rye of broad sweeps rather than the usual pinpoint, rapier thrusts. Technically not as good as barrel 22, but.... *50.8%*

291 Colorado Rye Whiskey White Dog Aged Less than a week, batch 10 **(86.5) n21 t21 f23 b21.5.** A much tamer version of the last one I got my hands on. The rye gets bullied by other factors more easily, too. The finish, though, is superb. *50.8% (101.7 proof)*

291 Colorado Whiskey Aspen Stave Finished rye malt mash, barrel no. 2 **(94) n23 t24 f23.5 b23.5.** A superb, enigmatic rye which ticks every box: they are obviously fast learners! *50.8%*

◇ **291 M Colorado Whiskey Rye Malt Mash Aged Less Than 2 Years** Aspen Stave Finished barrel no. 1, American oak barrel db **(95.5) n24** a dream rye aroma: malted rye at its most rich and thorough with no loss to its fruitier aspect. Big and beautiful; **t24** profound, grab-the-arm-of-your-chair delivery. The grain dominates over the oak in no uncertain terms and the sheer crunchiness of the rye is matched only by its concentrated flavour intensity. Needless to say, spices are soon being launched from every direction; **f23.5** a gorgeous dark chocolate mousse has rye stirred into it; **b24** the nose promises something quite immense. And not for a second does it let you down. A whiskey which needs not just a knife and fork, but a carving set, too...Bravo Distillery 291! *63% (126.1 proof)*

◇ **291 M Colorado Whiskey Rye Malt Mash Aged Less Than 2 Years** Aspen Stave Finished barrel no. 3, American oak barrel db **(86) n21.5 t22 f21 b21.5.** Quite dapper rye appears through the slight mustiness on both nose and delivery. A little murky by comparison to Barrel 1's outlandishly high standards. *63.1% (126.2 proof)*

◇ **291 M Colorado Whiskey Rye Malt Mash Aged Less Than 2 Years** Aspen Stave Finished batch no. 1, American oak barrels db **(92.5) n22** rye first and foremost with a lighter, crumbled clover freshness; **t24** superb delivery: the rye stands alone for the first five or six waves – as it should – and offers a more traditional, unmalted crispness before the more intense malt begins to show its hand; the spices hit just the right degree of intensity and with them, the juices open; **f23** the chocolate hinted at towards the middle spreads towards the end. A little feint tang, but all under control; **b23.5** a surprisingly subtle rye considering its undoubted intensity. *62.9% (125.9 proof). 190 bottles.*

◇ **291 M Colorado Whiskey Rye Malt Mash Aged Less Than 2 Years** Aspen Stave Finished barrel no. 5, American oak barrels db **(89.5) n22.5** rare to find a bourbon where the rye so dominates the sensory skyline. But a few feints apart, the intense fruitiness is unmistakable; **t23** fat, chewy, oily – perhaps a little too oily. Mocha with a little drop of rye tipped in; **f21.5** oily, still the residual salts and pretty dry; **b22.5** when they say there's a high rye content in the mash recipe, they just ain't kidding, nosiree! A slightly cleaner cut would have piled on the points... *50% (100 proof). 55 bottles*

American Whiskey Aged 3 months **(73)** n18 t19 f18 b18. Busy. Spices aplenty. But nothing sits right. *43% (86 proof)*

Bad Guy Bourbon aged 379 days barrel # 1 **(95.5)** n23.5 t24.5 f24 b24. Arguably the most astonishing whisky of its age worldwide of the year. That a whiskey just a year old can be this good is obscene. But just proves: the bad guys always win... *56.1%*

Black Mountain Colorado Bourbon aged 9 months barrel #1 **(87)** n22 t21.5 f22 b21.5. Oily and in your face, despite the big colour, it has been unable to entirely shrug of the white dog bark. That said, the sheer abandon of the cough sweet sugars combined with surging spice – with cinnamon and cloves prevalent - makes for gripping sipping. *46% (92 proof)*

DOWNSLOPE DISTILLING Centennial, Colorado.

Double Diamond aged 3 Years American/French oak batch RV-003 dist 1 June 2010 **(91.5)** n22.5 t22 f23 b24 the degree of oak is a challenge. But in the end you finish shaking your head in wonderment as to how so many vastly different and unlikely aspects of a whiskey somehow fit together. Good going, guys! 50.5% (101 proof)

DRY FLY DISTILLING Spokane, Washington

Dry Fly Bourbon 101 (88) n21.5 t23 f21.5 b22. A well made bourbon which, with a bit of extra complexity, would stand above some of its Kentucky colleagues. *50.5%*

Dry Fly Cask Strength Straight Wheat Whiskey (94.5) n23 t24 f23.5 b24 Quite beautiful whiskey. One every whisky lover should experience to further their understanding of this multi-faceted spirit. *60%*

Dry Fly Port Finish Wheat Whiskey (89) n22 t23 f22 b22. If you mixed whiskey and jam you might end up with this little charmer. *50% (100 proof)*

Dry Fly Straight Triticale Rye Wheat Hybrid (86) n22 t22 f21 b21. Pleasant and easy going. But very surprising degree of natural caramels fill in the gaps and shaves off the higher notes expected from the rye. *44% (88 proof)*

Dry Fly Washington Wheat Whiskey (89) n22 t22 f22.5 b22.5. Hugely impressive, well weighted and balanced and a much better use of wheat than bread, for instance... *40%*

EASTSIDE DISTILLING Portland, Oregon

Burnside Bourbon 4 Year Barrel-Aged bott 2012 **(92)** n24 t23.5 f22 b22.5. "Put some sideburns on your face!" screams the back label. Well, a whiskey far too gracious to put hairs on your chest though it would be a close shave to choose this or a Kentucky 4-y-o as one of the best young bourbon noses of the year...Just bristles with charm. *48%*

EDGEFIELD DISTILLERY Troutdale, Oregon.

Edgefield Hogshead Whisky 100% malted barley, batch 12-B **(94)** n23.5 t24 f23 b23.5 Been a little while since I lasted tasted Edgefield. At that time they were seriously getting their act together. Now they deserve star billing in any bar. This is sheer quality and even though the cut is very fractionally wide, the two years in new oak has ensured something bordering magnificence. *46%*

FEW SPIRITS DISTILLERY Evanston, Illinois.

FEW Bourbon Whiskey batch 13-808, aged in charred new oak barrels for less than four years db **(86)** n21 t22 f21.5 b21.5. A thick, chewy bourbon with a vague hint of botanicals on the nose and a delivery leaving little to the imagination. The small grains are busy while little has been spared on the liquorice and molasses content. Reduce the oils a little and this would be a belter. *46.5% WB15/377*

〜 **FEW Bourbon Whiskey** batch 15-57 db **(86.5)** n21.5 t22 f21.5 b21.5. Despite the house style of clattering oils, there is a delicious tenacity to the bigger liquorice-rich tannins which is thoroughly appealing. Not perfect, but not too shoddy, either. *46.5% (93 proof)*

FEW Bourbon Whiskey Cask Strength batch 14-62 db **(84.5)** n20 t22 f21 b21.5. A wider cut than usual has ramped up the sugars for maximum effect. Decidedly oily and no little butterscotch on the fade. *58.7% WB16/021*

FEW Rye Whiskey batch 13-910, aged in charred new oak barrels for less than four years db **(87)** n22 t22 f21.5 b21.5. Few! What a scorcher! Big fresh rye fills every crevice of the palate, the house style oils ensuring it hangs around, too. The buzzing spice at the finale is indicative of the wide-ish cut which ensures a busy tang to the salivating, ultra juicy rye. Still not quite one for the purist, but the entertainment level is high. *46.5% WB15/375*

〜 **FEW Rye Whiskey** batch 15-30 db **(85.5)** n20 t22.5 f21.5 b21.5. The first three or four mouthfuls might leave you pretty dazed. Even if you know and understand this distillery, as I do, you will not be quite prepared for this. Well certainly not the slightly cabbagey nose.

The delivery takes a little while to get to grips with. But, in time, you will begin to see how the bullet-hard rye notes come into play here. The finish returns to a slightly feinty structure. Definitely worth that ten minutes to see the rye in all its glory. *46.5% (93 proof)*

FEW Single Malt Whisky batch 10-13, aged in reused cooperage for one year db **(84.5) n21.5 t20 f22 b21.** This writing year, 2014, marks the 40th anniversary of when I first tasted an American single malt: it was in Maryland and had been made locally by a rye distillery. That was, I remember, a very simple, malty affair. This, by stark contrast, isn't. First you have to get through a nutty phase before the barley makes itself heard, but when it does, it is eloquent in its sheer maltiness. As usual, the oils have a big say. *46.5% WB15/376*

⚜ **FEW Single Malt Whiskey** batch 6/14, barrel no. 11-17 db **(81.5) n20 t20.5 f20.5 b20.5.** Massive nougat at play here. Few's whisky is hefty and oily on quiet days. Here, it fully pitches its full weight behind the major sugar, though the malt can be heard occasionally. *46.5% (93 proof). sc.*

FINGER LAKES DISTILLING Burdett, New York.

Glen Thunder Corn Whiskey **(92.5) n23.5 t23 f23 b23.** Beautifully distilled, copper rich, Formula 1 quality, absolutely classic corn white dog. *45% (90 proof)*

FLORIDA FARM DISTILLERS Umatilla, Florida

Palm Ridge Reserve Handmade Micro Batch Florida Whiskey orange and oak wood Less the 1 Year Old batch 29 **(94.5) n23 t24 f23.5 b24** I can see why everyone heads to Florida in the winter: obviously to try and grab one of the meager 6,000 bottles of this on offer each year. This is beautifully crafted, truly adorable whiskey where fruit appears to constantly have its hand on the tiller. And rather than blast in like a Hurricane from the sea, it breezes gently around the glass and palate with an easy elegance. I have relatives in Florida: about time I gave them another visit... *45% (90 proof)*

GARRISON BROTHERS Hye, Texas.

⚜ **Garrison Brothers Cowboy Bourbon Aged Four Years** corn harvest 2009, #1 panhandle yellow dent corn variety, dist 2009, bott 2015 **(96.5) n23.5** whichever way you sniff, the oak comes gunning for you: sweet, dry, salty, fruity (especially in terms of black cherry)... tannins in all forms and glories; **t24.5** good grief...!! I mean, heavens!! Surely this amount of beefcake, knuckle-dragging oak would be too much for even those who prefer their whiskey in a dirty glass. But just as you await a woody pummelling, the sugars arrive with a purpose and intensity that matches the grizzlier tannin blow for blow. When I say sugar, I mean toasted fudge, maple syrup bone-dry molasses and, inevitably, a dollop of full strength Manuka honey; **f24** don't bother with this one if you don't have half an hour to spare. The finish alone takes up a good eight or nine minutes. Outrageously elegant, given the tub-thumping enormity of all that had gone on before. And now we have a playing out of varying honey style, the Manuka dropping down a notch or two, ulmo offering a soothing intensity and then a lighter heather honey as the delicate spices soothe your shattered taste buds. Astonishing doesn't quite cover it...; **b24.5** I have recently returned from a tasting tour of China where a 23-year-old Kentucky bourbon was one of my staple props. But even that would have to bow before such elephantine oakiness as this. Four years in Texas evidently equate to 23 in Kentucky: there's a Geography lesson for you. Whiskeys from this distillery have absolutely delighted and astonished me in the past: this proves, indubitably, it was no fluke. If you didn't think Texas was on the world map of Great Whisky, it is now... *675% (135 proof)*

Garrison Brothers Texas Straight Bourbon 2010 Aged Two Years Spring 2013 **(91) n23 t23 f22 b23.** A fascinating bourbon, made from local organic corn, which for a two-year-old is simply brimming with personality. The intensity and balance of the sugars and more bitter toastiness is a constant delight. Still room for improvement, but just love this magnificent stuff. Mind you, still waiting for the Hye Rye... *47%*

Garrison Brothers Texas Straight Bourbon 2010 Aged Two Years dist 2010, bott Spring 2014 db **(91.5) n22.5 t23.5 f22.5 b23** Has not come close to outgunning their Cowboy bourbon which re-wrote the manual as far as micro distilleries are concerned. But there is still so much to savour here. Delicious. *47%.*

⚜ **Garrison Brothers Texas Straight Bourbon Single Barrel Aged Two Years** barrel no. 3804, corn harvest 2010, #1 panhandle white corn variety, dist 2011 **(94.5) n24** a truly classic bourbon aroma: intense black liquorice thickened by molasses and Manuka honey - all topped by a little bitumen; **t24** the thick corn oils ensure the silkiest of deliveries. The spirit may be young, but the oak impact belies its limited days in the barrel. Intense? Not half! But there is a surprising lightness of touch despite the uncompromising dark sugars at play and the ever thickening tannins; **f22.5** thins quite quickly as the youthfulness asserts itself. At last, a degree of vanilla-clad dryness, though not before the sugars have enjoyed one last oak-fuelled surge...; **b24** astonishing: you won't find another bourbon of this age showing such beauty, even in Kentucky. 47% (94 proof)

⬥ **Garrison Brothers Texas Straight Bourbon Aged Three Years** corn harvest 2011, #1 panhandle white corn variety, dist 2012, bott 2015 **(91.5) n23.5** polished oak floors; antique shops full of brown Victorian and Georgian furniture; muscovado sugars moving towards dried maple syrup and green tea...; **t23** a charmingly busy delivery: despite the reduction in strength, the corn oils still have enough depth to coat the palate and bring the light brown sugars alongside; never less than youthful...; **f22** a vague spiciness adds to the light sugars; **b23** a hushed whiskey leaving the youthfulness to be fully heard. 47% (94 proof)

Cowboy Bourbon Texas Straight Bourbon Whiskey Aged Three Years (96) n23.5 t24 f24 b24.5 I always know when I have a truly great whiskey on my hands: it takes every ounce of my professionalism to spit it out! This has, and make no mistake, raised the bar for bourbon made by the micro distillers: it is truly world class, three year old or not. In fact the name is a misnomer: there are no cowboys at work here. This is darned tootin' fine whiskey. Yesiree! 68%. 600 bottles.

GOLDEN NORTHWEST DISTILLERY Bow, Washington.
Golden Artisan Spirits Single Barrel Cask Strength (88) n20.5 t22.5 f23 b22 Much more like it! Not exactly textbook but excellent body and some lovely honey touches. 62.3%

GRAND TRAVERSE DISTILLERY Traverse City, Michigan
Bourbon Whiskey (88.5) n21 t22 f23 b22.5 an absolute charmer which just gets better as it goes along. 46% (92 proof)

Ole George Straight Rye Whiskey (80) n19 t21 f20 b20. Hard to mark this one. As a rye, it marks relatively low. As a gin, it would be higher. Not sure why, but there seems to be all kinds of botanical aromas and flavours involved here. Pleasant as a spirit – and I love the mouth feel. But the flavour make up is skewed. 46.5% (93 proof)

GREAT LAKES DISTILLERY Milwaukee, Wisconsin.
KinnicKinnic A Blend of American Whiskies (87) n21.5 t22.5 f21 b22. The bitterness is replaced by an extra dollop of nougat and honey. 43% (86 proof)

HAMILTON DISTILLERS Tuscon, Arizona.
⬥ **Whiskey Del Bac Classic Unsmoked Single Malt** batch US15-16, bott 19 Aug 15 db **(91) n23** major tannin infusion. But lightened by the more gentle end of the vanillins, as well as a biscuity maltiness; **t23** a mouth feel free of jagged inhospitality: this is rounded, embracing and welcoming. Huge, chewy vanilla toffee surge; **f22** wonder if they can keep that caramel in check as, spice apart, everything becomes a little too simplistic; **b23** these guys know how to make mighty fine whiskey. Literally, a cut above... 42% (84 proof)

⬥ **Whiskey Del Bac Clear Mesquite Smoked Single Malt** batch MC15-4, bott 2 Dec 15 db **(91) n21.5 t23 f23.5 b23.** I was in Arizona recently, but sadly didn't make it to this distillery. Shame: I would have loved to have seen how the smoking is carried out for one of the sweetest and most surprisingly soft, idiosyncratic and attractive white dogs currently barking. 45% (90 proof)

⬥ **Whiskey Del Bac Dorado Mesquite Smoked Single Malt** batch MC16-1, bott 29 Feb 16 db **(94) n23** lovely – and unique - mix of Fisherman's Friend cough sweets and concentrated liquorice; **t23.5** astonishingly soft delivery: the sugars burst out from every direction, mainly a mix of maple syrup doused in treacle; the smoke slowly thickens the plot; **f24** brilliant finish: the big sugary surge has halted. And one of the most complex finishes of the year has begun. Possibly the most delicate and teasing spices of the year, and a sublime juxtaposition between the soft, starchy oils and firmer tannins, all the while the sugars kissing and caressing...astonishing! **b23.5** dang! I'd sure like to see a bottle of this come sliding up to me next time I'm-a-drinkin' in the Crystal Palace Saloon Bar in Tombstone, yesiree! And I'd take my own dirty glass – one smoked with mesquite!! 45% (90 proof). ncf.

HIGH WEST DISTILLERY Park City, Utah.
High West Silver Oat (86) n20 t22 f22 b22. A white whiskey which at times struggles to find all the copper it needs. But so delicious is that sweet oat – a style that has enjoyed similar success in Austria – that some of the technical aberrations are forgiven. Soft and friendly. 40%

HILLROCK ESTATE DISTILLERY Hudson Valley, New York.

◇ **Hillrock Double Cask Rye Whiskey** American oak barrels, barrel no. 62, aged under 4 years db **(85.5) n21.5 t21.5 f21.5 b21.** A slightly untidy rye which I'm sure will improve as the distiller, stills and grain get better acquainted. Here, there are a host of vegetable notes, though the rye does have its moments. That distiller, by the way: Dave Pickerell. He'll go far.... 45%

◇ **Hillrock Double Cask Rye Whiskey** American oak barrels, barrel no. Port-4, aged under 4 years db **(88) n22.5** slightly fruity, but no doubting the grain type; **t21.5** takes a while to find its feet. But the rye really does come out fighting; **f22** excellent spice as a little tannin invades; **b22** a rare case of a Port finish working amid bourbon or rye, mainly because it eliminates the more aggressive vegetable notes and allows the attractive rye a relatively free hand. 45%

◇ **Hillrock Single Malt Whiskey** American oak barrels, finished in sherry casks, barrel no. HS-1, aged under 4 years db **(95.5) n23.5** a surprise, complimentary package of rich plummy fruit and acidic soot; **t24** beautiful dark sugars line up to make for a soft entrance, all revealing a more fruity aspect as they lighten. And, as they do, smoke gathers in force; the pace and weight of the spices is truly exceptional; **f24** a gorgeously creamy finale, with spices and smoky chocolate gathering; **b24** smoke and fruit rarely make happy bedfellows from a balancing viewpoint. Here they do, doubtless helped by the fact that, for once, the sherry butt does not possess a sulphur-stained edge. You won't get it until about the fifth mouthful: then is all clicks. The classiest of class acts. 48.2%

◇ **Hillrock Solera Aged Bourbon Whiskey** American oak barrels, finished in sherry casks, barrel no. 48 db **(89) n22.5** both fruit and spirit seem unusually compartmentalised; **t23** I'm assuming this is a rye-recipe mash as that grain does manage to punch through the half-hearted fruit; **f21.5** a little bit on the flat side, as fruit and grain cancel each other out. But the spices tumble about deliciously; **b22** a rare case of the wine finish working with a bourbon, but probably because the grape remains subtle. 48.2%

HOUSE SPIRITS DISTILLERY Portland, Oregon

Westward Oregon Straight Malt Whiskey 2 Years Old batch 1 **(92.5) n23** a coating of vanilla to the intense barley and maple syrup; **t23.5** superb degree of oils ensure the barley clings thickly to the plate. Ulmo honey and light hickory intermingle as the spices begin a gentle journey; **f23** the spices now fizz a little and a delicate, non-specific fruit tang attaches to the big barley; the vanillas are confident and creamy; just a tad too much lasting bitterness; **b23.5** two years old, perhaps. But absolute star quality with the barley pulsing at every turn: just so satisfyingly mouth-filling and palate teasing. Another great whiskey from Portland. 45%

IRON SMOKE WHISKEY Fairport, New York.

◇ **Iron Smoke Apple Wood Smoked Whiskey** batch no. 9, bott 4/2/16 db **(94.5) n23.5** just love the fact that the apple smoke contains both tannins and apple...and the grains are allowed the freedom to link with the tannins and form a bourbony undertone...; **t23.5** superb...for all the reasons stated on the nose. Very light textured, but wow! The complexity...! **f23.5** vanilla and butterscotch over bourbon-soaked spiced apple pie; **b24** an unconventional whiskey from Fairport. Though by no means the first apple wood smoked, it has less vigour than its Virginian forefather and no shortage of class...With it having a little more body than the skeletal 40%abv, handle with care as this would be too easy to get smashed out of your skull... Love it! 40% (80 proof)

KINGS COUNTY DISTILLERY Brooklyn, New York.

◇ **Kings County Distillery Bourbon Whiskey** aged one year or more, batch no. 128 db **(85.5) n22 t21.5 f21 b21.** Pleasant enough bourbon. But perhaps over-dependent on the brown sugars and tannin and does not yet have quite enough substance and complexity. Certainly has some spice, though! 45%

◇ **Kings County Distillery Bourbon Whiskey wine barrel finish,** aged one year or more, batch no. 128 db **(87.5) n21 t23.5 f21 b22.** Okay, so this isn't bourbon, even if they want to call it that. But they have selected some excellent wine barrels here...and the result is memorable. The nose is a bit stodgy and too tannin heavy. But the delivery is astonishing where the weight of oak, grain and fruit are in magnificent harmony. The midground is pure cappuccino – with a bite of accompanying fruitcake. Thins dramatically at the finish and loses balance. But, wow! Some fabulous moments! 45%

◇ **Kings County Distillery Peated Bourbon Whiskey** aged one year or more, batch no. p4 db **(94) n23.5** dark muscovado sugars mixed with orange peel, liquorice...and peat reek...!!! First time I came across something like this was in my own blending lab...probably about 25 years ago! **t24** adorable delivery: thick corn oil is awash with molten muscovado. The smoke keeps a respectful distance, but is there with the ever-thickening tannins; **f23** spices grow, the peat murmurs, the tannins throb quietly amid the residual sugars; **b23.5** no problem with this. You can use peat-smoked grain and still produce bourbon, which is how I assume this was produced. Just not a bourbon finished in a peated cask. That ain't bourbon. Whatever this is – and it appears to be the former – it is quite stunningly lovely. *45%*

◈ **Kings County Distillery Single Malt American whiskey** made from peated malt, aged two years or more, batch no. 1 db **(87) n21.5 t23 f21 b21.5.** A well made malt, apparently making full use of pre-used bourbon casks. Excellent structure with some toasted honeycomb running through the piece. The smoke is pretty well disguised, though may be evident in the gentle spice. Tires a little at the thin finish. *47%*

Kings County Moonshine Corn Whisky (92) n23 t23 f23 b23. Absolutely spot on corn whiskey: sweet, clean, berry-fruity, very well made; does exactly what it says on the tin. *40%* ⊙

KOVAL DISTILLERY Chicago, Illinois.

Koval Single Barrel Bourbon Whiskey cask no. 378 db **(89.5) n22.5** full on with the oils but also massive manuka honey, liquorice and rye influence, too; **t23** usual Koval whiskey pie in the face delivery: enormous toasty depth on delivery before a gentle spreading of the honey. Then it flares into an bourbon of huge intensity, with varying Demerara sugar notes heading in all directions; **f21** busily spiced but overly oily; **b22** as usual, the wide-ish cut has ensured maximum intensity. Some of the bourbon tones are about as classic Kentucky as they have so far achieved. *47%. sc.*

◈ **Koval Single Barrel Bourbon Whiskey** barrel no. 1|1JM9 db **(92) n23** these guys really know how to do small grains: complex! **t23.5** outstanding oil-grain mix, so the corn cannot dominate and a busy buzz keeps the palate on full alert; beautifully subtle chocolate orange marzipan nibbles with aplomb; **f22.5** more emphasis on the corn, though the tannins begin to make a mark; late, slightly milky molasses; **b23** a different style of bourbon to Kentucky, but this is not short on quality or complexity. Excellent. *47%*

◈ **Koval Single Barrel Four Grain Whiskey** barrel no. 2I0DM5 db **(96) n24.5** if all whiskies were this complex on the nose, not sure this book would ever get completed. Several points to focus on, each sharp as a knife. Though oat holds sway (and checking the label...yes oats are part of the mash bill...) there is a secondary intensity of light chocolate malt and fruity rye; astonishing layering of light sugars, crystallised golden syrup seemingly the anchor point; **t24** bloody hell...! Quite fantastic. Last year, I remember a jarring from the feints. Here there is no such problem: both earthy and ethereal in equal measure and as the oils spread, mainly of an oaty flavour, so too does the sharper, crisper rye; **f23** a few feinty notes at last collate, but the salivating quality of the grains is re-established at the last, helped by a few peppery spices; **b24.5** one of the most intriguing whiskies on the circuit! Last year didn't quite technically hit the heights, but this time round combines decent distillation with the mesmerising complexity of the grain. A very serious contender for US micro distillery whisky of the year. *47%*

Koval Single Barrel Four Grain Whiskey barrel no. 412. Mashbill: Oat, Malted Barley, Rye, Wheat db **(83) n20.5 t23 f19.5 b20**. The nougat and chocolate on the nose suggests we have a feinty beast at work here. And that sometimes spells good news on the palate – especially the delivery. And so it proves here, as the taste buds positively shrink under a barrage of intense flavour blows, softened only by basic sugars. Equally, the nose points to a finish that is likely to be rough hewn. And it doesn't disappoint. Or, rather, it does. But cherish that amazing delivery where the oats shine particularly brightly. And best take a seat while you encounter this briefly delicious grainy onslaught. *47%. sc.*

Koval Single Barrel Millet Whiskey db **(88) n22** the honeycomb and chocolate perhaps have more to do with the distillation technique and oak than the grain. For that, there appears to be a quite different sweet toastiness altogether; **t23** a beautiful and charming lift off: maple syrup sugars cascade into the much darker mooded oak-grain mix. These offer a flavour depth quite different to any other whisky type. The actual flavour itself cannot be compared exactly with another tasting experience: the grain has perhaps a vague oat porridge quality as its nearest marker. But this is deeper, with some of the smallest and most busy mini spices you'll ever encounter; **f21** a little bitter and oily as the sugars wear thin; **b22** I always wondered what my Myer's Parrot, Percy, sees in this stuff. If you want half an hour's peace and quiet, just hand him a small sprig of millet and he will munch contentedly on it, carefully inspecting, protecting and feasting on every single grain, not a single one seemingly wasted. Now I know. A gorgeously intense grain balances its unique flavour profile with delicate honey. Result: one happy palate. And one miserable parrot...for all his pleading he ain't getting his beak around this truly unique dram. *40%*

⬨ **Koval Single Barrel Rye Whiskey** barrel no. 8|1PM5 db **(88) n21** an odd mix of feints and business-like rye; **t22** salivating, of course, and boisterous when it gets to accentuating the grain; the sugars are dark and intent; **f22.5** settles on its best period when all quietens slightly into a more harmonious whole...and still quite juicy even late on; **b22.5** an extravagant whiskey, depending perhaps a little too much on a wide cut but still showing many a rye smile. 40%

KOZUBA & SONS DISTILLERY INC. St. Petersburg, Florida.

⬨ **Mr. Rye Straight Rye Malt Whisky** virgin American oak barrels db **(91) n23** big, impressive, unmistakable rye character, intensified and thickened by it being malt, so a little less crisp. Technically not quite perfect but the spices clear the nose beautifully; **t23.5** fabulous delivery! No prisoners taken, no shelter offered. Just pounding rye which offers a massive degree of layering; so many layers, in fact, almost impossible to count. Just so thick and chewy; **f22** the oils from the wide cut begin to create a bit of a slick; the spices carry on regardless; **b22.5** Okay, the cut has been maximised, but forgivably so. The quality of the rye malt is very high. 45%. ncf.

LAS VEGAS DISTILLERY Las Vegas, Nevada.

⬨ **Nevada 150 Bourbon Whiskey** American white oak barrels, aged 2 years, 4 months db **(92) n24** the quietest, most subtle bourbon on the market. The small grains can be heard only if you listen keenly. And so devoid are we of the usual background noise, even the barley makes its tentative presence felt...intriguing and fabulously sophisticated; **t22.5** light muscovado sugars lead the way, red liquorice and what appears to be rye are not far behind...all so gentle and clean; **f22.5** and now some spice...just! Outstanding vanilla fade with the small grains in close attendance; **b23.5** who would have thought that the loudest, brashest city in the world could conjure the most delicate, intricate and shy bourbon for many a year? Don't let this whisky fool you: it has much to say...but all in whispers... 45% (90 proof). 2,014 bottles.

LAWS WHISKEY HOUSE Denver, Colorado.

⬨ **A.D. Law Four Grain Straight Bourbon Aged No Less Than 3 Years** batch no. 1 db **(92) n23.5** bristling small grain embedded in a rich chocolate sauce. Chunky, with some lovely orange peel, too; **t23.5** a lot more powerful than your usual 47.5% bourbon, the main thrust coming from the direction of the oak as the tannins take a chocolatey grip. Elsewhere, the grains and spices buzz and bite; **f22** a busy whirring on the back of the throat suggests a broadish cut. But still a vaguely salivating quality persists; **b23** if your taste buds are a bit bored, then introduce them to this: grains rarely come busier or more confident. A bit oily from the very slightly wide cut. But this is superb whiskey demanding respect and attention 47.5%

⬨ **A.D. Law Four Grain Straight Bourbon Aged No Less Than 3 Years** batch no. 2 db **(94.5) n23 t24 f23.5 b24.** A better balanced version than Batch 1, as the slightly cleaner cut allows both the grain and oaks a far greater say, especially on the finish – where the tannins are quite sublime. A huge yet complex bourbon, cutting back on the citrus here, and one that long term lovers of Tom Moore Distillery will appreciate more than most. Confirms that truly classic bourbon is being made in Colorado...! 47.5%

⬨ **A.D. Law Four Grain Straight Bourbon Aged No Less Than 3 Years** batch no. 3 db **(85.5) n21 t22 f21 b21.5.** A clunky bottling which overdoes the oils all round. Need to get it cleaner and tighter like on Batch 2. Some inevitable chocolate, though of the tell-tale nougat variety... 47.5%

⬨ **A.D. Law Four Grain Straight Bourbon Aged No Less Than 3 Years** batch no. 4 db **(91.5) n21.5 t24 f23 b23.** A fascinating journey away from the initial oaky constraints on the nose to something which, on the palate, transforms into a bourbon not totally dissimilar to batch 1. The oils are positive here and harness all the chocolate intensity it possesses to maximum effect. For the first time, we have a mix of molasses and Demerara sugars not just in play but, at times, grabbing the steering wheel. Yummy barely covers it! 47.5%

⬨ **A.D. Law Four Grain Straight Bourbon Aged No Less Than 3 Years** batch no. 5 db **(93) n22.5 t24 f22.5 b24.** Another with the full emphasis on the busy grain. Still a generous cut which ushers in some extra blood orange, but the interplay between crisp, salivating grain and the sugar-coated, cocoa-enriched tannins is a delight. If only those oils could be contained slightly. 47.5%

⬨ **A.D. Law Four Grain Straight Bourbon Aged No Less Than 3 Years** batch no. 6 db **(86.5) n21 t22.5 f21 b22.** Back to a Tom Moore type grain-fest. Busy, complex but ultimately weighed down by just a little too much oil from the generous cut. Some excellent golden syrup on the salivating bits, though. 47.5%

◌◌◌ **A.D. Law Four Grain Straight Bourbon Aged No Less Than 3 Years** batch no. 7 db **(81) n20 t22 f19 b20.** A substantial bourbon which has gone a little heavy on the oil. Have to keep an eye on the cuts or, like here, the grains won't get a meaningful word in edgeways. A dose of ulmo honey does spring to the rescue. 47.5%

◌◌◌ **A.D. Law Origins Four Grain Straight Bourbon Bottled in Bond** barrel no. 1 db **(95) n23.5** an earthy aroma: heavy, though never quite pungent thanks to the neat interaction between the playful grain and the dry tannin. Lovely chocolate liquorice with the vaguest hint of molasses; **t24** the sugars, hiding away on the aroma, come out to play first on delivery. What a glorious juxtaposition between the intense, biting vanilla and tannin and spiced molasses and Manuka honey. A gorgeous blend of red and black liquorice paves the way to a rye-crisp intensity yet to be displayed in their standard four grain bottlings; **f23.5** long, with liquorice and delicate spice abounding; **b24** indubitably sublime bourbon. More ticks than there are boxes... 50%

◌◌◌ **A.D. Law Secale Cask Strength Straight Rye Whiskey Aged 3 Years** db **(86) n21 t22 f21.5 b21.5.** A muscular, husky rye. The oils come thick and fast, though the gently fruity message of the grain is not entirely overshadowed: indeed, this has the crispest rye of their bottlings thus far. A few nougat touches to this, though the tingling late spice does carry some Demerara. 55%

◌◌◌ **A.D. Law Secale Straight Rye Whiskey Aged 3 Years** batch no. 1 db **(87.5) n22 t22.5 f21.5 b21.5.** Rye tart? Or tart rye? No doubting the grain type: a brittle delivery on the palate which absolutely crash lands and shatters on the taste buds. The house style of chocolate mousse mashed into the heavy tannin and grain prevails, but the finish has a year or two's work perhaps to get those required sugars demanded by all great ryes into play. Takes a bit of time to tune into this, but worth twiddling the knobs. 50%

◌◌◌ **A.D. Law Secale Straight Rye Whiskey Aged 3 Years** batch no. 2 db **(82) n19 t21 f21 b21.** A gently feinty, nougat style not uncommon in the ryes of Austria. Needs some chewing. 50%

◌◌◌ **A.D. Law Secale Straight Rye Whiskey Aged 3 Years** batch no. 3 db **(84) n21 t22 f20 b21.** Good grief! The palate is absolutely coated in thick rye for an ungainly, rather unsettling experience. Make no mistake: this is huge whiskey where both the oils and rye refuse to take prisoners. Far from flawless, but the sheer concentrated oomph of the rye leaves you smacking your lips for quite some time. Some decent sugars on display in the middle period. 50%

LOST SPIRITS DISTILLERY Monterey County, California.
Leviathan III Under 4 Years db **(86) n21 t22 f22 b21.** Not sure I am a great fan of three things wishing to dominate at once: peat, fruit and oak. In the end there is too much cancelling each other out. Pleasant enough, though, and very sweet. 53%. sc.

Umami Under 4 Years Peat smoked barley fermented in salt water. db **(94) n23 t24 f23 b24** A chair with arm rests essential: you will be gripping them for dear life! If you are seeking a gentle, delicate little flower of a malt you have found the wrong bottle. This is a heat exuding missile...and your palate will be well and truly a-salted... 59%.

MISSISSIPPI RIVER DISTILLERY Le Claire, Indiana
Cody Road Bourbon 2013 Batch 1 **(91.5) n23.5 t23 f22 b23** You really don't need to be told this is a wheat recipe bourbon! A fabulously made whiskey of rare character. 45% (90 proof)

Cody Road Rye 2013 Batch 4 **(86.5) n23 t22.5 f20 b21.** The clean, fruity unambiguous rye on the nose is stunning. There is nothing too shoddy about the crisp, juicy grain on delivery, either. Just bitters out a little too enthusiastically from the midpoint onwards. 40%

MOYLAN'S DISTILLING COMPANY Petaluma, California.
Moylan's 2004 Cherry Wood Smoked Single Malt Cask Strength **(94) n24 t23.5 f23 b23.5** a top drawer, quite beautifully distilled and matured, malt which goes much easier on the smoke than you'd expect but is bubbling with personality...and quality. Bravo! 49.5%

◌◌◌ **Moylan's American Cask Strength Single Malt Whisky Aged 4 Years** finished in orange brandy, stout & French oak chardonnay barrels db **(80) n19 t23 f19 b19.** Ladies and Gentlemen of Moylan. I cannot fault you for your kaleidoscopic delivery which enthrals and entertains with a wild and delicious a cross section of fruity riches as you are likely to find. But remember: it is about balance. So don't lose sight of what a wide cut and hops from the stout can do... 58.7% (117.4 proof)

◌◌◌ **Moylan's American Single Malt Whisky Aged 4 Years** finished in orange brandy, stout & French oak chardonnay barrels db **(75.5) n18 t21.5 f18 b18.** The vital oils – and attendant sugars - have been destroyed by the water, allowing the hops far too great a domination. 43% (86 proof)

NELSON'S GREEN BRIER DISTILLERY Nashville, Tennessee.

◇◇ **Belle Meade Aged 9 Years Bourbon Finished in Oloroso Sherry Casks,** batch no. 2D **(83) n21 t22.5 f19.5 b20.** Remember: it ain't bourbon!! The sherry casks saw to that! And, sadly, they have dulled down the far richer – and spikier - elements of the bourbon. Lots of tannin and spice, but, ultimately, off the pace and lacking balance. 45.2% (90.4 proof). Bottled by Nelson's Green Brier Distillery.

◇◇ **Belle Meade Straight Bourbon Whiskey (92) n23.5** the rye positively trills: throws out all the fruit you would expect it to, landing softly in the vanilla; **t23** fabulous Demerara sugars at first, then into muscovado as the rye really takes hold; **f22.5** coffee cake...with chunky rye...!! **b23** a crisp, bright, beautifully made bourbon. The rye aspect of the recipe is pretty profound. 45.2% (90.4 proof). Bottled by Nelson's Green Brier Distillery.

◇◇ **Nelson's Green Brier Tennessee White Whiskey** distilled from Bourbon mash db **(94) n23 t23.5 f24 b23.5.** More green dog than white dog...! Beautifully distilled spirit using superbly judged cutting points. A wonderfully trained and friendly dog, be it white or green... Bravo, whoever is responsible for this: I'm genuinely impressed. 45.5% (91 proof)

NEW HOLLAND BREWING COMPANY Holland, Michigan.

◇◇ **Pitchfork Wheat Michigan-Grown Wheat Whiskey** aged 14 months, American oak barrels db **(93) n22.5** youthful but the oak has already dug deep to engineer an unlikely balance. A nutty fusion, something akin to a Maryland cookie; a few green apples confirm some youth; **t23.5** that is really impressive: the sugars arrive early for an early meet with the light, friendly tannins. It takes time for the expected spice onslaught from the wheat to arrive; some decent muscovado sugars in the mid-ground; **f23.5** less like a Maryland cookie now than a digestive – or even (milk) chocolate digestive. The spices have levelled out without becoming remotely dominant, the late buttery, butterscotch tart with the spices now in full flow is rather gorgeous; **b23.5** so love it! Like a digestive biscuit you want to dunk in your coffee...By far and away the best thing I have ever seen from this distillery: this really is top drawer microdistillery whiskey just brimming with flavours and personality. Genuinely impressed. 45% (90 proof)

◇◇ **Zeppelin Bend Straight Malt Whiskey** American oak barrels db **(84.5) n21 t21.5 f21 b21** The Zep is back!! Not seen it for a while and this is a new model. Actually, in some ways barely recognise it from the last one I saw about five years ago. Much more effervescent than before, though that curious hop note I remember not only persists but appears to have been upped slightly. 45% (90 proof).

PARLIAMENT DISTILLERY Sumner, Washington.

◇◇ **Ghost Owl Pacific Northwest Whisky** db **(88.5) n21.5** creamy fudge with a distant hint of treacle-sweetened nougat; a secondary line of greenish oakiness; **t22.5** no shortage of sugars as they don't just hit the ground running, but positively sprinting; silky, malty, gristy with a light citrus and muscovado feel; **f22** belatedly juicy before the vanillas arrive; **b22.5** on the sugary side of matters. But keeps just enough heavier tannin in reserve to ensure balance. 45% (90 proof)

◇◇ **Ghost Owl Pacific Northwest Rye Whisky** db **(94.5) n23** quite profound rye arriving alongside an unusual ashy dryness; **t23.5** superb delivery: almost rye concentrate, so profound is the grain. Crisp, teeth shattering stuff with the sugars restricted to a clipped roastiness amid the rye-style fruit; at times eye-wateringly sharp; **f24** a fabulous fade of complex cocoa notes, with a back story of molasses and vanilla; **b24** simply outstanding rye. Can't lose, really: my favourite grain (rye) being distilled in one of my favourite places on the planet (the Pacific north west of USA) and one of my favourite birds on the label (a barn owl). Actually, quite recently, I was doing some work in a lab at a distillery in India when I walked into a nearby wood to stretch my legs, rest my nose and enjoy 15 minutes of bird watching. There was suddenly a clattering above my head, strange shadows on the forest floor before me and then a crashing sound and soft thud. Astonishingly, a barn owl had fallen dead from the sky just three or four feet from where I stood. Spooky. And almost as dramatic as this stunning rye. 45% (90 proof)

PEACH STREET DISTILLERS Pallisade, Colorado.

Colorado Straight Bourbon Aged More Than Two Years batch 40 **(92.5) n22.5 t23.5 f23 b23.5** The last bottle I tasted was around the batch 20 mark and was an impressive intro to this distillery. Remarkably, this batch enjoys an almost identical thumb print. But now there is much more sharpness and definition. Superb! 46% (92 proof)

RANGER CREEK DISTILLING, San Antonio, Texas

◇ **Ranger Creek .36 Single Barrel Texas Straight Bourbon** aged 4 years, 6 months, barrel no. 506, 2015 vintage db **(89.5) n23.5** a gorgeous blood orange and liquorice broadside reveals a rich, oaky intent; the honey veritably drips off the nose..; **t23.5** a thick mouth feel, propped by starchy corn oil, ensures the vanillas and molasses stay long enough to be heard. Chewy, with a superb burnt fudge middle; **f20.5** thins out and becomes just a tad too tangy; **b22** rich and roasty, has many attributes that are prerequisite for fine bourbon. Finish flames out for reasons that are easier to spot in the white dog, but still give hefty clues here. Didn't get this on their bottlings of a few years back...though, still a bourbon to follow on the heels of a juicy rib-eye. 48% (96 proof). sc.

Ranger Creek .36 Texas Bourbon (93) n23 t23.5 f23 b23.5 I would so love to get back to Texas and have this wash down a plate-filling, half cooked ribeye. It's pretty obvious they have used small barrels to create a gentle giant like this – even before you find confirmation on the bottle. This comes under their Small Caliber series of whiskeys. Don't you believe it: this is a howitzer of a bourbon. 48% (96 proof)

◇ **Ranger Creek .36 Texas Bourbon** batch no. 530, Summer 2013 season db **(90.5) n21.5** not quite flawless, but the small grains are given a chance to speak their mind; **t23.5** whatever weaknesses are evident on the nose are washed away here with a volley of intense orangey blossom and ulmo honey tones, ably enforced with honeycomb. Truly beautiful...; **f22.5** a vanilla-lemon fade which has none of the drama of the delivery but reveals a more genteel side; **b23** boasts an array of stunning flavours which could shake the most jaded palate back into life. Lone star quality...! 48% (96 proof). Small Caliber Series.

◇ **Ranger Creek .36 White** db **(84) n21 t22 f20 b21**. A white dawg whose tail doesn't always wag. A deliciously jaw-dropping, juicy array of grain on delivery. But needs to get the copper content up to ensure a better pedigree. 50% (100 proof)

◇ **Ranger Creek .44 Texas Rye** aged 9 months, batch no. 10, Spring 2015 season db **(88) n21** a curious mix of youthful rye and unsalted celery; **t22.5** an engaging telling of a rye-rich tale, quietly at first - then with far more purpose and vigour as the sugars arrive to balance the crispness of the grain; **f22.5** a wonderfully long fade of warming spice and muscovado sugars; **b22** I hadn't read the label properly, so it was only on nosing and then delivery that the full impact of its relative youth became known. Holds up well, though. 47% (94 proof). Small Caliber Series.

Ranger Creek Rimfire Mesquite Smoked Texas Single Malt batch 1 **(85) n21.5 t22 f20.5 b21.** As I have never tasted anything smoked with mesquite before – especially whiskey – I will have to guess that it is the tree of the semi-desert which is imparting a strange, mildly bitter tang on the finish. Whether it is also responsible for the enormous degree of creamed toffee, I am also not sure. Enjoyable, fascinating even...but something the ol' taste buds need a bit of acclimatising to. 43% (86 proof)

◇ **Ranger Creek Rimfire Mesquite Smoked Texas Single Malt** aged 12 months, batch no. 12, Fall 2014 season db **(86.5) n20 t23 f21.5 b22.** Ah! Mesquite Smoked. The second time I've had a malt thus treated. And the first time was...yes, you guessed it: Ranger Creek! This is a better edition, where here they have gathered the sugars together, especially the toffees, in impressive fashion. 43% (86 proof). Small Caliber Series.

RANSON SPIRITS Sheridan, Oregon.

Ransom The Emerald 1865 Straight American Whiskey Batch 002 malted barley, unmalted barley, malted rye, malted oats. **(87.5) n22 t22.5 f21 b22.** The mash bill screams: "Irish whiskey". The oils found everyone screams: "Oi! Let those foreshots run another five minutes...!!!" If this was cleaned up a little we would have a whiskey everyone would be talking about. Because, taking the feints out of the equation, the interplay and weight of those complex grains really make for the most delicious experiences. Indeed, even with its faults, this provides one fabulous ride on the palate. On the cusp of being an American great. 43.8%

RESERVOIR DISTILLERY Richmond, Virginia.

◇ **Reservoir Distillery Bourbon Whiskey** batch 2, bott 2013 db **(93.5) n23.5** the small grains are waxing lyrical; **t23.5** the impact may not be quite as complex as the nose, but the follow-through – a series of mouth-watering, eye-watering, twists and squiggles on the palate – certainly is. The mid-ground is a lovely mix of mocha and gentle grain explosions; **f23** a soft vanilla thread, attached to a light molasses balancing act; **b23.5** this is all about the small grains: not sure if wheat and rye are both included, but wouldn't surprise me if they were. Complex and bitty only half covers it! *50% (100 proof)*

◈ **Reservoir Distillery Rye Whiskey** batch 2, bott 2016 db **(95.5) n24** this is impressive: the rye really does make its mark, in about three different strata. It is at once sharp, as well as rounded and enveloping, including an apple-like fruitiness. The third strata of rye is much more soft and absorbing: complex stuff; **t24** crisp at first, then melts into a beautiful, molten rye form: two toned, but every nuance is rye-related – astonishing; **f23.5** the oak interferes now and adds a further dimension of mocha complexity. The rye, though, remains at the steering wheel; **b24** there must be something in the DNA of the average Virginian in knowing how to make rye whiskey. I adore Richmond and I no less adore very good rye: indeed, I will always be proud to be its first advocate. I have some of my happiest memories of all time travelling in Virginia (the first time way back in 1967, now 50 years ago), and once with someone who was, still is and forever will be, very, very special. A truly great bitter-sweet whiskey to rekindle some beautiful, bitter-sweet memories... *50% (100 proof)*

◈ **Reservoir Distillery Wheat Whiskey** batch 5, bott 2015 db **(87.5) n21 t23 f21.5 b22.** Recovers superbly from a clumsy nose. The cut is just a little too generous. But the impact of the wheat is immediate on delivery and the grain unmistakable, combining some excellent spices with hickory and treacle follow-through. The big oils are never far away. *50% (100 proof)*

ROCK TOWN DISTILLERY Little Rock, Arkansas.

Rock Town 5th Anniversary Arkansas Straight Bourbon Whiskey #4 char white oak casks, bott Apr 15 db **(92) n22.5** busy spice, presumably wheat, and a mix of muscovado sugar and maple syrup. Heavy oils: signs of a generous cut; **t24** good grief! Probably the biggest whiskey I'll taste today. All kind of corn oils run rampant, though some enticing barley notes offer an unexpected salivating quality. The oak pounds hard, with some major liquorice notes; **f21** yes, a little too well oiled but the sugars fade gracefully; **b22.5** thought my taste buds were deceiving me on delivery with an unexpected barley kick. On inspection, it does boast 20% malted barley: intriguing as well as delicious. *50% (100 proof). ncf. 971 bottles.*

◈ **Rock Town 6th Anniversary Four Grain Sour Mash Bourbon Whiskey Aged 30 Months** db **(89) n22.5 t22.5 f22 b22.** A superb flavour combination. Interestingly, at 30 months old, this shows just how far this distillery has travelled in the improvement of its distillation techniques. Underlying the big wheat presence – which easily out-jousts the rye – are a few feints. Which simply push up the oil presence. *50%*

◈ **Rock Town Arkansas Bourbon Whiskey Aged 13 Months** batch no. 36 db **(88.5) n22.5 t22 f22 b22.** For a bourbon, this makes for a very presentable Corn Whiskey, or would have done had it been kept in the new oak a bit longer. *46% (92 proof)*

◈ **Rock Town Arkansas Bourbon Whiskey Flavour Grain Series Barley** db **(95) n23 t24 f24 b24.** Wow! That had me scampering to look for the sample bottle – Irish whiskey meets bourbon, I thought. And, indeed, 30% Arkansas unmalted barley in the recipe....corn, twice that amount. Totally magnificent. You can stop all the other whiskeys you do now and just concentrate on perfecting this stunner. Well, except your rye perhaps... The bite, the extraordinary dispersal of crisp sugars, the mouth-watering qualities, the spices, the chocolate....fabulous! *46% (92 proof)*

◈ **Rock Town Arkansas Bourbon Whiskey Flavour Grain Series Sorghum** db **(89.5) n21.5 t22.5 f22 b22.5.** Thick as a pea soup. Although the sorghum offers its own unique character, it also appears to have an effect on the texture, as well as the way in which the tannins lord it above the sugars. Substantial. *46% (92 proof)*

◈ **Rock Town Arkansas Hickory Smoked Whiskey Aged 11 Months** from wheat mash, used oak, batch no. 27 db **(84) n20.5 t21.5 b21.** Almost a bubble-gum character to this. The sweetness is unchecked by the insufficient tannin available. *45% (90 proof)*

Rock Town Arkansas Rye Single Barrel Reserve Bourbon Whiskey new charred oak barrels, barrel no. 22 db **(88.5) n21.5** feinty, as is the house style for their rye. But this one does appear to be distilled from rye concentrate...; **t23.5** good grief! I have picked myself off the floor after coming under attack from the most intense rye I have seen in years: I was wrong about their 4-year-old! And if the rye doesn't get you, the thick, tannin-rich oak certainly will; **f21.5** the tannins linger, clinging to the oils from the wide cut; **b22** ye gods! A veritable thug of a whiskey, which merrily beats your taste buds up without breaking sweat. Yet, so many intense rye moments to savour! *56.6%. ncf.*

◈ **Rock Town Arkansas Rye Whiskey Aged 15 Months** batch no. 14 db **(95.5) n24 t24 f23.5 b24.** The nose will give any rye lover a serious hard on, as the effect of the grain is entirely maxed out, leaving the sugars to fill in the cracks only. The delivery, likewise, is so full of that grain's unique fruity character, one can only swoon. Brilliant! *46% (92 proof)*

Rock Town Arkansas Single Barrel Reserve Hickory Smoked Whiskey new charred oak barrels, barrel no. 165 db **(89.5) n21.5** uncertain and nervous: the tobacco note doesn't know whether to advance or retreat; **t22.5** light molasses turn into sharper Demerara notes as the half-hearted tobacco note is finally crushed; **f23.5** sublime finish, wallowing in milk chocolate mousse; **b22** that's a lot better. Overcomes the tobacco moment with far more sugars than I have seen in the past. *56.2%. ncf.*

Rock Town Arkansas Single Barrel Reserve Hickory Smoked Whiskey new charred oak barrels, barrel no. 169 db **(90.5) n22.5** though thinner, the clarity of the sugar-smoke mix attracts; **t23** soft, melting sugars – then a wave of pugnacious oak. The smoke drifts in via the back door while the sugars make themselves at home; the bite suggests stills running a little warmly; **f22.5** buttery, lightly smoked pancake; **b22.5** a concept finally at ease with itself, though this is slightly more aggressive distillate. *55.9%. ncf.*

◈ **Rock Town Arkansas Single Barrel Reserve Hickory Smoked Whiskey Aged 20 Months** from wheat mash barrel no. 165 db **(90.5) n22.5 t23.5 f23.5 b22.5.** Well, I have to say this one got me running for my Bible thinking: "I'm sure I've tasted this before". And I discover I had – though at a weaker strength and probably younger. See last year's notes, though much more assertive and juicy now. *58.4%. sc.*

◈ **Rock Town Arkansas Single Barrel Reserve Hickory Smoked Whiskey Aged 22 Months** from wheat mash barrel no. 167 db **(88.5) n21.5 t22.5 f22 b22.5.** Soft and spicy in the wheated whisky style, though vanilla does take a surprising proportion of the attention. *58.5%. sc.*

◈ **Rock Town Arkansas Single Barrel Reserve Bourbon Whiskey Aged 15 Months** barrel no. 298 db **(91.5) n22.5 t23 f23 b23.** Well done, chaps. A lovely bourbon – except it is straight Corn Whiskey. Again, the wheat has a disproportionate say in both flavour and texture, though the corn is pretty full on. Superb balance of ulmo honey and spice. *57.4%. sc.*

◈ **Rock Town Arkansas Single Barrel Reserve Bourbon Whiskey Aged 15 Months** barrel no. 319 db **(89) n22 t23 f22 b22.** Beautifully distilled and the wheat involved, though not much, does a good Weetabix kind of job. One question though: how comes you call these single barrel bottlings bourbon? They contain 82% corn – anything over 80% corn and matured in virgin oak, as this is, makes it a Corn Whiskey... *55.4%. sc.*

◈ **Rock Town Arkansas Single Barrel Reserve Bourbon Whiskey Aged 15 Months** barrel no. 337 db **(94) n23.5 t24 f23 b23.5.** Another one where the 9% wheat outperforms the 82% corn. Exploding with character and flavour. And no little honey. Superb. *56.1%. sc.*

◈ **Rock Town Arkansas Single Barrel Reserve Rye Whiskey Aged 28 Months** barrel no. 39 db **(92.5) n22 t24.5 f23 b23.** Another example of how the distillery has taken giant strides in its ability to maximise the stills' potential. Some 88% rye at work here, yet has less effect than their 15 month 55% rye mentioned above as the slight feints undermine the rye's effect. Though, having said that, the delivery requires a seat with arm rests and straps... *58.4%. sc.*

Rock Town Four Grain Sour Mash Bourbon Whiskey new charred oak barrels db **(81) n20 t21 f20 b20.** Perhaps a tad too much sour in the sour mash... *46%*

Scotch Malt Whisky Society Cask B3.1 Aged 3 Years new charred oak, dist 15 Jul 11 **(93.5) n22.5** toasty, but never aggressively so as the house-style tannins queue quietly to have their say; **t23.5** chewy oils ensure maximum bang for your buck from the liquorice and molasses. The spices are far more up front than normal; **f23.5** ridiculously good age on this for such a youngster, as those toasty notes singing on the nose return for an encore; the lingering manuka honey-molasses and spice mix is mesmeric; **b24** as ever, Rock Town single barrel bourbon rocks... *53.9%. sc. 238 bottles.*

ROGUE SPIRITS Newport, Oregon

◈ **Rogue Chipotle Whiskey** ocean aged in oak barrels at least 6 months db **(84.5) n21.5 t22 f21 b20.** Peppery. Which, considering it has apparently been distilled with peppers, is hardly surprising. Interesting, chaps (especially with the countering honey). And entertaining. But using a vegetable disqualifies it from being a whiskey....!!! Does anyone happen to have a spare tortilla....? *40% (80 proof)*

◈ **Rogue Dead Guy Whiskey** ocean aged in oak barrels at least 1 year db **(86) n22.5 t22 f20.5 b21.** Ah, I remember this guy from a year or two back: I had a bone to pick with him about his finish. Well, not the preferred drink of the Grim Reaper now, and makes good use of its malty, peppery structure. The finish is still a bit tangy and salty. But a big improvement. *40% (80 proof)*

◈ **Rogue Farms Oregon Rye Whiskey** ocean aged in new oak barrels at least 4 months db **(74) n18 t21 f17 b18.** Rogue? You ain't joking... *40% (80 proof)*

◈ **Rogue Farms Oregon Single Malt Whiskey** ocean aged in oak barrels at least 3 months db **(81.5) n22 t22 f18 b19.5.** Malty, gristy and pleasant at first. But like many of their whiskeys, it feels as though the Pacific ocean has leaked into the cask. I'm not sure what "ocean-aged" means exactly, but whatever it is, I do wish they'd stop it... 40% (80 proof)

ROUGHSTOCK DISTILLERY Bozeman, Montana.

Montana Pure Malt db **(88.5) n21** no doubting the barley, but the sweetness of fried yam is a little unusual; **t22** oily, then a rich, vaguely spiced barley sugar coating; **f22** custard powder, then gristy duet of growing intensity; **b23** a rich offering where the barley is in deep, concentrated form. A better made spirit than its wheat whiskey, there appears to be tighter control of the stills. The result is a distinctive, confident and well-made malt which harmonises rather beautifully. 45% WB16/026

Montana Spring Wheat Whiskey db **(85.5) n21 t22 f21 b21.5**. Goes for the flavours in no half-hearted manner: the tobacco on the nose suggests the grains will be carried on big oils. And they really are, though the spices are subdued for a wheat whiskey while the sugars are broadcast widely. A genuine chewing whiskey! 45% WB16/025

Roughstock Black Label (92.5) n22.5 t23.5 f23 b23.5. A very beautiful malt whiskey very well made which underlines the happy marriage between barley and virgin oak. A stunner! 64%

ST GEORGE SPIRITS Alameda, California.

Breaking & Entering Bourbon New American charred oak, bott 08/08/2013 db **(82) n21.5 t21.5 f19 b20**. An arresting first attempt by St George. Vaguely butyric , but through the oils can be located some very decent bourbon strains. Needs a bit of tinkering, though. 43%. Batch no.130824/ 19900 bottles.

St Georges Single Malt Lot 12 bott 20/04/2012. db **(88.5) n22 t22.5 f22 b22**. Unquestionably their maltiest every offering, having now for the most part eschewed their traditional fruit style. Maybe the odd crack on the distillate is apparent, but the intensity of the barley more than compensates. 43%. Approximately 3,500 bottles.

St George's Single Malt Lot 14 db **(89) n22.5** an absent-minded sniff of this soon sent me to California: the apple-fruitiness really is unique among American whiskeys; **t22.5** dazzlingly fresh and eye-watering: the barley is delicate and easily absorbs the slightly overcooked gooseberry tart on offer; **f22** a whole plethora of vanillas; **b22** not quite so complex as some of their bottlings, but there is no getting away from their engaging and delicious house style. 43%

⬥ **St Georges Single Malt Lot 15** db **(89) n22** a malty theme with a distinct fruity undercurrent...hmmmm; **t22.5** juicy, firm, young and with a little bit of bite through the middle; **f22.5** vanilla, niggardly and troublesome spice and still that malty thread persists...; extra half mark for the mocha; **b22** hah! Even in the pitch dark, sitting in my garden on the first warm evening of the year with the church about to strike midnight, I know, St George, that this is your whiskey. Because, nobody – nobody, I tells yer!! - has this delicate fruity edge to the malt (I'm sure it is malt). So, although it is now too dark to even properly see the label in the dull glow of this computer, let alone read it, I am writing this in your pre-set space, just knowing it is you. Have to say, normally this distillery has a slightly more impressive tone: this is just a little too young and flaky – yet still great fun! 43%

SAINT JAMES SPIRITS Irwindale, California.

Peregrine Rock (83.5) n21 t20.5 f21.5 b20.5. Fruity and friendly, the wine and smoke combo work well-ish enough but the thumping oak injection highlights that maybe there isn't quite enough body to take in the aging. Perhaps less time in the barrel will reduce the bitter orange finale. 40%

SANTA FE SPIRITS Santa Fe, New Mexico.

Colkegan Single Malt Whisky once used American white oak batch no.2. db **(73) n18 t20 f17 b18**. I have been looking forward to seeing the latest from Santa Fe after encountering their strange Coyote whisky. This is another encounter which has me scratching my head wondering how some of the flavours were achieved – I really must get down to New Mexico to check this out: they are achieving results using just malt and oak I have never before seen. Can't say I go a bundle on the nose, or the finish come to that, with so much caramel and unidentified spice. Reminds me of some local whiskies I run across in India. 46%.

⬥ **Colkegan Single Malt Whiskey** American white oak barrels, batch 6 db **(88) n22.5** my word...! This time, the clarity of the distillate means there is no mistaking the mesquite smoking. For those who have never discovered that...think smoked almonds...; **t23** a cascade of brown sugars descend on the palate with a gristy maltiness in its wake...then the mesquite hits....and hits hard, with a smoky, spicy onslaught; **f21** perhaps just a tad too spicy...; **b21.5** the mesquite was a shock as I hadn't been forewarned and it's not on the front label. If I'd known, this would have been my last whiskey of the day. The way that mesquite is biting deep, it now is – an hour early...! *46% (92 proof)*

SPIRIT HOUND DISTILLERS Lyons, Colorado.

◇ **Spirit Hound Distillers Straight Malt Whisky 2 Years Old** batch 2 db **(93) n22.5** pretty solid and wonderfully clear barley at work: any interference comes not from so-so distillate – because this is obviously well made spirit - but decent quality tannins. Impressed...! **t24** that clarity of maltiness on the nose is concentrated into a breath-taking arrival. Again, the tannins are soon into action to offer a red-liquorice counter; **f23** long, though by no means overly oily. Superb late interplay between the milky malt, Manuka honey uncomplicated vanilla. Plus spice...; **b23.5** this particular spirit hound has already learned a few tricks when it comes to making very good whiskey. Well done, boy....!!! *62.05%*

STEIN DISTILLERY Joseph, Oregon.

Straight Rye Whiskey Aged 2 Years cask no. 7 **(88) n23 t22 f21 b22.** A whiskey which offers up the grains to the full spotlight. A little more care with the cut and we have something special on our hands. *40%*

STONE BARN BRANDYWORKS DISTILLERY Portland, Oregon.

Hard Eight Unoaked Rye Whiskey (86.5) **n22.5 t21.5 f21 b21.5.** The excellent fruity-rye nose does not quite show the width of the cut which creates a buzzing oiliness. Good brown sugar balance. *40%*

STRANAHAN DISTILLERY Denver, Colorado.

Stranahan's Colorado Whiskey Small Batch dist Dec 05, cask no. 225 **(94.5) n24 t23.5 f23 b24.** Absolutely magnificent; a malt which never stays still in the glass. By the way, boys: the message on the label to me brought a lump to my throat. Thank you. *47% (94 Proof). sc.*

Stranahan's Colorado Whiskey Batch #109 (92) n22 t23.5 f23 b23.5 Beautifully flighted malt with a rich seam of molassed sugars and raisins. Vanilla topping and spice. *47%*

Stranahan's Colorado Whiskey Batch #110 (91.5) **n22 t23 f23 b23.5** Lovely interplay between crispy grain and even crispier sugars. Two-toned . Juicy and gorgeously spiced. *47%*

Stranahan's Snowflake Cab Franc (95.5) n24 t24.5 f23 b24. A celebration of great whiskey, and a profound statement of what the small distilleries of the USA are capable of. *47%. sc.*

Stranahan's Snowflake Solitude dist Mar 08 **(93) n23 t23 f23.5 b23.5** I chose this as my 1,111th new whisky of the 2012 Bible, because there is a lot of ones in that. And when you spend three months on your own, virtually cut off from all others, one is number you get used to. So sampling a whisky called "Solitude" strikes home...whatever it tastes like. *47%. sc.*

Stranahan's Snowflake Tempranillo (91) n21.5 t22 f24 b23.5 A bold malt with a liquorice and greengage delivery backed by a big treacle middle. Molasses wherever you look! *47%. (94 Proof)*

SQUARE ONE BREWERY & DISTILLERY St. Louis, Missouri

J J Neukomm Missouri Malt Whisky Single Barrel (88.5) **n21 t23 f22 b22.5** it was like being transferred back to Sperryville, Virginia, where Copper Fox whiskey is made. The cherry wood smoked malt has a highly distinctive voice, and here it is again. Except this really does appear to have dark cherry notes at work on the palate. Annoyingly, although single barrel, there is no distinguishing reference number. *45% (90 proof)*

TACONIC DISTILLERY Stanfordville, New York.

◇ **Taconic Dutchess Private Reserve Straight Bourbon Whiskey** db (86) **n21.5 t22 f21 b21.5.** A pretty bourbon, with the sugars sitting in the right place, if sometimes over enthusiastically. Good spice balance, roastiness and generous oils. Also, some decent rye in that mash bill it seems. *45% (90 proof)*

◇ **Taconic Founder's Rye Whiskey** db (90.5) **n22.5** adorable floral notes attach to the unmistakable and pretty profound rye; **t23.5** yessss!! Fabulous delivery. Not a Kentucky style of rye, but so upfront with that grain that the fruit and peppery notes pour forth; a lovely blend of Manuka and ulmo honey in a four to one ratio; **f22** vanilla and spice all the way; **b22.5** well done, people of Taconic distillery. You sure know how to make a rye whiskey..! *45% (90 proof)*

TOM'S FOOLERY Chargin Falls, Ohio.

Tom's Foolery Ohio Straight Bourbon Whiskey aged 3 Years, batch 6, dist 2012 db **(83) n19 t22 f21 b21.** Not sure if Tom's fooling or feinted. Superb arrival on palate with some pretty smart spices, well backed up by maple syrup. But the cut needs to be narrowed considerably. 45% (90 proof)

Tom's Foolery Ohio Straight Rye Whiskey finished in an apple brandy barrel, aged 3 Years, batch 2, dist 2012 db **(92.5) n22.5** some serious rye notes chiming away; **t24** substantial rye impact. Arrives on two brain-exploding levels: Demerara sugar crunchy and salivating as a thicker, oil retained, chewy version. Truly superb...; **f22.5** the rye remains in crunchy mode, juicy and vaguely puckering. The Demerara sugars don't give up their ground, either. A little late extra fruit joins the fun; **b23.5** does finishing it in an apple brandy barrel mean this is a straight rye...? Either way, the extra fruit on top of the rye's already fruity nature appears to work. A beautifully vivid and memorable rye...which isn't quite as straight as Tom thinks... 45% (90 proof)

TRIPLE EIGHT DISTILLERY Nantucket, Massachusetts.

The Notch Aged 8 Years dist 2000, bott Aug 08 db **(93) n24 t23.5 f22.5 b23.** Very few distilleries make their international bow with a single malt this sublime and superbly constructed. $888 dollars a bottle it may be, but for a taste of America's very first island malt... well, is there really a price? A head turner of a whisky, and every time it's towards the glass. Do we have a world classic distillery in the making...? 44.4% (88.8 proof)

The Notch Aged 8 Years db **(95.5) n24.5 t24.5 f23 b23.5.** Only six bottles of this were produced for a special dinner at the distillery. It is possible one escaped. I admit I had a hand in putting this one together, selecting samples from about half a dozen casks on the warehouse and blending them to certain percentages. Perhaps the closest it might be compared to is a Cardhu, though with a touch extra fruit. For the doubters, proof that this distillery is quite capable of whisky of the very highest calibre. 40% (80 proof)

The Notch Aged 10 Years cask no. 009-025 dist 2001, bott 2011 db **(95.5) n23.5** I almost had to pinch myself here: there is an exotic fruit kick to this that one normally associates with ancient Speyside malt whiskies. Yet here it is, indubitably, after ten years on Nantucket... Just so obscenely elegant...; **t24.5** the clarity of the barley, the interplay between the top quality malt and the creamy, caressing layer of ulmo honey...good, grief...you could almost weep with joy; **f23.5** and now, a little predictably (though in a good way) the oak has just enough influence to take us into milky mocha territory. A light sprinkling of muscovado sugars adds some weight; and there is – and there had to be – the complex spice, too...; **b24** this is the 19th malt whisky I have tasted today. The previous 18 have been from Scotland. Yet this, unquestionably, is head and shoulders above them all. In fact, it is a good foot above most whiskies you will ever taste in your lifetime... 46%

The Notch Aged 12 Years cask no. 026-055 dist 2002, bott 2014 db **(96.5) n24** the extra two years in the cask has meant that where before we were in the land of the exotic fruit, now we are entering bourbon country...; **t24.5** spices arrive early, apparently loaded with liquorice and hickory. There is a small grain buzz to this while the sugars are deeper, darker and a little more subdued; **f23.5** toasty, outwardly dry, still spicy and still those dark, aged bourbon notes pick around; then the ulmo honey reveals it is still around after all these years; **b24.5** interesting to see this great whisky cope, as we all must do, with the passing of time. The quiet understatement and elegance of the 10-y-o has given way to a more brash and assertive, oak-stained version. Not that that is a criticism, as it does it with the usual Triple Eight panache. On the 8th of August 2008 (just two days after I had completed the 2009 Whisky Bible) I gave a speech at the distillery predicting that, from the samples I had tasted in their warehouses, this new venture was on course to be one of the great malt whisky distilleries of the world. I am heartened that, for once in my life, I got something right... 48%

TUTHILLTOWN SPIRITS Gardiner, New York.

Hudson Baby Bourbon Year 13 Batch E1 (86) n21 t21.5 f22 b21.5. A big, heavy duty bourbon. Feinty, though nothing like as oily as some previous bottlings I've encountered from these guys over the years. Enough toasted honeycomb and liquorice for this to make a few lovely noises. 46%. WB15/174

Hudson Four Grain Bourbon Year 13 Batch E1 (90.5) n22.5 t22 f23 b23 A really excellent whiskey, despite the odd technical weakness, which concentrates on complexity...and succeeds. An accomplished, big-hearted bourbon. 46%. WB15/175 **Hudson Manhattan Rye** pot-distilled from rye grain, year 13, batch E2 **(89) n23 t22.5 b22** Rich, dense and pretty impressive. 46% WB15/383

VAN BRUNT STILLHOUSE Brooklyn, New York.

◇ **Van Brunt Stillhouse American Whiskey** db **(80) n19 t20 f20.5 b20.5.** A hard one to categorise: it is whiskey and it is American. The main strand is attached to the vanilla and butterscotch tart, perhaps with a little liquorice squirted on for weight. *40%*

◇ **Van Brunt Stillhouse Bourbon** db **(81.5) n19 t21 f21 b20.5.** For a bourbon, this has a peculiarly malty kick to it. Distinct whiff of the hay ricks about this, before the fledgling liquorice becomes involved. *42%*

◇ **Van Brunt Stillhouse Rye** db **(86) n20.5 t22 f22 b21.5.** Technically wins few awards. But something, seemingly instinctually, seems to have dragged out the very best from this distillery with its rye. The oils are a bit of a problem, yet the grain rises above it enough to tap out a delightfully fruity and spicy message, and even confident enough to, late on, stray into mocha land.... *42%*

◇ **Van Brunt Stillhouse Single Malt** db **(69) n18 t18 f16 b17.** Sorry good people of Van Brunt. Just don't think single malt is your forte. Now the rye...that's another matter altogether... *42%*

WESTLAND DISTILLERY Seattle, Washington.

Westland American Single Malt Whiskey Peated bott Sept 15 db **(91.5) n23** a dry, powdery peatiness is enlivened by a sprig of mint; **t23** muscovado sugar melts on delivery, followed by lightly peated barley grist. After the dry nose, now attractively juicy; **f22.5** gently smoked vanilla; **b23** lightly peated, polite and safe.. The gristy sugars refuse to be thwarted. *46% (92 Proof). nc ncf.*

Westland American Single Malt Whiskey Sherry Wood bott Dec 14 db **(81) n20 t21 f20 b20.** Pleasant and fruity, but a certain bitter tang pervades on both nose and finish which do no favours. *46% (92 proof). nc ncf.*

Westland American Single Malt Whiskey Single Cask 115 Oregon oak cask, bott 2/10/15 db **(95.5) n24.5** give it a good 20 minutes in the glass and ensure it is at body temperature. What you will then find will be an aroma like no other whisky in this, and probably any other world. And for those of you who have been to Guyana and crawled around the warehouses there to sample the very finest aged Demerara rum, you will suddenly be transported back to South America...astonishing! **t24** again the sugars dominate. Not just any old sugars. But viscous Demerara and molasses; **f23.5** more big rummy tones...and warming, honeyed spice; **b23.5** the malt gets lost under the pungency of the massive oak influence. Oregon oak must contain more sugar compounds than any other tree on this planet. Not that I'm complaining... This is the perfect malt for rum lovers. *55% (110 proof). sc.*

Westland American Single Malt Whiskey Single Cask 118 Oregon oak cask, bott 2/10/15 db **(87.5) n23.5 t23 f20 b21.** Has just crossed that invisible line taking it from greatness – like cask 115 – to just very good. Too much tannin makes for a more sinewy and bitter experience, though the manuka honey delights. *55% (110 Proof). sc.*

Westland American Single Malt Whiskey Single Cask 177 ex-bourbon cask, bott 2/9/15 db **(94.5) n24** needs time to oxidise and warm in the glass to maximise the manuka honey at play; a little red liquorice and hickory hints at a light bourbon character, too; **t24.5** thick, powerful delivery with molasses and spices at the fore. A beautiful praline depth topped by an almost cake-like marzipan and honey frame. Calms slightly into a more Highland Park style heather honey-earthy character while the spices bubble along delightfully; **f22.5** bitters slightly at the death; **b23.5** bold, assertive single malt trying to stick to a honeyed theme. Fabulous quality! *62.5% (125 Proof). sc.*

Westland American Single Malt Whiskey Single Cask 187 ex-bourbon cask, bott 2/9/15 db **(92.5) n22.5** clean and gentle nose: old polished oak floors, with playful spice and a lick of acacia honey; **t23.5** and it is the honey which comes out quickest, never heavy or challenging: just adds a sweet sheen to the grassy, highly salivating barley; **f23** more heather honey now as a few spices buzz in. Very elegant oaky fade; **b23.5** hugely impressive single malt whisky where the emphasis is on clear honey... *62.5% (125 proof). sc.*

Westland American Single Malt Whiskey Single Cask 274 new oak cask, bott 2/10/15 db **(75.5) n18 t20.5 f18 b19.** A strange animal, this. Never sits right either on nose or finish, apart from an impressive malt hurrah soon after delivery (which itself is far from harmonious). And none of the new oak fingerprints I'd expect to find. By comparison with the usually high standards of this distillery, a real disappointment. *55% (110 Proof). sc.*

Westland American Single Malt Whiskey Single Cask 350 ex-bourbon cask, bott 2/10/15 db **(91) n22.5** malty, but also tangy. Not quite so honeyed as the norm...; **t23.5** until it hits the palate, where acacia honey is spread over digestive biscuit; soft oils, malt and spice flit around delightfully; **f22** some late cocoa on the dry-ish finish; **b23** a more sombre offering but excellent complexity. *62.5% (125 Proof). sc.*

⟡ **Westland American Single Malt Cask No. 606** db **(91.5) n23** big tannin kick: almost too big. You know those Bassett chocolate-coloured liquorice Allsorts. Crush one in your fingers, and that aroma is deliciously present here...; **t23.5** lush, with a big Manuka and heather-honey mix; the tannins again hit the palate hard and with oaky intent; **f22.5** vanilla aplenty; **b22.5** Westland really is like a box of chocolates: you just don't know... Here we have a honey-centred charmer. 578% (115.6 proof). nc ncf. 218 bottles.

⟡ **Westland American Single Malt Garryana 1/1** bott 18 Apr 2016 db **(91) n23** the most delicate smoky and nutty aroma bound in a light muscovado and oak wrapping; **t23.5** light sugars on delivery, as crunchy as you like: Demerara making way for the muscovado. The vanilla which follows really is complex stuff; the delicate phenolic anchor has hardly stirred; **f22** a little thin once the sugars have dissolved; **b22.5** a brittle but always delicious malt. 56.2% (112.4 proof). nc ncf.

⟡ **Westland American Single Malt Sherry Wood** db **(72) n18 t20 f16 b18**. Bitter and furry, disappointingly. 42% (92 proof). nc ncf.

WILLIE HOWELL SPIRITS
WH32137 (73.5) n15 t21 f18.5 b19. As big and intense as you'd expect from any spirit with a cut as wide as this. Very sweet corn oil ensures an uplifting body. 42.5%

WOODINVILLE WHISKEY CO. Woodinville, Washington
Mash Bill No 9 Bourbon Batch 2 **(90) n22 t23.5 f22 b22.5** a bourbon quite impossible not to love. Excellent fare from a new distillery to watch! 46%

WOODSTONE CREEK DISTILLERY Cincinnati, Ohio.
Woodstone Creek 10 Year Old Peated Malt (92) 24 23 22 23. Just read the previous tasting notes. There is nothing I can either add nor subtract. Quite, quite wonderful... 46.25%

WYOMING WHISKEY Kirby, Wyoming.
⟡ **Wyoming Barrel Strength Bourbon Whiskey** aged 5 Years, 8 months db **(95) n23.5** ticks plenty of boxes here for even the most hard line bourbon lover; **t24.5** oh, gosh! What a stunning volley of molasses and, presumably, rye as there is a real crisp, juicy quality to this delivery. Sets all your taste buds on edge and they are not given a chance to stand down, as the liquorice mounts up in extraordinary degrees; **f23** long, teasing, vanilla clad but with hickory aplenty; **b24** take a bow: absolutely superb bourbon! A micro distillery bourbon worth making a macro search for. 58% (116 proof)

⟡ **Wyoming Single Barrel Bourbon Whiskey** aged 5 Years db **(87.5) n22 t22 f21.5 b22**. A lovely bourbon, but certainly doesn't quite hit the heights of their monumental and landmark barrel strength bottling. I part suspect that has something to do with the strength: very possible that the essential oils that hold the whiskey together are broken down at 88 proof. Even so, the usual molasses and liquorice on display plus, briefly, some Manuka honey. 44% (88 proof). sc.

⟡ **Wyoming Small Batch Bourbon Whiskey** aged 5 Years db **(87) n21 t22.5 f21.5 b21.5**. A presentable bourbon, a little on the fatty side. But no denying the impact of the beautiful liquorice. Quietly impressive. 44% (88 proof)

YELLOW ROSE DISTILLING Houston, Texas.
⟡ **Yellow Rose Blended Whiskey** batch 39 **(81) n21 t19 f22 b19**. Wow...!! This is one sensationally sweet whiskey. Liqueur-like in composition, at least some vague spice moves in to compete with the concentrated maple syrup. At its best when a chocolate liqueur element boards the sugary party. 40%

⟡ **Yellow Rose Outlaw Bourbon Whiskey Over 6 Months** batch 24 db **(87) n20 t22.5 f23.5 b21**. The closest whiskey in style found to this anywhere in the world is European, where chestnut casks have been deployed for finishing (at least!). A tannin-dominated whiskey, where the normal liquorice and honey tones don't really apply, though close relatives may be found. Delicious when it settles down towards the end but, overall, little balance to be had. Very different...and like a yellow rose, grows on you. 46%

⟡ **Yellow Rose Straight Rye Whiskey** batch 26 **(79.5) n20 t21.2 f18 b20**. A distinctly oily gathering, though the sharper tones of the rye and headier tannins cancel each other out. Ultimately undone by a slight butyric note which does the whiskey, and drinker, few favours. 45%

YAHARA BAY DISTILLERY Madison, Wisconsin.
Sample No 1 (87) n22.5 t22 f20.5 b22. A disarmingly elegant whiskey. 40%

American/Kentucky Whiskey Blends

Ancient Age Preferred (73) n16.5 t19 f19.5 b18. A marginal improvement thanks mainly to a re-worked ripe corn-sweet delivery and the cocoa-rich finish. But still preferred, one assumes, by those who probably don't care how good this distillery's whisky can be... 40%

Beam's Eight Star (69.5) n17 t18 f17 b17.5. If you don't expect too much it won't let you down. 40%

Bellows (67) n17 t17.5 f16 b16.5 Just too thin. 40%

Calvert's Extra (79) n19 t20 f20 b20. Sweet and mega-toffeed. Just creaking with caramel but extra marks for the late spice. 40%

Carstair's White Seal (72) n16.5 t18.5 f19.5 b17.5 Possibly the cleanest blend about even offering a cocoa tang on the finale. Pleasant. 40%

◇ **The Hilhaven Lodge (88)** n21.5 slight bourbon; t23 an attractive walnut cake theme and a lovely honeyed-bourbon note which is in full salivation made; f21.5 much lighter with toffee and vanilla; b22 clean, juicy, easy drinking whiskey. 40% (80 proof)

Kentucky Dale (64) n16 t17 f15 b16. Thin and spineless, though soft and decently sweet on delivery. The grain spirit completely dominates. 40%

Kessler (84.5) n20 t21 f22 b21.5. "Smooth As Silk" claims the label. And the boast is supported by what is in the bottle: a real toffee-mocha charmer with a chewy, spicy depth. 40%

PM Deluxe (75) n18 t18 f19 b18. Pleasant moments as the toffee melts in the mouth. 40%

Sunny Brook (79.5) n20 t21 f19 b19.5. An entirely agreeable blend with toffee and lightly oiled nuts. Plus a sunny disposition... 40%

Straight Malt Whiskey

◇ **Parker's Heritage Collection Kentucky Straight Malt Whiskey Aged 8 Years** db **(93)** n23 blood orange, red liquorice and vanilla has the malt fighting to be heard above the lightly spiced din; t23.5 salivating from very first contact, as the barley makes an immediate impact. A superb gristy sweetness combines with Manuka honey and a salty tannin. Haven't seen the mash bill yet. But there must be corn in there, as the oiliness on which these sugars expand are unique to that sympathetic grain; f23 long, with that corn still holding the torch as a light molassed note busies itself with the spices; b23.5 from the distillery which brought you wheat whisky, now comes malt – Kentucky style. As delicious as it is fascinating. 54% (108 proof)

Whiskey Distilled From Bourbon Mash

Angels Envy Bourbon Finished in Port Barrels (84) n20 t22 f21 b21. Almost like a chocolate raisin candy and fruitcake. Silky textured and juicy. 43.3% (86.6 proof)

Angels Envy Cask Strength Bourbon Finished in Port Barrels Cask Strength (86.5) n21.5 t24 f20 b21. The problem with cask finishing most things, and bourbon in particular it seems, is that something is lost in the complexity - especially the small grain interaction, as well as balance between the spirit and oak - which is not quite compensated for with the lushness of extra fruit. Much better than the standard bottling, though, and the juiciness and cushioned enormity on delivery and spice at the midpoint is certainly worth discovering. 60.5%

Big Bottom Straight Bourbon Finished in Port Casks 91 (86.5) n21.5 t24 f20 b21. Subtract over enthusiastic toastiness and withering dryness and for a while we have a genuinely stunning mouth feel backed by spectacular spiced apricot and ulmo honey. The odd few moments of genius there. 45.5% (91 proof) ncf

Big Bottom Straight Bourbon Finished in Zinfandel Casks 91 (85) n21 t22 f21 b21. A flat nose and delivery comes alive about eight or nine flavour waves in when the fruit comes to a compromise with the grains. The burnt raisin finish is just a little too bitter. 45.5% ncf

Woodford Reserve Master's Collection Four Wood db **(78.5)** n20 t22.5 f18 b18. As much as they seem to want to kid us that this is bourbon – and let us be in no doubt: it isn't – it would help their misguided cause if whatever this was being offered proved an attractive experience. Apart from the immediate honey-rich delivery which is very pleasant indeed, the nose and finish have all the charisma of a 59-year-old train spotter going home to his empty house to make his sandwiches for the next day. Flat, characterless and spectacularly devoid of complexity. Basically, all the things bourbon cannot normally be accused of... 47.2% WB15/379

Whiskey Distilled From Malt Mash

Woodford Reserve Master's Collection Classic Malt distilled from a malt mash db **(79.5)** n20 t21 f19 b19.5. Ok. So let me get my head around this. If their label and neck blurb is to believed, a spirit distilled from malt in the US and placed into used casks is a "whiskey distilled from a malt mash" while, as written on another product, a bourbon transferred into used casks is a bourbon. That appears to be Woodford's stance. Sorry, guys. Don't buy that argument for a second. If anyone argued that there appears to be more politicising, tactical manoeuvring and precedential games being played here as there is careful fermentation, distilling and blending, it would be hard to disagree. Says it is malt. But doesn't help by saying malt what. Presumably barley, as the nose offers nothing other than freshly cut hay. Which in a Scotch or Irish might be regarded as a problem, often pointing an accusing finger at fermentation. Sadly, the drinking experience, as sweet as it is, doesn't get much better. *45.2% WB15/382*

Whiskey Distilled From Rye Mash

Angels Envy Rye Finished in Caribbean Rum Casks (78) n18.5 t20.5 f20 b19 Frankly, I was hardly expecting to have any teeth left after this sample. The hardest, most crisp of all whiskeys is rye. And if you want to give any whisk(e)y an extra degree of exoskeleton, then just finish it in a rum cask. And here we have the two together : yikes! Some twenty years ago I gave then Jack Daniel's blender Lincoln Henderson his first-ever taste of peated whisky: a Laphroaig. He hated it! I think he's waited a long time to return the compliment by showing me a style I did not know could exist. Beyond fascinating. Weird, even - hence the full tasting notes. One for the ladies with this liqueur-style smoothie. *50%.*

Other American Whiskey

❖ **1792 Port Finish Kentucky Straight Bourbon db (74) n19 t20 f18 b17.** What a waste of great bourbon. Flat and mind-bogglingly uninteresting. The great, aged whiskey of Barton is far too good for this kind of lemming-type nonsense. *44.45% (88.9 proof)*

Abraham Bowman Double Barrel Bourbon dist 12/06 bott 03/14. db **(85) n23 t23 f19 b20.** What does double barrel mean here? Well, in this instance thankfully it does not involve sherry or other wine casks. This is bourbon x2: the spirit is matured in virgin oak for a few years before being dumped into a fresh one. So this really is bourbon. If the great Truman Cox, the former distiller at Bowman, was still with us I'd have fun telling him why I think this is not something that has been done too often in the past. Not least because of the double dose of oak-induced sugars which means, sadly, a cloying, over-the-top sweetness and overall lack of charm and complexity. The saving grace on the palate is the delivery which packs enough spicily explosive punch to cut through the concentrated sugar candy to create something meaningful, if only temporarily so. The uncompromisingly dry finish is way off beam, so to speak, and even off-handedly bitter. One hundred proof, I'm afraid, that you can have too much of a good thing. If you do end up with a bottle, do make the most of the nose and test it only after it has aired and oxidised for about 20 minutes: it is like dipping your head into the spice cupboard in which the ginger has been knocked over and spilled. Ginger beer barrel...who needs it? *50%.*

Abraham Bowman Pioneer Spirit Coffee Finished Bourbon Release No. 11 dist 03/10/06, bott 4/10/15 db **(71) n19 t18 f17 b17.** Dry, aggressive, unbalanced...I think I'd rather just wake up and smell the whiskey... *67.3% (134.6 Proof)*

Abraham Bowman Pioneer Spirit 'Gingerbread Beer Finished Bourbon' charred white oak, dist 21/04/2006 bott 14/08/2013 db **(89) n22** most ginger cake lurks at ever corner of this dry, gently spiced nose...; **t22** again, a dry delivery with a build up of yapping if dull spice; big tannin signature though the hickory finds it hard to make its mark **f23** even drier – almost like toasted brown bread. The ginger, now more pronounced, shimmers...; **b22** as gingerbread beer finished whiskey goes, rates highly... *45%.*

Abraham Bowman Pioneer Spirit Vanilla Bean Flavored Whiskey dist 04/16/07, bott 11/03/14 db **(79) n21 t20 f19 b19.** Sharp, tangy and.... weird. Think I prefer my whiskey vanilla notes to come from the oak. *45% (90 Proof)*

Abraham Bowman Virginia Limited Edition Whiskey "Port Finished Borboun" dist 30/03/01 bott 17/08/13. db **(84.5) n20 t23 f20.5 b21.** I imagine this at one time was an entertaining bourbon. However, it reaches us as something of a dullard. The nose is instantly forgettable with the fruit and grains cancelling the other out; likewise the finish does little to stretch the imagination or taste buds other than some persistent spices. Only on delivery does this work as we are treated to a virtuoso display of dark sugars and jam vying for top spot. But the question needing answering for me is simple: why are the Americans trying to ape the Scots at a time when, quality-wise, Kentucky boots are firmly trod on kilted windpipes? *50%.*

◇◇◇ **Buffalo Trace Experimental Collection 100% French Oak Barrel Aged** dist 03/31/05, barrelled 04/01/05, bott 04/22/15, still proof: 140, entry proof: 125, warehouse/floor: K/8, rick/row/slot: 1/3/3, age at bottling: 10 Years, 0 Months, evaporation: 47% db **(90.5)** n23 low density rye and the sleepiest, vanilla oak...; icing sugar powdered onto the hickory; t23 curiously intense. The rye tries to get into full swing, but a thick barrage of tannin blocks its path f22 a curiously muted finale. Spices appear to be muzzled while the oak half roars, but then thinks twice; b22.5 a bourbon which, though delicious and technically faultless, appears to be working in slow motion...and with handcuffs and shackles. *45% (90 proof)*

◇◇◇ **Buffalo Trace Experimental Collection French Oak Barrel Head Aged** dist 03/31/05, barreled 04/01/05, bott 04/22/15, still proof: 140, entry proof: 125, warehouse/floor: K/8, rick/row/slot: 1/3/4, age at bottling: 10 Years, 0 Months, evaporation: 46% db **(95.5)** n24 the sexy clarity of the rye is perfectly matched by the gentle density of the liquorice-enriched oak; t24 crisp muscovado sugars in the greatest BT tradition wrap themselves around the brittle rye; the oak has a slight cough sweet intensity...; f23.5 creamy and dreamy. And so sweet to the very end...; b24 in so many ways, classic BT – especially of the rye recipe. *45% (90 proof)*

Buffalo Trace White Dog Mash #1 (93) n23 t23 f24 b23. Exceptionally high quality spirit, fabulously weighted, neither too sweet nor dry and with the distinctive cocoa character of the very best grain distillate. Beats the crap out of vodka. "White Dog" is the name for spirit which has run off the still but not yet been bottled: "New Make" in Scotland. It is not, therefore, whiskey as it has not been in any form of contact with oak. But what the hell... It must be at least 15 years ago that I told the old plant manager, Joe Darmond, that he should bottle this stuff as it would sell fast. BT brought it out initially for their distillery shop...and now it is in demand worldwide?! If you are reading this, what did I tell you? and about rye come to that! *62.5%*

High West Campfire rye, bourbon & Scotch malt, batch no. 3 **(93)** n23.5 t22.5 f23.5 b23.5. An enchanting, hugely complex dram...the sort of thing I conjure up in my tasting room every day, in fact, by mixing differing whisky styles from around the world. Here the rye dominates by some margin, creating the backbone on which the sweeter bourbon tones hang. The peated malt ensures a wonderful background rumble. Well blended...and great fun! *46%*

High West Son of Bourye blend of bourbon & rye **(95)** n23 t24.5 f23.5 b24 This son, presumably called Ryebon, is a stunningly stylish chap which comprehensively eclipses its lackluster parent... *46%*

High West Whiskey American Prairie Reserve Blend of Straight Bourbon batch 13DQ3 db **(91)** n22.5 warm and rich, there is an unusually heavy copper content; red currents sits well with the spiced honeycomb; the hefty tannins in a brand called Prairie Reserve add a degree of irony; t23 exceptionally dry, tingling delivery with the sugars apparent but usually keeping their distance; f23 cream fudge and a return to a heftier type of tannin; b23 not often you find a predominantly dry bourbon...must have something to do with the Prairie...which ten percent of post tax profit will help to preserve. *46%. ncf. WB15/177*

◇◇◇ **Jim Beam Double Oak** db **(86)** n22 t22.5 f20.5 b21. Attractive, caramel-soaked whiskey with a little too much fade after a big spice and liquorice delivery. *43%*

◇◇◇ **Knob Creek Smoked Maple (35)** n10 t10 f10 b5. How can this be called a " Kentucky straight bourbon"? What is straight about this? Am I missing something here? About 98% closer to maple syrup than bourbon, this would make a pleasant spread on your breakfast toast. It may be whiskey, Jim (Beam), but not as we know it. *45% (90 proof)*

Michter's No. 1 American Whiskey (84.5) n21 t21.5 f21 b21 Sugar-coated, oily and easy going. About as friendly as any whiskey you'll find this year *41.7%*

Michter's No. 1 Sour Mash (86) n22 t22 f21 b21 A pleasant, clean, light whiskey: perhaps too clean at times. Good mocha throughout, with the accent on the coffee. *43%*

WhistlePig Old World 12 Year Madeira Finish European casks **(88)** n21.5 hard, unyielding but attractive rye; t23.5 explosive delivery with spices going off like gelignite. But the sugars from the grain and yielding fruit form an unexpectedly attractive chocolatey mix; f21 on the short and thin side; bitters out; b22 not sure how this can be called a straight rye. But as a whiskey experience, certainly has its merits. *45%. (90 Proof)*

WhistlePig Old World 12 Year Port Finish European casks **(74)** n18 t20 f18 b18. Oily, dense and bitter *45%. (90 Proof)*

WhistlePig Old World 12 Year Sauternes Finish European casks **(79.5)** n21 t22.5 f18 b18. Has its brief moments of fun, mainly on delivery, when the rock-hard rye tries to keep out the surrounding, swamping fruit. But a very poor finish and very little balance throughout. *45%. (90 Proof)*

Canadian Whisky

The vastness of Canada is legendary. As is the remoteness of much of its land. Anyone who has not yet visited Gimli, which sits serenely on the shores of Lake Manitoba more or less bang in the middle of the country and in early Spring, venture a few miles out into the wilderness has missed a trick.

Because there, just a dozen miles from the remotest distillery of them all, Gimli, you can stand and listen to the ice crack with a clean, primeval crispness unlike any other thing you will have experienced; a sound once heard by the very first hunters who ventured into these uncharted wastes. And hear a distant loon call its lonely, undulating, haunting song, its notes skudding for miles along the ice and vanishing into the snow which surrounds you. Of all the places on the planet, it is the one where you will feel a sensation as close to nature - and insignificance - as you are likely to find.

It was also a place where I felt that, surely, great whisky should be made. But in the early days of the Gimli distillery there was a feeling of frustration by the blenders who used it. Because they were simply unable to recreate the depth and complexity of the legendary Crown Royal brand it had been built to produce in place of the old, now closed, distilleries to the east. When, in their lab, they tasted the new Crown Royal against the old there were furrowed brows, a slight shaking of heads and an unspoken but unmistakable feeling of hopeless resignation.

To understand why, we have to dispense with the nonsense which appears to have been trotted out by some supposed expert in Canadian whisky or other

Yukon

BRITISH COLUMBIA

ALBERTA

MANITOBA

Shelter Point   Okanagan
●Vancouver

Alberta
Highwood
Calgary

Palliser

Gimli

Key	
●	**Major Town or City**
♣	Distillery

who has, I have been advised by quite a few people I meet at my tastings, been writing somewhere that Canada has no history of blending from different distilleries. Certainly that is now the perceived view of many in the country. And it is just plain wrong: only a maniac would write such garbage as fact and completely undersell the provenance of Canadian whisky. Crown Royal, when in its pomp, was a meticulous blending of a number of different whiskies from the Seagram empire and by far the most complex distillery Canada had to offer.

The creases in the furrowed brows deepened as the end of the last century aproached. Because the key distilleries of LaSalle, Beupre and Waterloo were yielding the very last of their stocks, especially top quality pure rye, and although the much lighter make of Gimli was of a high standard, they had not yet been able to recreate the all round complexity as when adding the fruits of so many great distilleries together. The amount of experimentation with yeasts and distilling speeds and cutting times was a wonder to behold. But the race was on: could they produce the diversity of flavours to match the old, classic distilleries which were now not just closed but in some cases demolished before the final stocks ran dry?

When I had sat in the LaSalle blending lab for several days in the 1990s and worked my way through the near extinct whiskies in stock I recognised in Beupre a distillery which, had it survived, probably might have been capable of producing something as good, if not better, than anything else on this planet. And it was clear just what a vital contribution it made to Crown Royal's all round magnificence.

So I have monitored the Crown Royal brand with interest, especially since Gimli and the brand was acquired by Diageo 15 years ago. And anyone doubting that this really was a truly great whisky should have accompanied me when I visited the home of my dear and now sadly lost friend Mike Smith and worked our way through his astonishing Crown Royal collection which showed how the brand's taste profile had evolved through the ages.

And, at last, it appears all that hard work, all those early days of experimentation and fine tuning at Gimli have paid off. For while the standard Crown Royal brand doesn't yet quite live up to its starry past, they have unleashed upon us a whisky which dazzles, startles and engulfs you in its natural beauty like an early spring morning on Lake Manitoba.

The whisky is called Crown Royal Northern Harvest Rye. It is not only the best Canadian to be found in the market, it was last year's Jim Murray's World Whisky of the Year: batch L5085 N3 had redefined a nation's whisky.

The fact it should have achieved this at a time when Canadian whisky is at a nadir, with far too many brands dependent on adding too many unacceptble things as accepted flavouring agents, is providential. It shows that keeping the grains at a maximum and allowing them to be the flavouring agents - like Alberta Premium - is not just keeping true to the old Canadian traditions, but the way to go to drag it back onto the world's stage and give it a leading role. Walter Jonke and the other old Canadian blenders I knew understood this. Let this be a lesson to the present generation. And so many so-callled whisky experts.

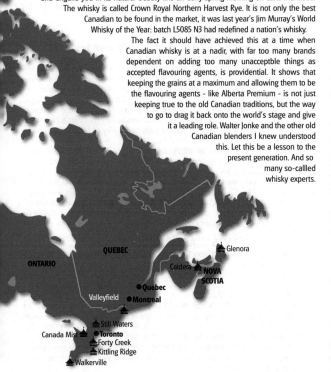

291

Jim Murray's Whisky Bible Canadian Whisky of the Year Winners	
2004	Seagram's VO
2005	Seagram's VO
2006	Alberta Premium
2007	Alberta Premium 25 Years Old
2008	Alberta Premium 25 Years Old
2009	Alberta Premium
2010	Wiser's Red Letter
2011	Crown Royal Special Reserve
2012	Crown Royal Special Reserve
2013	Materson's 10 Year Old Straight Rye
2014	Materson's 10 Year Old Straight Rye
2015	Materson's 10 Year Old Straight Rye
2016	Crown Royal Northern Harvest Rye
2017	Crown Royal Northern Harvest Rye

Canadian Single Malts
GLENORA
Glen Breton Rare Aged 10 Years bott 10 db **(89.5) n22 t23 f22 b22.5.** An impressive whisky: one of the best bottlings of this age for some while and showing the malt at full throttle. *43%*

HIGHWOOD DISTILLERS
◇ **Canadian Rockies 10 Year Old (84.5) n21.5 t22 f20.5 b20.5.** Resplendent in all its chewy one-dimensional caramel. *40%. Taiwan Exclusive.*

◇ **Canadian Rockies 21 Year Old (88) n22** so light, with a mix of apple crumble and vanilla ice cream; **t22** soft and simple as you like: vanilla and docile spice; **f22** more of the same...; **b22** not sure you can find a straighter, simpler whisky... *40%. Taiwan Exclusive.*

◇ **Canadian Rockies 21 Year Old (91.5) n22.5** the fruit here seems sharper all round; **t23.5** superb, juicy, tart delivery with a brittle element certainly not present in the Taiwan bottling; **f22.5** some busy spice makes the vanilla fade more interesting; **b23** surely it just can't be a matter of 6% abv. This has far more personality and joie de vivre. *46%. Canadian Exclusive.*

◇ **Canadian Rockies 34 Year Old (92.5) n23** the small grains leave the glass like tracer fire. Exceptionally sharp and revealing some superb, and unusual, caramelised eucalyptus notes; **t23** kerpow! Hits the palate like an express train running into buffers. Although caramel explodes everywhere, it is the shrapnel of crisp Demerara sugars which hit home with aplomb; **f23.5** long, with the spices now arriving to almost calm down proceedings! Superb oak-vanilla and Demerara mix, as those spices really take their job seriously; **b23** the most fun I've had with a 34-year-old Canadian for quite a few years now...though that was a little hotter than this... *79.3%. Taiwan Exclusive.*

OKANAGAN SPIRITS CRAFT DISTILLERY
Laird of Fintry Single Malt Whisky French & American oak. db **(84) n21 t22 f20 b21.** A tangy, aromatic whisky where the oak appears to have a disproportionate say. Interesting marmalade depth. *40%. First Batch. 264 bottles.*

PEMBERTON DISTILLERY
◇ **Pemberton Organic Single Malt Whisky 2010** ex-bourbon cask, cask no. 3, dist Oct 10, bott May 16 db **(88) n21.5** very young, with a slight nougat kick to the tight malt usually associated with German-style stills; **t22.5** exceptionally sweet as the grist gets to town. But there is a secondary, unique bubblegum and green leaf, even vaguely hoppy, edge to the light feints which intrigues; **f22** the wide cut is particularly effective here, garnering some serious oils and sugars; **b22** massively malty. And they really can claim their very own idiosyncratic style: deliciously different. *45.6%. nc ncf sc.*

◇◇ **Pemberton Organic Single Malt Whisky Lightly Peated 2011** ex-bourbon cask, cask no. 1, dist 2011, bott May 16 db **(84.5) n20.5 t22 f21 b21.** The mix of peat and nougat make slightly uncomfortable bedfellows. Apparently, the first ever peated malt from this distillery north of Whistler – a tough art to master. *45%. nc ncf sc.*

◇◇ **Pemberton Organic Single Malt Whisky Medium Peated 2012** ex-bourbon cask, cask no. 3, dist Aug 12, bott May 16 db **(87.5) n21 t22.5 f22 b22.** This one is all about the delivery: colossal barley on show despite the smoke. Again, a very wide cut from the stills means the oils tighten the sugars and experience and make for a challenging, tangy dram. *45.3%. nc ncf sc.*

POTTER DISTILLING CO.
Cadenhead's World Whiskies Canada Potter Distilling Co. Aged 24 Years Bourbon barrel, bott Feb 14 **(94.5) n23 t24 f23.5 b24** a true classic of the Canadian rye style...though of course without any rye at all. As a whisky, a little bit of a mystery. When at Potter distillers in British Columbia about 17 years ago, I remember they then had no maturing stock of their own as they did not distil large enough quantities. But they did have casks of maturing Canadian whisky they had bought in from the nearby Okanagan Distillery which, for a while, had made Canadian Club for the west coast and Far East market. No guarantees, but chances are it could be that – and they did make very good whisky there, evidenced by the outstanding old Bush Pilot single cask brand. *56.5%. 126 bottles. WB15/178*

SHELTER POINT DISTILLERY
◇◇ **Shelter Point Single Malt Whisky** db **(89.5) n22** huge malt signature with salt not far behind. Obviously young and has yet to shake off all its feints, but there is a delightful light squeeze of lime which helps open out the sugars; **t23** again, thick from a wide-ish cut from the still, but the oils serve only to ramp up the intensity of the juicy malt to extraordinary levels: almost like barley concentrate....; that secondary citrus note – closer to grapefruit now – ensures impressive layering; **f22.5** modest incursions by the oak help settle balance so now vanilla vies with malt for top spot. Still a little saltiness persists but it is the gathering, warming spices which grab most attention; **b22** a charming and very promising malt made by lovely people at a gorgeous distillery – and best when served very much at body temperature. I have been watching progress at Shelter Point – a remote distillery on Victoria Island in stunning British Columbia – since before it was actually built. And having looked at many of the early casks as they matured, I can tell you even better is to come, especially when more sugars are absorbed from the oak and a wider collection of barrels can be vatted for even greater complexity. Like the distillery, this is a whisky – even at this tender age - which just oozes personality. Congratulations to all concerned. *46%*

STILLWATERS DISTILLERY
Stalk & Barrel Single Malt Whisky cask 11 db **(87.5) n21.5 t22 f22 b22.** Attractively intense barley has all the space it requires to flourish thanks to a well distilled spirit impressively cut. Only a lack of complexity fails to crank the score a little higher. But if it's a malt whisky you want, with the accent on the malt, here's your man. *62.3%. sc.*

Stalk & Barrel Single Malt Whisky cask 13 db **(77) n20 t21 f17 b19.** Not quite the delight that is cask 11. Not sure if that is because the weaker strength means the water has broken up the oils a little bit too much for their own good, exposing a few feints. Or if the cut wasn't quite as carefully made this time round. Still plenty of malt to get on with, though. *46%. sc.*

YUKON BREWING
◇◇ **Two Brewers Yukon Single Malt Release 01 Classic** db **(86.5) n21 t21.5 f22.5 b21.5.** Not sure if I have come across a Canadian so steeped with rich cocoa from first moment to last. A pretty wide cut from the still can be thanked for this, as the thick finish on the tongue will testify. But I admit, I could easily enjoy this, especially the extraordinary and utterly delicious, top quality French praline on the finish. *46%*

◇◇ **Two Brewers Yukon Single Malt Release 02 Special Finishes** db **(80.5) n19 t21.5 f20 b20.** Sorry, chaps. You have some serious butyric going on there... *46%*

Canadian Blended Whisky
Alberta Premium (95.5) n24 t25 f22.5 b24 It has just gone 8am and the Vancouver Island sky is one of clear blue. My windows are open to allow in some chilly, early Spring air and, though only the first week of March, an American robin sits in the arbutus tree, resplendent in its now two-toned leaves, calling for a mate, as it has done since 5.15 this morning, his song blending with the lively trill of the house finches and the doleful, maritime anthem of the gull. It seems the natural environment of Alberta Premium, back here to its rye-studded best after

a couple I tasted socially in Canada last year appeared comparatively dull and restrained. I am tasting this from Bottle Lott No L93300197 and it is classic, generating all I expect and now demand. A national treasure. 40%

Alberta Premium 25 Years Old (95) n24 t23 f23 b25. Faultless. Absolutely nothing dominates. Yet every aspect has its moment of conquest and glory. It is neither bitter nor sweet, yet both. It is neither soft nor hard on the palate yet both elements are there. Because of the 100% rye used, this is an entirely new style of whisky to hit the market. No Canadian I know has ever had this uncompromising brilliance, this trueness to style and form. And, frightening to think, it could be improved further by bottling at least 46% and un-chillfiltered. For any whisky lover who ever thought Canadian was incapable of hitting the heights among the world's greats. 40%. Alberta Distillers.

Alberta Premium 30 Years (88.5) n23 t23.5 f20 b22. It doesn't take much to tip the balance of a whisky this delicate on the nose and delivery. Five extra years in the cask has nudged the oak just a little too far. However, savour the nose and delivery which are to die for. 40%

Alberta Premium Dark Horse (84) n18 t22 f22 b22. The blurb on the back says it is crafted for the "next generation of whisky connoisseur". Fine. But personally, I'd always shape a whisky for the true connoisseurs of today... I have not spoken to the blending team at Alberta to discuss this and, as the book has to be finished within a week or two, I won't get a chance. But this is the most extraordinary development in Canadian I have seen for a while. The nose is not great: it really does seem as though fruit cordial has been given the lead role. But the taste really does challenge, and I have to say there are many aspects I enjoy. It is as though some peated malt has been added to the mix as the finish does have distinctive smokiness. And the balance has been expertly worked to ensure the sugars don't dominate while the spices are persistent. But if it falls down anywhere, the over reliance on the fruit apart, it is the fact that Alberta makes the best spirit in Canada by a very great distance....yet someone has forgotten to ensure that fact is made clear in the taste and the nose especially. 45%

Alberta Rye Whisky Dark Batch Blended Rye (86) n19 t23 f22 b22. A veritable fruitcake of a whisky – and about as moist and sultana-laden as you'll ever find. Not sure about that bitter-tobacco most un-Canadian nose, though. 45% (90 Proof)

Alberta Springs Aged 10 Years (83) n21 t21 f20 b20. Really appears to have had a bit of a flavourectomy. Sweet but all traces of complexity have vanished. 40%.

Barton's Canadian 36 Months Old (78) n19 t20 f19 b20. Sweet, toffeed, easy-going. 40%

Bowman's Canadian Whisky (90.5) n22 t22 f23.5 b23. A delicious blend for chocoholics. 40%

Black Velvet (78) n18 t20 f20 b20. A distinctly off-key nose is compensated for by a rich corn and vanilla kick on the palate. But that famous spice flourish is a distant memory. Another big caramel number. 40%

◇ **Caldera Distilling Hurricane 5 Whisky** batch no. 0001 (87.5) n21.5 t22 f22 b22. Silky, soft. But lashings of toffee and sugars. Decent spices balance things up a little. 40% (80 proof)

Campbell & Cooper Aged a Minimum of 36 Months (84.5) n21.5 t22 f20 b21. Huge flavour profile. An orchard of oranges on the nose and profound vanilla on delivery. 40%

Canadian Club 100 Proof (89) n21 t23 f22 b23. If you are expecting this to be a high-octane version of the standard CC Premium, you'll be in for a shock. This is a much fruitier dram with an oilier body to absorb the extra strength. An entertaining blend. 50%.

◇ **Canadian Club 100% Rye** (92) n23 unmistakable pure rye grain but of the muted variety, rather than the chipped crunchy, fruity style. Slightly exotic, with a slight coconut and pineapple slant to the aroma, though the weightier oak plus some caramels offer good balance; t23.5 initially salivating as the rye bites, the delivery soon turns an oilier corner. The sugars are molassed, the grain are firm and increasingly toasty; f22.5 late liquorice and a little bitterness from both the tannins and caramels. Long and remains substantial; b23 will be interesting to see how this brand develops over the years. Rye is not the easiest grain to get right when blending differing ages and casks with varied histories: it is an art which takes time to perfect. This is a very attractive early bottling, though my money is on it becoming sharper in future vattings as the ability to show the grain above all else becomes more easily understood. Just so wonderful to see another excellent addition to the Canadian whisky lexicon. 40% (80 proof)

Canadian Club Chairman's Select 100% Rye (81.5) n21 t21.5 f20 b19. A bemusing whisky. The label proudly announces that here we have a whisky made from 100% rye. Great news: a Canadian eagerly anticipated. But the colour – a deep orange – looks a bit suspicious. And those fears prove well founded when the taste buds, as well as the nose, go looking for the rye influence in vain. Instead we have a massive toffee effect, offset by some busy spice. Colouring has ruined many a great whisky...and here we have a painful example. What a waste of good rye... 40%

Canadian Club Premium (92) n23 t22.5 f23 b23.5. A greatly improved whisky which now finds the fruit fitting into the mix with far more panache than of old. Once a niggardly whisky, often seemingly hell-bent on refusing to enter into any form of complexity: but not now! Great spices in particular. I'm impressed. 40%

Canadian Club Aged 6 Years (88.5) n21.5 t22 f22.5 b22.5. Not at all bad for a Canadian some purists turn their nose up at as it's designed for the American market. Just brimming with mouth-watering enormity and style. Dangerously moreish. 40%

Canadian Club Reserve Aged 10 Years (86) n20 t22 f21.5 b22. Odd cove, this. The nose is less than welcoming and offers a hotchpotch of somewhat discordant notes giving a jumbled message and less than well defined statement of intent. Decent delivery, though, shifting through the gears with some impressive and sultry fruit tying in well with a rare grain onslaught found in Canadian these days. The finish, though, just can't steer away from the rocks of bitterness, alas. Again, as so often appears to be the case with CC, the spices star. 40%

Canadian Club Classic Aged 12 Years (91.5) n22 t24 f21.5 b23.5. A confident whisky which makes the most of a honeycomb theme. 40%

Canadian Club Small Batch Classic 12 Aged 12 Years batch C12-020 (75.5) n21 t22.5 f15 b17. A syrupy whisky which talks a great game on the back label, but fails to deliver in reality. Big fruit, perhaps a little too heavily accented as other avenues of complexity are limited. The bitter, tangy finish is not great at all. 40%

Canadian Club Aged 20 Years (92.5) n24 t21 f23.5 b23. In previous years, CC20 has ranked among the worst whiskies I have tasted, not just in Canada, but the world. Their current bottling, though, is not even a distant relation. Sure, it has a big sherry investment. But the sheer elan and clever use of spice make this truly magnificent. Possibly the most pleasant surprise in my latest trawl through all Canada's whiskies. 40%

Canadian Club Sherry Cask batch no. SC-018 (76) n18 t20 f20 b18. Twice as strong as you can normally buy Sherry yet somehow has only half the body. As I say, I really don't know what to make of this. Nor do I get the point. 41.3%

Canadian Five Star Rye Whisky (83) n21 t22 f20 b20. An entirely tame, well behaved Canadian which celebrates the inherent sweetness of the species. That said, the immediate impact on the palate is pretty delicious with a quick, flash explosion of something spicy. But it is the deft, satin-soft mouthfeel which may impress most. 40%

Canadian Hunter (85.5) n20.5 t21 f22 b22. Remains truly Canadian in style. The toffee has diminished, allowing for more coffee and cocoa to ensure a delightful middle and finish. 40%

Canadian Mist (78) n19 t20.5 f18.5 b20. Much livelier than previous incarnations despite the inherent, lightly fruited softness. 40%

Canadian Pure Gold (82) n21.5 t20.5 f20 b20. Full-bodied and still a notably lush whisky. The pure gold may have more to do with the caramel than the years in cask but the meat of this whisky still gives you plenty to chew over. I especially enjoy the gradual building of spices. 40%

Canadian Spirit (78) n20 t20 f19 b19. A real toffee-fest with a touch of hard grain around the edges. 40%. Carrington Distillers (Alberta Distillers).

Caribou Crossing Single Barrel (84) n20 t22.5 f20 b21.5. While the nose offers an unholy battle between some apple-fruity rye notes and dry, dusty caramel, there is a real pulsating delivery with the sharper spices helped along the way by the silkiness of the body. Though the caramel offers a toffee-fudge backdrop, a countering dry date sweetness does more than enough to keep it at bay. However, the finish dulls out as the caramel gains the upper hand, though the twitching spices do ensure a light, throbbing beat. An enjoyable Canadian, undoubtedly, I am somewhat perplexed by it. There is no reference to the barrel number so you won't know if you are buying from different casks. Also, if it is single barrel what is the point of the caramel? If it is to make all the casks taste the same, or similar, then why not just blend them together. A badly missed opportunity. 40%. Sazerac.

Centennial 10 Year Limited Edition (88.5) n21.5 t23 f22 b22. Retains its usual honey-flavoured breakfast cereal style, but the complexity has increased. Busy and charming. 40%

Century Reserve 8 Years Old Premium (82) n20 t21 f20 b21. Clean vanilla caramel. 40%

Century Reserve Custom Blend 15 Years Plus (88.5) n21.5 t22 f23 b22. After two days of being ambushed in every direction, or completely steamrollered by Canadian caramel, my tastebuds are in total shock. Caramel kept to an absolute minimum so that it hardly registers at all. Charming and refined drinking. 40%

Century Reserve 21 Years Old (91.5) n23.5 t23 f23 b22. Quite beautiful, but a spirit that is as likely to appeal to rum lovers as whisky ones. 40%

Century Reserve Custom Blend lot no. 1525 (87) n21.5 t22 f21.5 b22. An enjoyable whisky which doesn't quite reach its full potential. 40%

Corby's Canadian 36 Months Old (85) n20 t21 f22 b22. Attractive with fine bitter-sweet balance and I love the late spice kick-back. 40%. Barton. Interesting label: as *a keen ornithologist, I had no idea there were parrots in Canada. Must be related to the Norwegian Blue.*

Crown Royal (86) n22 t23.5 f19.5 b21. The Crown has spoken and it has been decreed that this once ultra grainy old whisky is taking its massive move to a silky fruitiness as far as it can go. It was certainly looking that way last time out; on this re-taste (and a few I have unofficially tasted) there is now no room for doubt. If you like grape, especially the sweeter variety, you'll love this. The highpoint is the sublime delivery and starburst of spice. The low point? The buzzy, unhappy finale. The Grain Is Dead. Long Live The Grape! *40%*

Crown Royal Black (85) n22 t23 f18.5 b21.5. Not for the squeamish: a Canadian which goes for it with bold strokes from the off which makes it a whisky worth discovering. The finish needs a rethink, though. *45%*

◇ **Crown Royal Cornerstone Blend (85.5) n21 t22 f21 b21.5.** Something of a mishmash, where a bold spiciness appears to try to come to terms with an, at times, random fruity note. One of the most curious aspects of this quite different whisky is the way in which the weight of the body continues to change. Intriguing. *40.3% (80.6 proof)*

◇ **Crown Royal DeLuxe (91.5) n23.5** superbly crafted nose profile: crisp and flinty/ soft and yielding in equal measures, weight and pace. A little light pepper also counters the friendly sugars; **t23** the delivery is all about cracking, rock hard grains and fruity muscovado sugars. Some ripe pears sweeten further, though there is an oaky-caramel bitterness creeping in after the midpoint; **f22.5** mainly about the spiced vanilla; **b22.5** some serious blending went into this. Complex. *40% (80 proof)*

Crown Royal Cask No 16 Finished in Cognac Casks (85.5) n21.5 t21 f22 b21. Clean cut and very grapey. The nose is unique in the whisky world: it is one of Cognac. Otherwise struggles to really find its shape and rhythm. A perfect Canadian for those who prefer theirs with an air of grace and refinement but very limited depth. In fact, those who prefer a Cognac. *40%*

Crown Royal Hand Selected Barrel (90) n22 quintessential Canadian: corn oil and vanilla; **t23** concentrated corn oil relieved by ulmo honey, spice and the inevitable toffee; **f22.5** corn oil...and toffee. Thankfully the spice carries on buzzing; **b22.5** more Canadian than a punch in the kisser from an ice hockey player. *51.5%*

◇ **Crown Royal Hand Selected Barrel (94.5) n23.5** beautifully made and bursting with really high octane tannins, mainly around a deep vanilla. Lively, clean, with a gorgeous ice cream and muscovado sugar mix; **t24** ohhhh...!! So sensual. Corn oils, presumably, enriched in maple syrup at first before moving to a more earthy heather honey as the weight becomes far more of a factor; **f23.5** spices out to just the right degree. **b23.5** if this is a single barrel, it boasts extraordinary layering and complexity *51.5% (103 proof)*

Crown Royal Limited Edition (87) n22 t22.5 f20.5 b22. A much happier and productive blend than before with an attractive degree of complexity but the more bitter elements of the finish have been accentuated. *40%*

Crown Royal Northern Harvest Rye bott code L5085 N3 **(97.5) n25** the rye is not just profound and three dimensional, but has that extraordinary trick of allowing new elements to take their place: rarely does ulmo honey and manuka honey link arms when rye is around, but they do here, yet never for a second diminish the sharpness and presence of the grain; **t24.5** salivating and sensual on delivery, hardly for a second are we not reminded that rye is at work here. And it makes itself heard loudly through the stiff backbone from which all the softer, sugary notes emanate. Crunchy and at times bitter, though in a pleasant controlled way from the grain, rather than a questionable cask; **f23.5** quietens rapidly, though only for a moment or two before the spices begin to pulse again and vanillas take up their comfortable positions; **b24.5** this is the kind of whisky you dream of dropping into your tasting room. Rye, that most eloquent of grains, not just turning up to charm and enthral but to also take us through a routine which reaches new heights of beauty and complexity. To say this is a masterpiece is barely doing it justice. *45%*

◇ **Crown Royal Northern Harvest Rye** bott code L5099 **(94) n23** caramel plays a surprisingly leading role in this rye-swept drama. The sharpness of the grain, which helped carry all before it last year, here is blunted, though when its does finally come through it does so with restrained power, and some complimentary herbal and apple notes for good measure; **t24** ah here we go! Much more like it as the stunning good looks of last year's World Whisky of the Year come into focus on delivery, with a stunning salivating note for company. Moves swiftly into mocha mode and then begins to ship in friendly caramels; **f23.5** long, though the spices are not what are expected, nor the expected contrast between the brittle rye and later oils and caramels; **b23.5** superb whisky but just missing the magic of its all-conquering sister bottling. *45%.*

◇ **Crown Royal Northern Harvest Rye** bott code L5134 **(97) n24** much more like it: assertive, yet somehow relaxed and entreating. But here the rye glistens in the house three-dimensional style, at once bristling and bullish, yet kissing and caressing. The spices seem to have extra weight; **t24.5** mouth-watering as the rye hits the palate with the same force as the Demerera sugars. A real backbone to the rye which is in its crunchiest form, though with a few extra sugars up its sleeve from last year's winner; **f24** the spices assert themselves but without any force. The crisp rye and Demerara sugars, like the vanillas which have slowly assembled, seem to simply melt always leaving a spicy outline of where they once were; **b24.5** a close relation to last year's whisky sensation: Jim Murray's Whisky Bible World Whisky of the Year 2016. Not quite as truly incredible, but the link can very obvious and much more than bottling L5099 and a few others I have subsequently tasted, though not in controlled conditions like this. And, having just this moment tasted last year's winner, I can confirm that it is a close-ish miss. Absolutely brilliant and helps carry on the work of its sister bottling in waking up the world to how good the very top Canadian whiskies can be... *45%*.

Crown Royal Special Reserve (96) n24 a clean and attractively spiced affair with cinnamon and the faintest pinch of allspice leading the way: rye at work, one presumes; the fruit is clean and precise with weightier grape overshadowing a green apple freshness; **t24** a spicier element to the usual rye and fruit delivery, much more in keeping with the nose, but that fabulous, contrary mouth-feel of harder grain and softer fruit continues to do the business. The spices build slowly but with an impressive evenness and determination: one of the most outstanding Canadians on the palate of them all; **f24** the finish has been tidied up and with stunning effect: no more sawdust and eye-watering dryness. Both grain and soft fruit ensure a magnificently mouth-watering end to an amazing journey; **b24** complex, well weighted and simply radiant: it is like looking at a perfectly shaped, gossamer clad Deb at a ball. The ryes work astonishingly well here (they appear to be of the malted, ultra-fruity variety) and perhaps to best effect after Alberta Premium, though now it is a hard call between the two. *40%*

Crown Royal XR Extra Rare lot no. L7064 N4 **(93.5) n24 t23 f23 b23.5.** Just about identical to the previous bottle above. The only difference is on the finish where the rye, fortified with spice, decides to hang back and battle it out to the death; the toffee and vanilla make a controlled retreat. Either the same bottling with a slightly different stance after a few years in the bottle, or a different one of extraordinary high consistency. *40%*

Crown Royal XO (87.5) n22 t21 f22.5 b22. With an XO, one might have hoped for something eXtraOrdinary or at least eXOtic. Instead, we have a Canadian which carried on a little further where their Cask No 16 left off. Always a polite, if rather sweet whisky, it falls into the trap of allowing the Cognac casks a little too much say. Only on the finish, as the spices begin to find channels to flow into, does the character which, for generations, set Crown Royal apart from all other Canadians begin to make itself heard: complexity. *40% WB15/398*

Danfield's Limited Edition Aged 21 Years (95) n24 t24 f23.5 b23.5. A quite brilliant first-time whisky. The back label claims this to be small batch, but there is no batch number on the bottle, alas. Or even a visible bottling code. But this is a five star performer and one of this year's whiskies of the world. *40%*

Danfield's Private Reserve (84.5) n20 t21.5 f22 b21. A curious, non-committal whisky which improves on the palate as it goes along. An overdose of caramel (yawn!!) has done it no favours, but there is character enough for it to pulse out some pretty tasty spice. Seamless and silky, for all the toffee there underlying corn-rich clarity is a bit of a turn on. *40%*

8 Seconds Small Batch (86) n20 t22 f22.5 b21.5. Fruity, juicy, luxurious. Perhaps one of the few whiskies on the market anywhere in the world today which could slake a thirst. *40%*

Forty Creek Barrel Select (86.5) n21.5 t22 f21 b21.5. Thank goodness that the sulphur taint I had found on this in recent years has now vanished. A lush, enjoyable easy-goer, this juices up attractively at the start and ends with an almost sophisticated dry pithiness. *40%*

Forty Creek Confederation Oak Reserve lot 1867-B **(94.5) n23.5 t24 f23.5 b23.5.** Those who tasted the first batch of this will be intrigued by this follow up. The shape and intensity profile has been re-carved and all now fits together like a jigsaw. *40%*

Forty Creek Copper Pot Reserve (91.5) n23 t23.5 f22 b23. One of the beauties of John hall's whiskies at Forty Creek is that they follow no set pattern in the whisky would: they offer flavour profiles really quite different from anything else. That is why they are worth that bit of extra time for your palate to acclimatise. Here you are exceptionally well rewarded... *43%*

Forty Creek Double Barrel Reserve lot 247 **(86) n21.5 t22.5 f20.5 b21.5.** Juicy ride with plenty to savour early on. But something is slightly off balance about the finish. *40%*

Forty Creek Port Wood Reserve lot 61 **(95.5) n24.5** oh my word! Very highest quality Turkish Delight with some pretty top score chocolate; the fruit hangs off the frame full of juice and muscovado sugars. It demands spices...and gets them – with the right pizzazz! **t24** the delivery is pure silk in texture and the most stunning fruit and spice on delivery. Hard to know whether to suck as it melts in the mouth, or chew as the background depth is outrageously nutty, with more cocoa to thicken. It is the astonishing spice that really mesmerises, as it is of almost perfect intensity; **f23** dries into an attractive crushed grape pip dryness, again with the spices lingering; **b24** John P Hall has got his ducks in a row. Magnificent! *45%*

Forty Creek Three Grain (76) n19 t20 f18 b19. Not quite as well assembled as some Three grains I have come across over the last few years. There is a lopsidedness to this one: we know the fruit dominates (and I still haven't a clue why, when surely this of all whiskies, just has to be about the grains!) but the bitterness interferes throughout. If there have been sherry casks used here, I would really have a close look at them. *40%*

Fremont Mischief Whiskey batch MPJ-0803, bott 11 (77) n19 t20 f19 b19. Though this was from the Mischief distillery in Seattle, USA, the whiskey was produced in Canada. Overly sweet, overly toffeed and bereft of complexity. Like Alberta Springs on a very bad day. *40%*

Gibson's Finest Aged 12 Years (77) n18 t20 f19 b20. Unlike the Sterling, going backwards rather than forwards. This is way too syrupy, fruity and toffee impacted. Despite the very good spice, almost closer to a liqueur than a true whisky style. *40%*

Gibson's Finest Rare Aged 18 Years (95.5) n24 close your eyes and sniff and you would swear you have a bourbon-rye mix: simultaneously crisp and soft, the sharpness of the rye and apple-style fruitiness is sublime and as enticing as it gets; **t24.5** and a perfect transfer onto the palate: spectacularly juicy with all kinds of clean rye and corn notes bobbling around in a gorgeous gentle Demerara sugar backdrop; **f23.5** impressive vanilla and long strands of grain and bitter liquorice; **b23.5** so far ahead of both Sterling and the 12, it is hard to believe they are from the same stable. But make no mistake; this is pure thoroughbred: truly world class. *40%*

Gibson's Finest 100th Grey Cup Special Edition (87) n21 t23 f21 b22. When the label tells you there is a hint of maple, they aren't joking... *40%*

Gibson's Finest Canadian Whisky Bourbon Cask Rare Reserve (89) n23 t21 f23 b22. A much better version than the first bottling, the depth this time being massively greater. *40%*

Gibson's Finest Sterling (86.5) n22 t22.5 f20.5 b21.5. A massively improved Canadian that had me doing the equivalent of a tasting double take: had to look twice at this to check I had the right stuff! Much firmer now in all the right places with the corn making sweeping statements, the golden syrup melting into all the required crevices and spices exploding at the appropriate moments. Just need to sort the heavy toffee and bitter finish out and this would be up in the Canadian Premier League. *40%*

Gibson's New Oak (88) n22 t21 f23 b22. Distinctly different from any other Canadian doing the rounds: the oak influence makes a wonderful and clever impact. *40%*

Gooderham & Worts Four Grain blend no. A.A1129 (94) n23 complex. Four grains, indeed! Fruity, as so many Canadians today insist on being. But deeply complex tones abound, each understated and elegant. The rye just about shades it...; **t24** superb! So salivating! Deep and forever interweaving, the sturdier grains flip between offering a crisp fruitiness and a starker spiciness, especially as the wheat strikes home; the muscovado sugars pulse their fruity rhythm; **f23.5** now the wheat dominates as the spices begin to seriously warm up, radiating short, sharp pulses: love it! **b23.5** four there's a jolly good whisky...worts and all...! *44.4%*

Highwood Pure Canadian (84) n20 t21 f22 b21. A decent, ultra-clean Canadian with markedly more character than before. Certainly the caramel has been seriously reduced in effect and the wheat ensures a rather attractive spice buzz while the cane juice sweetness harmonises well. Perhaps most delightful is the wonderful and distinct lack of fruit. *40%*

Hiram Walker Special Old (93) n22.5 t24 f23 b23.5. Even with the extra degree of all-round harmony, this remains the most solid, uncompromising Canadian of them all. And I love it! Not least because this is the way Special old has been for a very long time with obviously no intentions of joining the fruity bandwagon. Honest, first class Canadian. *40%*

James Foxe (77.5) n20 t19.5 f19 b19. James could do with putting some weight on... *40%*

Lot No 40 Malted Rye Whisky (93) n24 t23.5 f22.5 b23 An old friend – almost a long lost son – has returned and has brightened up my glass with colossal Canadianness. This is of a style unique to this country, though here the high levels of oak have perhaps dimmed the flame of the rye slightly. Welcome home, my son...!!! *40%*

Masterson's 10 Year Old Straight Rye batch 003 (96.5) n24 t24 f24 b24.5 A magnificent whisky without any shadow of doubt. Rye is my favourite whisky type and this displays the style to a degree of excellence which is truly memorable in terms of a commercial bottling. Someone has done an outstanding job in selecting these casks. Interesting, however, that they don't actually state on the bottle that this is Canadian and confuse things a little further by spelling it "whiskey". My understanding is that this is unmalted rye from the outstanding Alberta Distillery in Calgary. What is certain is that this is a true classic of its style. And not so much Masterson's but Masterful. *45%*

McGuinness Silk Tassel (79.5) n20 t21 f19.5 b19. Silk or satin? The corn oils offer a delightful sheen but still the caramel is over enthusiastic. *40%*

McLoughlin and Steele Blended in the Okanagan Valley (87.5) n22 t22 f21.5 b22. As straight as a die: a Canadian Rye... without any discernible rye. *40%. McLoughlin and Steele.*

Mountain Rock (87) n22 t20.5 f22.5 b22. Still a soft Canadian cocking a melt-in-the-mouth snook at its name. But this time the fruit is just over anxious to be heard and a degree of its old stability has been eroded. *40%. Kittling Ridge.*

Okanagan Spirits Rye (88.5) n23 t22.5 f21 b22. A crisp, quite beautiful whisky with a youthful strain. Sort the thin finish out and we'd have something to really remember! Not, by the way, a whisky distilled at their new distillery. *40%*

Pendleton 1910 Aged 12 Years Rye (83) n21 t22 f20 b20. Pleasant enough. But if it wasn't for the small degree of spice pepping up this fruitfest, it would be all rather too predictable. *40%*

Pendleton Let'er Buck (91.5) n22.5 t23 f22.5 b23.5. A significantly improved whisky from the ultra-sweet, nigh on syrupy concoction of before. Here the surprisingly complex and sensual grains take star billing, despite the caramel: it almost makes a parody of being Canadian, so unmistakable is the style. For those who affectionately remember Canadian Club from 20-30 years ago, this might bring a moistening of the eye. *40% (80 proof). Hood River Distillers.*

Pendleton Midnight (78) n20 t21 f18 b19. Soft and soothing. But far more rampant fruit than grain. In fact, hard to detect the grain at all... *45% (90 Proof).*

Pike Creek (92) n22 an 'appeeling' nose: orange peel, mostly; **t23.5** so soft on delivery, you are not sure it has even arrived on your palate. The fruit flavours display first before moving into the realms of delicious chocolate mousse; **f23** more mousse, but now without the fruit; **b23.5** a whisky that is more effect over substance, for this really has to be the softest, silkiest world whisky of 2015. And if you happen to like your taste buds being pampered and chocolate is your thing, this Canadian has your name written all over it. *40%*

Pike Creek 10 Years Old finished in port barrels **(80) n21.5 t22.5 f17 b19.** The delivery is the highlight of the show by far as the fruit takes off backed by delicate spices and spongy softness. The nose needs some persuading to get going but when fully warmed, gives a preview of the delivery. The furry finish is a big disappointment, though. *40%*

Potter's Crown (83) n19 t21.5 f21.5 b21. Silky and about the friendliest and most inoffensive whisky on this planet. The dusty aroma and thick, chewy toffee backbone says it all but still impossible not to enjoy! *40%*

Potter's Special Old a blend of 5 to 11 year old rye whisky **(91) n23.5 t23 f22 b22.5.** More Canadian than a hockey punch-up – and, for all the spice, somewhat more gentle, too. *40%*

Rich and Rare (79) n20 t20 f20 b19. Simplistic and soft. One for toffee lovers. *40%*

Rich and Rare Reserve (86.5) n19.5 t21 f23.5 b22.5. Actually does what it says on the tin, certainly as to regard the "Rich" bit. But takes off when the finish spices up and even offers some ginger cake on the finale. Lovely stuff. *40%*

Royal Canadian (87.5) n22 t22.5 f21 b22. Now there's a whisky which is on the up. *40%*

Royal Canadian Small Batch (88) n22 t22.5 f21.5 b22. A big Canadian with a pleasing silk and steel pulse. *40%. Sazerac.*

Royal Reserve (84.5) n19 t22.5 f21.5 b21.5. No question that the delivery is much richer, fresher and entertaining than before with the spices, dovetailing with subtle fruit, ensuring a complexity previously lacking - especially at the death. Frustratingly, the caramel seems to be biting deeper on the nose, which has taken a backward step. A much more enjoyable and satisfying experience, though. *40%*

Royal Reserve Gold (94.5) n24 t23.5 f23 b24. Retains its position as a classy, classy Canadian that is an essay on balance. Don't confuse this with the much duller standard bottling: this has been moulded in recent years into one of the finest – and among its country's consumers - generally most underrated Canadians on the market. *40%*

Sam Barton Aged 5 Years (83.5) n19 t21.5 f22 b21. Sweet session whisky with a lovely maple syrup glow; some complexity on the finish. Friendly, hospitable: impossible not to like. *40%.*

Schenley Golden Wedding (92) n22 t24 f22 b23. Like a rare, solid marriage, this has improved over time. Always consistent and pleasant, there now appears to be a touch of extra age and maturity which has sent the complexity levels up dramatically. Quite sublime. *40%*

Schenley OFC (90) n22 t22.5 f23 b22.5. Notice anything missing from this whisky? Well the 8-year-old age statement has fallen off the label. But this is still a truly superb whisky which would benefit perhaps from toning down the degree of sweetness, but gets away with it in spectacular fashion thanks to those seductive oils. Not as complex as the magnificent old days, but a whisky that would have you demanding a refill nine time out of ten. *40%*

Seagram's Canadian 83 (86.5) n21 t22 f21.5 b22. A vastly improved blend which has drastically cut the caramel to reveal a melt-in-the-mouth, slightly crisp grain. There are some citrusy edges but the buttery vanilla and pleasing bite all go to make for a chic little number. *40%*

Seagram's VO (91) n22 t23.5 f22.5 b23. With a heavy heart I have to announce the king of rye-enriched Canadian, VO, is dead. Long live the corn-dominant VO. Over the years I have seen the old traditional character ebb away: now I have let go and have no option other than to embrace this whisky for what it has become: infinitely better than a couple of years back; not in the same league as a decade ago. But just taking it on face value, credit where credit is due. This is an enjoyably playful affair, full of vanilla-led good intention, corn and complexity. There is even assertive spice when needed and the most delicately fruity edge...though not rye-style. Thoughtfully blended and with no little skill, I am impressed. And look forward to seeing how this develops in future years. A treat which needs time to discover. *40%*

Still Waters Special 1+11 Blend batch 1204, bott 2012 **(92) n23.5 t23 f22.5 b23.** If the boys at Still Waters distillery end up with a whisky as enjoyable as this when theirs has matured, Canadian whisky will have flourished. *40%. 1200 bottles.*

Tangle Ridge Aged 10 Years (69) n18.5 t19.5 f15 b16. Decidedly less in your face than of old, unless you are thinking custard pies. For all the cleaned up aroma and early injection of spiced sultana, the uncompromisingly grim finish remains its usual messy self. An unpleasant reminder as to why I only taste this when it's Bible time... *40%*

Tesco Canadian Whisky (75) n18 t18 f20 b19. Sweet, clean, uninspiring. *40%*

Western Gold Canadian Whisky (91) n23 t23 f22.5 b22.5. Clean and absolutely classic Canadian: you can't ask for much more, really. *40%*

White Owl (77.5) n19 t19.5 f20 b19. White whisky: in others words, a whisky the same colour as water. To both nose and taste somewhat reminds me of the long gone Manx whisky which was casks of fully matured scotch re-distilled and bottled. Sweet and pleasant. But I doubt if connoisseurs will give two hoots... *40%*

Windsor (85.5) n21 t22 f21 b21.5. A whisky you could usually bet your week's wages on for consistency and depth. Here, though, the usual rye fruity, crispness has been dumbed down and though there are enough spices to make this a pleasant affair, the impact of the caramel is a tad too significant. The usual custard sweetness has also changed shape and dry vanilla at the death is the compromise. *40%*

Windsor (86) n20 t21 f23 b22. Pleasant but the majority of edges found on the Canadian edition blunted. Some outstanding, almost attritional, spice towards the middle and finale, though. Soft and desirable throughout: a kind of feminine version of the native bottling. *40%.*

J.P. Wiser's 18 Year Old db **(94) n22.5** dusty, fruity, busy. Soft, fruity sawdust to the sugars; **t24** excellent early bite, though the oils make their mark early. Salivating and silky despite the spice build and a little cocoa to accompany the fruit; **f23.5** comfortable, with a pleasing acceleration of spice; **b24** exceptionally creamy but maintains the required sharpness. *40%.*

J.P. Wiser's De Luxe (86) n20 t22.5 f21.5 b22. Still nothing like the classic, ultra-charming and almost fragile-delicate Wiser's of old. But this present bottling has got its head partly out of the sand by injecting a decently oaked spiciness to the proceedings and one might even fancy detecting shards of fruity- rye brightness beaming through the toffeed clutter. Definitely an impressive turn for the better and the kind of Canadian with a dangerous propensity to grow on you. If they had the nerve to cut the caramel, this could be a cracker... *40%*

J.P. Wiser's Double Still Rye (94) n23.5 the rye is gorgeously crisp, its natural fruity notes augmented by spearmint; **t23.5** every bit as salivating and full-flavoured as the nose predicts. Not as crunchy, maybe, until the Demerara sugars ram themselves home. But the spices arrive in the first few moments and continue building until they become quite a force; **f23.5** long, oily, with that spice still impacting positively; **b23.5** big, superb rye: a genuine triumph from Wiser's. *43.4%*

J.P. Wiser's Hopped Whisky (77) n18 t21 f19 b19. Sorry chaps: one has to draw the line somewhere. But, despite my deep love for great beer, as a whisky this really isn't my kind of thing. Oh, and by the way: been tasting this kind of thing from Germany for the last decade... *40%*

J.P. Wiser's Last Barrels Aged 14 Years (94.5) n24.5 I think I could nose this until the end of time: so complex are the oak notes and the way they merge or interplay with the corn and other grains, it is like watching a dance - a ballet more like – being played out before the nose...; as for the notes you can pick out...more than I have room or time for here. But Turkish delight, green tea, rye and mint are those which perhaps have the most telling influence; **t23.5** a two-toned delivery: sharp grain and sugar against a corn note of quicksand-ish qualities...; **f23.5** long – the corn oils ensure that – with fabulous development of vanilla; **b23.5** you don't need to be pulsing with rye to ensure a complex Canadian of distinction. *45%*

J.P. Wiser's Legacy (95) n24 t24.5 f22.5 b22.5. When my researcher got this bottle for me to taste, she was told by the Wiser's guy that I would love it, as it had been specially designed along the lines of what I considered essential attributes to Canadian whisky. Whether Mr Wiser was serious or not, such a statement both honoured and rankled slightly and made me entirely determined to find every fault with it I could and knock such impertinence down a peg or two. Instead, I was seduced like a 16-year-old virgin schoolboy in the hands of a 30-year-old vixen. An entirely disarming Canadian which is almost a whisky equivalent to the finest of the great French wines in its rich, unfolding style. Complex beyond belief, spiced almost to supernatural perfection, this is one of the great newcomers to world whisky in the last year. It will take a glass of true magnificence to outdo this for Canadian Whisky of the Year. 45%

J.P. Wiser's Red Letter 2014 Release Virgin Oak Finish (91) n22.5 t23.5 f22 b23 Top end Canadian still eschewing the busy grain route of when the brand was reintroduced in favour of a silkier profile. Less well defined but perhaps more easy-drinking for the masses. A letter always worth opening, though. 45%. ncf.

⋙ **J.P. Wiser's Red Letter 2015 Release** Virgin oak finish (90.5) n22.5 pithy fruit, like a mix of grape skins and pips have been introduced to add a dry, intense dimension to the sweeter muscovado and spice. Brave...; t22.5 their softest delivery yet! Too lightweight and soft to be even silky. Corn oils and ulmo honey offer a quicksand into which the heavier fruitier notes sink; f23 ablaze with spice...; b22.5 stubbornly refusing to return to its complex grain past, electing instead to stick to the silky route of more recent years. The sugars are kept in control – just. At times, a little touch and go: this style has been taken as safely as it can go... A backbone to this would be worth so many more points... 43.4%. ncf.

J.P. Wiser's Reserve (75) n19 t20 f18 b18. The nose offers curious tobacco while the palate is uneven, with the bitterness out of tandem with the runaway early sweetness. In the confusion the fruit never quite knows which way to turn. A once mighty whisky has fallen. And I now understand it might be the end of the line with the excellent Wiser's Small Batch coming in to replace it. So if you are a reserve fan, buy them up now. 43%

J.P. Wiser's Rye (84.5) n21 t22 f20.5 b21. Sweet, soft and easy going. The delivery is classic Canadian, with an enjoyable corn oil-vanilla oak mix which initially doesn't go easy on the sugars. The finish, though, is more brittle toffee. 40%

J.P. Wiser's Small Batch (90.5) n21.5 t24 f22 b23. A real oddity with the nose & taste on different planets. The fruity onslaught promised by the drab nose never materialises and instead we are treated to a rich, grainy explosion. It's the spices, though, that take the plaudits. 43.4%

J.P. Wiser's Special Blend (78) n19 t20 f19 b19. A plodding, pleasant whisky with no great desire to offer much beyond caramel. 40%

J.P. Wiser's Spiced Torched Toffee (35) n9 t9 f8 b9 Whisky by name and law. But an absurdly sweet liqueur indeed. As an adorer of true whisky all I can say is this is to Canadian what the Coen brothers' remake of The Ladykillers was to the 1955 Ealing original... 43%

J.P. Wiser's Spiced Whisky Vanilla db (51) n16 t12 f11 b12. The policy of the Whisky Bible is to not accept any spiced distillate as, by definition, being whisky. Only Canadian can escape that ban, as they are allowed to put up to 9.09% of whatever into their spirit and still call it whisky. That does not mean to say I am going to like it, though. And, believe me when I tell you I really can't stand this cloyingly sweet liqueur-like offering. Indeed, it may have "whisky" on the label, but this is about as much that great spirit as I am the next Hollywood pin up. 43%

⋙ **J.P. Wiser's Triple Barrel** (85.5) n22 t21.5 f21 b21. The barrels, whatever their number, appear to be no match for the big caramel theme. 40% (80 proof)

⋙ **WhistlePig 15 Year Old Straight Rye Whiskey** finished in Vermont Estate oak (90) n22 a musky nose, heavy and cumbersome in part. But also a thrilling spiciness at play before the grains become slightly more apparent; t23.5 juicy, crisp and with a barrage of muscovado sugar, moving slowly towards ulmo honey. Every salivating flavour profile is tracked by those warm and busy spices; f22 just a hint of bittering and tiredness. But those muscovado sugars are still clinging on; b22.5 distinctive and delicious. 46% (92 proof)

Canadian Wheat Whisky

Masterson's 12 Year Old Straight Wheat Whiskey batch 001 (92) n23 t23 f22.5 b23.5 Chose this as my 1,000th new whisk(e)y for Jim Murray WB 2015 because a couple of years back I uncorked their Rye...and tasted everything a great Canadian should be: indeed, it was a contender for my World Whisky of that year. Here I have their new wheat bottling. Not the blockbuster the rye bottling was: rye when distilled and matured to its fullest possibilities probably cannot be touched by any other grain. But this is a soft, melodious whisky, perfect for ending any day on a quiet high... 50% WB15/380

Japanese Whisky

How fitting that in the age when the sun never sets on where whisky is produced it is from the land of the Rising Sun that the finest can now be found.

Recently Japan, for the first time ever, won Jim Murray's World Whisky of the Year with its insanely deep and satisfying Yamazaki Sherry Cask(s) 2013, a result which caused predicted consternation among more than a few. And a degree of surprise in Japan itself. The industry followed that up last year by commanding 5th spot with a very different but truly majestic specimen of a malt showing a style unique to Japan. How impressive.

It reminded me of when, about 15 years ago, I took my old mate Michael Jackson and a smattering of non-friends on a tour of the Yoichi distillery on Hokkaido, pointing out to them that here was a place where a malt could be made to mount a serious challenge to the best being made anywhere in the world. While there, a local journalist asked me what Japanese distillers could learn from Scotland. I caused a bit of a sharp intake of breath – and a pathetically gutless but entirely characteristic denial of association by some whisky periodical executive or other who had a clear idea which side his bread was buttered – when I said it was the other way round: it was more what the Scots could learn from the Japanese.

The reason for that comment was simple: the extraordinary attention to detail and tradition that was paid by Japanese distillers, those at Yoichi in particular, and the touching refusal to cut costs and corners. It meant that it was the most expensive whisky in the world per unit of alcohol to produce. But the quality was astonishingly high – and that would, surely, eventually reap its rewards as the world learned to embrace malt whisky made away from the Highlands and islands of Scotland which, then, was still to happen. Ironically, it was the Japanese distillers' habit to ape most things Scottish – the reason why there is a near century-old whisky distilling heritage there in the first place - that has meant that Yoichi, or the magnificent Hakushu, has yet to pick up the Bible's World Whisky of the Year award I expected for them. Because, sadly, there have been too many bottlings over the last decade tainted by sherry butts brought from Spain after having been sulphur treated. So I was also pleasantly surprised when I first nosed – then nosed again in near disbelief – then tasted the Yamazaki 2013 sherry offering. There was not even the vaguest hint that a single one of the casks used in the bottling had been anywhere near a sulphur candle. The result: something as close to single malt perfection as you will have found in a good many years. A single malt which no Scotch can at the moment get anywhere near and, oddly, takes me back to the Macallans of 30 years ago.

A Japanese custom of refusing to trade with their rivals has not helped expand their export market. Therefore a Japanese whisky, if not made completely from home-distilled spirit, will instead contain a percentage of Scotch rather than whisky from fellow Japanese distillers. This, ultimately, is doing the industry no favours at all. The practice is partly down to the traditional work ethics of company loyalty and an inherent, and these days false, belief that Scotch whisky is automatically better than Japanese. Back in the late 1990s I planted the first seeds in trying to get rival distillers to discuss with each other the possibility of exchanging whiskies to ensure that their distilleries worked more economically. So it can only be hoped

Yamazaki

●Osaka

●Fukuoka

Jim Murray's Whisky Bible Japanese Whisky of the Year Winners	
2004	Pure Malt Black
2005	Nikka Single Cask Coffey Grain Whisky 1991
2006	The Cask of Hakusha 1989
2007	Nikka Single Cask Coffey Grain Whisky 1992
2008	Hanyu King of Diamonds
2009	Nikka Single Cask Coffey Grain Whisky 199
2010	TSMWS 116.4
2011	Karuizawa 1967 Vintage
2012	Hibiki Aged 21 Years
2013	Hanyu Final Vintage 2000
2014	SMWS Cask 116.17 (Yoichi) 25
2015	Yamazaki Single Malt Sherry 13
2016	Yamazaki Mizunara
2017	Yamazaki Single Malt Sherry 16

that the deserved lifting of the 2015 Jim Murray's Whisky Bible World Whisky of the Year crown, and the hitherto unprecedented international press it received coming from the east. Because unless you live in Japan, you are likely to see only a fraction of the fabulous whisky produced there. The Scotch Malt Whisky Society should have a special medal struck as they have helped in recent years with some memorable bottlings from Japan, single cask snapshots of the greatness that is still to be be fully explored and mapped. A two-pronged attack would be useful: one by whisky outlets to actively track down and stock the widest Japanese stock they can afford, though because of the clamour for all things Yamazaki this now at last appears to be hapening. And the distillers themselves, always on the conservative side of marketing, probably through a misplaced lack of belief, show us what they have.

And I don't mean just with malts. Because, even better still would be if the outside world could have at last access to the higher class blends produced there. But the Japanese whisky industry have themselves been slow coming forward. Just perhaps, with Yamazaki atop the world's whisky very own Mount Fuji, there are the first signs that they are at last ready to unleash upon us those hidden, majestic whiskies of Japan.

Single Malts
CHICHIBU

Chichibu 'On The Way' dist 2010 bott 2013 db (93) n23.5 t24 f22.5 b23. A malt which has already travelled far... 58.50%.

Chichibu 'The Peated' 2013 dist 2010 bott 2013 db (96.5) n24.5 t24.5 f23 b24.5 Clean, elegant, does exactly what it says on the tin...and a lot, lot more besides... 53.5%.

Chichubu Port Pipe dist 2009 bott 2013 db (66) n17 t18 f15 b16. A port pipe in an awful, off-key storm. 54.5%. Number One Drinks Company.

⬩ **ePower Chichibu Double Barrel** Mizunara heads hogshead & hard charred new barrels, dist 2012, bott 2015 (88) n21.5 off key: the various tones cannot find their own pitch...; t23.5 so enormous is the delivery, it is hard to know where to start. Probably the explosion of oak, which then leads to a stupendous sigh of varying sugars, though mainly differing muscovado types; f21 the discord on the nose is mirrored on the finish as it bitters out; b22 were it not for the spices, the sugars might have proved a little too much. Though not always hitting quite the right notes, this is big, profound malt. 61.1%

⬩ **Ichiro's Malt Chichibu Chibidaru** dist 2010, bott 2014 db (92) n22.5 husky malt: thick set with a mix of leather, dates and barley; t23.5 serious sugars arrive in an initial wave of dark muscovado; major oils ensure a big chewy depth; f23 long, as a malt with this amount of oil and sugar just must be; back to a few dried dates now, too. Lovely stuff...perfect for a cold night or even, perhaps, if you have a cold...; b23 this distillery certainly understands the meaning of "intense"... 53.5%. Number One Drinks Company.

Ichiro's Malt Chichibu Floor Malted 2009 (85.5) n22 t22.5 f20 b21. Big, pre-pubescent malt and barley statement, but barely in unison. Bitterness on the finish is unchecked. 50.5%.

Ichiro's Chichibu Peated 2009 (91.5) n23 t23.5 f22 b23. You can stand your chopsticks up in this one...works so beautifully in so many department. 50.5%

⬩ **Ichiro's Malt Chichibu Peated 2015** dist 2010, bott 2015 db (95) n23.5 so young and gristy! Yet meticulously clean and, with its light citrus touch, aligned in style to the south Islay malts; t24 or with this degree of oil, Caol lla....wow! f23.5 long, with the gristy sugars working a long rhythmic magic. The smoke remains intense; b24 had I tasted this blind, I would have mistaken it for an Islay. Quite sublimely made malt. As astonishing as it is beautiful... 62.5%. Number One Drinks Company.

Number One Asama 1999/2000 (71) n17 t19 f16 b19. Sulphured. 46%

FUJI GOTEMBA 1973. Kirin Distillers.

The Fuji Gotemba 15 Years Old db (92) n21 t23 f24 b24. Quality malt of great poise. 43%. Kirin.

HAKUSHU 1973. Suntory.

Hakushu Single Malt Whisky Aged 12 Years db (91.5) n22.5 t23.5 f22.5 b23. About identical to the 43.3% bottling. Please see those tasting notes for this little beauty. 43.5%

Hakushu Single Malt Aged 12 Years db (91) n22 t23 f23 b23. An even more lightly-peated version of the 40%, with the distillery's fabulous depth on full show. 43.3%

The Hakushu Single Malt Whisky Aged 15 Years Cask Strength db (95) n24 t23 f24 b24. Last time round I lamented the disappointing nose. This time perhaps only a degree of over eagerness from the oak has robbed this as a serious Whisky of the Year contender. No matter how you look at it, though, brilliant!! 56%

The Hakushu Single Malt Whisky Aged 25 Years db (93) n23 t24 f23 b23. A malt which is impossible not to be blown away by. 43%

The Hakushu Single Malt Whisky Sherry Cask bott 2014 db (96.5) n24.5 there we have it: a masterclass in what clean, untainted sherry butts are all about. A thousand levels of fruit intensity without a single off note – or even peculiar but unmistakable background hint of an off note which points to a sulphur problem at the very end of a whisky - when nearly all the other flavours have vanished. It is not there. The only problem, being over picky, is that the character of the distillery itself is hard to locate: the concentrated dates, plums and raisins, topped, naturally, with warming spice, means the malt itself has vanished somewhat...; t24 there we go. Find a comfortable chair for this one...it is going to take a very long time. Wave upon wave of fruitiness, all of varying degrees of intensity, roll and then crash over the palate. In its quiet moments, that's the odd toasted honeycomb mingling with butterscotch and vanilla bits – something other than fruit are apparent...; f24 long, elegant, gorgeously clean...but even more late toasted raisin...; **b24** theoretically, this should have been World Whisky of the Year. After all, Yamazaki – a distillery I regard as very slightly eclipsed in quality by Hakushu – won it last year using, like this, strictly unsulphured sherry butts. This is magnificent. One of the great whiskies of the year, for sure. However, the intensity of the grape has just strayed over that invisible line by a few molecules between being a vital cog and a shade too dominant. It is the finest of lines between genius and exceptional brilliance. *48%. ncf.*

Scotch Malt Whisky Society Cask 120.7 Aged 14 Years 1st fill Bota Corta, dist 30 Sept 99 **(95.5) n24 t25 f22.5 b24** If I ever developed a twitch, it will be from being told I am about to taste a whisky matured in some wine cask or other: over the years it has about the same effect as when Herbert Lom was told he would have to spend time with Inspector Clouseau. Here, though, my fears were unfounded. Over-aged for sure, but otherwise sweet as a nut. So good and so big, it is almost terrifying... *55.5%. sc. 517 bottles.*

Scotch Malt Whisky Society Cask 120.8 Aged 13 Years 2nd fill hogshead, dist 31 Dec 00 **(85.5) n21 t23 f20 b21.5**. Some typical Hakushu flourishes but done down by a disappointing cask which added too much tired tang than is appreciated. Unusually salty and sharp, this should have been destined for a blend. *63.1%. sc. 250 bottles.*

Suntory Pure Malt Hakushu Aged 20 Years db **(94) n23 t24 f23 b24**. A hard-to-find malt, but find it you must. Yet another huge nail in the coffin of those who purport Japanese whisky to be automatically inferior to Scotch. *56%*

HANYU

Ichiro's Malt Aged 20 Years (95.5) n24 t24 f23.5 b24. No this finish; no that finish. Just the distillery allowed to speak in its very own voice. And nothing more eloquent has been heard from it this year. Please, all those owning casks of Hanyu: for heaven's sake take note... *57.5%.*

Ichiro's Malt Aged 23 Years (92.5) n23 t23.5 f23 b23. A fabulous malt you take your time over. *58%*

KARUIZAWA 1955. Mercian.

Karuizawa Pure Malt Aged 17 Years db **(90) n20 t24 f23 b23**. Brilliant whisky beautifully made and majestically matured. Neither sweetness nor dryness dominates, always the mark of a quality dram. *40%*

The Spirit Of Asama sherry cask **(71.5) n17 t19 f17 b18.5**. Sulphur hit. *48%.*

The Spirit Of Asama sherry cask **(75) n18 t20 f18 b19**. Lots of sultanas. Sweet. Pleasant in part. But it isn't just Scotland suffering from poor sherry butts. *55%.*

Scotch Malt Whisky Society Cask 132.6 Aged 12 Years refill butt. diss 32 Dec 2000. **(84.5) n21 t23 f19 b21.5**. Fabulous delivery. Surprisingly youthful in some ways, with echoes of a new make maltiness, but there is a vividity to the barley which really deserves better than the nose appears a little perfunctory and dull and a finish which is disappointingly tangy. *63% nc ncf sc.*

KIRIN

Kirin 18 Years Old db **(86.5) n22 t22 f21.5 b21**. Unquestionably over-aged. Even so, still puts up a decent show with juicy citrus trying to add a lighter touch to the uncompromising, ultra dense oak. As entertaining as it is challenging. *43%. Suntory.*

KOMAGATAKE

Komagatake 1992 Single Cask American white oak cask, cask no. 1144, dist 1992, bott 2009 db **(93.5) n24.5 t23 f22.5 b23.5**. You know when you've had a glass of this: beautiful and no shrinking violet. *46%. Mars.*

MIYAGIKYO *(see Sendai)*

NIKKA *(Coffey Still)*

Nikka Whisky Single Coffey Malt 12 Years db **(97) n23.5 t25 f24 b24.5**. The Scotch Whisky Association would say that this is not single malt whisky because it is made in a Coffey still. When they can get their members to make whisky this stunning on a regular basis via their own pots and casks, then perhaps they should pipe up as their argument might then have a single atom of weight. *55%*

Scotch Malt Whisky Society Cask G12.1 Aged 11 Years re-charred hogshead, dist 6 Mar 03 (89.5) n22.5 whisky? Or toffee candy...? t23 silky-soft with only a nod towards the barley. Instead we are treated to the cream toffee and fudge; a short burst of spice offers some welcome pep; f22 more lightweight cream toffee; b22 coming via a Coffey still, the malt has been distilled to a high strength leaving more room to emphasis the barrel influence. The high degree of toffee shows it is mission accomplished. 58.9%. sc. 246 bottles.

SENDAI 1969. Nikka.

Scotch Malt Whisky Society Cask 124.4 Aged 17 Years 1st fill butt, dist 22 Aug 96 (94) n24 where do you start with the fruit, apart from prize Melton Hunt Cake? Certainly the dates are juicy and the sultanas a little burnt. I think there is some oak in there somewhere...; t24 brilliant delivery with sublime bitter-sweet toasty-roasty delivery. Yes, there is oak there, and it comes up as hickory straight after the burnt raisin on delivery; f23 still toasted – burnt toast, in fact. But with a plum jam (that's gone easy on the sugar) covering it thickly; b23 if there is a complaint to be made, it is that, at times, one might forget that this is a whisky at all, resembling instead a glass of highest quality oloroso. 60%. sc. 479 bottles.

Scotch Malt Whisky Society Cask 124.5 Aged 23 Years 1st fill hogshead, dist 12 Dec 90 (96) n23.5 countless layers: the majority oak-based, but so many hues and tones, ranging from chalky to sub-bourbon; big dry dates to spicy fruitcake – without the fruit but with plenty of molasses; t24.5 hold on tight: molasses concentrate has been dipped in tannin juice. Somehow, while the spices pepper you and the oak makes you draw breath, barley pops up out of nowhere for a juicy interlude...; f24 time and time again you think it is going OTT with the oak, then those molasses notes, as well as dark chocolate, intervene...brinkmanship of the sexiest kind...; b24 this isn't just how to grow old gracefully, but with style while making one hell of a statement! 66.7%. sc. 142 bottles.

SHINSHU MARS

Mars Whisky Single Malt Komagatake Sherry & American White Oak 2011 db (79.5) n19 t22 f18.5 b20. My heart bleeds, as the high class – and intensity – of the malt is outstanding. Sadly, the sherry butt does not match the excellence of the distillate and results in a Mars that is slightly out of orbit... 57%

SHIRAKAWA

Shirakawa 32 Years Old Single Malt (94) n23 t24 f23 b24. Just how big can an unpeated malt whisky get? The kind of malt that leaves you in awe, even when you thought you had seen and tasted them all. 55%. Takara.

WHITE OAK DISTILLERY

White Oak Akashi Single Malt Whisky Aged 8 Years bott 2007 db (74.5) n18.5 t19.5 f17.5 b19. Always fascinating to find a malt from one of the smaller distilleries in a country. And I look forward to tracking this one down and visiting, something I have yet to do. There is certainly something distinctly small still about his one, with butyric and feintiness causing damage to nose and finish. For all the early malty presence on delivery, some of the off notes are a little on the uncomfortable side. 40%

YAMAZAKI 1923. Suntory.

The Yamazaki Single Malt Whisky Aged 12 Years bott 2011 db (90) n23 t22 f22.5 b22.5. A complex and satisfying malt. 43%

The Yamazaki Single Malt Aged 18 Years db (96) n23 a sublime blend of Java and Sumatra coffees, enriched by vanilla and even toastier tannins. The sugars, a mix of treacle and maple syrup try not to steal the show, but nearly do...; t24.5 oh, oh, oh...!!!! Possibly the softest yet most compelling delivery this year: the grape is doused in busy, ever intensifying spice, the toasty vanillas in those subtle sugars spotted on the nose. Overripe plums, juicy dates, stewed prunes...and all the time the spice buzzes, the sugars salivate; f24 long, with just a slow wind down of the previously intense fruit notes. The juices just keep on gushing, but met almost perfectly with toasty, slightly milky mocha notes; the final strands are praline wafer...with chocolate fruit and nut, too; b24.5 for its strength, probably one of the best whiskies in the world. And one of the most brilliantly and sexily balanced, too... All told, one glass is equal to about 45 minutes of sulphur-free satisfaction... 43%

Suntory Pure Malt Yamazaki 25 Years Old db (91) n23 t23 f22 b23. Being matured in Japan, the 25 years doesn't have quite the same value as Scotland. So perhaps in some ways this can lay claim to be one of the most enormously aged, oak-laden whiskies that has somehow kept its grace and star quality. 43%

The Yamazaki Single Malt Whisky Mizunara Japanese oak cask, bott 2014 db (97) n25 the unmistakable and one off aroma of Japanese oak: a form of slightly aggressive bourbon where the spices are as busy as the light liquorice and hickory. But the malt has a massive presence, though you have to look for it first. The sugars are typically crisp for this style of oak and there is something of the Malteser chocolate candy about this, too: absolutely unique; t24 the sugars ram home first – a peculiar mix of crystallised heather and ulmo honey with molasses – but the sweetness immediately limited by the more toffeed and tannic qualities of the intense oak. Polite spices are not too far behind and they, too, have a vaguely American quality, only a little more prickly. A delicate oil ensures the sugars cover as much distance as possible; f23.5 late on, the spices pulse a backdrop to the vaguely bittering oak; b24.5 no other malt offers this flavour profile. And as there are now very few Japanese oak casks still in the industry it is a malt worthy of as long a time as you can afford it. A very special whisky of very high quality. 48%

The Yamazaki Single Malt Whisky Puncheon bott 2013 db (87) n22 t22 f21 b22. Not to be confused with former Millwall footballer Jason Puncheon who scored a hat-trick against Crystal Palace a couple of years back. Does not possess his guile, balance or explosive finish. Even so, a pleasant dram even if you'd like to see it do more than just offer a sugary glow offset by some half decent spices. 48%. ncf. WB15/179

The Yamazaki Single Malt Whisky Sherry Cask bott 2013 db (97.5) n24.5 when they say sherry, they are not joking: huge oloroso signature, nutty, thick, dry as rounded as a snooker ball. A nose that was not uncommon in the warehouses of Scotland three decades ago, but now as rare as...well, an unsulphured sherry butt...; t24.5 every bit as silky as the nose promises. The sugars, spices, plum walnut cake and moist Melton Hunt Cake combine for something rather special; f24 long, juicy dates, more walnuts, sultanas as big as a small planet...a light, teasing spice; b24.5 one of the first sherry casks I have seen from Japan not in any way, shape or form touched by sulphur for a very long time. It is as if the oloroso cask was still half filled with the stuff when they filled with Yamakazi spirit. If anyone wants to find out roughly what the first Macallan 10-year-old I had in 1975 tasted like, then grab a bottle of this... 48%. ncf. WB15/180

⟐ **Yamazaki Single Malt Sherry Cask 2016 Edition** db (96.5) n24.5 I was thinking: "I could nose this all day"...about half an hour ago... The richest, cleanest, most intense sherry with just enough tannin to poke its way through and ensure a more solid, spicy platform around which the bounteous fruit can hang; t24 dense, both from the rich, full-bodied distillate as well as the sherry concentrate. Imagine a fruitcake reduced and reduced again and then you have some idea what is going on here: there is not just intense grape at work but juicy dates, over-ripe figs and molasses enough to power a W C Fields sketch....; f24 not sure where the middle ends and the finish begins. Certainly dries as the tannins gather further momentum but always frust residue, withered and intense, is in close company; b24 a work of art. The oils, though, are markedly younger in style than the imperious 2013 edition. 48%

The Yamazaki Single Malt Whisky db (86) n22 t22 f21 b21. A tame, malty affair which, after the initial barley burst on delivery, plays safety first. 43%

Scotch Malt Whisky Society Cask 119.13 Aged 10 Years 1st fill barrel, dist 31 May 03 (94) n23 Brazil nut oil and toasted hazelnuts...getting the picture? t23.5 crisp muscovado sugar met head on by intense, peppery spice and caramelised biscuit; f24 at last the malt filters through...but still with a spicy guard. The tannins begin to get a bit toasty; b23.5 excellent distillate in a quality cask: can't go wrong! 60.2%. sc. 149 bottles.

Scotch Malt Whisky Society Cask 119.14 Aged 11 Years 1st fill Bota Corta, dist 30 Apr 03 (96.5) n24 big coffee overture...hang on, am I in Japan or Guyana here? This is virtually rum in style...! t24.5 more of the same: big fruit beginnings, juicy with a mix of dates and prunes. But in comes that Demerara spicy coffee kick...with toasty tannins drying out the middle ground; f24 ridiculously long. And with the fruit and coffee interweaving. Each time it looks like getting too bitter, somehow those sugars intervene...amazing! b24 tasted blind, I probably would have mistaken this for a the very highest quality – and very old - pot still Demerara rum. 53.9%. sc. 538 bottles.

YOICHI 1934. Nikka.

Yoichi Key Malt Aged 12 Years "Peaty & Salty" db (95) n23 t25 f23 b24. Of all the peated whiskies of the world, only Ardbeg can stand shoulder to shoulder with Yoichi when it comes to sheer complexity. Here is an astonishing example of why I rate Yoichi in the best five whiskies in the world. Forget the odd sulphur-tarnished bottling. Get Yoichi in its natural state with perfect balance between oak and malt and it delivers something approaching perfection. And this is just such a bottling. 55%. Nikka.

Yoichi 15 Years Old batch 06I08B db (**91.5**) n22 t23.5 f23 b23. For an early moment or two possibly one of the most salivating whiskies you'll get your kisser around this year. Wonderfully entertaining yet you still suspect that this is another Yoichi reduced in effect somewhat by either caramel and/or sherry. When it hits its stride, though, becomes a really busy whisky that gets tastebuds in a right lather. But I'm being picky as I know that this is one of the world's top five distilleries and am aware as anyone on this planet of its extraordinary capabilities. Great fun; great whisky – could be better still, but so much better than its siblings... 45%

Yoichi 20 Years Old db (**95**) n23 t23 f25 b24. I don't know how much they charge for this stuff but either alone or with mates get some for one hell of an experience. What makes it all the more remarkable is that there is a slight sulphury note on the nose: once you taste the stuff that becomes of little consequence. 52%. Nikka.

Scotch Malt Whisky Society Cask 116.17 Aged 25 Years First fill sherry butt, dist 20 Mar 1987, bott Sep 2012 (**96**) n24.5 t24.5 f23 b24. Not as mouth-puckering as I expected from the nose. This amazing this incredible celebration of all things oak works memorably well. 59.2%. nc ncf sc. 485 bottles.

Scotch Malt Whisky Society 116.18 Aged 18 Years refill butt, dist 2 Feb 94 (**89**) n23 t23 f21 b22. Not one of the truly great Yoichis in its traditional style but a salty, oaky beast of a malt. 64.4%. nc ncf sc. 410 bottles.

Scotch Malt Whisky Society Cask 116.19 Aged 20 Years virgin oak puncheon, dist 2 Feb 94 (**92**) n23 so much bourbon-style honey...the oak influence is majestic; t23.5 fizzing tannins scorch the palate. But those sublime sugars – the manuka honey in particular – kiss everything better; f22.5 bitters very slightly as those tannins take a stranglehold; b23 huh! Just shows what happens when you don't concentrate. Poured the whisky, half noticing the colour. Expected a big blast of sherry (or something adjacent and pretty unpleasant) and got this enormous kick of bourbon. Beautiful: suits the distillery style perfectly. 61.3%. sc.

Scotch Malt Whisky Society Cask 116.20 Aged 26 Years virgin oak puncheon, dist 7 Nov 87 (**82.5**) n20 t22 f20 b20.5. I'm sure some people will do cartwheels to celebrate this no holds barred malt. For me, simply too old: when you get this degree of eucalyptus on the nose and finish, it has gone way beyond its best before date. Decent sugars briefly on delivery and burnt ones at the death, plus the odd phenolic moment. But more like an over aged rum. 61.6%. sc.

Vatted Malts

All Malt (**86**) n22 t21 f21 b22. The best example by a mile of an almost unique style of vatted whisky: both malt and "grain" are distilled from entirely malted barley, identical to Kasauli malt whisky in India. Stupendous grace and balance. 40%. Nikka.

All Malt "Pure & Rich" (**89**) n22 t24 f21 b22. Not unlike some bottlings of Highland Park with its emphasis on honey. If they could tone down the caramel it'd really be up there. 40%. Nikka.

Hokuto Pure Malt Aged 12 Years (**86**) n20 t22 f22 b22. An oaky threat never materialises: excellent mixing. 40%. Suntory.

Ichiro's Malt Double Distilleries bott 2010 (**86.5**) n22.5 t22 f21 b21. Some imperious barley-rich honey reigns supreme until a bitter wood note bites hard. 46%. Venture Whisky Ltd.

Ichiro's Malt Mizunara Wood Reserve (**76**) n19 t21 f18 b19. I have my Reservations about the Wood, too... 46%. Venture Whisky Ltd.

Malt Club "Pure & Clear" (**83**) n21 t22 f20 b20. Another improved vatting, much heavier and older than before with bigger spice. 40%. Nikka.

Mars Maltage Pure Malt 8 Years Old (**84**) n20 t21 f21 b22. A very level, intense, clean malt with no peaks or troughs, just a steady variance in the degree of sweetness and oak input. Impossible not to have a second glass of. 43%. Mars.

Nikka Malt 100 The Anniversary Aged 12 Years (**73**) n18 t19 f18 b18. The depressing and deadly fingerprint of sulphur is all over this. Shame, as the spices excel. 40%

Nikka Pure Malt Aged 21 Years batch 08I18D db (**89**) n23 t22.5 f21.5 b22. By far the best of the set. 43%

Nikka Pure Malt Aged 17 Years batch 08I30B db (83) n21 t21 f20 b21. A very similar shape to the 12-years-old, but older - obviously. Certainly the sherry butts have a big say and don't always do great favours to the high quality spirit. 43%

Nikka Pure Malt Aged 12 Years batch 10I24C db (84) n21.5 t21 f20 b21.5 The nose may be molassed, sticky treacle pudding, but it spices up on the palate. The dull buzz on the finish also tells a tale. 40%

Pure Malt Black batch 02C58A (95) n24 t23 f23 b25. Well, if anyone can show me a better-balanced whisky than this you know where to get hold of me. You open a bottle of this at your peril: best to do so in the company of friends. Either way, it will be empty before the night is over. 43%. Nikka.

Pure Malt Black batch 06F54B (92) n24 t24 f21 b23. Not the finish of old, but everything else is present and correct for a cracker! 43%. Nikka.

Pure Malt Red batch 02C30B (86) n21 t21 f22 b22. A light malt that appears heavier than it actually is with an almost imperceptible oiliness. 43%. Nikka.

Pure Malt Red batch 06F54C (84) n21 t22 f20 b21. Oak is the pathfinder here, but the oily vanilla-clad barley is light and mouth-watering. 43%. Nikka.

Pure Malt White batch 02C30C (92) n23 t24 f22 b23. A big peaty number displaying the most subtle of hands. 43%. Nikka.

Pure Malt White batch 06J26 (91) n22 t23 f22 b24. A sweet malt, but one with such deft use of peat and oak that one never really notices. Real class. 43%

Pure Malt White batch 10F46C (90) n23 t23 f22 b22. There is a peculiarly Japanese feel to this delicately peated delight. 43%

Southern Alps Pure Malt (93) n24 t23 f22 b24. This is a bottle I have only to look at to start salivating. Sadly, though, I drink sparingly from it as it is a hard whisky to find, even in Japan. Fresh, clean and totally stunning, the term "pure malt" could not be more apposite. Fabulous whisky: a very personal favourite. 40%. Suntory.

Suntory Pure Malt Whisky Kiyosato Field Ballet 25th Anniversary (88) n23.5 gentle: over-ripe plums, green apple and red liquorice; t22.5 the malt surges on delivery for a very sharp introduction; soon calms down with a vague Indian candy sweetness and a more assertive bourbon style; goes tits up as the end approaches; f20 an annoying tang as the balance is compromised; b22 so frustrating: a whisky destined for greatness is side-tracked by some off-kilter casks. 48%

Super Nikka Vatted Pure Malt (76) n20 t19 f19 b18. Decent and chewy but something doesn't quite click with this one. 55.5%. Nikka.

Taketsuru Pure Malt 12 Years Old (80) n19 t22 f19 b20. For its age, heavier than a sumo wrestler. But perhaps a little more agile over the tastebuds. Lovely silkiness impresses, but lots of toffee. 40%. Nikka.

Taketsuru Pure Malt 17 Years Old (89) n21 t22 f23 b23 Not a whisky for the squeamish. This is big stuff – about as big as it gets without peat or rye. No bar shelf or whisky club should be without one. 43%. Nikka.

Taketsuru Pure Malt 21 Years Old (88) n22 t21 f22 b23. A much more civilised and gracious offering than the 17 year old: there is certainly nothing linear about the character development from Taketsuru 12 to 21 inclusive. Serious whisky for the serious whisky drinker. 43%. Nikka.

Zen (84) n19 t22 f22 b21. Sweet, gristy malt; light and clean. 40%. Suntory.

Japanese Single Grain
CHITA

Scotch Malt Whisky Society Cask G13.1 Aged 4 Years virgin oak puncheon, dist 31 Oct 10 (83) n22 t22 f19 b20. The first commercial bottling from this excellent grain distillery I have ever seen outside Japan. Sadly, though, hardly representative of many of the outstanding samples I have encountered in the tasting lab over the years, with some poor oak undermining the embracing softness of the grain itself. 58.3%. sc. 622 bottles.

Suntory Single Grain Chita Distillery db (92.5) n23.5 one of the typical characteristics of this distillery's nose, indeed its overall character, is its unusual ability to appear soft and yielding yet with a rod of iron at the very same time. It is this dual personality that can be both a blessing from heaven and a curse when blending. But as a single grain it works a treat as the complexity levels are upped immediately, allowing the vaguely bitter-sweet grain and oaks to perform their various tricks; maple syrup also lends a helping hand; t23 just like the nose, there is a bipolar feel to the shape of this grain, the delivery consumed by soft oils, yet a far more rigid note apparent, to which the oak appears to attach. The sugars – or light honey to be more precise – is in line with the silkier oils; **f22.5** soft oils persist but the oak turns a little bitter; **b23** now that's more like it! Far more down the track of the Chita I have tasted through the years than the SMWS bottling. Then again, this is the brand new official distillery version, so perhaps no surprises there... *43%. Available only in Nagoya Prefecture, Japan.*

KAWASAKI

Kawasaki Single Grain sherry butt, dist 1982, bott 2011 db **(95.5) n23.5 t24 f24 b24** My usual reaction to seeing the words "sherry" and "whisky" when in the context of Japanese whisky, is to feel the heart sinking like the sun. Sulphur is a problem that is no stranger to their whiskies. This, however, is a near perfect sherry butt, clean and invigorating. Grain or malt, it makes no difference: excellent spirit plus excellent cask equals (as often as not) magnificence. *65.5%.*

NIKKA

Nikka Coffey Grain Whisky db **(94.5) n24** molten muscovado sugar; **t24.5** soft oils carry the thinned golden syrup aloft. Almost a semi-liqueur, but with that indefinable whiskyness which sets it apart..; **f22.5** the slight bitterness of the cask jolts the serenity of the oily sugars; **b23.5** whisky, from any part of the globe, does not come more soft or silky than this... *45% WB15/401*

Scotch Malt Whisky Society Cask G11.1 Aged 14 Years re-charred hogshead, dist 1 Dec 99 **(94) n24** a delicious blend of creamy toffee and toasty, bourbon-style liquorice/hickory mix; **t23.5** huge delivery of intense, vanilla-daubed dark sugars – muscovado principally – with even a touch of treacle; **f23** the spices which had begun to form earlier are now in their element; **b23.5** an altogether more rousing experience than the Nikka Coffey Still malt, not least thanks to the big bourbon input and first grade spices. Brilliant! *576%. sc. 190 bottles.*

Blends

Black Nikka Aged 8 Years (82) n20 t21 f21 b20. Beautifully bourbony, especially on the nose. Lush, silky and great fun. Love it! 40%. Nikka.

The Blend of Nikka (90) n21 t23 f22 b24. An adorable blend that makes you sit up and take notice of every enormous mouthful. Classy, complex, charismatic and brilliantly balanced. 45%

Evermore (90) n22 t23 f22 b23. Top-grade, well-aged blended whisky with fabulous depth and complexity that never loses its sweet edge despite the oak. 40%. Kirin.

Ginko (78.5) n20.5 t20 f19 b19. Soft – probably too soft as it could do with some shape and attitude to shrug off the caramel. 46%. Number One Drinks Company.

Golden Horse Busyuu Deluxe (93) n22 t24 f23 b24. Whoever blended this has a genuine feel for whisky: a classic in its own right and one of astonishing complexity and textbook balance. 43%. Toa Shuzo. To celebrate the year 2000.

Hibiki (82) n20 t19 f23 b20. The grains here are fresh, forceful and merciless, the malts bouncing off them meekly. Lovely cocoa finish. A blend that brings a tear to the eye. Hard stuff – perfect after a hard day! Love it! 43%. Suntory.

Hibiki 50.5 Non Chillfiltered 17 Years Old (84) n22 t22 f20 b20. Pleasant enough in its own right. But against what this particular expression so recently was, hugely disappointing. Last year I lamented the extra use of caramel. This year it has gone through the roof, taking with it all the fineness of complexity that made this blend exceptional. Time for the blending lab to start talking to the bottling hall and sort this out. I want one of the great whiskies back...!! 50.5%. Suntory.

Hibiki Aged 30 Years (88) n21 t22 f22 b23. Still remains a very different animal from most other whiskies you might find: the smoke may have vanished somewhat but the sweet oakiness continues to draw its own unique map. 43%

Hokuto (86) n22 t24 f19 b21. A bemusing blend. At its peak, this is quite superb, cleverly blended whisky. The finish, though, suggests a big caramel input. If the caramel is natural, it should be tempered. If it is added for colouring purposes, then I don't see the point of having the whisky non-chillfiltered in the first place. 50.5%. ncf. Suntory.

Imperial (81) n20 t22 f19 b20. Flinty, hard grain softened by malt and vanilla but toffee dulled. 43%. Suntory.

Kakubin (92) n23 t23 f22 b24. Absolutely brilliant blend of stunningly refreshing and complex character. One of the most improved brands in the world. 40%. Suntory.

Kakubin Kuro 43° (89) n22 t23 f22 b22. Big, chewy whisky with ample evidence of old age but such is the intrusion of caramel it's hard to be entirely sure. *43%. Suntory.*

Kakubin New (90) n21 t24 f21 b24. Seriiously divine blending: a refreshing dram of the top order. *40%.*

Kirin Whisky Tarujuku 50° (93) n22.5 t24 f23 b23.5. A blend not afraid to make a statement and does so boldly. A sheer joy. *50%. Kirin Distillery Co Ltd.*

Master's Blend Aged 10 Years (87) n21 t23 f22 b21. Chewy, big and satisfying. *40%.*

New Kakubin Suntory *(see Kakubin New)*

Nikka Master Blend Blended Whisky 12 Years Old 70th Anniversary (94) n24 t23 f24 b23. An awesome blend swimming in top quality sherry. Perhaps a fraction too much sweetness on the arrival, but I am nit-picking. A blend for those who like their whiskies to have something to say. And this one just won't shut up. *58%. Nikka.*

Nikka Whisky Tsuru Aged 17 Years (94) n23 t24 f23 b24. Unmistakingly Tsuru in character, very much in line, profile-wise, with the original bottling and if the caramel was cut this could challenge as a world whisky of the year. *43%*

Robert Brown (91) n22.5 t23 f22.5 b23. Just love these clean but full-flavoured blends: a real touch of quality here. *43%. Kirin Brewery Company Ltd.*

Royal 12 Years Old (91) n23 t23 f22 b23. A splendidly blended whisky with complexity being the main theme. Beautiful stuff that appears recently to have, with the exception of the nose, traded smoke for grape. *43%*

Royal Aged 15 Years (95) n25 t24 f22 b24. Unquestionably one of the great blends of the world that can be improved only by a reduction of toffee input. Sensual blending that every true whisky lover must experience: a kind of Japanese Old Parr 18. *43%*

Shirokaku (79) n19 t21 f20 b19. Some over-zealous toffee puts a cap on complexity. Good spices, though. *40%. Suntory.*

Special Reserve 10 Years Old (94) n23 t24 f23 b24. A beguiling whisky of near faultless complexity. Blending at its peak. *43%. Suntory.*

Special Reserve Aged 12 Years (89) n21 t24 f21 b23. A tactile, voluptuous malt that wraps itself like a sated lover around the tastebuds, though the complexity is compromised very slightly by bigger caramel than the 10-y-o. *40%. Suntory.*

Suntory Old (87) n21 t24 f20 b22. A delicate and comfortable blend that just appears to have over-simplified itself on the finale. Delicious, but can be much better than this. *40%*

Suntory Old Mild and Smooth (84) n19 t22 f21 b22. Chirpy and lively around the palate, the grains soften the crisp malts wonderfully. *40%*

Suntory Old Rich and Mellow (91) n22 t23 f23 b23. A pretty malt-rich blend with the grains offering a fat base. Impressive blending. *43%*

Super Nikka (93) n23 t23 f23 b24. A very, very fine blend which makes no apology whatsoever for the peaty complexity of Yoichi malt. Now, with less caramel, it's pretty classy stuff. However, Nikka being Nikka you might find the occasional bottling that is entirely devoid of peat, more honeyed and lighter in style (21-22-23-23 Total 89 – no less a quality turn, obviously). Either way, an absolutely brilliant day-to-day, anytime, any place dram. One of the true 24-carat, super nova commonplace blends not just in Japan, but in the world. *43%. Nikka.*

Super Nikka Rare Old batch 02I18D **(90.5)** n22 t23 f22.5 b23. Beautiful whisky which just sings a lilting malty refrain. Strange, though, to find it peatless. *43%. Nikka.*

Torys (76) n18 t19 f20 b19. Lots of toffee in the middle and at the end of this one. The grain used is top class and chewy. *37%. Suntory.*

Torys Whisky Square (80) n19 t20 f21 b20. At first glance a very similar blend to Torys, but very close scrutiny reveals slightly more "new loaf" nose and a better, spicier and less toffeed finale. *37%.*

Tsuru (93) n23 t24 f22 b24. Gentle and beautifully structured, genuinely mouthwatering, more-ish and effortlessly noble. If they had the confidence to cut the caramel, this would be even higher up the charts as one of the great belons of the world. And with Japanese whisky becoming far more globally accepted and sought after, now would be a very good time to start. As it is, in my house we pass the ceramic Tsuru bottle as one does the ship's decanter. And it empties very quickly. *43%. Nikka.*

The Whisky (88) n22 t22 f21 b23. A rich, confident and well-balanced dram. *43%. Suntory.*

White (80) n19 t21 f20 b20. Boring nose but explodes on the palate for a fresh, mouth-watering classic blend bite. *40%. Suntory.*

Za (79) n19 t21 f19 b20. Some lively boisterous grain offers a suet-pudding chewiness. A little bitter on the finish. *40%. Suntory.*

European Whisky

The debate about what it means to be European was one that seemingly never ended. That was until June 23rd 2016 when the people of Britain firmly decided that it should and they weren't. By contrast, the discussion on how to define the character of a European whisky is only just beginning.

And as more and more distilleries open throughout mainland Europe, Scandinavia and the British Isles, the styles are becoming wider and wider.

Small distillers in mainland Europe, especially those in the Alpine area, share common ground with their US counterparts in often coming late into whisky. Their first love, interest and spirit had been with fruit brandies. It seemed that if something grew in a tree or had a stone when you bit into it, you could be pretty confident that someone in Austria or California was making a clear, eye-watering spirit from it somewhere.

So perhaps it is not surprising that the whiskies which each year seem now to get the highest and most consistent marks are those built purely with whisky in mind. Mackmyra in Sweden. Penderyn in Wales. The aged whiskies representing Gold Cock in the Czech Republic came from state-built distilleries when the land was still Czeckoslovakia. But, above all, it is becoming clear now that it is the English Whisky Company which has risen to the top and challenging all others to match the excellence of their malts. Norfolk may be most famous for its Christmas-culled poultry, but the whisky of St George's Distillery is no turkey.

To ram home this point they have, for the third year running walked off with wth European Whisky of the Year (Multiple Casks) and this year even wrestled the overall European Whisky of the Year off Kornog of France. There is a pattern now: the smaller distilleries of Langatun in Switzerland, Belgian Owl (an owl which has been growing in size in recent years) and Kornog are the ones you just know will give the serious players like St George's, Penderyn, Mackmyra and the medium-sized Stauning in Denmark a run for their money.

And there are new players on the scene, like the Cotswold Distillery just a short distance from me and The Lakes. Both in England, producing European whisky. How exciting. How ironic!

Jim Murray's Whisky Bible European Whisky of the Year Winners

	European Whisky Multiple Casks	European Whisky Single Cask
2004	Waldviester Hafer Whisky 2000	N/A
2005	Hessicher Whisky (German Bourbon-style Whisky)	N/A
2006	Swissky Exklusiv Abfullung	N/A
2007	Mackmyra Preludium 03 Svensk Single Malt Whisky	N/A
2008	Mackmyra Privus 03 Svensk Single Malt Whisky	N/A
2009	Old Buck 2nd Release (Finland)	N/A
2010	Santis Malt Highlander Dreifaltaigheit	Penderyn Port Wood Single Cask
2011	Mackmyra Brukswhisky	The Belgian Owl Aged 44 Months
2012	Mackmyra Moment "Urberg"	Penderyn Bourbon Matured S C
2013	Penderyn Portwood Swansea City Special	Hicks & Healey Cornish Whiskey 2004
2014	Mackmyra "Glod" (Glow)	Santis Malt Swiss Highlander
2015	English Whisky Co. Chapter 14 Not Peated	The Belgian Owl Single Malt '64 Months'
2016	English Whisky Co. Chapter 16	Kornog Chwee'hved 14 BC
2017	English Whisky Co. Chapter 14	Langatun 6YO Pinot Noir Cask

AUSTRIA

ACHENSEE'R EDELBRENNEREI FRANZ KOSTENZER Maurach. Working.

Whisky Alpin Grain Whisky Hafer db (86.5) n20.5 t23 f21 b22. A glutinous dram, full of thick wheat oils but a surprising lack of spice, though the little which forms works well within the hot cross bun sweetness. 40%

⟨⟩ **Whisky Alpin Grain Whisky Hafer** 3 Years Old bott code L1/2013 db (86) n21 t22.5 f21.5 b21. A distinctly bitter-sweet affair. Good body and molasses kick. 40%

Whisky Alpin Rye & Malt db (88) n22 t22 f22 b22. Needs to settle in the glass a little while for the malt to be at its best. But worth the wait. 40%

⟨⟩ **Whisky Alpin Single Malt Double Wood** 11 Years Old bott code L1/2005 db (83) n22.5 t23 f18 b21. Lime jelly with some of Lubek's top marzipan gets this off to a cracking start, but a sulphur flaw takes its toll. 40%

⟨⟩ **Whisky Alpin Single Malt Roggen 8 Years Old** bott code L2/2008 db (84) n19 t23.5 f20.5 b21. The marked beauty on the later stages of the delivery makes up for slap-dash oils from far too wide a cut on distillation. But for a few brief seconds simply marvel at just how intense that rye becomes and the astonishing marriage it has with a blend of honeys. Ulmo and acacia lead the field. 45%

⟨⟩ **Whisky Alpin Single Malt Sherry Cask Finish 8 Years Old** bott code L2/2008 db (83.5) n19 t22.5 f21.5 b21.5. Big on the nougat nose. But the grape and oils appear to flatten the remainder of this malt out. A brief juiciness which thoroughly, if briefly, entertains.... 40%

⟨⟩ **Whisky Alpin Single Malt Smoky Finish 5 Years Old** bott code L2/2011 db (88.5) n20.5 off beam, though the smoke is soothing; t22.5 begins with a kick of feints, but settles into a slow build up of cocoa. The smoke gets lost amid the milk chocolate...; f23.5 possibly the most chocolatey finish of all time. Chocolate praline wafers...; b22 An altogether more rounded whisky from them. Still technically fraught, but it is as though they have made this from smoked chocolate malt, because the degree of cocoa on this borders the bewildering... and beautiful! 42%

Whisky Alpin Single Rye Malt db (81) n19 t21 f20 b21. Creamy and spicy. Good Demerara sugar thread, but the rye itself struggles to convince. 45%

ALPEN WHISKY DISTILLERIE Frastanz, Working.

⟨⟩ **Alpenwhisky Single Malt** first fill rum casks, dist Aug 12, bott 22 Jan 16 db (89.5) n21 though matured in rum, the tannins come through like a rocket. A few feints aren't far behind but the overall molassed and liquorice effect isn't too bad; t23.5 this is big: very big! Hugely nutty at first, then so many layers of crisp, burnt sugar form like folds in a mountain...; f22 the feints return but enough sugar and vanilla to limit the damage; b23 if you are going to call yourself the Alps Distillery, then it is no bad idea to produce massive whisky. And they have done just that with no little panache and style. By no means technically perfect, and they can thank the sugars for keeping a tight hold of the feints, but the overall view is breath-taking... 55.4%

⟨⟩ **Alpenwhisky Single Malt** first fill sherry casks, dist Mar 11, bott 06 Jun 15 db (82.5) n19 t21.5 f21 b21. Very curious. The wide cut causes a few problems on the nose and, naturally, the finish. But the sherry cask is untainted and very decent quality. Sadly, the fruit is just a little too gentle to control the feints adequately: a bit like a five foot nothing policeman trying to apprehend a 6 foot 6 inch thug. As the distillery over time learns to tighten the cut points, this will shape up into a very impressive whisky. 45.8%

BRENNEREI GUGLHOF Hallein, Working.

⟨⟩ **Tauern Rogg Single Malt Whisky** Sauternes cask no. 93, dist 2011 db (88.5) n21 untidy but a little sherbet lemon keeps things fresh; t23 a typical wave of delightful, lightly honeyed sugars, tinged here with outrageously ripe greengages. Beautifully sweet but light and playful, even showing a degree of grist towards the late middle; f22 spices up as a light feint creeps in; b22.5 soft, sweet and satisfying. 42%. sc.

BRENNEREI ROSSETTI Kolsassberg, Working.

⟨⟩ **Rossetti Young & Fine Pure Single Malt** bott code L582 db (89.5) n22 orange blossom honey with a big tannin injection; t23 silky and much richer than expected: superb malt signature and a fabulously lush middle makes it impossible not to salivate; f22 a vague tang, though the sugars do a good job; b22.5 I remember well the previous Rossetti I tasted: a bit of a gaunt, pasty lad: youthful and undernourished. The boy has grown. Perhaps a slight buzz on the finish, but an altogether burlier and more rounded character altogether. 43.5%

BROGER PRIVATBRENNEREI Klaus, Working.

◆ **Broger Burn Out Single Malt Whisky** bott code L B0-12 db **(95) n23.5** good grief...!! Probably the most dense peat I have encountered this year: quite acrid and far from friendly or soothing. Anyone who has witnessed a barn burn down will immediately recognise this aroma...; **t24** dense doesn't quite cover it. But so much softer than you might imagine, helped along by an avalanche of sugars, most of them a molassed and muscovado variety. But there is a sub-strata of Demerara working underneath, just ensuring a subtle crispness to balance the candyfloss smoke; **f23.5** so long... Remains smoky, but now even more delicate, though the buzzing spices remind you of the peat fest which had just been conducted on your dazed palate; **b24** when I saw I was faced with six new samples of Broger, I strapped myself in. I remember from old, that this is a distillery of extremes, with wildly varying quality. So I went for this one first – taking the bull by the horns. Closed my eyes...took a mouthful...and lived! Actually, the label should be one of billowing smoke, as you want as little flame as possible when smoking malt. And perhaps one, also, of sugar cane. Because the Demerara on this is highly impressive. A very pleasant surprise. Oh, and didn't I mention it? This is a mini masterpiece... 42%

◆ **Broger Distiller's Edition Single Malt Whisky** Madeira cask db **(66) n16 t17 f16 b17.** Oh dear... The S word in abundance. 60.7%. 165 bottles.

◆ **Broger Medium Smoked Single Malt Whisky** bott code L MS-09 db **(94) n23.5** Arbroath Smokies at first, but as the glass warms, the sugars get a little more crisp. Except the acrid house style is a unique signature, here with a light thread of marmalade; **t23.5** the citrus arrives a step ahead of the smoke, though this appears diluted down by a fabulously malty, ulmo honey sweetness – so delicious...; **f23** spices arrive with grace and interweave with the smoked vanilla rather charmingly; **b24** there is no doubt that this distillery knows exactly how to make smoky whisky...because this is a very different, more subtle, style to their peated efforts. 42%

◆ **Broger Riebelmais Whisky** bott code L Wh-Bo09 db **(87.5) n22 t22 f21.5 b22.** An attractive whisky with some starchy elements. Good sugar balance and soft vanilla. Maybe needs to be a little less reduced to maximise the meagre oils. 42%

◆ **Broger Riebelmais Whisky** sherry cask, dist 2009, bott Dec 15 db **(91.5) n23.5** toasty and intense; a touch peppery with the sugars comfortably integrated with the flatter starches, almost like a roasted sweet potato; **t23** brilliantly different! Vivid honey and spice with that lovely oily undertone to soothe the palate; **f22** long and very toasty. **b23** there you go. There was me saying their Riebelmais needed to be closer to cask strength for it to maintain its integrity...and next sample up: Riebelmais at cask strength. Immediately the unbroken oils make their mark for a far more complete whisky. First came across this rare type of distillate maybe a dozen years ago – always works better at a fuller strength. 58%. sc.

◆ **Broger Triple Cask Single Malt Whisky** bott code L Wh-Tr09 db **(86.5) n21 t22 f21.5 b22.** By no means bad whisky: it is obviously well made distillate. But you can have too much of a good thing and here the sugars are just a tad too much in your face. Enjoyable, for sure. But just borderline liqueur... 42%

DACHSTEIN DESTILLERIE Radstadt. Working

Mandlbergut Rock Whisky 5 Years (82) **n20 t21.5 f20 b20.5.** Rock by name and nature. A massively crisp whisky, as though you are crunching on crystals of sugar and grains of barley. The slight tobacco note means it never quite gets into full song but if owners Bernhard and Doris perhaps slow the stills a tad and cut a little finer, they might have on their hands a rock of ages to come... db 40%.

DESTILLERIE GEORG HIEBL Haag. Working.

George Hiebl Mais Whisky 2004 db **(93) n23 t23.5 f23 b23.5.** More bourbon in character than some American bourbons I know...!! Beautifully matured, brilliantly matured and European whisky of the very highest order, Ye..haahhhh!! 43%

DESTILLERIE ROGNER Rappottenstein. Working.

Rogner Waldviertel Whisky 3/3 db **(86.5) n20 t22 f22.5 b22.** Plane sailing once you get past the tight nose. A beautiful display of crisp sugars and come-back-for more grainy juiciness. Lovable stuff, for all its gliches. 41.7%. ncf.

DESTILLERIE WEIDENAUER Kottes. Working

Waldviertler Classic Haferwhisky bottle code L05 db **(88) n21 t23.5 f21 b22.5.** A busy oat whisky of no little distinction, despite the lightest degree of butyric. Still, they have been making from this grain for a long time... 42%

Waldviertler Dinkelmalz Dinkelwhisky mit 2/3, bottle code L08 db **(83.5) n20 t22.5 f20 b21.** Big, boisterous and, at times, bruising. The spice is out in force, as you might expect. But despite the enormity of the character, the thicker-than-desired cut works against it – on the nose and finish especially. 42%

Waldviertler Dinkelwhisky bottle code L09 db **(94) n23 t23.5 f23.5 b24** A beautifully made and matured whisky. So, so subtle... 42%

Waldviertler Hafermalz Haferwhisky mit 2/3 bottle code L09 db **(91) n22 t23.5 f22.5 b23** Every last drop of flavour successfully extracted. Lovely! 42%

Waldviertler Limited Edition Hafermalz bottle code L08 db **(94) n22 t24.5 f23.5 b24** One of a type. Every whisky collector should hunt this down. Superb. 42%

Waldviertler Maiswhisky 100% Maisbrand, bottle code L09 db **(88.5) n21.5 t23 f22 b22.** A busy whisky with reasonable pretentions towards a bourbon style. 42%

Waldviertler Single Malt dunkel Hafer-Whisky bottle code L09 db **(81.5) n20 t22 f19 b20.5.** Massive flavours. But the over generous cut offers a metallic edge. 42%

DESTILLERIE WEUTZ St. Nikolai im Sausal. Working.
Franziska bott code. L070206/02 db The 5% elderflower means this is 100% not whisky. But a fascinating and eye-opening way to create a spirit very much in the young Kentucky rye style, especially in the nose. They certainly can do delicious... For the record, the scoring for enjoyment alone: **(93) n23.5 t23 f23.5 b23.** 48%. Malt refined with 5% elderflower.

DISTILLERY ZWEIGER Mooskirchen, Working.
⬥ **Zweiger Single Malt Whiskey Aged 4 Years Styrian oak** db **(89) n22** distinctly European wood effect: pungent tannins with a sharp citrus-saltiness; **t22.5** big delivery, again with the tannins right at the forefront. Shapes impressively as delicate maple syrup mixes with orange blossom honey to offer balance; **f22** some late red liquorice spices up; **b22.5** fascinating malt with the oak playing a far more entertaining part than the barley. 40%

LAVA BRÄU Feldbach, Working.
⬥ **Mehr Leben Brisky Single Malt Whisky** dist 2006, bott codeH 03|06 db **(87.5) n22.5 t22 f21 b22.** Lovely, fascinating nose, at times salty and sweaty, occasionally citrusy. And charmingly delicate on the palate, also, with a major citrus theme. 40.2%

⬥ **Mehr Leben Brisky Single Malt Whisky** dist 2009, bott code B 0509 db **(91.5) n23** so complex and just look at those varying weights. The house sweaty style is still evident but now with some mixed nuts and an almost creamy lime sharpness; **t23** salivating, fresh barley with a superb chocolate lime candy development; **f22.5** the oils from the distillate add length, a touch of spice and dryness... **b23** a bottle worth finding and savouring. Gorgeous! 40.8%

LEBE & GENIESSE Lagenrohr. Working
Bodding Lokn cask no. 8, dist 2010, bott 2014 db **(88) n22 t22.5 f21.5 b22.** Tight and toasty. But very young. 42%.

Bodding Lokn Double Cask French oak & oloroso sherry casks, cask no. 6/12, dist 2009, bott 2015 db **(91.5) n23** one very intense whisky: a happy combination of thick fruit, including slightly more subtle greengages, mixed in with some broad oak tones. A slightly wide cut adds a honey-nougat dimension...and extra weight; **t24** good grief! What a delivery!!! Massive sugars – mixing ulmo honey with acacia honey and maple syrup – have a secondary gristy barley effect and light grapey tones....; **f21.5** the feints bite back hard as some bitterness creeps in; **b23** having been knocking on the door, in terms of quality, I do believe they've cracked it! 42%. ncf sc.

Bodding Lokn Single Cask American white oak, cask no. 10, dist 2009, bott 2015 db **(88.5) n22** a tad feinty with plenty of nougat and molasses promised; **t22.5** yep, the feints first to show. But then a delightful mocha-vanilla-barley complexity takes hold; **f22** the outstanding dark sugars, like the minty cocoa, lingers; **b22** now that's better! If I remember correctly, these guys have tended in the past to bottle a little too young. I think this is older distillate. And though not as well made as their cleaner previous bottling, the extra time in the cask has resulted in far greater balance and complexity. 42%. sc.

MARILLENHOF DESTILLERIE KAUSL Mühldorf, Working.
Wachauer Whisky "G" Single Barrel Gerste (Barley) bott code L6WG db **(90.5) n22 t23 f22.5 b23.** Absolutely charming and well made malt. 40%

⬥ **Wachauer Whisky Kausl** bott code L: 13 WE db **(92) n22** good heavens! What a soup! As though freshly squeezed tannin has been liberally added to a plate of marmalade. And more than a pinch of black pepper to season it up a shade more...; **t23.5** a sensual, lush mouth feel. Gorgeously oily, though not from the cut: more the grain. Their oat whisky is the closest in style to this, though that lacks the fabulous marriage of citrus fruits and muscovado sugars - deeply impressive; **f23.5** long, with those spices now doing some sizzling and a wonderful creamy, citrus-edged mocha fade; **b23** Kausl appear to specialise in taking the tannin to the edge: the character is deep rooted in oak - literally - yet somehow they manage to get the intricacies of the grain - or perhaps grains - across. Brave. And either very lucky, or exceptionally skilful... Oh, and I say grains as I took the liberty to blend their four grains together and came up with something not entirely unlike this in style, complexity and balance - except perhaps slightly better and something over the 94 mark....(!!) An impressive distillery worthy of great praise, for sure. 40%

🔷 **Wachauer Whisky Kausl Single Pure G Barley** bott code L: 6WG db **(88) n21.5** a fraction too vividly oaky for comfort; **t22** again, a thumping blast of tannin, but after a while a satisfying degree of Demerara sugars break free from the woody grip **f22.5** settled and exceptionally pleasant finish. Medium length but the light molasses touch works superbly; **b22** barley may be behind the grain. But the oak leads in every direction. 40%

🔷 **Wachauer Whisky Kausl Single Pure H Oat** bott code L: 1WH db **(89) n22** thumping tannin, presumably from virgin oak, though in past years in Austria I have found this stunning effect from chestnut; also some dramatic, strangely angular bourbon notes with the liquorice pointy and jabbing at you; **t22** little surprise the tannin takes to the podium in first, second and third place. But, slowly, the sugars assemble with a charming maple syrup evolution as the oats finally get a word in; **f22.5** a degree of orange blossom honey infuse with the oaty oils; **b22.5** starting the day with some oats is supposed to be good for you. Usually my oat intake is at lunchtime when I mash up half a dozen or more oatcakes into mackerel and sometimes lighten with diced tomato. But if anyone is to ask me where you will find the best oat whisky, the answer has to be Austria. The startling intensity of the wood has an overbearing effect on the oats but the unique character of the grain shines through at the end. 40%

🔷 **Wachauer Whisky Kausl Single Pure Rye** bott code L: 9WR db **(90.5) n22** the rye is chunky and chases you with thick oils. The tannin prods, as part of a battering ram; all hardly subtle, but never less than enthralling...; **t23** much crisper now on delivery as the Demerara sugars click into place and that unique fruit element of the rye begins to radiate alongside the gentle spices; a backdrop of intense vanilla tries to distract, but fails; **f23** loads of natural caramels at play, but the rye enjoys an ever cleaner outlook; **b22.5** you may not be surprised that I left the rye as the last of their four grains. This is the hardest of them all to get right, and also offers the greatest reward if they can pull it off. In the end, it turned out they surpassed themselves: a full-flavoured, at times crisp and fruity success. 40%

🔷 **Wachauer Whisky Kausl Single Pure W Wheat** bott code L: 2WW db **(80) n19 t20 f21 b20.** Wheat is a hard grain to pull off at the best of times. But what appears to be a slight butyric note doesn't help the narrative and although it doesn't misfire quite so badly on the palate, the various constituents don't seem to gel too happily, either. 40%

MARKUS WIESER GMBH Woesendorf in der Wachau, Austria.

🔷 **Wieser Wahouua Single Malt WIESky American Oak** bott code L1115 db **(85.5) n21 t22 f21 b21.5.** Never a dull moment as the treacle and maple syrup mix join forces with a light spice to battle against some ungainly oils from the distillate. Always pleasant, but never convincing. 40%. nc.

🔷 **Wieser Wahouua Single Malt WIESky Pinot Noir** bott code L1015 db **(87) n21 t22 f22 b22.** A curious malt. Always soft, always polite and at times positively charming. But the fruit never makes much of a stand while the toffee has no such reservations. 40%. nc.

🔷 **Wieser Wahouua Single Malt WIESky Sherry Wood** bott code L1015 db **(82.5) n19 t21.5 f21 b21.** The sherry is absolutely clean and problem free. But the fruit has to work very hard to overcome the excesses of a wide cut. The result is predictably nutty and stilted. Soft throughout and not entirely unattractive once you are past the nose. 40%. nc.

MICHELEHOF Vorarlberg. Working.

Micheles Single Malt 6 Years Old 100% barley, dist 2008, bott code L8121 db **(78.5) n19 t21 f19 b19.5.** An oily, nutty affair which struggles hard to get over the effect of the wide cut. A few attractive salivating fudgy moments at about the halfway point. 43%

PETER AFFENZELLER Alberndorf in der Riedmark, Working.

🔷 **Peter Affenzeller Blended Whisky 7 Years Old** dist 2008, bott code: L-1015302 db **(86.5) n21.5 t22 f21.5 b21.5.** An exceptionally sweet blend, but spices emerge to tone down the threatening excess. Love the Lubek marzipan which surfaces on the nose especially. But overall, a surprising degree of youthfulness. 42%

⟐ **Peter Affenzeller Grain Whisky 5 Years Old** dist 2011, bott code: L-0841403 db **(90.5)** **n22.5** look at that gentle honey note: it sits well with the light oil and vaguely muscular tannin; **t22.5** retains the soft house style with the oils thickening by the moment. Superb sugar-spice combo of impressive pace and weight; **f22.5** long, with a light semolina and Demerara sugared porridge finale; **b23** it very much appears this distillery has moved up a notch of two in recent years. *42%*

⟐ **Peter Affenzeller Single Malt Whisky 7 Years Old** dist 2008, bott code: L-0841201 db **(95.5)** **n23.5** I didn't expect that! Don't remember Peter unleashing any form of a smoky whisky on us last time out. The phenols are as delicate as they are complex, playing reek-a-boo with the nutty tannins. The vaguest mix of Manuka honey and maple syrup ensures the overall picture is as fascinating as it is lovely; **t24.5** just superb. Not sure which impresses the most early on: the silkiness of the massaging oils or the stunning interplay between a slightly lethargic Highland Park-ish heather-honey and (no less Highland Park-ish) smoke which slowly transmogrifies into busy spices; **f23.5** a slow fade, with a vague tired oak tingle being more than matched by the thickening vanilla. That subtle smoke adds weight to the lingering honey; **b24** I defy any malt whisky lover, wherever you are in the world, not to entirely fall head over heals for this stunning whisky. *42%*

⟐ **Peter Affenzeller White Malzbrand** bott code: L-0821011 db **(89)** **n22 t22 f22.5 b22.5**. Beautifully cut new make: clean, with a fabulous slow burn of intensity. I'd expect a late spiced cocoa character, which is exactly what we get. Very acceptable copper content, too. Impressed: far more together than the last sample! *42%*

PFANNER Vorarlberg. Working.
Pfanner Single Malt dist 2009, bott code L 212 db **(74)** **n19 t20 f16.5 b18.5**. Nutty and some hefty feints late on puts a Pfanner in the works... *43%*

REISETBAUER Axberg, Thening. Working.
Reisetbauer Single Malt 7 Years Old Chardonnay and sweet wine cask, bott code LWH 099 db **(85.5)** **n19 t21 f23.5 b22**. A less than impressive nose is followed by a rocky delivery. But the panning out is truly spectacular as harmony is achieved with a rich honey and nougat mix, helped along with pecan nuts and figs. The finish is like a top rank trifle and fruitcake mix. A whisky of two halves. *43%*

⟐ **Reisetbauer Single Malt 7 Years Old** Chardonnay casks db **(84.5)** **n19 t23 f21 b21.5**. So weird!! On my final spit I thought: "I'm sure I've tasted this whisky before." And looking in last year's Bible, there it was. Though I gave bigger marks to the finale than the delivery. The 'G' Spot is the exact middle, when the fruit goes into delicious overdrive. Perhaps just three or four waves before where I noticed it last time. A varied dram, with a degree of brilliance - only too short in length. *43%*

⟐ **Reisetbauer Single Malt 12 Years Old** db **(86.5)** **n19 t23.5 f22 b22**. Presumably from the early days of the distillery when they hadn't quite got to grips with their cuts on the still. Recovers from a below-average nose to offer a sometimes sensational middle full of toffee and tannin and even a little Manuka honey. The heavier oils reassemble on the finale. *48%*

STBG BRAUEREI SCHLOSS STARKENBERG Tarrenz, Working.
⟐ **STGB Tiroler Single Malt Whisky Aged 3 Years** db **(94.5)** **n23.5** a vague phenolic note rises at a distance above the flat malty landscape and is then obscured by vanilla; **t23.5** stunningly sensual. Just as on the nose, the malt really covers all the ground the palate can see. And is so soft as to make you purr. Earthier notes, again very vaguely smoky, ensure there is a third dimension; **f23.5** it needs spices...and they arrive bang on schedule...; **b24** a charmingly relaxed single malt which has been beautifully crafted. You cannot really ask for more from a three-year-old single malt. *40%*

WHISKY-DESTILLERIE J. HAIDER Roggenreith. Working.
⟐ **Dark Single Malt J.H. Cask Strength** bott code L DSM 11 db **(94.5)** **n22.5** attractive yet not entirely happy, as a few feints get good coverage; but there is some malt in there, for sure...; **t24.5** ....and then this! Astonishing. Spellbinding. Almost redefining... Think of chocolate Malteisers candy on heat, absolutely concentrated to a point further than beyond your imagination. Yeah...? Well, you still don't have it...; **f24** now reduced down to sheer malt concentrate. With a little milky chocolate thrown in to dampen things slightly...; **b23.5** when it comes to almost bewildering intensity to a malt, this wonderful distillery is in a league of its own. Taste using the Murray Method to maximise the beauty. *64%*

Original Rye Whisky J.H. bott code L R 08 db **(92.5)** **n23** fantastic weight to this: the rye is no shrinking violet, yet can do nothing to prevent a significant earthy-cocoa backdrop, complete with the heftiest molasses imaginable; **t23.5** for all its brooding intensity on the nose, fair sparkles on the palate as the rye comes up trumps; **f23** duller, with a well balanced oak anchor at play; **b23** a true delight. 41%

⬦ **Original Rye Whisky J.H. Selection** bott code L R 05 db **(94)** **n23** none of the nougat but plenty of vanilla and crisp rye; degree of Jamaican rum in style; **t24** lively delivery with plenty of juice tripping off the grain. Eye-wateringly crisp, with a Demerara sweetness allied to muscovado fruit while the spices rant in opposition; **f23.5** long, lightly oiled and with a gorgeous light spice trail. A slow build up of cocoa still cannot dislodge the resident crisp rye; **b23.5** an assured and elegant rye of high quality. 46%

Pure Rye Malt bott code L PR 08 db **(93)** **n22 t24 f23.5 b23.5** Not a rye for the squeamish... even with its faults, something of a masterpiece. 41%

⬦ **Rare Selection Dark Rye Malt J.H** bott code L DRR 09 SG db **(93)** **n22.5** the house style of nougat has never been so richly bolstered by concentrated rye...wow! **t24** and there is no let up in that most distinct of grains. Though the mouth-feel is as friendly and yielding as they come, it is another matter when the rye really gets down to work. The intensity is immediate, thick and gives way to nothing; **f23** the rye is now on slow burn, some of the notes trailing off into a mint-chocolate fade; **b23.5** when this distillery gets its rye right, few distilleries in the world can match it for extracting every last nuance from the grain. Not a jot of elegance – just flavour power all the way. db 46%. sc.

Special Rye Malt Nougat bott code L SPR 08 db **(86.5)** **n20 t23 f21.5 b22**. Massive chocolate at play. But it is the intensity of the rye on delivery which impresses most. Huge feinty nougat on this. For those wishing to reduce the level of it and up the honey, place the tasting glass in a bowl of hot water and allow the feints to burn off. 41%

Special Single Malt Selection bott code L SSM 04 SL db **(82)** **n18 t22.5 f20.5 b21**. The butyric on the nose rather undoes the good of the nougat and honeycomb also visible. But a much better prospect on the palate, where the wide cut ensures maximum mocha. 46%

DESTILLERIE WEIDENAUER Kottes. Working.

Waldviertler Hafer-Malz (2007 Gold Medaille label on neck) db **(91)** **n22 t22.5 f23 b23.5.** One of those whiskies that just gets better the longer it stays on the palate. Also, a master class in achieving near perfection in the degree of sweetness generated. 42%

BELGIUM
THE BELGIAN OWL Grâce-Hollogne, Working.

The Belgian Owl Single Malt '8 Months' db **(85)** **n20 t21.5 f23 b20.5**. Typically imbalanced for its age with the first sugary tannins lurching about the malt both blindly and seemingly without a map. Good finish though to this sometimes lush piece. 70%.

The Belgian Owl Single Malt 36 Months 1st fill bourbon cask, bott code LB036068 db **(89.5)** **n23** lovely cross between banana and yam on toast – with a little side dish of ulmo honey; **t23.5** the malt arrives in all its gristy glory for a sweet delivery; still plenty of vanilla and banana doing the rounds; **f21** some toasty sugars but an unusual bitterness from the oak for this distillery – in the old Allied cask style; **b22** a beautiful box of Belgian tricks until the unscheduled bitterness arrives. 46%. nc ncf sc.

The Belgian Owl Single Malt 36 Months ex-Pedro Ximénez cask, bott code LB036069 db **(92.5)** **n22.5** toasty sugars abound like at a patisserie; the tightness of the sweetness tells you this is PX even before you get to inspect the label...; **t23.5** predictably crisp sugars, though softened by a demur gristiness which surprisingly over-rides the grape; **f23** a big spicy fanfare...; **b23.5** I'm not the greatest fan of PX in whisky, as it so often overwhelms and locks in the character of the distillery itself. But Belgian owl has such a strong personality, it appears more than able to look after itself, thus providing a wonderful two-toned soft-hard-soft-hard malt... 46%. nc ncf sc.

⬦ **The Belgian Owl Single Malt 36 Months** first fill bourbon cask, bott code LB036088 db **(85.5)** **n21 t22 f21 b21.5**. It seems only correct that, as the church clock strikes midnight and a tawny owl calls eerily to one of its young nearby, I should taste this. So it is obvious I give two hoots about a whisky which has always done exceptionally well in the Whisky Bible - and deservedly so. Not sure if this is distilled from their new (or do I mean old?) Caperdonich still. But it fails to grip and reveal the intensity of their older make, this emphasising the tender 36 months with its playful, citric and juicy maltiness, rather than the barley which, previously, was aflame with passion and desire to entertain. 46%. nc ncf.

The Belgian Owl Single Malt 40 Months 1st fill bourbon cask, bott code 4702028 db **(95)** **n23.5** quite massive: the tannins are there, in all their red liquorice glory. But there is a subtle, dry fruit note, also. The strength melts away into irrelevance, the malts grow substantially as the nose becomes accustomed...; **t23.5** such a soft, beautifully manicured delivery: the sugars range from muscovado to maple, with some decent grist thrown in; **f24** now into overdrive with the vanillas and mocha notes fully relaxed and integrated into the now lightly roasted malts – so complex and beautifully balanced; **b24** how can a whisky just 40 months old have morphed into so many flavours, even given this is from first-fill bourbon? Remains the world's most mind-blowing owl... *74.3%. nc ncf sc.*.

DESTILLERIE RADERMACHER Raeren, Working.

Lambertus Single Grain Aged 10 Years db **(44) n12 t12 f10 b10**. This is whisky...? Really???!!!!???? Well, that's what it says on the label, and this is a distillery I haven't got round to seeing in action (nor am I now very likely to be invited...). Let's check the label again... Ten years old...blah, blah. Single grain... blah, blah. But, frankly, this tastes like a liqueur rather than a whisky: the fruit flavours do not seem even remotely naturally evolved: synthetic is being kind. But apparently, this is whisky: I have re-checked the label. No mention of additives, so it must be. I am stunned. *40%*

IF GOULDYS FILLIERS DISTILLERY Deinze, Working.

Goldly's Belgian Double Still Whisky Aged 10 Years db **(88) n21.5 t23 f21.5 b22**. Having actually discovered this whisky before the distillers – I'll explain one day...!! – I know this could be a lot better. The caramel does great damage to the finish in particular, which should dazzle with its complexity. Even so, a lovely, high-class whisky which should be comfortably in the 90s but falls short. *40%*

Gouldys 12 Years Old Amontillado Finish First Release bott 2012 db **(89.5) n23.5 t22 f22 b22** A pleasant, gentle experience celebrating a non-sulphur involvement. But the grape influence is just a little too great even for the considerable character of Fillers' grain to show through to advantage. Easy does it, chaps. *43%. ncf nc. WB15/388*

Gouldys 12 Years Old Distillers Range cask no. 2600 db **(96) n24 t24.5 f23.5 b24** An essay in complexity. A faultless sherry butt influencing some of the best distillate in Europe: a triumph! *43.7%. ncf nc. WB15/390*

Gouldys 12 Years Old Manzilla Finish First Release bott 2012 db **(90) n23 t23 f23 b21** Another delightful whisky despite falling into the trap of overwhelming the grain with the grape. Pretty impossible not to love, though. *43%. ncf nc. WB15/389*

CZECH REPUBLIC
Single Malt
RUDOLF JELÍNEK DISTILLERY Vizovice, Working.

Gold Cock Single Malt Aged 12 Years "Green Feathers" bott 27/05/09 db **(89.5) n22 t23.5 f22 b22**. From my first ever malt-related trip to the Czech Republic nearly 20 years ago, it was always a pleasure to get hold of my Gold Cock. I was always told it went down a treat. And this is no exception. Not a particularly big whisky. But since when has size counted? *43%*

Gold Cock Single Malt Whisky 1992 Limited Release Whisky Festival.cz barrelled Jun 92, bott Apr 15 db **(97) n23.5** although it doesn't say on the label that this is from Czech oak...the intensity of the sugars, that magnificent mix between golden syrup, ulmo honey and manuka... I'd be pretty amazed if it wasn't; **t25** that has to be one of the most beautiful mouthfuls imaginable: golden Czech which, when you get your lips around it, makes your tongue explore its mysterious but inviting depths and then lick every last degree of juicy sweetness from the receptacle, nothing wasted as every last tingle of pleasure is sought and then extracted. A touch salty, and deliciously so, but it is that juicy sweetness, a result of the mature, rampant wood, which form thickening flavour layers, with that oaky hardness rhythmically interweaving with those gushing juices...in, out, in, out...so, so sensual...; **f24** really need a lie down after all that. Flickering spices kiss and tease while the echoes of that salt and sugar lingers on the taste buds seemingly forever; **b24.5** absolutely one of the great single barrels of the year. And, unquestionably, THE most sensual dram... *61.6%. ncf sc. 198 bottles.*

◈ **Gold Cock Single Malt Whisky 1992 Slivovitz Finish** Czech oak barrels db **(95) n24** this is truly brilliant: the nose has more layers than a Czech chicken shed. Sparkling spices, with a bit of niggardly bite and then a peck with black peppers. The malt does show briefly and then vanishes beneath a sharpened fruitiness...; **t24** three honeys hit the taste buds at the gallop: Manuka, ulmo and heather. Luckily the oak has plenty of chunky hickory notes to ensure the balance between sweet and dry is just about spot on; **f23.5** there is something closer to bourbon here as a few oils from a slightly wide cut that had been making discreet sounds on both the nose and delivery at last become powerful enough to make a mark of their own; good malt follow-through again ensures a bitter-sweet balance; **b23.5** Czech malt whisky. Matured in Czech oak. And finished in the wood that contained the Czech national spirit, slivovitz. Can you think of anything more beautiful and nakedly Czech than that? Well, I can. And I look forward to drinking it with her next time we meet... Czech-mate... *59.5%. nc ncf sc.*

 Gold Cock Single Malt Whisky Aged 24 Years 1992 Czech oak barrels, cask no. 505, dist 4/1992, bott 5/2016 db **(95.5) n23.5** light red liquorice mingles with rich malt; vaguely salty like a coastal distillery – some chance in the Czech Republic! But the local oak does offer a distinct saltiness which heightens all; **t24** what a monumental mixture of (black!) liquorice and Manuka honey: toasty and tasty from the first second; the oils are completely intact and brilliantly offer round every last bit of sugar going; the malt blasts out for a while to provide the juiciest of waves; spices are going strong by the midway point; **f24** the vanillas offer an almost apologetic simplicity to what had before been big stuff; but then is overwhelmed by the final distinct waves of the earlier enormity. And the spices are still radiating...; **b24** there is perhaps a one in three chance I tasted this whisky in the mid 1990s when it was only a nipper. In my 1997 Jim Murray's Complete Book of Whisky I wrote fondly of this maturing whisky as I was genuinely impressed. I see now I had good reason to be: it has navigated the passing years without hitting the rocks and passes no opportunity to radiate great personality. A bit like the wonderful people I met who made it... *61.5%. nc ncf sc. 246 bottles. Bottled for Black Stuff Irish Pub Olomouc.*

Gold Cock Single Malt Whisky Small Batch 1992 barrelled Jun 92, bott May 15 db **(94) n23** the spices tingle the nose; the slightly creamy sugars ensure depth; **t24** a volley of soft creamy sugars and honey (Demerara and ulmo in particular) – exactly like on the nose – bathe and massage the taste buds. And if it seems like Ambrosia, then in a way it is, as there is a milk-rice effect here which perfectly matches the ever-intensifying barley; **f23** just an apologetic degree of oaky bitterness creeps onto the scene, but those deft honey-sugar notes are in quickly to ensure a counter point; those gentle oils drift on forever ...; **b24** just as I was opening this bottle, I spotted a male green woodpecker on the lawn searching for ants, while just three feet above it a male great spotted woodpecker fed contentedly on nuts. And here was me about to taste a whisky derived from an oak which must, at one time or another, offered comfort to a black woodpecker or three; which, like the whisky, is found in the wonderful Czech Republic though not here. So I knew I was in for something different – and rather special – and I wasn't wrong. Because although the oak has maybe spent a season or two too long in the warehouse, the unique alignment of the sugars still ensures a malt of enormous character, quality and personality. *49.2%. ncf. 1,428 bottles.*

STOCK PLZEN - BOZKOV S.R.O. Plzeň, Working

Hammer Head 1989 db **(88.5) n22 t22.5 f22 b22.** Don't bother looking for complexity: this is one of Europe's maltiest drams...if not the maltiest... *40.7%*

Blends

Gold Cock Aged 3 Years "Red Feathers" bott 22/06/09 **(86) n22 t21 f21.5 b21.5.** Sensual and soft, this is melt-in-the-mouth whisky with a big nod towards the sweet caramels. *40%.*

Granette Premium (82) n21 t22 f19 b20. Lighter than the spark of any girl that you will meet in the Czech Republic. Big toffee thrust. *40%*

Printer's Aged 6 Years (86.5) n21.5 t22.5 f21 b21.5. Blended whisky is something often done rather well in the Czech Republic and this brand has managed to maintain its clean, malty integrity and style. Dangerously quaffable. *40%*

DENMARK
BRAENDERIET LIMFJORDEN Øster Assels, Working.

 Island of Mors Single Malt Danish Whisky db **(87) n21.5 t22 f22 b21.5.** A most curious – and delicious – whisky from Denmark. Though a single malt, it has the bite, underlying firmness, sliminess of body, and thick line of caramel which one normally associates with a blend. Some lovely spices at play, as well as malt, but just needs to complex out slightly. *46%. ncf. 462 bottles.*

BRAUNSTEIN DISTILLERY Køge, Working.

 Braunstein Danish Single Malt Cask Edition no. 2 db **(94) n23.5** youthful, attractively smoked bacon; even, though sharp and salty; clean, barley accented, with the sweetness veering towards banana and custard; **t23.5** beautifully textured and, despite its obvious lack of passing seasons, displays enough accomplished, intense gristy notes to make for one of the most impressively layered whiskies you'll find on mainland Europe. Initially supplemented by a light Demerara sweetness, then eventually heads deliciously towards a chocolate mint middle, but the peat is paying attention all the time; **f23** betrays its youth slightly. But, equally, the elegance is never in question; **b24** seriously high quality distillate that has been faithfully supported by good grade oak. Complex, satisfying, and for its obviously tender years, truly excellent malt. A welcome addition to the Scandinavian – and world! – whisky lexicon. *62.4%*

◈ **Braunstein Danish Single Malt Cask Edition no. 3** db (93) n22.5 t24 f23 b23.5. A very different experience to Edition No 2, with this being anchored not by peat but almost outrageous tannin and the astonishing sugar concentrate which accompanies it. For three, maybe four, glorious flavour waves the palate is almost swamped by oak at its most accomplished, yet still with good manners enough for the fresh gristy barley to also make a telling contribution. *62.3%*

◈ **Braunstein Danish Single Malt Cask Edition no. 5** db (89.5) n22 t22 f23 b22.5. Takes a little time to sort itself out and decide what it wants to say. A confusion of fruit and peat makes things a bit thick for a while: such is the over-exuberance of youth! Juicy and eventually less muggy and more impressively smoky. *60.8%*

◈ **Braunstein Danish Single Malt Cask Edition no. 6** db (94.5) n23.5 t23.5 f23.5 b24. What a class act this is! Everything beautifully weighted and measured: like a film star of the 1950s fitting perfectly into her tastefully revealing dress. The smoke appears to have been tailored with an unerring eye to allow both the highly sugared oak and more deftly sweetened barley to show its curves. A sublime layering of oil, and just the most playful of spice tingles – all softened by the most dazzling fruity muscovado sugars - really sets this off gloriously and papers over the youthful cracks expertly. What magnificence! *61.4%*

◈ **Braunstein Danish Single Malt Library Collection 10:2** db (89.5) n23 t23 f21.5 b22. Though initially an oily chap, perhaps not helped by the lower strength as the breakdown in its structure by the finale is pretty marked, as the powdery ending portrays. Even so, its youth does not deter the intense malt richness, nor the light smoke which offers useful weight. *43%*

◈ **Braunstein Danish Single Malt Library Collection 10:3** db (92) n23 t23 f22.5 b23.5. A comparative dullard by Braunstein's high standards. Yet still reeks of quality and class, even though the sharper edges have been rendered safe and flat by the big fruit injection.... and high water reduction. Silky soft, with a watered-down dark muscovado leaning. This allows the spices to come into their own late on, joining the intensifying cocoa with aplomb. Charming. *43%*

◈ **Braunstein Danish Single Malt Library Collection 11:2** db (87.5) n22 t22.5 f21 b22. A bit sharp and tangy in places, especially towards the end. Very youthful, but still excels in its big malt kick; though finds balance a little more elusive. *46%*

◈ **Braunstein Danish Single Malt Library Collection 14:2** db (91.5) n22 t22.5 f23.5 b23.5. No problems harnessing the dark, weighty sugars which ensures this malt is in for the long haul. A fruity fusillade on the nose but the delivery is divine: good oil structure, playful smoke and lovely tingling spice. All the time the barley thickens and the light ulmo and Manuka honey blend aid the growing spices. Complex and satisfying. *46%*

◈ **Braunstein Danish Single Malt Library Collection 15:1** db (91) n22.5 t23 f23.5 b22. Another Braunstein where a massive tannin injection offers the main theme throughout. Not sure how they do it, but for all the oak, the integrity of the barley remains undiminished. At times, the obvious youthfulness of the malt makes this seem like a marriage between teenager and pensioner. Lurches about the palate a bit with the vanilla and caramel-rich sugars always on hand to soothe any arguments. *46%*

◈ **Braunstein Danish Single Malt Cask Edition no. D28** db (94) n23.5 t23.5 f23 b24. Another big game malt from Braunstein. Not dissimilar in style to one of their malt cask collection: no. 6, I think. The smoke and oak appear to be dancing to the same tune and very much in step. Intense, the sugars are perhaps just a shade more weighted by vanilla with this one. Not a dram for those looking for a quiet few minutes... *61.4%*

◈ **Braunstein Danish Single Malt Library Collection e:7** db (89.5) n21 t23 f23 b22.5. A seriously odd whisky: unusually for this distillery, they have chosen to bottle at a point where the nose really is a stranger to harmonisation. Light smoke and jagged tannin juxtapose with the pithy fruit: they don't mix merrily. So they must have selected for the delivery, for this is absolutely stunning! While the nose is at odds, the sugars are all for one and one for all: gorgeous maple syrup with a touch of treacle thrown in. And a big spice bite to ram the intensity home. Some vague, estery, rummy notes emphasise the sugary input. Young, a little confused...but has so much to say. *60.2%*

Mikkeller Spirits Black Bourbon Cask (81) n20 t21 f20 b20. A peculiar whisky with a near apple brandy nose and all pervading fruit throughout. Perhaps been matured in a fruity atmosphere. But doesn't sit right. *43%*

Mikkeller Spirits Black Oloroso Cask (82) n21 t22 f19 b20. Again, closer to a fruit brandy than a single malt with apple outscoring the grape on points. The barley is nowhere to be seen. 43%

Mikkeller Spirits Black Rum Cask (86.5) n20 t22.5 f22 b22. The nose is almost identical to their bourbon cask. But the rum influence gives a sugary shield to the malt and keeps some of the fruit at bay. 43%

FARY LOCHAN DESTILLERI Give, Working.

◇ **Fary Lochan Danish Single Malt** batch 2, cask nos. 2011-04,09,11,12 & 13, filled 5 Nov 11, bott 27 Jan 16 db **(84) n21 t21 f21.5 b20.5**. A hugely promising whisky undone slightly by the width of the cut, which allows in a few too many heavy oils. There is no doubting the integrity of the barley and at times one hums with delight as its intensity hits the bullseye. But much peripheral bitterness needs to be trimmed away. 48%

◇ **Fary Lochan Vinter** batch 1 db **(86) n21.5 t22 f21 b21.5**. A more handsome malt here with the sugars happy to go hand-in-hand with the vivid barley and lively spice. Marked down, though, by a bitter shadow which has a vaguely hoppy edge to it. 54%

SMALL BATCH DISTILLERS Holstebro. Working

Peated first-fill 10L French oak casks db **(78.5) n21.5 t22 f17 b18**. A brave, one might say foolhardy, early bottling from a new distillery. Mixing peat and wine together is not always a winner even for well established distilleries, let alone a new one. Here, they have been caught out when the off-notes from the casks not only becomes apparent but damages the whisky severely, especially towards the furry, off-key finish. That said, the delivery has merits in its intensity. But a price is paid... 54%

Very Young Peated second-fill French oak casks db **(90) n23** some pretty full-on peat at work here: sharp, almost aggressive phenol only shadow-boxed by the oak; **t23** wine comes to the fore, catching the dryer edges of the peat for a puckering delivery. Intense stuff...; **f21** a slight flaw on the finale as the French oak does its worst. But enough peat around to repair the gouges; **b23** what a brilliant addition to the Scandinavian whisky lexicon! And recovery from their first disappointing attempt of peat and French oak. 62%

Young Rye first-fill Hungarian oak casks db **(74) n18 t21 f16 b18**. Probably the rye-est rye in the history of rye kind. I really must get to this distillery and sample the rye coming off the still: that would be a positive whisky experience the like of which even I have never encountered before. But I would also probably suggest, while there, that they seriously review – and then reboot - their wood policy. 62%

STAUNING WHISKEY Skjern, Working.

Brigantia 3 Years Old bott code L-12/12 db **(79) n19 t21 f19 b20**. Huge malt statement, as is the distillery style. But it appears someone decided to try and extract as much spirit as possible, because the cut seems to be a little too wide for comfort here: the oils are unforgiving. 43%

◇ **Stauning Danish Single Malt Virgin Oak 2010** bott Sept 15 db **(94) n22.5** a confusing – and confused – nose where neither the malt or massive sugars from the oak are prepared to give way to the other. A little time in the glass tames both sides slightly and it is the orange peel-led oak tannins which lead us to the spices; **t23.5** always youthful, the delivery is profound and lets rip with thickening tannins. The sugars, of the maple syrup variety, tinged slightly with molasses, offer an excellent counterweight; **f24** the earlier bickering ends and the finish is one very long fade of vividly spiced sugars and tannin; **b24** a malt which takes its time to find its feet. But once it has, it stands steadfast in its excellence. 49.5%

Stauning Peated 4th Edition dist 2011, bott 2014/10 db **(90.5) n22.5** a heavy distillate carries a lighter phenol. Sweet and dry run side by side and even occasionally merge; **t22.5** liquid Demerara sugar blinks first to let in the phenols which refuse to give up their position of power. A little ulmo honey and mocha ensure intensity and complexity; **f23** at first a bitter weakness. But this is overcome by the mind-boggling complexity of the sugar and smoky spice which soon overcomes any tannin negativity; **b22.5** clever harnessing of the sugars and smoke. 53.1%

Stauning 5th Edition Peated dist 2011, bott May 15 db **(93.5) n24** a stunning fanfare of peat: something like a mix between Laphroaig and Caol Ila in style...only with the odd hint of feint; **t23** and with those oils and sugars, a type of Caol Ila delivery and follow through. The vanilla-ulmo honey mix fills the gap before the finish brilliantly; **f23** sweet, oily and yet more soft honey. To be brutally technical, the feints, like the smoke, never quite goes away... but this is truly wonderful stuff; **b23.5** Danish peated whisky in full, confident stride. 51.1%

◈ **Stauning Peated 6th Edition** dist 2012, bott Jun 16 db **(95) n23.5** not your normal peat by any means. If it is Danish peat at play it wouldn't surprise me as the chemical make-up is distinct, with an almost smoked sausage style to this, with no little fatty gristle...; **t23.5** wonderful delivery of molten, almost porridge-like, sugars supplementing the major smoke. Supreme weight to the oils and spice, too, not dissimilar to wheated whiskies; **f23.5** long, chewy, distinctive and even a flash of late hickory; **b24.5** my God! When they say "peated", they bloody well mean peated...!!! So beautifully distilled: just makes technocrats like me purr...If you were not quite sure if Stauning qualifies as a Premier League distillery, this will most likely confirm it.. 51.5%

Stauning KAOS bott 2014/10 db **(89.5) n22.5** a slight feintiness dumbs down the more assured and better structured moments, especially with the light phenols and cranky grains; **t23** fabulously beautiful delivery: sharp as a surgeon's knife and almost as precise, the crispness to the grains ensure a big salivating factor; **f21.5** the feints on the nose return for a bitter, slightly oily finale; **b22.5** to entitle this whisky as Chaos is to do it a great disservice. Complex and challenging, for sure. Chaotic...never. 54.3%

◈ **Stauning KAOS** dist 2011-2013, bott Feb 16 db **(94.5) n23** first you are ware of the light feints, then the honey and...rye? Because of the feints, you have to look twice at the light smoke: is it there or not? It is...; **t24.5** just too ridiculously beautiful. Peated rye? Oily Demerara? Spiced acacia honey? Malted muscovado...? So many questions...so many confusing but magnificently delicious answers; **f23** long, with a spiced molassed fade. With smoked rye, of course....; **b24** an altogether better blending than their first attempt: indeed, rather well too layered and structured for true chaos... 46.5%

Stauning Peated Sherry Cask Finish dist 2011, bott 2014 db **(74.5) n19 t20.5 f17 b18.** Good, kind, talented people of Stauning Distillery. You took my advice many years ago, hopefully to your advantage. I hope you do so again now: please do NOT use sherry butts for your whisky, especially your peated version. It is far too risky for so little return...indeed, negative impact. 49.3%

◈ **Stauning Traditional 4th Edition 2010 Single Malt**, bott Sept 15 db **(87.5) n21.5 t22 f22 b22.** It is perhaps hard to imagine a malt whisky with more barley escaping from every pore. Indeed, there is something of the old English barley wine beer to this, though without the hop. But the slightly annoying oils attached to this – evidence of stretching the cut a little too far – tarnishes what might have been a golden cup. Highly entertaining, though far from perfect. 46.3%

Stauning Young Rye dist 2012, bott May 15 db **(89) n22** well it's young! And it's rye, for sure! Just a little too much nougat and tobacco has crept into this one; **t22.5** as oily and intense as you would expect from a wide cut involving a massive-flavoured grain; huge honey and spice, too, as the salivation levels keep on rising; **f22.5** dries, though the spices get serious; **b22** big and bruising...but so bloody tasty! 49.5%

◈ **Stauning Young Rye 2012**, bott Jun 15 db **(88.5) n22** sharp, punchy and spiced. The crisper rye notes reward some searching through the oils; **t23** thick, lush and a slow revelation of the dry, red-liquorice-tinged concentrated rye; **f21.5** just a shade too oily; **b22** a generous cut mean the heavier oils linger.... 51%

◈ **Stauning Young Rye** dist 2011-2013, bott Nov 15 db **(88) n21.5** thick with oils and even a hint of boiled brussels. Pretty opaque, though the rye can just be made out; **t23.5** emphasis on the early muscovado sugars, then an explosion of spice heralds in the profound rye; **f21** a tad dirty as the oils clog up a little; **b22** had the cut been a little less wide, this would have been a Stauning stunner. A fascinating mix of the brilliant and not so brilliant... 50%

◈ **Stauning Young Rye 2013**, bott Mar 16 db **(95) n23.5** profound American-style rye: clean, intense, bounding with threatening spices and cinnamon, too; **t24** clunking, crisp rye with the spice threat on the nose now a delicious reality. Gorgeous oils paint all the right spots and the dark muscovao sugars join with the rye in radiating a vague fruitiness; **f23.5** pounding spices with the multi-segmented rye still crisp and intact; **b24** so thick with rye, you have to floss your teeth afterwards... 50.1%

THY WHISKY Snedsted, Working.

◈ **Thy Whisky Single Malt Cask no. 2a Hawboen** db **(88) n21.5** warm pastry: custard tart straight out of the oven; **t22** eye-wateringly sharp delivery! A mass escape of early sugars – all of them dark – makes good the explosive tannin; a cream raspberry jam middle, not unlike that found in a Swiss Roll, develops out of seemingly nowhere; **f22.5** spices arrive early but are side-tracked by the growing complexity. They return for the finale in hearty fashion; **b22** not the type of malt you come across every day – or are likely to forget. At first, you sit there in stunned silence. Then you go back to it and discover that the dots join and, once acclimatised, the palate can identify a very enjoyable and complex whisky. If a little brash. 48%. ncf sc.

◈ **Thy Whisky Single Malt Cask no. 2b Fjordboen** db (86) n21 t22 f21.5 b21.5. Distinctly malty. Again the muscled tannin sports tattoos. 48%. ncf sc.

◈ **Thy Whisky Single Malt Cask no. 3 Kræn Kræmmer** db (93.5) n23.5 I haven't even looked at the label yet, but I'll bet my perfect parrot to a croaked canary that this is from sherry. And, not only that, as fresh a cask as you'll find this year. The grape is not just intense, but layered in its sweetness – and it is the sugars which really do shine. A fabulous mix of molasses and over-ripe crushed sultana, plus cider brandy and we have more Sussex Cake than Melton Hunt cake; oh...and there's warming spices, too...; t23.5 succulent delivery, but those spices now don't just explode but reach out into every crevice on the palate; improbably salivating and still malty despite the obvious attentions of the grape; f23 a more measured finale. The tones lower by small degrees; the relative youth of the spirit is, like on the very first hit, slightly more obvious now. But the fading mutterings of the fruit and spices can be heard for quite a while; b23.5 always great to happen across a non-sulphured sherry cask: well done people of Thy! This really is a beautiful malt. 57.7%. ncf sc.

ENGLAND

ADNAMS Saffron Walden. Working.

Adnams Southwold Triple Grain Whisky No 2 American oak, bott 2013 (87) n22 t22 f21 b22. For my 999th new whisky for Bible 2015 I wanted, as this book's custom dictates, to choose something a little unusual. And here we have the first-ever Suffolk whisky, made at one of my favourite breweries in the world, Adnams. Not sure what happened to the first bottling but I have the second. And beside me is Percy, my Meyers parrot born in Norfolk not far from the Suffolk border while this cask was maturing. The most remarkable thing to report is the nose. It is, and I really have to find out how, the closest whisky I have ever encountered on nose that matches a decent biryani in its subtle Asian spicy complexity. To taste it is a lot more straightforward: a tad feinty, but those oils conjure up the spices which sit well with the intense sugars. The finish, naturally enough, is a little bitter and foggy from the feints...but with no uncomfortable edges. For now I shall stick to their almost incomparable bitter beer. But I shall be keeping a close eye... 43%. ncf. WB15/407

COTSWOLDS DISTILLERY Shipton-on-Stour. Working.

Cotswolds Distillery 5 Months batch no. 04/2015, ex-oloroso sherry cask, bott 1 Sept 15 db (89.5) n21.5 t23.5 f22 b22.5. The fact that this is, thankfully, a clean sherry butt means we can spot some clues to the future style of this malt. It is clearly small still type, revelling in all its inherent intensity. But we can already see a confirmation of the new make: this a malt which likes to get off to a dramatic start, pitching all the elements of the flavour profile together in the first few moments before letting things unravel. At this age you let the odd jarring moment go, as all maturing spirit lacks a degree of couthness, with a degree of extra roughage from the extra copper. 63.5%. ncf.

Cotswolds Distillery 10 Months cask no. 32, ex-red wine cask, bott 1 Sept 15 db (91) n22 t23.5 f22.5 b23. This one, showing some of the first will-be whisky made at the distillery, has already begun to settle into a flavour rhythm. The body of the spirit is able to hold the powering fresh fruit with ease and allows the malt to interact from an early stage. Some very decent spices abound, though they have to work hard to get through the weightiness of the malt's weight. Again, a little sharpness at the finish: with the stills being brand new, that is entirely expected. Exceptionally promising malt from my neighbours just the other side of Banbury. 63.5%. ncf sc.

Cotswolds Distillery New Make batch no. 08/2015, bott 1 Sept 15 db (94) n23.5 t24 f23 b23.5. High quality new make still glistening with a coppery sheen on both nose and taste. And it is on delivery where it really stars, showing a gorgeous weight and great confidence as it maximises the malt. All spices and gristy sugars present and correct. The only thing missing is the usual cocoa dryness present on the finish of most good quality new makes. Maybe hiding behind the new still copper sharpness. 63.5%. ncf.

◈ **Cotswolds Distillery New Make Spirit** batch no. WC 22:2:2, dist 29 May 16, bott 11 Jul 16 db (89) n20 t23.5 f23 b22.5. Slightly different character to the last new make bottling I tasted from them. Here, they have allowed the cut to be just a little too wide, impacting on the nose. Though that can mean a massive personality on delivery, which is in evidence here. Loads of malt and chocolate notes later on, and astonishing sugars in between. Yummy doesn't quite cover it. Though with my blender's technical hat on, a few marks dropped. Anyway, thought I'd taste this English whisky – made just a short journey from my tasting room - on the very day our new Prime Minister, Theresa May, formed a brand new cabinet which includes the Whisky Bible's local MP as Environment Secretary: here's to you, Andrea! *63.5%*

◈ **Cotswolds Distillery Single Malt Spirit 20 Months** Old bourbon cask, cask no. 47, bott 11 Jul 16 db **(91) n21.5** still clings to its new makey aroma...; **t23** after an initial burst of slight feint we are almost overpowered by a glorious avalanche of intense, almost concentrated malty grist. The sugars are caught on an oily tide and crash relentlessly in to the spices; **f23.5** a stunning interplay between chocolate, vanilla and grist; **b23** coming along rather beautifully... *61.8%*

◈ **Cotswolds Distillery Single Malt Spirit 20 Months Old ex-red wine cask (shaved, toasted & recharred)**, cask no. 58, bott 11 Jul 16 db **(94) n22.5** very tight tannin: something more akin to lively bourbon than a single malt; **t24** oh, do I have to spit...? Really...? Damn it! This is so, so lovely. Salivating malt from the very first second. But the levels of tannin-enriched barley and the varying intensity of the sugars is mesmerising. A slick oiliness appears to attach itself to the more profound dark muscovdo; **f23.5** long, with a light citrus edging to the vanilla; a light hint of treacle towards the end just as the spices get serious; **b24** if they don't put the brakes on this, it'll be too old by the time it reaches 36 months. At this moment, simply stunning! *62.7%*

HEALEY'S CORNISH CYDER FARM Penhallow. Working.

Hicks & Healey Cornish Whiskey 2004 Cask #32 dist 13 Feb 04, bott Feb 12 db **(96) n24 t24.5 f23.5 b24.** I picked this one up absent-mindedly, nosed...and was carried to Cornwall. I knew what it was without even opening my eyes. Unmistakable. And just so stunningly beautiful... *60.2%. ncf.*

LAKES DISTILLERY Cumbria, Working.

◈ **The Lakes Malt Spirit** db **(90) n23 t22 f22.5 b22.5.** I have chosen this as the 999th new "whisky" for the 2017 Bible as a tribute to my dear old friend Harold Currie who was recently lost to us. Harold was behind the building of the Isle of Arran Distillery and a close bond, based mainly on mutual respect and fondness for the simple things in life – like St Mirren and football in general - formed between us. Both his sons played a part in getting this distillery off the ground, so though not yet a whisky, it is a special moment for me to taste their new-ish make. With the very first sip I ever have of this ground-breaking malt, I shall toast a very special old fiend: Harold Currie.... A lovely developing malt with a very puritanical cut ensuring the citrus has a big part to play. Massively promising as this is clean and characterful. But, my dear old friends, you have to bottle this stuff at something closer to cask strength: you have broken up the oils so we cannot quite see its full potential. *40%*

ST. GEORGE'S Rowdham. Working.

The English Whisky Co. Chapter 6 English Single Malt Not Peated ASB casks, cask no. 001, 002, 003, 004, dist May 09, bott Jan 13 db **(95) n23.5 t24 f23.5 b24.** Shows what maturing in truly great casks can do. Any more stylishly English and you'd think it was distilled in Jermyn Street... *46%. nc ncf.*

The English Whisky Co. Chapter 6 English Single Malt Not Peated ASB casks, cask no. 005, 006, 007, 008, dist May 09, bott Feb 13 db **(96) n24 t24 f24 b24.** You taste the Chapter 6 casks 1-4 and think it doesn't get any better...and then...this!!! Truly flawless distillate matured in high quality casks. Not just free of a single off note...free of a hint of a rumour of an off note. Truly sublime whisky showing that youth, when well brought up, can only delight. One of the finest examples of unpeated single malt whisky to have hit the market worldwide in the last three or four years... *46%. nc ncf.*

The English Whisky Co. Chapter 6 English Single Malt Not Peated ASB casks, cask no. 0193, 0194, dist Apr 10, bott Apr 13 db **(95) n23.5 t25 f23 b23.5.** I'm not sure if anything since Supertramp brought out Crime of the Century and Crisis What Crisis? back in the mid 1970s has two, or in this case three, back to back releases been so seamless or faultless. Let me say it and, as an Englishman, say it proudly: this whisky borders genius. *46%. nc ncf.*

T**he English Whisky Co. Chapter 6 Unpeated** cask no. 248, 249, 250, 251, dist Oct 10, bott Nov 13 db **(89.5) n22.5** a light honey thread distracts from the slightly new-makey breeze; **t22** outrageously juicy on delivery, but the malt is febrile and takes time to happily link with the oak; **f23** the slow pulsing of the dry cocoa is sublime though, unusually, this is from the spirit rather than the oak. Just how good the original spirit was becomes clear as the maltiness makes its mark; **b22** a very solid score, though anything under 90 seems like a failure for this particular distillery. A rare occurrence where the youth of the spirit and the influence of the oak have been detached. Still a thing of youthful beauty when all is said and done. *60.2%. WB15/183*

The English Whisky Co. Chapter 7 Rum Cask cask no. 765, 766, dist Oct 09, bott May 14 db **(92) n22.5** confidently crisp rum influence from the kickoff: a light, sugary shell encrusts the beautifully defined barley; **t23** mmmm...!! Such a glorious fanfare of intense barley on delivery, which intensifies even further with a chunky gristiness during the slow progression; **f23.5** quite wonderful finish: the rum remerges somewhat with a light sugary sheen to the charming chalky oak and citrus gristy mix; **b23** an essay in understated deliciousness. A near perfect use of delicate sugar. 46%. nc ncf. 550 bottles. WB15/188

The English Whisky Co. Chapter 7 Rum Cask cask no. 0765, 0766, dist Oct 09, bott May 14 db **(94) n23 t23.5 f24 b23.5.** Of all the English Whisky bottlings to its sister version (above), this is the closest in style despite the alcohol leap. Everything here, though, is more polished, concentrated and vivid....as you might expect. Quite superb. 59.9%. 96 bottles. WB15/187

The English Whisky Co. Chapter 7 Rum Finish ASB & rum casks, cask no. 0457, 0458, dist May 09, bott Apr 13 **(91.5) n22 t23.5 f23 b23.** You have to be confident when maturing in rum: this has a propensity to tighten a malt until little but the sugars are heard. This though is 92% proof that St George can slay that particular dragon. 46%. nc ncf.

The English Whisky Co. Chapter 7 Single Malt Rum Cask cask no. 0459 & 0461, dist May 09, bott Apr 15 db **(91.5) n22.5** the sugars are taught and allow the spices to slowly make their mark; **t24.5** amazing golden syrup notes on delivery and the first few waves, but enlivened with a spicy punctuation. A delivery of your dreams, where the malt also makes an impact, as does the Lubeck marzipan and chocolate; **f22** hardens and draws away from the more complex angles; bitters very slightly; **b22.5** there is quite a profound difference between the delivery and finish. 59.9%. nc ncf.

◈ **The English Whisky Co. Chapter 7** Rum Casks, cask no. 057, 059, 487 & 488, dist May 09, bott Feb 16 db **(92.5) n23** a tart, robust nose where the rum comes at you with minimum subtlety from the very start; **t23** startling clarity on delivery: a crispness reminiscent slightly of a youthful Glen Grant as the malt really does begin to magnify its intensity; **f23** clipped sugars, crisp and delicious. The spices and cocoa are as inevitable as they are teasing yet confident; **b23.5** you'll be hard pressed to find a better whisky to kick start an evening a tune up the taste buds before dinner. 46%. ncf nc.

The English Whisky Co. Chapter 9 Peated ASB casks, cask no. 064, 065, 066, 103, dist Oct 09, bott Feb 13 db **(92.5) n23.5 t23 f23 b23.** A growling, grumbling, curmudgeonly dram which wants to keep to a separate path from the sugars. 46%. nc ncf.

◈ **The English Whisky Co. Chapter 9** Peated cask no. 0201, 0202, 0203 & 0205, dist Apr 10, bott Jul 13 db **(94) n22.5** the peat has a vaguely ethereal feel. There is breakfast cereals at work here. Chocolate Rice Crispies are particularly prominent; a vague chocolate raisin element here, too; **t23.5** low level phenols on delivery with the grist really churning out the oily sugars. But, uniquely, as the phenols begin to gather then so too does the chocolate, almost blow for blow. Again, there is a non-specific fruitiness, perhaps erring towards plum or grape, which fills in the gaps with aplomb. Or is that a plum...? **f24,** so long. Here is a fabulous example of what non-chill-filtered whisky offers: every last trace and sinew is stretched by the oils; a vague fruitiness tries to speak above the noise of the phenols while all the time the cocoa assembles and thickens; **b24** not sure an English whisky has ever come across this chocolatey in the history of...well, English whisky. For those of you who have decided to give up sex, here's its replacement... 59.4%. ncf nc. 96 bottles.

◈ **The English Whisky Co. Chapter 9** Peated cask no. 354, 355, 356 & 577, dist Apr 13, bott May 16 db **(93) n22.5** youthful, for sure. But the slight squeeze of citrus both lightens yet complicates the character. The smoke is more than present, yet never allowed to remotely dominate; **t23.5** this is so clean, so crisp and expect my teeth to be gleaming by the time I have finished tasting this. The phenols are attached to some junior spices keen to flex their muscles. The juicy grist intervenes deliciously; **f23.5** for all the smoky presence, the citrus and juicy, grassy barley still lord it; **f23.5** it quite beggars belief that this is a 3-y-o whisky. Just so beautiful...this must be the mid cut of the very heart of the run... 46%. ncf nc.

The English Whisky Co. Chapter 11 Heavily Peated ASB casks, cask no. 0062, 0065, dist Apr 09, bott Jul 12 db **(81) n19 t22 f21 b19.** A rare blemish. This malt is very much less than the sum of its parts as not enough attention was made in balancing out the peats and the sugars. Brief harmony as the sugars and oils hit the palate, but on the nose and for long periods in the mouth this is a free for all: young malts are temperamental. And here the balance has not been found. 46%. nc ncf.

The English Whisky Co. Chapter 11 Heavily Peated ASB casks, cask no. 639, 640, 641 & 642, dist Mar 08, bott Nov 11 db **(91.5) n22.5 t23 f23 b23.** One of the sweetest English whiskies for the last century... 46%. nc ncf.

The English Whisky Co. Chapter 12 Single Malt Sherry Cask cask no. 0872, bott 2012 db **(94.5) n24 t24 f22.5 b24** An almost flawless sherry butt. Housing just about flawlessly-distilled whisky. The result is something a little special... 60.3%. nc ncf sc.

The English Whisky Co. Chapter 13 Dragon cask no.527, 528, 827, 830, dist 2008, bott 2013 db **(92.5) n23.5 t23.5 f22 b23.5** Take your time with this: like all the best whiskies, this is a moving target never sitting still and with so many elements camouflaged before being spotted. 49%. ncf nc. WB15/397

The English Whisky Co. Chapter 13 London db **(91) n22** a telling light furriness tells me to be on the lookout for more fruit characteristics, which are to be found, intriguingly, with a slightly salty tang. More herb garden than fruit, though the delicate molasses heads in the direction of a dry, two-days-on-the-plate Melton Hunt cake....; **t24** the spices rise early on an oily bed which makes for a friendly, though far from docile opening. A mix of malt, red liquorice and hickory forms the van of the attack but deeper fruitier notes rumble, especially the magnificent walnut and dates; **f22** spicy still but the dryness has an unwelcome catch, though a few chocolate fruit and nut notes repairs some of the damage; **b23** the nose suggests sherry butts at work here, as does the slightly furry finale. But this is a superficial wound and the overall composition is rather lovely. 45%. nc ncf. WB15/181

The English Whisky Co. Chapter 13 Letter Box db **(87) n21.5 t22.5 f21 b22.** How odd. Some of the characteristics found on their 2014 St George's day bottling can be found here, too. Except for this latest edition, those flatter notes are flatter still. No shortage of malt, mind. 45%. nc ncf.

⟐ **The English Whisky Co. Chapter 14** ASB Casks, cask no. 057, 059, 487 & 488, dist Sept 09, bott Jul 15 db **(94.5) n24** what a stunner: just the most playful peat at large, adding earthiness to the freshly pressed apples...and intense malt; **t23.5** creamy textured delivery with the malt thickening like a Bardstown Murray Maltshake; that gentle peat arrives in slightly prickly form; **f23** long and luxurious, with now a vanilla cream soda feel; **b24** only six years old! Boasts the complexity of a malt three times that age. Beautiful whisky: simple as! 46%. ncf nc.

⟐ **The English Whisky Co. Chapter 14** Not Peated cask no. 120, 121, 122 & 123, dist Apr 11, bott Jun 16 db **(96) n24** five years old....!!! Astonishing!! Yes, it is young, for sure. But the charm with which the lightest of acacia honey intermingles with gristy barley and thin layer of gooseberry jam...oh, my! So delicate one is frightened to nose slightly too hard....; **t24** soft, clean, gorgeously textured: the oils are fully rampant here having not been cut - yet all is perfectly weighted. Crisp and salivating barley arriving from the first moment pulse out a gentle sweetness which keeps in character with the nose; **f24** those oils take us into extra time. But the drier, chalky vanillas and cocoa merge with the barley to create an elegant and highly sophisticated finale; **b24** there are less than 200 bottles of this unambiguously world-class and faultless nectar, apparently. What a bugger...! 58.8%. ncf nc. 192 bottles.

The English Whisky Co. Chapter 14 Single Malt (unpeated) cask no. 205, 181, 182, 183, dist Apr 10, bott May 15 db **(92.5) n23** the oak plays little toffeed patterns upon the malt: soft and belying its age. The vanilla confirms more oak than usually seen from this distillery; **t23.5** a beautiful oily cushion offers a tapestry of intense malt and toffee apple; **f23** vanilla and butterscotch before a little toasted fudge begins to softly clear its throat...; **b23** how can a malt at nearly 60%abv be so silky soft and sexy? A ridiculously gentle and genteel whisky. 58.8%. nc ncf.

The English Whisky Co. Chapter 14 Not Peated cask no. 450, 451, 452, 453, dist Feb 09, bott May 14 db **(96) n24 t24.5 f23.5 b24** Any distiller in the world would give his right hand to lay claim to malt of such exceptionally high quality. 58.8%. 299 bottles. WB15/185

The English Whisky Co. Chapter 15 Single Malt Heavily Peated cask no. 041, 042, 043, 043, dist Sept 09, bott Sept 14 db **(94.5) n23.5** much more aggressive than the standard Peated bottling, not so much for the difference in strength, but the slightly more acidic anthracite kick to the peat; **t24** look for faults on the delivery for as long as you like: there aren't any! The oils and phenols are hand in glove, the chewability is off any known scales...; a little ulmo honey mixes with much broader muscovado, then an infusion of bewildering spices which swarm and warm; **f23.5** long; a little timber ensures extra ballast beyond the smoke; **b23.5** if all whiskies were like this, I'd never get this book finished: so easy to go off into another world as you explore the peaty complexity to its character. Just great stuff! 58.4%. nc ncf. 192 bottles.

The English Whisky Co. Chapter 15 English Single Malt (peated) db **(94.5) n23.5 t24 f23 b24.** If you could take that single flaw out of the equation, you'd have just about perfect whisky for a five-year-old. As it is, you'll just have to make do with bloody magnificent.... And make no mistake: this is no poor man's Islay. It stands up with the world's elite. 58.4%. nc ncf.

The English Whisky Co. Chapter 16 Single Malt Peated, Sherry Cask cask nos. 693 & 694, dist Nov 07, bott Sept 14 db **(95) n23** the peat, as welcoming as a feathered pillow, snuggles up first, prickly spices by its side. The soft grape sidles up beside the smoke and slowly begins to gently cloak it; **t24.5** oh...my...word...!!! The delivery stops you in your tracks. You sense the youth to this immediately, but that is immaterial. All that matters is the shape-shifting, forming and reforming with the interplay between the lush sherry and the toned, agile peat; beyond this mesmerising scene you might be able to focus also on the dates, sticky molasses and Zambian honey; **f23.5** so the odd furry note is there if you look for it (as I have to do). But the slowly unravelling of the grape must and dry peat soot is far more interesting and entertaining....; **b24** there are few occasions when sherry and peat travel comfortably together, hand-in-hand. But here is one, thanks to the softness (and general cleanness) of the grape and non-bombastic, embracing style of the peat. As gentle giants go, this is benign and enormous... *58.3%. nc ncf.*

⬦ **The English Whisky Co. Chapter 15 Heavily Peated** ASB casks, cask no. 180, 214, 215 & 216, dist May 10, bott Jan 16 db **(89.5) n22** for all its hefty peat overtones, remains bright, sharp and malt-laden; **t23** a delivery for peat freaks. The phenols gather immediately and form an early exclusive bond. Slowly lighter muscovado sugars break through as well as some pretty warming spice; a sprig of mint makes a surprising but welcome arrival at the midpoint; **f22.5** dries despite the oils and extra spoon-fulls of molassed, spiced vanilla; **b22** a rare whisky where the sum is less than the parts. Never finds a rhythm or narrative: it is like a series of disconnected stories are told on the palate. Yet many moments are superb. *46%. ncf nc.*

⬦ **The English Whisky Co. Chapter 15 Heavily Peated** cask no. 145, 146, 147 & 148, dist Feb 10, bott Sept 15 db **(95.5) n23.5** not usually a fan of fruit and peat. But here we have dates, citrus, spotted dog and compelling peat all working in unison with no single factor dominating; **t24** can this really be five years old? These must have been absolutely top casks at play here for the vanillins bind together the muscovado sugars as an almost perfect counterweight to the gorgeous oils which coat the palate with a fabulously weighted smokiness. Neither sweet nor dry – well, rather, both, but no domination. The spices prickle while the sugars slowly dissolve; **f24** ridiculously long. Unusually for a finish, the sugars multiply as a light gristiness combines with the persistent muscovado sugar. The phenols cling to the healthy oils and at the very death some genuine vanilla-clad age can be detected; the spices, which begin tentatively, finish with a degree of liquorice-laced panache; **b24** almost from the Lagavulian of vaguely fruity, pretty oily, intensely peaty school of malt whisky. Sublime. *58.4%. ncf nc. 192 bottles.*

⬦ **The English Whisky Co. Original** bourbon cask db **(89) n22.5** so light. The malt seems distracted by the gently encroaching vanillas and with the oils scuppered at this strength the daintier notes have a slight advantage; rarely does barley come much greener than this...; **t22.5** clean, soft, silky, exceptionally malty and then a surge of salivating gristly sweetness. It is like being licked to death by a neighbour's slobbering pet Labrador...; **f22** the vanilla and light citrus fade are entirely in keeping; **b22** when I first tasted this an odd thing happened. For a moment I thought I was tasting an old Scottish blend still in lab form and pre-bottled from over 25 years ago. I certainly didn't recognise it as Norfolk's finest. Pleasant, hugely enjoyable and friendly. But by EWC standards, pretty basic, too. *43%.*

⬦ **The English Whisky Co. Smokey** bourbon cask db **(93.5) n23** quite a different type of phenol here, sharp and acrid and not dissimilar to that found inside a crisp packet...; **t23** ridiculously soft delivery. Like their "Original" at 43% this has a curious and not unattractive feel of an old blend about it, the lightness of the body being in stark contrast to the weight of the peat. Sugars, of course, abound but in beautifully controlled form; **f23.5** now we hit super complexity as the phenols calm sufficiently for the light tannins and liquorice to make brilliant contrast to the glittering array of dark, toasty sugars; **b24** they could have also written "smoky bacon cask".... *43%.*

HRH Princess Charlotte of Cambridge db **(95) n23.5** youthful, but a lot more mature than Princess Charlotte. The barley is proud and unflustered and has taken on just enough positive from the oak to ensure a comfortable balance; **t24** sublime sugars lead from the start. An attractive almost Spey-style gristiness benefits from a sharper citrus edge, so, soon after delivery the salivation factor goes through the roof...; **f23.5** remains clean; perhaps a little bitterness creeping in from the cask. But the grist and vague heather-honey fade ensures it is kept in check with the most attractive and regal of finishes; **b24** to pay tribute to the latest member of the British royal family, I saved this as the 1,028th new and very last whisky for the 2016 Bible. Knowing first-hand her grandfather's taste for fine whisky, I am sure he will, like me, enjoy raising a glass of this most intensely malty bottling, which showcases the distillery in elegant style. *46%*

⬦ **Master of Malt Single Cask English Whisky Co. 5 Year Old** oloroso sherry cask, dist Apr 10, bott Feb 16 **(75) n18 t20 f18 b19**. God! If only those silly sods in Spain hadn't shoved a sulphur candle in this. Even through the murk, there are some sugars at work which astound. What a malt this might have been. Bollocks! *65.3%. sc.*

⬦ **Master of Malt Single Cask English Whisky Co. 5 Year Old Heavily Peated** bourbon cask, dist Jul 10, bott Feb 16 **(94) n23.5** technically, ticks so many boxes I've had to re-sharpen my pencil three times. A genuinely frugal cut, as the peat appears to be too unencumbered by the kind of notes you might expect from a malt of this tender age; **t24** massive. And yet, even so, the league in which the peat and molasses are in, and the way the grist is sprinkled all over the palate, makes for something a little special; **f23** the smoke drifts towards the finish line like an autumn leaf drifts towards the forest floor; **b23.5** you know when they say "heavily peated"...? Well, this is heavily peated...and, frankly, almost peerlessly made... *67.4%. sc.*

◇ **Master of Malt Single Cask English Whisky Co. 5 Year Old** oloroso sherry cask, dist Apr 10, bott Feb 16 **(75) n18 t20 f18 b19.** God! If only those silly sods in Spain hadn't shoved a sulphur candle in this. Even through the murk, there are some sugars at work which astound. What a malt this might have been. Bollocks! *65.3%. sc.*

◇ **Master of Malt Single Cask English Whisky Co. 7 Year Old** bourbon cask, cask no. B1/490, dist Aug 08, bott Feb 16 **(92.5) n23** a happy marriage of citrus and malt; the newlyweds are of tender years; **t23** good oils really nail the big malt statement to the wall. A lighter citrus sub-plot; decent spice, too; **f22.5** spiced vanilla; **b23** very similar to cask B1/491 except this appears slightly further down the road in terms of development. *67.2%. sc.*

◇ **Master of Malt Single Cask English Whisky Co. 7 Year Old** bourbon cask, cask no. B1/491, dist Aug 08, bott Feb 16 **(90.5) n23** incredible! You can play spot the citrus notes here, or, more simply, name the citrus notes you can't spot...; **t22.5** if the nose is youthful the delivery is almost embryonic. Yet the clarity of the barley and the cleanliness of that citrus astonishes; **f22** a vanilla tingle; **b22.5** still something of a new make feel to this. In a way, it's a shame it was bottled: I would have set this aside for another eight years at least, after which I think it would have thrust itself upon greatness... *67.3%. sc.*

Stephen Notman Whisky Live Taipei 2013 The English Whisky Co db **(95.5) n24 t24 f23.5 b24.** A ridiculously stunning cask which I selected from St George's to celebrate Stephen Notman's impressive five year stewardship of Whisky Live in Taipei... making this a very English Whisky affair. Bewildering and beguiling for a four-year-old, where the peat is confident yet elegent, the body crisp yet lush and the complexity and balance beyond comprehension for its age. It was a pleasure to help promote not just the best of Bristish, but truly world-class whisky to an appreciative Taiwanese audience. And just shows what magic happens when near perfect spirit meets a near perfect cask. *50.6%*

◇ **That Boutique-y Whisky Company English Whisky Co. 5 Year Old** batch 1 **(91) n22** like an old-fashioned Speysider with a few shards of smoke being found amid the intense malt; **t23** superb delivery: compact, thick and oily at first, then spreads out revealing its more fruity colours (muscovado sugars, to be more precise) like a naughty Victorian gal might have shown her ankles...; **f22.5** just too ridiculously long and well-weighted than any five-year-old malt has the remotest right to be...; **b23.5** how do you get a malt this young to perform so many adult tricks...? *49.5%. 964 bottles.*

Whisky Live Taipei 2013 Founders Release B1/416, dist 7/4/09 **(93) n23.5 t23 f23.5 b23.** Beautifully made; excellent sweetness and beautifully smoky. A quietly satisfying malt. *50.6%*

FINLAND
THE HELSINKI DISTILLING COMPANY Helsinki, Working.

◇ **The Helsinki Distilling Co White Dog 100% Rye** batch 5, dist 21 Oct 15, bott 16 Dec 15 db **(92.5) n23 t23 f23.5 b23.** A crisp, intense rye spirit which appears to achieve the goal that has been targeted. As well as the desired fruit note and spice, a little ulmo honey meanders around to sweeten the dose. I look forward to seeing its sister distillate make its mark over the forthcoming years. Impressive. *60.5%*

◇ **The Helsinki Distilling Co White Dog Straight Rye** batch 63, dist 15 Dec 15, bott 17 Dec 15 db **(88) n22 t22 f22 b22.** Seemingly, less copper contact here than with their batch 5 100% rye. Salivating and filled with burgeoning rye, a drier run with a bigger spice kick. Good powdered cocoa finale, as it should be. *60.5%*

◇ **The Helsinki Distilling Co Single Malt 2014 Prelude 1 Year Old** batch 5, cask no. 13-21, dist 01 Sept 14, bott 17 Dec 15 db **(91.5) n22 t23 f23.5 b23.** Just over a year old, yet dosed up with more tannin than some scotch malts see over 20 years... Presumably, either very small, heavily charred and/or virgin oak at play here. Delightfully distilled, the clarity of the spirit allows the oak extra dominance. But those rather angular molassed sugars, as well as the mocha, liquorice and toffee concentrate, work very well in tandem with the inevitable spices. By age, not actually whisky. But close your eyes and you'll never know: Fins aren't what they seem to be... *58%*

◇ **The Helsinki Distilling Co Single Malt 2015** batch 6, cask no. 15-SM5, dist 29 Jan 15, bott 02 Feb 15 db **(78.5) n19 t21 f19 b19.5.** Sweet: tick. Malty: tick. But that isn't quite enough when the copper has gone AWOL. *60.5%*

PANIMORAVINTOLA KOULU Turku, Working.

◈ **Sgoil Bourbon Cask 6 Years Old** (db (88) **n22.5** sultana fruit cake, sprinkled in fruity light muscovado sugar, ginger and nutmeg; **t22** distinctly doughy with a spiced spotted dog pudding feel; **f21.5** spiced ulmo honey does its best to overcome a nagging bitterness; **b22** not sure if you are meant to drink this or bake it... *59%. sc.*

◈ **Sgoil Sherry Cask** db **(90) n23** my parrot, Percy, would absolutely kill for these juicy, musky sapphire grapes; **t23.5** something of the Torqui about this delivery: fat, intense and purposeful, with a slow unravelling of herbs and spices as it dries in the same pace a striptease artist slowly reveals her hidden charms; **f21.5** annoyingly bitters at the death, despite all the fruity attention; **b22.5** sherry...and clean as a whistle! A sulphur-free dram from Finland. *59%. sc. 80 bottles.*

PANIMORAVINTOLA BEER HUNTER'S Pori. Working.

Old Buck cask no. 4, dist Mar 04, bott Apr 10 db **(95) n24 t23 f24 b24.** Just read the tasting notes to the second release because, a dose of what almost seems like corn oil and ancient Demerara rum combined apart, oh - and an extra dose of oak, there is barely any difference. I will never, ever forget how I got this sample: I was giving a tasting in Helsinki a few months back to a horseshoe-shaped audience and a chap who had been sitting to my right and joining in with all the fun introduced himself afterwards as I signed a book for him as non other than Mika Heikkinen, the owner and distiller of this glorious whisky. I had not been told he was going to be there. His actual, touchingly humble words were: "You might be disappointed: you may think it rubbish and give it a low score. It just means I have to do better next time." No, I am not disappointed: I am astonished. No, it isn't rubbish: it is, frankly, one of the great whiskies of the year. And if you can do better next time, then you are almost certainly in line for the Bible's World Whisky of the Year award. *70.6%*

TEERENPELI Tahti, Working.

Teerenpeli Single Malt Aged 8 Years oak cask db **(86) n21.5 t22 f21 b21.5.** Has moved on a notch or two from the five-year-old. A soft, simplistic experience, dependent on fudgy cream toffee and hazelnut. *43%*

◈ **Teerenpeli Single Malt 10 Year Old** bourbon & sherry casks db **(80) n20 t21 f19 b20.** Very hard to see what an average sherry butt can add to a malt as good as Teerenpeli's. And, sad to say, this is very average sherry wood, indeed... *43%*

◈ **Teerenpeli Single Malt Distiller's Choice Aura Porter-wood matured** db **(88.5) n22** a quite glorious layering of cocoa, walnut cake and malt. The sugars don't get all their own way, either...; hops....??? **t22.5** chewy, fat malt of considerable intensity alloyed with a vague bitterness; **f22** buttery finish, with the malt really upping the ante. And the hops even more...; **b22** before tasting this, I thought my researcher had accidentally added an "er " to Port Finish. Until I saw the colour...and discovered the lurking hops. As curious as it is tasty! *43%. sc. 426 bottles.*

Teerenpeli Single Malt Distiller's Choice HOSA 10 Year Old Black Cask Edition 2nd fill bourbon cask db **(94.5) n24** shadows, hints and whispers of delicate smoke, matched in subtlety by the deftness of the grain and sweetness of the butterscotch sugars; **t24** follows a silky road on the palate, bestowing along the way malty yet vaguely smoky kindnesses and gristy sugars which make a nonsense of the decade in the cask; **f23** long despite being slightly crystalline and crisp. The sugars harden slightly but work handsomely beside the vanilla thread; **b23.5** a distillery renowned for intensity shows it can do subtlety no less impressively *43% 672 bottles.*

◈ **Teerenpeli Single Malt Distiller's Choice KARHI** Madeira cask finish db **(92.5) n23** clean fruit - greengage and grape - slightly raised in profile by a hint of ginger and a pinch of salt; **t23.5** comfortable, silky and welcoming: the malt, aided by heather-honey, juts its chin proudly in every direction; **f23** a major late dose of tannin ensures the finale takes off beautifully; **b23** a delicious malt which, in the glass, has a habit of disappearing into Finnair... *43%. 1882 bottles. Duty Free Exclusive.*

◈ **Teerenpeli Single Malt Distiller's Choice RASI** Moscatel cask finish db **(93) n23.5** superb...! Faultlessly structured layering of outstanding weight: the fruit initially has the air of the substantial, but closer investigation reveals a much more delicate role played by the gently spiced grape; **t24** melt-in-the-mouth Demerara then gives way to juicy fruit candy...then that shadowy spice. Succulent, with the barley sugars never losing their way; **f22.5** dries almost over-emphatically at the chalky finish. But not before the fruit-layered malt says a classy farewell...; **b23** I see this distillery is giving up its reputation of offering some of the biggest whisky in the world for a more subtle approach... *43%. 2554 bottles. Duty Free Exclusive.*

Teerenpeli Single Malt Distiller's Choice Tallink Silja Edition Portwood Finish bourbon cask, finished in Port cask db **(93) n23.5** charming clarity with the Port influence more fulsome than just a finish; **t23.5** breathtaking juiciness: the barley is beautifully defined, the sugars no more than a background accompaniment; **f23** gentle grape keeps the oak involvement honest; **b23** typically Teerenpeli in its depth but now with well balanced fruitiness. *43% 1174 bottles.*

Teerenpeli Kaski Single Malt sherry cask db **(90.5) n23 t23.5 f21.5 b22.5.** A pristine sherry butt ensures massive fruit. Impressed. *43%*

FRANCE
Single Malt
DISTILLERIE ARTISANALE LEHMANN Obernai, Working.

◇ **Elsass Whisky Single Malt Whisky Alsacien Gold** db **(84.5) n21.5 t22 f20 b21.** The family of my old French girlfriend, Dominique, had an Alsacian. Dog, not whisky. And despite the breed's ferocious nature, I bonded with it more than any other dog before or since. For it was just a friendly as this caramel-rich offering. But had a lot more energy and personality. *40%. ncf.*

◇ **Elsass Whisky Single Malt Whisky Alsacien Origine** bott code. LF02 db **(83) n19 t22 f21 b21.** The soft feintiness on the nose warns of the riches of the oils to come. But before they reassemble on the finish, there is a lovely barley moment about two thirds of the way through the passage which does impress. *40%. ncf.*

◇ **Elsass Whisky Single Malt Whisky Alsacien Premium** db **(86) n20.5 t21.5 f22 b22.** This is about as close as you'll get to an abstract single malt. The early discordant notes of the distillate are thrown against the canvas of the malt, and then fruit is randomly hurled at it, making a juicy, then spicy, splash. The overall picture when you stand back is not at all bad. But getting there is a bit messy. *50%. ncf.*

DISTILLERIE BERTRAND Uberach, Working.

Uberach db **(77) n21 t19 f18 b19.** Big, bitter, booming. Gives impression something's happening between smoke and grape... whatever it is, there are no prisoners taken. *42.2%*

DISTILLERIE DE MONSIEUR BALTHAZAR Hérisson, Working.

◇ **Hedgehog Straight Whisky Bourbonnais** bott code. L2.16 db **(85.5) n20 t22.5 f21.5 b21.5.** You'd expect this to be a prickly little beast. Yet it is anything but: it celebrates the oils and honeys generated by the ample cut to the full and with only a minimum degree of spice. Eye-watering at its height, an unmistakable rye tartness maximises the flavour profile and dominates deliciously to the end. Get that cut a little tighter and what a magnificent whisky we would have here. *45%. ncf.*

DOMAINE DES HAUTES GLACES Saint-John-d'Hérans, Working.

◇ **Domaine des Hautes Glaces Flavis Single Cask Organic Whisky** db **(84.5) n21 t20 f22.5 b21.** Well, you can't say it doesn't have personality. Actually, the maltiness, which improves as it goes along, does hit impressive proportions. And the gathering cocoa also shows the oak plays an important part. But one or two verses of this are well out of tune. *46%. sc.*

◇ **Domaine des Hautes Glaces Moissons Single Malt Organic Whisky** db **(86.5) n20.5 t22 f22 b22.** Warming this to body temperature is vital as, when cool, it is not the most attractive proposition and scores badly. But when it is opened by body heat, the most delicate phenols show a subtlety and weight which were not before apparent, as do the tannins which reveal a more generous and inclusive element. The sugars are decidedly of an oaky bent with a dark toastiness which melt towards the tannins. *42%*

DISTILLERIE DES MENHIRS Bretagne, Working.

Eddu Gold db **(93) n22 t23 f24 b24.** Rarely do whiskies turn up in the glass so rich in character to the point of idiosyncrasy. Some purists will recoil from the more assertive elements. I simply rejoice. This is so proud to be different. And exceptionally good, to boot!! *43%*

Eddu Grey Rock db **(87.5) n21.5 t22 f22 b22.** A docile whisky reliant on friendly muscovado sugars which match the vanilla-oak very attractively. *40%*

Eddu Grey Rock Brocéliande db **(86.5) n22 t22.5 f20.5 b21.5.** Dense whisky which enjoys an enjoyable molassed fruitcake theme. A bit thin and wonky towards the finish. *40%*

Eddu Silver db **(81) n20 t22 f19 b20.** A curiosity of a whisky, though not up to the distillery's normal high standards. The base spirit hasn't been cut to advantage, so the feints tend to damage both nose and finish. Some astonishing sugars on deliver, though. *40%.*

Eddu Silver Broceliande db **(92.5) n23 t23 f23 b23.5** Pure silk. A beautiful and engaging experience. 40%.

DISTILLERIE DU PÉRIGOLD Sarlat, Working.
🔷 **Lascaw Aged 12 Years Blended Malt Whisky** bott 2-12-15 db **(87) n21 t22 f22 b22.** A very pleasant blend, very much of a Scotch style. Super soft, safe though sometimes juicy, this is perhaps held back by a constant caramel theme which tames the expected high points. 40%

DISTILLERIE GILBERT HOLL Ribeauvillé.
🔷 **Lac'Holl 15 Years Old Single Malt Whisky** db **(90.5) n23.5** beautiful. Delicate citrus and freshly plucked and squeezed grass. Freshly baked apple tart, too; **t22.5** superb clarity on delivery, just as the nose promised. Malty with a freshness which makes a mockery of the passing decade and a half, with a slow infusion of delicate vanilla; **f22** medium length, but the barley is almost three dimensional; light enough for the more bitter oak notes to carry through; **b22.5** such a rare display of barley and gristy sugars. Very impressive malt. And fabulously refreshing. 42%

🔷 **Lac'Holl Junior 13 Years Old Single Malt Whisky** db **(89) n22** usually a kind of green barley/tobacco note like this spells trouble. But there's a lovely diced coconut dipped in maple syrup secondary story, too...; **t22.5** ooh, so refreshing! The barley is being launched around the palate, again with a gorgeous maple syrup accompaniment; **f22** spices join the merry throng, plus slightly more bitter vanilla notes from the oak; **b22.5** wow!! Bursts from the glass with so much charisma and charm. Perhaps not technically the finest of all time, but such fun! Delicious!! 43%

🔷 **Lac'Holl Vieil Or 10 Years Old Single Malt Whisky** db **(92.5) n22.5** a mixed spice aroma more commonly found in a mainland Europe bakers than in a whisky. That said... wonderful! **t23.5** a fascinating delivery: both dry and sweet simultaneously! Seriously complex with those spices, the majority of them dry, really working overtime to keep in pace with the gristier malt; the mid-ground appears to be drifting off into orange blossom honey land...; **f23** long, with the sugars now in command; **b23.5** a malt which gives one's taste buds a real working over. Superb balance. 42%

DISTILLERIE GLANN AR MOR Larmor-Pleubian, Working.
Glann Ar Mor Maris Otter Barley 15 first fill bourbon cask db **(88.5) n21.5** a tad thin, a little feinty...but the barley is crisp and healthy; **t23** huge malt on delivery. For once, the ulmo honey takes a backseat to the barley which positively explodes on the palate, the grist taking its time to add a sweeter dimension. The oak is also firm, as the vanilla testifies; **f22** the traditional cocoa and fudge of slightly over cut malt..; **b22** as an Englishman, so warming to see the French embracing my country's most traditional and home-spun barley...and, certainly on the delivery at least, doing it proud. 46%. *Celtic Whisky Compagnie.*

🔷 **Glan Ar Mor Maris Otter Barley 03/16** db **(91.5) n22.5** beautifully rich barley with space enough for vanilla and light citrus; **t23** chunky malt, almost like a Russian doll of a whisky...malt, within malt, within malt...; **f23** desirable cocoa; the barley hangs on loud and clear, though; **b23** well done, chaps! One of the cleanest, barley-rich, malts I have ever tasted from the distillery: no feints...but plenty of faints...!! 46%

Glann Ar Mor Peated Gwech 15 BC db **(93) n23** crisp, nipping barley; firm, fresh oak and a pinch of salt: an embracing, vitalising mix; **t23.5** such clean malt! Oceans of vanilla are circumnavigated by a beautiful, eye-watering, salivating barley and ulmo honey mix; **f23** clean, tapering vanilla and ulmo honey; **b23.5** another very high class malt from these messieurs... 66.2%. *Celtic Whisky Compagnie.*

Glann Ar Mor Taol Esa 3ed Gwech 12 first fill bourbon barrel db **(76) n18 t20 f18 b18**. Sweet, oily, feinty. 46%. nc ncf. 674 bottles.

Glann Ar Mor Taol Esa 4ed Gewch 13 first fill bourbon barrel db **(78) n18 t21 f19 b20.** Looks like the distiller wanted to get as many flavours as he could from the cut. 46%.

Glann Ar Mor Taol Esa 2l Gwech 13 first fill barrel db **(73) n17 t19.5 f18 b18.5**. I had hoped the feints might have taken a backward step: they haven't. 46%. nc ncf. 955 bottles.

Glann Ar Mor Taol Esa 1an Gwech 14 first fill bourbon barrel db **(79) n18 t20 f21 b20.** Keeps up its feinty tradition. Ultra malty, though. 46%.

🔷 **Glan Ar Mor Taol Esa 4ed Gwech 15** db **(81) n19 t20 f21.5 b20.5**. Definitely a step in the right direction for the weakest of their brands. Loads of toffee and barley sugar at work. Still a bit messy, though. 46%

Kornog 2013 For The Auld Alliance first fill bourbon barrel db **(94.5)** n23 salty rock pools; t24 one of the most eye-wateringly intense deliveries produced by any European mainland distiller this year. The enormity of the barley is immeasurable, then ramped up even further by a big spoon-full of salt; entirely salivating and mind-blowing; f23.5 calms for the malt now to merely bathe in its own glow; some spices evolve but the usual mocha sweetness (and even a light hint of smoke) sees the malt out, perhaps helped along with gentle manuka honey; b24 an extraordinary whisky worthy of seeking and enjoying. In a style of its own. And when I say style...I mean style.... Specially tasted on 6th June 2014 to mark the 70th anniversary of the New Alliance... 58.7%.

⬗ **Kornog Oloroso Sherry Cask 15** db **(68)** n17 t18 f16 b17. Fails spectacularly on so many levels. 46%

⬗ **Kornog Pedro Ximenez Cask 15** db **(82.5)** n20 t21.5 f20 b21. A steady malt, a bit sticky in places – which is hardly a surprise. Also, feinty in parts. The barley shows good survival instincts, though, and battles through to the end. 46%

⬗ **Kornog Roc'h Hir** db **(95)** n23 the still has been shaped to accommodate the oils now, so the barley really does have a high value. A salty edge to the vanillas; t24.5 that is one stunning delivery: like a midsummer sunrise it arrives with a degree of eventually dazzling awe...; the mid-ground is like a library of oily cocoa types from around the world: I could taste this all day, every day...; f23.5 reverts to the vanilla, but not without a little molasses and mocha paste along the way...; b24 it appears that the days of feinty whisky from this distillery are just about over. This is a sophisticated malt and delicate enough to highlight any flaw. Beautifully distilled, superbly matured. Congratulations: this is high class whisky. 46%

Kornog Saint Erwan 2014 first fill bourbon barrel db **(88)** n23 t23 f20.5 b21.5 A slightly simplistic malt. But entirely charming. 50%.

Kornog Saint Erwan 2015 db **(84.5)** n21 t21.5 f21 b21. Butter smeared on the delicately smoked malt. Lovely sensations, but doesn't quite fire right. 50%. *Celtic Whisky Compagnie.*

⬗ **Kornog Saint Erwan 2016** db **(89)** n21.5 scary stuff! Something weirdly phenolic plays peek-a-boo amid the giant oak. Very dry and awkward...; t23.5 probably the ultimate of European oak-influenced whiskies. The tannins take you on a long journey involving honey and some pretty intense bourbon style notes. But it is the richness of the buttery oils which holds this together, as well as the treacle; f22 remains toasty, with just enough sugars; b22 a beast of a whisky. 50%

Kornog Saint Ivy 2015 db **(95.5)** n23.5 despite the oils, sharp, vaguely bourbony with a liquorice lead; t24 sacre bleu! Formidable...!!! The malt is, in the house style, rounded up and concentrated – guarded by a buttery spiciness. A sub plot of mocha but, beneath it all, the usual suspects of marzipan and ulmo honey. Massive....and increasingly oily! f24 long, with the rich oils squeezing every last drop of barley from the glass. Vanilla, butterscotch, red and black liquorice and dried ulmo tick every box...; b24 just love the liquorice theme. And the insane barley concentrate. A great malt looking for a deserving and receptive palate. There's a decent restaurant I have been known to frequent in central London this will do well in... 59.6%. *Celtic Whisky Compagnie.*

⬗ **Kornog Saint Ivy 2016** db **(93.5)** n21.5 a little warming, thin and clean, though you suspect the true character is yet to be revealed; t24 wow! Did I call that nose right...!! Salivating to the point of insanity, the taste buds are rocked by a series of malty explosions, backed up by the intense cocoa on the follow through; f24 a ridiculous finale which defies logic. Just how long can the oils keep those cocoa notes running for? So, so beautiful...; b24 another enormous, yet very pretty whisky from a distillery which is reaching superstar status. 59.1%

Kornog Single Malt Saint Ivy 2014 first fill bourbon barrel db **(94)** n23.5 t23 f23.5 b24 What an elegant and quite delightful whisky. 58.9%.

Kornog Taouarc'h Chwec'hved 14 BC db **(97)** n24 exceptional: despite the smoke, this is a very light aroma. The phenols are delicate, the citrus fragile. Also, a little nippy and busy, which works perfectly...; t24 just about faultless: a fabulous match between the peat and the ulmo honey and so light bodied (despite the oils) you can feel every nuance, every play being made; f24.5 one dreams of finishes like this. A backdrop of Lubeck's finest marzipan, a smattering of cocoa but that honey and smoke does things you can only pray for...; the remainder of this glass (usually poured away) will accompany me to bed tonight...and, for once, there will be no spitting...; b24.5 delicately distilled, marvellously matured...a triumph of the trade. One of the very best whiskies I have since the 2015 Bible. And confirmation, along with Seizud 14, that this distillery has entered true World Class status. 58.2%..

Kornog Taouarc'h Kentan db **(94.5)** n24 t24 f23 b23.5. Not sure there has been this number of perfectly rhapsodic notes coming out of France since Saint Sans was in his pomp... 57.1%

Kornog Taourc'h Kentan 13 BC first fill barrel db **(90)** n22 t22.5 f22 b23.5. As soft as sun cream being spread over you while basking on a French beach. 46%. nc ncf. 907 bottles.

Kornog Taouarc'h Kentan 14 BC db **(92)** n23 t22 f24 b23 Only the other day I was telling someone about how this distillery's peated malt has a distinctly Islay feel to it. Well, that was before I tasted this: a malt which has very much its own signature and provenance. Incidentally, I tasted this, with all the other Kornog whiskies, on 6th June 2014 to mark the 70th anniversary of the D-Day landings. My late father, after battling Rommel in Africa, was fighting in Italy at the time. So I will use this whisky – combining British influence with the peat, American oak and French water and craftsmanship – to toast all those who showed bravery beyond anything we can possibly imagine. And, in particular, those – on whichever side - who never returned to tell the tale... 46%.

Kornog Taouarc'h Seizued 14 BC db **(95)** n23 wispy smoke: first it's here, then it's not...; strands of peek-a-boo coconut; nipping, fizzing spices...; t23.5 a ridiculously beautiful delivery: gristy peat, where the sugars dissolve on your tongue like a lozenge. The house ulmo honey style remains as residue, as does the softest smoke imaginable; f24 long, sophisticated and delicate to the point of being too scared to move...but that smoke just lingers on...; b24.5 very rare that whiskies just get better and better on the palate. But here is one such case. A whisky of whispers and intrigue. 46%. Celtic Whisky Compagnie.

Kornog Taouarh'h Kentan 15 BC db **(94.5)** n23.5 another busy light peaty number, but now with a citrus hue; t24 the gristy sugars come out storming! Smoke, citrus, honey (ulmo, what else?), butterscotch...all left in their wake...; f23 the oak catches up with the grist, the phenols begins to pupate into something more tingling and spicy while a softer Werther's Original candy ups the creaminess; b24 a gentle giant of a malt: an exercise in restraint and balance. 46%. Celtic Whisky Compagnie.

◇ **Kornog Taouarc'h Kentan 16 BC** db **(94.5)** n24 I could almost mistake this for an Ardbeg: the peat is profound yet teasingly layered; the citrus weaves a thin but telling thread; light spices nip and nibble...astonishing...and not dissimilar to one of their bottlings of last year, if memory serves...; t23.5 what beautiful weight: oily and with some early heftiness. But it lightens as the smoke stretches further around the palate with the lightest touch of ulmo honey and spice; f23 buttery, with a mocha fade to the smoke; b24 this is serious malt. Unquestionably an equal to some of the peated beauties of Islay. 46%

100% Rye db **(85.5)** n21 t23 f20.5 b21. Massively flavoursome. Aided by a wide cut, the rye at first jolts then quietens as the delicious honey and fudge control the middle. As expected, a bitter finish. 46%. Celtic Whisky Compagnie.

DISTILLERIE GRALLET-DUPIC Rozelieures, Working.

◇ **G.Rozelieures Whisky De Lorraine Single Malt Whisky** bott code: L446 db **(87)** n21.5 t22.5 f21 b22. Exceptionally nutty. The blossoming of the sugars on delivery is always attractive, as are the complex nougat/caramel/cocoa tones. Though the feints are always a threat, the genteel pace and softness of the malt makes it well worth a look. 40%

◇ **G.Rozelieures Whisky De Lorraine Single Malt Whisky Fumé Collection** bott code: L415 db **(91.5)** n23 a very sensuous marriage of delicate smoke and moist fruitcake, complete with orange peel. Like whispers in the dark...; t24 you almost want to applaud the mouth feel alone: starts with a salivating intent, but soon thickens slightly into something a lot more in keeping with those sensual notes on the nose; f22 a slight flaw from a cask dries the malt rapidly; b22.5 but for a lingering off note, this would have scored very highly indeed. A vague smokiness gives this a lovely weight. 46%

◇ **G.Rozelieures Whisky De Lorraine Single Malt Whisky Rare Collection** bott code: L446 db **(88.5)** n19.5 feinty; vaguely copper-starved; t23.5 an amazing mix of golden syrup, liquorice, molasses and succulent dates make for one very memorable experience, especially when you consider the excellent balance offered by the spice; f22.5 dries, though there is a muscovado-date combination that ensures a comfortable finish; b23 one of the sweetest and most lush malts this year, but always delicious. 40%

◇ **G.Rozelieures Whisky De Lorraine Single Malt Whisky Tourbé Collection** bott code: L416 db **(92)** n22 the smokiest of their four bottlings on show here, though never dense; t23.5 the usual lush house style with a bombardment of sugars and spice. The smoke again, is present but remarkably laid back; f23 quite an oily fade with ulmo honey seeing off any late bitter incursions; b23.5 there is a feinty flaw to this, and even perhaps a slight lack of copper in the system; but the overall picture is a very pretty one. 46%

DISTILLERIE GUILLON Louvois, Working.
Guillon No. 1 Single Malt de la montagne de Reims db **(87) n22 t21 f22 b22.** Right. I'm impressed. Not exactly faultless, but enough life here really to keep the tastebuds on full alert; By and large well made and truly enjoyable. Well done, Les Chaps! *46%*

DISTILLERIE MEYER Hohwarth, Working.
Meyer's Le Whisky Alsacien Blend Superieur db **(90) n22.5** moist date and walnut cake; **t23** house style of yielding silk and then further fruit and nut tones, almost vaguely sherry trifle; **f22** more of the same, though just with the volume down slightly; **b22.5** not a whisky you can easilly say no to...Really charming. *40%*

Meyer's Le Whisky Alsacien Blend Superieur Pinot Noir Finish db **(83.5) n21.5 t21.5 f20 b21.** Slightly sticky on the palate as the fruit tries to take charge. Though pleasant, imbalanced somewhat by the late feints and lack of give from the grape. *40%*

Meyer's Le Whisky Alsacien Pur Malt No. 05169 db **(92) n22** a lovely fruit and nut overture with a decent spice buzz...; attractively soft; **t23.5** silky delivery, the early malt and building sugars do no more than kiss and caress. Salivating and fruity...and ridiculously soft; **f23** welcome spice to move things onto another level. But top rate vanilla, too. And that vague nuttiness re-emerges along with some molasses; **b23.5** my old Budgie, Borat, used to help himself to whatever whisky was going if no-one was watching. Sadly, he is no more and is buried in the garden overlooked by my tasting room. By contrast, my parrot, Percy, has never had a single drop of whisky in all his four years. Though he might be interested in this one, because he is a pure Meyer's. He has a sweet tooth, has Percy. Or do I mean beak? Anyway, I am sure he would bob his head up and down in appreciation of the sugary gristiness which pervades throughout this impressive dram. Who's a pretty whisky, then....? *40%*

Meyer's Whisky Alsacien Blend Superieur db **(88.5) n22.5 t22.5 f21.5 b22.** Impressively clean, barley-thick and confident: a delight. *40%*

DISTILLERIE WARENGHEM Lannion, Working.
Armorik db **(91) n23 t22 f23 b23.** I admit it; I blanched, when I first nosed this, so vivid was the memory of the last bottling. This, though ,was the most pleasant of surprises. Fabulous stuff: one of the most improved malts in the world. *40%*

Armorik Double Maturation finished in oloroso casks db **(75) n18.5 t20 f18 b18.5.** Dull and decidedly out of sorts. *46%. ncf.*

Armorik Millésime Matured for 10 Years cask no. 3261 db **(92) n22.5 t23 f23 b23.** Never quite know what you are going to get from these messieurs. Didn't expect this bottle of delights, I must say. The sweetness is a bit OTT at one point, but just copes. *56.1%. sc.*

Armorik Sherry Finish db **(92) n22.5 t23.5 f23 b23.5.** The first sherry finish today which has not had a sulphur problem...and I'm in my eighth working hour...! Bravo guys! If their Classic was a note on sophistication, then this was an essay. *40%*

DOMAINE MAVELA Aléria, Woring.
P&M Corsican Single Malt Whisky Aged 14 Years db **(92) n23.5** a kind of strange muscovado-laced tannin with a meaty duck l'orange...unique – and very attractive; **t23** an instant battle between the good sugars and evil oak. Both land telling wounds on the other and it is the molasses which retreat...; **f22.5** pretty bitter and dry as the tannins really squeeze hard, though at least offering some cocoa as compensation; also some oils from a once thick cut begin to accumulate...; **b23** as we are moving back to the earlier days of the distillery, you can pick out the odd technical flaw that appears to have been ironed out later down the line. But always entertaining and intriguing with its series of bold strokes from the chunky oak nose to the bittering finish. *42%*

KAERILIS Le Palais, Working.
Kaerilis Le Grand Dérangement 15 Ans db **(78) n18 t22 f19 b19.** A breakdown of the oils doesn't help reveal the weaknesses from the distillate. A must for fans de nougat. *43%. nc ncf sc.*

Kaerilis l'Aube du Grand Dérangement 15 Ans db **(83.5) n20 t22.5 f20 b21.** Misfires when the revs are up, but purrs for moment on two on delivery as the sugar and barley kicks in to delicious effect. An enigmatic fruitiness enriches. *57%. nc ncf sc.*

WAMBRECHIES DISTILLERY Wambrechies, Working.
Wambrechies Single Malt Aged 8 Years db **(83) n20 t21 f21 b21.** There's that aroma again, just like the 3-y-o. Except how it kind of takes me back 30 years to when I hitchhiked

across the Sahara. Some of the food I ate with the local families in Morocco and Algeria was among the best I have ever tasted. And here is an aroma I recognize from that time, though I can't say specifically what it is (tomatoes, maybe?). Attractive and unique to whisky, that's for sure. I rather like this malt. There is nothing quite comparable to it. One I need to investigate a whole lot more. 40%

UNSPECIFIED
Vicomte Single Malt Whisky Aged 8 Years Cognac barrels (86) n22 t22 f21 b21. Just like so much Cognac, this whisky has a distinctive toffee theme which makes for a rather too easy going malt. Just not enough peaks and troughs to add "interesting" to "enjoyable" in the description of this caramel-laden malt. From the attractive silky texture, I would not be surprised to learn the Cognac barrels in which this whisky laid were hand made by Asterix. 40% (80 proof)

Blends
◇ **Moon Harbour Pier 1 Sauternes cask finish** (86.5) n20 t22.5 f22 b22. A sticky toffee, chewy number with a beautiful flavour spike as the apricot on the Sauternes kicks in and lingers. Shame about the nose, though, which cannot disguise far from peerless malt. 45.8%. ncf.

P&M Blend Supérieur (82) n21 t21 f20 b20. Bitter and botanical, though no shortage of complexity. 40%. Mavela Distillerie.

P&M Whisky (89) n22 t23 f22 b22. No mistaking this is from a fruit distillery. Still quite North American, though. 40%

Vatted Malts
KAERILIS
Kaerilis Ster Vraz No 9 4 Year Old db (80) n22 t21 f18 b19. Plenty of salt and no little citrus. But undone by an oaky bitterness. 45%. nc ncf.

Kaerilis Ster Vraz No 9 4 Year Old db (87) n21.5 t23.5 f20 b22. What the hell was that...??? Something different, for sure. At its best, quite stunning. At its worst – at the death – hmmm, not great. Get your bucket and spade out for this one. 61.8%. nc ncf.

GERMANY
BAULAND BRENNEREI ALT ENDERLE ROSENBURG. WORKING.
Alt Enderle Neccarus 8 Years Old Single Malt Whisky db (90.5) n22 t23 f23 b22.5 A gently complex, delightful malt. Had it been scotch, I would have thought it was a coastal dram. Odd...! 43%

Alt Enderle Neccarus 12 Years Old Single Malt Whisky db (94) n23.5 t23.5 f23 b24 Technically, among the best malt I have ever encountered from Germany. 43%

Alt Enderle Neccarus 15 Years Old Port Fass Single Malt Whisky db (92.5) n23 another salty Neccarus: dry grape skin comes over in waves; t23.5 eye-watering fruit and saline mix; the sugars are subdues and of a fudgy style before mocha begins to soften the moment; f23 a lovely chocolate and raisin fade; b23 a chocolate mousse is on the loose. 51%

Alt Enderle Neccarus 15 Years Old Sherry Fass Single Malt Whisky db (86.5) n21 t22 f21.5 b22. Clean sherry. But, after the mouth-watering delivery, relatively sweet and simple with just not enough gear changes. Pleasant, if not up to the standard of the other Neccarus. 49%

BIRGITTA RUST PIEKFEINE BRÄNDE Bremen, Working.
◇ **Van Loon Single Malt Whisky** dist 2012, bott Jul 2015 db (84) n20 t22.5 f20 b21. Anyone who has had nougat filled to the brim with juicy raisins and diced nut will recognise this one. Messy beginning and end, but very decent middle. Like so many other European distilleries, must learn to be more ruthless with the cut. 48%. 1,200 bottles.

BRENNEREI DANNENMANN Owen. Working.
Danne's Single Grain Schwäbischer Whisky Vom Bellerhof dist 2006, bott L 0011 db (85) n21 t22 f21 b21. A rock hard whisky which crunches its way around the palate giving off flavours as flint might sparks. Eye-watering in places, though the rigid Demerara sugars are a treat. 43%

Danne's Single Grain Schwäbischer Whisky Vom Bellerhof dist 06, cask strength, bott 11 db (88.5) n22 t22.5 f22 b22 A good example of how reducing a whisky can damage it: compare this to the 43% version and here you see the oils unbroken and softening the flavour procession. 51.1%

Danne's Single Malt Schwäbischer Whisky Vom Bellerhof dist 09, bott code L 0017 db **(81) n19 t21.5 f20 b20.5.** A strange combination of nougat and thinness to the body: the over-widening of the cut usually results in nougat and heavy oils. Never finds a happy rhythm. *43%*

Danne's Single Malt Schwäbischer Whisky Vom Bellerhof dist 09, cask strength, bott code L 0017 db **(87) n20 t23 f22 b22.** A huge whisky which kicks a lot harder than its 55% abv. Works a lot better than its sister 43% bottling, making the most of the golden syrup and grist mix, and the spiced cocoa fade. Pretty enjoyable. *54.9%*

BRENNEREI FELLER Dietenheim-Regglisweiler, Working

Augutus Corado Single Grain Whisky Port Cask db **(83) n21.5 t23 f19 b20**. Unlike their Valerie Amorone cask, where the malt and grape are in perfect harmony, here we have a situation where the fruit influence has bullied the barley into submission. And, sadly, the port pipe appears to have been treated somewhere along the way, thus imparting a dull furriness to the finish in particular. *40%*

⟨⟩ **Augustus Single Grain Aged 5 Years** bott code los 1001 db **(87.5) n21.5 t22.5 f21 b22.** Exceptionally clean yet a little creamy; the greatest emphasis is on the thin sugars. Very enjoyable and charming, especially when those gentle spices arrive. But maybe just a little too genteel. *40%*

Valerie Amarone Single Malt Whisky 4 Years Old db **(95.5) n23** a thick, indulgent nose, brimming with spice and sherry trifle...; **t24.5** wow...!! What a delivery...what an astonishingly rich mouth feel. The grape is not just clean but absolutely layered with so many stratum of varying intensity and fruit significance that it is almost impossible to count...; **f23.5** long, with continuous spiced strands which almost refuse to fade; **b24.5** I think I'm in love with Valerie. *48%*

⟨⟩ **Valerie Amarone Cask Single Malt** bott code los 114 db **(95) n23** wow! Black cherry and molasses with a delicate nutty edge; **t24** so intense, this delivery, yet at the same time seemingly effortless and gossamer light. Yet, miraculously, there is still plenty of room for the grain and the sugars to poke through the grape. Wonderfully convoluted and complex, but best of all is the weight and balance. The coffee cake is expected but arrives early; spices... gentle, of course...; **f23.5** long, with the soft oils and the barley now every bit as confident as the warming fruit. Seriously high quality to the slightly understated end; **b24.5** Amorone comes from the Italian meaning "The Great Bitter." There is nothing bitter about this. But plenty that is great. So beautifully made and matured! *46%*

⟨⟩ **Valerie Sherry Cask Single Malt** bott code los 115 db **(86.5) n21 t22.5 f21 b22.** No sulphur, it seems. Yet for some reason this just doesn't get far off the ground. The nose is a bit dull while the palate seems to be under attack from a constant stream of caramel. By no means unpleasant and the immediate aftermath after the delivery is unquestionably the high point. But despite the active spices, never quite sits entirely right after that with the oils a little too aggressive. *46%*

Valerie Single Malt Whisky db **(92) n23** orange blossom honey and Turkish delight; malt grist can also be detected, alongside some guttural spices; **t23.5** a real sweetie, living up to the nose's promise. Abounds with diluted honey tones as well as thinned maple syrup and treacle. A little oak-induced toffee makes an entrance. One of the sweetest, yet entirely charming whiskies on the European scene; **f22** a little oily as the vague feints at last reveal themselves. But spices more than compensate; **b23.5** if this was named after someone called Valerie, then she should be thrilled and honoured, as she must be a sweet, well-balanced and beautiful lady... *48%*

BRENNEREI FRANK RODER Aalen - Wasseralfingen. Working.

Frank's Suebisch Cask Strength 2008 db **(91) n22 t23 f23 b23.** Frank has really got the hang of how to make the most of his still...a little stunner! And his cleanest yet. *57%*

Frank's Suebisch Single Grain 2007 db **(86.5) n21.5 t22 f21.5 b21.5.** Consistent, gristy, mouth-watering fare. Does not try to be spectacular. More dissolving sugars this time. *40%*

BRENNEREI HENRICH Kriftel, Hessia. Working.

Gilors Port Cask sherry, bott code L13033, dist 2010, bott 2013 db **(86) n20 t22 f22.5 b21.5.** Thoroughly enjoyable and full of depth and no little fruit and spice. But the wide cut, apparent in the sherry version, is not tamed in quite the same effortless way. *44%. sc.*

BRENNEREI HÖHLER Aarbergen, Kettenbach. Working.

Whesskey Hessischer Barley-Whisky bott code GW 01-15 db **(84) n19 t22 f21.5 b21.5.**
Follows a similar path to the corn whisky, except this has a dried grass/hay edge and never quite reaches those same heights of chocolatey deliciousness. 44%

Whesskey Hessischer Blend-Whisky bott code BW 01-15 db **(90.5) n23** a wonderful nose, with a Milky Bar nougat and milk chocolate lead and outstanding secondary Demerara sugars; **t22** rich from the off, with sugars linking early with spice to make for a massively busy start; **f23** chewy to the death with a little more nougat now coming in with toffee; the spices ramp up the ante...; **b22.5** a typical Hohler slightly flawed stunner. 44%

Whesskey Hessischer Corn-Whisky bott code MW 01-15 db **(87.5) n20.5 t22 f22 b22.**
Though the nose leaves you in no doubt about the feints at work, the beauty of the chocolate wafer and Nutella is there to be savoured. 44%

Whesskey Hessischer Rye-Malt-Whisky bott code MW 01-15 db **(84.5) n19 t22 f21.5 b22.** After the usual less than impressive nose, this is an earthy beast which grows on you. Hefty hardly touches it: the chunky sugars aids the clanking rye no end. 44%

Whesskey Hessischer Single Malt Whisky bott code CA 01-15 db **(81) n18.5 t21 f21 b20.5**. Despite the fact it has all kinds of flavour permutations, it is hard to get beyond the butyric. 44%

Whesskey Hessischer Whisky au Dinkel bott code DW 01-14 db **(86) n21 t21.5 f22 b21.5.**
Brimming with character, the oils ensure the flavours keep building to the sweet end. Gristy at times, then more spicy as the oils accumulate. Plenty of burnt fudge as it progresses. 40%

BRENNEREI MACK, Gütenbach. Working

Kilpen Single Malt Malt Whisky Single Barrel bott code L14092108 **(88) n21.5** the vague heaviness of the still is perfectly countered by toffee and dates; **t22.5** gorgeous spice and barley mix. The sugars are half Demerara and half molasses; **f22** more creamy toffee, but beautifully spiced up; **b22** attractively distilled and delightfully matured whisky. 40%

BRENNEREI ZIEGLER Freudenberg, North Württemberg. Working.

Aureum 1865 5 Year Old db **(87) n21.5 t22 f21.5 b22**. A tad feinty and nutty, but the huge barley makes this entertaining and sweet in all the right places. 43%

Aureum 1865 2008 Cask Strength db **(84.5) n21 t21.5 f21 b21**. A massive whisky, in no little part due to the very wide cut back in 2008. The usual nougat, hazelnut and cocoa gang up in the thick oils. 53.9%

Aureum 1865 Château Lafite Rothschild casks, dist 2008, bott 2015 db **(85) n20.5 t23 f20 b21.5**. Tight, hard, grapey, beautifully sweet on delivery but with some furriness. 47%

Aureum 1865 Grave Digger 6 Year Old db **(88) n22** salty and oily. Layers of molasses; **t22.5** a yielding delivery, soft with fertile malt. Mocha arrives early, a light feint buzz a little later; **f22** excellent spice; the mocha notes persist; **b22** this grave digger goes deep. 43%

DESTILLERIE HERMANN MÜHLHÄUSER Working.

Mühlhäuser Oberwalder Single Grain bott code L0612 db **(86.5) n22 t22 f21 b21.5.**
Enjoyable, showing sturdy and at times sophisticated oak and good early sugar structure. The grain is a bit on the shy side, though: may have had a better chance to shine at 46%. 40%

Mühlhäuser Schwäbischer Whisky aus Korn db **(90) n22.5 t23 f22 b22.5.** So different!
If you are into this, it'll be pastoral perfection. 40%

DESTILLERIE & BRENNEREI MICHAEL HABBEL Sprockhövel, Germany.

⬩ **Hillock 4 1/2-12** bott code L4512 db **(88.5) n23.5** good grief! Caol Ila? Bruichladdich...? What is going on? The acidity to the smoke has a distinct Islay air to it; and the citrus also adds to the Hebridean effect...I'm bemused...! **t22** okay, we are back in Germany again as the style on the delivery is way too fat and spicy for an Islay...indeed, the smoke has a bit of a battle to overcome the vague feints; **f21** quite a bit of nougat underlines the technical weakness. But still the cask works hard to ensure a soft phenolic kiss goodbye; **b22** on the nose I thought: wow! They've come up with a peatiness as close to an Islay style as I've ever seen in mainland Europe – watch out Scotland! Later I discovered that the whisky had been matured in ex-Islay casks. Either way, all rather lovely. 45%

DESTILLERIE RALF HAUER Bad Dürkheim, Working.

⬩ **Saillt Mór Pfälzer Eiche Single Malt Whisky** new Palatinate oak, dist 4-8 Sept 12, bott 2 Nov 2015 db **(94) n24** briny vanilla dipped in fabulous heather honey; **t23.5** superb barley fanfare which swiftly moves into the honey theme. Light, but the pacing of the sugars is superb; **f23** a tad tangy, but the sugars linger now closer towards custard cream biscuits; **b23.5** one of the most Scottish of all European malts, having something of a Dalwhinnie/Clynelish/Highland Park constitution. Or maybe constitution is not a good term to use regarding anything European at the moment... *46%*

DESTILLERIE THOMAS SIPPEL Weisenheim am Berg, Working.

⟐ **Palatinatus Single Malt Whisky** Port wood finish, dist 2011 db **(80) n19 t21 f20 b20.** A nougat bar dipped in Port...? Sometimes you just have to hold your hand up and say: well, I'm afraid that didn't quite work quite as we hoped. Here is one. Lovely bottle, though... *45%*

⟐ **Palatinatus Single Malt Whisky** German oak cask, dist 2012 db **(85.5) n20 t22 f22 b21.5.** Well, that was different! The sharp pungency of, presumably, the German oak, certainly offers a unique nose. And this transfers on to the palate, though the intense sugars – again, from the oak? – restore a degree of balance and even complexity as the juicier barley tones emerge. A truly unique malt that has been impressively distilled but offers just too vivid a flavour profile at times. Love the lemon on the early finish, mind.... *45%*

EDELBRÄENDE-SENFT Salem-Rickenbach. Working.

Senft Bodensee Whisky bott code L-SW39, dist Apr 12, bott Apr 15 db **(86) n21.5 t22 f21 b21.5.** Now come to expect the feints to be part of the make up! Here, they help generate an attractive toasted nuttiness which, with the slight nougat, toffee and late cocoa, kind of makes an acceptable whisky version of Topic candy...though it has rationed the sugars. *42%. nc.*

⟐ **Senft Bodensee Whisky** bott code L-SW41, dist 2012, bott 2016 db **(86.5) n20 t21 f23.5 b22.** You know with this distillery that feints and nougat are on the cards. Well, they don't disappoint but at least this bottling shows, after a so-so delivery, a fabulous finale where the high grade Venezuela cocoa is mixed beautifully with no lesser grade molasses. The spices sign the malt off with aplomb. *42%*

EDELBRENNEREI BISCHOF Wartmannsroth, Working.

⟐ **Stark & Eigenwillig Rebell Der Whisky Single Grain Chestnut Barrel Finish** db **(93) n23** a series of spices and sugars not normally associated with oak, especially the mix of praline and marzipan; **t23** seriously thick on the palate: again intense, vaguely nutty sugars moving towards a lighter Milky Way creaminess. The spices are precise, and also with a sweet edge; **f23.5** heavy tannin late on but this morphs into a series of rich, high quality cocoa notes, accompanied perfectly by molasses; **b23.5** I didn't need to be told chestnut maturation was involved here: just one sniff tells you all you need to know. *44%*

EDELBRENNEREI DIRKER Mömbris, Germany.

⟐ **Dirker Blended Whisky Aged 3 Years** bott code L L 15 db **(87.5) n21 t22.5 f22 b22.** Beautifully soft and viscous with a highly attractive fruit and nut theme. Even some rather excellent spices late on to keep the show going. Impressed. *45%*

⟐ **Dirker Whisky Aged 3 Years** bourbon cask, bott code L E 15 db **(81.5) n18 t22 f20.5 b21.** After the boiled sprouts, unfriendly nose, recovers quickly and nimbly on the palate. The burst of sugars and gristy oils attractively repairs some of the damage. *53%*

⟐ **Dirker Whisky Aged 4 Years** Sassicaia cask, bott code L A 16 db **(80.5) n18.5 t22.5 f19 b20.5.** A deeply frustrating whisky. This is one exceptionally beautiful cask at work here and - in the mid ground - offers all kinds of toffee apple and muscovado-sweetened mocha. Sadly, the initial spirit wasn't up to the barrel's standard. This really needs some cleaning up. *53%*

EIFEL DESTILLATE Koblenz, Working.

⟐ **Eifel Whisky 746.9. Single German Barley Malt Whisky 8 Years Old** db **(73) n17 t19 f18 b19.** I now have a bald patch where I have been scratching my head trying to work this one out. Wrong in so many ways. Yet the undertone has a rather charming fruity structure. *50%. sc.*

⟐ **Eifel Whisky Cask 99 Single German Barley Malt Whisky 5 Years Old** db **(62) n16 t16 f15 b15.** Just...aaaargghh! *57.5%. sc.*

⟐ **Eifel Whisky Einzelfass Single Malt 2016** American oak, ex-Bordeaux & Madeira casks, dist 2010 db **(89) n22** pungent, full throttle oak; something of the lightly burnt toast to this, perhaps with some peanut butter spread; **t22.5** silky but with intense burnt sugars. The malt struggles to make a coherent presence, but the vague burnt raisin and smouldering fruitcake does; **f22** calming butterscotch makes a softening contribution, but inadvertently ramps up the spices; **b22.5** a toast to your distillery! Or, to be more precise, a drink to your toasty oak... *50%. sc.*

◇ **Eifel Whisky Einzelfass Single Rye 2015** American oak, new bourbon & Bordeaux casks, dist 2009 db **(96) n23.5** love it! The rye is punching out a crisp, fruity message: the nature of the grain is unmistakable; curiously plummy, too, with a little over-ripe fig added for good measure; **t24.5** I don't believe it: the delivery is even better than the nose! So many layers, first of massive intensity, then softer, then larger, larger still, then soft...mesmeric! Unquestionably one of the best European ryes bottled this year with the grain both sending out stark, crunchy, sugary messages and a second fruit element, softer though, apparently carried on the Bordeaux cask; **f24** if you want a glorious spice ride, they rarely come more thrilling than this; **b24** quite brilliant! Magnificently distilled and beautifully matured. One of the European whiskies of the year with no doubt whatsoever. *50%. sc.*

◇ **Eifel Whisky Einzelfass Tripel Malt 2015** 1st fill bourbon casks, ruby Port cask finish, dist 2010 db **(93.5) n22.5** big 'n' toasty as appears to be the distillery style, but this also works its drier notes into a vaguely sweet molassed theme impressively; a distinct liquorice and hickory link to Kentucky; **t24** just a fantastic delivery. I don't think they could have got the impact of the Port to be better balanced had they tried for a thousand years. The fruit is both salivating and soft yet brittle at the very same moment; naturally the spices follow through, as expected; **f23** a little Jamaican Blue Mountain coffee shows just how delicate some of the notes can be among the more macho tannins and still chewy fruit; **b24** hearty handshakes, chaps, for a complex job exceptionally well done. *50%. sc.*

◇ **Eifel Whisky Einzelfass Malz & Rauch 2015** 1st fill bourbon casks, PX sherry cask finish, dist 2010 db **(89) n21.5** this could have been a really lovely peaty whisky. But the fruit has other ideas, trampling over the smoke with boots three sizes too big for it...; **t23.5** not sure whether to sit back and wait for the whisky to unfold, or simply wave a white flag and surrender now... Yes, I'll give you that for a few rather bedazzling moments the peat and grape do find an almost magical rhythm when they interlace and actually complement each other. But by the time you reach the mid-point, it has become unhinged with spices exploding with abandon; **f22** warming still, with the peat perhaps having the better of the finale moments; some decent cocoa and hickory; **b22** lurching, lumbering: the kind of whisky that Laurel and Hardy would love. Because, when you add in the cumbersome youthfulness, this is a fine mess....! What is it with pitting peat against PX? When will people learn that they simply never balance out. That all said, I am sure some will regard this one of their greatest ever whisky experiences. And were I not such a miserable old perfectionist, I might be one of them... *50%. sc.*

FEINDESTILLERIE BÜCHNER Langenbogen. Working

Büchner Single Malt db **(89) n22.5** superb malt: clean and alive with gristy sugars. Refreshing and sexy; **t22** light oils, but never enough to discourage the barley from showing to full effect; **f22.5** those oils confirm the wider cut, but celebrate their extra body with a malty, spicy display of defiance; **b22** a wonderfully characterful and enjoyable malt. *43%*

FINCH WHISKYDESTILLERIE Nellingen, Alb-Donau. Working.

Finch Schwäbischer Highland Whisky Barrel Proof bott Jan 15 db **(94) n23** intense manuka honey spread over mildly burnt toast: plenty of sugar at work...just most of it lightly incinerated; **t24** now that is beautiful in any language; by any standards. A delicate creaminess to the mouth feel helps ensure that lightly fried manuka honey clings to every crevice; there is also a dried dates toffeeness, yet without the whisky being particularly fruity; **f23.5** long, with the oils refusing to budge. Continuing waves of manuka break on the toasty, slightly overdone butterscotch tart shore; **b23.5** epic! *54%*

◇ **Finch Schwäbischer Highland Whisky Barrique R** bott code LA0004 db **(91.5) n23** what's not to like? Clean fruit and a degree of nuttiness turns this into light fruit cake; **t23.5** surprisingly compact: seemingly soft, but with a much richer yet firm fruit edge not unlike boiled candy cubes; spice, naturally and even the grain makes a juicy entrance before the oak intensifies; **f23** a lovely oak-spice fade, still with high grade fruit sticking to the sides; **b23.5** as beautifully in sync as Germany's midfield, *42%*

Finch Schwäbischer Highland Whisky Single Malt bott Oct 15 db **(76.5) n19 t21.5 f17 b19**. Too fruity and far too aggressively bitter: I assume a sherry cask is at work here somewhere. What a pity. *42%*

◇ **Finch Schwäbischer Highland Whisky Single Malt** bott code 1444LA0003 db **(78.8) n19 t21 f19 b19.5**. As I taste this, the German national anthem is being sung in the distant background on my radio as Germany take on Slovakia in the European Championships: how fitting! Sadly, this Finch is not singing anything like so impressively for, despite some attractive fudge, the oils are just a little too clunky and chunky. *42%*

Finch Schwäbischer Highland Whisky XS bott Oct 15 db (86) n22 t22 f20.5 b21.5. A pleasant, even whisky which hardly breaks sweat as it goes through the malty, occasionally sugar-laden motions. Ultra simplistic by Finch standards: a bird which sings only intermittently. 40%

GUTSBRENNEREI JOH. B. GEUTING Bocholt, Working.

◇ J.B.G Münsterländer Single Grain Whisky new American white oak cask no. JBG 20, dist 26 Apr 10, bott 18 Sept 15 db (86) n20 t22.5 f21.5 b22. A few gremlins in the distilling process can be heard on the nose. But the soft, yielding and wonderfully juicy delivery compensates to a major degree, as do the following cocoa notes which flourish before a clunkiness sets in. Some very good moments. 42%. sc.

◇ J.B.G Münsterländer Single Malt Whisky American white oak casks, cask nos. 40, 49 & 50, dist 22 Dec 11, bott 14 Mar 16 db (88) n21 a slight lack of copper is compensated by attractive light tannin; t23 chewy, sumptuous and salivating, the barley shows early before the chocolate nougat and liquorice make a delicious combination; f22 almost like chocolate coconut; b22 creaky at times, but the good bits are genuinely excellent. 43%

◇ J.B.G Münsterländer Single Malt Whisky bourbon barrels nos. 1, 23, 24, dist 5 Nov 10, bott 21 Mar 14 db (86.5) n22.5 t22 f20.5 b21.5. A very wide cut means that we have a bit of a heavyweight on our hands here. Thick in oils, though not short on either big bourbon richness nor, later, an intense mocha fade. A degree of dried molasses balances out the ultra dry notes trying to get a foothold. By no means technically perfect, but one you cannot help liking. 43%. 937 bottles.

◇ J.B.G Münsterländer Single Malt Whisky bourbon barrels, sherry oloroso cask finish, cask nos. JBG 96, 97, dist 21 Dec 11, bott 17 Mar 15 db (83) n21 t21.5 f20 b20.5. What with the density of the distillate from the over generous cut, and the (clean!) oloroso on top, reminds me of a cough syrup I used to take as a kid. 43%. 813 bottles.

HAMMERSCHMIEDE Zorge. Working.

The Glen Els Wayfare The Cask Strength bott code. L1587 db (93) n22.5 t23 f24 b23.5. Some kind of oily, hallucinogenic, sugar, cocoa and spice concoction which plays is played out at maximum volume. The word "big" hardly does it justice... 57.9%. nc ncf.

HAUSBRAUEREI ALTSTADTHOF Nürnberg, Working.

◇ Ayrer's Bourbon Barrel Aged Organic Single Malt db (87) n22.5 t22.5 f21 b21. A slightly wide cut here has undone some supreme work by the casks. And at 51% abv, close to a Kentucky 101, has just the right mouth feel for the light liquorice and ulmo honey on display. But when so little metal is apparent in the spirit, those cuts have to be as clean as a whistle. 51%

◇ Ayrer's PX Sherry Cask Finished Organic Single Malt dist 2009 db (90) n22 dates and sticky toffee – has to be PX! Sweet and a little sharp, too...; t22.5 a confused delivery as the tangy, fat spirit battles with the early aggression of the cask's sweeter tones. Middle delivery a lovely honey-roast sweet chestnut depth; f23 long, fabulously spiced and, at last, the malt has a say; a little mocha with a dollop of ulmo honey covers over the copper-starved finale; b22.5 always brave to use PX, as the intensity of the sugars can sometimes put the malt into the tightest of straight-jackets. However, this is fine, sulphur-free butt and is eventually relaxed enough for the malt to share equal billing once it finds its rhythm. 56%

◇ Ayrer's Red Organic Single Malt db (86) n21.5 t22 f21 b21.5. Quite dry and niggardly in places, a degree of chalkiness on the nose and delivery slightly undoing the sugars as they attempt to soar. Pleasant enough, but never quite gets into stride. 43%

◇ Ayrer's Red Organic Single Malt db (90.5) n22.5 distinctly rich with an appealing muscovado sugar fruitiness at play; t22.5 good oils on delivery guarantee the soft landing. Tannins offer a layered intensity and keep the sugars honest; f22.5 a genuinely delightful cocoa-spice interplay right through the long finale; b23 an impressive malt, probably benefitting from the full strength, as the unbroken oils play a leading role in length and balance. 58%

◇ Ayrer's White Organic Single Malt db (86) n21.5 t22 f21 b21.5. An attractive enough new make with good cut points, particularly hitting the heights with a big sugar surge in the mid-ground. But in this naked form, reveals a slight shortage of copper in the system. 46%

HINRICUS NOYTE´S-BRAUHAUS AM LOHBERG Wismar, Working.

◇ Baltach Wismarian Single Malt Whisky db (83) n20.5 t21 f20.5 b21. Needs a defter touch on the still to ensure those hefty oils don't get through. Some decent redeeming honey, though. Fascinating light curry on the nose! 43%

KAUZEN-BRÄU Ochsenfurt, Germany.

 Old Owl Single Malt Whisky dist Apr 12, bott Sept 15 db **(91)** n23.5 stunning! Anyone who remembers butterscotch tart for school dinners will be heading off down Memory Lane now....; some lovely ulmo honey softens the sweetness further; **t23** the barley stands up to be counted from the first moment. Juicy, with an intensifying grassy sweetness before the salty, biscuit middle arrives; **f22** really does dry as the salt becomes more dominating; **b22.5** a beautifully made and well matured whisky bursting with character, and a pretty unique one! 43%

KINZIGBRENNEREI MARTIN BROSAMER Biberach. Working.

Badischer Whisky Blended db **(87.5)** n21 t22.5 f22 b22. A little of the distillery's old nougat style shows its ankles, but otherwise, much cleaner with progressive sugars working in tandem with the growing, faintly wide-cut spice. Very pleasant. 42%

Biberacher Whisky Single Malt bott code L:MWJ15 db **(85)** n20 t22.5 f21 b21.5. A forthright, competent and confident delivery maximises every last degree of sugars in the grist for a sumptuous maltfest. The usual over–enthusiastic oils diminish the effect slightly on both nose and finish. 42%

Kinzigtäler Whisky Single Malt Smoke db **(88.5)** n21.5 maybe not technically on the money, but the pip-squeakingly dry smokiness also helps introduce a degree of cocoa to the scene; **t22.5** a little fat, as usual, but the sugars now have a third, more phenolic dimension and linger attractively; **f22** a rather lovely mix of chocolate and ginger cake; **b22.5** the phenols have much to say. 42%

Schwarzwälder Whisky Rye db **(81)** n19 t22 f20 b20. Few aromas are more scary in whisky than over-cut, feinty rye. Here it is in full, spoon-standing oiliness. Which means the flavours can also power through the roof. Not exactly for the purist. 42%

Single Barrel Whisky No. 5 -Select bott code L:5A14 db **(86)** n21.5 t22 f21 b21.5. An interesting battle between less than technically brilliant spirit and, evidently, some very decent oak. The spirit wins - or loses, if you see what I mean. But the strands of acacia honey and light liquorice are a joy. 40%

Single Barrel Whisky No. 8 -Select bott code L:8A14 db **(83.5)** n19 t21 f22 b21.5. Fruity nougat. There is a big sherry influence here which makes for an occasionally flat landscape with hills and valleys conspicuous by their absence. But no amount of clean fruit can entirely compensate for the enormity of the nougat. 40%

KLEINBRENNEREI FITZKE Herbolzheim-Broggingen. Working.

Derrina Einkorn-Malz Schwarzwälder Single Malt bott code L12010 **(83.5)** n20.5 t21.5 f20.5 b21. Where tobacco meet hay lofts. An impressive, even whisky in part with some decent sugar and barley. 43%

Derrina Gerstenmalz Buchenrauch Schwarzwälder Single Malt bott code L13211 **(88)** n21 earthy...complete with vegetables...and bubble gum; **t22.5** neutral at first, then some peculiar phenols and buzzing spices begin to make some interesting little speeches; **f22** long, an expansion of oils; very late on, some gorgeous liquorice and ulmo honey appear as if from nowhere; **b22.5** worth a revisit. On first impression...not happy with it, as the narrative appears incomprehensible and a little ugly. On second...the vague, weird smokiness and spice begins to grow on you. 43%

Derrina Gerstenmalz Torfrauch Stark Schwarzwälder Single Malt bott code L13111 **(77)** n19 t19 f20 b19. Despite the late injection of maple syrup and mocha, this one fails on many levels. 43%

 Derrina Grünkern Schwarzwälder Single Grain Whisky bott code L 11012 db **(88.5)** n22 a clever, busy nose with the early hint of honey met by a drier, crisper vanilla; **t22** sugars at a premium on delivery also. Vaguely juicy, but always brittle and firm. Even a vague hint of well-aged tannin, which is hardly expected; **f22** those tannins keep their shape to the end, allowing only a vague degree of liquorice; **b22.5** a carefully constructed, disciplined whisky. 43%

Derrina Hafer Schwarzwälder Single Grain bott code L6208 **(94)** n24 so many bourbon notes which win the heart: treacle and honeycomb plus the inevitable ulmo honey: magnificent! **t23** a heart-warming blend of what appears to be intense, salivating barley with crisper bourbon tones; fabulous weight and slow spice infusion; **f23.5** outstanding oils and a slow building of chocolate and hazelnut; the busy spice continue to pulse; **b23.5** voluptuously beautiful. 43%

 Derrina Hirse Schwarzwälder Single Grain Whisky bott code L 6512 db **(84)** n20 t21 f22 b21. Never quite finds its rhythm or style. From the horsebox hay nose to the unsynchronised sugars and wide-cut oils, the narrative is confused and of limited attractiveness. Still has the odd pleasant moment or two, though. 43%

Derrina Karamell-Malz Gerste Schwarzwälder Single Malt bott code L13411 **(87)** n21 t22 f22 b22. For those who like whisky with their nougat.. Bold, gristy sugars throughout. 43%

Derrina Karamell-Malz Roggen Schwarzwälder Single Malt bott code L13511 **(83.5)** n20 t21 f21.5 b21. For those who like whisky with their hay bales....Busy spices punctuates the barley sugar. Green doesn't quite over it... 43%

Derrina Karamell-Malz Weizen Schwarzwälder Single Malt bott code L13311 **(87.5)** n21 t22 f22 b22.5. Toffee nougat with an enjoyable barley and chocolate flourish. Really enjoyable. 43%

⬩ **Derrina Roggenmalz Schwarzwälder Single Malt Whisky** bott code L 5612 db **(95)** n23 a nose familiar to those of us who have blended in Canada: a malted rye of a similar style found out there, absolutely thick with chocolatey fruit notes and teasing spice; t24.5 massive; absolutely massive. Whoever decided on the cut points should get a medal as he or she has successfully taken it to the very limit to maximise the flavour spectrum. For some, maybe too oily. For me, a fabulous and rare chance to see an extraordinary range of sugar and honey notes, all of them of the dark variety; a fruity muscovado lording it above them all; f23.5 long, with the sugars still in control as the harder grain grinds a vaguely fruity finish out of nowhere; b24 this distillery should take a bow. They have produced a very high class rye whisky! 43%

Derrina Sorghum-Malz Schwarzwälder Single Malt bott code L10509 **(88.5)** n23.5 I know a lot of Germans settled in Kentucky... The bourbon influence of style is astonishing with honeycomb and liquorice leading the way with a touch of ulmo honey to soften; t22 light oils and heavy honey. A little feintiness hits the midground; f21 the earlier rhythm has been lost: goes slightly off course; b22 a hit and miss malt. But when it scores, it's a bullseye... 43%

⬩ **Derrina Triticale Schwarzwälder Single Grain Whisky** bott code L 10412 db **(89.5)** n22.5 a touch of nougat: a tad heavy and ungainly yet always attractive and welcoming; just the sexiest hint of bourbon topped with a little lime; t22 chewy start and gets progressively chewier! A mixed, indecipherable bag early on. But settles as the oils form into dark sugars, especially burnt fudge; f22.5 some complexity with the sugars and drier oak tones working well together; superb weight and a hint of butterscotch towards the very end as it lightens at last; b22.5 grows on you as the flavours open like a spring flower. 43%

KYMSEE WHISKY Grabenstätt, Working.

⬩ **Kymsee Der Chiemsee Single Malt Whisky** cask no. 2, dist Dec 2012 db **(87.5)** n21 t23 f22 b21.5. A fascinating malt. When sweet, it is very sweet with the molasses piled on thick. When it is bitter, it is so in a way which undermines the sweetness, rather than balancing with it. And the spices are borderline aggressive. Pleasant, and impressively distilled. But still a bit of an odd ball. 42%. sc.

MARDER EDELBRÄNDE Albbruck-Unteralpfen, Working.

⬩ **Marder Single Malt Whisky Aged 3 Years** bott 2015 db **(92)** n22.5 wow! Impressive! No off notes...no unacceptable feints, generally clean, yet bursting with a spiced maltiness and even a light smattering of marmalade...; t23.5 gorgeous mouth feel: beautifully weighted and oiled with a controlled intensity to the barley which revels in the light muscovado sugars without ever getting too sweet; throughout, there is a lovely sub-strata of hazelnut puree; f23 some heavier oils congregate, though the process is slow and a little mocha offsets the growing dryness; b23 very attractive whisky with plenty of character and complexity. 43%

MÄRKISCHE SPEZIALITÄTEN BRENNEREI Hagen. Working.

DeCavo Handcrafted Single Malt cask no. 9/2044 db **(91)** n22 That is one very malty aroma. Clean, too...; t23...and no less malty on delivery. Horlicks night drink with grass and maple syrup stirred in; f23 some light oaky vanillas while the spice is from the work of the stills. But the malt retains its dominance; b23 a whisky which puts the malt into single malt. 46%. sc.

⬩ **DeCavo Handcrafted Single Malt Höhlenwhisky** Fass-Nr. L 3 db **(89)** n22 creamy and nutty; t23.5 a real spiced gingerbread depth. Pretty well made and charmingly deployed flavour profile. The brown sugars go to town early and in earnest; f21 just a hint of feints on the Tunnock's Teacake finale; b22.5 certainly knows how to make an impact...! 43%. sc. 262 bottles.

⬩ **DeCavo Handcrafted Single Malt** Fass-Nr. L 13 db **(87)** n22 t22 f21 b22. A tame malt. First gristy, then a more complex development of vanilla and lighter, friendly sugars. 46%. sc.

DeCavo Handcrafted Single Malt Fass-Nr. L 13 db **(91)** n22 delicate vanilla and malt with an apologetic squeeze of lime; t23 intense malt on delivery with enough to spare to send gristy, barley-rich shockwaves and spasms over the taste buds for a little while. The oak generates plenty of spice to balance the big sugars; f23 for all the malty fudge, a degree of bitterness lingers, though without damaging the whole; b23 an astonishingly lush malt with an almost three dimensional sugar attack. Wow! *55%. sc.*

Edelsthal Moonshiner White Single Malt db **(88)** n19 t23 f23 b23. Now that is interesting stuff. The nose wins no beauty prizes. But there is no faulting the complexity and richness of the spirit on the palate, nor the astonishing degree of ulmo honey which somehow makes its way into the new make. Beyond the nose, very impressive, indeed. *50%*

Edelstahl Moonshiner White Single Malt bott code. L1/2015 db **(87)** n20.5 t23 f21.5 **b22.** The nose reveals just a little less copper than is desired, but the cut is a sound one: feint free and teaming with delicious, viscous malt and light ulmo honey. Attractive. *50%. sc.*

Tronje Von Hagen Single Malt Höhlenwhisky cask no. 2, bott 21 Aug 14 db **(94.5)** n23 honey roast almonds with Demerara sugar as a side dash...; **t24** brilliant delivery: you expect a brittle crispness to the sugars and they arrive early, but not before the lush, mouth-massaging and intense barley has already made its gristy presence felt: salivating and, as the spices arrive, invigorating...; **f23.5** chocolate honey fade with a little mint sprinkled in. But the spiced barley sugar carries on regardless; **b24** now, just how confident a whisky is that....? *55%. sc.*

NORDPFALZ BRENNEREI Höning. Working.

Taranis Pfälzer 3 Years Old Single Malt Whisky Amarone cask finished, dist Sept 11 db **(86)** n21 t22.5 f20.5 b22. A little feintier and thicker than last bottling. Even so, the quality of the wine cask is exceptional and makes best use of the nougat and toffee on show. *50.5%.*

Taranis Pfalzer 4 Years Old Single Malt Whisky Amarone Cask Finished dist Sept 09 db **(88.5)** n22 t23.5 f21 b22. Big and rather beautiful, in its own cumbersome way...especially in its delivery of fruit. *50.80%. 440 bottles.*

Taranis Pfälzer 5.5 Years Old Single Malt Whisky oloroso sherry cask, dist Sept 09 db **(85.5)** n19.5 t22.5 f22 b21.5. A clean oloroso butt. But one I have never before seen inject so much spice into: as though distilled from white pepper. The nose undermines the project by projecting the feints. But the lightning bolt delivery certainly ups the interest and some decent grape meanders to the gentler and much more sane finish. *50.7%. ncf. 480 bottles.*

NUMBER NINE SPIRITUOSENMANUFAKTUR
Leinefelde-Worbis, Working.

The Nine Springs Single Malt Whisky Aged 3 Years virgin oak cask, cask no. 2 db **(88.5)** n22 a few feints kicking around, plus the odd slightly mouldy tangerine; t22.5 beautiful arrival with the emphasis on Venezuelan cocoa. Clings to the roof of the mouth like a limpet...; f22 feinty Fox's Orange Cream biscuits...if they still do them...; b22 though the oak should be the driving force, the thick cut from the still means the distillate has its hands on the steering wheel. *45%. nc ncf sc.*

The Nine Springs Single Malt Whisky Aged 3 Years batch no. 1 db **(91)** n22.5 a plethora of healthy bourbon tones with the orange blossom honey and liquorice in harmony; t23 voluptuous and chewy, the delivery skirts around the rising chocolate orange and then focusses on the ever-intensifying tannins; f22.5 a little drier and the orange is discarded as the cocoa homes in; b23 for those who like their malt whiskies and be in touch with their bourbon side... *45%. nc ncf sc.*

SAUERLÄNDER EDELBRENNEREI Ruthen-Kallenhardt. Working.

Thousand Mountains Mc Raven Single Malt Whisky cask no. L1003 03.2012 db **(74.5)** n16 t21 f18.5 b19. A massively wide cut means this is a gluepot of a whisky. Best ignore the nose and concentrate on the delivery which has its magnificently sugared moments. But, as is to be expected, an oily, untamed beast. *46.2%*

SCHLENKERLA Bamberg, Working.

Schlenkerla db **(79.5)** n21 t18.5 f21 b19. Very much more like German lebkuchen biscuit/cake than whisky. Soft, vaguely phenolic, gingery and friendly – and the finish is surprisingly lovely, especially after the chaotic and confusing opening. A challenging whisky to say the least. *40%*

SEVERIN SIMON Alzenau-Michelbach, Aschaffenburg. Working.

Simon's Bavarian Pure Pott Still db **(86)** n21 t22 f21 b22. Always great to renew acquaintances with this idiosyncratic malt. I remember lots of pine last time out. Here the pine is remarkable for its almost lack of interest in this whisky after the nose. Which means this is a better bottling, with the malt – man marked by crisp sugars – having a much louder say than normal. Some soft, creamy toffee and nougat at play. But the spices and barley are most enjoyable. 40%

SLYRS Schliersee-Neuhaus. Working.

Slyrs Bavarian Single Malt Sherry Edition No. 1 finished in Oloroso, lot no. L00354, bott 2013 **(86) n20 t22 f22 b22.** Anyone out there who loves cream toffee and spice? This malt has your name on it. 46%

SPERBERS DESTILLERIE Rentweinsdorf, Working.

◇ **Sperbers Destillerie Malt Whisky Anno 2010** los-nr. 40 db **(86.5) n21.5 t22 f21.5 b21.5.** One gets the distinct feeling this was distilled to a pretty high strength before being put into cask. Hard to spot the malt, but plenty of tannins from the oak. Still, quite delicious! 59%

SPREEWÄLD BRENNEREI Schlepzig, Germany.

◇ **Spreewälder Sloupisti Single Malt Whisky** dist Oct 11, bott Mar 16 db **(94) n23** a dazzling nose: beautifully clean distillate – literally a cut above most German aromas – which allows the muscovado to really sparkle; the light acacia honey breeze is a sweet caress; **t23.5** fair crackles on the delivery: the sugars are massive, but the countering oaks ensure a beautifully balanced toastiness; still enough left in the tank for a salivating middle; **f24** some oils arrive from somewhere, so the finish now goes into warp drive: molasses, liquorice, light spice and Manuka honey all make guest appearances...; **b23.5** absolutely my best whisky of the day! And with its portrayal of a stork in a bow tie and top hat, probably the best label of the year! My kind of whisky; my kind of distillery...!! 68.5%

STEINHAUSER 1. BODENSEE-WHISKY-DESTILLERIE
Kressbronn, Working.

Brigantia 3 Years Old bott L-12/12 db **(79) n19 t21 f19 b20** Huge malt statement, as is the distillery style. But it appears someone decided to try and extract as much spirit as possible, because the cut seems to be a little too wide for comfort here: the oils are unforgiving. 43%

◇ **Brigantia Single Malt Whisky vom Bodensee 3 Years Old** bott code. 10/15 db **(75) n19 t19 f18 b19.** Sweet in part. But this distillery badly needs to get more copper into their spirit. 43%

WEINGUT MÖßLEIN Kolitzheim. Working.

Mößlein Grain Whisky 5 Years Old db **(87.5) n21.5 t22.5 f21.5 b22.** It's all about the oak. The tannins are the driving force for both the darker, more brooding phases – of which there are many - and the sugars. Some pleasant minty chocolate to be had if you look carefully enough. 41%

◇ **M Mößlein Fränkischer Grain Whisky 5 Jahre** fass nr. 4, bott code. L750 1 16 db **(83) n20 t21.5 f20.5 b21.** Soft and pleasant, though the odd gremlin comes through on the nose and finish. The generous cut ensures a vague nougat thread alongside the inevitable cocoa. 40.5%. sc.

Mößlein Single Malt Whisky 5 Years Old db **(77) n18.5 t20 f19 b19.5.** The early butyric makes it difficult for the malt to re-align to positive effect. 42%

◇ **M Mößlein Fränkischer Single Malt Whisky 5 Jahre** fass nr. 5, bott code. L730-1-15 db **(85) n21 t22 f21 b21.** More comfortable with the single malt than with the grain, though better cut point selection has helped. Even so, the oils are still big on this while the light liquorice works well with the buzzing spices. 41%. sc.

WHISKY-DESTILLERIE DREXLER Arrach, Working.

◇ **Drexler Arrach No 1 Single Cask Malt Whisky** sherry cask no. 76, dist Jan 12, bott Nov 15 db **(83) n21 t22 f19.5 b20.5.** Now there's a beast! The fact it starts off with a generous cut from the still, inclusive of some chunky oils, would normally be enough to keep the average palate quiet for a while. But when you then get a massive combination of bourbon-style oak and then lashings of fruit on top of even that, then it becomes challenging. Just a little too bitter towards the end, though. Not for the faint hearted. 46%. sc.

WHISKY-DESTILLERIE GRUEL Owen/Teck, Working.

◇ **Tecker Single Malt Whisky Port Cask Matured** db **(82.5) n19 t21.5 f21 b21.** A toffee-raisin whisky with a big degree of burnt sugar. 43%. ncf.

◈ **Tecker Single Grain Whisky Aged 5 Years** db **(84)** n21.5 t22 f20 b20.5. Somewhere in the five years between the ten and this five-year-old, someone appears to have made the cut a little wider. *40%. ncf.*

◈ **Tecker Single Grain Whisky Aged 10 Years** Chardonnay casks db **(93)** n23.5 complex and benefits from the lightness of touch of the bourbon-style red liquorice and diced green apple; **t23** every bit as salivating as the nose suggests, though the sugars are much more to the fore. The soft oil is almost perfect in weight and intensity, as are the pretty warming spices; like the nose, offers an intriguing hint of bourbon; **f23** ridiculously long. Brilliant spice alongside the clean, aged banana vanilla..; **b23.5** now, that is all rather beautiful... *53.2%. ncf.*

WHISKY DESTILLERIE LIEBL Bad Kötzting. Working.

Coillmór Bavarian Single Malt Bordeaux Cask cask no. 398, dist Oct 09 db **(87)** n21.5 t21.5 f22 b22. A stable bottling allowing the fruit to make the best use of the light nougat to offer a rich, rounded, lightly fruited malt. Well balanced, salivating and a joy to experience. *46%.*

Coillmór Bavarian Single Malt Port Cask 8 Years Old cask no. 351, dist 4 May 07 db **(79.5)** n21 t20 f19 b19.5. Even a Port cask has problems seeing off the excesses of the massively heavy nougat. Rough. *46%. 1080 bottles.*

Coillmór Bavarian Single Malt Alabanach Peat American oak, cask no. 47, dist 17 Jul 10 db **(81.5)** n20 t21 f20 b20.5. I'll give the peat from this distillery one thing: it really is idiosyncratic. No other smoked whisky is so jarring and a liquid antonym of "rounded". An absolute must for any serious collector or student of peated whisky. *46%. 392 bottles.*

Coillmór Bavarian Single Malt American Oak cask nos. 60,214,229,268339, dist May 10 db **(83)** n21 t20 f21 b21. A malt with a huge nougat input. Lots of toffee, but curiously little sweetness. *43%. 1895 bottles.*

Coillmór Bavarian Single Malt Distillers Edition Peated Oloroso Sherry Cask cask no. 81, dist 28 Aug 10 db **(80)** n20 t21 f19 b20. When you see peat and oloroso on the same whisky label, it tends to be a bottling you leave until the end of the day's work. If anything can hide sulphur until it is too late, it is peat. Too often have my taste buds been wrecked in this fashion. Well, my palate is still intact. Just. Though it was a close run thing: there is a buzz on the finish which might be the fault of the cask. But so clanking and grinding is the original course peat spirit, it is hard to tell. If you are simply a smoke head, then this really might just be a whisky right down your strasse. *46%. 895 bottles.*

WHISKY DESTILLERIE BLAUE MAUS Eggolsheim, Working.

Austrasier Single Cask Grain Whisky cask no. 2, dist May 08, bott Jun 15 db **(88.5)** n22 not dissimilar to a spice-seasoned cake baking; **t23** the softest delivery, then a slow rising of spiced – or is that herbed? – barley; **f21.5** just a little bitter towards the end as the spices and other tannins merge; **b22** few European whiskies come as flavoursome as this. *40%. sc.*

◈ **Blaue Maus Single Cask Malt Whisky** fass/los nr. 1, destilliert Feb 08, abgefüllt Apr 16 db **(86.5)** n21 t23 f21 b21.5. Perhaps a tad over-exuberant on the cut which impacts on both nose and finish. But the delivery and middle are a lush, honey-riddled treat. *40%. sc.*

◈ **Blaue Maus Single Cask Malt Whisky** fass/los nr. 2, destilliert Mar 06, abgefüllt May 16 db **(87)** n20.5 t22 f22.5 b22. The scary nose is compensated by a charming slow burn of light muscovado sugars and ulmo honey. The feinty bitters are kept in check. *40%. sc.*

◈ **Blaue Maus Single Cask Malt Whisky Fassstärke** fass/los nr. 1, destilliert Mar 00, abgefüllt May 16 db **(92)** n23 very similar to the salty symphony played out on the nose of one of Robert's Fasstarke's last year, unless my memory is really going. Here, a little more citrus has been squeezed in; **t22** a light feinty kick early on, then a succession of richer notes, vaguely veering towards a barley-intense middle; **f24** a really beautifully layered, relaxed finale with a playing out of Manuka honey and light mocha; **b23** a demure whisky for all its inner riches. The lack of spices is a surprise. *51.2%. sc.*

◈ **Blaue Maus Single Cask Malt Whisky Fassstärke** fass/los nr. 1, destilliert Feb 01, abgefüllt May 16 db **(94.5)** n23.5 wow! The cleanest grape-ish fruitiness, though this seems to be more about esters than the actual cask or grape. With the sharp, vaguely salty edge much more like an old island-matured rum; the bitter-dry balance could not be better; **t24** the first half dozen waves are normally found when working in the blending lab I know in Guyana. The sugars are rich and mildly toasty - a kind of treacle and maple syrup mix; **f23** long, languid and lush. Still no bitterness at play, even though the tannins have plenty about them; **b24** an exhibition of just how to control a sugar and honey-dominated whisky. *47.5%. sc.*

◈ **Blaue Maus Single Cask Malt Whisky Fassstärke** fass/los nr. 1, destilliert May 01, abgefüllt May 16 db **(89)** n23 a lower voltage dose of ester compared to the bottling above;

t23.5 sensual and chewy: ulmo honey meets concentrated malt head on with a slow vanilla middle; **f22.5** just light enough to show a little bit of gruff distillate, but the flavour intensity – especially from liquorice - never lets up; **b23** a kind of rum meets chocolate Liquorice Allsort. Just so much delicious character! 53.7%. sc.

Blaue Maus Single Cask Malt Whisky Fassstärke German oak casks, cask no. 1, dist Jun 98, bott May 15 db **(94) n22.5** whisky...? Pot still rum? A distillate of hay? Cream toffee concentrate...? **t24** though the feints are apparent early on, the oils drag with them a fascinating mix of copper and manuka honey. That is just the start. Next comes that mind-boggling, puzzling and mesmerising display of multi-layered, fizzing, buzzing biting spice...; **f23.5** here comes that toffee again. Though armed to the teeth in spices and ulmo honey; **b24** a sexy, subtle malt which seduces you from the moment the first sweet drop touches your lips... 57.5%. sc.

Blaue Maus Single Cask Malt Whisky Fassstärke German oak casks, cask no. 2, dist Jun 92, bott Jun 15 db **(92.5) n22** about as salty and coastal as a malt might get...in mainly land-locked Germany; **t24** the lush delivery defies the strength...though the peppery spices don't. The early exchanges are all about honey: on the fourth mouthful, I had counted five different styles at play: manuka and heather lead the way, though. Liquorice and hickory underline the vintage; **f23** dry, with the hickory taking control. A little maple syrup comes to the rescue; but those spices just nip and bite...; **b23.5** an exhausting whisky to taste: so much is happening, it is hard to know which bit to concentrate on... 48.7%. sc.

Blaue Maus Single Cask Malt Whisky dist Mar 15 db **(89.5) n23 t23 f21 b22.5**. The oils on the tail confirms the hint on the nose that this is a wide-ish cut. But absolutely bursting with delicious malty intent. 78.4%. sc.

Blaue Maus Single Cask Malt Whisky German oak casks, cask no. 2, dist Apr 07, bott Jun 15 db **(88) n21** usual array of household spices, including ginger; **t22.5** silky despite the low strength with a long cream toffee middle; below deck , the spices burn...; **f22.5** malt and toffee...so, so soft – like a feather run down the spine; **b22** the intensity of fire on the busiest of spice is unique to this distillery. 40%. sc.

Elbe 1 Single Cask Malt Whisky German oak casks, cask no. 2, dist Jun 06, bott Jun 15 db **(82) n20 t21 f20 b21**. A little too coppery and feinty for its own good. 40%. sc.

Grüner Hund Single Cask Malt cask no. 2, dist Jun 01 db **(79) n20 t19 f20 b20**. All kinds of German style biscuit spices. But the oil runs too deep. 40%. sc.

Grüner Hund Single Cask Malt Whisky German oak casks, cask no. 3, dist May 08, bott Jun 15 db **(90) n21** nougat and milk chocolate; **t23** beautiful oils and satisfying toasted honeycomb; **f23** long, lightly spiced with a return of cocoa but now with butterscotch tart; **b23** a satisfying malt full of clever, varying honey tones. 40%. sc.

◈ **Mary Read Single Cask Malt Whisky** fass/los nr. 3, destilliert May 08, abgefüllt Apr 16 db **(86.5) n18.5 t22.5 f23.5 b22.** Maybe just a touch more feinty than normal. But the delightful chocolate nut-led recovery, so soft and beautifully layered, is well worth the initial pain. 40%. sc.

Mary Read Single Cask Malt Whisky German oak casks, cask no. 3, dist May 07, bott Jun 15 db **(87) n20 t23 f22 b22.** The feinty, nutty nose never quite finds happiness. But the fizzing, spicy delivery is awash with dark honey. 40%. sc.

Old Fahr III dist Jul 02 db **(89) n22.5 t22 f22 b22.5.** A complex battle of a dram. 40%

◈ **Old Fahr Single Cask Malt Whisky** fass/los nr. 2, destilliert Apr 08, abgefüllt May 16 db **(88.5) n22** a lovely mix of nougat, ginger and orange blossom honey; **t23** wow, that ginger really does come out in force: some superb oils at play; **f21.5** a light maltiness finally appears; while the nougat re-emerges; a tad too dry on the finish perhaps; **b22** a tangy, complexly spiced whisky. 40%. sc.

◈ **Otto's Uisge Beatha Single Cask Malt Whisky** fass/los nr. 2, destilliert Oct 10, abgefüllt May 16 db **(94.5) n23.5** so sensual and smoky...wow! Very much the acrid bite of peat you get the morning after the crofter's fire has gone out...; the odd sinew of citrus...; **t24** if you think the nose is peaty....just get a load of that delivery and follow-through. I feel like I am in a warehouse on the south coast of Islay having just removed a bung from a cask and sampling the contents; the oils are quite superb here, accompanied by some decent molasses; **f23.5** long, ashy, a little salty with a late vanilla entrance; **b23.5** Robert has entered new territory with this: he has gone all Islay. Absolutely no trace of his usual house style. 55.6%. sc.

◈ **Spinnaker Single Cask Malt Whisky Fassstärke** fass/los nr. 1, destilliert Mar 01, abgefüllt May 16 db **(85) n21 t21 f21.5 b21.5.** Relatively disappointing. Last year's Spinnaker revelled in the rum-like house style. This is less composed and more sculpted by the feints, thus giving the late cocoa notes maximum voice. 48.1%. sc.

Spinnaker Single Cask Malt Whisky Fassstärke German oak casks, cask no. 3, dist May 07, bott Jun 15 db **(95) n23.5** all kinds of ginger-spiced tannins and a weird thick cut marmalade citrus note. At times, this appears to be an old pot still Demerara rum. Whatever, you get the feeling you might need seat belts for the delivery...; **t24** bloody hell...! I'm not wrong! Massive doesn't begin to cover it: the spices radiating from the tannins almost blast a hole through your head, from the direction of the roof of your mouth. This is hot: pure oaky spice. But there is a counter, and it is the thick molassed sugars leading the way....; **f23.5** dries enormously thanks to the oak. But some buttery burnt fudge soothes and kisses better; **b24** explosive. And a lesson in balance. *54.2%. sc.*

Spinnaker Single Cask Malt Whisky Fassstärke German oak casks, cask no. 1, dist Jun 88, bott Jun 15 db **(97) n23.5 t24.5 f24 b25** When fruit flies pass a few other malts to sup themselves to death in the same glass, you tend to know you are on to a winner. Rule of thumb means head for the sweetest around: for them to find sugars to die for in a 27-year-old German malt from which you can nearly spit the splinters takes some believing. The intense, but clever, balancing sugars in there really aren't an illusion. Amazing. Truly and so beautifully amazing...! The 700th new whisky tasted for the 2016 Whisky Bible. And if it doesn't win some kind of gong, then this has been one exceptional year!! *42.9%. sc.*

◇ **Sylter Watt Single Cask Malt Whisky Aged 7 Years** fass/los nr. 1, destilliert 2007 db **(83.5) n20 t21 f21.5 b21**. Curiously powdery, dry and spicy. Pretty feint heavy at times, though the sugars grow at a disarming rate. *42%. nc ncf sc.*

◇ **Sylter Watt Single Cask Malt Whisky Aged 7 Years** fass/los nr. 2, destilliert 2007 db **(86.5) n19.5 t22.5 f22 b22.5**. A pretty slinky whisky when it hits the palate. The nose has a curious cabbage and cucumber timbre, but once on board settles into a far more relaxed mode with light ulmo honey and various spices making for a delicious experience. *40%. sc.*

◇ **Sylter Tide Single Cask Malt Whisky** fass/los nr. 1, destilliert Jul 11, abgefüllt Mar 16 db **(92) n22.5** if this nose was any busier, it would collapse from exhaustion. Principally, some old fashioned Spanish orange on display alongside a much thicker malt nightcap...dreamy...; **t23** it noses thickly and arrives on the palate even thicker. We are back to Ovaltine, only in concentrated form...; **f23.5** healthy oils confirm the longevity of the finish: indeed, does it end at all? Still the intense malt dominates, though some drier tannin arrives to add some thrust; **b23** says "Single Malt"; and this is malt singularly... *40%. sc.*

◇ **Sylter Tide Single Cask Malt Whisky** fass/los nr. 2, destilliert Jul 11, abgefüllt May 16 db **(88) n22** liquorice, tannin and an earthy, vaguely medicinal aspect...; **t22** a real cough mixture zeal to this one...plenty of sugars have been stirred in to help it go down easier; **f22** intensely malty, but still that strangely cough sweet heaviness persists; **b22** to be taken three times a day after meals... *40.7%. sc.*

Sylter Watt Single Cask Malt Whisky Aged 7 Years lot no. 1, dist 2007, bott 15 May 15 **(92.5) n23.5** there we go: that unique arrangement of honey and old leather; **t23.5** soft, chewy, silky and the slow leeching of acacia honey, light liquorice and leather: simply one of the best things you'll ever taste in Germany...though I am always on the lookout for something new...; **f22** slightly more bitter as the feints catch up. But blood orange joins the malt for the finale; **b23.5** quite unmistakable. So delighted the 666th new whisky tasted for the 2016 Bible has turned out to be Devilishly good... *40%. Distilled at Whiskydestillerie Blaue Maus.*

Blends

Kahlgrund Whisky Blend (86.5) n21.5 t22 f21 b22. A well balanced, impressively weighted whisky full of enjoyable sugars. But definitely from the nougat school of German distilling. *46%*

ITALIAN
PUNI WHISKY DISTILLERY Glurns, Bozen, Working.

◇ **PUNI Alba 3 Year Old** batch no. 01/2015, marsala casks, finished in Islay casks db **(95) n23** takes a little bit of oxidisation and temperature warming to get the fruit and the smoke to quite sync. But when they do, we are treated to a delightful interplay of understated intensity and counterpoints; **t24** so, so soft. The delivery is a treat: an early flourish of lightly toasted sugars, a background maltiness, but the fruit picking up with a thickening of intensity and gathering dryness, the malt all the time weaving through the narrative; some red and black and liquorice mingle tantalisingly; **f23.5** long, with the smoke now making a mark, if only a light one; the oils now seem more assured; the malt, fittingly, has the final say...; **b24.5** funny how you think of Italy, and it is all about passion and fieriness – be it their football manager or volcanos. Yet here we have, for all this whisky's enormity, a tale played out in the cask of genteel elegance despite the high drama. You almost feel Italian whisky has come of age with an offering this complex and charming. *43%*

LATVIA
LATVIJAS BALZAMS Riga. Working.
L B Lavijas Balzams db (83) n20 t22 f20 b21. Soft and yielding on the palate, this is said to be made from Latvian rye, though of all the world's rye whiskies this really does have to be the softest and least fruity. I'll be astonished if there isn't a fair degree of thinning grain in there, too. 40%

LIECHTENSTEIN
TELSER DISTILLERY Triesen. Working.
Telsington V 4 Years Old Pinot Noir Cask db (88.5) n22 t22.5 f22 b22. An friendly satisfying malt. The pinot is a bit tight, but the fruit has just enough shine and clarity. 43.5%.

Telsington Moosalp Edition Single Malt Whisky bott 2014 db (92) n22.5 t23 f23.5 b23 benefitting from the use of an excellent cask, a big whisky from a little country. Very distinguished. Just like the Moosalp restaurant. 42%. 50 bottles.

Telsington VI Single Cask Malt, 5 Years Old Pinot Noir cask, Swiss oak db (94.5) n24 t23.5 f23 b24 I wonder if the chap at the top of the hill in that big castle above Vaduz has ever tasted this. For there is something effortlessly regal to this whisky. 43.5%. sc.

Telsington VII 5 Years Old Pinot Noir Finish db (73.5) n18 t20 f17.5 b18. A poor wine cask has strangled the life out of this one. A shame, as a few lovely mocha notes can be heard in the distance. Telser VI had to be better than this...where is it? 43.5%. sc.

Teslington Single Cask Malt Black Edition, 5 Years Old Pinot noir cask, French Oak db (86) n22.5 t22 f20 b21.5. The trouble, often, with French oak is that its tendency to dominate, even bully, shortens the complexity and ability to experience the full personality of the characters taking part. Sharp, sometimes shrill on the palate, it is certainly big. 43.5%. sc.

Telser Single Cask 100% Rye Malt, 2 Years Old db (89.5) n22.5 t23.5 f21.5 b22 a remarkably memorable first try at malted rye: had the cut been a tad narrower this would have been a very distinguished dram. 42%. sc.

Telsington Single Cask Rye Whisky Aged 3 Years Islay cask finish db (90) n23 t23 f20.5 b23.5 rye meets Islay, surely a match made in heaven as my two favourite whisky styles marry. I presume it had been in some kind of wine cask first, though, as there is high fruit dominance. Ticks many a box for me: well distilled, good fruit, firm grain and the most delicate smoke. Just a niggle on the finish, I fear. 42%

⬦ **Telser Liechtenstein Single Malt Whisky IX** - Pinot Noir Edition Aged 7 Years db (94.5) n23.5 one of the best wine cask noses I have encountered this year: crisp, firm and devoid of off notes. Neither sweet nor dry or, rather, both – equally. One of those ten minute noses which prevents you from moving on with the tasting...; t24 superb delivery with that same firm grape, initially firm, slightly tart and salivating but then softened massively by the texture of the intense malt; f23 a gentle spice fade respects both the fruit and malt camps; b24 the Burgundian edge to this is clean and almost fascinating: this distillery does Pinot Noir-matured malt probably better than any other in the world. A big treat from a small country. 42.5%. nc ncf.

LUXEMBOURG
DISTILLERIE DIEDENACKER Niederdonven. Working.
Diedenacker Number One Rye Malt 2008 Aged 5 Years db (86) n22 t22 f21 b21. Not quite hitting the heights of their first bottling, but the nut and nougat is balanced well by crystallised treacle. 42%. 450 bottles.

THE NETHERLANDS
ZUIDAM BAARLE Nassau. Working.
Millstone Barrel Proof Rye 2004 (92.5) n24 think of the most intense rye nose you can either imagine, or have experienced. Then double it....; t23.5 not just a massive rye surge – seemingly a mix of malted and unmalted due to the change in flavour profile – but a big dollop of acacia honey has been dropped on it to maximise the effect; strangely salty, too...; f22 the wide cut does a little damage as the oily bitterness creeps in. But the rye and honey still go the distance and find some marzipan as a late companion; b23 always a bottling I look forward to, as these Dutch guys know how to ramp up the rye. The nose (if you forgive the slightly wide cut!) is textbook and good to see them still flying their flag very high. 58.6%. The Whisky Exchange Exclusive. WB16/001

Millstone Aged 12 Years Sherry Cask dist 26 Feb 99, bott 22 Mar 13 db (95) n24 t23.5 f23.5 b24 After last year's disappointing sherry bottling, thought I'd need some Dutch courage to tackle this one. But, instead, an excellent cask at work here which ensures an overflow of character. Just underlines the difference between putting a good quality spirit into a less than impressive cask or filling into top quality oak So, so elegant... 46% WB15/399

Zuidam 2007 Dutch Rye virgin American oak barrel, cask no. 449, dist 07, bott 13 (**91.5**) **n24 t23 f22 b22.5.** Another impressive bottling from a distillery which proves it certainly knows how to make rye. 46%. sc. Distillery Region Netherlands.

SLOVAKIA
NESTVILLE DISTILLERY Hniezdne, Working.

⟨⟩ **Nestville Blended Whisky No. 1** db (**86**) **n21 t22 f21.5 b21.5.** Sweetens in the right places, dries when required. And is even salivating, too. A real lightweight, this. Though always easy, attractive and singing sweetly, the overall plumage is a little dull. 40%

⟨⟩ **Nestville Blended Whisky 6 Years Old** db (**91**) **n23** a sharp, almost rye-style nose with some distinct crisp fruit in ridiculously good harmony with the oak; **t23** a blend should always have a little bit of bite to ensure the grains don't render the creation too docile. This has it with freshly sharpened teeth which nibble naughtily. The slight Kentucky edge on the nose continues here as the sugars remain firm and precise; **f22** deft vanilla and a little maple syrup; **b23** blended, Slovak...it makes no difference: this is a beautifully constructed whisky. A genuine surprise package. 40%

⟨⟩ **Nestville Single Barrel Whisky 2009** dist May 09, bott 15 Dec 15 db (**92**) **n23** has some of the properties identified in their 6-year-old blend, especially that vaguely fruity rye-style kick. But much more tannin here. Clean, almost crystalline and boasting excellent light muscovado; **t23** possibly the softest mouth feel to any single cask I have tasted this week. Astonishing degree of sugar – like molten Demerara with some muscovado dissolving at the back of the palate. Toasty, crisp yet soft – makes for excellent balance; **f22.5** spiced vanilla all the way; **b23.5** a beautifully balanced whisky, not just in flavour but in the interplay between the soft and then hardening mouth feel. A winner all the way. Which, hopefully, Slovakia's football team against England won't be. And if they are – I'll toast their success with a glass of this excellence. 40%. sc.

SPAIN

DYC Aged 8 Years (**90**) **n22 t23 f22.5 b22.5.** I really am a sucker for clean, cleverly constructed blends like this. Just so enjoyable! 40%

DYC Selected Blended Whisky (**85.5**) **n21.5 t22 f21 b21.** One of the cleanest and perhaps creamiest whiskies in Europe. Some gooseberry, like the malt, occasionally drifts in, ramping up the flavour profile which is anything but taxing. 40%

DYC Single Malt Whisky Aged 10 Years (**91**) **n22** an aloof, stand-offish nose which reveals its malty and beautifully textured oak only when it gets to know you...; **t23** ridiculously clean at first, then a steady build up of malt, like cars at a traffic hold up. Oils slowly form and this introduces the oak, first apologetically...then with an integrated build up of vanillas; throughout there is a gorgeous backdrop of controlled sugars; **f23** a little spice begins to warm the cockles. The oak tones are pitch perfect, never too dry or heavy; late vanilla mingles contentedly with the malt; **b23** far more complex than it first seems. Like Segovia, where the distillery is based, worth exploring... 40%

SWEDEN
BOX DESTILLERI Bjärträ, Working.

⟨⟩ **BOX Early Days 001** 0ppm db (**91.5**) **n23** all the fingers point to rich malt. This is really well-made whisky...; **t23** sultry and simplistic, an oily gristiness releases the sugars with panache; a light muscovado edge; **f22.5** oily with more biscuit-style grain; **b23** for those who like their whisky malty and very well made. Almost modern classical Speyside style. 51.2%

⟨⟩ **BOX The Archipelago 2016** 41ppm db (**95**) **n23.5** few marriages I know are as comfortable and sound as this one between the chunky peat and chunkier oak...; the sub-plot is one of a herb garden...just after it has rained...; **t24** smoky, yes. But the real story is about the layering of the sugars: firstly bourbon-style tannin of maple syrup, liquorice and tangerine. Then a secondary wave of lighter notes, around Demerara, heather-honey and ulmo honey, all encased in slightly overcooked butterscotch tart; **f23.5** at last the spices arrive from the peat and tannins; dry, with a rare late insight into the spirit itself; **b24** another Box which ticks all the right complexity credentials. This is one bloody fantastic distillery. Boys, I'm checking BA flights to Stockholm now....and if I can fly to the standard of this whisky, it can only be First Class. 56.5%

◇ **BOX The Festival 2014** 35ppm db **(92) n22** such is the enormity of the tannin, that for a second it appears to be on course for a crash. But a subtle intervention of citrus amid the developing smoke acts like an airbag...; **t23.5** just try to get your head around this delivery: outrageous oak but all is buttressed by a smoky, blood orange sweetness, made all the more remarkable by the thickness of the oils; **f23.5** long, the tannins receding with liquorice and molasses arriving late on the scene. The smoke and spices look on from below and above accordingly; **b23** not sure whether to applaud loudly, wave a white flag or just go and lie down for a few minutes... *53.5%*

◇ **BOX The Festival 2015** 24ppm db **(92) n22** the peat appears ambushed by the enormity of the tannin; **t23** solid oak delivery, but immediately settles as the oils and light butterscotch usher in a delightful array of spices and smoke; **f23.5** very complex: the spices are at their busiest, the sugars at their politest and the ulmo honey at its gentlest; **b23.5** complex malt, really quite wonderfully distilled and matured to the brink...Curiously, although the lowest of the peated malt, the smoke here plays the biggest overall role of the three. *54.5%*

◇ **BOX The Messenger** 3ppm db **(87.5) n22 t21.5 f22 b22.** Juicy, malty, very well distilled. But perhaps too many fingerprints of an average old cask at play. Like Early Days, would still pass for a Speysider in a blind tasting... *48.4%*

GUTE DESTILLERI Havdhem, Working.

◇ **Gute Single Malt Whisky** db **(95.5) n24.5** the lightest smoke, very much Scottish in style, the acidity matching much that was found in the Highlands half a century ago. This infuses with astoundingly beautiful barley and strands of vanilla-rich tannin...one of the most Scottish experiences I have ever had outside a Highland dram...and so subtle...; **t24** ridiculously beautiful: the smoke, much more integrated than on the nose, drifts with poise and purpose around a palate already taking in the succulent barley and ulmo honey. There appears to be good age to this, or is it because this is such an old-fashioned, almost lost style...? **f23** every bit as delicate as the delivery: no bitterness, just an elegant, gradual fade which picks up on the spices, but cleverly, not to the detriment of any other character...; **b24** this is really quite weird. Back in the late 1970s and early 1980s, I used to comb old village stores looking for 1960s bottlings by Gordon and MacPhail single malts of Speyside and Highland whiskies as they were distilled just after the Second World War and early 1950s. Then, those whiskies had a little more smoke than was being used in the later 1950s. This malt has just hurled me back nearly 40 years. A malt very much in tune with a lost style in Scotland from some 60 years ago: I am stunned...!! *40%*

MACKMYRA Gästrikland. Working.

Mackmyra Moment "Malström" db **(96) n24 t24.5 f23.5 b24** more like "Femalstrom": very gentle and sexy..yet that self-assured power is always there: of its type an unequalled, and dominant malt. World class. *46.4%*

Mackmyra Moment "Mareld" (Sea Fire) bott code MM-013 db **(95) n23.5 t24 f23.5 b24.** Mesmerising. They say not all the wonders have been yet discovered from the sea. Here is one that apparently just has....A malt for people with time on their hands. Anything less than an hour will do you and the whisky a disservice... *52.2%. 1600 bottles.*

Mackmyra Midnattssol Single Malt Art No MC-002 db **(93.5) n23.5 t24 f23 b23.5** Fitting that this should be my 750th new whisky for the 2015 Bible: I had scheduled to hit that landmark by midsummer's day, but find myself tasting this just over two weeks later (thanks for nothing, the world's sulphured casks...!). However, this didn't drop into my lab until a few days ago, so it has worked out rather neatly. A silky number, this, with every character met by a calming influence. *46.1%*

Mackmyra Midvinter Single Malt Art No MC-001 db **(94.5) n23.5** fabulously delicate teasing of nutmeg, the lightest paprika and salted cashews...all with an undercurrent of malt, redcurrant and liquorice...wow! **t24** near perfect weight to the delivery with just-so oils filling the mouth and softening things all round: almost ridiculously soft. The spices on the nose buzz, test and tease. Again the malt comes through with clarity despite the hubbub surrounding it. Pretty salty, though the sugars take the strain, offering a slightly caramelled touch to absorb the growing oak; **f23** a little tangy as the oak gets to work; but a more buttery and traditional touch to this now; **b24** how fitting: probably the most Swedish of all the Mackmyra whiskies yet: reminds me of light-challenged days in that country when, at night, you would retreat to a restaurant and finish the evening with an aquavit, spiced to the owner's liking. The seasoning and smoking here takes us very close to that uniquely Swedish style. The sophistication takes the breath away... *46.1%*

Mackmyra Moment "Morgondagg" (Morning Dew) bott code MM-012 db **(93) n24 t23 f22.5 b23.5.** Another masterful Mackmyra experience. Above all, you get the feeling of a heavyweight pulling its punches... *51.1%. 1600 bottles.*

Mackmyra Moment "Rimfrost" db **(95.5) n24 t24 f23.5 b24.** I thought that they had got the name "Rimfrost" from sitting on a Stockholm park bench in the middle of a Swedish winter. Apparently not. *53.2%. 1,492 bottles.*

Mackmyra Reserve "Queen of Fucking Everything" recipe: Rök, Bourbon barrel, Cask no. 32, dist 24/03/2010, bott 04/09/2014 db **(94) n24** the casual observer may see nothing to excite them here; but wait awhile. Patience and warming in the hand is repaid handsomely as a complex map of interlocking strata comes into focus, the first contours being of a vague smoked bacon variety, perhaps mixed with delicately smoked Swiss cheese. Next, the mildly sweeter vanilla and butterscotch notes – tracing the influence of the oak – begin to surface. Yet the sugars, like the smoke, appear to be kept under a cloak, refusing to display to anyone not patient enough to find them...; **t24** a much more emboldened approach on delivery than the nose ever conveys. The smoke wafts with surprising weight early on and these are reinforced by oaky sugars, juicier and more profound. The smoke takes on several guises, though each relatively deep; the sugars are dark and play their part in the heaviness of the growing mocha personality; **f22.5** a tad too bitter for its own comfort zone. But the late, half-hidden spices remind you a degree of phenols are working in tandem with the sugars until very late on; **b23.5** after over 40 years of tasting whisky – some 25 of them professionally – this is the first time I have ever encountered a brand which includes in its title the word "Everything"... *53.4%*

NORRTELJE BRENNERI Norrtälje, Working.

⬧ **Roslags Whisky** dist 2009, batch 001 db **(85.5) n19 t22.5 f22 b22.** I doubt if ever I have nosed anything so identical to the haystacks I used to manoeuvre when I worked on a farm in my school holidays. And even the flavour has that unique half-forgotten timbre of how the bread to my sandwiches tasted when I had been handling the bales all day. Not sure if this is an astonishing addition to the European whisky lexicon, or its agricultural policy... That all said, definitely has something about it, and is rather gorgeously chewy, generously honeyed and very well spiced. *46%*

SMÖGEN WHISKY Hunnebostrand, Working.

Smögen Primör Svensk Single Malt Whisky db **(84.5) n21.5 t22 f20 b21.** Not the greatest fan of grape and smoky grist. This has its merits, though, as the fruit is succulent and the decent smoke cowers somewhat in its shadow. That said, the inevitable bitter furriness – hidden for the most part - rears its unwanted head. *63.7%*

⬧ **Smögen Primör Svensk Single Malt Whisky** bott 15 Nov 13 db **(85.5) n22.5 t21.5 f20.5 b21.** Well, it is smoky, alright: have no fear about that. But it is also fierce whisky, a little on the thin and hot side – as though the distiller was just letting the heat get a little too much to the stills. Enjoyable, though, and more than promising. *58%. Bottled for The Tasting Room, Norway.*

Smögen Svensk Single Malt Whisky Sherry Project 1:1 db **(89.5) n22.5** suety, sultana-ridden spotted dog pudding; **t22.5** eye-watering salivating from the grape covers over a slight distilling flaw; **f22** bitters very slightly but the spices make their mark; **b22.5** wow! A clean sherry butt! What a difference that makes to a malt. Not as well made as some of their other whiskies, but beautifully matured. *51.8%*

Smögen Svensk Single Malt Whisky Sherry Project 1:2 db **(94) n23.5** now that doesn't happen very often. First you get a clean sherry butt. Then high quality smoke. And the two seem meant for each other: love at first flight...; **t23.5** a rare malt where the smoke and grape are not only comfortable bedfellows but actually work in tandem to both ramp up the juiciness and then add a chewy weight by contrast; **f23** the ulmo honey comes in to compensate for the slight suety feel beginning to form on the finish; the smoke is now much quieter; **b24** what a fantastically clever whisky: you want to learn about balance and counter balance? Spend half an hour with this chap. A malt which fully maximises all its positives and papers over the cracks quite brilliantly. *55.7%*

⬧ **Smögen Svensk Single Malt Whisky Sherry Project 1:3** db **(88.5) n23.5** they do peat rather well: something of the smoky bacon style, with a degree of liquorice and the most vague of fruit notes; **t22** sugars line up early on, most of the muscovado variety. The smoke and grape make a joint entrance; **f21** thins out towards warm vanilla quite quickly; **b22** the grape has certainly taken some of the sting out of the distillate, which remains on the aggressive side. *53.7%*

⬧ **Smögen Svensk Single Malt Whisky Sherry Project 1:4** db **(90) n23** a thick, delightful nose in which the phenols are muscular but slightly outshone by the silkiness of the grape; **t23** a stinging, biting delivery as per the house style. This time, though, soothing fat sultana and an oilier smokiness absorbs some of the shockwaves...; **f21.5** back to a thinner constitution; **b22.5** the grape is overt and intent on issuing a fruity blanket. *57.2%*

Smögen Svensk Single Malt Whisky Single Cask cask no. 20/2011 db **(93.5) n23.5 t24 f22 b24** don't know whether to sit in shocked silence, or simply applaud. Tasted blind, I would have declared this young malt an Islay whisky. Truly astonishing single malt. *60.9%*

Smögen Svensk Single Malt Whisky Single Fresh Sauternes Barrique Cask, cask no. 7/2011, filled 11 Mar 11, bott 28 Mar 15 db **(95) n23.5 t24 f23.5 b24** Truly stunning. Sauternes, unsulphured like this, is unquestionably the most sympathetic of all wine barrels to mix with peat. And if you don't believe me, get your kisser around this gorgeous, naked Swede... *57.3%*

SPIRIT OF HVEN DISTILLERY Sankt Ibb, Working.

◇ **Spirit of Hven Organic Single Malt 7 Stars No. 4 Megrez** db **(94) n23** big malt, but so much more: a hefty cut, yet somehow doesn't send out a single negative feinty signal: some achievement! A serious degree of saltiness to this, too; **t24** about as round as any malt you'll taste this year on delivery. And if the barley comes across in a more concentrated malt form, I'd love to see it...; **f23.5** a vague tang, as the oak begins to gets its snout in the malty trough; lots of spiced vanilla and ulmo honey to compensate, though...; **b23.5** Hven sent! A malt which doesn't pull a single punch. *45%*

◇ **Spirit of Hven Organic Single Malt Tycho's Star** db **(88.5) n22.5** salty malt; **t22.5** anyone who loves fudge with an attitude – organic fudge at that – here's your perfect dram; **f21.5** spiced caramel; a little bit of a late tang **b22** delicious malt, but some serious caramels at play, too. *41.8%*

Spirit of Hven Sankt Claus db **(83.5) n22 t21 f20.5 b20.** Pungent, smoky fruit and nut on both nose and delivery. Thick bodied with a building spice, a rich whisky which seems ill-at-ease for, in the babble to say so much, little coherent is spoken at all. *53.2%. sc.*

Spirit of Hven Seven Stars Single Malt No. 3 Phecda db **(86.5) n21.5 t22 f21.5 b21.5.** A youthful, juicy whisky with a pleasing early weight if not depth. Malty, but there are some strange botanical messages being sent, especially those of a juniper bent. *45%*

Spirit of Hven Urania db **(95) n23.5** stunning gooseberry jam meets salty cashew cake; **t24** oh...one of the European deliveries of the year: silky soft and yielding, the clarity and juiciness of the malt is a joy to behold, the dignity of the ulmo honey and salted vanilla something to marvel at; **f23.5** long, charming, beautifully balanced and weighted, with all strands – including the understated spice – having equal shares in the grand finale; **b24** a soft, complex and truly beautiful whisky. *45%*

SWITZERLAND
ANDREAS VON OW DISTILLERY Busingen. Working.

Munot Malt dist Aug 10, bott 19 Sep 13 db **(87.5) n22 t22 f21.5 b22.** Sturdy and steady. The nose appears to offer more as a bourbon than malt and there is plenty of oak to chew on the palate. But the youthfulness is hinted at by firm oils and the light cocoa finish. *46%. sc.*

BAUERNHOF BRENNEREI LÜTHY Muhen, Working.

Herr Lüthy Pure Swiss No. 9 cask no. 502, dist 2011, bott 2014 db **(82.5) n19 t22 f20.5 b21.** For a three year old, shows potential, especially with some many mocha notes already to the fore. But the nose is a bit of a mess and a more precise maltiness would be useful. *43%. sc.*

◇ **Herr Lüthy Pure Swiss No. 10** cask no. 508, destilliert 2011, abgefüllt 2015 db **(89.5) n22.5** well made whisky: good clarity to the engaging fruitiness; **t23** attractive rye- and dark muscovado-style fruit and juiciness is matched by the inherent crispness. Excellent lift off...; **f21.5** much more attuned to the oak as it dries; **b22.5** a firm, impressively made and matured whisky worth finding. *43%*

BRAUEREI FALKEN Schaffhausen, Working.

◇ **Munot Malt Single Cask Limited Edition 2015** red wine cask no. 1-111 db **(87) n22 t21.5 f22 b21.5.** Has the thin feel of a whisky distilled initially to pretty high strength. The oak has by far the biggest script to learn here and only slowly does a balancing fruitiness emerge, though it remains gentle. Clean but warming. *57.1%. sc.*

◇ **Munot Malt Single Cask** red wine cask no. 1-288 db **(86) n22 t22 f21 b21.** Very similar to their Limited Edition with the trace barley showing upfront, even briefly in a salivating manner, only to vanish under the chalky vanilla and vague fruit. The strength reduction means the oils aren't around to lengthen the finale. Pleasant but seriously lightweight. *46%. sc.*

BRENNEREI HANS ERISMANN Bülach-Eschenmosen, Working.

◇ **Tsyri Zürcher Swiss Single Cask Malt Whisky Aged 5 Years** db (86) n21.5 t21.5 f21 b22. Quite a sharp, clean malt with tangy tannin. Big caramels soften the impact. The molasses do a good balancing job. 40%. sc.

BRENNEREI KOBELT Marbach, Working.

◇ **Glen Rhine Whiskey 2011/4J** db (85) n21.5 t22 f20 b21.5. A welter of sugary, soft, toffee tones with a squeeze of citrus to the malt to lightly freshen the experience. A vague burn on the finish. Pleasant and as untaxing as a Monaco bank account. 40%. sc. 181 bottles.

BRAUEREI LOCHER Appenzell. Working.

Säntis Malt Edition Alpstein No. VIII Aged 7 Years Pinot Noir finish, bott 09 May 14 db (93) n24 t23 f22.5 b23 Profound whisky, almost three dimensional. Every aspect of it comes at you in the most vivid form imaginable. 48%. 2000 bottles..

Säntis Malt Alpstein Edition No. X Aged 7 Years Merlot Finish, bott 16 Mar 15 db (89.5) n22 busy, deep spices with figs and greengages working overtime; t23.5 a volley of sugars on delivery are met by a salvo of spices; the fruit effect is pretty profound; f21.5 an annoying bitterness creeps into proceedings, though the spices carry on sizzling; b22.5 a complex malt that's not without its faults on maturation. But the fun element is far more important. 48%. 2,200 bottles.

Säntis Malt Himmelberg Edition oak beer casks, finished in wine casks db (88) n22 malt from the spirit? Or malt from the beer barrel, I wonder...Either way it is the mega intense fruit which balances out more comfortably; t22.5 powering sugars on delivery from a dessert wine type grape with light spices and a vague hop undertone; f21.5 a few extra hops from the beer barrel appear to blast their way through; b22 hmmm, make mine a pint...! 43%

Snow White Limited Edition No 2. Cherry Finish db (86) n21 t22 f21.5 b21.5. Dwarfed by the central European spices. At times tastes like a German, Austrian or Swiss Christmas cake. Add that to the sweetness and we have something a little more like a liqueur. 45%.

BRENNEREI SCHWAB Oberwil, Working.

◇ **Buechibärger Whisky Single Malt Fassstärke 2006** Chardonnas Fass Nr. 27 db (94.5) n23 if you are a fruit junky, get a fix of this: grapes on steroids with a touch of maple syrup just to thin things down slightly; t24 blisteringly eye-watering! Again, the grapes appear to have muscles as they lump their way around; f23.5 and after the bad cop comes the good one: as gentle a wind down of fruitcake and gristy malt as the delivery was abrasive; b24 a whisky to cherish... 55%. sc.

◇ **Buechibärger Whisky Single Malt Fassstärke 2009** Chardonnas Fass Nr. 34 db (75.5) n19 t19.5 f18 b19. The cask cannot entirely overcome the severe limitations of the distillate. 42%. sc.

BRENNEREI STADELMANN Altbüron, Working.

◇ **Luzerner Hinterländer Whiskey Nr. 6** db (89.5) n22 pretty clean distillate with a little Jaffa Cake sweetness which cuts through the heavier tones; t22 salivating, grassy barley with an intense gristy feel; f23 some quite wonderful lime pops up from somewhere to mingle beautifully with the malt and vanilla; remains juicy to the end; b22.5 unspectacular, but doesn't try to be a superstar. Just offers a lovely malty narrative without a cross word or hint of attitude. 40%

◇ **Luzerner Hinterländer Whiskey Nr. 7** db (91) n21.5 a huge blanket of caramel from the oak blocks out the lighter citrus; t23.5 fantastically soft and salivating on delivery: almost a barley sugar effect, with pure grist when you have sucked through to the middle; f23 the finish has just a sharper edge with the spices a little more vocal; b23 very much along the same lines as their Nr. 6 in many respects. Except this is softer still and, despite the restrictions of the natural caramel, has an extra degree of complexity. 40%

BRENNEREI-ZENTRUM BAUERNHO Zug. Working.

Swissky db (91) n23 t23 f22 b23. While retaining a distinct character, this is the cleanest, most refreshing malt yet to come from mainland Europe. Hats off to Edi Bieri for this work of art. Moving stuff. 42%

DESTILLERIE EGNACH Egnach. Silent.

Thursky db (93) n24 t23.5 f22.5 b23. Such a beautifully even whisky! I am such a sucker for that clean fruity-spice style. Brilliant! 40%

DISTILLERIE ETTER Zug, Working.

⬩ **Johnett Single Cask Swiss Single Malt Whisky Rum Trinidad Finish** cask no. 93, dist Aug 11, bott Jun 15 db **(95) n23** firm, as to be expected. But beyond the crispness of the sugar, a little spiced malt actually breathes the air; **t24** absolutely superb delivery: not sure I've ever enjoyed the start of a Trinidadian rum this much, let alone a German malt. Seriously compact and intense, the malt enjoys a genuinely salivating richness, which the sugars embolden rather than overpower. Quite a fantastic depth to this, one which has genuinely taken me aback...and delighted my taste buds in no small measure; as the malt opens up, it enters concentrated Malteser mode; **f23.5** long, spicy, toasty with a delicate muscovado thread. But it is those astonishing malts which continue to enthral; **b24.5** rum cask finishes seldom work because the hardness and occasional tartness of the sugar sends a force-field around the whisky which prevents it from opening up. Here, the opposite appears true, where the weaknesses found in their 2009 vintage appear to be sealed in, leaving the more complex notes a much freer hand. 51.1%. 280 bottles.

⬩ **Johnett Swiss Single Malt Whisky** 2009 dist May 09, bott Sept 15 db **(84) n20.5 t21.5 f21 b21.** Nutty, soft and welcoming, this focuses on the malt side of things: brimming with barley and even a smidgeon of ulmo honey. 44%. ncf.

DESTILLERIE HAGEN-RÜHLI Hüttwilen. Working.

Hagen's Best Whisky No. 2 lot no. 00403/04-03-08.08 db **(87) n19 t23.5 f22 b22.5.** Much more Swiss, small still style than previous bottling and although the nose isn't quite the most enticing, the delivery and follow through are a delight. Lovely whisky. 42%

DESTILLERIE MACARDO Strohwilen, Working.

⬩ **Macardo Distillers Selection 2016 Single Malt Double Cask** sherry & European oak casks db **(88) n21.5** a degree of bitterness from the distillate rather than cask; **t22.5** soft, juicy and embracing, the fruit gathers with intent; **f22** a few Manuka honey notes add a degree of life to the otherwise lethargic grape; **b22** a clean sherry butt. But it does make for a one-paced malt. 42%. 425 bottles.

⬩ **Macardo Swiss Single Malt Whisky** bourbon cask, dist 2009 db **(93.5) n23** excellent control of the tannin, the nose caressed by an almost soporific degree of ulmo honey...; **t23.5**...and it's that honey which lands gently to show first, making life very easy as the heavier tannin notes begin to gather. The malt, though, also has a voice and it is a placid and rather sexy one...; **f23.5** tannin, as tannin does, sticks limpet-like as the sugars dissolve, leaving the more weighty molasses and liquorice behind. But the soft oils ensure the light spices also remain and the elegance continues; **b23.5** a beautifully made and matured whisky: a credit to the distillery. And plucked from the warehouse not a day too soon. 42%

⬩ **Macardo Swiss Bourbon** dist 2009 db **(87.5) n22.5 t22.5 f21 b21.5.** If the Swiss had a navy and this was one of their ships, then it would be the one set on a straight course, never veering. There appears to be a rye involvement which attracts some delightful heather-honey with it, which is noticeable on both the nose and delivery. But the oak is perhaps just a little too determined to have the final say. 42%

⬩ **Macardo Seven Swiss Single Malt Whisky** dist 2008 db **(88) n21.5** crushed green acorn: sharp and distinctly autumnal; **t22.5** a welcome buttery delivery with a mix of Manuka honey and spice balancing impressively; **f22** swings back towards an oaky thickness, but just enough honey lingers, though now thinned to a maple syrup lightness; **b22** a testy, temperamental whisky with the oak stamping its feet. The honey doesn't let it get all its own way, thankfully. 47%

EDELBRENNEREI BRUNSCHWILER Oberuzwil, Working.

⬩ **B3 Fürsterländer Single Malt Whisky** Los Nr. 2015 db **(88.5) n22** an unusual mix of floral and nutty tones; **t22** a sweet, molassed beginning leads to a competent maltiness and intensifying spice; **f22** light spice, but nothing light about the late malt; **b22.5** does a great job of elevating the malt to prominence and keeping it there. Understatedly lovely. 40%

Brunschwiler B3 Single Malt db **(86.5) n22.5 t22 f20 b21.** Now, on the nose at least, a fruity fellow. But the bitterness on the finish is out of character with the otherwise charming sugars and even odd touch of ulmo honey. 40%

ETTER SOEHNE AG Zug. Working.

Johnett Whisky Swiss Single Malt Single Cask No 43 Pinot Noir barrel, dist May 10, bott Oct 14 db **(87.5) n22 t23.5 f20.5 b21.5.** As you know, I'm a man who likes a whisky to say what it has to say. However, this could do with a little less aggression when there is so much bitterness on the scene. That said, has some beautiful bourbon-style – or maybe rye - moments, really concentrating on the sugary crispness when it is there to be had. Sort the finish out, and you have a stunning whisky. 57.4%. ncf sc. 290 bottles.

FREIHOF BRAUEREI Gossau, Working.

◇ **Gossauer Single Malt Whisky** sherry cask no. 6, dist 23 Feb 13, bott 18 Jun 16 db (**92.5**) **n23.5** about as fruity a nose as you'll find: pure grape must in almost concentrated form; **t23** a calming delivery: soft, non-threatening and offering countless waves of rich Harvey's Bristol Cream style sherry. But the spices and sugars work in tandem, and even a little tannin finds its way into the mid-ground; not sure this could get any creamier...; **f23** possibly one of the most outrageously silky finishes this year; **b23** can't argue with that: a clean cask and a profusion of fruit. 43%. sc. 50 bottles.

HIGHGLEN WHISKY DISTILLERY Santa Maria Val Müstair, Working.

◇ **HighGlen Raetia Prima Single Malt Swiss Whisky** db (**92**) **n22.5** for connoisseurs of oaky aromas: a sawdust and molasses blend; **t23** the sugars arrive first, second and third. A heady mix of treacle, tannin and Manuka honey. A few strands of unspecified citrus lightens things to a minor degree; a brief burst of spice soon peters out; **f23.5** head into liquorice territory, but this is thick, sticky stuff; **b23** worth getting a spoon for this. Amazing! 54.9%. 25 bottles.

◇ **HighGlen Raetia Secunda Single Malt Swiss Whisky** db (**93**) **n23.5** soothing in its voluptuousness: a big barley wine depth with fragments of salt, tannin and caramelised fruit; **t24** enormous. But from the moment it hits the palate, the juices flow. Fruit and nut toffee, though the fruit appears more muscovado sugar based; **f22** dark fudge but with a vaguely bitter trail; **b23.5** magnificent whisky of Alpine beauty. 64.1%. 30 bottles.

◇ **HighGlen Raetia Terza Single Malt Swiss Whisky** db (**88**) **n22** soft, easy going malt aside from the semi-hoppy style bitterness; **t23** sits prettily on the palate: a degree of gristy sweetness balances out with the German caramelised biscuit; **f21** a vaguely nagging bitterness; **b22** another mainly sweet malt, but this time barley-based and less oak oriented. 58.5%. 64 bottles.

HUMBEL DISTILLERY Stetten Aargau, Working.

◇ **OURBEER Aged 36 Months Single Malt Whisky Tokaj Finish** dist 2002 db (**88.5**) **n22** a degree of feints at work, but the thick sugar malt lessens the impact; **t22** a fleeting glimpse of malt vanishes under an avalanche of not unpleasant muscovado sugars; **f22.5** a little spice and vanilla pushes the complexity up significantly; **b22** a friend of mine who lives just a few villages from me was one of the people who successfully got Tokaj wine back on the map and he was a little surprised when I told him that for the whisky lover that has been something of a mixed blessing: most Tokay-finished or matured casks have been wrecked beyond redemption by sulphur. Thankfully, not this offering. Though, like its distant cousin, PX, the improbable intensity of the sugars do restrict the overall development of the malt. 50%

OURBEER Single Malt Whisky dist 10, bott 23 Jul 14 db (**82**) **n20 t21.5 f20 b20.5**. A pretty unique aroma and flavour profile, strongly scented with spiced citrus and with a late herbal tang to the standard toffee. 43%

KOBELT Marbach, St. Gallen. Working.

Glen Rhine Whiskey db (**88**) **n21 t22.5 f21.5 b22.** Try and pick your way through this one...can't think of another whisky in the world with that kind of fingerprint. 40%. Corn & barley.

LANGATUN DISTILLERY Langenthal, Kanton Bern. Working.

Langatun 10 Years Langatun Distillery Single Malt Whisky Châteuaneuf-du-Pape cask, cask no. 5, dist Mar 08, bott Mar 15 db (**96.5**) **n23.5 t24 f24.5 b24.5** Just a few miles from where this distillery, with its ancient walls and in the shadow of a medaeval schloss, now sits is the old town of Langenthal. But it is ancient village of Aarwangen that provides the perfect setting now, with the distillery close to the river from which the community takes its name and where, if you are lucky like me, you might even spot a Hoopoe on its summer visit. And with outstanding cheese made there as well, it is some kind of whisky heaven which the gods have sprinkled a little magic on. 49.12%. nc. 499 bottles.

Langatun Jacob's Dream Single Malt Whisky pinot noir cask, cask no. 97, dist 23 Mar 09, bott 15 Jun 15 db (**92.5**) **n23.5** despite the grape, it is the youthful malt which can be detected first, the wine mounting soft sultana incursions until it finally takes command...; **t24** both malt and grape are neck and neck out of the trap, though the intensity of the fruitcake concentrates the mind ahead of the barley; major Christmas cake/fruitcake influence but the mid-ground celebrates the gentle influence beginning with spice and moving onto a more vanilla-buttery aspect; **f22** a little bitterness just becomes slightly entangled; **b23** quite astonishing how this malt has the presence to comfortably fit into the shoes of such big wine casks.

Langatun Old Bear Châteauneuf-du-Pape cask, dist Apr 08, bott Jan 12, bott code L1201 db **(96) n24 t24 f23.5 b24.5.** Whisky for the gods... 64%

◇ **Langatun Old Bear Single Malt** bott code L 0116 db **(88) n21.5** a vague feinty note is soon over-run by some lovely vanillas and a crispy smoked bacon thread; **t22.5** that's more like it: lashings of malt, accompanied by light gingerbread; **f22** one could become addicted to chocolate just from this finish alone; **b22** Langatun whisky is such a force of nature, it doesn't seem natural to taste it much below natural strength, let alone at 40%. 40%

◇ **Langatun Old Deer Single Malt** bott code L 0116 db **(87.5) n21.5 t22.5 f21.5 b22.** This is one of the great distilleries of Europe, make no mistake. But here the cut strays just onto the wide side of things, though it is still brimming with hay and marmalade notes. The sugars are of the heather-honey variety. But those feints, a rarity - a collectors' item - for Langatun, just stifle the overall complexity. 40%

◇ **Langatun Old Deer Cask Strength Single Malt** bott code L 0116 db **(95.5) n24** faultless fruit: a muscovado sweetness mixing in light fruit and spice with the dense malt. Just so purringly harmonious; **t24** that density doesn't let up. Except it is a wall of malt which confronts the taste buds, not unlike an old fashioned English barley wine. Even so, still ridiculously salivating with the fruit again arriving as though part of the muscovado plot. Chewy, and gets chewier still as the tannins, deep and cocoa-rich, begin to arrive; **f23.5** long, with a lovely liquorice depth. But that malt just keeps on stewing...; **b24** now that is what I was expecting...not the character of the 40% bottling. This is, quite simply, brilliant. 62.1%

Langatun Old Mustang Bourbon 4 Year Old recipe: 60% corn, 40% barley malt db **(95.5) n23.5** a beautifully busy nose where the malt appears to be lifted onto a plinth by the corn oil. Clean and makes the most of the genteel sugars and intensifying tannins; **t24** just brilliant....!! The delivery is couched in corn oil, which ensures the softest possible landing on the palate, but soon makes way for a brilliant array of manuka and ulmo honey as the richer, toastier notes and the more subtle barley notes merge effortlessly; **f24** long, with growing spices. Firms up as the darker sugars crystallise, which throws it into a fascinating juxtaposition with the swamp-soft corn; **b24** this is Switzerland's answer to bourbon whiskey. Soon there will be a new Canton of Kentucky...yessirree!! Or at least there deserves to be in honour of this great whisky. 62.1%

◇ **Langatun Single Malt Whisky 6 Year Old** Pinot Noir cask, cask no. 98, dist 18 Sept 09, bott 11 Nov 15 db **(96.5) n23.5** the Pinot barely gets a meaningful look in as the malt and tannins dance a sugary jig. Muscovado sugars account mainly for the fruit...; **t25** dazzling! As though there is a rye component to this, as it is firm, crisp, ultra-juicy, fruity and just simply bloody fantastic! Just one of the worldwide deliveries of the year, for sure...; **f23.5** an injection of vanilla and spice ensures the fade doesn't lose its ability to astound; **b24.5** when last at this distillery in Switzerland, I spotted, quite amazingly, the exceptionally rare and bizarre hoopoe, having flown in probably from the Arab lands. While tasting this, I have been serenaded by not one but two song thrush: no less amazing because in my third summer here until now, 49 different species had visited, but none a song thrush. Its sister mistle thrush, yes. As well as cousins redwing and blackbird. But never a song thrush. Until today, where now there are two competing with each other for the song most beautifully delivered. And here we have a whisky in stunning harmony just like those two magnificent birds...and a whole lot rarer. 62.3%. nc sc. 100 bottles.

Langatun Relocation Whisky 7 Year Old bourbon cask, dist 11 Jan 08, bott 21 Jan 15 db **(91.5) n22.5** a gorgeous and intense mix of concentrated barley, oak-drawn caramel and hazelnuts; **t23** early sugars plus plenty of oil, but it is the richness of the malt which dominates; **f23.5** long, and now those sugars – especially the weightier muscovado ones – begin to move towards ulmo honey and then, inevitably gristy malt; **b23** about as intense as an elegant malt can be. A really beautiful barley experience. 49.12%

Langatun Winter Wedding Single Malt Whisky Châteauneuf-du-Pape, Chardonnay & sherry casks, batch no. L 0614, dist Oct 09, bott Jan 15 db **(94.5) n23.5** such weight: amazed my glass isn't cracking under the strain! There is an ashy quality to the grape must; both intricately sweet and dry...great balance and depth; **t24** not sure a delivery can be much thicker or weightier than this, yet still have enough about it for you to be able to pick out its individual characteristics. Immense depth, but the fruit seems to sit on top aloof: juicy, grapey and untouched. Beneath, the smokier notes have sunk to the bottom, but there is a layer of barley to ensure a juicy liveliness; **f23** a trail of spices that carry on as long as the taste buds are able to detect anything from this malt...and that, despite some late furriness, is for a very long time! **b24** oh, and by the way: not only is this a truly great malt, but this has to be the best and most ingenious clasp I have ever seen to open a bottle of whisky! *46%. nc.*

RUGENBRAU AG Matten bei Interlaken. Working.

Interlaken Swiss Highland Single Malt "Classic" oloroso sherry butt db **(95) n23.5 t24 f23 b24.** Hugely impressive. I have long said that the finest whiskies made on mainland Europe are to be found in Switzerland. Game, set and match... *46%*

Top Of Europe Swiss Highland Single Malt "Ice Label" bott 2011 **(93.5) n23 t24 f23 b23.5.** I get a lot of stick for heaping praise on European whisky. OK, there is the odd technical flaw in the distillation – though in some ways it works to its advantage. But how many casks do you find like this in Scotland? For sheer quality of its output, this distillery must rate as high as an Alpine peak... *58.9%. sc.*

SANTISBLICK DESTILLERIE Niederbüren, Working.

Single Malt Madeira cask, bott code 91 von 300 db **(34) n1 t16 f8 b9.** This, without question, offers the scariest nose I have ever encountered on a commercially bottled whisky. Appallingly aggressive, I'll make this the last whisky I'll taste today (at least) - for I know I will regret it and my senses will need time to recover. Nosed at a safe distance, if such a thing exists, it appears to have been matured in a petrol barrel, though closer, braver inspection suggests it is peat of some sort at work. The palate gives some lie to this terrifying aroma, as my teeth still seem to be intact. Some burnt fudge running alongside the "smoke" makes the delivery not only bearable but for a few moments quite acceptable. But the finish, by contrast, is dry and after a short while you feel your tongue aflame...and it takes a while to put out the blaze. The Swiss are known as a peaceful people with a history of neutrality. Hardly surprising: with stocks of this stuff at hand, it is unlikely anyone will ever dare invade. *48%*

◈ **Santisblick Single Malt im Vieille Prune Fass ausgereift** bott code 266 von 500 db **(90) n22** candy store nutty nougat and chocolate; **t23.5** astonishingly salivating as, presumably, barley is ramped up to the highest degree. The juiciness is compounded by the warming spice. The mid-ground appears to be spiced chocolate massively laden with molasses and muscovado...; **f22.5** not an easy act to follow and retreats to a more oily, nougaty stance, though the grain does also have a say; **b22** wow! Generates flavour like a dynamo churns out electricity... As a fatalist, few things scare me. Heights. Electricity. Angela Merkel. Oh, and as an ornithologist, Australian and Indian snakes. That's about it. Except, probably the name "Santisblick." Some years ago I tried two of their whiskies and I still am receiving counselling to this day. They were memorably awful, but I remember them so vividly as they still reappear in my worst whisky nightmares. So you will not be surprised that I approached these two whiskies of theirs as a bomb disposal officer might when he's aware that the device before him has already stopped ticking. It crossed my mind to contact the nearest high contamination unit to see if I could handle these in a sealed container via attached rubber gloves. But then realised that might present a problem when it came to nosing. So, as I so often do for the readers of this annual publication, I put my self-interest and safety aside and poured the sample into my glass, unprotected, in my tasting room. And do you know what? In the intervening years, the people of Santisblick have learned how to make a decent whisky....Well, almost.... *48%*

◈ **Santisblick 3 Jahre alt, im Sherryass ausgereift** bott code 447 von 600 db **(60) n22.5 t22.5 f5 b10** The delivery has a fabulous density to the dark muscovado fruitiness and structured malt; some spices begin to take off. But the finish shows its fabled fiery harshness of before. My taste buds were burning from this one some 24 hours after tasting. *43%*

Whisky 3 Years Old bourbon cask, bott code L-130001 db **(83.5) n21 t22 f21.5 b19.** An odd but attractive whisky where the maltiness has been ramped up to nuclear strength. Best of all, though, is the body and overall mouth feel which is highly satisfying. A peculiar experience, though. *43%*

Whisky 3 Years Old sherry cask, bott code 83 von 300 db **(59) n13 t18 f12 b15.** Probably the weirdest sherry matured whisky I have ever encountered. Words fail me for the nose and finish, the former being unreal and the latter being only too real in its grimness. *43%*

SPEZIALITÄTENBRENNEREI ZÜRCHER Port, Working.

◈ **Single Lakeland Malt Whisky Anniversary Edition 8 Years Old** Oloroso sherry casks, dist July 06, bott Aug 14 db **(86) n21 t23 f21.5 b21.5.** Annoyingly, a vague bitterness off-balances the malt after a pretty impressive start. Cream sherry doesn't come any creamier than this, nor more interesting with the early spices. But the malt is entirely lost under the sea of grape. Decent mid-range sugars, though, before that bitter cask note kicks in. *45%*

◈ **Single Lakeland Malt Whisky 6 Years Old** Oloroso sherry casks, dist Oct 09, bott Nov 15 db **(91) n22** mainly healthy oloroso at work: real depth to the aroma beyond the fruitcake feel; **t24** possibly one of the best oloroso casks found on mainland Europe: has the all-round game plan to include the best of the oak as well as varying levels of sultana; **f22** just a slight sulphur prickle, but no major damage done...; **b23** oh, a virtually sulphur-free sherry butt or two can make such a wonderful difference... *42%*

⬦ **Weidhöfler Single Malt Whisky** sherry casks, dist 05 May 11 db **(87.5) n22 t22.5 f21 b22.** Some sharp, lively fruit – not unlike pastels – on the nose, the delivery is much fatter and flatter. There are a few wonderful moments where the grape offers up its head in a defiant, bright-eyed pose, before dull vanillas flatten it. *41%. 114 bottles.*

WEINGUT CLERC BAMERT Ruteli im Buobental. Working.

Weingut Clerc Bamert Whisky Finest Pure Malt 8 Years Old db **(87) n22 t22 f21 b22.** Splutters and misfires on the finish, though not as badly as the single engine plane that has just gone, worryingly, overhead. Elsewhere some lovely malt, black cherry and caramel makes for a soft landing. *40%. sc nc.*

WHISKY CASTLE Elfingen, Working.

⬦ **Castle Hill Single Malt Doublewood** cask no. 492, dist Feb 08 db **(86) n21 t22 f21.5 b21.5.** Double wood, but only half the normal fun. Soft and seemingly alluring on delivery. Yet curiously flat in part and full of caramel. And a slight bitter tone, too. *43%. sc.*

⬦ **Whisky Castle Single Malt Edition Käser** cask no. 468 db **(93) n22** huge seems inadequate, but it will have to do. Despite the enormity, the weight is beautifully even and offers up equal amounts of grain and oak...and that means a lot! **t24** enters into overdrive as the red liquorice and muscovado sugars surge like an avalanche onto the palate. Naturally, spices are immense, yet fit into the Brobdingnagian scheme of things; the intense sugars extracted from the oak almost defy description; **f23.5** toasty, but forever moving towards a mix of mocha and praline; **b23.5** immense, magisterial and a castle for which there is no breaching... *68%. sc.*

⬦ **Whisky Castle Single Malt Family Reserve** cask no. 17 db **(91) n22** a teasing smokiness unsettles and interrupts the big oaky speech; **t23** oh..yes! A delivery of satin with some high flying crisped maple syrup – and the inevitable oaky spice the nose promised; **f22.5** much drier, with that vague smokiness still nagging at the death. Chewy, long and very satisfying; **b23.5** it is a great many years now since I met the lovely family who are behind the Family Reserve at Whisky Castle. I was highly impressed with their whisky then; I am impressed now: this is a beautifully and very carefully distilled without a single trace of feints. So I selected this as the malt of choice prior to Switzerland playing France in the European Championships. I think it will score a lot higher than the boys in red. *43%. sc.*

⬦ **Whisky Castle Single Malt Oloroso** cask no. 494, dist Mar 08 db **(84.5) n21 t23 f19.5 b21.** When they say Oloroso, they really aren't joking. The fruit pours from this like water from a spring. Rich, intense and about as sherry trifle as you'll ever get, too. But, alas, a light but discordant note troubles the serenity of what would have been something a little bit special. Bugger...! *48%. sc.*

⬦ **Whisky Castle Single Malt Smoke Barley** cask no. 489, dist Jan 07 db **(85.5) n21.5 t21 f22 b21.** Is it the youth? The vague feints, maybe? Either way, something doesn't quite ring true. And for all the smoky bacon on steroids, and the delicious sugars which fall into place and make sense only in the final chapter, you still can't help thinking that it is hard to interpret the overall picture. *43%. sc.*

Unspecified Swiss

⬦ **ORMA Swiss Whisky Single Malt** cask no. 12-1 **(71) n16 t19 f20 b18.** Presumably a smoky malt of some sort; at least I hope it is. Sadly, neither attractive nor friendly with the malt failing to find a meaningful narrative or balance until right at the very end. *44%. sc.*

⬦ **ORMA Swiss Whisky Single Malt Zernez Edition** cask no. 12-2 **(80) n21 t22 f18 b19.** Well, this is a very game whisky not frightened to stamp its unique personality over the palate. Some softening fruit, but not enough to keep the more thuggish elements of the distillate at bay. *46%. sc. 188 bottles.*

Vatted Malts

The Swiss Malt (95.5) n23 t24 f24 b24.5. Sumptuous and the stuff for late night naval gazing. When Orson Welles, as Harry Lime in the immortal Third Man, made a disparaging summary of all Switzerland's achievements over the centuries as the invention of the cuckoo clock, it was obvious he had never tasted this. A whisky the Swiss distilling nation can be rightly proud of. *50.2%. From 20 Swiss Distillers. 175 miniatures.*

WALES

PENDERYN Penderyn. Working.

Penderyn bott code 092909 **(93.5) n23 t23.5 f24 b23.** Just couldn't have been more Welsh than any potential offSpring of Catherine Zeta Jones by Tom Jones, conceived while "How Green Is My Valley" was on the DVD player and a Shirley Bassey CD playing in the background. And that after downing three pints of Brains bitter after seeing Swansea City play Cardiff City at the Liberty Stadium, before going home to a plate of cawl while watching Wales beating England at rugby live on BBC Cymru. Yes, it is that unmistakably Penderyn; it is that perfectly, wonderfully and uniquely Welsh. *46%. ncf.*

Penderyn 41 db **(91.5) n22 t23 f24 b22.5.** Don't think for one moment it's the reduction of strength that makes this work so well. Rather, it is the outstanding integration of the outlandishly good Madeira casks with the vanilla. At usual strength this would have scored perhaps another couple of points. Oh, the lucky French for whom this was designed... *41%*

Penderyn Bourbon Matured Single Cask cask no. 227B, dist 06 db **(89.5) n22 t23 f22 b22.5.** Definitely a much bigger Penderyn than you might be used to, and that is only partly because of the cask. *62%. ncf sc.*

Penderyn Bourbon Matured Single Cask dist 2000 **(96) n24 t24.5 f23.5 b24.** Penderyn as rarely seen, even by me. This is as old a Welsh whisky that has been bottled in living memory. And it is one that will live in the memory of this current generation. For I have encountered very few whiskies which revels in a controlled sweetness on so many levels. This is so good, it is frightening. *61.2%*

◇ **Penderyn Celt** bott code. 53003 db **(94.5) n23** anyone who has stood on a windy beach while peat reek has been blown towards you from an old, nearby cottage will immediately have a sense of deja-vu...; **t24** so soft, so clean, so subtle, so gristy...just so damn good...! **f23.5** bitters out very slightly as the oak begins to get a grip, a touch of spice makes a vaguely stinging entry. But the barley has such a big say here...; **b24** another Penderyn which works so beautifully. Congratulations on another cracking brand! This will be my whisky of choice when watching Wales' next European Championship game – against England. Though I will also make a vatting of this and some St George's...believe me, even if the game disappoints, the whisky won't...! *41%. ncf.*

◇ **Penderyn Celt** bott code. 60402 db **(91) n22** dry vanilla with a peaty afterthought; **t23** good oils intensify as the barley and vanilla forge a rich partnership. The smoke arrives alongside the spices; **f23** long, sweet as a little smoked ulmo honey coats the palate. The spices continue to tease; **b23** delicious, but a slightly subdued version of the previous bottling. *41%. ncf.*

Penderyn Celt Peated bott Jul 15 db **(82.5) n21 t22 f19.5 b20.** Very curious one, this. Much oiler than the norm. But what makes it so unusual for a Penderyn is that, for whatever reason, it is a malt which fails to find its equilibrium. Whether it is the light smoke at fault, it is difficult to say. *41%. ncf.*

Penderyn Icons of Wales Dylan Thomas Sherrywood db **(91) n21.5** chalky, perhaps a tad too astringent and dry; **t24** the delivery is a complete contrast to the aroma: immediately sweet and superbly weighted. Lush without being oily, sultanas abound to magnificent effect; **f23** now reverts to something between the nose and delivery: delicate and dry, with vanillas handily placed but the fruit always pushing, probing and allowing in a little ulmo honey at the end; **b23** from an unpromising start comes something of a tone poem. *41%. ncf. WB15/402*

◇ **Penderyn Legend** bott code. 52951 db **(92.5) n23** an upped fruitcake depth to this, with a chalky-vanilla sub-plot; **t23** lush, juicy and satisfying delivery; a lovely light muscovado arrival early on, but this tails off to leave a gentle trifle mid-ground; **f23** a beautiful spiced chocolate mint fade; **b23.5** tasting this after Wales' historic and merited 2-1 victory over Slovakia, perhaps this should be called the Gareth Bale Edition. As it happens, I was dining with the Southampton chairman the day Bale made his professional first team debut, which happened to be against my side Millwall. "Look out for our young, full back, Jim. We have very high hopes for him," he confided. Who would have thought....? *41%. ncf.*

◇ **Penderyn Legend** bott code. 53097 db **(91) n22** a tad thin and just a little too dry for greatness; **t23** again, an austere delivery, in keeping with the nose, but suddenly the oils find each other and the malt fattens out to fine effect. The fruit also manages to find its voice; **f23** surprisingly long after the half-hearted start. Lovely fruit and nut notes flit in and out with the persistent vanilla and the spices come into their own; **b23** so, equally, we must call this the Robson-Kanu bottling. A lovely build up in parts, though a bit ragged and off the shin of the ball. But still finishes to great effect.... *41%. ncf.*

Penderyn Legend bott Feb 15 db **(89.5) n22** enough oil on the nose to offer a sheen to the fruit amid austere oak; **t23** delicate and delightful. A vague layering of ulmo honey creates the sweet backdrop to the house pithy style, though some lemon peel helps, too; **f22** vague fruitcake but bolstered with late but telling spice; **b22.5** you wonder at times if it has the strength to get up the hill. But it surprises. *41%. ncf.*

Penderyn Legend bott Mar 15 db **(89) n21** dry and fragile; **t21.5** simple sugars with the odd juicy moment to ensure levity; **f23.5** ahhhh...! Now this is worth opening a bottle for. Seriously complex and understated, it is like a very dry chocolate fruit and nut...with the sugars at a minimum; **b23** for the occasional fruit notes which introduce themselves to your taste buds, though only muttering their names, frugality of flavour is the name of the game. But there is enough subtlety and late cocoa to make this enjoyable. Even sophisticated. *41%. ncf.*

Penderyn Legend bott Apr 15 db **(85) n21 t22.5 f20.5 b21.** A little too dull and simplistic by Penderyn's high standards. Pleasant, certainly. But the caramels at the end make for uninspiring whisky. *41%. ncf..*

Penderyn Madeira bott Jan 15 db **(95) n23** exceptionally fruity and intense so far as Penderyn noses go: the oak offers the usual dry vanilla and the pith is there, too. But the deluge of subtle fruit notes is stirring; **t24.5** one of the best Penderyn madeira bottling deliveries of all time: the mix of ulmo honey, over-ripe greengages and complex vanilla and butterscotch is ridiculously beautiful; **f23.5** long, thanks to a little extra oil, with the honey and sugar lasting the pace for much longer than usual; **b24** standard Penderyn...but on steroids. All its normal attributes are present and correct. But simply magnified several times... *46%. ncf.*

Penderyn Madeira bott Feb 15 db **(90.5) n22** extra dry thanks to the crushed pips; **t23.5** juicy delivery with pear and acacia honey, then wanders off into a sawdusty desert; **f22** good sugars linger to balance the oak; **b23** a much more recognisably standard, complex but dry version without all the twiddly fruity bits of the previous bottling. *46%. ncf.*

Penderyn Madeira bott Mar 15 db **(93.5) n23** grapefruit amid the pith and sawdust; **t23.5** the sugars show early, then a blend of ulmo and heather honeys allow the malt ample scope to develop; juicy and grassy in the middle-ground; **f23** long, with the vanilla – usually dominant at this time – upstaged by the lingering honey and delicate spices; **b23.5** a luxurious model, a bit closer in style to the Jan 15 bottling than the Feb 15. Effortlessly sexy stuff... *46%.*

◈ **Penderyn Madeira Finish** bott code. 53162 db **(89.5) n22.5** emphasis on the fruit: a distinct boiled candy aspect; **t22** surprisingly thin delivery, though it builds as the sugars gather. A light muscovado theme becomes a fraction plumier; **f22.5** an unusual vanilla and malt fade: unusual, as the spices are pretty subdued; **b22.5** much softer and less stark version of Penderyn with the sugars guaranteeing a juicier journey. *46%. ncf.*

◈ **Penderyn Madeira Finish** bott code. 53436 db **(94) n22.5** pithy fruit and a chalky vanilla-gristiness...; **t23.5** beautiful oils pull together the weightier fruit moments and the bigger concentrated vanillas. Just love the way the spices break free and pepper the taste buds with studied determination; **f24** a spot-on finish. A little toffee enters the fray, but that appears to balance beautifully with the fruit, while mocha and muscovado sugar join the spices to bring up the rear; **b24** despite the sugars, more in tune with the drier house style than the previous two bottlings; *46%. ncf.*

◈ **Penderyn Madeira Finish** bott code 61403 **(94) n23.5** a degree of black cherry amid the drier fluffy vanilla; **t24** possibly one of the softest deliveries of all time from Wales: certainly one of the most lusciously fruity from their Madeira finish brand. Both salivating yet weighty, with an extra lick of oil to emphasise the thicker fruit notes; **f23** the spices have delayed their entry until late on; **b23.5** a distinctively lush bottling. *46%*

◈ **Penderyn Madeira Finish** bott 6 Aug 15 db **(95) n23.5** charmingly chalky. The fruit is no more than a gentle breeze; just enough tannin to suggest a Kentucky link; **t23.5** subtle sugars have a molassed hue; big vanilla but with a vaguely fruity gait; the malt offers a juicy edge; **f23.5** a slow burn of spice fits sublimely with the light cocoa development. An earthier fruitiness grumbles on the lower notes; **b24.5** such a lovely style of whisky which begins almost as a whisper but builds, almost imperceptibly, into something of substance, never losing its balance along the way. *46%. ncf.*

◈ **Penderyn Madeira Finish** bott 7 Sept 15 db **(89) n22.5** an impressive mallow and fruit interplay; **t22** a more toffeed delivery, chewy and soft with the fruit and early spice; slightly oilier than the norm; **f22** dries and spices up significantly; the cocoa makes a later than usual entrance; **b22.5** a starker Penderyn than most and just about the perfect pre-dinner dram, especially if Welsh lamb is on the menu... *46%. ncf.*

◈ **Penderyn Myth** bott code. 52853 db **(95) n23.5** as though a slightly salty, coastal wind is blowing towards you, though from a fruitcake bakery; a few other subtle notes creep in, apart from the diced nuts. And they include gentle bourbon-style liquorice...; **t23.5** so, so soft... Vanilla, a hint of lemon drizzle cake; a touch of the Eccles cake; **f24** oh, the spices, the spices... A continuing pattering of tiny pin-pricks on the palate ensure the fruit doesn't make the proceedings all too processional; lovely butterscotch and vanilla on the fade also. But the weight and pace, especially as the mocha evolves, is sublime...; **b24** one of the most subtle and most beautifully balanced Penderyns of all time. Had it been at 46% with a longer finale, would have been one of the distillery's highest scorers ever. *41%. ncf.*

◈ **Penderyn Myth** bott code. 53306 db **(93.5) n23** much more accent on a bourbon style, with the fruit side-lined to a plummy sub-plot; **t23** busy, vaguely puckering delivery. Begins with a fruity edge but soon dries off and concentrates on the house-style spice; **f23.5** more relaxed, with some oils at work, maximising the light muscovado sugars; **b24** yeth, much more a hit than a myth... 41%. ncf.

Penderyn Myth bott Oct 14 db **(86.5) n21.5 t22.5 f21 b21.5**. Light, at times pretty dry and flits around the palate: perhaps should have been called Penderyn Moth. 41%. ncf.

Penderyn Peated bott 1 Dec 14 db **(91) n22** outwardly dry, but a subplot of delicate sugars and phenols intrigue; **t23.5** one of the softest and most silky deliveries from Penderyn: a bed of oil allow the honey and lazy smoke to fall onto the palate without any shockwaves; **f22.5** long, drying, even with a tangy sharpness. The phenols, half-hearted at their liveliest, allow the spices to take over for the remainder of the flight; **b23** a gentle Penderyn with little more than a sprinkling of smoke... 46%. ncf.

◇ **Penderyn Peated** bott code. 53032 db **(94) n23** unmistakably Penderyn: that unique little chalky catch to the nose, around which the light peat has a comparatively lofty presence; **t24** gentle as she goes: the delivery is the usual whispers and suggestions; the oak is present but only barely, the sugars offer an equally deft touch – never for a moment over doing it. The mid-ground has a touch of praline, though gently smoked, too...; **f23** not sure how a malt so light has such a long finish – defies the laws of whisky...; **b24** as Wales are, within the next hour, kicking off their first competitive Finals since 1958, I thought I would show solidarity with them by today tasting Penderyn. Even though I have a fair chunk of Welsh blood – my father's mother's family originate from Pembroke Dock – that has not coloured my view that this is another absolutely beautiful, subtle whisky with the most sexy, teasing smokiness on the market. Just hope Wales perform half as well as this accomplished malt. Not that I have anything against the lovely people of Slovakia, especially those in the gorgeous city of Bratislava: the Taff versus the Danube. No contest... 46%. ncf.

◇ **Penderyn Peated** bott code. 60292 db **(89.5) n22.5** light, big vanilla frame on which the smoke is slightly dwarfed; **t22.5** noticeably thinner than bottling 53032, with the sugars playing a deeper, more intense role as the smoke again holds back from full commitment; **f22** medium length, with the spices building attractively; **b22.5** very much a subdued version of their other Peated bottling this year. Attractive and worth spending a night with; but nothing like so beautiful. 46%. ncf.

Penderyn Portwood Single Cask cask no PT72 db **(96.5) n24.5 t24.5 f23 b24.5** the Penderyn Port Wood single cask bottling has now been carved in stone as one of the world's great whiskies; it's unveiling each year one of the stratospheric moments in the world whisky calendar. And yet again, it lives up to its own ridiculously high reputation. If I find a better single cask than this for the 2016 Bible it will be of the proportions of a Cecil B DeMille epic... 59%. ncf sc.

◇ **Penderyn Portwood** bott code 615121 db **(91) n22.5** many of the Madeira wood characteristics, except the grape is more heavily slapped on here; **t23** some early profound sugars soften into a light muscovado style; **f22.5** unusual for any whisky to be quite so salivating towards the finish. The late spice and cocoa does no harm at all; **b23** a striking Penderyn where the flavours sometimes come across more vividly than usual. 46%. ncf sc.

◇ **Penderyn Portwood Single Cask PT165** db **(95) n23.5** rich fruitcake, especially nutty with a playful spice nip; **t24.5** silky delivery with the spices arriving thick and fast in a thicker still oiliness. A kind of mocha Swiss roll and walnut cake blend, enhanced by dark muscovado fruitiness, with the grape skin getting a bit more intense as we move towards the finish; **f23** much less volumous as the vanilla moves in to gain control and ensure a slightly drier finish than initially seemed possible; **b24** this is the last of the bottlings sent to me from Penderyn. And I have to say that since the distillery first opened, this has been the best year so far with the most consistent and attractive whiskies I have yet encountered from them. Always one of the highlights of the year, Penderyn, and so pleased they have enhanced their reputation further. 46%. ncf sc.

Penderyn Rich Oak db **(93) n23** dry, toasty...curiously showing a flavour signal normally broadcast by a German-type still; sandalwood and oak shavings seem to generate the gentle spice; **t24** decidedly nutty yet enriched by a gorgeous array of sugars, ranging from watered-down maple syrup through to molasses via Demerara; **f23** dries quickly again and we are back to the vanilla and butterscotch compounds, as well as Brazil nut oil; **b23** a curious, even unique, line-up of flavours makes for a massively enjoyable and occasionally head-scratching experience. 50%. ncf. 1,113 bottles.

◇ **Penderyn Single Cask PT9 LMDW Vintage 2003** db **(96) n24** the marriage of the tannins takes some unravelling: blood orange, malty maple syrup, treacle...these can be stripped away without too many difficulties. The ulmo honey and dark muscovado sugars are harder to prise apart...; **t23.5** after the profound nose comes the extraordinary, eye-wateringly intense delivery. Exactly the same as the nose, except much more red liquorice; **f24** dries as the vanillas take up residence and even a little hickory formulates with the mocha; **b24.5** in the bottle, the whisky looks as though this could be attached to a transfusion unit. There again, this really is the blood of life... Amazing! 58%. ncf sc.

⬩⬩⬩ **Penderyn That Try** bott code. 60403 db **(91.5) n22.5** the vaguest smoke ensures a degree of ballast for an otherwise ethereal aroma; **t23.5** surprising sugars – actually, closer to ulmo honey – get caught up in a thickish delivery; spices rant early but are mollified by that honey and increasing soft vanilla; **f22.5** long, vaguely austere with the most deft of smoky touches to accompany the vanilla; **b23.5** delicate and, for the strength, this is surprisingly oily and fat. And now after THAT try, surely they are going to have to bring out THAT goal...will it be Bale's – the first in a Welsh finals game since Pele scored for Brazil in 1958? Or is it still to come after I tasted this...and maybe against England... *41%. ncf. 50 bottles.*

British Blends

The One British Blended Whisky (84.5) n22 t21.5 f20 b21. Although it doesn't say so on the bottle, I understand this is made from a blend of malts from England, Ireland, Scotland and Wales. It says "blend" which implies the use of grain, though this is probably not so...another example of the confusion caused by the brainless and arrogant change of terminology from "vatted" to denote a blend of malts insisted upon by the Scotch Whisky Association. Not yet checked, but would have thought that as not scotch, they still would have been entitled to call it a vatting. The mind boggles over what they will do with this whisky if Scotland votes for independence in a few weeks' times. Doubtless the SWA will make some kind of noise... Anyway, back to the action. The label does claim this is a whisky of "intriguing complexity". If true, the term will have to be redefined. The nose, sure enough, does offer just enough smoky and citrus twists and turns to wonder what will happen next. But the delivery on the palate is a disappointment, with any complexity desired submerged under a welter of dull caramels. Just too flat and soft for its own good: back to the drawing board....and possibly without scotch... *40% WB15/406*

European Blends

⬩⬩⬩ **Black Mountain Excellence Whisky Selection No. 1 (85) n21.5 t22 f20.5 b21.** Thin, delicate, clean, toffeed and with an early sweet peak. *42%*

⬩⬩⬩ **Black Mountain Premium Whisky Sélection No. 2 (85.5) n21 t21.5 f22 b21.** Just like the No 1 bottling, this is grain dominant and simplistic. Though less sweet and more vigorously spiced throughout. Not at all unpleasant. *40%*

MISCELLANEOUS

⬩⬩⬩ **Michel Couvreur Blossoming 14 Year Old Single Malt Whisky** sherry cask **(75) n18 t20 f18 b19.** The thing that blossoms most is a bitterness from the sherry cask. *45%*

⬩⬩⬩ **Michel Couvreur Candid 8 Year Old Single Malt Whisky** sherry cask **(90) n22** a distinctly Islay kick to this: as well as smoky bacon; **t22.5** a bit like washing down your smoky bacon with a mouthful of sherry; **f23** a degree of ulmo honey to finish – most unexpected; **b22.5** the smoke wins the arm-wrestle with the grape. *49%*

⬩⬩⬩ **Michel Couvreur Couvruer's Clearach 3 Year Old Single Malt Cereal Spirit** sherry cask **(89) n22** almost closer to a bottle of sherry than whisky: exceptionally clean rich grape; **t23** again, the sweet grape makes an immediate and profound impact; spices rumble along; **f22** dries, but not seemingly due to any oak; good cocoa fade; **b22** a seriously odd whisky, but hard not to enjoy. *43%*

⬩⬩⬩ **Michel Couvreur Intravagan'za 3 Year Old Single Malt Cereal Spirit** sherry cask **(84.5) n21 t22 f20.5 b21.** Another oddball experience. Again, the sherry dominates virtually all aspects and holds too tight a noose around the grain's neck. *50%*

⬩⬩⬩ **Michel Couvreur Overaged 12 Year Old Blended Malt Whisky (87.5) n21.5 t22 f22 b22.** Attractive, with no shortage of molasses. Heavy, chewy, hints of Fisherman's Friend and also possession a surprisingly delicate grassy maltiness. *43%*

⬩⬩⬩ **Michel Couvreur Special Vatting 12 Year Old Blended Malt Whisky** sherry cask **(77) n18 t20 f19 b19.** Not the kindest of sherry casks... *45%*

⬩⬩⬩ **Michel Couvreur Spirale 26 Year Old Single Malt Whisky** Jura Vin de Paille finish **(88) n22** a few flighty spices; **t22** here we go again: grape! But at least there is a spicy side-line to keep interest alive; **f22** wow, I think I'm getting a little bit of tannin coming through...; **b22** pretty one-dimensional. But that dimension, luckily, happens to be pretty enjoyable. *47%*

⬩⬩⬩ **Michel Couvreur Very Sherried 25 Year Old Single Malt Whisky** sherry cask **(86.5) n22 t22 f21.5 b21.** No off-notes from the sherry here. But the strange thing about this malt is that the grape is so single-minded and bossing proceedings with such dominance, it is hard to recognise the quarter of a century of maturation. A whisky with such a lack of balance is always a bit unnerving, especially when the sugars – or date concentrate - are so cloying. *45%*

Nomad Outland Whisky (82) n21 t22 f20 b19. The entire shape of the whisky is lost under the tsunami of the PX casks. So first comes the scary sugars...followed by a very bitter finish with no happy midpoint. All-in-all, I have tasted whisky liqueurs less sweet than this... *41.3% WB16/006*

Deciphered and Distilled. The Bible's European Guide to Whisky Labels

English	German	French
Malt	Malz	Malt
Grain	Getreide	céréales
Wheat	Weizen	blé
Barley	Gerste	orge
Rye	Roggen	seigle
Spelt	Dinkel	épeautre
Corn	Mais	maïs
Oat	Hafer	avoine
Peated	getorft	tourbé
Smoked	geraucht	fumé
Organic	biologisch	biologique
Cask	Fass	fût
Matured in/Aged in	gereift in	vieilli en
Finish	Nachreifung	déverdissage
Double Maturation	Zweitreifung	deuxième maturation
Oak	Eiche	chêne
Toasted	wärmebehandelt	grillé
Charred	ausgeflammt, verkohlt	carbonisé
Years	Jahre	ans
Months	Monate	mois
Days	Tage	journées
Chill Filtration	Kühlfiltration	filtration à froid
Non Chill Filtered	nicht kühlgefiltert	non filtré à froid
No Colouring	nicht gefärbt	non coloré
Cask Srength	Fassstärke	brut du fût
Single Cask	Einzelfass	single cask
Cask No.	Fass-Nummer	numéro du fût
Batch	Charge	Lot/charge
Distillation Date	Destillations-Datum	date de distillation
Bottling Date	Abfüll-Datum	date de mise en bouteille
Alcohol by Volume/abv	Volumenprozente/% vol.	teneur en alcool/abv
Proof (American)	amerikanische Einheit für % vol.	unité américaine

Danish	Dutch	Swedish
Malt	Gerst	Malt
Korn	graan	säd
hvede	tarwe	vete
byg	gerst	korn
rug	rogge	råg
spelt	spelt	speltvete
majs	mais	majs
havre	haver	havre
tørv	geturfd	torvrökt
røget	gerookt	rökt
organisk	biologisch/organisch	ekologisk
fad	vat	fat
modning i	gerijpt in	mognad på/lagrad på
finish	narijping/finish	slutlagrat
dobbelt modning	dubbele rijping	dubbellagrat
egetræ	eik	ek
ristet	getoast	rostad
forkullet	gebrand	kolad
år	jaren	år
måned	maanden	månader
dage	dagen	dagar
kold filtrering	koude-filtratie	kylfiltrering
ikke kold filtreret	niet koud gefilterd	ej kylfiltrerad
ikke farvet	niet bijgekleurd	inga färgämnen
fadstyrke	vatsterkte	fatstyrka
enkelt fad	enkel vat	enkelfat
fad nr.	vat nummer	fatnummer
parti/batch	serie/batch	batch
destillations dato	distillatie datum	destilleringsdatum
aftapnings dato	bottel datum	buteljeringsdatum
volumenprocent	alcoholpercentage/% vol	volymprocent/% vol.
Proof	amerikaanse aanduiding voor % vol	Amerikanska proof

World Whiskies

I have long said that whisky can be made just about anywhere in the world; that it is not writ large in stone that it is the inalienable right for just Scotland, Ireland, Kentucky and Canada to have it all to themselves. And so, it seems, it is increasingly being proved. Perhaps only sandy deserts and fields of ironstone can prevent its make physically and Islam culturally, though even that has not been a barrier to malt whisky being distilled in both Pakistan and Turkey. While not even the world's highest mountains or jungle can prevent the spread of barley and copper pot.

Outside of North America and Europe, whisky's traditional nesting sites, you can head in any direction and find it being made. South America may be well known for its rum, but in the south of Brazil, an area populated by Italian and German settlers many generations back, malt whisky is thriving. It can now also be found in even more lush and tropical climes with Taiwan and Thailand leading the way.

Japan has long represented Asia with distinction and whisky-making there is in such an advanced state and at a high standard Jim Murray's Whisky Bible has given it its own section - and World Whisky of the Year for 2015!. But while neighbouring South Korea has ended its malt distilling venture, further east, and at a very unlikely altitude, Nepal has forged a small industry to team up, geographically, with fellow malt distillers India and Pakistan. The main malt whisky from this region making inroads in world markets is India's Amrut single malt.

Actually, inroads is hardly doing them justice. Full-bloodied trailblazing, more like. So good now is their whisky they were, with their fantastically complex brand, Fusion deservedly awarded Jim Murray's Whisky Bible 2010 Third Finest Whisky in the World. That represented a watershed not just for the distillery, but Indian whisky as a whole and in a broader sense the entire world whisky movement: it proved beyond doubt that excellent distilling and maturation wherever you are on this planet will be recognised and rewarded. Following hard on Amrut's tail is the ever-improving and high-flavoured malt from the Paul John distillery in Goa.

But it is Taiwan which again takes the plaudits with their fabulous distillery Kavalan. Bible winner again for 2017. Their third title in four years. Literally, world class.

Jim Murray's Whisky Bible World Whiskies of the Year Winners		
	Asian Whisky	Southern Hemisphere Whisky
2004-09	N/A	N/A
2010	Amrut Fusion	N/A
2011	Amrut Intermediate Sherry Matured	N/A
2012	Amrut Two Continents 2nd Edition	Kavalan Solist Fino Single Cask
2013	N/A	Sullivan's Cove Single Cask HH0509
2014	Kavalan Podium Single Malt	Timboon Single Malt Whisky
2015	Kavalan Single Malt Whisky	NZ Willowbank 1988 25 years Old
2016	Amrut Greedy Angels 46%	Heartwood Port 71.3%
2017	Kavalan Solist Moscatel	Heartwood Any Port in a Storm

ARGENTINA
Blends
Breeders Choice (84) n21 t22 f21 b20. A sweet blend using Scottish malt and, at the helm, an unusually lush Argentinian grain. *40%*

AUSTRALIA
BAKERY HILL North Bayswater, Working.

‹› **Bakery Hill Classic Malt** cask no. 1015 db **(91.5)** n23 t23 f22.5 b23. A beautiful malt for sure. Compared to its cask strength sister bottling, this has a far more sawdusty, dry feel though the cocoa finale is an extra bonus. *46%*

‹› **Bakery Hill Classic Malt** cask no. 1015 db **(95)** n23.5 distinctly plummy with a real spotted dog suet pudding and raisin feel; t24 more suet, but now with muscovado sugars exploding on juicy, fruity impact with gristy barley; f23.5 settles as the oils lighten and the butterscotch begins to play a part; b24 emphasis on a fruit character, but always stunningly subtle in its execution. But it pays off because it never falls out of sync or balance. *60%*

‹› **Bakery Hill Classic Malt** cask no. 1415 db **(93.5)** n23 t23 f24 b23.5. As the 60% version below, except here there is far less emphasis on the light phenols and more, especially late on, on the bready sugars. *46%*

‹› **Bakery Hill Classic Malt** cask no. 1415 db **(94.5)** n23.5 talk about complex! The most gentle, apologetic peats have entered the fray here to ensure an anchor to the more ethereal citrus and barley. A little minty, too; t24 wow! Now that is some delivery. The playful phenols and the sugars are in breathtaking harmony while the oils ensures the most comfortable silky cushion; f23.5 those sugars have no problem staying the course; b23.5 this is the seventh Bakery Hill whisky I have tasted today. And in the many years I have been sampling this stuff, I cannot remember when I was faced with such a long line of outstanding whisky from this Melbourne distillery. This is truly stunning malt, the light smokiness doing it no harm whatsoever. *60%*

‹› **Bakery Hill Classic Malt** cask no. 3115 db **(92)** n22.5 t23.4 f22.5 b23.5. Markedly more conservative than the sister bottling below with far less emphasis on the citrus and more on a gristy maltiness. The oils do stay remarkably intact and even aid the complexity of the delivery. *46%*

‹› **Bakery Hill Classic Malt** cask no. 3115 db **(91.5)** n23 a lovely parade of varied citrus notes, including orange blossom honey; t23 a distinct suet-type greasiness to the punchy delivery; the malt comes through loud and clear on about the sixth wave; those citrus notes hang about to excellent effect; f22.5 a charming malt and vanilla fade; b23 another malt which has no compunction about hitting hard. Bruising and delightful. *60%*

‹› **Bakery Hill Peated Malt** cask no. 0315 db **(91)** n22.5 t23 f22.5 b23. As below, but without quite building the same intensity. Still a treat. *46%*

‹› **Bakery Hill Peated Malt** cask no. 0315 db **(93)** n23.5 seriously subtle: the smoke creeps up and mugs you...; t23 an oilier malt this, allowing a gentle peatiness to gather and form into something a lot more telling, though never getting heavy with it. The interplay between vanilla and Manuka honey is impressive; f23 very long: a dull spice buzz accompanies the fading peat; b23.5 every last drop of oil is extracted for maximum complexity and effect. Lovely stuff! *60%*

‹› **Bakery Hill Peated Malt** cask no. 0715 db **(90)** n22.5 t22 f23 b22.5 As below, except the lack of oils does rip away a degree of the sweetness and durability. *46%*

‹› **Bakery Hill Peated Malt** cask no. 0715 db **(91.5)** n23 adore that nose: some real attitude alongside the devilish peat; curiously salty with something of the coast about it; t22.5 a beautiful bite on delivery: very similar to Teacher's in its heyday. The body is essentially thin, but there are just enough oils for the coating to contain a degree of light honey; f23 more vanilla and greater complexity. The smoke sticks; b23 Bakery Dave still knows how to treat us to a rip-roaring, snorting smoky one. What fun! And really does have a touch of the Teacher's about it – which even for malt is a serious compliment. *59%*

‹› **Bakery Hill Peated Malt** cask no. 104 db **(90.5)** n22 another one with a hint of Teacher's: Dave, are you sure you haven't been on holiday to Ardmore distillery, mate...? t22.5 sticks to that blended Scotch-style roughness which, frankly, I adore. Superb mix of smoke and oils with a train of varied sugars, some of them gristy; f23 long, the oils now radiating some vanilla picked up along the way; b23 give yourself a good 20 minutes with this one, using the Murray method. You will be rewarded... *52%*

⬧ **Bakery Hill Double Wood** cask no. 3159 db **(84.5) n21 t21.5 f21 b21**. Pleasant. Apart from a slight bum note on the nose, nothing particularly wrong with this. Just a bit dull and uninteresting I'm afraid, the whole experience being a little too flat. **46%**

⬧ **Bakery Hill Double Wood** cask no. 4477 db **(87.5) n21.5 t22 f22 b22**. Lightly smoked, possibly to the extent it may not have meant to be. Even more lightly fruity. But a little bit of cancelling out on both sides here – so often the case. Juicy when it needs to be **46%**

⬧ **Bakery Hill Double Wood cask** no. 4905 db **(82) n18.5 t22 f20.5 b21**. About as subtle as a fruity custard pie in the face. For a few moments, the delivery is a grapey delight, but too much bubblegum at play. Compared to the brilliance of the other Bakery Hill whiskies, the Double Wood range doesn't quite measure up, alas. *52%*

BELGROVE DISTILLERY Tasmania, Working.

Belgrove Distillery Rye Whisky 100% Rye Aged 3 Years ex-Overeem French oak Port cask, bott 22 Jun 15 db **(94.5) n23.5** no doubting the grain of choice: bristles with a rigid determination. Perhaps a little nougat in the mix from the cut, but my word...that rye...!!! **t24.5** that is just one fantastic delivery. Perhaps the most concentrated rye arrival I have tasted for a couple of years from any part of the world. Just so sharp, almost three dimensional. On one hand crisp and jagged, as the best rye whiskies should be, but also a more oily, softer, less fruity version underneath; brittle dark sugars at every turn; **f23** takes some time for those light nougaty feints to eat through. Until then, the rye and accompanying sugars – now joined by some biting spices - continue their remarkable show...; **b23.5** what a memorable rye. The grain leads on both nose and delivery in the same way Watson leads with his pads. *61%. ncf.*

⬧ **Belgrove Distillery Rye Whisky 100% Rye** Pinot Noir cask, bott 22 Feb 16 db **(94) n24** if you like your rye dry, peppery and alive with tart English scrumpy, look no further. And if you prefer the rye slightly flattened by extra fruit...; **t23.5** the peppers on the nose aren't ornamental, and kick in early here to maximum, salivating effect. The rye rises to speak but is soon heckled to near silence by the profound grape...and apple! **f23** dry still while the spices whittle away; superb late cocoa, too; **b23.5** really excellent rye. Not sure I would have selected a Pinot cask, though, as the rye naturally offers fruitiness galore. Still, as a distiller, I doff my hat to you, Peter Bignell. Because, when all is said and done, it works rather brilliantly. *57%. ncf.*

HEARTWOOD DISTILLERS Tasmania, Working.

The Good Convict Port cask, cask no. HH0543, dist Nov 00, bott Jun 15 db **(96) n24 t24 f24 b24** No problems with this cask. Has done its time, and has come away even and rounded. Massively impressive distilling and maturation: just beautiful! *71.3%. sc. 100 bottles.*

⬧ **Heartwood Any Port in a Storm** Port cask, cask no. HH 593 (95%) & LD 644 (5%), Summer batch, bott Dec 15 **(96) n24** just get that light spice nip to that fruit: so clever. Some seriously dry dates: an almost identical smell to those I used to buy as they dried by the side of the desert (as opposed to dessert) roads of Niger in the 1970s. Plenty of over-ripe banana. No hiding the cocoa here, either; **t24** salivating, juicy fruit. The malt, amazingly, remains intact on a slightly higher flavour level; **f24** Lubek marzipan in a high cocoa chocolate; long with just the right amount of oils; **b24** another stunningly massive malt from Heartwood. One of the world's great single casks of the year for sure. *69.1%. 160 bottles.*

Heartwood The Beagle 3 Tasmania Vatted Malt Whisky nine Lark & Tasmania Distillery casks, bott May 15 **(95.5) n23.5 t24 f24 b24** A more clotted version of Beagle 2. *68.4%. 220 bottles.*

Heartwood Convict Resurrection American oak Port, cask no. HH0239, dist Mar 00, bott Dec 14 **(82.5) n22.5 t22 f19 b19**. From the crème brûlée nose to the sherry (well, port!) trifle delivery, we know we are in for fruity beast. But, sadly, there is a mildly off-key dullness present which means a balance is never quite achieved. *72%*

Heartwood Devil in the Detail bourbon cask, cask no. HH0244, dist Apr 00, bott May 15 db **(95.5) n23.5** arely do you encounter a malt whisky that is so...malty! Supremely distilled; **t24** a kind of George T Stagg delivery, except it is concentrated malt which is burrowing into your taste buds like a drill might burrow into the earth looking for oil; the sugar seems to be a mixture of grist on steroids and light, buttery tannins in pure, concentrated form; **f24** long, with probably the most complete set of sugars you could ask for. The vanilla and ulmo honey is in near perfect harmony; **b24** probably did the enamel on my teeth few favours, but did my heart good. Magnificent malt! *73.5%. 152 bottles.*

⬧ **Heartwood Dregs Volume 1 Tasmanian Vatted Malt Whisky** distilled at Lark and Tasmania Distillery, bott Jan 16 **(89) n22** a suety, fruity mish-mash; **t22.5** pretty sharp fruit brings a tear to the eye; a little biting, too; **f22** a decent chocolate mousse fade; **b22.5** pleasant and juicy but comes across as slightly less well-structured than it might. *66.1%. 110 bottles.*

⬦ **Heartwood Spiritual Journey** sherry cask no. LD300, dist Apr 07, bott Mar 16 **(94)** **n23.5** the peat bludgeons you; the fruit softens you to death; **t24** I know some will adore this and talk lovingly of it until their tongues fall out. But I always have a slight problem with big grape and peat together as the wall of flavour can sometimes be a little too big to scale; still, the juiciness is almost unparalleled; even I, the biggest peat/sherry sceptic living, am arm-wrestled by the sheer enormity and seduced by the sexiest of shapes, into admitting that this is...bloody brilliant...; **f22.5** seemingly tones down like a spent force, though, in reality, that finale still has more muscle than about 95% of all whiskies out there; oh, and then there is the late choc ice...; **b24** when I read "sherry" on a Scotch, Irish and Japanese, my heart sinks and I bring the glass to my nose as might a man bring a gun to his head, with five loaded chambers and one empty. With Oz whisky, though, sulphur is never, thankfully, an issue. *67.9%. 100 bottles.*

HELLYERS ROAD Tasmania, Working.

⬦ **Hellyers Road 2002** 1st fill bourbon barrels, dist 14 Nov 02, bott 24 Apr 15 db **(87) n22** **t22.5 f21 b22.** A characterful malt which has come a long way since that first copper-starved distillate was made. Plenty of lime and light muscovado sugars have added a zappy mouth-watering quality to enjoy. Even some chocolate milkshake towards the finish. Impressive. *46.2%. nc ncf. 1,500 bottles. Bottled for the Swedish Whisky Federation.*

Hellyers Road Single Malt Whisky 12 Year Old Original db **(84.5) n19 t22 f21.5 b22.** Forget the nose and get stuck into the massive malt. *46.2%.*

Hellyers Road Single Malt Whisky Henry's Legacy 'The Gorge' db **(83) n21.5 t21 f20** **b20.5.** Eye-wateringly sharp in places, its best bits hang on a vaguely smoky, molasses-sweetened coffee note. *46.2%.*

Hellyers Road Single Malt Whisky Original db **(84) n20.5 t22 f20.5 b21.** Bolstered on last year's bottling thanks to a profound malt surge on delivery. Citrus fruity in part, but both nose the tingle at the finish demands more copper. *46.2%.*

Hellyers Road Single Malt Whisky Port Matured db **(88) n22.5** spiced, juicy fruitcake; **t23** superb delivery with the grape ripping home onto the throat with spice, then soothing and kissing better with its salivating freshness; **f20.5** a tad off key but the spices are busy and biting; **b22** without question the direction this distillery should take. Some wonderful moments. *46.2%.*

Hellyers Road Single Malt Whisky Port Matured db **(89.5) n23** the fruit is meticulously layered, almost prim. This lightness allows the odd off note from the spirit to pass through, but it is hardly noticeable, so complex are the varied grape tones; **t23** fabulous. That complexity on the nose is more than matched by the fruit on delivery, offering a delightful juiciness with further hints of honeydew melon and mocha; **f21** a few gremlins from the spirit do get through, but still the depth of the mocha and the light layering of muscovado sees it through; **b22.5** an absolutely top dog wine cask has done a splendid job on this malt. Impressive. And, what's more, Australia haven't lost a wicket – and even scored 28 runs - in all the time it took me to taste this... *48.9%*

Hellyers Road Single Malt Whisky Saint Valentine's Peak db **(85.5) n22.5 t22 f20 b21.** Regular readers of Jim Murray's Whisky Bible know that I traditionally taste the Australian whisky during the First Test of an Ashes series, if one is being played – which seems like every six months in recent years. So it is fitting that St Valentine's on the day of a massacre – the Aussies are currently 128-6 in their second innings, still needing almost 300 more runs to win. This malt has done a lot better than Clarke's sorry mob. Still pretty rough towards the finish, the gorgeous fruit effect on the nose works well into the delivery. At least the last embers show some coffee cake attractiveness. Now, I'd better hurry up with the remaining Aussie whiskies before Broad and Co bring the game to an early close on just the 4th day... *60.1%*

LARK DISTILLERY Tasmania, Working.

The Beagle Tasmanian Vatted Malt Whisky batch no. 2, bott Aug 14 db **(95) n23** a beautiful mix of sultana and Dundee cake...with a dollop of treacle for good measure; **t24** the enormity of the grape, the alcohol, the spice...it fair takes your breath away: no raisins come more succulent, no spice busier, no oak any more vanilla-bound; **f23.5** huge toastiness now: the dryness is profound. But the fruit and sugars from the cake not only offer the perfect balance, but have legs enough to make the finish two or three times the length of most other whiskies..; **b24.5** another ridiculously fine whisky from Australia. *68.3%. 160 bottles.*

◇◇◇ **Lark Distillery Limited Release Heavily Peated** cask no. LD670 db **(89.5) n22** light, malty, oily...and somewhat shy when it comes to phenols...; **t23.5** hugely attractive array of thick malty notes, thickening further as the ulmo and Manuka honey makes a pretty impact; **f22** fades as the oils take hold; **b22** I think Bill's having a lark: as heavy peated whiskies go, this is pretty, well...not heavily peated... 46%. sc.

◇◇◇ **Lark Distillery Limited Release Heavily Peated** cask no. LD690 db **(90.5) n23** a very different aroma: like a musky cherry cake with molasses by the ladle; **t23** ok, yes, the feints arrive thick and fast. But my word, someone knows brinkmanship when it comes to their still, for the cut insures a massive personality, one that needs a blowtorch to cut through. A huge surge of juicy malt hits hard; then, as it progresses, far more fruit and nut with, presumably, peat offering a dusky backdrop **f22** the oils insure a presence for the longest of finishes; **b22.5** fabulous, heavy duty whisky where, bizarrely, in the scheme of things, peat is at a premium... 61.6%. sc.

The Lark Distillery Single Malt Whisky Cask Strength port cask, cask no. 473, bott 2014 db **(94) n24 t24 f22.5 b23.5** And I'd always thought Hobart was a friendly town... 58%.

The Lark Distillery Single Malt Whisky Distiller's Selection sherry barrel aged, cask no. 475, bott 2014 db **(88.5) n23 t22 f21.5 b22** Don't go looking for complexity or a quickened pulse. A Steady Eddie dram 46%.

The Lark Distillery Single Malt Whisky Limited Release sherry cask, bott 2014 db **(86) n21.5 t23 f20 b21.5.** Big fruit and nut ensemble. Not quite Lark's finest ever distillate, mind. 52.1%

The Lark Distillery Single Malt Whisky Limited Release 2nd fill sherry cask, cask no. 689 db **(95) n23.5 t23 f24 b24** Not quite sure how he did it, but my old mate Bill Lark has gone and produced flavour profile not quite like anything else I have found on this planet. The malt and oak, perhaps with still influence, but probably through the youth of the distillate, have forged a nose in particular which needs as much time as you can spare to unravel. What great fun! And probably the best young whisky in the world. 63.3%. 35 bottles.

The Lark Distillery Single Malt Whisky Single Cask Port barrel aged, cask no. 516, bott 2014 db **(90) n23 t23 f22 b22** An entertaining dram which doesn't always balance out the way it was probably planned but gets there in the end. 43%.

LIMEBURNERS ALbany, Working.

Limeburners Single Malt Whisky Barrel M23 bott no. 78 db **(90.5) n22.5 t23.5 f22 b22.5.** First time I've tasted anything from this Western Australian mob. G'day fellas! I have to admit, thought it might have been from France at first, as the aroma on nosing blind reminded me of brandy. And not without good reason, it transpires. This no age statement malt spent an unspecified amount of time in American brandy cask before being finished in bourbon casks. Does it work? Yes it does. But now that's torn it lads. You are supposed to start off with a bloody horrible whisky and get better. Now you have gone and made a rod for your own back. Good on you! 61%

Limeburners Single Malt Whisky Peated Barrel M58 ex-bourbon American oak cask db **(89) n22.5 t23.5 f21 b22.** Taken aback when I nosed this: saw the Limeburners tag, but hadn't spotted the style. The smoke gave me a jolt: not seen this from these guys before. Peatburners, more like...and an attractive smoky style the like of which I have never encountered before. 48%. ncf. 133 bottles.

Limeburners Single Malt Whisky M64 Muscat Finish db **(92) n23.5 t23 f22.5 b23.** Macho malt keeps in touch with its feminine side. Tasty and beautifully made. 61%. ncf.

Limeburners Single Malt Whisky Barrel M79 ex-bourbon American oak cask and finished in an old Australian sherry cask db **(93.5) n23 t24 f23 b23.5.** A rare exhibition of a happy marriage between bourbon cask and sherry. 61%. ncf. 113 bottles.

Limeburners Single Malt Whisky Barrel M91 ex-bourbon American oak barrique and finished in an old Australian sherry cask db **(80) n19 t21 f20 b20.** The stale tobacco on the nose and rumbling, off key finish says something about the feints involved. The delicious clarity of the fruit is a tick for the "sherry" cask. 43%. ncf. 355 bottles.

OLD HOBART DISTILLERY Tasmania, Working.

Overeem Bourbon Cask Matured Cask Strength cask no. OHD065 db **(93) n23.5 t23 f22.5 b23.5** As though someone has exploded a vanilla pod in the centre of an oak tree. Supremely beautiful texture. 60%

Overeem Port Cask Matured cask no. OHD026 db **(94.5) n23.5 t23.5 f23.5 b24** Oh! Had only this been at cask strength!!! A joyous experience. 43%

Overeem Sherry Cask Matured cask no. OHD030 db **(90.5) n22 t23 f22.5 b23** for a 43% malt, this has some serious depth and complexity. Impressive stuff. But from this great Down Under distillery, what do you expect....? *43%*

Overeem Sherry Cask Matured Cask Strength cask no. OHD032 db **(87.5) n22 t21.5 f22 b22.** No complaints from me about the silky texture of the fruit, or the mouth-watering qualities and spice. But, despite the cocoa finish, all seems just a little too manicured. *60%*

◇ **Overeem Single Malt Whisky Port Cask Matured** cask no. OHD-096 db **(84) n21 t21.5 f20.5 b21.** Big, but doesn't have the excellence of the Port cask as in OHD-104 to get away with a few technical frailties. *43%. sc.*

◇ **Overeem Single Malt Whisky Port Cask Matured** cask no. OHD-104 db **(91.5) n22.5** rich, hefty, oily cocoa with more than the odd raisin chucked in for good measure; not short on nuts either, especially walnuts; **t23** huge, lush delivery. So oily, including some naughty but nice feints, and the chocolate soon takes up the mid-ground; **f23** more chocolate fruit and nut **b23** just dig that chocolate, digger...! *43%. sc.*

◇ **That Boutique-y Whisky Company Overeem** batch 2 **(89.5) n22** a sliver of grapefruit in the barley; **t23** juicy delivery, as light as your first love's kiss and falls into full malt mode; **f22** gentle vanilla; **b22.5** for those who think Oz whiskies tend to be full on, bruising buggers, cop a load of this... *52.9%. 75 bottles.*

REDLANDS ESTATE DISTILLERY Tasmania, Working.

◇ **Redlands Estate Single Malt** Whisky Pinot cask, cask no. RD008#14, bott 18 Dec 15 **(89.5) n22.5** despite the obvious Pinot undercurrent, the main structure is centred around the tannins, which offer a red liquorice deftness; **t22.5** fat, chewy and rich with grape skin and spice; **f22** sensual and dry with a big vanilla contribution; **b22.5** a lovely bottling, but not often you see a whisky take more from the tannin than the freely available wine... *46%. sc.*

SHENE ESTATE DISTILLERY Tasmania, Working.

◇ **Mackey Tasmanian Single Malt First Release Aged 6 Years** Port cask 001, bott 2015 db **(89) n22** though the cask is clean, there is a rare tightness on the nose and it takes some persuasion for the fruit to reveal its spicy charms; the malt is distinctly grassy; **t23** the delivery is the highlight, for the sugars are soon unlocked to reveal ulmo honey and dark muscovado sugars; the middle bitters slightly and spices up further; **f21.5** vaguely bitter spices play us out; **b22.5** as a first release, the distillers can hold their heads very high... *49%. sc. 125 bottles.*

◇ **Mackey Tasmanian Single Malt Aged 6 Years** Port cask 002, bott 2015 db **(94.5) n23** a voluptuous, plummy fruitiness combines with heather honey; **t24** brilliant! A sublime delivery where the impact of the fruit is clean and telling. Spices are soon out of their traps and chase the sugar candy fruit round the palate; **f23.5** darker, deeper, a dash drier with black cherry merging with molasses; **b24** some seriously fast learning here because, for a second bottling, this is stunning. Uncharacteristically subtle for an Australian... *49%. sc. 151 bottles.*

SMALL CONCERN DISTILLERY Tasmania, Working.

Cadenhead's Authentic Collection Cradle Mountain Aged 18 Years (81) n20 t22 f20 b19. A nutty monster of a malt. A strange nougat-like note really is packed with hazelnuts. Sadly, the fruit and the grain have yet to find a way to achieve harmony. *52.9%*

Cradle Mountain Pure Tasmanian Malt db **(87) n21 t22 f21 b23.** A knock-out malt from a sadly now lost distillery in Tasmania. Faultlessly clean stuff with lots of new oak character but sufficient body to guarantee complexity. *43%*

SOUTHERN COAST DISTILLERS Adelaide, Working.

Southern Coast Single Malt Batch 003 db **(79.5) n18 t19 f23 b19.5.** Third time unlucky. Lots of oils and berserk honey. But too feinty, though this went to some finishing school, believe me...! *46%. ncf.*

Southern Coast Single Malt Batch 004 db **(82.5) n20 t22 f20.5 b20.** An earthy, slightly musty dram with a pleasing essence of honey but struggles to find structure or balance. *46%*

Southern Coast Single Malt Batch 005 db **(83.5) n21.5 t22 f20 b20.** Starts off like a Jack Hobbs or Brian Lara or Alec Stewart taking the Aussie quick bowling apart. There is even an unusual, but mightily attractive, sweetened Vegemite hint to this (not as strange as it sounds, actually). But the middle stump is removed by the hefty finish: the cricketing equivalent of an ungainly, head-up hoick to cow corner.... *46%*

Southern Coast Single Malt Batch 006 db **(95) n24 t24 f23.5 b24.** When I saw these Southern Coast Whiskies before me, my eyes lit up. Here was my journey to Demerara. Much cheaper and less problem-riddled than any trip I normally make to Guyana..and with less chance of coming away with my normal stomach complaint. Batches 4 and 5 let me down. But Batch 6.... even the sun has come out for the first time in three days as I nose this... Georgetown, here I come... 46%

TASMAN DISTILLERY Tasmania, Working.

Great Outback Rare Old Australian Single Malt db (92) n24 t24 f21 b23. What can you say? An Australian whisky distillery makes a malt to grace the world's stage. But you can't find it outside of Australia. This will have to be rectified. 40%

TASMANIA DISTILLERY Tasmania, Working.

⬥ **Sullivan's Cove 2000 American Oak Single Cask** cask no. HH0332, dist 02 Jun 00, bott 28 Jan 16 (90.5) n22.5 charming, uncomplicated but well-constructed malt; t23 intense malt kick off then a barley sugar follow-through; f22.5 vanilla and malt; b22.5 well, that was malty! 47.5%. sc.

⬥ **Sullivan's Cove 2000 American Oak Single Cask** cask no. HH0354, dist 13 Jun 00, bott 27 Jan 16 (86) n21.5 t22 f21 b21.5. Another big malty job. But a niggardly cask suppresses complexity. 47.5%. sc.

⬥ **Sullivan's Cove 2000 French Oak Single Cask** cask no. HH00419, dist 04 Aug 00, bott 27 Nov 15 (92) n23 a mix of demerara and muscovado sugars charge at full speed alongside the tannin; t23.5 the impact defies the abv. Big and bruising, a curious fruitcake shape appears – especially when the molasses turn up; f22.5 drier, with big vanilla emphasis; b23 just a series of very positive confident notes somehow finding a very pleasant tune. 47.5%. sc.

Sullivan's Cove American Oak Single Cask cask no. HH0047, dist 9 Nov 99, bott 30 Apr 14 db (95.5) n24 hard to imagine a malt whisky being more malt whiskier...the nose celebrates outstanding distilling and classic maturation in a fine cask. The barley is multi-faceted and just about perfectly balanced between barley intensity and the use of deft, still slightly gristy, sugars. The oak chimes in with delicious butterscotch and even a hint of ginger; t24 few distilleries go weight on delivery better than this one. The intensity of the barley deserves a medal alone, its balance with the gentle vanilla-led oak a bar; f23.5 long, with a light smattering of cocoa yet the barley still feigns to have a degree of youth...even now; b24 exemplary malt whisky: absolutely beautiful. 47.5%

Sullivan's Cove American Oak Single Cask cask no. HH00460,dist 5 Sep 00, bott 30 Apr 14 db (92) n23 fabulous mix of ulmo and heather honey really allows the barley to show in a bright light; t22.5 intense barley from the moment it hits the palate and doesn't cease as the early cocoa arrives; f23 the spices have been busy from early on but come into their own here. German caramelized biscuit meets Weetabix and malt cereal as the Demerara sugars gain hold; b23.5 out malts many a Scottish malt distillery. A lovely barrel, complimenting top quality distillate. An assured and wonderfully paced dram of great confidence. 47.5%

Sullivans Cove Double Cask batch DC74, youngest cask 21 Oct 00, bott 13 May 14 db (85) n21.5 t23 f19.5 b21.5. Tasting this while England are recovering from a bright start by the Australians to the first Ashes test. A disappointing finish...and I'm not just talking about in the days play for England. Furry and not remotely right. 40%. 1307 bottles.

Sullivans Cove French Oak Cask cask no. HH386, dist 28 Jul 00, bott 17 Feb 15 db (94) n23 the tannins are up for a battle. Sharp spices and punchy Demerara sugars offer full support; t24 now that is quite beautiful. The malt melts early in the proceedings, accompanied by those sugars. But it's the intensity of the mildly belligerent tannins and the way the dovetail with the Demerara and maple syrup which really wins you heart; f23 a long, oak-laden fade. The vanilla runs into butterscotch while the spices carry just getting hotter...; b24 a massive whisky which maximises the tannins and sugars yet never faintly goes OTT. Beautiful. 47.5%. 461 bottles.

⬥ **Sullivan's Cove French 2000 Oak Single Cask** cask no. HH0400, dist 21 Jul 00, bott 25 Nov 15 (91) n22 a butterscotch/crème brule welcome; t23 ka-powww! The spices fly in like a swarm of pissed off hornets: where the hell did they come from...? Beyond this, the malt carries on serenely; f23 genteel butterscotch and vanilla...; b23 the sleepy nose offers no hints at the spicy onslaught to follow. 47.5%. sc.

Sullivans Cove Winterfeast Special Issue batch no. WF2 db (84.5) n21 t21.5 f21 b21. Almost as dull as Glen McGrath's BBC Test Match Special radio summarising. More of a toffee fest than a Winter's Feast. Shame, because tasting S C whisky is always one of my highlights of the year. 48%

⤜ **Tasmanian Independent Bottlers Single Bourbon Cask 1999** cask no. HH177, dist Nov 99, bott Nov 12 **(91) n22.5 t23 f22.5 b23.** Just the most beautiful essay in intense malt. I swear to you, although I'm not remotely a gambling man, I would wager £5,000 that if I grabbed ten scotch whisky blenders and presented this to them as a Scotch single malt, there would not be a single dissenting voice. Watch your backs, Scotland...! *46%. sc.*

TIMBOON RAILWAY SHED DISTILLERY Victoria, Working.

Timboon Single Malt Whisky 2010 dist 05/09/10, bott 03/06/15 db **(96) n24** in the words of Twin Peaks: "it is happening...again..." Just one nose of this and you are transported into a different whisky world which makes the hairs stand on the back of your neck. There is nothing else like it: fruit, grapes especially, including pips, skins and most else, in the most marvellously clean yet concentrated form. Scary...; **t24** hold on to your bar stools, folks! The fruit is going in! Drier than previous bottlings maybe, but never reaches bitter; the sugars (which pitch up early) wear tin helmets as grape explodes all around. But there is enough tannin, spice, lazy molasses and inevitable cocoa to crank up the complexity and ensure balance..; **f24** just more of the same. Forever...; **b24** how can any critic fault a whisky this magnificent and mega...? A late night dram...but don't leave it too late to give it the full half hour treatment it deserves. *69%*

Timboon Single Malt Whisky 2015 dist 31/05/15, bott 03/06/15 db **(92.5) n23 t24.5 f22 b23.** When the label says "oak barrel matured" they may be stretching a point. Or, more likely, having a bit of a laugh. For this has spent precisely one month in the cask, perhaps just about long enough to perceive the most pathetic colouration discernible to the naked eye. That said...what magnificent jazzed up new make this is. Whoever is distilling this stuff knows exactly what the hell they are doing! The nose is rich and a tad earthy (maybe some stainless steel in the still somewhere?) but so, so malty. It is the delivery and immediate follow through which blows you away, though. In every sense. Fabulous gristy sugars peddling as hard as they can to last into the distance. Love it. *70.8%c.*

TIN SHED DISTILLING COMPANY Adelaide, Working.

Iniquity Single Malt Port casks Batch 001 db **(94) n23** if I say the nose is huge, I am telling only half the story: we have dates, plums, walnuts, raisins...; **t23.5** just as silky on the palate as the nose promises: an intense Cadbury's Fruit and Nut feel to this one; **f23.5** a predictably long finish, with the spice joining in the rich, fruity fun...; **b24** a gorgeous experience and quite a start for this new distillery: they will have to work overtime to keep this standard up. *46%. ncf.*

Iniquity Single Malt Port casks Batch 002 db **(87) n21 t23 f21 b22.** A sharper, less inclusive bottling than Batch 1. Still profound, silky fruit: a truly lip-smacking start. But a metallic note creeps in later on. *46%. ncf.*

Iniquity Single Malt Port casks Batch 003 rum cask finished db **(85) n20 t22.5 f21.5 b21.5.** Tin shed loads of personality once you get away from the confused nose. As time allows the glass to settle, the butyric decreases and a degree of South American-style rum begins to make a shout. But it's all a right hubbub and bloody confused. The finish is usually where you get confirmation of all not being quite right with the world and, sure enough, a slightly non-coppery tone emerges. All that said, the delivery is a celebration of all things sugar and entirely enjoyable. Get the feeling, though, that these stills would make better rum than whisky. *46%. ncf.*

⤜ **Iniquity Single Malt Batch 004** db **(89) n22.5** every nuance of caramel has been dragged out of the oak to sit shoulder to shoulder with the intense malt; **t22** a little ulmo honey goes a long way...yet still it is pure malt which fills in every last gap; **f22.5** never seen malt travel so far...; **b22** a distillery which has long fascinated me, and I am so frustrated I still haven't been able to find the time to visit. This is their maltiest offering so far...by a distance. *46%. ncf.*

⤜ **Iniquity Single Malt Batch 005** db **(82.3) n20.5 t21 f20.5 b20.5.** Malty, nutty but way too feinty, Not a patch on Batch 004. *46%. ncf.*

Vatted Malts

⤜ **Heartwood 2 of /3 Tasmanian Malt Whisky** distilled at Lark 8 & 6 Years and Tasmania Distillery 16 Years, Port, peated & sherry casks, bott Apr 16 **(95.5) n23.5** somehow, the delicate smoke seems to emphasise the impact of the pithy fruit; **t24** obviously designed for maximum impact: and it achieved it with 100% success. One of the great Ozzy deliveries of the year, so complex in smoke and grape interplay that you don't really notice the abv; **f24** like breaking into a bar of fruit and nut chocolate. Superb...; **b24** make no mistake: the vatting of these casks from these two distilleries and over such wide ages really is a work of art: a study of fruit, as well. 68.1%. 189 bottles.

Tasmanian Double Malt Whisky Unpeated (87.5) n22 t22 f21.5 b22. Not a chance of getting bored with this guy. A sweet tooth would be useful. 43%. The Nant Distillery.

Unspecified Grain

◈ **3Souls Small Batch Australian Single Malt Whisky Batch 1** new American oak cask, cask no. SC30, dist Jul 08, bott Aug 15 (87.5) n21.5 t23 f21 b22. A sturdy malt displaying a degree of bitterness on both nose and finish. But the parade of sugars, some of them thick honey textured – is a treat on delivery. 46.7%. sc.

◈ **3Souls Small Batch Australian Single Malt Whisky Batch 2** Port cask, cask no. SC35, dist Oct 09, bott Aug 15 (90.5) n22 estery: closer to a Jamaican rum; t23 this one's not mucking about! Thumping fruit totally fills the mouth with creamy, plummy riches; a light but effective spicy substrata also makes its point; f22.5 long, with a distinct Victoria sponge quality; b23 apparently, an unspecified Australian. If the finish was anything to go by, made in Victoria, I'd say.... 46.3%. sc.

◈ **3Souls Small Batch Australian Single Malt Whisky Batch 3** Pedro Ximenez cask, cask no. SC41, dist Dec 10, bott Aug 15 (79) n20 t21 f19 b19. Either too sweet or too bitter. Like many a PX whisky, comes to a sticky end... 52.1%. sc.

BRAZIL
HEUBLEIN DISTILLERY
Durfee Hall Malt Whisky db (81) n18 t22 f20 b21. Superbly made whisky; the intensity of the malt is beautifully layered without ever becoming too sweet. Very light bodied and immaculately clean. Good whisky by any standards. 43%

UNION DISTILLERY
Barrilete db (72) n18 t19 f18 b17. Nothing particularly wrong with it technically; it just lacks vitality. Thin but extremely malt intense. 39.1%

Blends
Cockland Gold Blended Whisky (73) n18 t18 f19 b18. Silky caramel. Traces of malt there, but never quite gets it up. 38%. Fante.

Drury's Special Reserve (86.5) n21.5 t22 f21 b22. Deceptively attractive, melt-in-the-mouth whisky; at times clean, regulation stuff, but further investigation reveals a honeycomb edge which hits its peak in the middle ground when the spices mix in beautifully. One to seek out and savour when in Brazil. 40%. Campari, Brasil.

Gold Cup Special Reserve (84.5) n21 t22.5 f20 b21. Ultra soft, easily drinkable and, at times, highly impressive blend which is hampered by a dustiness bestowed upon it by the nagging caramels on both nose and finish. Some lovely early honey does help lift it, though, and there is also attractive Swiss roll jam towards the finish. Yet never quite gets out of third gear despite the most delicate hint of smoke. 39%. Campari, Brasil.

Gran Par (77) n19.5 t22 f17.5 b18. The delivery is eleven seconds of vaguely malty glory. The remainder is thin and caramelled with no age to live up to the name. And with Par in the title and bagpipes and kilt in the motif, how long before the SWA buys a case of it...? 39%

Green Valley Special Reserve batch 07/01 (70) n16 t19 f17 b18. A softly oiled, gently bitter-sweet blend with a half meaty, half boiled sweet nose. An unusual whisky experience. 38.1%.

Malte Barrilete Blended Whisky batch 001/03 (76) n18 t20 f19 b19. This brand has picked up a distinctive apple-fruitiness in recent years and some extra oak, too. 39.1%.

Natu Nobilis (81.5) n22.5 t20 f19 b20. The nose boasts a genuinely clean, Speyside-style malt involvement. But to taste is much more non-committal with the soft grain dominating and the grassy notes restricted the occasional foray over the tastebuds. Pleasant, but don't expect a flavor fest. 39%. Pernod Ricard, Brasil.

Natu Nobilis Celebrity (86) n22.5 t22 f20.5 b21. A classy blend with a decent weight and body, yet never running to fat. Some spice prickle ensures the flavor profile never settles in a neutral zone and the charming, citrus-domiated malt on the nose is immediately found on the juicy delivery. A cut above the standard Natu Nobilis and if the finish could be filled out with extra length and complexity, we'd have an exceptionally impressive blend on our hands. Another blend to seek out whenever in Brazil. 39%. Pernod Ricard, Brasil.

O Monge batch 02/02 (69) n17 t18 f17 b17. Poor nose but it recovers with a malty mouth arrival but the thinness of the grain does few favours. 38.5%. Union Distillery.

Old Eight Special Reserve (85.5) n20 t21 f22.5 b22. Traditionally reviled by many in Brazil, I can assure you that the big bite followed by calming soft grains is exactly what you need after a day's birding in the jungle. *39%. Campari, Brasil.*

Pitt's (84) n21 t20 f22 b21. The pits it certainly aint!! A beautifully malted blend where the barley tries to dominate the exceptionally flinty grain whenever possible. Due to be launched later in 2004, this will be the best Brazil has to offer – though some fine tuning can probably improve the nose and middle even further and up the complexity significantly. I hope, when I visit the distillery early in 2005, I will be able to persuade them to offer a single malt: on this evidence it should, like Pitt's, be an enjoyable experience and perfect company for any World Cup finals. *40%. Busnello Distillery.*

Wall Street (84) n23 t22 f19 b20. Fabulous nose with a sexy citrus-light smoke double bill. And the arrival on the palate excels, too, with a rich texture and confident delivery of malt, again with the smoke dominating. But falls away rather too rapidly as the grains throw the balance out of kilter and ensures too much bitter oak late on. *38%. Pernod Ricard, Brasil.*

BHUTAN

K5 Premium Spirit Himalayan Whisky bott 2013 (88) n22 t23 f21 b22 Absolutely nothing wrong with the Bhutan grain but more judicious cask selection (i.e remove the odd one or two sub-standard Scotch barrels) and this really could be an irresistible little charmer. As a first attempt, really impressive. This whisky is a mix of Scotch malt and grain made in Bhutan. So it was fitting that seeing as parts of that mysterious, land-locked mountainous country rises to some 23,000 feet, I was just slightly above that height when I first learned of the whisky. While on board a flight to Asia I witnessed the brand's manager trying to talk an airline into carrying it. He then assured me I'd love it. Actually, clean that malt up a bit and I really could! *40%*

INDIA
AMRUT DISTILLERY

Amrut Fusion batch no. 01, bott Mar 09 db (97) n24 t24 f24 b25. One of the most complex and intriguing new whiskies of 2010 that needs about two days and half a bottle to get even close to fathoming. Not exactly a textbook whisky, with a few edges grinding together like tectonic plates. And there is even odd note, like the fruit and a kind of furry, oaky buzz, which I have never seen before. But that is the point of whiskies like this: to be different, to offer a unique slant. But, ultimately, to entertain and delight. And here it ticks all boxes accordingly. To the extent that this has to be one of the great whiskies found anywhere in the world this year. And the fact it is Indian? Irrelevant: from distillation to maturation this is genius whisky, from whichever continent... *50%*

Amrut Fusion batch 10, bott Mar 11 db (94.5) n24 t24 f22.5 b23.5. Superb whisky, though to be plotted on a different map to the now legendary Whisky Bible award-winning Batch 1. This is a much more delicate affair: more hints and shadows rather than statements and substance. Still, though, a fabulous malt whisky in Amrut's best style. *50%. nc.*

Amrut Greedy Angels 10 Years Old batch no. 1, bott Sept 14 db (96.5) n24.5 t24 f23.5 b24.5 when I visited my first Indian distillery, some 20 years ago, the last thing I thought I would ever experience would be a native malt reaching double figures in age. All those I tasted showed decline to the point of undrinkability at only half that age. However, cellared warehousing and far more judicial oak selection means that not only is there now an Indian malt whisky reaching double figures in age, it has reached a stage of magnificence on its maturation road. I first tasted this at the distillery itself in the Spring of 2015. But waited until August 2015, making this the second to last whisky sampled for the 2016 Bible, before officially reviewing it under neutral conditions in the UK. What is apparent is that wherever in the world you experience this, you are being royally entertained - bewitched and mesmerised, to be nearer the truth - by one of the most remarkable whiskies of all time. *46%. 284 bottles.*

Amrut Greedy Angels 10 Years Old batch no. 1, bott Sept 14 db (96) n24 t24 f24 b24. As above. Except at this strength it is all a little oilier; tighter in its delivery and demeanour, with a bit more shouting where there were once whispers. All the same flavours are present and correct, though they all rush through at a greater pace to get to the finale. Beautiful, salivating...and dazzlingly brilliant. *71%*

Amrut Greedy Angels dist 3 Oct 04, bott 15 Nov 12 db (96) n25 t24 f23 b24. So here we have it: an 8-year-old Indian whisky. Matured in a cellar, luckily, but still has the hallmarks often seen on certain Speysiders in their late 30s...a series of Caperdonichs from about five or six years ago spring to mind. Except their noses were never this good: in fact, few whiskies have ever been better – it is certainly unsurpassed this year...worldwide. A true whisky great of the last decade. *50%*

Amrut Naarangi batch no. 1, bott Dec 14 db **(94) n23** thick, intense sherry...plus. If you think you are detecting a strange, vaguely sharp, blood orange undertone, you might well be...; **t23.5** a no less intense delivery with the grape almost boasting a six pack. But as the sherry effect takes a breather, the vague orangeyness reappears and then vanishes almost as fast as a general fruitcake countenance takes effect; **f24** at last the malt – quite young at times - relaxes and the fruit, a little spent by now, makes way for much softer, less egotistical sugars, muscovado leading the pack. The vanilla has a light ulmo honey tinge while the spices now begin to make a beautifully timed impact; **b23.5** the first sherry I know of worldwide which has had orange peel added to it in the butt to help infuse delicate citrus flavour to the maturing whisky which was to follow. Oddly enough, the whisky is in its element when the fruit levels have receded... *50%. 900 bottles.*

Amrut 100 Peated Single Malt ex-bourbon/virgin oak barrels db **(92) n23 t23 f23.5 b22.5**. Ironically, though one of the older whiskies to come from this distillery, the nose shows a little bit of youth. A quite different style from Amrut's other peated offerings and it was obviously intended. Further proof that this distillery has grown not only in stature but confidence. And with very good reason. *57.1%. nc ncf.*

JOHN DISTILLERIES

Paul John Brilliance db **(94.5) n23.5 t24 f23.5 b23.5** Yet another astonishing malt from India. *46%*

◇ **Paul John Brilliance** batch no. 3, bott July 16 db **(94) n24** the burgeoning house style of orange blossom honey is brought out to the full here, giving an almost phenolic density to this – even though there is no peat. The light liquorice from the ex-bourbon casks joins the vanilla and sugars dealt out by the oak in equal measure; **t24** this was a malt designed to get the most out of the barley and here the juices arrive in force and early on. Much less copper than the first bottling, showing this relatively new distillery is moving on, but the spices and light mocha make a handsome contribution; **f22.5** perhaps more on sugars late on, but the gently oiled malt continues to pulse away with panache; **b23.5** it is impossible not to be impressed. Complexity is the key word here. And though it has moved on a little – mainly through tannin – from its earliest rendition, the layering and structure remains superb. The tail needs a little attention, but I am being ultra-strict: this is excellent whisky and make no mistake. *46%*

Paul John Edited db **(96.5) n24.5 t24.5 f23.5 b24** A new Indian classic: a sublime malt from the subcontinent. To be more precise: a world classic! Think of Ardmore at its most alluring: one of Scotland's finest and most complex single malts, yet somehow possessing a saltiness and depth more befitting Islay. Then stir in a small degree of ulmo honey and bourbon-style hickory and liquorice. Plus subtle chocolate mint. And there you have it...the smoke drifting around stirring up spicy tales of the east. A world class whisky to be talked about with reverence without doubt... *52.9%*

Paul John Indian Single Malt Bold batch no. 01 db **(95.5) n23.5** the smoke tries to rule the roost, but it is not allowed: a dizzying array of manuka honey, prickly spice and bourbonesque red liquorices make sure of that; **t24** melt-in-the mouth-malt: a silky delivery – what else do you expect from India? – is shaped again by that oak-studded honey. But just as it begins to break up on the palate and lighten, a hefty second wave of spice and then thick, cloudy smoke coat the roof of the mouth, leaving tide marks of dry molasses, peaty soot and a degree of copper in its wake: absolutely delicious...; **f23.5** a tad lighter on the finish with the copper really now making an impact. A gorgeous smoked mocha is given a third dimension by the busy, delicate and intricate spices; meanwhile the molasses have time to linger and morph into mocha; **b24.5** one of the most weighty and chewable Indian whiskies of all time – yet it is not just about peat. So many elements to this, you expect a bottle to weigh the equivalent of a block of lead. This truly great whisky, so complex and absorbing, needs a good 20 minutes minimum of your time to adequately explore. *46%*

◇ **Paul John Mars Orbiter** db **(95) n24** here's a fabulous example of how tannins can be used to maximum effect without the oak overwhelming the more subtle aspects of the vatting. So fabulously toasty where the smokiness and sweetness become blurred as the muscovado sugars move into something closer to dank orange blossom honey...; **t23.5** beautifully lush delivery where the tannins are straining at the leash but kept at bay by several waves of intense maltiness; again the sugars and tannins appear to harmonise rather than, as Mars might prefer, go to war; **f23.5** long, with myriad spices trailing the tannins like comet dust. All the while the toasty sugars hold their line and nerve...; **b24** we have lift off!! Out of this world whisky! *57.8%*

◇ **Paul John Olorosso Sherry Cask Finish** db (94.5) n23.5 evidence of the grape arrives early: clean and well structured. As spices form around it, it opens out to become more rounded and confident, even allowing vanilla to play an important role: intriguing! t23.5 the delivery is soft and immediately salivating. Again, the fruit shows its hand quickly enough with an overly moist Melton Hunt Cake feel, as the raisins begin to feel a little more toasty and the molasses take up residence; f23.5 spiced orange peel melds into the growing mocha as the intensity fails to diminish; b24 oh, for the rare joy of a sulphur-free malt. And as complex a one as this, to boot. 57.4%. ncf.

Paul John Single Malt Cask No 161 Non Peated (94) n22.5 t24.5 f23 b24. A malt which has much to say but does so with a quiet intensity. This really is a class act... 57%

Paul John Single Malt Single Cask No 164 Non Peated (96) n24 t24 f24 b24. It is hardly believable that this is a three year old single malt: the unstinting high humidity of Goa and even higher temperature, perhaps helped along by three months of monsoons, appears to have given this whisky a degree of complexity which, even in Kentucky, it might have taken a dozen years to compile. This is single malt, but one with a hint of paradise...57%

Paul John Peated Single Malt db (89) n23 t22 f21.5 b22.5. A delicately peaty guy which gangs up on you slowly. The smoke-infused layering of sugars is the star turn, though. 55.5%

Paul John Single Malt Cask No 692 Peated db (95.5) n24 t23.5 f24 b24. Hard to believe a whisky apparently so young in years can offer such complexity. But that's Goa for you... 58.5%

Paul John Single Malt Cask No 777 Peated db (95) n23.5 t24 f23.5 b24. A Paul John which tries to offer as much delicate honey as the peat will allow. Something of rare, understated beauty. And though I often fly 777s, few take off as well as this and here there is no need for a seat belt... 59.7%

Paul John Single Malt Cask No 780 Peated db (96) n24 t24 f24 b24. Warning. If you are a bit of a dithering, wishy-washy whisky drinker, don't go anywhere near this stuff: this bottling is for serious whisky drinkers only... 57.3%

Paul John Single Malt Cask No 784 Peated db (95.5) n23.5 t23.5 f24.5 b24. The understated smoke ensures an elegant yet chewy experience. 59.2%

Paul John Single Malt Cask No 1444 Non Peated db (95.5) n23.5 t24 f24 b24 Among the most intensely malty Indian whiskies ever to have been bottled. Quite superb. 59.7%

◇ **Paul John Single Cask No 1833** db (95.5) n23.5 such an earthy nose: there are even hints of stewed (unsalted) celery and battles between dry molasses and spices. This is one very intense malt whisky; t24 unlike on the nose, the sugars are not only first out the traps, but second and third, also. The first to arrive is splendid gristy maltiness which sets the tone. Just behind comes ulmo honey with its subtle vanillas followed by a liquorice-treacle mix. Slowly the mouth is filled by a gently spiced smokiness, so subtle that those simply concentrating on the sugars may not be aware of its intensifying effect; f24 the oils are so softly spoken early on, you hardly notice the way they gently carry the narrative beyond the gathering tannins right through to the finish...which is a long way away; b24 just....wow! A cask with more star quality than a Bollywood Blockbuster...and, for all its enormity, a whole lot more subtlety and finesse, also... 60.5%. sc.

Paul John Single Malt Cask No 1844 Non Peated db (94.5) n23 t24 f23.5 b24 Let someone taste this blind, tell them it is three years old...and see their reaction. A big malt showing elegance and good grace throughout. 60.5%

Paul John Single Malt Cask No 1846 Non Peated db (96) n23.5 t23 f25 b24.5 A very deep, complex whisky with many hills and canyons to explore. The finish orbits and often touches perfection. A profound malt. 60.8%

Paul John Single Malt-Classic (Un Peated) db (95) n23.5 an essay in complexity: softly sizzling lightly salted bacon mingles easily with tannins. The barley, offering the vaguest hint of grist, is almost in pastel, so delicate is it, with the deftest touch of citrus and moist syrup cake; t24 much more salivating on delivery than might be expected: the barley shows early and with pride. A bourbony manuka, honey-liquorice mix makes for an attractive spine with toasted honeycomb arriving in the mid ground; f23.5 an elegant finish again with the barley chirping surprisingly brightly on the oak branches. The tannins remain checked and under control with juicy Demerara tones ensuring the softest and friendliest of finishes; b24 further evidence that Indian whisky is on the rise. Just so charming...and irresistible. 55.2%

Paul John Select Cask Peated (96) n24 a sexy, sultry, sympathetic exhibition of smoke on varying levels...though all of them soft. A tantalising chocolate mint hangs of the embers, which glow both sweet and dry. Peated whisky from outside Islay rarely comes as complex and beautiful as this, or as deliciously gristy; t24 a massive delivery. Massive yet tender and subtle. How does that happen? Again, cocoa quickly fills the middle but there is more than enough molasses to counter. The weight and depth are spot on, as are the spices which get off to a delicate start but soon get into the swing of things; **f24** long, fabulously oiled and just-so amounts of gristy sugars clinging to the smoke. As charming and impressionistic as an Indian kitchen fire wafting its smoke over a remote village in the nearby valleys; **b24** a peated malt whisky which will make a few people sit up and take even further notice of Indian whisky. World class... *46%*

⬦ **That Boutique-y Whisky Company Paul John Batch 1 (95) n24** the smoke, through serious maturation, has now moved into a stunningly structured herbal nature with lavender and mint being found among the phenols; **t24** such a brilliant mouth feel: soft without being oily, the smoke has less of an impact than on the nose thanks to the assuredness of the blend of maple syrup and treacle. Amazingly, a little malt gristiness can still be found about halfway through...; **f23** still the tannins are tamed by dark sugars, though the spice now has a constant rumble...; **b24** a sublime peated malt from India. Knowing exactly how limited stocks are of this sub-Continental liquid gold dust, I'm amazed they let this go! Still, if it helps more people discover just how magnificent this distillery is and, with Amrut, the indisputable high position of top Indian malt, then so much the better. *55.5%. 148 bottles.*

⬦ **That Boutique-y Whisky Company Paul John 6 Year Old Batch 2 (89) n22.5** vanilla and full blooded oak, though the sugars offer a safe buffer; **t23** big, salivating malt, again with a big vanilla kick fused with a light lemon drizzle cake. The oak is encroaching by the second, though...; **f21.5** the tannins overpower the remaining sugars for a slightly bitter finale; **b22** a substantial malt feeling its age: six years in India is probably closer to about 35-40 years in Scotland. As a single malt, attractive and intriguing, as this malt is moving into a previously unknown phase, though obviously tiring. Within part of a creation, a blender's delight... *54.7%. 173 bottles.*

PONDA DISTILLERY

Stillman's Dram Single Malt Whisky Limited Edition bourbon cask no. 11186-90 **(94) n23 t23 f24 b24.** Well, I thought I had tasted it all with the Amrut cask strength. And then this arrived at my lab...!! I predicted many years back that India would dish out some top grade malt before too long. But I'd be stretching the truth if I said I thought it would ever be this good... *42.8%. McDowell & Co Ltd, India.*

Blends

Peter Scot Malt Whisky (84) n20 t21 f22 b21. Enjoyable balance between sweetness and oak and entertainingly enlivened by what appears to be some young, juicy malt. *42.8%.*

Rendezvous (95.5) n24 t24 f23.5 b24.5. A new Indian classic. A sublime malt from the subcontinent. *46%*

Royal Stag Barrel Select batch 212, bott 17 Feb 12 **(75.5) n20.5 t19 f17 b18.** Thin and sweet. But should be shot to put it out of its misery. *42.8% Mix of Scotch malt and India grain spirit.*

Seagram's Blenders Pride Reserve Collection (77) n19 t20 f19 b19. Way too reliant on the grain and the malt submerged under the caramel. Soft, clean and painfully non-committal. *42.8%. Mix of Scotch malt and India grain spirit.*

Signature (81.5) n22.5 t22 f17.5 b19.5. Excellent, rich nose & delivery helped along with a healthy display of peat reek. But more attention has to be paid to the brutally thin finish. *42.8%*

NEW ZEALAND
THE NEW ZEALAND WHISKY COMPANY

The New Zealand Whisky Collection 25 Years Old Single Malt dist in Dunedin, matured in Oamaru, Ex-Bourbon casks **(94.5) n23** attractive apples and intense malt; the most distant peat reek imaginable; **t24** the malt strikes early as it fully engulfs the palate: excellent balance as the vanilla begins to merge before those exotic fruits – the proud mark of great age – begin to form and delight. And then, just like on the nose, a mirage of delicate smoke shimmers on the horizon; **f23.5** a long, slightly oily finale, full of decent oaky, exotic tones... and still the lightly spiced hint of distant smoke; **b24** around the time this was made, some of the malt was very lightly peated. Though it doesn't mention so on the bottle, I strongly suspect that – after 25 years wear and tear in the cask – this is one of them. Seriously charming malt. And historic – and for me, at least, as one of the very few to see it in operation – touchingly memorable. *46%*

The New Zealand Whisky Collection Doublewood 15 Years Old American oak, finished in French oak ex New Zealand red wine barrels **(81.5) n20 t21 f20 b20.5.** A curiously thin whisky offering little above the clean fruit. *40%*

The New Zealand Whisky Collection Oamaruvian 16 Years Old American oak, finished in French oak ex New Zealand red wine barrels, cask no. 328, bott July 15 **(87)** n21.5 t21.5 f22.5 b21.5. A similar cove to their 58.4% bottling. Actually, I take my hats off to the boys on this one: they started with something pretty ordinary and have turned it through the employment of exceptionally fine casks into a spirit worthy of investigation. Still not a great whisky - in fact far, far closer in personality to a column still rum - but for those who love to see a big clean fruity spirit, then they will enjoy this. The spices are pretty major and the late chocolate liqueur finale is very pleasant. However, the complete lack of body to the spirit base means this can never qualify as a great whisky. Good try, though. *57%*

The New Zealand Whisky Collection Oamaruvian 16 Years Old American oak, finished in French oak ex New Zealand red wine barrels, cask no. 544, bott July 15 **(86.5)** n22 t21 f22.5 b21. I think I know what this spirit is. The guys who now own the barrels have done a great job in trying to turn it into something profound and have come pretty close. The problem is that the original grain spirit was distilled to such high strength and so bereft of body and personality, rather than add anything to the mix it is just a case of the alcohol turning up the volume on the absolutely sublime wine casks. However, just adore the chocolate raisin on the finish and worth trying out for that alone. *58.4%*

The New Zealand Whisky Collection South Island Single Malt Aged 23 Years ex bourbon casks **(92)** n22.5 a tiring, Puffing Billy of a nose where big, but friendly, tannins more or less obliterate any malt still hanging around. Just moving into the exotic fruit phase...; t23 beautifully soft and welcoming on the palate. The oak has backed off slightly for a while, allowing the sugars a clear run. Lots of vanilla, hazelnuts and spice...and even a hint of growing salt; f23 yes, now pretty salty and a little honey seeps into the proceedings; the spices are a last gasp from the cask...; b23 a slightly stuttering malt, but no off notes and when it does click it does so quite beautifully. *40%*

The New Zealand Whisky Collection 1987 24 Year Old Single Malt dist in Dunedin **(84.5)** n21.5 t22 f20 b21. "Not Aged in French Oak" announces the back label, pricking one's curiosity. A bit like the old comedy sketch with a bored pilot (John Cleese, who else?) telling the passengers, out of nowhere, "hello, this is your captain speaking: there is absolutely no cause for alarm....the engines are NOT on fire." That, of course, was in a different, more innocent and enjoyable world than today, pre 9/11. As, indeed, is this whisky...made when there was little interest in World Whisky and the Willowbank Distillery in Dunedin in particular. This may not be the finest bottling from the distillery and, with its fruitiness and bitter finish, unrepresentative of the house style. *43%*

⬩⬩ **The New Zealand Whisky Collection 1987 Single Malt Aged 27 Years** dist in Dunedin, American oak casks **(89)** n22.5 an attractive combination of apple strudel and ulmo honey; t22.5 surprisingly light bodied: the vanillas make a very early charge; some tangy spices generate a degree of juiciness; f22 evidence of drying, budding malt; b22 by no means the most complicated malt but enjoys a series of pleasant moments. *43%*

The New Zealand Whisky Collection 1992 21 Year Old Single Malt (91.5) n22.5 a non-specific fruitiness – halfway between grape and exotic – ensures a very soft aroma; t23.5 mouth-watering delivery with an exotic fruit and crème brûlée mix I have never quite tasted before from this distillery; the early sugars are tinged with muscovado sugars; f22.5 creamy textured, but late on, the malt and spices emerge; some late tannins leave you in no doubt of the antiquity; b23 an odd fruitiness has crept into this one somehow. Delightfully pleasant, but still a bit of a shame to see the complex grain and oak tones, which I know can be quite magnificent from this distillery, somewhat obscured. Probably just down to age. Still a joy, though. *50.7%. sc.*

⬩⬩ **The New Zealand Whisky Collection South Island Single Malt Aged 25 Years** dist in Dunedin, American oak, ex-Bourbon casks **(85.5)** n21.5 t21.5 f21 b21.5. Wow! This malt has taken a surprising direction in the 25 years since it was made. When, back in 1994, I tasted samples from a vast cross section of the maturing casks at the distillery in the days it was still working (and looked somewhat different to the charming picture on the inside back label) it had a far more compact, malt intense nature. This has opened and thinned out with a big vanilla input while the oak has kept a discreet distance. *40%*

The New Zealand Whisky Collection Willowbank 1988 25 Years Old cask no. 64, bott 3/13 **(96.5)** n24 t24.5 f23.5 b24.5 When I first encountered this whisky it would have been a six-year-old and the Dunedin distillery had a very uncertain future. Question marks hung over the quality of the stock, so they were a bit surprised when I assured them that the vast majority of what they were making was of very decent to high standard. Who then would have thought that some two decades on I would be tasting this as one of the most delicate and sophisticated and complex 25-year-olds imaginable? Only the untidy finish shows the distillery's Achilles: low copper content. On the other hand, it also ensured that it would never be short of character. One of the most poignant and enjoyable whiskies of the year. And memories of the only distillery I ever visited and then took a five minute drive to watch penguins surface from the sea... 55.1%. sc. WB15/396

THE SOUTHERN DISTILLING CO LTD

The Coaster Single Malt Whiskey batch no. 2356 (85) n20 t22 f21 b22. Distinctly small batch and sma' still with the accent very much on honey. Nosed blind I might have mistaken as Blue Mouse whisky from Germany: certainly European in style. Recovers well from the wobble on the nose and rewards further investigation. 40%

The MacKenzie Blended Malt Whiskey (85) n20 t22 f21 b22. A vaguely spicier, chalkier, mildly less honeyed version of Coaster. Quite banana-laden nose. 40%

THOMSON WILLOWBANK

Thomson Single Malt 10 Years Old ex-bourbon barrel (71) n18.5 t19 f16.5 b17. The sugars are working hard. But have nothing to work with. 40%. Thomson Whisky.

Thomson Single Malt 18 Years Old (77) n19.5 t20 f18.5 b19. Pleasant, sweet but absolutely no body whatsoever. 46%. sc. Thomson Whisky.

Thomson Single Malt 21 Years Old (84) n21 t22.5 f20.5 b20. Bit of a bimbo whisky: looks pretty and outwardly attractive but has picked up very little in its 21 years... 46%. sc.

Thomson Whisky Two Tone European oak & American white oak (86) n22 t22 f21 b21. This one had promise. Started full of intent on both nose and delivery, boasting attractive citrus notes. But after a quick rush of clear honey, thins out like the most basic of blends. 40%

WILSON DISTILLERY

Cadenhead's World Whiskies Lammerlaw Aged 10 Years bourbon, bott 07 (91.5) n22 t23.5 f23 b23. Stunning bottlings like this can only leave one mourning the loss of this distillery. 48.9%

Blends

Kiwi Whisky (37) n2 t12 f11 b12. Strewth! I mean, what can you say? Perhaps the first whisky containing single malt offering virtually no nose at all and the flavour appears to be grain neutral spirit plus lashings of caramel and (so I am told) some Lammerlaw single malt. The word bland has been redefined. As has whisky. 40%.

Wilson's Superior Blend (89) n22 t23 f21 b23. Apparently has a mixed reception in its native New Zealand but I fail to see why: this is unambiguously outstanding blended whisky. On the nose you expect a mouthwatering mouthful and it delivers with aplomb. Despite this being a lower priced blend it is, intriguingly, a marriage of 60% original bottled 10-y-o Lammerlaw and 40% old Wilson's blend, explaining the high malt apparent. Dangerous and delicious and would be better still at a fuller strength...and with less caramel. 37.5%.

MISCELLANEOUS

The New Zealand Whisky Collection Doublewood Aged 16 Years (87.5) n22 t22 f22.5 b21. Light, silky, fruity and an all-round lovely experience. But as a whisky leaves one somewhat frustrated as it is a bit of a one trick pony with variation and complexity very much at a premium. 40%.

SOUTH AFRICA
JAMES SEDGWICK DISTILLERY

Three Ships 10 Years Old db (83) n21 t21 f20 b21. Seems to have changed character, with more emphasis on sherry and natural toffee. The oak offers a thrusting undercurrent. 43%

Three Ships Aged 10 Years Single Malt Limited Edition db (91) n22.5 t22.5 f23 b23.5. If you are looking for a soft, sophisticated malt whose delicate fingers can sooth your troubled brow, then don't bother with this one. On the other hand, if you are looking for a bit of rough, some entertaining slap and tickle: a slam-bam shag of a whisky - a useful port in a storm - then your boat may just have sailed in... Beware: an evening with this and you'll be secretly coming back for more... 43%

Bain's Cape Mountain Single Grain Whisky db (85.5) n21 t22 f21 b21.5. A lively, attractively structured whisky with more attitude than you might expect. Some lovely nip and bite despite the toffee and surprising degree of soft oils. 43%

Blends

Drayman's Solera (86) n19 t22 f23 b22. For a change, the label gets it spot on with its description of chocolate orange: it is there in abundance. If they can get this nose sorted they would be on for an all round impressive dram. As it is, luxuriate in the excellent mouthfeel and gentle interplay between malt and oak. Oh and those chocolate oranges... *43%.*

Harrier (78) n20 t20 f19 b19. Not sure what has happened to this one. Has bittered to a significant degree while the smoke has vanished. A strange, almost synthetic, feel to this now. *43%. South African/Scotch Whisky.*

Knights (83) n20.5 t21 f20 b20.5. While the Harrier has crashed, the Knights is now full of promise. Also shows the odd bitter touch but a better all-round richer body not only absorbs the impacts but radiates some malty charm. *43%. South African/Scotch Whisky.*

Knights Aged 3 Years (87) n22 t22 f22 b22. This now appears to be 100% South African whisky if I understand the label correctly: "Distilled Matured and Bottled in South Africa." A vast improvement on when it was Scotch malt and South African grain. Bursting with attitude and vitality. When next in South Africa, this will be my daily dram for sure. Love it. *43%.*

Three Ships Bourbon Cask Finish (90) n22 t23 f22.5 b22.5. A soft, even whisky which enjoys its finest moments on delivery. Clean with a pressing, toasty oakiness to the sweeter malt elements. Always a delight. *43%*

Three Ships Premium Select Aged 5 Years (93) n23 t23.5 f23 b23.5. What a fabulous whisky. The blender has shown a rare degree of craft to make so little smoke do so much. Bravo! *43%. James Sedgwick Distillery.*

Three Ships Select (81) n19 t21 f20 b21. Busy and sweet. But I get the feeling that whatever South African malt may be found in Knights does a better job than its Scotch counterpart here. *43%. James Sedgwick Distillery.*

TAIWAN
KAVALAN DISTILLERY

Kavalan Distillery Reserve peaty cask, dist 2007, bott 23 Jan 2015 db **(95)** n23.5 the smoke is little more than a tease, a blink and you miss the wisp of phenol; creamy malt with stuttering sugars; t24.5 much more assured peat on delivery: the smoke maybe delicate but has enough about it meet the barley face to face; toasty tannins steal the scenes in the second and third act but never completely eclipse the crunchy malt; for a few moments the oil let rise to impressive, yet deliciously manageable heights upping the intensity further; f23 a long trail of spiced tannin: amazingly salivating even to the toasty death; b24 what a crackerjack cask this malt spent seven worthwhile and highly active and productive years maturing in. Starts so quietly, then becomes pretty loud. *55%.*

Kavalan Single Malt Amontillado Sherry Cask cask no. S100623016A db **(97)** n24 t24.5 f24 b24.5 Given the right bottling, Amontillado is probably my favourite sherry style. How many times, though, have I discovered its delicate, complex, understated nature perfectly transferred onto a singe malt? In some 35 years, this must be only the fourth or fifth time, and I doubt any quite displayed such truth to its style, such panache. Forget the unique and intriguing bottle design (though it is hard!). This is a classic whisky on so many levels that it will stay indelibly stamped on both taste buds and memory. What a magnificent whisky experience this is...!!! *56.3%. sc. 744 bottles. Limited edition 2014_1402.*

Kavalan Single Malt Manzanilla Sherry Cask cask no. S100716002A db **(95.5)** n23 the fruit needs a little coaxing as it grips, limpet-like to a drier, pithy, oak-drenched style; t24 likewise, the delivery is reserved and then...oh, my word! The shackles are suddenly bust open ad he spices escape en masse. At the same moment the juicy elements of the grape gush forward, as if from nowhere and engulf the palate. Eye-watering and emphatic...; f24 the palate is coated with the light oils required spread the fruit and spices into the furthermost corners; slows as the oak regains a slightly nervous foothold..; b24.5 a mouth-watering jape from Kavalan. The nose appears a tad tight and introverted. But as it relaxes on the palate it certainly lets the malt the freedom to take on the grape. Or is it the other way round? A sublime surprise package.... *57.8%. sc. 744 bottles. Limited edition 2014_1402.*

Kavalan Solist Fino Sherry Cask db cask no. S060814021 **(97)** n24.5 t24 f24 b24.5. It might be argued that the one and only thing that makes this exceptional is the quality of the cask, rather than the actual malt it contains. Well, let me set the record straight in this one. Earlier this week I made a very rare escape from my tasting room and visited the Royal Albert Hall for the 34th Prom of the 2011 season. The highlight of the evening was Camille Saint-Saens Symphony No 3 – "Organ". Now some critics, when they can find time to extract themselves from their own rear ends, dismiss this as a commoners' piece; something to amuse the plebeian. What they appear to not have is neither the wit nor humanity to understand that Saint-Saens sewed into this work a degree of such subtle shade and emotion, especially in the less dramatic second movement, that it can, when treated correctly, affect those capable of normal warmth and feeling. With so many nerve endings tingling and nowhere to go Saint-Saens seemingly recognised that he required something profound – in this case the organ – to create a backbone. And someone able to use it to maximum effect. And there we had it the other day: the Royal Albert Hall's awe-inspiring organ, and Thomas Trotter to make it come alive: The Solist. And this is what we have here: a perfect fino sherry selected by the maestro Dr Jim Swan. But able to display its full magnificence only because the host spirit is so beautifully composed. Good whisky is, without question, a work of art; great whisky is a tone poem. And here, I beg to insist, is proof. *58.4%. nc ncf sc. 513 bottles.*

◈ **Kavalan Solist Port** cask, cask no. 0 090617023A db **(93.5) n23.5** a curious nutty note far more often associated with a fresh sherry butt than Port pipe. But nutty and dry it is, as well as sophisticated and endearingly complex. Just love that hint of high cherry content fruitcake, too; **t24** the fruit drips off the tongue as the palate is awash with a resounding moist fruitcake intensity. Spices and molasses arrive on cue; a little resin fills in gaps in the midpoint region; **f22.5** dips towards a slight dryness which is a tad out of keeping with the more balanced nose and delivery; **b23.5** but for those subtle sugars this would be a brute of a whisky. One for those who prefer their fruitcakes fruity... *58.6%. nc ncf sc. 175 bottles.*

◈ **Kavalan Solist Moscatel** cask, cask no. S100623024A db **(94.5) n24** dry enough thanks to that unique feel of ancient molasses; indeed, there is a peculiar rum shape to this. The sweetness does balance in a muscovado kind of way, but it is almost too subtle for words: beautiful...; **t23.5** and it's muscovado which kicks in first, offering a gentle fruitiness which allows the malt a salivating view. Some resounding tannin hits the halfway point, but the delicate fruity sugars cope easily; **f23** now just a suggestion of spice to add to the tannin. Long, drying and satisfying; **b24** a big malt, but so subtle with it, too. Superb! *55.6%. nc ncf sc. 491 bottles.*

Other Brands Available In Taiwan

Eagle Leader Storage Whisky (81.5) n20 t21 f21 b20.5. Attractively smoky with a surprisingly long finish for a whisky which initially seem to lack body. By no means straightforward, but never less than pleasant. *40%*

Golden Hill Single Malt (75) n18 t20 f19 b18. An unwieldy heavyweight. *40%*

Good Deer (in Chinese Characters) *see McAdams Rye Whisky*

McAdams Rye Whisky bott Nov 09 **(85.5) n21 t22 f21.5 b21.5.** Thoroughly delicious stuff absolutely brimming with juicy, crisp grain notes. The body is lightly oiled and shapely while the finish is sweet and attractive. The odd green apple note, too. *40%. Note: Says it's made in Taiwan, but possesses a maple leaf on the label.*

Sea Pirates (77) n18 t21 f19 b19. More Johnny Depp than Errol Flynn. Attractive smoke, though. *40%*

URUGUAY

Dunbar Anejo 5 Anos (85.5) n20 t22.5 f21.5 b21.5. A clean, mouth-wateringly attractive mix where the grain nips playfully and the Speyside malts are on best salivating behaviour. Decently blended and boasting a fine spice prickle, too. *40%*

Seagram's Blenders Pride (83) n20.5 t22 f20b20.5. The busy, relatively rich delivery contrasts with the theme of the silky grains and caramel. Easy drinking. *40%*

MISCELLANEOUS

◈ **Precinct No. 6 Kentucky Sour Mash** spirits distilled from 50% corn & 50% cane, batch no. 2 db **(60) n12 t18 f14 b16.** If you were to say, this seems like half whisky and half rum, you'd be right. Because it is both. And neither. Similar to so-called and self-styled "whiskies" of the Far East and some South American countries where either cane or molasses is used. Except this has much more oak involvement and spice. *478% (95.6 proof).*

CROSS-COUNTRY VATTED WHISKIES

Diggers & Ditch Doublemalt Spirit of the Anzacs (82.5) n21 t21 f20 b20.5. Soft, fruity but never quite gets it together. Always too thin and shapeless. I'll give it a D. *45%. A blend of New Zealand & Australian whisky.*

Jim Beam Kentucky Dram (89) n22.5 t22.5 f21.5 b22.5 There may be some of you reading this who will remember tastings I did 15 or 20 years ago where, for fun and to show balancing effects, I vatted bourbon with smoky Scotch. At last someone has done it commercially. I suspect this is more for the American palate as the peat has been used sparingly. *40% (80 Proof)*

Slàinte

It seems as though you can't have a Bible without a whole lot of begetting. And without all those listed below – herds of whiskybeast roaming Drafrica – this Jim Murray's Whisky Bible 2017 would never have been begot at all. A huge amount of blood, sweat and tears go into the production of each edition, more than anyone not directly involved could even begin to comprehend. So, as usual, I must thank my amazing team: Vincent Flint-Hill, Billy Jeffrey, Robin Pulford, David Rankin and Cate Crawshaw. Special thanks to Julia Nourney for contacting the distilleries of Europe on my behalf gathering samples, and overseeing the new European dictionary. Once again, extra special thanks to the unfailing, glass half full support of Paul and Denise Egerton, Pete and Linda Mayne and David Hartley and Julie Barrie who, collectively, kept me going and laughing when, as ever, the weight of whisky and expectation seemed - and was - so daunting. As well as to Mr. and Mrs. Murray of the classic Super Sausage Cafe on the A5 near Towcester whose delicious non-spiced sausage sandwiches have no equal - even when refrigerated in my lab. As always, a massive hug to Heiko Thieme. And, finally, thanks to those below who have provided assistance and samples for the 2013 Bible onwards. For all those who have assisted in the previous decade, we remain indebted.

Mitch Abate; Andrew Abela; Emma Alessandrini; Mary Allison; Mike Almy; Ally Alpine; Nicole Anastasi; Tommy Andersen; Wayne Anderson; Kristina Anerfält-Jansson; Jane & Martin Armstrong; Hannah Arnold; Teemu Artukka; Kevin Atchinson; Ryan Baird; David Bakery; Duncan Baldwin; Clare Banner; Steve Beam; Stefan Beck; Jan Beckers; Kirsteen Beeston; Becky Bell; Annie Bellis; Sigurd Belsnes; Franz Benner; Alexander Berger; John Bernasconi; Barry Bernstein; Stuart Bertra; Jodi Best; Marilena Bidaine; Peter Bignell; Menno Bijmolt; Sonat Birknecker Hart; Franziska Bishof; Rich Blair; Olivier Blanc; Elisabeth Blum; René Bobrink; Andreas Boessow; Anna Boger; Hans Bol; Mark Boley; Yvonne Bonner; Etienne Bouillon; Borat, Birgit Bornemeier; Kev & Karen Bowler; Phil Brandon; Caroline Brel; Stephen Bremner; Rebecca Brennan; Stephanie Bridge; Chris Brown; James Brown; Sara Browne; Michael Brzozowski; Alexander Buchholz; Ryan Burchett; Amy Burgess; Euan Campbell; Nathan Campbell; Kimla Carsten; Lauren Casey-Haiko; Bert Cason; Stuart Cassells; Jim Caudill; Danilo Cembrero; Lisa Chandler; Yuseff Cherney; Julia Christian; Morten Christensen; Claire Clark; Nick Clark; Joseph Clarkson; Fredi Clerc; Dr Martin Collis; Brian Cox; Jason Craig; David Croll; Nathan Currie; Larry Currier; Benjamin Curtis; Danni Cutten; Mike DaRe; Alan Davis; Stephen Davies; Alasdair Day; Dick & Marti; Scott Dickson; Martin Diekmann; Dixon Dedman; Paul Dempsey; Lauren Devine; Marie-Luise Dietich; Rob Dietrich; Arno Josef Dirker; Caroline Docherty; Angela D'Orazio; Jean Donnay; Tim Duckett; Camille Duhr-Merges; Mariette Duhr-Merges; Gemma Duncan; Christophe Dupic; Jens Drewitz; Jochen Druffel; Michael D'souza; Kellie Du; Jonas Ebensperger; Ray Edwards; Carsten Ehrlich; Ben Ellefsen; Rebecca Elliott-Smith; Lucie Ellis; Thimo Elz; Maximilian Engel; Camilla Ericsson; Beanie Espey; James Espey; Brad Estabrooke; Patrick Evans; Jennifer Eveleigh; Selim Evin; Thomas Ewers; Charlotte Falconer; Lauren Fallert; Bruce Farquhar; David Faverot; Joanna Fearnside; Walter Fitzke; Roland Feller; Andrea Ferrari; Holly Forbes; Tricia Fox; Jean-Arnaud Frantzen; Hans-Gerhard Fink; David Fitt; Kent Fleischman; Martyn Flynn; Danny Gandert; Arno Gänsnamtel; Patrick Garcia; Dan Garrison; Ralph Gemmel; Stefanie Geuting; Carole Gibson; Jonathan Gibson; John Glaser; John Glass; Emily Glynn; Emma Golds; Rodney Goodchild; Jonathon Gordan; Tomer Goren; Lawrence Graham; Kelly Greenawalt; Hannah Gregory; Andrew Grey; George Grindlay; Rebecca Groom; Jason Grossmiller; Jan Groth; Viele Grube; Immanuel Gruel; Katia Guidolin; Josh Hafer; Jasmin Haider; Jamie Hakim; Georgina Hall; Georges Hannimann; Scott E Harris; Alistair Hart; Andrew Hart; Donald Hart; Stuart Harvey; Ralf Hauer; Elizabeth Haw; Steve Hawley; Ailsa Hayes; Ross Hendry; Lianne Herbruck; Thomas Herbruck; Jason Himstedt; Roland Hinterreiter; Tom Holder; Bernhard Höning; Jason Horn; Emma Hurley; Alex Huskingson; Thomas B. Ide; Jill Inglis; Rachel Showalter Inman; Hannah Irwin; Kai Ivalo; Richard Jansson; Amelia James; Ulrich Jakob; Andrew Jarrell; Michael John; Celine Johns; Eamonn Jones; Robert Joule; Aista Jukneviciute; Raphael Käser; Alfred Kausl; Christina Kavanaugh; Serena Kaye; Colin Keegan; Kai Kilpinen; Daniel Kissling; Sara Klingberg; Franz Kostenzer; Matt Kozuba; Martina Krainer; Larry Krass; Armin Krister; Karen Kushner; Sophie Lambert-Russell; Ryan Lang; Oliver Lange; Jürgen Laskowski; Sebastian Lauinger; Alan Laws; Darren Leitch; Christelle Le Lay; Cédric Leprette; Eiling Lim; Bryan Lin; Lars Lindberger; Mark T Litter; Steven Ljubicic; Alistair Longwell; Dorene Lorenz; Claire Lormier; Sarah Loughton; C. Mark McDavid; Jane Macduff; Myriam Mackenzie; Damian & Madeleine Mackey; John Maclellan; Derek Mair; Dennis Malcolm; Jari Mämmi; Sarah Manning; Stefan Marder; Ole Mark; Amaury Markey; Tim Marwood; Jennifer

Masson; Gregor Mathieson; Leanne Matthews; Josh Mayr; Roxane Mazeaude; Stephen R McCarthy; Mark McDavid; Angela Mcilrath; Catherine McKay; Jonny McMillan; Douglas McIvor; Heinz Meistermann; Uwe Meuren; Raphael Meuwly; Maggie Miller; Tatsuya Minagawa; Euan Mitchell; Jacqueline Mitchell; Paul Mitchell; Jeroen Moernaut; Stephan Mohr; Henk Mol; Nick Morgan; Celine Moran; Maggie Morri; Brendan J. Moylan; Miroslav Motyčka; Fabien Mueller; Mike Müller; Michael Myers; Simone Nagel; Arthur Nägele; Andrew Nelstrop; Sandra Neuner; Alex Nicol; Jane Nicol; Jennifer Nicol; Thorsten Niesner; Zack Nobinger; Soren Norgaard; Julia Nourney; Nathan Nye; Tom O'Connor; Richard Oldfield; Jonas Östberg; Casey Overeem; Ted Pappas; Lauri Pappinen; Richard Parker; Katie Partridge; Sanjay Paul; Percy; Jörg Pfeiffer; Alexandra Piciu; Amy Preske; Phil Prichard; George Quiney; Rachel Quinn; George Racz; Robert Ransom; Nidal Ramini; Sarah Rawlingson; Julie Holl Rebsomen; Michael Reckhard; Guy Rehorst; Michel Reick; Lutz Reifferscheid; Marco Reiner; Drexler Reinhard; Carrie Revell; Frederic Revol; Kay Riddoch; Massimo Righi; Nicol von Rijbroek; Karen Ripley; Patrick Roberts; James Robertson; Dr. Torsten Römer; Anton Rossetti; David Roussier; Ronnie Routledge; Stephane Rouveyrol; Matthias Rosinski; Ken Rose; Michal Rusiňak; Jim Rutledge; Caroline Rylance; Simi Sagoo; Paloma Salmeron Planells; Jasmine Sangria; Carla Santoni; Colette Savage; John Savage-Onstwedder; Kirsty Saville; Manuela Savona; Ian Schmidt; Fred Heinz Schober; Lorien Schramm; Becky Schultz; Birgitta Schulze van Loon; Chris Seale; Mick & Tammy Secor; Marina Sepp; Paul Shand; Mike Sharples; Rubyna Sheikh; Caley Shoemaker; Lauren Shayne Mayer; Jamie Siefken; Peter Siegenthaler; Silke; Sam Simmons; Alastair Sinclair; Sukhinder Singh; Thomas Sippel; Thomas Smidt-Kjaerby; Aidan Smith; Barbara Smith; Gigha Smith; Phil Smith; Gunter Sommer; Oliver Späth; Cat Spencer; Colin Spoelma; Alexander Springensguth; Jolanda Stadelmann; Stauning; Silvia Steck; Jeremy Stephens; Hawley Steve; Vicky Stevens; Karen Stewart; Jakob Stjernholm; Katy Stollery; Greg Storm; Jarret Stuart; Jason Stubbs; Nicki Sturzaker; Peter Summer; Henning Svoldgaard; Tom Swift; Daniel Szor; Solene Tailland; Shoko Takagi; Chip Tate; Marko Tayburn; Emily Tedder; Marcel Telser; Celine Tetu; Sarah Thacker; Laura Thomson; Brian Toft; Jarrett Tomal; Katy Took; Hamish Torrie; Louise Towers; Hope Trawick; Matthias Trum; Anne Ulrich; Jens Unterweger; Richard Urquhart; Stuart Urquhart; CJ Van Dijk; Adam Vincent; Mariah Veis; Aurelien Villefranche; Lorraine Waddell; Emma Ware; Micheal Wells; Arne Wesche; Anna Wilson; Nick White; Peter White; Robert Whitehead; Stephanie Whitworth; Daniel Widmer; Markus Wieser; James Wills; Rinaldo Willy; Arthur Winning; Ellie Winters; Stephen Worrall; Kate Wright; Frank Wu; Tom Wyss; Junko Yaguchi; Kiyoyuki Yoshimura; Bettina Zannier; Jörg Zahorodnyj; Ruslan Zamoskovny; Ulrich Jakob Zeni; Rama Zuniga; Ernst Zweiger; Руслан Замосковный. And, as ever, in warm memory of Mike Smith.